CORPORATE FINANCE
EUROPE

CORPORATE FINANCE
EUROPE

by

ADRIAN BUCKLEY
Cranfield School of Management
Cranfield University

STEPHEN A. ROSS
Yale University

RANDOLPH W. WESTERFIELD
University of Southern California

JEFFREY F. JAFFE
The Wharton School
University of Pennsylvania

London • New York • St Louis • San Francisco • Auckland • Bogotá • Caracas
Lisbon • Madrid • Mexico • Milan • Montreal • New Delhi • Panama • Paris
San Juan • São Paulo • Singapore • Sydney • Tokyo • Toronto

Published by
McGRAW-HILL Publishing Company
Shoppenhangers Road, Maidenhead, Berkshire, SL6 2QL, England
Telephone 01628 502500
Facsimile 01628 770224

The LOC data for this book has been applied for and may be obtained from the Library of Congress, Washington, D.C.

A catalogue record for this book is available from the British Library.

ISBN 0256 20399 7

McGraw-Hill

A Division of The McGraw·Hill Companies

12345 CUP 21098

Typeset by Mackreth Media Services, Hemel Hempstead
Printed and bound in Great Britain at the University Press, Cambridge

Contents

About the Authors   xiii

Preface   xv

PART I

Overview   1

1   Foundation to European Corporate Finance   3
    1.1   European Equity Market   3
    1.2   Companies in Britain   10
    1.3   Companies in Germany   12
    1.4   Companies in France   14
    1.5   Companies in the Netherlands   16
    1.6   Corporate Governance and Corporate Finance   18
    1.7   European Corporate Reporting   20
    1.8   European Corporate Tax Systems   25
    1.9   Summary and Conclusions   27
    Appendix 1A   A Summary of the EU's Fourth Directive   27
    Appendix 1B   A Summary of the EU's Seventh Directive   28

2   Introduction to Corporate Finance   29
    2.1   What Is Corporate Finance?   30
    2.2   Corporate Securities as Contingent Claims on Total Firm Value   35
    2.3   The Corporate Firm   36
    2.4   Goals of the Corporate Firm   40
    2.5   Financial Markets   42
    2.6   Outline of the Text   44

3   Accounting Statements and Cash Flow   45
    3.1   The Balance Sheet   45
    3.2   The Profit and Loss Account (also called Income Statement)   48
    3.3   Net Working Capital   50
    3.4   Financial Cash Flow   51
    3.5   Summary and Conclusions   53
    Appendix 3A   Financial Statement Analysis   56
    Appendix 3B   Statement of Cash Flow   62

PART II

Value and Capital Budgeting — 65

4   Financial Markets and Net Present Value: First Principles of Finance — 67
4.1   The Financial Market Economy — 68
4.2   The Competitive Market — 70
4.3   The Basic Principle — 72
4.4   Illustrating the Investment Decision — 72
4.5   Corporate Investment Decision-Making — 75
4.6   Summary and Conclusions — 77

5   Net Present Value — 78
5.1   The One-Period Case — 78
5.2   The Multiperiod Case — 82
5.3   Compounding Periods — 90
5.4   Simplifications — 94
5.5   What Is a Firm Worth? — 104
5.6   Summary and Conclusions — 106

6   How to Value Bonds and Shares — 111
6.1   Definition and Example of a Bond — 111
6.2   How to Value Bonds — 111
6.3   Bond Concepts — 115
6.4   The Present Value of Ordinary Shares — 117
6.5   Estimates of Parameters in the Dividend-Discount Model — 121
6.6   Growth Opportunities — 124
6.7   The Dividend-Growth Model and the NPVGO Model (Advanced) — 128
6.8   Price-Earnings Ratio — 130
6.9   Summary and Conclusions — 133
Appendix 6A   The Term Structure of Interest Rates Spot Rates and Yield to Maturity — 137

7   Some Other Investment Rules — 146
7.1   Why Use Net Present Value? — 146
7.2   The Payback Period Rule — 147
7.3   The Discounted Payback Period Rule — 150
7.4   The Average Accounting Return — 150
7.5   The Internal Rate of Return — 153
7.6   Problems with the IRR Approach — 156
7.7   The Profitability Index — 165
7.8   The Practice of Capital Budgeting — 168
7.9   Summary and Conclusions — 168

8   Net Present Value and Capital Budgeting — 174
8.1   Incremental Cash Flows — 174
8.2   The Baldwin Company: An Example — 176
8.3   Inflation and Capital Budgeting — 182
8.4   Investments of Unequal Lives: The Equivalent Annual Cost Method — 184
8.5   Summary and Conclusions — 189

9   Strategy and Analysis in Using Net Present Value   **193**
   9.1   Corporate Strategy and Positive NPV   193
   9.2   Decision Trees   195
   9.3   Sensitivity Analysis, Scenario Analysis and Break-even Analysis   197
   9.4   Options   204
   9.5   Summary and Conclusions   206

PART **III**

Risk   **209**

10   Capital Market Theory: An Overview   **211**
   10.1   Returns   212
   10.2   Holding-Period Returns   216
   10.3   Return Statistics in the USA   221
   10.4   Average Stock Returns and Risk-Free Returns in the USA   222
   10.5   Risk Statistics in the USA   223
   10.6   The Discount Rate for Risky Projects   225
   10.7   Risk and Beta   228
   10.8   British Evidence   229
   10.9   European Returns   231
   10.10   Summary and Conclusions   234
   Appendix 10A   The Historical Market Risk Premium: The Very Long Run   236

11   Return and Risk: The Capital-Asset-Pricing Model (CAPM)   **238**
   11.1   Individual Securities   238
   11.2   Expected Return, Variance and Covariance   239
   11.3   The Return and Risk for Portfolios   244
   11.4   The Efficient Set for Two Assets   249
   11.5   The Efficient Set for Many Securities   253
   11.6   Diversification: An Example   257
   11.7   Riskless Borrowing and Lending   260
   11.8   Market Equilibrium   264
   11.9   Relationship between Risk and Expected Return (CAPM)   268
   11.10   Summary and Conclusions   271
   Appendix 11A   Is Beta Dead?   275

**12   An Alternative View of Risk and Return: The Arbitrage
       Pricing Theory**   **277**
   12.1   Factor Models: Announcements, Surprises and Expected Returns   278
   12.2   Risk: Systematic and Unsystematic   279
   12.3   Systematic Risk and Betas   280
   12.4   Portfolios and Factor Models   284
   12.5   Betas and Expected Returns   288
   12.6   The Capital-Asset-Pricing Model and the Arbitrage Pricing Model   291
   12.7   Parametric Approaches to Asset Pricing   292
   12.8   Summary and Conclusions   294

13   Risk, Return and Capital Budgeting   **299**
   13.1   The Cost of Equity Capital   300
   13.2   Determinants of Beta   305

13.3	Extensions of the Basic Model	308
13.4	Summary and Conclusions	312
Appendix 13A	Tax Systems and Capital Budgeting	314

PART IV

Capital Structure and Dividend Policy   317

14	**Corporate Financing Decisions and Efficient Capital Markets**	**319**
14.1	Can Financing Decisions Create Value?	319
14.2	A Description of Efficient Capital Markets	322
14.3	The Different Types of Efficiency	325
14.4	The Evidence	330
14.5	Implications for Corporate Finance	338
14.6	Summary and Conclusions	341

15	**Long-Term Financing: An Introduction**	**344**
15.1	Ordinary Shares	344
15.2	Corporate Long-Term Debt: The Basics	349
15.3	Preference Shares	352
15.4	Patterns of Financing	354
15.5	Summary and Conclusions	355

16	**Capital Structure: Basic Concepts**	**357**
16.1	The Capital-Structure Question and the Pie Theory	357
16.2	Maximizing Firm Value versus Maximizing Shareholder Interests	358
16.3	Can an Optimal Capital Structure Be Determined?	360
16.4	Financial Leverage and Firm Value: An Example	362
16.5	Modigliani and Miller: Proposition II (No Taxes)	366
16.6	Taxes	374
16.7	Summary and Conclusions	384

17	**Capital Structure: Limits to the Use of Debt**	**388**
17.1	Costs of Financial Distress	388
17.2	Description of Costs	391
17.3	Can Costs of Debt Be Reduced?	395
17.4	Integration of Tax Effects and Financial Distress Costs	396
17.5	Shirking and Perquisites: A Note on Agency Cost of Equity	399
17.6	Growth and the Debt-Equity Ratio	400
17.7	How Firms Establish Capital Structure	402
17.8	Financial Distress, Bankruptcy and Reorganization	404
17.9	Summary and Conclusions	406

18	**Valuation and Capital Budgeting for the Levered Firm**	**408**
18.1	Adjusted-Present-Value Approach	408
18.2	Flow-to-Equity Approach	410
18.3	Weighted-Average-Cost-of-Capital Method	412
18.4	A Comparison of the APV, FTE and WACC Approaches	413
18.5	Capital Budgeting for Projects that Are Not Scale-Enhancing	416
18.6	APV Example	418
18.7	Beta and Leverage	421

18.8   Summary and Conclusions   423
        Appendix 18A   The Adjusted-Present-Value Approach to Valuing
                            Leveraged Buyouts   426

19   **Dividend Policy: Why Does It Matter?**   **431**
        19.1   Different Types of Dividends   431
        19.2   Standard Method of Cash Dividend Payment   432
        19.3   The Benchmark Case: An Illustration of the Irrelevance of
                Dividend Policy   433
        19.4   Taxes, Issuance Costs and Dividends   438
        19.5   Expected Return, Dividends and Personal Taxes   441
        19.6   Real-World Factors Favouring a High-Dividend Policy   444
        19.7   A Resolution of Real-World Factors?   446
        19.8   What We Know and Do Not Know about Dividend Policy   448
        19.9   Summary and Conclusions   450

PART V

Long-Term Financing   **453**

20   **Issuing Equity Securities to the Public**   **455**
        20.1   How Shares are Issued to the Public   455
        20.2   The Cost of New Issues   459
        20.3   Rights   460
        20.4   The Announcement of New Equity and the Value of the Firm 464
        20.5   Venture Capital   465
        20.6   Bonus Issues or Scrip Issues   466
        20.7   Summary and Conclusions   466

21   **Long-Term Debt**   **468**
        21.1   Long-Term Debt: A Review   468
        21.2   The Public Issue of Bonds   469
        21.3   Bond Refunding   473
        21.4   Bond Ratings   477
        21.5   Some Different Types of Bonds   481
        21.6   Direct Placement Compared to Public Issues   484
        21.7   Summary and Conclusions   485

22   **Options and Corporate Finance**   **487**
        22.1   Options   487
        22.2   Call Options   488
        22.3   Put Options   490
        22.4   Writing Options   491
        22.5   Reading the *Financial Times*   493
        22.6   Combinations of Options   493
        22.7   Valuing Options   496
        22.8   An Option-Pricing Formula   501
        22.9   An Option-Pricing Table   509
        22.10   Stocks and Bonds as Options   510
        22.11   Capital-Structure Policy and Options   516
        22.12   Investment in Real Projects and Options   517
        22.13   Summary and Conclusions   520

23   Warrants and Convertibles   **524**
   23.1   Warrants   524
   23.2   The Difference between Warrants and Call Options   526
   23.3   Warrant Pricing and the Black–Scholes Model (Advanced)   528
   23.4   Convertible Bonds   530
   23.5   The Value of Convertible Bonds   530
   23.6   Reasons for Issuing Warrants and Convertibles   533
   23.7   Why Are Warrants and Convertibles Issued?   536
   23.8   Conversion Policy   538
   23.9   Summary and Conclusions   539

24   Leasing   **542**
   24.1   Leasing—The Basics   542
   24.2   European Lease Accounting   545
   24.3   The Cash Flows of Leasing   547
   24.4   A Detour on Discounting and Debt Capacity with Corporate Taxes   549
   24.5   NPV Analysis of the Lease-versus-Buy Decision   551
   24.6   Debt Displacement and Lease Valuation   552
   24.7   Does Leasing Ever Pay: The Base Case   556
   24.8   Reasons for Leasing   557
   24.9   Some Unanswered Questions   560
   24.10 Summary and Conclusions   561
          Appendix 24A   APV Approach to Leasing   563

PART VI

Financial Planning, Short-Term Finance and Working Capital Management   565

25   Corporate Financial Models and Long-Term Planning   **567**
   25.1   What Is Corporate Financial Planning?   567
   25.2   A Financial-Planning Model: The Ingredients   568
   25.3   What Determines Growth?   571
   25.4   Some Caveats of Financial-Planning Models   575
   25.5   Summary and Conclusions   576

26   Short-Term Finance and Planning   **578**
   26.1   Tracing Cash and Net Working Capital   579
   26.2   Defining Cash in Terms of Other Elements   580
   26.3   The Operating Cycle and the Cash Cycle   582
   26.4   Some Aspects of Short-Term Financial Policy   585
   26.5   Cash Budgeting   590
   26.6   The Short-Term Financial Plan   593
   26.7   Managing the Collection and Disbursement of Cash   595
   26.8   Summary and Conclusions   597

27   Credit Management   **600**
   27.1   Terms of the Sale   601
   27.2   The Decision to Grant Credit: Risk and Information   605
   27.3   Optimal Credit Policy   608
   27.4   Credit Analysis   609

27.5 Collection Policy   610
27.6 How to Finance Trade Credit   612
27.7 Summary and Conclusions   613

PART VII

Special Topics   615

28 **Mergers and Acquisitions**   617
28.1   The Basic Forms of Acquisition   618
28.2   Accounting for Acquisitions   620
28.3   Determining the Synergy from an Acquisition   622
28.4   Source of Synergy from Acquisitions   623
28.5   Calculating the Value of the Firm after an Acquisition   627
28.6   A Cost to Shareholders from Reduction in Risk   628
28.7   Two 'Bad' Reasons for Mergers   631
28.8   The NPV of a Merger   632
28.9   Defensive Tactics   636
28.10 Some Evidence on Acquisitions   638
28.11 Summary and Conclusions   640

29 **International Corporate Finance and Derivative Securities**   644
29.1   The Foreign Exchange Markets   645
29.2   Eurocurrency Markets   646
29.3   Currency Calculations   647
29.4   Foreign Exchange Quotations   654
29.5   International Investment Decisions   658
29.6   International Financing Decisions   663
29.7   Derivatives and Hedging of Risk   666
29.8   Summary and Conclusions   669
       Appendix 29A A Deductive Proof of the Four-Way Equivalence Model 672

30 **The Road to Economic and Monetary Union**   677
30.1   Principal Features of the EMS   677
30.2   Economic and Monetary Union   678
30.3   Summary and Conclusions   683

Appendix A Mathematical Tables   685

Appendix B Selected Answers to End-of-Chapter Problems   703

Glossary   707

Subject Index   721

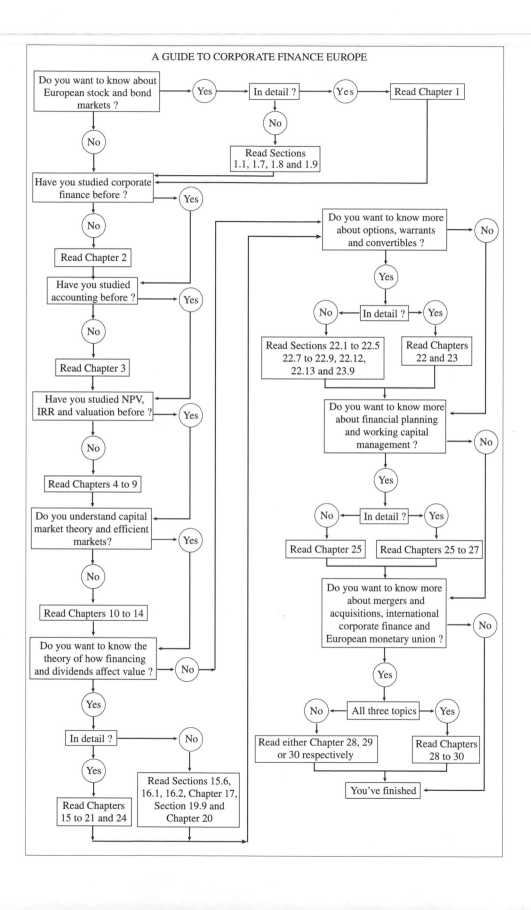

A GUIDE TO CORPORATE FINANCE EUROPE

About the Authors

Adrian Buckley, *Cranfield School of Management, Cranfield University* Adrian Buckley is Professor of International Finance at Cranfield University. Before taking up an academic career, Dr Buckley qualified as a chartered accountant and was a management consultant, an investment banker and a corporate treasurer. He has been a visiting professor in every continent in the world and obtained his doctorate in international finance and international business from the Free University, Amsterdam following earlier UK degrees. Adrian Buckley has been a recent contributor to such journals as the *European Journal of Finance*, the *European Management Journal* and the *Journal of General Management*. His research interests are in the areas of international capital budgeting, corporate valuation and real operating options.

Stephen A. Ross, *Yale University* Stephen Ross is presently the Sterling Professor of Economics and Finance at Yale University. One of the most widely published authors in finance and economics, Professor Ross is recognized for his work in developing the Arbitrage Pricing Theory. He has also made substantial contributions to the discipline through his research in signalling, agency theory, options, and the theory of the term structure of interest rates. Previously the president of the American Finance Association, he serves as an associate editor of the *Journal of Finance* and the *Journal of Economic Theory*. He is co-chairman of Roll and Ross Asset Management Corporation.

Randolph W. Westerfield, *University of Southern California* Randolph Westerfield is the Dean of the University of Southern California School of Business Administration and holder of the Robert R. Dockson Dean's Chair of Business Administration.

Dr Westerfield came to USC from the Wharton School, University of Pennsylvania, where he was Chairman of the Finance Department and Senior Associate at the Rodney I. White Center for Financial Research. He has taught at Stanford University, The Claremont Graduate School, and the University of Lisbon.

His research interests are in corporate financial policy, investment management and analysis, mergers and acquisition, and pension fund management. Dr Westerfield has served as a member of the Continental Bank (Philadelphia) trust committee. He has also been a consultant to a number of corporations, including AT&T, Mobil Oil and Pacific Enterprises, as well as to the United Nations and the US Departments of Justice and Labor. Dr Westerfield is the author of more than 30 monographs and articles. He has served as a member of the editorial review board of the *Journal of Banking and Finance* and the *Financial Review*.

Jeffrey F. Jaffe, *The Wharton School, University of Pennsylvania*   Jeffrey F. Jaffe has been a frequent contributor to finance and economic literature in such journals as the *Quarterly Economic Journal*, *The Journal of Finance*, *The Journal of Financial and Quantitative Analysis*, and *The Financial Analysts' Journal*. His best-known work concerns insider trading, where he showed both that corporate insiders earn abnormal profits from their trades and that regulation has little effect on these profits. He has also made contributions concerning initial public offerings, regulation of utilities, the behaviour of market makers, the fluctuation of gold prices, the theoretical effect of inflation on the interest rate, the empirical effect of inflation on capital asset prices, the relationship between small capitalization stocks and the January effect, and the capital structure decision.

Preface

The teaching and practice of corporate finance within Europe have become more challenging than ever before. The last several years have seen fundamental changes in financial markets and financial instruments. Scarcely a day goes by without an announcement in the financial press about such matters as takeovers, foreign exchange losses, financial restructuring, initial public offerings, bankruptcy and derivatives. The theory and practice of corporate finance have been moving ahead with speed. And so, too, has the breadth of teaching of corporate finance around Europe. To a significant extent, though, this has been hampered by the absence of a text focused upon Europe and providing European examples. This book is the first textbook on corporate finance specifically aimed at an audience of Europeans who are looking beyond their country towards, at least, the boundaries of their own continent. With physical mobility and mobility of ideas so much greater nowadays, it is felt that a text that strides across Europe is more than overdue.

New developments in European money place new burdens on the teaching of corporate finance. On the one hand, the changing world of finance makes it more difficult to keep materials up to date. On the other hand, the teacher must distinguish the permanent from the temporary, and avoid the temptation to follow fads. In this text, we emphasize the modern fundamentals of the theory of finance and make the theory come to life with many numerical examples. All too often, the beginning student views corporate finance as a collection of unrelated topics that are unified largely because they are bound together between the covers of one book. Our aim is to present European corporate finance as the working of a small number of integrated and powerful ideas, theories and intuitions.

Our Intended Audience

This book has been written for core course and intermediate-level courses in corporate finance at universities and business schools in Europe on undergraduate programmes and on MBA-level courses.

We assume that most students either will have taken or will concurrently be taking courses in accounting, statistics and economics. This exposure will help students understand some of the more difficult material. However, the book is self-contained. A prior knowledge of these areas is not essential. The only mathematics prerequisite is basic algebra.

Attention to Pedagogy

We see three keys to good pedagogy in a corporate finance text: (1) extensive examples, questions and problems; (2) consistency in the level of difficulty; and (3) conceptual coherence.

There is room for both easy and difficult textbooks in corporate finance. Of course, good textbooks should not shift haphazardly from difficult to easy, and vice versa. Our objective is to write a text that is consistently moderate in difficulty. Our book is designed for two audiences—the intermediate undergraduate and the MBA. Therefore our objective has been to write a book with sufficient flexibility to be taught to both of these audiences. We have written the core material on value, risk, capital budgeting, and capital structure at a consistently moderate level of difficulty. Some chapters can be omitted without loss of continuity for a more introductory level treatment. More specialized chapters, such as those on options, warrants and convertibles, and mergers and acquisitions, may be covered in more advanced courses. We indicate how the reader might abridge *Corporate Finance Europe* to a relatively simple overview of the topic of finance later in this preface.

We have found that many textbooks lack conceptual coherence. We attempt to use consistently the intuitions of arbitrage, net present value, efficient markets, and options throughout the book. We have also attempted to enliven some of the conceptual material by including recent results from modern financial research—mainly from the USA. This research has at times raised more questions than answers; therefore we have presented some of the puzzles, anomalies and unresolved questions of corporate finance. We hope that this will stimulate the curiosity of students and motivate them to work harder to grasp the complexities of modern corporate finance.

Study Features

Getting the theory and concepts current and up-to-date is only one phase of developing a corporate finance text. To be an effective teaching tool, the text must present the theory and concepts in a coherent way that can be easily learned. With this in mind, we have included several study features:

1. *Concept Questions*   After each major section in a chapter is a unique learning tool called 'Concept Questions'. Concept Questions point to essential material and allow students to test their recall and comprehension periodically.
2. *Key Terms*   Students will note that important words are highlighted in **boldface** type the first time they appear. They are also listed at the end of the chapter along with the page number on which they first appear. New words appear in *italics* when they are first mentioned. Both key terms and new words are defined in the glossary at the end of the text.
3. *Demonstration problems*   Throughout the text we have provided worked-out examples to give students a clear understanding of the logic and structure of the solution process.
4. *Boxed material*   Interesting concepts and topics are examined and expanded in boxes.

5. *Problem sets* Because problems are so critical to a student's learning, at the end of each chapter we present problems which have been thoroughly reviewed and class-tested. The problem sets are graded for difficulty, moving from easier problems, intended to build confidence and skill, to more difficult problems that are designed to challenge the enthusiastic student. Problems have been grouped according to the concepts they test. We provide answers to selected problems at the end of the book.

6. *Enumerated chapter summaries* At the end of each chapter a numbered summary provides a quick review of key concepts in the chapter.

7. *Text signposts* At the end of this preface we present a suggested route through the text which should appeal to the student wishing to focus upon the bare essentials of corporate finance. This should enable this book to be used as a basic text as well as at an intermediate to advanced level.

Supplementary Materials

For the use of instructors in corporate finance there is an *Instructor's Manual*. This contains mission statements for each chapter in the book which may help lecturers with ideas on context and teaching. It also includes answers to the Text Problems and Concept Questions. Also provided is a test bank of multiple-choice questions for most chapters.

International Currency Codes

Given that this book concerns corporate finance in Europe, one of the problems that we have had to confront concerns the currency in which we explain concepts and set questions. Sticking with one European currency, say the German mark, would be inappropriate and our text would tend to become *Corporate Finance Germany*. So we have decided to use different currencies for different examples. Sometimes we use the German mark, sometimes the British pound, sometimes the Italian lira, sometimes the Swiss franc and so on. But even this presents problems. Sometimes the Swiss franc is abbreviated to FS, sometimes to Sfr. Sometimes the Dutch guilder is referred to as Fl and sometimes as NFl. To overcome this problem we have resorted to the use of ISO codes of international currency identification, sometimes referred to as SWIFT codes. According to this, the Swiss franc is identified as CHF, the Dutch guilder is identified as NLG and so on. To avoid confusion and ensure that the student is aware of these codes, a list of selected European currency codes appears below—and the US dollar is also referred to because we use it in some examples too. Note that we also use the proposed European common currency of the Euro; one Euro equals one ECU (European currency unit), a basket currency of European foreign exchange based on a fixed percentage of most EU currencies and equal, at the time of writing, to about US dollars 1.1.

Corporate Finance Europe: The Essentials

Our main audience for *Corporate Finance Europe* is intended to be intermediate undergraduate and MBA students. But we would like to feel sure that this textbook is not ruled out in terms of use at basic undergraduate and basic MBA levels. To this end, we set out below a scheme of suggested reading which is designed to communicate a

Country	Currency	Code
Austria	Schilling	ATS
Belgium	Belgian franc	BEF
Czech Republic	Koruna	CZK
Denmark	Danish krone	DKK
Finland	Finnish markka	FIM
France	French franc	FRF
Germany	Deutschemark	DEM
Greece	Drachma	GRD
Hungary	Forint	HUF
Iceland	Icelandic krona	ISK
Ireland	Punt	IEP
Israel	Shekel	ILS
Italy	Lira	ITL
Luxembourg	Luxembourg franc	LUF
Malta	Maltese lira	MTL
Netherlands	Guilder	NLG
Norway	Norwegian krone	NOK
Poland	Zloty	PLZ
Portugal	Escudo	PTE
Romania	Leu	ROL
Spain	Peseta	ESB
Sweden	Swedish krona	SEK
Switzerland	Swiss franc	CHF
Turkey	Turkish lira	TRL
United Kingdom	Pound sterling	GBP
United States	US dollar	USD
European currency unit	ECU	XEU

firm foundation in corporate finance without too many of the difficulties associated with the subject. Our suggested study scheme is as follows:

- Chapter 1   Read sections 1.1 and 1.7 to 1.9 inclusive
- Chapters 2 to 11 inclusive in their entirety
- Chapters 13 and 14 in their entirety
- Chapter 15   Read section 15.6
- Chapter 16   Read sections 16.1, 16.2 and 16.7
- Chapter 17   Read in its entirety
- Chapter 19   Read section 19.9
- Chapter 20   Read in its entirety
- Chapter 22   Read sections 22.1 to 22.5 inclusive in their entirety, read Sections 22.7, 22.8, 22.9, 22.12 and 22.13
- Chapter 25   Read in its entirety
- Chapter 30   Read in its entirety

Acknowledgements

We are outstandingly indebted to Liz Tribe who has pieced together, typed and corrected the English relating to *Corporate Finance Europe*. This has been a mammoth task which has been completed with great cheerfulness and a good sense of humour. Many thanks. Errors that remain must be debited, though, to the authors' account. Please mail details of errors found to Professor Adrian Buckley, Cranfield School of Management, Cranfield University, Cranfield, Bedfordshire, MK43 0AL, UK.

We are also grateful to the support of our publishers in easing the gestation of this text particularly, in various ways, and at various times, to Cathy Peck, to Alfred Waller and to Alastair Lindsay. Again many thanks.

Adrian Buckley
Stephen Ross
Randolph Westerfield
Jeffrey Jaffe

How to make *Corporate Finance Europe* Easy

Our main audience for *Corporate Finance Europe* is intended to be intermediate undergraduate and MBA students. But we would like to feel sure that this textbook is not ruled out in terms of use at basic undergraduate and basic MBA levels. To this end, we set out below a scheme of suggested reading which is designed to communicate a firm foundation in corporate finance without too many of the difficulties associated with the subject. Our suggested study scheme is as follows:

- Chapter 1   Read sections 1.1 and 1.7 to 1.9 inclusive
- Chapters 2 to 11 inclusive in their entirety
- Chapters 13 and 14 in their entirety
- Chapter 15   Read section 15.6
- Chapter 16   Read sections 16.1, 16.2 and 16.7
- Chapter 17   Read in its entirety
- Chapter 19   Read section 19.9
- Chapter 20   Read in its entirety
- Chapter 22   Read sections 22.1 to 22.5 inclusive in their entirety, read
                Sections 22.7, 22.8, 22.9, 22.12 and 22.13
- Chapter 25   Read in its entirety
- Chapter 30   Read in its entirety

We are aware that the wording here is exactly as it is in the preface. Why? Just in case you, the student, missed it. We really want to help you to find an easy way through *Corporate Finance Europe*.

PART I

Overview

1 Foundation to European Corporate Finance   3
2 Introduction to Corporate Finance   29
3 Accounting Statements and Cash Flow   45

To present a unified and logical theory of corporate finance is a complicated task in itself. To present it within the confines of European corporate finance is doubly complicated because European finance is not homogeneous. In particular, the role of the stock exchange varies from country to country, accounting rules differ within Europe and tax systems vary across frontiers.

In Chapter 1, we focus upon these issues and attempt to point out the major differences which confront the student of finance within a European framework. We would stress that these differences are very important and should always be borne in mind by readers as they, hopefully, progress through this text. The approach which we have adopted in this book substantially assumes that stock markets play a major role in the financial life of European countries. However, as the reader will learn, this importance differs from one European country to another. In Britain, for example, it is outstandingly important. In Greece, Austria and Portugal, its relevance is at the opposite extreme.

To engage in business the financial managers of a firm must find answers to three kinds of important questions. First, what long-term investments should the firm take on? This is the capital budgeting decision. Second, how can cash be raised for the required investments? We call this the financing decision. Third, how will the firm manage its day-to-day cash and financial affairs? These decisions involve short-term finance and concern net working capital.

In Chapter 2, we discuss these important questions, briefly introducing the basic ideas of this book and describing the nature of the modern corporation and why it has emerged as the leading form of the business firm. The chapter discusses the goals of the modern corporation. Though the goals of shareholders and managers may not always be the same, conflicts are usually resolved in favour of the shareholders. Finally, the chapter reviews some of the salient features of modern financial markets. This preliminary material will be familiar to students who have some background in accounting, finance and economics.

Chapter 3 examines the basic accounting statements. It is review material for students with an accounting background. We describe the balance sheet and the income statement. The point of the chapter is to show the ways of converting data from accounting statements into cash flow. Understanding how to identify cash flow from accounting statements is especially important for later chapters on capital budgeting.

Foundation to European Corporate Finance

In introducing the topic of European corporate finance, we are immediately confronted with a very substantial problem, namely that European finance is not homogeneous—far from it. The stock market plays a bigger part in some countries than others; shareholder returns as a corporate goal are emphasized to different extents in different European countries; corporate governance differs across borders; takeovers are more prevalent in some territories than in others; accounting rules are different and so are tax systems; banks play greater roles in some countries compared to others and they operate in varying ways in various European countries. But not everything is different. There are a lot of factors that are common across borders. Anyway, let us confront the problems head on and examine the differences. In this respect we focus, first of all, upon European stock markets.

1.1   European Equity Market

In this section, we present a brief overview of European equity markets. Immediately, Table 1.1, which summarizes **equity market capitalization** (the total value of all of companies' ordinary shares in terms of their stock market value) and turnover of the major exchanges in Europe and shows US and Japanese data for comparison, tells an interesting story. Note that the data in the table relate to 1994. London and Luxembourg can be seen to have equity capital market capitalizations in excess of their local gross domestic product (GDP)—a feature not achieved in New York or Tokyo, although almost achieved in Switzerland. This characteristic of equity investment is not apparent elsewhere in the EU—it is nowhere near achieved in France or Germany, for example. Similarly, on the criterion of annual stock market turnover of domestic equities as a percentage of GDP, London figures show a total of almost 50 per cent, far outstripping both New York and Tokyo,[1] to say nothing of its European peers. On this point, the large European economies of France and Germany show, respectively, 15 per cent and 30 per cent. In general, compared to London the equity markets of continental Europe play a far more limited role. To some extent, the high market capitalization and relatively high liquidity (as a percentage of GDP) of the Dutch market could, as of 1994, be attributed, primarily, to a small number of very large multinational firms. Royal Dutch Shell alone accounted for 34 per cent of total capitalization. And Shell plus four other large international Dutch companies had 33 per cent of the turnover. Over the three years from

---

[1] Tokyo figures for market capitalization may be around 50 per cent overstated due to cross-shareholdings among Japanese quoted companies.

TABLE 1.1   EU versus US and Japanese Equity Markets—end 1994

Market	Listed companies Domestic	Listed companies Foreign	Domestic market capitalization in millions of ECUs*	Domestic market capitalization as % of GDP	Annual turnover In millions of ECUs* Domestic	Annual turnover In millions of ECUs* Foreign	Annual turnover In millions of ECUs* Total	as % of GDP Domestic
Amsterdam	317	215	182,492	68.10	72,251	158	72,409	26.96
Athens	165	0	11,678	18.45	4,293	0	4,293	6.78
Brussels	155	141	68,583	37.09	10,477	3,130	13,608	5.67
Copenhagen	243	10	38,343	31.89	24,082	488	24,570	20.03
Dublin	56	9	16,003	37.87	3,945	0	3,945	9.34
Germany	423	227	388,024	23.30	509,408	14,833	524,240	30.59
Helsinki	65	0	33,936	43.38	11,194	2	11,196	14.31
Lisbon	83	0	11,890	16.66	3,195	0	3,195	4.48
London	1,747	462	932,018	112.72	391,635	463,063	854,698	47.37
Luxembourg	55	217	23,127	208.47	862	19	881	7.77
Madrid	375	4	126,401	32.26	43,631	14	43,645	11.14
Milan	219	4	147,511	17.73	121,835	53	121,888	14.64
Paris	459	195	367,939	34.20	161,662	3,228	164,890	15.03
Stockholm	106	8	97,106	61.14	66,733	58	66,791	42.02
Vienna	94	41	23,521	14.74	7,065	251	7,316	4.43
EU major markets	**4,562**	**1,533**	**2,468,572**	**41.49**	**1,432,268**	**485,297**	**1,917,565**	**24.07**
New York	1,689	216	3,460,354	63.90	1,884,429	202,511	2,086,940	34.80
Nasdaq**	4,577	325	644,661	11.90	1,115,319	63,784	1,179,103	20.60
Tokyo	1,651	110	2,926,215	77.13	713,244	614	713,857	18.80
Switzerland	217	243	204,626	93.20			176,171	

* At the time of writing one USD is equal to about 0.9 ECU.

** National Association of Security Dealers Automated Quotations—a US computerized system providing prices on around 4,000 unlisted stocks provided by nearly 500 firms making markets in such securities.

Source: *London Stock Exchange Quality of Markets Review* (Summer 1995); *European Stock Exchange Statistics, FESE* (1994 Annual report); Datastream; Nasdaq.

1994, estimates indicate that the share of number of deals (not value) of Amsterdam equity turnover accounted for by private individual investors, as opposed to financial institutions, has increased from 25 per cent to around 40 per cent. Moving on to Sweden, measured against GDP, it is characterized by a relatively large and (as we shall see in Table 1.3) active stock market despite heavily concentrated ownership.

Note that if Table 1.1 were redrafted on the basis of stock market levels as at the middle of 1997, the figures for domestic market capitalization to GDP would all (except Japan) be some 50 per cent or more higher than those shown. Thus, London would be around 170 per cent, Amsterdam 145 per cent, Stockholm 110 per cent, Germany approaching 40 per cent, Paris 45 per cent, New York over 100 per cent, and so on. Clearly the European countries with substantial equity market cultures can be seen to include Britain, Switzerland, Luxembourg, the Netherlands and Sweden.

Look further at Table 1.1 and London's importance is seen not just in terms of shares in domestic companies, but in terms of foreign equities too. London actually trades a greater worth of foreign stocks than British. Obviously we would hypothesize a different focus in terms of the role of stock market quoted equities in corporate finance across Europe. As we shall see, this first difference has interesting repercussions in financial management. The underlying story of the first table can be told in picture form—see Figure 1.1.

FIGURE 1.1   Market Capitalization, 1994

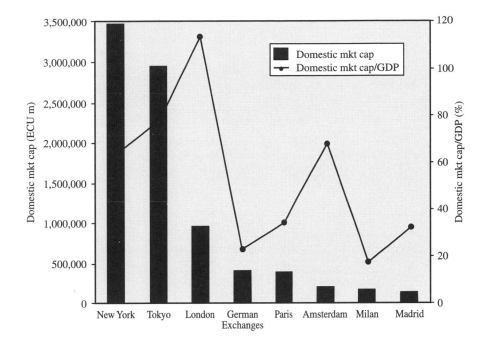

Lest the above statistics are criticized, it has to be admitted that some caution is necessary in comparing data. For example, London foreign equity turnover is inflated by double-counting of trades which are actually executed through the domestic market trading systems. German domestic turnover is artificially boosted by such factors as the commission arrangements on floor trading, which encourage multiple intermediation of trades. And similar caveats abound for other countries too. But there can be little doubt that the conclusions about relative magnitudes apply.

Table 1.2 widens the perspective to the world's 20 largest markets, indicating the percentage of world market capitalization represented by each for selected years between 1982 and 1994. Figures 1.2 and 1.3 show these data in graphical form, for 1985 and 1994. Europe's total share of world market capitalization has declined very slightly, while that accounted for by the Asian Tiger economies has risen considerably, although largely (over the long run) at the expense of North America. But Europe remains the generator of some 20 per cent of world equity turnover—significant indeed, although a long way behind the USA.

What about ownership in European firms? Although data are somewhat frail and hardly fully comparable, Table 1.3 summarizes a number of studies of ownership of equity in non-financial corporations in six European countries plus the USA and Japan. Of course, given that the studies underpinning data in the table are not comparable, very firm conclusions cannot be confidently drawn. Despite this, the high concentration of ownership in continental European and Scandinavian countries, compared with the UK, Japan and the USA is clear. Generally the high ownership concentration countries are those where the equity market is less cultivated. It has been reported that 79 and 85 per cent, respectively, of local companies quoted on the stock exchange in France and Germany, respectively, had a single investor with stakes larger than 25 per cent—the corresponding figure for the UK is only 16 per cent of companies. The overwhelming majority of listed companies in continental Europe are

TABLE 1.2   **Percentage Shares of World Market Capitalization, 1982–94**

	1982	*1985*	*1988*	*1991*	*1994*
USA	53.27	47.55	27.92	37.07	42.89
Japan	16.69	22.12	43.20	29.99	20.52
UK	7.45	8.02	8.07	9.54	7.74
Canada	4.24	3.62	2.53	2.36	4.34
Germany	2.83	4.40	2.72	3.74	3.20
France	1.83	1.96	2.53	3.44	3.06
Switzerland	1.70	2.15	1.65	1.97	2.59
Hong Kong	0.00	0.88	0.88	1.18	1.82
Taiwan	0.00	0.00	1.28	0.92	1.71
South Africa	3.95	1.26	1.34	1.23	1.48
Netherlands	2.06	1.36	1.46	1.09	1.36
Australia	1.70	1.57	1.56	1.38	1.29
Korea	0.22	0.17	1.01	0.72	1.27
Malaysia	0.69	0.55	0.25	0.42	1.25
Italy	0.85	1.57	1.56	1.57	1.23
Brazil	0.51	0.97	0.33	0.33	0.97
Sweden	0.85	1.27	0.97	1.28	0.91
Singapore	0.98	0.49	0.49	0.79	0.85
Mexico	0.18	0.09	0.27	0.77	0.77
Thailand	0.00	0.00	0.00	0.21	0.75
Total	100.00	100.00	100.00	100.00	100.00

Source: Fédération Intérnationale des Bourses de Valeurs.

FIGURE 1.2   **Percentage of World Market Capitalization, 1985**

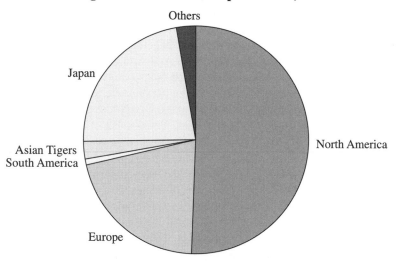

closely held. And, although comparisons over time are not always available, the evidence for France, Germany and Sweden shows an increase in ownership concentration over the 'seventies and 'eighties. Establishing the identity of controlling holders is often difficult in many countries, however, the continuing importance of families in the control of corporations is one of the central features distinguishing the continental European business environment from those of the UK and the USA. This concentration of ownership is related to liquidity in local equity markets and to the willingness of firms to list on public stock exchanges.

FIGURE 1.3   Percentage of World Market Capitalization, 1994

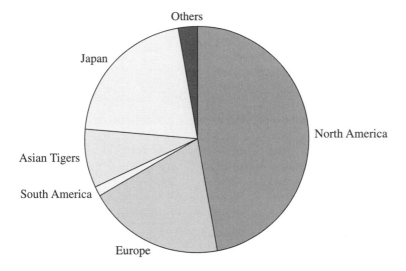

TABLE 1.3   Ownership Concentration in Listed Firms in Various Countries (the Largest Owner's Share)

	(1)	*(2)*	*(3)*	*(4)*	*(5)*	*(6)*	*(7)*	*(8)*
Largest owner's share	*France (1982)*	*Germany (1985)*	*Italy (1993)*	*Spain (1990)*	*Sweden (1987)*	*UK (1990)*	*Japan (1983)*	*US (1981)*
> 50	55	66	89	49	42	5	5	9
30–50			9		31	29	70	29
25–30	42	23		49	12			
20–25								
15–20			2		11	27		10
10–15		12				30		29
5–10	2			2	4	9	25	23
< 5								

In practically all European countries, **institutional investors** (pension funds, insurance companies, investment trusts and similar investment companies) have, over the recent past, become more important at the expense of private individuals—see Table 1.4. However, the types of institutions holding shares, and possibly exercising control, are different. In the UK, the growth of pension funds over the past two decades has been spectacular. The strong portfolio orientation of institutional investors in the UK contrasts sharply with the control orientation of this investor group in, for example, Germany. This difference in the orientation of institutional investors is, as we shall see, closely linked to the functioning of financial markets.

There are also differences in the nature of the market for corporate control—mergers and acquisitions. In the UK, hostile takeovers mounted via purchases in the official stock market play an important role in the world of business. In continental Europe, such transactions are rare. In Germany and in the Netherlands, no truly hostile takeover attempt has succeeded, and this is largely true for Belgium too. Sweden experienced four successful hostile offers during the 'eighties, a period of substantial local corporate

TABLE 1.4   Ownership of Listed Equities in Various Countries by Sector (as of 31 December)

		Private individuals	Non-financial corporations	Government institutions	Financial institutions	Foreign owners
France	1977	41	20	3	24	12
	1992	34	21	2	23	20
Germany	1970	29	41	11	11	8
	1993	17	39	3	29	12
Italy	1993	32	22	28	14	4
UK	1969	50	5	3	36	6
	1993	19	2	1	62	16
Japan	1970	40	23	0	34	3
	1993	20	28	1	43	8
USA	1991	51	15	0	28	6
	1993	48	9	0	37	6

restructuring. Reversing past passivity, the French authorities have, over the past decade, made a point of activating the market for corporate control and a considerable number of takeovers have taken place against the will of incumbent management. But, in general, takeovers in continental Europe are used as a mechanism to withdraw firms from the stock exchange rather than as a means of changing control. Most control-related trades in continental Europe occur in large blocks of shares outside official markets.

Pension funds also have different levels of importance in the pattern of investment in different European countries. Table 1.5 shows contrasting pension fund asset levels in 11 European countries—they represent a very high percentage of GDP in the Netherlands, Britain and Ireland. Large variations are apparent on this score, with UK pension fund assets amounting to 82 per cent of GDP, a figure only exceeded in Europe by the Netherlands. The colossal contrast of Germany and France, where pension fund assets amount to only 6 per cent and 3 per cent of GDP, respectively, is a marked one. In the European Union (EU) foreign assets as a percentage of pension fund investments are concentrated in the UK, Irish, Belgian and Dutch funds—such

TABLE 1.5   Assets of Pensions Funds in Various EU Countries—end 1993 (US$ bn)

	Pension fund assets (end-1993) $ bn	% of GDP	% of pension fund assets held in foreign assets
UK	717	82	31
Germany	106	6	8
Netherlands	261	85	21
Sweden (1991)	39	16	1
Denmark	26	19	4
Ireland	18	44	41
France	41	3	2
Italy	12	1	4
Belgium	7	3	37
Spain	10	2	10
Portugal	5	7	10

Note: Includes only independent (private- and public-sector) funded schemes.
Source: European Federation for Retirement Provision/EU Committee.

TABLE 1.6   **Pension Funds' Portfolio Distributions in Various EU Countries (percentage allocations), 1992**

	Equities	Fixed income	Property	Liquidity and deposits
UK	80	11	6	3
Germany	6	80	13	1
Netherlands	24	60	14	2
Sweden	2	90	2	6
Denmark	19	67	12	2
Ireland	66	24	7	3
France	20	67	11	2
Italy	14	72	10	4
Belgium	31	50	8	11
Spain	3	94	2	1
Portugal	18	58	5	19

Source: European Federation for Retirement Provision/EU Committee.

investment is itself limited by regulation for funds in some countries, such as Germany. Equity holdings of pension funds seem to vary from 80 per cent of the portfolio in the UK to 6 per cent in Germany and to only 2 per cent in Sweden (see Table 1.6). Apart from the UK and Ireland, the lion's share of pension fund portfolios is invested in fixed income investments.

Estimates of **real total returns** (return in terms of dividends—and the like—and capital gains versus initial investment with inflationary effects taken out of the equation) and their standard deviations, based on work by Davis,[2] over the period from 1967 to 1990 are shown in Table 1.7. European equity shares have, over long periods, achieved real returns of between 6.3 per cent per annum and 9.5 per cent per annum in most European markets, although with a standard deviation of some 20 per cent plus. First-class US equities display similar long-run returns and standard deviations.

TABLE 1.7   **Local Currency Real Returns on Pension Funds' Portfolios in Various EU Countries—1967–1990**

	UK	Germany	Netherlands	Sweden	Denmark	Ireland	France	Italy	Belgium
Figures in percentages									
Estimated portfolio real return	5.8 (12.5)	5.1 (4.4)	4.0 (6.0)	0.2 (7.6)	3.6 (12.7)	5.0 (11.9)	n/a n/a	n/a n/a	n/a n/a
Inflation (CPI)	8.9 (5.3)	3.5 (2.1)	4.9 (3.1)	8.1 (2.7)	7.7 (3.2)	10.0 (6.0)	7.1 (4.1)	11.3 (5.9)	5.5 (3.2)
Returns on:									
Loans	1.4 (5.0)	5.3 (1.9)	3.8 (3.6)	3.4 (3.1)	6.1 (3.6)	n/a n/a	2.6 (3.2)	2.7 (3.7)	n/a n/a
Mortgages	2.0 (5.2)	4.7 (1.4)	4.3 (2.6)	2.6 (3.0)	5.8 (3.7)	n/a n/a	3.7 (2.6)	n/a n/a	n/a n/a
Equities	8.1 (20.3)	9.5 (20.3)	7.9 (28.2)	8.4 (23.3)	7.0 (27.5)	8.5 (25.9)	9.4 (26.9)	4.0 (35.9)	6.3 (16.7)
Bonds	−0.5 (13.0)	2.7 (14.9)	1.0 (13.1)	−0.9 (8.5)	3.4 (16.1)	−0.1 (15.3)	1.0 (13.1)	−0.2 (18.3)	1.3 (11.7)
Short-term assets	1.7 (4.9)	3.1 (2.1)	1.6 (4.0)	1.3 (3.5)	1.6 (1.8)	n/a n/a	2.4 (3.4)	−2.2 (4.2)	n/a n/a
Property	6.7 (11.4)	4.5 (2.9)	4.6 (15.0)	n/a n/a	n/a n/a	n/a n/a	n/a n/a	n/a n/a	n/a n/a
Foreign bonds	−0.1 (15.0)	3.0 (11.2)	−0.7 (11.2)	−0.2 (12.6)	−2.0 (11.6)	−1.4 (11.4)	−0.2 (12.8)	−1.5 (10.7)	0.2 (11.1)
Foreign equities	7.0 (16.2)	10.4 (13.5)	6.6 (14.4)	7.1 (14.0)	5.5 (14.3)	5.9 (14.2)	7.0 (13.5)	6.0 (12.5)	7.5 (13.7)

Notes: (i) Figures in brackets represent standard deviations of annual real total returns in local currency.
        (ii) Returns include both capital gains and dividends, interest or rental income.
Source: Davis (1995).[2]

---

[2] E. P. Davis, (1995). *Pension Funds. Retirement-Income Insurance and Capital Markets: An International Perspective,* Oxford: Oxford University Press.

Asset returns, both absolute and relative to other assets, are a key influence in the structure of any portfolio. Risk reduction is the main motivation for portfolio diversification. International diversification can offer a better risk/return trade-off by reducing the impact of the domestic economic cycle. In a longer-term context, international investment in countries with a relatively young population may be a reasonable ploy to ensure adequate returns to pensioners in countries with an ageing population. Foreign asset holdings have grown sharply through the 'eighties in the UK, since the abolition of exchange controls, and in Ireland. Dutch and Belgian funds have long held a significant proportion of assets abroad. For funds in Belgium, Ireland, and the Netherlands, international investment is particularly attractive owing to the large volume of pension fund assets compared with the size of domestic security and property markets, and the thinness and lack of diversification of local equity markets. Risk aversion of trustees or managers may limit portfolio distribution of assets. It may also play a role in many countries in limiting international investment.

The United Kingdom, Irish, Belgian and Dutch funds tend to index retirement pensions, although there is no legal obligation to do so. Also, indexation promises are made by the Swedish national plan. Hence the need for pension fund managers in these countries to seek a degree of inflation protection. Funds in these countries hold a significant proportion of equities and international assets. In the UK, where bond-holding is low, fixed income securities form a relatively low proportion of pension fund portfolios. However, this is not so in Germany with its recent history of a far lower inflation rate.

So we see the strong differences in the level of interest in equity markets being reflected in patterns of company ownership concentration and in differing patterns of influence of pension funds. And, of course, company law in different European countries has created different modes of company structure—this topic is examined for a handful of countries with a view to familiarizing readers with their diverse structures. But inevitably it is impossible to focus on all European countries and the examination is restricted to the UK, Germany, France and the Netherlands.

Concept Questions

- What factors contribute to making British equity market capitalization to GDP so much higher than most of its European peers?
- How should total real returns on shares be measured?

1.2   Companies in Britain

The dominant business entity in Britain is the limited liability company—that is a company limited by shares. A limited liability company may be incorporated as either a private or a public concern, the latter having the right to issue securities to the public. Both public and private companies must have at least two shareholders, and public companies must have at least two directors, although private companies need have only one director. For a limited liability company to be incorporated as a public entity, it must have a minimum share capital of GBP50,000 and include Public Limited Company (or plc) in its name. A private company is subject to no minimum capital requirement and must include the word Limited (or Ltd) at the end of its name. In the UK, the practice is for shares to be issued in registered, rather than bearer, form. This is the case for both public and private companies. **Registered shares** have the name and address of the holder, together with the number of shares held, documented with the company or its agent. Transfer of shares from one party to another is documented in the company's Register of Members. By contrast, the ownership of **bearer shares** usually takes place by transfer of the share certificate; the company does not have a full documented list of shareholders. The practice in most continental European countries is for shares to be issued in bearer form. To ensure security, it is usually the case that bearer shares have to be placed with an authorized depository. Generally, on payment of a dividend, the depository, on behalf of the owner of shares, exchanges a voucher attached to the share certificate for the actual dividend cheque. Similar practices apply, in terms of registered and bearer forms, with respect to debt that is listed on a stock exchange.

London has long been one of the financial capitals of the world with a market capitalization that makes it Europe's largest equity market. As we have seen, market capitalization is over 100 per cent of the British gross domestic product. The main securities exchange in the UK is The London Stock Exchange. Since 1973, it has been electronically integrated with the securities exchanges of a number of other cities across the country, making it a network rather than a single exchange. The London Stock Exchange lists around 7,000 securities (one company may have half a dozen securities listed), many of which are issued by foreign companies, and it has developed and maintained sophisticated mechanisms of disclosure to protect the interest of both large and small investors.

Companies must fulfil a number of stringent requirements to be granted a full listing on The London Stock Exchange. The securities to be listed must have a minimum initial capitalization of GBP700,000, and at least 25 per cent of any class of issued equity capital must be held by the public. With its application for listing, the company must submit a variety of financial data, including audited financial statements. These should consist of the company's most recent balance sheet, its income statement, and a statement of cash flows. After it is granted a listing, the company must publish audited annual financial statements within six months of its year-end and unaudited interim statements semi-annually. It must also release on a timely basis important ancillary information, such as preliminary profit announcements, details of major transactions, explanation of departures from standard accounting practices and particulars concerning borrowings. The London Stock Exchange reserves the right to publish information itself or to suspend a listing if it deems a company's public financial disclosures to be inadequate.

Securities deregulation in the UK reached significant levels in October 1986 with the Big Bang, as it was termed. This included a broad range of measures, such as abolishing minimum commission rates, admitting international firms to membership on The London Stock Exchange, abandoning the mandatory separation of broking and jobbing (that is, dealing) functions, and introducing an electronic trading system allowing off-floor trading. It was hoped that these changes would improve London's competitive edge as a trading centre. In its first year, the market's capacity rose fivefold, costs doubled, and fee levels halved. But in October 1987, with the crash of Black Monday, turnover collapsed. Though it is now back to pre-1987 levels, the market still has too much capacity. Following the Big Bang, the winners are undoubtedly the institutional investors who have seen commission rates on large bargains in well-traded shares pared sharply. Although not directly a consequence of the Big Bang, Table 1.8 shows the diminishing role of the individual investor in British equities.

Nowadays the securities industry in the UK is overseen by a group of rather too many self-regulatory organizations (SROs) that answer to the Securities and Investments Board (SIB), a watchdog agency with an ambiguous legal status. A clear question is

TABLE 1.8   British Share Ownership Profile

Share owner	1969(%)	1989(%)	1993(%)
Pension funds	9.0	30.6	34.2
Insurance companies	12.2	18.6	17.3
Other financial institutions	14.7	9.3	10.3
Individuals	49.5	22.9	19.3
Public sector	2.6	2.0	1.3
Commercial sector	5.4	3.8	1.5
Overseas	6.6	12.8	16.1
Total	100.0	100.0	100.0

whether the system would function better with fewer regulatory bodies. Overlap between watchdogs has created excessive confusion and it also increases the risk of a small, weak regulatory body becoming too close to those it is supposedly policing.

1.3   Companies in Germany

German law recognizes two types of limited liability companies—these are the Aktiengesellschaft (AG) and the Gesellschaft mit beschränkter Haftung (GmbH). The first of these, the AG, is almost analogous to the publicly held corporation in the USA or the plc in the UK. It is the only business entity in Germany whose shares may be traded on a stock exchange. The second, the GmbH, is analogous to a privately held corporation. It is generally chosen by those owners, such as families, who wish to retain a measure of privacy and close personal control over their businesses.

An AG must have at least five shareholders at the time of its formation, but afterwards a smaller number of shareholders is permissible. It must possess a minimum share capital of DEM100,000 (about GBP43,000) with at least 25 per cent of this amount paid in. The AG is governed by two bodies. These are the board of management, which oversees the day-to-day operations, and the supervisory board, which advises management on behalf of the shareholders and employees. Although the views of the supervisory board carry considerable weight with management, it usually does not possess the legal power to direct the company.

The supervisory board is first appointed by the founder, and thereafter by the shareholders' meeting. German law requires that one-third (in smaller companies) to one-half (in companies with more than 2,000 employees) of the members of the supervisory board to be elected by employees—the others are elected by shareholders. The German supervisory board is thus an institution geared towards binding together parties with potential conflicts of interest. Confrontation is limited by the fact that each group holds a veto over the election of the other's representatives. This tends to deter both sides from nominating controversial or provocative candidates.

Representation of the employees' posts is generally taken by senior employees, and the chairman is elected by the shareholders and has a casting vote. The supervisory board generally includes professional advisors to the company, such as lawyers and accountants, as well as representatives from banks and other firms with which the corporation has a business relationship. Clearly, a large proportion of the members of the supervisory board is appointed under German law, not under the corporation's own internal rules. The supervisory board, in turn, appoints the executive board. Once appointed, the executive board enjoys a high degree of managerial autonomy, although the most important decisions must be confirmed by either the supervisory board and/or a general meeting of shareholders.

Plants with more than five employees are required by law to have a works' council, which must be consulted with regard to recruitment, dismissals and changes in working practice. There is also an economic council—half of whose members are appointed by the supervisory board, and half by the works' council. This has only limited functions. Trade unions have considerable influence in the election of both the members of the works' council and the employee representatives on the supervisory board. Unions normally nominate a number of candidates, and the personnel director is often a trade unionist.

There are fewer than 700 quoted companies in Germany, compared with well over 2,000 in the UK. There is also a different structure of share ownership to that in the UK (see Table 1.9). The tabulation indicates that institutional funds exert relatively little influence over board policy in Germany. Institutional funds hold some 6 per cent of shares in Germany compared with 64 per cent in the UK. Maybe this feature is influential in the fact that German dividend levels have lagged behind earnings growth over time. In this regard, the term distributable profits is more narrowly defined than in the UK, where all aggregate undistributed profits after tax are available for dividend. In Germany, a certain proportion of profits must be retained to build up a legal reserve, equal to 10 per cent of nominal capital.

TABLE 1.9   Ownership Structure of German and UK Companies

	Germany (%)	UK (%)
Foreigners	20	17
Private investors	20	19
Banks	8	–
Other corporates	39	–
Investment funds	3	47
Insurance companies	3	17
State and local government	7	–
Total	100	100

Also, in Germany, corporate cross-holdings are common—see the total of 39 per cent in Table 1.9. Corporate shareholders' interests are concerned with strategic, long-term considerations rather than dividend growth or capital appreciation. There is only a duty to disclose such a holding if it exceeds 25 per cent, with a further obligation to notify the authorities if the holding is more than 50 per cent. Commercial banks are also significant investors in equities in Germany. Banks and corporate shareholders exert great influence. Also, banks exercise proxy voting rights over many private client shares deposited with them. Most shares in Germany are in bearer form (as opposed to registered) and are deposited with commercial banks. German investment companies and pension funds have remained, predominantly, in bonds and property, not equities. As borne out by Table 1.6, a German pension fund would be unlikely to hold more than 10 per cent of its portfolio in equities.

In Germany, the focus upon shareholder value as a standard for business performance is not widespread—unlike the UK and the USA—but it is growing. Also, hostile takeovers are not typical. There is some evidence that the structure of share ownership is changing in favour of investment institutions and this may ultimately lead to the spread of contested takeovers.

Banks play a strong central role in providing capital to German companies—not only via lending but also through purchasing shares. When a German company seeks financing, its bank may lend money or buy shares, depending on the immediate financial position of the venture as well as its long-term outlook. Consequently, many German banks have built up sizeable shareholdings in non-financial companies. Deutsche Bank, for example, has significant equity interests in a number of public companies outside of the banking industry, including a 24 per cent stake in Daimler-Benz plus significant interests in several dozen privately-held companies. These equity holdings enable German banks to wield an unusual amount of influence over the policies of their clients. This influence is reflected in the composition of the supervisory boards of many companies.

The power of German banks and the presence of their representatives on the supervisory boards of major companies have important implications for financial practices in Germany. Most important of these is that banks have access to inside information on company operations and therefore they do not have to depend on published financial statements as their major source of information. Because their largest shareholders also tend to be both lenders and insiders, German companies have relatively little incentive to develop the extensive—and expensive—financial reporting systems that firms in English-speaking countries find necessary to attract and hold equity market investors. Although the disclosure standards governing German financial reporting are more sophisticated than those in countries still dominated by family-owned business cartels, such as Italy, they are not as detailed and extensive as those in countries with strong public capital markets and a long tradition of financial stewardship, such as the UK. Given this, plus the fact that, under German corporate law, the principle is to protect the creditors and not the shareholders, it is not surprising that the German equity markets are underdeveloped by international standards.

Germany has eight stock exchanges. The Frankfurt exchange, with about 70 per cent of the volume of all trading throughout German, is the largest, with the other seven operating as regional exchanges. In a move to create a world-class, primary exchange, the Deutsche Borse was created in early 1993. It serves as a holding company for the eight exchanges and has the Frankfurt exchange as its centre. In spite of the global importance of the German economy, the total capitalization of the German stock market is only 23 per cent of its gross domestic product, as compared to 64 per cent in the USA, 77 per cent in Japan, and well over 100 per cent in the UK. In 1994, less then 700 companies were listed on German exchanges as compared to about 6,500 in the USA, 1,700 in Japan, and 2,200 in the UK. Only about 6 per cent of German adults directly owned company shares (compared to 35 per cent in the USA and around 20 per cent in the UK) despite an average household savings rate of 13 per cent, well beyond that of the average US household. Equally surprising is the fact that it was only in 1994 that Germany made insider trading a criminal offence. Moreover, it is only recently, with a concern for investor fairness protection in mind, that the banks have been required to establish Chinese walls between their trading and corporate finance departments. Clearly, Germany lacks a strong equity culture like that of the USA, Japan or the UK.

1.4   Companies in France

In France, the public company is termed a *société anonyme* (SA), while the private company is called a *société à responsabilité limitée*. But it is not in such definitions that the singular characteristics of French companies and business resides. It is, rather, in the impact of France's distinct culture; we return to this in the paragraphs following the next.

One of the main features of the French system is the absence of a diverse investment community. The state, banks, and corporate management hold the controlling interest in the French corporate governance structure. In this respect, the French system departs not only from the Anglo-American model, but also from the German model, too. The majority of French companies are either state-controlled or owned by families or management. Although, like many other European countries, France is experiencing privatization, its top 50 industrial, commercial and service companies break down as to 12 state-controlled, 17 management-controlled, 14 family-controlled and managed, 3 family-controlled (but with outside management) and 4 subsidiaries.

Probably, in no other modern industrialized country, except Japan, does the state play as powerful a role as it does in France. This may, in part, be due to the long French tradition of encouraging the nation's finest minds into the civil service, via the educational system of the Grandes Ecoles. Since the Second World War, when the state stepped in to rebuild France's economy, the French intellectual élite (represented by both civil servants and industrial managers) has been intimately involved in the formation and direction of industry. So important did the civil service become in the creation of business that private groups, seeking to compete, recruited the same Grandes Ecoles/civil-servant types who were familiar with the corridors of state power. Thus, the managers who run the largest companies, the bankers who provide them with capital and the government officials who oversee them, are all drawn from the same educational background and all share the same goal of keeping French industry very much in French hands.

The state's strong role in the economy (termed *dirigisme*) is one of the main factors affecting business in France. Though the state is becoming less *dirigiste*, it has been active in forcing mergers and restructurings in state-owned industries for policy purposes and keeping many key industries firmly under government control. But the results have been mixed. France has enjoyed some notable successes (for example, nuclear power) but it has had its failures (for example, computers and consumer electronics). The government had substantial holdings in cars, steel, insurance and banking and had a monopoly in most public utilities, rail, coal, tobacco, radio and television—although privatization is changing that to some extent.

The French state's motivation is to keep what it perceives as key industries in French hands and under French control. Traditionally, this was achieved simply by keeping such industries nationalized. However, following the privatization drive, a *noyeau dur* (hard core) of management-friendly shareholders has emerged. These hard-core holding groups undertook not to sell their controlling blocks for a period of five years without the company's approval. Thus Banque Nationale de Paris (BNP), which was privatized in December 1993 (with an overwhelming stake of individual shareholders with tiny holdings), has 16 friendly institutional shareholders who in total own 30 per cent of BNP's shares. Half of such shares are held by Union des Assurances de Paris (UAP), a state-owned insurer.

Even in non-state-owned companies, the government plays a powerful role. The state protects industry in other ways. For instance, any EU company buying a fifth of the capital of a French firm needs clearance from the government. Also, there is a tangled web of relationships among directors, managers and government. In private companies, directors and executives shuttle back and forth between the private and public sector. Many of the top people in the finance ministry move across to jobs in state-owned and private companies (the French call this *pantouflage*—meaning putting on one's slippers). In 1992, *pantouflage* became so common that the government introduced new rules to stem the tide of people leaving the civil service.

The state's control over private companies also extends indirectly through the banking system. France's financial institutions (banks and insurance companies) are leading providers of capital to French industry, and now account for one-twentieth of the Bourse's capitalization. However, many of the banks are state owned, or heavily state influenced. Banks are informed, long-term shareholders who have played a strong role in protecting French companies from takeover. Through the above, and many other mechanisms, the state exerts a good deal of influence over private, or recently privatized, companies. France has developed a complex system of cross-shareholdings. Not unlike the Japanese *keiretsu*, this is called the *verrouillage* system, in which shares are parked with friendly companies and accounts for an estimated two-thirds of the shares traded on French stock exchanges—the Bourses.

France has been said to be the only Western country where one man, the President-Director-General (PDG), determines the strategy of the company, executes that strategy and controls it, without the countervailing power of the board of directors. The PDG has virtual control over the board of directors from their selection to their functional specialism and roles. It is regarded as bad form for the board to take a vote on a management decision, since it shows that the PDG has lost the confidence of the board. The PDG tends to be responsible for day-to-day operations as well as the long-term strategic direction of the company. If the PDG seeks advice on a major strategic move, he is as likely to go to the state or state banks as he is to go to the board.

Given that even privately owned companies tend to be in the hands of controlling blocks, director selection usually takes the interests of the few large shareholders into account. Even though the PDG has absolute power over the board and its selection, he would invariably pay close attention to the wishes of his owners in choosing new board members. And it is worth noting that the largest banks are represented on the boards of most sizeable companies.

Rules governing the structure and composition of French boards are complicated. For example, French companies may choose between two methods of board governance. They may adopt either a unitary boardroom structure, like an Anglo-American model, or a two-tier structure, as in German companies.

Under the unitary structure, there is a single administrative board called the *counseil d'administration*. There must be a minimum of three members but no more than twelve. Up to four executives may serve, though their number must not make up more than one-third of the board. Two staff representatives must also serve on the board, one representing the executives, one the other employees, though they are not counted as full directors. On top of this there are non-executive representatives.

With the two-tiered structure, there is an executive committee (*directoire*) and a supervisory board (*counseil de surveillance*) that oversees the activities of the executive committee. This structure is similar to the German system—as is the role of the banks in providing finance for business. Most French companies opt for the single-tier system—the Anglo-American model.

1.5   Companies in the Netherlands

The most important forms of business organization in the Netherlands are the *naamloze vennootschap* (NV) or public company and the *besloten vennootschap met beperkte aansprakelijheid* (BV) or private company. In 1993, there were about 1,800 NVs and over 191,000 BVs. Other forms of enterprise characterize Dutch business, including sole proprietorships, civil partnerships, general partnerships, limited partnerships, cooperative and mutual guarantee associations. These forms are not dealt with here.

Large (*structuur*) companies, whether NVs or BVs, must have a board of management directors (*Raad van bestuur*) and a supervisory board (*Raad van commissarissen*) of at least three persons (no maximum number is set). For other companies, a supervisory board is optional. Three interested parties—the general meeting of shareholders, the works' council (*Ondernemingsraad*) and the board of managerial directors—may recommend appointees to the supervisory board. The former two must be informed who is chosen, and have rights of objection and appeal. It is the supervisory board which appoints the board of managerial directors and adopts the accounts and submits them to the shareholders' meeting, the works council and the local trade registry. The Dutch system of two-tier boards is similar to the systems operating in Germany and (partially) in France.

A large (*structuur*) company is one which satisfies all the following criteria:

- It has issued share capital and reserves (at the time of writing) totalling at least 25 million guilders.
- It, or any other company in which it holds at least half of the issued share capital directly or indirectly for its own benefit, has, pursuant to a legal obligation, formed a works' council.
- It, or any other such company, taken together, employ, as a rule, at least 100 persons in the Netherlands.

Both NVs and BVs must deposit for public inspection, within eight days of their being approved by the annual general meeting, a copy of their annual accounts, directors' report and supplementary information at the trade registry at which they are registered.

As in France and Germany, most listed shares in the Netherlands are in bearer, rather than registered, form. The shares of BVs cannot be listed and cannot be in bearer form. As well as ordinary shares, Dutch companies may have fixed dividend preference shares and priority shares (*Prioriteitsaandelen*). *Prioriteitsaandelen* are peculiar to Dutch law and have the effect of strengthening the power of founding shareholders and directors against takeover bids.

Dutch companies raise funds both by share and loan issues on the Amsterdam Stock Exchange and from the commercial banks in the form of short- and medium-term loans. Of course, many of the larger Dutch-based multinationals have to look outside of domestic financial sources to fund their needs. Although over 300 domestic companies are listed, dealings are dominated by the five major multinational companies (Akzo Nobel, Hoogovens, Philips, Royal Dutch Shell and Unilever) which account for about 50 per cent of the market capitalization and turnover. Despite the governance system resembling the German/French in terms of supervisory boards, the banking/finance system is otherwise fairly Anglo-American, except for the relative absence of hostile takeovers.

Concept Questions

- What is the difference between registered shares and bearer shares?
- Does the bearer form of shareholding make it easier or more difficult to mount hostile takeovers? Why? (Hint: In a hostile takeover, the bidder offers to buy the shares from existing shareholders. The bidder may also wish to build up a significant holding before bidding.)

1.6   Corporate Governance and Corporate Finance

A summary of the names used in some EU countries for private and public companies appears in Table 1.10. Different company law regulations apply to private and public companies; different rules of corporate governance apply.

TABLE 1.10   EU Private and Public Companies

	Private	*Public*
Denmark	Anspartsselkab (ApS)	Aktieselskab (AS)
Belgium, France and Luxembourg	Société à responsabilité limitée (Sarl)	Société anonyme (SA)
Germany	Gesellschaft mit beschränkter Haftung (GmbH)	Aktiengesselschaft (AG)
Greece	Etairia periorismenis efthynis (EPE)	Anonymos etairia (AE)
Italy	Societá a responsibilitá limitata (SRL)	Societá per azioni (SpA)
Netherlands and Belgium	Besloten vennootschap (BV)	Naamloze vennootschap (NV)
Portugal	Sociedade por quotas (Lda)	Sociedade anónima (SA)
Spain	Sociedad de responsibildad limitada (SRL)	Sociedad anónima (SA)
UK and Ireland	Private limited company (Ltd)	Public limited company (PLC)

The term **corporate governance** is concerned with how a company is directed and controlled and, in particular, with the role of the directorate and the need for ensuring that there is an effective framework for accountability of directors to owners. Corporate governance and financial market liquidity are important topics in the finance literature, but they have traditionally been addressed independently of each other. Here we attempt to link the two. The starting point of the corporate governance literature is the agency problem of capitalism. This concerns the credibility problem facing firms when they seek to convince outside investors to contribute funds. In its most extreme form, the agency problem is about how to ensure that management does not steal investors' contributed resources or pay themselves undeserved handsome salaries, and so on. The role of corporate governance is to ensure that resources are not dissipated, but applied effectively into profitable investment opportunities. There are two generic approaches to the classic agency problem: either key investors are given influence over strategic decisions in the firm (control-oriented finance) or management finds ways of committing to efficient actions and to shares in the proceeds from these actions (arm's-length finance).

Under control-oriented finance, investor intervention is typically based on a control block of equity or a position as exclusive or dominant creditor. Intervention may take many forms, from vetoing or blocking inefficient investment decisions, or using a voting majority to oust incumbent management.

Under arm's-length finance, investors do not intervene in the company, at least not as long as payment obligations are met. Intervention, if it occurs, typically involves some external mechanism such as renegotiation of corporate control, or court proceedings in the case of bankruptcy. The firm attempts to commit itself to behave efficiently and repay investors, and in the meantime it may provide collateral in the form of contingent property rights to individual well-specified assets or cash flows.

The basic issue of these two approaches to the agency problems is the same—how to convince investors that they will be repaid in the future. But the choice of ownership structure has important implications for the way in which the problem is addressed. In the case of control-oriented finance, control is concentrated from the outset, but in the arm's-length case, we rely on the accumulation of controlling stakes, and this, in turn, presupposes the existence of a liquid market through which this is facilitated in the marketplace.

Systems where control-oriented finance dominates can be expected to be associated with more concentrated ownership structures at the level of the individual firm and with less liquid capital markets. Control-oriented financial systems breed control-oriented investors. The market for corporate control (takeovers) operates outside of the public stock exchanges in the form of occasional trades in large blocks.

Arm's-length systems have dispersed ownership of both debt and equity, and more liquid capital markets. Investors are oriented towards holding portfolios of securities and the market for corporate control operates over public stock markets and this is seen as an important mechanism for the correction of managerial failure. Table 1.11 summarizes hypothesized and observed contrasting characteristics of control-oriented and arm's-length types of financial systems.

TABLE 1.11   Characteristics of Control-oriented and Arm's-length Financial Systems

	Type of financial system	
	Control-oriented	*Arm's-length*
Share of control-oriented finance in capital markets	High	Low
Financial markets	Small, less liquid	Large, highly liquid
Number of firms listed on exchanges	Small	Large
Ownership of debt and equity	Concentrated	Dispersed
Investor orientation	Control-oriented	Portfolio-oriented
Turnover of control blocks	Very low	Relatively high
Dominant agency conflict	Controlling vs. minority shareholders	Shareholders vs. management
Influence of board of directors	Less important	Important
Role of hostile takeovers	Very limited	Potentially important

Although the link between corporate finance and governance, on the one hand, and corporate law and securities regulation on the other, is still poorly understood, a recent survey of the corporate governance literature, by Shleifer and Vishny argues that concentration of ownership is an unavoidable outcome of shortcomings in the legal system.[3] In the absence of well-functioning securities regulation, concentration of ownership is the only way to surmount the agency problem referred to above. Shleifer

---

[3] A. Shleifer and R. Vishny (1995). 'A Survey of Corporate Governance'. Paper presented at the Nobel Symposium on 'Law and Finance' in Stockholm.

and Vishny imply that ownership and control patterns are ultimately determined by existing laws. On this front, it is not a coincidence that continental Europe has a legal system founded on codified Roman law, whereas the legal systems of England and the USA are rooted in common law. This distinction is worth further comment.

Some countries have a legal system which relies upon a limited amount of statute law and a large amount of case law built up in the courts, supplementing the statutes. Such a common law system is the case in England. It is hence less abstract than codified law. A common law rule seeks to provide an answer to a specific case rather than to formulate a general rule for the future. Although this common law system emanates from England, it is found in similar forms in many countries influenced by England. For example, the federal law of the United States, the laws of Ireland, India and Australia are, to a greater or lesser extent, modelled on English common law. Other counties have a system of law which is based on the Roman civil law as compiled by Justinian in the sixth century and subsequently developed, at least in Europe, by continental European élites. Here, rules are linked to ideas of justice and morality and they become doctrine and codified in laws. The above distinction has important implications for company law or commercial codes. Table 1.12 illustrates the way in which developed countries' legal systems fall into these two categories.

TABLE 1.12   Western Legal Systems

Common law	*Codified Roman law*
England and Wales	France
Ireland	Italy
United States	Germany
Canada	Spain
Australia	Netherlands
New Zealand	Portugal
	Japan (commercial)

Note: The laws of Scotland, Israel and South Africa, among others, tend to embody elements of both systems.

Nobes and Parker note the relevance of the above classification in terms of its impact for company accounting; they state that in Germany accounting is 'to a large extent a branch of company law'.[4] The fact that England and Wales and continental Europe fall in opposite camps in Table 1.12 may partially explain differences in corporate governance and also in financial reporting techniques.

Concept Questions

- What is the agency problem of capitalization?
- What are the key differences between control-orientated finance and arms'-length finance?

1.7   European Corporate Reporting

Of course, in any discussion of corporate finance across borders, differences in financial reporting of company performance is an important topic—this is so at the current time in Europe, although moves are afoot towards harmonization. Following

---

[4]C. Nobes and R. Parker (1995). *Comparative International Accounting,* 4th edition, Prentice Hall.

earlier work by Nair and Frank,[5] Nobes and Parker propose a hierarchy model of financial reporting. Their classification of 14 countries is interesting and is summarized in Figure 1.4. By and large, the countries to the right in Figure 1.4 can be characterized by legal systems derived from codified Roman law (see Table 1.12) and those to the left are mainly rooted in common law. Particularly relevant in Figure 1.4 are the various sources of driving force discernible from country to country, for example, the influence of the tax system, and so on. Of course, further territories could be added:

- Singapore, Hong Kong and Malaysia, under UK Influence
- Korea, near Japan
- Switzerland and Austria, close to Germany
- Denmark, close to the Netherlands

FIGURE 1.4   A Suggested Classification of Accounting Systems in some Developed Western Countries in 1980

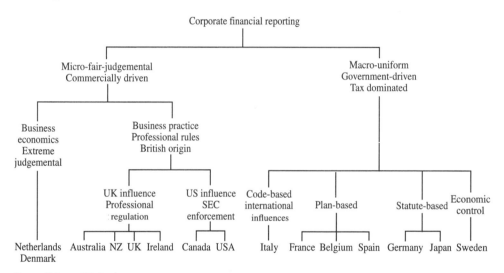

Source: Nobes and Parker.[4]

Nobes suggests some refinement to the above hierarchical model and notes that EU harmonization of accounting (see later in this chapter) may be in the process of reducing variations in Figure 1.4.[6] For example, since 1980 France has moved, somewhat, towards the left of the classification in Figure 1.4. Sweden has reduced the influence of taxation on financial reporting since the late 'eighties moving it, like France, a little towards the left. Similar movement is evident for Italy and Spain.

All the European countries in Figure 1.4, except the UK, Ireland, Denmark and the Netherlands, appear to the right of the tabulation. Were one to wish to put typical accounts from countries on the right hand side on to a UK-style basis, a number of adjustments would be required. In general terms, according to Alexander and Nobes, these would embrace the following:[7]

[5] R.D. Nair and W.G. Frank (1980). 'The impact of disclosure and measurement practices on international accounting classifications', *Accounting Review,* July.

[6] C. Nobes (1992). *International Classification of Financial Reporting,* London: Routledge.

[7] D. Alexander and C. Nobes (1994). *A European Introduction to Financial Accounting,* Prentice Hall.

- Conservatism   Increase net asset values
- Historic cost   Increase net asset values
- LIFO   Increase inventory values for some countries
- Consolidation   Beware lack of consolidation
- Associated companies Increase net assets and profit where the equity method
                        of accounting is not used
- R & D   Decrease net assets by any capitalized amounts.
                        Adjust profits appropriately
- Leases   Increase fixed assets and liabilities where leases are
                        not capitalized
- Pensions   Examine carefully. Extract any pension provisions
                        from shareholders' funds
- Provisions   Increase shareholders' funds by portion of general
                        provisions
- Tax   Decrease depreciation where caused by tax

Of course, it is currently impossible to achieve precise international comparisons of earnings and net asset figures. This does not mean that users of financial statements should give up. Approximate adjustments and informed questions, like those referred to in the previous paragraph, provide rather general guidelines towards comparison. Steps are afoot to harmonize European accounting although it seems that the path is likely to be a long one.

European Union company law and financial reporting harmonization is proposed in its Fourth Directive. Provisions laid down in a directive are binding on all companies once the directive is written into national law. However, each country is free to choose the form and method of implementation and also to modify options for specific requirements. Even after directives have been written into law, the latter must still be interpreted and applied at the level of the member state. The adoption of a directive on accounting by all EU member states does not guarantee accounting uniformity if directives are not uniformly interpreted. The EC's Fourth Directive (ratified in 1978) was concerned with EU company law harmonization. Specifying the form and content of annual financial statements, the Fourth Directive represents an important compromise between the legalistic approach to accounting and financial reporting prevalent in continental Europe and the case-precedent approach prevailing in the United Kingdom. Although fairly detailed, the Fourth Directive still permits many alternative treatments and permits member states of the EU various options upon implementation, for example, according to the Directive:

- Intangible assets, such as goodwill, formation and start-up expenses, and research and development costs, may be amortized through the income statement over a period of five years, or written off immediately to reserves or amortized through the income statement over its estimated useful life.
- Inventories may be valued at the lower of cost or market value. Member States may allow actual cost, FIFO, LIFO, weighted average or a similar cost method, or a combination of these methods.
- Assets may be valued at historic cost. However, companies are also allowed to undertake revaluations and adjust asset values accordingly. Assets may also be adjusted for inflation using the following bases—revaluation of tangible and financial fixed assets, replacement cost for plant, equipment, and inventories, and valuation of all financial statement items by a method 'designed to recognize the effects of inflation'.

- The Fourth Directive is silent on a number of measurement issues for which authoritative guidance is sorely needed, including foreign-currency translation, accounting changes, prior period adjustments, related party transactions, leases, long-term contracts, capitalization of interest costs, accounting for deferred taxes, pensions and other retirement benefits, discontinued operations and earnings per share.

Financial disclosure options are a common feature of the Fourth Directive, for example, while sales revenues must be broken down by product and line of business and geographical area, companies are permitted to omit this information if its nature is deemed to be seriously prejudicial to the company. A summary of the EU's Fourth Directive appears in Appendix 1A to this chapter,

According to a study by Choi and Bavishi, conducted two years after ratification of the Fourth Directive, major differences in reporting were found among reporting entities in Belgium, Denmark, France, Germany, Ireland, Italy, the Netherlands, Norway, Spain, Switzerland and the United Kingdom.[8] Accounting measurements for which major practice differences were observed included foreign consolidations, business combinations, leases, pensions, defined taxes, use of discretionary reserves, asset revaluations, and foreign-currency translation and transactions.

On the question of consolidation of accounts of reporting entities, the European Commission spent numerous years of heated debate. Its Seventh Directive was adopted by the EU and the Board of Ministers in 1983. To comply with the directive establishing basic rules for preparing consolidated statements, member states were required to enact legislation by the end of 1987 that would take effect no later than 1990. Any EU parent companies falling under the provisions of the Seventh Directive were to begin, if they were not already doing so, preparing consolidated statements for financial years beginning in 1990. A brief summary of the content of this latter directive appears in Appendix 1B of this chapter.

Despite this movement towards harmonization in European accounting, the need for continued caution in terms of inferences drawn from published accounts across Europe is borne out by a study by Simmonds and Azières.[9] They subjected exactly similar business happenings to different European accounting interpretations. Accounts were prepared in each of seven European countries on the most likely basis, the lowest permitted basis and the highest permitted basis, with the astonishing results detailed in Table 1.13. In Germany, profit ranged from ECU 27 million to ECU 140 million while the UK range was from ECU 171 million to ECU 194 million. The most likely reported profit ranged from ECU 131 million for Spain to ECU 192 million in Britain. Clearly, perfect harmonization is a long way off.

In this very area, Blake and Amat[10] cite further evidence based on a report by the London stockbroking firm, Smithers & Co., who reckon that, using national income accounts to estimate a 'true' income figure to compare with company accounts in each country, a ratio of true to published profits is computable for five countries as to:

- Japan   1.69
- USA   0.77
- UK   0.75
- France   0.84
- Germany   1.00

---

[8] F.D. Choi and V.B. Bavishi (1983). 'International accounting standards: issues needing atttention', *Journal of Accountancy*, **155** (3), 62–68.

[9] A. Simmonds and O. Azières (1989). *Accounting for Europe—Success by 2000 AD?*, Touche Ross.

[10] J. Blake and O. Amat (1993). *European Accounting*, London: Pitman.

TABLE 1.13   **Ranges of Profit Interpretations for Same Set of Events in Various EU Countries**

	Most likely (ECU m)	Lowest permitted (ECU m)	Highest permitted (ECU m)
Belgium	135	90	193
Germany	133	27	140
Spain	131	121	192
France	149	121	160
Italy	174	167	193
Netherlands	140	76	156
UK	192	171	194

Source: Adapted from Simmonds and Azières.[9]

The above represents factors by which company accounts should be adjusted to make them comparable from country to country. Weetman and Gray, in an exercise concerning accounting practices in the UK, the USA, the Netherlands and Sweden, found UK accounts to be significantly less conservative than those in the USA.[11] Swedish accounts appeared more conservative, and Dutch accounts less conservative, than those in the USA, although not to any statistically significant extent. Of course, the mere passage of time and the evolution of new accounting standards, especially in the UK, has made the above evidence *passé*—but the word of caution about comparisons needs to be restated and always borne in mind.

Having given this caveat, Table 1.14 throws up some interesting evidence on the extent of the use of debt across European frontiers. It shows average debt to capital employed ratios in Europe, according to Tucker.[12] It might be interesting to speculate as to the extent to which the divergences—from 55 per cent for Switzerland to 20 per cent for the UK—flow from different corporate governance systems, banking relationships and financial reporting policies. Certainly the presence of bankers as insiders in a number of European countries might well be consistent with higher debt levels than elsewhere.

TABLE 1.14   **European Gearing Ratios of Companies**

Country	Debt to debt plus equity
Switzerland	0.55
Belgium	0.51
Italy	0.45
Ireland	0.40
Denmark	0.34
France	0.34
Germany	0.30
Sweden	0.27
Netherlands	0.26
Spain	0.25
UK	0.20

Source: Tucker.[12]

---

[11] P. Weetman and S.J. Gray (1991). 'A comparative international analysis of the impact of accounting principles on profits: the USA versus the UK, Sweden and the Netherlands', *Accounting and Business Research,* Autumn, 363–379.

[12] J. Tucker (1994). 'Capital structure: an econometric perspective on Europe' *in* J. Pointon (ed.), *Issues in Business Taxation,* Avebury.

1.8   European Corporate Tax Systems

Different corporate tax systems across boundaries create another problem in European corporate finance. Essentially, the problem arises, not from differences in rate, but from differences emanating from the use of the classical system versus the imputation system. How each works precisely is well summarized in Nobes and Parker[4] from which Table 1.15 is adapted—their text includes more numerical examples assuming different dividend payout rates. So, what is the essential difference between the two systems?

Under a classical system, corporate tax is borne, in the usual way, by the company. But, on payment of a dividend to shareholders, the gross amount of the dividend is subjected to further tax deduction, usually representing shareholder tax at the basic tax rate. Thus, the dividend received by the shareholder is net of both corporate tax and shareholder basic rate tax. Higher levels of tax on the dividend may subsequently be collected from the shareholder to the extent that he or she falls into high tax brackets. But note particularly the incidence of double taxing.

The imputation tax system is designed to eliminate this double taxing effect. Under it, like the classical tax system, the company pays corporation tax. But when it pays a dividend, the dividend is looked upon as a net dividend and no further shareholder tax is paid, until higher rate calculations are made. The dividend is, though, said to be net of an imputed tax (the tax credit) and it is, of course, the net

TABLE 1.15   Classical and Imputation Systems

		Classical £	*Imputation* £
Company			
income (say)		10,000	10,000
corporation tax (40%)		4,000	(52%) 5,200
Distributable income		6,000	4,800
distribution (say) gross		2,000	
less income tax deducted at source (30%)	600		
	net 1,400		net dividend 1,400
retained income		4,000	3,400
Shareholders (basic rate)			
dividend: cash received		1,400	1,400
income tax deducted at source		600	0
tax credit received ($^3/_7$)		0	600
gross dividend		2,000	'grossed up' 2,000 dividend
income tax liability (30%)		600	600
less tax already deducted		600	0
less tax credit		0	600
tax due		0	0
Total tax	(4,000 + 600)	4,600	5,200

Source: Nobes and Parker.[4]

dividend plus this imputed tax credit which are added together for purposes of income calculation for higher level tax rate calculation, to give the gross dividend.

Table 1.15 shows how, in summary, the two tax systems contrast in their working. In Table 1.15, it is assumed that there is a basic rate of income tax, which is the marginal rate for a majority of taxpayers. It has been assumed that this is 30 per cent, that the classical system corporate tax rate is 40 per cent, and that the imputation rate is 52 per cent, as was the case in the UK between 1973 and 1983. For simplicity, accounting and taxable income are taken as being equal. The tax credit is assumed to be 30/70 or 3/7. Note that the bottom line total tax figure in Table 1.15 may show a higher total for the imputation tax system or for the classical tax system dependent upon assumptions about whether dividend payout is high or low.

Although it may not be immediately evident how this creates problems, it will become apparent later in the text. Note that nowadays the Netherlands, Denmark, Belgium, Luxembourg and the USA use the classical tax system. The UK, France, Germany, Ireland, Italy, Portugal, Spain, Australia and New Zealand employ the imputation system. Rates of tax in the early 'nineties and the system employed are summarized in Table 1.16.

TABLE 1.16   Corporation Tax Systems and Main Rates in Various EU Countries and the USA—early 'nineties

Country	System	Corporation Tax rate (%)	Tax credit as % of dividend
Belgium	Classical (1989 onwards) (Imputation 1963–89)	39	–
Denmark	Classical (1991 onwards) (Imputation 1977–91)	38	–
France	Imputation (1965 onwards)	42	50
Germany	Imputation (1977 onwards)	50 and 36*	56.25
Ireland	Imputation (1976 onwards)	40	$33\frac{1}{3}$
Italy	Imputation (1977 onwards)	48	56.25
Luxembourg	Classical	44	–
Netherlands	Classical	35	–
Portugal	Imputation (1989 onwards)	36	19.7
Spain	Imputation (1986 onwards)	35	10
UK	Imputation (1973 onwards)	33	$33\frac{1}{3}$
USA	Classical	35	–

Note: Withholding taxes ignored throughout.

* Plus a business tax of 5 per cent. Note that Germany has a split rate system in which distributed profits are subject to a lower rate than those retained in the business.

On the topic of corporate taxes, it is worth noting that most tax regimes have statutory rules for depreciation allowances in computing profit for tax purposes. Referring back to Figure 1.4, it is worth noting that most of the countries to the right side in that figure tend to use tax depreciation in their published accounts as the amortization charge for reporting purposes.

Usually, companies making losses are allowed to set off such losses against immediately past profits or to carry them forward against future profits, but rules vary. A sample of a few international regulations on this point are shown in Table 1.17. Although the EU has plans for harmonization of tax systems and rates, this is an area which is conspicuous for its lack of progress, rather than any observable move towards coordination.

TABLE 1.17   Carry Back and Carry Forward for Tax Losses in Various Countries (years)

	Carry back	*Carry forward*
UK	3	No limit
USA	3	15
France	3	5
Germany	2	No limit
Netherlands	3	8
Japan	1	5

1.9   Summary and Conclusions

1. European corporate finance differs in many ways from one country within Europe to another. In the UK, there is a far greater emphasis upon stock market sourced equity finance than in other countries. France and Germany, for example, rely to a greater extent upon bank borrowing.
2. Corporate governance is concerned with how a company is directed and controlled and how a framework for accountability of directors to owners is established.
3. Control-oriented finance and arm's-length finance are important contrasting systems of corporate governance which probably have their roots in different legal systems.
4. Different corporate governance systems, contrasting legal frameworks and cultures, together with differing orientations towards stock market finance have created accounting reporting systems which vary sharply across Europe. Countries with a greater reliance on stock market equity finance seem to have looser rules on reporting profit to investors.
5. Like its contrasting accounting rules, European countries have different tax systems, too. Despite lip-service (and some slow shoe-shuffling) on harmonization of accounting and tax systems, there is arguably a lack of real convergence on these aspects of European business.

KEY TERMS

Equity market capitalization   3
Institutional investors   7
Real total returns   9

Registered shares   10
Bearer shares   11
Corporate governance   18

APPENDIX 1A

A SUMMARY OF THE EU'S FOURTH DIRECTIVE

- Article 1 states that the directive relates to public and private companies throughout the European Union, except that member states need not apply the provisions to banks, insurance companies and other financial institutions.
- Article 2 defines the annual accounts to which it refers as the balance sheet, profit and loss account, and notes.
- Articles 3–7 contain general provisions about the consistency and detail of the formats for financial statements. Some items cannot be omitted and corresponding figures for the previous year must be shown.
- Articles 8–10 detail two formats for balance sheets: horizontal or vertical. One or both may be allowed by member states.
- Articles 11 and 12 allow member states to permit small companies to publish considerably abridged balance sheets.

- Articles 15–21 concern the definition and disclosure of assets and liabilities.
- Articles 22–26 specify four formats for profit and loss accounts that member states may choose.
- Article 27 allows member states' medium-sized companies (defined in the Directive) to avoid disclosure of the items making up gross profit.
- Articles 28–30 contain definitions relating to the profit and loss accounts.
- Articles 31 and 32 provide general rules of valuation.
- Article 33 examines the Directive's stance toward accounting for inflation or for specific price changes.
- Articles 34–42 relate to detailed valuation and disclosure requirements for various balance sheet items.
- Articles 43–46 concern the disclosures that are obligatory in the annual report, including the notes to the accounts. Small companies (defined in the Directive) may be partially exempted.
- Articles 47–51 relate to the audit and publication of accounts. Member states may exempt small companies from publishing profit and loss statements. Medium-sized companies may abridge their balance sheets and notes.
- Articles 52–62 deal with the implementation of the Directive and with transitional problems, particularly those relating to consolidation (see Appendix 1.2 below).

APPENDIX 1B

A SUMMARY OF THE EU's SEVENTH DIRECTIVE

- Articles 1–4 require limited companies, or the equivalent, to draw up consolidated accounts that include subsidiaries, irrespective of their location.
- Article 5 allows member states to exempt financial holding companies that neither manage their subsidiaries nor take part in board appointments.
- Article 6 allows member states to exempt medium-sized and small groups, using the criteria of the Fourth Directive and assuming that no listed company is included.
- Articles 7–11 exempt a company from the requirement to consolidate its own subsidiaries if it is itself a wholly owned subsidiary of an EU company.
- Article 12 allows member states to require consolidation when companies are managed by the same persons.
- Articles 13–15 allow various subsidiaries to be excluded from the consolidation on immateriality grounds.
- Article 16 requires that consolidated accounts shall be clear and shall give a true and fair view.
- Article 17 requires the Fourth Directive's formats to be used, suitably amended.
- Article 18 requires complete consolidation.
- Article 19 requires there to be a once-and-for-all calculation of goodwill based on fair values at the date of first consolidation or at the date of purchase.
- Article 20 relates to accounting for takeovers.
- Articles 21–23 require minority interest to be shown separately, and 100 per cent of income of consolidated companies to be included.
- Articles 24–28 require consistency, elimination of intragroup items, use of the parent's year-end as the group's year-end, and disclosure of information to enable meaningful comparisons to be made through time.
- Article 29 requires the valuation rules of the Fourth Directive to be used and uniform rules to be used for the consolidation of all subsidiaries.
- Articles 30 and 31 require goodwill on consolidation to be depreciated or to be written off immediately against reserves.
- Article 32 allows member states to require or permit proportional consolidation for joint ventures.
- Article 33 requires associated companies to be recorded as a single item, initially valued at cost or at the proportion of net assets.
- Articles 34–36 specify the number of disclosures relating to group companies and consolidation methods.
- Articles 37 and 38 deal with publication and audit.
- Articles 39–51 deal with transitional and enabling provisions.

Introduction to Corporate Finance

Although the topic of corporate finance is extensive, its basic concerns can be expressed relatively simply:

1. What long-term investment strategy should a company take on?
2. How can cash be raised for the required investments?
3. How much short-term cash flow does a company need to pay its bills?

These are not the only questions that can be raised regarding corporate finance. They are, however, among the most important questions and, taken in order, they provide a rough outline of the present book.

One way that companies raise cash to finance their investment activities is by selling or 'issuing' securities. The securities, sometimes called *financial instruments* or *claims*, may be roughly classified as *equity* or *debt*, sometimes called *shares* (*stocks* in the USA) or *bonds*, respectively. The difference between equity and debt is a basic distinction in the modern theory of finance. All securities of a firm are claims that depend on or are contingent on the value of the firm.[1] In Section 2.2 we show how debt and equity securities depend on the firm's value, and we describe them as different contingent claims.

In Section 2.3 we discuss different organizational forms and the pros and cons of the decision to become a corporation.

In Section 2.4 we take a close look at the goals of the corporation and discuss why maximizing shareholder wealth is likely to be the primary goal of the corporation. Throughout the rest of the book, we assume that the firm's performance depends on the value it creates for its shareholders. Shareholders are made better off when the value of their shares is increased by the firm's decisions.

A company raises cash by issuing securities to the financial markets. Some idea of the value of outstanding securities traded in European financial markets was given in Chapter 1. In Section 2.5 we describe some of the basic features of the financial markets. Roughly speaking, there are two basic types of financial markets: the money markets and the capital markets. The last section of the chapter provides an outline of the rest of the book.

---

[1] We tend to use the words firm, company, and business interchangeably. However, there is a difference between a firm and a corporation. We discuss this difference in Section 2.3.

2.1   What Is Corporate Finance?

Suppose you decide to start a firm to make tennis balls. To do this, you hire managers to buy raw materials, and you assemble a workforce that will produce and sell finished tennis balls. In the language of finance, you make an investment in assets such as inventory, machinery, land and labour. The amount of cash you invest in assets must be matched by an equal amount of cash raised by financing. When you begin to sell tennis balls, your firm will generate cash. This is the basis of value creation. The purpose of the firm is to create value for you, the owner. The value is reflected in the framework of the simple balance-sheet model of the firm.

The Balance-Sheet Model of the Firm

Suppose we take a financial snapshot of the firm and its activities at a single point in time. Figure 2.1 shows a graphic conceptualization of the balance sheet, and it will help introduce you to corporate finance.

The assets of the firm are on the lefthand side of the balance sheet. These assets can be thought of as current and fixed. *Fixed assets* are those that will last a long time, such as a building. Some fixed assets are tangible, such as machinery and equipment. Other fixed assets are intangible, such as patents, trademarks and the quality of management. The other category of assets, *current assets*, comprises those that have short lives, such as inventory. The tennis balls that your firm has made but has not yet sold are part of its inventory. Unless you have overproduced, they will leave the firm shortly.

Before a company can invest in an asset, it must obtain financing, which means

FIGURE 2.1   **The Balance-Sheet Model of the Firm**

Total value of assets   **Total value of the firm
to investors**

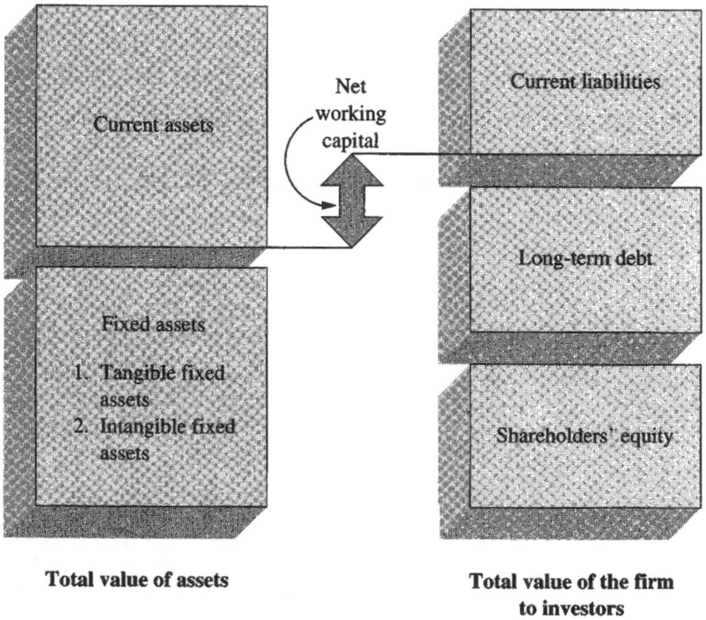

Lefthand side, total value of assets. Righthand side, total value of the firm to investors, which determines how the value is distributed.

that it must raise the money to pay for the investment. The forms of financing are represented on the righthand side of the balance sheet. A firm will issue (sell) pieces of paper called *debt* (loan agreements) or *equity shares* (share certificates—sometimes called stock certificates). Just as assets are classified as long-lived or short-lived, so too are liabilities. A short-term debt is called a *current liability*. Short-term debt represents loans and other obligations that must be repaid within one year. Long-term debt is debt that does not have to be repaid within one year. Shareholders' equity represents the difference between the value of the assets and the debt of the firm. In this sense it is a residual claim on the firm's assets.

From the balance-sheet model of the firm it is easy to see why finance can be thought of as the study of the following three questions:

1. In what long-lived assets should the firm invest? This question concerns the lefthand side of the balance sheet. Of course, the type and proportions of assets the firm needs tend to be set by the nature of the business. We use the terms **capital budgeting** and *capital expenditure* to describe the process of making and managing expenditures on long-lived assets.

2. How can the firm raise cash for required capital expenditures? This question concerns the righthand side of the balance sheet. The answer to this involves the firm's **capital structure**, which represents the proportions of the firm's financing from current and long-term debt and equity.

3. How should short-term operating cash flows be managed? This question concerns the upper portion of the balance sheet. There is a mismatch between the timing of cash inflows and cash outflows during operating activities. Furthermore, the amount and timing of operating cash flows are not known with certainty. The financial managers must attempt to manage the gaps in cash flow. From an accounting perspective, short-term management of cash flow is associated with a firm's **net working capital**. Net working capital is defined as current assets minus current liabilities. From a financial perspective, the short-term cash flow problem comes from the mismatching of cash inflows and outflows. It is the subject of short-term finance.

Capital Structure

Financing arrangements determine how the value of the firm is sliced up. The persons or institutions that buy debt from the firm are called *creditors*.[2] The holders of equity shares are called *shareholders*.

Sometimes it is useful to think of the firm as a pie. Initially, the size of the pie will depend on how well the firm has made its investment decisions. After a firm has made its investment decisions, it determines the value of its assets (e.g. its buildings, land and inventories).

The firm can then determine its capital structure. The firm might initially have raised the cash to invest in its assets by issuing more debt than equity; now it can consider changing that mix by issuing more equity and using the proceeds to buy back some of its debt. Financing decisions like this can be made independently of the original investment decisions. The decisions to issue debt and equity affect how the pie is sliced.

The pie we are thinking of is depicted in Figure 2.2. The size of the pie is the

---

[2] We tend to use the words creditors, debtholders, and bondholders interchangeably. In later chapters we examine the differences among the kinds of creditors. In algebraic notation, we will usually refer to the firm's debt in terms of the letter B (for bondholders).

FIGURE 2.2   Two Pie Models of the Firm

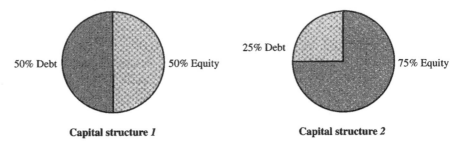

Capital structure *1*   Capital structure *2*

value of the firm in the financial markets. We can write the value of the firm, *V* as

$$V = B + S$$

where *B* is the value of the debt and *S* is the value of the equity. The pie diagram considers two ways of slicing the pie: 50 per cent debt and 50 per cent equity, and 25 per cent debt and 75 per cent equity. The way the pie is sliced could affect its value. If so, the goal of the financial manager will be to choose the ratio of debt to equity that makes the value of the pie—that is, the value of the firm, *V*—as large as it can be.

The Financial Manager

In large firms the finance activity is usually associated with a top officer of the firm, such as the finance director, the corporate treasurer and some lesser officers. We think that the most important job of a financial manager is to create value from the firm's capital budgeting, financing and liquidity activities. How do financial managers create value?

1. The firm should try to buy assets that generate more cash than they cost.
2. The firm should sell bonds and stocks and other financial instruments that raise more cash than they cost.

Thus, the firm must create more cash flow than it uses. The cash flow paid to bondholders and stockholders of the firm should be higher than the cash flows put into the firm by the bondholders and stockholders. To see how this is done, we can trace the cash flows from the firm to the financial markets and back again.

The interplay of the firm's finance with the financial markets is illustrated in Figure 2.3. The arrows in Figure 2.3 trace cash flow from the firm to the financial markets and back again. Suppose we begin with the firm's financing activities. To raise money the firm sells debt and equity shares to investors in the financial markets. This results in cash flows from the financial markets to the firm (*A*). This cash is invested in the investment activities of the firm (*B*) by the firm's management. The cash generated by the firm (*C*) is paid to shareholders and bondholders (*F*). The shareholders receive cash in the form of dividends; the bondholders who lent funds to the firm receive interest and, when the initial loan is repaid, principal. Not all of the firm's cash is paid out. Some is retained (*E*) and some is paid to the government as taxes (*D*).

Over time, if the cash paid to shareholders and bondholders (*F*) is greater than the cash raised in the financial markets (*A*), value will be created.

Identification of Cash Flows

Unfortunately, it is not all that easy to observe cash flows directly. Much of the

FIGURE 2.3   Cash Flows between the Firm and the Financial Markets

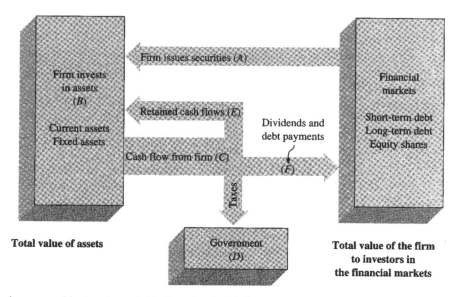

A. Firm issues securities to raise cash (the financing decision).
B. Firm invests in assets (capital budgeting).
C. Firm's operations generate cash flow.
D. Cash is paid to government as taxes.
E. Retained cash flows are reinvested in firm.
F. Cash is paid out to investors in the form of interest and dividends.

information we obtain is in the form of accounting statements, and much of the work of financial analysis is to extract cash flow information from accounting statements. The following example illustrates how this is done.

● Example

The Midland Company is a British firm which refines and trades gold. At the end of the year it sold 4,000 ounces of gold for GBP1 million. The company had acquired the gold for GBP900,000 at the beginning of the year. The company paid cash for the gold when it was purchased. Unfortunately, it has yet to collect from the customer to whom the gold was sold. The following is a standard accounting of Midland's financial circumstances at year-end:

THE MIDLAND COMPANY
Accounting View
Profit and Loss Account
Year Ended December 31

Sales	GBP1,000,000
−Costs	−900,000
Profit	GBP 100,000

By generally accepted accounting principles (GAAP), the sale is recorded even though the customer has yet to pay. It is assumed that the customer will pay soon. From the accounting perspective, Midland seems to be profitable. The perspective of corporate finance is different. It focuses on cash flows:

THE MIDLAND COMPANY
Cash Flow View
Cash Flow Statement
Year Ended December 31

Cash inflow	0
Cash outflow	−GBP900,000
	−GBP900,000

The perspective of corporate finance is interested in whether cash flows are being created by the gold-trading operations of Midland. Value creation depends on cash flows. For Midland, value creation depends on whether and when it actually receives GBP1 million. ●

Timing of Cash Flows

The value of an investment made by the firm depends on the timing of cash flows. One of the most important assumptions of finance is that individuals prefer to receive cash flows earlier rather than later. One pound sterling received today is worth more than one pound sterling received next year. This time preference plays a role in share and bond prices.

● Example

The Midland Company is attempting to choose between two proposals for new products. Both proposals will provide cash flows over a four-year period and will initially cost GBP10,000. The cash flows from the proposals are as follows:

Year	New product A	New product B
1	0	GBP4,000
2	0	4,000
3	0	4,000
4	GBP20,000	4,000
Total	GBP20,000	GBP16,000

At first it appears that new product *A* would be best. However, the cash flows from proposal B come earlier than those of *A*. Without more information we cannot decide which set of cash flows would create the most value to the bondholders and shareholders. It depends on whether the value of getting cash from *B* up front outweighs the extra total cash from *A*. Bond and share prices reflect this preference for earlier cash, and we will see how to use them to decide between *A* and *B*. ●

Risk of Cash Flows

The firm must consider risk. The amount and timing of cash flows are not usually known with certainty. Most investors have an aversion to risk.

● Example

The Midland Company is considering expanding operations overseas. It is evaluating the Netherlands and Japan as possible sites. The Netherlands is considered to be relatively safe, whereas operating in Japan is seen as very risky. In both cases, the company would close down operations after one year.

After doing a complete financial analysis, Midland has come up with the following pound sterling cash flows of the alternative plans for expansion under three equally likely scenarios-pessimistic, most likely and optimistic:

	Pessimistic	*Most likely*	*Optimistic*
Netherlands	GBP75,000	GBP100,000	GBP125,000
Japan	GBP0	GBP150,000	GBP200,000

If we ignore the pessimistic scenario, perhaps Japan is the better alternative. When we take the pessimistic scenario into account, the choice is unclear. Japan appears to be riskier, but it also offers a higher expected level of cash flow. What is risk and how can it be defined? We must try to answer this important question. Corporate finance cannot avoid coping with risky alternatives, and much of our book is devoted to developing methods for evaluating risky opportunities. ●

Concept Questions

- What are three basic questions of corporate finance?
- Describe capital structure.
- List the three reasons why value creation is difficult to identify in advance.

2.2   Corporate Securities as Contingent Claims on Total Firm Value

What is the essential difference between debt and equity? The answer can be found by thinking about what happens to the payoffs to debt and equity when the value of the firm changes.

The basic feature of debt is that it is a promise by the borrowing firm to repay a fixed pound (or mark or dollar, etc.) amount by a certain date.

● Example

The Officer Company promises to pay GBP100 to the Brigham Insurance Company at the end of one year. This is a debt of the Officer Company. Holders of the Officer Company's debt will receive GBP100 if the value of the Officer Company's assets is equal to or more than GBP100 at the end of the year.

Formally, the debtholders have been promised an amount F at the end of the year. If the value of the firm, X, is equal to or greater than F at year-end, debtholders will get F. Of course, if the firm does not have enough to pay off the promised amount, the firm will be 'broke'. It may be forced to liquidate its assets for whatever they are worth, and the bondholders will receive X. Mathematically this means that the debtholders have a claim to X or F, whichever is smaller. Figure 2.4 illustrates the general nature of the payoff structure to debtholders.

Suppose at year-end the Officer Company's value is equal to GBP100. The firm has promised to pay the Brigham Insurance Company GBP100, so the debtholders will get GBP100.

Now suppose the Officer Company's value is GBP200 at year-end and the debtholders are promised GBP100. How much will the debtholders receive? It should be clear that they will receive the same amount as when the Officer Company was worth GBP100.

Suppose the firm's value is GBP75 at year-end and debtholders are promised GBP100. How much will the debtholders receive? In this case the debtholders will get GBP75. ●

FIGURE 2.4   Debt and Equity as Contingent Claims

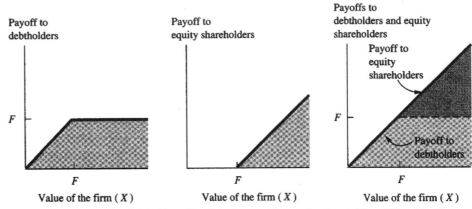

F is the promised payoff to debtholders. $X - F$ is the payoff to equity shareholders if $X - F > 0$. Otherwise the payoff is 0.

The shareholders' claim on firm value at the end of the period is the amount that remains after the debtholders are paid. Of course, shareholders get nothing if the firm value is equal to or less than the amount promised to the debtholders.

● Example
The Officer Company will sell its assets for GBP200 at year-end. The firm has promised to pay the Brigham Insurance Company GBP100 at that time. The stockholders will get the residual value of GBP100. ●

Algebraically, the stockholders' claim is $X - F$ if $X > F$ and zero if $X \leq F$. This is depicted in Figure 2.4. The sum of the debtholders' claim and the stockholders' claim is always the value of the firm at the end of the period.

The debt and equity securities issued by a firm derive their value from the total value of the firm. In the words of finance theory, debt and equity securities are **contingent claims** on the total firm value.

When the value of the firm exceeds the amount promised to debtholders, the shareholders obtain the residual of the firm's value over the amount promised the debtholders, and the debtholders obtain the amount promised. When the value of the firm is less than the amount promised the debtholders, the shareholders receive nothing and the debtholders get the value of the firm.

Concept Questions
- What is a contingent claim?
- Describe equity and debt as contingent claims.

2.3   The Corporate Firm

The firm is a way of organizing the economic activity of many individuals, and there are many reasons why so much economic activity is carried out by firms and not by individuals. The theory of firms, however, does not tell us much about why most large firms are corporations rather than any of the other legal forms that firms can assume.

A basic problem of the firm is how to raise cash. The corporate form of business, that is, organizing the firm as a corporation, is the standard method for solving problems encountered in raising large amounts of cash. However, business can take other forms. In this section we consider the three basic legal forms of organizing firms, and we see how firms go about the task of raising large amounts of money under each form.

The Sole Proprietorship

A **sole proprietorship** is a business owned by one person. Suppose you decide to start a business to produce mousetraps. Going into business is simple: You announce to all who will listen, 'Today I am going to build a better mousetrap'.

Most large cities require that you obtain a business licence. Afterwards you can begin to hire as many people as you need and borrow whatever money you require. At year-end all the profits and the losses will be yours.

Here are some factors that are important in considering a sole proprietorship:

1. The sole proprietorship is the cheapest to form. No formal charter is required, and few government regulations must be satisfied.
2. A sole proprietorship pays no corporate income taxes. All profits of the business are taxed as individual income.
3. The sole proprietorship has unlimited liability for business debts and obligations. No distinction is made between personal and business assets.
4. The life of the sole proprietorship is limited by the life of the sole proprietor.
5. Because the only money invested in the firm is the proprietor's, the equity money that can be raised by the sole proprietor is limited to the proprietor's personal wealth.

The Partnership

Any two or more persons can get together and form a **partnership**. In general, partnerships fall into two categories: (1) general partnerships and (2) limited partnerships. But there are further variants in different European countries—see, for example, Chapter 1.

In a *general partnership* all partners agree to provide some fraction of the work and cash and to share the profits and losses. Each partner is liable for the debts of the partnership. A partnership agreement specifies the nature of the arrangement. The partnership agreement may be an oral agreement or a formal document setting forth the understanding.

Limited partnerships permit the liability of some of the partners to be limited to the amount of cash each has contributed to the partnership. Limited partnerships usually require that (1) at least one partner be a general partner and (2) the limited partners do not participate in managing the business. Here are some things that are important when considering a partnership:

1. Partnerships are usually inexpensive and easy to form. In complicated arrangements, including general and limited partnerships, written documents are required. Business licences and filing fees may be necessary.
2. General partners have unlimited liability for all debts. The liability of limited partners is usually limited to the contribution each has made to the partnership. If one general partner is unable to meet his or her commitment, the shortfall must be made up by the other general partners.

3. The general partnership is terminated when a general partner dies or withdraws (but this is not so for a limited partner). It is difficult for a partnership to transfer ownership without dissolving. Usually, all general partners must agree. However, limited partners may sell their interest in a business.
4. It is difficult for a partnership to raise large amounts of cash. Equity contributions are limited to a partner's ability and desire to contribute to the partnership. Many companies, such as Apple Computer, start life as a proprietorship or partnership, but at some point they need to convert to corporate form.
5. Income from a partnership is taxed as personal income to the partners.
6. Management control resides with the general partners. Usually a majority vote is required on important matters, such as the amount of profit to be retained in the business.

It is very difficult for large business organizations to exist as sole proprietorships or partnerships. The main advantage is the cost of getting started. Afterward, the disadvantages, which may become severe, are (1) unlimited liability, (2) limited life of the enterprise and (3) difficulty of transferring ownership. These three disadvantages lead to (4) the difficulty of raising cash.

The Company

Of the many forms of business enterprise, the **company** (or **corporation**) is by far the most important. It is a distinct legal entity. As such, a company can have a name and enjoy many of the legal powers of natural persons. For example, companies can acquire and exchange property. Companies can enter into contracts and may sue and be sued. For jurisdictional purposes, the company is a citizen of its state of incorporation. (It cannot vote, however.)

Starting a company is more complicated than starting a proprietorship or partnership. The incorporators must prepare articles of incorporation and a set of bylaws. The articles of incorporation (or articles of association) normally include the following in most countries:

1. Name of the company
2. Intended life of the company if it is finite. Usually it has no time limit. In other words, it is forever
3. Business purpose
4. Number of shares that the company is authorized to issue, with a statement of limitations and rights of different classes of shares
5. Nature of the rights granted to shareholders
6. Number of members of the initial board of directors

The bylaws (called the memorandum of association in some countries) are the rules to be used by the company to regulate its own existence, and they concern its shareholders, directors and officers. Bylaws range from the briefest possible statement of rules for the company's management to hundreds of pages of text.

In its simplest form, the company comprises sets of distinct interests—the shareholders (the owners), the directors, the corporation officers (the top management) and the employees. Usually, the shareholders control, although indirectly, the corporation's policies and activities. The shareholders elect a board of directors, who in turn appoint top management. Top management serves as corporate officers, recruits and motivates employees and manages the operation of the company.

The separation of ownership from management gives the corporation several advantages over proprietorships and partnerships:

1. Because ownership in a corporation is represented by shares, ownership can be readily transferred to new owners. Because the company exists independently of those who own its shares, there is no limit to the transferability of shares as there is in partnerships.
2. The corporation has unlimited life. Because the company is separate from its owners, the death or withdrawal of an owner does not affect its existence. The company can continue after the original owners have withdrawn.
3. The shareholders' liability is limited to the amount invested in the ownership shares. For example, if a shareholder purchased DEM10,000 in shares of a company, the potential loss would be DEM10,000. In a partnership, a general partner with a DEM10,000 contribution could lose the DEM10,000 plus any other indebtedness of the partnership.

Limited liability, ease of ownership transfer, and perpetual succession are the major advantages of the corporation form of business organization. These give the company an enhanced ability to raise cash.

There is, however, one great disadvantage to incorporation. The government taxes corporate income as well as personal incomes, including dividend income. This can result in double taxation for shareholders when compared to proprietorships and partnerships. Clearly, the exact tax implications and relative advantages and disadvantages will vary from one European country to another depending upon the local tax legislation.

A summary of how partnerships and companies compare with each other in terms of their legal status, in most European countries, is set out in Table 2.1.

TABLE 2.1   A Comparison of Partnership and Companies in Most European Countries

	Company	*Partnership*
Liquidity and marketability	Ordinary shares can be listed on stock exchange.	Units are subject to substantial restrictions on transferability. There is usually no established trading market for partnership units
Voting rights	Usually each ordinary share entitles each holder to one vote per share on matters requiring a vote and on the election of the directors. Directors determine top management	Voting in accordance with partnership agreement
Taxation	Companies may have double taxation; corporate income is taxable, and dividends to shareholders are also taxable.	Partnerships are not taxable. Partners pay taxes on appropriate proportional share of partnership income
Liability	Shareholders are not personally liable for obligations of the company	General partners usually have unlimited liability. Limited Partners are not liable for obligations of partnerships beyond the amounts of their limited commitment
Continuity of existence	Companies have perpetual life.	Partnerships have limited life

Concept Questions

- Define a proprietorship, a partnership and a corporation.
- What are the advantages of the corporate form of business organization?

2.4   Goals of the Corporate Firm

What is the primary goal of the corporation? The traditional answer is that managers in a corporation make decisions for the shareholders of the corporation. However, it is impossible to give a definitive answer to this important question, first of all, because the corporation is an artificial being, not a natural person and, second, because in many instances, especially where companies are not quoted on stock exchanges, family owners may place employees' interest as stakeholders at a significant level. Furthermore, it is difficult to generalize across European borders—note all of the differences referred to in Chapter 1.

In short, goals may vary according to international corporate culture and according to who precisely owns and controls the corporation. In this matter, the **set-of-contracts viewpoint** is relevant. This viewpoint suggests the corporate firm will attempt to maximize the shareholders' wealth in the firm by taking actions that increase the current value per share of existing stock.

Agency Costs and the Set-of-Contracts Perspective

The set-of-contracts theory of the firm states that the firm can be viewed as a set of contracts.[3] One of the contract claims is a residual claim (equity) on the firm's assets and cash flows. The equity contract can be defined as a principal–agent relationship. The members of the management team are the agents, and the equity investors (shareholders) are the principals. It is assumed that the managers and the shareholders, left alone, will each attempt to act in their own self-interest.

The shareholders, however, can discourage the managers from diverging from the shareholders' interests by devising appropriate incentives for managers and then monitoring their behaviour. Doing so, unfortunately, is complicated and costly. The costs of resolving the conflicts of interest between managers and shareholders are special types of costs called *agency costs*. These costs are defined as the sum of (1) the monitoring costs of the shareholders and (2) the incentive fees paid to the managers. It can be expected that contracts will be devised that will provide the managers with appropriate incentives to maximize the shareholders' wealth. Thus, the set-of-contracts theory suggests that the corporate firm will usually act in the best interests of shareholders. However, agency problems can never be perfectly solved, and managers may not always act in the best interests of shareholders. As a consequence shareholders may experience residual losses. *Residual losses* are the lost wealth of the shareholders due to divergent behaviour of the managers.

Managerial Goals

Managerial goals may be different from those of shareholders. What will managers maximize if they are left to pursue their own goals rather than shareholders' goals?

---

[3] M. C. Jensen and W. Meckling (1976). 'Theory of the Firm: Managerial Behaviour, Agency Costs and Ownership Structure', *Journal of Financial Economics,* **3**.

Williamson proposes the notion of *expense preference*.[4] He argues that managers obtain value from certain kinds of expenses. In particular, company cars, office furniture, office location and funds for discretionary investment have value to managers beyond that which comes from their productivity.

Donaldson conducted a series of interviews with the chief executives of several large companies.[5] He concluded that managers are influenced by two basic underlying motivations:

1. *Survival* Organizational survival means that management will always try to command sufficient resources to avoid the firm's going out of business.
2. *Independence and self-sufficiency* This is the freedom to make decisions without encountering external parties or depending on outside financial markets. The Donaldson interviews suggested that managers do not like to issue new shares of stock. Instead, they like to be able to rely on internally generated cash flow.

These motivations lead to what Donaldson concludes is the basic financial objective of managers: the maximization of corporate wealth. Corporate wealth is that wealth over which management has effective control; it is closely associated with corporate growth and corporate size. Corporate wealth is not necessarily shareholder wealth. Corporate wealth tends to lead to increased growth by providing funds for growth and limiting the extent to which new equity is raised. Increased growth and size are not necessarily the same thing as increased shareholder wealth.

Separation of Ownership and Control

Some people argue that shareholders do not completely control the corporation. They argue that shareholder ownership is too diffuse and fragmented for effective control of management.[6] A striking feature of the modern large corporation is the diffusion of ownership among thousands of investors.

One of the most important advantages of the corporate form of business organization is that it allows ownership of shares to be transferred. The resulting diffuse ownership, however, brings with it the separation of ownership and control of the large corporation. The possible separation of ownership and control raises an important question: Who controls the firm?

Do Shareholders Control Managerial Behaviour?

The claim that managers can ignore the interests of shareholders is deduced from the fact that ownership in large corporations is widely dispersed. As a consequence, it is often claimed that individual shareholders cannot control management. There is some merit in this argument, but it is too simplistic.

The extent to which shareholders can control managers depends on (1) the costs of monitoring management, (2) the costs of implementing the control devices and (3) the benefits of control.

---

[4] O. Williamson (1963). 'Managerial Discretion and Business Behaviour', *American Economic Review* **53**.

[5] G. Donaldson (1984). *Managing Corporate Wealth: The Operations of a Comprehensive Financial Goals System*, New York: Praeger.

[6] Recent work by Gerald T. Garvey and Peter L. Swan (1994). 'The Economics of Corporate Governance: Beyond the Mashallian Firm', *Journal of Corporate Finance* **1**, surveys literature on the stated assumption of shareholder maximization.

When a conflict of interest exists between management and shareholders, who wins? Does management or do the shareholders control the firm? There is no doubt that ownership in large corporations is diffuse when compared to the closely held corporation. However, several control devices used by shareholders bond management to the self-interest of the former.

1. Shareholders determine the membership of the board of directors by voting. Thus, shareholders control the directors, who, in turn, select the management team.
2. Contracts with management and arrangements for compensation, such as stock option plans, can be made so that management has an incentive to pursue the goal of the shareholders. Another device is called *performance shares*. These are shares of stock given to managers on the basis of performance as measured by earnings per share and similar criteria.
3. If the price of a firm's shares drops too low because of poor management, the firm may, although not in European countries, be acquired by a group of shareholders, by another firm or by an individual. This is called a *takeover*. In a takeover, the top management of the acquired firm may find itself out of a job. This puts pressure on the management to make decisions in the stockholders' interests. Fear of a takeover gives managers an incentive to take actions that will maximize stock prices.
4. Competition in the managerial labour market may force managers to perform in the best interest of shareholders. Otherwise they will be replaced. Firms willing to pay the most will lure good managers. These are likely to be firms that compensate managers based on the value they create.

The available evidence and theory are consistent with the ideas of shareholder control and shareholder value maximization. However, there can be no doubt that at times corporations pursue managerial goals at the expense of shareholders. There is also evidence that the diverse claims of customers, vendors and employees must frequently be considered in the goals of the corporation.

Concept Questions

- What are the two types of agency costs?
- How are managers bonded to shareholders?
- Can you recall some managerial goals?
- What is the set-of-contracts perspective?

2.5   Financial Markets

As indicated in Section 2.1, firms offer two basic types of securities to investors. Debt securities are contractual obligations to repay corporate borrowing. *Equity securities* are ordinary shares (sometimes also called common shares) stock that represent non-contractual claims to the residual cash flow of the firm. Issues of debt and shares that are publicly sold by the firm are then traded on the financial markets.

The financial markets are composed of the **money markets** and the **capital markets**. Money markets are the markets for debt securities that pay off in the short term (usually less than one year). Capital markets are the markets for long-term debt and for equity shares.

The term *money market* applies to a group of loosely connected markets. They are dealer markets. Dealers are firms that make continuous quotations of prices for which they stand ready to buy and sell money-market instruments for their own inventory and at their own risk. Thus, the dealer is a principal in most transactions. This is different from a stockbroker acting as an agent for a customer in buying or selling common stock on most stock exchanges; an agent does not actually acquire the securities.

At the core of the money markets are the money-market banks (these are usually the larger banks), government securities dealers (some of which are the large banks), commercial-paper dealers (firms which trade corporate and similar IOUs) and a large number of money brokers. Money brokers specialize in finding short-term money for borrowers and placing money for lenders. The financial markets can be classified further as the *primary market* and the *secondary markets*.

Primary and Secondary Markets

The primary market is used when governments and corporations initially sell securities as new issues. Corporations engage in two types of primary-market sales of debt and equity: public offerings and private placements.

Most publicly offered corporate debt and equity come to the market underwritten by a syndicate of investment banking firms. The *underwriting* syndicate buys the new securities from the firm for the syndicate's own account and resells them at a higher price.

After debt and equity securities are originally sold, they are traded in the secondary markets—either stock exchanges, where quoted equities are traded, or in dealer markets.

Most debt securities are traded in dealer markets. The many bond dealers communicate with one another by telecommunications equipment—wires and telephones. Investors get in touch with dealers when they want to buy or sell, and they can negotiate a deal.

Listing

Firms that want their equity shares to be traded on a stock exchange must apply for listing. To be listed on the particular stock exchange concerned, a company is usually expected to satisfy certain minimum requirements relating to the following:

1. Demonstrated earning power in terms of profits being above a certain specified level.
2. Net tangible assets above another specified level.
3. A market value for publicly held shares in excess of prescribed level.
4. A specified minimum level of shares outstanding.
5. A minimum level in terms of number of shareholders.

Clearly, such requirements vary from one national stock exchange in Europe to another.

Concept Questions

- Distinguish between money markets and capital markets.
- What is listing?
- What is the difference between a primary market and a secondary market?

2.6   Outline of the Text

Now that we have taken a quick tour through corporate finance, we can take a closer look at the structure of this book. It is divided into seven parts. The long-term investment decision is covered first. Financing decisions and working capital are covered next. Finally a series of special topics is covered. Here are the seven parts:

Part 1 Overview
Part 2 Value and Capital Budgeting
Part 3 Risk
Part 4 Capital Structure and Dividend Policy
Part 5 Long-Term Financing
Part 6 Financial Planning and Short-Term Finance
Part 7 Special Topics

Part 2 describes how investment opportunities are valued in financial markets. This part contains the basic theory. Because finance is a subject that builds understanding from the ground up, the material is very important. The most important concept in Part 2 is *net present value* (NPV). We develop the net-present-value rule into a tool for valuing investment alternatives. We discuss general formulas and apply them to a variety of different financial instruments.

Part 3 introduces basic measures of risk. The capital-asset pricing model (CAPM) and the arbitrage pricing theory (APT) are used to devise methods for incorporating risk in valuation. As part of this discussion, we describe the famous beta coefficient. Finally, we use the above pricing models to handle capital budgeting under risk.

Part 4 examines two interrelated topics: capital structure and dividend policy. Capital structure is the extent to which the firm relies on debt. It cannot be separated from the amount of cash dividends the firm decides to pay out to its equity shareholders.

Part 5 concerns long-term financing. We describe the securities that corporations issue to raise cash, as well as the mechanics of offering securities for a public sale. Here we discuss call provisions, warrants, convertibles and leasing.

Part 6 is devoted to financial planning and short-term finance. The first chapter describes financial planning. Next we focus on managing the firm's current assets and current liabilities. We describe aspects of the firm's short-term financial management. A separate chapter on credit management is included.

Part 7 covers two important special topics: mergers and international corporate finance, including European Economic and Monetary Union.

KEY TERMS

Capital budgeting 31	Partnership 37
Capital structure 31	Corporation 38
Net working capital 31	Set-of-contracts viewpoint 40
Contingent claims 36	Money markets 42
Sole proprietorship 37	Capital markets 42

CHAPTER 3

Accounting Statements and Cash Flow

Chapter 3 describes the basic accounting statements used for reporting corporate activity. The focus of the chapter is the practical details of cash flow. It will become obvious to you in the next few chapters that knowing how to determine cash flow helps the financial manager make better decisions. Students who have had accounting courses will not find the material new and can think of it as a review with an emphasis on finance. We discuss cash flow further in later chapters. We assume that readers have already studied at least a core course in accounting, hence we present an overview here rather than a detailed explanation.

3.1 The Balance Sheet

The **balance sheet** is an accountant's snapshot of the firm's accounting value on a particular date, as though the firm stood momentarily still. The balance sheet has two sides: on the left are the assets and on the right the *liabilities* and *shareholders' equity*. The balance sheet states what the firm owns and how it is financed. The accounting definition that underlies the balance sheet and describes the balance is

$$\text{Assets} = \text{Liabilities} + \text{Shareholders' equity}$$

We have put a three-line equality in the balance equation to indicate that it must always hold, by definition. In fact, the shareholders' equity is *defined* to be the difference between the assets and the liabilities of the firm. In principle, equity is what the shareholders would have remaining after the firm discharged its obligations. Shareholders' equity is sometimes called stockholders' equity or just plain equity.

Table 3.1 gives the 19X2 and 19X1 balance sheet for the fictitious UK Composite Corporation. The assets in the balance sheet are listed in order by the length of time it normally takes an ongoing firm to convert them to cash. The asset side depends on the nature of the business and how management chooses to conduct it. Management must make decisions about cash versus marketable securities, credit versus cash sales, whether to make or buy commodities, whether to lease or purchase items, the types of business in which to engage, and so on. The liabilities and the stockholders' equity are listed in the order in which they must be paid.

The liabilities and shareholders' equity side reflects the types and proportions of financing, which depend on management's choice of capital structure, as between debt and equity and between current debt and long-term debt.

When analysing a balance sheet, the financial manager should be aware of three concerns: accounting liquidity, debt versus equity and value versus cost.

TABLE 3.1   **The Balance Sheet of the UK Composite Corporation**

UK COMPOSITE CORPORATION
Balance Sheet
19X2 and 19X1
(in GBP millions)

Assets	19X2	19X1		Liabilities (debt) and Shareholders' Equity	19X2	19X1
Fixed assets:				**Shareholders' equity:**		
Property, plant and equipment	GBP1,423	GBP1,274		Ordinary shares (GBP1 nominal value)	GBP55	GBP32
Less accumulated depreciation	(550)	(460)		Capital reserve	347	327
				Accumulated retained earnings	390	347
Net property, plant and equipment	873	814		Less treasury shares[1]	(26)	(20)
Intangible assets and others	245	221		Total equity	766	686
Total fixed assets	1,118	1,035				
				Preferred shares	39	39
					805	725
Current assets:				**Current liabilities:**		
Inventory	269	280		Trade creditors	213	197
Trade debtors	294	270		Debt payable within 12 months	50	53
Cash and equivalents	140	107		Accrued expenses	223	205
Other	58	50		Total current liabilities	486	455
Total current assets	761	707				
				Long-term liabilities:		
				Deferred taxes	117	104
				Long-term debt	471	458
				Total long-term liabilities	588	562
Total assets	GBP1,879	GBP1,742		Total liabilities and shareholders' equity	GBP1,879	GBP1,742

[1] Repurchase of its own shares by a company is allowed in some, but by no means all, European countries. In some countries, shares repurchased may subsequently be reissued; in such countries repurchased shares appear on the balance sheet as treasury shares. In reality, in the UK, shares repurchased may not (at the current time) be reissued. Hence, the picture given in Table 3.1 would not occur in the UK; the treasury shares would, in fact, be deducted from issued ordinary share capital.

Accounting Liquidity

Accounting liquidity refers to the ease and quickness with which assets can be converted to cash. *Current assets* are the most liquid and include cash and those assets that will be turned into cash within a year from the date of the balance sheet. *Trade debtors*, also called *accounts receivable* in some countries, is the amount not yet collected from customers for goods or services sold to them (after adjustment for potential bad debts). *Inventory*, also called *stocks* in many countries, is composed of raw materials to be used in production, work in process and finished goods. *Fixed assets* are the least liquid kind of asset. Tangible fixed assets include property, plant and equipment. These assets do not convert to cash from normal business activity, and they are not usually used to pay expenses such as salaries.

Some fixed assets are not tangible. Intangible assets have no physical existence, but can be very valuable. Examples of intangible assets are the value of a trademark or the value of a patent or even a brandname. The more liquid a firm's assets, the less likely the firm is to experience problems meeting short-term obligations. Thus, the probability that a firm will avoid financial distress can be linked to the firm's liquidity. Unfortunately, liquid assets frequently have lower rates of return than fixed assets; for example, cash generates no investment income. To the extent to which a firm invests in liquid assets, it sacrifices an opportunity to invest in more profitable investment vehicles.

Debt versus Equity

Liabilities are obligations of the firm that require a payout of cash within a stipulated time period. Many liabilities involve contractual obligations to repay a stated amount and interest over a period. Thus, liabilities are debts and are frequently associated with nominally fixed cash burdens, called *debt service*, that put the firm in default of a contract if they are not paid. *Shareholders'* (or *stockholders'*) *equity* is a claim against the firm's assets that is residual and not fixed. In general terms, when the firm borrows, it gives the bondholders first claim on the firm's cash flow.[2] Bondholders can sue the firm if the firm defaults on its bond contracts. This may lead the firm to declare itself bankrupt. Shareholders' equity is the residual difference between assets and liabilities:

$$\text{Assets} - \text{Liabilities} = \text{Shareholders' equity}$$

This is the shareholders' share in the firm stated in accounting terms. The accounting value of shareholders' equity increases when retained earnings are added. This occurs when the firm retains part of its earnings instead of paying them out as dividends.

Value versus Cost

The accounting value of a firm's assets is frequently referred to as the *book value* of the assets.[3] Under **generally accepted accounting principles (GAAP)**, which vary from one European country to another (see Chapter 1), financial statements of firms usually carry the assets at cost.[4] Thus the term *book value* is unfortunate. It specifically says 'value',

---

[2] Bondholders are investors in the firm's debt. They are creditors of the firm. In this discussion, the term *bondholder* means the same thing as *creditor*.

[3] Confusion often arises because many financial accounting terms have the same meaning. This presents a problem with jargon for the reader of financial statements. For example, the following terms usually refer to the same thing: assets minus liabilities, net worth, equity, shareholders' equity, stockholders' equity, owner's equity and equity value.

[4] In most countries, GAAP requires assets to be carried at the lower of cost or market value. In most instances cost is lower than market value.

when in fact the accounting numbers are based on cost. This misleads many readers of financial statements to think that the firm's assets are recorded at true market values. *Market value* is the price at which willing buyers and sellers trade the assets. It would be only a coincidence if accounting value and market value were the same. In fact, one of management's principal jobs is to create a value for the firm that is higher than its cost.

Many people use the balance sheet, but the information each may wish to extract may not be the same. A banker may look at a balance sheet for evidence of accounting liquidity and working capital. A supplier may also note the size of accounts payable and therefore the general promptness of payments. Many users of financial statements, including managers and investors, want to know the value of the firm, not its cost. This is not found on the balance sheet. In fact, many of the true resources of the firm do not appear on the balance sheet: good management, proprietary assets, favourable economic conditions, and so on.

Concept Questions

- What is the balance-sheet equation?
- What three things should be kept in mind when looking at a balance sheet?

3.2   The Profit and Loss Account (also called Income Statement)

The **profit and loss account** or **income statement** measures performance over a specific period of time, say, a year. The accounting definition of income is

$$\text{Revenue} - \text{Expenses} \equiv \text{Income}$$

If the balance sheet is like a snapshot, the income statement is like a video recording of what the people did between two snapshots. Table 3.2 gives the income statement for the UK Composite Corporation for 19X2.

TABLE 3.2   The Income Statement of the UK Composite Corporation

UK COMPOSITE CORPORATION Income Statement 19X2 (in GBP millions)	
Total operating revenues	GBP2,262
Cost of goods sold	(1,655)
Selling, general and administrative expenses	(327)
Depreciation	(90)
Operating income	190
Other income	29
Earnings before interest and taxes	219
Interest expense	(49)
Pretax income	170
Taxes	(84)
Current: GBP71	
Deferred: GBP13	
Net income	GBP86
Retained earnings: GBP43	
Dividends: GBP43	

The income statement usually includes several sections. The operations section reports the firm's revenues and expenses from principal operations. Among other things, the non-operating section of the income statement includes all financing costs, such as interest expense. Usually, a second section reports as a separate item the amount of taxes levied on income. The last item on the income statement is the bottom line, or net income. Net income is frequently expressed per ordinary share (or per unit of common stock[5]), that is, earnings per share.

When analysing an income statement, the financial manager should keep in mind GAAP, non-cash items, time and costs.

Generally Accepted Accounting Principles

Revenue is, in most European countries, recognized in the profit and loss account (called income statement in many countries) when the earnings process is virtually completed and an exchange of goods or services has occurred. Therefore, the unrealized appreciation in owning property will not be recognized as income. This provides a device for smoothing income by selling appreciated property at a convenient time. For example, if the firm owns a tree farm that has doubled in value, then, in a year when its earnings from other businesses are down, it can raise overall earnings by selling some trees. The matching principle of GAAP dictates that revenues be matched with expenses. Thus, income is reported when it is earned, or accrued, even though no cash flow has necessarily occurred (for example, when goods are sold for credit, sales and profits are reported).

Non-cash Items

The economic value of assets is intimately connected to their future incremental cash flows. However, cash flow does not appear on an income statement. There are several *non-cash items* that are expenses against revenues, but do not affect cash flow. The most important of these is *depreciation*. Depreciation reflects the accountant's estimate of the cost of equipment used up in the production process.[6] For example, suppose an asset with a five-year life and no resale value is purchased for GBP1,000. According to accountants, the GBP1,000 cost must be expensed over the useful life of the asset. If straight-line depreciation is used, there will be five equal instalments and GBP200 of depreciation expense will be incurred each year. From a finance perspective, the cost of the asset is the actual negative cash flow incurred when the asset is acquired (that is, GBP1,000, *not* the accountant's smoothed GBP200-per-year depreciation expense).

Another non-cash expense is *deferred taxes*. Deferred taxes result from differences between accounting income and true taxable income.[7] Notice that the accounting tax shown on the profit and loss account of UK Composite Corporation is GBP84 million. It can be broken down as current taxes and deferred taxes. The current tax portion is actually paid to the tax authorities. The deferred tax portion is not. However, the

---

[5] Common stock unit is a term more frequently used in the USA. It means the same as an ordinary share.

[6] In many European countries the depreciation charge that appears in the profit and loss account is exactly the same as that which is allowed for purposes of tax computation. This is particularly true in those countries categorized as tax-dominated (see Chapter 1).

[7] This arises in countries where the accounting depreciation charge is different from tax depreciation in the profit and loss account. One situation in which taxable income may be lower than accounting income is when the firm is entitled to use accelerated depreciation expense procedures, but uses straight-line procedures for reporting purposes.

theory is that if taxable income is less than accounting income in the current year, it will be more than accounting income later on. Consequently, the taxes that are not paid today or in the very near future (say within one year) will have to be paid sometime in the future. They thus represent a deferred liability of the firm. This shows up on the balance sheet as deferred tax liability. From the cash flow perspective, though, deferred tax is not a cash outflow in the current year.

Time and Costs

It is often useful to think of all of future time as having two distinct parts, the *short run* and the *long run*. The short run is that period of time in which certain equipment, resources, and commitments of the firm are fixed; but it is long enough for the firm to vary its output by using more labour and raw materials. The short run is not a precise period of time that will be the same for all industries. However, all firms making decisions in the short run have some fixed costs, that is, costs that will not change because of the fixed commitments. In real business activity, examples of fixed costs are bond interest, overhead and property taxes. Costs that are not fixed are variable. Variable costs change as the output of the firm changes; some examples are raw materials and wages for labourers on the production line.

In the long run, all costs are variable.[8] In published financial statements, accountants do not distinguish between variable costs and fixed costs.[9] Instead, accounting costs usually fit into a classification that distinguishes product costs from period costs. Product costs are the total production costs incurred during a period—raw materials, direct labour and manufacturing overhead—and are reported in the profit and loss account as cost of goods sold. Both variable and fixed costs are included in product costs. Period costs are costs that are allocated to a time period; they are called *selling*, *general* and *administrative expenses*. One such period cost would be the chief executive's salary.

Concept Questions

- What is the income statement equation?
- What are three things to keep in mind when looking at an income statement?
- What are non-cash expenses?

3.3   Net Working Capital

Net working capital is current assets minus current liabilities. Net working capital is positive when current assets are greater than current liabilities. This means the cash that will become available over the next 12 months is greater than the cash that must be paid out. The net working capital of the UK Composite Corporation is GBP275 million in 19X2 and GBP252 million in 19X1:

	Current assets (GBP millions)	−	Current liabilities (GBP millions)	=	Net working capital (GBPmillions)
19X2	GBP761	−	GBP486	=	GBP275
19X1	707	−	455	=	252

---

[8] When one famous economist was asked about the difference between the long run and the short run, he said, 'In the long run we are all dead'.

[9] Although they do, of course, in management accounts.

In addition to investing in fixed assets (i.e., capital spending), a firm can invest in net working capital. This is called the *change in net working capital*. The **change in net working capital** in 19X2 is the difference between the net working capital in 19X2 and 19X1; that is, GBP275 million − GBP252 million = GBP23 million. The change in net working capital is usually positive in a growing firm.

Concept Questions

- What is net working capital?
- What is the change in net working capital?

3.4   Financial Cash Flow

Perhaps the most important item that can be extracted from financial statements is the actual **cash flow**. There is an accounting statement called the *statement of cash flows*. This statement helps to explain the change in accounting cash and equivalents, which for UK Composite is GBP33 million in 19X2. (See Appendix 3B.) Notice in Table 3.1 that cash and equivalents increases from GBP107 million in 19X1 to GBP140 million in 19X2. However, we will look at cash flow from a different perspective, the perspective of finance. In finance, the value of the firm is its ability to generate financial cash flow. (We will talk more about financial cash flow in Chapter 8.)

The first point we should mention is that cash flow is not the same as net working capital. For example, increasing stocks or inventory requires using cash. Because both stocks or inventories and cash are current assets, this does not affect net working capital. In this case, an increase in a particular net working capital account, such as inventory, is associated with decreasing cash flow.

Just as we established that the value of a firm's assets is always equal to the value of the liabilities and the value of the equity, the cash flows from the firm's assets (that is, its operating activities), CF(A), must equal the cash flows to the firm's creditors, CF(B), and equity investors, CF(S):

$$CF(A) \equiv CF(B) + CF(S)$$

The first step in determining cash flows of the firm is to figure out the *cash flow from operations*. As can be seen in Table 3.3, operating cash flow is the cash flow generated by business activities, including sales of goods and services. Operating cash flow reflects tax payments, but not financing, capital spending or changes in net working capital.

(in GBP millions)	
Earnings before interest and taxes	GBP219
Depreciation	90
Current taxes	(71)
Operating cash flow	GBP238

Another important component of cash flow involves *changes in fixed assets*. For example, if company A, a broadly based fuel conglomerate sells its coal-mining operations to company B, it will generate cash flow. The net change in fixed assets

TABLE 3.3   **Financial Cash Flow of the UK Composite Corporation**

UK COMPOSITE CORPORATION
Financial Cash Flow
19X2
(in GBP millions)

Cash flow of the firm	
Operating cash flow	GBP238
(Earnings before interest and taxes plus depreciation minus taxes)	
Capital spending	(173)
(Acquisition of fixed assets minus sales of fixed assets)	
Additions to net working capital	(23)
Total	42
Cash flow to investors in the firm	
Debt	36
(Interest plus retirement of debt minus long-term debt financing)	
Equity	6
(Dividends plus repurchase of equity minus new equity financing)	
Total	GBP42

equals sales of fixed assets minus the acquisition of fixed assets. The result is the cash flow used for capital spending:

Acquisition of fixed assets	GBP198
Sales of fixed assets	(25)
Capital spending	GBP173

Cash flows are also used for making investments in net working capital. In the UK Composite Corporation in 19X2, additions to net working capital are

Additions to net working capital	GBP23

Total cash flows generated by the firm's assets are the sum of

Operating cash flow	GBP238
Capital spending	(173)
Additions to net working capital	(23)
Total cash flow of the firm	GBP42

The total outgoing cash flow of the firm can be separated into cash flow paid to creditors and cash flows paid to stockholders. The cash flow paid to creditors represents a regrouping of the data in Table 3.3 and an explicit recording of interest expense. Creditors are paid an amount generally referred to as *debt service*. Debt service is interest payments plus repayments of principal—that is, retirement (often called 'amortization') of debt.

An important source of cash flow is from selling new debt. Thus, an increase in long-term debt is the net effect of new borrowing and repayment of maturing obligations plus interest expense.

Cash flow paid to creditors
(GBP millions)

Interest	GBP49
Retirement of debt	73
Debt service	122
Proceeds from long-term debt sales	(86)
Total	GBP36

Cash flow of the firm also is paid to the shareholders. It is the net effect of paying dividends plus repurchasing outstanding shares and issuing new shares of the company.

Cash flow to shareholders
(GBP millions)

Dividends	GBP43
Repurchase of shares	6
Cash to shareholders	49
Proceeds from new share issue	(43)
Total	GBP6

Some important observations can be drawn from our discussion of cash flow:

1. Several types of cash flow are relevant to understanding the financial situation of the firm. **Operating cash flow**, defined as earnings before interest and depreciation minus taxes, measures the cash generated from operations not counting capital spending or working capital requirements. It should usually be positive; a firm is in trouble if operating cash flow is negative for a long time because the firm is not generating enough cash to pay operating costs. **Total cash flow of the firm** includes adjustments for capital spending and additions to net working capital. It will frequently be negative. When a firm is growing at a rapid rate, the spending on inventory and fixed assets can be higher than cash flow from sales.
2. Net income is not cash flow. The net income of the UK Composite Corporation in 19X2 was GBP86 million, whereas cash flow was GBP42 million. The two numbers are not usually the same. In determining the economic and financial condition of a firm, cash flow is more revealing.

Concept Questions

- How is cash flow different from changes in net working capital?
- What is the difference between operating cash flow and total cash flow of the firm?

3.5   Summary and Conclusions

Besides introducing you to corporate accounting, the purpose of this chapter has been to teach you how to determine cash flow from the accounting statements of a typical company.

1. Cash flow is generated by the firm and paid to creditors and shareholders. It can be classified as:
   a. Cash flow from operations
   b. Cash flow from changes in fixed assets
   c. Cash flow from changes in working capital
2. Calculations of cash flow are not difficult, but they require care and particular attention to detail in properly accounting for noncash expenses such as depreciation and deferred taxes. It is especially important that you do not confuse cash flow with changes in net working capital and net income.

KEY TERMS

Balance sheet 45	Non-cash items 49
Generally accepted accounting principles (GAAP) 47	Change in net working capital 51
	Cash flow 51
Profit and loss account 48	Operating cash flow 53
Income statement 48	Total cash flow of the firm 53

QUESTIONS AND PROBLEMS

The Balance Sheet

3.1 Prepare a December 31 balance sheet using the following data (figures in DEM)

Cash	4,000
Patents	82,000
Accounts payable	6,000
Accounts receivable	8,000
Taxes payable	2,000
Machinery	34,000
Bonds payable	7,000
Accumulated retained earnings	6,000
Capital surplus	19,000

The nominal value of the company's ordinary shares is DEM100.

3.2 The following table presents the long-term liabilities and stockholders' equity of Ajaxco NV of one year ago (all figures in Dutch guilders, NLG).

Long-term debt	50,000,000
Preferred shares	30,000,000
Ordinary shares	100,000,000
Retained earnings	20,000,000

During the past year, Ajaxco issued NLG10 million of new ordinary shares. The firm generated NLG5 million of net income and paid NLG3 million of dividends. Construct today's balance sheet that reflects the changes that occurred at Ajaxco NV during the year.

The Income Statement

3.3 Prepare a profit and loss account using the following data (all figures in Irish punts, IEP).

Sales	500,000
Cost of goods sold	200,000
Administrative expenses	100,000
Interest expense	50,000

The firm's tax rate is 34 per cent.

3.4 The Flying Lion Co. plc reported the following data on the income of one of its divisions. Flying Lion Co. has other profitable divisions (all figures in British pounds, GBP).

	19X2	19X1
Net sales	800,000	500,000
Cost of goods sold excluding depreciation	560,000	320,000
Operating expenses excluding depreciation	75,000	56,000
Depreciation	300,000	200,000
Tax rate (%)	30	30

a. Prepare an income statement for each year.
b. Determine the operating cash flow during each year.
Assume that accounting and tax depreciation are equal.

Financial Cash Flow

3.5 What are the differences between accounting profit and cash flow?

3.6 During 1997, the Senbet Discount Tyre Company had gross sales of GBP1 million. The firm's cost of goods sold and selling expenses were GBP300,000 and GBP200,000, respectively. These figures do not include depreciation. Senbet also had bonds payable of GBP1 million. These bonds carried an interest rate of 10 per cent. Depreciation was GBP100,000. Senbet's tax rate in 1995 was 35 per cent.
a. What was Senbet's net operating income?
b. What were the firm's earnings before taxes?
c. What was Senbet's net income?
d. What was Senbet's operating cash flow?

3.7 Accountants at Lebeouf SA have prepared the following financial statements for year-end 19X2 (all figures French francs, FRF, million).

LEBEOUF SA
Profit and Loss Account
19X2

Revenue	400
Expenses	250
Depreciation	50
Net income	100
Dividends	50

LEBEOUF SA
Balance Sheets
December 31

	19X2	19X1
Assets		
Net fixed assets	200	100
Current assets	150	100
Total assets	350	200
Liabilities and Equity		
Shareholders' equity	200	150
Long-term debt	75	0
Current liabilities	75	50
Total liabilities and equity	350	200

a. Determine the change in net working capital in 19X2.
b. Determine the cash flow during the year 19X2.

APPENDIX 3A

FINANCIAL STATEMENT ANALYSIS

The objective of this appendix is to show how to rearrange information from financial statements into financial ratios that provide information about five areas of financial performance:

1. *Short-term solvency*—the ability of the firm to meet its short-run obligations
2. *Activity*—the ability of the firm to control its investment in assets
3. *Financial leverage* (sometimes also called *financial gearing*)—the extent to which a firm relies on debt financing
4. *Profitability*—the extent to which a firm is profitable
5. *Value*—the value of the firm

   Financial statements cannot provide the answers to the preceding five measures of performance. However, management must constantly evaluate how well the firm is doing, and financial statements provide useful information. The financial statements of the UK Composite Corporation, which appear in Tables 3.1, 3.2 and 3.3, provide the information for the examples that follow. (Monetary values are given in GBP millions.)

Short-Term Solvency

Ratios of short-term solvency measure the ability of the firm to meet recurring financial obligations (that is, to pay its bills). To the extent a firm has sufficient cash flow, it will be able to avoid defaulting on its financial obligations and thus avoid experiencing financial distress. Accounting liquidity measures short-term solvency and is often associated with net working capital, the difference between current assets and current liabilities. Recall that current liabilities are debts that are due within one year from the date of the balance sheet. The basic source from which to pay these debts is current assets.
   The most widely used measures of accounting liquidity are the current ratio and the quick ratio.

Current Ratio   To find the current ratio, divide current assets by current liabilities. For the UK Composite Corporation, the figure for 19X2 is:

$$\text{Current ratio} = \frac{\text{Total current assets}}{\text{Total current liabilities}} = \frac{761}{486} = 1.57$$

   If a firm is having financial difficulty, it may not be able to pay its bills (accounts payable) on time or it may need to extend its borrowings from its bankers. As a consequence, current liabilities may rise faster than current assets and the current ratio may fall. This may be the first sign of financial trouble. Of course, a firm's current ratio should be calculated over several years for historical perspective, and it should be compared to the current ratios of other firms with similar operating activities.

Quick Ratio (also called *Acid Test Ratio*)   The quick ratio is computed by subtracting inventories from current assets and dividing the difference (called *quick assets*) by current liabilities:

$$\text{Quick ratio} = \frac{\text{Quick assets}}{\text{Total current liabilities}} = \frac{492}{486} = 1.01$$

Quick assets are those current assets that are quickly convertible into cash. Inventories are the least liquid current assets. Many financial analysts believe it is important to determine a firm's ability to pay off current liabilities without relying on the sale of inventories.

Activity

Ratios of activity are constructed to measure how effectively the firm's assets are being managed. The level of a firm's investment in assets depends on many factors. For example, a toy firm might have a large stock of toys at the peak of the Christmas season; yet that same inventory in January would be undesirable. How can the appropriate level of investment in assets be measured? One logical starting point is to compare assets with sales for the year to arrive at turnover. The idea is to find out how quickly assets are used to generate sales.

Total Asset Turnover   The total asset turnover ratio is determined by dividing total operating revenues for the accounting period by the average of total assets. The total asset turnover ratio for the UK Composite Corporation for 19X2 is:

$$\text{Total asset turnover} = \frac{\text{Total operating revenues}}{\text{Total assets (average)}} = \frac{2,262}{1,810.5} = 1.25$$

$$\text{Average total assets} = \frac{1,879 + 1,742}{2} = 1,810.5$$

This ratio is intended to indicate how effectively a firm is using its assets. If the asset turnover ratio is high, the firm is presumably using its assets effectively in generating sales. If the ratio is low, the firm is not using its assets up to their capacity and must either increase sales or dispose of some of the assets. One problem in interpreting this ratio is that it is maximized by using older assets because their accounting value is lower than newer assets. Also, firms with relatively small investments in fixed assets, such as retail and wholesale trade firms, tend to have high ratios of total asset turnover when compared with firms that require a large investment in fixed assets, such as manufacturing firms.

Receivables Turnover (also called ***Debtors Turnover***)   The ratio of receivables turnover is calculated by dividing sales by average receivables during the accounting period. If the number of days in the year (365) is divided by the receivables turnover ratio, the average collection period can be determined. Net receivables are used for these calculations.[10] The receivables turnover ratio and average collection period for the UK Composite Corporation are:

$$\text{Receivables turnover} = \frac{\text{Total operating revenues}}{\text{Receivables average}} = \frac{2,262}{282} = 8.02$$

$$\text{Average receivables} = \frac{294 + 270}{2} = 282$$

$$\text{Average collection period} = \frac{\text{Days in period}}{\text{Receivables turnover}} = \frac{365}{8.02} = 45.5 \text{ days}$$

The receivables turnover ratio and the average collection period provide some information on the success of the firm in managing its investment in accounts receivable. The actual value of these ratios reflects the firm's credit policy. If a firm has a liberal credit policy, the amount of its receivables will be higher than would otherwise be the case.

Inventory Turnover (also called ***Stock Turnover***)   The ratio of inventory turnover is calculated by dividing the cost of goods sold by average inventory. Because inventory is always stated in terms of historical cost, it must be divided by cost of goods sold instead of sales (sales include a margin for profit and are not commensurate with inventory). The number of days in the year divided by the ratio of inventory turnover yields the ratio of days in inventory. The ratio of days in inventory is the number of days it takes to get goods produced and sold; it is called shelf life for retail and wholesale trade firms. The inventory ratios for the UK Composite Corporation are:

$$\text{Inventory turnover} = \frac{\text{Cost of goods sold}}{\text{Inventory (average)}} = \frac{1,655}{274.5} = 6.03$$

---

[10] Net receivables are determined after an allowance for potential bad debts.

$$\text{Average inventory} = \frac{269 + 280}{2} = 274.5$$

$$\text{Days in inventory} = \frac{\text{Days in period}}{\text{Inventory turnover}} = \frac{365}{6.03} = 60.5 \text{ days}$$

The inventory ratios measure how quickly inventory is produced and sold. They are significantly affected by the production technology of goods being manufactured. It takes longer to produce a gas turbine engine than a loaf of bread. The ratios are also affected by the perishability of the finished goods. A large increase in the ratio of days in inventory could suggest an ominously high inventory of unsold finished goods or a change in the firm's product mix to goods with longer production periods.

The method of inventory valuation can materially affect the computed inventory ratios. Thus, financial analysts should be aware of the different inventory valuation methods and how they might affect the ratios.

Financial Leverage (also called Financial Gearing)

Financial leverage is related to the extent to which a firm relies on debt financing rather than equity. Measures of financial leverage are tools in determining the probability that the firm will default on its debt contracts. The more debt a firm has, the more likely it is that the firm will become unable to fulfil its contractual obligations. In other words, too much debt can lead to a higher probability of insolvency and financial distress.

On the positive side, debt is an important form of financing, and provides a significant tax advantage because interest payments are tax deductible. If a firm uses debt, creditors and equity investors may have conflicts of interest. Creditors may want the firm to invest in less risky ventures than those the equity investors prefer.

Debt Ratio   The debt ratio is calculated by dividing total debt by total assets. We can also use several other ways to express the extent to which a firm uses debt, such as the debt–equity ratio and the equity multiplier (that is, total assets divided by equity). The debt ratios for the UK Composite Corporation for 19X2 are:

$$\text{Debt ratio} = \frac{\text{Total debt}}{\text{Total assets}} = \frac{1{,}074}{1{,}879} = 0.57$$

$$\text{Debt-equity ratio} = \frac{\text{Total debt}}{\text{Total equity}} = \frac{1{,}074}{805} = 1.33$$

$$\text{Equity multiplier} = \frac{\text{Total assets}}{\text{Total equity}} = \frac{1{,}879}{805} = 2.33$$

Debt ratios provide information about protection of creditors from insolvency and the ability of firms to obtain additional financing for potentially attractive investment opportunities. However, debt is carried on the balance sheet simply as the unpaid balance. Consequently, no adjustment is made for the current level of interest rates (which may be higher or lower than when the debt was originally issued) or risk. Thus, the accounting value of debt may differ substantially from its market value. Some forms of debt may not appear on the balance sheet at all, such as pension liabilities or, in some countries, lease obligations.

Interest Coverage   The ratio of interest coverage is calculated by dividing earnings (before interest and taxes) by interest. This ratio emphasizes the ability of the firm to generate enough income to cover interest expense. This ratio for the UK Composite Corporation is:

$$\text{Interest coverage} = \frac{\text{Earnings before interest and taxes}}{\text{Interest expense}} = \frac{219}{49} = 4.5$$

Interest expense is an obstacle that a firm must surmount if it is to avoid default. The ratio of interest coverage is directly connected to the ability of the firm to pay interest. However, it would probably make sense to add depreciation to income in computing this ratio and to include other financing expenses, such as payments of principal and lease payments.

A large debt burden is a problem only if the firm's cash flow is insufficient to make the required debt service payments. This is related to the uncertainty of future cash flows. Firms with predictable cash flows are frequently said to have more debt capacity than firms with high, uncertain cash flows, therefore, it makes sense to compute the variability of the firm's cash flows. One possible way to do this is to calculate the standard deviation of cash flows relative to the average cash flow.

Profitability

One of the most difficult attributes of a firm to conceptualize and to measure is profitability. In a general sense, accounting profits are the difference between revenues and costs. Unfortunately, there is no completely unambiguous way to know when a firm is profitable. At best, a financial analyst can measure current or past accounting profitability. Many business opportunities, however, involve sacrificing current profits for future profits. For example, all new products require large start-up costs and, as a consequence, produce low initial profits. Thus, current profits can be a poor reflection of true future profitability. Another problem with accounting-based measures of profitability is that they ignore risk. It would be false to conclude that two firms with identical current profits were equally profitable if the risk of one was greater than the other.

The most important conceptual problem with accounting measures of profitability is they do not give us a benchmark for making comparisons. In general, a firm is profitable in the economic sense only if its profitability is greater than investors can achieve on their own in the capital markets.

Profit Margin   Operating profit margins are computed by dividing operating profits by total operating revenue. Thus they express profits as a percentage of total operating revenue. The most important margin is the profit margin. The profit margin for the UK Composite Corporation is:

$$\text{Profit margin} = \frac{\text{Operating income}}{\text{Total operating revenue}} = \frac{190}{2,262} = 0.084 \ (8.4\%)$$

In general, profit margins reflect the firm's ability to produce a product or service at a low cost or a high price. Trade firms tend to have low margins and service firms tend to have high margins.

For some purposes, the net of tax margin is calculated. This ratio is based upon profit after interest and tax divided by total operating revenue or turnover.

Return on Assets   One common measure of managerial performance is the ratio of income to average total assets, both before tax and after tax. These ratios for the UK Composite Corporation for 19X2 are:

$$\frac{\text{Net return}}{\text{on assets}} = \frac{\text{Net income}}{\text{Average total assets}} = \frac{86}{1,810.5} = 0.0475 \ (4.75\%)$$

$$\frac{\text{Gross return}}{\text{on assets}} = \frac{\text{Earnings before interest and tax}}{\text{Average total assets}} = \frac{219}{1,810.5} = 0.121 \ (12.1\%)$$

One of the most interesting aspects of return on assets (ROA) is how some financial ratios can be linked together to compute ROA. One implication of this is usually referred to as the *DuPont system of financial control*. This system highlights the fact that ROA can be expressed in terms of the profit margin and asset turnover. The basic components of the system are as follows:

$$\text{ROA} = \qquad \text{Profit margin} \qquad \times \qquad \text{Asset turnover}$$

$$\text{ROA (net)} = \frac{\text{Net income}}{\text{Total operating revenue}} \times \frac{\text{Total operating revenue}}{\text{Average total assets}}$$

$$0.0475 = \quad\quad 0.038 \quad\quad \times \quad\quad 1.25$$

$$\text{ROA (gross)} = \frac{\text{Earnings before interest and taxes}}{\text{Total operating revenue}} \times \frac{\text{Total operating revenue}}{\text{Average total assets}}$$

$$0.121 = \quad\quad 0.097 \quad\quad \times \quad\quad 1.25$$

Firms can increase ROA by increasing profit margins or asset turnover. Of course, competition limits their ability to do so simultaneously. Thus, firms tend to face a trade-off between turnover and margin. In the retail trade, for example, mail-order outfits have low margins and high turnover whereas high-quality jewellery stores have high margins and low turnover.

It is often useful to describe financial strategies in terms of margins and turnover. Suppose a firm selling pneumatic equipment is thinking about providing customers with more liberal credit terms. This will probably decrease asset turnover (because receivables would increase more than sales). Thus, the margins will have to go up to keep ROA from falling.

Return on Equity   This ratio (ROE) is defined as net income (after interest and taxes) divided by average common stockholders' equity, which for the UK Composite Corporation is:

$$\text{ROE} = \frac{\text{Net income}}{\text{Average shareholders' equity}} = \frac{86}{765} = 0.11 \ (11\%)$$

$$\text{Average shareholders' equity} = \frac{805 + 725}{2} = 765$$

The most important difference between ROA and ROE is due to financial leverage. To see this, consider the following breakdown of ROE:

$$\text{ROE} = \text{After tax profit margin} \ \times \ \text{Asset turnover} \ \times \ \text{Equity multiplier}$$

$$= \frac{\text{Net income}}{\text{Total operating revenue}} \times \frac{\text{Total operating revenue}}{\text{Average total assets}} \times \frac{\text{Average total assets}}{\text{Average shareholders' equity}}$$

$$0.11 = \quad\quad 0.038 \quad\quad \times \quad\quad 1.25 \quad\quad \times \quad\quad 2.36$$

From the preceding numbers, it would appear that financial leverage always magnifies ROE. Actually, this occurs only when ROA (gross) is greater than the interest rate on debt.

Payout Ratio   The payout ratio is the proportion of net income paid out in cash dividends. For the UK Composite Corporation,

$$\text{Payout ratio} = \frac{\text{Cash dividends}}{\text{Net income}} = \frac{43}{86} = 0.5$$

The *retention ratio* for the UK Composite Corporation is:

$$\text{Retention ratio} = \frac{\text{Retained earnings}}{\text{Net income}} = \frac{43}{86} = 0.5$$

$$\text{Retained earnings} = \text{Net income} - \text{Dividends}$$

The Sustainable Growth Rate

One ratio that is very helpful in financial analysis is called the sustainable growth rate. It is the maximum rate of growth a firm can maintain without increasing its financial leverage and using internal equity only. The precise value of sustainable growth can be calculated as

$$\text{Sustainable growth rate} = \text{ROE} \times \text{Retention ratio}$$

For the UK Composite Company, ROE is 11 per cent. The retention ratio is $\frac{1}{2}$ so we can calculate the sustainable growth rate as

$$\text{Sustainable growth rate} = 0.11 \left(\tfrac{1}{2}\right) = 5.5\%$$

The UK Composite Corporation can expand at a maximum rate of 5.5 per cent per year with no external equity financing or without increasing financial leverage. (We discuss sustainable growth in Chapters 6 and 25.)

Market Value Ratios

We can learn many things from a close examination of balance sheets and income statements. However, one very important characteristic of a firm that cannot be found on an accounting statement is its market value.

Market Price The market price of an ordinary share is the price that buyers and sellers establish when they trade the share. The market value of the equity of a firm is the market price of a share per ordinary share multiplied by the number of shares outstanding.

Sometimes the words 'fair market value' are used to describe market prices. *Fair market value* is the amount at which ordinary shares would change hands between a willing buyer and a willing seller, both having knowledge of the relevant facts. Thus, market prices give guesses about the true worth of the assets of a firm. In an efficient stock market, market prices reflect all relevant facts about firms, and thus market prices reveal the true value of the firm's underlying assets.

The market value of British Telecom is many times greater than that of Orange. This may suggest nothing more than the fact that British Telecom is a bigger firm than Orange (hardly a surprising revelation). Financial analysts construct ratios to extract information that is independent of a firm's size.

Price-to-Earnings (P/E) Ratio One way to calculate the P/E ratio is to divide the current market price by the earnings per share for the latest year. Average P/E ratios for the same industry may vary from country to country reflecting not only different growth prospects but also different accounting conventions in reporting profit—remember Table 1.12.

Usually, firms with higher growth prospects have higher P/E ratios, all other things being equal.

Dividend Yield The dividend yield is calculated by annualizing the last observed dividend payment of a firm and dividing by the current market price:

$$\text{Dividend yield} = \frac{\text{Dividend per share}}{\text{Market price per share}}$$

Dividend yields are related to investor perceptions of future growth prospects for firms. Firms with high growth prospects will generally have lower dividend yields. Dividend yield is generally calculated using dividend before tax per share divided by market price per share.

Market-to-Book (M/B) Value and the Q ratio The market-to-book value ratio is calculated by dividing the market price per share by the book value per share. There is another ratio, called *Tobin's* Q, that is very much like the M/B ratio. Tobin's Q ratio divides the market value of all of the firm's debt plus equity by the estimated replacement value of the firm's assets. Calculating replacement values generally relies upon indices of replacement cost to book cost. The Q ratio differs from the M/B ratio in that the Q ratio uses market value of the debt plus equity. It also uses the replacement value of all assets and not the historical cost value.

It should be obvious that if a firm has a Q ratio above 1 it has an incentive to invest that is probably greater than a firm with a Q ratio below 1. Firms with high Q ratios tend to be those firms with attractive investment opportunities or a significant competitive advantage.

Summary and Conclusions

Much research indicates that accounting statements provide important information about the value of the firm. Financial analysts and managers learn how to rearrange financial statements to squeeze out the maximum amount of information. In particular, analysts and managers use financial ratios to summarize the firm's liquidity, activity, financial leverage and profitability. When possible, they also use market values. This appendix describes the most popular financial ratios. You should keep in mind the following points when trying to interpret financial statements:

1. Measures of profitability such as return on equity suffer from several potential deficiencies as indicators of performance. They do not take into account the risk or timing of cash flows.
2. Financial ratios are linked to one another. For example, return on equity is determined from the profit margins, the asset turnover ratio and the financial leverage.

APPENDIX 3B

STATEMENT OF CASH FLOW

There is an accounting statement called the statement of cash flow. This statement helps explain the change in accounting cash, which for UK Composite is GBP33 million in 19X2. It is very useful in understanding financial cash flow. Notice in Table 3.1 that cash increases from GBP107 million in 19X1 to GBP140 million in 19X2.

The first step in determining the change in cash is to figure out cash flows from operating activities. This is the cash flow that results from the firm's normal activities of producing and selling goods and services. The second step is to make an adjustment for cash flow from investing activities. The final step is to make an adjustment for cash flows from financing activities. Financing activities are the net payments to creditors and owners (excluding interest expense) made during the year.

The three components of the statement and cash flows are determined below.

Cash Flow from Operating Activities

To calculate cash flow from operating activities we start with net income. Net income can be found on the income statement and is equal to GBP86 million. We now need to add back non-cash expenses and adjust for changes in current assets and liabilities (other than cash). The result is cash flow from operating activities.

UK COMPOSITE CORPORATION
CASH FLOW FROM OPERATING ACTIVITIES
19X2

Net income	86
Depreciation	90
Deferred taxes	13
Change in assets and liabilities	
Accounts receivable	(24)
Inventories	11
Accounts payable	16
Accrued expense	19
Notes payable	(3)
Other	(8)
Cash flow from operating activities	199

Cash Flow from Investing Activities

Cash flow from investing activities involves changes in capital assets: acquisition of fixed assets and sales of fixed assets (i.e. net capital expenditures). The result for UK Composite is below.

UK COMPOSITE CORPORATION
CASH FLOW FROM INVESTING ACTIVITIES
19X2

Acquisition of fixed assets	(198)
Sales of fixed assets	25
Cash flow from investing activities	**(173)**

Cash Flow from Financing Activities

Cash flows to and from creditors and owners include changes in equity and debt.

UK COMPOSITE CORPORATION
CASH FLOW FROM FINANCING ACTIVITIES
19X2

Retirement of debt (includes notes)	(73)
Proceeds from long-term debt sales	86
Dividends	(43)
Repurchase of stock	(6)
Proceeds from new stock issue	43
Cash flows from financing activities	**7**

The statement of cash flows is the addition of cash flows from operations, cash flows from investing activities, and cash flows from financing activities, and is produced in Table 3B.1. There is a close relationship between the official accounting statement called the statement of cash flows and the total cash flow of the firm used in finance. The difference between cash flow from financing activities and total cash flow of the firm (see Table 3.3) is interest expense.

TABLE 3B.1   Statement of Consolidated Cash Flows of the UK Composite Corporation

UK COMPOSITE CORPORATION
STATEMENT OF CASH FLOWS
19X2
(in GBP millions)

Operations	
Net income	86
Depreciation	90
Deferred taxes	13
Changes in assets and liabilities	
Accounts receivable	(24)
Inventories	11
Accounts payable	16
Accrued expenses	19
Debt payable	(3)
Other	(8)
Total cash flow from operations	**199**

(continued)

TABLE 3B.1   *(concluded)*

Investing activities	
Acquisitions of fixed assets	(198)
Sales of fixed assets	25
Total cash flow from investing activities	(173)
Financing activities	
Retirement of debt (including notes)	(73)
Proceeds of long-term debt	86
Dividends	(43)
Repurchase of shares	(6)
Proceeds from new share issues	43
Total cash flow from financing activities	7
Change in cash (on the balance sheet)	33

PART II   Value and Capital Budgeting

4   Financial Markets and Net Present Value: First Principles of Finance   67
5   Net Present Value   78
6   How to Value Bonds and Shares   111
7   Some Other Investment Rules   146
8   Net Present Value and Capital Budgeting   174
9   Strategy and Analysis in Using Net Present Value   193

Firms and individuals invest in a large variety of assets. Some are real assets, such as machinery and land, and some are financial assets, such as stocks and bonds. The object of the investment is to maximize the value of the investment. In the simplest terms, this means to find assets that have more value to the firm than they cost. To do this, we need a theory of value. We develop a theory of value in Part II.

Finance is the study of markets and instruments that deal with cash flows over time. In Chapter 4 we describe how financial markets allow us to determine the value of financial instruments. We study some stylized examples of money over time, and show why financial markets and financial instruments are created. We introduce the basic principles of rational decision-making. We apply these principles to a two-period investment. Here we introduce one of the most important ideas in finance: net present value (NPV). We show why net present value is useful and the conditions that make it applicable.

In Chapter 5, we extend the concept of net present value to more than one time period. The mathematics of compounding and discounting is presented. In Chapter 6 we apply net present value to bonds and shares. This is a very important chapter because net present value can be used to determine the value of a wide variety of financial instruments.

Although we have made a strong case for using the NPV rule in Chapters 4 and 5, Chapter 7 presents four other rules: the payback period rule, the average accounting return rule (ARR), the internal rate of return (IRR) and the profitability index. Each of these alternatives has some redeeming features, but they are not sufficient to replace the NPV rule.

In Chapter 8, we analyse how to estimate the cash flows required for capital budgeting. We start the chapter with a discussion of the concept of incremental cash flows—the difference between the cash flows for the firm with and without the project. Chapter 9 focuses on assessing the reliability and reasonableness of estimates of NPV. The chapter introduces techniques for dealing with uncertain incremental cash flows in capital budgeting, including break-even analysis, decision trees, and sensitivity analysis.

<table>
<tr><td>CHAPTER
4</td><td># Financial Markets and Net Present Value: First Principles of Finance</td></tr>
</table>

Finance refers to the process by which special markets deal with cash flows over time. These markets are called financial markets. Making investment and financing decisions requires an understanding of the basic economic principles of financial markets. This introductory chapter describes a financial market as one that makes it possible for individuals and corporations to borrow and lend. As a consequence, financial markets can be used by individuals to adjust their patterns of consumption over time and by corporations to adjust their patterns of investment spending over time. The main point of this chapter is that individuals and corporations can use the financial markets to help them make investment decisions. We introduce one of the most important ideas in finance: net present value.

By far the most important economic decisions are those that involve investments in real assets. We don't mean savings decisions, which are decisions not to consume some of this year's income, but decisions regarding actual investments: building a machine or a whole factory or a McDonald's, for example. These decisions determine the economic future for a society. Economists use the word 'capital' to describe the total stock of machines and equipment that a society possesses and uses to produce goods and services. Investment decisions are decisions about whether or not to increase this stock of capital.

The investment decisions made today determine how much additional capital the society will add to its current stock of capital. That capital can then be used in the future to produce goods and services for the society. Some of the forms that capital takes are obvious, like steel mills and computers. But many kinds of capital are things that you probably never would have thought of as part of a country's capital stock. Public roads, for example, are a form of capital, and the decisions to build them are investment decisions. Perhaps most important, the decision you are making to invest in an education is no different in principle from these other investment decisions. Your decision to invest in education is a decision to build your human capital, just as a company's decision to build a new factory is a decision to invest in physical capital.[1] The total of all the capital possessed by a society is a measure of its wealth. The

---

[1] If you have any doubt about the importance of human capital as part of a country's wealth, think about the conditions of Germany and Japan at the end of the Second World War. The physical capital of those countries had been destroyed, and even the basic social capital like roads, sewer systems and factories was in rubble. Even though these countries might have appeared to be economically crippled beyond repair, a look below the surface would have revealed a different picture. A huge part of the wealth of those countries consisted of the human capital inherent in their literate and skilled populations. Building on this substantial base of capital by a long-term policy of investment has brought those two countries to a very high standard of living.

purpose of this chapter is to develop the basic principles that guide rational investment decision-making. We show that a particular investment decision should be made if it is superior to available alternatives in the financial markets.

4.1   The Financial Market Economy

Financial markets develop to facilitate borrowing and lending between individuals. Here we talk about how this happens. Suppose we describe the economic circumstances of two people, Tom and Lesley. Both Tom and Lesley have current income of GBP100,000. Tom is a very patient person, and some people call him a miser. He wants to consume only GBP50,000 of current income and save the rest. Lesley is a very impatient person, and some people call her extravagant. She wants to consume GBP150,000 this year. Tom and Lesley have different intertemporal consumption preferences.

Such preferences are personal matters and have more to do with psychology than with finance. However, it seems that Tom and Lesley could strike a deal: Tom could give up some of his income this year in exchange for future income that Lesley can promise to give him. Tom can *lend* GBP50,000 to Lesley, and Lesley can *borrow* GBP50,000 from Tom.

Suppose that they do strike this deal, with Tom giving up GBP50,000 this year in exchange for GBP55,000 next year. This is illustrated in Figure 4.1 with the basic cash flow time chart, a representation of the timing and amount of the cash flows. The cash flows that are received are represented by an arrow pointing up from the point on the time line at which the cash flow occurs. The cash flows paid out are represented by an arrow pointing down. In other words, for each GBP Tom trades away or lends, he gets a commitment to get it back as well as to receive 10 per cent more.

In the language of finance, 10 per cent is the annual rate of interest on the loan. When a pound is lent out, the repayment of GBP1.10 can be thought of as being made up of two parts. First, the lender gets the pound back; that is the *principal repayment.* Second, the lender receives an *interest payment*, which is GBP0.10 in this example.

Now, not only have Tom and Lesley struck a deal, but, as a by-product of their

---

FIGURE 4.1   **Tom's and Lesley's Cash Flow**

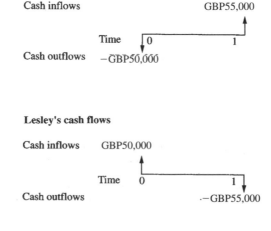

bargain, they have created a financial instrument—the IOU. This piece of paper entitles whoever receives it to present it to Lesley in the next year and redeem it for GBP55,000. Financial instruments that entitle whoever possesses them to receive payment are called *bearer instruments* because whoever bears them can use them. Presumably there could be more such IOUs in the economy written by many different lenders and borrowers like Tom and Lesley.

Of course, if you have lent some money this year and expect to be repaid next year, you are indifferent to who pays you back, as long as you get your money. In a completely honest society where people borrow only when they are certain that they will be able to repay the loan, lenders can be assured that the IOUs they hold will be repaid. Similarly, if the society is not entirely peopled by honest folks, governments can impose penalties to discourage individuals from borrowing when they do not have the ability to repay their loans. In either of these worlds, however, if the lenders are sure that the loans will be repaid, it follows that the lenders will not care whose loans they actually are holding.

Even in a virtuous society, people can make honest mistakes. Individuals may borrow in the full expectation that they will be able to fulfil the terms of their contracts, but circumstances may prevent them from doing so. More important, both the lender and the borrower may recognize there is some possibility that the loan will not be repaid. In this case, there must be provisions in the contract to cover such a possibility. We defer our discussion of these possibilities until later in the book. For the present we assume that we are dealing with risk-free bonds, that is, IOUs or bonds that are sure to be repaid.

The Anonymous Market

If the borrower does not care whom he has to pay back, and if the lender does not care whose IOUs he is holding, we could just as well drop Tom's and Lesley's names from their contract. All we need is a record book, in which we could record the fact that Tom has lent GBP50,000 and Lesley has borrowed GBP50,000 and that the term of the loan, the interest rate, is 10 per cent. Perhaps another person could keep the records for borrowers and lenders, for a fee, of course. In fact, and this is one of the virtues of such an arrangement, Tom and Lesley wouldn't even have to meet. Instead of needing to find and trade with each other, they could each trade with the record keeper. The record keeper could deal with thousands of such borrowers and lenders, none of whom would need to meet the other.

Institutions that perform this sort of market function, matching borrowers and lenders or traders, are called **financial intermediaries**. Stockbrokers and banks are examples of financial intermediaries in our modern world. A bank's depositors lend the bank money, and the bank makes loans from the funds it has on deposit. In essence, the bank is an intermediary between the depositors and the ultimate borrowers. To make the market work, we must be certain that the market clears. By *market clearing* we mean that the total amount that people like Tom wish to lend to the market, say GBP11 million, equals the total amount that people like Lesley wish to borrow.

Market Clearing

If the lenders wish to lend more than the borrowers want to borrow, then presumably the interest rate is too high. Because there would not be enough borrowing for all of the lenders at, say, 15 per cent, there are really only two ways that the market could be made to clear. One is to ration the lenders. For example, if the lenders wish to lend

GBP20 million when interest rates are at 15 per cent and the borrowers wish to borrow only GBP8 million, the market could take, say, 8/20 of each pound, or GBP0.40, from each of the lenders and distribute it to the borrowers. This is one possible scheme for making the market clear, but it is not one that would be sustainable in a free and competitive marketplace. Why not?

To answer this important question, let's go back to our lender, Tom. Tom sees that interest rates are 15 per cent and, not surprisingly, rather than simply lending the GBP50,000 that he was willing to lend when rates were 10 per cent, Tom decides that at the higher rates he would like to lend more, say, GBP80,000. But since the lenders want to lend more money than the borrowers wanted to borrow, the record keepers tell Tom that they won't be able to take all of his GBP80,000; rather, they will take only 40 per cent of it, or GBP32,000. With the interest rate at 15 per cent, people are not willing to borrow enough to match up with all of the loans that are available at that rate.

Tom is not very pleased with that state of affairs, but he can do something to improve his situation. Suppose that he knows that Lesley is borrowing GBP20,000 in the market at the 15 per cent interest rate. That means that Lesley must repay GBP20,000 on her loan next year plus the interest of 15 per cent of GBP20,000, or $0.15 \times GBP20,000 = GBP3,000$. Suppose that Tom goes to Lesley and offers to lend her the GBP20,000 for 14 per cent. Lesley is happy because she will save 1 per cent on the deal and will need to pay back only GBP2,800 in interest next year. This is GBP200 less than if she had borrowed from the record keepers. Tom is happy, too, because he has found a way to lend some of the money that the record keepers would not take. The net result of this transaction is that the record keepers have lost Lesley as a customer. Why should she borrow from them when Tom will lend her the money at a lower interest rate?

Tom and Lesley are not the only ones cutting side deals in the marketplace, and it is clear that the record keepers will not be able to maintain the 15 per cent rate. The interest rate must fall if they are to stay in business.

Suppose, then, that the market clears at the rate of 10 per cent. At this rate the amount of money that the lenders wish to lend, GBP11 million, is exactly equal to the amount that the borrowers desire. We refer to the interest rate that clears the market, 10 per cent in our example, as the **equilibrium rate of interest.**

In this section, we have shown that in the market for loans, bonds or IOUs are traded. These are *financial instruments*. The interest rate on these loans is set so that the total demand for such loans by borrowers equals the total supply of loans by lenders. At a higher interest rate, lenders wish to supply more loans than are demanded, and if the interest rate is lower than this equilibrium level, borrowers demand more loans than lenders are willing to supply.

Concept Questions

- What is an interest rate?
- What are institutions that match borrowers and lenders called?
- What do we mean when we say a market clears? What is an equilibrium rate of interest?

4.2   The Competitive Market

In modern financial markets, the total amount of borrowing and lending is not GBP11 million; rather, it is closer to several trillions of US dollars. In such a huge market, no one investor or even any single company can have a significant effect (although a government might). We assume, then, in all of our subsequent discussions and analyses that the financial market is competitive. By that we mean no individuals or firms think they have any effect whatsoever on the interest rates that they face no matter how much borrowing, lending or investing they do. In the language of economics, individuals who respond to rates and prices by acting as though they have no influence on them are called *price takers*, and this assumption is sometimes called the *price-taking assumption*. It is the condition of **perfectly competitive financial markets** (or, more simply, *perfect markets*). The following conditions are likely to lead to this:

1. Trading is costless. Access to the financial markets is free.
2. Information about borrowing and lending opportunities is available.
3. There are many traders, and no single trader can have a significant impact on market prices.

How Many Interest Rates are there in a Competitive Market?

An important point about this one-year market is that if credit risk is ignored, only one interest rate can be quoted in the market at any one time. Suppose that some competing record keepers decide to set up a rival market. To attract customers, their business plan is to offer lower interest rates, say, 9 per cent. Their business plan is based on the hope that they will be able to attract borrowers away from the first market and soon have all of the business.

Their business plan will work, but it will do so beyond their wildest expectations. They will indeed attract the borrowers, all GBP11 million worth of them! But the matter doesn't stop there. By offering to borrow and lend at 9 per cent when another market is offering 10 per cent, they have created the proverbial money machine.

The world of finance is populated by sharp-eyed inhabitants who would not let this opportunity slip by them. Any one of these, whether a borrower or a lender, would go to the new market and borrow everything he could at the 9 per cent rate. At the same time he was borrowing in the new market, he would also be striking a deal to lend in the old market at the 10 per cent rate. If he could borrow GBP100 million at 9 per cent and lend it at 10 per cent, he would be able to net 1 per cent, or GBP1 million, next year. He would repay the GBP109 million he owed to the new market from the GBP110 million he receives when the 10 per cent loans he made in the original market are repaid, pocketing GBP1 million.

This process of striking a deal in one market and an offsetting deal in another simultaneously and at more favourable terms is called *arbitrage*, and doing it is called arbitraging. Of course, someone must be paying for all of this free money, and it must be the record keepers because the borrowers and the lenders are all making money. Our intrepid entrepreneurs will lose their proverbial shirts and go out of business. The moral of this is clear: As soon as different interest rates are offered for essentially the same risk-free loans, arbitrageurs will take advantage of the situation by borrowing at the low rate and lending at the high rate. The gap between the two rates will be closed quickly, and for all practical purposes there will be only one rate available in the market.

Concept Questions

- What is the most important feature of a competitive financial market?
- What conditions are likely to lead to this?

4.3   The Basic Principle

We have already shown how people use the financial markets to adjust their patterns of consumption over time to fit their particular preferences. By borrowing and lending, they can greatly expand their range of choices. They need only to have access to a market with an interest rate at which they can borrow and lend.

In the previous section, we saw how these savings and consumption decisions depend on the interest rate. The financial markets also provide a benchmark against which proposed investments can be compared, and the interest rate is the basis for a test that any proposed investment must pass. The financial markets give the individual, the corporation, or even the government a standard of comparison for economic decisions. This benchmark is critical when investment decisions are being made.

The way we use the financial markets to aid us in making investment decisions is a direct consequence of our basic assumption that individuals can never be made worse off by increasing the range of choices open to them. People can always make use of the financial markets to adjust their savings and consumption by borrowing or lending. An investment project is worth undertaking only if it increases the range of choices in the financial markets. To do this the project must be at least as desirable as what is available in the financial markets.[2] If it were not as desirable as what the financial markets have to offer, people could simply use the financial markets instead of undertaking the investment. This point will govern us in all of our investment decisions. It is the *first principle of investment decision-making*, and it is the foundation on which all of our rules are built.

Concept Question

- Describe the basic financial principle of investment decision-making.

4.4   Illustrating the Investment Decision

Consider a person with income of GBP50,000 this year and GBP60,000 next year facing a financial market in which the interest rate is 10 per cent. But, at that moment, the person has no investment possibilities beyond the 10 per cent borrowing and lending that is available in the financial market. Suppose that we give this person the chance to undertake an investment project that will require a GBP30,000 outlay of cash this year and that will return GBP40,000 to the investor next year.

Combining the investment decision and the income flows, the person faces a net position promising GBP20,000 this year and GBP100,000 next year. These amounts would be available for consumption. But suppose that our individual wanted to consume the maximum possible this year. If he did not take the investment, he would be able to consume the GBP50,000 of income this year and would be able to borrow an amount now and consume that too and repay the borrowing from next year's income. Since the interest rate is stated as 10 per cent, the amount of the borrowing would be GBP54,545. This would give rise to an interest cost of GBP5,455 and the borrowing plus interest could be repaid out of next year's income of GBP60,000. So total consumption this year could equal GBP104,545.

---

[2] You might wonder what to do if an investment is as desirable as an alternative in the financial markets. In principle, if there is a tie, it doesn't matter whether or not we take on the investment. In practice, we've never seen an exact tie.

With the investment, and using a similar logic to that in the last paragraph, consumption this year would be only GBP20,000 in respect of this year's income minus the investment outlay but, in addition, we could borrow GBP90,909 on the expectation of receiving GBP100,000 next year—this GBP100,000 would comprise GBP60,000 of income plus GBP40,000 from the investment. The total amount available for consumption today would be GBP110,909 made up as follows:

$$\text{GBP50,000} - \text{GBP30,000} + (\text{GBP60,000} + \text{GBP40,000})/(1 + 0.1)$$

$$= \text{GBP20,000} + \text{GBP100,000}/(1.1)$$

$$= \text{GBP110,909}$$

The additional consumption available this year from undertaking the investment and using the financial market is the difference between the consumption amounts as of now, that is:

$$\text{GBP110,909} - \text{GBP104,545} = \text{GBP6,364}$$

This difference is an important measure of what the investment is worth to the person. It answers a variety of questions. For example, it is the answer to the question: How much money would we need to give the investor this year to make him just as well off as he is with the investment?

We could also ask a different question: How much money would we need to give the investor next year to make him just as well off as he is with the investment?

Rather than beginning the analysis with the assumption that all consumption occurs as of now, we will reverse the process and assume that all consumption occurs next year. On this basis, without the investment, the individual will have GBP50,000 this year, which he could deposit with a bank for a year at 10 per cent interest. In addition, he will have GBP60,000 of income arising next year. But given that this latter sum arises next year, it will not attract any interest if we are undertaking the analysis as of next year. So the total available for consumption next year will total:

$$\text{GBP50,000} \times (1.1) + \text{GBP60,000} = \text{GBP115,000}$$

With the effects of the investment decision, his position would be different. He would only have a net GBP20,000 this year, but would have an amount of GBP100,000 (income of GBP60,000 plus investment proceeds of GBP40,000) next year. Clearly, the GBP20,000 would be available for deposit at 10 per cent interest for one whole year, but the GBP100,000 (which arises next year) would not earn any interest were we to undertake our calculations as of next year. In fact, the total amount available for consumption next year will total:

$$\text{GBP20,000} \times (1.1) + \text{GBP100,000} = \text{GBP122,000}$$

The difference between this amount and GBP115,000 is

$$\text{GBP122,000} - \text{GBP115,000} = \text{GBP7,000}$$

which is the answer to the question of how much we would need to give the person next year to make him as well off as he is with the investment.

There is a simple relationship between these two numbers. If we multiply GBP6,364 by 1.1 we get GBP7,000. Consider why this must be so. The GBP6,364 is the amount of extra cash we must give the person this year to substitute for having the investment. In a financial market with a 10 per cent rate of interest, however, GBP1 this year is worth exactly the same as GBP1.10 next year. Thus, GBP6,364 this year is the same as GBP6,364 × 1.1 next year. In other words, the person does not care whether he has the investment, GBP6,364, this year or GBP6,364 × 1.1 next year. But we already showed that the investor is equally willing to have the investment and to have GBP7,000 next year. This must mean that

$$GBP6,364 \times 1.1 = GBP7,000$$

Now we can show you how to evaluate the investment opportunity on a stand alone basis. Here are the relevant facts: The individual must give up GBP30,000 this year to get GBP40,000 next year. These cash flows are illustrated in Figure 4.2.

FIGURE 4.2   Cash Flows for the Investment Project

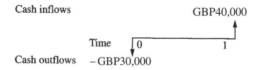

The investment rule that follows from the previous analysis is the net-present-value (NPV) rule. Here we convert all consumption values to the present and add them up:

$$\text{Net present value} = -GBP30,000 + GBP40,000 \times (1/1.1)$$
$$= -GBP30,000 + GBP36,364$$
$$= GBP6,364$$

The future amount, GBP40,000, is called the *future value* (FV).

The net present value of an investment is a simple criterion for deciding whether or not to undertake an investment. The NPV answers the question of how much cash an investor would need to have today as a substitute for making the investment. If the net present value is positive, the investment is worth taking on because doing so is essentially the same as receiving a cash payment equal to the net present value. If the net present value is negative, taking on the investment today is equivalent to giving up some cash today, and the investment should be rejected.

We use the term *net present value* to emphasize that we are already including the current cost of the investment in determining its value and not simply what it will return. For example, if the interest rate is 10 per cent and an investment of GBP30,000 today will produce a total cash return of GBP40,000 in one year's time, the *present value* of the GBP40,000 by itself is

$$GBP40,000/1.1 = GBP36,364$$

but the *net present value* of the investment is GBP36,364 minus the original investment:

Net present value = GBP36,364 − GBP30,000 = GBP6,364

The present value of a future cash flow is the value of that cash flow after considering the appropriate market interest rate. The net present value of an investment is the present value of the investment's future cash flows, minus the initial cost of the investment. We have just decided that our investment is a good opportunity. It has a positive net present value because it is worth more than it costs.

In general, the above can be stated in terms of the **net-present-value rule:**

> An investment is worth making if it has a positive NPV. If an investment's NPV is negative, it should be rejected.

Concept Questions

- Give the definitions of net present value, future value and present value.
- What information does a person need to compute an investment's net present value?

4.5 Corporate Investment Decision-Making

Up to now, everything we have done has been from the perspective of the individual investor. How do corporations and firms make investment decisions? Aren't their decisions governed by a much more complicated set of rules and principles than the simple NPV rule that we have developed for individuals?

We return to questions of corporate decision-making and corporate governance later in the book, but it is remarkable how well our central ideas and the NPV rule hold up even when applied to corporations.

Suppose that firms are just ways in which many investors can pool their resources to make large-scale business decisions. Suppose, for example, that you own 1 per cent of some firm. Now suppose that this firm is considering whether or not to undertake some investment. If that investment passes the NPV rule, that is, if it has a positive NPV, then 1 per cent of that NPV belongs to you. If the firm takes on this investment, the value of the whole firm will rise by the NPV and your investment in the firm will rise by 1 per cent of the NPV of the investment. Similarly, the other shareholders in the firm will profit by the firm taking on the positive NPV project because the value of their shares in the firm will also increase. This means that the shareholders in the firm will be unanimous in wanting the firm to increase its value by taking on the positive NPV project. If you follow this line of reasoning, you will also be able to see why the shareholders would oppose the firm taking on any projects with a negative NPV because this would lower the value of their shares.

One common objection to this line of reasoning is that people differ in their tastes and that they would not necessarily agree to take on or reject investments by the NPV rule. For instance, suppose that you and we each own some shares in a company. Further, suppose that we are older than you and might be anxious to spend our money. Being younger, you might be more patient than we are and more willing to wait for a good long-term investment to pay off.

Because of the financial markets we all agree that the company should take on investments with positive NPVs and reject those with negative NPVs. If there were no financial markets, then, being impatient, we might want the company to do little or no investing so that we could have as much money as possible to consume now, and, being patient, you might prefer the company to make some investments. With financial markets, we are both satisfied by having the company follow the NPV rule.

Suppose that the company takes on a positive NPV investment. Let us assume that this investment has a net payoff of GBP1 million next year. That means that the value of the company will increase by GBP1 million next year and, consequently, if you own 1 per cent of the company's shares, the value of your shares will increase by 1 per cent of GBP1 million, or GBP10,000, next year. Because you are patient, you might be prepared to wait for your GBP10,000 until next year. Being impatient, we do not want to wait, and, with financial markets, we do not need to wait. We can simply borrow against the extra GBP10,000 we will have tomorrow and use the loan to consume more today.

In fact, if there is also a market for the firm's shares, we do not even need to borrow. After the company takes on a positive NPV investment, our shares in the company increase in value today. This is because owning the shares today entitles investors to their portion of the extra GBP1 million the company will have next year. This means that the shares would rise in value today by the present value of GBP1 million. Because you want to delay your consumption, you could wait until next year and sell your shares then to have extra consumption next year. Being impatient, we might sell our shares now and use the money to consume more today. If we owned 1 per cent of the company's shares, we could sell our shares for an extra amount equal to the present value of GBP10,000.

In reality, shareholders in big companies do not vote on every investment decision, and the managers of big companies must have rules that they follow. We have seen that all shareholders in a company will be made better off—no matter what their levels of patience or impatience—if these managers follow the NPV rule. This is a marvellous result because it makes it possible for many different owners to delegate decision-making powers to the managers. They need only to tell the managers to follow the NPV rule, and if the managers do so they will be doing exactly what the stockholders want them to do. Sometimes this form of the NPV rule is stated as having the managers maximize the value of the company. As we argued, the current value of the shares of the company will increase by the NPV of any investments that the company undertakes. This means that the managers of the company can make the shareholders as well off as possible by taking on all positive NPV projects and rejecting projects with negative NPVs.

Separating investment decision-making from the owners is a basic requirement of the modern large firm. The separation theorem in financial markets says that all investors will want to accept or reject the same investment projects by using the NPV rule, regardless of their personal preferences. Investors can delegate the operations of the firm and require that managers use the NPV rule. Of course, much remains for us to discuss about this topic. For example, what ensures that managers will actually do what is best for their stockholders?

We discussed this possibility in Chapter 2, and we take up this interesting topic later in the book. For now, though, we no longer will consider our perspective to be that of the lone investor. Instead, we will use the NPV rule for companies as well as for investors. The analysis we have presented has been restricted to risk-free cash flows in one time period. However, these ideas can be derived for risky cash flows that extend beyond one period.

Concept Question

- In terms of the net-present-value rule, what is the essential difference between the individual and the corporation?

4.6   Summary and Conclusions

Finance is a subject that builds understanding from the ground up. Whenever you come up against a new problem or issue in finance, you can always return to the basic principles of this chapter for guidance.

1. Financial markets exist because people want to adjust their consumption over time. They do this by borrowing and lending.
2. Financial markets provide the key test for investment decision-making. Whether a particular investment decision should or should not be taken depends only on this test: If there is a superior alternative in the financial markets, the investment should be rejected; if not, the investment is worth taking. The most important thing about this principle is that the investor need not use his or her preferences to decide whether the investment should be taken. Regardless of the individual's preference for consumption this year versus next, regardless of how patient or impatient the individual is, making the proper investment decision depends only on comparing it with the alternatives in the financial markets.
3. The net present value of an investment helps us make the comparison between the investment and the financial market. If the NPV is positive, our rule tells us to undertake the investment. This illustrates the second major feature of the financial markets and investment. Not only does the NPV rule tell us which investments to accept and which to reject, the financial markets also provide us with the tools for actually acquiring the funds to make the investments. In short, we use the financial markets to decide both what to do and how to do it.
4. The NPV rule can be applied to corporations as well as to individuals. The separation theorem developed in this chapter says that all of the owners of the firm would agree that the firm should use the NPV rule even though each might differ in personal tastes for consumption and savings.

In the next chapter, we learn more about the NPV rule by using it to examine a wide array of problems in finance.

KEY TERMS

Financial intermediaries   69
Equilibrium rate of interest   70

Perfectly competitive financial market   71
Net present value rule   75

Net Present Value

We now examine one of the most important concepts in all of corporate finance, the relationship between one pound or mark today and one pound or mark respectively in the future. Consider the following example. A firm is contemplating investing DEM1 million in a project that is expected to pay out DEM200,000 per year for nine years. Should the firm accept the project? At first glance, one might say yes since total inflows of DEM1.8 million (= DEM200,000 × 9) are greater than DEM1 million outflow. However, the DEM1 million is paid out *immediately*, whereas the DEM200,000 per year is received in the future. Also, the immediate payment is known with certainty, whereas the later inflows can only be estimated. Thus, we need to know the relationship between a DEM today and a (possibly uncertain) DEM in the future before deciding on the project.

This relationship is called the *time-value-of-money concept*. It is important in such areas as capital budgeting, lease versus buy decisions, accounts receivable analysis, financing arrangements, mergers and pension funding.

The basics are presented in this chapter. We begin by discussing two fundamental concepts, future value and present value. Next, we treat simplifying formulas, such as perpetuities and annuities.

5.1 The One-Period Case

● **Example**

Don Simkowitz is trying to sell a piece of agricultural land. Yesterday, he was offered GBP10,000 for the property. He was about ready to accept the offer when another individual offered him GBP11,424. However, the second offer was to be paid a year from now. Don has satisfied himself that both buyers are honest and financially solvent, so he has no fear that the offer he selects will fall through. These two offers are pictured as cash flows in Figure 5.1. Which offer should Mr Simkowitz choose?

Mike Tuttle, Don's financial advisor, points out that if Don takes the first offer, he could invest the GBP10,000 in the bank at an insured rate of 12 per cent. At the end of one year, he would have

$$\underset{\substack{\text{Return of}\\\text{principal}}}{\text{GBP10,000}} + \underset{\text{Interest}}{0.12 \times \text{GBP10,000}} = \text{GBP10,000} \times 1.12 = \text{GBP11,200}$$

Because this is less than the GBP11,424 Don could receive from the second offer, Mr

FIGURE 5.1   **Cash Flow for Mr Simkowitz's Sale**

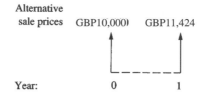

Tuttle recommends that he take the latter. This analysis uses the concept of **future value** or **compound value**, which is the value of a sum after investing over one or more periods. The compound or future value of GBP10,000 is GBP11,200. ●

An alternative method employs the concept of **present value**. One can determine present value by asking the following question: How much money must Don put in the bank today so that he will have GBP11,424 next year? We can write this algebraically as

$$\text{PV} \times 1.12 = \text{GBP}11,424 \tag{5.1}$$

We want to solve for present value (PV), the amount of money that yields GBP11,424 if invested at 12 per cent today. Solving for PV, we have

$$\text{PV} = \frac{\text{GBP}11,424}{1.12} = \text{GBP}10,200$$

The formula for PV can be written as

Present Value of Investment:

$$\text{PV} = \frac{C_1}{1 + r}$$

where C_1 is cash flow at date 1, r is the appropriate interest rate. The rate of r is the return that Don Simkowitz requires on his land sale. It is sometimes referred to as the discount rate.

Present value analysis tells us that a payment of GBP11,424 to be received next year has a present value of GBP10,200 today. In other words, at a 12 per cent interest rate, Mr Simkowitz could not care less whether you gave him GBP10,200 today or GBP11,424 next year. If you gave him GBP10,200 today, he could put it in the bank and receive GBP11,424 next year.

Because the second offer has a present value of GBP10,200, whereas the first offer is for only GBP10,000, present value analysis also indicates that Mr Simkowitz should take the second offer. In other words, both future value analysis and present value analysis lead to the same decision. As it turns out, present value analysis and future value analysis must always lead to the same decision.

As simple as this example is, it contains the basic principles that we will be working with over the next few chapters. We now use another example to develop the concept of net present value.

● **Example**
Louisa Dice is thinking about investing in a piece of land in North Holland that costs NLG85,000. She is certain that next year the land will be worth NLG91,000, a sure

NLG6,000 gain. Given that the guaranteed interest rate in the bank is 10 per cent, should she undertake the investment in land? Ms Dice's choice is described in Figure 5.2 with the cash flow time chart.

FIGURE 5.2   Cash Flows for Land Investment

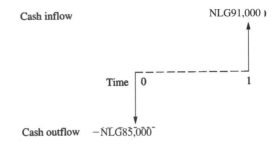

A moment's thought should be all it takes to convince her that this is not an attractive business deal. By investing NLG85,000 in the land, she will have NLG91,000 available next year. Suppose, instead, that she puts the same NLG85,000 into the bank. At the interest rate of 10 per cent, this NLG85,000 would grow to

$$(1 + 0.10) \times \text{NLG85,000} = \text{NLG93,500}$$

next year.

It would be foolish to buy the land when investing the same NLG85,000 in the financial market would produce an extra NLG2,500 (that is, NLG93,500 from the bank minus NLG91,000 from the land investment). This is a future-value calculation.

Alternatively, she could calculate the present value of the sale price next year as

$$\text{Present value} = \frac{\text{NLG91,000}}{1.10} = \text{NLG82,727.27}$$

Since the present value of next year's sales price is less than this year's purchase price of NLG85,000, present-value analysis also indicates that she should not purchase the property. ●

Frequently, business people want to determine the exact cost or benefit of a decision. The decision to buy this year and sell next year can be evaluated as

Net Present Value of Investment:

$$-\text{NLG2,273} = \underset{\substack{\text{Cost of land} \\ \text{today}}}{-\text{NLG85,000}} + \underset{\substack{\text{Present value of} \\ \text{next year's sales price}}}{\text{NLG91,000}/1.10} \qquad (5.2)$$

The formula for NPV can be written as

$$\text{NPV} = \quad -\text{Cost} \quad + \text{PV}$$

Equation (5.2) says that the value of the investment is $-$NLG2,273, after stating all the benefits and all the costs as of date 0. We say that $-$NLG2,273 is the **net present**

value (NPV) of the investment. That is, NPV is the present value of future cash flows minus the present value of the cost of the investment. Because the net present value is negative, Louisa Dice should not purchase the land.

Both the Simkowitz and the Dice examples deal with perfect certainty. That is, Don Simkowitz knows with perfect certainty that he could sell his land for GBP11,424 next year. Similarly, Louisa Dice knows with perfect certainty that she could receive NLG91,000 for selling her land. Unfortunately, business people frequently do not know future cash flows. This uncertainty is treated in the next example.

● **Example**

Artwerk GmbH is a firm that speculates in modern paintings. The manager is thinking of buying an original modern painting for DEM400,000 with the intention of selling it at the end of one year. The manager expects that the painting will be worth DEM480,000 in one year. The relevant cash flows are depicted in Figure 5.3.

FIGURE 5.3   Cash Flows for Investment in Painting

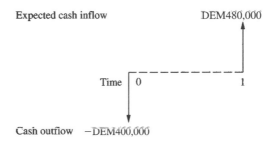

Of course, this is only an expectation—the painting could be worth more or less than DEM480,000. Suppose the guaranteed interest rate granted by banks is 10 per cent. Should the firm purchase the piece of art?

Our first thought might be to discount at the interest rate, yielding

$$\frac{\text{DEM480,000}}{1.10} = \text{DEM436,364}$$

Since DEM436,364 is greater than DEM400,000, it looks at first glance as if the painting should be purchased. However, 10 per cent is the return one can earn on a riskless investment. Because the painting is quite risky, a higher discount rate is called for. The manager chooses a rate of 25 per cent to reflect this risk. In other words, he argues that a 25 per cent expected return is fair compensation for an investment as risky as this painting.

The present value of the painting becomes

$$\frac{\text{DEM480,000}}{1.25} = \text{DEM384,000}$$

Thus, the manager believes that the painting is currently overpriced at DEM400,000 and does not make the purchase. ●

The above analysis is typical of decision-making in today's corporations, though real-world examples are, of course, much more complex. Unfortunately, any example with risk poses a problem not faced by a riskless example. In an example with riskless cash flows, the appropriate interest rate can be determined by simply checking with a few banks.[1] The selection of the discount rate for a risky investment is quite a difficult task. We simply don't know at this point whether the discount rate on the painting should be 11 per cent, 25 per cent, 52 per cent or some other percentage.

Because the choice of a discount rate is so difficult, we merely wanted to broach the subject here. The rest of the chapter reverts to examples under perfect certainty. We must wait until the specific material on risk and return is covered in later chapters before a risk-adjusted analysis can be presented.

Concept Questions

- Define future value and present value.
- How does one use net present value when making an investment decision?

5.2   The Multiperiod Case

The previous section presented the calculation of future value and present value for one period only. We will now perform the calculations for the multiperiod case.

Future Value and Compounding

Suppose an individual were to make a loan of GBP1. At the end of the first year, the borrower would owe the lender the principal amount of GBP1 plus the interest on the loan at the interest rate of r. For the specific case where the interest rate is, say, 9 per cent, the borrower owes the lender

$$GBP1 \times (1 + r) = GBP1 \times 1.09 = GBP1.09$$

At the end of the year, though, the lender has two choices. She can either take the GBP1.09—or, more generally, $(1 + r)$—out of the capital market, or she can leave it in and lend it again for a second year. The process of leaving the money in the capital market and lending it for another year is called **compounding**.

Suppose that the lender decides to compound her loan for another year. She does this by taking the proceeds from her first one-year loan, GBP1.09, and lending this amount for the next year. At the end of next year, then, the borrower will owe her

$$GBP1 \times (1 + r) \times (1 + r) = GBP1 \times (1 + r)^2 = 1 + 2r + r^2$$

$$GBP1 \times (1.09) \times (1.09) = GBP1 \times (1.09)^2 = GBP1 + GBP0.18 + GBP0.0081$$

$$= GBP1.1881$$

This is the total she will receive two years from now by compounding the loan.

In other words, the capital market enables the investor, by providing a ready opportunity for lending, to transform GBP1 today into GBP1.1881 at the end of two years. At the end of three years, the cash will be $GBP1 \times (1.09)^3 = GBP1.2950$.

The most important point to notice is that the total amount that the lender receives

---

[1] In Chapter 10, we discuss estimation of the riskless rate in more detail.

is not just the GBP1 that she lent out plus two years' worth of interest on GBP1:

$$2 \times r = 2 \times GBP0.09 = GBP0.18$$

The lender also gets back an amount r^2, which is the interest in the second year on the interest that was earned in the first year. The term, $2 \times r$, represents **simple interest** over the two years, and the term, r^2, is referred to as the *interest on interest*. In our example this latter amount is exactly

$$r^2 = (GBP0.09)^2 = GBP0.0081$$

When cash is invested at **compound interest**, each interest payment is reinvested. With simple interest, the interest is not reinvested. Benjamin Franklin's statement, 'Money makes money and the money that money makes makes more money,' is a colourful way of explaining compound interest. The difference between compound interest and simple interest is illustrated in Figure 5.4. In this example, the difference does not amount to much because the loan is for GBP1. If the loan were for GBP1 million, the lender would receive GBP1,188,100 in two years' time. Of this amount, GBP8,100 is interest on interest. The lesson is that those small numbers beyond the decimal point can add up to large amounts when the transactions are for large amounts. In addition, the longer-lasting the loan, the more important interest on interest becomes.

The general formula for an investment over many periods can be written as

Future Value of an Investment:

$$FV = C_0 \times (1 + r)^T$$

FIGURE 5.4   **Simple and Compound Interest**

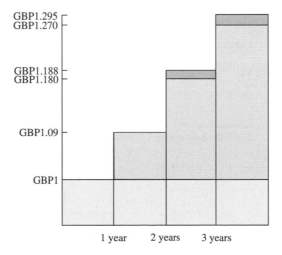

The darker shaded area indicates the difference
between compound and simple interest. The difference
is substantial over a period of many years or decades.

where C_0 is the cash to be invested at date 0, r is the interest rate, and T is the number of periods over which the cash is invested.

● Example

Jan Vink has put NLG5000 in a savings account at the First Bank of Utrecht. The account earns 7 per cent, compounded annually. How much will Jan Vink have at the end of three years?

$$NLG5000 \times 1.07 \times 1.07 \times 1.07 = NLG5000 \times (1.07)^3 = NLG6125.2$$

Figure 5.5 illustrates the growth of Jan Vink's account. ●

FIGURE 5.5   Jan Vink's Savings Account

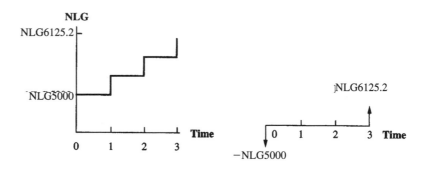

● Example

Pat Green invested GBP1,000 in shares of the SDH Company. On this amount, the company pays a current dividend of GBP20, which is expected to grow by 20 per cent per year for the next two years. What will the dividend of the SDH Company be after two years?

$$GBP20 \times (1.20)^2 = GBP28.8$$

Figure 5.6 illustrates the increasing value of SDH's dividends. ●

The two previous examples can be calculated in any one of three ways. The computations could be done by hand, by calculator or with the help of a table. The

---

FIGURE 5.6   The Growth of the SDH Dividends

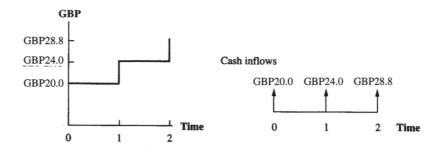

appropriate table is Table A.3, which appears in the back of this book. This table presents *Future values of USD1 at the end of T periods*. Of course, you can use the table for any currency you like—just substitute GBP or NLG or DEM for dollars. But for convenience, and also to avoid any single European currency, we refer to dollars in the tables at the back of the book. The table is used by locating the appropriate interest rate on the horizontal and the appropriate number of periods on the vertical.

For example, Jan Vink would look at the following portion of Table A.3:

	Interest rate		
Period	6%	7%	8%
1	1.0600	1.0700	1.0800
2	1.1236	1.1449	1.1664
3	1.1910	1.2250	1.2597
4	1.2625	1.3108	1.3605

He could calculate the future value of his NLG5000 as

$$
\begin{array}{ccccc}
\text{NLG5000} & \times & 1.2250 & = & \text{NLG6125.0} \\
\text{Initial} & & \text{Future value} & & \\
\text{investment} & & \text{of NLG1} & &
\end{array}
$$

In the example concerning Jan Vink, we gave you both the initial investment and the interest rate and then asked you to calculate the future value. Alternatively, the interest rate could have been unknown, as shown in the following example.

● **Example**

Michael Duffy, who recently won GBP10,000 in the lottery, wants to buy a car in five years. Michael estimates that the car will cost GBP16,105 at that time. His cash flows are displayed in Figure 5.7.

──────────

FIGURE 5.7   **Cash Flows for Purchase of Michael Duffy's Car**

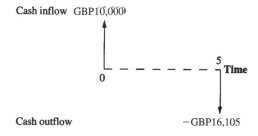

What interest rate must he earn to be able to afford the car?

The ratio of purchase price to initial cash is

$$
\frac{\text{GBP16,105}}{\text{GBP10,000}} = 1.6105
$$

Thus, he must earn an interest rate that allows GBP1 to become GBP1.6105 in five years. Table A.3 tells us that an interest rate of 10 per cent will allow him to purchase the car.

One can express the problem algebraically as

$$GBP10,000 \times (1 + r)^5 = GBP16,105$$

where r is the interest rate needed to purchase the car. Because GBP16,105/GBP10,000 = 1.6105, we have

$$(1 + r)^5 = 1.6105$$

Either the table or any sophisticated hand calculator solves[2] for r. ●

The Power of Compounding: A Digression

Most people who have had any experience with compounding are impressed with its power over long periods of time. Take the stock market, for example. Ibbotson and Sinquefield have calculated that the US stock market as a whole had approximately a 10 per cent rate of return per year from 1926 through 1994.[3] A return of this magnitude may not appear to be anything special over, say, a one-year period. However, one dollar placed in these stocks at the beginning of 1926 would have been worth USD810.54 at the end of 1994.

The example illustrates the great difference between compound and simple interest. At 10 per cent, simple interest on USD1 is 10c a year. Simple interest over 69 years is USD6.90 (69 × USD0.10). That is, an individual withdrawing 10c every year would have withdrawn USD6.90 (69 × USD0.10) over 69 years. This is quite a bit below the USD810.54 that was obtained by reinvestment of all principal and interest.

The results are more impressive over even longer periods of time. A person with no experience in compounding might think that the value of USD1 at the end of 138 years would be twice the value of USD1 at the end of 69 years, if the yearly rate of return stayed the same. Actually the value of USD1 at the end of 138 years would be the square of the value of USD1 at the end of 69 years. That is, if the annual rate of return remained the same, a USD1 investment in common stocks should be worth USD656,975.09 [USD1 × (810.54 × 810.54)].

A few years ago an archaeologist unearthed a relic stating that Julius Caesar lent the Roman equivalent of one penny to someone. Since there was no record of the penny ever being repaid, the archaeologist wondered what the interest and principal would be if a descendant of Caesar tried to collect from a descendant of the borrower in the twentieth century. The archaeologist felt that a rate of 6 per cent might be appropriate. To his surprise, the principal and interest due after more than 2,000 years was far greater than the entire wealth on earth.

Present Value and Discounting

We now know that an annual interest rate of 9 per cent enables the investor to transform FRF1 today into FRF1.1881 two years from now. In addition, we would like

---

[2] Conceptually, we are taking the fifth roots of both sides of the equation. That is,

$$r = \sqrt[5]{1.6105} - 1$$

[3] *Stocks, Bonds, Bills and Inflation* [SBBI]. 1994 Yearbook, Ibbotson Associates, Chicago, 1994.

to know:

> How much would an investor need to lend today so that she could receive FRF1 two years from today?

Algebraically, we can write this as

$$PV \times (1.09)^2 = FRF1 \tag{5.3}$$

In (5.3), PV stands for present value, the amount of money we must lend today in order to receive FRF1 in two years' time.

Solving for PV in (5.3), we have

$$PV = \frac{FRF1}{1.1881} = FRF0.84$$

This process of calculating the present value of a future cash flow is called **discounting**. It is the opposite of compounding. The difference between compounding and discounting is illustrated in Figure 5.8.

FIGURE 5.8   **Compounding and Discounting**

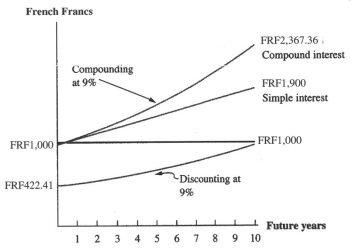

The top line shows the growth of the FRF1,000 at compound interest with the funds invested at 9 per cent: FRF1,000 × (1.09)^{10} = FRF2,367.36. Simple interest is shown on the next line. It is FRF1,000 + 10 × (FRF1,000 × 0.09) = FRF1,900. The bottom line shows the discounted value of FRF1,000 if the interest rate is 9 per cent.

To be certain that FRF0.84 is in fact the present value of FRF1 to be received in two years, we must check whether or not, if we loaned out FRF0.84 and rolled over the loan for two years, we would get exactly FRF1 back. If this were the case, the capital markets would be saying that FRF1 received in two years' time is equivalent to having FRF0.84 today. Checking with the exact numbers, we get

$$FRF0.84168 \times 1.09 \times 1.09 = FRF1$$

In other words, when we have capital markets with a sure interest rate of 9 per cent, we are indifferent between receiving FRF0.84 today or FRF1 in two years. We have no reason to treat these two choices differently from each other, because if we had FRF0.84 today and loaned it out for two years, it would return FRF1 to us at the end of that time. The value 0.84 [1/(1.09)^2] is called the **present value factor**. It is the factor used to calculate the present value of a future cash flow.

● Example

Pierre Dumas will receive FRF10,000 three years from now. Pierre can earn 8 per cent on his investments, and so the **appropriate discount rate** is 8 per cent. What is the present value of his future cash flow?

$$PV = FRF10,000 \times \left(\frac{1}{1.08}\right)^3$$

$$= FRF10,000 \times 0.7938$$

$$= FRF7,938$$

Figure 5.9 illustrates the application of the present value factor to Pierre's investment.

FIGURE 5.9   Discounting Pierre Dumas's Opportunity

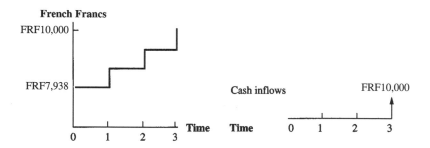

When his investments grow at an 8 per cent rate of interest, Pierre Dumas is equally inclined toward receiving FRF7,938 now and receiving FRF10,000 in three years' time. After all, he could convert the FRF7,938 he receives today into FRF10,000 in three years by lending it at an interest rate of 8 per cent.

Pierre Dumas could have reached his present value calculation in one of three ways. The computation could have been done by hand, by calculator, or with the help of Table A.1, which appears at the back of this book. This table presents *present value of USD1 to be received after T periods*. The table is used by locating the appropriate interest rate on the horizontal and the appropriate number of periods on the vertical. For example, Pierre Dumas would look at the following portion of Table A.1:

Period	Interest rate		
	7%	*8%*	*9%*
1	0.9346	0.9259	0.9174
2	0.8734	0.8573	0.8417
3	0.8163	0.7938	0.7722
4	0.7629	0.7350	0.7084

The appropriate present value factor is 0.7938. ●

In the above example, we gave both the interest rate and the future cash flow. Alternatively, the interest rate could have been unknown.

● **Example**
A customer of the Chaffkin Corp. wants to buy a tugboat today. Rather than paying immediately, he will pay GBP50,000 in three years. It will cost the Chaffkin Corp. GBP38,610 to build the tugboat immediately. The relevant cash flows to Chaffkin Corp. are displayed in Figure 5.10. By charging what interest rate would the Chaffkin Corp. neither gain nor lose on the sale?

FIGURE 5.10   **Cash Flows for Tugboat**

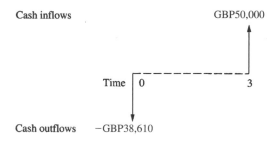

The ratio of construction cost to sale price is

GBP38,610/GBP50,000 = 0.7722

We must determine the interest rate that allows GBP1 to be received in three years to have a present value of GBP0.7722. Table A.1 tells us that 9 per cent is that interest rate.[4] ●

Frequently, an investor or a business will receive more than one cash flow. The present value of the set of cash flows is simply the sum of the present values of the individual cash flows. This is illustrated in the following example.

● **Example**
Klaus Seeler has won a prize in the lottery and will receive the following set of cash flows over the next two years:

Year	*Cash flow*
1	DEM2,000
2	DEM5,000

---
[4] Algebraically, we are solving for *r* in the equation:

$$\frac{GBP50,000}{(1+r)^3} = GBP38,610$$

or, equivalently,

$$\frac{GBP1}{(1+r)^3} = GBP0.7722$$

Klaus can currently earn 6 per cent in his passbook savings account, and so, the appropriate discount rate is 6 per cent. The present value of the cash flows is

Year	Cash flow	×	Present value factor	=	Present value
1	DEM2,000	×	$1/1.06 = 0.943$	=	DEM1,887
2	DEM5,000	×	$(1/1.06)^2 = 0.890$	=	DEM4,450
			Total		DEM6,337

In other words, Klaus Seeler is equally inclined towards receiving DEM6,337 today and receiving DEM2,000 and DEM5,000 over the next two years. ●

The Algebraic Formula

To derive an algebraic formula for net present value of a cash flow, recall that the PV of receiving a cash flow one year from now is

$$PV = C_1/(1 + r)$$

and the PV of receiving a cash flow two years from now is

$$PV = C_2/(1 + r)^2$$

We can write the NPV of a *T*-period project as

$$NPV = -C_0 + \frac{C_1}{1 + r} + \frac{C_2}{(1 + r)^2} + \cdots + \frac{C_T}{(1 + r)^T} = C_0 + \sum_{i=1}^{T} \frac{C_i}{(1 + r)}$$

The initial flow, $-C_0$, is assumed to be negative because it represents an investment. The term $\sum$ is shorthand for the sum of the series.

Concept Questions

- What is the difference between simple interest and compound interest?
- What is the formula for the net present value of a project?

5.3   Compounding Periods

So far we have assumed that compounding and discounting occur yearly. Sometimes compounding may occur more frequently than just once a year. For example, imagine that a bank pays a 10 per cent interest rate 'compounded semiannually'. This means that a NLG1,000 deposit in the bank would be worth NLG1,000 × 1.05 = NLG1,050 after six months, and NLG1,050 × 1.05 = NLG1,102.50 at the end of the year.

The end-of-the-year wealth can be written as[5]

$$NLG1,000\left(1 + \frac{0.10}{2}\right)^2 = NLG1,000 \times (1.05)^2 = NLG1,102.50$$

Of course, a NLG1,000 deposit would be worth NLG1,100 (NLG1,000 × 1.10) with

---

[5] In addition to using a calculator, one can still use Table A.3 when the compounding period is less than a year. Here, one sets the interest rate at 5 per cent and the number of periods at two.

yearly compounding. Note that the future value at the end of one year is greater with semiannual compounding than with yearly compounding. With yearly compounding, the original NLG1,000 remains the investment base for the full year. The original NLG1,000 is the investment base only for the first six months with semiannual compounding. The base over the second six months is NLG1,050. Hence, one gets interest on interest with semiannual compounding.

Because NLG1,000 × 1.1025 = NLG1,102.50, 10 per cent compounded semiannually is the same as 10.25 per cent compounded annually. In other words, a rational investor could not care less whether she is quoted a rate of 10 per cent compounded semiannually, or a rate of 10.25 per cent compounded annually.

Quarterly compounding at 10 per cent yields wealth at the end of one year of

$$\text{NLG1,000}\left(1 + \frac{0.10}{4}\right)^4 = \text{NLG1,103.81}$$

More generally, compounding an investment m times a year provides end-of-year wealth of

$$C_0\left(1 + \frac{r}{m}\right)^m \tag{5.4}$$

where C_0 is one's initial investment and r is the **stated annual interest rate**. The stated annual interest rate is the annual interest rate without consideration of compounding.

● **Example**

What is the end-of-year wealth if Jane Christine receives a 24 per cent rate of interest compounded monthly on a GBP1 investment?

Using Eq. (5.4), her wealth is

$$\text{GBP1}\left(1 + \frac{0.24}{12}\right)^{12} = \text{GBP1} \times (1.02)^{12}$$
$$= \text{GBP1.2682}$$

The annual rate of return is 26.82 per cent. This annual rate of return is called the **effective annual interest rate**. Due to compounding, the effective annual interest rate is greater than the stated annual interest rate of 24 per cent. Algebraically, we can rewrite the effective annual interest rate as

Effective Annual Interest Rate:

$$\left(1 + \frac{r}{m}\right)^m - 1 \tag{5.5}$$

Students are often bothered by the subtraction of 1 in (5.5). Note that end-of-year wealth is composed of both the interest earned over the year and the original principal. We remove the original principal by subtracting one in (5.5). ●

● **Example**

If the stated annual rate of interest, 8 per cent, is compounded quarterly, what is the effective annual rate of interest?

Using (5.5), we have

$$\left(1 + \frac{r}{m}\right)^m - 1 = \left(1 + \frac{0.08}{4}\right)^4 - 1 = 0.0824 = 8.24\%$$

Referring back to our original example where $C_0 = $ NLG1,000 and $r = $ 10%, we can generate the following table:

C_0	Compounding frequency (m)	C_1	Effective annual interest rate = $\left(1 + \frac{r}{m}\right)^m - 1$
NLG1,000	Yearly ($m = 1$)	NLG1,100.00	0.10
1,000	Semiannually ($m = 2$)	1,102.50	0.1025
1,000	Quarterly ($m = 4$)	1,103.81	0.10381
1,000	Daily ($m = 365$)	1,105.16	0.10516 ●

Compounding over Many Years

Formula (5.4) applies for an investment over one year. For an investment over one or more (T) years, the formula becomes

Future Value with Compounding:

$$\text{FV} = C_0\left(1 + \frac{r}{m}\right)^{mT} \tag{5.6}$$

● **Example**

Juan Porras is investing ESB5,000 at 12 per cent per year, compounded quarterly for five years. What is his wealth at the end of five years?

Using (5.6), his wealth is

$$\text{ESB5,000} \times \left(1 + \frac{0.12}{4}\right)^{4 \times 5} = \text{ESB5,000} \times (1.03)^{20} = \text{ESB5,000} \times 1.8061$$
$$= \text{ESB9,030.50} \qquad ●$$

Continuous Compounding (Advanced)

The previous discussion shows that one can compound much more frequently than once a year. One could compound semiannually, quarterly, monthly, daily, hourly, each minute or even more often. The limiting case would be to compound every infinitesimal instant, which is commonly called **continuous compounding**. Surprisingly, banks and other financial institutions frequently quote continuously compounded rates, which is why we study them.

Though the idea of compounding this rapidly may boggle the mind, a simple formula is involved. With continuous compounding, the value at the end of T years is expressed as

$$C_0 \times e^{rT} \tag{5.7}$$

where C_0 is the initial investment, r is the stated annual interest rate, and T is the number of years over which the investment runs. The number e is a constant and is approximately equal to 2.718. It is not an unknown like C_0, r, and T.

● **Example**

Linda Bennett invested GBP1,000 at a continuously compounded rate of 10 per cent for one year. What is the value of her wealth at the end of one year?

From formula (5.7) we have

$$\text{GBP1,000} \times e^{0.10} = \text{GBP1,000} \times 1.1052 = \text{GBP1,105.20}$$

This number can easily be read from Table A.5 at the end of this book. One merely sets r, the value on the horizontal dimension, to 10 per cent and T, the value on the vertical dimension, to 1. For this problem, the relevant portion of the table is

Continuously compounded rate (r)

Period	9%	10%	11%
1	1.0942	1.1052	1.1163
2	1.1972	1.2214	1.2461
3	1.3100	1.3499	1.3910

Note that a continuously compounded rate of 10 per cent is equivalent to an annually compounded rate of 10.52 per cent. In other words, Linda Bennett could not care less whether her bank quoted a continuously compounded rate of 10 per cent or a 10.52 per cent rate, compounded annually. ●

● **Example**

Linda Bennett's brother, Bruce, invested GBP1,000 at a continuously compounded rate of 10 per cent for 2 years.

The appropriate formula here is

$$\text{GBP1,000} \times e^{0.10 \times 2} = \text{GBP1,000} \times e^{0.20} = \text{GBP1,221.40}$$

Using the portion of the table of continuously compounded rates reproduced above, we find the value to be 1.2214. ●

Figure 5.11 illustrates the relationship among annual, semiannual, and continuous compounding. Semiannual compounding gives rise to both a smoother curve and a higher ending value than does annual compounding. Continuous compounding has both the smoothest curve and the highest ending value of all.

FIGURE 5.11   Annual, Semiannual and Continuous Compounding

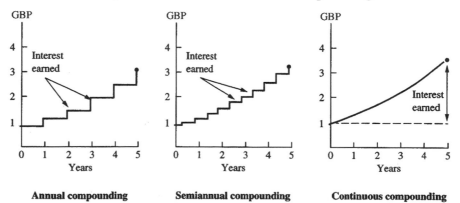

● **Example**

The national lottery is going to pay you GBP1,000 at the end of four years. If the annual continuously compounded rate of interest is 8 per cent, what is the present value of this payment?

$$\text{GBP}1{,}000 \times \frac{1}{e^{0.08 \times 4}} = \text{GBP}1{,}000 \times \frac{1}{1.3771} = \text{GBP}726.16 ●$$

Concept Questions

- What is a stated annual interest rate?
- What is an effective annual interest rate?
- What is the relationship between the stated annual interest rate and the effective annual interest rate?
- Define continuous compounding.

5.4   Simplifications

The first part of this chapter has examined the concepts of future value and present value. Although these concepts allow one to answer a host of problems concerning the time value of money, the human effort involved can frequently be excessive. For example, consider a bank calculating the present value on a 20-year monthly mortgage. Because this mortgage has 240 (20 × 12) payments, a lot of time is needed to perform a conceptually simple task.

Because many basic finance problems are potentially so time-consuming, we search out simplifications in this section. We provide simplifying formulas for four classes of cash flow streams:

- ● Perpetuity
- ● Growing perpetuity
- ● Annuity
- ● Growing annuity

Perpetuity

A **perpetuity** is a constant stream of cash flows without end. If you are thinking that perpetuities have no relevance to reality, it will surprise you that there is a well-known case of an unending cash flow stream: the British bonds called *consols*. An investor purchasing a consol is entitled to receive yearly interest from the British government forever.

How can the price of a consol be determined? Consider a consol that pays a coupon of C dollars each year and will do so forever. Simply applying the PV formula gives us

$$\text{PV} = \frac{C}{1 + r} + \frac{C}{(1 + r)^2} + \frac{C}{(1 + r)^3} + \cdots$$

where the dots at the end of the formula stand for the infinite string of terms that continues the formula. Series like that are called geometric series. It is well known that even though they have an infinite number of terms, the whole series has a finite sum because each term is only a fraction of the preceding term. Before turning to our calculus books, though, it is worth going back to our original principles to see if a bit of financial intuition can help us find the PV.

The present value of the consol is the present value of all of its future coupons. In other words, it is an amount of money that, if an investor had it today, would enable him to achieve the same pattern of expenditures that the consol and its coupons would. Suppose that an investor wanted to spend exactly C dollars each year. If he had the consol, he could do this. How much money must he have today to spend the same amount? Clearly, he would need exactly enough so that the interest on the money would be C dollars per year. If he had any more, he could spend more than C dollars each year. If he had any less, he would eventually run out of money spending C dollars per year.

The amount that will give the investor C dollars each year, and therefore the present value of the consol, is simply

$$PV = \frac{C}{r} \tag{5.8}$$

To confirm that this is the right answer, notice that if we lend the amount C/r, the interest it earns each year will be

$$\text{Interest} = \frac{C}{r} \times r = C$$

which is exactly the consol payment.[6] To sum up, we have shown that for a consol

Formula for Present Value of Perpetuity:

$$PV = \frac{C}{1 + r} + \frac{C}{(1 + r)^2} + \frac{C}{(1 + r)^3} + \cdots$$
$$= \frac{C}{r}$$

It is comforting to know how easily we can use a bit of financial intuition to solve this mathematical problem.

● Example
Consider a perpetuity paying GBP100 a year. If the relevant interest rate is 8 per cent, what is the value of the consol?

Using (5.8), we have

$$PV = \frac{GBP100}{0.08} = GBP1{,}250$$

---

[6] We can prove this by looking at the PV equation:

$$PV = C/(1 + r) + C/(1 + r)^2 + \cdots$$

Let $C/(1 + r) = a$ and $1/(1 + r) = x$. We now have
$$PV = a(1 + x + x^2 \ldots) \tag{1}$$

Next we can multiply by x:
$$xPV = ax + ax^2 + \cdots \tag{2}$$

Subtracting (2) from (1) gives
$$PV(1 - x) = a$$

Now we substitute for a and x and rearrange:
$$PV = C/r$$

Now suppose that interest rates fall to 6 per cent. Using (5.8), the value of the perpetuity is

$$PV = \frac{GBP100}{0.06} = GBP1,666.67$$

Note that the value of the perpetuity rises with a drop in the interest rate. Conversely, the value of the perpetuity falls with a rise in the interest rate. ●

Growing Perpetuity

Imagine an apartment building where cash flows to the landlord after expenses will be DEM100,000 next year. These cash flows are expected to rise at 5 per cent per year. If one assumes that this rise will continue indefinitely, the cash flow stream is termed a **growing perpetuity**. The relevant interest rate is 11 per cent. Therefore, the appropriate discount rate is 11 per cent and the present value of the cash flows can be represented as

$$PV = \frac{DEM100,000}{1.11} + \frac{DEM100,000(1.05)}{(1.11)^2} + \frac{100,000(1.05)^2}{(1.11)^3} + \cdots$$

$$+ \frac{100,000(1.05)^{N-1}}{(1.11)^N} + \cdots$$

Algebraically, we can write the formula as

$$PV = \frac{C}{1 + r} + \frac{C(1 + g)}{(1 + r)^2} + \frac{C(1 + g)^2}{(1 + r)^3} + \cdots + \frac{C(1 + g)^{N-1}}{(1 + r)^N} + \cdots \qquad (5.9)$$

where C is the cash flow to be received one period hence, g is the rate of growth per period, expressed as a percentage, and r is the appropriate discount rate.

Fortunately, (5.9) reduces to the following simplification:[7]

Formula for Present Value of Growing Perpetuity:

$$PV = \frac{C}{r - g} \qquad (5.10)$$

From (5.10), the present value of the cash flows from the apartment building is

$$\frac{DEM100,000}{0.11 - 0.05} = DEM1,666,667$$

---

[7] PV is the sum of an infinite geometric series:

$$PV = a(1 + x + x^2 + \cdots)$$

where $a = C/(1 + r)$ and $x = (1 + g)/(1 + r)$. Previously we showed that the sum of an infinite geometric series is $a/(1 - x)$. Using this result and substituting for a and x, we find

$$PV = C/(r - g)$$

Note that this geometric series converges to a finite sum only when x is less than 1. This implies that the growth rate, g, must be less than the interest rate, r.

There are three important points concerning the growing perpetuity formula:

1. *The Numerator*   The numerator in (5.10) is the cash flow one period hence, not at date 0. Consider the following example:

● Example

Beckenbauer AG is *just about* to pay a dividend of DEM3.00 per share. Investors anticipate that the annual dividend will rise by 6 per cent a year forever. The applicable interest rate is 11 per cent. What is the price of the share today?

The numerator in formula (5.10) is the cash flow to be received next period. Since the growth rate is 6 per cent, the dividend next year is DEM3.18 (DEM3.00 $\times$ 1.06). The price of the share today is

$$\text{DEM66.60} \quad = \quad \underset{\substack{\text{Imminent} \\ \text{dividend}}}{\text{DEM3.00}} \quad + \quad \underset{\substack{\text{Present value} \\ \text{of all dividends} \\ \text{beginning a year} \\ \text{from now}}}{\frac{\text{DEM3.18}}{0.11 - 0.06}}$$

The price of DEM66.60 includes both the dividend to be received immediately and the present value of all dividends beginning a year from now. Formula (5.10) only makes it possible to calculate the present value of all dividends beginning a year from now. Be sure you understand this example; test questions on this subject always seem to trip up a few of our students. ●

2. *The Interest Rate and the Growth Rate*   The interest rate r must be greater than the growth rate g for the growing perpetuity formula to work. Consider the case in which the growth rate approaches the interest rate in magnitude. Then the denominator in the growing perpetuity formula gets infinitesimally small and the present value grows infinitely large. The present value is in fact undefined when r is less than g.

3. *The Timing Assumption*   Cash generally flows into and out of real-world firms both randomly and nearly continuously. However, formula (5.10) assumes that cash flows are received and disbursed at regular and discrete points in time. In the example of the apartment, we assumed that the net cash flows of DEM100,000 only occurred once a year. In reality, rent cheques are commonly received every month. Payments for maintenance and other expenses may occur any time within the year.

The growing perpetuity formula of (5.10) can be applied only by assuming a regular and discrete pattern of cash flow. Although this assumption is sensible because the formula saves so much time, the user should never forget that it is an *assumption*. This point will be mentioned again in the chapters ahead.

A few words should be said about terminology. Authors of financial textbooks generally use one of two conventions to refer to time. A minority of financial writers treat cash flows as being received on exact *dates*, for example date 0, date 1 and so forth. Under this convention, date 0 represents the present time. However, because a year is an interval, not a specific moment in time, the great majority of authors refer to cash flows that occur at the end of a year (or alternatively, the end of a period). Under this *end-of-the-year* convention, the end of year 0 is the present, the end of year 1 occurs one period hence, and so on. (The beginning of year 0 has already passed and is not generally referred to.)[8]

The interchangeability of the two conventions can be seen from the following chart:

Date 0	Date 1	Date 2	Date 3 . . .
= Now			
End of year 0	End of	End of	End of
= Now	year 1	year 2	year 3 . . .

We strongly believe that the *dates convention* reduces ambiguity. However, we use both conventions because you are likely to see the *end-of-year convention* in later courses. In fact, both conventions may appear in the same example for the sake of practice.

Annuity

An **annuity** is a level stream of regular payments that lasts for a fixed number of periods. Not surprisingly, annuities are among the most common kinds of financial instruments. The pensions that people receive when they retire are often in the form of an annuity. Leases, mortgages and pension plans are also annuities.

To figure out the present value of an annuity, we need to evaluate the following equation:

$$\frac{C}{1+r} + \frac{C}{(1+r)^2} + \frac{C}{(1+r)^3} + \cdots + \frac{C}{(1+r)^T}$$

The present value of only receiving the coupons for T periods must be less than the present value of a consol, but how much less? To answer this, we have to look at consols a bit more closely.

Consider the following time chart:

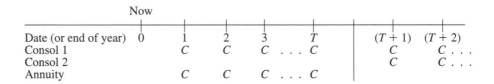

Date (or end of year)	Now 0	1	2	3	T	(T + 1)	(T + 2)
Consol 1		C	C	C . . .	C	C	C . . .
Consol 2						C	C . . .
Annuity		C	C	C . . .	C		

Consol 1 is a normal consol with its first payment at date 1. The first payment of consol 2 occurs at date $T + 1$.

The present value of having a cash flow of C at each of T dates is equal to the present value of consol 1 minus the present value of consol 2. The present value of consol 1 is given by

$$PV = \frac{C}{r} \qquad (5.11)$$

Consol 2 is just a consol with its first payment at date $T + 1$. From the perpetuity formula, this consol will be worth C/r at date T.[9] However, we do not want the value at

---

[8] Sometimes financial writers merely speak of a cash flow in year x. Although this terminology is ambiguous, such writers generally mean the *end of year x*.

[9] Students frequently think that C/r is the present value at date $T + 1$ because the consol's first payment is at date $T + 1$. However, the formula values the annuity as of one period prior to the first payment.

date T. We want the value now; in other words, the present value at date 0. We must discount C/r back by T periods. Therefore, the present value of consol 2 is

$$PV = \frac{C}{r}\left[\frac{1}{(1+r)^T}\right] \tag{5.12}$$

The present value of having cash flows for T years is the present value of a consol with its first payment at date 1 minus the present value of a consol with its first payment at date $T + 1$. Thus, the present value of an annuity is formula (5.11) minus formula (5.12). This can be written as

$$\frac{C}{r} - \frac{C}{r}\left[\frac{1}{(1+r)^T}\right]$$

This simplifies to

Formula for Present Value of Annuity:[10, 11]

$$PV = C\left[\frac{1}{r} - \frac{1}{r(1+r)^T}\right] \tag{5.13}$$

● **Example**

Bruno Gerard has just won a prize in the lottery, paying CHF50,000 a year for 20 years. He is to receive his first payment a year from now. Imagine that the state bills this as the million franc prize because CHF1,000,000 = CHF50,000 × 20. If the interest rate is 8 per cent, what is the true value of the prize?

Formula (5.13) yields

$$\begin{array}{c}\text{Present value of}\\\text{million franc prize}\end{array} = \text{CHF50,000} \times \left[\frac{1}{0.08} - \frac{1}{0.08(1.08)^{20}}\right]$$

$$\qquad\qquad\qquad\quad \text{Periodic payment} \qquad\qquad \text{Annuity factor}$$

$$= \text{CHF50,000} \quad \times \quad 9.8181$$

$$= \text{CHF490,905}$$

Rather than being overjoyed at winning the million francs, Bruno feels somewhat dumbfounded. Rather than a prize of CHF1 million, he has calculated its present value as CHF490,905.[12] ●

The term we use to compute the value of the stream of level payments, C, for T years is called an **annuity factor**. The annuity factor in the current example is 9.8181. Because the annuity factor is used so often in PV calculations, we have included it in Table A.2 at the back of this book. The table gives the values of these factors for a range of interest rates, r, and maturity dates, T.

---

[10] This can also be written as

$$C[1 - 1/(1+r)^T]/r$$

[11] We can also provide a formula for the future value of an annuity.

$$FV = C[(1+r)^T/r - 1/r]$$

[12] To solve this problem on a common type HP-12C financial calculator, you should do the following:

a. Enter the payment 50,000 and press 'PMT'.

b. Enter the interest rate at $r = 10$ and press 'T' per year

c. Enter the number of periods as 20 and press N.

d. Finally, press PV to solve.

The annuity factor as expressed in the brackets of (5.13) is a complex formula. For simplification, we may from time to time refer to the annuity factor as

$$A_r^T \qquad (5.14)$$

That is, expression (5.14) stands for the present value of $1 a year for T years at an interest rate of r.

Our experience is that annuity formulas are not hard, but tricky, for the beginning student. We present four tricks below.

Trick 1: A Delayed Annuity   One of the tricks in working with annuities or perpetuities is getting the timing exactly right. This is particularly true when an annuity or perpetuity begins at a date many periods in the future. We have found that even the brightest beginning student can make errors here. Consider the following example.

• Example

Danielle Caravello will receive a four-year annuity of ESB500,000 per year, beginning at date 6. If the interest rate is 10 per cent, what is the present value of her annuity?

This situation can be graphed as:

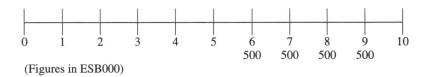

(Figures in ESB000)

The analysis involves two steps:

1. Calculate the present value of the annuity using (5.13). This is

Present Value of Annuity at Date 5 (ESB000):

$$ESB500 \left[\frac{1}{0.10} - \frac{1}{0.10(1.10)^4} \right] = ESB500 \times A_{0.10}^4$$
$$= ESB500 \times 3.1699$$
$$= ESB1,584.95$$

Note that ESB1,584,950 represents the present value at *date 5*.

Students frequently think that ESB1,584,950 is the present value at date 6, because the annuity begins at date 6. However, our formula values the annuity as of one period prior to the first payment. This can be seen in the most typical case where the first payment occurs at date 1. The formula values the annuity as of date 0 here.

2. Discount the present value of the annuity back to date 0. That is

Present Value at Date 0:

$$\frac{ESB1,584,950}{(1.10)^5} = ESB984,130$$

Again, it is worth while mentioning that, because the annuity formula brings Danielle's annuity back to date 5, the second calculation must discount over the remaining 5 periods. The two-step procedure is graphed in Figure 5.12.

FIGURE 5.12   **Discounting Danielle Caravello's Annuity (ESB000)**

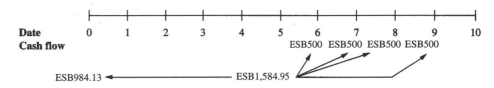

Step One: Discount the four payments back to date 5 by using the annuity formula.
Step Two: Discount the present value at date 5 (ESB1,584.95) back to present value at date 0.

Trick 2: Annuity in Advance   The annuity formula of (5.13) assumes that the first annuity payment begins a full period hence. This type of annuity is frequently called an *annuity in arrears*. What happens if the annuity begins today, in other words, at date 0? ●

● **Example**
In a previous example, Bruno Gerard received CHF50,000 a year for 20 years from the lottery. In that example, he was to receive the first payment a year from the winning date. Let us now assume that the first payment occurs immediately. The total number of payments remains 20.

Under this new assumption, we have a 19-date annuity with the first payment occurring at date 1—plus an extra payment at date 0. The present value is

$$\begin{array}{ccc} \text{CHF 50,000} & + & \text{CHF50,000} \times A^{19}_{0.08} \\ \text{Payment at date 0} & & \text{19-year annuity} \end{array}$$

$$= \text{CHF50,000} + \text{CHF50,000} \times 9.6036$$

$$= \text{CHF530,180}$$

CHF530,180, the present value in this example, is greater than CHF490,905, the present value in the earlier lottery example. This is to be expected because the annuity of the current example begins earlier. An annuity with an immediate initial payment is called an annuity in advance. Always remember that formula (5.13), as well as Table A.2 at the end of this book, refers to an *annuity in arrears*. ●

Trick 3: The Infrequent Annuity   The following example treats an annuity with payments occurring less frequently than once a year.

● **Example**
Ms Ann Chen receives an annuity of GBP450, payable once every two years. The annuity stretches out over 20 years. The first payment occurs at date 2, that is, two years from today. The annual interest rate is 6 per cent.

The trick is to determine the interest rate over a two-year period. The interest rate over two years is

$$1.06 \times 1.06 - 1 = 12.36\%$$

That is, GBP100 invested over two years will yield GBP112.36.

What we want is the present value of a GBP450 annuity over 10 periods, with an interest rate of 12.36 per cent per period. This is

$$\text{GBP450}\left[\frac{1}{0.1236} - \frac{1}{0.1236 \times (1.1236)^{10}}\right] = \text{GBP450} \times A^{10}_{0.1236} = \text{GBP2,505.57}$$

Trick 4: Equating Present Value of Two Annuities   The following example equates the present value of inflows with the present value of outflows.

• Example

Harold and Helen Nash are saving for the university education of their newborn daughter, Susan. The Nashes estimate that university expenses will run GBP30,000 per year when their daughter gets to university in 18 years. They reckon the annual interest rate over the next few decades will be 14 per cent. How much money must they deposit in the bank each year so that their daughter will be completely supported through four years at university?

To simplify the calculations, we assume that Susan is born today. Her parents will make the first of her four annual tuition payments on her 18th birthday. They will make equal bank deposits on each of her first 17 birthdays, but no deposit at date 0. This is illustrated as

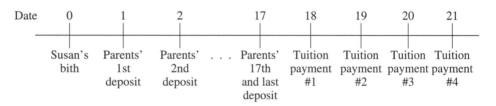

Helen and Harold Nash will be making deposits to the bank over the next 17 years. They will be withdrawing GBP30,000 per year over the following four years. We can be sure they will be able to withdraw fully GBP30,000 per year if the present value of the deposits is equal to the present value of the four GBP30,000 withdrawals.

This calculation requires three steps. The first two determine the present value of the withdrawals. The final step determines yearly deposits that will have a present value equal to that of the withdrawals.

1. We calculate the present value of the four years at college using the annuity formula.

$$\text{GBP30,000} \times \left[\frac{1}{0.14} - \frac{1}{0.14 \times (1.14)^4}\right] = \text{GBP30,000} \times A^4_{0.14}$$
$$= \text{GBP30,000} \times 2.9137 = \text{GBP87,411}$$

We assume that Susan enters university on her 18th birthday. Given our discussion in Trick 1 above, GBP87,411 represents the present value at date 17.

2. We calculate the present value of the college education at date 0 as

$$\frac{\text{GBP87,411}}{(1.14)^{17}} = \text{GBP9,422.91}$$

3. Assuming that Helen and Harold Nash make deposits to the bank at the end of each of the 17 years, we calculate the annual deposit that will yield a present value of all deposits of GBP9,422.91. This is calculated as

$$C \times A^{17}_{0.14} = \text{GBP9,422.91}$$

Since $A_{0.14}^{17} = 6.3729$,

$$C = \frac{\text{GBP9,422.91}}{6.3729} = \text{GBP1,478.59}$$

Thus, deposits of GBP1,478.59 made at the end of each of the first 17 years and invested at 14 per cent will provide enough money to make tuition payments of GBP30,000 over the following four years. ●

An alternative method would be to (1) calculate the present value of the tuition payments at Susan's 18th birthday and (2) calculate annual deposits such that the future value of the deposits at her 18th birthday equal the present value of the tuition payments at that date. Although this technique can also provide the right answer, we have found that it is more likely to lead to errors. Therefore, we only equate present values in our presentation.

Growing Annuity

Cash flows in business are very likely to grow over time, due either to real growth or to inflation. The growing perpetuity, which assumes an infinite number of cash flows, provides one formula to handle this growth. We now consider a **growing annuity**, which is a *finite number* of growing cash flows. Because perpetuities of any kind are rare, a formula for a growing annuity would be useful indeed. The formula is[13]

Formula for Present Value of Growing Annuity:

$$\overline{PV} = C\left[\frac{1}{r-g} - \frac{1}{r-g} \times \left(\frac{1+g}{1+r}\right)^T\right] \qquad (5.15)$$

where, as before, C is the payment to occur at the end of the first period, r is the interest rate, g is the rate of growth per period, expressed as a percentage and T is the number of periods for the annuity.

● **Example**
Walter Maxwell, an MBA student about to finish his course, has just been offered a job at GBP50,000 a year. He anticipates his salary increasing by 9 per cent a year until his retirement in 40 years. Given an interest rate of 20 per cent, what is the present value of his life-time salary?

---

[13] This can be proved as follows. A growing annuity can be viewed as the difference between two growing perpetuities. Consider a growing perpetuity A, where the first payment of C occurs at date 1. Next, consider growing perpetuity B, where the first payment of $C(1 + g)^T$ is made at date $T + 1$. Both perpetuities grow at rate g. The growing annuity over T periods is the difference between annuity A and annuity B. This can be represented as:

Date	0	1	2	3	...	T	$T+1$	$T+2$	$T+3$	
Perpetuity A	C	$C \times (1+g)$	$C \times (1+g)^2$	...	$C \times (1+g)^{T-1}$		$C \times (1+g)^T$	$C \times (1+g)^{T+1}$	$C \times (1+g)^{T+2}$	...
Perpetuity B							$C \times (1+g)^T$	$C \times (1+g)^{T+1}$	$C \times (1+g)^{T+2}$	...
Annuity	C	$C \times (1+g)$	$C \times (1+g)^2$	...	$C \times (1+g)^{T-1}$					

The value of perpetuity A is
$$\frac{C}{r-g}$$
The value of perpetuity B is
$$\frac{C \times (1+g)^T}{r-g} \times \frac{1}{(1+r)^T}$$
The difference between the two perpetuities is given by (5.15).

We simplify by assuming he will be paid his GBP50,000 salary exactly one year from now, and that his salary will continue to be paid in annual instalments. The appropriate discount rate is 20 per cent. From (5.15), the calculation is

Present value
of Walter's $= \text{GBP50,000} \times \left[\dfrac{1}{0.20 - 0.09} - \dfrac{1}{0.20 - 0.09}\left(\dfrac{1.09}{1.20}\right)^{40}\right] = \text{GBP444,832}$
lifetime salary

Though the growing annuity is quite useful, it is more tedious than the other simplifying formulas. Whereas most sophisticated calculators have special programs for perpetuity, growing perpetuity and annuity, there is no special program for growing annuity. Hence, one must calculate all the terms in (5.15) directly. ●

● **Example**
In a previous example, Harold and Helen Nash planned to make 17 identical payments in order to fund the college education of their daughter, Susan. Alternatively, imagine that they planned to increase their payments at 4 per cent per year. What would their first payment be?

The first two steps of the previous Nash family example showed that the present value of the university costs was GBP9,422.91. These two steps would be the same here. However, the third step must be altered. Now we must ask: 'How much should their first payment be so that, if payments increase by 4 per cent per year, the present value of all payments will be GBP9,422.91?'

We set the growing-annuity formula equal to GBP9,422.91 and solve for C.

$$C\left[\frac{1}{r-g} - \frac{1}{r-g}\left(\frac{1+g}{1+r}\right)^{T}\right] = C\left[\frac{1}{0.14-0.04} - \frac{1}{0.14-0.04}\left(\frac{1.04}{1.14}\right)^{17}\right]$$

$$= \text{GBP9,422.91}$$

Here, $C = \text{GBP1,192.78}$. Thus, the deposit on their daughter's first birthday is GBP1,192.78, the deposit on the second birthday is GBP1,240.49 ($1.04 \times$ GBP1,192.78), and so on. ●

Concept Questions

- What are the formulas for perpetuity, growing perpetuity, annuity, and growing annuity?
- What are three important points concerning the growing-perpetuity formula?
- What are four tricks concerning annuities?

5.5   What Is a Firm Worth?

Suppose you are in the business of trying to determine the value of small companies. (You are a business appraiser.) How can you determine what a firm is worth? The lesson you learn from this chapter is that the present value of a firm depends upon its future cash flows.

Let us consider the example of a firm that is expected to generate net cash flows (cash inflows minus cash outflows) of CHF5 million in the first year and CHF2 million for each of the next five years. The firm can be sold for CHF10 million seven years from now. The owners of the firm would like to be able to make 10 per cent on their investment in the firm.

The value of the firm is found by multiplying the net cash flows by the appropriate present-value factor. The value of the firm is simply the sum of the present values of the individual net cash flows.

The present value of the net cash flows is given below:

The Present Value of the Firm

End of Year	Net cash flow of the firm (CHF million)	Present value factor (10%)	Present value of net cash flows (CHF million)
1	5	0.90909	4.54545
2	2	0.82645	1.65290
3	2	0.75131	1.50262
4	2	0.68301	1.35502
5	2	0.62092	1.24184
6	2	0.56447	1.12894
7	10	0.51315	5.13158
		Present value of firm	16.56935

We can also use the simplifying formula for an annuity to give us

$$\frac{CHF5}{1.1} + \frac{(2 \times A^5_{0.10})}{1.1} + \frac{10}{(1.1)^7} = CHF16.56935 \text{ million}$$

Suppose you have the opportunity to acquire the firm for CHF12 million. Should you acquire the firm? The answer is yes because the NPV is positive.

$$NPV = PV - Cost$$

$$CHF4.56935 = CHF16.56935 - CHF12.000 \text{ (million)}$$

The incremental value (NPV) of acquiring the firm is CHF4.56935 million.

● **Example**

Trojan Pizza is contemplating investing NLG1 million in four new outlets in Amsterdam. Hans Lo, the firm's Chief Financial Officer (CFO), has estimated that the investments will pay out cash flows of NLG200,000 per year for nine years and nothing thereafter. (The cash flows will occur at the end of each year and there will be no cash flow after year 9.) Hans Lo has determined that the relevant discount rate for this investment is 15 per cent. This is the rate of return that the firm can earn at comparable projects. Should Trojan Pizza make the investments in the new outlets?

The decision can be evaluated as:

$$NPV = -NLG1,000,000 + \frac{NLG200,000}{1.15} + \frac{NLG200,000}{(1.15)^2} + \cdots + \frac{NLG200,000}{(1.15)^9}$$

$$= -NLG1,000,000 + 200,000 \times A^9_{0.15}$$

$$= -NLG45,683.22$$

Trojan Pizza should not make the investment because the NPV is −NLG45,683.22. If Trojan Pizza requires a 15 per cent rate of return, the new outlets are not a good investment. ●

5.6   Summary and Conclusions

1. Two basic concepts, *future value* and *present value*, were introduced in the beginning of this chapter. With a 10 per cent interest rate, an investor with GBP1 today can generate a future value of GBP1.10 in a year, GBP1.21 [GBP1 $\times$ $(1.10)^2$] in two years and so on. Conversely, present-value analysis places a current value on a later cash flow. With the same 10 per cent interest rate, a pound to be received in one year has a present value of GBP0.909 (GBP1/1.10) in year 0. A pound to be received in two years has a present value of GBP0.826 [GBP1/$(1.10)^2$].

2. One commonly expresses the interest rate as, say, 12 per cent per year. However, one can speak of the interest rate as 3 per cent per quarter. Although the stated annual interest rate remains 12 per cent (3 per cent $\times$ 4), the effective annual interest rate is 12.55 per cent [$(1.03)^4 - 1$]. In other words, the compounding process increases the future value of an investment. The limiting case is continuous compounding, where funds are assumed to be reinvested every infinitesimal instant.

3. A basic quantitative technique for financial decision-making is net-present-value analysis. The net-present-value formula for an investment that generates cash flows (C_i) in future periods is

$$\text{NPV} = -C_0 + \frac{C_1}{(1 + r)} + \frac{C_2}{(1 + r)^2} + \cdots + \frac{C_N}{(1 + r)^N} = -C_0 + \sum_{i=1}^{N} \frac{C_i}{(1 + r)^i}$$

The formula assumes that the cash flow at date 0 is the initial investment (a cash outflow).

4. Frequently, the actual calculation of present value is long and tedious. The computation of the present value of a long-term mortgage with monthly payments is a good example of this. We presented four simplifying formulas:

$$\textbf{Perpetuity:} \quad \text{PV} = \frac{C}{r}$$

$$\textbf{Growing perpetuity:} \quad \text{PV} = \frac{C}{r - g}$$

$$\textbf{Annuity:} \quad \text{PV} = C\left[\frac{1}{r} - \frac{1}{r \times (1 + r)^T}\right]$$

$$\textbf{Growing annuity:} \quad \text{PV} = C\left[\frac{1}{r - g} - \frac{1}{r - g} \times \left(\frac{1 + g}{1 + r}\right)^T\right]$$

5. We stressed a few practical considerations in the application of these formulas:

   a. The numerator in each of the formulas, C, is the cash flow to be received one *full period hence*.

   b. Cash flows are generally irregular in practice. To avoid unwieldy problems, assumptions to create more regular cash flows are made both in this textbook and in the real world.

   c. A number of present value problems involve annuities (or perpetuities) beginning a few periods hence. Students should practice combining the annuity (or perpetuity) formula with the discounting formula to solve these problems.

   d. Annuities and perpetuities may have periods of every two or every *n* years, rather than once a year. The annuity and perpetuity formulas can easily handle such circumstances.

   e. One frequently encounters problems where the present value of one annuity must be equated with the present value of another annuity.

KEY TERMS

Future value   79
Compound value   79
Present value   79
Net present value   80
Compounding   82

Simple interest   83
Compound interest   83
Discounting   87
Present value factor   88
Appropriate discount rate   88

Stated annual interest rate 91   Growing perpetuity 96
Effective annual interest rate 91   Annuity 98
Continuous compounding 92   Annuity factor 99
Perpetuity 94   Growing annuity 103

QUESTIONS AND PROBLEMS—IGNORE TAXATION THROUGHOUT

The Multiperiod Case

5.1 Compute the future value of GBP1,000, annually compounded for
   a. 10 years at 5 per cent.
   b. 10 years at 7 per cent.
   c. 20 years at 5 per cent.
   d. Why is the interest earned in part *c* not twice the amount earned in part *a*?

5.2 Calculate the present value of the following cash flows discounted at 10 per cent.
   a. DEM1,000 received seven years from today.
   b. DEM2,000 received one year from today.
   c. DEM500 received eight years from today.

5.3 Would you rather receive CHF1,000 today or CHF2,000 in 10 years if the discount rate is 8 per cent?

5.4 The government has issued a bond. It will pay NLG1,000 in 25 years. The bond will pay no interim coupon payments. What is the present value of the bond if the discount rate is 10 per cent?

5.5 It is estimated that a firm has a pension liability that will require the payment of CHF1.5 million 27 years from today. If the firm can invest in a risk-free security that has a stated annual interest rate of 8 per cent, how much must the firm invest to be able to make the CHF1.5 million payment?

5.6 You have won a new kind of prize in the national lottery. Lottery officials offer you the choice of the following alternative payouts:
   Alternative 1: GBP10,000 one year from now.
   Alternative 2: GBP20,000 five years from now.
   Which should you choose if the discount rate is
   a. 0 per cent?
   b. 10 per cent?
   c. 20 per cent?
   d. What rate makes the options equally attractive to you?

5.7 You are selling your flat. Jan de Boer has offered you NLG115,000. He will pay you immediately. Mark van Breukelen has offered you NLG150,000, but he cannot pay you until three years from today. The relevant interest rate is 10 per cent. Ignoring any bad debt risk, which offer should you choose?

5.8 Suppose you bought a bond that will pay DEM1,000 in 20 years. No additional payments will be made. If the appropriate discount rate for the bond is 8 per cent,
   a. What is the current price of the bond?
   b. What will the price be 10 years from today?
   c. What will the price be 15 years from today?

5.9 Suppose you place NLG1,000 in an account at the end of each of the next four years. If the account earns 12 per cent, how much will be in the account at the end of seven years? (Hint: See footnote 11.)

5.10 Ann Woodhouse is considering the purchase of a house in Geneva. She expects that she will own the house for 10 years and then sell it for CHF5 million. What is the most she would be willing to pay for the house if the appropriate discount rate is 12 per cent?

5.11 You have the opportunity to make an investment that costs GBP900,000. If you make this investment now, you will receive GBP120,000 one year from today, GBP250,000 and GBP800,000 two and three years from today, respectively. The appropriate discount rate for this investment is 12 per cent.
   a. Should you make the investment?

    b. What is the NPV of this opportunity?

    c. If the discount rate is 11 per cent, should you invest? Compute the NPV to support your answer.

5.12 You have the opportunity to invest in a machine that will cost NLG340,000. The machine will generate cash flows of NLG100,000 at the end of each year and require maintenance costs of NLG10,000 at the beginning of each year. If the economic life of the machine is five years and the relevant discount rate is 10 per cent, should you buy the machine? What if the relevant discount rate is 9 per cent?

5.13 Today a firm signed a contract to sell a capital asset for GBP90,000. The firm will receive payment five years from today. The asset costs GBP60,000 to produce.
    a. If the appropriate discount rate is 10 per cent, is the firm making a profit on this item?
    b. At what appropriate discount rate will the firm break even?

5.14 Your aunt owns an auto dealership. She promised to give you GBP3,000 in trade-in value for your car when you graduate one year from now, while your roommate offered you GBP3,500 for the car now. The prevailing interest rate is 12 per cent. If the future value of benefit from owning the car for one year is expected to be GBP1,000, should you accept your aunt's offer?

Compounding Periods

5.15 What is the future value three years hence of DEM1,000 invested in an account with a stated annual interest rate of 8 per cent,
    a. compounded annually?
    b. compounded semiannually?
    c. compounded monthly?
    d. compounded continuously?
    e. Why does the future value increase as the compounding period shortens?

5.16 Compute the future value of NLG1,000 continuously compounded for
    a. 5 years at 12 per cent.
    b. 3 years at 10 per cent.
    c. 10 years at 5 per cent.
    d. 8 years at 7 per cent.

5.17 Calculate the present value of CHF5,000 in 12 years at a stated annual interest rate of 10 per cent, compounded quarterly.

5.18 Bank Amsterdam offers a 4.1 per cent interest rate, compounded quarterly, while BankUtrecht offers a 4.05 per cent interest rate, compounded monthly. In which bank should you deposit your money? Both banks are equally good credit risks.

Perpetuities and Growing Perpetuities

5.19 The prevailing interest rate is 15 per cent. What is the price of a consol bond that pays GBP120 annually?

5.20 A prestigious investment bank designed a new security that pays a quarterly dividend of DEM10 permanently. What is the price of the security if the stated annual interest rate is 12 per cent?

5.21 World Computing is expected to initiate its quarterly dividend of NLG1 five years from today and the dividend is expected to remain constant permanently. What is the price of a World Computing share if the required annual interest rate is 15 per cent?

5.22 Assuming an interest rate of 10 per cent, calculate the present value of the following streams of yearly payments:
    a. ESB1,000 per year forever, with the first payment one year from today.
    b. ESB500 per year forever, with the first payment two years from today.
    c. ESB2,420 per year forever, with the first payment three years from today.

5.23 Given an interest rate of 10 per cent per year, what is the value at date $t = 5$ (i.e., the end of year 5) of a perpetual stream of DEM120 annual payments starting at date $t = 9$?

5.24 Vogts AG paid a DEM3 dividend yesterday. If the firm raises its dividend at 5 per cent every year and the appropriate discount rate is 12 per cent, what is the price of Vogts shares?

5.25 In its most recent corporate report, de Hooch NV apologized to its stockholders for not paying a dividend. The report states that management will pay a NLG1 dividend next year. That dividend will grow at 4 per cent every year thereafter. If the appropriate discount rate is 10 per cent, how much are you willing to pay for a share of de Hooch NV?

5.26 Mark Weinstein has been working on an advanced technology in laser eye surgery. The technology is expected to be available to the medical industry two years from today and will generate annual income of CHF200,000 growing at 5 per cent perpetually. What is the present value of the technology if the discount rate is 10 per cent?

Annuities and Growing Annuities

5.27 Banque Nova has offered you three different types of loans with an annual interest rate of 16 per cent. How much will you have borrowed today if the loan requires
a. an annual payment of FRF1,200 for 5 years?
b. a quarterly payment of FRF300 for 10 years?
c. a monthly payment of FRF100 for 15 years?

5.28 Should you buy an asset that will generate income of FRF1,200 per year for eight years? The price of the asset is FRF6,200 and the appropriate annual interest rate is 10 per cent.

5.29 What is the present value of end-of-year cash flows of NLG2,000 per year, with the first cash flow received three years from today and the last one 22 years from today? Use a discount rate of 8 per cent.

5.30 What is the value of a 15-year annuity that pays DEM500 a year? The annuity's first cash flow is at the end of year 6 and the appropriate annual interest rate is 12 per cent for years 1 through 5 and 15 per cent thereafter.

5.31 You are offered the opportunity to buy a bond for NLG12,800. The bond is certain to pay NLG2,000 at the end of each of the next 10 years. If you buy the bond, what rate of interest will you receive?

5.32 You need CHF25,000 five years from now. You budget to make equal payments at the end of every year into an account that pays a stated annual interest rate of 7 per cent. (Hint: See footnote 11.)
a. What are your annual payments?
b. Your uncle died and left you CHF20,000. How much of it must you put into the same account as a lump sum today to meet your goal?

5.33 Nancy Ferris bought an apartment in London for GBP120,000. She paid 15 per cent down and agreed to pay the balance in 20 equal annual instalments that are to include principal plus 10 per cent interest on the declining balance. What are the equal instalments?

5.34 Jacques Ferguson has signed a three-year contract to work for a computer software company. He expects to receive a basic salary of CHF5,000 a month and a bonus of CHF10,000 at year-end. All payments are made at the end of periods. What is the present value of the contract if the discount rate is 12 per cent?

5.35 Peter Green bought a GBP15,000 Renault Laguna with 20 per cent down and financed the rest with a four-year loan at 8 per cent annual interest rate. What is his monthly payment if he starts the payment one month after the purchase?

5.36 Your company is considering leasing a FRF120,000 piece of equipment for the next 10 years. The annual lease payments of FRF15,000 are due at the beginning of each year. The lease includes an option for your company to buy the equipment for FRF25,000 at the end of the leasing period. Should your company accept the lease offer if the appropriate discount rate is 8 per cent a year?

5.37 You are saving for your retirement. You have decided that one year from today you will place 2 per cent of your annual salary in an account which will earn 8 per cent per year. Your salary is GBP50,000, but it will grow at 4 per cent per annum throughout your career. How much money will you have for your retirement, which will begin in 40 years?

5.38   You must decide whether or not to purchase new capital equipment. The cost of the machine is NLG5,000. It will yield the following amounts of income. The appropriate discount rate is 10 per cent.

Year	Cash flow
1	NLG700
2	900
3	1,000
4	1,000
5	1,000
6	1,000
7	1,250
8	1,375

Should you purchase the equipment?

5.39   Ms Adams has received a job offer from a large investment bank as an assistant to the vice president. Her basic salary will be GBP35,000. She will receive her first annual salary payment one year from the day she begins to work. In addition, she will get an immediate GBP10,000 bonus for joining the company. Her salary will grow at 4 per cent each year. Each year she will receive a bonus equal to 10 per cent of her salary. Ms Adams is expected to work for 25 years. What is the present value of the offer if the appropriate discount rate is 12 per cent?

What Is a Firm Worth?

5.40   Simplified Publishing BV is trying to decide whether or not to revise its popular textbook *Financial Psychoanalysis in Europe*. The firm has estimated that the revision will cost NLG40,000. Cash flows from increased sales will be NLG10,000 in the first year. These cash flows will increase by 7 per cent per year. The book will go out of print five years from now. Assume the initial cost is paid now and all revenues are received at the end of each year. If the company requires a 10 per cent return from such an investment, should it undertake the revision?

5.41   Consider a firm that is expected to generate a net cash flow of CHF10,000 at the end of the first year. The cash flows will increase by 3 per cent a year for seven years and then the firm will be sold for CHF120,000. The relevant discount rate for the firm is 11 per cent. What is the present value of the firm?

5.42   The management of New Project is trying to decide whether or not to undertake the following investment:
        Cost: GBP5 million
        After-tax cash flows: GBP1 million per year for 7 years
        Risk level: an appropriate discount rate of 8 per cent per year
        Help the management make its decision by computing the NPV of the project. Should the management undertake the project?

CHAPTER
6

How to Value Bonds and Shares

The previous chapter discussed the mathematics of compounding, discounting and present value. We also showed how to value a firm. We now use the mathematics of compounding and discounting to determine the present values of financial obligations of the firm, beginning with a discussion of how bonds are valued. Since the future cash flows of bonds are known, application of net-present-value techniques is fairly straightforward. The uncertainty of future cash flows makes the pricing of stocks according to NPV more difficult.

6.1 Definition and Example of a Bond

A bond is a certificate showing that a borrower owes a specified sum. In order to repay the money, the borrower has agreed to make interest and principal payments on designated dates. For example, imagine that Kreuger Enterprises just issued 100,000 bonds for DEM1,000 each, where the bonds have a coupon rate of 5 per cent and a maturity of two years. Interest on the bonds is to be paid yearly. This means that:

1. DEM100 million (100,000 × DEM1,000) has been borrowed by the firm.
2. The firm must pay interest of DEM5 million (5 per cent × DEM100 million) at the end of one year.
3. The firm must pay both DEM5 million of interest and DEM100 million of principal at the end of two years.

We now consider how to value a few different types of bonds.

6.2 How to Value Bonds

Pure Discount Bonds

The **pure discount bond** is perhaps the simplest kind of bond. It promises a single payment, say DEM1, at a fixed future date. If the payment is one year from now, it is called a *one-year discount bond*; if it is two years from now, it is called a *two-year discount bond*, and so on. The date when the issuer of the bond makes the last payment is called the **maturity date** of the bond, or just its *maturity* for short. The bond is said to mature or *expire* on the date of its final payment. The payment at maturity (DEM1 in this example) is termed the bond's **face value**.

Pure discount bonds are often called zero-coupon bonds or zeros to emphasize the fact that the holder receives no cash payments until maturity. We will use the terms *zero* and *discount* interchangeably to refer to bonds that pay no coupons.

The first row of Figure 6.1 shows the pattern of cash flows from a four-year pure discount bond. Note that the face value, F, is paid when the bond expires in the 48th month. There are no payments of either interest or principal prior to this date.

In the previous chapter, we indicated that one discounts a future cash flow to determine its present value. The present value of a pure discount bond can easily be determined by the techniques of the previous chapter. For short, we sometimes speak of the *value* of a bond instead of its present value.

FIGURE 6.1   Different Types of Bonds: C, Coupon Paid Every 6 Months, F, Face Value at Year 4 (maturity for pure discount and coupon bonds)

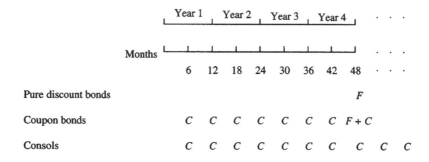

Consider a pure discount bond that pays a face value of f in T years, where the interest rate is r in each of the T years. (We also refer to this rate as the *market interest rate*.) Because the face value is the only cash flow that the bond pays, the present value of this face amount is

Value of a Pure Discount Bond:

$$PV = \frac{F}{(1 + r)^T}$$

The present value formula can produce some surprising results. Suppose that the interest rate is 10 per cent. Consider a bond with a face value of DEM1 million that matures in 20 years. Applying the formula to this bond, its PV is given by

$$PV = \frac{DEM1\ million}{(1.1)^{20}}$$
$$= DEM148{,}644$$

or only about 15 per cent of the face value.

Level-Coupon Bonds

Many bonds, however, are not of the simple, pure discount variety. Typical bonds issued by either governments or corporations offer cash payments not just at maturity, but also at regular times in between. For example, payments on many corporate bonds are made every six months until the bond matures. These payments are called the **coupons** of the bond. The middle row of Figure 6.1 illustrates the case of a four-year, *level-coupon bond*: the coupon, C, is paid every six months and is the same throughout the life of the bond.

Note that the face value of the bond, F, is paid at maturity (end of year 4). F is sometimes called the *principal* or the *denomination*. Bonds typically have face values of GBP100 or DEM1,000, and so on, though this can vary with the type of bond.

As we mentioned above, the value of a bond is simply the present value of its cash flows. Therefore, the value of a level-coupon bond is merely the present value of its stream of coupon payments plus the present value of its repayment of principal. Because a level-coupon bond is just an annuity of C each period, together with a payment at maturity of DEM1,000, the value of a level-coupon bond is

Value of a Level-Coupon Bond:

$$PV = \frac{C}{1+r} + \frac{C}{(1+r)^2} + \cdots + \frac{C}{(1+r)^T} + \frac{DEM1,000}{(1+r)^T}$$

where C is the coupon and the face value, F, is DEM1,000. The value of the bond can be rewritten as

Value of a Level-Coupon Bond:

$$PV = C \times A_r^T + \frac{DEM1,000}{(1+r)^T}$$

As mentioned in the previous chapter, A_r^T is the present value of an annuity of DEM1 per period for T periods at an interest rate per period of r.

● **Example**

Suppose it is November 1997 and we are considering a government bond. We see in the *Financial Times* some 13*s* of November 2001. This is jargon that means the annual coupon rate is 13 per cent.[1] The face value is GBP100, implying that the yearly coupon is GBP13 (13% × GBP100). Interest is paid each May and November, implying that the coupon every six months is GBP6.50 (GBP13/2). The face value will be paid out in November 2001, four years from now. By this we mean that the purchaser obtains claims to the following cash flows:

5/98	11/98	5/99	11/99	5/00	11/00	5/01	11/01
GBP6.50	GBP6.50	GBP6.50	GBP6.50	GBP6.50	GBP6.50	GBP6.50	GBP6.50+ GBP100

If the stated annual interest rate in the market is 10 per cent per year, what is the present value of the bond?

Our work on compounding in the previous chapter showed that the interest rate over any six-month interval is one-half of the stated annual interest rate. In the current example, this semiannual rate is 5 per cent (10%/2). Since the coupon payment in each six-month period is GBP6.50, and there are eight of these six-month periods from

---

[1] The coupon rate is specific to the bond. The coupon rate indicates what cash flow should appear in the numerator of the NPV equation. The coupon rate does not appear in the denominator of the NPV equation.

November 1997 to November 2001, the present value of the bond is

$$PV = \frac{GBP6.50}{1.05} + \frac{GBP6.50}{(1.05)^2} + \cdots + \frac{GBP6.50}{(1.05)^8} + \frac{GBP100}{(1.05)^8}$$

$$= (GBP65 \times A_{0.05}^8) + GPB1,000/(1.05)^8$$

$$= (GBP6.50 \times 6.463) + (GBP100 \times 0.677)$$

$$= GBP42.0095 + GBP67.70$$

$$= GBP109.71$$

Traders will generally quote the bond as 109.71,[2] indicating that it is selling at 109.71 per cent of its face value. Even if the bond had a face value of DEM1,000, the practice would be for it to be quoted at 109.71. This implies 109.71 per cent of its face value of DEM1,000. •

At this point, it is worth while to relate the above example of bond-pricing to the discussion of compounding in the previous chapter. At that time we distinguished between the stated annual interest rate and the effective annual interest rate. In particular, we pointed out that the effective annual interest rate is

$$(1 + r/m)^m - 1$$

where r is the stated annual interest rate and m is the number of compounding intervals. Since $r = 10$ per cent and $m = 2$ (because the bond makes semiannual payments), the effective annual interest rate is

$$(1 + 0.10/2)^2 - 1 = (1.05)^2 - 1 = 10.25\%$$

In other words, because the bond is paying interest twice a year, the bondholder earns a 10.25 per cent return when compounding is considered.[3]

One final note concerning level-coupon bonds: Although the above example concerns government bonds, corporate bonds are identical in form. For example, Held AG may have an $8\frac{1}{2}$ per cent bond maturing in 2006. This means that Held AG will make semiannual payments of DEM42.50 ($8\frac{1}{2}\%/2 \times$ DEM1,000) between now and 2006 for each face value amount of DEM1,000.

Consols

Not all bonds have a final maturity date. As we mentioned in the previous chapter, consols are bonds that never stop paying a coupon, have no final maturity date and therefore never mature. Thus, a consol is a perpetuity. In the eighteenth century the Bank of England issued such bonds, called English consols. These were bonds that the Bank of England guaranteed would pay the holder a cash flow forever! Through wars and depressions, the Bank of England continued to honour this commitment, and you

---

[2] Bond prices are actually quoted in 32nds of a currency unit (such as pound or mark), so a quote this precise would not be given.

[3] For an excellent discussion of how to value semiannual payments, see J. T. Lindley, B. P. Helms and M. Haddad (1987). 'A Measurement of the Errors in Intra-Period Compounding and Bond Valuation', *The Financial Review*, **22**, February. We benefited from several conversations with the authors of the above article.

can still buy such bonds in London today. The US government also once sold consols to raise money to build the Panama Canal. Even though these US bonds were supposed to last forever and to pay their coupons forever, don't go looking for any. There is a special clause in the bond contract that gives the government the right to buy them back from the holders, and that is what the US government has done. Clauses like that are *call provisions*, and we study them later.

An important example of a consol, though, is called *preferred stock*. Preferred stock is stock that is issued by corporations and that provides the holder a fixed dividend in perpetuity. If there were never any question that the firm would actually pay the dividend on the preferred stock, such stock would in fact be a consol.

These instruments can be valued by the perpetuity formula of the previous chapter. For example, if the marketwide interest rate is 10 per cent, a consol with a yearly interest payment of GBP5 is valued at

$$\frac{\text{GBP5}}{0.10} = \text{GBP50}$$

Concept Questions

- Define pure discount bonds, level-coupon bonds and consols.
- Contrast the stated interest rate and the effective annual interest rate for bonds paying semiannual interest.

6.3 Bond Concepts

We complete our discussion on bonds by considering two concepts concerning them. First, we examine the relationship between interest rates and bond prices. Second, we define the concept of yield to maturity.

Interest Rates and Bond Prices

The above discussion on level-coupon bonds allows us to relate bond prices to interest rates. Consider the following example.

● Example

The interest rate is 10 per cent. A two-year bond with a 10 per cent coupon pays interest of DEM100 (DEM1,000 × 10%). For simplicity, we assume that the interest is paid annually. The bond is priced at its face value of DEM1,000:

$$\text{DEM1,000} = \frac{\text{DEM100}}{1.10} + \frac{\text{DEM1,000} + \text{DEM100}}{(1.10)^2}$$

If the interest rate unexpectedly rises to 12 per cent, the bond sells at

$$\text{DEM966.20} = \frac{\text{DEM100}}{1.12} + \frac{\text{DEM1,000} + \text{DEM100}}{(1.12)^2}$$

Because DEM966.20 is below $1,000, the bond is said to sell at a **discount**. This is a sensible result. Now that the interest rate is 12 per cent, a newly issued bond with a 12 per cent coupon rate will sell at DEM1,000. This newly issued bond will have coupon payments of DEM120 (0.12 × DEM1,000). Because our bond has interest payments of only DEM100, investors will pay less than DEM1,000 for it.

If interest rates fell to 8 per cent, the bond would sell at

$$\text{DEM1,035.67} = \frac{\text{DEM100}}{1.08} + \frac{\text{DEM1,000} + \text{DEM100}}{(1.08)^2}$$

Because DEM1,035.67 is above DEM1,000, the bond is said to sell at a **premium.** •

Thus, we find that bond prices fall with a rise in interest rates and rise with a fall in interest rates. Furthermore, the general principle is that a level-coupon bond sells in the following ways:

1. At the face value of DEM1,000 if the coupon rate is equal to the marketwide interest rate.
2. At a discount if the coupon rate is below the marketwide interest rate.
3. At a premium if the coupon rate is above the marketwide interest rate.

The Present Value Formulas for Bonds

Pure Discount Bonds

$$\text{PV} = \frac{F}{(1 + r)^T}$$

Level-Coupon Bonds

$$\text{PV} = C\left[\frac{1}{r} - \frac{1}{r \times (1 + r)^T}\right] + \frac{F}{(1 + r)^T} = C \times A_r^T + \frac{F}{(1 + r)^T}$$

Consols

$$\text{PV} = \frac{C}{r}$$

Yield to Maturity

Let's now consider the previous example in reverse. If our bond is selling at DEM1,035.67, what return is a bondholder receiving? This can be answered by considering the following equation:

$$\text{DEM1,035.67} = \frac{\text{DEM100}}{1 + y} + \frac{\text{DEM1,000} + \text{DEM100}}{(1 + y)^2}$$

The unknown, y, is the rate of return that the holder is earning on the bond. Our earlier work implies that $y = 8$ per cent. Thus, traders state that the bond is yielding an 8 per cent return. Bond traders also state that the bond has a **yield to maturity** of 8 per cent.

Concept Questions

- What is the relationship between interest rates and bond prices?
- How does one calculate the yield to maturity on a bond?

6.4 The Present Value of Ordinary Shares

Dividends versus Capital Gains

Our goal in this section is to value ordinary shares. We learned in the previous chapter that an asset's value is determined by the present value of its future cash flows. A share provides two kinds of cash flows. First, most shares pay dividends on a regular basis. Second, the shareholder receives the sale price when he or she sells the shares. Thus, in order to value ordinary shares, we need to answer an interesting question: Is the value of a share equal to

1. the discounted present value of the sum of next period's dividend plus next period's share price, or
2. the discounted present value of all future dividends?

This is the kind of question that students would love to see on a multiple choice exam, because both (1) and (2) are right.

To see that (1) and (2) are the same, let's start with an individual who will buy the stock and hold it for one year. In other words, he or she has a one-year *holding period*. In addition, he or she is willing to pay P_0 for the stock today. That is, he or she calculates

$$P_0 = \frac{\text{Div}_1}{1 + r} + \frac{P_1}{1 + r} \tag{6.1}$$

Div_1 is the dividend paid at year-end and P_1 is the price at year's end. P_0 is the PV of the ordinary share investment. The term in the denominator, r, is the discount rate of the share. It will be equal to the interest rate in the case where the share is riskless. It is likely to be greater than the interest rate in the case where the share is risky.

That seems easy enough, but where does P_1 come from? P_1 is not pulled out of thin air. Rather, there must be a buyer at the end of year 1 who is willing to purchase the stock for P_1. This buyer determines price by

$$P_1 = \frac{\text{Div}_2}{1 + r} + \frac{P_2}{1 + r} \tag{6.2}$$

Substituting the value of P_1 from (6.2) into equation (6.1) yields

$$P_0 = \frac{1}{1 + r}\left[\text{Div}_1 + \left(\frac{\text{Div}_2 + P_2}{1 + r}\right)\right]$$

or

$$= \frac{\text{Div}_1}{1 + r} + \frac{\text{Div}_2}{(1 + r)^2} + \frac{P_2}{(1 + r)^2} \tag{6.3}$$

We can ask a similar question for (6.3): Where does P_2 come from? An investor at the end of year 2 is willing to pay P_2 because of the dividend and stock price at year 3. This process can be repeated *ad nauseam*.[4] At the end, we are left with

---

[4] This procedure reminds us of the physicist lecturing on the origins of the universe. He was approached by an elderly gentleman in the audience who disagreed with the lecture. The attendee said that the universe rests on the back of a huge turtle. When the physicist asked what the turtle rested on, the gentleman said another turtle. Anticipating the physicist's objections, the attendee said, 'Don't tire yourself out, young fellow. It's turtles all the way down.'

$$P_0 = \frac{Div_1}{1+r} + \frac{Div_2}{(1+r)^2} + \frac{Div_3}{(1+r)^3} + \cdots = \sum_{t=1}^{\infty} \frac{Div_t}{(1+r)^t} \qquad (6.4)$$

Thus the value of a firm's ordinary share to the investor is equal to the present value of all of the expected future dividends.

This is a very useful result. A common objection to applying present value analysis to shares is that investors are too shortsighted to care about the long-run stream of dividends. These critics argue that an investor will generally not look past his or her time horizon. Thus, prices in a market dominated by short-term investors will reflect only near-term dividends. However, our discussion shows that a long-run dividend-discount model holds, even when investors have short-term time horizons. Although an investor may want to cash out early, he or she must find another investor who is willing to buy. The price this second investor pays is dependent on dividends *after* his or her date of purchase.

Valuation of Different Types of Stocks

The above discussion shows that the value of the firm is the present value of its future dividends. How do we apply this idea in practice? Equation (6.4) represents a very general model and is applicable regardless of whether the level of expected dividends is growing, fluctuating or constant. The general model can be simplified if the firm's dividends are expected to follow some basic patterns: (1) zero growth, (2) constant growth, and (3) differential growth. These cases are illustrated in Figure 6.2.

FIGURE 6.2   Zero-Growth, Constant-Growth, and Differential-Growth Practices

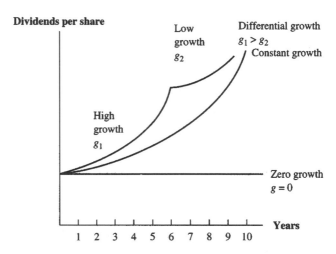

Dividend-growth models

Zero growth: $P_0 = \dfrac{Div}{r}$

Constant growth: $P_0 = \dfrac{Div}{r - g}$

Differential growth: $P_0 = \displaystyle\sum_{t=1}^{T} \frac{Div\,(1+g_1)^t}{(1+r)^t} + \frac{\dfrac{Div_{T+1}}{r - g_2}}{(1+r)^T}$

Case 1 (Zero Growth)

The value of a stock with a constant dividend is given by

$$P_0 = \frac{\text{Div}_1}{1 + r} + \frac{\text{Div}_2}{(1 + r)^2} + \cdots = \frac{\text{Div}}{r}$$

Here it is assumed that $\text{Div}_1 = \text{Div}_2 = \cdots = \text{Div}$. This is just an application of the perpetuity formula of the previous chapter.

Case 2 (Constant Growth)

Dividends grow at rate g, as follows:

End of year	1	2	3	4	...
Dividend	Div	Div$(1 + g)$	Div$(1 + g)^2$	Div$(1 + g)^3$	

Note that Div is the dividend at the end of the *first* period.

• Example

Hampshire Products will pay a dividend of 4 pence per share a year from now. Financial analysts believe that dividends will rise at 6 per cent per year for the foreseeable future. What is the dividend per share at the end of each of the first five years?

End of Year	1	2	3	4	5
Dividend	4p	4p × (1.06) = 4.24p	4p × (1.06)² = 4.4944p	4p × (1.06)³ = 4.7641p	4p × (1.06)⁴ = 5.0499p

The value of an ordinary share with dividends growing at a constant rate is

$$P_0 = \frac{\text{Div}}{1 + r} + \frac{\text{Div}(1 + g)}{(1 + r)^2} + \frac{\text{Div}\,(1 + g)^2}{(1 + r)^3} + \frac{\text{Div}(1 + g)^3}{(1 + r)^4} + \cdots$$

$$= \frac{\text{Div}}{r - g}$$

where g is the growth rate. Div is the dividend on the stock at the end of the first period. This is the formula for the present value of a growing perpetuity, which we derived in the previous chapter. •

• Example

Suppose an investor is considering the purchase of a share of Bayern AG. The stock will pay a DEM3 dividend a year from today. (Note that we use the terms 'share' and 'stock' interchangeably. Some countries tend to use more frequently the former description; some the latter). His dividend is expected to grow at 10 per cent per year ($g = 10\%$) for the foreseeable future. The investor thinks that the required return (r) on this stock is 15 per cent, given her assessment of Bayern AG's risk. (We also refer to r as the discount rate of the stock.) What is the value of a share of Bayern AG's shares?

Using the constant growth formula of case 2, we assess the value to be DEM60:

$$\text{DEM60} = \frac{\text{DEM3}}{0.15 - 0.10}$$

P_0 is quite dependent on the value of g. If g had been estimated to be 12.5 per cent, the value of the share would have been

$$DEM120 = \frac{DEM3}{0.15 - 0.125}$$

The stock price doubles (from DEM60 to DEM120) when g only increases 25 per cent (from 10 per cent to 12.5 per cent). Because of P_0's dependency on g, one must maintain a healthy sense of scepticism when using this constant growth of dividends model.

Furthermore, note that P_0 is equal to infinity when the growth rate, g, equals the discount rate, r. Because share prices do not grow infinitely, an estimate of g greater than r implies an error in estimation. More will be said of this point later. ●

Case 3 (Differential Growth)

In this case, an algebraic formula would be too unwieldy. Instead, we present examples.

● Example

Consider the stock of Elixir AG, which has a new back-rub ointment and is enjoying rapid growth. The dividend a year from today will be DEM1.15. During the next four years, the dividend will grow at 15 per cent per year (g_1 = 15 per cent). After that, growth (g_2) will be equal to 10 per cent per year. Can you calculate the present value of the stock if the required return (r) is 15 per cent?

Figure 6.3 displays the growth in the dividends. We need to apply a two-step process to discount these dividends. We first calculate the net present value of the dividends growing at 15 per cent per annum. That is, we first calculate the present value of the dividends at the end of each of the first five years. Second, we calculate the present value of the dividends beginning at the end of year 6.

FIGURE 6.3   Growth in Dividends for Elixir AG

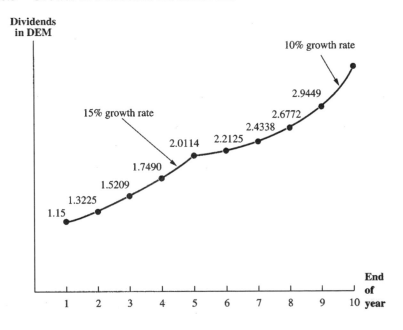

Calculate Present Value of First Five Dividends   The present value of dividend payments in years 1 through 5 is as follows:

Future year	Growth rate (g_1)	Expected dividend (DEM)	Present value (DEM)
1	0.15	1.15	1
2	0.15	1.3225	1
3	0.15	1.5209	1
4	0.15	1.7490	1
5	0.15	2.0114	1
Years 1–5	The present value of dividends = DEM5		

The growing-annuity formula of the previous chapter could normally be used in this step. However, note that dividends grow at 15 per cent, which is also the discount rate. Since $g = r$, the growing-annuity formula cannot be used in this example.

Calculate Present Value of Dividends Beginning at End of Year 6   This is the procedure for deferred perpetuities and deferred annuities that we mentioned in the previous chapter. The dividends beginning at the end of year 6 are

End of year	6	7	8	9
Dividend (DEM)	$Div_5 \times (1 + g_2)$ 2.0114×1.10 $= 2.2125$	$Div_5 \times (1 + g_2)^2$ $2.0114 \times (1.10)^2$ $= 2.4338$	$Div_5 \times (1 + g_2)^3$ $2.0114 \times (1.10)^3$ $= 2.6772$	$Div_5 \times (1 + g_2)^4$ $2.0114 \times (1.10)^4$ $= 2.9449$

As stated in the previous chapter, the growing-perpetuity formula calculates present value as of one year prior to the first payment. Because the payment begins at the end of year 6, the present value formula calculates present value as of the end of year 5.

The price at the end of year 5 is given by

$$P_5 = \frac{Div_6}{r - g_2} = \frac{DEM2.2125}{0.15 - 0.10}$$
$$= DEM44.25$$

The present value of P_5 at the end of year 0 is

$$\frac{P_5}{(1 + r)^5} = \frac{DEM44.25}{(1.15)^5} = DEM22$$

The present value of all dividends as of the end of year 0 is DEM27 (DEM22 + DEM5). ●

6.5   Estimates of Parameters in the Dividend-Discount Model

The value of the firm is a function of its growth rate, g, and its discount rate, r. How does one estimate these variables?

Where Does *g* Come From?

The previous discussion on stocks assumed that dividends grow at the rate g. We now want to estimate this rate of growth. Consider a business whose earnings next year are expected to be the same as earnings this year unless a *net investment* is made. This situation is likely to occur, because net investment is equal to gross, or total, investment less depreciation. A net investment of zero occurs when *total investment* equals depreciation. If total investment is equal to depreciation, the firm's physical plant is maintained, consistent with no growth in earnings.

Net investment will be positive only if some earnings are not paid out as dividends, that is, only if some earnings are retained.[5] This leads to the following equation:

$$
\underset{\text{Increase in earnings}}{\underbrace{\begin{array}{c}\text{Earnings}\\\text{next}\\\text{year}\end{array} = \begin{array}{c}\text{Earnings}\\\text{this}\\\text{year}\end{array} + \begin{array}{c}\text{Retained}\\\text{earnings}\\\text{this year}\end{array} \times \begin{array}{c}\text{Return on}\\\text{retained}\\\text{earnings}\end{array}}} \qquad (6.5)
$$

The increase in earnings is a function of both the *retained earnings* and the *return on the retained earnings*.

We now divide both sides of (6.5) by earnings this year, yielding

$$
\frac{\text{Earnings next year}}{\text{Earnings this year}} =
$$

$$
\frac{\text{Earnings this year}}{\text{Earnings this year}} + \left(\frac{\begin{array}{c}\text{Retained earnings}\\\text{this year}\end{array}}{\text{Earnings this year}}\right) \times \begin{array}{c}\text{Return on}\\\text{retained}\\\text{earnings}\end{array} \qquad (6.6)
$$

The lefthand side of (6.6) is simply one plus the growth rate in earnings, which we write as $1 + g$.[6] The ratio of retained earnings to earnings is called the **retention ratio**. Thus, we can write

$$
1 + g = 1 + \text{Retention ratio} \times \text{Return on retained earnings} \qquad (6.7)
$$

It is difficult for a financial analyst to determine the return to be expected on currently retained earnings, because the details on forthcoming projects are not generally public information. However, it is frequently assumed that the projects selected in the current year have an anticipated return equal to returns from projects in other years. Here, we can estimate the anticipated return on current retained earnings by the historical **return on equity** or ROE. After all, ROE is simply the return on the firm's entire equity, which is the return on the cumulation of all the firm's past projects.[7]

From (6.7), we have a simple way to estimate growth:

Formula for Firm's Growth Rate:

$$
g = \text{Retention ratio} \times \text{Return on retained earnings} \qquad (6.8)
$$

---

[5] We ignore the possibility of the issuance of shares or bonds in order to raise capital. These possibilities are considered in later chapters.

[6] Previously g referred to growth in dividends. However, the growth in earnings is equal to the growth rate in dividends in this context, because as we will presently see, the ratio of dividends to earnings is held constant.

[7] Students frequently wonder whether return on equity (ROE) or return on assets (ROA) should be used here. ROA and ROE are identical in our model because debt financing is ignored. However, most real-world firms have debt. Because debt is treated in later chapters, we are not yet able to treat this issue in depth now. Suffice it to say that ROE is the appropriate rate, because both ROE for the firm as a whole and the return to equity holders from a future project are calculated after interest has been deducted.

● **Example**

Pagemaster Enterprises plc has just reported earnings of GBP2 million. It plans to retain 40 per cent of its earnings. The historical return on equity (ROE) was 0.16, a figure that is expected to continue into the future. How much will earnings grow over the coming year?

We first perform the calculation without reference to (6.8). Then we use (6.8) as a check.

Calculation without Reference to (6.8)   The firm will retain GBP800,000 (40% × GBP2 million). Assuming that historical ROE is an appropriate estimate for future returns, the anticipated increase in earnings is

$$GBP800{,}000 \times 0.16 = GBP128{,}000$$

The percentage growth in earnings is

$$\frac{\text{Change in earnings}}{\text{Total earnings}} = \frac{GBP128{,}000}{GBP2 \text{ million}} = 0.064$$

This implies that earnings in one year will be GBP2,128,000 (GBP2,000,000 × 1.064).

Check Using Equation (6.8)   We use g = Retention ratio × ROE. We have

$$g = 0.4 \times 0.16 = 0.064 \; ●$$

Where Does r Come From?

In this section, we want to estimate r, the rate used to discount the cash flows of a particular stock. There are two methods developed by academics. We present one method below, but must defer the second until we give it extensive treatment in later chapters.

The first method begins with the concept that the value of a growing perpetuity is

$$P_0 = \frac{\text{Div}}{r - g}$$

Solving for r, we have

$$r = \frac{\text{Div}}{P_0} + g \tag{6.9}$$

As stated earlier, Div refers to the dividend to be received one year hence.

Thus, the discount rate can be broken into two parts. The ratio, Div/P_0, places the dividend return on a percentage basis, frequently called the *dividend yield*. The second term, g, is the growth rate of dividends.

Because information on both dividends and stock price is publicly available, the first term on the righthand side of (6.9) can be easily calculated. The second term on the righthand side, g, can be estimated from (6.8).

● **Example**

Pagemaster Enterprises plc, the company examined in the previous example, has 1,000,000 shares outstanding. The shares are selling at GBP10. What is the required return on the shares?

Because the retention ratio is 40 per cent, the **payout ratio** is 60 per cent (1 − Retention ratio). The payout ratio is the ratio of dividends/earnings. Because earnings a year from now will be GBP2,128,000 (GBP2,000,000 × 1.064), dividends will be GBP1,276,800 (0.60 × GBP2,128,000). Dividends per share will be GBP1.28 (GBP1,276,800/1,000,000). Given our previous result that $g = 0.064$, we calculate r from (6.9) as follows:

$$0.192 = \frac{GBP1.28}{GBP10.00} + 0.064 \ \bullet$$

A Healthy Sense of Scepticism

It is important to emphasize that our approach merely *estimates* g; our approach does not *determine* g precisely. We mentioned earlier that our estimate of g is based on a number of assumptions. For example, we assume that the return on reinvestment of future retained earnings is equal to the firm's past ROE. We assume that the future retention ratio is equal to the past retention ratio. Our estimate for g will be off if these assumptions prove to be wrong.

Unfortunately, the determination of r is highly dependent on g. For example, if g is estimated to be 0, r equals 12.8 per cent (GBP1.28/GBP10.00). If g is estimated to be 12 per cent, r equals 24.8 per cent (GBP1.28/GBP10.00 + 12%). Thus, one should view estimates of r with a healthy sense of scepticism.

Because of the above, some financial economists generally argue that the estimation error for r or a single security is too large to be practical. Therefore, they suggest calculating the average r for an entire industry. This r would then be used to discount the dividends of a particular stock in the same industry.

One should be particularly sceptical of two polar cases when estimating r for individual securities. First, consider a firm currently paying no dividend. The stock price will be above zero because investors believe that the firm may initiate a dividend at some point or the firm may be acquired at some point. However, when a firm goes from no dividends to a positive number of dividends, the implied growth rate is *infinite*. Thus, equation (6.9) must be used with extreme caution here, if at all—a point we emphasize later in this chapter.

Second, we mentioned earlier that the value of the firm is infinite when g is equal to r. Because prices for stocks do not grow infinitely, an analyst whose estimate of g for a particular firm is equal to or above r must have made a mistake. Most likely, the analyst's high estimate for g is correct for the next few years. However, firms simply cannot maintain an abnormally high growth rate *forever*. The analyst's error was to use a short-run estimate of g in a model requiring a perpetual growth rate.

6.6 Growth Opportunities

We previously spoke of the growth rate of dividends. We now want to address the related concept of growth opportunities. Imagine a company with a level stream of earnings per share in perpetuity. The company pays all of these earnings out to stockholders as dividends. Hence,

$$EPS = Div$$

where EPS is *earnings per share* and Div is dividends per share. A company of this type is frequently called a *cash cow*.

From the perpetuity formula of the previous chapter, the value of a share of stock is:

Value of a Share when Firm Acts as a Cash Cow:

$$\frac{EPS}{r} = \frac{Div}{r}$$

where r is the discount rate on the firm's stock.

The above policy of paying out all earnings as dividends may not be the optimal one. Many firms have *growth* opportunities, that is, opportunities to invest in profitable projects. Because these projects can represent a significant fraction of the firm's value, it would be foolish to forgo them in order to pay out all earnings as dividends.

While firms frequently think in terms of a *set* of growth opportunities, let's focus on only one opportunity, that is, the opportunity to invest in a single project. Suppose the firm retains the entire dividend at date 1 in order to invest in a particular capital budgeting project. The net present value *per share* of the project as of date 0 is *NPVGO*, which stands for the *net present value (per share) of the growth opportunity*.

What is the price of a share at date 0 if the firm decides to take on the project at date 1? Because the per share value of the project is added to the original share price, the share price must now be:

Share Price after Firm Commits to New Project:

$$\frac{EPS}{r} + NPVGO \tag{6.10}$$

Thus, equation (6.10) indicates that the price of a share of stock can be viewed as the sum of two different items. The first term (EPS/r) is the value of the firm if it rested on its laurels, that is, if it simply distributed all earnings to the stockholders. The second term is the *additional value* if the firm retains earnings in order to fund new projects.

● **Example**

Sarro Shipping NV expects to earn NLG1 million per year in perpetuity if it undertakes no new investment opportunities. There are 100,000 shares outstanding, so earnings per share equal NLG10 (NLG1,000,000/100,000). The firm will have an opportunity at date 1 to spend NLG1,000,000 in a new marketing campaign. The new campaign will increase earnings in every subsequent period by NLG210,000 (or NLG2.10 per share). This is a 21 per cent return per year on the project. The firm's discount rate is 10 per cent. What is the value per share before and after deciding to accept the marketing campaign?

The value of a share of Sarro Shipping before the campaign is

Value of a Share of Sarro when Firm Acts as a Cash Cow:

$$\frac{EPS}{r} = \frac{NLG10}{0.1} = NLG100$$

The value of the marketing campaign as of date 1 is

Value of Marketing Campaign at Date 1:

$$-NLG1,000,000 + \frac{NLG210,000}{0.1} = NLG1,100,000 \tag{6.11}$$

Because the investment is made at date 1 and the first cash inflow occurs at date 2, equation (6.11) represents the value of the marketing campaign as of date 1. We determine the value at date 0 by discounting back one period as follows:

Value of Marketing Campaign at Date 0:

$$\frac{\text{NLG1,100,000}}{1.1} = \text{NLG1,000,000}$$

Thus, NPVGO per share is NLG10 (NLG1,000,000/100,000).

The price per share is

$$\text{EPS}/r + \text{NPVGO} = \text{NLG100} + \text{NLG10} = \text{NLG110} \bullet$$

The calculation can also be made on a straight net-present-value basis. Because all the earnings at date 1 are spent on the marketing effort, no dividends are paid to shareholders at that date. Dividends in all subsequent periods are NLG1,210,000 (NLG1,000,000 + NLG210,000). In this case, NLG1,000,000 is the annual dividend when Sarro is a cash cow. The additional contribution to the dividend from the marketing effort is NLG210,000. Dividends per share are NLG12.10 (NLG1,210,000/100,000). Because these dividends start at date 2, the price per share at date 1 is NLG121 (NLG12.10/0.1). The price per share at date 0 is NLG110 (NLG121/1.1).

Note that value is created in this example because the project earned a 21 per cent rate of return when the discount rate was only 10 per cent. No value would have been created had the project earned a 10 per cent rate of return. The NPVGO would have been zero, and value would have been negative had the project earned a percentage return below 10 per cent. The NPVGO would be negative in that case.

Two conditions must be met in order to increase value.

1. Earnings must be retained so that projects can be funded.[8]
2. The projects must have positive net present value.

Surprisingly, a number of companies seem to invest in projects known to have *negative* net present values. For example, Jensen has pointed out that, in the late 1970s, oil companies and tobacco companies were flush with cash.[9] Due to declining markets in both industries, high dividends and low investment would have been the rational action. Unfortunately, a number of companies in both industries reinvested heavily in what were widely perceived to be negative NPVGO projects. A study by McConnell and Muscarella documents this perception.[10] They find that, during the 1970s, the stock prices of oil companies generally decreased on the days that announcements of increases in exploration and development were made.

Given that NPV analysis (such as that presented in the previous chapter) is common knowledge in business, why would managers choose projects with negative NPVs? One conjecture is that some managers enjoy controlling a large company. Because paying dividends in lieu of reinvesting earnings reduces the size of the firm, some managers find it emotionally difficult to pay high dividends.

---

[8] Later in the text we speak of issuing shares or debt in order to fund projects.

[9] M. C. Jensen (1986), 'Agency Costs of Free Cash Flows, Corporate Finance and Takeovers', *American Economic Review,* May.

[10] J. J. McConnell and C. J. Muscarella (1985), 'Corporate Capital Expenditure Decisions and the Market Value of the Firm', *Journal of Financial Economics* **14**.

Growth in Earnings and Dividends versus Growth Opportunities

As mentioned earlier, a firm's value increases when it invests in growth opportunities with positive NVPGOs. A firm's value falls when it selects opportunities with negative NVPGOs. However, dividends grow whether projects with positive NPVs or negative NPVs are selected. This surprising result can be explained by the following example.

● **Example**

Supermarchets de France SA will earn FRF1 million a year in perpetuity if it pays out all its earnings as dividends. However, the firm plans to invest 20 per cent of its earnings in projects that earn 10 per cent per year. The discount rate is 18 per cent. An earlier formula tells us that the growth rate of dividends is

$$g = \text{Retention ratio} \times \text{Return on retained earnings} = 0.2 \times 0.10 = 2\%$$

For example, in this first year of the new policy, dividends are FRF800,000 $((1 - 0.2) \times \text{FRF1,000,000})$. Dividends next year are FRF816,000 (FRF800,000 $\times$ 1.02). Dividends the following year are FRF832,323 [FRF800,000 $\times (1.02)^2$] and so on. Because dividends represent a fixed percentage of earnings, earnings must grow at 2 per cent a year as well.

However, note that the policy reduces value because the rate of return on the projects of 10 per cent is less than the discount rate of 18 per cent. That is, the firm would have had a higher value at date 0 if it had a policy of paying all its earnings out as dividends. Thus, a policy of investing in projects with negative NPVs, rather than paying out earnings as dividends, will lead to growth in dividends and earnings, but will reduce value. ●

Dividends or Earnings: Which to Discount?

As mentioned earlier, this chapter applied the growing-perpetuity formula to the valuation of shares. In our application, we discounted dividends, not earnings. This is sensible since investors select a share for what they can get out of it. They only get two things out of a share: dividends and the ultimate sales price, which is determined by what future investors expect to receive in dividends.

The calculated share price would be too high were earnings to be discounted instead of dividends. As we saw in our estimation of a firm's growth rate, only a portion of earnings goes to the shareholders as dividends. The remainder is retained to generate future dividends. In our model, retained earnings are equal to the firm's investment. To discount earnings instead of dividends would be to ignore the investment that a firm must make today in order to generate future returns.

The No-Dividend Firm

Students frequently ask the following question: If the dividend-discount model is correct, why aren't no-dividend companies selling at zero? This is a good question and gets at the goals of the firm. A firm with many growth opportunities is faced with a dilemma. The firm can pay out dividends now, or it can forgo dividends now so that it can make investments that will generate even greater dividends in the future.[11] This is often a painful choice, because a strategy of dividend deferment may be optimal yet unpopular among certain shareholders.

---

[11] A third alternative is to issue shares so that the firm has enough cash both to pay dividends and to invest. This possibility is explored in a later chapter.

Many firms choose to pay no dividends—and these firms sell at positive prices. Rational shareholders believe that they will either receive dividends at some point or they will receive something just as good. That is, the firm will be acquired in a merger, with the shareholders receiving either cash or shares at that time.

Of course, the actual application of the dividend-discount model is difficult for firms of this type. Clearly, the model for constant growth of dividends does not apply. Though the differential growth model can work in theory, the difficulties of estimating the date of first dividend, the growth rate of dividends after that date, and the ultimate merger price make application of the model quite difficult in reality.

Empirical evidence suggests that firms with high growth rates are likely to pay lower dividends, a result consistent with the above analysis. For example, consider McDonald's Corporation. The company started in the 1950s and grew rapidly for many years. It paid its first dividend in 1975, though it was a billion-dollar company (in both sales and market value of stockholder's equity) prior to that date. Why did it wait so long to pay a dividend? It waited because it had so many positive growth opportunities, that is, additional locations for new hamburger outlets, of which to take advantage.

Utilities—electricity companies and water companies, for example—are an interesting contrast because, as a group, they have few growth opportunities. Because of this, they pay out a large fraction of their earnings in dividends. Some have payout ratios of over 90 per cent in some countries.

6.7   The Dividend-Growth Model and the NPVGO Model (Advanced)

This chapter has revealed that the price of a share in a firm is the sum of its price as a cash cow plus the per-share value of its growth opportunities. The Sarro Shipping example illustrated this formula using only one growth opportunity. We also used the growing-perpetuity formula to price a stock with a steady growth in dividends. When the formula is applied to stocks, it is typically called the *dividend-growth model*. A steady growth in dividends results from a continual investment in growth opportunities, not just investment in a single opportunity. Therefore, it is worth while to compare the dividend-growth model with the *NPVGO model* when growth occurs through continual investing.

● Example
South Holland Book Publishers has EPS of NLG10 at the end of the first year, a dividend-payout ratio of 40 per cent, a discount rate of 16 per cent, and a return on its retained earnings of 20 per cent. Because the firm retains some of its earnings each year, it is selecting growth opportunities each year. This is different from Sarro Shipping, which had a growth opportunity in only one year. We wish to calculate the price per share using both the dividend-growth model and the NPVGO model. ●

The Dividend-Growth Model

The dividends at date 1 are $0.40 \times$ NLG10 = NLG4 per share. The retention ratio is 0.60 $(1 - 0.40)$, implying a growth rate in dividends of 0.12 (0.60×0.20).

From the dividend-growth model, the price of a share of stock is

$$\frac{\text{Div}}{r - g} = \frac{\text{NLG4}}{0.16 - 0.12} = \text{NLG100}$$

The NPVGO Model

Using the NPVGO model, it is more difficult to value a firm with growth opportunities each year (like South Holland) than a firm with growth opportunities in only one year (like Sarro). In order to value according to the NPVGO model, we need to calculate on a per-share basis (1) the net present value of a single growth opportunity, (2) the net present value of all growth opportunities, and (3) the stock price if the firm acts as a cash cow, that is, the value of the firm without these growth opportunities. The value of the firm is the sum of (2)+ (3).

1. *Value per Share of a Single Growth Opportunity*   Out of the earnings per share of NLG10 at date 1, the firm retains NLG6 (0.6 × NLG10) at that date. The firm earns NLG1.20 (NLG6 × 0.20) per year in perpetuity on that NLG6 investment. The NPV from the investment is

Per-Share NPV Generated from Investment at Date 1:

$$- NLG6 + \frac{NLG1.20}{0.16} = NLG1.50 \qquad (6.12)$$

That is, the firm invests NLG6 in order to reap NLG1.20 per year on the investment. The earnings are discounted at 0.16, implying a value per share from the project of NLG1.50. Because the investment occurs at date 1 and the first cash flow occurs at date 2, NLG1.50 is the value of the investment at *date 1*. In other words, the NPV from the date 1 investment has *not* yet been brought back to date 0.

2. *Value per Share of All Opportunities*   As pointed out earlier, the growth rate of earnings and dividends is 12 per cent. Because retained earnings are a fixed percentage of total earnings, retained earnings must also grow at 12 per cent a year. That is, retained earnings at date 2 are NLG6.72 (NLG6 × 1.12), retained earnings at date 3 are NLG7.5264 [NLG6 × (1.12)²], and so on.

Let's analyse the retained earnings at date 2 in more detail. Because projects will always earn 20 per cent per year, the firm earns NLG1.344 (NLG6.72 × 0.20) in each future year on the NLG6.72 investment at date 2.

The NPV from the investment is

NPV per Share Generated from Investment at Date 2:

$$- NLG6.72 + \frac{NLG1.344}{0.16} = NLG1.68 \qquad (6.13)$$

NLG1.68 is the NPV as of date 2 of the investment made at date 2. The NPV from the date 2 investment has *not* yet been brought back to date 0.

Now consider the retained earnings at date 3 in more detail. The firm earns NLG1.5053 (NLG7.5264 × 0.20) per year on the investment of NLG7.5264 at date 3.

The NPV from the investment is

NPV per Share Generated from Investment at Date 3:

$$- NLG7.5264 + \frac{NLG1.5053}{0.16} = NLG1.882 \qquad (6.14)$$

From (6.12), (6.13) and (6.14), the NPV per share of all of the growth opportunities, discounted back to date 0, is

$$\frac{\text{NLG1.50}}{1.16} + \frac{\text{NLG1.68}}{(1.16)^2} + \frac{\text{NLG1.882}}{(1.16)^3} + \cdots \qquad (6.15)$$

Because it has an infinite number of terms, this expression looks quite difficult to compute. However, there is an easy simplification. Note that retained earnings are growing at 12 per cent per year. Because all projects earn the same rate of return per year, the NPVs in (6.12), (6.13) and (6.14) are also growing at 12 per cent per year. Hence, we can rewrite (6.15) as

$$\frac{\text{NLG1.50}}{1.16} + \frac{\text{NLG1.50} \times 1.12}{(1.16)^2} + \frac{\text{NLG1.50} \times (1.12)^2}{(1.16)^3} + \cdots$$

This is a growth perpetuity whose value is

$$\text{NPVGO} = \frac{\text{NLG1.50}}{0.16 - 0.12} = \text{NLG37.50}$$

Because the first NPV of NLG1.50 occurs at date 1, the NPVGO is NLG37.50 as of date 0. In other words, the firm's policy of investing in new projects from retained earnings has an NPV of NLG37.50.

3. **Value per Share if Firm Is a Cash Cow**   We now assume that the firm pays out all of its earnings as dividends. The dividends would be NLG10 per year in this case. Since there would be no growth, the value per share would be evaluated by the perpetuity formula:

$$\frac{\text{Div}}{r} = \frac{\text{NLG10}}{0.16} = \text{NLG62.50}$$

Summation

Formula (6.10) states that value per share is the value of a cash cow plus the value of the growth opportunities. This is

$$\text{NLG100} = \text{NLG62.50} + \text{NLG37.50}$$

Hence, value is the same whether calculated by a discounted-dividend approach or a growth-opportunities approach. The share prices from the two approaches must be equal, because the approaches are different yet equivalent methods of applying concepts of present value.

6.8   Price-Earnings Ratio

We argued earlier that one should not discount earnings in order to determine price per share. Nevertheless, financial analysis frequently relate earnings and price per share, as made evident by their heavy reliance on the price-earnings (or P/E) ratio.

Our previous discussion stated that

$$\text{Price per share} = \frac{\text{EPS}}{r} + \text{NPVGO}$$

Dividing by EPS yields

$$\frac{\text{Price per share}}{\text{EPS}} = \frac{1}{r} + \frac{\text{NPVGO}}{\text{EPS}}$$

The lefthand side is the formula for the price-earnings ratio. The equation shows that the P/E ratio is related to the net present value of growth opportunities. As an example, consider two firms, each having just reported earnings per share of GBP1. However, one firm has many valuable growth opportunities, while the other firm has no growth opportunities at all. The firm with growth opportunities should sell at a higher price, because an investor is buying both current income of GBP1 and growth opportunities. Suppose that the firm with growth opportunities sells for GBP16 and the other firm sells for GBP8. The GBP1 earnings per share number appears in the denominator of the P/E ratio for both firms. Thus, the P/E ratio is 16 for the firm with growth opportunities, but only 8 for the firm without the opportunities.

This explanation seems to hold fairly well in the real world. Electronic and other high-tech stocks generally sell at very high P/E ratios (or *multiples*, as they are often called) because they are perceived to have high growth rates. In fact, some technology stocks sell at high prices even though the companies have never earned a profit. The P/E ratios of these companies are infinite. Conversely, railroads, utilities and steel companies sell at lower multiples because of the prospects of lower growth.

Of course, the market is merely pricing *perceptions* of the future, not the future itself. We will argue later in the text that the stock market generally has realistic perceptions of a firm's prospects. However, this is not always true. In the late 1960s, many electronics firms were selling at multiples of 90 times earnings. The high perceived growth rates did not materialize, causing great declines in stock prices during the early 1970s. In earlier decades, fortunes were made in America in stocks like IBM and Xerox, because the high growth rates were not anticipated by investors.

One of the most puzzling phenomena to many investors has been the high P/E ratios in the Japanese stock market. The average P/E ratio for the Tokyo Stock Exchange has varied between 40 and 70 in recent years, while Europe and America averages have been much lower (see Table 6.1). Our formula indicates that Japanese companies have been perceived to have great growth opportunities. However, commentators have frequently suggested that investors in the Japanese markets have been overestimating these growth prospects.[12] This point (at least to some extent) has been borne out with the passage of time.

There are two additional factors explaining the P/E ratio. The first is the discount rate, r. The above formula shows that the P/E ratio is *negatively* related to the firm's discount rate. We have already suggested that the discount rate is positively related to the stock's risk or variability. Thus, the P/E ratio is negatively related to the stock's risk. To see that this is a sensible result, consider two firms, *A*

---

[12] It has been suggested that Japanese companies use more conservative accounting practices, thereby creating higher P/E ratios. This point, which will shortly be examined for firms in general, appears to explain only a small part of Japan's high multiples.

TABLE 6.1   **International P/E Ratios (1st January 1998)**

	Dividend yield (%)	P/E ratio		Dividend yield (%)	P/E ratio
Australia	3.54	18.7	Netherlands	2.13	21.4
Belgium	2.25	16.6	New Zealand	4.02	18.1
China	1.21	70.9	Norway	1.94	14.4
Denmark	1.26	21.6	Singapore	2.34	14.5
France	2.42	17.9	South Africa	3.14	12.6
Germany	1.42	20.5	Spain	2.29	21.7
Hong Kong	3.63	10.6	Sweden	1.78	21.8
Ireland	2.22	19.2	Switzerland	1.04	23.9
Italy	1.80	21.6	UK	3.23	19.4
Japan	0.97	40.3	USA	1.55	25.1

Source: *Financial Times,* January 2, 1998.

and *B*, behaving as cash cows. The stock market *expects* both firms to have annual earnings of DEM1 per share forever. However, the earnings of firm *A* are known with certainty while the earnings of firm *B* are quite variable. A rational stockholder is likely to pay more for a share of firm *A* because of the absence of risk. If a share of firm *A* sells at a higher price and both firms have the same EPS, the P/E ratio of firm *A* must be higher.

The second additional factor concerns the firm's choice of accounting methods. Under accounting rules, companies in most countries are given a fair amount of leeway. For example, consider inventory accounting where either *FIFO* (first in–first out) or *LIFO* (last in–first out) may be used—this is the case in the USA, although in the UK virtually all companies use FIFO (only FIFO is allowed for UK tax purposes). In an inflationary environment, FIFO accounting shows the cost of inventory highly and hence inflates reported earnings. Inventory is valued according to less recent costs under LIFO, implying that reported earnings are lower here than they would be under FIFO. Thus, LIFO profit accounting is a more conservative method than FIFO. Similar accounting leeway exists for construction costs (*completed-contracts* versus *percentage-of-completion methods*) and depreciation (*accelerated depreciation* versus *straight-line depreciation*) and in other areas too—see Chapter 1.

As an example, consider two identical firms, *C* and *D*. *Firm C* uses LIFO and reports earnings of USD2 per share. Firm *D* uses the less conservative accounting assumptions of FIFO and reports earnings of USD3 per share. The market knows that both firms are identical and prices both at USD18 per share. This price-earnings ratio is 9 (USD18/USD2) for firm *C* and 6 (USD18/USD3) for firm *D*. Thus, the firm with the more conservative principles has the higher P/E ratio.

This last example depends on the assumption that the market sees through differences in accounting treatments. A significant portion of the academic community believes that the market sees through virtually all accounting differences. These academics are adherents of the hypothesis of *efficient capital markets*, a theory that we explore in great detail later in the text. Though many financial people might be more moderate in their beliefs regarding this issue, the consensus view is certainly that many of the accounting differences are seen through. Thus, the proposition that firms with conservative accountants have high P/E ratios is widely accepted.

This discussion argued that the P/E ratio is a function of three different factors. A company's ratio or multiple is likely to be high if (1) it has many growth opportunities,

(2) it has low risk and (3) it is accounted for in a conservative manner. While each of the three factors is important, it is our opinion that the first factor is much more so. Thus, our discussion of growth is quite relevant in understanding price-earnings multiples.

Concept Question

• What are the three factors determining a firm's P/E ratio?

6.9 Summary and Conclusions

In this chapter we use general present-value formulas from the previous chapter to price bonds and shares.

1. Pure discount bonds and perpetuities can be viewed as the polar cases of bonds. The value of a pure discount bond (also called a zero-coupon bond, or simply a zero) is

$$PV = \frac{F}{(1 + r)^T}$$

The value of a perpetuity (also called a consol) is

$$PV = \frac{C}{r}$$

2. Level-payment bonds can be viewed as an intermediate case. The coupon payments form an annuity and the principal repayment is a lump sum. The value of this type of bond is simply the sum of the values of its two parts.

3. The yield to maturity on a bond is that single rate that discounts the payments on the bond to its purchase price.

4. A share can be valued by discounting its dividends. We mention three types of situations:
   a. The case of zero growth of dividends.
   b. The case of constant growth of dividends.
   c. The case of differential growth.

5. An estimate of the growth rate of a share is needed for formulas (*4b*) or (*4c*) above. A useful estimate of the growth rate is

$$g = \text{Retention ratio} \times \text{Return on retained earnings}$$

6. It is worth while to view a share as the sum of its worth if the company behaves like a cash cow (the company does no investing) and the value per share of its growth opportunities. We write the value of a share as

$$\frac{\text{EPS}}{r} + \text{NPVGO}$$

We show that, in theory, share price must be the same whether the dividend-growth model or the above formula is used.

7. From accounting, we know that earnings are divided into two parts: dividends and retained earnings. Most firms continually retain earnings in order to create future dividends. One should not discount earnings to obtain price per share since part of earnings must be reinvested. Only dividends reach the shareholders and only they should be discounted to obtain share price.

8. We suggested that a firm's price-earnings ratio is a function of three factors:
   a. The per-share amount of the firm's valuable growth opportunities.
   b. The risk of the share.
   c. The type of accounting method used by the firm.

KEY TERMS

Pure discount bond 111	Premium 116
Maturity date 111	Yield to maturity 116
Face value 111	Retention ratio 122
Coupons 113	Return on equity 122
Discount 115	Payout ratio 124

QUESTIONS AND PROBLEMS

How to Value Bonds

6.1 What is the present value of a 10-year, pure discount bond that pays NLG1,000 at maturity to yield the following rates?
  a. 5 per cent
  b. 10 per cent
  c. 15 per cent

6.2 A bond with the following characteristics is available.
  Principal: NLG1,000
  Term to maturity: 20 years
  Coupon rate: 8 per cent
  Semiannual payments
  Calculate the price of the bond if the stated annual interest rate is:
  a. 8 per cent
  b. 10 per cent
  c. 6 per cent

6.3 Consider a bond with a face value of DEM1,000. The coupon is paid semiannually and the market interest rate (effective annual interest rate) is 12 per cent. How much would you pay for the bond if
  a. the coupon rate is 8 per cent and the remaining time to maturity is 20 years?
  b. the coupon rate is 10 per cent and the remaining time to maturity is 15 years?

6.4 A firm has issued an 8 per cent, 20-year bond that pays interest semiannually. If the market prices the bond to yield an effective annual rate of 10 per cent, what is the price of the bond?

6.5 A bond is sold at DEM923.14 (below its par value of DEM1,000). The bond has 15 years to maturity and investors require a 10 per cent yield on the bond. What is the coupon rate for the bond if the coupon is paid semiannually?

6.6 You have just purchased a newly issued DEM1,000 five-year XYZ AG bond at par. This five-year bond pays DEM60 in interest semiannually. You are also considering the purchase of another XYZ bond that returns DEM30 in semiannual interest payments and has six years remaining before it matures. This bond has a face value of DEM1,000.
  a. What is effective annual return on the five-year bond?
  b. Assume that the rate you calculated in part (*a*) is the correct rate for the bond with six years remaining before it matures. What should you be willing to pay for that bond?
  c. How will your answer to part (*b*) change if the five-year bond pays DEM40 in semiannual interest?

Bond Concepts

6.7 Consider two bonds, bond *A* and bond *B*, with equal coupon rates of 10 per cent and the same face values of DEM1,000. The coupons are paid annually for both bonds. Bond *A* has 20 years to maturity while bond *B* has 10 years to maturity.
  a. What are the prices of the two bonds if the relevant market interest rate is 10 per cent?
  b. If the market interest rate increases to 12 per cent, what will be the prices of the two bonds?
  c. If the market interest rate decreases to 8 per cent, what will the prices of the two bonds be?

6.8 *a*. If the market interest rate (the required rate of return that investors demand) unexpectedly increases, what effect would you expect it to have on the prices of long-term bonds? Why?
  b. What would be the effect of the rise in the interest rate on the general level of stock prices? Why?

6.9 Consider a bond, which pays an NLG80 coupon annually and has a face value of NLG1,000. Calculate the yield to maturity if the bond has
   a. 20 years remaining to maturity and it is sold at NLG1,200.
   b. 10 years remaining to maturity and it is sold at NLG950.

The Present Value of Ordinary Shares

6.10 World Wide plc, is expected to pay a per-share dividend of 30 pence next year. It also expects that this dividend will grow at a rate of 8 per cent in perpetuity. What price would you expect to see for World Wide shares if the appropriate discount rate is 12 per cent?

6.11 Marie Dupont purchased the ordinary shares of Sudest SA, which are currently being sold at FRF50 per share. The company will pay a dividend of FRF2 per share a year from today, FRF2.5 per share two years from today, and FRF3 per share three years from today. If Marie Dupont requires an annual return of 10 per cent and intends to sell her shares three years from now, how much does she expect to receive?

6.12 An ordinary share pays a current dividend of ESB2. The dividend is expected to grow at an 8 per cent annual rate for the next three years; then it will grow at 4 per cent in perpetuity. The appropriate discount rate is 12 per cent. What is the theoretical price of this share?

6.13 Suppose that a shareholder has just paid SEK50 per share for an XYZ Company share. The stock will pay a dividend of SEK2 per share in the upcoming year. This dividend is expected to grow at an annual rate of 10 per cent for the indefinite future. The shareholder felt that the price she paid was an appropriate price, given her assessment of XYZ's risks. What is the annual required rate of return of this shareholder?

6.14 Lebrun SA has just paid a FRF3 dividend per share. The share is currently being sold at FRF40. Investors expect that Lebrun's dividend will grow at a constant rate indefinitely. What growth rate is expected by investors if they require
   a. 8 per cent return on the stock?
   b. 10 per cent return on the stock?
   c. 15 per cent return on the stock?

6.15 Consider the stock of Davidson Company plc that will pay an annual dividend of GBP2 in the coming year. The dividend is expected to grow at a constant rate of 5 per cent permanently. The market requires 12 per cent return on the company.
   a. What is the current price of the stock?
   b. What should the share price be 10 years from today?

6.16 Easy Type plc is one of a myriad of companies selling word processor programs. Their newest program will cost GBP5 million to develop. First-year net cash flows will be GBP2 million. As a result of competition, profits will fall by 2 per cent each year. All cash inflows will occur at year-end. If the market discount rate is 14 per cent, what is the value of this new program?

6.17 Whizzkids AG is experiencing a period of rapid growth. Earnings and dividends are expected to grow at a rate of 18 per cent during the next two years, 15 per cent in the third year, and at a constant rate of 6 per cent thereafter. Whizzkids' last dividend, which has just been paid, was DEM1.15. If the required rate of return on the stock is 12 per cent, what is the price of the stock today?

6.18 Allen NV is expected to pay an equal amount of dividends at the end of the first two years. Thereafter the dividend will grow at a constant rate of 4 per cent indefinitely. Its shares are currently traded at NLG30. What is the expected dividend per share for the next year if the required rate of return is 12 per cent?

6.19 The Highest Potential plc will pay a quarterly dividend of GBP1 per share at the end of each of the first 12 quarters. Subsequently, the dividend will grow at a quarterly rate of 0.5 per cent indefinitely. The appropriate rate of return on the stock is 10 per cent. What, theoretically, is the current share price?

Estimates of Parameters in the Dividend-Discount Model

6.20 The newspaper reported last week that Swiss Enterprises earned CHF20 million. The report also stated that the firm's return on equity remains on its historical trend of 14 per cent. Swiss Enterprises retains 60 per cent of its earnings. What is the firm's growth rate of earnings? What will next year's earnings be?

6.21 McKenna Enterprises has just reported earnings of IEP10 million, and it plans to retain 75 per cent of its earnings. The company has 1.25 million shares outstanding. The stock is selling at IEP30. The historical return on equity (ROE) of 12 per cent is expected to continue in the future. What is the required rate of return on the stock?

Growth Opportunities

6.22 Rite Bite Enterprises plc sells toothpicks. Gross revenues last year were GBP3 million, and total costs were GBP1.5 million. Rite Bite has 1 million shares outstanding. Gross revenues and costs are expected to grow at 5 per cent per year. Rite Bite pays no income taxes, and all earnings are paid out as dividends.

  a. If the appropriate discount rate is 15 per cent and all cash flows are received at the year-end, what is the price per share of Rite Bite stock?

  b. The chief executive of Rite Bite decided to institute a policy to produce toothbrushes. The project requires an immediate outlay of GBP15 million. In one year, another outlay of GBP5 million will be needed. The year after that, net cash inflows will be GBP6 million. This profit level will be maintained in perpetuity. What effect will undertaking this project have on the price per share of Rite Bite Enterprises?

6.23 Zurich Electronics expects to earn CHF100 million per year in perpetuity if it does not undertake any new projects. The firm has an opportunity that requires an investment of CHF15 million today and CHF5 million in one year. The new investment will begin to generate additional annual earnings and cash of CHF10 million two years from today in perpetuity. The firm has 20 million shares outstanding, and the required rate of return on the share is 15 per cent.

  a. What is the price of the share if the firm does not undertake the new project?

  b. What is the value of the growth opportunities resulting from the new project?

  c. What is the price of the share if the firm undertakes the new project?

6.24 Holmes Fixtures plc expects net cash flows of GBP50,000 by the end of this year. Net cash flows will grow 3 per cent if the firm makes no new investments. Peggy Holmes, the chief executive of the firm, has the opportunity to add a line of kitchen and bathroom cabinets to the business. The immediate outlay for this opportunity is GBP100,000, and the net cash flows from the line will begin one year from now. The cabinet business will generate GBP32,000 in additional net cash flows. These net cash flows will also grow at 3 per cent. The firm's discount rate is 13 per cent, and 200,000 shares of Holmes Fixtures plc are outstanding.

  a. What is the theoretical price per share of Holmes Fixtures without the cabinets line?

  b. What is the value of the growth opportunities that the cabinet line offers?

  c. Once Holmes Fixtures adds the cabinet line, what is the theoretical price of its shares?

6.25 Bayern Ski AG has reported earnings of DEM8 million. It is expected that earnings will grow at 3 per cent each year in perpetuity if the firm undertakes no new investment opportunities. There are 2 million shares outstanding. The firm has a new project that needs an immediate investment of DEM3 million. The new project will produce annual earnings of DEM1.5 million in each of the next 20 years. Shareholders of the firm require 12 per cent return on the share.

  a. What is the theoretical price of the share if the firm does not undertake the new project?

  b. Is it worthwhile to undertake the new project? Calculate the NPV of the new project.

  c. What is the price of the share if the firm undertakes the new project?

6.26 Special Info plc just reported earnings of GBP1.5 million. The firm will retain 40 per cent of its earnings. The historic return on equity (ROE) was 15 per cent, and this figure is expected to continue into the future. The firm has 300,000 shares outstanding. The appropriate discount rate on the stock is 13 per cent.

  a. What is the firm's growth rate of earnings?

  b. What is the price of the share?

  c. The firm has an opportunity to invest in a new project. The project requires an initial investment of GBP1.2 million today, and it will generate additional cash earnings in the next 10 years. The first additional annual earnings of GBP0.3 million will begin one year from now and grow at 10 per cent each year thereafter. Calculate the NPV of the new project.

  d. What will the price of the stock be if the firm undertakes the new project?

APPENDIX 6A

THE TERM STRUCTURE OF INTEREST RATES SPOT RATES AND YIELD TO MATURITY

In the main body of this chapter, we have assumed that the interest rate is constant over all future periods. In reality, interest rates vary through time. This occurs primarily because inflation rates are expected to differ through time.

To illustrate, we consider two zero-coupon bonds. Bond A is a one-year bond and bond B is a two-year bond. Both have face values of DEM1,000. The one-year interest rate, r_1, is 8 per cent. The two-year interest rate, r_2, is 10 per cent. These two rates of interest are examples of spot rates. Perhaps this inequality in interest rates occurs because inflation is expected to be higher over the second year than over the first year. The two bonds are depicted in the following time chart.

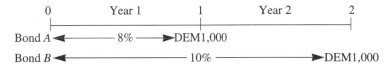

We can easily calculate the present value for bond A and bond B as

$$PV_A = DEM925.93 = \frac{DEM1,000}{1.08}$$

$$PV_B = DEM826.45 = \frac{DEM1,000}{(1.10)^2}$$

Of course, if PV_A and PV_B were observable and the spot rates were not, we could determine the spot rates using the PV formula, because

$$PV_A = DEM925.93 = \frac{DEM1,000}{(1 + r_1)} \rightarrow r_1 = 8\%$$

and

$$PV_B = DEM826.45 = \frac{DEM1,000}{(1 + r_2)^2} \rightarrow r_2 = 10\%$$

Now we can see how the prices of more-complicated bonds are determined. Try to do the next example. It illustrates the difference between spot rates and yields to maturity.

● Example

Given the spot rates, r_1 equals 8 per cent and r_2 equals 10 per cent, what should a 5 per cent coupon, two-year bond cost? The cash flows C_1 and C_2 are illustrated in the following time chart.

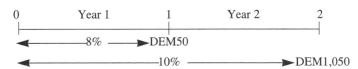

The bond can be viewed as a portfolio of zero-coupon bonds with one- and two-year maturities. Therefore

$$PV = \frac{DEM50}{1 + 0.08} + \frac{DEM1,050}{(1 + 0.10)^2} = DEM914.06 \qquad (A.1)$$

We now want to calculate a single rate for the bond. We do this by solving for y in the following equation:

$$DEM914.06 = \frac{DEM50}{1 + y} + \frac{DEM1,050}{(1 + y)^2} \qquad (A.2)$$

In (A.2), y equals 9.95 per cent. As mentioned in the chapter, we call y the *yield to maturity* of the bond. Solving for y for a multiyear bond is generally done by means of trial and error.[13] While this can take much time with paper and pencil, it is virtually instantaneous on a hand-held calculator.

It is worth while to contrast equation (A.1) and (A.2). In (A.1), we use the marketwide spot rates to determine the price of the bond. Once we get the bond price, we use (A.2) to calculate its yield to maturity. Because equation (A.1) employs two spot rates whereas only one appears in (A.2), we can think of yield to maturity as some sort of average of the two spot rates.[14]

Using the above spot rates, the yield to maturity of a two-year coupon bond whose coupon rate is 12 per cent and PV equals DEM1,036.73 can be determined by

$$\text{DEM}1,036.73 = \frac{\text{DEM}120}{1 + r} + \frac{\text{DEM}1,120}{(1 + r)^2} \rightarrow r = 9.89\%$$

As these calculations show, two bonds with the same maturity will usually have different yields to maturity if the coupons differ. ●

Graphing the Term Structure   The **term structure** describes the relationship of spot rates with different maturities. Figure 6A.1 graphs a particular term structure. In Figure 6A.1 the spot rates are increasing with longer maturities, that is, $r^3 > r^2 > r^1$. Graphing the term structure is easy if we can observe spot rates. Unfortunately, this can be done only if there are enough zero-coupon government bonds.

FIGURE 6A.1   The Term Structure of Interest Rates

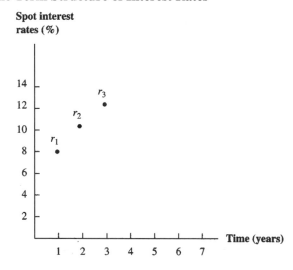

A given term structure, such as that in Figure 6A.1, exists for only a moment in time, say, 10.00 a.m., July 30, 1997. Interest rates are likely to change in the next minute, so that a different (though quite similar) term structure would exist at 10.01 a.m.

Concept Question

• What is the difference between a spot interest rate and the yield to maturity?

Explanations of the Term Structure

Figure 6A.1 showed one of many possible relationships between the spot rate and maturity. We now want to explore the relationship in more detail. We begin by defining a new term, the forward

---

[13] The quadratic formula may be used to solve for y for a two-year bond. However, formulas generally do not apply for longer-term bonds.

[14] Yield to maturity is not a simple average of r_1 and r_2. Rather, financial economists speak of it as a time-weighted average of r_1 and r_2.

rate. Next, we relate this forward rate to future interest rates. Finally, we consider alternative theories of the term structure.

Definition of Forward Rate   Earlier in this appendix, we developed a two-year example where the spot rate over the first year is 8 per cent and the spot rate over the two years is 10 per cent. Here, an individual investing DEM1 in a two-year zero-coupon bond would have DEM1 $\times$ $(1.10)^2$ in two years.

In order to pursue our discussion, it is worth while to rewrite[15]

$$\text{DEM1} \times (1.10)^2 = \text{DEM1} \times 1.08 \times 1.1204 \tag{A.3}$$

Equation (A.3) tells us something important about the relationship between one- and two-year rates. When an individual invests in a two-year zero-coupon bond yielding 10 per cent, his wealth at the end of two years is the same as if he received an 8 per cent return over the first year and a 12.04 per cent return over the second year. This hypothetical rate over the second year, 12.04 per cent, is called the *forward rate*. Thus, we can think of an investor with a two-year zero-coupon bond as getting the one-year spot rate of 8 per cent and *locking in* 12.04 per cent over the second year. This relationship is presented in Figure 6A.2.

FIGURE 6A.2   Breakdown of a Two-Year Spot Rate into a One-Year Spot Rate and Forward Rate over the Second Year

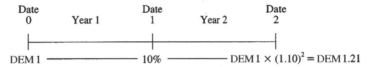

	Date 0		Date 1		Date 2

DEM 1 ———————— 10% ———————— DEM 1 $\times (1.10)^2$ = DEM 1.21

With a two-year spot rate of 10 per cent, investor in two-year bond receives DEM 1.21 at date 2.

This is the same return *as if* investor received the spot rate of 8 per cent over the first year and 12.04 per cent return over the second year.

DEM 1 — 8% — DEM 1.08 — 12.04% — DEM 1 $\times$ 1.08 $\times$ 1.1204 = DEM 1.21

Because both the one-year spot rate and the two-year spot rate are known at date 0, the forward rate over the second year can be calculated at date 0.

More generally, if we are given spot rates, r_1 and r_2, we can always determine the forward rate, f_2, such that:

$$(1 + r_2)^2 = (1 + r_1) \times (1 + f_2) \tag{A.4}$$

We solve for f_2, yielding:

$$f_2 = \frac{(1 + r_2)^2}{1 + r_1} - 1 \tag{A.5}$$

● **Example**

If the one-year spot rate is 7 per cent and the two-year spot rate is 12 per cent, what is f_2?

We plug in (A.5), yielding

$$f_2 = \frac{(1.12)^2}{1.07} - 1 = 17.23\%$$

Consider an individual investing in a two-year zero-coupon bond yielding 12 per cent. We say

---

[15] 12.04 per cent is equal to $(1.10)^2/1.08 - 1$ when rounding is performed after four digits.

it is as if he receives 7 per cent over the first year and simultaneously locks in 17.23 per cent over the second year. Note that both the one-year spot rate and the two-year spot rate are known at date 0. Because the forward rate is calculated from the one-year and two-year spot rates, it can be calculated at date 0 as well.

Forward rates can be calculated over later years as well. The general formula is

$$f_n = \frac{(1 + r_n)^n}{(1 + r_{n-1})^{n-1}} - 1 \tag{A.6}$$

where f_n is the forward rate over the nth year, r_n is the n-year spot rate, and r_{n-1} is the spot rate for $n - 1$ years. ●

● Example
Assume the following set of rates:

Year	Spot rate
1	5%
2	6
3	7
4	6

What are the forward rates over each of the four years?

The forward rate over the first year is, *by definition*, equal to the one-year spot rate. Thus, we do not generally speak of the forward rate over the first year. The forward rates over the later years are

$$f_2 = \frac{(1.06)^2}{1.05} - 1 = 7.01\%$$

$$f_2 = \frac{(1.07)^3}{(1.06)^2} - 1 = 9.03\%$$

$$f_2 = \frac{(1.06)^4}{(1.07)^3} - 1 = 3.06\%$$

An individual investing DEM1 in the two-year zero-coupon bond receives DEM1.1236 [DEM1 × (1.06)²] at date 2. He can be viewed as receiving the one-year spot rate of 5 per cent over the first year and receiving the forward rate of 7.01 per cent over the second year. An individual investing DEM1 in a three-year zero-coupon bond receives DEM1.2250 [DEM1 × (1.07)³] at date 3. She can be viewed as receiving the two-year spot rate of 6 per cent over the first two years and receiving the forward rate of 9.03 per cent over the third year. An individual investing DEM1 in a four-year zero-coupon bond receives DEM1.2625 [DEM1 × (1.06)⁴] at date 4. He can be viewed as receiving the three-year spot rate of 7 per cent over the first three years and receiving the forward rate of 3.06 per cent over the fourth year.

Note that all of the four spot rates in this problem are known at date 0. Because the forward rates are calculated from the spot rates, they can be determined at date 0 as well. ●

The material in this appendix is likely to be difficult for a student exposed to term structure for the first time. It helps to state what the student should know at this point. Given equations (A.5) and (A.6), a student should be able to calculate a set of forward rates given a set of spot rates. This can simply be viewed as a mechanical computation. In addition to the calculations, a student should understand the intuition of Figure 6A.2.

We now turn to the relationship between the forward rate and the expected spot rates in the future.

Estimating the Price of a Bond at a Future Date   In the example from the body of this chapter, we considered zero-coupon bonds paying DEM1,000 at maturity and selling at a discount prior to maturity. We now wish to change the example slightly. Now, each bond initially sells at par so that its payment at maturity is above DEM1,000.[16] Keeping the spot rates at 8 per cent and 10 per cent, we have

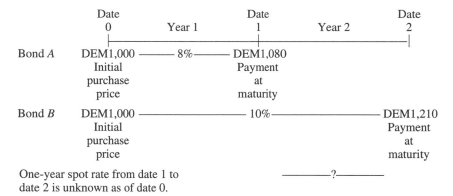

The payments at maturity are DEM1,080 and DEM1,210 for the one- and two-year zero-coupon bonds, respectively. The initial purchase price of DEM1,000 for each bond is determined as

$$DEM1,000 = \frac{DEM1,080}{1.08}$$

$$DEM1,000 = \frac{DEM1,210}{(1.10)^2}$$

We refer to the one-year bond as bond *A* and the two-year bond as bond *B*, respectively.

There will be a different one-year spot rate when date 1 arrives. This will be the spot rate from date 1 to date 2. We can also call it the spot rate over year 2. This spot rate is not known as of date 0. For example, should the rate of inflation rise between date 0 and date 1, the spot rate over year 2 would likely be high. Should the rate of inflation fall between date 0 and date 1, the spot rate over year 2 would likely be low.

Now that we have determined the price of each bond at date 0, we want to determine what the price of each bond will be at date 1. The price of the one-year bond (bond *A*) must be DEM1,080 at date 1, because the payment at maturity is made then. The hard part is determining what the price of the two-year bond (bond *B*) will be at that time.

Suppose we find that, on date 1, the one-year spot rate from date 1 to date 2 is 6 per cent. We state that this is the one-year spot rate over year 2. This means that I can invest DEM1,000 at date 1 and receive DEM1,060 (DEM1,000 × 1.06) at date 2. Because one year has already passed for bond *B*, the bond has only one year left. Because bond *B* pays DEM1,210 at date 2, its value at date 1 is

$$DEM1,141.51 = \frac{DEM1,210}{1.06} \tag{A.7}$$

Note that no one *knew* ahead of time the price that bond *B* would sell for on date 1, because no one knew that the one-year spot rate over year 2 would be 6 per cent.

Suppose the one-year spot rate beginning at date 1 turned out not to be 6 per cent, but to be 7 per cent instead. This means that I can invest DEM1,000 at date 1 and receive DEM1,070 (DEM1,000 × 1.07) at date 2. In this case, the value of bond *B* at date 1 would be

$$DEM1,130.84 = \frac{DEM1,210}{1.07} \tag{A.8}$$

Finally, suppose that the one-year spot rate at date 1 turned out to be neither 6 per cent nor 7 per cent, but 14 per cent instead. This means that I can invest DEM1,000 at date 1 and receive DEM1,140 (DEM1,000 × 1.14) at date 2. In this case, the value of bond *B* at date 1 would be

$$DEM1,061.40 = \frac{DEM1,210}{1.14}$$

---

[16] This change in assumptions simplifies our presentation, but does not alter any of our conclusions.

The above possible bond prices are represented in Table 6A.1. The price that bond B will sell for on date 1 is not known before date 1 since the one-year spot rate prevailing over year 2 is not known until date 1.

It is important to reemphasize that, although the forward rate is known at date 0, the one-year spot rate beginning at date 1 is *unknown* ahead of time. Thus, the price of bond B at date 1 is unknown ahead of time. Prior to date 1, we can speak only of the amount that bond B is *expected* to sell for on date 1. We write this as[17]

The Amount that Bond B Is Expected to Sell for on Date 1:

$$\frac{DEM1,210}{1 + \text{Spot rate expected over year 2}} \tag{A.9}$$

It is worth while making two points now. First, because each individual is different, the expected value of bond B differs across individuals. Later, we will speak of a consensus expected value across investors. Second, equation (A.9) represents one's forecast of the price that the bond will be selling for on date 1. The forecast is made ahead of time, that is, on date 0.

TABLE 6A.1   Price of Bond B at Date 1 as a Function of Spot Rate over Year 2

Price of bond B at Date 1	Spot rate over Year 2
$DEM1,141.51 = \dfrac{DEM1,210}{1.06}$	6%
$DEM1,130.84 = \dfrac{DEM1,210}{1.07}$	7%
$DEM1,061.40 = \dfrac{DEM2,210}{1.14}$	14%

The Relationship between Forward Rate over Second Year and Spot Rate Expected over Second Year

Given a forecast of bond B's price, an investor can choose one of two strategies at date 0:

I. Buy a one-year bond. Proceeds at date 1 would be

$$DEM1,080 = DEM1,000 \times 1.08 \tag{A.10}$$

II. Buy a two-year bond, but sell at date 1. His expected proceeds would be

$$\frac{DEM1,000 \times (1.10)^2}{1 + \text{Spot rate expected over year 2}} \tag{A.11}$$

Given our discussion of forward rates, we can rewrite (A.11) as

$$\frac{DEM1,000 \times 1.08 \times 1.1204}{1 + \text{Spot rate expected over year 2}} \tag{A.12}$$

(Remember that 12.04 per cent was the forward rate over year 2; i.e. $f_2 = 12.04\%$.)

Under what condition will the return from strategy I equal the expected return from strategy II? In other words, under what condition will formula (A.10) equal formula (A.12)?

The two strategies will yield the same expected return only when

$$12.04\% = \text{Spot rate expected over year 2} \tag{A.13}$$

---

[17] Technically, equation (9) is only an approximation due to *Jensen's inequality*. That is, expected values of DEM1,210/1 + Spot rate > DEM1,210/ 1 + Spot rate expected over year 2. However, we ignore this very minor issue in the rest of the analysis.

In other words, if the forward rate equals the expected spot rate, one would expect to earn the same return over the first year whether one

1. invested in a one-year bond, or
2. invested in a two-year bond but sold after one year.

The Expectations Hypothesis

Equation (A.13) seems fairly reasonable, that is, it is reasonable that investors would set interest rates in such a way that the forward rate would equal the spot rate expected by the marketplace a year from now.[18] For example, imagine that individuals in the marketplace do not concern themselves with risk. If the forward rate, f_2, is less than the spot rate expected over year 2, individuals desiring to invest for one year would always buy a one-year bond. That is, our work above shows that an individuals investing in a two-year bond, but planning to sell at the end of one year would expect to earn less than if they simply bought a one-year bond.

Equation (A.13) was stated for the specific case where the forward rate was 12.04 per cent. We can generalize this to:

Expectations Hypothesis:

$$f_2 = \text{Spot rate expected over year 2} \tag{A.14}$$

Equation (A.14) says that the forward rate over the second year is set to the spot rate that people expect to prevail over the second year. This is called the *expectations hypothesis*. It states that investors will set interest rates such that the forward rate over the second year is equal to the one-year spot rate expected over the second year.

Liquidity-Preference Hypothesis

At this point, many students think that equation (A.14) *must* hold. However, note that we developed (A.14) by assuming that investors were risk-neutral. Suppose, alternatively, that investors are adverse to risk.

Which strategy would appear more risky for an individual who wants to invest for one year?

 I. Invest in a one-year bond.
 II. Invest in a two-year bond, but sell at the end of one year.

Strategy (I) has no risk because the investor knows that the rate of return must be r_1. Conversely, strategy (II) has much risk; the final return is dependent on what happens to interest rates.

Because strategy (II) has more risk than strategy (I), no risk-averse investor will choose strategy (II) if both strategies have the same expected return. Risk-averse investors can have no preference for one strategy over the other only when the expected return on strategy (II) is *above* the return on strategy (I). Because the two strategies have the same expected return when f_2 equals the spot rate expected over year 2, strategy (II) can only have a higher rate of return when

Liquidity-Preference Hypothesis:

$$f_2 > \text{Spot rate expected over year 2} \tag{A.15}$$

That is, in order to induce investors to hold the riskier two-year bonds, the market sets the forward rate over the second year to be above the spot rate expected over the second year. Equation (A.15) is called the *liquidity-preference* hypothesis.

We developed the entire discussion by assuming that individuals are planning to invest over one year. We pointed out that for these types of individual, a two-year bond has extra risk because it must be sold prematurely. What about those individuals who want to invest for two years? (We call these people investors with a two-year *time horizon*.)

---

[18] Of course, each individual will have different expectations, so (A.13) cannot hold for all individuals. However, financial economists generally speak of a *consensus* expectation. This is the expectation of the market as a whole.

They could choose one of the following strategies:

III. Buy a two-year zero-coupon bond.
IV. Buy a one-year bond. When the bond matures, they immediately buy another one-year bond.

Strategy (III) has no risk for an investor with a two-year time horizon, because the proceeds to be received at date 2 are known as of date 0. However, strategy (IV) has risk since the spot rate over year 2 is unknown at date 0. It can be shown that risk-averse investors will prefer neither strategy (III) nor strategy (IV) over the other when

$$f_2 < \text{Spot rate expected over year 2} \qquad \text{(A.16)}$$

Note that the assumption of risk aversion gives contrary predictions. Relationship (A.15) holds for a market dominated by investors with a one-year time horizon. Relationship (A.16) holds for a market dominated by investors with a two-year time horizon. Financial economists have generally argued that the time horizon of the typical investor is generally much shorter than the maturity of typical bonds in the marketplace. Thus, economists view (A.15) as the best depiction of equilibrium in the bond market with *risk-averse* investors.

However, do we have a market of risk-neutral investors or risk-averse investors? In other words, can the expectations hypothesis of equation (A.14) or the liquidity-preference hypothesis of equation (A.15) be expected to hold? As we will learn later in this book, economists view investors as being risk-averse for the most part. Yet economists are never satisfied with a casual examination of a theory's assumptions. To them, empirical evidence of a theory's predictions must be the final arbiter.

There has been a great deal of empirical evidence on the term structure of interest rates. Unfortunately (perhaps fortunately for some students), we will not be able to present the evidence in any detail. Suffice it to say that, in our opinion, the evidence supports the liquidity-preference hypothesis over the expectations hypothesis. One simple result might give students the flavour of this research. Consider an individual choosing between one of the following two strategies:

I. Invest in a one-year bond.
II'. Invest in a 20-year bond but sell at the end of one year.

(Strategy (II') is identical to strategy (II), except that a 20-year bond is substituted for a two-year bond.)

The expectations hypothesis states that the expected returns on both strategies are identical. The liquidity-preference hypothesis states that the expected return on strategy (II') should be above the expected return on strategy (I). Though no one knows what returns are actually expected over a particular time period, actual returns from the past may allow us to infer expectations. The results in the USA from January 1926 to now are illuminating. The average yearly return on strategy (I) is 3.7 per cent and 5.4 per cent on strategy (II') over this time period.[19,20] This evidence is generally considered to be consistent with the liquidity-preference hypothesis and inconsistent with the expectations hypothesis.

Concept Questions

- Define the forward rate.
- What is the relationship between the one-year spot rate, the two-year spot rate, and the forward rate over the second year?
- What is the expectations hypothesis?
- What is the liquidity-preference hypothesis?

---

[19] Taken from *Stocks, Bonds, Bills and Inflation Yearbooks,* Chicago: Ibbotson Associates. Ibbotson Associates annually updates work by Roger G. Ibbotson and Rex A. Sinquefield.

[20] It is important to note that strategy (II') does not involve buying a 20-year bond and holding it to maturity. Rather, it consists of buying a 20-year bond and selling it one year later, that is, when it has become a 19-year bond. This round-trip transaction occurs 70 times in the 70-year sample from January 1926 to December 1995.

QUESTIONS AND PROBLEMS

A.1 The appropriate discount rate for cash flows received one year from today is 10 per cent. The appropriate annual discount rate for cash flows received two years from today is 11 per cent.
a. What is the price of a two-year bond, relative to its nominal value, that pays an annual coupon of 6 per cent?
b. What is the yield to maturity of this bond?

CHAPTER
7

Some Other Investment Rules

Chapter 5 examined the relationship between one unit of currency today and one unit of currency in the future. For example, a corporate project generating a set of cash flows can be valued by discounting these flows, an approach called the *net-present-value* (NPV) approach. While we believe that the NPV approach is the best one for evaluating capital budgeting projects, our treatment would be incomplete if we ignored alternative methods. This chapter examines these alternative methods. We first consider the NPV approach as a benchmark. Next we examine three alternatives—payback, accounting rates of return, and internal rate of return.

7.1 Why Use Net Present Value?

Before examining competitors of the NPV approach, we should ask: 'Why consider using NPV in the first place?' Answering this question will put the rest of this chapter in a proper perspective. There are actually a number of arguments justifying the use of NPV, and you may have already seen the detailed one of Chapter 4. We now present one of the simplest justifications through an example.

● **Example**
The Alpha Company is considering investing in a riskless project costing GBP100. The project pays GBP107 at date 1 and has no other cash flows. The managers of the firm might contemplate one of two strategies:

1. Use GBP100 of corporate cash to invest in the project. The GBP107 will be paid as a dividend in one period.
2. Forgo the project and pay the GBP100 of corporate cash as a dividend today.

If strategy 2 is employed, the shareholder might deposit the dividend in the bank for one period. Because the project is riskless and lasts for one period, the shareholder would prefer strategy 1 if the bank interest rate was below 7 per cent. In other words, the shareholder would prefer strategy 1 if strategy 2 produced less than GBP107 by the end of the year. ●

The comparison can easily be handled by NPV analysis. If the interest rate is 6 per cent, the NPV of the project is

$$GBP0.94 = -\,GBP100 + \frac{GBP107}{1.06}$$

Because the NPV is positive, the project should be accepted. Of course, a bank interest rate above 7 per cent would cause the project's NPV to be negative, implying that the project should be rejected.

Thus, our basic point is:

> Accepting positive NPV projects benefits the shareholders.

Although we used the simplest possible example, the results could easily be applied to more plausible situations. If the project lasted for many periods, we would calculate the NPV of the project by discounting all the cash flows. If the project were risky, we could determine the expected return on a stock whose risk is comparable to that of the project. This expected return would serve as the discount rate.

Having shown that NPV is a sensible approach, how can we tell whether alternative approaches are as good as NPV? The key to NPV is its three attributes:

1. *NPV Uses Cash Flows* Cash flows from a project can be used for other corporate purposes (e.g. dividend payments, other capital-budgeting projects or payments of corporate interest). By contrast, earnings are an artificial construct. While earnings are useful to accountants, they should not be used in capital budgeting because they do not represent cash.
2. *NPV Uses All the Cash Flows of the Project* Other approaches ignore cash flows beyond a particular date; beware of these approaches.
3. *NPV Discounts the Cash Flows Properly* Other approaches may ignore the time value of money when handling cash flows. Beware of these approaches as well.

7.2 The Payback Period Rule

Defining the Rule

One of the most popular alternatives to NPV is the **payback period rule**. Here is how the payback period rule works.

Consider a project with an initial investment of −DEM50,000. Cash flows are DEM30,000, DEM20,000 and DEM10,000 in the first three years, respectively. These flows are illustrated in Figure 7.1. A useful way of writing down investments like the preceding is with the notation:

$$(-\text{DEM}50,000, \text{DEM}30,000, \text{DEM}20,000, \text{DEM}10,000)$$

The minus sign in front of the DEM50,000 reminds us that this is a cash outflow for the investor, and the commas between the different numbers indicate that they are received—or if they are cash outflows, that they are paid out—at different times. In this example we are assuming that the cash flows occur one year apart, with the first one occurring the moment we decide to take on the investment.

The firm receives cash flows of DEM30,000 and DEM20,000 in the first two years, which add up to the DEM50,000 original investment. This means that the firm has recovered its investment within two years. In this case two years is the *payback period* of the investment.

FIGURE 7.1   Cash Flows of an Investment Project

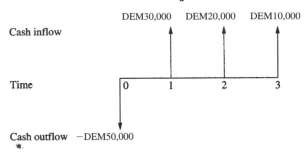

The payback period rule for making investment decisions is simple. A particular cutoff time, say two years, is selected. All investment projects that have payback periods of two years or less are accepted and all of those that pay off in more than two years, if at all, are rejected.

Problems with the Payback Method

There are at least three problems with the payback method. To illustrate the first two problems, we consider the three projects in Table 7.1. All three projects have the same three-year payback period, so they should all be equally attractive—right?

Actually, they are not equally attractive, as can be seen by a comparison of different *pairs* of projects.

TABLE 7.1   Expected Cash Flows for Projects *A* through *C* (DEM)

Year	A	B	C
0	−100	−100	−100
1	20	50	50
2	30	30	30
3	50	20	20
4	60	60	60,000
Payback period (years)	3	3	3

Problem 1   Timing of Cash Flows within the Payback Period
Let us compare project *A* with project *B*. In years 1 through 3, the cash flows of project *A* rise from DEM20 to DEM50 while the cash flows of project *B* fall from DEM50 to DEM20. Because the large cash flow of DEM50 comes earlier with project *B*, its net present value must be higher. Nevertheless, we saw above that the payback periods of the two projects are identical. Thus, a problem with the payback period is that it does not consider the timing of the cash flows within the payback period. This shows that the payback method is inferior to NPV because, as we pointed out earlier, the NPV approach *discounts the cash flows properly.*

Problem 2   Payments after the Payback Period
Now consider projects *B* and *C*, which have identical cash flows within the payback period. However, project *C* is clearly preferred because it has the cash flow of DEM60,000 in the fourth year. Thus, another problem with the payback method is that

it ignores all cash flows occurring after the payback period. This flaw is not present with the NPV approach because, as we pointed out earlier, the NPV approach *uses all the cash flows of the project*. The payback method forces managers to have an artificially short-term orientation, which may lead to decisions not in the shareholders' best interests.

Problem 3: Arbitrary Standard for Payback Period

We do not need to refer to Table 7.1 when considering a third problem with the payback approach. When a firm uses the NPV approach, it can go to the capital market to get the discount rate. There is no comparable guide for choosing the payback period, so the choice is arbitrary to some extent.

Managerial Perspective

The payback rule is often used by large and sophisticated companies when making relatively small decisions. The decision to build a small warehouse, for example, or to pay for a tune-up for a truck is the sort of decision that is often made by lower-level management. Typically a manager might reason that a tune-up would cost, say, DEM200, and if it saved DEM120 each year in reduced fuel costs, it would pay for itself in less than two years. On such a basis the decision would be made.

Although the treasurer of the company might not have made the decision in the same way, the company endorses such decision-making. Why would upper management condone or even encourage such retrograde activity in its employees? One answer would be that it is easy to make decisions using the payback rule. Multiply the tune-up decision into 50 such decisions a month, and the appeal of this simple rule becomes clearer.

Perhaps most important though, the payback rule also has some desirable features for managerial control. Just as important as the investment decision itself is the company's ability to evaluate the manager's decision-making ability. Under the NPV rule, a long time may pass before one may decide whether or not a decision was correct. With the payback rule, we know in two years whether the manager's assessment of the cash flows was correct. It has also been suggested that firms with very good investment opportunities, but no available cash may justifiably use the payback method. For example, the payback method could be used by small, privately held firms with good growth prospects, but limited access to the capital markets. Quick cash recovery may enhance the reinvestment possibilities for such firms.

Notwithstanding all of the preceding rationale, it is not surprising to discover that as the decision grows in importance, which is to say when firms look at bigger projects, the NPV becomes the order of the day. When questions of controlling and evaluating the manager become less important than making the right investment decision, the payback period is used less frequently. For the big-ticket decisions, such as whether or not to buy a big machine, build a factory or acquire a company, the payback rule is seldom used.

Summary of the Payback Period Rule

To summarize, the payback period is not the same as the NPV rule and is therefore conceptually wrong. With its arbitrary cutoff date and its blindness to cash flows after this date, it can lead to some flagrantly foolish decisions if it is used too literally. Nevertheless, because it is so simple, companies often use it as a screen for making the myriad of minor investment decisions they continually face.

Although this means that you should be wary of trying to change rules like the payback period when you encounter them in companies, you should probably be careful not to fall into the sloppy financial thinking they represent. After this course you would do your company a disservice if you ever used the payback period instead of the NPV when you had a choice.

Concept Questions

- List the problems of the payback period rule.
- What are some advantages?

7.3   The Discounted Payback Period Rule

Aware of the pitfalls of the payback approach, some decision makers use a variant called the **discounted payback period rule**. Under this approach, we first discount the cash flows. Then we ask how long it takes for the discounted cash flows to equal the initial investment.

For example, suppose that the discount rate is 10 per cent and the cash flows on a project are given by

$$(-GBP100, GBP50, GBP50, GBP20)$$

This investment has a payback period of two years, because the investment is paid back in that time.

To compute the project's discounted payback period, we first discount each of the cash flows at the 10 per cent rate. In discounted terms, then, the cash flows look like

$$(-GBP100, GBP50/1.1, GBP50/(1.1)^2, GBP20/(1.1)^3)$$

$$= (-GBP100, GBP45.45, GBP41.32, GBP15.03)$$

The discounted payback period of the original investment is simply the payback period for these discounted cash flows. The payback period for the discounted cash flows is slightly less than three years, since the discounted cash flows over the three years are GBP101.80 (GBP45.45 + GBP41.32 + GBP15.03). As long as the cash flows are positive, the discounted payback period will never be smaller than the payback period, because discounting will lower the cash flows.

At first glance the discounted payback may seem like an attractive alternative, but on closer inspection we see that it has some of the same major flaws as the payback. Like payback, discounted payback first requires us to make a somewhat magical choice of an arbitrary cutoff period, and then it ignores all of the cash flows after that date.

If we have already gone to the trouble of discounting the cash flows, any small appeal to simplicity or to managerial control that payback may have, has been lost. We might just as well add up the discounted cash flows and use the NPV to make the decision. Although discounted payback looks a bit like the NPV, it is just a poor compromise between the payback method and the NPV.

7.4   The Average Accounting Return

Defining the Rule

Another attractive and fatally flawed approach to making financial decisions is the **average accounting return (AAR)**. The average accounting return is the average project earnings after taxes and depreciation, divided by the average book value of the investment during its life. In spite of its flaws, the average accounting return method is worth examining because it is used frequently in the real world.

● Example

Consider a company that is evaluating whether or not to buy a store in a newly built mall. The purchase price is DEM500,000. We will assume that the store has an estimated life of five years and will need to be completely scrapped or rebuilt at the end of that time. The projected yearly sales and expense figures are shown in Table 7.2. ●

TABLE 7.2   Projected Yearly Revenue and Costs for Average Accounting Return (DEM)

	Year 1	Year 2	Year 3	Year 4	Year 5
Revenue	433,333	450,000	266,667	200,000	133,333
Expenses	200,000	150,000	100,000	100,000	100,000
Before-tax cash flow	233,333	300,000	166,667	100,000	33,333
Depreciation	100,000	100,000	100,000	100,000	100,000
Earnings before taxes	133,333	200,000	66,667	0	−66,667
Taxes $(T_c = 0.25)$*	33,333	50,000	16,667	0	−16,667
Net income	100,000	150,000	50,000	0	−50,000

$$\text{Average net income} = \frac{(100,000 + 150,000 + 50,000 + 0 - 50,000)}{5} = 50,000$$

$$\text{Average investment} = \frac{500,000 + 0}{2} = 250,000$$

$$\text{AAR} = \frac{\text{DEM}50,000}{\text{DEM}250,000} = 20\%$$

*Corporate tax rate = T_c. We assume for simplicity that 25 per cent is the operative rate. We also assume that accounting and tax depreciation are on an equal five-year straight-line allowance method. We simplify, of course. Different European countries have different tax rules (see Chapter 1). The tax rebate in year 5 of − DEM16,667 occurs if the rest of the firm is profitable. Here, the loss in the project reduces taxes of entire firm.

It is worth looking carefully at Table 7.2. In fact, the first step in any project assessment is a careful look at the projected cash flows. When the store starts up, it is estimated that first-year sales will be DEM433,333 and that, after expenses, the before-tax cash flow will be DEM233,333. After the first year, sales are expected to rise and expenses are expected to fall, resulting in a before-tax cash flow of DEM300,000. After that, competition from other stores and the loss in novelty will drop before-tax cash flow to DEM166,667, DEM100,000 and DEM33,333 respectively, in the next three years.

To compute the AAR on the project, we divide the average net income by the average amount invested. This can be done in three steps.

Step One: Determining Average Net Income   The net income in any year is the net cash flow minus depreciation and taxes. Depreciation is *not* a cash outflow.[1] Rather, it is a charge reflecting the fact that the investment in the store becomes less valuable every year.

---

[1] Depreciation will be treated in more detail in the next chapter.

We assume the project has a useful life of five years, at which time it will be worthless. Because the initial investment is DEM500,000, and because it will be worthless in five years, we will assume that it loses value at the rate of DEM100,000 each year. This steady loss in value of DEM100,000 is called *straight-line depreciation*. We subtract both depreciation and taxes from before-tax cash flow to derive the net income, as shown in Table 7.2. The net income over the five years is DEM100,000 in the first year, DEM150,000 in year 2, DEM50,000 in year 3, zero in year 4 and −DEM50,000 in the last year. The average net income over the life of the project is therefore

Average Net Income:

[DEM100,000 + DEM150,000 + DEM50,000 +
$$\text{DEM0} + (-\text{DEM50,000})]/5 = \text{DEM50,000}$$

Step Two: Determining Average Investment   We stated earlier that, due to depreciation, the investment in the store becomes less valuable every year. Because depreciation is DEM100,000 per year, the value at the end of year zero is DEM500,000, the value at the end of year 1 is DEM400,000 and so on. What is the average value of the investment over the life of the investment?

The mechanical calculation is

Average Investment:

(DEM500,000 + DEM400,000 + DEM300,000 +
$$\text{DEM200,000} + \text{DEM100,000} + \text{DEM0})/6 = \text{DEM250,000} \tag{7.1}$$

We divide by 6 and not 5, because DEM500,000 is what the investment is worth at the beginning of the five years and DEM0 is what it is worth at the beginning of the sixth year. In other words, there are six terms in the parenthesis of equation (7.1).

Step Three: Determining AAR   The average return is simply

$$\text{AAR} = \frac{\text{DEM50,000}}{\text{DEM250,000}} = 20\%$$

If the firm had a targeted accounting rate of return greater than 20 per cent, the project would be rejected, and if its targeted return were less than 20 per cent, it would be accepted.

Average Accounting Return before Tax

Sometimes average accounting return is stated on a before tax basis (the term average return on capital is used). As far as the calculations derived from Table 7.2 are concerned, the top half of the ARR calculation (the numerator) becomes DEM66,667 given by

$$(\text{DEM133,333} + 200,000 + 66,667 + 0 - 66,667)/5$$

Of course, the bottom half of the calculation remains DEM250,000 giving an ARR (before tax) of 26.67%.

Analysing the Average Accounting Return Method

By now you should be able to see what is wrong with the AAR method of making investment decisions.

The first, most important flaw in the AAR method is that it does not use the right raw materials. It uses the net income figures and the book value of the investment (from the accountant's books) to figure out whether to take the investment. Conversely, the NPV rule *uses cash flows.*

Second, AAR takes no account of timing. In the previous example, the AAR would have been the same if the income in the first year had swapped places with the income in the last year. However, delaying the DEM133,333 pre-tax (DEM100,000 net of tax) inflow for five years would have made the investment less attractive under the NPV rule as well as by the common sense of the time value of money. That is, the NPV approach *discounts properly.*

Third, just as the payback period requires an arbitrary choice of a cutoff date, the AAR method offers no guidance on what the right targeted rate of return should be. It could be the discount rate in the market. But then again, because the AAR method is not the same as the present value method, it is not obvious that this would be the right choice.

Like the payback method, the AAR (and variations of it) is frequently used as a 'backup' to discounted cash flow methods. Perhaps this is so because it is easy to calculate and uses accounting numbers readily available from the firm's accounting system.

Concept Questions

- What are the three steps in calculating AAR?
- What are some flaws with the AAR approach?

7.5   The Internal Rate of Return

Now we come to the most important alternative to the NPV approach, the internal rate of return, universally known as the IRR. The IRR is about as close as you can get to the NPV without actually being the NPV. The basic rationale behind the IRR is that it tries to find a single number that summarizes the merits of a project. That number does not depend on the interest rate that prevails in the capital market. That is why it is called the internal rate of return; the number is internal or intrinsic to the project and does not depend on anything except the cash flows of the project.

For example, consider the simple project ($-$GBP100, GBP110) in Figure 7.2. For a given rate, the net present value of this project can be described as

$$\text{NPV} = -\text{GBP}100 + \frac{\text{GBP}110}{1 + r} \qquad (7.2)$$

where r is the discount rate.

What must the discount rate be to make the NPV of the project equal to zero?

We begin by using an arbitrary discount rate of 0.08, which yields

$$\text{GBP}1.85 = -\text{GBP}100 + \frac{\text{GBP}110}{1.08} \qquad (7.3)$$

FIGURE 7.2   **Cash Flows for a Simple Project**

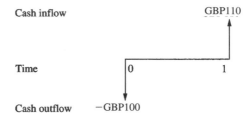

Since the NPV in equation (7.3) is positive, we now try a higher discount rate, say, 0.12. This yields

$$-\text{GBP}1.79 = -\text{GBP}100 + \frac{\text{GBP}110}{1.12} \qquad (7.4)$$

Since the NPV in equation (7.4) is negative, we lower the discount rate to, say, 0.10. This yields

$$0 = -\text{GBP}100 + \frac{\text{GBP}110}{1.10} \qquad (7.5)$$

This trial-and-error procedure tells us that the NPV of the project is zero when r equals 10 per cent.[2] Thus, we say that 10 per cent is the project's **internal rate of return** (IRR). In general, the IRR is the rate that causes the NPV of the project to be zero. The implication of this exercise is very simple. The firm should be equally willing to accept or reject the project if the discount rate is 10 per cent. The firm should accept the project if the discount rate is below 10 per cent. The firm should reject the project if the discount rate is above 10 per cent.

The general investment rule is clear:

> Accept the project if IRR is greater than the discount rate. Reject the project if IRR is less than the discount rate.

We refer to this as the **basic IRR rule**. Now we can try the more complicated example in Figure 7.3.

As we did in equations (7.3) to (7.5), we use trial and error to calculate the internal rate of return. We try 20 per cent and 30 per cent, yielding

FIGURE 7.3   **Cash Flows for a More Complex Project**

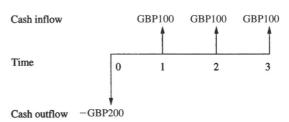

---

[2] Of course, we could have directly solved for r in equation (7.2) after setting NPV equal to zero. However, with a long series of cash flows, one cannot generally directly solve for r. Instead, one is forced to use a trial-and-error method similar to that in (7.3), (7.4) and (7.5).

Discount rate	NPV
20%	GBP10.65
30	−18.39

After much more trial and error, we find that the NPV of the project is zero when the discount rate is 23.37 per cent. Thus, the IRR is 23.37 per cent. With a 20 per cent discount rate the NPV is positive and we would accept it. However, if the discount rate were 30 per cent, we would reject it.

Algebraically, IRR is the unknown in the following equation:[3]

$$0 = -\text{GBP}200 + \frac{\text{GBP}100}{1 + \text{IRR}} + \frac{\text{GBP}100}{(1 + \text{IRR})^2} + \frac{\text{GBP}100}{(1 + \text{IRR})^3}$$

Figure 7.4 illustrates what it means to find the IRR for a project. The figure plots the NPV as a function of the discount rate. The curve crosses the horizontal axis at the IRR of 23.37 per cent because this is where the NPV equals zero.

FIGURE 7.4   Net Present Value (NPV) and Discount Rates for a More Complex Project

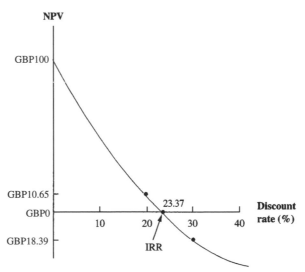

The NPV is positive for discount rates below the IRR and negative for discount rates above the IRR.

It should also be clear that the NPV is positive for discount rates below the IRR and negative for discount rates above the IRR. This means that if we accept projects like this one when the discount rate is less than the IRR, we will be accepting positive NPV projects. Thus, the IRR rule will coincide exactly with the NPV rule.

If this were all there were to it, the IRR rule would always coincide with the NPV rule. This would be a wonderful discovery because it would mean that just by

---

[3] One can derive the IRR directly for a problem with an initial outflow and either one or two subsequent inflows. In the case of two subsequent inflows, the quadratic formula is needed. In general, however, only trial and error will work for an outflow and three or more subsequent inflows. Hand calculators calculate IRR by trial and error, though at lightning speed.

computing the IRR for a project we would be able to tell where it ranks among all of the projects we are considering. For example, if the IRR rule really works, a project with an IRR of 20 per cent will always be at least as good as one with an IRR of 15 per cent.

But the world of finance is not so kind. Unfortunately, the IRR rule and the NPV rule are the same only for simple examples like the ones above. Several problems with the IRR occur in more complicated situations.

Concept Question

• How does one calculate the IRR of a project?

7.6   Problems with the IRR Approach

Definition of Independent and Mutually Exclusive Projects

An **independent project** is one whose acceptance or rejection is independent of the acceptance or rejection of other projects. For example, imagine that McDonald's is considering putting a hamburger outlet on a remote island. Acceptance or rejection of this unit is likely to be unrelated to the acceptance or rejection of any other restaurant in their system. The remoteness of the outlet in question ensures that it will not pull sales away from other outlets.

Now consider the other extreme, **mutually exclusive investments**. What does it mean for two projects, A and B, to be mutually exclusive? You can accept A or you can accept B or you can reject both of them, but you cannot accept both of them. For example, A might be a decision to build an apartment house on a corner lot that you own, and B might be a decision to build a movie theatre on the same lot.

We now present two general problems with the IRR approach that affect both independent and mutually exclusive projects. Next, we deal with two problems affecting mutually exclusive projects only.

Two General Problems Affecting Both Independent and Mutually Exclusive Projects

We begin our discussion with project A, which has the following cash flows:

$$(-DEM100, DEM130)$$

The IRR for project A is 30 per cent. Table 7.3 provides other relevant information on

TABLE 7.3   The Internal Rate of Return and Net Present Value

	Project A			Project B			Project C		
Dates	*0*	*1*	*2*	*0*	*1*	*2*	*0*	*1*	*2*
Cash flows	−DEM100	DEM130		DEM100	−DEM130		−DEM100	DEM230	−DEM132
IRR		30%			30%		10%	and	20%
NPV @ 10%		DEM18.2			−DEM18.2			0	
Accept if market rate		< 30%			> 30%		> 10%	but	< 20%
Financing or investing		Investing			Financing			Mixture	

FIGURE 7.5   **Net Present Value and Discount Rates for Projects *A*, *B*, and *C***

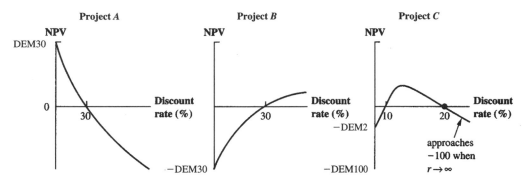

Project *A* has a cash outflow at date 0 followed by a cash inflow at date 1. Its NPV is negatively related to the discount rate.
Project *B* has a cash inflow at date 0 followed by a cash outflow at date 1. Its NPV is positively related to the discount rate.
Project *C* has two changes of sign in its cash flows. It has an outflow at date 0, an inflow at date 1 and an outflow at date 2. Projects with more than one change of sign can have multiple rates of return.

the project. The relationship between NPV and the discount rate is shown for this project in Figure 7.5. As you can see, the NPV declines as the discount rate rises.

Problem 1: Investing or Financing?

Now consider project *B*, with cash flows of

$$(\text{DEM}100, -\text{DEM}130)$$

These cash flows are exactly the reverse of the flows for project *A*. In project *B*, the firm receives funds first and then pays out funds later. While unusual, projects of this type do exist. For example, consider a corporation conducting a seminar where the participants pay in advance. Because large expenses are frequently incurred at the seminar date, cash inflows precede cash outflows.

Consider our trial-and-error method to calculate IRR:

$$-\text{DEM}4 = +\text{DEM}100 - \frac{\text{DEM}130}{1.25}$$

$$\text{DEM}0 = +\text{DEM}100 - \frac{\text{DEM}130}{1.30}$$

$$\text{DEM}3.70 = +\text{DEM}100 - \frac{\text{DEM}130}{1.35}$$

As with project *A*, the internal rate of return is 30 per cent. However, notice that the net present value is negative when the discount rate is *below* 30 per cent. Conversely, the net present value is positive when the discount rate is above 30 per cent. The decision rule is exactly the opposite of our previous result. For this type of a project, the rule is

Accept the project when IRR is less than the discount rate. Reject the project when IRR is greater than the discount rate.

This unusual decision rule follows from the graph of project *B* in Figure 7.5. The curve is upward sloping, implying that NPV is *positively* related to the discount rate.

The graph makes intuitive sense. Suppose that the firm wants to obtain DEM100 immediately. It can either (1) conduct project *B* or (2) borrow DEM100 from a bank. Thus, the project is actually a substitute for borrowing. In fact, because the IRR is 30 per cent, taking on project *B* is tantamount to borrowing at 30 per cent. If the firm can borrow from a bank at, say, only 25 per cent, it should reject the project. However, if a firm can only borrow from a bank at, say, 35 per cent, it should accept the project. Thus, project *B* will be accepted if and only if the discount rate is *above* the IRR.[4]

This should be contrasted with project A. If the firm has DEM100 of cash to invest, it can either (1) conduct project *A* or (2) lend DEM100 to the bank. The project is actually a substitute for lending. In fact, because the IRR is 30 per cent, taking on project *A* is tantamount to lending at 30 per cent. The firm should accept project *A* if the lending rate is below 30 per cent. Conversely, the firm should reject project *A* if the lending rate is above 30 per cent.

Because the firm initially pays out money with project *A*, but initially receives money with project *B*, we refer to project *A* as an investing-type project and project *B* as a financing-type project. Investing-type projects are the norm. Because the IRR rule is reversed for a financing-type project, we view this type of project as a problem—unless it is understood properly.

Problem 2: Multiple Rates of Return
Suppose the cash flows from a project are

$$(-DEM100, DEM230, -DEM132)$$

Because this project has a negative cash flow, a positive cash flow and another negative cash flow, we say that the project's cash flows exhibit two changes of sign or 'flip-flops.' While this pattern of cash flows might look a bit strange at first, many projects require outflows of cash after some receiving inflows. An example would be a strip-mining project. The first stage in such a project is the initial investment in excavating the mine. Profits from operating the mine are received in the second stage. The third stage involves a further investment to reclaim the land and satisfy the requirements of environmental-protection legislation. Cash flows are negative at this stage.

Projects financed by lease arrangements also produce negative cash flows followed by positive ones. We study leasing carefully in a later chapter, but for now we will give you a hint. Using leases for financing can sometimes bring substantial tax advantages. These advantages are often sufficient to make an otherwise bad investment have positive cash flows following an initial outlay. But after a while the tax advantages decline or run out. The cash flows turn negative when this occurs.

It is easy to verify that this project has not one but two IRRs, 10 per cent and 20 percent.[5] In a case like this, the IRR does not make any sense. What IRR are we to use,

---

[4] This paragraph implicitly assumes that the cash flows of the project are risk-free. In this way, we can treat the borrowing rate as the discount rate for a firm needing DEM100. With risky cash flows, another discount rate would be chosen. However, the intuition behind the decision to accept when IRR is less than the discount rate would still apply.

[5] The calculations are

$$-DEM100 + DEM230/1.1 - DEM132/(1.1)^2$$
$$0 = -DEM100 + DEM209.09 - DEM109.09$$

and

$$-DEM100 + DEM230/1.2 - DEM132/(1.2)^2$$
$$0 = -DEM100 + DEM191.67 - DEM91.67$$

Thus, we have multiple rates of return.

10 per cent or 20 per cent? Because there is no good reason to use one over the other, IRR simply cannot be used here.

Of course, we should not feel too worried about multiple rates of return. After all, we can always fall back on NPV. Figure 7.5 plots the NPV for this project *C* as a function of the different discount rates. As it shows, the NPV is zero at both 10 per cent and 20 per cent. Furthermore, the NPV is positive for discount rates between 10 per cent and 20 per cent and negative outside of this range.

This example generates multiple internal rates of return because both an inflow and an outflow occur after the initial investment. In general, these flip-flops or changes in sign produce multiple IRRs. In theory, a cash flow stream with *M* changes in sign can have up to *M* positive internal rates of return.[6] As we pointed out, projects whose cash flows change sign repeatedly can occur in the real world.

Are We Ever Safe from the Multiple-IRR Problem?   If the first cash flow for a project is negative—because it is the initial investment—and if all of the remaining flows are positive, there can be only a single, unique IRR, no matter how many periods the project lasts. This is easy to understand by using the concept of the time value of money. For example, it is easy to verify that project *A* in Table 7.3 has an IRR of 30 per cent, because using a 30 per cent discount rate gives

$$NPV = -DEM100 + DEM130/(1.3)$$
$$= 0$$

How do we know that this is the only IRR? Suppose that we were to try a discount rate greater than 30 per cent. In computing the NPV, changing the discount rate does not change the value of the initial cash flow of −DEM100 because that cash flow is not discounted. But raising the discount rate can only lower the present value of the future cash flows. In other words, because the NPV is zero at 30 per cent, any increase in the rate will push the NPV into the negative range. Similarly, if we try a discount rate of less than 30 per cent, the overall NPV of the project will be positive. Though this example has only one positive flow, the above reasoning still implies a single, unique IRR if there are many inflows (but no outflows) after the initial investment.

If the initial cash flow is positive—and if all of the remaining flows are negative—there can only be a single, unique IRR. This result follows from reasoning similar to that above. Both these cases have only one change of sign or flip-flop in the cash flows. Thus, we are safe from multiple IRRs whenever there is only one sign change in the cash flows.

---

[6] Those of you who are steeped in algebra might have recognized that finding the IRR is like finding the root of a polynomial equation. For a project with cash flows of $(C_0, \ldots, C_T)$, the formula for computing the IRR requires us to find the interest rate, *r*, that makes
$$NPV = C_0 + C_1/(1 + r) + \cdots + C_T/(1 + r)^T = 0$$
If we let the symbol *x* stand for the discount factor,
$$x = 1/(1 + r)$$
then the formula for the IRR becomes
$$NPV = C_0 + C_1 x + C_2 x^2 + \cdots + C_T x^T = 0$$
Finding the IRR, then, is the same as finding the roots of this polynomial equation. If a particular value x^* is a root of the equation, then, because
$$x = 1/(1 + r)$$
it follows that there is an associated IRR:
$$r^* = (1/x^*) - 1$$
From the theory of polynomials, it is well known that an *n*th order polynomial has *n* roots. Each such root that is positive and less than 1 can have a sensible IRR associated with it. Applying Descartes' rule of signs gives the result that a stream of *n* cash flows can have up to *M* positive IRRs, where *M* is the number of changes of sign for the cash flows.

General Rules   The following chart summarizes our rules:[7]

Flows	*Number of IRRs*	*IRR criterion*	*NPV criterion*
First cash flow is negative and all remaining cash flows are positive	1	Accept if IRR > r Reject if IRR < r	Accept if NPV > 0 Reject if NPV < 0
First cash flow is positive and all remaining cash flows are negative	1	Accept if IRR < r Reject if IRR > r	Accept if NPV > 0 Reject if NPV < 0
Some cash flows after first are positive and some cash flows after first are negative	May be more than 1	No valid IRR	Accept if NPV > 0 Reject if NPV < 0

Note that the NPV criterion is the same for each of the three cases. In other words, NPV analysis is always appropriate. Conversely, the IRR can be used only in certain cases. When it comes to NPV, the preacher's words, 'You just can't lose with the stuff I use', clearly apply.

Problems Specific to Mutually Exclusive Projects

As mentioned earlier, two or more projects are mutually exclusive if the firm can, at most, accept only one of them. We now present two problems dealing with the application of the IRR approach to mutually exclusive projects. These two problems are quite similar, though logically distinct.

The Scale Problem

A professor we know motivates class discussions on this topic with the statement: 'Students, I am prepared to let one of you choose between two mutually exclusive 'business' propositions. Opportunity 1—You give me CHF1 now and I'll give you CHF1.50 back at the end of the class period. Opportunity 2—You give me CHF10 and I'll give you CHF11 back at the end of the class period. You can only choose one of the two opportunities. And you cannot choose either opportunity more than once. I'll pick the first volunteer.'

Which would you choose? The correct answer is opportunity 2.[8] To see this, look at the following chart:

	Cash flow at beginning of class	*Cash flow at end of class (90 minutes later)*	*NPV*[9]	*IRR*
Opportunity 1	−CHF1	+CHF1.50	CHF0.50	50%
Opportunity 2	−10	+11.00	1.00	10

---

[7] IRR stands for internal rate of return, NPV stands for net present value and r stands for discount rate.

[8] The professor uses real money here. Though many students have done poorly on the professor's exams over the years, no student ever chose opportunity 1. The professor claims that his students are 'money players'.

[9] We assume a zero rate of interest because his class lasted only 90 minutes. It just seemed like a lot longer.

As we have stressed earlier in the text, one should choose the opportunity with the highest NPV. This is opportunity 2 in the example. Or, as one of the professor's students explained it: 'I'm bigger than the professor, so I know I'll get my money back. And I have CHF10 in my pocket right now so I can choose either opportunity. At the end of the class, I'll be able to play four rounds of my favourite electronic game with opportunity 2 and still have my original investment, safe and sound.[10] The profit on opportunity 1 buys only two rounds.'

We believe that this business proposition illustrates a defect with the internal rate of return criterion. The basic IRR rule says take opportunity 1, because the IRR is 50 per cent. The IRR is only 10 per cent for opportunity 2.

Where does IRR go wrong? The problem with IRR is that it ignores issues of scale. While opportunity 1 has a greater IRR, the investment is much smaller. In other words, the high percentage return on opportunity 1 is more than offset by the ability to earn at least a decent return[11] on a much bigger investment under opportunity 2.

Since IRR seems to be misguided here, can we adjust or correct it? We illustrate how in the next example.

● Example

Stanley Jaffe and Sherry Lansing have just purchased the rights to *Corporate Finance Europe: The Motion Picture*.[12] They will produce this major motion picture on either a small budget or a big budget. The estimated cash flows are

	Cash flow at date 0	Cash flow at date 1	NPV @ 25%	IRR
Small budget	−USD10 million	USD40 million	USD22 million	300%
Large budget	−25 million	65 million	27 million	160

Because of high risk, a 25 per cent discount rate is considered appropriate. Sherry wants to adopt the large budget because the NPV is higher. Stanley wants to adopt the small budget because the IRR is higher. Who is right? ●

For the reasons espoused in the classroom example above, NPV is correct. Hence, Sherry is right. However, Stanley is very stubborn where IRR is concerned. How can Sherry justify the large budget to Stanley using the IRR approach?

This is where incremental IRR comes in. She calculates the incremental cash flows from choosing the large budget instead of the small budget as

	Cash flow at date 0 (in USD million)	Cash flow at date 1 (in USD million)
Incremental cash flows from choosing large budget instead of small budget	−25 − (−10) = −15	65 − 40 = 25

This chart shows that the incremental cash flows are −USD15 million at date 0 and

---

[10] At press time for this text, electronic games cost USD0.25 apiece.

[11] A 10 per cent return is more than decent over a 90 minute interval!

[12] We use dollars here to reflect the nature of the Hollywood potential of this proposition. Hollywood thinks dollars.

USD25 million at date 1. Sherry calculates incremental IRR as

Formula for Calculating the Incremental IRR:

$$0 = -\text{USD15 million} + \frac{\text{USD25 million}}{1 + \text{IRR}}$$

IRR equals 66.67 per cent in this equation. Sherry says that the **incremental IRR** is 66.67 per cent. Incremental IRR is the IRR on the incremental investment from choosing the large project instead of the small project.

In addition, we can calculate the NPV of the incremental cash flows:

NPV of Incremental Cash Flows:

$$-\text{USD15 million} + \frac{\text{USD25 million}}{1.25} = \text{USD5 million}$$

We know the small-budget picture would be acceptable as an independent project since its NPV is positive. We want to know whether it is beneficial to invest an additional USD15 million in order to make the large-budget picture instead of the small-budget picture. In other words, is it beneficial to invest an additional USD15 million in order to receive an additional USD25 million next year? First, the above calculations show the NPV on the incremental investment to be positive. Second, the incremental IRR of 66.67 per cent is higher than the discount rate of 25 per cent. For both reasons, the incremental investment can be justified. The second reason is what Stanley needed to hear to be convinced. Hence, the large-budget movie should be made.

In review, we can handle this example (or any mutually exclusive example) in one of three ways:

1. Compare the NPVs of the two choices. The NPV of the large-budget picture is greater than the NPV of the small-budget picture, that is, USD27 million is greater than USD22 million.
2. Compare the incremental NPV from making the large-budget picture instead of the small-budget picture. Because incremental NPV equals USD5 million, we choose the large-budget picture.
3. Compare the incremental IRR to the discount rate. Because the incremental IRR is 66.67 per cent and the discount rate is 25 per cent, we take the large-budget picture.

All three approaches always give the same decision. However, we must not compare the IRRs of the two pictures. If we did we would make the wrong choice, that is, we would accept the small-budget picture.

One final note here. Students often ask which project should be subtracted from the other in calculating incremental flows. Notice that we are subtracting the smaller project's cash flows from the bigger project's cash flows. This leaves an outflow at date 0. We then use the basic IRR rule on the incremental flows.[13]

---

[13] Alternatively, we could have subtracted the larger project's cash flows from the smaller project's cash flows. This would have left an inflow at date 0, making it necessary to use the IRR rule for financing situations. This would work but we find it more confusing.

The Timing Problem

Below we illustrate another, but very similar, problem with using the IRR approach to evaluate mutually exclusive projects.

● Example

Suppose that the Kaufold Company has two alternative uses for a warehouse. It can store toxic waste containers (investment *A*) or electronic equipment (investment *B*). The cash flows are as follows:

					NPV			
Year:	*0*	*1*	*2*	*3*	*@ 0%*	*@ 10%*	*@ 15%*	*IRR*
Investment *A*	−GBP10,000	GBP10,000	GBP1,000	GBP1,000	GBP2,000	GBP669	GBP109	16.04%
Investment *B*	−10,000	1,000	1,000	12,000	4,000	751	−484	12.94

We find that the NPV of investment *B* is higher with low discount rates, and the NPV of investment *A* is higher with high discount rates. This is not surprising if you look closely at the cash flow patterns. The cash flows of *A* occur early, whereas the cash flows of B occur later. If we assume a high discount rate, we favour investment *A* because we are implicitly assuming that the early cash flow (for example, GBP10,000 in year 1) can be reinvested at that rate. Because most of investment *B*'s cash flows occur in year 3, *B*'s value is relatively high with low discount rates. ●

The patterns of cash flow for both projects appear in Figure 7.6. Project *A* has an NPV of GBP2,000 at a discount rate of zero. This is calculated by simply adding up the cash flows without discounting them. Project *B* has an NPV of GBP4,000 at the zero rate. However, the NPV of project *B* declines more rapidly as the discount rate increases than does the NPV of project *A*. As we mentioned above, this occurs because the cash flows of *B* occur later. Both projects have the same NPV at a discount rate of 10.55 per cent. The IRR for a project is the rate at which the NPV equals zero. Because the NPV of *B* declines more rapidly, *B* actually has a lower IRR.

FIGURE 7.6   Net Present Value and the Internal Rate of Return for Mutually Exclusive Projects

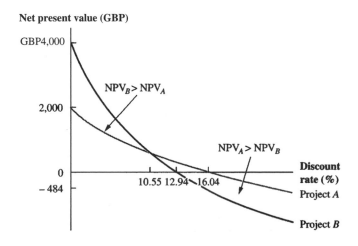

As with the movie example presented above, we can select the better project with one of three different methods:

1. *Compare NPVs of the Two Projects*   Figure 7.6 aids our decision. If the discount rate is below 10.55 per cent, one should choose project *B* because *B* has a higher NPV. If the rate is above 10.55 per cent, one should choose project *A* because *A* has a higher NPV.

2. *Compare Incremental IRR to Discount Rate*   The above method employed NPV. Another way of determining that *B* is a better project is to subtract the cash flows of *A* from the cash flows of *B* and then to calculate the IRR. This is the incremental IRR approach we spoke of earlier.

The incremental cash flows are

**NPV of Incremental
Cash Flows**

Year	0	1	2	3	Incremental IRR	@ 0%	@ 10%	@ 15%
B − A	0	−GBP9,000	0	GBP11,000	10.55%	GBP2,000	GBP83	−GBP593

This chart shows that the incremental IRR is 10.55 per cent. In other words, the NPV on the incremental investment is zero when the discount rate is 10.55 per cent. Thus, if the relevant discount rate is below 10.55 per cent, project *B* is preferred to project *A*. If the relevant discount rate is above 10.55 per cent, project *A* is preferred to project *B*.[14]

3. *Calculate NPV on Incremental Cash Flows*   Finally, one could calculate the NPV on the incremental cash flows. The chart that appears with the previous method displays these NPVs. We find that the incremental NPV is positive when the discount rate is either 0 per cent or 10 per cent. The incremental NPV is negative if the discount rate is 15 per cent. If the NPV is positive on the incremental flows, one should choose *B*. If the NPV is negative, one should choose *A*.

In summary, the same decision is reached whether one (*a*) compares the NPVs of the two projects, (*b*) compares the incremental IRR to the relevant discount rate or (*c*) examines the NPV of the incremental cash flows. However, as mentioned earlier, one should not compare the IRR of project *A* with the IRR of project *B*.

We suggested earlier that one should subtract the cash flows of the smaller project from the cash flows of the bigger project. What do we do here since the two projects have the same initial investment? Our suggestion in this case is to perform the subtraction so that the first non-zero cash flow is negative. In the Kaufold Company example, we achieved this by subtracting *A* from *B*. In this way, we can still use the basic IRR rule for evaluating cash flows.

The above examples illustrate problems with the IRR approach in evaluating

---

[14] In this example, we first showed that the NPVs of the two projects are equal when the discount rate is 10.55 per cent. We next showed that the incremental IRR is also 10.55 per cent. This is not a coincidence; this equality must always hold. The incremental IRR is the rate that causes the incremental cash flows to have zero NPV. The incremental cash flows have zero NPV when the two projects have the same NPV.

mutually exclusive projects. Both the professor–student example and the motion-picture example illustrate the problem that arises when mutually exclusive projects have different initial investments. The Kaufold Company example illustrates the problem that arises when mutually exclusive projects have different cash flow timing. When working with mutually exclusive projects, it is not necessary to determine whether it is the scale problem or the timing problem that exists. Very likely both occur in any real-world situation. Instead, the practitioner should simply use either an incremental IRR or an NPV approach.

Redeeming Qualities of the IRR

The IRR probably survives because it fills a need that the NPV does not. People seem to want a rule that summarizes the information about a project in a single rate of return. This single rate provides people with a simple way of discussing projects. For example, one manager in a firm might say to another, 'Remodelling the clerical wing has a 20 per cent IRR'.

To their credit, however, companies that employ the IRR approach seem to understand its deficiencies. For example, companies frequently restrict managerial projections of cash flows to be negative at the beginning and strictly positive later. Perhaps, then, the ability of the IRR approach to capture a complex investment project in a single number and the ease of communicating that number explain the survival of the IRR.

A Test

To test your knowledge, consider the following two statements:

1. You must know the discount rate to compute the NPV of a project but you compute the IRR without referring to the discount rate.
2. Hence, the IRR rule is easier to apply than the NPV rule because you don't use the discount rate when applying IRR.

The first statement is true. The discount rate is needed to *compute* NPV. The IRR is *computed* by solving for the rate where the NPV is zero. No mention is made of the discount rate in the mere computation. However, the second statement is false. In order to *apply* IRR, you must compare the internal rate of return with the discount rate. Thus, the discount rate is needed for making a decision under either the NPV or IRR approach.

Concept Questions

- What is the difference between independent projects and mutually exclusive projects?
- What are two problems with the IRR approach that apply to both independent and mutually exclusive projects?
- What are two additional problems applying only to mutually exclusive projects?

7.7 The Profitability Index

Another method that is used to evaluate projects is called the **profitability index.** It is the ratio of the present value of the future expected cash flows after initial investment divided by the amount of the initial investment. The profitability index can be represented as

$$\begin{array}{c} \text{Profitability} \\ \text{index} \\ \text{(PI)} \end{array} = \frac{\text{PV of cash flows } \textit{subsequent} \text{ to initial investment}}{\text{Initial investment}}$$

● **Example**

Brown Smith plc, applies a 12 per cent cost of capital to two investment opportunities.

Project	Cash flows (GBP000,000)			PV @12% of cash flows subsequent to initial investment (GBP000,000)	Profitability index	NPV @ 12% (GBP000,000)
	C_0	C_1	C_2			
1	−20	70	10	70.5	3.53	50.5
2	−10	15	40	45.3	4.53	35.3

For example, the profitability index is calculated for project 1 as follows. The present value of the cash flows *after* the initial investment are

$$\text{GBP}70.5 = \text{GBP}70/1.12 + \text{GBP}10/(1.12)^2 \tag{7.6}$$

The profitability index is calculated by dividing the result of equation (7.6) by the initial investment of GBP20. This yields

$$3.53 = \text{GBP}70.5/\text{GBP}20$$

We consider three possibilities:

1. *Independent Projects*   We first assume that we have two independent projects. According to the NPV criterion, both projects should be accepted since NPV is positive in each case. The NPV is positive whenever the profitability index (PI) is greater than one. Thus, the *PI decision rule* is

   > Accept an independent project if PI > 1.
   > Reject if PI < 1.

2. *Mutually Exclusive Projects*   Let us assume that you can now only accept one project. NPV analysis says accept project 1 because this project has the bigger NPV. Because project 2 has the higher PI, the profitability index leads to the wrong selection.

   The problem with the profitability index for mutually exclusive projects is the same as the scale problem with the IRR that we mentioned earlier. Project 2 is smaller than project 1. Because the PI is a ratio, this index misses the fact that project 1 has a larger investment than project 2 has. Thus, like IRR, PI ignores differences of scale for mutually exclusive projects.

   However, like IRR, the flaw with the PI approach can be corrected using incremental analysis. We write the incremental cash flows after subtracting project 2 from project 1 as follows:

Project	Cash flows (GBP000,000)			PV @ 12% of cash flows subsequent to initial investment (GBP000,000)	Profit-ability index	NPV @ 12% (GBP000,000)
	C_0	C_1	C_2			
1 − 2	−10	55	−30	25.2	2.52	15.2

Because the profitability index on the incremental cash flows is greater than 1.0, we should choose the bigger project, that is, project 1. This is the same decision we get with the NPV approach.

3. *Capital Rationing.* The two cases above implicitly assumed that the firm could always attract enough capital to make any profitable investments. Now we consider the case when a firm does not have enough capital to fund all positive NPV projects. This is the case of **capital rationing.**

Imagine that the firm has a third project, as well as the first two. Project 3 has the following cash flows:

Project	Cash flows (GBP000,000)			PV @ 12% of cash flows subsequent to initial investment (GBP000,000)	Profit-ability index	NPV @ 12% (GBP000,000)
	C_0	C_1	C_2			
3	−10	−5	60	43.4	4.34	33.4

Further, imagine that (*a*) the projects of Brown Smith plc, are independent, but (*b*) the firm has only GBP20 million to invest. Because project 1 has an initial investment of GBP20 million, the firm cannot select both this project and another one. Conversely, because projects 2 and 3 have initial investments of GBP10 million each, both these projects can be chosen. In other words, the cash constraint forces the firm to choose either project 1 or projects 2 and 3.

What should the firm do? Individually, projects 2 and 3 have lower NPVs than project 1 has. However, when the NPVs of projects 2 and 3 are added together, they are higher than the NPV of project 1. Thus, common sense dictates that projects 2 and 3 shall be accepted.

What does our conclusion have to say about the NPV rule or the PI rule? In the case of limited funds, we cannot rank projects according to their NPVs. Instead, we should rank them according to the ratio of present value to initial investment. This is the PI rule. Both project 2 and project 3 have higher PI ratios than does project 1. Thus, they should be ranked ahead of project 1 when capital is rationed.

The usefulness of the profitability index under capital rationing can be explained in military terms. The Pentagon in the USA speaks highly of a weapon with a lot of 'bang for the buck'. In capital budgeting, the profitability index measures the bang (the dollar return) for the buck invested. Hence, it is useful for capital rationing.

It should be noted that the profitability index does not work if funds are also limited beyond the initial time period. For example, if heavy cash outflows elsewhere in the firm were to occur at date 1, project 3 might need to be rejected. In other words, the profitability index cannot handle capital rationing over multiple time periods.

Concept Questions

- How does one calculate a project's profitability index?
- How is the profitability index applied to independent projects, mutually exclusive projects and situations of capital rationing?

7.8   The Practice of Capital Budgeting

Not all firms use capital budgeting procedures based on discounted cash flows. Some firms use the payback method, and others use the accounting-rate-of-return method. In numerous recent surveys in Western Europe and the USA (but not in Japan), the most frequently used capital budgeting technique is the discounted cash flow method. The next most widely used capital budgeting technique is the payback method with the average-accounting-return method next in importance.

The use of quantitative techniques in capital budgeting varies with the industry. As one would imagine, firms that are better able to precisely estimate cash flows are more likely to use NPV. For example, estimation of cash flow in certain aspects of the oil business is quite feasible. Because of this, energy-related firms were among the first to use NPV analysis. Conversely, the cash flows in the motion-picture business are very hard to project. The grosses of the great hits like *Rocky*, *Star Wars*, *ET,* and *Fatal Attraction* were far, far greater than anyone imagined. The big failures like *Heaven's Gate* and *Waterworld* were unexpected as well. Because of this, NPV analysis receives relatively minor weight in the movie business.

How does Hollywood perform capital budgeting? The information that a studio uses to accept or reject a movie idea comes from the pitch. An independent movie producer schedules an extremely brief meeting with a studio to pitch his or her idea for a movie. Consider the following four paragraphs of quotes concerning the pitch from the thoroughly delightful book, *Reel Power*:[15]

> 'They [studio executives] don't want to know too much', says Ron Simpson. 'They want to know concept. . . . They want to know what the three-liner is, because they want it to suggest the ad campaign. They want a title. . . . They don't want to hear any esoterica. And if the meeting lasts more than five minutes, they're probably not going to do the project'.

> 'A guy comes in and says this is my idea: "*Jaws* on a spaceship"', says writer Clay Frohman (*Under Fire*). 'And they say, "Brilliant, fantastic". Becomes *Alien*. That is *Jaws* on a spaceship, ultimately. . . . And that's it. That's all they want to hear. Their attitude is "Don't confuse us with the details of the story".'

> . . . Some high-concept stories are more appealing to the studios than others. The ideas liked best are sufficiently original that the audience will not feel it has already seen the movie, yet similar enough to past hits to reassure executives wary of anything too far-out. Thus, the frequently used shorthand: It's *Flashdance* in the country (*Footloose*) or *High Noon* in outer space (*Outland*).

> '. . . One gambit not to use during a pitch', says executive Barbara Boyle, 'is to talk about big box-office grosses your story is sure to make. Executives know as well as anyone that it's impossible to predict how much money a movie will make, and declarations to the contrary are considered pure malarkey'.

7.9   Summary and Conclusions

1. In this chapter we cover different investment decision rules. We evaluate the most popular alternatives to the NPV: the payback period, the accounting rate of return, the internal rate of return and the profitability index. In doing so, we learn more about the NPV.

2. While we find that the alternatives have some redeeming qualities, when all is said and done, they are not the NPV rule; for those of us in finance, that makes them decidedly second-rate.

---

[15] Mark Litwak (1986), *Reel Power: The Struggle for Influence and Success in the New Hollywood*, New York: Morrow, pp. 73, 74 and 77.

3. Of the competitors to NPV, IRR must be ranked above either payback or accounting rate of return. In fact, IRR always reaches the same decision as NPV in the normal case where the initial outflows of an independent investment project are only followed by a series of inflows.

4. We classified the flaws of IRR into two types. First, we considered the general case applying to both independent and mutually exclusive projects. There appeared to be two problems here:
   a. Some projects have cash inflows followed by one or more outflows. The IRR rule is inverted here:
   One should accept when the IRR is below the discount rate.
   b. Some projects have a number of changes of sign in their cash flows. Here, there are likely to be multiple internal rates of return. The practitioner must use NPV here.

   Clearly, (*b*) is a bigger problem than (*a*). A new IRR criterion is called for with (*a*). No IRR criterion at all will work under (*b*).

5. Next, we considered the specific problems with the NPV for mutually exclusive projects. We showed that, either due to differences in size or in timing, the project with the highest IRR need not have the highest NPV. Hence, the IRR rule should not be applied. (Of course, NPV can still be applied.)

   However, we then calculated incremental cash flows. For ease of calculation, we suggested subtracting the cash flows of the smaller project from the cash flows of the larger project. In that way, the incremental initial cash flow is negative.

   One can correctly pick the better of two mutually exclusive projects in three other ways:
   a. Choose the project with the highest NPV.
   b. If the incremental IRR is greater than the discount rate, choose the bigger project.
   c. If the incremental NPV is positive, choose the bigger project.

6. We describe capital rationing as a case where funds are limited to a fixed dollar amount. With capital rationing the profitability index is a useful method of adjusting the NPV.

KEY TERMS

Payback period rule 147
Discounted payback period rule 150
Average accounting return 150
Internal rate of return 154
Basic IRR rule 154

Independent project 156
Mutually exclusive investments 156
Incremental IRR 162
Profitability index 165
Capital rationing 167

QUESTIONS AND PROBLEMS

The Payback Period Rule

7.1 Swiss Miss has the following projects.

Year	Project A	Project B
0	−CHF7,500	−CHF5,000
1	4,000	2,500
2	3,500	1,200
3	1,500	3,000

a. Suppose Swiss Miss's cutoff payback period is two years. Which of these two projects should be chosen?
b. Suppose Swiss Miss uses the NPV rule to rank these two projects. If the appropriate discount rate is 15 per cent, which project should be chosen?

7.2 Suppose de Grauw invests BEF1 million today on a new construction project. The project will generate annual cash flows of BEF150,000 in perpetuity. The appropriate annual discount rate for the project is 10 per cent.

a. What is the payback period for the project? If de Grauw desires to have a 10-year payback period, should the project be adopted?

b. What is the discounted payback period for the project?

c. What is the NPV of the project?

The Average Accounting Return

7.3 The annual, end-of-year, book-investment accounts for the machine whose purchase your firm is considering are shown below.

	Purchase date	Year 1	Year 2	Year 3	Year 4
Gross investment	SEK16,000	SEK16,000	SEK16,000	SEK16,000	SEK16,000
Less: accumulated depreciation	0	4,000	8,000	12,000	16,000
Net investment	SEK16,000	SEK12,000	SEK8,000	SEK4,000	SEK0

If the firm purchases this machine, you can expect it to generate, on average, SEK4,500 per year in additional income.

a. What is the average accounting return for this machine?

b. What three flaws are inherent in this decision rule?

The Internal Rate of Return

7.4 Compute the internal rate of return on a project with the following cash flows.

Year	Cash flows (FRF)
0	−3,000
1	2,500
2	1,000

7.5 Italco has a project with the following cash flows.

Year	Cash flows (ITL000)
0	−4,000
1	2,000
2	1,500
3	1,000

a. Compute the internal rate of return on the project.

b. Suppose the discount rate is 8 per cent. Should the project be adopted by Italco?

7.6 Compute the internal rate of return for the cash flows of the following two projects.

	Cash flows (DEM000)	
Time	A	B
0	−200	−150
1	200	50
2	800	100
3	−800	150

7.7 Suppose you are offered ESB5,000,000 today and obligated to make scheduled payments as follows:

Year	Cash flows (ESB000)
0	5,000
1	−2,500
2	−2,000
3	−1,000
4	−1,000

a. What is the IRRs of this offer?

b. If the appropriate discount rate is 10 per cent, should you accept this offer?

c. If the appropriate discount rate is 20 per cent, should you accept this offer?

d. What is the corresponding NPV of the project if the appropriate discount rate is 10 per cent and 20 per cent, respectively? Are the choices under the NPV rule consistent with those of the IRR rule?

7.8 As the treasurer of London Express, you are offered the following two mutually exclusive projects.

Year	Project A	Project B
0	−GBP5,000	−GBP100,000
1	3,500	65,000
2	3,500	65,000

a. What are the IRRs of these two projects?

b. If you are told only the IRRs of the projects, which would you choose?

c. What did you ignore when you made your choice in part (b)?

d. How can the problem be remedied?

e. Compute the incremental IRR for the projects.

f. Based on your answer to part (e), which project should you choose?

g. Suppose you have determined that the appropriate discount rate for these projects is 15 per cent. According to the NPV rule, which of these two projects should be adopted?

7.9 Consider two streams of cash flows, A and B. Cash flow A consists of GBP5,000 starting three years from today and growing at 4 per cent in perpetuity. Cash flow B consists of −GBP6,000 starting two years from today and continuing in perpetuity. Assume the appropriate discount rate is 12 per cent.

a. What is the present value of each stream?

b. What is the IRR of a project C, which is a combination of projects A and B; that is, $C = A + B$?

c. If it is assumed that the discount rate is always positive, what is the rule related to IRR for assessing project C that would correspond to the NPV rule?

7.10 Consider a Danish firm confronted with two projects. Project A involves an investment of DKK1 million, and project B involves an investment of DKK2 million. Both projects have a unique internal rate of return of 20 per cent. Is the following statement true or false? Explain your answer.

For any discount rate between 0 per cent and 20 per cent, inclusive, project B has an NPV twice as great as that of project A.

The Profitability Index

7.11 Suppose the following two mutually exclusive investment opportunities are available to the DeAngelo Firm. The appropriate discount rate is 10 per cent.

Year	Project Alpha (ITL000)	Project Beta (ITL000)
0	−500	−2,000
1	−300	−300
2	700	1,800
3	600	1,700

a. What is the NPV of project alpha and project beta?

b. Which project would you recommend for the DeAngelo Firm?

7.12 The firm for which you work must choose between the following two mutually exclusive projects. The appropriate discount rate for the projects is 10 per cent.

	C_0	C_1	C_2	Profitability index	NPV
A	−GBP1,000	GBP1,000	GBP500	1.32	GBP322
B	−500	500	400	1.57	285

The firm chose to undertake A. At a luncheon for shareholders, the manager of a pension fund that owns a substantial amount of the firm's shares asked you why the firm chose project A instead of project B when B is more profitable.

How would you justify your firm's action? Are there any circumstances under which the pension fund manager's argument could be correct?

7.13 The treasurer of Davids NV has projected the cash flows of project A, B and C as follows. Suppose the relevant discount rate is 12 per cent a year.

Year	Project A	Project B	Project C
0	−NLG100,000	−NLG200,000	−NLG100,000
1	70,000	130,000	75,000
2	70,000	130,000	60,000

a. Compute the profitability indices for each of the three projects.
b. Compute the NPVs for each of the three projects.
c. Suppose these three projects are independent. Which projects should Davids accept based on the profitability index rule?
d. Suppose these three projects are mutually exclusive. Which project should Davids accept based on the profitability index rule?
e. Suppose Davids' budget for these projects is NLG300,000. The projects are not divisible. Which projects should Davids accept?

Comparison of Investment Rules

7.14 Define each of the following investment rules. In your definition state the criteria for accepting or rejecting an investment under each rule.
a. Payback period
b. Average accounting return
c. Internal rate of return
d. Profitability index
e. Net present value

7.15 Consider the following cash flows of two mutually exclusive projects for the *Irish Clarion and Daily News*.

Year	New Sunday early edition (IEP000)	New Saturday late edition (IEP000)
0	−1,200	−2,100
1	600	1,000
2	550	900
3	450	800

a. Based on the payback period rule, which project should be chosen?
b. Suppose there is no corporate tax and the cash flows above are income before the depreciation. The firm uses a straight-line depreciation method (i.e. equal amounts of depreciation in each year). What is the average accounting return for each of these two projects?
c. Which project has a greater IRR?
d. Based on the incremental IRR rule, which project should be chosen?

7.16 Consider the following cash flows on two mutually exclusive projects that require an annual return of 15 per cent. Working in the financial planning department for the London Leisure and Recreational Company Ltd, you are trying to compare different investment criteria to arrive at a sensible choice of these two projects.

Year	Deepwater fishing	New submarine ride
0	−GBP600,000	−GBP1,800,000
1	270,000	1,000,000
2	350,000	700,000
3	300,000	900,000

a. Based on the discounted payback period rule, which project should be chosen?

b. If your decision rule is to accept the project with a greater IRR, which project should you choose?

c. Since you are fully aware of the IRR rule's scale problem, you calculate the incremental IRR for the cash flows. Based on your computation, which project should you choose?

d. To be prudent, you compute the NPV for both projects. Which project should you choose? Is it consistent with the incremental IRR rule?

CHAPTER
8

Net Present Value and Capital Budgeting

Previous chapters discussed the basics of capital budgeting and the net present value approach. We now want to move beyond these basics into the real-world application of these techniques. We want to show you how to use discounted cash flow (DCF) analysis and net present value (NPV) in capital budgeting decision-making.

In this chapter, we show how to identify the relevant cash flows of a project, including initial investment outlays, requirements for working capital and operating cash flows. We look at the effects of depreciation and taxes. We examine the impact of inflation on interest rates and on a project's discount rate, and we show why inflation must be handled consistently in NPV analysis.

8.1 Incremental Cash Flows

Cash Flows—Not Accounting Income

You may not have thought about it, but there is a big difference between corporate finance courses and financial accounting courses. Techniques in corporate finance generally use cash flows, whereas financial accounting generally stresses income or earnings numbers. Certainly, our text has followed this tradition since our net-present-value techniques discounted cash flows, not earnings. When considering a single project, we discounted the cash flows that the firm receives from the project. When valuing the firm as a whole, we discounted dividends—not earnings—because dividends are the cash flows that an investor receives.

There are many differences between earnings and cash flows. In fact, much of a standard financial accounting course delineates these differences. Because we have no desire to duplicate such course material, we merely discuss one example of the differences. Consider a firm buying a building for CHF100,000 today. The entire CHF100,000 is an immediate cash outflow. However, assuming straight-line depreciation over 20 years, only CHF5,000 (CHF100,000/20) is considered an accounting expense in the current year. Current earnings are thereby reduced only by CHF5,000. The remaining CHF95,000 is expensed over the following 19 years.

Because the seller of the property demands immediate payment, the cost at date 0 of the project to the firm is CHF100,000. Thus, the full CHF100,000 figure should be viewed as an immediate outflow for capital budgeting purposes. This is not merely our opinion, but the unanimous verdict of both academics and practitioners.

In addition, it is not enough to use cash flows. In calculating the NPV of a project, only cash flows that are *incremental* to the project should be used. These cash flows are the changes in the firm's cash flows that occur as a direct consequence of accepting the project. That is, we are interested in the difference between the cash flows of the firm with the project and the cash flows of the firm without the project.

The use of incremental cash flows sounds easy enough, but pitfalls abound in the real world. In this section, we describe how to avoid some of the pitfalls of determining incremental cash flows.

Sunk Costs

A **sunk cost** is a cost that has already occurred. Because sunk costs are in the past, they cannot be changed by the decision to accept or reject the project. Just as we 'let bygones be bygones', we should ignore such costs. Sunk costs are not incremental cash outflows.

• Example
The General Milk Company plc is currently evaluating the NPV of establishing a line of chocolate milk. As part of the evaluation the company had paid a consulting firm GBP100,000 to perform a test-marketing analysis. This expenditure was made last year. Is this cost relevant for the capital budgeting decision now confronting the management of General Milk Company?

The answer is no. The GBP100,000 is not recoverable, so the GBP100,000 expenditure is a sunk cost, or spilled milk. Of course, the decision to spend GBP100,000 for a marketing analysis was a capital budgeting decision itself and was perfectly relevant before it was sunk. Our point is that once the company incurred the expense, the cost became irrelevant for any future decision. •

Opportunity Costs

Your firm may have an asset that it is considering selling, leasing, or employing elsewhere in the business. If the asset is used in a new project, potential revenues from alternative uses are lost. These lost revenues can meaningfully be viewed as costs. They are called **opportunity costs** because, by taking the project, the firm forgoes other opportunities for using the assets.

• Example
Suppose Berger Trading GmbH has an empty warehouse in Munich that can be used to store a new line of electronic pinball machines. The company hopes to market the machines to affluent Bavarian consumers. Should the cost of the warehouse and land be included in the costs associated with introducing a new line of electronic pinball machines?

The answer is yes. The use of a warehouse is not free; it has an opportunity cost. The cost is the cash that could be raised by the company if the decision to market the electronic pinball machines were rejected and the warehouse and land were put to some other use (or sold). If so, the NPV of the alternative uses becomes an opportunity cost of the decision to sell electronic pinball machines. •

Side-Effects

Another difficulty in determining incremental cash flows comes from the side effects of the proposed project on other parts of the firm. The most important side effect is **erosion**. Erosion is the cash flow transferred to a new project from customers and sales of other products of the firm. Erosion is sometimes also called cannibalization.

● **Example**

Suppose Innovative Motors AG is determining the NPV of a new convertible sports car. Some of the customers who would purchase the car are owners of Innovative Motors' compact sedan. Are all sales and profits from the new convertible sports car incremental?

The answer is no because some of the cash flow represents transfers from other elements of Innovative Motors' product line. This is erosion, which must be included in the NPV calculation. Without taking erosion into account, Innovative Motors might erroneously calculate the NPV of the sports car to be, say, DEM100 million. If Innovative Motors' managers recognized that half the customers are transfers from the sedan and that lost sedan sales have an NPV of −DEM150 million, they would see that the true NPV is −DEM50 million (DEM100 million − DEM150 million). ●

Concept Questions

- What are the three difficulties in determining incremental cash flows?
- Define sunk costs, opportunity costs and side effects.

8.2   The Baldwin Company: An Example

We next consider the example of a proposed investment in machinery and related items. Our example involves the Baldwin Company and coloured bowling balls.

The Baldwin Company, originally established in 1962 to make footballs, is now a leading producer of tennis balls, footballs, golf balls, cricket balls and sundry others. In 1970 the company introduced 'High Flite', its first line of high-performance golf balls. The Baldwin management has sought opportunities in whatever businesses seem to have some potential for cash flow. In 1993, Bill Meadows, chief executive of the Baldwin Company, identified another segment of the sports ball market that looked promising, and that he felt was not adequately served by larger manufacturers. That market was for brightly coloured bowling balls. He believed that it would be difficult for competitors to take advantage of this opportunity based on style and appearance because of Baldwin's cost advantages and because of its ability to use its highly developed marketing skills.

As a result, in late 1994 the Baldwin Company decided to evaluate the marketing potential of brightly coloured bowling balls. The results of the market research were much better than expected and supported the conclusion that the brightly coloured bowling ball could achieve a 10 to 15 per cent share of the market. Some people at Baldwin complained about the cost of the test marketing, which was GBP250,000. However, Meadows argued that it was a sunk cost and should not be included in project evaluation.

In any case, the Baldwin Company is now considering investing in a machine to produce bowling balls. They would be produced in a building owned by the firm and located near London. This building, which is vacant, and the land can be sold to net GBP150,000 after taxes. The book value of this property, the original purchase price of the property less depreciation, is zero and so is the tax written down value.

Working with his staff, Meadows is preparing an analysis of the proposed new product. He summarizes his assumptions as follows: The cost of the new machine is GBP100,000. The machine has an estimated market value at the end of five years of GBP30,000. Production by year during the five-year life of the machine is expected to be as follows: 5,000 units, 8,000 units, 12,000 units, 10,000 units, and 6,000 units. The price of bowling balls in the first year will be GBP20. The bowling ball market is highly competitive, so Meadows believes that the price of bowling balls will increase at only 2 per cent per year, as compared to the anticipated general inflation rate of 5 per cent. Conversely, the plastic used to produce bowling balls is rapidly becoming more expensive. Because of this, production cash outflows are expected to grow at 10 per cent per year. First-year production costs will be GBP10 per unit. Meadows has determined, based upon Baldwin's taxable income, that the appropriate incremental corporate tax rate in the bowling ball project is 33 per cent.

Net working capital is defined as the difference between current assets and current liabilities. Baldwin finds that it must maintain an investment in working capital. Like any manufacturing firm, it will purchase raw materials before production and sale, giving rise to an investment in inventory. It will maintain cash as a buffer against unforeseen expenditures. Its credit sales will generate accounts receivable. Management believes that the investment in the different items of working capital totals GBP10,000 in year 0, rises somewhat in the early years of the project, and falls to GBP0 by the project's end. In other words, the investment in working capital is completely recovered by the end of the project's life.

Projections based on these assumptions and Meadow's analysis appear in Tables 8.1 through 8.4. In these tables all cash flows are assumed to occur at the *end* of the year. Because of the large amount of data in these tables, it is important to see how the tables are related. Table 8.1 shows the basic data for both investment and income. Supplementary schedules on operations and depreciation, as presented in Tables 8.2 and 8.3, help explain where the numbers in Table 8.1 come from. Our goal is to obtain projections of cash flow. The data in Table 8.1 are all that is needed to calculate the relevant cash flows, as shown in Table 8.4.

TABLE 8.1   The Worksheet for Cash Flows of the Baldwin Company (GBP thousands). (All cash flows occur at the *end* of the year.)

	Year 0	Year 1	Year 2	Year 3	Year 4	Year 5	Year 6
Investment related:							
(1) Bowling ball machine	−100.00					30.00*	−2.09*
(2) Tax depreciation (called capital allowances)		25.00	18.75	14.06	10.55	7.91	
(3) Adjusted basis of machine after depreciation (end of year)		75.00	56.25	42.19	31.64	23.73	
(4) Opportunity cost (warehouse)	−150.00					150.00	
(5) Net working capital (end of year)	10.00	10.00	16.32	24.97	21.22	0	
(6) Change in net working capital	−10.00		−6.32	−8.65	3.75	21.22	
(7) Total cash flow of investment [(1) + (4) + (6)]	−260.00		−6.32	−8.65	3.75	201.22	−2.09
Incomes related:							
(8) Sales revenues		100.00	163.20	249.72	212.20	129.80	
(9) Operating costs excluding depreciation		50.00	88.00	145.20	133.10	87.84	
(10) Tax depreciation (as per line (2))		25.00	18.75	14.06	10.55	7.91	
(11) Income before taxes [(8) − (9) − (10)]		25.00	56.45	90.46	68.55	34.15	
(12) Tax at 33%			8.25	18.63	29.85	22.62	11.27
(13) Income after taxes [(11) − (12)]		25.00	48.20	71.83	38.70	11.53	−11.27

* We assume that the ending market value of the capital investment at year 5 is GBP30 (in thousands). Capital gain is the difference between ending market value and the written down tax value of the machine. This written down value, see line (3), is GBP23.73. The capital gain is GBP30 − 23.73 = 6.27. We will assume the incremental corporate tax rate for Baldwin on this project is 33 per cent. Capital gains are, for simplification purposes, subjected to tax at 33 per cent— that is, GBP2.09. This gives net proceeds of GBP27.91 (GBP30 − 2.09). But the capital gains tax would be paid in year 6. In the UK, all tax items occur in the year following, see line (12). In reality the position in the UK is more complex with the capital gain (GBP6.27), in fact, reducing the written-down book value for tax purposes of all plant and machinery.

TABLE 8.2   Operating Revenues and Costs of the Baldwin Company

(1) Year	(2) Production	(3) Price	(4) Sales revenues	(5) Cost per unit	(6) Operating costs
1	5,000	GBP20.00	GBP100,000	GBP10.00	GBP50,000
2	8,000	20.40	163,200	11.00	88,000
3	12,000	20.81	249,720	12.10	145,200
4	10,000	21.22	212,200	13.31	133,100
5	6,000	21.65	129,900	14.64	87,840

Prices rise at 2% a year.
Unit costs rise at 10% a year.

TABLE 8.3   Incremental Cash Flows for the Baldwin Company (GBP thousands)

Year	Accounting depreciation*	Tax written-down value	Tax depreciation[†]
0		100,000	25,000
1	20,000	75,000	18,750
2	20,000	56,250	14,062
3	20,000	42,188	10,547
4	20,000	31,641	7,910
5	20,000	23,731	

* Assume a write-down using straight-line depreciation to zero. At the end of year 5, the written-down value will be zero. This means that when the machine is sold off for GBP30,000, there will be a pre-tax profit on sale appearing in year 5 accounts of GBP30,000.
   [†] British tax depreciation (called capital allowances) amounts to 25 per cent on a reducing balance method for plant and machinery (and 4 per cent per annum straight line on original cost in respect of buildings—they are written down to zero after 25 years) and is first available in the year in which the cost is incurred. But the cash flow effect is deferred for a year because, in the UK, tax on profits in year 1 are paid in year 2 and so on.

TABLE 8.4   Incremental Cash Flows for the Baldwin Company (GBP thousands)

	Year 0	Year 1	Year 2	Year 3	Year 4	Year 5	Year 6
(1) Sales revenue [line 8, Table 8.1]		100.00	163.20	249.72	212.20	129.90	
(2) Operating costs [line 9, Table 8.1]		−50.00	−88.00	−145.20	−133.10	−87.84	
(3) Taxes [line 12, Table 8.1]			−8.25	−18.63	−29.85	−22.62	−11.27
(4) Cash flow from operations [(1) − (2) − (3)]		50.00	66.95	85.89	49.25	19.44	−11.27
(5) Total cash flow of investment [line 7, Table 8.1]	−260.00		−6.32	−8.65	3.75	201.22	−2.09
(6) Total cash flow of project [(4) + (5)]	−260.00	50.00	60.63	77.24	53.00	220.66	−13.36

NPV @ 4%   128.54
       10%   59.25
       15%   15.71
       20%   −21.76

An Analysis of the Project

Investments

The investment outlays required for the project are summarized in the top segment of Table 8.1. They consist of three parts:

1. *The Bowling Ball Machine*   The purchase requires a cash outflow of GBP100,000 at year 0. The firm realizes a cash inflow when the machine is sold in year 5. These cash flows are shown in line 1 of Table 8.1. As indicated in the footnote to the table, taxes are incurred when the asset is sold.

2. *The Opportunity Cost of Not Selling the Warehouse*   If Baldwin accepts the bowling-ball project, it will use a warehouse and land that could otherwise be sold. The estimated sales price of the warehouse and land is therefore included as an opportunity cost, as presented in line 4. Opportunity costs are treated as cash flows for purposes of capital budgeting. However, the expenditures of GBP250,000 for test marketing are not included. The tests occurred in the past and should be viewed as a sunk cost.

3. *The Investment in Working Capital*   Required working capital appears in line 5. Working capital rises over the early years of the project as expansion occurs. However, all working capital is assumed to be recovered at the end, a common assumption in capital budgeting. In other words, all inventory is sold by the end, the cash balance maintained as a buffer is liquidated, and all accounts receivable are collected. Increases in working capital in the early years must be funded by cash generated elsewhere in the firm. Hence, these increases are viewed as cash outflows. Conversely, decreases in working capital in the later years are viewed as cash inflows. All of these cash flows are presented in line 6. A more complete discussion of working capital is provided later in this section. The total cash flow from the above three investments is shown in line 7.

Income and Taxes

Next, the determination of income is presented in the bottom segment of Table 8.1. While we are ultimately interested in cash flow—not income—we need the income calculation in order to determine taxes. Lines 8 and 9 of Table 8.1 show sales revenues and operating costs, respectively. The projections in these lines are based on the sales revenues and operating costs computed in columns 4 and 6 of Table 8.2. The estimates of revenues and costs follow from assumptions made by the corporate planning staff at Baldwin. In other words, the estimates critically depend on the fact that product prices are projected to increase at 2 per cent per year and costs are projected to increase at 10 per cent per year.

Taxation is complicated and rules vary from one European country to another. In the UK, profits in year 1 are taxed, but the tax is actually paid in year 2. And so on, with one year in arrear. Furthermore, in the UK different rules apply for tax depreciation as opposed to accounting depreciation charges. There are statutory legal rules for determining tax depreciation. Amounts charged in the profit and loss account for depreciation have to be added back and replaced by what legal rules insist is tax depreciation. This is based on a 25 per cent writing-down allowance on a reducing balance method for plant, machinery and vehicles. For buildings, the tax allowance is 4 per cent per annum straight line on cost. Thus writing buildings down to zero over 25 years. But the point to bear in mind is that the practice in the UK is for tax depreciation to be different from depreciation in the profit and loss account. This is not the case in Germany and France, for example, where the practice is that the accounting depreciation is deliberately put on to the same footing as for tax purposes. Indeed, if companies deviate from this, they may run the risk of having their tax depreciation disregarded by tax authorities.

Table 8.3 details tax depreciation and income before taxes is calculated in line 11 of Table 8.1. Taxes are provided in line 12 of this table, and net income is calculated in line 13.

The Baldwin example can easily be reworked to provide for tax environments other than those in the UK. In the main, this will involve a different percentage applied in calculating tax depreciation and, in most countries, the tax is not lagged one year—thus tax on year 1 profits is paid in year 1, tax on year 2 profits is paid in year 2 and so on. Clearly, the combined effect would be to impact bottom line project cash flow were the Baldwin example reworked to allow for location elsewhere in Europe.

Cash Flow
Cash flow is finally determined in Table 8.4. We begin by reproducing lines 8, 9 and 12 in Table 8.1 as lines 1, 2 and 3 in Table 8.4. Cash flow from operations, which is sales minus both operating costs and taxes, is provided in line 4 of Table 8.4. Total investment cash flow, taken from line 7 of Table 8.1, appears as line 5 of Table 8.4. Cash flow from operations plus total cash flow of the investment equals total cash flow of the project, which is displayed as line 6 of Table 8.4. The bottom of the table presents the NPV of these cash flows for different discount rates.

Net Present Value
It is possible to calculate the NPV of the Baldwin bowling ball project from these cash flows. As can be seen at the bottom of Table 8.4, the NPV is GBP59,250 if 10 per cent is the appropriate discount rate and −GBP21,760 if 20 per cent is the appropriate discount rate. If the discount rate is 17.1 per cent, the project will have a zero NPV. In other words, the project's internal rate of return is 17.1 per cent. If the discount rate of the Baldwin bowling ball project is above 17.1 per cent, it should not be accepted because its NPV would be negative.

A Note on Net Working Capital

The investment in net working capital is an important part of any capital budgeting analysis. While we explicitly considered net working capital in lines 5 and 6 of Table 8.1, students may be wondering where the numbers in these lines came from. An investment in net working capital arises whenever (1) raw materials and other inventory are purchased prior to the sale of finished goods, (2) cash is kept in the project as a buffer against unexpected expenditures and (3) credit sales are made, generating an accounts receivable rather than cash. (The investment in net working capital is offset to the extent that purchases are made on credit, that is, when an accounts payable is created.) This investment in net working capital represents a cash outflow, because cash generated elsewhere in the firm is tied up in the project.

To see how the investment in net working capital is built from its component parts, we focus on year 1. We see in Table 8.1 that Baldwin's managers predict sales in year 1 to be GBP100,000 and operating costs to be GBP50,000. If both the sales and costs were cash transactions, the firm would receive GBP50,000 (GBP100,000 − GBP50,000).

However, the managers:

1. Forecast that GBP9,000 of the sales will be on credit, implying that cash

receipts in year 1 will be only GBP91,000 (GBP100,000 − GBP9,000). The accounts receivable of GBP9,000 will be collected in year 2.
2. Believe that they can defer payment on GBP3,000 of the GBP50,000 of costs, implying that cash disbursements will be only GBP47,000 (GBP50,000 − GBP3,000). Of course, Baldwin will pay off the GBP3,000 of accounts payable in year 2.
3. Decide that inventory of GBP2,500 should be left on hand at year 1 to avoid *stockouts* (that is, running out of inventory) and other contingencies.
4. Decide that cash of GBP1,500 should be earmarked for the project at year 1 to avoid running out of cash.

Thus, net working capital in year 1 is

GBP9,000	−	GBP3,000	+	GBP2,500	+	GBP1,500	=	GBP10,000
Accounts receivable		Accounts payable		Inventory		Cash		Net working capital

Because GBP10,000 of cash generated elsewhere in the firm must be used to offset this requirement for net working capital, Baldwin's managers correctly view the investment in net working capital as a cash outflow of the project. As the project grows over time, needs for net working capital increase. *Changes* in net working capital from year to year represent further cash flows, as indicated by the negative numbers for the first few years of line 6 of Table 8.1. However, in the declining years of the project, net working capital is reduced—ultimately to zero. That is, accounts receivable are finally collected, the project's cash buffer is returned to the rest of the corporation and all remaining inventory is sold off. This frees up cash in the later years, as indicated by positive numbers in years 4 and 5 on line 6.

Typically, corporate worksheets (such as Table 8.1) treat net working capital as a whole. The individual components of working capital (receivables, inventory, etc.) do not generally appear in the worksheets. However, the reader should remember that the working capital numbers in the worksheets are not pulled out of thin air. Rather, they result from a meticulous forecast of the components, just as we illustrated for year 1.

Interest Expense

It may have bothered you that interest expense was ignored in the Baldwin example. After all, many projects are at least partially financed with debt, particularly a bowling ball machine that is likely to increase the debt capacity of the firm. As it turns out, our approach of assuming no debt financing is rather standard in the real world. Firms typically calculate a project's cash flows under the assumption that the project is financed only with equity. Any adjustments for debt financing are reflected in the discount rate, not the cash flows. The treatment of debt in capital budgeting will be covered in depth later in the text. Suffice it to say at this time that the full ramifications of debt financing are well beyond our current discussion.

Concept Questions

- What are the items leading to cash flow in any year?
- Why did we determine income when NPV analysis discounts cash flows, not income?
- Why is working capital viewed as a cash outflow?

8.3   Inflation and Capital Budgeting

Inflation is an important fact of economic life, and it must be considered in capital budgeting. We begin our examination of inflation by considering the relationship between interest rates and *inflation*.

Interest Rates and Inflation

Suppose that the one-year interest rate that the bank pays is 10 per cent. This means that an individual who deposits GBP1,000 at date 0 will get GBP1,100 (GBP1,000 × 1.10) in one year. While 10 per cent may seem like a handsome return, one can only put it in perspective after examining the rate of inflation.

Suppose that the rate of inflation is 6 per cent over the year and it affects all goods equally. For example, a restaurant that charges GBP1.00 for a burger at date 0 charges GBP1.06 for the same burger at the end of the year. You can use your GBP1,000 to buy 1,000 burgers at date 0. Alternatively, if you put all of your money in the bank, you can buy 1,038 (GBP1,100/GBP1.06) burgers at date 1. Thus, you are only able to increase your burger consumption by 3.8 per cent by lending to the bank. Since the prices of all goods rise at this 6 per cent rate, lending lets you increase your consumption of any single good or any combination of goods by only 3.8 per cent. Thus, 3.8 per cent is what you are *really* earning through your savings account, after adjusting for inflation. Economists refer to the 3.8 per cent number as the **real interest rate.** Economists refer to the 10 per cent rate as the **nominal interest rate** or simply the *interest rate*. The above discussion is illustrated in Figure 8.1.

We have used an example with a specific nominal interest rate and a specific inflation rate. In general, the formula between real and nominal cash flows can be written as

$$1 + \text{Nominal interest rate} = (1 + \text{Real interest rate}) \times (1 + \text{Inflation rate})$$

Rearranging terms, we have

$$\text{Real interest rate} = \frac{1 + \text{Nominal interest rate}}{1 + \text{Inflation}} - 1 \qquad (8.1)$$

The formula indicates that the real interest rate in our example is 3.8 per cent (1.10/1.06 − 1).

FIGURE **8.1**   **Calculation of Real Rate of Interest**

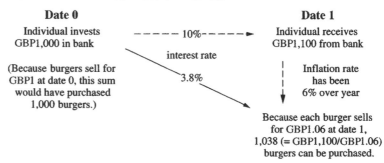

Burger is used as an illustrative good. 1,038 burgers can be purchased on date 1 instead of 1,000 burgers at date 0. Real interest rate = 1,038/1,000 − 1 = 3.8 per cent.

The above formula determines the real interest rate precisely. The following formula is an approximation:

$$\text{Real interest rate} \cong \text{Nominal interest rate} - \text{Inflation rate} \qquad (8.2)$$

The symbol '$\cong$' indicates that the equation is approximately true. This latter formula calculates the real rate in our example as:

$$4\% = 10\% - 6\%$$

The student should be aware that, while equation (8.2) may seem more intuitive than equation (8.1), (8.2) is only an approximation.

Cash Flow and Inflation

The above analysis defines two types of interest rates, nominal rates and real rates, and relates them through equation (8.1). Capital budgeting requires data on cash flows as well as on interest rates. Like interest rates, cash flows can be expressed in either nominal or real terms.

A cash flow is expressed in nominal terms if the actual dollars to be received (or paid out) are given. A cash flow is expressed in real terms if the current or date 0 purchasing power of the cash flow is given. Like most definitions, these definitions are best explained by examples.

● Example
Burrows Publishing has just purchased the rights to the next book of famed romantic novelist Barbara Musk. Still unwritten, the book should be available to the public in four years. Currently, romantic novels sell for GBP10.00 in hardcover. The publishers believe that inflation will be 6 per cent a year over the next four years. Since romantic novels are so popular, the publishers anticipate that the prices of romantic novels will rise about 2 per cent per year more than the inflation rate over the next four years. Not wanting to overprice, Burrows anticipates pricing the novel at GBP13.60 [$(1.08)^4 \times$ GBP10.00] four years from now. The firm anticipates selling 100,000 copies.

The expected cash flow in the fourth year of GBP1.36 million (GBP13.60 $\times$ 100,000) is a **nominal cash flow**. That is because the firm expects to receive GBP1.36 million at that time. In other words, a nominal cash flow reflects the actual pounds, dollars, marks or whatever to be received in the future.

We determine the purchasing power of GBP1.36 million in four years as

$$\text{GBP1.08 million} = \frac{\text{GBP1.36 million}}{(1.06)^4}$$

The figure GBP1.08 million is a **real cash flow** since it is expressed in terms of date 0 purchasing power. Extending our burger example, the GBP1.36 million to be received in four years will only buy 1.08 million burgers because the price of a burger will rise from GBP1 to GBP1.26 [GBP1 $\times (1.06)^4$] over the period. ●

Discounting: Nominal or Real?

Our previous discussion showed that interest rates can be expressed in either nominal or real terms. Similarly, cash flows can be expressed in either nominal or real terms.

Given these choices, how should one express interest rates and cash flows when performing capital budgeting?

Financial practitioners correctly stress the need to maintain consistency between cash flows and discount rates. That is,

> *Nominal* cash flows must be discounted at the *nominal* rate.
> *Real* cash flows must be discounted at the *real* rate.

Because both approaches, handled correctly, always yield the same result, which one should be used? Students will be happy to learn the following rule: Use the approach that is simpler. Firms will often forecast unit sales per year. They can easily convert these forecasts to real quantities by multiplying expected unit sales each year by the product price at date 0. (This assumes that the price of the product rises at exactly the rate of inflation.) Once a real discount rate is selected, NPV can easily be calculated from real quantities. Conversely, nominal quantities complicate the example, because the extra step of converting all real cash flows to nominal cash flows must be taken.

Concept Questions

- What is the difference between the nominal and the real interest rate?
- What is the difference between nominal and real cash flows?

8.4   Investments of Unequal Lives: The Equivalent Annual Cost Method

Suppose a firm must choose between two machines of unequal lives. Both machines can do the same job, but they have different operating costs and will last for different time periods. A simple application of the NPV rule suggests that we should take the machine whose costs have the lower present value. This could lead to the wrong decision, though, because the lower-cost machine may need to be replaced before the other one. If we are choosing between two mutually exclusive projects that have different lives, the projects must be evaluated on an equal-life basis. In other words, we must devise a method that takes into account all future replacement decisions. We first discuss the classic *replacement-chain* problem. Next, a more difficult replacement decision is examined.

Replacement Chain

- **Example**

Amstel Athletic Club must choose between two mechanical tennis-ball throwers. Machine *A* costs less than machine *B*, but does not last as long. The cash outflows from the two machines are:

Machine	\multicolumn{5}{c}{Date}
	0	1	2	3	4
A	NLG500	NLG120	NLG120	NLG120	
B	600	100	100	100	NLG100

Machine *A* costs NLG500 and lasts three years. There will be maintenance expenses of NLG120 to be paid at the end of each of the three years. Machine *B* costs NLG600 and lasts four years. There will be maintenance expenses of NLG100 to be paid at the end of each of the four years. We place all costs in *real* terms, an assumption greatly simplifying the analysis. Revenues per year are assumed to be the same, regardless of machine, so they are ignored in the analysis. Note that all numbers in the above chart are *outflows*. ●

To get a handle on the decision, we take the present value of the costs of each of the two machines:

$$\text{Machine } A: \quad \text{NLG798.42} = \text{NLG500} + \frac{\text{NLG120}}{1.1} + \frac{\text{NLG120}}{(1.1)^2} + \frac{\text{NLG120}}{(1.1)^3}$$

$$\tag{8.3}$$

$$\text{Machine } B: \quad \text{NLG916.99} = \text{NLG600} + \frac{\text{NLG100}}{1.1} + \frac{\text{NLG100}}{(1.1)^2} + \frac{\text{NLG100}}{(1.1)^3} + \frac{\text{NLG100}}{(1.1)^4}$$

Machine *B* has a higher present value of outflows. A naive approach would be to select machine *A* because of the lower outflows. However, machine *B* has a longer life so perhaps its cost per year is actually lower. How might one properly adjust for the difference in useful life when comparing the two machines? We present two methods.

1. *Matching Cycles*   Suppose that we run the example for 12 years. Machine *A* would have four complete cycles in this case and machine *B* would have three, so a comparison would be appropriate. Consider machine *A*'s second cycle. The replacement of machine *A* occurs at date 3. Thus, another NLG500 must be paid at date 3 with the yearly maintenance cost of NLG120 payable at dates 4, 5, and 6. Another cycle begins at date 6 and a final cycle begins at date 9. Our present value analysis of (8.3) tells us that the payments in the first cycle are equivalent to a payment of NLG798.42 at date 0. Similarly, the payments from the second cycle are equivalent to a payment of NLG798.42 at date 3. Carrying this out for all four cycles, the present value of all costs from machine *A* over 12 years is

Present Value of Costs of Machine *A* over 12 Years:

$$\text{NLG2,188} = \text{NLG798.42} + \frac{\text{NLG798.42}}{(1.10)^3} + \frac{\text{NLG798.42}}{(1.10)^6} + \frac{\text{NLG798.42}}{(1.10)^9} \quad (8.4)$$

Now consider machine *B*'s second cycle. The replacement of machine *B* occurs at date 4. Thus, another NLG600 must be paid at this time, with yearly maintenance costs of NLG100 payable at dates 5, 6, 7 and 8. A third cycle completes the 12 years. Following our calculations for machine *A*, the present value of all costs from machine *B* over 12 years is

Present Value of Costs of Machine *B* over 12 Years:

$$\text{NLG1,971} = \text{NLG916.99} + \frac{\text{NLG916.99}}{(1.10)^4} + \frac{\text{NLG916.99}}{(1.10)^8}$$

Because both machines have complete cycles over the 12 years, a comparison of 12-year costs is appropriate. The present value of machine *B*'s costs is lower than the present value of machine *A*'s costs over the 12 years, implying that machine *B* should be chosen.

While the above approach is straightforward, it has one drawback: Sometimes the number of cycles is high, demanding an excessive amount of calculating time. For example, if machine C lasts for seven years and machine D lasts for 11 years, these two machines must be compared over a period of 77 (7×11) years. And if machines C, D and E are compared, where machine E has a four-year cycle, a complete set of cycles occurs over 308 ($7 \times 11 \times 4$) years. Therefore, we offer the following alternative approach.

2. *Equivalent Annual Cost*   Equation (8.3) showed that payments of (NLG500, NLG120, NLG120, NLG120) are equivalent to a single payment of NLG798.42 at date 0. We now wish to equate the single payment of NLG798.42 at date 0 with a three-year annuity. Using techniques of previous chapters, we have

$$\text{NLG}798.42 = C \times A_{0.10}^{3}$$

$A_{0.10}^{3}$ is an annuity of NLG1 a year for three years, discounted at 10 per cent. C is the unknown—the annuity payment per year that causes the present value of all payments to equal NLG798.42. Because $A_{0.10}^{3}$ equals 2.4869, C equals NLG321.05 (NLG798.42/2.4869). Thus, a payment stream of (NLG500, NLG120, NLG120, NLG120) is equivalent to annuity payments of NLG321.05 for three years. Of course, this calculation assumes only one cycle of machine A. Use of machine A over many cycles is equivalent to annual payments of NLG321.05 for an indefinite period into the future. We refer to NLG321.05 as the equivalent annual cost of machine A.

Now let us turn to machine B. We calculate its equivalent annual cost from

$$\text{NLG}916.99 = C \times A_{0.10}^{4}$$

Because $A_{0.10}^{4}$ equals 3.1699, C equals NLG916.99/3.1699, or NLG289.28.

The following chart facilitates a comparison of machine A with machine B.

Date	0	1	2	3	4	5	
Machine *A*	NLG321.05	NLG321.05	NLG321.05	NLG321.05	NLG321.05	. . .
Machine *B*	289.28	289.28	289.28	289.28	289.28	. . .

Repeated cycles of machine A give rise to yearly payments of NLG321.05 for an indefinite period into the future. Repeated cycles of machine B give rise to yearly payments of NLG289.28 for an indefinite period into the future. Clearly, machine B is preferred to machine A.

So far, we presented two approaches: matching cycles and equivalent annual costs. Machine B was preferred under both methods. The two approaches are simply different ways of presenting the same information so that, for problems of this type, the same machine *must* be preferred under both approaches. In other words, use whichever method is easier for you since the decision will always be the same.

Assumptions in Replacement Chains
Strictly speaking, the two approaches make sense only if the time horizon is a multiple of 12 years. However, if the time horizon is long, but not known precisely, these approaches should still be satisfactory in practice.

The problem comes in if the time horizon is short. Suppose that the Downtown Athletic Club knows that a new machine will come on the market at date 5. The machine will be incredibly cheap and virtually maintenance-free, implying that it will replace either machine *A* or machine *B* immediately. Furthermore, its cheapness implies no salvage value for either *A* or *B*.

The relevant cash flows for *A* and *B* are

Date	*0*	*1*	*2*	*3*	*4*	*5*
Machine *A*	NLG500	NLG120	NLG120	NLG120 + NLG500	NLG120	NLG120
Machine *B*	600	100	100	100	100 + 600	100

Note the double cost of machine *A* at date 3. This occurs because machine *A* must be replaced at that time. However, maintenance costs still continue, because machine *A* remains in service until the day of its replacement. Similarly, there is a double cost of machine *B* at date 4.

Present values are

Present Value of Costs of Machine *A*:

$$\text{NLG1,331} = \text{NLG500} + \frac{\text{NLG120}}{1.10} + \frac{\text{NLG120}}{(1.10)^2} + \frac{\text{NLG620}}{(1.10)^3} + \frac{\text{NLG120}}{(1.10)^4} + \frac{\text{NLG120}}{(1.10)^5}$$

Present Value of Costs of Machine *B*:

$$\text{NLG1,389} = \text{NLG600} + \frac{\text{NLG100}}{1.10} + \frac{\text{NLG100}}{(1.10)^2} + \frac{\text{NLG100}}{(1.10)^3} + \frac{\text{NLG700}}{(1.10)^4} + \frac{\text{NLG100}}{(1.10)^5}$$

Thus, machine *B* is more costly. Why is machine *B* more costly here when it is less costly under strict replacement-chain assumptions? Machine *B* is hurt more than machine *A* by the termination at date 5 because *B*'s second cycle ends at date 8 while *A*'s second cycle ends at date 6.

One final remark: Our analysis of replacement chains applies only if one anticipates replacement. The analysis would be different if no replacement were possible. This would occur if the only company that manufactured tennis-ball throwers just went out of business and no new producers are expected to enter the field. In this case, machine *B* would generate revenues in the fourth year whereas machine *A* would not. In that case, simple net present value analysis for mutually exclusive projects including both revenues and costs would be appropriate.

The General Decision to Replace

The previous analysis concerned the choice between machine *A* and machine *B*, both of which were new acquisitions. More typically, firms must decide when to replace an existing machine with a new one. The analysis is actually quite straightforward. First, one calculates the equivalent annual cost (EAC) for the new equipment. Second, one calculates the yearly cost for the old equipment. This cost likely rises over time because the machine's maintenance expense should increase with age. Replacement should occur right before the cost of the old equipment exceeds the EAC on the new equipment. As with much else in finance, an example clarifies this criterion better than further explanation.

● **Example**

Consider the situation of BIKE. BIKE is contemplating whether to replace an existing machine or to spend money overhauling it. BIKE currently pays no taxes. The replacement machine costs DEM9,000 now and requires maintenance of DEM1,000 at the end of every year for eight years. At the end of eight years it would have a salvage value of DEM2,000 and would be sold. The existing machine requires increasing amounts of maintenance each year, and its salvage value falls each year, as shown:

Year	Maintenance	Salvage
Present	DEM0	DEM4,000
1	1,000	2,500
2	2,000	1,500
3	3,000	1,000
4	4,000	0

The existing machine can be sold for DEM4,000 now. If it is sold in one year, the resale price will be DEM2,500, and DEM1,000 must be spent on maintenance during the year to keep it running. The machine will last for four more years before it falls apart. If BIKE faces an opportunity cost of capital of 15 per cent, when should it replace the machine?

Equivalent Annual Cost of New Machine   The present value of the cost of the new replacement machine is as follows:

$$PV_{costs} = DEM9,000 + DEM1,000 \times A_{0.15}^8 - \frac{DEM2,000}{(1.15)^8}$$

$$= DEM9,000 + DEM1,000 \times (4.4873) - DEM2,000 \times (0.3269)$$

$$= DEM12,833$$

Notice that the DEM2,000 salvage value is an inflow. It is treated as a negative number in the above equation because it *offsets* the cost of the machine.

The EAC of a new replacement machine equals

$$PV/\text{8-year annuity factor at } 15\% = \frac{PV}{A_{0.15}^8} = \frac{DEM12,833}{4.4873} = DEM2,860$$

Cost of Old Machine   The cost of keeping the existing machine one more year includes the following:

1. The opportunity cost of not selling it now (DEM4,000)
2. Additional maintenance (DEM1,000)
3. Salvage value (DEM2,500)

Thus, the PV of the costs of keeping the machine one more year and selling it equals

$$DEM4,000 + DEM1,000/1.15 - DEM2,500/1.15 = DEM2,696$$

While we normally express cash flows in terms of present value, the analysis to come is made easier if we express the cash flow in terms of its future value one year from now. This future value is

$$DEM2,696 \times 1.15 = DEM3,100$$

In other words, the equivalent cost of keeping the machine for one year is DEM3,100 at the end of the year.

Making the Comparison   If we replace the machine immediately, we can view our annual expense as DEM2,860, beginning at the end of the year. This annual expense occurs forever, if we replace the new machine every eight years.

This cash flow stream can be written as

	Year 1	*Year 2*	*Year 3*	*Year 4*	...
Expenses from replacing machine immediately	DEM2,860	DEM2,860	DEM2,860	DEM2,860	...

If we replace the old machine in one year, our expense from using the old machine for that final year can be viewed as DEM3,100, payable at the end of the year. After replacement, we can view our annual expense as DEM2,860, beginning at the end of two years. This annual expense occurs forever, if we replace the new machine every eight years. This cash flow stream can be written as

	Year 1	*Year 2*	*Year 3*	*Year 4*	...
Expenses from using old machine for one year and then replacing it	DEM3,100	DEM2,860	DEM2,860	DEM2,860	...

BIKE should replace the old machine immediately in order to minimize the expense at year 1.

One caveat is in order. Perhaps the old machine's maintenance is high in the first year, but drops after that. A decision to replace immediately might be premature in that case. Therefore, we need to check the cost of the old machine in future years. The cost of keeping the existing machine a second year is

$$\text{PV of costs at time 1} = \text{DEM2,500} + \frac{\text{DEM2,000}}{1.15} - \frac{\text{DEM1,500}}{1.15} = \text{DEM2,935}$$

which has future value of DEM3,375 (DEM2,935 × 1.15).

The costs of keeping the existing machine for years 3 and 4 are also greater than the EAC of buying a new machine. Thus, BIKE's decision to replace the old machine immediately still is valid. ●

Concept Questions

- What is the equivalent annual cost method of capital budgeting?
- Can you list the assumptions that we must make to use EAC?

8.5   Summary and Conclusions

This chapter discusses a number of practical applications of capital budgeting.

1. Capital budgeting must be placed on an incremental basis. This means that sunk costs must be ignored, while both opportunity costs and side-effects must be considered.
2. Inflation must be handled consistently. One approach is to express both cash flows and the discount rate in nominal terms. The other approach is to express both cash flow and the discount rate in real terms. Because either approach yields the same NPV calculation, the simpler method should be used. The simpler method will generally depend on the type of capital budgeting problem.

3. In the Baldwin case, we computed NPV using the following two steps:
   a. Calculate the net cash flow from all sources for each period.
   b. Calculate the NPV using the cash flows calculated above.
   Alternatively, we might have used the following two steps:
   a. Calculate the present value of each source, for example, revenues, costs, taxes.
   b. Add the present value across the different sources (including initial investment) in order to get NPV.
   The second approach allows three benefits. Simplifying formulas can often be used. Nominal cash flows and real cash flows can be handled in the same example. Cash flows of varying risk can be used in the same example.

KEY TERMS

Sunk cost 175	Real interest rate 182
Opportunity cost 175	Nominal interest rate 182
Erosion 175	Nominal cash flow 183
Net working capital 177	Real cash flow 183

QUESTIONS AND PROBLEMS

NPV and Capital Budgeting

8.1 Which of the following cash flows should be treated as incremental cash flows when computing the NPV of an investment?
   a. The reduction in the sales of the company's other products.
   b. The expenditure on plant and equipment.
   c. The cost of research and development undertaken in connection with the product during the past three years.
   d. The annual depreciation expense.
   e. Dividend payments.
   f. The resale value of plant and equipment at the end of the project's life.
   g. Salary and medical costs for production employees on leave.

8.2 The Best Manufacturing Company is considering a new investment. Financial projections for the investment are tabulated below. (Cash flows are in GBP thousands and the corporate tax rate is 34 per cent.)

	Year 0	Year 1	Year 2	Year 3	Year 4
Sales revenue		7,000	7,000	7,000	7,000
Operating costs		2,000	2,000	2,000	2,000
Investment	10,000				
Depreciation		2,500	2,500	2,500	2,500
New working capital (end of year)	200	250	300	200	0

   a. Compute the incremental net income of the investment.
   b. Compute the incremental cash flows of the investments.
   c. Suppose the appropriate discount rate is 12 per cent. What is the NPV of the project?

8.3 XOX International has land in Europe that is expected to produce average annual profits of GBP800,000 in real terms forever. XOX has no depreciable assets and is an all-equity firm with 200,000 shares outstanding. The appropriate discount rate for its share is 12 per cent. XOX has an investment opportunity with a gross present value of GBP1 million. The investment requires a GBP400,000 outlay now. XOX has no other investment opportunities. Assume that all cash flows are received at the end of each year. What is the theortetical price per share of XOX?

Capital Budgeting with Inflation

8.4 Consider the following cash flows on two mutually exclusive projects.

Year	Project A	Project B
0	$-$CHF40,000	$-$CHF50,000
1	20,000	10,000
2	15,000	20,000
3	15,000	40,000

Cash flows of project *A* are expressed in real terms, while those of project *B* are expressed in nominal terms. The appropriate nominal discount rate is 15 per cent, and the inflation is 4 per cent. Which project should you choose?

8.5 Sanders Enterprises has been considering the purchase of a new manufacturing facility for CHF120,000. The facility is to be depreciated for tax on a seven-year basis. It is expected to have no value after seven years. Operating revenues from the facility are expected to be CHF50,000 in the first year. The revenues are expected to increase at the inflation rate of 5 per cent. Production costs in the first year are CHF20,000, and they are expected to increase at 7 per cent per year. The real discount rate for risky cash flows is 14 per cent, while the nominal riskless interest rate is 10 per cent. The corporate tax rate is 34 per cent. Tax payments are not to be lagged. Should the company accept the suggestion?

8.6 Tilkowski GmbH runs a small manufacturing operation. For this year, it expects to have real net cash flows of DEM120,000. Tilkowski GmbH is an ongoing operation, but it expects competitive pressures to erode its (inflation-adjusted) net cash flows at 6 per cent per year. The appropriate real discount rate for Tilkowski is 11 per cent. All net cash flows are received at year-end. What is the present value of the net cash flows from Tilkowski's operations?

8.7 Biological Insect Control plc (BIC) has hired you as a consultant to evaluate the NPV of their proposed toad ranch. BIC plans to breed toads and sell them as ecologically desirable insect-control mechanisms. They anticipate that the business will continue in perpetuity. Following negligible start-up costs, BIC will incur the following nominal cash flows at the end of the year:

Revenues	GBP150,000
Labour costs	80,000
Other costs	40,000

The company will lease machinery from a firm for GBP20,000 per year. (The lease payment starts at the end of year 1.) The payments of the lease are fixed in nominal terms. Sales will increase at 5 per cent per year in real terms. Labour costs will increase at 3 per cent per year in real terms. Other costs will decrease at 1 per cent per year in real terms. The rate of inflation is expected to be 6 per cent per year. The real rate of discount for revenues and costs is 10 per cent. The lease payments are risk-free; therefore, they must be discounted at the risk-free rate. The real risk-free rate is 7 per cent. There are no taxes. All cash flows occur at year-end. What is the NPV of BIC's proposed toad farm today?

8.8 A machine that lasts four years has the following net cash outflows. DEM12,000 is the cost of purchasing the machine, and DEM6,000 is the annual year-end operating cost. At the end of four years, the machine is sold for DEM2,000; thus, the cash flow at year four, C_4, is only DEM4,000.

C_0	C_1	C_2	C_3	C_4
DEM12,000	DEM6,000	DEM6,000	DEM6,000	DEM4,000

The cost of capital is 6 per cent. What is the present value of the costs of operating a series of such machines in perpetuity?

Replacement with Unequal Lives

8.9 Office Automation NV is obliged to choose between two copiers, XX40 or RH45. XX40 costs less than RH45, but its economic life is shorter. The costs and maintenance expenses of these two copiers are given as follows. These cash flows are expressed in real terms.

Copier	Year 0	Year 1	Year 2	Year 3	Year 4	Year 5
XX40	NLG700	NLG100	NLG100	NLG100		
RH45	NLG900	NLG110	NLG110	NLG110	NLG110	NLG110

The inflation rate is 5 per cent and the nominal discount rate is 14 per cent. Assume that revenues are the same regardless of the copier and that whichever copier the company chooses, it will buy the model forever. Which copier should the company choose? Ignore taxes and depreciation.

8.10 Fibre Glasses must choose between two kinds of facilities. Facility I costs CHF2.1 million and its economic life is 7 years. The maintenance costs for facility I are CHF60,000 per year. Facility II costs CHF2.8 million and it lasts 10 years. The annual maintenance costs for facility II are CHF100,000 per year. Both facilities are fully depreciated for tax purposes by the straight-line method. The facilities have no values after their economic lives. The corporate tax rate is 34 per cent. Revenues from the facilities are the same. The company is assumed to earn a sufficient amount of revenues to generate tax shields from depreciation. If the appropriate discount rate is 10 per cent, which facility should Fibre Glasses choose? Do not lag taxes.

CHAPTER 9

Strategy and Analysis in Using Net Present Value

The previous chapter discussed how to identify the incremental cash flows involved in capital budgeting decisions. In this chapter, we look more closely at what it is about a project that produces a positive net present value (NPV). The process of asking about the sources of positive NPV in capital budgeting is often referred to as *corporate strategy analysis*. We talk about corporate strategy analysis in the first part of the chapter. Next, we consider several analytical tools that help managers deal with the effects of uncertainty on incremental cash flows. The concepts of decision trees, scenario analysis and break-even analysis are discussed.

9.1 Corporate Strategy and Positive NPV

The intuition behind discounted cash flow analysis is that a project must generate a higher rate of return than the one that can be earned in the capital markets. Only if this is true will a project's NPV be positive. A significant part of corporate strategy analysis is seeking investment opportunities that can produce positive NPV.

Simple 'number crunching' in a discounted cash flow analysis can sometimes erroneously lead to a positive NPV calculation. In calculating discounted cash flows, it is always useful to ask: What is it about this project that produces a positive NPV? or: where does the positive NPV in capital budgeting come from? In other words, we must be able to point to the specific sources of positive increments to present value in doing discounted cash flow analysis. In general, it is sensible to assume that positive NPV projects are hard to find and that most project proposals are 'guilty until proven innocent'.

Here are some ways that firms create positive NPV:

1. Be the first to introduce a new product.
2. Further develop a core competency to produce goods or services at lower cost than competitors.
3. Create a barrier that makes it difficult for other firms to compete effectively.
4. Introduce variations on existing products to take advantage of unsatisfied demand.
5. Create product differentiation by aggressive advertising and marketing networks.
6. Use innovation in organizational processes to do all of the above.
7. Extend competencies in the home market to overseas.

This is undoubtedly a partial list of potential sources of positive NPV. However, it is important to keep in mind the fact that positive NPV projects are not commonplace. Our basic economic intuition should tell us that it will be harder to find positive NPV projects in a competitive industry than a non-competitive industry. Positive NPV is usually associated with what economists call market imperfections.

Now we ask another question: How can someone find out whether a firm is obtaining positive NPV from its operating and investment activities? First we talk about how share prices are related to long-term and short-term decision-making. Next we explain how managers can find clues in share price behaviour on whether they are making good decisions.

Corporate Strategy and the Stock Market

There should be a connection between the stock market and capital budgeting. If a firm invests in a project that is worth more than its cost, the project will produce positive NPV, and the firm's stock price should go up. However, the popular financial press frequently suggests that the best way for a firm to increase its share price is to report high short-term earnings. As a consequence, it is often said that some firms tend to reduce capital expenditures and research and development in order to increase short-term profits and stock prices. Moreover, it is claimed that UK and American firms that have valid long-term goals and undertake long-term capital budgeting at the expense of short-term profits are hurt by short-sighted stock market reactions. Sometimes institutional investors are blamed for this state of affairs. By contrast, Japanese firms are said to have a long-term perspective and make the necessary investments in research and development to provide a competitive edge against British and US firms.

Of course, these claims rest, in part, on the assumption that the UK and US stock markets systematically overvalue short-term earnings and undervalue long-term earnings. The available evidence does not confirm this. McConnell and Muscarella looked closely at the effect of corporate investment on the market value of equity.[1] They found that, for most US industrial firms, announcements of increases in planned capital spending were associated with significant increases in the market value of the common stock (an American term meaning ordinary shares) and that announcements of decreases in capital spending had the opposite effect. The McConnell and Muscarella research suggests that the US stock market pays close attention to corporate capital spending and it reacts positively to firms making long-term investments.

In another highly regarded study, Woolridge studied the stock market reaction to the strategic capital spending programs of several hundred US firms.[2] He looked at firms announcing joint ventures, research and development spending, new-product strategies and capital spending for expansion and modernization. He found a strong positive stock reaction to these types of announcements. This finding provides significant support for the notion that the stock market encourages managers to make long-term strategic investment decisions in order to maximize shareholders' value. It strongly opposes the viewpoint that markets and managers are myopic.

---

[1] John J. McConnell and Chris J. Muscarella (1985), 'Corporate capital expenditure decisions and the market value of the firm', *Journal of Financial Economics*, September, pp. 399–422.

[2] J. Randall Woolridge (1988), 'Competitive decline: Is a myopic stock market to blame', *Journal of Applied Corporate Finance*, Spring, pp. 26–36. Another interesting study has been conducted by Su Han Chan, John Martin and John Kensinger (1990), 'Corporate research and development expenditures and share value', *Journal of Financial Economics*, **26**, pp. 255–76. They report that the share-price responses to announcements of increased research and development are significantly positive, even when the firm's earnings were decreasing.

Concept Questions

- What are the ways a firm can create positive NPV projects?
- What NPV would you expect to accrue from investment in a project in what economists call a perfect market? Why?

9.2   Decision Trees

We have considered potential sources of value in NPV analysis. Now our interest is in coming up with estimates of NPV for a proposed project. A fundamental problem in NPV analysis is dealing with uncertain future outcomes. Furthermore, there is usually a sequence of decisions in NPV project analysis. This section introduces the device of **decision trees** for identifying the sequential decisions in NPV analysis.

Imagine you are the treasurer of the Solar Electronics Corporation (SEC), and the engineering group has recently developed the technology for solar-powered jet engines. The jet engine is to be used with 150-passenger commercial airplanes. The marketing staff has proposed that SEC develop some prototypes and conduct test marketing of the engine. A corporate planning group, including representatives from production, marketing and engineering, has recommended that the firm go ahead with the test and development phase. They estimate that this preliminary phase will take a year and will cost GBP100 million. Furthermore, the group believes there is a 75 per cent chance that the reproduction and marketing tests will prove successful.

Based on its experience in the industry, the company has a fairly accurate idea of how much the development and testing expenditures will cost. Sales of jet engines, however, are subject to (1) uncertainty about the demand for air travel in the future, (2) uncertainty about future oil prices, (3) uncertainty about SEC's market share for engines for 150-passenger planes and (4) uncertainty about the demand for 150-passenger planes relative to other sizes. Future oil prices will have a substantial impact on when airlines replace their existing fleets of Boeing 727 jets, because the 727s are much less fuel efficient compared with the new jets that will be produced over the next five years.

If the initial marketing tests are successful, SEC can acquire some land, build several new plants, and go ahead with full-scale production. This investment phase will cost GBP1,500 million. Production will occur over the next five years. The preliminary cash flow projection appears in Table 9.1. Should SEC decide to go ahead with investment and production on the jet engine, the NPV at a discount rate of 15 per cent (in millions) is

$$\text{NPV} = -\text{GBP1,500} + \sum_{t=1}^{5} \frac{\text{GBP900}}{(1.15)^t}$$

$$= -\text{GBP1,500} + \text{GBP900} \times A_{0.15}^5$$

$$= \text{GBP1,517}$$

Note that the NPV is calculated as of date 1, the date at which the investment of GBP1,500 million is made. Later we bring this number back to date 0.

If the initial marketing tests are unsuccessful, SEC's GBP1,500 million investment has an NPV of −GBP3,611 million. This figure is also calculated as of date 1.

Figure 9.1 displays the problem concerning the jet engine as a decision tree. If SEC decides to conduct test marketing, there is a 75 per cent probability that the test marketing will be successful. If the tests are successful, the firm faces a second

TABLE 9.1   **Cash Flow Forecasts for Solar Electronics Corporation's Jet Engine Base Case (millions)***

Investment	Year 1	Year 2
Revenues		GBP6,000
Variable costs		(3,000)
Fixed costs		(1,791)
Depreciation		(300)
Pretax profit		909
Tax ($T_c = 0.34$)		(309)
Net profit		GBP600
Cash flow		GBP900
Initial investment costs	− GBP1,500	

* Assumptions: (1) Investment is depreciated in years 2 through 6 using the straight-line method; (2) tax rate is 34 per cent on pretax profit; (3) the company receives no tax benefits on initial development costs.

decision: whether to invest GBP1,500 million in a project that yields GBP1,517 million NPV or to stop. If the tests are unsuccessful, the firm faces a different decision: whether to invest GBP1,500 million in a project that yields −GBP3,611 million NPV or to stop.

As can be seen from Figure 9.1, SEC has the following two decisions to make:

1. Whether to test and develop the solar-powered jet engine.
2. Whether to invest for full-scale production following the results of the test.

One makes decisions in reverse order with decision trees. Thus, we analyse the second-stage investment of GBP1,500 million first. If the tests are successful, it is obvious that SEC should invest, because GBP1,517 million is greater than zero. Just as obviously, if the tests are unsuccessful, SEC should not invest.

FIGURE 9.1   **Decision Tree (GBP millions) for SEC**

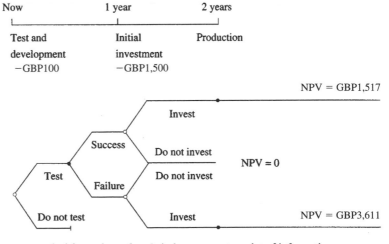

Open circles represent decision points; closed circles represent receipt of information.

Now we move back to the first stage where the decision boils down to a simple question: Should SEC invest GBP100 million now to obtain a 75 per cent chance of GBP1,517 million one year later? The expected payoff evaluated at date 1 (in millions) is

$$\begin{pmatrix} \text{Expected} \\ \text{payoff} \end{pmatrix} = \begin{pmatrix} \text{Probability} \\ \text{of} \\ \text{sucess} \end{pmatrix} \times \begin{pmatrix} \text{Payoff} \\ \text{if} \\ \text{successful} \end{pmatrix} + \begin{pmatrix} \text{Probability} \\ \text{of} \\ \text{failure} \end{pmatrix} \times \begin{pmatrix} \text{Payoff} \\ \text{if} \\ \text{failure} \end{pmatrix}$$

$$= (0.75 \times \text{GBP1,517}) + (0.25 \times \text{GBP0})$$

$$= \text{GBP1,138}$$

The NPV of testing computed at date 0 (in millions) is

$$\text{NPV} = -\text{GBP100} + \frac{\text{GBP1,138}}{1.15}$$
$$= \text{GBP890}$$

Thus, the firm should test the market for solar-powered jet engines.

Warning 1   We have used a discount rate of 15 per cent for both the testing and the investment decisions. Perhaps a higher discount rate should have been used for the initial test-marketing decision, which is likely to be riskier than the investment decision.

Warning 2   It was assumed that after making the initial investment to produce solar engines and then being confronted with a low demand, SEC could lose money. This worst-case scenario leads to an NPV of −GBP3,611 million. This is an unlikely eventuality. Instead, it is more plausible to assume that SEC would try to sell its initial investment-patents, land, buildings, machinery and prototypes—for GBP1,000 million. For example, faced with low demand, suppose SEC could scrap the initial investment. In this case, it would lose GBP500 million of the original investment. This is much better than what would happen if it produced the solar-powered jet engines and generated a negative NPV of GBP3,611 million. It is hard for decision trees to capture all of the managerial options in changing environments.

Concept Questions

- What is a decision tree?
- What are two potential problems in using decision trees?

9.3   Sensitivity Analysis, Scenario Analysis and Break-even Analysis

One thrust of this book is that NPV analysis is a superior capital-budgeting technique. In fact, because the NPV approach uses cash flows rather than profits, uses all the cash flows and discounts the cash flows properly, it is hard to find any theoretical fault with it. However, in our conversations with practical business people, we hear the phrase 'a false sense of security' frequently. These people point out that the documentation for capital-budgeting proposals is often quite impressive. Cash flows are projected down to the last thousand pounds, marks or lira (or even the last pound, mark or lira) for each year (or even each month). Opportunity costs and side-effects are handled quite properly. Sunk costs are ignored—also quite properly. When a high net present value appears at the bottom, one's temptation is immediately to say yes. Nevertheless, the projected cash flow often goes unmet in practice, and the firm ends up with a money loser.

Sensitivity Analysis and Scenario Analysis

How can the firm get the net-present-value technique to live up to its potential? One approach is **sensitivity analysis** (also known as *what-if analysis* and *bop*[3] analysis). This approach examines how sensitive a particular NPV calculation is to changes in underlying assumptions. We illustrate the technique with Solar Electronics' solar-powered jet engine from the previous section. As pointed out earlier, the cash flow forecasts for this project appear in Table 9.1. We begin by considering the assumptions underlying revenues, costs, and after-tax cash flows shown in the table.

Revenues

Sales projections for the proposed jet engine have been estimated by the marketing department as

Number of jet engines sold	=	Market share	×	Size of jet engine market
3,000	=	0.30	×	10,000

Sales revenues	=	Number of jet engines sold	×	Price per engine
GBP6,000 million	=	3,000	×	GBP2 million

Thus, it turns out that the revenue estimates depend on three assumptions.

1. Market share
2. Size of jet engine market
3. Price per engine

Costs

Financial analysts frequently divide costs into two types: variable costs and fixed costs. **Variable costs** change as the quantity of output changes, and they are zero when production is zero. Costs of direct labour and raw materials are usually variable. It is common to assume that variable costs are proportional to production. A typical variable cost is one that is constant per unit of output. For example, if direct labour is variable and one unit of final output requires GBP10 of direct labour, then 100 units of final output should require GBP1,000 of direct labour.

Fixed costs are not dependent on the amount of goods or services produced during the period. Fixed costs are usually measured as costs per unit of time, such as rent per month or salaries per year. Naturally, fixed costs are not fixed forever. They are only fixed over a predetermined time period.

---

[3] Bop stands for best, optimistic, pessimistic.

Variable costs per unit produced have been estimated by the engineering department at GBP1 million. Fixed costs are GBP1,791 million per year. The cost breakdowns are

Variable cost	=	Variable cost per unit	×	Number of jet engines sold
GBP3,000 million	=	GBP1 million	×	3,000
Total cost before taxes	=	Variable cost	+	Fixed cost
GBP4,791 million	=	GBP3,000 million	+	GBP1,791 million

The above estimates for market size, market share, price, variable cost and fixed cost, as well as the estimate of initial investment, are presented in the middle column of Table 9.2. These figures represent the firm's expectations or best estimates of the different parameters. For purposes of comparison, the firm's analysts prepared both optimistic and pessimistic forecasts for the different variables. These are also provided in the table.

Standard sensitivity analysis calls for an NPV calculation for all three possibilities of a single variable, along with the expected forecast for all other variables. This procedure is illustrated in Table 9.3. For example, consider the NPV calculation of GBP8,154 million provided in the upper righthand corner of this table. This occurs when the

TABLE 9.2   Different Estimates for Solar Electronics' Solar Plane

Variable	Pessimistic	Expected or best	Optimistic
Market size (per year)	5,000	10,000	20,000
Market share	20%	30%	50%
Price	GBP1.9 million	GBP2 million	GBP2.2 million
Variable cost (per plane)	GBP1.2 million	GBP1 million	GBP0.8 million
Fixed cost (per year)	GBP1,891 million	GBP1,791 million	GBP1,741 million
Investment	GBP1,900 million	GBP1,500 million	GBP1,000 million

TABLE 9.3   NPV Calculations as of Date 1 (in GBP millions) for the Solar Plane Using Sensitivity Analysis

Variable	Pessimistic	Expected or best	Optimistic
Market size	−GBP1,802*	GBP1,517	GBP8,154
Market share	−GBP696*	GBP1,517	GBP5,942
Price	GBP853	GBP1,517	GBP2,844
Variable cost	GBP189	GBP1,517	GBP2,844
Fixed cost	GBP1,295	GBP1,517	GBP1,628
Investment	GBP1,208	GBP1,517	GBP1,903

Under sensitivity analysis, one input is vaired while all other inputs are assumed to meet their expectation. For example, an NPV of −GBP1,802 occurs when the pessimistic forecast of 5,000 is used for market size. However, the expected forecasts form Table 9.2 are used for all other variableswhen −GBP1,802 is generated.

* We assume that the other divisions of the firm are profitable, implying that a loss on this project can offset income elsewhere in the firm. The firm reports a loss to the inland revenue in these two cases. Thus, the loss on the project generates a tax rebate to the firm.

optimistic forecast of 20,000 units per year is used for market size. However, the expected forecasts from Table 9.2 are employed for all other variables when the GBP8,154 million figure is generated. Note that the same number of GBP1,517 million appears in each row of the middle column of Table 9.3. This occurs because the expected forecast is used for the variable that was singled out, as well as for all other variables.

A table such as Table 9.3 can be used for a number of purposes. First, taken as a whole, the table can indicate whether NPV analysis should be trusted. In other words, it reduces the false sense of security we spoke of earlier. Suppose that NPV is positive when the expected forecast for each variable is used. However, further suppose that every number in the pessimistic column is wildly negative and every number in the optimistic column is wildly positive. Even a single error in this forecast greatly alters the estimate, making one leery of the net-present-value approach. A conservative manager might well scrap the entire NPV analysis in this case. Fortunately, this does not seem to be the case in Table 9.3, because all but two of the numbers are positive. Managers viewing the table will likely consider NPV analysis to be useful for the solar-powered jet engine.

Second, sensitivity analysis shows where more information is needed. For example, error in the investment appears to be relatively unimportant because even under the pessimistic scenario, the NPV of GBP1,208 million is still highly positive. By contrast, the pessimistic forecast for market share leads to a negative NPV of −GBP696 million, and a pessimistic forecast for market size leads to a substantially negative NPV of −GBP1,802 million. Because the effect of incorrect estimates on revenues is so much greater than the effect of incorrect estimates on costs, more information on the factors determining revenues might be needed.

Unfortunately, sensitivity analysis suffers from some drawbacks. For example, sensitivity analysis may unwittingly *increase* the false sense of security among managers. Suppose all pessimistic forecasts yield positive NPVs. A manager might feel that there is no way the project can lose money. Of course, the forecasters may simply have an optimistic view of a pessimistic forecast. To combat this, some companies do not treat optimistic and pessimistic forecasts subjectively. Rather, their pessimistic forecasts are always, say, 20 per cent less than expected. Unfortunately, the cure in this case may be worse than the disease, because a deviation of a fixed percentage ignores the fact that some variables are easier to forecast than others.

In addition, sensitivity analysis treats each variable in isolation when, in reality, the different variables are likely to be related. For example, if ineffective management allows costs to get out of control, it is likely that variable costs, fixed costs and investment will all rise above expectation at the same time. If the market is not receptive to a solar plane, both market share and price should decline together.

Managers frequently perform **scenario analysis**, a variant of sensitivity analysis, to minimize this problem. Simply put, this approach examines a number of different likely scenarios, where each scenario involves a confluence of factors. As a simple example, consider the effect of a few airline crashes. These crashes are likely to reduce flying in total, thereby limiting the demand for any new engines. Furthermore, even if the crashes did not involve solar-powered aircraft, the public could become more adverse to any innovative and controversial technologies. Hence, SEC's market share might fall as well. Perhaps the cash flow calculations would look like those in Table 9.4 under the scenario of a plane crash. Given the calculations in the table, the NPV (in millions) would be

$$-GBP2{,}023 = -GBP1{,}500 - GBP156 \times A_{0.15}^{5}$$

A series of scenarios like this might illuminate issues concerning the project better than a standard application of sensitivity analysis would.

TABLE 9.4 Cash Flow Forecast (in GBP millions) under the Scenario of a Plane Crash *

Investment	Year 1	Years 2–6
Revenues		2,800
Variable costs		−1,400
Fixed costs		−1,791
Depreciation		−300
Pretax profit		−691
Tax ($T_c = 0.34$)†		235
Net profit		−456
Cash flow		−156
Initial investment costs	−1,500	

* Assumptions are: Market size 7,000 (70 per cent of expectation); Market share 20 per cent (2/3 of expectation).

Forecasts for all other variables are the expected forecasts as given in Table 9.2.

† Tax loss offsets income elsewhere in firm.

Break-Even Analysis

Our discussion of sensitivity analysis and scenario analysis suggests that there are many ways to examine variability in forecasts. We now present another approach, **break-even analysis**. As its name implies, this approach determines the sales needed to break even. The approach is a useful complement to sensitivity analysis, because it also sheds light on the severity of incorrect forecasts. We calculate the break-even point in terms of both accounting profit and present value.

Accounting Profit

Net profit under four different sales forecasts is

Unit sales	Net profit (GBP millions)
0	−1,380
1,000	−720
3,000	600
10,000	5,220

A more complete presentation of costs and revenues appears in Table 9.5.

TABLE 9.5 Revenues and Costs of Project under Different Sales Assumptions (GBP millions, except unit sales)

Year 1		Years 2–6							
Initial investment	Annual unit sales	Revenues	Variable costs	Fixed costs	Depreci-ation	Taxes* ($T_c = 0.34$)	Net profits	Operating cash flows	NPV (evaluated date 1)
GBP1,500	0	GBP0	GBP0	−GBP1,791	−GBP300	GBP711	−GBP1,380	−GBP1,080	−GBP5,120
1,500	1,000	2,000	−1,100	−1,791	−300	371	−720	−420	−2,908
1,500	3,000	6,000	−3,000	−1,791	−300	−309	600	900	1,517
1,500	10,000	20,000	−10,000	−1,791	−300	−2,689	5,220	5,520	17,004

*Loss is incurred in the first two rows. For tax purposes, this loss offsets income elsewhere in the firm.

FIGURE 9.2   **Break-even Point Using Accounting Numbers**

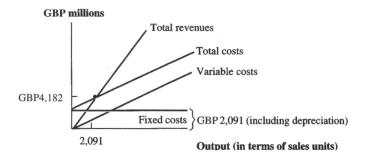

We plot the revenues, costs and profits under the different assumptions about sales in Figure 9.2. The revenue and cost curves cross at 2,091 jet engines. This is the break-even point, in other words, the point where the project generates no profits or losses. As long as sales are above 2,091 jet engines, the project will make a profit.

This break-even point can be calculated very easily. Because the sales price is GBP2 million per engine and the variable cost is GBP1 million per engine,[4] the after-tax difference per engine is

$$(\text{Sales price} - \text{Variable cost}) \times (1 - T_c)$$

$$= (\text{GBP2 million} - \text{GBP1 million}) \times (1 - 0.34) = \text{GBP0.66 million}$$

where T_c is the corporate tax rate of 34 per cent. This after-tax difference is called the **contribution margin** because it is the amount that each additional engine contributes to after-tax profit.

Fixed costs are GBP1,791 million and depreciation is GBP300 million, implying that the after-tax sum of these costs is

$$(\text{Fixed costs} + \text{Depreciation}) \times (1 - T_c)$$

$$= (\text{GBP1,791 million} + \text{GBP300 million}) \times (1 - 0.34) = \text{GBP1,380 million}$$

That is, the firm incurs costs of GBP1,380 million, regardless of the number of sales. Because each engine contributes GBP0.66 million, sales must reach the following level to offset the above costs:

Accounting Profit Break-even Point:

$$\frac{(\text{Fixed costs} + \text{Depreciation}) \times (1 - T_c)}{(\text{Sales price} - \text{Variable costs}) \times (1 - T_c)} = \frac{\text{GBP1,380 million}}{\text{GBP0.66 million}} = 2,091$$

Thus, 2,091 engines is the break-even point required for an accounting profit.

Present Value

As we have stated many times in the text, we are more interested in present value than we are in net profits. Therefore, we must calculate the present value of the cash flows.

---

[4] Though the previous section considered both optimistic and pessimistic forecasts for sales price and variable cost, break-even analysis only works with the expected or best estimates of these variables.

Given a discount rate of 15 per cent, we have

Unit sales	NPV (GBP millions)
0	−5,120
1,000	−2,908
3,000	1,517
10,000	17,004

These NPV calculations are reproduced in the last column of Table 9.5. We can see that the NPV is negative if SEC produces 1,000 jet engines and positive if it produces 3,000 jet engines. Obviously, the zero NPV point occurs between 1,000 and 3,000 jet engines.

The present value break-even point can be calculated very easily. The firm originally invested GBP1,500 million. This initial investment can be expressed as a five-year equivalent annual cost (EAC), determined by dividing the initial investment by the appropriate five-year annuity factor:

$$
\begin{aligned}
EAC &= \frac{\text{Initial investment}}{\text{5-year annuity factor at 15\%}} \\
&= \frac{\text{Initial investment}}{A^5_{0.15}} \\
&= \frac{\text{GBP1,500 million}}{3.3522} = \text{GBP447.5 million}
\end{aligned}
$$

Note that the EAC of GBP447.5 million is greater than the yearly depreciation of GBP300 million. This must occur since the calculation of EAC implicitly assumes that the GBP1,500 million investment could have been invested at 15 per cent.

After-tax costs, regardless of output, can be viewed as

$$
\text{GBP1,528 million} = \text{GBP447.5 million} + \text{GBP1,791 million} \times 0.66 - \text{GBP300 million} \times 0.34
$$

$$
= EAC + \text{Fixed costs} \times (1 - T_c) - \text{Depreciation} \times T_c
$$

That is, in addition to the initial investment's equivalent annual cost of GBP447.5 million, the firm pays fixed costs each year and receives a depreciation tax shield each year. The depreciation tax shield is written as a negative number because it offsets the costs in the equation. Because each plane contributes GBP0.66 million to after-tax profit, it will take the following sales to offset the above costs:

Present Value Break-Even Point:

$$
\frac{EAC + \text{Fixed costs} \times (1 - T_c) - \text{Depreciation} \times T_c}{(\text{Sales price} - \text{Variable costs}) \times (1 - T_c)} = \frac{\text{GBP1,528 million}}{\text{GBP0.66 million}} = 2,315
$$

Thus, 2,315 planes is the break-even point from the perspective of present value.

Why is the accounting break-even point different from the financial break-even point? When we use accounting profit as the basis for the break-even calculation, we subtract depreciation. Depreciation for the solar-jet-engines project is GBP300 million. If 2,091 solar jet engines are sold, SEC will generate sufficient revenues to cover the GBP300 million depreciation expense plus other costs. Unfortunately, at this level of sales SEC will not cover the economic opportunity costs of the GBP1,500 million laid out for the investment. If we take into account that the GBP1,500 million could have been invested at 15 per cent, the true annual cost of the investment is GBP447.5 million and not GBP300 million. Depreciation understates the true costs of recovering the initial investment. Thus, companies that break even on an accounting basis are really losing money. They are losing the opportunity cost of the initial investment.

Concept Questions

- What is a sensitivity analysis?
- Why is it important to perform a sensitivity analysis?
- What is a break-even analysis?
- Describe how sensitivity analysis interacts with break-even analysis.

9.4   Options

The analysis we have presented so far is static. In fact, standard NPV analysis is somewhat static. Because corporations make decisions in a dynamic environment, they have options that should be considered in project valuation.

The Option to Expand

One of the most important options is the option to expand when economic prospects are good. The option to expand has value. Expansion pays off if demand is high. Recall the Solar Electronics Corporation (SEC) in Section 9.2. SEC's expenditure on the test marketing program buys an option to produce new jet engines. This turned out to be a very valuable option. SEC had the option to produce new jet engines depending on the results of the test marketing.

There are many real-world examples. In 1977 Saab was the first car maker to introduce turbo-charged automobile engines in its gasoline model. Sales of the Saab 900 almost doubled after the introduction. In response to this high demand, Saab has increased its capacity and entered into joint ventures with other car makers to increase production. Now many automobile manufacturers use turbo chargers.

The Option to Abandon

The option to close a facility also has value. The SEC would not have been obligated to produce jet engines if the test marketing results had been negative. Instead, SEC had the option to abandon the jet engine project if the results had been bad.

Take the case of General Motors (GM). On December 19, 1991, GM announced plans to close 21 factories and cut 74,000 jobs by the end of 1995. It said that it also intended to sell non-auto assets. Faced with low demand for its automobiles, GM decided to scrap the investment it had made in automobile manufacturing capacity, and it will likely lose much of its original investment in the 21 factories. However, this outcome is much better than would have occurred if GM continued to operate these factories in a declining auto market. On the day the factory closing was announced, GM's stock was marginally down by USD0.125 (from USD27.875 to USD27.75). The stock market reaction was a signal that GM had waited too long to close its factories and that the declining demand GM was encountering was greater than expected. However, the market was relieved that GM had finally abandoned money-losing factories.

Corporations frequently make changes in their plans when confronted with changing market conditions. One of the most stunning reversals in marketing history occurred on June 10, 1985, when Coca-Cola publicly apologized for scrapping 'old' Coke, a 99-year-old product. Henceforth, the company said, the 'old' Coca-Cola would be revived as 'Coca-Cola Classic'. By reviving the old Coke, the Coca-Cola Company undid an abandonment decision that had taken four-and-a-half years of planning and market research. Coke's original plan to abandon the old Coke and to replace it with new Coke was intended to break what for several years had been Pepsi's biggest advantage in the market: its ability to win taste contests. However, Coca-Cola's decision after two months to revive the old Coke came because of the unwillingness of a large number of consumers to go along with the idea of a new Coke.

Discounted Cash Flows and Options

Conventional NPV analysis discounts a project's cash flows estimated for a certain project life. The decision is whether to accept the project or reject it. In practice, managers can expand or contract the scope of a project at various moments over its life. In theory, all such managerial options should be included in the project's value.

The market value of the project (M) will be the sum of the NPV of the project without options to expand or contract and the value of the managerial options (Opt):

$$M = \text{NPV} + \text{Opt}$$

● **Example**

Imagine two ways of producing Frisbees. Method A uses a conventional machine that has an active secondary market. Method B uses highly specialized machine tools for which there is no secondary market. Method B has no salvage value, but is more efficient. Method A has a salvage value, but is inefficient.

If production of Frisbees goes on until the machines used in methods A and B are used up, the NPV of B will be greater than that of A. However, if there is some possibility that production of Frisbees will be stopped before the end of the useful life of the Frisbee-making machines, method A is better. Method A's higher value in the secondary market increases its NPV relative to B's. ●

Robichek and Van Horne and Dye and Long were among the first to recognize the abandonment value in project analysis.[5] More recently, Myers and Majd constructed a model of abandonment based on an American put option with varying dividend yields and an uncertain exercise price.[6] They present a numerical procedure for calculating abandonment value in problems similar to that of the Frisbee-making machine.

Brennan and Schwartz use a gold mine to illustrate the value of managerial operations.[7] They show that the value of a gold mine will depend on management's ability to shut it down if the price of gold falls below a certain point, and the ability to reopen it subsequently if conditions are right. They show that valuation approaches that ignore these managerial options are likely to substantially underestimate the value of the project.

---

[5] A. Robichek and J. Van Horne (1967), 'Abandonment value and capital budgeting', *Journal of Finance*, December; and E. Dye and H. Long (1969), 'Abandonment value and capital budgeting: Comment', *Journal of Finance*, March.

[6] S. C. Myers and S. Majd (1985), 'Calculating abandonment value using option pricing theory', Unpublished manuscript, June.

[7] M. J. Brennan and E. S. Schwartz (1985), 'A new approach to evaluating natural resource investments', *Midland Corporate Finance Journal*, **3**, Spring.

There are both qualitative and quantitative approaches to adjusting for option value in capital budgeting decisions. Most firms use qualitative approaches, such as subjective judgment. However, quantitative approaches are gaining acceptance. We talk about the quantitative approaches in Chapter 22.

9.5   Summary and Conclusions

This chapter discusses a number of practical applications of capital budgeting.

1. In Chapter 8, we observed how the net-present-value rule in capital budgeting is used. In Chapter 9, we ask about the sources of positive net present value and we explain what managers can do to create positive net present value.

2. Though NPV is the best capital-budgeting approach conceptually, it has been criticized in practice for providing managers with a false sense of security. Sensitivity analysis shows NPV under varying assumptions, giving managers a better feel for the project's risks. Unfortunately, sensitivity analysis modifies only one variable at a time, while many variables are likely to vary together in the real world. Scenario analysis considers the joint movement of the different factors under different scenarios (e.g. war breaking out or oil prices skyrocketing). Finally, managers want to know how bad forecasts must be before a project loses money. Break-even analysis calculates the sales figure at which the project breaks even. Though break-even analysis is frequently performed on an accounting profit basis, we suggest that a net-present-value basis is more appropriate.

3. We talk about hidden options in doing discounted cash flow analysis of capital budgeting. We discuss the option to expand and the option to abandon.

KEY TERMS

Decision trees	195	Scenario analysis	200
Sensitivity analysis	198	Break-even analysis	201
Variable costs	198	Contribution margin	202
Fixed costs	198		

QUESTIONS AND PROBLEMS

Decision Trees

9.1 Bayern Electronix GmbH has developed a new type of VCR. If the firm directly goes to the market with the product, there is only a 50 per cent chance of success. On the other hand, if the firm conducts test marketing of the VCR, it will take a year and will cost DEM2 million. Through the test marketing, however, the firm is able to improve the product and increase the probability of success to 75 per cent. If the new product proves successful, the present value (at the time when the firm starts selling it) of the payoff is DEM20 million, while, if it turns out to be a failure, the present value of the payoff is DEM5 million. Should the firm conduct test marketing or go directly to the market? The appropriate discount rate is 15 per cent.

9.2 The marketing manager for a growing consumer products firm is considering launching a new product. To determine consumers' interest in such a product, the manager can conduct a focus group that will cost NLG120,000 and has a 70 per cent chance of correctly predicting the success of the product, or hire a consulting firm that will research the market at a cost of NLG400,000. The consulting firm boasts a correct assessment record of 90 per cent. Of course going directly to the market with no prior testing will be the correct move 50 per cent of the time. If the firm launches the product, and it is a success, the payoff will be NLG1.2 million. Which action will result in the highest expected payoff for the firm?

9.3 Holland Bikes NV is noticing a decline in sales due to the increase of lower-priced import products from the Far East. The finance director is considering a number of strategies to maintain its market share. The options he sees are the following:

- Price the products more aggressively, resulting in a NLG1.3 million decline in cash flows. The likelihood that Holland Bikes will lose no cash flows to the imports is 55 per cent; there is a 45 per cent probability that they will lose only NLG550,000 in cash flows to the imports.
- Hire a lobbyist to convince the regulators that there should be import tariffs placed upon overseas manufacturers of bicycles. This will cost Holland Bikes NLG800,000 and will have a 75 per cent success rate, that is, no loss in cash flows to the importers. If the lobbyists do not succeed, Holland Bikes will lose NLG2 million in cash flows.

As the assistant to the CFO, which strategy would you recommend to your boss?

Accounting Break-even Analysis

9.4 Samuelson plc has invested in a facility to produce calculators. The price of the machine is GBP600,000 and its economic life is five years. The machine is fully depreciated by the straight-line method and will produce 20,000 units of calculators in the first year. The variable production cost per unit of the calculator is GBP15, while fixed costs are GBP900,000. Corporate tax rate for the company is 30 per cent. What should the sales price per unit of the calculator be for the firm to have a zero profit? Do not bother to lag tax.

9.5 You are considering investing in a fledgling company that cultivates abalone for sale to local restaurants. The proprietor says he'll return all profits to you after covering operating costs and his salary. How many abalone must be harvested and sold in the first year of operations for you to get any payback? (Assume no depreciation.)

Price per adult abalone	= GBP2.00
Variable costs	= GBP0.72
Fixed costs	= GBP300,000
Salaries	= GBP40,000
Tax rate	= 35%

How much profit will be returned to you if he sells 300,000 abalone? Do not lag tax.

Present Value Break-even Analysis

9.6 Using the information in the problem above, what is the present value break-even point if the discount rate is 15 per cent, initial investment is GBP140,000, and the life of the project is seven years? Assume a straight-line depreciation method with a zero salvage value.

9.7 Kids & Toys GmbH has purchased a DEM200,000 machine to produce toy cars. The machine will be fully depreciated by the straight-line method for its economic life of five years and will be worthless after its life. The firm expects that sales price of the toy is DEM25, while its variable cost is DEM5. The firm should also pay DEM350,000 as fixed costs each year. The corporate tax rate for the company is 25 per cent, and the appropriate discount rate is 12 per cent. What is the present value break-even point?

Scenario Analysis

9.8 You are the financial analyst for a manufacturer of tennis rackets that has identified a graphite-like material that it is considering using in its rackets. Given the following information about the results of launching a new racket, will you undertake the project? (Assumptions: tax rate = 40 per cent, effective discount rate = 13 per cent, depreciation = CHF300,000 per year, and production will occur over the next five years only.)

	Pessimistic		Expected		Optimistic	
Market size	110,000		120,000		130,000	
Market share		22%		25%		27%
Price	CHF	115	CHF	120	CHF	125
Variable costs	CHF	72	CHF	70	CHF	68
Fixed costs	CHF	850,000	CHF	800,000	CHF	750,000
Investment	CHF1,500,000		CHF1,500,000		CHF1,500,000	

9.9 What would happen to the analysis done above if your competitor introduces a graphite composite that is even lighter than your product? What factors would this likely effect? Do an NPV analysis assuming market size increases (due to more awareness of graphite-based rackets) to the level predicted by the optimistic scenario, but your market share decreases to the pessimistic level (due to competitive forces). What does this tell you about the relative importance of market size versus market share?

PART III

Risk

10 Capital Market Theory: An Overview   211
11 Return and Risk: The Capital-Asset-Pricing Model (CAPM)   238
12 An Alternative View of Risk and Return: The Arbitrage Pricing Theory   277
13 Risk, Return, and Capital Budgeting   299

This part of the book examines the relationship between expected return and risk for portfolios and individual assets. When capital markets are in equilibrium, they determine a trade-off between expected return and risk. The return that shareholders can expect to obtain in the capital markets is the one they will require from firms when the firms evaluate risky investment projects. The shareholders' required return is the firm's cost of equity capital.

Chapter 10 examines the modern history of capital markets. A central fact emerges: the return on risky assets has been higher on average than the return on risk-free assets. This fact supports the perspective for our examination of risk and return. In Chapter 10, we introduce several key intuitions of modern finance and show how they can be useful in determining a firm's cost of capital.

Chapters 11 and 12 contain more advanced discussions of risk and expected return. The chapters are self-contained and elaborate on the material in Chapter 10.

Chapter 11 shows what determines the relationship between return and risk for portfolios. The model of risk and expected return used in the chapter is called the *capital-asset-pricing model* (CAPM).

Chapter 12 examines risk and return from another perspective: the arbitrage pricing theory (APT). This approach yields insights that one cannot get from the CAPM. The key concept is that the total risk of individual stocks can be divided into two parts: systematic and unsystematic. The fundamental principle of diversification is that, for highly diversified portfolios, unsystematic risk disappears; only systematic risk survives.

The section on risk finishes with a discussion in Chapter 13 on estimating a firm's cost of equity capital and some of the problems that are encountered in doing so.

Capital Market Theory: An Overview

The previous chapters of this book handled capital budgeting with riskless cash flows. These cash flows should be discounted at the riskless rate of interest. Because most capital-budgeting projects involve risky flows, a different discount rate must be used. The next four chapters are devoted to determining the discount rate for risky projects.

Past experience indicates that students find the following material among the most difficult in the entire book. Because of this, we always teach the material by presenting the results and conclusions first. By seeing where we are going ahead of time, it is easier to absorb the material when we get there. First, let us look at a synopsis of the four chapters.

1. Because our ultimate goal is to discount risky cash flows, we must first find a way to measure risk. In the current chapter, we measure the variability of a share by the variance or standard deviation of its returns. If an individual holds only *one* security, the variance or standard deviation of the security would be the appropriate measure of risk.

2. Because investors generally hold diversified portfolios, we are interested in the *contribution* of a security to the risk of the entire portfolio. Because much of an individual security's variance is dispersed in a large diversified portfolio, neither the security's variance nor its standard deviation can be viewed as the security's contribution to the risk of a large portfolio. Rather, this contribution is best measured by the security's *covariance* with the other securities in the portfolio. As an example, consider a stock whose returns are high when the portfolio's returns are low—and vice versa. This stock has negative covariance with the portfolio. In other words, it acts as a hedge, implying that the stock actually tends to reduce the risk of the portfolio. However, the stock could have a high variance, implying high risk for an investor holding only this security.

3. We talk about diversification and the related concept beta in the present chapter. The next chapter more fully develops the concept of *beta* (β). We argue that beta is the appropriate measure of the contribution of a security to the risk of a large portfolio.

4. Investors will only hold a risky security if its expected return is high enough to compensate for its risk. Given the above, the expected return on a security should be positively related to the security's beta. We introduce you to some of

these ideas in the present chapter. In Chapter 11, we develop more fully the following equation:

Expected return on security

= Risk free rate + Beta × (Expected return on market portfolio − Risk free rate)

Because the term in parentheses on the righthand side is positive, this equation says that the expected return on a security is a positive function of its beta. This equation is frequently referred to as the *capital-asset-pricing model* (CAPM).

5. We derive the relationship between risk and return in a different manner in Chapter 12. However, many of the conclusions are quite similar. This chapter is based on *arbitrage pricing theory* (APT).

6. The theoretical ideas in Chapters 10, 11 and 12 are quite intellectually challenging. Fortunately, Chapter 13, which applies the above theory to the selection of discount rates, is much simpler. In a world where (a) a project has the same risk as the firm and (b) the firm has no debt, the expected return on the stock should serve as the project's discount rate. This expected return is taken from the capital-asset-pricing model, as presented above.

Because we have a long road ahead of us, the maxim that any journey begins with a single step applies here. We start with the perhaps mundane calculation of a security's return.

10.1   Returns

Cash Returns on Shares

Suppose the Video Concept AG has several thousand shares outstanding and you are a shareholder. Further, suppose that you purchased some of the shares in the company at the beginning of the year; it is now year-end and you want to figure out how well you have done your investment. The return you get on an investment in shares, like that in bonds or any other investment, comes in two forms.

First, over the year most companies pay dividends to shareholders. As the owner of shares in Video Concept AG, you are a part owner of the company. If the company is profitable, it generally distributes some of its profits to the shareholders. Therefore, as the owner of shares of stock, you will receive some cash, called a *dividend*, during the year.[1] This cash is the *income component* of your return. In addition to the dividends, the other part of your return is the *capital gain*—or, if it is negative, the *capital loss* (negative capital gain)—on the investment.

For example, suppose we are considering the cash flows of the investment in Figure 10.1 and you purchased 100 shares at the beginning of the year at a price of DEM37 per share. Your total investment, then, would be

$$C_0 = DEM37 \times 100 = DEM3,700$$

Suppose that over the year the shares paid a dividend of DEM1.85 per share. During

---

[1] In fact, companies often continue to pay dividends even when they have lost money during the year. These dividends are part of the return that shareholders require to keep them from selling their shares of stock.

FIGURE 10.1   Returns

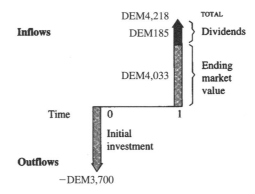

the year, then, you would have received income of

$$\text{Div} = \text{DEM}1.85 \times 100 = \text{DEM}185$$

Suppose, lastly, that at the end of the year the market price of the shares is DEM40.33 per share. Because the shares increased in price, you have a capital gain of

$$\text{Gain} = (\text{DEM}40.33 - \text{DEM}37) \times 100 = \text{DEM}333$$

The capital gain, like the dividend, is part of the return that shareholders require to maintain their investment in Video Concept AG. Of course, if the price of Video Concept shares had dropped in value to, say, DEM34.78, you would have recorded a capital loss of

$$\text{Loss} = (\text{DEM}34.78 - \text{DEM}37) \times 100 = -\text{DEM}222$$

The total return on your investment is the sum of the income and the capital gain or loss on the investment:

$$\text{Total return} = \text{Dividend income} + \text{Capital gain (or loss)}$$

(From now on we will refer to *capital losses* as *negative capital gains* and not distinguish them.) In our first example, then, the total return is given by

$$\text{Total return} = \text{DEM}185 + \text{DEM}333 = \text{DEM}518$$

Notice that if you sold the shares at the end of the year, your total amount of cash would be the initial investment plus the total return. In the preceding example, then, you would have

$$\text{Total cash if shares are sold} = \text{Initial investment} + \text{Total return}$$
$$= \text{DEM}3,700 + \text{DEM}518$$
$$= \text{DEM}4,218$$

As a check, notice that this is the same as the proceeds from the sale of shares plus the dividends:

$$\begin{aligned}
\text{Proceeds from share sale} &+ \text{Dividends} \\
&= \text{DEM40.33} \times 100 + \text{DEM185} \\
&= \text{DEM4,033} + \text{DEM185} \\
&= \text{DEM4,218}
\end{aligned}$$

Suppose, however, that you hold your Video Concept shares and don't sell them at year-end. Should you still consider the capital gain as part of your return? Does this violate our previous present value rule that only cash matters?

The answer to the first question is a strong yes, and the answer to the second question is an equally strong no. The capital gain is every bit as much a part of your return as is the dividend, and you should certainly count it as part of your total return. That you have decided to hold on to the stock and not sell or *realize* the gain or the loss in no way changes the fact that, if you wanted to, you could get the cash value of the stock.[2]

Percentage Returns

It is more convenient to summarize the information about returns in percentage terms than in dollars, because the percentages apply to any amount invested. The question we want to answer is: How much return do we get for each dollar invested? To find this out, let t stand for the year we are looking at, let P_t be the price of the stock at the beginning of the year, and let Div_{t+1} be the dividend paid on the stock during the year. Consider the cash flows in Figure 10.2.

In our example, the price at the beginning of the year was DEM37 per share and the dividend paid during the year on each share was DEM1.85. Hence the percentage of income return,[3] sometimes called the *dividend yield*, is

$$\text{Dividend yield} = \text{Div}_{t+1}/P_t = \text{DEM1.85}/\text{DEM37} = 0.05 = 5\%$$

Capital gain is the change in the price of the stock divided by the initial price. Letting P_{t+1} be the price of the stock at year-end, the capital gain can be computed

$$\begin{aligned}
\text{Capital gain} = (P_{t+1} - P_t)/P_t &= (\text{DEM40.33} - \text{DEM37})/\text{DEM37} \\
&= \text{DEM3.33}/\text{DEM37} \\
&= 0.09 \\
&= 9\%
\end{aligned}$$

---

[2] After all, you could always sell the shares at year-end and immediately buy them back. As we previously computed, the total return on the investment would be DEM518 before you bought the stock back. The total amount of cash you would have at year-end would be this DEM518 plus your initial investment of DEM3,700. You would not lose this return when you bought back 100 shares. In fact, you would be in exactly the same position as if you had not sold the shares (assuming, of course, that there are no tax consequences and no brokerage commissions from selling the shares).

[3] We will use 0.05 and 5 per cent interchangeably. Keep in mind that, although $(0.05)^2 = 0.0025$, $(5^2)\% = 25\%$. Thus, it is important to keep track of parentheses so that decimal points land where they belong.

FIGURE 10.2   Percentage Returns

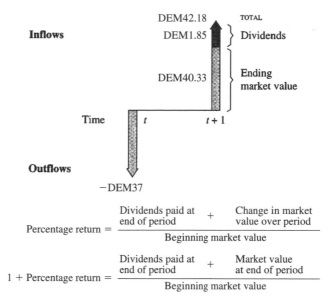

$$\text{Percentage return} = \frac{\begin{array}{c}\text{Dividends paid at} \\ \text{end of period}\end{array} + \begin{array}{c}\text{Change in market} \\ \text{value over period}\end{array}}{\text{Beginning market value}}$$

$$1 + \text{Percentage return} = \frac{\begin{array}{c}\text{Dividends paid at} \\ \text{end of period}\end{array} + \begin{array}{c}\text{Market value} \\ \text{at end of period}\end{array}}{\text{Beginning market value}}$$

Combining these two results, we find that the total returns on the investment in Video Concept stock during the year, which we will label R_{t+1}, was

$$R_{t+1} = \frac{\text{Div}_{t+1}}{P_t} + \frac{P_{t+1} - P_t}{P_t}$$

$$= 5\% + 9\%$$

$$= 14\%$$

From now on we will refer to returns in percentage terms.

● **Example**

Suppose a share begins the year with a price of NLG25 per share and ends with a price of NLG35 per share. During the year it paid a NLG2 dividend per share. What are its dividend yield, its capital gain, and its total return for the year? We can imagine the cash flows in Figure 10.3.

FIGURE 10.3   Cash Flow—an Investment Example

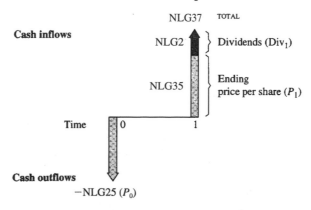

$$R_1 = \frac{\text{Div}_1}{P_0} + \frac{P_1 - P_0}{P_0}$$

$$= \frac{\text{NLG2}}{\text{NLG25}} + \frac{\text{NLG35} - \text{NLG25}}{\text{NLG25}} = \frac{\text{NLG12}}{\text{NLG25}}$$

$$= 8\% + 40\% = 48\%$$

Thus, the stock's dividend yield, its capital gain, and its total return are 8 per cent, 40 per cent, and 48 per cent, respectively. ●

Suppose you had NLG5,000 to invest. The total dollar return you would have received on an investment in the stock is NLG5,000 × 1.48 = NLG7,400. If you know the total return on the stock, you do not need to know how many shares you would have had to purchase to figure out how much money you would have made on the NLG5,000 investment. You just use the total return.[4]

Concept Questions

• What are the two parts of total return?
• Why are unrealized capital gains or losses included in the calculation of returns?
• What is the difference between a dollar return and a percentage return?

10.2   Holding-Period Returns

The most famous set of studies dealing with rates of return on ordinary shares, bonds, and Treasury bills has been conducted in the USA by Roger Ibbotson and Rex Sinquefield.[5] There are other studies for European countries and we will present the essence of those later, but because of its extensive and pioneering nature, we start with the Ibbotson and Sinquefield studies. They present year-by-year historical rates of return for the following five important types of financial instruments in the United States:

1. *Common Stocks*   (The term common stock is the American equivalent of ordinary shares.) The common-stock portfolio is based on the Standard &

---

[4] Consider the shares in the previous example. We have ignored the question of when during the year you receive the dividend. Does it make a difference? To explore this question, suppose first that the dividend is paid at the very beginning of the year, and you receive it the moment after you have purchased the shares. Suppose, too, that interest rates are 10 per cent, and that immediately after receiving the dividend you loan it out. What will be your total return, including the loan proceeds, at the end of the year?

Alternatively, instead of loaning out the dividend you could have reinvested it and purchased more of the shares. If that is what you do with the dividend, what will your total return be? (Warning: This does not go on forever, and when you buy more shares with the cash from the dividend on your first purchase, you are too late to get yet another dividend on the new shares.)

Finally, suppose the dividend is paid at year-end. What answer would you get for the total return?

As you can see, by ignoring the question of when the dividend is paid when we calculate the return, we are implicitly assuming that it is received at the end of the year and cannot be reinvested during the year. The right way to figure out the return on a share is to determine exactly when the dividend is received and to include the return that comes from reinvesting the dividend on the shares. This gives a pure share return without confounding the issue by requiring knowledge of the interest rate during the year.

[5] *Stocks, Bonds, Bills and Inflation*: *Yearbooks*, published annually updating data, by Roger G. Ibbotson and Rex A. Sinquefield, Chicago: Ibbotson Associates. All rights reserved.

Poor's (S&P) composite index. At present, the S&P composite includes 500 of the largest (in terms of market value) stocks in the United States.

2. *Small-Capitalization Stocks*   This is a portfolio composed of the bottom fifth of stocks traded on the New York Stock Exchange in which stocks are ranked by market value (i.e. the price of the stock multiplied by the number of shares outstanding).

3. *Long-Term Corporate Bonds*   This is a portfolio of high-quality corporate bonds with a 20-year maturity.

4. *Long-Term US Government Bonds*   This is a portfolio of US government bonds with a maturity of 20 years.

5. *US Treasury Bills*   This is a portfolio of Treasury bills of three-month maturity.

None of the returns is adjusted for taxes or transactions costs. In addition to the year-by-year returns on financial instruments, the year-to-year change in the consumer price index is computed. This is a basic measure of inflation. Year-by-year real returns can be calculated by subtracting annual inflation.

Before looking closely at the different portfolio returns, we graphically present the returns and risks available from US capital markets in the 69-year period from 1926–94. Figure 10.4 shows the growth of USD1 invested at the beginning of 1926. Notice that the vertical axis is logarithmic, so that equal distances measure the same number of percentage changes. The figure shows that if USD1 were invested in common stocks and all dividends were reinvested, the dollar would have grown to USD810.54 by the end of 1994. The biggest growth was in the small-stock portfolio. If USD1 were invested in small stocks during the 69-year period, the investment would have grown to USD2,842.77. However, when you look carefully at Figure 10.4, you can see great variability in the returns on small stocks, especially in the earlier part of the period. A dollar in long-term government bonds was very stable as compared with USD1 in common stocks. Figures 10.5 to 10.8 plot each year-to-year percentage return as a vertical bar drawn from the horizontal axis for common stocks, for small-company stocks, for long-term bonds and Treasury bills and for inflation, respectively.

Figure 10.4 gives the total value of a dollar investment in the stock market from 1926 through 1994. In other words, it shows what the total return would have been if the dollar had been left in the stock market and if each year the dividends from the previous year had been reinvested in more stock. If R_t is the return in year t (expressed in decimals), the total you would have from year 1 to year T is the product of the returns in each of the years:

$$(1 + R_1) \times (1 + R_2) \times \cdots \times (1 + R_t) \times \cdots \times (1 + R_T)$$

For example, if the returns were 11 per cent, −5 per cent and 9 per cent in a three-year period, an investment of USD1 at the beginning of the period would be worth

$$(1 + R_1) \times (1 + R_2) \times (1 + R_3) = (\text{USD1} + 0.11) \times (\text{USD1} - 0.05) \times (\text{USD1} + 0.09)$$

$$= \text{USD1.11} \times \text{USD0.95} \times \text{USD1.09}$$

$$= \text{USD1.15}$$

at the end of the three years. Notice that 0.15 or 15 per cent is the total return and that it includes the return from reinvesting the first-year dividends in the stock market for two more years and reinvesting the second-year dividends for the final year. The 15 per cent is called a three-year **holding-period return**.

FIGURE 10.4   A USD1 Investment in Different Types of Portfolios in the USA 1926–1994 (year-end 1925 = USD1.00)

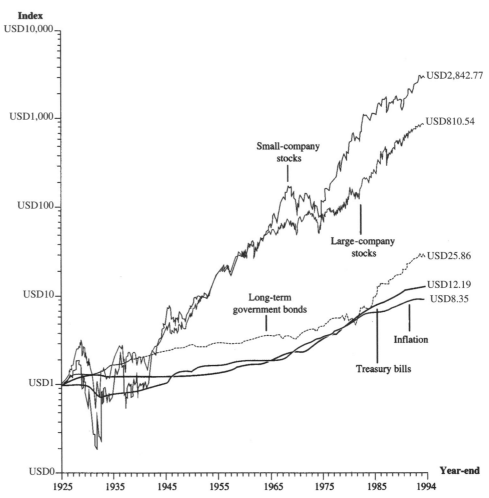

FIGURE 10.5   Year-by-Year Total Returns on Common Stocks in the USA

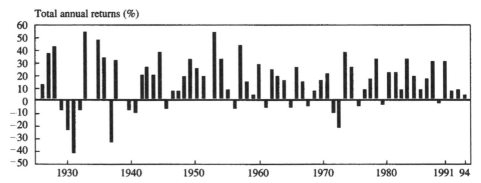

FIGURE 10.6   Year-by-Year Total Returns on Small-Company Stocks in the USA

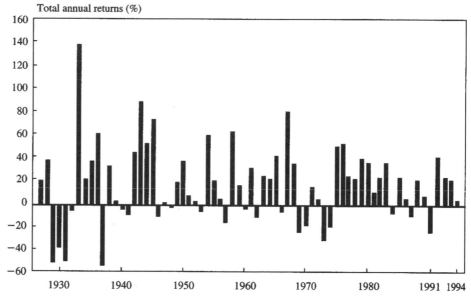

FIGURE 10.7   Year-by-Year Total Returns on Bonds and Bills in the USA

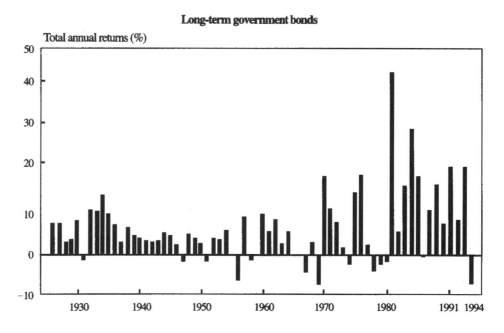

(Continued overleaf)

FIGURE **10.7**   *(concluded)*

US Treasury bills

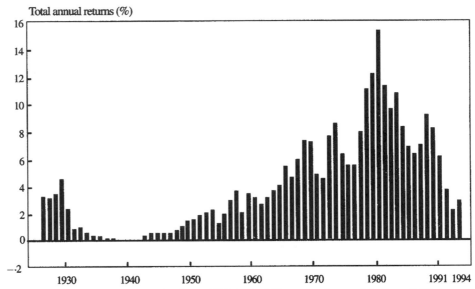

FIGURE **10.8**   **Year-by-Year US Inflation**

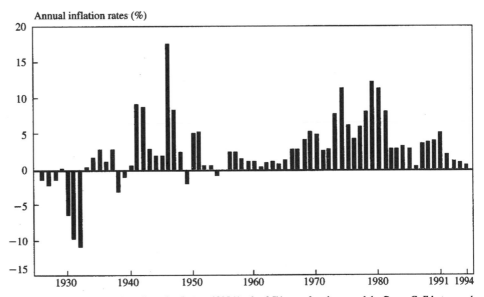

10.3 Return Statistics in the USA

The history of capital-market returns is too complicated to be handled in its undigested form. To use the history, we must first find some manageable ways of describing it, dramatically condensing the detailed data into a few simple statements.

This is where two important numbers summarizing the history come in. The first and most natural number we want to find is some single measure that best describes the past annual returns on the stock market. In other words, what is our best estimate of the return that an investor could have realized in a particular year over the 1926–94 period? This is the *average return*.

Figure 10.9 plots the histogram of yearly USA stock market returns. This plot is the **frequency distribution** of the numbers. The height of the graph gives the number of sample observations in the range on the horizontal axis.

Given a frequency distribution like that in Figure 10.9, we can calculate the **average** or **mean** of the distribution. To compute the arithmetic average of the distribution, we add up all of the values and divide by the total (T) number (69 in our case because we have 69 years of data). The bar over the R is used to represent the mean, and the formula is the ordinary formula for the average:

$$\text{Mean} = \bar{R} = \frac{(R_1 + \cdots + R_T)}{T}$$

The arithmetic mean of the 69 annual returns from 1926–94 is 12.2 per cent.

FIGURE 10.9 Histogram of Returns on Common Stocks, 1926–1994

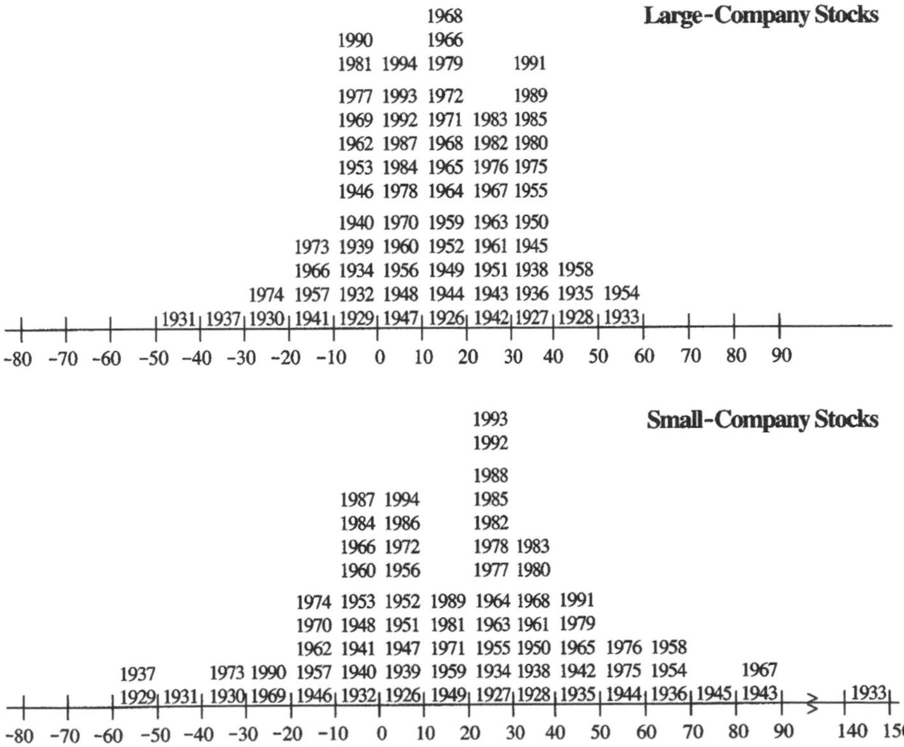

Redrawn from *Stocks, Bonds, Bills, and Inflation: 1995 Yearbook,*™ annual updates work by Roger G. Ibbotson and Rex A. Sinquefield (Chicago: Ibbotson Associates).

- **Example**

The returns on common stock from 1926 to 1929 are 0.1162, 0.3749, 0.4361 and −0.0840, respectively. (Or, 11.62 per cent, 37.49 per cent, 43.61 per cent and minus 8.40 per cent respectively.) The average or mean return over these four years is

$$\bar{R} = \frac{0.1162 + 0.3749 + 0.4361 - 0.0840}{4} = 0.2108 \quad \bullet$$

10.4   Average Stock Returns and Risk-Free Returns in the USA

Now that we have computed the average return on the stock market, it seems sensible to compare it with the returns on other securities. The most obvious comparison is with the low-variability returns in the government-bond market. These are free of most of the volatility we see in the stock market.

The government borrows money by issuing bonds, which the investing public holds. As we discussed in an earlier chapter, these bonds come in many forms, and the ones we will look at here are called *Treasury bills* or *T-bills*. Once a week, the US government sells some bills at an auction. A typical bill is a pure discount bond that will mature in a year or less. Because the government can raise taxes to pay for the debt it incurs—a trick that many of us would like to be able to perform—this debt is virtually free of risk of default. Thus we will call this the risk-free return over a short time (one year or less).[6]

An interesting comparison, then, is between the virtually risk-free return on T-bills and the very risky return on common stocks. This difference between risky returns and risk-free returns is often called the *excess return on the risky asset*. It is called *excess* because it is the additional return resulting from the riskiness of common stocks and is interpreted as a **risk premium.**

Table 10.1 shows the average stock return, bond return, T-bill return and inflation rate for the period from 1926 through 1994. From this, we can derive excess returns. We can see that the average excess return for common stocks for the entire period was 8.5 per cent (12.2% − 3.7%).

One of the most significant observations of stock market data is this long-run excess of the stock return over the risk-free return. An investor for this period was rewarded for investment in the stock market with an extra or excess return over what would have been achieved by simply investing in T-bills.

Why was there such a reward? Does it mean that it never pays to invest in T-bills, and that someone who invested in them instead of in the stock market needs a course in finance? A complete answer to these questions lies at the heart of modern finance, and Chapter 11 is devoted entirely to this.

Part of the answer, however, can be found by looking more closely at Table 10.1. We see that the standard deviation of T-bills is substantially less than that of common stocks. This suggests that the risk of T-bills is less than that of common stocks. Because the answer turns on the riskiness of investments in common stock, we now turn our attention to measuring this risk.

Concept Questions

- What is the major observation about capital markets that we will seek to explain?
- What does the observation tell us about investors for the period from 1926 through 1994?

---

[6] A Treasury bill with a 90-day maturity is risk-free only during that particular time period.

TABLE 10.1   **Total US Annual Returns, 1926–1994**

Series	Arithmetic Mean	Risk Premium (relative to US Treasury bills)	Standard Deviation	Distribution
Common Stocks	12.2%	8.5%	20.3%	
Small Company Stocks	17.4	13.7	34.6	*
Long-Term Corporate Bonds	5.7	2.0	8.4	
Long-Term Government Bonds	5.2	1.5	8.8	
Intermediate-Term Government Bonds	5.2	1.5	5.7	
US Treasury Bills	3.7		3.3	
Inflation	3.2		4.6	

-90%   0%   90%

*The 1993 small-company stock total return was 142.90 per cent.
Modified from *Stocks, Bonds, Bills, and Inflation: 1995 Yearbook*,™ annual updates work by Roger G. Ibbotson and Rex A. Sinquefield (Chicago: Ibbotson Associates). All rights reserved.

10.5   Risk Statistics in the USA

The second number that we use to characterize the distribution of returns is a measure of the risk in returns. There is no universally agreed-upon definition of risk. One way to think about the risk of returns on common stock is in terms of how spread-out the frequency distribution in Figure 10.9 is.[7] The spread or dispersion of a distribution is a measure of how much a particular return can deviate from the mean return. If the distribution is very spread out, the returns that will occur are very uncertain. By contrast, a distribution whose returns are all within a few percentage points of each other is tight, and the returns are less uncertain. The measures of risk we will discuss are variance and standard deviation.

Variance

The **variance** and its square root, the **standard deviation**, are the most common

[7] Several condensed frequency distributions are also in the extreme right column of Table 10.1.

measures of variability or dispersion. We will use Var and σ^2 to denote the variance and SD and σ to represent the standard deviation; σ is, of course, the Greek letter sigma.

● **Example**

The returns on US common stocks from 1926–29 is (in decimals) 0.1162, 0.3749, 0.4361 and −0.0840, respectively (see previous example). The variance of this sample is computed as

$$\text{Var} = \frac{1}{T-1}\,(R_1 - \bar{R})^2 + (R_2 - \bar{R})^2 + (R_3 - \bar{R})^2 + (R_4 - \bar{R})^2$$

$$0.0578 = \tfrac{1}{3}[(0.1162 - 0.2108)^2 + (0.3749 - 0.2108)^2$$
$$+ (0.4361 - 0.2108)^2 + (-0.0840 - 0.2108)^2]$$

$$\text{SD} = \sqrt{0.578} = 0.2405 \text{ (i.e. 24.05\%)} \quad ●$$

This formula tells us just what to do: Take the T individual returns $(R_1, R_2, \ldots)$ and subtract the average return $\bar{R}$, square the result, and add them up. Finally, this total must be divided by the number of returns less one $(T - 1)$. The standard deviation is always just the square root of the variance.

Using the actual stock returns for the 69-year period from 1926 through 1994 in the above formula, the resulting standard deviation of stock returns is 20.3 per cent. The standard deviation is the standard statistical measure of the spread of a sample, and it will be the measure we use most of the time. Its interpretation is facilitated by a discussion of the normal distribution.

Normal Distribution and Its Implications for Standard Deviation

A large enough sample drawn from a **normal distribution** looks like the bell-shaped curve drawn in Figure 10.10. As you can see, this distribution is symmetric about its mean, not skewed, and it has a much cleaner shape than the actual distribution of yearly returns drawn in Figure 10.9.[8] Of course, if we had been able to observe stock market returns for 1,000 years, we might have filled in a lot of the jumps and jerks in Figure 10.9 and had a smoother curve.

In traditional classical statistics the normal distribution plays a central role, and the standard deviation is the usual way to represent the spread of a normal distribution. For the normal distribution, the probability of having a return that is above or below the mean by a certain amount depends only on the standard deviation. For example, the probability of having a return that is within one standard deviation of the mean of the distribution is approximately 0.68 or $\tfrac{2}{3}$, and the probability of having a return that is within two standard deviations of the mean is approximately 0.95.

The 20.3 per cent standard deviation we found for stock returns from 1926 through 1994 can now be interpreted in the following way: if stock returns are roughly normally distributed, the probability that a yearly return will fall within 20.3

---

[8] Some people define risk as the possibility of obtaining a return below the average. Some measures of risk, such as *semivariance*, use only the negative deviations from the average return. However, for symmetric distributions, such as the normal distribution, this method of measuring downside risk is equivalent to measuring risk with deviations from the mean on both sides.

FIGURE 10.10   **The Normal Distribution**

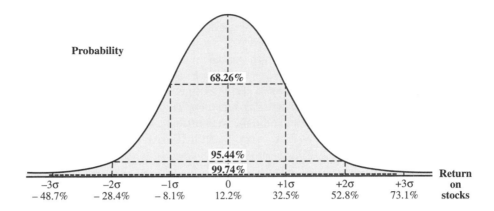

per cent of the mean of 12.2 per cent will be approximately $\frac{2}{3}$. That is, about $\frac{2}{3}$ of the yearly returns will be between -8.1 per cent and $+32.5$ per cent. (Note that -8.1% = 12.2% $-$ 20.3% and 32.5% = 12.2% $+$ 20.3%.) The probability that the return in any year will fall within two standard deviations is about 0.95. That is, about 95 per cent of yearly returns will be between -28.4 per cent and 52.8 per cent.

The distribution in Figure 10.10 is a theoretical distribution, sometimes called the *population*. There is no assurance that the actual distribution of observations in a given sample will produce a histogram that looks exactly like the theoretical distribution. We can see how messy the actual frequency function of historical observations is by observing Figure 10.9. If we were to keep on generating observations for a long enough period of time, however, the aberrations in the sample would disappear, and the actual historical distribution would start to look like the underlying theoretical distribution.

This points out that sampling error exists in any individual sample. In other words, the distribution of the sample only approximates the true distribution; we always measure the truth with some error. For example, we do not know what the true expected return was for common stocks in the 69-year history. However, we are sure that 12.2 per cent is very close to it.

Concept Questions

• What is the definition of sample estimates of variance and standard deviation?
• How does the normal distribution help us interpret standard deviation?

10.6   The Discount Rate for Risky Projects

We can now consider the discount rate for risky projects.

The Case Where Risk Is the Same as the Market

Let us suppose there is a non-financial investment in the USA that has the same risk as the S&P composite index. We will frequently call the S&P composite the *market portfolio of risky assets*.[9] What return should we require on this investment? We should use the current expected return on the market portfolio as our discount rate because this is the return that we would need to give up if we took on our proposed project instead of investing in the S&P. Financial economists frequently view the expected return on the market portfolio as

Expected return on market portfolio = Risk-free rate + Expected risk premium

Here, the expected return on the market is expressed as the sum of the risk-free rate and the expected *risk premium*. This risk premium is simply compensation for the risk that investors in the market portfolio bear.

Because the expected return on the market portfolio is made up of two parts, let us try to estimate both of them. The risk-free rate is easy to estimate. If the *Wall Street Journal (WSJ)* tells us that the current rate for one-year Treasury bills is 7 per cent, it is quite plausible to set the risk-free rate at 7 per cent. The expected risk premium is much more difficult to estimate, because expected returns or premiums are obviously not provided in the *WSJ*. Alternative methods such as surveying finance professors (or students, for that matter) would probably yield meaningless results.

Instead, we get our estimate of the risk premium from the past. Table 10.1 shows us that the average return on common stocks from 1926 to 1994 was 12.2 per cent, and the average return on US Treasury bills over the same period was 3.7 per cent. The historical risk premium is 8.5 per cent (12.2% − 3.7%). Financial economists argue that the historical risk premium is our best predictor of the expected risk premium in the future.[10] Thus, given the T-bill rate of 7 per cent, they would calculate the expected return on the market as

$$\begin{matrix} \text{Expected return} \\ \text{on the market} \end{matrix} = \begin{matrix} \text{Current risk-free} \\ \text{rate} \end{matrix} + \begin{matrix} \text{Historical} \\ \text{risk premium} \end{matrix}$$
$$15.5\% = 7\% + 8.5\%$$

Therefore, the discount rate on the risky non-financial investment is 15.5 per cent.

The Case Where Risk Is Different from the Market

The above discussion concerned a project with risk *equal* to that of the market. How does one determine the discount rate of a project whose risk *differs* from that of the market? A possible relationship is provided in Figure 10.11, where the discount rate is positively related to the project's risk. This is plausible because we argued in earlier chapters that both individuals and firms demand a high expected return on a project with high risk.

In its present form, this graph is of *some* use; a manager could easily employ it in an *ad hoc* fashion. The manager would decide whether a project has more or less risk than that of the market. If the project's risk were judged to be high, the manager would choose a discount rate higher than the market's expected return. Conversely, if the project's risk were judged to be low, the manager would choose a discount rate lower

---

[9] Strictly speaking, the S&P index is not the market portfolio because it does not include all risky assets, such as real estate. However, economists generally argue that it is an acceptable proxy for the market. In addition, it is much easier to construct than a more realistic portfolio including assets not traded in a central marketplace.

[10] Some people may not agree with this. However, if risk today is about the same as it has been over the last 69 years and individuals' distaste for risk is about the same, the historical risk premium will be a good estimate of the future risk premium.

FIGURE 10.11 **Relationship between the Project's Discount Rate and its Risk**

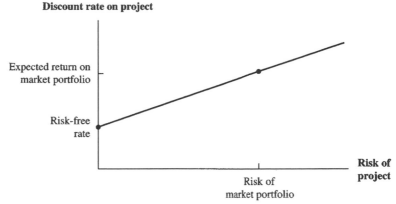

The discount rate on a project is positively related to the project's risk.

than that of the market as a whole. We used the term *ad hoc* because we need to answer a question before applying the graph in a precise manner. The question is this: What is the appropriate measure of risk?

The question may surprise you, because the standard deviation of the project's return may seem the obvious choice for the project's risk measure. However, financial economists disagree. They point out that a diversified investor is not concerned with the risk of any individual asset. Rather, the investor cares about the effect of the asset on the risk of the entire portfolio.

● Example

Diversified Industries is considering an investment in either a gold-mining venture or a utility franchise. At a meeting of the board of directors, Dr Katherine Russell argues that the cash flows from a gold-mining operation are inherently quite variable. Thus, a high discount rate should be applied to these flows. Because a typical utility is less volatile, a low discount rate is appropriate.

Another director, Dr Jacques Breakstone, disagrees. He states that the firm itself is diversified and most of the firm's stockholders are diversified. He argues that gold prices generally rise during inflationary times, just when stock prices tend to fall. Gold prices fall in deflationary times, just when stock prices tend to rise. Thus, he argues that a gold-mining venture is a hedge against both the firm's other assets and the stockholders' other investments. When the rest of the economy is doing well, gold is doing poorly—and vice versa. Because the gold venture is inherently a hedge, it does not add to the risk of a large portfolio. Conversely, utility investments do well when other assets do well and do poorly when other assets do poorly. The utility franchise adds to the risk of a large portfolio. Therefore, Dr Breakstone wants a higher discount rate for the utility franchise. ●

Modern portfolio theory agrees with Dr Breakstone. According to financial economists, any asset must be viewed as part of a portfolio. The asset's risk is the contribution to the variability of the portfolio. Because standard deviation and variance treat an asset in isolation, we must move to statistical measures relating one asset to another. We now turn to beta and diversification, the building blocks of modern portfolio theory.

Concept Question

- How can financial managers use the history of capital markets to estimate the required rate of return on nonfinancial investments with the same risk as the average common stock?

10.7   Risk and Beta

Diversification

This chapter has looked closely at the historical risk and return of highly diversified portfolios typified by the S&P composite index. We found that the historical standard deviation of the S&P composite is 20.3 per cent. However, the historical standard deviations of individual common stocks are much higher than 20.3 per cent. In fact, the average historical standard deviation of individual stocks is closer to 50 per cent.

The difference between the standard deviation of an individual stock and the standard deviation of a portfolio or an index is due to the well-known phenomenon of *diversification*. With diversification, individual risky stocks can be combined in such a way that a combination of individual securities (i.e. a portfolio) is almost always less risky than any one of the individual securities. Risk elimination is possible because the returns on individual securities are not usually perfectly correlated to each other. A certain amount of risk is 'diversified away.'

Diversification is very effective at reducing risk. However, the risk of holding common stock cannot be completely eliminated by diversification. We have seen that the risk (e.g. the standard deviation) of the S&P composite portfolio, which includes 500 individual stocks, is still very high when compared to US Treasury securities. In fact, diversification makes measuring the risk of an individual security very difficult. The reason is that we are not so much interested in the standard deviation of an individual security as we are in the impact of an individual standard deviation on the risk of a portfolio.

Most individuals and institutions hold portfolios, not single, securities. Conceptually, the risk of an individual security is related to how the risk of a portfolio changes when the security is added to it. It turns out that the standard deviation of an individual stock is not a good measure of how the standard deviation of a portfolio changes when an individual stock is added to it. Therefore, the standard deviation of an individual security is not a good measure of its risk if most investors hold diversified portfolios.

In the next chapter, we formally show that a security with a high standard deviation need not have a high impact on the standard deviation of a large portfolio. Conversely, a security with a low standard deviation may actually have a high impact on a large portfolio's standard deviation. This apparent paradox is actually the basis of the famous capital-asset-pricing model.

Beta

The capital-asset-pricing model (CAPM) shows that the risk of an individual security is well represented by its **beta** coefficient.[11] In statistical terms the beta tells us the tendency of an individual stock to covary with the market (e.g. the S&P composite

---

[11] Statistically, *beta* is defined as the covariance of the return of an individual stock with the 'market proxy' portfolio return divided by the variance of the market's proxy return.

index). A stock with a beta of 1 tends to move up and down in the same percentage as the market. Stocks with a beta coefficient less than 1 tend to move in percentage terms less than the market. Similarly, a stock with a beta that is higher than 1 will tend to move up and down more than the market. In other words, beta measures the responsiveness of the return on an individual security to the return on the market portfolio.

The expected return on a security is positively related to the security's risk, since investors will only take on extra risk if they receive extra compensation. The CAPM implies that beta, not standard deviation, is the appropriate measure of risk. This insight allows us to calculate the expected return on an individual security as follows:

$$\begin{matrix} \text{Expected return} \\ \text{on individual} \\ \text{security} \end{matrix} = \begin{matrix} \text{Current risk} \\ \text{security} \end{matrix} + \left(\begin{matrix} \text{Beta of} \\ \text{a security} \end{matrix} \times \begin{matrix} \text{Historical market} \\ \text{risk premium} \end{matrix} \right)$$

● Example
Suppose the current risk-free rate is 7 per cent and the historical market risk premium is 8.5 per cent. If the beta of the Campbell Soup company is 0.8, what is its expected return? Using the CAPM, we find that the expected return for the Campbell Soup Company is

$$= 7\% + (0.8 \times 8.5\%)$$
$$= 13.8\% \quad ●$$

For students who want to know more about risk and expected return, we will talk much more about CAPM and beta in Chapter 11. We now turn to European evidence on equity returns. We look first at UK data, for no better reason than the fact that researchers in the UK have undertaken studies over very long periods comparable to Ibbotson and Sinquefield's work in the USA.

10.8   British Evidence

There have been various studies of achieved rates of return from equities and government securities in Britain. These include work in the 'sixties and early 'seventies on ordinary share investment by Merrett and Sykes,[12] investigations of achieved excess returns on UK equities up to the late 'seventies by Dimson and Brealey[13] and Dimson and Marsh,[14] a similar study of long run returns from investing in government securities and ordinary shares up to the mid-Eighties by Allen, Day, Kwiatowski and Hirst[15] and, like the Ibbotson Associates' annual update of US returns, BZW (the London-based stockbrokers) produce an annual update of returns earned from investment.

---

[12] A. J. Merrett and A. Sykes (1963). 'Return on equities and fixed interest securities, 1919–1963', *District Bank Review,* December. A. J. Merrett and A. Sykes (1966). 'Return on equities and fixed interest securities, 1919–1966', *District Bank Review,* June, 29-44. A. J. Merrett and A. Sykes (1973). *The Finance and Analysis of Capital Projects,* 2nd edn, London: Longman.

[13] E. Dimson and R. A. Brealey (1978). 'The premium on UK equities', *Investment Analyst,* December, 14–18.

[14] E. Dimson and P. Marsh (1982). 'Calculating the cost of capital', *Long Range Planning,* **15** (2), 112–120.

[15] D. E. Allen, R. E. Day, J. Kwiatowski and I. R. C. Hirst (1987). 'Equity, gilts, treasury bills and inflation', *Investment Analyst,* January, 11–18.

The Merrett and Sykes studies focused upon real returns accruing from UK equity investment in net of tax terms. They focused upon the market return net of tax and in real terms rather than upon the risk premium. They found fairly substantial standard deviations in outturns over different holding periods. However, in geometric mean terms, their results over the period from 1919–71 suggest a real, net of tax return of just over 7.75 per cent, more than 1 per cent higher than compatible returns from US investment. But the lion's share of this UK return accrued in the early years of this holding period. This is shown in the summary of Merrett and Sykes' findings which appears in Table 10.2. If these findings were to perpetuate in the future, it would be logical to expect that a UK company with a beta of 1.0 would yield a real, net of tax, return of between 7.5 per cent and 8 per cent to shareholders in the long run. The caveats raised in the section relating to US returns would be equally applicable to UK corporate returns.

TABLE 10.2   **UK and US Equity Returns in Real Terms and Net of Shareholder Tax 1919–71**

	UK returns (%)			USA returns (%)		
Period	*Tax exempt*	*Tax at standard rate (capital gains tax excluded)*	*Period*	*Tax exempt*	*Tax at 25% (capital gains tax excluded)*	
1919–39	12.1	10.5	1919–39	7.8	6.5	
1926–39	10.6	6.4	1926–39	7.0	5.7	
1949–66	7.3	5.4	1949–66	14.1	12.7	
1949–71	6.6	4.5	1949–71	12.4	10.8	
1949–72	7.4	5.3				
1926–66	6.2	4.5	1926–66	7.5	6.5	
1919–71	10.2	7.8	1919–71	7.7	6.5	

Source: Merrett and Sykes (1973).[12]

Dimson and Marsh computed returns to investment in UK equities in a similar manner to Ibbotson Associates in the USA. In other words, they calculated an arithmetic average of the risk premium based on equity returns minus the treasury bill rate for individual years. For relatively long periods, beginning in 1919 and ending at January 1, 1980, the value of the risk premium appears to be around 8.75 per cent gross of taxes and about 8 per cent on an after-tax basis. Dimson and Marsh did their computation on a net of tax basis because the structure of UK tax makes this the relevant rate, under the imputation tax system, to build into calculations of the required equity cost of capital.

The difference of less than 1 per cent between gross and net, rather than 25 per cent of 8.75 per cent (25 per cent being the approximate basic rate of UK tax), arises because the excess return comprises capital gain and dividend, and these sources of increment have been taxed differently. Given that the magnitude of dividend yields in many countries is fairly close, a conversion from gross to net would frequently involve a difference of a similar absolute amount. Dimson and Marsh's findings on the value of the UK **equity risk premium** (the return, in terms of dividends and capital gains, from equity investment less the risk-free return, measured as the return from holding government securities) for periods up to 1980 are summarized in Table 10.3.

Allen, Day, Kwiatowski and Hirst reported UK returns in a format fairly similar to Ibbotson Associates' US studies. And BZW publish annual returns for UK investment

TABLE 10.3 **The Equity Risk Premium in the UK from 1919–80**

	$(R_M - R_F)$	
Period to 1.1.80	*Gross of tax %*	*Net of tax %*
1919–	8.7	8.1
1930–	8.3	7.7
1940–	8.8	8.3
1950–	9.6	9.6

Source: Dimson and Marsh (1982).[14]

over the long run from 1919. Most of these data are presented in arithmetic mean terms. Findings for the UK are summarized in Table 10.4. It should be mentioned that data in Table 10.3 and in Table 10.4 show slightly different equity risk premium data from 1919 onwards. This is because the former table shows returns with 1980 as a terminating date while the latter derives its equity risk premium from a range with various terminating years.

TABLE 10.4 **Total Annual Returns from UK Investment Over Long Run from 1919**

	Geometric mean (%)	*Arithmetic mean (%)*	*Standard deviation (%)*
Ordinary shares	11.4 to 11.8	13.5 to 14.4	26
Long-term government bonds	5.2 to 5.6	5.7 to 61.1	8.2
3 month government bills	4.6 to 5.3	4.6 to 5.3	4.4
Inflation	4.1 to 4.4	4.3 to 4.6	
$R_M - R_F$ (based on long-term government bonds)	6.2	8.4	
$R_M - R_F$ (based on 3 month government bills)	6.6	9.0	

Source: BZW and Allen, Day, Kwiatowski and Hirst (1987).[15]

Note that if we compare the two exhibits of US and UK returns, we find that the total return, the real return and the value of the risk premium is higher for the UK. Such higher returns may be due to an increased risk premium related to increasing unexpected inflation. But we really cannot be sure that this is the ultimate explanation. Suffice to say that the risk premium is higher in the UK than in the USA.

10.9 European Returns

Unfortunately, we do not have a complete picture of levels of the equity risk premium in continental European stock markets for seventy to eighty year periods. Various researchers have studied such markets but their results have not coincided in terms of periods covered. Clearly, were we to wish to compare and contrast European returns, it would be useful if they covered the same time period. Fortunately, Davis[16] has collected such information for the period from 1967–90 using the Bank of International Settlements macroeconomic database. Some of the most interesting findings of his work are summarized in Table 10.5. The data in the table are in real terms and in local currency, but no allowance has been made for taxation or transaction costs. The calculations are based on annual holding-period returns and therefore include capital gains and losses as well as dividends. Notable features of the data are that the highest returns—and the biggest risks—are offered by equities, followed by property. Generally, bonds offer a much lower real return, as one would expect. The highest bond returns have accrued in Germany and Denmark—significantly higher than in other countries. Of course, Germany had the lowest and least volatile inflation rate and a very strong culture of bond investment (rather than equity investment). Note that in Table 10.5 bonds show annual standard deviation figures because returns are measured year by year and in real terms (that is, with inflation, year by year, disaggregated). Were the bonds held from issue to maturity, naturally, their overall money terms return would not be volatile.

Perhaps, though, even returns over 23 years—as in Table 10.5—represent too short a time horizon from which to draw firm conclusions. This period would have included, for most European countries, many years of exchange controls that would have prevented international portfolio optimization and created segmented capital markets. Note also that the US return figure for equities is far below the long run Ibbotson and Sinquefield figures—see Table 10.1. Despite this, the European domestic real return from equities seems, generally, to be in a band between 6 and 10 per cent per annum, which is not too far away from the long-run real return on US common stocks as shown in Table 10.1. Certainly, as the academic study of financial management expands, we can expect a complete tableau of long-run returns from Europe and from around the world to emerge. In the meantime, while our picture is an incomplete one, we feel that it would be wise to conclude that long run returns among developed countries, after adjusting for inflation, risk and possible tax effects, should tend towards equality. If this were not so, investors would rush to invest where returns appeared high. In so doing, they would inflate prices which would depress returns for subsequent, less quick-moving investors. This process of arbitrage (buying assets in one market while simultaneously selling them in another) should force returns towards each other in terms of their achieved returns. This conclusion leads to the view that a risk premium based on the Ibbotson and Sinquefield data would be relatively appropriate for most developed European countries, although, as research develops, we may find that the use of a country-based beta would be called for in moving from the US risk premium to, for example, the French figure. But work in this area is by no means complete as yet. It is being developed from the pioneering work of Solnik.[17] Were it found to be sustained, the idea of a link between different countries' levels of risk premium would follow and this relationship would be expressed in the country beta. From the country beta for France, for example, the risk premium for France could be estimated. From this, the required return on equity investment in Carrefour SA, the French supermarket group, could be estimated by reference to Carrefour's beta.

[16] E. P. Davis (1995). *Pension Funds. Retirement-Income Insurance and Capital Markets: An International Perspective*, Oxford: Oxford University Press.

[17] B. Solnik, (1973) 'A note on the validity of the random walk for European stock prices', *Journal of Finance*, **28**, 1151–59. B. Solnik (1974). 'Why not diversify internationally rather than domestically?', *Financial Analysts Journal*, **30** (4), 48–54. B. Solnik (1988), *International Investments*, Addison-Wesley, Reading, MA.

TABLE 10.5   Local Currency Real Returns on Financial Assets Portfolios in Various EU Countries and the USA—1967–90

	UK	Germany	Netherlands	Sweden	Denmark	Ireland	France	Italy	Belgium	USA
Figures in percentages										
Real returns on domestic equities	8.1 (20.3)	9.5 (20.3)	7.9 (28.2)	8.4 (23.3)	7.0 (27.5)	8.5 (25.9)	9.4 (26.9)	4.0 (35.9)	6.3 (16.7)	4.7 (14.4)
Real returns on domestic bonds	−0.5 (13.0)	2.7 (14.9)	1.0 (13.1)	−0.9 (8.5)	3.4 (16.1)	−0.1 (15.3)	1.0 (13.1)	−0.2 (18.3)	1.3 (11.7)	−0.5 (14.3)
Real returns on domestic property	6.7 (11.4)	4.5 (2.9)	4.6 (15.0)	n/a n/a	n/a n/a	n/a n/a	n/a n/a	n/a n/a	n/a n/a	3.4 (6.4)
Inflation (CPI)	8.9 (5.3)	3.5 (2.1)	4.9 (3.1)	8.1 (2.7)	7.7 (3.2)	10.0 (6.0)	7.1 (4.1)	11.3 (5.9)	5.5 (3.2)	5.8 (3.0)

Notes: (i) Figures in brackets represent standard deviations of annual real total returns in local currency.
(ii) Returns include both capital gains and dividends, interest or rental income.
Source: Davis (1995).[16]

10.10   Summary and Conclusions

The statistical measures in this chapter are necessary building blocks for the material of the next three chapters.

1. Standard deviation and variance measure the variability of the return on an individual security. We will argue that standard deviation and variance are appropriate measures of the risk of an individual security if an investor's portfolio is composed of that security only.

2. Most investors hold portfolios and, as a consequence, the variance (or standard deviation) is not a good measure of an individual security's risk. Beta is a better measure. Beta reflects the responsiveness of an individual security to movements in the market portfolio.

KEY TERMS

Capital gain   214
Holding-period return   217
Frequency distribution   221
Average (mean)   221
Risk premium   222
Variance   223

Standard deviation   223
Normal distribution   224
Diversification   228
Beta   228
Equity risk premium   230

QUESTIONS AND PROBLEMS

Returns

10.1   Last year, you bought 500 shares of Tweede El Dee (the company with operations in the Netherlands, Spain, Wales and Scotland) at NLG37 per share. You have received total dividends of NLG1,000 during the year. Currently, Tweede El Dee stock sells for NLG38.
   a. How much did you earn in capital gains?
   b. What was your total guilder return?
   c. What was your percentage return?

10.2   Mr Alexander Bell invested USD10,400 in 200 shares of First Industries stock a year ago and has received total dividends of USD600 during the period. He sold the stock today at USD54.25.
   a. What was his total dollar return?
   b. What was his capital gain?
   c. What was his percentage return?
   d. What was the stock's dividend yield?

10.3   Suppose a share had an initial price of DEM42 per share. During the year, the stock paid a dividend of DEM2.40 per share. At the end of the year, the price is DEM31 per share. What is the percentage return on this share in market terms?

10.4   Suppose the current interest rate on US Treasury bills is 6.2 per cent. Ibbotson and Sinquefield found the average return on Treasury bills from 1926 through 1994 to be 3.7 per cent. The average return on common stock during the same period was 12.2 per cent. Given this information, what is the current expected return on common stocks?

10.5   Two stocks, Koke and Pepsee, had the same prices two years ago. During the last two years, Koke's stock price had first increased by 10 per cent and then dropped by 10 per cent, while Pepsee's stock price had first dropped by 10 per cent and then increased by 10 per cent. Do these two stocks have the same prices today? Explain.

Average Returns, Expected Returns and Variance

10.6   During the past seven years, the returns on a portfolio of long-term corporate bonds were the following:

Year	Long-term corporate bonds
−7	−2.6%
−6	−1.0
−5	43.8
−4	4.7
−3	16.4
−2	30.1
Last	19.9

   a. Calculate the average return for long-term corporate bonds over this period.
   b. Calculate the variance and the standard deviation of the returns for long-term corporate bonds during this period.

10.7   The following are the returns during the past seven years on a market portfolio of common stocks and on Treasury bills.

Year	Common stocks	Treasury bills
−7	32.4%	11.2%
−6	−4.9	14.7
−5	21.4	10.5
−4	22.5	8.8
−3	6.3	9.9
−2	32.2	7.7
Last	18.5	6.2

   The realized risk premium is the return on the common stocks less the return on the Treasury bills.
   a. Calculate the realized risk premium of common stocks over T-bills in each year.
   b. Calculate the average risk premium of common stocks over T-bills during the period.
   c. Is it possible that this observed risk premium can be negative? Explain.

10.8   The following data are the returns for 1980 through 1986 on five types of capital-market instruments: common stocks, small-capitalization stocks, long-term corporate bonds, long-term US government bonds, and US Treasury bills.

Year	Common stock	Small stocks	Long-term corporate bonds	Long-term government bonds	US Treasury bills
1980	0.3242	0.3988	−0.0262	−0.0395	0.1124
1981	−0.0491	0.1388	−0.0096	0.0185	0.1471
1982	0.2141	0.2801	0.4379	0.4035	0.1054
1983	0.2251	0.3967	0.0470	0.0068	0.0880
1984	0.0627	−0.0667	0.1639	0.1543	0.0985
1985	0.3216	0.2466	0.3090	0.3097	0.0772
1986	0.1847	0.0685	0.1985	0.2444	0.0616

   Calculate the average return and variance for each type of security.

Return and Risk Statistics

10.9   Ibbotson and Sinquefield have reported the returns on small company stocks and US Treasury bills for the period 1986–91 as follows.

Year	Small-company stocks	US Treasury bills
1986	6.85%	6.16%
1987	−9.30	5.47
1988	22.87	6.35
1989	10.18	8.37
1990	−21.56	7.81
1991	44.63	5.60

   a. Calculate the average returns on small company stocks and US Treasury bills.
   b. Calculate the variances and standard deviations of the returns on small company stocks and US Treasury bills.
   c. Compare the returns and risks of these two types of securities.

10.10 Suppose International Trading Company's stock returns follow a normal distribution with a mean of 17.5 per cent and a standard deviation of 8.5 per cent. What is the range of returns in which about 95 per cent of International Trading's stock returns are located?

Expected Returns and Beta

10.11 The Alpha firm makes pneumatic equipment. Its beta is 1.2. The market risk premium is 8.5 per cent, and the current risk-free rate is 6 per cent. What is the expected return for the Alpha firm?

10.12 Suppose the beta for the RossCo is 0.80. The risk-free rate is 6 per cent, and the market risk premium is 8.5 per cent. What is the expected return for the RossCo?

10.13 The risk-free rate is 8 per cent. The beta for the Jordan Company is 1.5, and the expected return of the market is 15 per cent. What is the expected return for the Jordan Company?

Risk and Beta

10.14 Suppose the market risk premium is 7.5 per cent and the risk-free rate is 3.7 per cent. The expected return of TriStar Textiles is 14.2 per cent. What is the beta for TriStar Textiles?

APPENDIX 10A

THE HISTORICAL MARKET RISK PREMIUM: THE VERY LONG RUN

The data in Chapter 10 indicate that the returns on common stock have historically been much higher than the returns on short-term government securities. This phenomenon has bothered economists, since it is difficult to justify why large numbers of rational investors purchase the lower yielding bills and bonds.

   In 1985 Mehra and Prescott published a very influential US paper that showed that the historical returns for common stocks are far too high when compared to the rates of return on short-term government securities.[18] They point out that the difference in returns (frequently called the *market risk premium for equity*) implies a very high degree of risk aversion on the part of investors. Since the publication of the Mehra and Prescott research, financial economists have tried to explain the so-called equity risk premium puzzle. The high historical equity risk premium is especially intriguing compared to the very low historical rate of return on Treasury securities. This seems to imply behaviour that has not actually happened. For example, if people have been very risk-averse and historical borrowing rates have been low, it suggests that persons should have been willing to borrow in periods of economic uncertainty and downturn to avoid the possibility of a reduced standard of living. However, we do not observe increased borrowing in recessions.

   The equity risk premium puzzle of Mehra and Prescott has been generally viewed as an unexplained paradox. However, recently, Jeremy Siegel has shown that the historical risk premium

---

[18] Rajnish Mehra and Edward C. Prescott (1995). 'The equity premium: A puzzle', *Journal of Monetary Economics* **15**, 145–61.

may be substantially lower than previously realized (see Table 10A.1). He shows that while the risk premium averaged 8.5 per cent from 1926–94, it averaged only 1.4 per cent from 1802–70, and 4.4 per cent from 1871–1925.[19] It is puzzling that the trend has been rising over the last 200 years. It has been especially high since 1926. However, the key point is that historically the risk premium has been lower than in more recent times, and we should be somewhat cautious about assumptions we make about the current risk premium.

TABLE 10A.1

	1802–1870	*1871–1925*	*1926–94*	*Overall 1902–90*
Common stock	6.8	8.5	12.2	9.2
Treasury bills	5.4	4.1	3.7	4.4
Risk premium	1.4	4.4	8.5	4.8

[19] Jeremy J. Siegel (1994). *Stocks for the Long Run*, Burr Ridge, Ill.: Irwin.

Return and Risk: The Capital-Asset-Pricing Model (CAPM)

The previous chapter achieved three purposes. First, we acquainted you with some of the history of US and European capital markets. Second, we presented statistics such as expected return, variance, standard deviation and beta. Third, we discussed a simplified model of the discount rate on a risky project.

However, we pointed out that the above model was *ad hoc* in nature. We now present a carefully reasoned approach to calculating the discount rate on a risky project. Chapter 11 examines the risk and the return of individual securities when these securities are part of a large portfolio. While this investigation is a necessary stepping-stone to discounting projects, corporate projects are not considered here. Rather, a treatment of the appropriate discount rate for capital budgeting is reserved for Chapter 13.

The crux of the current chapter can be summarized as follows: An individual who holds one security should use expected return as the measure of the security's return. Standard deviation or variance is the proper measure of the security's risk. An individual who holds a diversified portfolio cares about the *contribution* of each security to the expected return and the risk of the portfolio. It turns out that a security's expected return is the appropriate measure of the security's contribution to the expected return on the portfolio. However, neither the security's variance nor the security's standard deviation is an appropriate measure of a security's contribution to the risk of a portfolio. The contribution of a security to the risk of a portfolio is best measured by beta.

11.1 Individual Securities

In the first part of Chapter 11, we will examine the characteristics of individual securities. In particular, we will discuss:

1. *Expected Return* This is the return that an individual expects a share to earn over the next period. Of course, because this is only an expectation, the actual return may be either higher or lower. An individual's expectation may simply be the average return per period a security has earned in the past. Alternatively, it may be based on a detailed analysis of a firm's prospects, on some computer-based model, or on special (or inside) information.

2. *Variance and Standard Deviation*   There are many ways to assess the volatility of a security's return. One of the most common is variance, which is a measure of the squared deviations of a security's return from its expected return. Standard deviation, which is the square root of the variance, may be thought of as a standardized version of the variance.

3. *Covariance and Correlation*   Returns on individual securities are related to one another. Covariance is a statistic measuring the interrelationship between two securities. Alternatively, this relationship can be restated in terms of the correlation between the two securities. Covariance and correlation are building blocks to an understanding of the beta coefficient.

11.2   Expected Return, Variance and Covariance

Expected Return and Variance

Suppose financial analysts believe that there are four equally likely states of the economy: depression, recession, normal and boom times. The returns on the Supertech Company are expected to follow the economy closely, while the returns on the Slowgrow Company are not. The return predictions are given below:

	Supertech Returns R_{At}	Slowgrow Returns R_{Bt}
Depression	−20%	5%
Recession	10	20
Normal	30	−12
Boom	50	9

Variance can be calculated in four steps. An additional step is needed to calculate standard deviation. (The calculations are presented in Table 11.1.) The steps are:

1. Calculate the expected return:

Supertech:

$$\frac{-0.20 + 0.10 + 0.30 + 0.50}{4} = 0.75 = 17.5\% = \bar{R}_A$$

Slowgrow:

$$\frac{0.20 + 0.20 - 0.12 + 0.09}{4} = 0.055 = 5.5\% = \bar{R}_B$$

2. For each company, calculate the deviation of each possible return from the company's expected return given above. This is presented in the third column of Table 11.1.
3. The deviations we have calculated are indications of the dispersion of returns. However, because some are positive and some are negative, it is difficult to work with them in this form. For example, if we were to simply add up all the deviations for a single company, we would get zero as the sum.

    To make the deviations more meaningful, we multiply each one by itself. Now all the numbers are positive, implying that their sum must be positive as well. The squared deviations are presented in the last column of Table 11.1.

TABLE 11.1   Calculating Variance and Standard Deviation

(1) State of economy	(2) Rate of return	(3) Deviation from expected return	(4) Squared value of deviation
	Supertech*	**(Expected return = 0.175)**	
	R_{At}	$(R_{At} - \bar{R}_A)$	$(R_{At} - \bar{R}_A)^2$
Depression	−0.20	−0.375	0.140625
		$(= -0.20 - 0.175)$	$[= (-0.375)^2]$
Recession	0.10	−0.075	0.005625
Normal	0.30	0.125	0.015625
Boom	0.50	0.325	0.105625
			0.267500
	Slowgrow†	**(Expected return = 0.055)**	
	R_{Bt}	$(R_{Bt} - \bar{R}_B)$	$(R_{Bt} - \bar{R}_B)^2$
Depression	0.05	−0.005	0.000025
		$(= 0.05 - 0.055)$	$[= (-0.005)^2]$
Recession	0.20	0.145	0.021025
Normal	−0.12	−0.175	0.030625
Boom	0.09	0.035	0.001225
			0.052900

$$*\bar{R}_A = \frac{-0.20 + 0.10 + 0.30 + 0.50}{4} = 0.175 = 17.5\%$$

$$\text{Var}(R_A) = \sigma_A^2 = \frac{0.2675}{4} = 0.066875$$

$$\text{SD}(R_A) = \sigma_A = \sqrt{0.066875} = 0.2586 = 25.86\%$$

$$†\bar{R}_B = \frac{0.05 + 0.20 - 0.12 + 0.09}{4} = 0.055 = 5.5\%$$

$$\text{Var}(R_B) = \sigma_B^2 = \frac{0.0529}{4} = 0.013225$$

$$\text{SD}(R_B) = \sigma_B = \sqrt{0.013225} = 0.1150 = 11.50\%$$

4. For each company, calculate the average squared deviation, which is the variance:[1]

Supertech:

$$\frac{0.140625 + 0.005625 + 0.015625 + 0.105625}{4} = 0.066875$$

Slowgrow:

$$\frac{0.000025 + 0.021025 + 0.030625 + 0.001225}{4} = 0.013225$$

Thus, the variance of Supertech is 0.066875, and the variance of Slowgrow is 0.013225.

---

[1] In this example, the four states give rise to four *possible* outcomes for each stock. Had we used past data, the outcomes would have actually occurred. In that case, statisticians argue that the correct divisor is $N - 1$, where N is the number of observations. Thus the denominator would be 3 (4 − 1) in the case of past data, not 4. Note that the example in Section 10.5 involved past data and we used a divisor of $N - 1$. While this difference causes grief to both students and textbook writers, it is a minor point in practice. In the real world, samples are generally so large that using N or $N - 1$ in the denominator has virtually no effect on the calculation of variance.

5. Calculate standard deviation by taking the square root of the variance:

Supertech:

$$\sqrt{0.066875} = 0.2586 = 25.86\%$$

Slowgrow:

$$\sqrt{0.013225} = 0.1150 = 11.50\%$$

Algebraically, the formula for variance can be expressed as

$$\text{Var}(R) = \text{Expected value of } (R - \bar{R})^2$$

where $\bar{R}$ is the security's expected return and R is the actual return.

A look at the four-step calculation for variance makes it clear why it is a measure of the spread of the sample of returns. For each observation, one squares the difference between the actual return and the expected return. One then takes an average of these squared differences. Squaring the differences makes them all positive. If we used the differences between each return and the expected return and then averaged these differences, we would get zero because the returns that were above the mean would cancel the ones below.

However, because the variance is still expressed in squared terms, it is difficult to interpret. Standard deviation has a much simpler interpretation, which was provided in Section 10.5. Standard deviation is simply the square root of the variance. The general formula for the standard deviation is

$$\text{SD}(R) = \sqrt{\text{Var}(R)}$$

Covariance and Correlation

Variance and standard deviation measure the variability of individual stocks. We now wish to measure the relationship between the return on one stock and the return on another. To make our discussion more precise, we need a statistical measure of the relationship between two variables. Enter **covariance** and **correlation**.

Covariance and correlation measure how two random variables are related. We explain these terms by extending the Supertech and Slowgrow example presented earlier in this chapter.

● **Example**

We have already determined the expected returns and standard deviations for both Supertech and Slowgrow earlier in the chapter. (The expected returns are 0.175 and 0.055 for Supertech and Slowgrow, respectively. The standard deviations are 0.2586 and 0.1150, respectively.) In addition, we calculated for each firm the deviation of each possible return from the expected return. Using these data, covariance can be calculated in two steps. An extra step is needed to calculate correlation.

1. For each state of the economy, multiply Supertech's deviation from its expected return and Slowgrow's deviation from its expected return together. For example, Supertech's rate of return in a depression is −0.20, which is −0.375 (−0.20 − 0.175) from its expected return. Slowgrow's rate of return in a depression is 0.05, which is −0.005 (0.05 − 0.055) from its expected return.

Multiplying the two deviations together yields 0.001875 [(−0.375) × (−0.005)]. The actual calculations are given in the last column of Table 11.2.

This procedure can be written algebraically as

$$(R_{At} - \bar{R}_A) \times (R_{Bt} - \bar{R}_B) \tag{11.1}$$

where R_{At} and R_{Bt} are the returns on Supertech and Slowgrow in state t. $\bar{R}_A$ and $\bar{R}_B$ are the expected returns on the two securities.

TABLE 11.2   Calculating Covariance and Correlation

State of economy	Rate of return of Supertech R_{At}	Deviation from expected return $(R_{At} - \bar{R}_A)$	Rate of return of Slowpoke R_{Bt}	Deviation from expected return $(R_{Bt} - \bar{R}_B)$	Product of deviations $(R_{At} - \bar{R}_A) \times (R_{Bt} - \bar{R}_B)$
		(Expected return = 0.175)		(Expected return = 0.055)	
Depression	−0.20	− 0.375 (= −0.20 − 0.175)	0.05	−0.005 (= 0.05 − 0.055)	0.001875 (= −0.375 × −0.005)
Recession	0.10	−0.075	0.20	0.145	− 0.010875 (= −0.75 × 0.145)
Normal	0.30	0.125	−0.12	−0.175	−0.021875 (= 0.125 × −0.175)
Boom	0.50	0.325	0.09	0.035	0.011375 (= 0.325 × 0.035)
	0.70		0.22		− 0.0195

$$\sigma_{AB} = \text{Cov}(R_A, R_B) = \frac{-0.0195}{4} = -0.004875$$

$$\rho_{AB} = \text{Corr}(R_A, R_B) = \frac{\text{Cov}(R_A, R_B)}{\text{SD}(R_A) \times \text{SD}(R_B)} = \frac{-0.004875}{0.2586 \times 0.1150} = -0.1639$$

2. Calculate the average value of the four states in the last column. This average is the covariance. That is,[2]

$$\sigma_{AB} = \text{Cov}(R_A, R_B) = \frac{-0.0195}{4} = -0.004875 \bullet$$

Note that we represent the covariance between Supertech and Slowgrow as either Cov(R_A, R_B) or σ_{AB}. Equation (11.1) illustrates the intuition of covariance. Suppose Supertech's return is generally above its average when Slowgrow's return is above its average, and Supertech's return is generally below its average when Slowgrow's return is below its average. This is indicative of a positive dependency or a positive relationship between the two returns. Note that the term in equation (11.1) will be *positive* in any state where both returns are above their averages. In addition, equation (11.1) will still be *positive* in any state where both terms are *below* their averages. Thus, a positive relationship between the two returns will give rise to a positive calculation for covariance.

[2] As with variance, we divide by N (4 in this example) because the four states give rise to four *possible* outcomes. However, had we used past data, the correct divisor would be $N - 1$ (3 in this example).

Conversely, suppose Supertech's return is generally above its average when Slowgrow's return is below its average, and Supertech's return is generally below its average when Slowgrow's return is above its average. This is indicative of a negative dependency or a negative relationship between the two returns. Note that the term in equation (11.1) will be negative in any state where one return is above its average and the other return is below its average. Thus, a negative relationship between the two returns will give rise to a negative calculation for covariance.

Finally, suppose there is no relation between the two returns. In this case, knowing whether the return on Supertech is above or below its expected return tells us nothing about the return on Slowgrow. In the covariance formula, then, there will be no tendency for the terms to be positive or negative, and on average they will tend to offset each other and cancel out. This will make the covariance zero.

Of course, even if the two returns are unrelated to each other, the covariance formula will not equal zero exactly in any actual history. This is due to sampling error; randomness alone will make the calculation positive or negative. But for a historical sample that is long enough, if the two returns are not related to each other, we should expect the formula to come close to zero.

The covariance formula seems to capture what we are looking for. If the two returns are positively related to each other, they will have a positive covariance, and if they are negatively related to each other, the covariance will be negative. Last, and very important, if they are unrelated, the covariance should be zero.

The formula for covariance can be written algebraically as

$$\sigma_{AB} = \text{Cov}(R_A, R_B) = \text{Expected value of } [(R_A - \bar{R}_A) \times (R_B - \bar{R}_B)]$$

where $\bar{R}_A$ and $\bar{R}_B$ are the expected returns for the two securities, and R_A and R_B are the actual returns. The ordering of the two variables is unimportant. That is, the covariance of A with B is equal to the covariance of B with A. This can be stated more formally as $\text{Cov}(R_A, R_B) = \text{Cov}(R_B, R_A)$ or $\sigma_{AB} = \sigma_{BA}$.

The covariance we calculated is -0.004875. A negative number like this implies that the return on one stock is likely to be above its average when the return on the other stock is below its average, and vice versa. However, the size of the number is difficult to interpret. Like the variance figure, the covariance is in squared deviation units. Until we can put it in perspective, we don't know what to make of it.

3. We solve the problem by computing the correlation. To do this, we divide the covariance by the standard deviations of both of the two securities. For our example, we have:

$$\rho_{AB} = \text{Corr}(R_A, R_B) = \frac{\text{Cov}(R_A, R_B)}{\sigma_A \times \sigma_B} = \frac{-0.004875}{0.2568 \times 0.1150} = -0.1639 \qquad (11.2)$$

where σ_A and σ_B are the standard deviations of Supertech and Slowgrow, respectively. Note that we represent the correlation between Supertech and Slowgrow either as $\text{Corr}(R_A, R_B)$ or ρ_{AB}. As with covariance, the ordering of the two variables is unimportant. That is, the correlation of A with B is equal to the correlation of B with A. More formally, $\text{Corr}(R_A, R_B) = \text{Corr}(R_B, R_A)$ or $\rho_{AB} = \rho_{BA}$.

Because the standard deviation is always positive, the sign of the correlation between two variables must be the same as that of the covariance between the two variables. If the correlation is positive, we say that the variables are *positively correlated*; if it is negative, we say that they are *negatively correlated*; and if it is zero, we say that they are *uncorrelated*. Furthermore, it can be proved that the correlation is always between $+1$ and -1. This is due to the standardizing procedure of dividing by the two standard deviations.

We can compare the correlation between different pairs of securities. For example, assume that the correlation between company A and company B is much higher than the correlation between company A and company C. Hence, we can state that the first pair of securities is more interrelated than the second pair.

Figure 11.1 shows the three benchmark cases for two assets, A and B. The figure shows two assets with return correlations of $+1$, -1 and 0. This implies perfect positive correlation, perfect negative correlation and no correlation, respectively. The graphs in the figure plot the separate returns on the two securities through time.

FIGURE 11.1   Examples of Different Correlation Coefficients. The Graphs in the Figure Plot the Separate Returns on the Two Securities through Time.

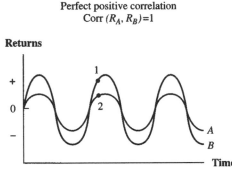

Perfect positive correlation
Corr $(R_A, R_B) = 1$

Both the return on security A and the return on security B are higher than average at the same time. Both the return on security A and the return on security B are lower than average at the same time.

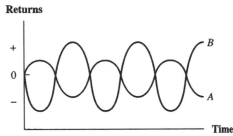

Perfect negative correlation
Corr $(R_A, R_B) = -1$

Security A has a higher-than-average return when security B has a lower-than-average return, and vice versa.

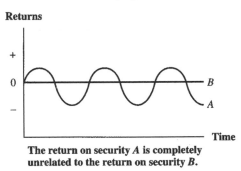

Zero correlation
Corr $(R_A, R_B) = 0$

The return on security A is completely unrelated to the return on security B.

11.3   The Return and Risk for Portfolios

Suppose that an investor has estimates of the expected returns and standard deviations on individual securities and the correlations between securities. How then does the investor choose the best combination or **portfolio** of securities to hold? Obviously, the investor would like a portfolio with a high expected return and a low standard deviation of return. It is therefore worth while to consider:

1. The relationship between the expected return on individual securities and the expected return on a portfolio made up of these securities.
2. The relationship between the standard deviations of individual securities, the correlations between these securities, and the standard deviation of a portfolio made up of these securities.

Relevant Data from Example of Supertech and Slowgrow

Item	Symbol	Value
Expected return on Supertech	$\overline{R}_{\text{Super}}$	0.175 = 17.5%
Expected return on Slowgrow	$\overline{R}_{\text{Slow}}$	0.055 = 5.5%
Variance of Supertech	σ^2_{Super}	0.066875
Variance of Slowgrow	σ^2_{Slow}	0.013225
Standard deviation of Supertech	σ_{Super}	0.2586 = 25.86%
Standard deviation of Slowgrow	σ_{Slow}	0.1150 = 11.50%
Covariance between Supertech and Slowgrow	$\sigma_{\text{Super,Slow}}$	−0.004875
Correlation between Supertech and Slowgrow	$\rho_{\text{Super,Slow}}$	−0.1639

The Example of Supertech and Slowgrow

In order to analyse the above two relationships, we will use the same example of Supertech and Slowgrow that was presented previously. The relevant data are as follows.[3]

The Expected Return on a Portfolio

The formula for expected return on a portfolio is very simple:

> The expected return on a portfolio is simply a weighted average of the expected returns on the individual securities.

● Example

Consider Supertech and Slowgrow. From the above box, we find that the expected returns on these two securities are 17.5 per cent and 5.5 per cent, respectively.

The expected return on a portfolio of these two securities alone can be written as

$$\text{Expected return on a portfolio} = X_{\text{Super}} (17.5\%) + X_{\text{Slow}} (5.5\%) = \overline{R}_P$$

where X_{Super} is the percentage of the portfolio in Supertech and X_{Slow} is the percentage of the portfolio in Slowgrow. If the investor with DEM100 invests DEM60 in Supertech and DEM40 in Slowgrow, the expected return on the portfolio can be written as

$$\text{Expected return on portfolio} = 0.6 \times 17.5\% + 0.4 \times 5.5\% = 12.7\%$$

---

[3] See Tables 11.1 and 11.2 for actual calculations.

Algebraically, we can write

$$\text{Expected return on portfolio} = X_A \overline{R}_A + X_B \overline{R}_B = \overline{R}_P \qquad (11.3)$$

where X_A and X_B are the proportions of the total portfolio in the assets A and B, respectively. (Because our investor can only invest in two securities, $X_A + X_B$ must equal 1 or 100 per cent.) $\overline{R}_A$ and $\overline{R}_B$ are the expected returns on the two securities. ●

Now consider two stocks, each with an expected return of 10 per cent. The expected return on a portfolio composed of these two stocks must be 10 per cent, regardless of the proportions of the two stocks held. This result may seem obvious at this point, but it will become important later. The result implies that you do not reduce or *dissipate* your expected return by investing in a number of securities. Rather, the expected return on your portfolio is simply a weighted average of the expected returns on the individual assets in the portfolio.

Variance and Standard Deviation of a Portfolio

The Variance

The formula for the variance of a portfolio composed of two securities, A and B, is

The Variance of the Portfolio:

$$\text{Var(portfolio)} = X_A^2 \sigma_A^2 + 2X_A X_B \sigma_{A,B} + X_B^2 \sigma_B^2$$

Note that there are three terms on the righthand side of the equation. The first term involves the variance of A (σ_A^2), the second term involves the covariance between the two securities ($\sigma_{A,B}$), and the third term involves the variance of B (σ_B^2). (It should be noted that $\sigma_{A,B} = \sigma_{B,A}$. That is, the ordering of the variables is not relevant when expressing the covariance between two securities.)

The formula indicates an important point. The variance of a portfolio depends on both the variances of the individual securities and the covariance between the two securities. The variance of a security measures the variability of an individual security's return. Covariance measures the relationship between the two securities. For given variances of the individual securities, a positive relationship or covariance between the two securities increases the variance of the entire portfolio. A negative relationship or covariance between the two securities decreases the variance of the entire portfolio. This important result seems to square with common sense. If one of your securities tends to go up when the other goes down, or vice versa, your two securities are offsetting each other. You are achieving what we call a *hedge* in finance, and the risk of your entire portfolio will be low. However, if both your securities rise and fall together, you are not hedging at all. Hence, the risk of your entire portfolio will be higher.

The variance formula for our two securities, Super and Slow, is

$$\text{Var(portfolio)} = X^2_{\text{Super}} \sigma^2_{\text{Super}} + 2X_{\text{Super}} X_{\text{Slow}} \sigma_{\text{Super,Slow}} + X^2_{\text{Slow}} \sigma^2_{\text{Slow}} \qquad (11.4)$$

Given our earlier assumption that an individual with DEM100 invests DEM60 in Supertech and DEM40 in Slowgrow, $X_{\text{Super}} = 0.6$ and $X_{\text{Slow}} = 0.4$. Using this assumption and the relevant data from the box above, the variance of the portfolio is

$$\begin{aligned} 0.023851 &= 0.36 \times 0.066875 \\ &+ 2 \times [0.6 \times 0.4 \times (-0.004875)] + 0.16 \times 0.013225 \end{aligned} \qquad (11.4')$$

The Matrix Approach

Alternatively, equation (11.4) can be expressed in the following matrix format:

	Supertech	Slowgrow
Supertech	$X^2_{Super}\sigma^2_{Super}$ $0.024075 = 0.36 \times 0.066875$	$X_{Super}X_{Slow}\sigma_{Super,Slow}$ $-0.00117 = 0.6 \times 0.4 \times (-0.004875)$
Slowgrow	$X_{Super}X_{Slow}\sigma_{Super,Slow}$ $-0.00117 = 0.6 \times 0.4 \times (-0.004875)$	$X^2_{Slow}\sigma^2_{Slow}$ $0.002116 = 0.16 \times 0.013225$

There are four boxes in the matrix. We can add the terms in the boxes to obtain equation (11.4), the variance of a portfolio composed of the two securities. The term in the upper lefthand corner involves the variance of Supertech. The term in the lower righthand corner involves the variance of Slowgrow. The other two boxes contain the term involving the covariance. These two boxes are identical, indicating why the covariance term is multiplied by 2 in equation (11.4).

At this point, students often find the box approach to be more confusing than equation (11.4). However, the box approach is easily generalized to more than two securities, a task we perform later in this chapter.

Standard Deviation of a Portfolio

Given (11.4′), we can now determine the standard deviation of the portfolio's return. This is

$$\sigma_P = \text{SD (portfolio)} = \sqrt{\text{Var(portfolio)}} = \sqrt{0.023851} \qquad (11.5)$$

$$= 0.1544 = 15.44\%$$

The interpretation of the standard deviation of the portfolio is the same as the interpretation of the standard deviation of an individual security. The expected return on our portfolio is 12.7 per cent. A return of -2.74 per cent ($12.7\% - 15.44\%$) is one standard deviation below the mean and a return of 28.14 per cent ($12.7\% = 15.44\%$) is one standard deviation above the mean. If the return on the portfolio is normally distributed, a return between -2.74 per cent and $+28.14$ per cent occurs about 68 per cent of the time.[4]

The Diversification Effect

It is instructive to compare the standard deviation of the portfolio with the standard deviation of the individual securities. The weighted average of the standard deviations of the individual securities is

$$\text{Weighted average of standard deviations} = X_{Super}\sigma_{Super} = X_{Slow}\sigma_{Slow} \qquad (11.6)$$

$$0.2012 = 0.6 \times 0.2586 + 0.4 \times 0.115$$

One of the most important results in this chapter relates to the difference between (11.5) and (11.6). In our example, the standard deviation of the portfolio is less than a weighted average of the standard deviations of the individual securities.

---

[4] There are only four equally probable returns for Supertech and Slowgrow, so neither security possesses a normal distribution. Thus, probabilities would be slightly different in our example.

We pointed out earlier that the expected return on the portfolio is a weighted average of the expected returns on the individual securities. Thus, we get a different type of result for the standard deviation of a portfolio than we do for the expected return on a portfolio.

It is generally argued that our result for the standard deviation of a portfolio is due to diversification. For example, Supertech and Slowgrow are slightly negatively correlated ($\rho = -0.1639$). Supertech's return is likely to be a little below average if Slowgrow's return is above average. Similarly, Supertech's return is likely to be a little above average if Slowgrow's return is below average. Thus, the standard deviation of a portfolio composed of the two securities is less than a weighted average of the standard deviations of the two securities.

The above example has negative correlation. Clearly, there will be less benefit from diversification if the two securities exhibited positive correlation. How high must the positive correlation be before all diversification benefits vanish?

To answer this question, let us rewrite (11.4) in terms of correlation rather than covariance. The covariance can be rewritten as[5]

$$\sigma_{Super,Slow} = \rho_{Super,Slow}\sigma_{Super}\sigma_{Slow} \tag{11.7}$$

The formula states that the covariance between any two securities is simply the correlation between the two securities multiplied by the standard deviations of each. In other words, covariance incorporates both (1) the correlation between the two assets and (2) the variability of each of the two securities as measured by standard deviation.

From our calculations earlier in this chapter we know that the correlation between the two securities is -0.1639. Given the variances used in equation (11.4'), the standard deviations are 0.2586 and 0.115 for Supertech and Slowgrow, respectively. Thus, the variance of a portfolio can be expressed as

$$\begin{array}{l}\text{Variance of the} \\ \text{portfolio's return}\end{array} = X^2_{Super}\sigma^2_{Super} + 2X_{Super}X_{Slow}\rho_{Super,Slow}\sigma_{Super}\sigma_{Slow} + X^2_{Slow}\sigma^2_{Slow} \tag{11.8}$$

$$0.023851 = 0.36 \times 0.066875 + 2 \times 0.6 \times 0.4 \times (-0.1639)$$
$$\times 0.2586 \times 0.115 + 0.16 \times 0.013225$$

The middle term on the right-hand side is now written in terms of correlation, ρ, not covariance.

Suppose $\rho_{Super,Slow} = 1$, the highest possible value for correlation. Assume all the other parameters in the example are the same. The variance of the portfolio is

Variance of the portfolio's return = 0.040466

$$= 0.36 \times 0.066875 + 2 \times (0.6 \times 0.4 \times 1 \times 0.2586 \times 0.115) + 0.16 \times 0.013225$$

The standard deviation is

Standard variation of portfolio's return = $\sqrt{0.040466}$ = 0.2012 = 20.12% (11.9)

Note that (11.9) and (11.6) are equal. That is, the standard deviation of a portfolio's return is equal to the weighted average of the standard deviations of the individual returns when $\rho = 1$. Inspection of (11.8) indicates that the variance and hence the standard deviation of the portfolio must drop as the correlation drops below 1. This leads to:

---

[5] As with covariance, the ordering of the two securities is not relevant when expressing the correlation between the two securities. That is, $\rho_{Super,Slow} = \rho_{Slow,Super}$.

As long as ρ < 1, the standard deviation of a portfolio of two securities is *less* than the weighted average of the standard deviations of the individual securities.

In other words, the diversification effect applies as long as there is less than perfect correlation (as long as ρ < 1). Thus, our Supertech–Slowgrow example is a case of overkill. We illustrated diversification by an example with negative correlation. We could have illustrated diversification by an example with positive correlation—as long as it was not perfect positive correlation.

Concept Questions

- What are the formulas for the expected return, variance and standard deviation of a portfolio of two assets?
- What is the diversification effect?
- What are the highest and lowest possible values for the correlation coefficient?

11.4   The Efficient Set for Two Assets

Our results on expected returns and standard deviations are graphed in Figure 11.2. In the figure, there is a dot labelled Slowgrow and a dot labelled Supertech. Each dot represents both the expected return and the standard deviation for an individual security. As can be seen, Supertech has both a higher expected return and a higher standard deviation.

FIGURE 11.2   Expected Return and Standard Deviation for Supertech, Slowgrow, and a Portfolio Composed of 60 Per cent in Supertech and 40 Per cent in Slowgrow

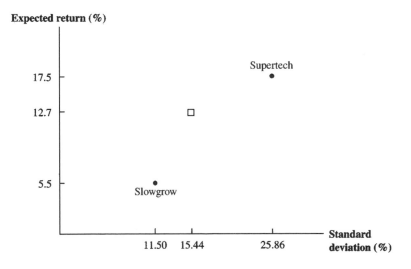

The box or □ in the graph represents a portfolio with 60 per cent invested in Supertech and 40 per cent invested in Slowgrow. You will recall that we have previously calculated both the expected return and the standard deviation for this portfolio.

The choice of 60 per cent in Supertech and 40 per cent in Slowgrow is just one of an infinite number of portfolios that can be created. The set of portfolios is sketched by the curved line in Figure 11.3.

Consider portfolio *1*. This is a portfolio composed of 90 per cent Slowgrow and 10 per cent Supertech. Because it is weighted so heavily toward Slowgrow, it appears close to the Slowgrow point on the graph. Portfolio *2* is higher on the curve because it is composed of 50 per cent Slowgrow and 50 per cent Supertech. Portfolio *3* is close to the Supertech point on the graph because it is composed of 90 per cent Supertech and 10 per cent Slowgrow.

FIGURE 11.3   Set of Portfolios Composed of Holdings in Supertech and Slowgrow (Correlation between the two securities is −0.16)

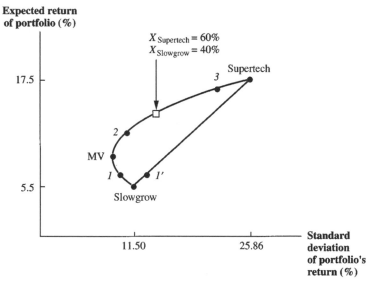

Portfolio *1* is composed of 90 per cent Slowgrow and 10 per cent Supertech ($\rho = -0.16$).
Portfolio *2* is composed of 50 per cent Slowgrow and 50 per cent Supertech ($\rho = -0.16$).
Portfolio *3* is composed of 10 per cent Slowgrow and 90 per cent Supertech ($\rho = -0.16$).
Portfolio *1'* is composed of 90 per cent Slowgrow and 10 per cent Supertech ($\rho = 1$).
Point MV denotes the minimum variance portfolio. This is the portfolio with the lowest possible variance. By definition, the same portfolio must also have the lowest possible standard deviation.

There are a few important points concerning this graph.

1.   We argued that the diversification effect occurs whenever the correlation between the two securities is below 1. The correlation between Supertech and Slowgrow is −0.1639. The diversification effect can be illustrated by comparison with the straight line between the Supertech point and the Slowgrow point. The straight line represents points that would have been generated had the correlation coefficient between the two securities been 1. The diversification effect is illustrated in the figure since the curved line is always to the left of the straight line. Consider point *1'*. This represents a portfolio composed of 90 per cent in Slowgrow and 10 per cent in Supertech *if* the correlation between the two were exactly 1. We argue that there is no diversification effect if $\rho = 1$. However, the diversification effect applies to the curved

line, because point *1* has the same expected return as point *1'* but has a lower standard deviation. (Points *2'* and *3'* are omitted to reduce the clutter of Figure 11.3.)

Though the straight line and the curved line are both represented in Figure 11.3, they do not simultaneously exist in the same world. *Either* $\rho = -0.1639$ and the curve exists *or* $\rho = 1$ and the straight line exists. In other words, though an investor can choose between different points on the curve if $\rho = -0.1639$, she cannot choose between points on the curve and points on the straight line.

2.   The point MV represents the minimum variance portfolio. This is the portfolio with the lowest possible variance. By definition, this portfolio must also have the lowest possible standard deviation. (The term *minimum variance portfolio* is standard in the literature, and we will use that term. Perhaps minimum standard deviation would actually be better, because standard deviation, not variance, is measured on the horizontal axis of Figure 11.3.)

3.   An individual contemplating an investment in a portfolio of Slowgrow and Supertech faces an **opportunity set** or **feasible set** represented by the curved line in Figure 11.3. That is, he can achieve any point on the curve by selecting the appropriate mix between the two securities. He cannot achieve any points above the curve because he cannot increase the return on the individual securities, decrease the standard deviations of the securities or decrease the correlation between the two securities. Neither can he achieve points below the curve because he cannot lower the returns on the individual securities, increase the standard deviations of the securities or increase the correlation. (Of course, he would not want to achieve points below the curve, even if he were able to do so.)

Were he relatively tolerant of risk, he might choose portfolio *3*. (In fact, he could even choose the end point by investing all his money in Supertech.) An investor with less tolerance for risk might choose point *2*. An investor wanting as little risk as possible would choose MV, the portfolio with minimum variance or minimum standard deviation.

4.   Note that the curve is backward bending between the Slowgrow point and MV. This indicates that, for a portion of the feasible set, standard deviation actually decreases as one increases expected return. Students frequently ask: 'How can an increase in the proportion of the risky security, Supertech, lead to a reduction in the risk of the portfolio?'

This surprising finding is due to the diversification effect. The returns on the two securities are negatively correlated with each other. One security tends to go up when the other goes down and vice versa. Thus, an addition of a small amount of Supertech acts as a hedge to a portfolio composed only of Slowgrow. The risk of the portfolio is reduced, implying backward bending. Actually, backward bending always occurs if $\rho \leq 0$. It may or may not occur when $\rho > 0$. Of course, the curve bends backward only for a portion of its length. As one continues to increase the percentage of Supertech in the portfolio, the high standard deviation of this security eventually causes the standard deviation of the entire portfolio to rise.

5.   No investor would want to hold a portfolio with an expected return below that of the minimum variance portfolio. For example, no investor would choose portfolio *1*. This portfolio has less expected return, but more standard deviation than the minimum variance portfolio has. We say that portfolios such as portfolio *1* are *dominated* by the minimum variance portfolio. Though the entire curve from Slowgrow to Supertech is called the *feasible set*, investors only consider the curve from MV to Supertech. Hence, the curve from MV to Supertech is called the **efficient set**.

Figure 11.3 represents the opportunity set where $\rho = -0.1639$. It is worth while to examine Figure 11.4, which shows different curves for different correlations. As can be seen, the lower the correlation, the more bend there is in the curve. This indicates that the diversification effect rises as ρ declines. The greatest bend occurs in the limiting case where ρ = −1. This is perfect negative correlation. While this extreme case where ρ = −1 seems to fascinate students, it has little practical importance. Most pairs of securities exhibit positive correlation. Strong negative correlation, let alone perfect negative correlation, is an unlikely occurrence indeed.[6]

FIGURE 11.4   Opportunity Sets Composed of Holdings in Supertech and Slowgrow

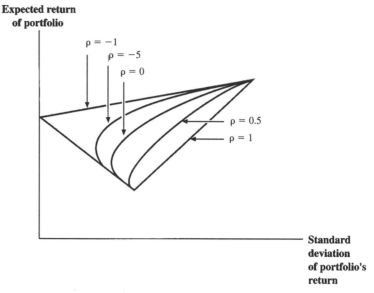

Each curve represents a different correlation. The lower the correlation, the more bend in the curve.

The graphs we examined are not mere intellectual curiosities. Rather, efficient sets can easily be calculated in the real world. As mentioned earlier, data on returns, standard deviations and correlations are generally taken from past observations, though subjective notions can be used to calculate the values of these statistics as well. Once the statistics have been determined, any one of a whole host of software packages can be purchased to generate an efficient set. However, the choice of the preferred portfolio within the efficient set is up to you. As with other important decisions such as what job to choose, what house or car to buy or how much time to allocate to this course, there is no computer program to choose the preferred portfolio.

An efficient set can be generated where the two individual assets are portfolios themselves. For example, the two assets in Figure 11.5 are a diversified portfolio of American stocks and a diversified portfolio of foreign stocks. Expected returns, standard deviations and the correlation coefficient were calculated over the recent past. No subjectivity entered the analysis. The US stock portfolio with a standard deviation of about 0.173 is less risky than the foreign stock portfolio, which has a standard deviation of about 0.222. However, combining a small percentage of the foreign stock portfolio

---

[6] A major exception occurs with derivative securities. For example, the correlation between a stock and a put on the stock is generally strongly negative. Puts will be treated later in the text.

FIGURE 11.5   Return/Risk Trade-off for World Stocks: Portfolio of US and Foreign Stocks

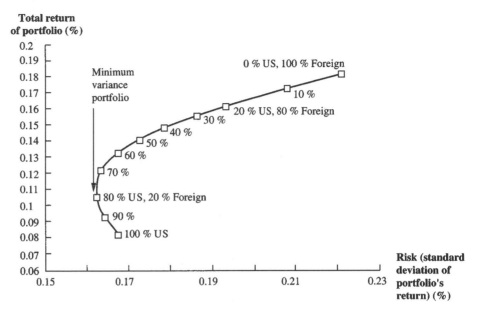

with the US portfolio actually reduces risk, as can be seen by the backward-bending nature of the curve. In other words, the diversification benefits from combining two different portfolios more than offset the introduction of a riskier set of stocks into one's holdings. The minimum variance portfolio occurs with about 80 per cent of one's funds in American stocks and about 20 per cent in foreign stocks. Addition of foreign securities beyond this point increases the risk of one's entire portfolio.

The backward-bending curve in Figure 11.5 is important information that has not bypassed money managers. In recent years, pension-fund and mutual-fund managers in the United States and elsewhere have sought out investment opportunities overseas. Another point worth pondering concerns the potential pitfalls of using only past data to estimate future returns. The stock markets of many foreign countries have had phenomenal growth in the past 25 years. Thus, a graph such as Figure 11.5 makes a large investment in these foreign markets seem attractive. However, because abnormally high returns cannot be sustained forever, some subjectivity must be used when forecasting future expected returns.

Concept Question

• What is the relationship between the shape of the efficient set for two assets and the correlation between the two assets?

11.5   The Efficient Set for Many Securities

The previous discussion concerned two securities. We found that a simple curve sketched out all the possible portfolios. Because investors generally hold more than two securities, we should look at the same curve when more than two securities are held. The shaded area in Figure 11.6 represents the opportunity set or feasible set when many securities are considered. The shaded area represents all the possible

FIGURE 11.6   The Feasible Set of Portfolios Constructed from Many Securities

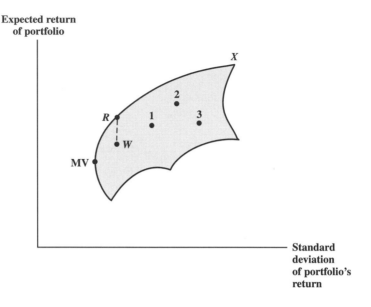

combinations of expected return and standard deviation for a portfolio. For example, in a universe of 100 securities, point 1 might represent a portfolio of, say, 40 securities. Point 2 might represent a portfolio of 80 securities. Point 3 might represent a different set of 80 securities, or the same 80 securities held in different proportions, or something else. Obviously, the combinations are virtually endless. However, note that all possible combinations fit into a confined region. No security or combination of securities can fall outside of the shaded region. That is, no one can choose a portfolio with an expected return above that given by the shaded region because the expected returns on individual securities cannot be altered. Furthermore, no one can choose a portfolio with a standard deviation below that given in the shady area. Perhaps more surprisingly, no one can choose an expected return below that given in the curve. In other words, the capital markets actually prevent a self-destructive person from taking on a guaranteed loss.[7]

So far, Figure 11.6 is different from the earlier graphs. When only two securities are involved, all the combinations lie on a single curve. Conversely, with many securities the combinations cover an entire area. However, notice that an individual will want to be somewhere on the upper edge between MV and X. The upper edge, which we indicate in Figure 11.6 by a thick curve, is called the *efficient set*. Any point below the efficient set would receive less expected return and the same standard deviation as a point on the efficient set. For example, consider R on the efficient set and W directly below it. If W contains the risk you desire, you should choose R instead in order to receive a higher expected return.

In the final analysis, Figure 11.6 is quite similar to Figure 11.3. The efficient set in Figure 11.3 runs from MV to Supertech. It contains various combinations of the securities Supertech and Slowgrow. The efficient set in Figure 11.6 runs from MV to X. It contains various combinations of many securities. The fact that a whole shaded

---

[7] Of course, someone dead set on parting with his money can do so. For example, he can trade frequently without purpose, so that commissions more than offset the positive expected returns on the portfolio.

area appears in Figure 11.6, but not in Figure 11.3, is just not an important difference; no investor would choose any point below the efficient set in Figure 11.6 anyway.

We mentioned before that an efficient set for two securities can be traced out easily in the real world. The task becomes more difficult when additional securities are included because the number of observations grows. For example, using subjective analysis to estimate expected returns and standard deviations for, say, 100 or 500 securities may very well become overwhelming, and the difficulties with correlations may be greater still. There are almost 5,000 correlations between pairs of securities from a universe of 100 securities.

Though much of the mathematics of efficient-set computation had been derived in the 1950s,[8] the high cost of computer time restricted application of the principles. In recent years, the cost has been drastically reduced. A number of software packages allow the calculation of an efficient set for portfolios of moderate size. By all accounts these packages sell quite briskly, so that our discussion above would appear to be important in practice.

Variance and Standard Deviation in a Portfolio of Many Assets

We earlier calculated the formulas for variance and standard deviation in the two-asset case. Because we considered a portfolio of many assets in Figure 11.6, it is worth while to calculate the formulas for variance and standard deviation in the many-asset case. The formula for the variance of a portfolio of many assets can be viewed as an extension of the formula for the variance of two assets.

To develop the formula, we employ the same type of matrix that we used in the two-asset case. This matrix is displayed in Table 11.3. Assuming that there are N assets, we write the numbers 1 through N on the horizontal axis and 1 through N on the vertical axis. This creates a matrix of $N \times N = N^2$ boxes.

Consider, for example, the box with a horizontal dimension of 2 and a vertical dimension of 3. The term in the box is $X_3 X_2 \text{Cov}(R_3, R_2)$. X_3 and X_2 are the percentages of the entire portfolio that are invested in the third asset and the second asset,

---

TABLE 11.3 **Matrix Used to Calculate the Variance of a Portfolio**

Stock	1	2	3	...	N
1	$X_1^2\sigma_1^2$	$X_1 X_2 \text{Cov}(R_1, R_2)$	$X_1 X_3 \text{Cov}(R_1, R_3)$		$X_1 X_N \text{Cov}(R_1, R_N)$
2	$X_2 X_1 \text{Cov}(R_2, R_1)$	$X_2^2\sigma_2^2$	$X_2 X_3 \text{Cov}(R_2, R_3)$		$X_2 X_N \text{Cov}(R_2, R_N)$
3	$X_3 X_1 \text{Cov}(R_3, R_1)$	$X_3 X_2 \text{Cov}(R_3, R_2)$	$X_3^2\sigma_3^2$		$X_3 X_N \text{Cov}(R_3, R_N)$
.					
.					
.					
N	$X_N X_1 \text{Cov}(R_N, R_1)$	$X_N X_2 \text{Cov}(R_N, R_2)$	$X_N X_3 \text{Cov}(R_N, R_3)$		$X_N^2\sigma_N^2$

σ_i is the standard deviation of stock i.
$\text{Cov}(R_i, R_j)$ is the covariance between stock i and stock j.
Terms involving the standard deviation of a single security appear on the diagonal. Terms involving covariance between two securities appear off the diagonal.

---

[8] The classic treatise is H. Markowitz (1959), *Portfolio Selection*, New York: Wiley. Markowitz won the Nobel prize in economics in 1990 for his work on modern portfolio theory.

respectively. For example, if an individual with a portfolio of GBP1,000 invests GBP100 in the second asset, $X_2 = 10\%$ (GBP100/GBP1,000). Cov(R_3, R_2) is the covariance between the returns on the third asset and the returns on the second asset. Next, note the box with a horizontal dimension of 3 and a vertical dimension of 2. The term in the box is $X_2 X_3$ Cov(R_2, R_3). Because Cov(R_3, R_2) = Cov(R_2, R_3), both boxes have the same value. The second security and the third security make up one pair of stocks. In fact, every pair of stocks appears twice in the table, once in the lower lefthand side and once in the upper righthand side.

Suppose that the vertical dimension equals the horizontal dimension. For example, the term in the box is $X_1^2\sigma_1^2$ when both dimensions are one. Here, σ_1^2 is the variance of the return on the first security.

Thus, the diagonal terms in the matrix contain the variances of the different stocks. The off-diagonal terms contain the covariances. Table 11.4 relates the numbers of diagonal and off-diagonal elements to the size of the matrix. The number of diagonal terms (number of variance terms) is always the same as the number of stocks in the portfolio. The number of off-diagonal terms (number of covariance terms) rises much faster than the number of diagonal terms. For example, a portfolio of 100 stocks has 9,900 covariance terms. Since the variance of a portfolio's returns is the sum of all the boxes, we have:

> The variance of the return on a portfolio with many securities is more dependent on the covariances between the individual securities than on the variances of the individual securities.

Concept Questions

- What is the formula for the variance of a portfolio for many assets?
- How can the formula be expressed in terms of a box or matrix?

TABLE 11.4   Number of Variance and Covariance Terms as a Function of the Number of Stocks in the Portfolio

Number of stocks in portfolio	Total number of terms	Number of variance terms (number of terms on diagonal)	Number of covariance terms (number of terms off diagonal)
1	1	1	0
2	4	2	2
3	9	3	6
10	100	10	90
100	10,000	100	9,900
.	.	.	.
.	.	.	.
.	.	.	.
N	N^2	N	$N^2 - N$

In a large portfolio, the number of terms involving covariance between two securities is much greater than the number of terms involving vartiance of a single security.

11.6   Diversification: An Example

The above point can be illustrated by altering the matrix in Table 11.3 slightly. Suppose that we make the following three assumptions:

1. All securities possess the same variance, which we write as $\overline{\text{var}}$. In other words, $\sigma_i^2 = \overline{\text{var}}$ for every security.
2. All covariances in Table 11.3 are the same. We represent this uniform covariance as $\overline{\text{cov}}$. In other words, $\text{cov}(R_i, R_j) = \overline{\text{cov}}$ for every pair of securities. It can easily be shown that $\overline{\text{var}} > \overline{\text{cov}}$.
3. All securities are equally weighted in the portfolio. Because there are N assets, the weight of each asset in the portfolio is $1/N$. In other words, $X_i = 1/N$ for each security i.

Table 11.5 is the matrix of variances and covariances under these three simplifying assumptions. Note that all of the diagonal terms are identical. Similarly, all of the off-diagonal terms are identical. As with Table 11.3, the variance of the portfolio is the sum of the terms in the boxes in Table 11.5. We know that there are N diagonal terms involving variance. Similarly, there are $N \times (N - 1)$ off-diagonal terms involving covariance. Summing across all the boxes in Table 11.5, we can express the variances of the portfolio as

$$
\underset{\substack{\text{Variance} \\ \text{of} \\ \text{portfolio}}}{} = \underset{\substack{\text{Number of} \\ \text{diagonal} \\ \text{terms}}}{N} \times \underset{\substack{\text{Each} \\ \text{diagonal} \\ \text{term}}}{\left(\frac{1}{N^2}\right)\overline{\text{var}}} + \underset{\substack{\text{Number of} \\ \text{off-diagonal} \\ \text{term}}}{N(N-1)} \times \underset{\substack{\text{Each} \\ \text{off-diagonal} \\ \text{term}}}{\left(\frac{1}{N^2}\right)\overline{\text{cov}}}
$$

(11.10)

$$
= \left(\frac{1}{N}\right)\overline{\text{var}} + \left(\frac{N^2 - N}{N^2}\right)\overline{\text{cov}}
$$

$$
= \left(\frac{1}{N}\right)\overline{\text{var}} + \left(1 - \frac{1}{N}\right)\overline{\text{cov}}
$$

Equation (11.10) expresses the variance of our special portfolio as a weighted sum of the average security variance and the average covariance.[9] The intuition is confirmed when we increase the number of securities in the portfolio without limit. The variance of the portfolio becomes

$$
\text{Variance of portfolio (when } N \to \infty) = \overline{\text{cov}} \tag{11.11}
$$

This occurs because (1) the weight on the variance term, $1/N$, goes to 0 as N goes to infinity, and (2) the weight on the covariance term, $1 - 1/N$, goes to 1 as N goes to infinity.

Formula (11.11) provides an interesting and important result. In our special portfolio, the variances of the individual securities completely vanish as the number of securities becomes large. However, the covariance terms remain. In fact, the variance

---

[9] Equation (11.10) is actually a weighted average of the variance and covariance terms because the weights, $1/N$ and $1 - 1/N$, sum to 1.

TABLE 11.5   **Matrix Used to Calculate the Variance of a Portfolio When (a) All Securities Possess the Same Variance, Which We Represent as $\overline{var}$; (b) All Pairs of Securities Possess the Same Covariance, Which We Represent as $\overline{cov}$; (c) All Securities Are Held in the Same Proportion, Which is $1/N$**

Stock	1	2	3	...	N
1	$(1/N^2)\overline{var}$	$(1/N^2)\overline{cov}$	$(1/N^2)\overline{cov}$		$(1/N^2)\overline{cov}$
2	$(1/N^2)\overline{cov}$	$(1/N^2)\overline{var}$	$(1/N^2)\overline{cov}$		$(1/N^2)\overline{cov}$
3	$(1/N^2)\overline{cov}$	$(1/N^2)\overline{cov}$	$(1/N^2)\overline{var}$		$(1/N^2)\overline{cov}$
.					
.					
.					
N	$(1/N^2)\overline{cov}$	$(1/N^2)\overline{cov}$	$(1/N^2)\overline{cov}$		$(1/N^2)\overline{var}$

of the portfolio becomes the average covariance, $\overline{cov}$. One often hears that one should diversify. In other words, you should not put all your eggs in one basket. The effect of diversification on the risk of a portfolio can be illustrated in this example. The variances of the individual securities are diversified away, but the covariance terms cannot be diversified away.

The fact that part, but not all, of one's risk can be diversified away should be explored. Consider Mr Smith, who brings GBP1,000 to the roulette table at a casino. It would be very risky if he put all his money on one spin of the wheel. For example, imagine that he put the full GBP1,000 on red at the table. If the wheel showed red, he would get GBP2,000, but if the wheel showed black, he would lose everything. Suppose, instead, he divided his money over 1,000 different spins by betting GBP1 at a time on red. Probability theory tells us that he could count on winning about 50 per cent of the time. This means that he could count on pretty nearly getting all his original GBP1,000 back.[10] In other words, risk is essentially eliminated with 1,000 different spins.

Now, let's contrast this with our stock market example, which we illustrate in Figure 11.7. The variance of the portfolio with only one security is, of course, $\overline{var}$ because the variance of a portfolio with one security is the variance of the security. The variance of the portfolio drops as more securities are added, which is evidence of the diversification effect. However, unlike Mr Smith's roulette example, the portfolio's variance can never drop to zero. Rather it reaches a floor of $\overline{cov}$, which is the covariance of each pair of securities.[11]

Because the variance of the portfolio asymptotically approaches $\overline{cov}$, each additional security continues to reduce risk. Thus, if there were neither commissions nor other transactions costs, it could be argued that one can never achieve too much diversification. However, there is a cost to diversification in the real world. Commissions per dollar invested fall as one makes larger purchases in a single stock.

---

[10] This ignores the casino's cut.

[11] Though it is harder to show, this risk reduction effect also applies to the general case where variances and covariances are *not* equal.

FIGURE 11.7   **Relationship between the Variance of a Portfolio's Return and the Number of Securities in the Portfolio***

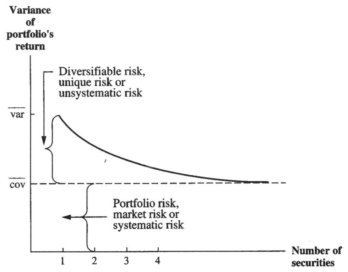

*This graph assumes
  a. All securities have constant variance, var.
  b. All securities have constant covariance, cov.
  c. All securities are equally weighted in portfolio.
The variance of a portfolio drops as more securities are added to the portfolio. However, it does not drop to zero. Rather, $\overline{cov}$ serves as the floor.

Unfortunately, one must buy fewer shares of each security when buying more and more different securities. Comparing the costs and benefits of diversification, Meir Statman argues that a portfolio of about 30 stocks is needed to achieve optimal diversification.[12]

We mentioned earlier that $\overline{var}$ must be greater than $\overline{cov}$. Thus, the variance of a security's return can be broken down in the following way:

$$
\begin{array}{ccc}
\text{Total risk of} & & \text{Unsystematic or} \\
\text{individual security} \;=\; & \text{Portfolio risk} \;+\; & \text{diversifiable risk} \\
(\overline{var}) & (\overline{cov}) & (\overline{var}-\overline{cov})
\end{array}
$$

Total risk, which is $\overline{var}$ in our example, is the risk that one bears by holding on to one security only. *Portfolio risk* is the risk that one still bears after achieving full diversification, which is $\overline{cov}$ in our example. Portfolio risk is often called **systematic** or **market risk** as well. **Diversifiable**, **unique**, or **unsystematic risk** is that risk that can be diversified away in a large portfolio, which must be $(\overline{var}-\overline{cov})$ by definition.

To an individual who selects a diversified portfolio, the total risk of an individual security is not important. When considering adding a security to a diversified portfolio, the individual cares about that portion of the risk of a security that cannot be diversified away. This risk can alternatively be viewed as the *contribution* of a security to the risk of an entire portfolio. We will talk later about the case where securities make different contributions to the risk of the entire portfolio.

---

[12] M. Statman (1987), How Many Stocks Make a Diversified Portfolio? *Journal of Financial and Quantitative Analysis*, September.

Risk and the Sensible Investor

Having gone to all this trouble to show that unsystematic risk disappears in a well-diversified portfolio, how do we know that investors even want such portfolios? Suppose they like risk and don't want it to disappear?

We must admit that, theoretically at least, this is possible, but we will argue that it does not describe what we think of as the typical investor. Our typical investor is **risk-averse**. Risk-averse behaviour can be defined in many ways, but we prefer the following example: A fair gamble is one with zero expected return; a risk-averse investor would prefer to avoid fair gambles.

Why do investors choose well-diversified portfolios? Our answer is that they are risk-averse, and risk-averse people avoid unnecessary risk, such as the unsystematic risk on a stock. If you do not think this is much of an answer to why investors choose well-diversified portfolios and avoid unsystematic risk, consider whether you would take on such a risk. For example, suppose you had worked all summer and had saved GBP5,000, which you intended to use for your university expenses. Now, suppose someone came up to you and offered to flip a coin for the money: heads, you would double your money and tails, you would lose it all.

Would you take such a bet? Perhaps you would, but most people would not. Leaving aside any moral question that might surround gambling, and recognizing that some people would take such a bet, it's our view that the average investor would not.

To induce the typical risk-averse investor to take a fair gamble, you must sweeten the pot. For example, you might need to raise the odds of winning from 50–50 to 70–30 or higher. The risk-averse investor can be induced to take fair gambles only if they are sweetened so that they become unfair to the investor's advantage.

Concept Questions

- What are the two components of the total risk of a security?
- Why doesn't diversification eliminate all risk?

11.7   Riskless Borrowing and Lending

Figure 11.6 assumes that all the securities on the efficient set are risky. Alternatively, an investor could easily combine a risky investment with an investment in a riskless or risk-free security, such as an investment in Treasury bills. This is illustrated in the following example.

● Example

Ms Bagwell is considering investing in the ordinary shares of Merville Company. In addition, Ms Bagwell will either borrow or lend at the risk-free rate. The relevant parameters are

	Ordinary Shares of Merville	*Risk-Free Asset*
Expected return	14%	10%
Standard deviation	0.20	0

Suppose Ms Bagwell chooses to invest a total of GBP1,000, GBP350 of which is to be invested in the ordinary shares of Merville Company and GBP650 placed in the risk-free asset. The expected return on her total investment is simply a weighted average of the two returns:

> Expected return on portfolio
> composed of one riskless $= 0.114 = 0.35 \times 0.14 + 0.65 \times 0.10$ (11.12)
> and one risky asset

Because the expected return on the portfolio is a weighted average of the expected return on the risky asset (Merville Company) and the risk-free return, the calculation is analogous to the way we treated two risky assets. In other words, equation (11.3) applies here.

Using equation (11.4), the formula for the variance of the portfolio can be written as

$$X^2_{\text{Merville}}\sigma^2_{\text{Merville}} + 2X_{\text{Merville}}X_{\text{Risk-free}}\sigma_{\text{Merville, Risk-free}} + X^2_{\text{Risk-free}}\sigma^2_{\text{Risk-free}}$$

However, by definition, the risk-free asset has no variability. Thus, both $\sigma_{\text{Merville, Risk-free}}$ and $\sigma^2_{\text{Risk-free}}$ are equal to zero, reducing the above expression to

> Variance of portfolio
> composed of one riskless $= X^2_{\text{Merville}}\sigma^2_{\text{Merville}} = (0.35)^2 \times (0.20)^2 = 0.0049$ (11.13)
> and one risky asset

The standard deviation of the portfolio is

> Standard deviation of portfolio
> composed of one riskless $= X_{\text{Merville}}\sigma_{\text{Merville}} = 0.35 \times 0.20 = 0.07$ (11.14)
> and one risky asset

The relationship between risk and expected return for one risky and one riskless asset can be seen in Figure 11.8. Ms Bagwell's split of 35–65 per cent between the two assets is represented on a *straight* line between the risk-free rate and a pure investment

---

FIGURE 11.8   Relationship between Expected Return and Risk for a Portfolio of One Risky Asset and One Riskless Asset

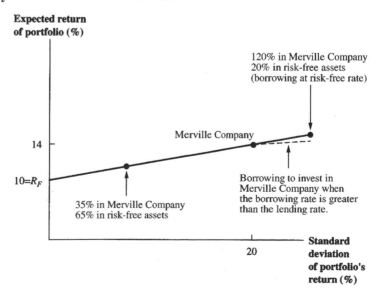

in Merville Company. Note that, unlike the case of two risky assets, the opportunity set is straight, not curved.

Suppose that, alternatively, Ms Bagwell borrows GBP200 at the risk-free rate. Combining this with her original sum of GBP1,000, she invests a total of GBP1,200 in the Merville Company. Her expected return would be

$$\begin{matrix} \text{Expected return on portfolio} \\ \text{formed by borrowing} \\ \text{to invest in risky asset} \end{matrix} = 14.8\% = 1.20 \times 0.14 + (-0.2) \times 0.10$$

Here, she invests 120 per cent of her original investment of GBP1,000 by borrowing 20 per cent of her original investment. Note that the return of 14.8 per cent is greater than the 14 per cent expected return on Merville Company. This occurs because she is borrowing at 10 per cent to invest in a security with an expected return greater than 10 per cent.

The standard deviation is

$$\begin{matrix} \text{Standard deviation of portfolio formed} \\ \text{by borrowing to invest in risky asset} \end{matrix} = 0.24 = 1.20 \times 0.2$$

The standard deviation of 0.24 is greater than 0.20, the standard deviation of the Merville Company, because borrowing increases the variability of the investment. This investment also appears in Figure 11.8.

So far, we have assumed that Ms Bagwell is able to borrow at the same rate at which she can lend. Now let us consider the case where the borrowing rate is above the lending rate. The dotted line in Figure 11.8 illustrates the opportunity set for borrowing opportunities in this case. The dotted line is below the solid line because a higher borrowing rate lowers the expected return on the investment. ●

The Optimal Portfolio

The previous section concerned a portfolio formed between one riskless asset and one risky asset. In reality, an investor is likely to combine an investment in the riskless asset with a portfolio of risky assets. This is illustrated in Figure 11.9.

Consider point Q, representing a portfolio of securities. Point Q is in the interior of the feasible set of risky securities. Let us assume that the point represents a portfolio of 30 per cent in company A, 45 per cent in company B, and 25 per cent in company C—each of companies A, B and C are first-class equity shares. Individuals combining investments in Q with investments in the riskless asset would achieve points along the straight line from R_F to Q. We refer to this as line I. For example, point I represents a portfolio of 70 per cent in the riskless asset and 30 per cent in stocks represented by Q. An investor with GBP100 choosing point I as his portfolio would put GBP70 in the risk-free asset and GBP30 in Q. This can be restated as GBP70 in the riskless asset, GBP9 (0.3 × GBP30) in company A, GBP13.50 (0.45 × GBP30) in company B and GBP7.50 (0.25 × GBP30) in company C. Point 2 also represents a portfolio of the risk-free asset and Q, with more (65 per cent) being invested in Q.

Point 3 is obtained by borrowing to invest in Q. For example, an investor with GBP100 of his own would borrow GBP40 from the bank in order to invest GBP140 in Q. This can be stated as borrowing GBP40 and contributing GBP100 of one's own money in order to invest GBP42 (0.3 × GBP140) in company A, GBP63 (0.45 × GBP140) in company B and GBP35 (0.25 × GBP140) in company C.

FIGURE 11.9   Relationship between Expected Return and Standard Deviation for an Investment in a Combination of Risky Securities and the Riskless Asset

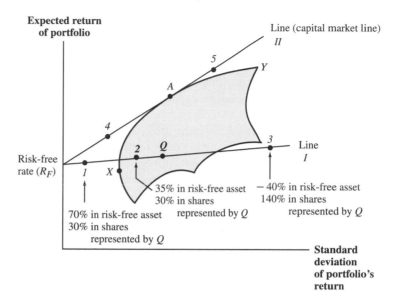

The above investments can be summarized as:

	Point Q	*Point 1* *(lending GBP70)*	*Point 2* *(borrowing GBP40)*
Company A	GBP30	GBP9	GBP42
Company B	45	13.50	63
Company C	25	7.50	35
Risk-free	0	70.00	−40
Total investment	GBP100	GBP100.00	GBP100

Though any investor can obtain any point on line *I*, no point on the line is optimal. To see this, consider line *II*, a line running from R_F through *A*. Point *A* represents a portfolio of risky securities. Line *II* represents portfolios formed by combinations of the risk-free asset and the securities in *A*. Points between R_F and *A* are portfolios in which some money is invested in the riskless asset and the rest is placed in *A*. Points past *A* are achieved by borrowing at the riskless rate to buy more of *A* than one could with one's original funds alone.

As drawn, line *II* is tangent to the efficient set of risky securities. Whatever point an individual can obtain on line *I*, he can obtain a point with the same standard deviation and a higher expected return on line *II*. In fact, because line *II* is tangent to the efficient set, it provides the investor with the best possible opportunities. In other words, line *II*, which is frequently called the **capital market line**, can be viewed as the efficient set of *all* assets, both risky and riskless. An investor with a fair degree of risk aversion might choose a point between R_F and *A*, perhaps point *4*. An individual with less risk aversion might choose a point closer to *A* or even beyond *A*. For example, point *5* corresponds to an individual borrowing money to increase his investment in *A*.

The graph illustrates an important point. With riskless borrowing and lending, the portfolio of *risky* assets held by any investor would always be point *A*. Regardless of the investor's tolerance for risk, he would never choose any other point on the efficient set of risky assets (represented by curve *XAY*) nor any point in the interior of the feasible region. Rather, he would combine the securities of *A* with the riskless assets if he had high aversion to risk. He would borrow the riskless asset to invest more funds in *A* had he low aversion to risk.

This result establishes what financial economists call the **separation principle**. That is, the investor makes two separate decisions:

1.　After estimating (*a*) the expected return and variances of individual securities, and (*b*) the covariances between pairs of securities, the investor calculates the efficient set of risky assets, represented by curve *XAY* in Figure 11.9. He then determines point *A*, the tangency between the risk-free rate and the efficient set of risky assets (curve *XAY*). Point *A* represents the portfolio of risky assets that the investor will hold. This point is determined solely from his estimates of returns, variances, and covariances. No personal characteristics, such as degree of risk aversion, are needed in this step.

2.　The investor must now determine how he will combine point *A*, his portfolio of risky assets, with the riskless asset. He could invest some of his funds in the riskless asset and some in portfolio *A*. He would end up at a point on the line between R_F and *A* in this case. Alternatively, he could borrow at the risk-free rate and contribute some of his own funds as well, investing the sum in portfolio *A*. He would end up at a point on line *II* beyond *A*. His position in the riskless asset, that is, his choice of where on the line he wants to be, is determined by his internal characteristics, such as his ability to tolerate risk.

Concept Questions

- What is the formula for the standard deviation of a portfolio composed of one riskless and one risky asset?
- How does one determine the optimal portfolio among the efficient set of risky assets?

11.8　Market Equilibrium

Definition of the Market-Equilibrium Portfolio

The above analysis concerns one investor. His estimates of the expected returns and variances for individual securities and the covariances between pairs of securities are his and his alone. Other investors would obviously have different estimates of the above variables. However, the estimates might not vary much, because all investors would be forming expectations from the same data on past price movement and other publicly available information.

Financial economists often imagine a world where all investors possess the same estimates on expected returns, variances, and covariances. Though this can never be literally true, it can be thought of as a useful simplifying assumption in a world where investors have access to similar sources of information. This assumption is called **homogeneous expectations**.[13]

If all investors have homogeneous expectations, Figure 11.9 would be the same for all individuals. That is, all investors would sketch out the same efficient set of risky

---

[13] The assumption of homogeneous expectations states that all investors have the same beliefs concerning returns, variances, and covariances. It does not say that all investors have the same aversion to risk.

assets because they would be working with the same inputs. This efficient set of risky assets is represented by the curve *XAY*. Because the same risk-free rate would apply to everyone, all investors would view point *A* as the portfolio of risky assets to be held.

This point *A* takes on great importance because all investors would purchase the risky securities that it represents. Those investors with a high degree of risk aversion might combine *A* with an investment in the riskless asset, achieving point *4*, for example. Others with low aversion to risk might borrow to achieve, say, point *5*. Because this is a very important conclusion, we restate it:

> In a world with homogeneous expectations, all investors would hold the portfolio of risky assets represented by point *A*.

If all investors choose the same portfolio of risky assets, it is possible to determine what that portfolio is. Common sense tells us that it is a market-valued weighted portfolio of all existing securities. It is the **market portfolio**.

In practice, financial economists use a broad-based index such as the FTSE 100 (100 top British quoted companies) as a proxy for the market portfolio. Of course all investors do not hold the same portfolio in practice. However, we know that a large number of investors hold diversified portfolios, particularly when mutual funds or pension funds are included. A broad-based index is a good proxy for the highly diversified portfolios of many investors.

Definition of Risk When Investors Hold the Market Portfolio

The previous section states that many investors hold diversified portfolios similar to broad-based indices. This result allows us to be more precise about the risk of a security in the context of a diversified portfolio.

Researchers have shown that the best measure of risk of a security in a large portfolio is the beta of the security. The definition of beta is

$$\beta_i = \frac{\text{Cov}(R_i, R_M)}{\sigma^2(R_M)} \qquad (11.15)$$

where $\text{Cov}(R_i, R_M)$ is the covariance between the return on asset *i* and the return on the market portfolio and $\sigma^2(R_M)$ is the variance of the market. Though both $\text{Cov}(R_i, R_M)$ and β_i can be used as measures of the contribution of security *I* to the risk of the market portfolio, β_i is much more common. As we will show, the basic intuition of beta is that it measures the sensitivity of a change in the return of an individual security to the change in return of the market portfolio. One useful property is that the average beta across all securities, when weighted by the proportion of each security's market value to that of the market portfolio, is 1. That is,

$$\sum_{i=1}^{N} X_i \beta_i = 1 \qquad (11.16)$$

Beta as a Measure of Responsiveness

The previous discussion shows that the beta of a security is the standardized covariance between the return on the security and the return on the market. Though this explanation is 100 per cent correct, it is not likely to be 100 per cent intuitively appealing to anyone other than a statistician. Luckily, there is a more intuitive explanation for beta. We present this explanation through an example.

● Example

Consider the following possible returns on both the shares of Jelco and on the market:

State	Type of economy	Return on market (%)	Return on Jelco (%)
I	Bull	15	25
II	Bull	15	15
III	Bear	−5	−5
IV	Bear	−5	−15

Though the return on the market has only two possible outcomes (15% and −5%), the return on Jelco has four possible outcomes. It is helpful to consider the expected return on a security for a given return on the market. Assuming each state is equally likely, we have

Type of economy	Return on market (%)	Expected return on Jelco (%)
Bull	15%	$20\% = 25\% \times \frac{1}{2} + 15\% \times \frac{1}{2}$
Bear	−5%	$-10\% = -5\% \times \frac{1}{2} + (-15\%) \times \frac{1}{2}$

Jelco responds to market movements because its expected return is greater in bullish states than in bearish states. We now calculate exactly how responsive the security is to market movements. The market's return in a bullish economy is 20 per cent [15% − (−5%)] greater than the market's return in a bearish economy. However, the expected return on Jelco in a bullish economy is 30 per cent [20% − (−10%)] greater than its expected return in a bearish state. Thus, Jelco has a responsiveness coefficient of 1.5 (30%/20%).

This relationship appears in Figure 11.10. The returns for both Jelco and the market in each state are plotted as four points. In addition, we plot the expected return on the security for each of the two possible returns on the market. These two points, which we designate by X, are joined by a line called the **characteristic line** of the security. The slope of the line is 1.5, the number calculated in the previous paragraph. This responsiveness coefficient of 1.5 is the beta of Jelco.

The interpretation of beta from Figure 11.10 is intuitive. The graph tells us that the returns on Jelco are magnified 1.5 times over those of the market. When the market does well, Jelco's shares are expected to do even better. When the market does poorly, Jelco's shares are expected to do even worse. Now imagine an individual with a portfolio near that of the market who is considering the addition of Jelco to his portfolio. Because of Jelco's *magnification factor* of 1.5, he will view this stock as contributing much to the risk of the portfolio. We showed earlier that the beta of the average security in the market is 1. Jelco contributes more to the risk of a large, diversified portfolio than does an average security because Jelco is more responsive to movements in the market. ●

Further insight can be gleaned by examining securities with negative betas. One should view these securities as either hedges or insurance policies. The security is

FIGURE 11.10   Performance of Jelco and the Market Portfolio

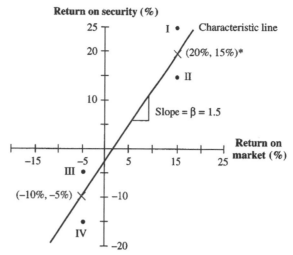

The two points marked X represent the expected return on Jelco for each possible outcome of the market portfolio. The expected return on Jelco is positively related to the return on the market. Because the slope is 1.5, we say that Jelco's beta is 1.5. Beta measures the responsiveness of the security's return to movement in the market.

*(20%, 15%) refers to the point where the return on the security is 20 per cent and the return on the market is 15 per cent.

expected to do well when the market does poorly and vice versa. Because of this, adding a negative beta security to a large, diversified portfolio actually reduces the risk of the portfolio.[14]

A Test

We have put these questions on past corporate finance examinations:

1. What sort of investor rationally views the variance (or standard deviation) of an individual security's return as the security's proper measure of risk?
2. What sort of investor rationally views the beta of a security as the security's proper measure of risk?

A proper answer might be something like the following:

> A rational, risk-averse investor views the variance (or standard deviation) of her portfolio's return as the proper measure of the risk of her portfolio. If for some reason or another the investor can hold only one security, the variance of that security's return becomes the variance of the portfolio's return. Hence, the variance of the security's return is the security's proper measure of risk.
>
> If an individual holds a diversified portfolio, she still views the variance (or standard deviation) of her portfolio's return as the proper measure of the risk of her portfolio. However, she is no longer interested in the variance of each individual security's return. Rather, she is interested in the contribution of an individual security to the variance of the portfolio.
>
> Under the assumption of homogeneous expectations, all individuals hold the market portfolio. Thus, we measure risk as the contribution of an individual security to the variance of

---

[14] Unfortunately, empirical evidence shows that virtually no stocks have negative betas.

the market portfolio. This contribution, when standardized properly, is the beta of the security. While very few investors hold the market portfolio exactly, many hold reasonably diversified portfolios. These portfolios are close enough to the market portfolio so that the beta of a security is likely to be a reasonable measure of its risk.

Concept Questions

- If all investors have homogeneous expectations, what portfolio of risky assets do they hold?
- What is the formula for beta?
- Why is beta the appropriate measure of risk for a single security in a large portfolio?

11.9   Relationship between Risk and Expected Return (CAPM)

It is commonplace to argue that the expected return on an asset should be positively related to its risk. That is, individuals will hold a risky asset only if its expected return compensates for its risk. In this section, we first estimate the expected return on the stock market as a whole. Next, we estimate expected returns on individual securities.

Expected Return on Market

Financial economists frequently argue that the expected return on the market can be represented as:

$$\overline{R}_M = R_F + \text{Risk premium}$$

In words, the expected return on the market is the sum of the risk-free rate plus some compensation for the risk inherent in the market portfolio. Note that the equation refers to the *expected* return on the market, not the actual return in a particular month or year. Because stocks have risk, the actual return on the market over a particular period can, of course, be below R_F, or can even be negative.

Since investors want compensation for risk, the risk premium is presumably positive. But exactly how positive is it? It is generally argued that the best estimate for the risk premium in the future is the average risk premium in the past. As reported in Table 10.1, Ibbotson and Sinquefield found that the expected return on common stocks was 12.2 per cent over 1926–94. The average risk-free rate over the same time interval was 3.7 per cent. Thus, the average difference between the two was 8.5 per cent (12.2%–3.7%). Financial economists in the USA use this as the best estimate of the difference to occur in the future. In the UK the figure is around 9 per cent. In Germany it is near 9 per cent. For the meantime, we will use an average difference between the expected return on ordinary shares and the risk-free rate of 8.5 per cent for all of Europe. We will use this figure frequently in this text.

For example, if the risk-free rate, generally estimated by the yield on a one-year Treasury bill, is 4 per cent, the expected return on the market is

$$12.5\% = 4\% + 8.5\%$$

Expected Return on Individual Security

Now that we have estimated the expected return on the market as a whole, what is the expected return on an individual security? We have argued that the beta of a security is

FIGURE 11.11   **Relationship between Expected Return on a Individual Security and Beta of the Security**

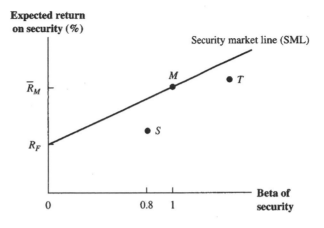

the appropriate measure of risk in a large, diversified portfolio. Since most investors are diversified, the expected return on a security should be positively related to its beta. This is illustrated in Figure 11.11.

Actually, financial economists can be more precise about the relationship between expected return and beta. They posit that, under plausible conditions, the relationship between expected return and beta can be represented by the following equation:[15]

Capital-Asset-Pricing Model

$$\bar{R} \quad = \quad R_F \quad + \quad \beta \quad \times \quad (\bar{R}_M - R_F)$$

| Expected return on a security | $=$ | Risk-free rate | $+$ | Beta of the security | $\times$ | Difference between expected return on market and risk-free rate | (11.17) |

This formula, which is called the **capital-asset-pricing model** (or the CAPM for short), implies that the expected return on a security is linearly related to its beta. Since the average return on the market has been higher than the average risk-free rate over long periods of time, $\bar{R}_M - R_F$ is presumably positive. Thus, the formula implies that the expected return on a security is *positively* related to its beta. The formula can be illustrated by assuming a few special cases:

- *Assume that* $\beta = 0$. Here $\bar{R} = R_F$, that is, the expected return on the security is equal to the risk-free rate. Because a security with zero beta has no relevant risk, its expected return should equal the risk-free rate.
- *Assume that* $\beta = 1$. Equation (11.17) reduces to $\bar{R} = \bar{R}_M$, that is, the expected return on the security is equal to the expected return on the market. This makes sense since the beta of the market portfolio is 1.

Formula (11.17) can be represented graphically by the upward-sloping line in Figure 11.11. Note that the line begins at R_F and rises to $\bar{R}_M$ when beta is 1. This line is frequently called the **security market line** (SML).

---

[15] This relationship was first proposed independently by John Lintner and William F. Sharpe.

As with any line, the SML has both a slope and an intercept. R_F, the risk-free rate, is the intercept. Because the beta of a security is the horizontal axis, $R_M - R_F$ is the slope. The line will be upward-sloping as long as the expected return on the market is greater than the risk-free rate. Because the market portfolio is a risky asset, theory suggests that its expected return is above the risk-free rate. In addition, the evidence is of an average return around 8.5 per cent above the risk-free rate.

● **Example**

The shares of Aardvark Enterprises has a beta of 1.5 and that of Zebra Enterprises has a beta of 0.7. The risk-free rate is 7 per cent, and the difference between the expected return on the market and the risk-free rate is 8.5 per cent. The expected returns on the two securities are:

Expected Return for Aardvark:

$$19.75\% = 7\% + (1.5 \times 8.5\%)$$

(11.18)

Expected Return for Zebra:

$$12.95\% = 7\% + (0.7 \times 8.5\%) \quad ●$$

Three additional points concerning the CAPM should be mentioned:

1. *Linearity* The intuition behind an upwardly sloping curve is clear. Because beta is the appropriate measure of risk, high-beta securities should have an expected return above that of low-beta securities. However, both Figure 11.11 and equation (11.17) show something more than an upwardly sloping curve; the relationship between expected return and beta corresponds to a *straight* line.

It is easy to show that the line of Figure 11.11 is straight. To see this, consider security *S* with, say, a beta of 0.8. This security is represented by a point below the security-market line in the figure. Any investor could duplicate the beta of security *S* by buying a portfolio with 20 per cent in the risk-free asset and 80 per cent in a security with a beta of 1. However, the homemade portfolio would itself lie on the SML. In other words, the portfolio dominates security *S* because the portfolio has a higher expected return and the same beta.

Now consider security *T* with, say, a beta greater than 1. This security is also below the SML in Figure 11.11. Any investor could duplicate the beta of security *T* by borrowing to invest in a security with a beta of 1. This portfolio must also lie on the SML, thereby dominating security *T*.

Because no one would hold either *S* or *T*, their stock prices would drop. This price adjustment would raise the expected returns on the two securities. The price adjustment would continue until the two securities lay on the security market line. The above example considered two overpriced stocks and a straight SML. Securities lying above the SML are *underpriced*. Their prices must rise until their expected returns lie on the line. If the SML is itself curved, many stocks would be mispriced. In equilibrium, all securities would be held only when prices changed so that the SML became straight. In other words, linearity would be achieved.

2. *Portfolios as well as securities* Our discussion of the CAPM considered individual securities. Does the relationship in Figure 11.11 and equation (11.17) hold for portfolios as well?

Yes. To see this, consider a portfolio formed by investing equally in our two securities, Aardvark and Zebra. The expected return on the portfolio is

Expected Return on Portfolio:

$$16.35\% = 0.5 \times 19.75\% + 0.5 \times 12.95\% \tag{11.19}$$

The beta of the portfolio is simply a weighted average of the two securities. Thus we have

Beta of Portfolio:

$$1.1 = 0.5 \times 1.5 + 0.5 \times 0.7$$

Under the CAPM, the expected return on the portfolio is

$$16.35\% = 7\% + (1.1 \times 8.5\%) \tag{11.20}$$

Because the expected return in (11.19) is the same as the expected return in (11.20), the example shows that the CAPM holds for portfolios as well as for individual securities.

3. *A potential confusion.*   Students often confuse the SML in Figure 11.11 with the capital market line (line *II* in Figure 11.9). Actually, the lines are quite different. The capital market line traces the efficient set of portfolios formed from both risky assets and the riskless asset. Each point on the line represents an entire portfolio. Point *A* is a portfolio composed entirely of risky assets. Every other point on the line represents a portfolio of the securities in *A* combined with the riskless asset. The axes on Figure 11.9 are the expected return on a *portfolio* and the standard deviation of a *portfolio*. Individual securities do not lie along line *II*.

The SML in Figure 11.11 relates expected return to beta. Figure 11.11 differs from Figure 11.9 in at least two ways. First, beta appears in the horizontal axis of Figure 11.11, but standard deviation appears in the horizontal axis of Figure 11.9. Second, the SML in Figure 11.11 holds both for all individual securities and for all possible portfolios, whereas line *II* (the capital market line) in Figure 11.9 holds only for efficient portfolios.

Concept Questions

- Why is the SML a straight line?
- What is the capital-asset pricing model?
- What are the differences between the capital market line and the security market line?

11.10   Summary and Conclusions

This chapter sets forth the fundamentals of modern portfolio theory. Our basic points are these:

1. This chapter shows us how to calculate the expected return and variance for individual securities, and the covariance and correlation for pairs of securities. Given these statistics, the expected return and variance for a portfolio of two securities A and B can be written as

$$\text{Expected return on portfolio} = X_A \bar{R}_A + X_B \bar{R}_B$$

$$\text{Var(portfolio)} = X_A^2 \sigma_A^2 + 2 X_A X_B \sigma_{AB} + X_B^2 \sigma_B^2$$

2. In our notation, X stands for the proportion of a security in one's portfolio. By varying X, one can trace out the efficient set of portfolios. We graphed the efficient set for the two-asset case as a curve, pointing out that the degree of curvature or bend in the graph reflects the diversification effect: the lower the correlation between the two securities, the greater the bend. Without proof, we stated that the general shape of the efficient set holds in a world of many assets.

3. Just as the formula for variance in the two-asset case is computed from a 2×2 matrix, the variance formula is computed from an $N \times N$ matrix in the N-asset case. We show that, with a large number of assets, there are many more covariance terms than variance terms in the matrix. In fact, the variance terms are effectively diversified away in a large portfolio but the covariance terms are not. Thus, a diversified portfolio can only eliminate some, but not all, of the risk of the individual securities.

4. The efficient set of risky assets we spoke of earlier can be combined with riskless borrowing and lending. In this case, a rational investor will always choose to hold the portfolio of risky securities represented by point A in Figure 11.9. Then he can either borrow or lend at the riskless rate to achieve any desired point on the capital market line.

5. The contribution of a security to the risk of a large, well-diversified portfolio is proportional to the covariance of the security's return with the market's return. This contribution, when standardized, is called the beta. The beta of a security can also be interpreted as the responsiveness of a security's return to that of the market.

6. The CAPM states that

$$\bar{R} = R_F + \beta(\bar{R}_M - R_F)$$

In other words, the expected return on a security is positively (and linearly) related to the security's beta.

KEY TERMS

Covariance 241	Risk-averse 260
Correlation 241	Capital market line 263
Portfolio 244	Separation principle 264
Opportunity (feasible) set 251	Homogeneous expectations 264
Efficient set 251	Market portfolio 265
Systematic (market) risk 259	Characteristic line 266
Diversifiable (unique)	Capital-asset-pricing model 269
(unsystematic) risk 259	Security market line 269

QUESTIONS AND PROBLEMS

Expected Return, Variance and Covariance

11.1 Ms Sharp thinks that the distribution of rates of return on Q Co is as follows.

State of economy	Probability of state occurring	Q Co shares return (%)
Depression	0.10	−4.5%
Recession	0.20	4.4
Normal	0.50	12.0
Boom	0.20	20.7

a. What is the expected return for the shares of Q Co?

b. What is the standard deviation of returns for Q Co?

11.2 Suppose you have invested only in two shares, A and B. You expect that returns on the shares depend on the following three states of economy, which are equally likely to happen.

State of economy	Return on share A (%)	Return on share B (%)
Bear	6.3%	−3.7%
Normal	10.5	6.4
Bull	15.6	25.3

    a. Calculate the expected return of each share.
    b. Calculate the standard deviation of returns of each share.
    c. Calculate the covariance and correlation between the two shares.

11.3 Henri can invest in Highbull shares or Slowbear shares. His projection of the returns on these two shares is as follows:

State of economy	Probability of state occurring	Return on highbull shares (%)	Return on Slowbear shares (%)
Recession	0.25	−2.0%	5.0%
Normal	0.60	9.2	6.2
Boom	0.15	15.4	7.4

    a. Calculate the expected return of each share.
    b. Calculate the standard deviation of return of each share.
    c. Calculate the covariance and correlation between the two shares.

Portfolios

11.4 A portfolio consists of 120 shares of Atlas, which sell for NLG50 per share, and 150 shares of Beta, which sell for NLG20 per share. What are the weights of the two stocks in this portfolio?

11.5 Security *F* has an expected return of 12 per cent and a standard deviation of 9 per cent per year. Security *G* has an expected return of 18 per cent and a standard deviation of 25 per cent per year.
    a. What is the expected return on a portfolio composed of 30 per cent of security *F* and 70 per cent of security *G*?
    b. If the correlation coefficient between the returns of *F* and *G* is 0.2, what is the standard deviation of the portfolio?

11.6 Suppose the expected returns and standard deviations of shares *A* and *B* are $\bar{R}_A = 0.15$, $\bar{R}_B = 0.25$, $\sigma_A = 0.1$, and $\sigma_B = 0.2$ respectively.
    a. Calculate the expected return and standard deviation of a portfolio that is composed of 40 per cent *A* and 60 per cent *B* when the correlation coefficient between the shares is 0.5.
    b. Calculate the standard deviation of a portfolio that is composed of 40 per cent *A* and 60 per cent *B* when the correlation coefficient between the stocks is − 0.5.
    c. How does the correlation coefficient affect the standard deviation of the portfolio?

11.7 Suppose Janet Smith holds 100 shares of Macrosoft and 300 shares of Intelligence. Macrosoft is currently sold at DEM80 per share, while Intelligence is sold at DEM40. The expected return of Macrosoft stock is 15 per cent, while that of Intelligence stock is 20 per cent. The standard deviation of Macrosoft is 8 per cent, while that of Intelligence is 20 per cent. The correlation coefficient between the stocks is 0.38.
    a. Calculate the expected return and standard deviation of her portfolio.
    b. Today she sold 200 shares of Intelligence to pay her tuition fees. Calculate the expected return and standard deviation of her new portfolio.

11.8 Consider the possible rates of return that you might obtain over the next year. You can invest in stock *U* or stock *V*.

State of economy	Probability of state occurring	Stock U return if state occurs (%)	Stock V return if state occurs (%)
Recession	0.2	7%	−5%
Normal	0.5	7	10
Boom	0.3	7	25

    a. Determine the expected return, variance and the standard deviation for stock *U* and stock *V*.

b. Determine the covariance and correlation between the returns of stock *U* and stock *V*.

c. Determine the expected return and standard deviation of an equally weighted portfolio of stock *U* and stock *V*.

11.9   Suppose there are only two stocks in the world: stock *A* and stock *B*. The expected returns of these two stocks are 10 per cent and 20 per cent, while the standard deviations of the stocks are 5 per cent and 15 per cent, respectively. The correlation coefficient of the two stocks is zero.

a. Calculate the expected return and standard deviation of a portfolio that is composed of 30 per cent *A* and 70 per cent *B*.

b. Calculate the expected return and standard deviation of a portfolio that is composed of 90 per cent *A* and 10 per cent *B*.

c. Suppose you are risk averse. Would you hold 100 per cent stock *A*? How about 100 per cent stock *B*?

11.10   If a portfolio has a positive weight for each asset, can the expected return on the portfolio be greater than the return on the asset in the portfolio that has the highest return? Can the expected return on the portfolio be less than the return on the asset in the portfolio with the lowest return? Explain.

11.11   Ms Maple is considering two securities, *A* and *B*, and the relevant information is given below:

State of economy	Probability	Return on security A (%)	Return on security B (%)
Bear	0.4	3.0%	6.5%
Bull	0.6	15.0	6.5

a. Calculate the expected returns and standard deviations of the two securities.

b. Suppose Ms Maple invested CHF2,500 in security *A* and CHF3,500 in security *B*. Calculate the expected return and standard deviation of her portfolio.

c. Suppose Ms Maple borrowed from her friend 40 shares of security *B*, which is currently sold at CHF50, and sold all shares of the security. (She promised her friend to pay back in a year with the same number of shares of security *B*.) Then she bought security *A* with the proceeds obtained in the sales of security *B* shares and the cash of CHF6,000 she owned. Calculate the expected return and standard deviation of the portfolio.

11.12   A broker has advised you not to invest in oil industry stocks because, in her opinion, they are far too risky. She has shown you evidence of how wildly the prices of oil stocks have fluctuated in the recent past. She demonstrated that the standard deviation of oil stocks is very high relative to most stocks. Do you think the broker's advice is sound for a risk-averse investor like you? Why or why not?

The CAPM

11.13   *a.* Draw the security market line for the case where the market-risk premium is 5 per cent and the risk-free rate is 7 per cent.

b. Suppose that an asset has a beta of −1 and an expected return of 4 per cent. Plot it on the graph you drew in part (*a*). Is the security properly priced? If not, explain what will happen in this market.

c. Suppose that an asset has a beta of 3 and an expected return of 20 per cent. Plot it on the graph you drew in part (*a*). Is the security properly priced? If not, explain what will happen in this market.

11.14   A stock has a beta of 1.8. A security analyst who specializes in studying this stock expects its return to be 18 per cent. Suppose the risk-free rate is 5 per cent and the market-risk premium is 8 per cent. Is the analyst pessimistic or optimistic about this stock relative to the market's expectations?

11.15   Suppose the expected return on the market is 13.8 per cent and the risk-free rate is 6.4 per cent. Solomon shares have a beta of 1.2.

a. What is the expected return on the Solomon shares?

b. If the risk-free rate decreases to 3.5 per cent, what is the expected return on the Solomon shares?

11.16   The expected return on a portfolio that combines the risk-free asset and the asset at the point of tangency to the efficient set is 25 per cent. The expected return was calculated under the following assumptions:

> The risk-free rate is 5 per cent.
> The expected return on the market portfolio of risky assets is 20 per cent.
> The standard deviation of the efficient portfolio is 4 per cent.

In this environment, what expected rate of return would a security earn if it had a 0.5 correlation with the market and a standard deviation of 2 per cent?

11.17   Suppose the current risk-free rate is 7.6 per cent. Potpourri shares have a beta of 1.7 and an expected return of 16.7 per cent. (Assume the CAPM is true.)

    a. What is the risk premium on the market?

    b. Magnolia Industries shares have a beta of 0.8. What is the expected return on the Magnolia shares?

    c. Suppose you have invested GBP10,000 in both Potpourri and Magnolia, and the beta of the portfolio is 1.07. How much did you invest in each stock? What is the expected return on the portfolio?

11.18   Suppose the risk-free rate is 6.3 per cent and the market portfolio has an expected rate of return of 14.8 per cent. The market portfolio has a variance of 0.0121. Portfolio *Z* has a correlation coefficient with the market of 0.45 and a variance of 0.0169. According to the CAPM, what is the expected rate of return on portfolio *Z*?

11.19   The following data have been developed for the Durham Company.

> Variance of market returns = 0.04326
> Covariance of the returns on Durham and the market = 0.0635
> Suppose the market risk premium is 9.4 per cent and the expected return on Treasury bills is 4.9 per cent.

    a. Write the equation of the security market line.

    b. What is the required return of Durham Company?

11.20   Johnson Paint shares have an expected return of 19 per cent with a beta of 1.7, while Williamson Tile shares have an expected return of 14 per cent with a beta of 1.2. Assume the CAPM is true. What is the expected return on the market? What is the risk-free rate?

11.21   Is the following statement true or false? Explain.

> A risky security cannot have an expected return that is less than the risk-free rate because no risk-averse investor would be willing to hold this asset in equilibrium.

APPENDIX 11A

IS BETA DEAD?

The capital-asset-pricing model represents one of the most important advances in financial economics. It is clearly useful for investment purposes, since it shows how the expected return on an asset is related to its beta. In addition, we will show in Chapter 13 that it is useful in corporate finance, since the discount rate on a project is a function of the project's beta. However, one must never forget that, as with any other model, the CAPM is not revealed truth but, rather, a construct to be empirically tested.

The first empirical tests of the CAPM occurred over 20 years ago and were quite supportive. Using data from the 'thirties to the 'sixties, researchers showed that the average return on a portfolio of stocks was positively related to the beta of the portfolio,[16] a finding consistent with the CAPM. Though some evidence in these studies was less consistent with the CAPM,[17] financial economists were quick to embrace the CAPM following these empirical papers.

While a large body of empirical work developed in the following decades, often with varying

---

[16] Perhaps the two most well-known papers were: F. Black, M. C. Jensen and M. S. Scholes (1972) 'The capital asset pricing model: Some empirical tests', in M. Jensen (ed.) *Studies in the Theory of Capital Markets*, New York: Praeger. E. F. Fama and J. MacBeth, 'Risk, return and equilibrium: Some empirical tests', *Journal of Political Economy*, **8**, 607–36.

[17] For example, the studies suggest that the average return on a zero-beta portfolio is above the risk-free rate, a finding inconsistent with the CAPM.

results, the CAPM was not seriously called into question until recently. Two papers by Fama and French[18] (yes, the same Fama whose joint paper in 1973 with James MacBeth supported the CAPM) present evidence inconsistent with the model. Their work has received a great deal of attention, both in academic circles and in the popular press, with newspaper articles displaying headlines such as 'Beta Is Dead'. These papers make two related points. First, they conclude that the relationship between average return and beta is weak over the period from 1941–90, and virtually non-existent from 1963–90. Second, they argue that the average return on a security is negatively related to both the firm's price-to-earnings (P/E) ratio and the firm's market value-to-book value (M/B) ratio. These contentions, if confirmed by other research, would be quite damaging to the CAPM. After all, the CAPM states that the expected returns on stocks should be related only to beta, and not to other factors such as P/E and M/B.

However, a number of researchers have criticized the Fama–French papers. While we avoid an in-depth discussion of the fine points of the debate, we mention a few issues. First, although Fama and French cannot reject the hypothesis that average returns are unrelated to beta, one can also not reject the hypothesis that average returns are related to beta exactly as specified by the CAPM. In other words, while 50 years of data seem like a lot, they may simply not be enough to test the CAPM properly. Second, the result with P/E and M/B may be due to a statistical fallacy called a hindsight bias.[19] Third, P/E and M/B are merely two of an infinite number of possible factors. Thus, the relationship between average return and both P/E and M/B may be spurious, being nothing more than the result of data dredging. Fourth, average returns are positively related to beta over the period from 1927–90. There appears to be no compelling reason for emphasizing a shorter period than this one. Fifth, average returns are actually positively related to beta over shorter periods when annual data, rather than monthly data, are used to estimate beta.[20] There appears to be no compelling reason for preferring either monthly data over annual data or vice versa. Thus, we believe that, while the results of Fama and French are quite intriguing, they cannot be viewed as the final word.

---

[18] E. F. Fama and K. R. French (1992). 'The cross-section of expected stock returns', *Journal of Finance*, **47**, 427–66; E. F. Fama and K. R. French (1993). 'Common risk factors in the returns on stocks and bonds', *Journal of Financial Economics*, **17**, 3–56.

[19] For example, see W. J. Breen and R. A. Koraczyk (1993), 'On selection biases in book-to-market based tests of asset pricing models', unpublished paper, Northwestern University, November; S. P. Kothari, J. Shanken and R. G. Sloan (1994). 'Another look at the cross-section of expected stock returns', unpublished paper, University of Rochester, February.

[20] Points 4 and 5 are addressed in the Kothari, Shanken and Sloan paper.

An Alternative View of Risk and Return: The Arbitrage Pricing Theory

The previous two chapters mentioned the obvious fact that returns on securities are variable. This variability is measured by variance and by standard deviation. Next, we mentioned the somewhat less obvious fact that the returns on securities are interdependent. We measured the degree of interdependence between a pair of securities by covariance and correlation. This interdependence led to a number of interesting results. First, we showed that diversification in stocks can eliminate some, but not all, risk. By contrast, we showed that diversification in a casino can eliminate all risk. Second, the interdependence of returns led to the capital-asset-pricing model (CAPM). This model posits a positive (and linear) relationship between the beta of a security and its expected return.

The CAPM was developed in the early 'sixties.[1] An alternative to the CAPM, called the *arbitrage pricing theory* (APT), has been developed more recently.[2] For our purposes, the differences between the two models stem from the APT's treatment of the interrelationship among the returns on securities.[3] The APT assumes that returns on securities are generated by a number of industrywide and marketwide factors. Correlation between a pair of securities occurs when these two securities are affected by the same factor or factors. By contrast, though the CAPM allows correlation among securities, it does not specify the underlying factors causing the correlation.

Both the APT and the CAPM imply a positive relationship between expected return and risk. In our (perhaps biased) opinion, the APT allows this relationship to be developed in a particularly intuitive manner. In addition, the APT views risk more generally than just the standardized covariance or beta of a security with the market portfolio. Therefore, we offer this approach as an alternative to the CAPM.

---

[1] In particular, see J. Treynor (1961). 'Toward a theory of the market value of risky assets', unpublished manuscript; W. F. Sharpe (1964). 'Capital asset prices: A theory of market equilibrium under conditions of risk', *Journal of Finance*, September; and J. Lintner (1965). 'The valuation of risky assets and the selection of risky investments in stock portfolios and capital budgets', *Review of Economics and Statistics*, February.

[2] See S. A. Ross (1976). 'The arbitrage theory of capital asset pricing', *Journal of Economic Theory*, December.

[3] This is by no means the only difference in the assumptions of the two models. For example, the CAPM usually assumes either that the returns on assets are normally distributed or that investors have quadratic utility functions. The APT does not require either assumption. While this and other differences are quite important in research, they are not relevant to the material presented in our text.

12.1   Factor Models: Announcements, Surprises and Expected Returns

We learned in the previous chapter how to construct portfolios and how to evaluate their returns. We now step back and examine the returns on individual securities more closely. By doing this we will find that the portfolios inherit and alter the properties of the securities they comprise.

To be concrete, let us consider the return on the shares of a company called Flyers Pharmaceuticals plc (Flyers). What will determine this stock's return in, say, the coming month?

The return on any stock traded in a financial market consists of two parts. First, the *normal* or *expected* return from the stock is the part of the return that shareholders in the market predict or expect. It depends on all of the information shareholders have that bears on the stock, and it uses all of our understanding of what will influence the stock in the next month.

The second part is the *uncertain* or *risky return* on the stock. This is the portion that comes from information that will be revealed within the month. The list of such information is endless, but here are some examples:

- News about Flyers Pharmaceuticals plc research.
- Government figures released on the gross national product (GNP).
- Results of the latest arms-control talks.
- Discovery that a rival's product has been tampered with.
- News that Flyers Pharmaceuticals' sales figures are higher than expected.
- A sudden drop in interest rates.
- The unexpected retirement of Flyers Pharmaceuticals' founder and president.

A way to write the return on Flyers' shares in the coming month, then, is

$$R = \bar{R} + U$$

where R is the actual total return in the month, $\bar{R}$ is the expected part of the return, and U stands for the unexpected part of the return.

Some care must be exercised in studying the effect of these and other news items on the return. For example, the government might give us GNP or unemployment figures for this month, but how much of that is new information for shareholders? Surely at the beginning of the month shareholders will have some idea or forecast of what the monthly GNP will be. To the extent to which the shareholders had forecast the government's announcement, that forecast should be factored into the expected part of the return as of the beginning of the month, $\bar{R}$. On the other hand, insofar as the announcement by the government is a surprise, and to the extent to which it influences the return on the stock, it will be part of U, the unanticipated part of the return.

As an example, suppose shareholders in the market had forecast that the GNP increase this month would be 0.5 per cent. If GNP influences our company's shares, this forecast will be part of the information shareholders use to form the expectation, $\bar{R}$, of monthly return. If the actual announcement this month is exactly 0.5 per cent, the same as the forecast, then the shareholders learned nothing new, and the announcement is not news. It is like hearing a rumour about a friend when you knew it all along. Another way of saying this is that shareholders had already discounted the announcement. This use of the word *discount* is different from that in computing present value, but the spirit is similar. When we discount a dollar in the future, we say that it is worth less to us because of the time value of money. When we discount an announcement or a news item in the future, we mean that it has less impact on the market because the market already knew much of it.

On the other hand, suppose the government announced that the actual GNP increase during the year was 1.5 per cent. Now shareholders have learned something, that the increase is one percentage point higher than they had forecast. This difference between the actual result and the forecast, one percentage point in this example, is sometimes called the *innovation* or *surprise*.

Any announcement can be broken into two parts, the anticipated or expected part and the surprise or innovation:

$$\text{Announcement} = \text{Expected part} + \text{Surprise}$$

The expected part of any announcement is part of the information the market uses to form the expectation, $\bar{R}$, of the return on the stock. The surprise is the news that influences the unanticipated return on the stock, U.

To take another example, if shareholders knew in January that the president of a firm was going to resign, the official announcement in February will be fully expected and will be discounted by the market. Because the announcement was expected before February, its influence on the stock will have taken place before February. The announcement itself in February will contain no surprise, and the stock's price should not change at all at the announcement in February.

When we speak of news, then, we refer to the surprise part of any announcement and not the portion that the market has expected and therefore has already discounted.

Concept Questions

- What are the two basic parts of a return?
- Under what conditions will some news have no effect on common stock prices?

12.2   Risk: Systematic and Unsystematic

The unanticipated part of the return, that portion resulting from surprises, is the true risk of any investment. After all, if we had already got what we had expected, there would be no risk and no uncertainty.

There are important differences, though, among various sources of risk. Look at our previous list of news stories. Some of these stories are directed specifically at Flyers Pharmaceuticals, and some are more general. Which of the news items are of specific importance to Flyers?

Announcements about interest rates or GNP are clearly important for nearly all companies, whereas the news about Flyers' chief executive, its research, its sales, or the affairs of a rival company are of specific interest to Flyers. We will divide these two types of announcements and the resulting risk, then, into two components: a systematic portion, called *systematic risk*, and the remainder, which we call *specific* or *unsystematic risk*. The following definitions describe the difference:

- A *systematic* risk is any risk that affects a large number of assets, each to a greater or lesser degree.
- An *unsystematic risk* is a risk that specifically affects a single asset or a small group of assets.[4]

---

[4] In the previous chapter, we briefly mentioned that unsystematic risk is risk that can be diversified away in a large portfolio. This result will also follow from the present analysis.

Uncertainty about general economic conditions, such as GNP, interest rates, or inflation, is an example of systematic risk. These conditions affect nearly all stocks to some degree. An unanticipated or surprise increase in inflation affects wages and the costs of the supplies that companies buy, the value of the assets that companies own and the prices at which companies sell their products. These forces, to which all companies are susceptible, are the essence of systematic risk.

In contrast, the announcement of a small oil strike by a company may very well affect that company alone or a few other companies. Certainly, it is unlikely to have an effect on the world oil market. To stress that such information is unsystematic and affects only some specific companies, we sometimes call it an idiosyncratic risk.

The distinction between a systematic risk and an unsystematic risk is never as exact as we make it out to be. Even the most narrow and peculiar bit of news about a company ripples through the economy. It reminds us of the tale of the war that was lost because one horse lost a shoe; even a minor event may have an impact on the world. But this degree of hair-splitting should not trouble us as much. We may not be able to define a systematic risk and an unsystematic risk exactly, but we know them when we see them.

This permits us to break down the risk of Flyers' shares into its two components: the systematic and the unsystematic. As is traditional, we will use the Greek epsilon, ϵ, to represent the unsystematic risk and write

$$R = \bar{R} + U$$
$$= \bar{R} + m + \epsilon$$

where we have used the letter m to stand for the systematic risk. Sometimes systematic risk is referred to as *market risk*. This emphasizes the fact that m influences all assets in the market to some extent.

The important point about the way we have broken the total risk, U, into its two components, m and ϵ, is that ϵ, because it is specific to the company, is unrelated to the specific risk of most other companies. For example, the unsystematic risk on Flyers' shares, ϵ_F, is unrelated to the unsystematic risk of Daimler-Benz, ϵ_D. The risk that Flyers' shares will go up or down because of a discovery by its research team—or its failure to discover something—probably is unrelated to any of the specific uncertainties that affect Daimler-Benz shares.

Using the terms of the previous chapter, this means that the unsystematic risks of Flyers' shares and Daimler-Benz shares are unrelated to each other, or uncorrelated. In the symbols of statistics,

$$\text{Corr}(\epsilon_F, \epsilon_D) = 0$$

Concept Questions

- Describe the difference between systematic risk and unsystematic risk.
- Why is unsystematic risk sometimes referred to as *idiosyncratic* risk?

12.3   Systematic Risk and Betas

The fact that the unsystematic parts of the returns on two companies are unrelated to each other does not mean that the systematic portions are unrelated. On the contrary, because both companies are influenced by the same systematic risks, individual companies' systematic risks and therefore their total returns will be related.

For example, a surprise about inflation will influence almost all companies to some extent. How sensitive is Flyers' shares return to unanticipated changes in inflation? If Flyers' shares tend to go up on news that inflation is exceeding expectations, we would say that it is positively related to inflation. If the shares go down when inflation exceeds expectations and up when inflation falls short of expectations, it is negatively related. In the unusual case where a share's return is uncorrelated with inflation surprises, inflation has no effect on it.

We capture the influence of a systematic risk like inflation on a share by using the **beta coefficient**. The beta coefficient, β, tells us the response of the shares' return to a systematic risk. In the previous chapter, beta measured the responsiveness of a security's return to a specific risk factor, the return on the market portfolio. We used this type of responsiveness to develop the capital-asset-pricing model. Because we now consider many types of systematic risks, our current work can be viewed as a generalization of our work in the previous chapter.

If a company's shares are positively related to risk of inflation, that stock has a positive inflation beta. If it is negatively related to inflation, its inflation beta is negative, and if it is uncorrelated with inflation, its inflation beta is zero.

It is not hard to imagine shares with positive and negative inflation betas. The stock of a company owning gold mines will probably have a positive inflation beta because an unanticipated rise in inflation is usually associated with an increase in gold prices. On the other hand, an automobile company facing stiff foreign competition might find that an increase in inflation means that the wages it pays are higher, but that it cannot raise its prices to cover the increase. This profit squeeze, as the company's expenses rise faster than its revenues, would give its shares a negative inflation beta.

Some companies that have few assets and that act as brokers—buying items in competitive markets and reselling them in other markets—might be relatively unaffected by inflation, because their costs and their revenues would rise and fall together. Their stock would have an inflation beta of zero.

Some structure is useful at this point. Suppose we have identified three systematic risks on which we want to focus. We may believe that these three are sufficient to describe the systematic risks that influence stock returns. Three likely candidates are inflation, GNP, and interest rates. Thus, every stock will have a beta associated with each of these systematic risks: an inflation beta, a GNP beta, and an interest-rate beta. We can write the return on the stock, then, in the following form:

$$R = \bar{R} + U$$
$$= \bar{R} + m + \epsilon$$
$$= \bar{R} + \beta_I F_I + \beta_{GNP} F_{GNP} + \beta_r F_r + \epsilon$$

where we have used the symbol β_I to denote the share's inflation beta, β_{GNP} for its GNP beta, and β_r to stand for its interest-rate beta. In the equation, F stands for a surprise, whether it be in inflation, GNP or interest rates.

Let us go through an example to see how the surprises and the expected return add up to produce the total return, R, on a given stock. To make it more familiar, suppose that the return is over a horizon of a year and not just a month. Suppose that at the beginning of the year, inflation is forecast to be 5 per cent for the year, GNP is forecast to increase by 2 per cent and interest rates are expected not to change. Suppose the stock we are looking at has the following betas:

$$\beta_I = 2$$
$$\beta_{GNP} = 1$$
$$\beta_r = -1.8$$

The magnitude of the beta describes how great an impact a systematic risk has on a share's returns. A beta of $+1$ indicates that the share's return rises and falls one for one with the systematic factor. This means, in our example, that because the shares have a GNP beta of 1, it experiences a 1 per cent increase in return for every 1 per cent surprise increase in GNP. If its GNP beta were -2, it would fall by 2 per cent when there was an unanticipated increase of 1 per cent in GNP, and it would rise by 2 per cent if GNP experienced a surprise 1 per cent decline.

Finally, let us suppose that during the year the following occurs: inflation rises by 7 per cent, GNP rises by only 1 per cent, and interest rates fall by 2 per cent. Last, suppose we learn some good news about the company, perhaps that it is succeeding quickly with some new business strategy, and that this unanticipated development contributes 5 per cent to its return. In other words,

$$\epsilon = 5\%$$

Let us assemble all of this information to find what return the stock had during the year.

First, we must determine what news or surprises took place in the systematic factors. From our information we know that

$$\text{Expected inflation} = 5\%$$
$$\text{Expected GNP change} = 2\%$$

and

$$\text{Expected change in interest rates} = 0\%$$

This means that the market had discounted these changes, and the surprises will be the difference between what actually takes place and these expectations:

$$
\begin{aligned}
F_I &= \text{Surprise in inflation} \\
&= \text{Actual inflation} - \text{Expected inflation} \\
&= 7\% - 5\% \\
&= 2\%
\end{aligned}
$$

Similarly,

$$
\begin{aligned}
F_{GNP} &= \text{Surprise in GNP} \\
&= \text{Actual GNP} - \text{Expected GNP} \\
&= 1\% - 2\% \\
&= -1\%
\end{aligned}
$$

and

$$
\begin{aligned}
F_r &= \text{Surprise in change in interest rates} \\
&= \text{Actual change} - \text{Expected change} \\
&= -2\% - 0\% \\
&= -2\%
\end{aligned}
$$

The total effect of the systematic risks on the share return, then, is

$$m = \text{Systematic risk portion of return}$$
$$= \beta_I F_I + \beta_{GNP} F_{GNP} + \beta_r F_r$$
$$= [2 \times 2\%] + [1 \times (-1\%)] + [(-1.8) \times (-2\%)]$$
$$= 6.6\%$$

Combining this with the unsystematic risk portion, the total risky portion of the return on the share is

$$m + \epsilon = 6.6\% + 5\% = 11.6\%$$

Last, if the expected return on the share for the year was, say, 4 per cent, the total return from all three components will be

$$R = \bar{R} + m + \epsilon$$
$$= 4\% + 6.6\% + 5\%$$
$$= 15.6\%$$

The model we have been looking at is called a **factor model**, and the systematic sources of risk, designated F, are called the factors. To be perfectly formal, a *k-factor model* is a model where each share's return is generated by

$$R = \bar{R} + \beta_1 F_1 + \beta_2 F_2 + \cdots + \beta_k F_k + \epsilon$$

where ϵ is specific to a particular share and uncorrelated with the ϵ term for other shares. In our preceding example, we had a three-factor model. We used inflation, GNP and the change in interest rates as examples of systematic sources of risk, or factors. Researchers have not settled on what is the correct set of factors. Like so many other questions, this might be one of those matters that never are laid to rest.

In practice, researchers frequently use a one-factor model for returns. They do not use all of the sorts of economic factors we used previously as examples; instead, they use an index of stock market returns—like the S&P 500 in the USA—as the single factor. Using the single-factor model we can write returns as

$$R = \bar{R} + \beta(R_{S\&P500} - \bar{R}_{S\&P500}) + \epsilon$$

Where there is only one factor (the returns on the S&P 500 portfolio index), we do not need to put a subscript on the beta. In this form (with minor modifications) the factor model is called a **market model**. This term is employed because the index that is used for the factor is an index of returns on the whole (stock) market. The market model is written as

$$R = \bar{R} + \beta(R_M - \bar{R}_M) + \epsilon$$

where R_M is the return on the market portfolio.[5] The single β is called the *beta coefficient.*

---

[5] Alternatively, the market model could be written as

$$R = \alpha + \beta R_M + \epsilon$$

Here alpha (α) is an intercept term equal to $\bar{R} - \beta \bar{R}_M$.

Concept Questions

- What is an inflation beta? A GNP beta? An interest-rate beta?
- What is the difference between a *k*-factor model and the market model?
- Define the beta coefficient.

12.4   Portfolios and Factor Models

Now let us see what happens to portfolios of stocks when each of the stocks follows a one-factor model. For purposes of discussion, we will take the coming one-month period and examine returns. We could have used a day or a year or any other time period. If the period represents the time between decisions, however, we would rather it be short than long, and a month is a reasonable time frame to use.

We will create portfolios from a list of N stocks, and we will use a one-factor model to capture the systematic risk. The ith stock in the list will therefore have returns

$$R_i = \bar{R}_i + \beta_i F + \epsilon_i \tag{12.1}$$

where we have subscripted the variables to indicate that they relate to the ith stock. Notice that the factor F is not subscripted. The factor that represents systematic risk could be a surprise in GNP, or we could use the market model and let the difference between the market return and what we expect that return to be, $R_{Mkt} - \bar{R}_{Mkt}$, be the factor. In either case, the factor applies to all of the shares.

The β_i is subscripted because it represents the unique way the factor influences the ith stock. To recapitulate our discussion of factor models, if β_i is zero, the returns on the ith stock are

$$R_i = \bar{R}_i + \epsilon_i$$

In words, the ith stock's returns are unaffected by the factor, F, if β_i is zero. If β_i is positive, positive changes in the factor raise the ith stock's returns, and declines lower them. Conversely, if β_i is negative, its returns and the factor move in opposite directions.

Figure 12.1 illustrates the relationship between a stock's excess returns, $R_i - \bar{R}_i$ and the factor F for different betas, where $\beta_i > 0$. The lines in Figure 12.1 plot equation (12.1) on the assumption that there has been no unsystematic risk. That is, $\epsilon_i = 0$. Because we are assuming positive betas, the lines slope upward, indicating that the return on the stock rises with F. Notice that if the factor is zero ($F = 0$), the line passes through zero on the *y*-axis.

Now let us see what happens when we create stock portfolios where each stock follows a one-factor model. Let X_i be the proportion of security i in the portfolio. That is, if an individual with a portfolio of GBP100 wants GBP20 in British Telecom, we say $X_{BT} = 20\%$. Because the X's represent the proportions of wealth we are investing in each of the stocks, we know that they must add up to 100 per cent or 1. That is,

$$X_1 + X_2 + X_3 + \cdots + X_N = 1$$

We know that the portfolio return is the weighted average of the returns on the

FIGURE 12.1   The One-Factor Model

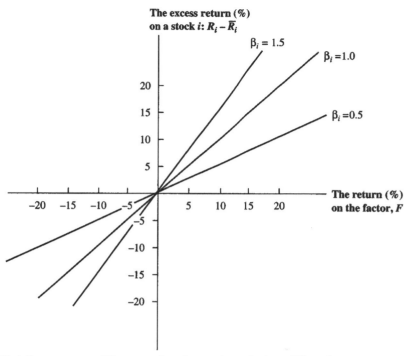

Each line represents a different security, where each security has a different beta.

individual assets in the portfolio:

$$R_P = X_1 R_1 + X_2 R_2 + X_3 R_3 + \cdots + X_N R_N \tag{12.2}$$

Equation (12.2) expresses the return on the portfolio as a weighted average of the returns on the individual assets. We saw from equation (12.1) that each asset, in turn, is determined by both the factor F and the unsystematic risk of ϵ_i. Thus, by substituting equation (12.1) for each R_i in equation (12.2), we have

$$R_P = \underset{\text{(Return on stock } 1)}{X_1(\bar{R}_1 + \beta_1 F + \epsilon_1)} + \underset{\text{(Return on stock } 2)}{X_2(\bar{R}_2 + \beta_2 F + \epsilon_2)}$$

$$+ \underset{\text{(Return on stock } 3)}{X_3(\bar{R}_3 + \beta_3 F + \epsilon_3)} + \cdots + \underset{\text{(Return on stock } N)}{X_N(\bar{R}_N + \beta_N F + \epsilon_N)} \tag{12.3}$$

Equation (12.3) shows us that the return on a portfolio is determined by three sets of parameters:

1. The expected return on each individual security, $\bar{R}_i$.
2. The beta of each security multiplied by the factor F.
3. The unsystematic risk of each individual security, ϵ_i.

We express equation (12.3) in terms of these three sets of parameters as

Weighted Average of Expected Returns:

$$R_P = X_1\overline{R}_1 + X_2\overline{R}_2 + X_3\overline{R}_3 + \cdots + X_N\overline{R}_N$$

(Weighted Average of Betas)F:

$$+ (X_1\beta_1 + X_2\beta_2 + X_3\beta_3 + \cdots + X_N\beta_N)F \qquad (12.4)$$

Weighted Average of Unsystematic Risks:

$$+ X_1\epsilon_1 + X_2\epsilon_2 + X_3\epsilon_3 + \cdots + X_N\epsilon_N$$

This rather imposing equation is actually straightforward. The first row is the weighted average of each security's expected return. The items in the parentheses of the second row represent the weighted average of each security's beta. This weighted average is, in turn, multiplied by the factor F. The third row represents a weighted average of the unsystematic risks of the individual securities.

Where does uncertainty appear in equation (12.4)? There is no uncertainty in the first row because only the expected value of each security's return appears there. Uncertainty in the second row is reflected by only one item, F. That is, while we know that the expected value of F is zero, we do not know what its value will be over a particular time period. Uncertainty in the third row is reflected by each unsystematic risk, ϵ_i.

Portfolios and Diversification

In the previous sections of this chapter, we expressed the return on a single security in terms of our factor model. Portfolios were treated next. Because investors generally hold diversified portfolios, we now want to know what equation (12.4) looks like in a large or diversified portfolio.[6]

As it turns out, something unusual occurs to equation (12.4), the third row actually *disappears* in a large portfolio. To see this, consider the gambler of the previous chapter who divides GBP1,000 by betting on red over many spins of the roulette wheel. For example, he may participate in 1,000 spins, betting GBP1 at a time. Though we do not know ahead of time whether a particular spin will yield red or black, we can be confident that red will win about 50 per cent of the time. Ignoring the house take, the investor can be expected to end up with just about his original GBP1,000.

Though we are concerned with shares, not roulette wheels, the same principle applies. Each security has its own unsystematic risk, where the surprise for one share is unrelated to the surprise of another share. By investing a small amount in each security, the weighted average of the unsystematic risks will be very close to zero in a large portfolio.[7]

Although the third row completely vanishes in a large portfolio, nothing unusual occurs in either row 1 or row 2. Row 1 remains a weighted average of the expected returns on the individual securities as securities are added to the portfolio. Because there is no uncertainty at all in the first row, there is no way for diversification to cause this row to vanish. The terms inside the parentheses of the second row remain a

---

[6] Technically, we can think of a large portfolio as one where an investor keeps increasing the number of securities without limit. In practice, *effective* diversification would occur if at least a few dozen securities were held.

[7] More precisely, we say that the weighted average of the unsystematic risk approaches zero as the number of equally weighted securities in a portfolio approaches infinity.

weighted average of the betas. They do not vanish, either, when securities are added. Because the factor F is unaffected when securities are added to the portfolios, the second row does not vanish.

Why does the third row vanish while the second row does not, though both rows reflect uncertainty? The key is that there are many unsystematic risks in row 3. Because these risks are independent of each other, the effect of diversification becomes stronger as we add more assets to the portfolio. The resulting portfolio becomes less and less risky, and the return becomes more certain. However, the systematic risk, F, affects all securities because it is outside the parentheses in row 2. Because one cannot avoid this factor by investing in many securities, diversification does not occur in this row.

● **Example**

The above material can be further explained by an example similar in spirit to the diversification example of the previous chapter. We keep our one-factor model, but make three specific assumptions:

1. All securities have the same expected return of 10 per cent. This assumption implies that the first row of equation (12.4) must also equal 10 per cent because this row is a weighted average of the expected returns of the individual securities.
2. All securities have a beta of 1. The sum of the terms inside parentheses in the second row of (12.4) must equal 1 because these terms are a weighted average of the individual betas. Since the terms inside the parentheses are multiplied by F, the value of the second row is $1 \times F = F$.
3. In this example, we focus on the behaviour of one individual, Walter V. Bagehot, a new observer of the economic scene. Mr Bagehot decides to hold an equally weighted portfolio. That is, the proportion of each security in his portfolio is $1/N$. ●

We can express the return on Mr Bagehot's portfolio as

Return on Walter V. Bagehot's Portfolio:

$$R_P = 10\% + F + \frac{1}{N}\,\epsilon_1 + \frac{1}{N}\,\epsilon_2 + \frac{1}{N}\,\epsilon_3 + \cdots + \frac{1}{N}\,\epsilon_N \qquad (12.4')$$

| From row 1 of (12.4) | From row 2 of (12.4) | From row 3 of (12.4) |

We mentioned above that, as N increases without limit, row 3 of (12.4) vanishes. Thus, the return to Walter Bagehot's portfolio when the number of securities is very large is

$$R_P = 10\% + F \qquad (12.4'')$$

The key to diversification is exhibited in (12.4″). The unsystematic risk of row 3 vanishes,[8] while the systematic risk of row 2 remains.

---

[8] The variance of row 3 is

$$\frac{1}{N^2}\,\sigma_\epsilon^2 + \frac{1}{N^2}\,\sigma_\epsilon^2 + \frac{1}{N^2}\,\sigma_\epsilon^2 + \cdots + \frac{1}{N^2}\,\sigma_\epsilon^2 = \frac{1}{N^2}\,N\sigma_\epsilon^2$$

where σ_ϵ^2 is the variance of each ϵ. This can be written as σ_ϵ^2/N, which tends to 0 as N goes to infinity.

This is illustrated in Figure 12.2. Systematic risk, captured by variation in the factor *F*, is not reduced through diversification. Conversely, unsystematic risk diminishes as securities are added, vanishing as the number of securities becomes infinite. Our result is analogous to the diversification example of the previous chapter. In that chapter, we said that undiversifiable or systematic risk arises from positive covariances between securities. In this chapter, we say that systematic risk arises from a common factor *F*. Because a common factor causes positive covariances, the arguments of the two chapters are parallel.

FIGURE 12.2   Diversification and the Portfolio Risk for an Equally Weighted Portfolio

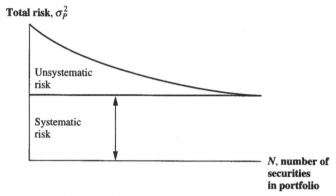

Total risk decreases as the number of securities in the portfolio rises. This drop occurs only in the unsystematic-risk component. Systematic risk is unaffected by diversification.

Concept Questions

• How can the return on a portfolio be expressed in terms of a factor model?
• What risk is diversified away in a large portfolio?

12.5   Betas and Expected Returns

The Linear Relationship

We have argued many times that the expected return on a security compensates for its risk. In the previous chapter, we showed that market beta (the standardized covariance of the security's returns with those of the market) was the appropriate measure of risk under the assumptions of homogeneous expectations and riskless borrowing and lending. The capital-asset-pricing model, which posited these assumptions, implied that the expected return on a security was positively (and linearly) related to its beta. We will find a similar relationship between risk and return in the one-factor model of this chapter.

We begin by noting that the relevant risk in large and well-diversified portfolios is all systematic because unsystematic risk is diversified away. An implication is that, when a well-diversified shareholder considers changing her holdings of a particular stock, she can ignore the security's unsystematic risk.

Notice that we are not claiming that shares, like portfolios, have no unsystematic risk. Neither are we saying that the unsystematic risk of a share will not affect its returns. Shares do have unsystematic risk, and their actual returns do depend on the unsystematic risk. Because this risk washes out in a well-diversified portfolio, however, shareholders can ignore this unsystematic risk when they consider whether or not to add a stock to their portfolio. Therefore, if shareholders are ignoring the unsystematic risk, only the systematic risk of a share can be related to its *expected* return.

This relationship is illustrated in the security market line of Figure 12.3. Points *P*, *C*, *A* and *L* all lie on the line emanating from the risk-free rate of 10 per cent. The points representing each of these four assets can be created by combinations of the risk-free rate and any of the other three assets. For example, since *A* has a beta of 2.0 and *P* has a beta of 1.0, a portfolio of 50 per cent in asset *A* and 50 per cent in the riskless rate has the same beta as asset *P*. The risk-free rate is 10 per cent and the expected return on security *A* is 35 per cent, implying that the combination's return of 22.5 per cent [(10% + 35%)/2] is identical to security *P*'s expected return. Because security *P* has both the same beta and the same expected return as a combination of the riskless asset and security *A*, an individual is equally inclined to add a small amount of security *P* and to add a small amount of this combination to her portfolio. However, the unsystematic risk of security *P* need not be equal to the unsystematic risk of the combination of security *A* and the risk-free rate because unsystematic risk is diversified away in a large portfolio.

FIGURE 12.3   A Graph of Beta and Expected Return for Individual Stocks under the One-Factor Model

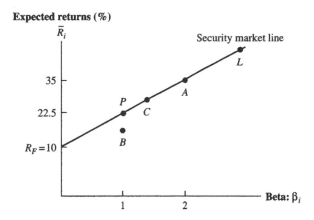

Of course, the potential combinations of points on the security market line are endless. One can duplicate *P* by combinations of the risk-free rate and either *C* or *L* (or both of them). One can duplicate *C* (or *A* or *L*) by borrowing at the risk-free rate to invest in *P*. The infinite number of points on the security market line that are not labelled can be used as well.

Now consider security *B*. Because its expected return is below the line, no investor would hold it. Instead, the investor would prefer security *P*, a combination of security *A* and the riskless asset or some other combination. Thus, security *B*'s price is too high. Its price will fall in a competitive market, forcing its expected return back up to the line in equilibrium.

We know that a line can be described algebraically from two points. Because we know that the return on any zero-beta asset is R_F and the expected return on the asset is $\bar{R}_1$, it can easily be shown that

$$\bar{R} = R_F + \beta(\bar{R}_1 - R_F) \tag{12.5}$$

The Market Portfolio and the Single Factor

In the CAPM, the beta of a security measures the security's responsiveness to movements in the market portfolio. In the one-factor model of the APT, the beta of a security measures its responsiveness to the factor. We now relate the market portfolio to the single factor.

A large, diversified portfolio has no unsystematic risk because the unsystematic risks of the individual securities are diversified away. Assuming enough securities so that the market portfolio is fully diversified, and assuming that no security has a disproportionate market share, this portfolio is fully diversified and contains no unsystematic risk. In other words, the market portfolio is perfectly correlated with the single factor, implying that the market portfolio is really a scaled-up or scaled-down version of the factor. After scaling properly, we can treat the market portfolio as the factor itself.

The market portfolio, like every security or portfolio, lies on the security market line. When the market portfolio is the factor, the beta of the market portfolio is 1 by definition. This is shown in Figure 12.4. (We deleted the securities and the specific expected returns from Figure 12.3 for clarity; the two graphs are otherwise identical.) With the market portfolio as the factor, equation (12.5) becomes

$$\bar{R} = R_F + \beta(\bar{R}_M - R_F)$$

where $\bar{R}_M$ is the expected return on the market. This equation shows that the expected return on any asset, $\bar{R}$, is linearly related to the security's beta. The equation is identical to that of the CAPM, which we developed in the last chapter.

Concept Question

- What is the relationship between the one-factor model and the CAPM?

FIGURE 12.4   A Graph of Beta and Expected Return for Individual Stocks under the One-Factor Model

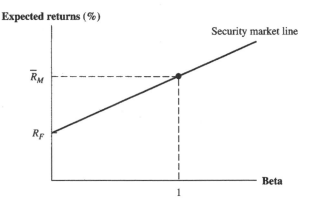

The factor is scaled so that it is identical to the market portfolio. The beta of the market portfolio is 1.

12.6 The Capital-Asset-Pricing Model and the Arbitrage Pricing Model

The CAPM and the APT are alternative models of risk and return. It is worth while to consider the differences between the two models, both in terms of pedagogy and in terms of application.

Differences in Pedagogy

We feel that the CAPM has at least one strong advantage from the student's point of view. The derivation of the CAPM necessarily brings the reader through a discussion of efficient sets. This treatment—beginning with the case of two risky assets, moving to the case of many risky assets and finishing when a riskless asset is added to the many risky ones—is of great intuitive value. This sort of presentation is not as easily accomplished with the APT.

However, the APT has an offsetting advantage. The model adds factors until the unsystematic risk of any security is uncorrelated with the unsystematic risk of every other security. Under this formulation, it is easily shown that (1) unsystematic risk steadily falls (and ultimately vanishes) as the number of securities in the portfolio increases, but (2) the systematic risks do not decrease. This result was also shown in the CAPM, though the intuition was cloudier because the unsystematic risks could be correlated across securities.

Differences in Application

One advantage of the APT is that it can handle multiple factors while the CAPM ignores them. Although the bulk of our presentation in this chapter focuses on the one-factor model, a multifactor model is probably more reflective of reality. That is, one must abstract from many marketwide and industrywide factors before the unsystematic risk of one security becomes uncorrelated with the unsystematic risks of other securities. Under this multifactor version of the APT, the relationship between risk and return can be expressed as:

$$\overline{R} = R_F + (\overline{R}_1 - R_F)\beta_1 + (\overline{R}_2 - R_F)\beta_2 + (\overline{R}_3 - R_F)\beta_3 + \cdots + (\overline{R}_K - R_F)\beta_K \quad (12.6)$$

In this equation, β_1 stands for the security's beta with respect to the first factor, β_2 stands for the security's beta with respect to the second factor, and so on. For example, if the first factor is GNP, β_1 is the security's GNP beta. The term $\overline{R}_1$ is the expected return on a security (or portfolio) whose beta with respect to the first factor is 1 and whose beta with respect to all other factors is zero. Because the market compensates for risk, $(\overline{R}_1 - R_F)$ will be positive in the normal case.[9] (An analogous interpretation can be given to $\overline{R}_2$, $\overline{R}_3$, and so on.)

The equation states that the security's expected return is related to the security's factor betas. The intuition in equation (12.6) is straightforward. Each factor represents risk that cannot be diversified away. The higher a security's beta with regard to a particular factor is, the higher is the risk that the security bears. In a rational world, the expected return on the security should compensate for this risk. The above equation states that the expected return is a summation of the risk-free rate plus the compensation for each type of risk that the security bears.

---

[9] Actually, $(\overline{R}_i - R_F)$ could be negative in the case where factor i is perceived as a hedge of some sort.

As an example, consider a study where the factors were monthly growth in industrial production (IP), change in expected inflation (ΔEI), unanticipated inflation (UI), unanticipated change in the risk premium between risky bonds and default-free bonds (URP), and unanticipated change in the difference between the return on long-term government bonds and the return on short-term government bonds (UBR).[10] Using the period 1958–84, the empirical results of the US study indicated that the expected monthly return on any share, $\bar{R}_S$, can be described as

$$\bar{R}_S = 0.0041 + 0.0136\beta_{IP} - 0.0001\beta_{\Delta EI} - 0.0006\beta_{UI} + 0.0072\beta_{URP} - 0.0052\beta_{UBR}$$

Suppose a particular share had the following betas: $\beta_{IP} = 1.1$, $\beta_{\Delta EI} = 2$, $\beta_{UI} = 3$, $\beta_{URP} = 0.1$, $\beta_{UBR} = 1.6$. The expected monthly return on that security would be

$$\bar{R}_S = 0.0041 + 0.0136 \times 1.1 - 0.0001 \times 2$$
$$- 0.0006 \times 3 + 0.0072 \times 0.1 - 0.0052 \times 1.6 = 0.0095$$

Assuming that a firm is unlevered and that one of the firm's projects has risk equivalent to that of the firm, this value of 0.0095 (i.e. 95 per cent) can be used as the monthly discount rate for the project. (Because annual data are often supplied for capital budgeting purposes, the annual rate of 0.120 $[(1.0095)^{12} - 1]$ might be used instead.)

Because many factors appear on the righthand side of equation (12.5), the APT formulation has the potential to measure expected returns more accurately than does the CAPM. However, as we mentioned earlier, one cannot easily determine which are the appropriate factors. The factors in the above study were included for reasons of both common sense and convenience. They were not derived from theory.

12.7 Parametric Approaches to Asset Pricing

Empirical Models

The CAPM and the APT by no means exhaust the models and techniques used in practice to measure the expected return on risky assets. Both the CAPM and the APT are *risk-based models*. They each measure the risk of a security by its beta(s) on some systematic factor(s), and they each argue that the expected excess return must be proportional to the beta(s). As we have seen, this is intuitively appealing and has a strong basis in theory, but there are alternative approaches.

Most of these alternatives can be lumped under the broad heading of parametric or **empirical** methods. The word *empirical* refers to the fact that these approaches are based less on some theory of how financial markets work and more on simply looking for regularities and relations in the past history of market data. In these approaches the researcher specifies some parameters or attributes associated with the securities in question and then examines the data directly for a relation between these attributes and expected returns. For example, an extensive amount of research has been done on whether the expected return on a firm is related to its size. Is it true that small firms have higher average returns than large firms? Researchers have also examined a variety of accounting measures such as the ratio of the price of a stock to the accounting earnings, the P/E ratio, and the closely related ratio of the market value of

---

[10] N. Chen, R. Roll and S. Ross (1986). 'Economic forces and the stock market', *Journal of Business*, July.

the stock to the book value of the company, the M/B ratio. Here it might be argued that companies with low P/Es or low M/Bs are 'undervalued' and can be expected to have higher returns in the future.

To use the empirical approach to determine the expected return, we would estimate the following equation:

$$\bar{R}_i = k_{P/E} \, (P/E)_i + k_{M/B}(M/B)_i + k_{size}(size)_p$$

where $\bar{R}_i$ is the expected return of firm i, and where the k's are coefficients that we estimate from stock market data. Notice that this is the same form as equation (12.6) with the firm's attributes in place of betas and with the k's in place of the excess factor portfolio returns.

When tested with data, these parametric approaches seem to do quite well, and when comparisons are made between using parameters and using betas to predict stock returns, the parameters, such as P/E and M/B, seem to work better. There are a variety of possible explanations for these results, and the issues have certainly not been settled. Critics of the empirical approach are sceptical of what they call *data mining*. The particular parameters that researchers work with are often chosen because they have been shown to be related to returns. For instance, suppose that you were asked to explain the change in intelligence test scores over the past 40 years in some particular country. Suppose that to do this you searched through all of the data series you could find. After much searching, you might discover, for example, that the change in the scores was directly related to the rabbit population in England. We know that any such relation is purely accidental, but if you search long enough and have enough choices, you will find something even if its not really there. It's a bit like staring at clouds. After a while you will see clouds that look like anything you want, clowns, bears, or whatever, but all you are really doing is data mining.

Needless to say, the researchers on these matters defend their work by arguing that they have not mined the data and have been very careful to avoid such traps by not snooping at the data to see what will work.

Of course, as a matter of pure theory, since anyone in the market can easily look up the P/E ratio of a firm, one would certainly not expect to find that firms with low P/Es did better than firms with high P/Es simply because they were undervalued. In an efficient market, such public measures of undervaluation would be quickly exploited and would not expect to last.

Perhaps a better explanation for the success of empirical approaches lies in a synthesis of the risk-based approaches and the empirical methods. In an efficient market, risk and return are related, hence perhaps the parameters or attributes which appear to be related to returns are also better measures of risk. For example, if we were to find that low P/E firms outperformed high P/E firms and that this was true even for firms that had the same beta(s), then we have at least two possible explanations. First, we could simply discard the risk-based theories as incorrect. Furthermore, we could argue that markets are inefficient and that buying low P/E stocks provides us with an opportunity to make higher than predicted returns. Second, we could argue that both views of the world are correct and that the P/E is really just a better way to measure systematic risk, i.e. beta(a), than directly estimating beta from the data.

Style Portfolios

In addition to its use as a platform for estimating expected returns, stock attributes are also widely used as a way of characterizing money management styles. For example, a portfolio that has a P/E ratio much in excess of the market average might be characterized as a high P/E or a **growth** stock **portfolio**. Similarly, a portfolio made up of stocks with an average P/E less than that for a market index might be characterized as a low P/E or a **value portfolio**.

To evaluate how well a portfolio manager is doing, often their performance is compared with the performance of some basic indexes. For example, the portfolio returns of a manager who purchases large British stocks might be compared against the performance of the FTSE-100 Index. In such a case the FTSE-100 is said to be the **benchmark** against which their performance is measured. Similarly, an international manager might be compared against some index of international stocks. In choosing an appropriate benchmark, care should be taken to identify a benchmark that contains only those types of stocks that the manager targets as representative of his or her style and that are also available to be purchased. A manager who was told not to purchase any stocks in the FTSE-100 Index would not consider it legitimate to be compared against the FTSE-100.

Increasingly, too, managers are compared not only against an index, but also against a peer group of similar managers. The performance of a fund that advertises itself as a growth fund might be measured against the performance of a large sample of similar funds. For instance, the performance over some period commonly is assigned to quartiles. The top 25 per cent of the funds are said to be in the first quartile, the next 25 per cent in the second quartile, the next 25 per cent in the third quartile, and the worst-performing 25 per cent of the funds in the last quartile. If the fund we are examining happens to have performance that falls in the second quartile, then we speak of it as a second quartile manager.

Similarly, we call a fund that purchases low M/B stocks a value fund and would measure its performance against a sample of similar value funds. These approaches to measuring performance are relatively new, and they are part of an active and exciting effort to refine our ability to identify and use investment skills.

Concept Questions

- Empirical models are sometimes called factor models. What is the difference between a factor as we have used it previously in this chapter and an attribute as we use it in this section?
- What is data mining and why might it overstate the relation between some stock attribute and returns?
- What is wrong with measuring the performance of a U.S. growth stock manager against a benchmark composed of English stocks?

12.8   Summary and Conclusions

The previous chapter developed the capital-asset-pricing model (CAPM). As an alternative, this chapter develops the arbitrage pricing theory (APT).

1. The APT assumes that stock returns are generated according to factor models. For example, we might describe a stock's return as

$$R = \bar{R} = \beta_I F_I + \beta_{GNP} F_{GNP} + \beta_r F_r + \epsilon$$

The three factors F_I, F_{GNP}, and F_r represent systematic risk because these factors affect many securities. The term ϵ is considered an unsystematic risk because it is unique to each individual security.

2. For convenience, we frequently describe a security's return according to a one-factor model:

$$R = \bar{R} = \beta F + \epsilon$$

3. As securities are added to a portfolio, the unsystematic risks of the individual securities offset each other. A fully diversified portfolio has no unsystematic risk, but still has systematic risk. This result indicates that diversification can only eliminate some, but not all, of the risk of individual securities.

4. Because of this, the expected return on a stock is positively related to its systematic risk. In a one-factor model, the systematic risk of a security is simply the beta of the CAPM. Thus, the implications of the CAPM and the one-factor APT are identical. However, each security has many risks in a multifactor model. The expected return on a security is positively related to the beta of the security with each factor.

5. Empirical or parametric models that capture the relations between returns and stock attributes such as P/E or M/B ratios can be estimated directly from the data without any appeal to theory. These ratios are also used to measure the style of a portfolio manager and to construct benchmarks and samples against which they are measured.

KEY TERMS

Beta coefficient 281	Growth portfolios 294
Factor model 283	Value portfolios 294
Market model 283	Benchmark 294
Empirical model 292	

QUESTIONS AND PROBLEMS

Factor Models and Risk

12.1 You own shares in the Lewis-Striden Drug Company. Suppose you expected the following events to occur last month.

  a. The government would announce that real GNP would have grown 1.2 per cent during the previous quarter. The returns of Lewis-Striden are positively related to real GNP.

  b. The government would announce that inflation over the previous quarter was 3.7 per cent. The returns of Lewis-Striden are negatively related to inflation.

  c. Interest rates would rise 2.5 percentage points. The returns of Lewis-Striden are negatively related to interest rates.

  d. The president of the firm will announce his retirement. The retirement will be effective six months from the announcement day. The president is well liked; in general he is considered an asset to the firm.

  e. Research data will conclusively prove the efficacy of an experimental drug. Completion of the efficacy testing means the drug will be on the market soon.

  Suppose the following events actually occurred.

  a. The government announced that real GNP grew 2.3 per cent during the previous quarter.

  b. The government announced that inflation over the previous quarter was 3.7 per cent.

  c. Interest rates rose 2.1 percentage points.

  d. The chief executive of the firm died suddenly of a heart attack.

  e. Research results in the efficacy testing were not as strong as expected. The drug must be tested another six months and the efficacy results must be resubmitted to the regulatory authorities.

  f. Lab researchers had a breakthrough with another drug.

  g. A competitor announced that it will begin distribution and sale of a medicine that will compete directly with one of Lewis-Striden's top-selling products.

   i. Discuss how each of the actual occurrences affects the returns on your Lewis-Striden shares.

   ii. Which events represent systematic risk?

   iii. Which events represent unsystematic risk?

12.2 Suppose a three-factor model is appropriate to describe the returns of a share. Information about those three factors is presented in the following chart. Suppose this is the only information you have concerning the factors.

Factor	Beta of factor	Expected value	Actual value
GNP	0.042	GBP4,416	GBP4,480
Inflation	−1.40	3.1%	4.3%
Interest rate	−0.67	9.5%	11.8%

  a. What is the systematic risk of the stock return?
  b. Suppose unexpected bad news about the firm was announced that dampens the returns by 2.6 percentage points. What is the unsystematic risk of the share return?
  c. Suppose the expected return of the share is 9.5 per cent. What is the total return on this share?

12.3 The following three shares are available in the market.

	Expected return (%)	Beta
Share *A*	10.5	1.20
Share *B*	13.0	0.98
Share *C*	15.7	1.37
Market	14.2	1.00

Assume the market model is valid.
  a. Write the market-model equation for each share.
  b. What is the return on a portfolio that is 30 per cent share *A*, 45 per cent share *B*, and 25 per cent share *C*?
  c. Suppose the return on the market is 15 per cent and there are no unsystematic surprises in the returns.
   i. What is the return on each stock?
   ii. What is the return on the portfolio?

12.4 You are forming an equally weighted portfolio of shares. There are many shares that all have the same beta of 0.84 for factor 1 and the same beta of 1.69 for factor 2. All stocks also have the same expected return of 11 per cent. Assume a two-factor model describes the returns on each of these shares.
  a. Write the equation of the returns on your portfolio if you place only five shares in it.
  b. Write the equation of the returns on your portfolio if you place in it a very large number of shares that all have the same expected returns and the same betas.

The APT
12.5 There are two stock markets, each driven by the same common force F with an expected value of zero and standard deviation of 10 per cent. There is a large number of securities in each market; thus, you can invest in as many stocks as you wish. Due to restrictions, however, you can invest in only one of the two markets. The expected return on every security in both markets is 10 per cent.
   The returns for each security i in the first market are generated by the relationship

$$R_{1i} = 0.10 + 1.5F + \epsilon_{1i}$$

where ϵ_{1i} is the term that measures the surprises in the returns of stock i in market one. These surprises are normally distributed; their mean is zero. The returns for security j in the second market are generated by the relationship

$$R_{2j} = 0.10 + 0.5F + \epsilon_{2j}$$

where ϵ_{2j} is the term that measures the surprises in the returns of stock j in market two. These surprises are normally distributed; their mean is zero. The standard deviation of ϵ_{1i} and ϵ_{2j} for any two stocks, i and j, is 20 per cent.
  a. If the correlation between the surprises in the returns of any two stocks in the first market is zero, and if the correlation between the surprises in the returns of any two stocks in the

second market is zero, in which market would a risk-averse person prefer to invest? (Note: The correlation between ϵ_{1i} and ϵ_{1j} for any i and j is zero, and the correlation between ϵ_{2i} and ϵ_{2j} for any i and j is zero.)

b. If the correlation between ϵ_{1i} and ϵ_{1j} in the first market is 0.9 and the correlation between ϵ_{2i} and ϵ_{2j} in the second market is zero, in which market would a risk-averse person prefer to invest?

c. If the correlation between ϵ_{1i} and ϵ_{1j} in the first market is zero and the correlation between ϵ_{2i} and ϵ_{2j} in the second market is 0.5, in which market would a risk-averse person prefer to invest?

d. In general, what is the relationship between the correlations of the disturbances in the two markets that would make a risk-averse person equally willing to invest in either of the two markets?

12.6 Assume that the following market model adequately describes the return-generating behaviour of risky assets.

$$R_{it} = \alpha_i + \beta_i R_{Mt} + \epsilon_{it}$$

where

$$R_{it} = \text{The return for the } i\text{th asset at time } t$$

and

$$R_{mt} = \text{The return on a portfolio containing all risky assets in some proportion, at time } t$$

$$R_{mt} \text{ and } \epsilon_{it} \text{ are statistically independent.}$$

Suppose the following data are true.

Asset	β_i	$E(R_i)$	$Var(\epsilon_i)$
A	0.7	8.41%	1.00%
B	1.2	12.06%	1.44%
C	1.5	13.95%	2.25%
$Var(R_{Mt}) = 1.21\%$			

a. Calculate the standard deviation of returns for each asset.

b. Assume short selling is allowed.

  i. Calculate the variance of return of three portfolios containing an infinite number of asset types A, B or C, respectively.

  ii. Assume: $R_F = 3.3\%$ and $\bar{R}_M = 10.6\%$. Which asset will not be held by rational investors?

  iii. What equilibrium state will emerge such that no arbitrage opportunities exist? Why?

12.7 Assume that the returns of individual securities are generated by the following two-factor model:

$$R_{it} = E(R_{it}) + \beta_{i1}F_{1t} + \beta_{i2}F_{2t}$$

R_{it} is the return for security i at time t. F_{1t} and F_{2t} are market factors with zero expectation and zero covariance. In addition, assume that there is a capital market for four securities, where each one has the following characteristics:

Security	β_1	β_2	$E(R_{it})$
1	1.0	1.5	20%
2	0.5	2.0	20
3	1.0	0.5	10
4	1.5	0.75	10

The capital market for these four assets is perfect in the sense that there are no transactions costs and short sales can take place.

a. Construct a portfolio containing (long or short) securities *1* and *2*, with a return that does not depend on the market factor, F_{1t}, in any way. (Hint: Such a portfolio will have $\beta_1 = 0$.) Compute the expected return and β_2 coefficient for this portfolio.

b. Following the procedure in (*a*), construct a portfolio containing securities *3* and *4* with a return that does not depend on the market factor, F_{1t}. Compute the expected return and β_2 coefficient for this portfolio.

c. Consider a risk-free asset with expected return equal to 5 per cent, $\beta_1 = 0$, and $\beta_2 = 0$. Describe a possible arbitrage opportunity in such detail that an investor could implement it.

d. What effect would the existence of these kinds of arbitrage opportunities have on the capital markets for these securities in the short and long run? Graph your analysis.

Risk, Return and Capital Budgeting

Our text has devoted a number of chapters to net-present-value (NPV) analysis. We pointed out that a pound or mark (or whatever) to be received in the future was worth less than a pound or mark (or whatever) received today for two reasons. First, there is the simple time-value-of-money argument in a riskless world. If you have a pound today, you can invest it in the bank and receive more than a pound by some future date. Second, a risky pound is worth less than a riskless pound. Consider a firm expecting a GBP1 cash flow. If actuality exceeds expectations (revenues are especially high or expenses are especially low), perhaps GBP1.10 or GBP1.20 will be received. If actuality falls short of expectations, perhaps only GBP0.80 or GBP0.90 will be received. This risk is unattractive to the typical firm.

Our work on NPV allowed us to precisely value riskless cash flows. That is, we discounted by the riskless interest rate. However, because most real-world cash flows in the future are risky, business demands a procedure for discounting risky cash flows. This chapter applies the concept of net present value to risky cash flows. Let us review what previous work in the text has to say about NPV. In earlier chapters, we learned that the basic NPV formula for an investment that generates cash flows (C_t) in future periods is

$$\text{NPV} = C_0 + \sum_{t=1}^{T} \frac{C_t}{(1+r)^t}$$

For risky projects, expected incremental cash flows $\bar{C}_t$ are placed in the numerator, and the NPV formula becomes

$$\text{NPV} = C_0 + \sum_{t=1}^{T} \frac{\bar{C}_t}{(1+r)^t}$$

In this chapter, we will learn that the discount rate used to determine the NPV of a risky project can be computed from the CAPM (or APT). For example, if an all-equity firm is seeking to value a risky project, such as renovating a warehouse, the firm will determine the required return, r_S, on the project by using the SML. We call r_S the firm's **cost of equity** capital.

When firms finance with both debt and equity, the discount rate to use is the project's overall cost of capital. The overall cost of capital is a weighted average of the cost of debt and the cost of equity.

13.1   The Cost of Equity Capital

Whenever a firm has extra cash, it can take one of two actions. On the one hand, it can pay out the cash immediately as a dividend. On the other hand, the firm can invest extra cash in a project, paying out the future cash flows of the project as dividends. Which procedure would the shareholder prefer? If a shareholder can reinvest the dividend in a financial asset (a share or bond) with the same risk as that of the project, the shareholder would desire the alternative with the highest expected return. In other words, the project should be undertaken only if its expected return is greater than that of a financial asset of comparable risk. This is illustrated in Figure 13.1. This discussion implies a very simple capital-budgeting rule: the discount rate of a project should be the expected return on a financial asset of comparable risk.

FIGURE 13.1   Choices of a Firm with Extra Cash

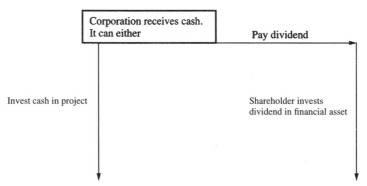

Shareholder wants the firm to invest in a project only if the expected return on the project is at least as great as that of a financial asset of comparable risk.

From the firm's perspective, the expected return is the cost of equity capital. If we use the CAPM model for returns, the expected return on the stock will be

$$\overline{R} = R_F - \beta \times (\overline{R}_M - R_F) \tag{13.1}$$

where R_F is the risk-free rate and $\overline{R}_M - R_F$ is the difference between the expected return on the market portfolio and the riskless rate. This difference is often called the expected excess market return.[1]

---

[1] Of course, we can use the k-factor APT model (Chapter 12) and estimate several beta coefficients. However, for our purposes it is sufficient to estimate a single beta.

We now have the tools to estimate a firm's cost of equity capital. To do this, we need to know three things:

- The risk-free rate, R_F
- The market-risk premium, $\overline{R}_M - R_F$
- The company beta, β_i

● Example

Suppose the stock of the Quatram Company, a publisher of college textbooks, has a beta (β) of 1.3. The firm is 100 per cent equity financed, that is, it has no debt. Quatram is considering a number of capital-budgeting projects that will double its size. Because these new projects are similar to the firm's existing ones, the average beta on the new projects is assumed to be equal to Quatram's existing beta. What is the appropriate discount rate for these new projects, assuming a market-risk premium of 8.5 per cent?

Now we can estimate the cost of equity r_s for Quatram as

$$r_s = 7\% + (8.5\% \times 1.3)$$
$$= 7\% + 11.05\%$$
$$= 18.05\%$$

Two key assumptions were made in this example. (1) The beta risk of the new projects is the same as the risk of the firm, and (2) the firm is all-equity financed. Given these assumptions, it follows that the cash flows of the new projects should be discounted at the 18.05 per cent rate. ●

● Example

Suppose Alpha Air Freight is an all-equity firm with a beta of 1.21. Further suppose the market-risk premium is 8.5 per cent, and the risk-free rate is 6 per cent. We can determine the expected return on the common stock of Alpha Air Freight by using the SML of equation (13.1). We find that the expected return is

$$6\% + (1.21 \times 8.5\%) = 16.3\%$$

Because this is the return that shareholders can expect in the financial markets on a stock with a β of 1.21, it is the return they expect on Alpha Air Freight's stock.

Further suppose Alpha is evaluating the following non-mutually exclusive projects:

Project	Project's beta (β)	Project's expected cash flows next year	Project's internal rate of return	Project's NPV when cash flows are discounted at 16.3%	Accept or reject
A	1.21	GBP140	40%	GBP20.4	Accept
B	1.21	GBP120	20%	GBP 3.2	Accept
C	1.21	GBP110	10%	–GBP 5.4	Reject

Each project initially costs GBP100. All projects are assumed to have the same risk as the firm as a whole. Because the cost of equity capital is 16.3 per cent, projects in an all-equity firm are discounted at this rate. Projects *A* and *B* have positive NPVs, and *C* will have a negative NPV. Thus, only *A* and *B* will be accepted.[2] This is illustrated in Figure 13.2. ●

In the last example we assumed that the company beta was known. Of course, beta must be estimated in the real world. We pointed out earlier that the beta of a security is the standardized covariance of a security's return with the return on the market portfolio. The formula for security *i*, first given in Chapter 11, is

$$\text{Beta of security } i = \frac{\text{Cov}(R_i, R_M)}{\text{Var}(R_M)} = \frac{\sigma_{i,M}}{\sigma_M^2}$$

In words, the beta is the covariance of a security with the market, divided by the variance of the market. Because we calculated both covariance and variance in earlier chapters, calculating beta involves no new material.

● Example (Advanced)

Suppose we sample the returns on the stock of the General Tool Company and the returns on the market index for four years. They are tabulated as follows:

Year	General Tool Company R_G	Market index R_M
1	−10%	−40%
2	3	−30
3	20	10
4	15	20

We can calculate beta in six steps.
   1. Calculate average return on each asset:

Average Return on General Tool:

$$\frac{-0.10 + 0.03 + 0.20 + 0.15}{4} = 0.07 \ (7\%)$$

---

[2] In addition to the SML, the dividend-valuation model presented earlier in the text can be used to represent the firm's cost of equity capital. Using this model, the present value (*P*) of the firm's expected dividend payments can be expressed as

$$P = \frac{\text{Div}_1}{(1 + r_S)} + \frac{\text{Div}_2}{(1 + r_S)^2} + \cdots + \frac{\text{Div}_N}{(1 + r_S)^N} + \cdots \tag{a}$$

where r_S is the required return of shareholders and the firm's cost of equity capital. If the dividends are expected to grow at a constant rate, *g*, equation (a) reduces to

$$P = \frac{\text{Div}_1}{r_S - g} \tag{b}$$

Equation (b) can be reformulated as

$$r_S = \frac{\text{Div}_1}{P} + g \tag{c}$$

We can use equation (c) to estimate r_S. Div_1/P is the dividend yield expected over the next year. An estimate of the cost of equity capital is determined from an estimate of Div_1/P and *g*.

The dividend-valuation model is generally considered both less theoretically sound and more difficult to practically apply than the SML. Hence, examples in this chapter calculate cost of equity capital using the SML approach.

FIGURE 13.2   Using the Security-Market Line to Estimate the Risk-Adjusted Discount Rate for Risky Projects

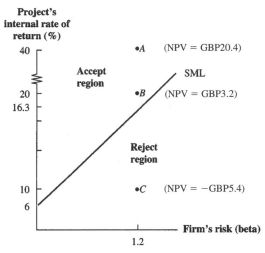

The diagonal line represents the relationship between the cost of equity capital and the firm's beta. An all-equity firm should accept a project whose internal rate of return is greater than the cost of equity capital, and should reject a project whose internal rate of return is less than the cost of equity capital. (The above graph assumes that all projects are as risky as the firm.)

Average Return on Market Portfolio:

$$\frac{-0.40 - 0.30 + 0.10 + 0.20}{4} = -0.10 \ (-10\%)$$

2. For each asset, calculate the deviation of each return from the asset's average return determined above. This is presented in columns 3 and 5 of Table 13.1.
3. Multiply the deviation of General Tool's return by the deviation of the market's return. This is presented in column 6. This procedure is analogous to our calculation of covariance in an earlier chapter. The procedure will be used in the numerator of the beta calculation.
4. Calculate the squared deviation of the market's return. This is presented in column 7. This procedure is analogous to our calculation of variance in Chapter 9. The procedure will be used in the denominator of the beta calculation.
5. Take the sum of column 6 and the sum of column 7. They are

Sum of Deviation of General Tool Multiplied by Deviation of Market Portfolio:

$$0.051 + 0.008 + 0.026 + 0.024 = 0.109$$

Sum of Squared Deviation of Market Portfolio:

$$0.090 + 0.040 + 0.040 + 0.090 = 0.260$$

TABLE 13.1 Calculating Beta

(1) Year	(2) Rate of return on General Tool (R_G)	(3) General Tool's deviation from average return* $(R_G - \bar{R}_G)$	(4) Rate of return on market portfolio	(5) Market portfolio's deviation from average return† $(R_M - \bar{R}_M)$	(6) Deviation of General Tool multiplied by deviation of market portfolio	(7) Squared deviation of market portfolio
1	−0.10	−0.17 (−0.10 − 0.07)	−0.40	−0.30	0.051 [(−0.17) × (−0.30)]	0.090 [(−0.30) × (−0.30)]
2	0.03	−0.04	−0.30	−0.20	0.008	0.040
3	0.20	0.13	0.10	0.20	0.026	0.040
4	0.15	0.08	0.20	0.30	0.024	0.090
	Avg = 0.07		Avg = −0.10		Sum: 0.109	Sum: 0.260

Beta of General Tool: $0.419 = \dfrac{0.109}{0.260}$.

  * Average return for General Tool is 0.07.
  † Average return for market is −0.10.

6. The beta is the sum of column 6 divided by the sum of column 7. This is

Beta of General Tool:

$$0.419 = \frac{0.109}{0.260} \quad \bullet$$

Concept Questions

• How does one calculate the discount rate from the beta?
• What are the two key assumptions we used when calculating the discount rate?
• What are the six steps needed to calculate beta?

Measuring Company Betas

The basic method of measuring company betas is to estimate:

$$\frac{\text{Cov}(R_{it}, R_{Mt})}{\text{Var}(R_{Mt})}$$

Using $t = 1, 2, \ldots, T$ observations.

Problems

1. Betas may vary over time.
2. The sample size may be inadequate.
3. Betas are influenced by changing financial leverage and business risk.

Solutions

1. Problems 1 and 2 (above) can be moderated by more sophisticated statistical techniques.
2. Problem 3 can be lessened by adjusting for changes in business and financial risk.
3. Look at average beta estimates of several comparable firms in the industry.

13.2   Determinants of Beta

The regression analysis approach in the previous section doesn't tell us where beta comes from. The beta of a stock does not come out of thin air. Rather, it is determined by the characteristics of the firm. We consider three factors: the cyclical nature of revenues, operating leverage and financial leverage.

Cyclicality of Revenues

The revenues of some firms are quite cyclical. That is, these firms do well in the expansion phase of the business cycle and do poorly in the contraction phase. Empirical evidence suggests high-tech firms, retailers and automotive firms fluctuate with the business cycle. Firms in industries such as utilities, railways and food are less dependent upon the cycle. Because beta is the standardized covariability of a stock's return with the market's return, it is not surprising that highly cyclical stocks have high betas.

It is worth while to point out that cyclicality is not the same as variability. For example, a movie-making firm has highly variable revenues because hits and flops are not easily predictable. However, because the revenues of a studio are more dependent on the quality of its releases than upon the phase of the business cycle, motion-picture companies are not particularly cyclical. In other words, stocks with high standard deviations need not have high betas, a point we have stressed before.

Operating Leverage

We distinguished fixed costs from variable costs earlier in the text. At that time, we mentioned that fixed costs do not change as quantity changes. Conversely, variable costs increase as the quantity of output rises. This difference between variable and fixed costs allows us to define operating leverage.

● Example

Consider a firm that can choose either technology A or technology B when making a particular product. The relevant differences between the two technologies are displayed below:

Technology A	*Technology B*
Fixed cost: DEM1,000/year	Fixed cost: DEM2,000/year
Variable cost: DEM8/unit	Variable cost: DEM6/unit
Price: DEM10/unit	Price: DEM10/unit
Contribution margin: DEM2 (DEM10 − DEM8)	Contribution margin: DEM4 (DEM10 − DEM6)

Technology *A* has lower fixed costs and higher variable costs than does technology *B*. Perhaps technology *A* involves less mechanization than does *B*. Or the equipment in *A* may be leased whereas the equipment in *B* must be purchased. Alternatively, perhaps technology *A* involves few employees but many subcontractors, whereas *B* involves only highly skilled employees who must be retained in bad times. Because technology *B* has both lower variable costs and higher fixed costs, we say that it has higher **operating leverage**.[3]

---

[3] The actual definition of operating leverage is

$$\frac{\text{Change in EBIT}}{\text{EBIT}} \times \frac{\text{Sales}}{\text{Change in sales}}$$

where EBIT is the earnings before interest and taxes. That is, operating leverage measures the percentage change in EBIT for a given percentage change in sales or revenues. It can be shown that operating leverage increases as fixed costs rise and as variable costs fall.

Figure 13.3 graphs costs under both technologies. The slope of each total-cost line represents variable costs under a single technology. The slope of *A*'s line is steeper, indicating greater variable costs.

Because the two technologies are used to produce the same products, a unit price of DEM10 applies for both cases. We mentioned in an earlier chapter that contribution margin is the difference between price and variable cost. It measures the incremental profit from one additional unit. Because the contribution margin in *B* is greater, its technology is riskier. An unexpected sale increases profit by DEM2 under *A*, but increases profit by DEM4 under *B*. Similarly, an unexpected sale cancellation reduces profit by DEM2 under *A*, but reduces profit by DEM4 under *B*. This is illustrated in Figure 13.4. This figure shows the change in earnings before interest and taxes for a given change in volume. The slope of the righthand graph is greater, indicating that technology *B* is riskier. ●

The cyclicality of a firm's revenues is a determinant of the firm's beta. Operating leverage magnifies the effect of cyclicity on beta. As mentioned earlier, business risk is generally defined as the risk of the firm without financial leverage. Business risk depends both on the responsiveness of the firm's revenues to the business cycle and on the firm's operating leverage.

FIGURE 13.3   Illustration of Two Different Technologies

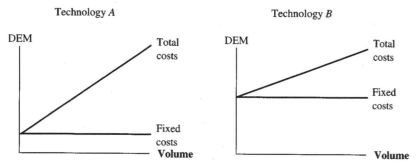

Technology *A* has higher variable costs and lower fixed costs than does technology *B*. Technology *B* has higher operating leverage.

FIGURE 13.4   Illustration of the Effect of a Change in Volume on the Change in Earnings before Interest and Taxes (EBIT)

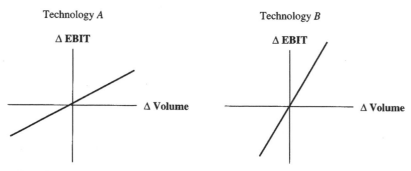

Technology *B* has lower variable costs than *A*, implying a higher contribution margin. The profits of the firm are more responsive to changes in volume under technology *B* than under *A*.

While the above discussion concerns firms, it applies to projects as well. If one cannot estimate a project's beta in another way, one can examine the project's revenues and operating leverage. Those projects whose revenues appear strongly cyclical and whose operating leverage appears high are likely to have high betas. Conversely, weak cyclicality and low operating leverage implies low betas. As mentioned earlier, this approach is unfortunately qualitative in nature. Because start-up projects have little data, quantitative estimates of beta are generally not feasible.

Financial Leverage and Beta

As suggested by their names, operating leverage and financial leverage are analogous concepts. Operating leverage refers to the firm's fixed costs of *production*. Financial leverage is the extent to which a firm relies on debt; a levered firm is a firm with some debt in its capital structure. Because a *levered* firm must make interest payments regardless of the firm's sales, financial leverage refers to the firm's fixed costs of *finance*.

Consider our discussion in Section 11.8 concerning the beta of Jelco. In that example, we estimated beta from the returns of Jelco *stock*. Similarly, we estimated General Tool's beta in Section 13.1 from stock returns. Thus, in each case, we estimated the firm's stock or **equity beta**. One will generally be estimating the equity beta in the real world, since beta is typically estimated from returns on stock. Actually, a firm has an asset beta as well as an equity beta. As the name suggests, the **asset beta** is the beta of the assets of the firm. The asset beta may also be thought of as the beta of the common stock had the firm been financed with only equity.

Imagine an individual who owns all of the firm's debt and all of its equity. In other words, this individual owns the entire firm. What is the beta of her portfolio of the firm's debt and equity?

As with any portfolio, the beta of this portfolio is a weighted average of the betas of the individual items in the portfolio. Hence, we have

$$\beta_{\text{Asset}} = \frac{\text{Debt}}{\text{Debt} + \text{Equity}} \times \beta_{\text{Debt}} + \frac{\text{Equity}}{\text{Debt} + \text{Equity}} \times \beta_{\text{Equity}} \qquad (13.2)$$

where β_{Equity} is the beta of the equity of the *levered* firm. Notice that the beta of debt is multiplied by Debt/(Debt + Equity), the percentage of debt in the capital structure. Similarly, the beta of equity is multiplied by the percentage of equity in the capital structure. Because the portfolio contains both the debt of the firm and the equity of the firm, the beta of the portfolio is the *asset beta*. As we said above, the asset beta can also be viewed as the beta of the common stock had the firm been all-equity.

The beta of debt is very low in practice. If we make the commonplace assumption that the beta of debt is zero, we have

$$\beta_{\text{Asset}} = \frac{\text{Equity}}{\text{Debt} + \text{Equity}} \times \beta_{\text{Equity}} \qquad (13.3)$$

Because Equity/(Debt + Equity) must be below 1 for a levered firm, it follows that $\beta_{\text{Asset}} < \beta_{\text{Equity}}$. Rearranging the above equation, we have

$$\beta_{\text{Equity}} = \beta_{\text{Asset}} \left(1 + \frac{\text{Debt}}{\text{Equity}} \right)$$

The equity beta will always be greater than the asset beta with financial leverage.[4]

Concept Questions

- What are determinants of equity betas?
- What is the difference between an asset beta and an equity beta?

13.3 Extensions of the Basic Model

The Firm versus the Project: *Vive la Difference*

We now assume that the risk of a project differs from that of the firm, while going back to the all-equity assumption. We began the chapter by pointing out that each project should be paired with a financial asset of comparable risk. If a project's beta differs from that of the firm, the project should be discounted at the rate commensurate with its own beta. This is a very important point because firms frequently speak of a *corporate discount rate*. (*Hurdle rate, cutoff rate, benchmark*, and *cost of capital* are frequently used synonymously.) Unless all projects in the corporation are of the same risk, choosing the same discount rate for all projects is incorrect.

● Example

D. D. Ronnelley Co., a publishing firm, may accept a project in computer software. Noting that computer software companies have high betas, the publishing firm views the software venture as more risky than the rest of its business. It should discount the project at a rate commensurate with the risk of software companies. For example, it might use the average beta of a portfolio of publicly traded software firms. Instead, if all projects in D. D. Ronnelley Co. were discounted at the same rate, a bias would result. The firm would accept too many high-risk projects (software ventures) and reject too many low-risk projects (books and magazines). This point is illustrated in Figure 13.5. ●

The D. D. Ronnelley example assumes that the proposed project has identical risk to that of the software industry, allowing the industry beta to be used. However, the beta of a new project may be greater than the beta of existing firms in the same industry because the very newness of the project is likely to increase its responsiveness to economywide movements. For example, a start-up computer venture may fail in a recession, while IBM will still be around. Conversely, in an economywide expansion, the venture may grow much faster than the old-line computer firms.

Fortunately, a slight adjustment is all that is needed here. The new venture should be assigned a somewhat higher beta than that of the industry to reflect added risk. The adjustment is necessarily *ad hoc*, so no formula can be given. Our experience indicates that this approach is widespread in practice today.

However, a problem does arise for the rare project constituting its own industry. For example, consider the firms providing consumer shopping by television. Only a very few such firms have publicly traded shares. So, any beta estimate will be suspect.

---

[4] It can be shown that the relationship between a firm's asset beta and its equity beta with corporate taxes is

$$\beta_{\text{Equity}} = \beta_{\text{Asset}} \left[1 + (1 - T_C) \frac{\text{Debt}}{\text{Equity}} \right]$$

See Chapter 18 for more details.

FIGURE 13.5   Relationship between the Firm's Cost of Capital and the Security Market Line

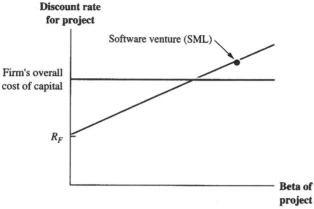

Use of a firm's cost of capital may lead to incorrect capital-budgeting decisions. Projects with high risk should be discounted at a high rate. By using the firm's cost of equity, the firm is likely to accept too many high-risk projects.

Projects with low risk should be discounted at a low rate. By using the firm's cost of capital, the firm is likely to reject too many low-risk projects.

What beta should be used in the rare case when an industrywide beta is not appropriate? One approach, which considers the determinants of the project's beta, was treated earlier in this chapter. Unfortunately, that approach is only qualitative in nature.

The Cost of Capital with Debt

Section 13.1 showed how to choose the discount rate when a project is all-equity financed. In this section, we discuss an adjustment when the project is financed with both debt and equity.

Suppose a firm uses both debt and equity to finance its investments. If the firm pays r_B for its debt financing and r_S for its equity, what is the overall or average cost of its capital? The cost of equity is r_S, as discussed in earlier sections. The cost of debt is the firm's borrowing rate, r_B. If a firm uses both debt and equity, the cost of capital is a weighted average of each. This works out to be

$$\frac{S}{S+B}r_S + \frac{B}{S+B}r_B$$

The weights in the formula are, respectively, the proportion of total value represented by the equity

$$\frac{S}{S+B}$$

and the proportion of total value represented by debt

$$\frac{B}{S+B}$$

This is only natural. If the firm had issued no debt and was therefore an all-equity firm, its average cost of capital would equal its cost of equity, r_S. At the other extreme, if the firm had issued so much debt that its equity was valueless, it would be an all-debt firm, and its average cost of capital would be its cost of debt, r_B.

Of course, interest is tax deductible at the corporate level (to be treated in more detail in Chapter 16). The after-tax cost of debt is

$$\text{Cost of debt (after corporate tax)} = r_B \times (1 - T_C)$$

Assembling these results, we get the average cost of capital (after tax) for the firm:

$$\text{Average cost of capital} = \left(\frac{S}{S + B}\right) \times r_S + \left(\frac{B}{S + B}\right) \times r_B \times (1 - T_C) \qquad (13.4)$$

Because the average cost of capital is a weighting of its cost of equity and its cost of debt, it is usually referred to as the **weighted average cost of capital** r_{WACC}, and from now on we will use this term.

● Example

We can compute the r_{WACC} for a firm in Denmark whose debt has a market value of DEK40 million and whose shares have a market value of DEK60 million (3 million outstanding shares each selling for DEK20 per share). The firm pays a 15 per cent rate of interest on its new debt and has a beta of 1.41. The corporate tax rate is 34 per cent. (Assume that the SML holds, that the risk premium on the market is 8.5 per cent and that the current Treasury bill rate is 11 per cent.)

To compute the r_{WACC} using equation (13.4), we must know (1) the after-tax cost of debt, $r_B \times (1 - T_C)$, (2) the cost of equity, r_S, and (3) the proportions of debt and equity used by the firm. These three values are computed below.

1. The pretax cost of debt is 15 per cent, implying an after-tax cost of 9.9 per cent [$15\% \times (1 - 0.34)$].

2. The cost of equity capital is computed by using the SML:

$$\begin{aligned} r_S &= R_F + \beta \times [\overline{R}_M - R_F] \\ &= 11\% + 1.41 \times 8.5\% \\ &= 23.0\% \end{aligned}$$

3. The proportions of debt and equity are computed from the market values of debt and equity. Because the market value of the firm is DEK100 million (DEK40 million + DEK60 million), the proportions of debt and equity are 40 and 60 per cent, respectively.

The cost of equity, r_S, is 23.0 per cent, and the after-tax cost of debt, $r_B \times (1 - T_C)$, is 9.9 per cent. B is DEK40 million and S is DEK60 million. Therefore,

$$\begin{aligned} r_{\text{WACC}} &= \frac{B}{B + S} \times r_B \times (1 - T_C) + \frac{S}{B + S} \times r_S \\ &= \left(\frac{40}{100} \times 9.9\%\right) + \left(\frac{60}{100} \times 23.0\%\right) = 17.8\% \end{aligned}$$

This procedure is presented in chart form below:

(1) *Financing components*	*(2)* *Market values*	*(3)* *Weight*	*(4)* *Cost of capital (after corporate tax)*	*(5)* *Weighted cost of capital*
Debt	DEK40,000,000	0.40	$15\% \times (1 - 0.34) = 9.9\%$	4.0%
Equity	DEK60,000,000	0.60	$11\% + 1.41 \times 8.5\% = 23.0\%$	13.8%
	DEK100,000,000	1.00		17.8%

The weights we used in the previous example were market-value weights. Market-value weights are more appropriate than book-value weights because the market values of the securities are closer to the actual dollars that would be received from their sale. ●

● **Example**
Suppose that a Danish firm has a current debt-equity ratio of 0.6, a cost of debt of 15.15 per cent, and a cost of equity of 20 per cent. The corporate tax rate is 34 per cent.

Our first step calls for transforming the debt-to-equity (*B/S*) ratio to a debt-to-value ratio. A *B/S* ratio of 0.6 implies 6 parts debt for 10 parts equity. Since value is equal to the sum of the debt plus the equity, the debt-to-value ratio is $6/(6 + 10) = 0.375$.

Similarly, the equity-to-value ratio is $10/(6 + 10) = 0.625$. The r_{WACC} will then be

$$r_{WACC} = \left(\frac{S}{S + B}\right) \times r_S + \left(\frac{B}{S + B}\right) \times r_B \times (1 - T_C)$$

$$= 0.625 \times 20\% + 0.375 \times 15.15\% \times (0.66) = 16.25\%$$

Suppose the firm is considering taking on a warehouse renovation that is expected to yield cost savings of DEK12 million a year for six years. Using the NPV equation and discounting the six years of expected cash flows from the renovation at the r_{WACC}, we have[5]

$$NPV = -DEK50 + \frac{DEK12}{(1 + r_{WACC})} + \ldots + \frac{DEK12}{(1 + r_{WACC})^6}$$

$$= -DEK50 + DEK12 \times A^6_{1625}$$

$$= -DEK50 + (12 \times 3.66)$$

$$= -DEK6.07$$

Should the firm take on the warehouse renovation? The project has a negative NPV using the firm's r_{WACC}. This means that the financial markets offer superior projects in the same risk class (namely, the firm's risk class). The answer is clear: The firm should reject the project. ●

---

[5] This discussion of WACC has been based on perpetual cash flows. However, an important paper by J. Miles and R. Ezzel (1980) 'The weighted average cost of capital, perfect capital markets and project life: A clarification', *Journal of Financial and Quantitative Analysis*, September, shows that the WACC is appropriate even when cash flows are not perpetual.

13.4 Summary and Conclusions

Earlier chapters on capital budgeting assumed that projects generate riskless cash flows. The appropriate discount rate in that case is the riskless interest rate. Of course, most cash flows from real-world capital-budgeting projects are risky. This chapter discusses the discount rate when cash flows are risky.

1. A firm with excess cash can either pay a dividend or make a capital expenditure. Because stockholders can reinvest the dividend in risky financial assets, the expected return on a capital-budgeting project should be at least as great as the expected return on a financial asset of comparable risk.
2. The expected return on any asset is dependent upon its beta. Thus, we showed how to estimate the beta of a stock. The appropriate procedure employs regression analysis on historical returns.
3. We considered the case of a project whose beta risk was equal to that of the firm. If the firm is unlevered, the discount rate on the project is equal to

$$R_F + \beta \times (\bar{R}_M - R_F)$$

where $\bar{R}_M$ is the expected return on the market portfolio and R_F is the risk-free rate. In words, the discount rate on the project is equal to the CAPM's estimate of the expected return on the security.
4. If the project's beta differs from that of the firm, the discount rate should be based on the project's beta. The project's beta can generally be estimated by determining the average beta of the project's industry.
5. The beta of a company is a function of a number of factors. Perhaps the three most important are

   • Cyclicality of revenues
   • Operating leverage
   • Financial leverage

6. Sometimes one should not use the average beta of the project's industry as an estimate of the beta of the project. In this case, one can estimate the project's beta by considering the project's cyclicality of revenues and its operating leverage. This approach is qualitative in nature.
7. If a firm uses debt, the discount rate to use is the r_{WACC}. In order to calculate r_{WACC}, the cost of equity and the cost of debt applicable to a project must be estimated. If the project is similar to the firm, the cost of equity can be estimated using the SML for the firm's equity. Conceptually, a dividend-growth model could be used as well, though it is likely to be far less accurate in practice.

KEY TERMS

Cost of equity   300
Operating leverage   305
Equity beta   307

Asset beta   307
Weighted average cost
   of capital (r_{WACC})   310

QUESTIONS AND PROBLEMS

Beta and the Cost of Equity

13.1 Furniture Depot NV, is an all-equity firm with a beta of 0.95. The market-risk premium is 9 per cent and the risk-free rate is 5 per cent. The company must decide whether or not to undertake the project that requires an immediate investment of NLG1.2 million and will generate annual after-tax cash flows of NLG340,000 at year-end for 5 years. If the project has the same risk as the firm as a whole, should Furniture Depot undertake the project?

13.2 The correlation between the returns on Ceramics Craftsman plc, and the returns on the UK equity market 0.675. The variance of the returns on Ceramics Craftsman plc, is 0.004225, and the variance of the returns on the UK equity market is 0.001467. What is the beta of Ceramics Craftsman shares?

13.3 The returns from the past 12 quarters on Travis Manufacturing and the market are listed below.

Travis	Market
−0.009	0.023
0.051	0.058
−0.001	−0.020
−0.045	−0.050
0.085	0.071
0.000	0.012
−0.080	−0.075
0.020	0.050
0.125	0.120
0.110	0.049
−0.100	−0.030
0.040	0.028

a. What is the beta of Travis Manufacturing shares?
b. Is Travis's beta higher or lower than the beta of the average stock?

13.4 The following table lists possible rates of return on two risky assets, M and J. The table also lists their joint probabilities, that is, the probability that they will occur simultaneously.

R_M	R_J	$Prob(R_M, R_J)$
0.16	0.16	0.10
0.16	0.18	0.06
0.16	0.22	0.04
0.18	0.18	0.12
0.18	0.20	0.36
0.18	0.22	0.12
0.20	0.18	0.02
0.20	0.20	0.04
0.20	0.22	0.04
0.20	0.24	0.10

a. List the possible values for R_M and the probabilities that correspond to those values.
b. Compute the following items for R_M.
   i. expected value
   ii. variance
   iii. standard deviation
c. List the possible values for R_J and the probabilities that correspond to those values.
d. Compute the following items for R_J.
   i. expected value
   ii. variance
   iii. standard deviation
e. Calculate the covariance and correlation coefficient of R_M and R_J.
f. Assume M is the market portfolio. Calculate the beta coefficient for security J.

13.5 If you use the stock beta and the security market line to compute the discount rate for a project, what assumptions are you implicitly making?

13.6 Atlantic Cosmetics is evaluating a project to produce a perfume line. Atlantic currently produces no-body scent products. Atlantic Cosmetics is an all-equity firm.
a. Should Atlantic Cosmetics use its stock beta to evaluate the project?
b. How should Atlantic Cosmetics compute the beta to evaluate the project?

13.7 The following table lists possible rates of return on Blue Jay shares and debt, and on the market portfolio. The corporate tax rate is 35 per cent. The corresponding probabilities are also listed.

State	Probability	Return on equity (%)	Return on debt (%)	Return on the market (%)
1	0.1	3%	8%	5%
2	0.3	8	8	10
3	0.4	20	10	15
4	0.2	15	10	20

     a. What is the beta of Blue Jay debt?

     b. What is the beta of Blue Jay shares?

     c. If the debt-to-equity ratio of Blue Jay is 0.5, what is the asset beta of Blue Jay?

13.8 Is the discount rate for the projects of a levered firm higher or lower than the cost of equity computed using the security market line? Why? (Consider only projects that have similar risk to that of the firm.)

13.9 What factors determine the beta of a share? Define and describe each.

Weighted Average Cost of Capital

13.10 The equity beta for National Napkin Company is 1.29. National Napkin has a debt-to-equity ratio of 1.0. The expected return on the market is 13 per cent. The risk-free rate is 7 per cent. The cost of debt capital is 7 per cent. The corporate tax rate is 35 per cent.

     a. What is National Napkin's cost of equity?

     b. What is National Napkin's weighted average cost of capital?

13.11 Calculate the weighted average cost of capital for the Luxury Porcelain Company. The book value of Luxury's outstanding debt is GBP60 million. Currently, the debt is trading at 120 per cent of book value and is priced to yield 12 per cent. The 5 million outstanding shares of Luxury Porcelain are selling for GBP20 per share. The required return on Luxury stock is 18 per cent. The tax rate is 25 per cent.

13.12 M. Silberman Co. has 20 million shares outstanding that are currently being sold for DEM25 per share. The firm's debt is publicly traded at 95 per cent of its face value of DEM180 million. The cost of debt is 10 per cent and the cost of equity is 20 per cent. What is the weighted average cost of capital for the firm? Assume the corporate tax rate is 40 per cent.

13.13 Bosman NV is considering a new project that costs BEF25 million. The project will generate after tax (year-end) cash flows of BEF7 million for five years. The firm has a debt-to-equity ratio of 0.75. The cost of equity is 15 per cent and the cost of debt is 9 per cent. The corporate tax rate is 35 per cent. It appears that the project has the same risk of the overall firm. Should Bosman take on the project?

APPENDIX 13A

TAX SYSTEMS AND CAPITAL BUDGETING

The specification of the cost of equity capital in terms of being before shareholder tax or after shareholder tax is a problem which has to be confronted in capital budgeting in Europe. The argument that is advanced here critically pivots about whether the required return is stated for a company located in a country under the imputation tax system or under the classical tax system. The rationale is as follows. The UK, Germany, France, Spain and many of the countries in the European Union have adopted the imputation tax system. If a basic rate tax-paying shareholder achieves a gross of tax return equal to the risk-free return plus the excess return, he would be due to pay tax on this. Under the imputation system, a company is first of all subject to corporation tax, but on payment of a dividend, no further tax is paid by the company—although, in the UK, advance corporation tax is paid. The dividend is said to be net of a tax credit, the amount of which varies from country to country and from time to time. It is usually (but not always) represented by the basic personal tax rate. Assuming a 25 per cent basic tax rate (and a tax credit at this rate), a dividend of 75 would, for purposes of shareholder income, count as a gross amount of 100 with tax of 25 credited as already paid. In other words, the dividend paid would effectively be net of personal tax at the basic rate.

The cost of equity capital is normally viewed as a shareholder opportunity cost. To compare a gross return achieved from R_F plus $(\bar{R}_M - R_F)$ to a net of tax dividend received from a company is clearly illogical. We must apply tax to the risk-free return plus the excess return. This leads us towards an estimate of the cost of equity capital under the imputation system as:

$$R_F(1 - T_p) + \beta\,(\bar{R}_M - R_F)\,(1 - T_p)$$

where R_F and $(\bar{R}_M - R_F)$ are both quoted gross and T_p is the personal tax rate. Remember that this is the rate that the company must earn on equity financed investment to meet equity investors' requirements. This should be the approach used in countries with imputation tax systems (see Chapter 1).

It contrasts with the classical tax system, which is effective in the USA, Belgium, Denmark, Luxembourg and the Netherlands. Under the classical tax system, the company pays tax on its income. Upon payment of a dividend, it further deducts shareholder tax at the standard rate and remits this to the tax authorities. Thus a gross return of $R_F + (\bar{R}_M - R_F)$ achieved from investment in the stock market directly contrasts to a dividend return before the deduction of shareholder tax by the company. Both of such receipts would be subject to shareholder tax. Thus when we calculate $R_F + \beta(\bar{R}_M - R_F)$ on a gross of tax basis, this is directly comparable (in tax terms) to the return received from a company before shareholder dividend tax. In order to specify a bottom line required return for companies to achieve before shareholder dividend tax, we should do so using the gross of tax value of R_F plus $\beta(\bar{R}_M - R_F)$. Under the classical tax system, an estimate of the cost of equity capital would be:

$$R_F + \beta(\bar{R}_M - R_F)$$

where R_F and $(\bar{R}_M - R_F)$ are expressed gross of personal tax. This approach is the logical one to use in the USA and those European (and other) countries which use a classical system of corporation tax. These conclusions are congruent with those of Ashton.[6]

---

[6] D. J. Ashton (1989), 'The cost of capital and the imputation tax system', *Journal of Business Finance and Accounting,* Spring, 75–88.

PART IV

Capital Structure and Dividend Policy

14 Corporate-Financing Decisions and Efficient Capital Markets   319
15 Long-Term Financing: An Introduction   344
16 Capital Structure: Basic Concepts   357
17 Capital Structure: Limits to the Use of Debt   388
18 Valuation and Capital Budgeting for the Levered Firm   408
19 Dividend Policy: Why Does It Matter?   431

Part II discussed the capital-budgeting decisions of the firm. We argued that the objective of the firm should be to create value from its capital-budgeting decisions. To do this the firm must find investments with a positive net present value. In Part IV we concentrate on financing decisions. As with capital-budgeting decisions, the firm seeks to create value with its financing decisions. To do this the firm must find positive NPV financing arrangements. However, financial markets do not provide as many opportunities for positive NPV transactions as do non-financial markets. We show that the sources of NPV in financing are taxes, bankruptcy costs, and agency costs.

Chapter 14 introduces the concept of efficient markets, where current market prices reflect available information. We describe several forms of efficiency: the weak form, the semistrong form, and the strong form. The chapter offers a number of important lessons for the corporate financial manager in understanding the logic behind efficient financial markets.

In Chapter 15 we describe the basic types of long-term financing: common stock, preferred stock and bonds. We then briefly analyse the major trends and patterns of long-term financing.

We consider the firm's overall capital-structure decision in Chapters 16 and 17. In general, a firm can choose any capital structure it desires: common stocks, bonds, preferred stocks, and so on. How should a firm choose its capital structure? Changing the capital structure of the firm changes the way the firm pays out its cash flows. Firms that borrow pay lower taxes than firms that do not. Because of corporate taxes, the value of a firm that borrows may be higher than the value of one that does not. However, with costly bankruptcy, a firm that borrows may have lower value. The combined effects of taxes and bankruptcy costs can produce an optimal capital structure.

Chapter 18 discusses capital budgeting for firms with some debt in their capital structures. It extends some of the material of Chapter 13. This chapter presents three alternative valuation methods: the weighted-average-cost-of-capital approach, the flows-to-equity approach, and the adjusted-present-value approach.

We discuss dividend policy in Chapter 19. It seems surprising that much empirical evidence and logic suggest that dividend policy does not matter. There are some good reasons for firms to pay low levels of dividends: lower taxes and costs of issuing new equity. However, there are also some good reasons to pay high levels of dividends: to reduce agency costs and to satisfy low-tax, high-income clientele.

CHAPTER

14 Corporate Financing Decisions and Efficient Capital Markets

The section on value concentrated on the firm's capital-budgeting decisions—the lefthand side of the balance sheet of the firm. This chapter begins our analysis of corporate-financing decisions—the righthand side of the balance sheet. We take the firm's capital-budgeting decision as fixed in this section of the text.

The point of this chapter is to introduce the concept of *efficient capital markets* and its implications for corporate finance. Efficient capital markets are those in which current market prices reflect available information. This means that current market prices reflect the underlying present value of securities, and there is no way to make unusual or excess profits by using the available information.

This concept has profound implications for financial managers, because market efficiency eliminates many value-enhancing strategies of firms. In an efficient market, positive NPV opportunities can't exist. In particular, we show that in an efficient market

1. Financial managers cannot time issues of bonds and stocks.
2. A firm can sell as many shares or bonds as it wants without fear of depressing price.
3. Share and bond markets cannot be affected by firms artificially increasing earnings (that is, cooking the books).

Ultimately, whether or not capital markets are efficient is an empirical question. We describe several of the important studies that have been carried out to examine efficient markets.

14.1 Can Financing Decisions Create Value?

Earlier parts of the book show how to evaluate projects according to the net-present-value criterion. The real world is a competitive one where projects with positive net present value are not always easy to come by. However, through hard work or through good fortune, a firm can identify winning projects. For example, to create value from capital-budgeting decisions, the firm is likely to

1. Locate an unsatisfied demand for a particular product or service.
2. Create a barrier to make it more difficult for other firms to compete.
3. Produce products or services at lower cost than competition.
4. Be the first to develop a new product.

The next five chapters concern financing decisions. Typical financing decisions include how much debt and equity to sell, what types of debt and equity to sell, and when to sell debt and equity. Just as the net-present-value criterion was used to evaluate capital-budgeting projects, we now want to use the same criterion to evaluate financing decisions.

Though the procedure for evaluating financing decisions is identical to the procedure for evaluating projects, the results are different. It turns out that the typical firm has many more capital-expenditure opportunities with positive net present value than financing opportunities with positive net present values. In fact, we later show that some plausible financial models imply that no valuable financial opportunities exist at all.

Though this dearth of profitable financing opportunities will be examined in detail later, a few remarks are in order now. We maintain that there are basically three ways to create valuable financing opportunities:

1. *Fool Investors*   Assume that a firm can raise capital either by issuing shares or by issuing a more complex security, say, a combination of shares and warrants. Suppose that, in truth, 100 shares are worth the same as 50 units of our complex security. If investors have a misguided, overly optimistic view of the complex security, perhaps the 50 units can be sold for more than the 100 shares of stock can. Clearly this complex security provides a valuable financing opportunity because the firm is getting more than fair value for it.

Financial managers try to package securities to receive the greatest value. A cynic might view this as attempting to fool investors. However, empirical evidence suggests that investors cannot easily be fooled. Thus, one must be sceptical that value can easily be created.

The theory of efficient capital markets expresses this idea. In its extreme form, it says that all securities are appropriately priced at all times, implying that the market as a whole is very shrewd indeed. Thus, corporate managers should not attempt to create value by fooling investors. Instead, managers must create value in other ways.

2. *Reduce Costs or Increase Subsidies*   We show later in the book that certain forms of financing have greater tax advantages than other forms. Clearly, a firm packaging securities to minimize taxes can increase firm value. In addition, any financing technique involves other costs. For example, investment bankers, lawyers and accountants must be paid. A firm packaging securities to minimize these costs can also increase its value. Finally, any financing vehicle that provides subsidies is valuable. This last possibility is illustrated below.

● Example

Suppose Bailey Electronics Company is thinking about relocating its plant from the UK to Poland where labour costs are lower. In the hope that it can stay in the UK, the company has submitted an application to a UK government department to issue GBP2 million in special five-year, tax-exempt industrial bonds (these are incidentally fictitious just in case you think you've missed an opportunity). The coupon rate on these industrial bonds in the UK is currently 5 per cent. This is an attractive rate because the normal cost of debt capital for Bailey Electronics Company is 10 per cent. What is the NPV of this potential financing transaction?

If the application is accepted and the industrial revenue bonds are issued by the Bailey Electronics Company, the NPV is

$$\text{NPV} = \text{GBP2,000,000} - \left[\frac{\text{GBP100,000}}{1.1} + \frac{\text{GBP100,000}}{(1.1)^2} \right.$$
$$\left. + \frac{\text{GBP100,000}}{(1.1)^3} + \frac{\text{GBP100,000}}{(1.1)^4} + \frac{\text{GBP2,100,000}}{(1.1)^5} \right]$$
$$= \text{GBP2,000,000} - \text{GBP1,620,921}$$
$$= \text{GBP379,079}$$

This transaction has a positive NPV. The Bailey Electronics Company obtains subsidized financing where the amount of the subsidy is GBP379,079. ●

3. *Create a New Security*   There has been a surge in financial innovation in recent years. For example, in a speech on financial innovation, Merton Miller asked the rhetorical question, 'Can any twenty-year period in recorded history have witnessed even a tenth as much new development?'[1] Where corporations once issued only straight debt and straight ordinary shares, they now issue zero-coupon bonds, adjustable-rate notes, floating-rate notes, putable bonds, credit-enhanced debt securities, receivable-backed securities, adjusted-rate preferred stock, convertible adjustable preferred stock, auction-rate preferred stock, single-point adjustable-rate stock, convertible exchangeable preferred stock, adjustable-rate convertible debt, zero-coupon convertible debt—to name just a few!

Though the advantage of each instrument is different, one general theme is that these new securities cannot easily be duplicated by combinations of existing securities.[2] Thus, a previously unsatisfied clientele may pay extra for a specialized security catering to its needs. For example, putable bonds let the purchaser sell the bond at a fixed price back to the firm. This innovation creates a price floor, allowing the investor to reduce his or her downside risk. Perhaps risk-averse investors or investors with little knowledge of the bond market would find this feature particularly attractive.

Companies gain from developing unique securities by issuing these securities at high prices. However, we believe that the value captured by the innovator is small in the long run because the innovator usually cannot patent or copyright his idea. Soon, many firms are issuing securities of the same kind, forcing prices down as a result.[3]

---

[1] M. Miller (1986) 'Financial Innovation: The last twenty years and the next', *Journal of Financial and Quantitative Analysis*, December. Actually, financial innovation has occurred even more rapidly in the years following Miller's speech.

[2] Another theme is that many of these new securities are specifically designed to reduce either the investor's or the issuing corporation's taxes. This theme is part of (2) above: reduce costs or increase subsidies.

[3] Most financial innovations originally come from investment banks and are then sold to firms. Peter Tufano (1990) 'Financial innovation and first-mover advantages', *Journal of Financial Economics*, **25**, 213–40, looked at 58 financial innovations (including original-issue deep-discount bonds) to examine how well investment banks are compensated for developing new financial products. He finds investment banks underwrite significantly more public offerings of the products they create. His study does not directly address the question of whether investment banks or corporations obtain most of the benefits of new financial products. However, it is clear that investment banks benefit substantially from creating new products.

Raj Varma and Donald Chambers (1990) 'The role of financial innovation in raising capital', *Journal of Financial Economics*, **26**, 289–98, look at how firms have benefited from issuing original issue deep-discount bonds after TEFRA. They report no gains.

This brief introduction sets the stage for the next five chapters of the book. The rest of this chapter examines the efficient-capital-markets hypothesis. We show that if capital markets are efficient, corporate managers cannot create value by fooling investors. This is quite important, because managers must create value in other, perhaps more difficult, ways. The following four chapters concern the costs and subsidies of various forms of financing. A discussion of new financing instruments is postponed until later chapters of the text.

Concept Question

- List the three ways financing decisions can create value.

14.2   A Description of Efficient Capital Markets

An efficient capital market is one in which stock prices fully reflect available information. To illustrate how an efficient market works, suppose the F-stop Camera Company (FCC) is attempting to develop a camera that will double the speed of the auto-focusing system now available. FCC believes this research has positive NPV. The value of the new auto-focusing system will depend on demand for cameras at the time of the discovery, as well as on many other factors.

Now consider a share of stock in FCC. What determines the willingness of investors to hold shares of FCC at a particular price? One important factor is the probability that FCC will be the company to develop the new auto-focusing system first. In an efficient market we would expect the price of the shares of FCC to increase if this probability increases.

Suppose a well-known engineer is hired by FCC to help develop the new auto-focusing system. In an efficient market, what will happen to FCC's share price when this is announced? If the well-known scientist is paid a salary that fully reflects his or her contribution to the firm, the price of the shares will not necessarily change. Suppose, instead, that hiring the scientist is a positive NPV transaction. In this case, the price of shares in FCC will increase because the market for scientists is imperfect and FCC can pay the scientist a salary below his or her true value to the company.

When will the increase in the price of FCC's shares take place? Assume that the hiring announcement is made in a press release on Wednesday morning. In an efficient market, the price of shares in FCC will immediately adjust to this new information. Investors should not be able to buy the stock on Wednesday afternoon and make a profit on Thursday. This would imply that it took the stock market a day to realize the implication of the FCC press release. The efficient-market hypothesis predicts that the price of FCC shares on Wednesday afternoon will already reflect the information contained in the Wednesday morning press release.

The **efficient-market hypothesis** (EMH) has implications for investors and for firms.

- Because information is reflected in prices immediately, investors should only expect to obtain a normal rate of return. Awareness of information when it is released does an investor no good. The price adjusts before the investor has time to trade on it.
- Firms should expect to receive the *fair* value for securities that they sell. Fair means that the price they receive for the securities they issue is the present

value. Thus, valuable financing opportunities that arise from fooling investors are unavailable in efficient capital markets.

Some people spend their entire careers trying to pick shares that will outperform the average. For any given share, they can learn not only what has happened in the past to the share price and dividends, but also what the company earnings have been, how much debt it owes, what taxes it pays, what businesses it is in, what market share it has for its products, how well it is doing in each of its businesses, what new investments it has planned, how sensitive it is to the economy, and so on.

If you want to learn about a given company and its shares, an enormous amount of information is available to you. The preceding list only scratches the surface; we haven't even included the information that only insiders know. **Inside information** is information possessed by people in special positions inside the company, such as the major officers of the company or people farther down in the company who might be aware of some special discovery or new development.

Not only is there a lot to know about any given company, there is also a powerful motive for doing so: the profit motive. If you know more about a company than other investors in the marketplace, you can profit from that knowledge by investing in the company's shares if you have good news or selling it if you have bad news.

There are other ways to use your information. If you could convince investors that you have reliable information about the fortunes of companies, you might start a newsletter and sell investors that information. You could even charge a varying rate depending on how fresh the information is. You could sell the monthly standard report for a subscription price of CHF100 per year, but for an extra CHF300 a subscriber could get special interim once-a-week reports. For CHF5,000 per year you could offer to telephone the customer as soon as you had a new idea or a new piece of information. This may sound a bit farfetched, but it is what many sellers of market information actually do.

The logical consequence of all of this information being available, studied, sold, and used in an effort to make profits from stock market trading is that the market becomes *efficient*. A market is efficient with respect to information if there is no way to make unusual or excess profits by using that information. When a market is efficient with respect to information, we say that prices *incorporate* the information. Without knowing anything special about a stock, an investor in an efficient market expects to earn an equilibrium required return from an investment, and a company expects to pay an equilibrium cost of capital.[4]

● Example
Suppose IBM announces it has invented a microprocessor that will make its computer 30 times faster than existing computers. The price of a share of IBM should increase immediately to a new equilibrium level. ●

Figure 14.1 presents several possible adjustments in stock prices. The solid line represents the path taken by the stock in an efficient market. In this case, the price adjusts immediately to the new information so that no further changes take place in the price of the stock. The dotted line depicts a delayed reaction. Here it takes the market 30 days to fully absorb the information. Finally, the broken line illustrates an

---

[4] In Chapter 11 we analyse how the required return on a risky asset is determined.

overreaction and subsequent correction back to the true price. The broken line and the dotted line show the paths that the stock price might take in an inefficient market. If the price of the stock takes several days to adjust, trading profits would be available to investors who bought at the date of the announcement and sold once the price settled back to the equilibrium.[5]

Concept Question

• Can you define an efficient market?

FIGURE 14.1   Reaction of Share Price to New Information in Efficient and Inefficient Markets

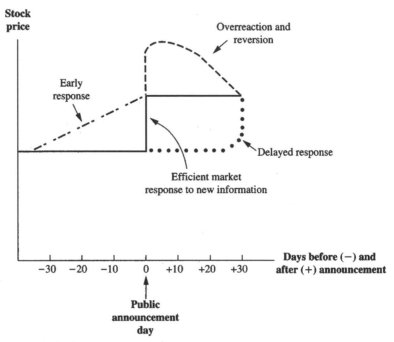

Efficient-market response: The price instantaneously adjusts to and fully reflects new information; there is no tendency for subsequent increases and decreases.
Early response: New information is leaked and price responds before public dissemination.
Delayed response: The price partially adjusts to the new information; 30 days elapse before the price completely reflects the new information.
Overreaction: The price overadjusts to the new information; there is a bubble in the price sequence.

---

[5] Now you should understand the following short story. A student was walking down the hall with his finance professor when they both saw a $20 bill on the ground. As the student bent down to pick it up, the professor shook his head slowly and, with a look of disappointment on his face, said patiently to the student, 'Don't bother. If it was really there, someone else would have already picked it up.'

   The moral of the story reflects the logic of the efficient-market hypothesis: if you think you have found a pattern in stock prices or a simple device for picking winners, you probably have not. If there were such a simple way to make money, someone else would have found it before. Furthermore, if people tried to exploit the information, their efforts would become self-defeating and the pattern would disappear.

14.3   The Different Types of Efficiency

In our previous discussion, we assumed that the market responds immediately to all available information. In actuality, certain information may affect stock prices more quickly than other information. To handle differential response rates, researchers separate information into different types. The most common classification system speaks of three types: information on past prices, publicly available information and all information. The effect of these three information sets on prices is examined below.[6]

The Weak Form

Imagine a trading strategy that recommends buying a share when it has gone up three days in a row and recommends selling a share when it has gone down three days in a row. This strategy only uses information on past prices. It does not use any other information, such as earnings forecasts, merger announcements, or money-supply figures. A capital market is said to be *weakly efficient* or to satisfy **weak-form efficiency** if it fully incorporates the information in past stock prices. Thus, the above strategy would not be able to generate profits if weak-form efficiency holds.

Often weak-form efficiency is represented mathematically as

$$P_t = P_{t-1} + \text{Expected return} + \text{Random error}_t \qquad (14.1)$$

Equation (14.1) says that the price today is equal to the sum of the last observed price plus the expected return on the stock plus a random component occurring over the interval. The last observed price could have occurred yesterday, last week or last month, depending on one's sampling interval. The expected return is a function of a security's risk and would be based on the models of risk and return in previous chapters. The random component is due to new information on the stock. It could be either positive or negative and has an expectation of zero. The random component in any one period is unrelated to the random component in any past period. Hence, this component is not predictable from past prices. If stock prices follow (14.1), they are said to follow a **random walk**.

Weak-form efficiency is about the weakest type of efficiency that we would expect a financial market to display because historical price information is the easiest kind of information about a share to acquire. If it were possible to make extraordinary profits simply by finding the patterns in the share price movements, everyone would do it, and any profits would disappear in the scramble.

The effect of competition can be seen in Figure 14.2. Suppose the price of a share displayed a cyclical pattern, as indicated by the wavy curve. Shrewd investors would buy at the low points, forcing those prices up. Conversely, they would sell at the high points, forcing prices down. Through competition, the cyclical regularities would be eliminated, leaving only random fluctuations.

By denying that future market movements can be predicted from past movements, we are denying the profitability of a host of techniques falling under the heading of technical analysis. The term **technical analysis** refers to attempts to predict the future from the patterns of past price movements. Furthermore, we are denigrating the work of all of their followers, who are called *technical analysts*.

---

[6] This is due to H. V. Roberts (1959) 'Stock market 'patterns' and financial analysis: Methodological suggestions', *Journal of Finance* , March.

FIGURE 14.2   Investor Behaviour Tends to Eliminate Cyclical Patterns

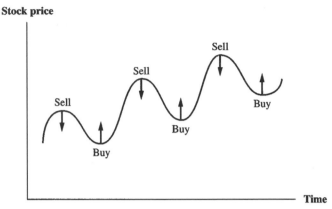

If a share's price has followed a cyclical pattern, the pattern will be
quickly eliminated in an efficient market. A random pattern will
emerge as investors buy at the trough and sell at the peak of a cycle.

To provide some flavour to technical analysis, consider two commonly used
approaches. First, many technical analysts believe that share prices are likely to follow
a head-and-shoulders pattern. This is presented in the lefthand side of Figure 14.3. An
analyst at point *A*, anticipating a head-and-shoulders pattern, might very well buy the
stock and hopefully hold it for a short-term gain. An analyst at point *B*, anticipating the
completion of the pattern, would sell the stock short.

Second, other analysts believe that stocks making three tops are likely to fall in
price. This pattern is presented in the righthand side of Figure 14.3. An analyst who, at
point *C*, discovers that a triple-tops pattern has occurred, might sell the stock.

At this point, one might wonder why anyone would restrict his or her information
to the set of past prices. Surprisingly, many technical analysts do just that, saying that
all relevant information on a security's future price movement is contained in the

FIGURE 14.3   Two Widely Believed Technical Patterns

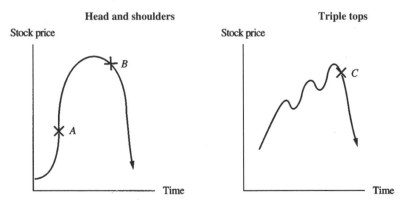

Technical analysts frequently claim that the price of a share is likely to follow a
head-and-shoulders pattern or a triple-tops pattern. According to a technical analyst,
if a head-and-shoulders pattern can be identified early enough, an investor might
like to buy at point *A* and sell at point *B*. A triple-tops pattern occurs when three
highs are followed by a precipitous drop. If a triple-tops pattern can be identified
early enough, an investor might like to sell at point *C*.

security's past movement. Other information is considered distracting. John Magee,[7] one of the most renowned of technical analysts, took this approach to an extreme. He reportedly worked on his stock market charts in an office with boarded-up windows. To him, weather was superfluous information that could only impede his task of share selection.

The Semistrong and Strong Forms

If weak-form efficiency is controversial, even more contentious are the two stronger types of efficiency, **semistrong-form efficiency** and **strong-form efficiency**. A market is semistrong-form efficient if prices reflect (incorporate) all publicly available information, including information such as published accounting statements for the firm as well as historical price information. A market is strong-form efficient if prices reflect all information, public or private.

The information set of past prices is a subset of the information set of publicly available information, which, in turn, is a subset of all information. This is shown in Figure 14.4. Thus, strong-form efficiency implies semistrong-form efficiency, and semistrong-form efficiency implies weak-form efficiency. The distinction between semistrong-form efficiency and weak-form efficiency is that semistrong-form efficiency requires not only that the market be efficient with respect to historical price information, but that all of the information available to the public be reflected in price.

FIGURE 14.4   **Relationship among Three Different Information Sets**

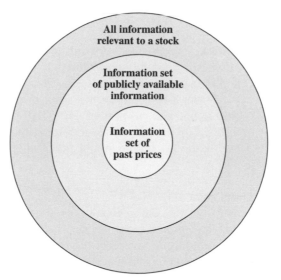

The information set of past prices is a subset of the information set of publicly available information, which in turn is a subset of all information. If prices reflect only information on past prices, the market is weak-form efficient. If prices reflect all publicly available information, the market is semistrong-form efficient. If prices reflect all information, both public and private, the market is strong-form efficient.

---

[7] J. Magee and R. D. Edwards (1985) *Technical Analysis of Stock Trends*, 5th edn, Stock Trends Service, is considered by many to be the bible of technical analysis.

For example, suppose that a company tried the following scheme: whenever it observed that its stock price had risen, the company sold some shares of stock. A market that was only weak-form efficient, and not semistrong-form efficient would still prevent such a scheme from generating positive NPV. According to weak-form efficiency, a recent price rise does not imply that the stock is overvalued.

As another example, suppose a company combines historical information with inside accounting information. One resulting strategy would be to buy back shares of stock before reporting that its earnings had risen. In this way, it could repurchase shares at low prices and sell them at higher prices later on. Because the company has inside information about its own earnings, this strategy is possibly profitable even if the semistrong version of the efficient-market hypothesis holds.

At the furthest end of the spectrum is strong-form efficiency, which incorporates the other two types of efficiency. This form says that anything that is pertinent to the value of the stock and that is known to at least one investor is, in fact, fully incorporated into the stock value. A strict believer in strong-form efficiency would deny that an insider who knew whether a company mining operation had struck gold could profit from that information. Such a devotee of the strong-form efficient-market hypothesis might argue that as soon as the insider tried to trade on his or her information, the market would recognize what was happening and the price would shoot up before he or she could buy any of the stock. Alternatively, sometimes believers in strong-form efficiency take the view that there are no such things as secrets and that as soon as the gold is discovered, the secret gets out.

Are the hypotheses of semistrong-form efficiency and strong-form efficiency good descriptions of how markets work? Expert opinion is divided here. The evidence in support of semistrong-form efficiency is, of course, more compelling than that in support of strong-form efficiency, and for many purposes it seems reasonable to assume that the market is semistrong-form efficient. The extreme of strong-form efficiency seems more difficult to accept. Before we look at the evidence on market efficiency, we will summarize our thinking on the versions of the efficient-market hypothesis in terms of basic economic arguments.

One reason to expect that markets are weak-form efficient is that it is so cheap and easy to find patterns in stock prices. Anyone who can program a computer and knows a little bit of statistics can search for such patterns. It stands to reason that if there were such patterns, people would find and exploit them, in the process causing them to disappear.

Semistrong-form efficiency, though, uses much more sophisticated information and reasoning than weak-form efficiency. An investor must be skilled at economics and statistics, and steeped in the idiosyncrasies of individual industries and companies and their products. Furthermore, to acquire and use such skills requires talent, ability and time. In the jargon of the economist, such an effort is costly and the ability to be successful at it is probably in scarce supply.

As for strong-form efficiency, this is just farther down the road than semistrong-form efficiency. It is difficult to believe that the market is so efficient that someone with true and valuable inside information cannot prosper by using it. It is also difficult to find direct evidence concerning strong-form efficiency. What we have tends to be unfavourable to this hypothesis of market efficiency.

Some Common Misconceptions about the Efficient-Market Hypothesis

No idea in finance has attracted as much attention as that of efficient markets, and not all of the attention has been flattering. To a certain extent this is because much of the criticism has been based on a misunderstanding of what the hypothesis does and does not say. We illustrate three misconceptions below.

The Efficacy of Dart Throwing

When the notion of market efficiency was first publicized and debated in the popular financial press, it was often characterized by the following quote: ' . . . throwing darts at the financial page will produce a portfolio that can be expected to do as well as any managed by professional security analysts'.[8] This is almost, but not quite, true.

All the efficient-market hypothesis really says is that, on average, the manager will not be able to achieve an abnormal or excess return. The excess return is defined with respect to some benchmark expected return that comes from the security market line of Chapter 11 (SML). The investor must still decide how risky a portfolio he or she wants and what expected return it will normally have. A random dart thrower might wind up with all of the darts sticking into one or two high-risk shares that deal in genetic engineering. Would you really want all of your stock investments in two such shares? (Beware, though, a professional portfolio manager could do the same.)

The failure to understand this has often led to a confusion about market efficiency. For example, sometimes it is wrongly argued that market efficiency means that it does not matter what you do because the efficiency of the market will protect the unwary. However, someone once remarked, 'The efficient market protects the sheep from the wolves, but nothing can protect the sheep from themselves'.

What efficiency does say is that the price that a firm will obtain when it sells a share is a fair price in the sense that it reflects the value of that share given the information that is available about it. Shareholders need not worry that they are paying too much for a share with a low dividend or some other characteristic, because the market has already incorporated it into the price. We sometimes say that the information has been *priced out*.

Price Fluctuations

Much of the public is sceptical of efficiency because stock prices fluctuate from day to day. However, this price movement is in no way inconsistent with efficiency, because a share in an efficient market adjusts to new information by changing price. In fact, the absence of price movements in a changing world might suggest an inefficiency.

Shareholder Disinterest

Many laypersons are sceptical that the market price can be efficient if only a fraction of the outstanding shares changes hands on any given day. However, the number of traders in a share on a given day is generally far less than the number of people following the share. This is true because an individual will trade only when his or her appraisal of the value of the share differs enough from the market price to justify incurring brokerage commissions and other transactions costs. Furthermore, even if the number of traders following a share is small relative to the number of outstanding shareholders, the share can be expected to be efficiently priced as long as a number of interested traders use the publicly available information. That is, the share price can reflect the available information even if many shareholders never follow the share and are not considering trading in the near future, and even if some shareholders trade with little or no information. Thus, the empirical findings suggesting that the stock market is predominantly efficient need not be surprising.

---

[8] B. G. Malkiel (1990) *A Random Walk Down Wall Street*, 5th college edn, New York: Norton.

Concept Questions

- Can you describe the three forms of the efficient-market hypothesis?
- What kinds of things could make markets inefficient?
- Does market efficiency mean you can throw darts at a *Wall Street Journal* listing of New York Stock Exchange stocks to pick a portfolio?
- What does it mean to say the price you pay for a stock is fair?

14.4   The Evidence

The record on the efficient-market hypothesis is extensive, and in large measure it is reassuring to advocates of the efficiency of markets. The studies done by academicians fall into broad categories. First, there is evidence as to whether changes of share prices are random. Second are event studies. Third is the record of professionally managed investment firms.

The Weak Form

The random-walk hypothesis, as expressed in equation (14.1), implies that a share's price movement in the past is unrelated to its price movement in the future. The work of Chapter 10 allows us to test this implication. In that chapter, we discussed the concept of correlation between the returns on two different shares. For example, the correlation between the return on General Motors and the return on Ford is likely to be high because both shares are in the same industry. Conversely, the correlation between the return on General Motors and the return on the share of, say, a European fast-food chain is likely to be low.

Financial economists frequently speak of **serial correlation**, which involves only one security. This is the correlation between the current return on a security and the return on the same security over a later period. A positive coefficient of serial correlation for a particular stock indicates a tendency toward *continuation*. That is, a higher-than-average return today is likely to be followed by higher-than-average returns in the future. Similarly, a lower-than-average return today is likely to be followed by lower-than-average returns in the future.

A negative coefficient of serial correlation for a particular share indicates a tendency toward *reversal*. A higher-than-average return today is likely to be followed by lower-than-average returns in the future. Similarly, a lower-than-average return today is likely to be followed by higher-than-average returns in the future. Both significantly positive and significantly negative serial-correlation coefficients are indications of market inefficiencies; in either case, returns today can be used to predict future returns.

Serial correlation coefficients for share returns near zero would be consistent with the random-walk hypothesis. Thus, a current share return that is higher than average is as likely to be followed by lower-than-average returns as by higher-than-average returns. Similarly, a current share return that is lower than average is as likely to be followed by higher-than-average returns as by lower-than-average returns.

Figure 14.5 shows the serial correlation for daily stock-price changes for nine stock markets. These coefficients indicate whether or not there are relationships between yesterday's return and today's return. For example, Germany's coefficient of 0.08 is slightly positive, implying that a higher-than-average return today makes a higher-than-average return tomorrow slightly more likely. Conversely, Belgium's coefficient is slightly negative, implying that a lower-than-average return today makes a higher-than-average return tomorrow slightly more likely.

FIGURE 14.5   **Testing the Random-Walk Hypothesis**

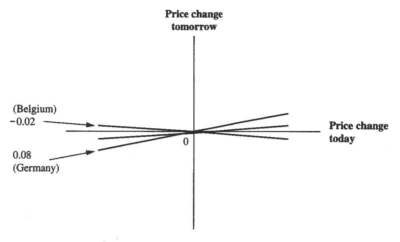

The serial correlation for nine stock markets:

US	0.03	UK	0.08	Switzerland	0.01	France	−0.01	Sweden	0.06
Italy	−0.02	Germany	0.08	Netherlands	0.03	Belgium	−0.02		

Germany's coefficient of 0.08 is slightly positive, implying that a positive return today makes a positive return tomorrow slightly more likely. Belgium's coefficient is negative, implying that a negative return today makes a positive return tomorrow slightly more likely. However, the coefficients are so small relative to estimation error and to transaction costs that the results are generally considered to be consistent with efficient capital markets.

Data from B. H. Solnik (1973). 'A note on the validity of the random walk for European stock prices.' *Journal of Finance,* December.

However, because correlation coefficients can, in principle, vary between −1 and 1, the reported coefficients are quite small. In fact, the coefficients are so small relative to both estimation errors and to transactions costs that the results are generally considered to be consistent with weak-form efficiency.

The weak form of the efficient-market hypothesis has been tested in many other ways as well. Our view of the literature is that the evidence, taken as a whole, is strongly consistent with weak-form efficiency.[9]

This finding raises an interesting thought: If price changes are truly random, why do so many believe that prices follow patterns? The work of Harry Roberts suggests that most people simply do not know what randomness looks like. For example,

---

[9] Work by A. Lo and C. MacKinlay (1988) 'Stock market prices do not follow random walks: Evidence from a simple specification test', *Review of Financial Studies*, **1**, 41–66; J. Conrad and G. Kaul (1988) 'Time-variation in expected returns', *Journal of Business*, **61**, 409–25; J. Boudoukh, M. Richardson and R. Whitelaw (1994) 'A tale of three schools: Insights on autocorrelations of short-horizon stock returns', *Review of Financial Studies*, **7** (Fall) 539–73; and K. French and R. Roll (1986) 'Stock return variances: The arrival of information and the reaction of traders', *Journal of Financial Economics*, **17**, 5–26, suggests that there may be a small amount of negative autocorrelation in daily stock market returns. However, it is a very small part of the overall variance of stock returns, and, for the most part, can be ignored.

There is much recent evidence that expected returns on ordinary shares vary over time—perhaps in predictable ways. The work of D. Keim and R. Stambough (1986) 'Predicting returns in stock and bond markets', *Journal of Financial Economics*, **17**; and Nai-Fu Chen (1991) 'Financial investment opportunities and the macroeconomy', *Journal of Finance*, **46**, 529–54, seems to suggest that expected return can be predicted. C. Harvey (1991). 'The world price of covariance risk', *Journal of Finance*, **46**, 111–57, suggests some common variation in expected returns across countries. This evidence is not inconsistent with efficient markets.

FIGURE 14.6   **Simulated and Actual Share-Price Returns**

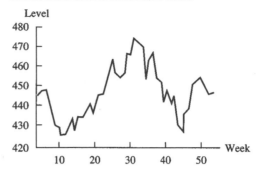

A. Simulated market levels for 52 weeks

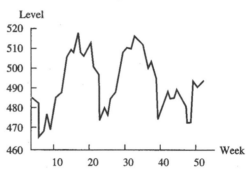

B. Friday closing levels: Dow Jones Industrial Index
December 30, 1955, to December 28, 1956

From H. Roberts (1959). 'Stock market patterns and financial analysis: Methodological suggestions'.
Journal of Finance, March.

consider Figure 14.6. The top graph was generated by computer using random numbers and equation (14.1). Because of this it must follow a random walk. Yet, we have found that people examining the chart continue to see patterns. Different people will see different patterns and will forecast different future price movements. However, in our experience, viewers are all quite confident of the patterns they see.

Next, consider the bottom graph, which tracks actual movements in the market index in the USA. This graph may look quite nonrandom to some, suggesting weak-form inefficiency. However, it also bears a close visual resemblance to the simulated series above, and statistical tests indicate that it indeed behaves like a purely random series. Thus, in our opinion, people claiming to see patterns in stock-price data are probably seeing optical illusions.

The Semistrong Form

The semistrong form of the efficient-market hypothesis implies that prices should reflect all publicly available information. We present two types of tests of this form.

Event Studies

A way to think of the tests of the semistrong form is to examine the following system of relationships:

Information released at time $t - 1 \rightarrow Ar_{t-1}$
Information released at time $t \rightarrow AR_t$
Information released at time $t + 1 \rightarrow Ar_{t+1}$

where AR stands for a share's abnormal return and where the arrows indicate that the return in any time period is related only to the information released during that period. The abnormal return (AR) of a given share on a particular day can be measured by subtracting the market's return on the same day (R_m) from the actual return (R) of the share on that day:[10]

$$AR = R - R_m$$

According to the efficient-market hypothesis, a share's abnormal return at time t, AR_t, should reflect the release of information at the same time, t. Any information released before then, though, should have no effect on abnormal returns in this period, because all of its influence should have been felt before. In other words, an efficient market would already have incorporated previous information into prices. Because a share's return today cannot depend on what the market does not yet know, the information that will be known only in the future cannot influence the share's return either. Hence the arrows point in the direction that is shown, with information in any one time period affecting only that period's abnormal return. *Event studies* are statistical studies that examine whether the arrows are as shown or whether the release of information influences returns on other days.

The first, and perhaps the best-known, event study was conducted by Fama, Fisher, Jensen and Roll, who studied 940 share splits in the USA.[11] Figure 14.7 shows their plot of the *cumulative abnormal return* (CAR) for the share-split sample. Compare the CAR with the plots in Figure 14.1. Positive abnormal returns were observed before the share split, probably because firms tend to split in good times. In addition, positive abnormal returns were observed around the time the split was announced. Fama *et al.* suggested that share splits released information to the market, perhaps as signals of future dividend increases. After the split, they observed no further tendency for the CAR to increase. This is consistent with efficient financial markets. To see this, note that investors could profit by buying shares on the split date, if the CAR continued to rise after that date.

Over the years this type of methodology has been applied to a large number of events. Announcements of dividends, earnings, mergers, capital expenditures, and new issues of shares are a few examples of the vast literature in the area.[12] Although there are exceptions, the event-study tests generally support the view that the market is semistrong-form (and therefore also weak-form) efficient. In fact, the tests even tend to support the view that the market is gifted with a certain amount of foresight. By this we mean that news tends to leak out and be reflected in share prices even before the official release of the information.

---

[10] The abnormal return can also be measured by using the market model. In this case the abnormal return is

$$AR = R - (\alpha + \beta R_m)$$

[11] E. F. Fama, L. Fisher, M. C. Jensen and R. Roll (1969) 'The adjustment of stock prices to new information', *International Economics Review*, **10**, February, 1–31.

[12] In academic finance nothing is ever completely resolved, and some event studies suggest that stock market prices respond to information too slowly for the market to be efficient. For example, E. Barlow (1992) 'Patterns in unexpected earnings as an explanation for post-announcement drift', *The Accounting Review*, July, pp. 610–22, suggests that the market doesn't respond properly to corporate earnings announcements. He found some delay in share-price responses.

FIGURE 14.7   **Abnormal Returns for Companies Announcing Share Splits**

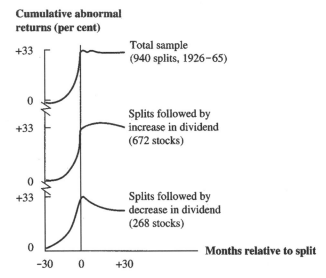

Cumulative abnormal returns rise prior to month of split. Very
likely this occurs because splits take place in good times, that is,
they take place *following* a rise in stock price. Abnormal returns are
flat after month of split, a finding consistent with efficient capital
markets.

Redrawn from E. F. Fama, L. Fisher, M. C. Jensen and R. Roll
(1969). 'The adjustment of stock prices to new information',
International Economic Review **10**, 1–31.

The Record of Mutual Funds

A mutual fund (a US term) refers to a managed investment fund, the shares in which
are sold to investors. If the market is efficient in the semistrong form, then no matter
what publicly available information mutual-fund managers rely on to pick shares, their
average returns should be the same as those of the average investor in the market as a
whole. We can test efficiency, then, by comparing the performance of these
professionals with that of a market index.

As you might imagine, the studies differ in their particular samples of mutual-
fund performance, and they differ in their use of statistics. Because the object of the
studies is to detect abnormal performance, it is not surprising that they employ
different theories for determining what normal performance is. But the general
conclusion of all the theories is the same—there is no evidence from US research
that the funds outperform suitably selected indices. The most common index of
market performance is the Standard & Poor's (S&P) composite index. Ignoring
some small costs of trading, a big investor could achieve the S&P 500 return by
buying the same shares in the same proportion as the index, that is, by *buying the
index*.[13]

---

[13] Recent work by G. Brinson, R. Hood and G. Beebower (1986) 'Determinants of portfolio
performance', *The Financial Analysts Journal*, **43**, July/August, 39–44; S. Berkowitz, L. Finnery, and D.
Logue (1988) *The Investment Performance of Corporate Pension Plans*, New York: Quorom; and E.
Elton, M. Gruber, S. Das and M. Hlavka (1993) 'Efficiency with costly information: A reinterpretation of
evidence for managed portfolios', *Review of Financial Studies*, **6**, (1), show that professional investors do
not have superior stock and bond selection skills.

Perhaps nothing rankles successful stock market investors more than to have some professor tell them that they are not necessarily smart, just lucky. However, the view that mutual-fund managers, on average, have no special ability to beat the stock market indices is largely supported by the evidence. This does not mean that no individual investor can beat the market average or that he or she lacks a special insight, only that proof seems difficult to find.

By and large, mutual-fund managers rely on publicly available information. Thus the finding that they do not outperform the market indices is consistent with semistrong-form and weak-form efficiency. This does not imply that mutual funds are bad investments for individuals. Though these funds fail to achieve better returns than some indices of the market, they do permit the investor to buy a portfolio that has a large number of stocks in it (the phrase 'a well-diversified portfolio' is often used). They might also be very good at providing a variety of services such as keeping custody and records of all of the shares.

Perhaps it is worth mentioning in the wake of some of the scandals in the City of London and on Wall Street, that the evidence on mutual funds derives from funds which are available to the public—we are not looking at in-house funds which investment banks may run for their own staff. The City of London cynic might be inclined to the view that there is so much evidence of less than ethical practices (for example, in a BBC television programme—*Naked City*, November 6, 1996—an ex-trader said that 'the good deals were for us, the bad ones we stuffed our clients for' and there are many, many more) that it is hardly surprising if public funds fail to beat the market, it's the private funds that we should be looking at.

Some Contrary Views

Although the bulk of the evidence supports the view that markets are efficient, we would not be fair if we did not note the existence of contrary results. We begin with three areas of academic research.

1. *Size* Chapter 10 showed that shares with small market capitalization companies outperformed shares with large **market capitalizations**[14] over the period from 1926 to the present. The difference in returns is perhaps 5 per cent per year. While much of the differential performance is merely compensation for the extra risk of small shares, a number of researchers have argued that not all of it can be explained by risk differences.[15] In addition, Donald Keim[16] presented evidence that most of the 5 per cent per year difference in performance occurs in the month of January.

2. *Time Anomalies* After Keim's surprising results in January, researchers examined returns over various units of time. For example, studies indicate that average share returns in January are higher than in other months for both large and small capitalization securities. Across days of the week, share returns are highest on Wednesdays and Fridays and are lowest on Mondays.[17] In fact, average share returns in

---

[14] Market capitalization is the price per share multiplied by the number of shares outstanding.

[15] See R. W. Banz (1981) 'The relationship between return and market value of common stocks', *Journal of Financial Economics*, March, and M. R. Reinganum (1981) 'Misspecification of capital asset pricing: Empirical anomalies based on earnings yields and market values', *Journal of Financial Economics*, March.

[16] D. B. Keim (1983) 'Size-related anomalies and stock return seasonality: Further empirical evidence', *Journal of Financial Economics*, June.

[17] M. R. Gibbons and P. Hess (1981) 'Day of the week effects and asset returns', *Journal of Business*.

the United States have been negative on Mondays over most of the twentieth century. Average stock returns are significantly higher over the first half of the month than they are over the second half of the month.[18] Returns are particularly high on the day before a holiday.[19]

The evidence on time anomalies is quite convincing, with results being replicated in other time periods and in other countries. However, the implications are few because the return differences do not exceed transition costs. For example, an individual who bought a share every Tuesday morning and sold the share every Friday evening in order to avoid the negative Monday return would have a lower return after commissions than an individual who bought the same share and held it for months or years without trading.

3. *Value versus Glamour*   At least two papers by Fama and French observed that stocks with low price-to-book ratios and/or low price-to-earnings ratios (generally called value stocks) outperform stocks with high ratios (glamour stocks).[20] The results of Lakonishok, Vishny, and Schleifer[21] suggest that the difference in average return between value stocks and glamour stocks may differ by as much as 8 per cent per year. Because the return difference is so large and because the above ratios can be obtained so easily for individual shares, the results may constitute substantive evidence against market efficiency. However, a number of recent papers suggest that the unusual returns are due to biases in the commercial databases, not to a true inefficiency.[22] Since the debate revolves around the details of data collection, we will not pursue the issue further. However, it is safe to say that no conclusion is warranted at this time. As with so many other topics in finance and economics, further research is needed.

In addition, the stock market crash of October 19, 1987, is extremely puzzling. The stockmarkets for most of the world dropped between 20 per cent and 25 per cent on a Monday following a weekend during which little surprising news was released. A drop of this magnitude for no apparent reason is not consistent with market efficiency. Because the crash of 1929 is still an enigma, it is doubtful that the more recent debacle will be explained anytime soon. The comments of an eminent historian in the 1970s are apt here. When asked what, in his opinion, the effect of the French Revolution of 1789 was, he replied that it was too early to tell.

Perhaps the two stock market crashes are evidence consistent with the **bubble theory** of speculative markets. That is, security prices sometimes move wildly above their true values. Eventually prices fall back to their original level, causing great losses for investors. The tulip craze of the seventeenth century in the Netherlands and the

---

[18] R. A. Ariel (1987) 'A monthly effect on stock returns', *Journal of Financial Economics*.

[19] R. A. Ariel (1990) 'High stock returns before holidays: Existence and evidence on possible causes', *Journal of Finance*, December.

[20] The two most well-known papers in the area are E. F. Fama and K. R. French (1992) 'The cross-section of expected stock returns', *Journal of Finance*, June, and E. F. Fama and K. R. French (1993) 'Common risk factors in the returns on stocks and bonds', *Journal of Financial Economics*, February.

[21] J. Lakonishok, R. W. Vishny and A. Schleifer (1993) 'Contrarian investment, extrapolation and risk', National Bureau of Economic Research Working Paper, May.

[22] For example, see S. P. Kothari, J. Shanken and R. G. Sloan (1994) 'Another look at the cross-section of expected stock returns', unpublished paper, University of Rochester, February, and W. J. Breen and R. A. Korajczyk (1993) 'On selection biases in book-to-market based tests of asset pricing models', unpublished paper, Northwestern University, November.

South Sea Bubble in England the following century are perhaps the two best-known bubbles. In the first episode, tulips rose to unheard-of prices. For example:

> A single bulb of the Haarlem species was exchanged for twelve acres of building ground. . . . Another variety fetched 4,600 florins, a new carriage and two gray horses, plus nine complete sets of harnesses. A bulb of the Viceroy species commanded the sum of all the following items in exchange: seventeen bushels of wheat, thirty-four bushels of rye, four fat oxen, eight fat swine, twelve fat sheep, two hogshead of wine, four tons of beer, two tons of butter, 1,000 pounds of cheese, a complete bed, a suit of clothes, and a silver drinking cup thrown in for good measure.[23]

It seems speculative fervour hit England a century later. Fantastic schemes of all types were paraded before a public eager to invest. Most of them provided good evidence for the dictums: 'A sucker is born every minute' and 'A fool and his money are soon parted'.

According to Malkiel,

> The prize, however, must surely go to the unknown soul who started 'A Company for carrying on an undertaking of great advantage, but nobody to know what it is.' The prospectus promises unheard-of rewards. At nine o'clock in the morning, when the subscription books opened, crowds of people from all walks of life practically beat down the doors in an effort to subscribe. Within five hours a thousand investors handed over their money for shares in the company. Not being greedy himself, the promoter promptly closed up shop and set off for the Continent. He was never heard from again.[24]

The Strong Form

Even the strongest adherents to the efficient-market hypothesis would not be surprised to find that markets are inefficient in the strong form. After all, if an individual has information that no one else has, it is likely that he or she can profit from it.

A group of studies of strong-form efficiency has investigated insider trading in the USA. Insiders in firms have access to information that is not generally available. But if the strong form of the efficient-market hypothesis holds, they should not be able to profit by trading on their information. A US government agency, the Securities and Exchange Commission, requires insiders in companies to reveal any trading they might do in their own company's stock. By examining the record of such trades, we can see whether they made abnormal returns. A number of studies support the view that these trades were abnormally profitable. Thus, strong-form efficiency does not seem to be substantiated by US evidence.[25]

Of course, it has to be said, that insider dealing is not, in fact, illegal in all European countries. In one or two, it may not be a norm but is practised, although under the mask of relative secrecy. That continental European rules lag behind those in the USA and UK is borne out by the observation that it was only as recently as 1994 that insider trading became illegal in Germany.

---

[23] B. G. Malkiel (1996) *A Random Walk Down Wall Street*, 6th edn, New York: Norton.

[24] B. G. Malkiel (1996) *A Random Walk Down Wall Street.*, 6th edn, New York: Norton.

[25] J. Jaffe (1974) 'Special information and insider trading', *Journal of Business*, J. E. Finnerty (1976) 'Insiders and market efficiency', *Journal of Finance*; and H. N. Seyhun (1986) 'Insiders' profits, costs of trading and market efficiency', *Journal of Financial Economics*.

14.5   Implications for Corporate Finance

Accounting and Efficient Markets

The accounting profession provides firms with a significant amount of leeway in their reporting practices. For example, companies may value inventory according to different methods. They may choose either the percentage-of-completion or the completed-contract method for construction projects. They may depreciate physical assets in different ways.

Accountants have frequently been accused of misusing this leeway in the hopes of boosting earnings and share prices. However, accounting choice should not affect share price if two conditions hold. First, enough information must be provided in the annual report so that financial analysts can construct earnings under the alternative accounting methods. This appears to be the case for many, though not necessarily all, accounting choices. For example, most skilled analysts can create *pro forma* financial statements under different assumptions about depreciation and inventory valuation. Second, the market must be efficient in the semistrong form. In other words, the market must appropriately use all of this accounting information in determining the market price.

Of course, the issue of whether accounting choice affects share price is ultimately an empirical matter. A number of US academic papers have addressed this issue. Kaplan and Roll found that the switch from accelerated to straight-line depreciation generally did not significantly affect share prices.[26] They found that a switch would increase accounting earnings, but had no effect on share prices.

Several other accounting procedures have been studied. Hong, Kaplan, and Mandelker found no evidence that the US stock market was affected by the artificially higher earnings reported using the pooling method, compared to the purchase method, for reporting mergers and acquisitions.[27] Biddle and Lindahl found that firms switching from FIFO to the LIFO method of costing inventory experienced an increase in stock price.[28] Such a change would tend to depress reported earnings (in an inflationary era) on a one-year basis, but would lower tax payable and thus increase cash generation. This is to be expected in inflationary environments because LIFO inventory costing can reduce taxes, compared to FIFO inventory costing. They found that the larger the tax decrease resulting from the use of LIFO, the greater was the increase in stock price. In summary, the empirical evidence suggests that accounting changes do not fool the market.[29] Whether this is equally so in the UK, Germany or the Netherlands is an empirical question. If share analysis is less sophisticated in these countries, perhaps the market might be fooled. Clearly, this is an area particularly ripe for research.

Of course, the semistrong form of the efficient-capital-markets hypothesis does not imply that share price is invariant to every accounting decision. Price is likely to be affected if a company were either to withhold useful information or to provide incorrect or positively fraudulent information.

---

[26] R. S. Kaplan and R. Roll (1972) 'Investor evaluation of accounting information: Some empirical evidence', *Journal of Business*, **45**, April.

[27] H. Hong, R. S. Kaplan, and G. Mandelker (1978) 'Pooling vs. purchase: The effects of accounting for mergers on stock prices', *Accounting Review*, **53**.

[28] G. C. Biddle and F. W. Lindahl (1982) 'Stock price reactions to LIFO adoptions: The association between excess returns and LIFO tax savings', *Journal of Accounting Research*.

[29] These excellent studies are slightly off the mark for our purposes. They test the hypothesis that, in aggregate, stock prices are invariant to accounting changes. The efficient-market hypothesis actually makes a stronger statement. As long as earnings can be reconstructed under alternative accounting methods, each stock should be unaffected by a change in accounting.

Timing of Issuance of Financing

Imagine a firm whose managers are contemplating the date to issue equity. This decision is frequently called the timing decision. If managers believe that their shares are overpriced, they are likely to issue equity immediately. Of course, issuance of such equity must be to third parties to create value for shareholders prior to the issue. If the overpriced issue is made to existing shareholders, the total wealth of the existing shareholders is, in total, unaffected.

Where the issue is to the third parties, value creation occurs for the shareholders prior to the issue because they are selling shares for more than they are worth. Conversely, if the managers believe that their shares are underpriced, they are more likely to wait, hoping that the share price will eventually rise to its true value.

However, if markets are efficient, securities are always correctly priced. Since efficiency implies that shares always sell for their true worth, the timing decision becomes unimportant. Figure 14.8 shows three possible share price adjustments to the issuance of new shares. Of course, market efficiency is ultimately an empirical issue. And there is the question of inside information. Thus, markets may be efficient in the semistrong sense, but not in the strong sense. It may be that inefficiency in the strong sense would lead managers to time issuance of shares—especially to third parties.

A well-known study in the USA by Roger Ibbotson[30] examined share price performance after firms had an initial public offering (IPO), i.e. after they issued shares for the first time. The study found that, on average, shares experienced zero abnormal returns in the five years immediately following IPOs. This result was taken as convincing evidence that shares are correctly priced at the time of issuance.[31]

FIGURE 14.8   Three Share-Price Adjustments

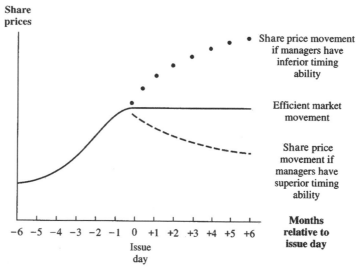

Studies show that shares are more likely to be issued after share prices have increased.

[30] R. G. Ibbotson (1975) 'Price performance of common stock new issues', *Journal of Financial Economics*, September.

[31] Actually, initial public offerings tend to rise on the day of issuance. However, this is likely due to certain reasons concerning the issuing process and not due to an inefficiency. For example, see R. G. Ibbotson, *op. cit.*

However, a recent paper has called US market efficiency into question. Loughran and Ritter[32] present evidence that annual returns over the five years following an IPO are, on average, approximately 7 per cent less for the issuing company than the return on a non-issuing company of similar market capitalization. In addition, Loughran and Ritter examine seasoned equity offerings (SEO), i.e. publicly traded companies that issue additional shares. They find that, over the five years following an SEO, the annualized return on the issuing firm's stock is, on average, 8 per cent less than the return on a comparable non-issuing company. The evidence of the Loughran and Ritter paper suggests that corporate managers issue shares when the are overpriced. In other words, they are successfully able to time the market.

If firms can time the issuance of shares, perhaps they can also time the repurchase of shares. Here, a firm would like to repurchase when its shares are undervalued. Lakonishok and Vermaelen[33] find that share returns of US repurchasing firms are abnormally high in the two years following the repurchase, suggesting that timing is effective here.

As is always the case, empirical research is never ultimately settled. However, in our opinion, the evidence of the Loughran and Ritter paper and the Lakonishok and Vermaelen paper, taken together, suggest that managers successfully engage in timing. These papers, if they stand the test of time, constitute evidence against market efficiency. But given that it is managers who are acting to exploit any inefficiency, it may merely reflect inefficiency in the strong form, because managers have inside information.

Price-Pressure Effects

Suppose a firm wants to sell a large block of shares. Can it sell as many shares as it wants without depressing the price? If capital markets are efficient, a firm should be able to sell as many shares as it desires without the depressing price. Scholes was one of the first to examine this question empirically in the USA.[34] He found that the market's ability to absorb large blocks of shares was virtually unlimited. His findings were surprising to real-world practitioners, because the sale of large blocks of shares is generally believed temporarily to depress the price of a company's shares.

Conversely, Kraus and Stoll, using intra-day prices, found clear evidence of a price-pressure effect in the USA.[35] However, the effects were very small—less than 1 per cent. Finally, Dann, Mayers, and Robb, using transactions data, determined that prices in the USA fell by an average of 4.5 per cent and recovered within 15 minutes.[36,37]

---

[32] T. Loughran and J. R. Ritter (1995) 'The timing and subsequent performance of new issue', *Journal of Finance*.

[33] J. Lakonishok and T. Vermaelen (1990) 'Anomalous price behaviour around repurchase tender offers', *Journal of Finance*, June.

[34] M. Scholes (1972) 'The market for securities: Substitution versus price pressure and the effects of information on share prices', *Journal of Business*, April.

[35] A. Kraus and H. R. Stoll (1972) 'Price impacts of block trading on the New York Stock Exchange', *Journal of Finance*, **27**, 542.

[36] L. Dann, D. Mayers and R. Robb (1977) 'Trading rules, large blocks and the speed of adjustment', *Journal of Financial Economics*.

[37] Robert Holthausen, Richard Leftwich and David Mayers (1990) 'Large-block transactions, the speed of response, and temporary and permanent stock price effects', *Journal of Financial Economics*, **26**, 71–95, find that prices adjust within at most three trades. However, most of the overall effect is permanent indicating a price–pressure effect. The magnitude appears to be small (less than 0.25 per cent). However, the sales impact is likely to be a function of firm size. Donald Keim (1994) 'The upstairs market for large block transitions: Analysis and measurement of price effects', unpublished paper, University of Pennsylvania, September, find an average price impact of almost 3 per cent for a group of low-capitalization stocks.

The Dann, Mayers, and Robb finding suggests that the sellers of shares pay a large cost when issuing equity. The controversy is important. If new issues of equity cannot be sold at prevailing market prices, the reduction in price must be included as a cost of raising external equity. Unfortunately, future research is needed to resolve the conflicting results presented above.

Efficient-Market Hypothesis: A Summary

Does Not Say
Prices are uncaused.
Investors are foolish and too stupid to be in the market.
All shares have the same expected returns.
Investors should throw darts to select stocks.
There is no upward trend in share prices.

Does Say
Prices reflect underlying value.
Financial managers cannot time stock and bond sales.
Sales of stock and bonds will not depress prices.
You cannot cook the books.

Why Doesn't Everybody Believe It?
There are optical illusions, mirages and apparent patterns in charts of stock market returns.
The truth is less interesting.
There is evidence against efficiency:
  • Seasonality
  • Insider trading
  • Excess stock-price volatility.
The tests of market efficiency are weak.

Three Forms
Weak form (random walk): Prices reflect past prices; chartism (technical analysis) is useless.
Semistrong form: Prices reflect all public information; most financial analysis is useless.
Strong form: Prices reflect all that is knowable; nobody consistently makes superior profits.

Concept Question

• What are three implications of the efficient-market hypothesis for corporate finance?

14.6   Summary and Conclusions

1. An efficient financial market processes the information available to investors and incorporates it into the prices of securities. This has two general implications. First, in any given time period, a stock's abnormal return can depend on information or news received by the market in that period. Second, an investor who uses the same information as the market cannot expect to earn abnormal returns. In other words, systems for playing the market are doomed to fail.

2. What information does the market use to determine prices? The weakest form of the efficient-market hypothesis says that the market uses the past history of prices and is therefore efficient with respect to these past prices. This implies that stock selection based on patterns of past stock-price movements is not better than random stock selection.

3. A stronger theory of efficiency is semistrong-form efficiency, which argues that the market uses all publicly available information. If the market has already used all of this information and it is now reflected in the prices of stocks, investors will not be able to outperform the market by using the same information.

4. The strongest theory of efficiency, strong-form efficiency, argues that the market has available to it and uses all of the information that anybody knows about stocks, even inside information.

5. The evidence from different financial markets supports weak-form and semistrong-form efficiency, but not strong-form efficiency. This is no consolation to the army of investors that uses publicly available information in attempts to beat the market.

6. In our study of efficient markets we stress the importance of distinguishing between the actual return on a stock and the expected return. The difference is called the *abnormal return* and comes from the release of news to the market.

7. Not everybody believes the efficient-market hypothesis. It is a misunderstood theory. The boxed material , before this summary, shows the essence of what it does and does not say.

8. Three implications of efficient markets for corporate finance are listed below:
   a. The price of a company's stock cannot be affected by a change in accounting.
   b. Finance managers cannot time issues of stocks and bonds using publicly available information.
   c. A firm can sell as many bonds or shares of stock as it desires without depressing prices. There is conflicting empirical evidence on both point *b* and point *c*.

KEY TERMS

Efficient-market hypothesis 322	Semistrong-form efficiency 327
Inside information 323	Strong-form efficiency 327
Weak-form efficiency 325	Serial correlation 330
Random walk 325	Market capitalization 335
Technical analysis 325	Bubble theory 336

QUESTIONS AND PROBLEMS

Can Financing Decisions Create Value?

14.1 *a.* What rule should a firm follow when making financing decisions?
   b. How can firms create valuable financing opportunities?

A Description of Efficient Capital Markets

14.2 Define the three forms of market efficiency.

14.3 Which of the following statements are true about the efficient-market hypothesis?
   a. It implies perfect forecasting ability.
   b. It implies that prices reflect all available information.
   c. It implies an irrational market.
   d. It implies that prices do not fluctuate.
   e. It results from keen competition among investors.

14.4 Aerotech GmbH, a German aerospace-technology research firm, announced this morning that it has hired the world's most knowledgeable and prolific space researchers. Before today, Aerotech's shares had been selling for DEM100.
   a. What do you expect will happen to Aerotech's shares?
   b. Consider the following scenarios:
      i. The share price jumps to DEM118 on the day of the announcement. In subsequent days it floats up to DEM123 then falls back to DEM116.
      ii. The share price jumps to DEM116 and remains there.
      iii. The share price gradually climbs to DEM116 over the next week.
   Which scenario(s) indicate market efficiency? Which do not? Why?

14.5 When the 56-year-old founder of Gulf & Western, Inc., died of a heart attack, the stock price jumped from USD18.00 a share to USD20.25, a 12.5 per cent increase. This is evidence of market inefficiency, because an efficient stock market would have anticipated his death and adjusted the price beforehand. Is this statement true or false? Explain.

14.6 Newtech plc is going to adopt a new chip testing device that can greatly improve its production efficiency. Do you think the lead engineer of this device can profit from purchasing the firm's stock before the news release on the implementation of the new technology? What if you rush to call your broker to buy the stock right after you learn of the announcement in the *Financial Times*?

14.7   In a recent discussion with you, your broker commented that well-managed firms are not necessarily more profitable than firms with average management. To convince you of this, she presented you with evidence from a recent study conducted by the firm for which she works. The study examined the returns on 17 small manufacturing firms that, eight years earlier, an industry magazine had listed as the best-managed small manufacturers in the country. In the eight years since the publication of that issue of the magazine, the 17 firms have not earned more than the market. Your broker concluded that if they were well-managed, they should have produced better-than-average returns. Do you agree with your broker?

14.8   Many investors (sometimes called technical analysts) claim to observe patterns in stock market prices. Is technical analysis consistent with EMH? If the share price follows a random-walk model, can technical analysts systematically profit from trading rules based on patterns in the historical share prices? If so, what form of market efficiency is violated?

The Evidence

14.9   Suppose the market is semistrong-form efficient. Can you expect to earn excess returns if you make trades based on:
   a. Your broker's information about record earnings for a share?
   b. Rumours about a merger of a firm?
   c. Yesterday's announcement of a successful test of a new product?

14.10   Consider an efficient capital market in which a particular macroeconomic variable that influences your firm's net earnings is positively serially correlated. Would you expect price changes in your stock to be serially correlated? Why or why not?

14.11   Although mutual-fund managers frequently claim that they have investing strategies, under the EMH mutual fund managers should obtain the same returns after adjusting for the risk level of their respective investments. Therefore, we can simply pick mutual funds at random. Is this statement true or false? Explain.

CHAPTER
15

Long-Term Financing: An Introduction

This chapter introduces the basic sources of long-term financing: ordinary shares, preference shares and long-term debt. Later chapters discuss these topics in more detail. Perhaps no other area of corporate finance is more perplexing to new students of finance than corporate securities, such as shares, bonds and debentures. Whereas the concepts are simple and logical, the language is strange and unfamiliar.

The purpose of this chapter is to describe the basic features of long-term financing. We begin with a look at ordinary shares, preference shares and long-term debt, and then briefly consider patterns of the different kinds of long-term financing. Discussion of non-basic forms of long-term finance, such as convertibles, is reserved for later chapters.

15.1 Ordinary Shares

The term **ordinary shares** (typically called common stock in the USA) has a less than precise meaning. It usually is applied to shares that have no special preference either in dividends or in bankruptcy. A description of the ordinary shares of the Boots Company, a UK-based retail company, is present in the box on the next page.

Owners of ordinary shares in a company are referred to as *shareholders* or *stockholders*. They receive share certificates for the *shares* they own (although computerized company registers with ownership certified therein is an innovation which is occurring in the UK). There is usually a stated value on each share certificate called the *par value*. However, in some countries some shares have no-par value. The nominal or par value of each share of nominal value of The Boots Company is 25p.

The total nominal par value, called the issued capital, is the number of shares issued multiplied by the nominal value of each share. The issued capital of The Boots Company is 949 million shares × 25p = GBP237.2 million.

THE BOOTS COMPANY PLC
Share Capital and Other Shareholders' Equity
March 31, 1995
(in millions)

Ordinary shares, 25 nominal value, authorized 1,200,000,000 shares in 1995:

Issued 949 million shares	GBP237.2
Share premium account	219.0
Revaluation reserve	310.7
Other reserve	24.0
Retained earnings	1216.0
Equity shareholders' funds	2006.9

Authorized versus Issued Ordinary Shares

Ordinary shares are the fundamental ownership units of the company. The articles of association of a new company must state the number of ordinary shares that the company (or corporation) is authorized to issue.

The board of directors of the company, after a vote of the shareholders, can amend the articles of association (or incorporation) to increase the number of shares authorized; there is no limit to the number of shares that can be authorized. In 1995 The Boots Company had authorized 1200 million shares and had issued 949 million shares. There is no requirement that all of the authorized shares actually be issued. There are no legal limits to authorizing shares.

Share Premium Account

Share premium account refers to amounts of directly contributed equity capital in excess of the nominal value.

● Example
Suppose 100 ordinary shares have a nominal value of GBP2 each and are sold to shareholders for GBP10 per share. The share premium would be (GBP10 − GBP2) × 100 = GBP8 × 100 = GBP800, and the total nominal value would be GBP2 × 100 = GBP200. What difference does it make if the total capital contribution is reported as nominal value or capital surplus? ●

In most European countries, virtually none.

The share premium account of The Boots Company is GBP219.0 million. This figure indicates that the price of new shares issued by The Boots Company has exceeded the nominal value and the difference has been entered as *share premium account*. In most countries shares cannot be issued below their nominal or par value, implying that capital in excess of nominal value cannot be negative.

Revaluation Reserve

In some countries, but not all, companies may (if economic circumstances justify it) write up the value of assets in excess of original cost. This frequently happens in respect of land ownership. To balance the books, land would be increased on the assets side of the balance sheet and a revaluation reserve would be created on the equity and liabilities side of the balance sheet. This Revaluation Reserve is not a realized profit as such and cannot be distributed through the profit and loss account as dividend to shareholders. The Boots Company has a Revaluation Reserve of GBP310.7 million.

Retained Earnings

The Boots Company usually pays out slightly more than half of its net income as dividends, the rest is retained in the business and is called **retained earnings**. The cumulative amount of retained earnings (since original incorporation) was GBP1,216.0 million in 1995.

The sum of the nominal value, share premium account, other reserves and accumulated retained earnings is called shareholders' funds, or sometimes merely equity, which is often referred to as the **book value** of equity. The book value represents the amount contributed directly and indirectly to the company by equity investors.

● Example

Suppose Western Redwood plc was formed in 1906 with 10,000 shares issued and sold at its GBP1 nominal value. Because the shares were sold for GBP1, the first balance sheet showed a zero amount for share premium account. By 1996 the company had become very profitable and had retained profits of GBP100,000. The stockholders' equity of Western Redwood in 1996 is as follows:

WESTERN REDWOOD PLC
Shareholders' Funds
31 December 1996

Ordinary shares GBP nominal 10,000 shares outstanding	GBP10,000
Share premium account	0
Retained earnings	100,000
Total shareholders' equity	GBP110,000

$$\text{Book value per share} = \frac{\text{GBP110,000}}{10,000} = \text{GBP11}$$

Suppose the company has profitable investment opportunities and decides, in January 1997, to sell 10,000 shares of new shares. The current market price is GBP20 per share. The effect of the sale of stock on the balance sheet will be

WESTERN REDWOOD PLC
Shareholders' Funds

Ordinary shares, GBP1 nominal, 20,000 shares outstanding	GBP20,000
Share premium account (GBP20 – GBP1) × 10,000 shares	190,000
Retained earnings	100,000
Total shareholders' equity	GBP310,000

$$\text{Book value per share} = \frac{\text{GBP310,000}}{20,000} = \text{GBP15.50}$$

What happened?

1. Because 10,000 shares of new shares were issued with nominal value of GBP1, the nominal value rose GBP10,000.

2. The total amount raised by the new issue was GBP20 $\times$ 10,000 = GBP200,000, and GBP190,000 was entered as share premium.
3. The book value per share increased because the market price of the new shares was higher than the book value of the old. ●

Market Value, Book Value, and Replacement Value

The **book value** of The Boots Company's equity in 1995 was GBP2006.9 million. This figure is based on the number of shares outstanding. The company had issued 1045 million shares and bought back 96 million shares (you can't tell this from our summarized figures in the book), so that the total number of outstanding shares was 1045 million $-$ 96 million = 949 million. The shares bought back are called *treasury stock* in the USA and in some other countries.

The book value per share was equal to

$$\frac{\text{Total ordinary shareholders' equity}}{\text{Shares outstanding}} = \frac{\text{GBP2006.9 million}}{949 \text{ million}} = \text{GBP2.11}$$

The Boots Company is a publicly owned company. Its ordinary shares trade on the London Stock Exchange, and thousands of shares change hands every day. The recent market price of The Boots Company was around GBP6 per share. Thus the market price was above the book value.

In addition to market and book values, you may hear the term *replacement value*. This refers to the current cost of replacing the assets of the firm. Market, book and replacement value for an asset are equal at the time when a firm purchases that asset. After that time, these values will diverge. The *market-to-book-value* ratio of ordinary shares and *Tobin's Q* (market value of assets/replacement value of assets) introduced in the appendix to Chapter 3 are, in some ways, indicators of the success of the firm. A market-to-book or Tobin's Q ratio greater than one indicates the firm has done well with its investment decisions.

Shareholders' Rights

The structure of companies in many countries assumes that shareholders elect directors who in turn elect corporate officers—more generally, the management—to carry out their directives. It is the right to elect the directors of the corporation by vote that constitutes the most important control device for shareholders.

In most countries, directors are usually elected (or their continuing appointment is confirmed) each year at an annual meeting by a vote of the holders of a majority of shares who are present and entitled to vote. The exact mechanism for electing differs among different companies and countries.

● **Example**
Imagine that a company has two shareholders: Smith with 25 shares and Marshall with 75 shares. Both want to be on the board of directors. Marshall does not want Smith to be a director. Let us assume that there are four directors to be elected and each shareholder nominates four candidates. ●

Cumulative Voting
In many European countries, cumulative voting is permitted. The effect of **cumulative voting** is to permit minority participation. If cumulative voting is permitted, the total

number of votes that each shareholder may cast is determined first. That number is usually calculated as the number of shares (owned or controlled) multiplied by the number of directors to be elected. Each shareholder can distribute these votes as he or she wishes over one or more candidates. Smith will get $25 \times 4 = 100$ votes, and Marshall is entitled to $75 \times 4 = 300$ votes. If Smith gives all his votes to himself, he is assured of a directorship. It is not possible for Marshall to divide 300 votes among the four candidates in such a way as to preclude Smith's election to the board.

Straight Voting

If **straight voting** is permitted, Smith may cast 25 votes for each candidate and Marshall may cast 75 votes for each. As a consequence, Marshall will elect all of the candidates.

Straight voting can freeze out minority shareholders; that is the reason many countries have mandatory cumulative voting. In countries where cumulative voting is mandatory, devices have been worked out to minimize its impact. One such device is to *stagger* the voting for the board of directors. Staggering permits a fraction of the directorships to come to a vote at a particular time. It has two basic effects:

1. Staggering makes it more difficult for a minority to elect a director when there is cumulative voting.
2. Staggering makes successful takeover attempts less likely by making the election of new directors more difficult.

Proxy Voting

A **proxy** is the legal grant of authority by a shareholder to someone else to vote his or her shares. For convenience, the actual voting in large public companies is usually done by proxy.

Many companies such as The Boots Company have hundreds of thousands of shareholders. Shareholders can come to the annual meeting and vote in person, or they can transfer their right to vote to another party by proxy.

Obviously, management always tries to get as many proxies transferred to it as possible. However, if shareholders are not satisfied with management, an outside group of shareholders can try to obtain as many votes as possible via proxy. They can vote to replace management by adding enough directors. This is called a *proxy fight*, and is most common in the USA.

Other Rights

In addition to the right to vote for directors, ordinary shareholders usually have the following rights:

1. The right to share proportionally in dividends paid.
2. The right to share proportionally in assets remaining after liabilities have been paid in a liquidation.
3 The right to vote on matters of great importance to shareholders, such as a takeover.
4. The right to share proportionally in any new shares sold. This is called the *preemptive right* and will be discussed in later chapters.

Dividends

A distinctive feature of companies is that they issue shares and are authorized by law to pay dividends to the holders of those shares. **Dividends** paid to shareholders represent a return on the capital directly or indirectly contributed to the company by the shareholders. The payment of dividends is usually, legally, at the discretion of the board of directors.

Here are some important characteristics of dividends which apply in most countries:

1. Unless a dividend is declared by the board of directors of a company, it is not a liability of the company. A company cannot *default* on an undeclared dividend. As a consequence, companies cannot become *bankrupt* because of non-payment of dividends. The amount of the dividend—and even whether or not it is paid— are decisions based on the business judgement of the board of directors.
2. The payment of dividends by the company is not a business expense. Dividends are not deductible for corporate tax purposes. In short, dividends are paid out of after-tax profits of the company.
3. Dividends received by individual shareholders are, for the most part, considered ordinary income by the tax authorities and are therefore fully taxable.

Classes of Shares

Some firms issue more than one class of ordinary share. The classes are usually created with unequal voting rights. For example, The Ford Motor Company has Class B common stock, which is not publicly traded (it is held by Ford family interests and trusts). This class has about 40 per cent of the voting power, but these shares comprise only about 15 per cent of the total outstanding stock.

Many companies issue dual classes of ordinary shares. The reason has to do with control of the firm. Management of a firm can raise equity capital by issuing non voting ordinary shares while maintaining voting control. This practice is very usual in many European countries. Thus, managerial vote ownership is an important element of corporate control structure.

In the USA, Lease, McConnell and Mikkelson found the market prices of stocks with superior voting rights to be about 5 per cent higher than the prices of otherwise identical stocks with inferior voting rights.[1] However, DeAngelo and DeAngelo[2] found some evidence that the market value of differences in voting rights may be much higher when control of the firm is involved and at risk.

Concept Questions

- What is a company's book value?
- What rights do stockholders have?
- What is a proxy?

15.2   Corporate Long-Term Debt: The Basics

Securities issued by corporations may be classified roughly as *equity* securities and *debt* securities. The distinction between equity and debt is basic to much of the modern theory and practice of corporate finance.

---

[1] R. C. Lease, J. J. McConnell, and W. H. Mikkelson (1983) 'The market value of control in publicly traded corporations', *Journal of Financial Economics*, April.

[2] H. DeAngelo and L. DeAngelo (1985) 'Managerial ownership of voting rights: A study of public corporations with dual classes of common stock', *Journal of Financial Economics*, **14**.

At its crudest level, debt represents something that must be repaid; it is the result of borrowing money. When corporations borrow, they promise to make regularly scheduled interest payments and to repay the original amount borrowed (that is, the *principal*). The person or firm making the loan is called a *creditor* or *lender*.

Interest versus Dividends

The company borrowing the money is called a *debtor* or *borrower*. The amount owed to the creditor is a liability of the company; however, it is a liability of limited value. The company can legally default at any time on its liability (for example, by not paying interest) and hand over the assets to the creditors.[3] This can be a valuable option. The creditors benefit if the assets have a value greater than the value of the liability, but this would happen only if management were foolish. On the other hand, the company and the equity investors benefit if the value of the assets is less than the value of the liabilities, because equity investors are able to walk away from the liabilities and default on their payment.

From a financial point of view, the main differences between debt and equity are the following:

1. Debt is not an ownership interest in the firm. Creditors do not usually have voting power. The device used by creditors to protect themselves is the loan contract (sometimes called the *indenture*).
2. The company's payment of interest on debt is considered a cost of doing business and is (in most countries) fully tax deductible. Thus interest expense is paid out to creditors before the corporate tax liability is computed. Dividends on ordinary shares and preferred shares are paid to shareholders after the tax liability has been determined. Dividends are considered a return to shareholders on their contributed capital. Because interest expense can be used to reduce taxes, the government (in its role as the tax authority) is providing a direct tax subsidy on the use of debt when compared to equity. This point is discussed in detail in the next two chapters.
3. Unpaid debt is a liability of the firm. If it is not paid, the creditors can legally claim the assets of the firm. This action may result in *liquidation* and *bankruptcy*. Thus, one of the costs of issuing debt is the possibility of *financial failure*, which does not arise when equity is issued.

Is It Debt or Equity?

Sometimes it is not clear whether a particular security is debt or equity. For example, suppose a 50-year bond is issued with interest payable solely from corporate income if, and only if, earned, and repayment is subordinate to (that is, comes after) all other debts of the business. Companies are very adept at creating hybrid securities that look like equity but are called *debt*. Obviously, the distinction between debt and equity is important for tax purposes. When corporations try to create a debt security that is really equity, they are trying to obtain the tax benefits of debt while eliminating its bankruptcy potential.

---

[3] In practice, creditors can make a claim against the assets of the firm and a court will administer the legal remedy.

Basic Features of Long-Term Debt

Long-term corporate debt usually is denominated in units of 100 or 1,000 or even 10,000 or 100,000 units of local currency called the *principal* or *face value*. Long-term debt is a promise by the borrowing firm to repay the principal amount by a certain date, called the *maturity date*. Long-term debt almost always has a par value equal to the face value, and debt price is often expressed as a percentage of the par value. For example, it might be said that General Motors debt is selling at 90, which means that a bond with a par value of USD1,000 can be purchased for USD900. In this case the debt is selling at a discount because the market price is less than the par value. Debt can also sell at a premium with respect to par value. The borrower using long-term debt generally pays interest at a rate expressed as a fraction of par value. Thus, at USD1,000 par value, General Motors' 7 per cent debt means that USD70 of interest is paid to holders of the debt, usually in semiannual instalments (for example, USD35 on June 30 and December 31). The payment schedules are in the form of coupons that are detached from the debt certificates and sent to the company for payment. However, some companies debt attracts mere payment without this need. The company simply pays interest to the registered holder of the debt securities.

Different Types of Debt

Typical debt securities are called *notes*, *debentures*, or *bonds*. A debenture is usually an unsecured corporate debt (although in some countries it can be secured or unsecured), whereas a bond is usually secured by a charge on some corporate property. However, in common usage, the word bond is used indiscriminately and often refers to both secured and unsecured debt. A note usually refers to a short-term obligation with a maturity of less than five years but frequently much less.

Debentures and bonds are long-term debt. *Long-term* debt is any obligation that is payable more than one year from the date it was originally issued. Sometimes long-term debt—debentures and bonds—is called *funded debt*. Debt that is due in less than one year is accounted for as a current liability and is sometimes called *unfunded debt*. Some debt is perpetual and has no specific maturity. This type of debt is referred to as a *consol*.

Repayment

Long-term debt is typically repaid in regular amounts over the life of the debt. The payment of long-term debt by instalments is called *amortization*. At the end of the amortization the entire indebtedness is said to be *extinguished*. Amortization may be arranged by a *sinking fund*. Each year the company places money into a fund which earns interest and the accumulated money is used to buy back the debt.

Debt may be extinguished before maturity by a call option possessed by the company. Most corporate long-term is *callable*. These are debentures or bonds for which the firm has the right to pay a specific amount, the *call price*, to retire (extinguish) the debt before the stated maturity date. The call price is always higher than the par value of the debt. Debt that is callable at 105 is debt that the firm can buy back from the holder at a price of, for example, GBP105 for GBP100 of nominal value per debenture or bond, regardless of what the market value of the debt might be. Call prices are always specified when the debt is originally issued. However, lenders may be given a 5-year to 10-year call-protection period during which the debt cannot be called.

Seniority

In general terms **seniority** indicates preference in position over other lenders. Some debt is **subordinated**. In the event of default, holders of subordinated debt must give preference to other specified creditors. Usually, this means that the subordinated lenders will be paid off only after the specified creditors have been compensated. However, debt cannot be subordinated to equity.

Security

Security is a form of charge or attachment to property. It provides that the property can be sold in the event of default to satisfy the debt for which security is given. A mortgage is used for security on tangible property; for example, debt can be secured by mortgages on real property. Holders of such debt have prior claim on the mortgaged assets in case of default. Debentures may be secured by a mortgage. If mortgaged property is sold in the event of default, the proceeds are first applied to settle the debt due to the creditors holding the mortgage.

Indenture

The written agreement between the corporate debt issuer and the lender, setting forth maturity date, interest rate and all other terms, is called an *indenture*. We treat this in detail in later chapters. For now, we note that

1. The indenture completely describes the nature of the indebtedness.
2. It lists all restrictions placed on the firm by the lenders. These restrictions are placed in *restrictive covenants*.

Some typical restrictive covenants are the following:

1. Restrictions on further indebtedness.
2. A maximum on the amount of dividends that can be paid.
3. A minimum level of working capital.
4. Maintenance of certain levels of balance sheet or income statement ratio, such as debt to equity, interest cover or current ratio, and so on.

Concept Questions

- What is corporate debt? Describe its general features.
- Why is it sometimes difficult to tell whether a particular security is debt or equity?

15.3   Preference Shares

Preference shares represent quasi-equity of a company. It is different from ordinary share capital because it has preference over ordinary shares in payment of dividends and in the assets of the corporation in the event of liquidation. *Preference* means only that the holder of the preferred share must receive a dividend (in the case of an ongoing firm) before holders of ordinary shares are entitled to anything.

Stated Value

Preferred shares have a stated nominal value, perhaps GBP1 per share. The dividend preference is described in terms of pounds per share. For example, a company's 5 per cent preference shares indicates a dividend yield of 5 per cent of stated nominal value, for example GBP1.

Cumulative and Non-cumulative Dividends

A preferred dividend is not like interest on a bond. The board of directors may decide not to pay the dividends on preferred shares, and their decision may not have anything to do with current net income of the company. Dividends payable on preference shares are either *cumulative* or *non-cumulative*. If preferred dividends are cumulative and are not paid in a particular year, they will be carried forward. Usually, both the cumulated (past) preferred dividends plus the current preferred dividends must be paid before the ordinary shareholders can receive anything. Unpaid preferred dividends are not debts of the firm. Directors elected by the shareholders can defer preferred dividends indefinitely. However, if this happens

1. Ordinary shareholders must forgo dividends.
2. Though holders of preferred shares do not always have voting rights, they will typically be granted these rights if preferred dividends have not been paid for some time.

Because preference shareholders (sometimes synonymously called preferred stockholders) receive no interest on the cumulated dividends, some have argued that firms have an incentive to delay paying preferred dividends.

Are Preference Shares Really Debt?

A good case can be made that preference shares are really debt in disguise. Preferred shareholders receive a stated dividend only, and if the company is liquidated, preferred shareholders get a stated maximum value although they usually rank behind secured and unsecured creditors, but before ordinary shareholders. Some new issues of preferred stock have had obligatory sinking funds.

Equity versus Debt

Feature	Equity	Debt
Income	Dividends	Interest
Tax Status	Dividends taxed as personal income. Dividends are not a business expense.	Interest is taxed as personal income. Interest is a business expense and companies can deduct interest when computing corporate tax liability.
Control	Ordinary shares and preference shares usually having voting rights.	Control is exercised with loan agreement
Default	Firms cannot become bankrupt for nonpayment of dividends.	Unpaid debt is a liability of the firm. Non-payment may result in liquidation or bankruptcy.
Bottom line:	Tax status favours debt, but default favours equity. Control features of debt and equity are different, but one is not better than the other.	

For all these reasons, preferred stock seems like debt, but, unlike debt, preferred stock dividends cannot be deducted as interest expense when determining taxable corporate income. From the individual investor's point of view, preferred dividends are ordinary income for tax purposes.

Concept Questions

* What are preference shares?
* Do you think they are more like debt or equity?

15.4   Patterns of Financing

Firms use cash flow for capital spending and new working capital. Typically, firms spend about 80 per cent of cash flow on capital spending and 20 per cent on new working capital. **Internal financing** comes from internally generated cash flow and is defined as net income plus depreciation minus dividends. External financing is net new debt and new shares of equity net of buy-backs.

Several features of long-term financing are apparent from data on company cash flows.

1. Internally generated cash flow has dominated as a source of financing. Typically, between 60 and 80 per cent of long-term financing comes from cash flows that companies generate from operations.
2. A financial deficit is created where uses of financing exceed internally generated sources.

In general, the financial deficit is covered by (1) borrowing and (2) issuing new equity, the two sources of external financing.

In a USA survey conducted by Gordon Donaldson on the way firms establish long-term financing strategies,[4] he found

1. The first form of financing used by firms for positive NPV projects is internally generated cash flow (that is net income plus depreciation minus dividends).
2. As a last resort a firm will use externally generated cash flow. First, debt is used. Ordinary shares are used last.

TABLE 15.1   International Financing Patterns: 1990–1992 (sources of funds as a percent of total sources)

	USA	Japan	UK	Germany	France
Internally generated funds	82.8	71.3	68.3	65.5	54.0
Externally generated funds	17.2	28.7	31.7	34.5	46.0
Increase in long-term debt	17.4	21.6	7.4	31.4	6.9
Increase in short-term debt	−3.7	−0.1	6.1	—	10.6
Increase in share issue	3.5	7.1	16.9	—	12.4

----

[4] G. G. Donaldson (1961) *Corporate Debt Capacity: A Study of Corporate Debt Policy and Determination of Corporate Debt Capacity*, Boston: Harvard Graduate School of Business Administration. See also S. C. Myers (1984) 'The capital structure puzzle', *Journal of Finance*, July.

These observations, when taken together, suggest a **pecking order** to long-term financing strategy. At the top of the pecking order is using internally generated cash flow, and at the bottom is issuing new equity.

Concept Questions

- What is the difference between internal financing and external financing?
- What are the major sources of corporate financing?
- What factors influence a firm's choices of external versus internal equity financing?
- What pecking order can be observed in the historical patterns of long-term financing?

15.5   Summary and Conclusions

The basic sources of long-term financing are long-term debt, preferred stock and ordinary shares. This chapter describes the essential features of each.

1. We emphasize that ordinary shareholders have
   - Residual risk and return in a company.
   - Voting rights.
   - Limited liability if the company elects to default on its debt and must transfer some or all of the assets to the creditors.
2. Long-term debt involves contractual obligations set out in indentures. There are many kinds of debt, but the essential feature is that debt involves a stated amount that must be repaid. Interest payments on debt are considered a business expense and are tax deductible.
3. Preferred stock has some of the features of debt and some of the features of ordinary shares. Holders of preferred stock have preference in liquidation and in dividend payments compared to holders of ordinary shares.
4. Firms need financing for capital expenditures, working capital and other long-term uses. Most of the financing is provided from internally generated cash flow. Only about 25 per cent of financing comes from new debt and new external equity.

KEY TERMS

Ordinary shares 344	Dividends 348
Share premium account 345	Seniority 352
Retained earnings 346	Subordinated 352
Book value 346	Preference shares 352
Cumulative voting 347	Internal financing 354
Straight voting 348	Pecking order 355
Proxy 348	

QUESTIONS AND PROBLEMS

Ordinary Shares

15.1 Below are the equity accounts for Kerch Manufacturing Ltd.

Ordinary shares, GBP2 nominal value	GBP135,430
Share premium	203,145
Retained earnings	2,370,025
Total	GBP2,708,600

- *a.* How many shares are outstanding?
- *b.* At what average price were the shares sold?
- *c.* What is the book value of Kerch per share?

15.2 Eastern plc shareholders' funds for last year are presented below:

Ordinary shares GBP1 nominal, 500 shares outstanding	(1)
Share premium	GBP50,000
Retained earnings	100,000
Total	(2)

a. Fill in the missing numbers.

b. Eastern decided to issue 1,000 new shares. The current price is GBP30 per share. Show the effects of the new issue upon the equity accounts.

Preference Shares

15.3 What are the differences between preference shares and debt?

Patterns of Financing

15.4 What are the main differences between corporate debt and equity? Why do some firms try to issue equity in the guise of debt?

CHAPTER 16
Capital Structure: Basic Concepts

Previous chapters of this book examined the capital-budgeting decision. We pointed out that this decision concerns the lefthand side of the balance sheet. The last two chapters began our discussion of the capital-structure decision,[1] which deals with the righthand side of the balance sheet.

In general, a firm can choose any capital structure that it wants. It can issue floating-rate preferred stock, warrants, convertible bonds, caps and collars. It can arrange lease financing, bond swaps and forward contracts. Because the number of instruments is so large, the variations in capital structures are endless. We simplify the analysis by considering only ordinary shares and straight debt in this chapter. The 'bells and whistles', as they are called, must await later chapters of the text.

Our points of focus in this chapter are basic. First, we discuss the capital-structure decision in a world with neither taxes nor other capital-market imperfections. Surprisingly, we find that the capital-structure decision is a matter of indifference in this world. We next argue that there is a quirk in the tax codes of most countries that subsidizes debt financing. Finally, we show that an increase in the firm's value from debt financing leads to an increase in the value of the equity.

16.1 The Capital-Structure Question and the Pie Theory

How should a firm choose its debt–equity ratio? More generally, what is the best capital structure for the firm? We call our approach to the capital-structure question the **pie model**. If you are wondering why we chose this name, just take a look at Figure 16.1. The pie in question is the sum of the financial claims of the firm, debt and equity in this case. We *define* the value of the firm to be this sum. Hence, the value of the firm, V, is

$$V \equiv B + S \qquad (16.1)$$

where B is the market value of the debt and S is the market value of the equity. Figure 16.1 presents two possible ways of slicing this pie between stock and debt: 40 per cent–60 per cent and 60 per cent–40 per cent. If the goal of the management of the firm is to make the firm as valuable as possible, then the firm should pick the debt-equity ratio that makes the pie—the total value, V—as big as possible.

---

[1] It is conventional to refer to choices regarding debt and equity as *capital-structure decisions*. However, the term *financial-structure decisions* would be more accurate, and we use the terms interchangeably.

FIGURE 16.1   Two Pie Models of Capital Structure

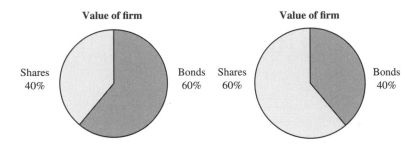

This discussion begs two important questions:

1. Why should the shareholders in the firm care about maximizing the value of the entire firm? After all, the value of the firm is, by definition, the sum of both the debt and the equity. Instead, why should the shareholders not prefer the strategy that maximizes their interests only?
2. What is the ratio of debt to equity that maximizes the shareholders' interests?

Let us examine each of the two questions in turn.

Concept Question

• What is the pie model of capital structure?

16.2   Maximizing Firm Value versus Maximizing Shareholder Interests

The following example illustrates that the capital structure that maximizes the value of the firm is the one that financial managers should choose for the shareholders.

● Example

Suppose the market value of the J. J. Smith Company is GBP1,000. The company currently has no debt, and each of J. J. Smith's 100 shares of stock sells for GBP10. A company such as J. J. Smith with no debt is called an *unlevered* company. Further, suppose that J. J. Smith plans to borrow GBP500 and pay the GBP500 proceeds to shareholders as an extra cash dividend of GBP5 per share. After the issuance of debt, the firm becomes *levered*. The investments of the firm will not change as a result of this transaction. What will the value of the firm be after the proposed restructuring?

Management recognizes that, by definition, only one of three outcomes can occur from restructuring. Firm value after restructuring can be either (1) greater than the original firm value of GBP1,000, (2) equal to GBP1,000 or (3) less than GBP1,000. After consulting with investment bankers, management believes that restructuring will not change firm value more than GBP250 in either direction. Thus, they view firm values of GBP1,250, GBP1,000 and GBP750 as the relevant range. The original capital structure and these three possibilities under the new capital structure are presented below.

	No debt (original capital structure)	Value of debt plus equity after payment of dividend (three possibilities)		
		I	*II*	*III*
Debt	0	GBP500	GBP500	GBP500
Equity	GBP1,000	750	500	250
Firm value	GBP1,000	GBP1,250	GBP1,000	GBP750

Note that the value of equity is below GBP1,000 under any of the three possibilities. This can be explained in one of two ways. First, the chart shows the value of the equity *after* the extra cash dividend is paid. Since cash is paid out, a dividend represents a partial liquidation of the firm. Consequently, there is less value in the firm for the equityholders after the dividend payment. Second, in the event of a future liquidation, shareholders will be paid only after bondholders have been paid in full. Thus, the debt is an encumbrance of the firm, reducing the value of the equity.

Of course, management recognizes that there are infinite possible outcomes. The above three are to be viewed as representative outcomes only. We can now determine the payoff to shareholders under the three possibilities:

	Payoff to shareholders after restructuring		
	I	*II*	*III*
Capital gains	−GBP250	−GBP500	−GBP750
Dividends	500	500	500
Net gain or loss to shareholders	GBP250	0	−GBP250

No one can be sure ahead of time which of the three outcomes will occur. However, imagine that managers believe that outcome *I* is most likely. They should definitely restructure the firm because the shareholders would gain GBP250. That is, although the price of the shares declines by GBP250 to GBP750, they receive GBP500 in dividends. Their net gain is GBP250 = −GBP250 + GBP500. Also, notice that the value of the firm would rise by GBP250.

Alternatively, imagine that managers believe that outcome *III* is most likely. In this case, they should not restructure the firm because the shareholders would expect a GBP250 loss. That is, the shares fall by GBP750 to GBP250 and they receive GBP500 in dividends. Their net loss is −GBP250 = −GBP750 + GBP500. Also, notice that the value of the firm would fall by GBP250.

Finally, imagine that the managers believe that outcome *II* is most likely. Restructuring would not affect the shareholders' interest because the net gain to shareholders in this case is zero. Also, notice that the value of the firm is unchanged if outcome *II* occurs. ●

This example explains why managers should attempt to maximize the value of the firm. In other words, it answers question (1) in Section 16.1. In this example, changes in capital structure benefit the shareholders *if and only if* the value of the firm increases. Conversely, these changes hurt the shareholders if and only if the value of the firm decreases. This result holds generally for capital-structure changes of many different types.[2] Thus, managers should choose the capital structure that they believe

---

[2] This result may not hold exactly in the more complex case where debt has a significant possibility of default. Issues of default are treated in the next chapter.

will have the highest firm value because this capital structure is most beneficial to the firm's shareholders.

Note, however, that the example does not tell us which of the three outcomes is most likely to occur. Thus, it does not tell us whether debt should be added to J. J. Smith's capital structure. In other words, it does not answer question (2) in Section 16.1. This second question is treated in the next section.

Concept Question

• Why should financial managers choose the capital structure that maximizes the value of the firm?

16.3   Can an Optimal Capital Structure Be Determined?

Modigliani and Miller: Proposition I (No Taxes)

The previous section shows that the capital structure producing the highest firm value is the one most beneficial to the shareholders. In the present section, we would have liked to determine the particular capital structure that produces the highest firm value. Unfortunately, as you will see, we are unable to do this. Modigliani and Miller (MM) have a convincing argument that a firm cannot change the total value of its outstanding securities by changing the proportions of its capital structure. In other words, the value of the firm is always the same under different capital structures. In still other words, no capital structure is any better or worse than any other capital structure for the firm's stockholders. This rather pessimistic result is the famous **MM Proposition I**.[3]

To see how the MM Proposition I works, consider an unlevered firm that generates expected earnings of *Earn* per year. The firm does not retain any earnings, so its earnings are all paid out as dividends. The value of this unlevered firm is denoted as V_U. Further consider an individual buying 15 per cent of the company. He pays $0.15V_U$ initially and expects to receive $0.15Earn$ as dividends each year. This transaction can be illustrated as follows:

Strategy I (buying 15 per cent of unlevered firm)

Initial investment	Expected dividend per year
$0.15V_U$	$0.15Earn$

Now consider a levered firm, i.e. a firm with both stock and debt in its capital structure. The value of the shares are denoted by S_L, and the value of the bonds is denoted B. As mentioned earlier, the value of the firm is, by definition, the sum of its shares plus its bonds. Thus, the value of the levered firm, V_L, is equal to $S_L + B$. Except for the difference in capital structure, we assume that this firm is identical to the unlevered firm above. This means that the levered firm is expected to generate yearly earnings before interest payments of *Earn*. Now assume that the bondholders receive interest payments of *Int*, implying that the shareholders expect to receive annual dividends of (*Earn – Int*). A person buying 15 per cent of the stock of this

---

[3] The original paper appeared in 1958: F. Modigliani and M. Miller (1958) 'The cost of capital, corporation finance and the theory of investment', *American Economic Review*, June.

levered firm pays $0.15S_L$ initially and expects to receive $0.15(Earn - Int)$ each year. This transaction can be illustrated as:

Strategy II (buying 15 per cent of the stock of the levered firm)

Initial investment	*Expected dividend per year*
$0.15S_L$	$0.15(Earn - Int)$

Strategy II is more risky than strategy I because strategy II involves corporate leverage. This difference in risk occurs because bondholders receive their interest in full before the shareholders receive anything. (Much more will be said on the effect of leverage on risk later in this chapter.)

Now consider Robert Heiler, an arbitrageur, who is contemplating a third, and more complex, strategy. He plans to:

1. Borrow 0.15BL from a bank.
2. Use the borrowed proceeds plus his own funds to buy 15 per cent of the shares of the unlevered firm.

This strategy is illustrated as follows:

Strategy III (buying 15 per cent of the shares of the unlevered firm by a combination of one's own funds plus personal borrowing)

Initial investment	*Expected net dividend per year after payment of interest*
$0.15V_U - 0.15B_L$	$0.15Earn - 0.15Int$

Note that it costs $0.15V_U$ to buy 15 per cent of the unlevered firm. However, since our arbitrageur borrows $0.15B_L$, he only pays the difference, $0.15V_U - 0.15B_L$, out of his own pocket. Also, his expected net dividends per year is $0.15Earn - 0.15Int$ because he must pay interest on the money he borrowed.[4]

Now let us compare strategy III with strategy II, the comparison that Modigliani and Miller use to establish their important capital proposition I. We compare both the expected net dividends per year and the initial investments of the two strategies. Notice that the expected net dividends each period are equal for the two strategies.

The initial investments of the two strategies are:

Initial investment of strategy II	*Initial investment of strategy III*
$0.15S_L$	$0.15V_U - 0.15B_L$

Because the net dividends on the two strategies are identical, the initial investments *must* be identical as well. Otherwise, one investment would be cheaper than the other, and no rational person would buy the expensive asset. Consequently, its price would then fall until the two initial investments became equal.

Inspection of the two initial investments above indicates that equality of initial

---

[4] We are assuming that an individual can borrow at the same interest rate as the firm. Though many students believe that this assumption is unrealistic, we show later that it is quite plausible in the real world.

investment occurs when $V_U = S_L + B_L$. Since $S_L + B_L$ is equal to V_L by definition, equality of initial investment occurs when $V_U = V_L$. This proves that

> MM proposition I (no taxes): the value of the unlevered firm is the same as the value of the levered firm, that is $V_L = V_U$.

Though this discussion may strike you as mathematical, the intuition can be explained as follows. Suppose that our result did not hold. For example, suppose that the value of the levered firm were actually greater than the value of the unlevered firm, that is, $V_L > V_U$. Our arbitrageur, Mr Heiler, could borrow on his own account and invest in the shares of the unlevered company. He would get the same net dividend each year as if he had invested in the levered firm. However, his cost would be less because $V_L > V_U$. The strategy would not be unique to him. Given $V_L > V_U$, no rational individual would ever invest in the levered firm. Anyone desiring shares in the levered firm would get the same cash return more cheaply by borrowing to finance a purchase of the unlevered firm's shares. The equilibrium result would be, of course, that the value of the levered firm would fall and the value of the unlevered firm would rise until $V_L = V_U$. At this point, individuals would be indifferent between strategy II and strategy III.

This is perhaps the most important example in all of corporate finance. In fact, it is considered the beginning point of modern managerial finance. Before MM, the effect of leverage on the value of the firm was considered complex and convoluted. Modigliani and Miller show a blindingly simple result: if levered firms are priced too high, rational investors will simply borrow on personal account to buy shares in unlevered firms. This substitution is oftentimes called *homemade leverage*. As long as individuals borrow (and lend) on the same terms as the firm, they can duplicate the effects of corporate leverage on their own.

The above example shows that leverage does not affect the value of the firm. Since we showed earlier that shareholders' welfare is directly related to the firm's value, the example indicates that changes in capital structure cannot affect the shareholders' welfare.

Concept Questions

- State MM Proposition I. What are its assumptions?
- How can a shareholder undo a firm's financial leverage?

16.4   Financial Leverage and Firm Value: An Example

Trans Euro Company currently has no debt in its capital structure. The chief financial officer, Ms Morris, is considering issuing debt to buy back some of its equity. Both its current and proposed capital structures are presented in Table 16.1. The firm's assets are GBP8,000,000. There are 400,000 shares of the all-equity firm, implying a market value per share of GBP20. The proposed debt issue is for GBP4,000,000, leaving GBP4,000,000 in equity. The interest rate is 10 per cent.

Ms Morris believes the firm's shareholders will be better off with a debt issue. To justify her conclusion, she has prepared Table 16.2, which shows both the company's current structure and its proposed structure under three different, *equally probable* economic scenarios. Ms Morris is ultimately interested in comparing both return on

TABLE 16.1   Financial Structure of Trans Euro Company

	Current	Proposed
Assets	GBP8,000,000	GBP8,000,000
Debt	0	GBP4,000,000
Equity (market and book)	GBP8,000,000	GBP4,000,000
Interest rate	10%	10%
Market value/share	GBP20	GBP20
Shares outstanding	400,000	200,000

The propsed capital structure has leverage, whereas the current structure is all equity.

TABLE 16.2   Alternative Capital Structure for Trans Euro Company

	Current structure: No debt			Proposed structure: Debt = GBP4,000,000		
	Recession	Expected	Expansion	Recession	Expected	Expansion
Return on assets (ROA)	5%	15%	25%	5%	15%	25%
Earnings before interest (EBI)	GBP400,000	GBP1,200,000	GBP2,000,000	GBP400,000	GBP1,200,000	GBP2,000,000
Interest	0	0	0	GBP400,000	GBP400,000	GBP400,000
Earnings after interest	GBP400,000	GBP1,200,000	GBP2,000,000	0	GBP800,000	GBP1,600,000
Return on equity (ROE) = Earnings after interest/Equity	5%	15%	25%	0	20%	40%
Earnings per share (EPS)	GPB1.00	GBP3.00	GBP5.00	0	GBP4.00	GBP8.00

When EBI is high, Trans Euro has higher EPS and ROE with the proposed structure than with the current structure. When EBI is low, Trans Euro has lower EPS and ROE with the proposed structure. Thus, the equityholders bear more risk with the proposed structure.

equity (ROE) and earnings per share (EPS) under the two capital structures. ROE is the ratio of earnings after interest to equity. Under the current capital structure, ROE is expected to be 15 per cent (= GBP1,200,000/GBP8,000,000). Under the current capital structure, EPS is expected to be GBP3 (= GBP1,200,000/400,000), where 400,000 is the number of shares outstanding.

She concludes from her analysis that

1. The effect of financial leverage depends on the company's earnings before interest. If earnings before interest is equal to GBP1,200,000, the return on equity (ROE) is higher under the proposed structure. If earnings before interest is equal to GBP400,000, the ROE is higher under the current structure.

This is represented in a graph of hers, which we have reproduced as Figure 16.2. The solid line represents the case of no leverage. The line begins at the origin, indicating that earnings per share (EPS) would be zero if earnings before interest (EBI) were zero. The EPS rises in tandem with a rise in EBI.

FIGURE 16.2   **Financial Leverage: EPS and EBI for the Trans Euro Company**

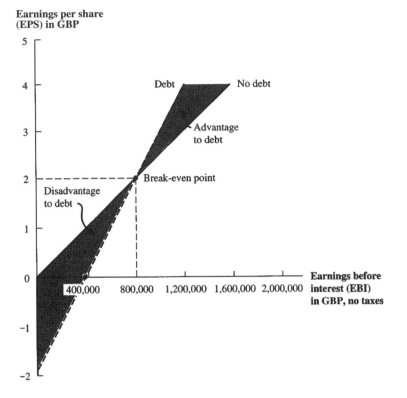

The dotted line represents the case of GBP4,000,000 of debt. Here, EPS is negative if EBI is zero. This follows because GBP400,000 of interest must be paid regardless of the firm's profits.

Now consider the slopes of the two lines. The slope of the dotted line (the line with debt) is higher than the slope of the solid line. This occurs because the levered firm has *fewer* shares of stock outstanding than does the unlevered firm. Therefore, any increase in EBI leads to a greater rise in EPS for the levered firm because the earnings increase is distributed over fewer shares of stock.

Because the dotted line has a lower intercept, but a higher slope, the two lines must intersect. The *break-even* point occurs at GBP800,000 of EBI. Were earnings before interest to be GBP800,000, both firms would produce GBP2 of earnings per share (EPS). Because GBP800,000 is break-even, earnings above GBP800,000 lead to greater EPS for the levered firm. Earnings below GBP800,000 lead to greater EPS for the unlevered firm.

2. Because expected earnings before interest is GBP1,200,000, she reasons that the shareholders are better off under the proposed capital structure.

Mr Siegel, a financial consultant hired by the Trans Euro Company, argues that the analysis in point (1) is correct, but the conclusion in point (2) is incorrect. He states that the shareholders of Trans Euro can borrow on personal account if they want to duplicate the company's proposed financial leverage. The consultant considers an investor who would buy 100 shares of the proposed levered equity. Alternatively, the investor could buy 200 shares of the unlevered firm, partially financing his purchase by borrowing GBP2,000. Both the cost and the payoff from the two strategies will be the same. Thus, Mr Siegel concludes that Trans Euro is neither helping nor hurting its shareholders by restructuring. In other words, the investor is not receiving anything from corporate leverage that he or she could not achieve on his or her own. His calculations are presented in Table 16.3.

His assistant, Stuart Weiss, then stated, 'This is nothing more than a discussion of the Modigliani–Miller relationship. Because individuals can create homemade leverage, there is no need for corporate leverage.' He then related the story of the world's stupidest criminal. It seems someone hijacked a commercial airplane, commanding it to go to London Heathrow. However, London Heathrow was the scheduled destination anyway. Mr Weiss concluded, 'The hijacker's action neither helped nor hurt the passengers. Similarly, a change in corporate leverage can neither help nor hurt the shareholders.'

TABLE 16.3 Payoff and Cost to Shareholders of Trans Euro Company under the Proposed Structure and under the Current Structure with Homemade Leverage

Trans Euro: proposed capital structure

	Recession	*Expected*	*Expansion*
EPS (taken from last line of Table 16.2)	GBP0	GBP4	GBP8
Earnings per 100 shares	GBP0	GBP400	GBP800

Initial cost = 100 shares @ GBP20/share = GBP2,000

Homemade leverage by shareholders of Trans Euro

	Recession	*Expected*	*Expansion*
Earnings per 200 shares in current Trans Euro	GBP1 × 200 = GBP200	GBP3 × 200 = GBP600	GBP5 × 200 = GBP1,000
Interest at 10% on GBP2,000	−GBP200	−GBP200	−GBP200
Net	GBP0	GBP400	GBP800

Initial cost = 200 shares @ GBP20/share − GBP2,000 = GBP2,000
                    Cost of shares   Cost of debt

Investor receives the same payoff whether she (1) buys shares in a levered corporation or (2) buys shares in an unlevered firm and borrows on personal account. Her initial investment is the same in either case. Thus, the firm neither helps nor hurts her by adding debt to capital structure.

A Key Assumption

The MM result hinges on the assumption that individuals can borrow as cheaply as corporations. If, alternatively, individuals can only borrow at a higher rate, one can easily show that corporations can increase firm value by borrowing.

Is this assumption of equal borrowing costs a good one? Individuals who want to buy shares and borrow can do so by establishing a loan account with a banker. Under this arrangement, the banker lends the individual a portion of the purchase price. For example, the individual might buy GBP10,000 of shares by investing GBP6,000 of her own funds and borrowing GBP4,000 from the banker. Should the shares be worth GBP9,000 on the next day, the individual's net worth or equity in the account would be GBP5,000 = GBP9,000 − GBP4,000.[5]

---
[5] We are ignoring the one-day interest charge on the loan.

The banker fears that a sudden price drop will cause the equity in the individual's account to be negative, implying that the banker may not get the loan repaid in full. To guard against this possibility, the banker may hold the shares as collateral.

By contrast, companies frequently borrow using illiquid assets (e.g., plant and equipment) as collateral. The costs to the lender of initial negotiation and ongoing supervision, as well as of working out arrangements in the event of financial distress, can be quite substantial. Thus, it is difficult to argue that individuals must borrow at higher rates than corporations—all other things being equal.

This is, of course, the argument of MM Proposition I.

Concept Questions

- Describe financial leverage.
- What is levered equity? How can a shareholder of Trans Euro undo the company's financial leverage?

16.5   Modigliani and Miller: Proposition II (No Taxes)

At a corporate meeting where both Ms Morris and Mr Siegel presented their viewpoints, a corporate officer said, 'Well, maybe it doesn't matter whether the company or the individual levers—as long as some leverage takes place. Leverage benefits investors. After all, the investor's expected return rises with the amount of leverage present.' He then pointed out that, from Table 16.2, the expected return on unlevered equity is 15 per cent while the expected return on levered equity is 20 per cent.

Mr Siegel replied, 'Not necessarily. Though the expected return rises with leverage, the *risk* rises as well.' Mr Siegel's point can be seen from an examination of Table 16.2. With earnings before interest (EBI) varying between GBP400,000 and GBP2,000,000, earnings per share (EPS) for the shareholders of the unlevered firm vary between GBP1.00 and GBP5.00. EPS for the shareholders of the levered firm vary between GBP0 and GBP8.00. This greater range for the EPS of the levered firm implies greater risk for the levered firm's shareholders. In other words, levered shareholders have better returns in good times than do unlevered shareholders but have worse returns in bad times. Table 16.2 also shows greater range for the ROE of the levered firm's shareholders. The above interpretation concerning risk applies here as well.

The same insight can be taken from Figure 16.2. The slope of the line for the levered firm is greater than the slope of the line for the unlevered firm. This also means that the levered shareholders have better returns in good times than do unlevered shareholders, but have worse returns in bad times, implying greater risk with leverage. In other words, the slope of the line measures the risk to shareholders, since the slope indicates the responsiveness of ROE to changes in firm performance (earnings before interest).

Since levered equity has greater risk, it should have greater expected returns as compensation. The market only *requires* a 15 per cent expected return for the unlevered equity, but it requires a 20 per cent expected return for the levered equity.

This type of reasoning allows us to develop **MM Proposition II**. Here, MM argue that the expected return on equity is positively related to leverage, because the risk of equity increases with leverage.

To develop this position recall from Chapter 13 that the firm's weighted average cost of capital, r_{WACC}, can be written as:[6]

$$\frac{B}{B + S} \times r_B + \frac{S}{B + S} \times r_S \tag{16.2}$$

where

> r_B is the interest rate, also called the cost of debt
> r_S is the expected return on equity, also called the *cost of equity* or the *required return on equity*
> r_{WACC} is the firm's weighted average cost of capital
> B is the value of debt
> S is the value of stock or equity.

Formula (16.2) is quite intuitive. It simply says that a firm's weighted average cost of capital is a weighted average of its cost of debt and its cost of equity. The weight applied to debt is the proportion of debt in the capital structure, and the weight applied to equity is the proportion of equity in the capital structure. Calculations of r_{WACC} from (16.2) for both the unlevered and the levered firm are presented in Table 16.4.

An implication of MM Proposition I is that r_{WACC} is a constant for a given firm, regardless of the capital structure.[7] For example, Table 16.4 shows that r_{WACC} for Trans Euro is 15 per cent, with or without leverage.

Let us now define r_0 to be the *cost of capital for an all-equity firm*. For the Trans Euro Company, r_0 is calculated as:

$$r_0 = \frac{\text{Expected earnings to unlevered firm}}{\text{Unlevered equity}} = \frac{\text{GBP1,200,000}}{\text{GBP8,000,000}} = 15\%$$

As can be seen from Table 16.4, r_{WACC} is equal to r_0 for Trans Euro. In fact, r_{WACC} must always equal r_0 in a world without corporate taxes.

TABLE 16.4   Cost of Capital Calculations for Trans Euro

$r_{\text{WACC}} = \dfrac{B}{B + S} \times r_B + \dfrac{S}{B + S} \times r_S$	
Unlevered firm:	$15\% = \dfrac{0}{\text{GBP8,000,000}} \times 10\%{*} + \dfrac{\text{GBP8,000,000}}{\text{GBP8,000,000}} \times 15\%{\dagger}$
Levered firm:	$15\% = \dfrac{\text{GBP4,000,000}}{\text{GBP8,000,000}} \times 10\%{*} + \dfrac{\text{GBP4,000,000}}{\text{GBP8,000,000}} \times 20\%{\ddagger}$

*10% is the interest rate.

†From the 'expected' column in Table 16.2, we learn that expected earnings after interest for the unlevered firm are GBP1,200,000. From Table 16.1, we learn that equity for the levered firm is GBP8,000,000. Thus, r_S for the unlevered firm is:

$$\frac{\text{Expected earnings after interest}}{\text{Equity}} = \frac{\text{GBP1,200,000}}{\text{GBP8,000,000}} = 15\%.$$

‡From the 'expected' column in Table 16.2, we learn that expected earnings after interest for the levered firm are GBP800,000. From Table 16.1, we learn that equity for the levered firm is GBP4,000,000. Thus, r_S for the levered firm is:

$$\frac{\text{Expected earnings after interest}}{\text{Equity}} = \frac{\text{GBP800,000}}{\text{GBP4,000,000}} = 20\%.$$

---

[6] Since we do not have taxes here, the cost of debt is r_B, not $r_B(1 - T_C)$ as it was in Chapter 13.

[7] This statement holds in a world of no-taxes. It does not hold in a world with taxes, a point to be brought out later in this chapter (see Figure 16.6).

Proposition II states the expected return on equity, r_S, in terms of leverage. The exact relationship, derived by setting $r_{WACC} = r_0$ and then rearranging (16.2), is[8]

MM Proposition II (no taxes):

$$r_S = r_0 + \frac{B}{S}(r_0 - r_B) \qquad (16.3)$$

Equation (16.3) states that the required return on equity is a linear function of the firm's debt–equity ratio. Examining formula (16.3), we see that if r_0 exceeds the debt rate, r_B, then the cost of equity increases with increases in the debt–equity ratio, B/S.[9] Note that equation (16.3) holds for Trans Euro in its levered state:

$$0.20 = 0.15 + \frac{GBP4,000,000}{GBP4,000,000}(0.15 - 0.10)$$

Figure 16.3 graphs formula (16.3). As you can see, we have plotted the relation between the cost of equity, r_S, and the debt–equity ratio, B/S, as a straight line. What we witness in (16.3) and illustrate in Figure 16.3 is the effect of leverage on the cost of equity. As the firm raises the debt–equity ratio, each dollar of equity is levered with additional debt. This raises the risk of equity and therefore the required return, r_S, on the equity.

Figure 16.3 also shows that r_{WACC} is unaffected by leverage, a point we made above.

Example Illustrating Proposition I and Proposition II

● Example

Luteran Motors plc, an all-equity firm, has expected earnings of GBP10 million per year in perpetuity. The firm pays all of its earnings out as dividends, so that the GBP10 million may also be viewed as the shareholders' expected cash flow. There are 10 million shares outstanding, implying expected annual cash flow of GBP1 per share. The cost of capital for this unlevered firm is 10 per cent. In addition, the firm will soon

---

[8] This can be derived from (16.2) by setting $r_{WACC} - r_0$

$$\frac{B}{B+S}r_B + \frac{S}{B+S}r_S = r_0 \qquad (16.2)$$

Multiplying both sides by $(B + S)/S$ yields:

$$\frac{B}{S}r_B + r_S = \frac{B+S}{S}r_0$$

We can rewrite the righthand side as

$$\frac{B}{S}r_B + r_S = \frac{B}{S}r_0 + r_0$$

Moving $(B/S)\,r_B$ to the righthand side and rearranging yields:

$$r_S = r_0 + \frac{B}{S}(r_0 - r_B) \qquad (16.3)$$

[9] Normally, r_0 should exceed r_B. That is, because even unlevered equity is risky, it should have an expected return greater than that on riskless debt.

FIGURE 16.3   The Cost of Equity, the Cost of Debt, and the Weighted Average Cost of Capital: MM Proposition II with No Corporate Taxes

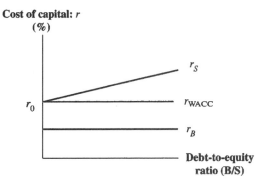

$$r_S = r_0 + (r_0 - r_B)B/S$$

r_S is the cost of equity

r_B is the cost of debt

r_0 is the cost of capital for an all-equity firm

r_{WACC} is a firm's weighted average cost of capital. In a world with no taxes, r_{WACC} for a levered firm is equal to r_0.

The cost of equity capital, r_S is positively related to the firm's debt–equity ratio. The firm's weighted average cost of capital, r_{WACC}, is invariant to the firm's debt–equity ratio.

build a new plant for GBP4 million. The plant is expected to generate additional cash flow of GBP1 million per year. These figures can be described as

Current company	*New plant*
Cash flow: GBP10 million	Initial outlay: GBP4 million
Number of outstanding shares: 10 million	Additional annual cash flow: GBP1 million

The project's net present value is

$$-\text{GBP4 million} + \frac{\text{GBP1 million}}{0.1} = \text{GBP6 million}$$

assuming that the project is discounted at the same rate as the firm as a whole. Before the market knows of the project, the *market-value* balance sheet of the firm is

LUTERAN MOTORS
Market-value balance sheet (all equity)

Old assets: $\dfrac{\text{GBP10million}}{0.1} = \text{GBP100 million}$	Equity: GBP100 million (10 million shares)

The value of the firm is GBP100 million, because the cash flow of GBP10 million per year is capitalized at 10 per cent. A share sells for GBP10 (GBP100 million/10 million) because there are 10 million shares outstanding. ●

The market-value balance sheet is a useful tool of financial analysis. Because students are often thrown off guard by it initially, we recommend extra study here. The key is that the market-value balance sheet has the same form as the balance sheet that accountants use. That is, assets are placed on the lefthand side whereas liabilities and owners' equity are placed on the righthand side. In addition, the lefthand side and the righthand side must be equal. The difference between a market value balance sheet and the accountant's balance sheet is in the numbers. Accountants value items in terms of historical cost (original purchase price less depreciation), whereas financial people value items in terms of market value.

The firm will either issue GBP4 million of equity or debt. Let us consider the effect of equity and debt financing in turn.

Share Financing

Imagine that the firm announces that, in the near future, it will raise GBP4 million in equity in order to build a new plant. The share price, and therefore the value of the firm, will rise to reflect the positive net present value of the plant. According to efficient markets, the increase occurs immediately. That is, the rise occurs on the day of the announcement, not on the date of either the onset of construction of the power plant or the forthcoming share offering. The market-value balance sheet becomes

LUTERAN MOTORS
Market-value balance sheet
(upon announcement of equity issue to construct plant)

Old assets	GBP100 million	Equity	GBP106 million (10 million shares)
NPV of plant: $-\text{GBP4 million} + \dfrac{\text{GBP1 million}}{0.1} = 6 \text{ million}$			
Total assets	GBP106 million		

Note that the NPV of the plant is included in the market-value balance sheet. Because the new shares have not yet been issued, the number of outstanding shares remains 10 million. The price per share has now risen to GBP10.60 (GBP106 million/10 million) to reflect news concerning the plant.

Shortly thereafter, GBP4 million of shares are issued or *floated*. Because the shares are selling at GBP10.60 per share, 377,358 (GBP4 million/GBP10.60) shares are issued. Imagine that funds are put in the bank *temporarily* before being used to build the plant. The market-value balance sheet becomes

LUTERAN MOTORS
Market-value balance sheet
(upon issuance of stock but before construction begins on plant)

Old assets	GBP100 million	Equity	GBP110 million (10,377,358 shares)
NPV of plant:	6 million		
Proceeds from new issue of shares (currently invested in bank)	4 million		
Total asset	GBP110 million		

The number of shares outstanding is now 10,377,358 because 377,358 new shares were issued. The price per share is GBP10.60 (GBP110,000,000/10,377,358). Note that the price has not changed. This is consistent with efficient capital markets, because share price should only move due to new information.

Of course, the funds are placed in the bank only temporarily. Shortly after the new issue, the GBP4 million is given to a contractor who builds the plant. To avoid problems in discounting, we assume that the plant is built immediately. The balance sheet then becomes

LUTERAN MOTORS
Market-value balance sheet
(upon completion of the plant)

Old assets	GBP100 million	Equity	GBP110 million
			(10,377,358 shares)
PV of plant:	$\dfrac{\text{GBP1 million}}{0.1} = 10$ million		
Total assets	GBP110 million		

Though total assets do not change, the composition of the assets does change. The bank account has been emptied to pay the contractor. The present value of cash flows of GBP1 million a year from the plant are reflected as an asset worth GBP10 million. Because the building expenditures of GBP4 million have already been paid, they no longer represent a future cost. Hence, they no longer reduce the value of the plant. According to efficient capital markets, the price per share remains GBP10.60.

The expected yearly cash flow from the firm is GBP11 million, GBP10 million of which comes from the old assets and GBP1 million from the new. The expected return to equityholders is

$$r_S = \frac{\text{GBP11 million}}{\text{GBP110 million}} = 0.10$$

Because the firm is all equity, $r_S = r_0 = 0.10$.

Debt Financing

Alternatively, imagine that the firm announces that, in the near future, it will borrow GBP4 million at 6 per cent to build a new plant. This implies yearly interest payments of GBP240,000 (GBP4,000,000 $\times$ 6%). Again, the share price rises immediately to reflect the positive net present value of the plant. Thus, we have

LUTERAN MOTORS
Market value balance sheet
(upon announcement of debt issue to construct plant)

Old assets	GBP100 million	Equity	GBP106 million
			(10 million shares)
NPV of plant:			
$-\text{GBP4 million} + \dfrac{\text{GBP1 million}}{0.1} = 6$ million			
Total assets	GBP106 million		

The value of the firm is the same as in the equity financing case because (1) the same plant is to be built and (2) MM prove that debt financing is neither better nor worse than equity financing.

At some point, GBP4 million of debt is issued. As before, the funds are placed in the bank temporarily. The market-value balance sheet becomes

LUTERAN MOTORS
Market-value balance sheet
(upon debt issuance but before construction begins on plant)

Old assets	GBP100 million	Debt	GBP4 million
NPV of plant	6 million	Equity	106 million
			(10 million shares)
Proceeds from debt issue (currently invested in bank)	4 million		
Total assets	GBP110 million	Debt plus equity	GBP110 million

Note that debt appears on the right-hand side of the balance sheet. The share price is still GBP10.60, in accordance with our discussion of efficient capital markets.

Finally, the contractor receives GBP4 million and builds the plant. The market value balance sheet becomes

LUTERAN MOTORS
Market-value balance sheet
(upon completion of the plant)

Old assets	GBP100 million	Debt	GBP4 million
PV of plant	10 million	Equity	106 million
			(10 million shares)
Total assets	GBP110 million	Debt plus equity	GBP110 million

The only change here is that the bank account has been depleted to pay the contractor. The equityholders expect yearly cash flow after interest of

$$\underset{\substack{\text{Cash flow on}\\\text{old assets}}}{\text{GBP10,000,000}} + \underset{\substack{\text{Cash flow on}\\\text{new assets}}}{\text{GBP1,000,000}} - \underset{\substack{\text{Interest:}\\\text{GBP4 million} \times 6\%}}{\text{GBP240,000}} = \text{GBP10,760,000}$$

The equityholders expect to earn a return of

$$\frac{\text{GBP10,760,000}}{\text{GBP106,000,000}} = 10.15\%$$

This return of 10.15 per cent for levered equityholders is higher than the 10 per cent return for the unlevered equityholders. This result is sensible because, as we argued earlier, levered equity is riskier. In fact, the return of 10.15 per cent should be exactly what the MM Proposition II predicts. This prediction can be verified by plugging values into

$$r_S = r_0 + \frac{B}{S} \times (r_0 - r_B) \tag{16.3}$$

We obtain

$$10.15\% = 10\% + \frac{\text{GBP4,000,000}}{\text{GBP106,000,000}} \times (10\% - 6\%)$$

This example was useful for two reasons. First, we wanted to introduce the concept of market-value balance sheets, a tool that will prove useful elsewhere in the text. Among other things, this technique allows one to calculate the price per share of a new issue of stock. Second, the example illustrates three aspects of Modigliani and Miller:

1. The example is consistent with MM Proposition I because the value of the firm is GBP110 million after either equity or debt financing.
2. Students are often more interested in stock price than in firm value. We show that the share price is always GBP10.60, regardless of whether debt or equity financing is used.
3. The example is consistent with MM Proposition II. The expected return to equityholders rises from 10 to 10.15 per cent, just as formula (16.3) states. This rise occurs because the equityholders of a levered firm face more risk than do the equityholders of an unlevered firm.

MM: An Interpretation

The Modigliani–Miller results indicate that managers of a firm cannot change its value by repackaging the firm's securities. Though this idea was considered revolutionary when it was originally proposed in the late 1950s, the MM model and arbitrage proof have since met with wide acclaim.[10]

It is argued by MM that the firm's overall cost of capital cannot be reduced as debt is substituted for equity, even though debt appears to be cheaper than equity. The reason for this is that, as the firm adds debt, the remaining equity becomes more risky. As this risk rises, the cost of equity capital rises as a result. The increase in the cost of the remaining equity capital offsets the higher proportion of the firm financed by low-cost debt. In fact, MM prove that the two effects exactly offset each other, so that both the value of the firm and the firm's overall cost of capital are invariant to leverage.

An interesting analogy to food is used by MM. They consider a dairy farmer with two choices. On the one hand, he can sell whole milk. On the other hand, by skimming he can sell a combination of cream and low-fat milk. Though the farmer can get a high price for the cream, he gets a low price for the low-fat milk, implying no net gain. In fact, imagine that the proceeds from the whole-milk strategy were less than those from the cream–low-fat-milk strategy. Arbitrageurs would buy the whole milk, perform the skimming operation themselves, and resell the cream and low-fat milk separately. Competition between arbitrageurs would tend to boost the price of whole milk until proceeds from the two strategies became equal. Thus, the value of the farmer's milk is invariant to the way in which the milk is packaged.

Food found its way into this chapter earlier, when we viewed the firm as a pie.[11] According to MM, the size of the pie does not change, no matter how shareholders and bondholders divide it. They say that a firm's capital structure is irrelevant; it is what it is by some historical accident. The theory implies that firms' debt–equity ratios could be anything. The latter are what they are because of whimsical and random managerial decisions about how much to borrow and how much stock to issue.

---

[10] Both Merton Miller and Franco Modigliani were awarded separate Nobel Prizes, in part for their work on capital structure.

[11] Other authors have also brought food into discussions on capital structure. For example, Stewart Myers (1983) 'The search for optimal capital structure', *Midland Corporate Finance Journal*, Spring, used chicken. Abstracting from the extra costs in cutting-up poultry, he argues that all of the chicken parts should, in sum, sell for no more than a whole chicken.

Although scholars are always fascinated by far reaching theories, students are perhaps more concerned with real-world applications. Do real-world managers follow MM by treating capital-structure decisions with indifference? Unfortunately for the theory, virtually all companies in certain industries, such as banking, choose high debt–equity ratios. Conversely, companies in other industries, such as pharmaceuticals, choose low debt–equity ratios. In fact, almost any industry has a debt–equity ratio to which companies in that industry adhere. Thus, companies do not appear to be selecting their degree of leverage in a frivolous or random manner. Because of this, financial economists (including MM themselves) have argued that real-world factors may have been left out of the theory.

Though many of our students have argued that individuals can only borrow at rates above the corporate borrowing rate, we disagreed with this argument earlier in the chapter. But when we look elsewhere for unrealistic assumptions in the theory, we find two.[12]

1. Taxes were ignored.
2. Bankruptcy costs and other agency costs were not considered.

We will turn to taxes shortly. Bankruptcy costs and other agency costs will be treated in the next chapter.

Concept Questions

• Why does the expected return on equity rise with firm leverage?
• What is the exact relationship between the expected return on equity and firm leverage?
• How are market-value balance sheets set up?

16.6   Taxes

The Basic Insight

The previous part of this chapter showed that firm value is unrelated to debt in a world without taxes. We now show that, in the presence of corporate taxes, the firm's value is positively related to its debt. The basic intuition can be seen from a pie chart, such as the one in Figure 16.4. Consider the all-equity firm on the left. Here, both equityholders and the tax authorities have claims on the value of the firm. The value of the all-equity firm is, of course, that part of the pie owned by the equityholders. The proportion going to taxes is simply a cost.

The pie on the right for the levered firm shows three claims: equityholders, debtholders and taxes. The value of the levered firm is the sum of the value of the debt and the value of the equity. In selecting between the two capital structures in the picture, a financial manager should select the one with the highest value. Assuming that the total area is the same for both pies,[13] value is maximized for that capital structure paying the least in taxes. In other words, the manager should choose the capital structure that the tax authorities hate the most.

We will show that, due to a quirk in most countries' tax laws, the proportion of the

---

[12] MM were aware of both of these issues, as can be seen in their original paper.
[13] Under the MM propositions developed earlier, the two pies should be of the same size.

In Professor Miller's Words . . .

The Modigliani–Miller results are not easy to understand fully. This point is related in a story told by Merton Miller.[14]

'How difficult to summarize briefly the contribution of the [Modigliani–Miller] papers was brought home to me very clearly last October after Franco Modigliani was awarded the Nobel Prize in Economics in part—but, of course, only in part—for the work in finance. The television camera crews from our local stations in Chicago immediately descended upon me. "We understand", they said, "that you worked with Modigliani some years back in developing these M and M theorems and we wonder if you could explain them briefly to our television viewers".'

'"How briefly?" I asked.

'"Oh, take ten seconds", was the reply.

'Ten seconds to explain the work of a lifetime! Ten seconds to describe two carefully reasoned articles, each running to more than thirty printed pages and each with sixty or so long footnotes! When they saw the look of dismay on my face, they said, "You don't have to go into details. Just give us the main points in simple, common-sense terms".

'The main point of the first or cost-of-capital article was, in principle at least, simple enough to make. It said that in an economist's ideal world of complete and perfect capital markets and with full and symmetric information among all market participants, the total market value of all the securities issued by a firm was governed by the earning power and risk of its underlying real assets and was independent of how the mix of securities issued to finance it was divided between debt instruments and equity capital. . . .

'Such a summary, however, uses too many shorthanded terms and concepts, like perfect capital markets, that are rich in connotations to economists but hardly so to the general public. So I thought, instead, of an analogy that we ourselves had invoked in the original paper. . . .

'"Think of the firm", I said, "as a gigantic tub of whole milk. The farmer can sell the whole milk as is. Or he can separate out the cream and sell it at a considerably higher price than the whole milk would bring. (That's the analog of a firm selling low-yield and hence high-priced debt securities.) But, of course, what the farmer would have left would be skim milk with low butterfat content and that would sell for much less than whole milk. That corresponds to the levered equity. The M and M proposition says that if there were no costs of separation (and, of course, no government dairy support programs), the cream plus the skim milk would bring the same price as the whole milk".

'The television people conferred among themselves and came back to inform me that it was too long, too complicated, and too academic.

'"Don't you have anything simpler?" they asked. I thought of another way that the M and M proposition is presented these days, which emphasizes the notion of market completeness and stresses the role of securities as devices for 'partitioning' a firm's payoffs in each possible state of the world among the group of its capital suppliers.

'"Think of the firm", I said, "as a gigantic pizza, divided into quarters. If now you cut each quarter in half in eighths, the M and M proposition says that you will have more pieces but not more pizza".

'Again there was a whispered conference among the camera crew, and the director came back and said:

'"Professor, we understand from the press release that there were two M and M propositions. Can we try the other one?"

[Professor Miller tried valiantly to explain the second proposition, though this was apparently even more difficult to get across. After his attempt:]

'Once again there was a whispered conversation. They shut the lights off. They folded up their equipment. They thanked me for giving them the time. They said that they'd get back to me. But I knew that I had somehow lost my chance to start a new career as a packager of economic wisdom for TV viewers inconvenient ten-second bites. Some have the talent for it . . . and some just don't.'

---

[14] Taken from *GSB Chicago*, University of Chicago, Autumn, 1986.

FIGURE 16.4   Two Pie Models of Capital Structure under Corporate Taxes

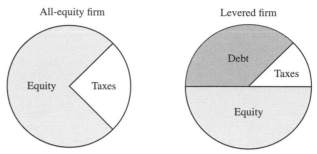

All-equity firm   Levered firm

The levered firm pays less than does the all-equity firm. Thus, the sum
of the debt plus the equity of the levered firm is greater than the equity
of the unlevered firm.

pie allocated to taxes is less for the levered firm than it is for the unlevered firm. Thus,
managers should select high leverage.

The Quirk in the Tax Rules

● Example

The Water Products Company is evaluating two financing plans. The Water Products
Company has a corporate tax rate, T_C, of 35 per cent and expected earnings before
interest and taxes (EBIT) of GBP1 million. Under plan *I*, Water Products has no debt
in its capital structure. Under plan *II*, the company would have GBP4,000,000 of debt,
B. The cost of debt, r_B, is 10 per cent.

The chief financial officer for Water Products makes the following calculations:

	Plan I	*Plan II*
Earnings before interest and corporate taxes (EBIT)	GBP1,000,000	GBP1,000,000
Interest ($r_B B$)	0	(400,000)
Earnings before taxes (EBT) = (EBIT − $r_B B$)	1,000,000	600,000
Taxes ($T_C = 0.35$)	(350,000)	(210,000)
Earnings after corporate taxes (EAT) = [(EBIT − $r_B B$) × (1 − T_C)]	650,000	390,000
Total cash flow to both shareholders and bondholders [EBIT × (1 − T_C) + $T_C r_B B$]	GBP650,000	GBP790,000

The most relevant numbers for our purposes are the two on the bottom line. Here,
we see that more cash flow reaches the owners of the firm (both shareholders and
bondholders) under plan *II*. The difference is GBP140,000 = GBP790,000 −
GBP650,000. It does not take one long to realize the source of this difference. The tax
authority receives less taxes under plan *II* (GBP210,000) than it does under plan *I*
(GBP350,000). The difference here is GBP140,000 = GBP350,000 − GBP210,000.

This difference[15] occurs because the tax authorities treat interest differently than

---

[15] Note that shareholders actually receive more under Plan I (GBP650,000) than under Plan II
(GBP390,000). Students are often bothered by this since it seems to imply that shareholders are better off
without leverage. However, remember that there are more shares outstanding in Plan I than in Plan II. A
full-blown model would show that earnings *per share* are higher with leverage.

they do earnings going to shareholders. Interest totally escapes corporate taxation, whereas earnings after interest, but before corporate taxes (EBT), are taxed at the 35 per cent rate. We can express this relationship algebraically below.

We will assume in this discussion that all cash flows are constant (that is, perpetual without growth). If EBIT is the total cash flow of the firm before interest and taxes, and if we ignore the effect of depreciation and other items such as taxes, then the taxable income of an all-equity firm is simply

$$EBIT$$

For an all-equity firm, total taxes are

$$EBIT \times T_C$$

where T_C is the corporate tax rate. Earnings after corporate taxes are

$$EBIT \times (1 - T_C) \tag{16.4}$$

For a levered firm, taxable income is

$$EBIT - r_B B$$

Total taxes in a levered firm are

$$T_C \times (EBIT - r_B B)$$

Cash flow going to the shareholders in a levered firm is

$$EBIT - r_B B - T_C \times (EBIT - r_B B) = (EBIT - r_B B) \times (1 - T_C)$$

Cash flow going to both the shareholders and the bondholders in a levered firm is

$$EBIT \times (1 - T_C) + T_C r_B B \tag{16.5}$$

which quite explicitly depends on the amount of debt financing.

The key can be seen by comparing the difference between expressions (16.4) and (16.5). The difference, $T_C r_B B$, is the extra cash flow going to **investors** in the levered firm. We use the term *investors* to mean both shareholders and bondholders. It is also the extra funds not going to the tax authorities.

Let us calculate this difference for Water Products:

$$T_C r_B B = 35\% \times 10\% \times GBP4,000,000 = GBP140,000$$

This is the same number that we calculated above. ●

Value of the Tax Shield

The discussion above shows a tax advantage to debt or, equivalently, a tax disadvantage to equity. We now want to value this advantage. We previously said that the cash flow of the levered firm in each period is greater than the cash flow of the unlevered firm by

$$T_C r_B B \qquad (16.6)$$

Expression (16.6) is often called the tax shield from debt.

As long as the firm expects to be in a positive tax bracket, we can assume that the cash flow in expression (16.6) has the same risk as the interest on the debt. Thus, its value can be determined by discounting at the interest rate, r_B. Assuming that the cash flows are perpetual, the value of the tax shield is

$$\frac{T_C r_B B}{r_B} = T_C B$$

Value of the Levered Firm

We have just calculated the present value of the tax shield from debt. Our next step is to calculate the value of the levered firm. We showed above that the after-tax cash flow to the shareholders in the levered firm is

$$\text{EBIT} \times (1 - T_C) + T_C r_B B \qquad (16.5)$$

The first term in expression (16.5) is the after-tax cash flow in the unlevered firm. The value of an unlevered firm (that is, a firm with no debt) is the present value of $\text{EBIT} \times (1 - T_C)$,

$$V_U = \frac{\text{EBIT} \times (1 - T_C)}{r_0}$$

where

$$V_U = \text{Present value of an unlevered firm}$$
$$\text{EBIT} \times (1 - T_C) = \text{Firm cash flows after corporate taxes}$$
$$T_C = \text{Corporate tax rate}$$
$$r_0 = \text{The cost of capital to an all-equity firm. As can be seen from the formula, } r_0 \text{ now discounts after-tax cash flows.}$$

The second part of the cash flows, $T_C r_B B$, is the tax shield. To determine its value, the tax shield should be discounted at r_B.

As a consequence, we have[16]

MM Proposition I (corporate taxes):

$$V_L = \frac{\text{EBIT} \times (1 - T_C)}{r_0} + \frac{T_C r_B B}{r_B} \qquad (16.7)$$
$$= V_U + T_C B$$

---

[16] This relationship holds when the debt level is assumed to be constant through time. A different formula would apply if the debt–equity ratio was assumed to be a constant over time. For a deeper treatment of this point, see J. A. Miles and J. R. Ezzel (1980) 'The weighted average cost of capital, perfect capital markets and project life', *Journal of Financial and Quantitative Analysis,* September.

Equation (16.7) is MM Proposition I under corporate taxes. The first term in equation (16.7) is the value of the cash flows of the firm with no debt tax shield. In other words, this term is equal to V_U, the value of the all-equity firm. The value of the firm is the value of an all-equity firm plus T_CB, the tax rate times the value of the debt. T_CB is the present value of the tax shield in the case of perpetual cash flows.[17]

The Water Products example reveals that, because the tax shield increases with the amount of debt, the firm can raise its total cash flow and its value by substituting debt for equity. We now have a clear example of why the capital structure does matter: By raising the debt–equity ratio, the firm can lower its taxes and thereby increase its total value. The strong forces that operate to maximize the value of the firm would seem to push it toward an all-debt capital structure.

● Example

Divided Airlines is currently an unlevered firm. It is considering a capital restructuring to allow GBP200 of debt. The company expects to generate GBP153.85 in cash flows before interest and taxes, in perpetuity. The corporate tax rate is 35 per cent, implying after-tax cash flows of GBP100. Its cost of debt capital is 10 per cent. Unlevered firms in the same industry have a cost of equity capital of 20 per cent. What will the new value of Divided Airlines be?

The value of Divided Airlines will be equal to[18]

$$
\begin{aligned}
V_L &= \frac{\text{EBIT} \times (1 - T_c)}{r_0} + T_CB \\
&= \frac{\text{GBP100}}{0.20} + (0.35 \times \text{GBP200}) \\
&= \text{GBP500} + 70 \\
&= \text{GBP570}
\end{aligned}
$$

Because $V_L = B + S$, the value of levered equity, S, is equal to GBP570 − GBP200 = GBP370. The value of Divided Airlines as a function of leverage is illustrated in Figure 16.5. ●

---

[17] The following example calculates the present value if we assume the debt has a finite life. Suppose the Eastville Company has GBP1 million in debt with an 8 per cent coupon rate. If the debt matures in two years and the cost of debt capital, r_B, is 10 per cent, what is the present value of the tax shields if the corporate tax rate is 35 per cent? The debt is amortized in equal instalments over two years.

Year	Loan balance	Interest	Tax shield	Present value of tax shield
0	GBP1,000,000			
1	GBP500,000	GBP80,000	0.35 × GBP80,000	GBP25,454.54
2	0	GBP40,000	0.35 × GBP40,000	11,570.25
				GBP37,024.79

The present value of the tax savings is

$$
\text{PV} = \frac{0.35 \times \text{GBP80,000}}{1.10} + 0.35 \times \frac{\text{GBP40,000}}{(1.10)^2} = \text{GBP37,024.79}
$$

The Eastville Company's value is higher than that of a comparable unlevered firm by GBP37,024.79.

[18] Note that, in a world with taxes, r_0 is used to discount *after-tax* cash flows.

Expected Return and Leverage under Corporate Taxes

MM Proposition II under no taxes posits a positive relationship between the expected return on equity and leverage. This result occurs because the risk of equity increases with leverage. The same intuition also holds in a world of corporate taxes. The exact formula is[19]

MM Proposition II (corporate taxes):

$$r_S = r_0 + \frac{B}{S} \times (1 - T_C) \times (r_0 - r_B) \tag{16.8}$$

Applying the formula to Divided Airlines, we get

$$r_S = 0.2351 = 0.20 + \frac{200}{370} \times (1 - 0.35) \times (0.20 - 0.10)$$

This calculation is illustrated in Figure 16.6.

We can check this calculation by discounting at r_S to determine the value of the levered equity. The algebraic formula for levered equity is

$$S = \frac{(\text{EBIT} - r_B B) \times (1 - T_C)}{r_S} \tag{16.9}$$

The numerator is the expected cash flow to levered equity after interest and taxes. The denominator is the rate at which the cash flow to equity is discounted.

---

[19] This relationship can be shown as follows: Given MM Proposition I under taxes, a levered firm's market-value balance sheet can be written as

V_U = Value of unlevered firm	B = Debt
$T_C B$ = tax shield	S = Equity

The value of the unlevered firm is simply the value of the assets without benefit of leverage. The balance sheet indicates that the firm's value increases by $T_C B$ when debt of B is added. The expected cash flow *from* the lefthand side of the balance sheet can be written as

$$V_U r_0 + T_C B r_B \tag{a}$$

Because assets are risky, their expected rate of return is r_0. The tax shield has the same risk as the debt, so its expected rate of return is r_B.

The expected cash *to* bondholders and shareholders together is

$$S r_S + B r_B \tag{b}$$

Expression (b) reflects the fact that stock earns an expected return of r_S and debt earns the interest rate r_B.

Because all cash flows are paid out as dividends in our no-growth perpetuity model, the cash flows going into the firm equal those going to stakeholders. Hence (a) and (b) are equal:

$$S r_S + B r_B = V_U r_0 + T_C B r_B \tag{c}$$

Dividing both side of (c) by S, subtracting $B r_B$ from both sides, and rearranging yields

$$r_S = \frac{V_U}{S} \times r_0 - (1 - T_C) \times \frac{B}{S} r_B$$

Because the value of the levered firm V_L, equals $V_U + T_C B = B + S$, it follows that $V_U = S + (1 - T_C) \times B$. This can be rewritten as

$$r_S = \frac{S + (1 - T_C) \times B}{S} \times r_0 - (1 - T_C) \times \frac{B}{S} r_B \tag{d}$$

Bringing the terms involving $(1 - T_C) \times \frac{B}{S}$ together produces (16.8).

FIGURE 16.5 The Effect of Financial Leverage on Firm Value: MM with Corporate Taxes in the Case of Divided Airlines

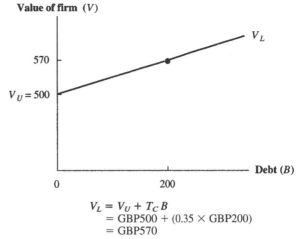

$$V_L = V_U + T_C B$$
$$= GBP500 + (0.35 \times GBP200)$$
$$= GBP570$$

Debt reduces Divided's tax burden. As a result, the value of the firm is positively related to debt.

FIGURE 16.6 The Effect of Financial Leverage on the Cost of Debt and Equity Capital

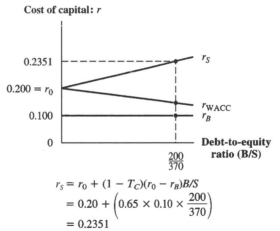

$$r_S = r_0 + (1 - T_C)(r_0 - r_B)B/S$$
$$= 0.20 + \left(0.65 \times 0.10 \times \frac{200}{370}\right)$$
$$= 0.2351$$

Financial leverage adds risk to the firm's equity. As compensation, the cost of equity rises with the firm's risk.

For Divided Airlines we get[20]

$$\frac{(GBP153.85 - 0.10 \times GBP200)\,(1 - 0.35)}{0.2351} = GBP370 \qquad (16.9')$$

the same result we obtained earlier.

---

[20] The calculation suffers slightly from rounding error because we only carried the discount rate, 0.2351, out to four decimal places.

The Weighted Average Cost of Capital r_{WACC} and Corporate Taxes

In Chapter 13, we defined the weighted average cost of capital (with corporate taxes) as

$$r_{WACC} = \frac{B}{V_L} r_B (1 - T_C) + \frac{S}{V_L} r_S$$

For Divided Airlines, r_{WACC} is equal to

$$r_{WACC} = \left(\frac{200}{570} \times 0.10 \times 0.65\right) + \left(\frac{370}{570} \times 0.2351\right) = 0.1754$$

Divided Airlines has reduced its r_{WACC} from 0.20 (with no debt) to 0.1754 with reliance on debt. This result is intuitively pleasing because it suggests that, when a firm lowers its r_{WACC}, the firm's value will increase. Using the r_{WACC} approach, we can confirm that the value of Divided Airlines is GBP570.

$$V_L = \frac{EBIT \times (1 - T_C)}{r_{WACC}}$$
$$= GBP570$$

Share Price and Leverage under Corporate Taxes

At this point, students often believe the numbers—or at least are too intimidated to dispute them. However, they think we have asked the wrong question. 'Why are we choosing to maximize the value of the firm?', they will say. 'If managers are looking out for the shareholder's interest, why aren't they trying to maximize share price?' If this question occurred to you, you have come to the right section.

Our response is twofold. First, we showed in Section 16.1 that the capital structure that maximizes firm value is also the one that most benefits the interests of the shareholders.[21]

However, that general explanation is not always convincing to students. As a second procedure, we calculate the stock price of Divided Airlines both before and after the exchange of debt for shares. We do this by presenting a set of market-value balance sheets. The market-value balance sheet for the company in its all-equity form can be represented as

DIVIDED AIRLINES
Market-value balance sheet (all-equity firm)

Physical assets: $\dfrac{GBP153.85}{0.20} \times (1 - 0.35) = GBP500$	Equity GBP500 (100 shares)

Assuming that there are 100 shares outstanding, each share is worth GBP5 = GBP500/100.

Next imagine that the company announces that, in the near future, it will issue GBP200 of debt to buy back GBP200 of shares. We know from our previous discussion that the value of the firm will rise to reflect the tax shield of debt. According to efficient capital markets, the increase occurs immediately. That is, the rise occurs on

---

[21] At that time, we pointed out that this result may not exactly hold in the more complex case where debt has a significant possibility of default. Issues of default are treated in the next chapter.

the day of the announcement, not on the date of the debt-for-equity exchange. The market-value balance sheet now becomes

DIVIDED AIRLINES
Market-value balance sheet
(upon announcement of debt issue)

Physical assets	GBP500	Equity	GBP570
			(100 shares)
Present value of tax shield: $T_cB = 35\% \times GBP200 =$	70		
Total Assets	GBP570		

Note that the debt has not yet been issued. Therefore, only equity appears on the righthand side of the balance sheet. Each share is now worth GBP570/100 = GBP5.70, implying that the shareholders have benefited by GBP70. The equityholders gain because they are the owners of a firm that has improved its financial policy.

The introduction of the tax shield to the balance sheet is frequently perplexing to students. Although physical assets are tangible, the ethereal nature of the tax shield bothers many students. However, remember that an asset is any item with value. The tax shield has value because it reduces the stream of future taxes. The fact that one cannot touch the shield in the way that one can touch a physical asset is a philosophical, not a financial, consideration.

At some point, the exchange of debt for equity occurs. Debt of GBP200 is issued, and the proceeds are used to buy back shares. How many shares are repurchased? Because shares are now selling at GBP5.70 each, the number of shares that the firm acquires is GBP200/GBP5.70 = 35.09. This leaves 64.91 (100 − 35.09) shares of stock outstanding. The market-value balance sheet is now

DIVIDED AIRLINES
Market-value balance sheet
(after exchange has taken place)

Physical assets	GBP500	Equity	GBP370
		(100 − 35.09 = 64.91 shares)	
Present value of tax shield	70	Debt	200
Total assets	GBP570	Debt plus equity	GBP570

Each share is worth GBP370/64.91 = GBP5.70 after the exchange. Notice that the share price does not change on the exchange date. As we mentioned above, the share price moves on the date of the announcement only. Because the shareholders participating in the exchange receive a price equal to the market price per share after the exchange, they do not care whether they exchange their shares or not.

This example was provided for two reasons. First, it shows that an increase in the value of the firm from debt financing leads to an increase in the price of the shares. In fact, the shareholders capture the entire GBP70 tax shield. Second, we wanted to provide more work with market-value balance sheets.

Concept Questions

- What is the quirk in the tax code making a levered firm more valuable than an otherwise-identical unlevered firm?
- What is MM Proposition I under corporate taxes?
- What is MM Proposition II under corporate taxes?

16.7   Summary and Conclusions

1. We began our discussion of capital-structure policy by arguing that the particular capital structure that maximizes the value of the firm is also the one that provides the most benefit to the stockholders.
2. In a world of no taxes, the famous Proposition I of Modigliani and Miller proves that the value of the firm is unaffected by the debt-to-equity ratio. In other words, financial policy is a matter of indifference in that world. The authors obtain their results by showing that either a high or a low corporate ratio of debt to equity can be offset by homemade leverage. The result hinges on the assumption that individuals can borrow at the same rate as corporations, an assumption we believe to be quite plausible.
3. MM's Proposition II in a world without taxes states

$$r_S = r_0 + \frac{B}{S}(r_0 - r_B)$$

This implies that the expected rate of return on equity (also called the *cost of equity* or the *required return on equity*) is positively related to the firm's leverage. This makes intuitive sense, because the risk of equity rises with leverage, a point illustrated by the different sloped lines of Figure 16.2.
4. While the above work of MM is quite elegant, it does not explain the empirical findings on capital structure very well. They imply that the capital-structure decision is a matter of indifference, while the decision appears to be a weighty one in the real world. To achieve real-world applicability, we next considered corporate taxes.
5. In a world with corporate taxes but no bankruptcy costs, firm value is an increasing function of leverage. The formula for the value of the firm is

$$V_L = V_U + T_C B$$

Expected return on levered equity can be expressed as

$$r_S = r_0 + (1 - T_C) \times (r_0 - r_B) \times \frac{B}{S}$$

Here, value is positively related to leverage. This result implies that firms should have a capital structure almost entirely composed of debt. Because real-world firms select more moderate levels of debt, the next chapter considers modifications to the results of this chapter.

KEY TERMS

Pie model   357
MM Proposition I   360
MM Proposition II   366

Investors   377
MM Proposition I (corporate taxes)   378
MM Proposition II (corporate taxes)   380

QUESTIONS AND PROBLEMS

Capital Structure without Taxes

16.1 Nadus GmbH and Logis GmbH are identical in every way except their capital structures. Nadus, an all-equity firm, has 5,000 shares outstanding; each share sells for DEM20. Logis uses leverage in its capital structure. The market value of Logis debt is DEM25,000. Logis's cost of debt is 12 per cent. Each firm is expected to have earnings before interest of DEM350,000. Neither firm pays taxes.

Suppose you want to purchase the same portion of the equity of each firm. Assume you can borrow money at 12 per cent.
a. What is the value of Nadus's shares?
b. What is the value of Logis's shares?

    c. What will your costs and returns be if you buy 20 per cent of each firm's equity?

    d. Which investment is riskier? Why?

    e. Construct an investment strategy for Nadus shares that replicates the investment returns of Logis shares.

    f. What is the value of Logis GmbH?

    g. If the value of Logis's assets is DEM135,000 and you can invest up to 20 per cent of the Logis shares, what should you do?

16.2 Acetate NV has ordinary shares with a market value of NLG20 million and debt with a market value of NLG10 million. The cost of the debt is 14 per cent. The current Treasury-bill rate is 8 per cent, and the expected market premium is 10 per cent. The beta on Acetate's equity is 0.9.

    a. What is Acetate's debt–equity ratio?

    b. What is the firm's overall required return?

16.3 You invest BEF100,000 in the shares of the Liana SA. To make the investment, you borrowed BEF75,000 from a friend at a cost of 10 per cent. You expect your equity investment to return 20 per cent. There are no taxes. What would your return be if you did not use leverage?

16.4 Two Spanish companies, Levered SA and Unlevered SA, are identical companies with identical business risk. Their earnings are perfectly correlated. Each company is expected to earn ESB96 million per year in perpetuity, and each company distributes all its earnings. Levered's debt has a market value of ESB275 million and provides a return of 8 per cent. Levered's shares sell for ESB100 per share, and there are 4.5 million outstanding shares. Unlevered has only 10 million outstanding shares worth ESB80 each. Unlevered has no debt. There are no taxes. Which share is the better investment?

16.5 Veblen GmbH and Knight GmbH are identical in every respect except that Veblen is not levered. The market value of Knight's 6 per cent bonds is DEM1 million. The financial statistics for the two firms appear below. Neither firm pays taxes.

	Veblen	*Knight*
Net operating income	DEM2,300,000	DEM2,300,000
Interest on debt	0	60,000
Earnings available to common stock	DEM2,300,000	DEM2,240,000
Required return on equity	0.125	0.140
Market value of shares	DEM2,400,000	DEM1,714,000
Market value of debt	0	DEM1,000,000
Market value of the firm	DEM2,400,000	DEM2,714,000
Overall required return	0.125	0.110
Debt–equity ratio	0	0.584

    a. An investor who is also able to borrow at 6 per cent owns DEM10,000 worth of Knight shares. Can he increase his net return by borrowing money to buy Veblen shares? If so, show the strategy.

    b. According to Modigliani and Miller, what kind of investors will attempt this strategy? When will the process cease?

16.6 Rayburn Manufacturing plc is currently an all-equity firm. The firm's equity is worth GBP2 million. The cost of that equity is 18 per cent. Rayburn pays no taxes. Rayburn plans to issue GBP400,000 in debt and to use the proceeds to repurchase shares. The cost of debt is 10 per cent.

    a. After Rayburn repurchases the shares, what will the firm's overall costs of capital be?

    b. After the repurchase, what will the cost of equity be?

    c. Explain your result in (*b*).

16.7 Stam NV has 250,000 outstanding shares that sell for NLG20 per share. Stam NV currently has no debt. The appropriate discount rate for the firm is 15 per cent. Stam's earnings last year were NLG750,000. The management expects that if no changes affect the assets of the firm, the earnings will remain NLG750,000 in perpetuity. Stam pays no taxes. Stam plans to buy out a competitor's business at a cost of NLG300,000. Once added to Stam's current business, the competitor's facilities will generate earnings of NLG120,000 in perpetuity. The competitor has the same risk as Stam NV.

    a. Construct the market-value balance sheet for Stam before the announcement of the acquisition is made.

    b. Suppose Stam uses equity to fund the purchase.
      i. According to the efficient-market hypothesis, what will happen to Stam's price?
      ii. Construct the market-value balance sheet as it will look after the announcement.
      iii. How many shares would Stam sell?
      iv. Once Stam sells the new shares, how will its accounts look?
      v. After the purchase is finalized, how will the market-value balance sheet look?
      vi. What is the return to Stam's equityholders?

    c. Suppose Stam uses 10 per cent debt to fund the purchase.
      i. Construct the market-value balance sheet as it will look after the announcement.
      ii. Once Stam sells the bonds, how will its accounts look?
      iii. What is the cost of equity?
      iv. Explain any difference in the cost of equity between the two plans.
      v. Use MM Proposition II to verify the answer in (*iii*).

    d. Under each financing plan, what is the price of Stam shares after the takeover?

16.8 Gulf SA is a French electric utility that is planning to build a new conventional power plant. The company has traditionally paid out all earnings to the shareholders as dividends, and financed capital expenditures with new issues of ordinary shares. There is no debt or preferred stock presently outstanding. Data on the company and the new power plant follow. Assume all earnings streams are perpetuities.

Company Data
Current annual earnings: FRF27 million
Number of outstanding shares: 10 million

New Power Plant
Initial outlay: FRF20 million
Added annual earnings: FRF3 million

Management considers the power plant to have the same risk as existing assets. The current required rate of return on equity is 10 per cent. Assume there are no taxes and no costs of bankruptcy.

    a. What will the total market value of Gulf SA be if ordinary shares are issued to finance the plant?

    b. What will the total market value of the firm be if FRF20 million in bonds with an interest rate of 8 per cent are issued to finance the plant? Assume the bonds are perpetuities.

    c. Suppose Gulf SA issues the bonds. Calculate the rate of return required by shareholders after the financing has occurred and the plant has been built.

16.9 Suppose there are no taxes, no transaction costs and no costs of financial distress. In such a world, are the following statements true, false, or uncertain? Explain your answers.

    a. If a firm issues equity to repurchase some of its debt, the price of the remaining shares will rise because those shares are less risky.

    b. Moderate borrowing does not significantly affect the probability of financial distress or bankruptcy. Hence, moderate borrowing will not increase the required return on equity.

16.10 *a.* List the three assumptions that lie behind the Modigliani–Miller theory.

    b. Briefly explain the effect of each upon the conclusions of the theory for the real world.

Capital Structure with Corporate Taxes

16.11 The market value of a firm with NLG500,000 of debt is NLG1,700,000. EBIT are expected to be a perpetuity. The pretax interest rate on debt is 10 per cent. The company is in the 34 per cent tax bracket. If the company were 100 per cent equity financed, the equityholders would require a 20 per cent return.

    a. What would the value of the firm be if it was financed entirely with equity?

    b. What is the net income to the shareholders of this levered firm?

16.12 An all-equity firm is subject to a 30 per cent corporate tax rate. Its equityholders require a 20 per cent return. The firm's initial market value is GBP3,500,000, and there are 175,000 shares outstanding. The firm issues GBP1 million of bonds at 10 per cent and uses the proceeds to repurchase ordinary shares. Assume there is no change in the costs of financial distress for the firm. According to MM, what is the new market value of the equity of the firm?

16.13 Streiber Publishing NV, an all-equity firm, generates perpetual earnings before interest and taxes (EBIT) of NLG2.5 million per year. Streiber's after-tax, all-equity discount rate is 20 per cent. The company's tax rate is 34 percent.
   a. What is the value of Streiber Publishing?
   b. If Streiber adjusts its capital structure to include NLG600,000 of debt, what is the value of the firm?
   c. Explain any difference in your answers.
   d. What assumptions are you making when you are valuing Streiber?

16.14 Olbet plc, is a non-growth company in the 35 per cent tax bracket. Olbet's perpetual EBIT is GBP1.2 million per annum. The firm's pretax cost of debt is 8 per cent and its interest expense per year is GBP200,000. Company analysts estimate that the unlevered cost of Olbet's equity is 12 per cent.
   a. What is the value of this firm?
   b. What does the calculation in (*a*) imply about the correct level of debt?
   c. Is the conclusion correct? Why or why not?

16.15 Green Manufacturing plc, plans to announce that it will issue GBP2,000,000 of perpetual bonds. The bonds will have a 6 per cent coupon rate. Green Manufacturing currently is an all-equity firm. The value of Green's equity is GBP10,000,000 and there are 500,000 shares outstanding. After the sale of the bonds, Green will maintain the new capital structure indefinitely. The expected annual pretax earnings of Green are GBP1,500,000. Those earnings are also expected to remain constant into the foreseeable future. Assume that Green is in a 40 per cent tax bracket (if such existed).
   a. What is Green's current overall required return?
   b. Construct Green Manufacturing's market-value balance sheet as it looks before the announcement of the debt issue.
   c. What is the market-value balance sheet after the announcement?
   d. How many shares will Green retire?
   e. What will the accounts show after the restructuring has taken place?
   f. What is Green's cost of equity after the capital restructuring?

Capital Structure: Limits to the Use of Debt

One question that might be asked is: 'Does the MM theory with taxes predict the capital structure of typical firms?' The answer is, unfortunately, 'No.' The theory states that $V_L = V_U + T_C B$. According to this equation, one can always increase firm value by increasing leverage, implying that firms should issue maximum debt. This is inconsistent with the real world, where firms generally employ only moderate amounts of debt.

However, the MM theory tells us *where to look* when searching for the determinants of capital structure. For example, the theory ignores bankruptcy and its attendant costs. Because these costs are likely to get out of hand for a highly levered firm, the moderate leverage of most firms can now easily be explained.

In addition, the MM theory ignores personal taxes. In the real world, the *personal* tax rate on interest might be higher than the *effective* personal tax rate on equity distributions. This would mean that the personal tax penalties to bondholders would offset the tax benefits to debt at the corporate level. Even when bankruptcy costs are ignored, this idea can be shown to imply that there is an optimal amount of debt for the economy as a whole. The implications of bankruptcy costs and personal taxes are examined in this chapter.

17.1 Costs of Financial Distress

Bankruptcy Risk or Bankruptcy Cost?

As mentioned throughout the previous chapter, debt provides tax benefits to the firm. However, debt puts pressure on the firm, because interest and principal payments are obligations. If these obligations are not met, the firm may risk some sort of financial distress. The ultimate distress is *bankruptcy*, where ownership of the firm's assets is legally transferred from the shareholders to the bondholders. These debt obligations are fundamentally different from stock obligations. While shareholders like and expect dividends, they are not legally entitled to dividends in the way bondholders are legally entitled to interest and principal payments.

We show below that bankruptcy costs, or more generally financial distress costs, tend to offset the advantages to debt. We begin by positing a simple example of bankruptcy. All taxes are ignored to focus only on the costs of debt.

● Example
The Knight Company plc plans to be in business for one more year. It forecasts a cash flow of either GBP100 or GBP50 in the coming year, each occurring with 50 per cent probability. The firm has no other assets. Previously issued debt requires payments of

GBP49 of interest and principal The Day Company plc has identical cash flow prospects, but has GBP60 of interest and principal obligations. The cash flows of these two firms can be represented as

	KNIGHT CO.		DAY CO.	
	Boom times (prob. 50%)	*Recession* (prob. 50%)	*Boom times* (prob. 50%)	*Recession* (prob. 50%)
Cash flow	GBP100	GBP50	GBP100	GBP50
Payment of interest and principal on debt	49	49	60	50
Distribution to shareholders	GBP51	GBP1	GBP40	0

For Knight Company in both boom times and recession, and for Day Company in boom times, cash flow exceeds interest and principal payments. In these situations, the bondholders are paid in full and the shareholders receive any residual. However, the most interesting of the four columns involves Day Company in a recession. Here, the bondholders are owed GBP60, but the firm has only GBP50 in cash. Since we assumed that the firm has no other assets, the bondholders cannot be satisfied in full. If bankruptcy occurs, the bondholders will receive all of the firm's cash, and the shareholders will receive nothing. Importantly, the shareholders do not have to come up with the additional GBP10 (= GBP60 − GBP50). Corporations have limited liability in the UK and most other countries, implying that bondholders cannot sue the shareholders for the extra GBP10.[1]

We assume that (1) both bondholders and shareholders are risk-neutral and (2) the interest rate is 10 per cent. Due to this risk neutrality, cash flows to both stockholders and bondholders are to be discounted at the 10 per cent rate.[2] We can evaluate the debt, the equity and the entire firm for both Knight and Day as follows;

$$S_{\text{KNIGHT}} = \text{GBP23.64} = \frac{\text{GBP51} \times 1\frac{1}{2} + \text{GBP1} \times \frac{1}{2}}{1.10} \qquad S_{\text{DAY}} = \text{GBP18.18} = \frac{\text{GBP40} \times \frac{1}{2} + 0 \times \frac{1}{2}}{1.10}$$

$$B_{\text{KNIGHT}} = \text{GBP44.54} = \frac{\text{GBP49} \times \frac{1}{2} + \text{GBP49} \times \frac{1}{2}}{1.10} \qquad B_{\text{DAY}} = \text{GBP50} \quad = \frac{\text{GBP60} \times \frac{1}{2} + \text{GBP50} \times \frac{1}{2}}{1.10}$$

$$V_{\text{KNIGHT}} = \text{GBP68.18} \qquad\qquad\qquad\qquad V_{\text{DAY}} = \text{GBP68.18}$$

Note that the two firms have the same value, even though Day runs the risk of bankruptcy. Furthermore, notice that Day's bondholders are valuing the bonds with

---

[1] These are situations where the limited liability of companies can be 'pierced'. Typically, fraud or misrepresentation must be present. And, of course, lenders can protect themselves by seeking guarantees, for example from directors. Of course, this assumes that such directors are creditworthy individuals.

[2] Normally, one assumes that investors are averse to risk. In that case, the cost of debt capital, r_B, is less than the cost of equity capital, r_S, which rises with leverage as shown in the previous chapter. In addition, r_B may rise when the increase in leverage allows the possibility of default.

For simplicity, we assume risk neutrality in this example. This means that investors are indifferent to whether risk is high, low or even absent. Here, $r_S = r_B$, because risk-neutral investors do not demand compensation for bearing risk. In addition, neither r_S nor r_B rises with leverage. Because the interest rate is 10 per cent, our assumption of risk neutrality implies that $r_S = 10\%$ as well.

Though financial economists believe that investors are risk-averse, they frequently develop examples based on risk-neutrality to isolate a point unrelated to risk. This is our approach, because we want to focus on bankruptcy costs—not bankruptcy risk. The same qualitative conclusions from this example can be drawn in a world of risk aversion, albeit with much more difficulty for the reader. Having said all this students will be well advised always to assume that r_S is greater than r_B.

their eyes open. Though the promised payment of principal and interest is GBP60, the bondholders are willing to pay only GBP50. Hence, their *promised* return or yield is

$$\text{GBP60/GBP50} - 1 = 20\%$$

Day's debt can be viewed as a *junk bond*, because the probability of default is so high. As with all junk bonds, bondholders demand a high promised yield.

Day's example is not realistic because it ignores an important cash flow to be discussed below. A more realistic set of numbers might be

DAY COMPANY

	Boom times (prob. 50%)	Recession (prob. 50%)	
Earnings	GBP100	GBP50	$S_{\text{DAY}} = \text{GBP18.18} = \dfrac{\text{GBP40} \times \frac{1}{2} + 0 \times \frac{1}{2}}{1.10}$
Debt repayment	60	35	$B_{\text{DAY}} = \text{GBP43.18} = \dfrac{\text{GBP60} \times \frac{1}{2} + \text{GBP35} \times \frac{1}{2}}{1.10}$
Distribution to shareholders	GBP40	0	$V_{\text{DAY}} = \text{GBP61.36}$

Why do the bondholders receive only GBP35 in a recession? If cash flow is only GBP50, bondholders will be informed that they are not paid in full. These bondholders are likely to hire lawyers to negotiate or even to sue the company. Similarly, the firm is likely to hire lawyers to defend itself. Further costs will be incurred if the case gets to a bankruptcy court. These fees are always paid before the bondholders get paid. Thus, we are assuming that bankruptcy costs total GBP15 (GBP50 − 35).

The value of the firm is now GBP61.36, an amount below the GBP68.18 figure calculated earlier. By comparing Day's value in a world with no bankruptcy costs to Day's value in a world with these costs, we conclude

> The possibility of bankruptcy has a negative effect on the value of the firm. However, it is not the *risk* of bankruptcy itself that lowers value. Rather it is the *costs* associated with bankruptcy that lower value.

The explanation follows from our pie example. In a world of no bankruptcy costs, the bondholders and the shareholders share the entire pie. However, bankruptcy costs eat up some of the pie in the real world, leaving less for the shareholders and bondholders.

Because the bondholders are aware that they receive little in a recession, they pay a low price. In this case, their promised return is

$$\frac{\text{GBP60}}{\text{GBP43.18}} - 1 = 39.0\%$$

The bondholders are paying a fair price if they are realistic about both the probability and the cost of bankruptcy. It is the *shareholders* who bear these future bankruptcy costs. To see this, imagine that Day Company was originally an all-equity firm. The shareholders want the firm to issue debt with a promised payment of GBP60 and use the proceeds to pay a dividend. If there had been no bankruptcy costs, our results show that bondholders would pay GBP50 to purchase the debt with a promised payment of GBP60. Hence, a dividend of GBP50 could be paid to the shareholders. However, if bankruptcy costs exist, bondholders would only pay GBP43.18 for the debt. In that case, only a dividend of GBP43.18 could be paid to the shareholders. Because the dividend is less when bankruptcy costs exist, the shareholders are hurt by bankruptcy costs. ●

Concept Questions

* What does risk neutrality mean?
* Can one have bankruptcy risk without bankruptcy costs?
* Why do we say that shareholders bear bankruptcy costs?

17.2   Description of Costs

The above example showed that bankruptcy costs can lower the value of the firm. In fact, the same general result holds even if a legal bankruptcy is prevented. Thus, *financial distress* costs may be a better phrase than *bankruptcy costs*. It is worth while to describe these costs in more detail.

Direct Costs of Financial Distress: Legal and Administrative Costs of Liquidation or Reorganization

As mentioned earlier, lawyers are involved throughout all the stages before and during bankruptcy. With fees often in the hundreds of pounds an hour, these costs can add up quickly. A wit once remarked that bankruptcies are to lawyers what blood is to sharks. In addition, administrative and accounting fees can substantially add to the total bill. And if a trial takes place, we must not forget expert witnesses. Each side may hire a number of these witnesses to testify about the fairness of a prepared settlement. Their fees can easily rival those of lawyers or accountants. (However, we personally look upon these witnesses more kindly, because they are frequently drawn from the ranks of finance professors.)

These direct costs have recently been estimated in the USA. While large in absolute amount, they are actually small as a percentage of firm value. White, Altman and Weiss estimated the direct costs of financial distress to be about 3 per cent of the market value of the firm.[3] In a study of direct financial distress costs of 20 railroad bankruptcies, Warner found that net financial distress costs were, on average, 1 per cent of the market value of the firm seven years before bankruptcy and were somewhat larger percentages as bankruptcy approached (for example, 2.5 per cent of the market value of the firm three years before bankruptcy).[4] Note that all of these estimates derive from US data.

---

[3] M. J. White (1983) 'Bankruptcy costs and the new bankruptcy code', *Journal of Finance*, May; and E. I. Altman (1984) 'A further empirical investigation of the bankruptcy cost question', *Journal of Finance*, September. More recently, Lawrence A. Weiss (1990) 'Bankruptcy resolution: Direct costs and violation of priority of claims', *Journal of Financial Economics*, **27**, estimates that direct costs of bankruptcy are 3.1 per cent of the value of the firm. Ferris, Jayaraman, and Makhija (1993) 'Direct costs of bankruptcy: Evidence from filings of liquidations and reorganizations by small firms, 1981–1991', unpublished manuscript, Georgia Institute of Technology, report very high direct cost in smaller firms. At initiation of bankruptcy, the direct costs are about 28 per cent of assets.

[4] J. B. Warner (1977) 'Bankruptcy costs: Some evidence', *Journal of Finance*, May.

Indirect Costs of Financial Distress

Impaired Ability to Conduct Business

Bankruptcy hampers conduct with customers and suppliers. Sales are frequently lost because of both fear of impaired service and loss of trust. Buyers question whether parts and servicing would be available were a supplier to fail. Sometimes the taint of impending bankruptcy is enough to drive customers away. Though these costs clearly exist, it is quite difficult to estimate them. Some investigations have estimated that both direct and indirect costs are frequently greater than 20 per cent of firm value. But, at the other extreme, there are investigations which put such total costs far lower.

Agency Costs

When a firm has debt, conflicts of interest arise between shareholders and bondholders. Because of this, shareholders are tempted to pursue selfish strategies. These conflicts of interest, which are magnified when financial distress is incurred, impose **agency costs** on the firm. We describe three kinds of selfish strategies that shareholders use to hurt the bondholders and help themselves. These strategies are costly because they will lower the market value of the whole firm.

Selfish Investment Strategy 1: Incentive to Take Large Risks Firms near bankruptcy often take great chances, because they feel that they are playing with someone else's money. To understand this, imagine a levered firm considering two *mutually exclusive* projects: a low-risk one and a high-risk one. There are two equally likely outcomes: recession and boom. The firm is in such dire straits that should a recession hit, it will come near to bankruptcy with one project and actually fall into bankruptcy with the other. The cash flows for the firm if the low-risk project is taken can be described as

Low-Risk Project

	Probability	Value of firm	=	Stock	+	Bonds
Recession	0.5	DEM100	=	0	+	DEM100
Boom	0.5	DEM200	=	DEM100	+	DEM100

If recession occurs, the value of the firm will be DEM100, and if boom occurs, the value of the firm will be DEM200. The expected value of the firm is DEM150 (0.5 $\times$ DEM100 + 0.5 $\times$ DEM200).

The firm has promised to pay bondholders DEM100. Shareholders will obtain the difference between the total payoff and the amount paid to the bondholders. In other words, the bondholders have the prior claim on the payoffs, and the shareholders have the residual claim.

Now suppose that another, riskier project can be substituted for the low-risk project. The payoffs and probabilities are as follows:

High-Risk Project

	Probability	Value of firm	=	Stock	+	Bonds
Recession	0.5	DEM50	=	0	+	DEM50
Boom	0.5	DEM240	=	DEM140	+	DEM100

The expected value of the *firm* is DEM145 (0.5 × DEM50 + 0.5 × DEM240), which is lower than the expected value of the firm with the low-risk project. Thus, the low-risk project would be accepted if the firm were all equity. However, note that the expected value of the *shares* is DEM70 (0.5 × 0 + 0.5 × DEM140) with the high-risk project, but only DEM50 (0.5 × 0 + 0.5 × DEM100) with the low-risk project. Given the firm's present levered state, shareholders will select the high-risk project.

The key is that, relative to the low-risk project, the high-risk project increases firm value in a boom and decreases firm value in a recession. The increase in value in a boom is captured by the shareholders, because the bondholders are paid in full (they receive DEM100) regardless of which project is accepted. Conversely, the drop in value in a recession is lost by the bondholders, because they are paid in full with the low-risk project, but receive only DEM50 with the high-risk one. The shareholders will receive nothing in a recession anyway, whether the high-risk or low-risk project is selected. Thus, financial economists argue that shareholders expropriate value from the bondholders by selecting high-risk projects.

A story, perhaps apocryphal, illustrates this idea. It seems that Federal Express was near financial collapse within a few years of its inception. The founder, Frederick Smith, took USD20,000 of corporate funds to Las Vegas in despair. He won at the gaming tables, providing enough capital to allow the firm to survive. Had he lost, the banks would simply have received USD20,000 less when the firm reached bankruptcy.

Selfish Investment Strategy 2: Incentive to Underinvest   Shareholders of a firm with a significant probability of bankruptcy often find that new investment helps the bondholders at the shareholders' expense. The simplest case might be a property owner facing imminent bankruptcy. If he took GBP100,000 out of his own pocket to refurbish the building, he could increase the building's value by, say, GBP150,000. Though this investment has a positive net present value, he will turn it down if the increase in value cannot prevent bankruptcy. 'Why', he asks, 'should I use my own funds to improve the value of a building that the bank will soon repossess?'

This idea is formalized by the following simple example. Consider a firm with NLG4,000 of principal and interest payments due at the end of the year. It will be pulled into bankruptcy by a recession because its cash flows will be only NLG2,400 in that state. The firm's cash flows are presented in the lefthand side of Table 17.1. The firm could avoid bankruptcy in a recession by raising new equity to invest in a new project. The project costs NLG1,000 and brings in NLG1,700 in either state, implying a positive net present value. Clearly, it would be accepted in an all-equity firm.

TABLE 17.1   Example Illustrating Incentive to Underinvest

	Firm without Project		Firm with Project	
	Boom	*Recession*	*Boom*	*Recession*
Firm cash flows	NLG5,000	NLG2,400	NLG6,700	NLG4,100
Bonholders' claim	4,000	2,400	4,000	4,000
Shareholders' claim	NLG1,000	0	NLG2,700	NLG100

The project has positive NPV. However, much of its value is captured by bondholders. Rational managers, acting in the shareholders' interest, will reject the project.

However, the project hurts the shareholders of the levered firm. To see this, imagine the old shareholders contribute the NLG1,000 *themselves*.[5] The expected value of the shareholders' interest without the project is NLG500(0.5 × NLG1,000 + 0.5 × NLG0). The expected value with the project is NLG1,400(0.5 × NLG2,700 + 0.5 × NLG100). The shareholders' interest rises by only NLG900(NLG1,400 − NLG500) while costing NLG1,000.

The key is that the shareholders contribute the full NLG1,000 investment, but the shareholders and bondholders *share* the benefits. The shareholders take the entire gain if boom times occur. Conversely, the bondholders reap most of the cash flow from the project in a recession.

The discussion of selfish strategy 1 is quite similar to the discussion of selfish strategy 2. In both cases, an investment strategy for the levered firm is different from the one for the unlevered firm. Thus, leverage results in distorted investment policy. Whereas the unlevered company always chooses projects with a positive net present value, the levered firm may deviate from this policy.

Selfish Investment Strategy 3: Milking the Property   Another strategy is to pay out extra dividends or other distributions in times of financial distress, leaving less in the firm for the bondholders. This is known as *milking the property*, a phrase taken from real estate. Strategies 2 and 3 are very similar. In strategy 2, the firm chooses not to raise new equity. Strategy 3 goes one step further, because equity is actually withdrawn through the dividend.

Summary of Selfish Strategies

The above distortions occur only when there is a probability of bankruptcy or financial distress. Thus, these distortions *should not* affect, say, Deutsche Telekom because bankruptcy is not a realistic possibility for a blue-chip firm such as that. In other words, Deutsche Telekom's debt is virtually risk-free, regardless of the projects it accepts. Because the distortions are related to financial distress, we have included them in our discussion of the 'Indirect Costs of Financial Distress'.

Who pays for the cost of selfish investment strategies? We argue that it is ultimately the shareholders. Rational bondholders know that, when financial distress is imminent, they cannot expect help from shareholders. Rather, shareholders are likely to choose investment strategies that reduce the value of the bonds. Bondholders protect themselves accordingly by raising the interest rate that they require on the bonds. Because the shareholders must pay these high rates, they ultimately bear the costs of selfish strategies. The relationship between shareholders and bondholders is very similar to the relationship between Erroll Flynn and David Niven, good friends and movie stars in the 1930s. Niven reportedly said that the good thing about Flynn was that you knew exactly where you stood with him. When you needed his help, you could always count on him to let you down.

Concept Questions

- What is the main direct cost of financial distress?
- What are the indirect costs of financial distress?
- Who pays the costs of selfish strategies?

---

[5] The same qualitative results will obtain if the NLG1,000 is raised from new shareholders. However, the arithmetic becomes much more difficult since we must determine how many new shares are issued.

17.3   Can Costs of Debt Be Reduced?

Each of the costs of financial distress we mentioned above is substantial in its own right. The sum of them may well affect debt financing severely. Thus, managers have an incentive to reduce these costs. We now turn to some of their methods. However, it should be mentioned at the outset that methods below can, at most, reduce the costs of debt. They cannot *eliminate* them entirely.

Protective Covenants

Because the shareholders must pay higher interest rates as insurance against their own selfish strategies, they frequently make agreements with bondholders in hopes of lower rates. These agreements, called **protective covenants**, are incorporated as part of the loan document (or *indenture*) between shareholders and bondholders. The covenants must be taken seriously since a broken covenant can lead to default. Protective covenants can be classified into two types: negative covenants and positive covenants.

A **negative covenant** limits or prohibits actions that the company may take. Here are some typical negative covenants:

1. Limitations are placed on the amount of dividends a company may pay.
2. The firm may not pledge any of its assets to other lenders.
3. The firm may not merge with another firm.
4. The firm may not sell or lease its major assets without approval by the lender.
5. The firm may not issue additional long-term debt.

A **positive covenant** specifies an action that the company agrees to take or a condition the company must abide by. Here are some examples:

1. The company agrees to maintain its working capital at a minimum level.
2. The company must furnish periodic financial statements to the lender.

These lists of covenants are not exhaustive. We have seen loan agreements with more than 30 covenants.

Smith and Warner, in the USA, examined public issues of debt in 1975 and found that 91 per cent of the bond indentures included covenants that restricted the issuance of additional debt, 23 per cent restricted dividends, 39 per cent restricted mergers and 36 per cent limited the sale of assets.[6]

Protective covenants should reduce the costs of bankruptcy, ultimately increasing the value of the firm. Thus, shareholders are likely to favour all reasonable covenants. To see this, consider three choices by shareholders to reduce bankruptcy costs.

1. *Issue No Debt*   Because of the tax advantages to debt, this is a very costly way of avoiding conflicts.
2. *Issue Debt with No Restrictive and Protective Covenants*   In this case, bondholders will demand high interest rates to compensate for the unprotected status of their debt.
3. *Write Protective and Restrictive Covenants into the Loan Contracts*   If the covenants are clearly written, the creditors may receive protection without large costs being imposed on the shareholders. They will happily accept a lower interest rate.

---

[6]C. W. Smith and J. B. Warner (1979) 'On financial contracting: An analysis of bond covenants', *Journal of Financial Economics*, **7**.

TABLE 17.2   Loan Covenants

Covenant type	Shareholder action or firm circumstances	Reason for covenant
Financial-statement signals 1. Working capital requirement 2. Interest coverage 3. Minimum net worth	As firm approaches financial distress, shareholders may want firm to make high-risk investments	Shareholders lose value before bankruptcy; bondholders hurt much more in bankruptcy than shareholders (limited liability); bondholders hurt by *distortion of investment that leads to increases in risk*
Restrictions on asset disposition 1. Limit dividends 2. Limit sale of assets 3. Collateral and mortgages	Shareholders attempt to transfer corporate assets to themselves	Limits the ability of shareholders to transfer assets to themselves and to *underinvest*
Restrictions on switching assets	Shareholders attempt to increase risk of firm	Increased firm risk helps shareholders; bondholders hurt by *distortion of investment that leads to increases in risk*
Dilution 1. Limit on leasing 2. Limit on further borrowing	Shareholders may attempt to issue new debt of equal or greater priority	Restricts *dilution of the claim of existing bondholders*

Thus, bond covenants, even if they reduce flexibility, can increase the value of the firm. They can be the lowest-cost solution to the shareholder–bondholder conflict. A list of typical bond covenants and their uses appears in Table 17.2.

Consolidation of Debt

One reason bankruptcy costs are so high is that different creditors (and their lawyers) fight with each other. This problem can be alleviated by proper arrangement of bondholders and shareholders. For example, perhaps one or, at most, a few lenders can shoulder the entire debt. Should financial distress occur, negotiating costs are minimized under this arrangement. In addition, bondholders can purchase stock as well. In this way, shareholders and debtholders are not pitted against each other, because they are not separate entities. This appears to be the approach in Japan where large banks generally take significant stock positions in the firms to which they lend money.[7] Debt–equity ratios in Japan are far higher than those in most of the rest of the world.

17.4   Integration of Tax Effects and Financial Distress Costs

Modigliani and Miller argue that the firm's value rises with leverage in the presence of corporate taxes. Because this implies that all firms should choose maximum debt, the theory does not predict the behaviour of firms in the real world. Other authors have suggested that bankruptcy and related costs reduce the value of the levered firm.

The integration of tax effects and distress costs appears in Figure 17.1. The diagonal straight line in the figure represents the value of the firm in a world without bankruptcy costs. The ∩-shaped curve represents the value of the firm with these costs. The ∩-shaped curve rises as the firm moves from all-equity to a small amount of debt. Here, the present value of the distress costs is minimal because the probability of distress is so small. However, as more and more debt is added, the present value of these costs rises at an *increasing* rate. At some point, the increase in the present value

---

[7] Legal limitations may prevent this practice in some countries in the world.

FIGURE 17.1 The Optimal Amount of Debt and the Value of the Firm

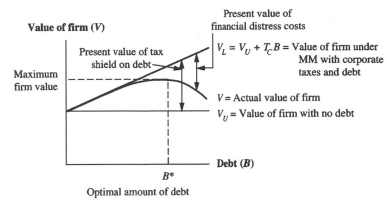

The tax shield increases the value of the levered firm. Financial distress costs lower the value of the levered firm. The two offsetting factors produce an optimal amount of debt at B^*.

---

of these costs from an additional dollar of debt equals the increase in the present value of the tax shield. This is the debt level maximizing the value of the firm and is represented by B^* in Figure 17.1. In other words, B^* is the optimal amount of debt. Bankruptcy costs increase faster than the tax shield beyond this point, implying a reduction in firm value from further leverage.

The above discussion presents two factors that affect the degree of leverage. Unfortunately, no formula exists at this time to exactly determine the optimal debt level for a particular firm. This is because bankruptcy costs cannot be expressed in a precise way. The last section of this chapter offers some rules of thumb for selecting a debt–equity ratio in the real world.

Pie Again

Critics of the MM theory often say that MM fails when we add such real-world issues as taxes and bankruptcy costs. Taking that view, however, blinds critics to the real value of the MM theory. The pie approach offers a more constructive way of thinking about these matters and the role of capital structure.

Taxes are just another claim on the cash flows of the firm. Let G (for government and taxes) stand for the market value of the government's claim to the firm's taxes. Bankruptcy costs are also another claim on the cash flows. Let us label their value with an L (for lawyers?). The bankruptcy costs are cash flows paid from the firm's cash flows in a bankruptcy. The cash flows to the claim L rise with the debt–equity ratio.

The pie theory says that all of these claims are paid from only one source, the cash flows (CF) of the firm. Algebraically, we must have

CF = Payments to shareholders
        +
    Payments to bondholders
        +
    Payments to the government
        +
    Payments to lawyers
        +
    Payments to any and all other claimants to the cash flows of the firm

Figure 17.2 shows the new pie. No matter how many slices we take, and no matter who gets them, they must still add up to the total cash flow. The value of the firm, V_T, is unaltered by the capital structure. Now, however, we must be broader in our definition of the firm's value

$$V_T = S + B + G + L$$

We previously wrote the firm's value as

$$S + B$$

when we ignored taxes and bankruptcy costs.

FIGURE 17.2   The Pie Model with Real-World Factors

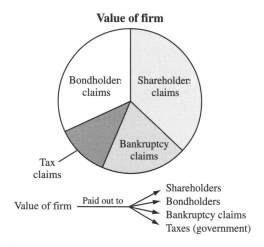

The essence of MM intuition and theory is that: V is V(CF) and depends on the total cash flow of the firm. The capital structure cuts it into slices. There is, however, an important difference between claims such as those of shareholders and bondholders on the one hand and those of government and potential litigants in lawsuits on the other. The first set of claims are **marketed claims**, and the second set are **non-marketed claims**. One difference is that the marketed claims can be bought and sold in financial markets, and the nonmarketed claims cannot.

When we speak of the value of the firm, generally we are referring just to the value of the marketed claims, V_M, and not the value of non-marketed claims, V_N. What we have shown is that the total value,

$$V_T = S + B + G + L$$
$$= V_M + V_N$$

is unaltered. But, as we saw, the value of the marketed claims, V_M, can change with changes in the capital structure in general and the debt–equity ratio in particular.

By the pie theory, any increase in V_M must imply an identical decrease in V_N. In an efficient market we showed that the capital structure will be chosen to maximize the value of the marketed claims, V_M. We can equivalently think of the efficient market as working to minimize the value of the non-marketed claims, V_N. These are taxes and bankruptcy costs.

Concept Questions

- List all the claims to the firm's assets.
- Describe marketed claims and nonmarketed claims.
- How can a firm maximize the value of its marketed claims?

17.5   Shirking and Perquisites: A Note on Agency Cost of Equity

The chapter has focused on agency costs of debt so far. However, we would be remiss if we failed to mention an important agency cost of equity. A discussion of this cost of equity is contained in a well-known quote from Adam Smith:[8]

> The directors of such [joint-stock] companies, however, being the managers of other people's money than of their own, it cannot well be expected that they should watch over it with the same anxious vigilance with which the partners in a private copartnery frequently watch over their own. Like the stewards of a rich man, they are apt to consider attention to small matters as not for their master's honour, and very easily give themselves a dispensation from having it. Negligence and profusion, therefore, must always prevail, more or less, in the management of the affairs of such a company.

This elegant prose can be restated in modern-day vocabulary. An individual will work harder for a firm if he or she is one of its owners than if he or she is just an employee. In addition, the individual will work harder if he or she owns a large percentage of the company than if he or she owns a small percentage. This idea has an important implication for capital structure, which we illustrate with the following example.

● Example

Ms Pagell is an owner-entrepreneur running a computer-services firm worth DEM1 million. She currently owns 100 per cent of the firm. Because of the need to expand, she must raise another DEM2 million. She can either issue DEM2 million of debt at 12 per cent interest or issue DEM2 million in shares. The cash flows under the two alternatives are presented below:

	Debt Issue				**Share Issue**			
	Cash flow	*Interest*	*Cash flow to equity*	*Cash flow to Ms Pagell (100% of equity)*	*Cash flow*	*Interest*	*Cash flow to equity*	*Cash flow to Ms Pagell ($33\frac{1}{3}$ of equity)*
6-hour days	DEM300,000	DEM240,000	DEM60,000	DEM60,000	DEM300,000	0	DEM300,000	DEM100,000
10-hour days	400,000	240,000	160,000	160,000	400,000	0	400,000	133,333

Like any entrepreneur, Ms Pagell can choose the degree of intensity with which she works. In our example, she can either work a 6- or a 10-hour day. With the debt issue, the extra work brings her DEM100,000 (DEM160,000 − DEM60,000) more

---

[8] Adam Smith, *Enquiry into the Nature and Causes of the Wealth of Nations* [1776], Oxford University Press, as quoted in M. C. Jensen and W. Meckling (1978) 'Theory of the firm: Managerial behaviour, agency costs, and ownership structure', *Journal of Financial Economics*, **3**.

income. However, with a share issue she retains only a one-third interest in the equity. Thus, the extra work brings her only DEM33,333 (DEM133,333 − DEM100,000). Being only human, she is likely to work harder if she issues debt. In other words, she has more incentive to *shirk* if she issues equity.

In addition, she is likely to obtain more *perquisites* (a big office, a company car, more expense-account meals) if she issues shares. If she is a one-third shareholder, two-thirds of these costs are paid for by the other shareholders. If she is the sole owner, any additional perquisites reduce her equity stake. Thus, as the firm issues more equity, she will increase both leisure time and work-related perquisites. The leisure time and work-related amenities are called agency costs, because managers of the firm are agents of the shareholders.[9] ●

Who bears the burden of these agency costs? If the new shareholders invest with their eyes open, they do not. Knowing that Ms Pagell may work short hours, they will pay only a low price for the shares. Thus, it is the owner who is hurt by agency costs. However, Ms Pagell can protect herself to some extent. Just as shareholders reduce bankruptcy costs through protective covenants, an owner may allow monitoring by new shareholders. However, though proper reporting and surveillance may reduce the agency costs of equity, these techniques are unlikely to eliminate them.

Effect of Agency Costs of Equity on Debt–Equity Financing

Before our discussion of agency costs of equity in the current section, we stated that the change in the value of the firm when debt is substituted for equity is the difference between (1) the tax shield on debt minus (2) the increase in the costs of financial distress (including the agency costs of debt). Now, the change in the value of the firm is (1) the tax shield on debt plus (2) the reduction in the agency costs of equity minus (3) the increase in the costs of financial distress (including the agency costs of debt). The optimal debt–equity ratio would be higher in a world with agency costs of equity than in a world without these costs. However, because the agency costs of debt are so significant, the costs of equity do not imply 100 per cent debt financing.

Concept Questions

- What are agency costs?
- Why are shirking and perquisites considered an agency cost of equity?
- How do agency costs of equity affect the firm's debt-equity ratio?

17.6   Growth and the Debt–Equity Ratio

While the trade-off between the tax shield and bankruptcy costs (as illustrated in Figure 17.1) is the 'standard model' of capital structure, it has its critics. For example, some point out that bankruptcy costs in the real world appear to be much smaller than the tax subsidy. Thus, the model implies that the optimal debt/value ratio should still be near 100 per cent, an implication at odds with reality.[10]

---

[9] As previously discussed, agency costs are generally defined as the costs from the conflicts of interest among shareholders, bondholders and managers.

[10] See Merton Miller's Presidential Address to the American Finance Association, reprinted as 'Debt and taxes', *Journal of Finance*, May.

An important new idea is that growth implies significant equity financing, even in a world with low bankruptcy costs.[11] To explain the idea, we first consider an example of a no-growth firm. Next, we examine the effect of growth on firm leverage.

No-Growth

Imagine a world of perfect certainty[12] where a firm has earnings before interest and taxes (EBIT) of GBP100. In addition, the firm has issued GBP1000 of debt at an interest rate of 10 per cent, implying interest payments of GBP100 per year. The cash flows to the firm are:

Date	1	2	3	4 ...
Earnings before interest and taxes (EBIT)	GBP100	GBP100	GBP100	GBP100 ...
Interest	−100	−100	−100	−100 ...
Taxable income	0	0	0	0

The firm has issued just enough debt so that all EBIT is paid out as interest. Since interest is tax-deductible, the firm pays no taxes. In this example, the equity is worthless because shareholders receive no cash flows. Since debt is worth GBP1,000, the firm is also valued at GBP1,000. Therefore, the debt-to-value ratio is 100 per cent (= GBP1,000/GBP1,000).

Had the firm issued less than GBP1,000 of debt, the company would have positive taxable income and, consequently, would have ended up paying some taxes. Had the firm issued more than GBP1,000 of debt, interest would have exceeded EBIT, causing default. Consequently, the optimal debt-to-value ratio is 100 percent.

Growth

Now imagine another firm that also has EBIT of GBP100 at date 1 but is growing at 5 per cent per year.[13] To eliminate taxes, this firm also wants to issue enough debt so that interest equals EBIT. Since EBIT is growing at 5 per cent per year, interest must also grow at this rate. This is achieved by increasing debt by 5 per cent per year.[14] The debt and income levels are:

Date	0	1	2	3	4 ...
Debt	GBP1,000	GBP1,050	GBP1,102.50	GBP1,157.63 ...	
New debt issued		50	52.50	55.13 ...	
EBIT		GBP100	GBP105	GBP110.25	GBP115.76 ...
Interest		−100	−105	−110.25	−115.76 ...
Taxable income		GBP0	GBP0	GBP0	GBP0

Note that interest on a particular date is always 10 per cent of the debt on the previous date. Debt is set so that interest is exactly equal to EBIT. As in the no-growth case, the levered firm has the maximum amount of debt at each date. Default would occur if interest payments were increased.

---

[11] This new idea is introduced and analysed in J. L. Berens and C. L. Cuny (1993) 'Inflation, growth and capital structure', unpublished paper, University of California at Irvine, June.

[12] The same qualitative results occur under uncertainty, though the mathematics is more troublesome.

[13] For simplicity, assume that growth is achieved without earnings retention. The same conclusions would be reached with retained earnings, though the arithmetic would become more involved. Of course, growth without earnings retention is less realistic than growth with retention.

[14] Since the firm makes no real investment, the new debt is used to buy back shares.

Because growth is 5 per cent per year, the value of the firm is:[15]

$$V_{firm} = \frac{GBP100}{0.10 - 0.05} = GBP2,000$$

The equity at date 0 is the difference between the value of the firm at that time, GBP2,000, and the debt of GBP1,000. Hence, equity must be equal to GBP1,000[16] implying a debt-to-value ratio of 50 per cent (= GBP1,000/GBP2,000). Note the important difference between the no-growth and the growth example. The no-growth example has no equity; the value of the firm is simply the value of the debt. With growth, there is equity as well as debt.

As we mentioned earlier, any further increase in debt would lower the value of the firm in a world with bankruptcy costs. Thus, with growth, the optimal amount of debt is less than 100 per cent. Note, however, that bankruptcy costs need not be as large as the tax subsidy. In fact, even with infinitesimally small bankruptcy costs, firm value would decline if promised interest rose above GBP100 in the first year. The key to this example is that *today's* interest is set equal to *today's* income. While the introduction of future growth opportunities increases firm value, it does not increase the current level of debt needed to shield today's income from today's taxes. Since equity is the difference between firm value and debt, growth increases the value of equity.

The above example captures an essential feature of the real world: growth. The same conclusion is reached in a world of inflation but no growth opportunities.[17] The result of this section, that 100 per cent debt financing is suboptimal, holds whether growth opportunities and/or inflation are present. Since most firms have growth opportunities, and since inflation has been with us for most of this century, this section's example is based on realistic assumptions. The basic point is this: high-growth firms will have lower debt ratios than low-growth firms.

Concept Question

- How do growth opportunities decrease the advantage of debt financing?

17.7   How Firms Establish Capital Structure

The theories of capital structure are among the most elegant and sophisticated in the field of finance. Financial economists should (and do!) pat themselves on the back for contributions in this area. However, the practical applications of the theories are less

---

[15] The firm can also be valued by a variant of (16.7):

$$V_L = V_U + PVTS$$
$$= \frac{GBP100(1 - T_C)}{0.10 - 0.05} + \frac{T_C \times GBP100}{0.10 - 0.05} = GBP2,000$$

Because of firm growth, both V_U and $PVTS$ are growing perpetuities.

[16] Students are often surprised that equity has value when taxable income is zero. Actually, the equityholders are receiving cash flow each period, since new debt is used to buy back shares.

[17] Notice that we restricted the debt to bonds with level coupon payments. Suppose, instead, that the firm had begun at date 0 by issuing debt-carrying coupons of GBP105 in year one, GBP110.25 in year 2, GBP115.76 in year 3, and so on. Since there is no uncertainty in our example, these coupons are just the annual EBIT of the firm. At an interest rate of 10 per cent such a bond would carry a price of GBP2,000, which is the entire value of the firm. Thus, the proceeds from the bond issue would equal the value of the firm and the firm would be capitalized as an all-debt firm. Keep in mind that the important feature of debt is that it is a contractual commitment by the firm to make scheduled payments to the holder. While these payments are usually in the form of level coupons, they also may vary over time.

than fully satisfying. Consider that our work on net present value produced an exact formula for evaluating projects. Conversely, the most we can say on capital structure is provided in Figure 17.1; the optimal capital structure involves a trade-off between taxes and costs of debt. No exact formula is available for evaluating the optimal debt–equity ratio. However there is evidence that firms behave as if they had target debt–equity ratios.[18] From a theoretical perspective and from empirical research, we present four important factors in the final determination of a target debt–equity ratio:

1. *Taxes*   If a company has (and will continue to have) taxable income, an increased reliance on debt will reduce taxes paid by the company and increase taxes paid by some bondholders. If corporate tax rates are higher than bondholder tax rates, there is value from using debt.

2. *Types of Assets*   Financial distress is costly, with or without formal bankruptcy proceedings. The costs of financial distress depend on the types of assets that the firm has. For example, if a firm has a large investment in land, buildings, and other tangible assets, it will have smaller costs of financial distress than a firm with a large investment in research and development. Research and development typically has less resale value than land; thus, most of its value disappears in financial distress.

3. *Uncertainty of Operating Income*   Firms with uncertain operating income have a high probability of experiencing financial distress, even without debt. Thus, these firms must finance mostly with equity. For example, pharmaceutical firms with most of their value deriving from R&D have uncertain operating income because no one can predict whether today's research will generate new drugs. Consequently, these firms issue relatively little debt. By contrast, the operating income of utilities generally has little uncertainty. Relative to other industries, utilities should use a great deal of debt.

4. *Pecking Order and Financial Slack*[19]   We first talked about the idea of a pecking order in our discussion of the financing patterns of firms in Chapter 15. The pecking-order theory states that firms prefer internal equity (i.e. retained earnings) to external financing. And, if funding requirements exceed retained earnings, debt issues are preferred to equity issues. This pecking order can be explained by two factors.

   ● External financing is expensive because of the large fees paid to investment bankers.
   ● It is hard for shareholders accurately to price external equity when managers know more about the firm than shareholders ('asymmetric information'). This may lead to a reluctance of shareholders to accept new equity issues.

   If firms prefer retained earnings over external financing, they may use less debt than is implied by taxes and financial distress costs. This is particularly true for highly profitable firms where retained earnings are likely to exceed funding requirements.

---

[18] The classic studies showing that firms have target debt ratios are P. Marsh (1981) 'The choice between equity and debt: An empirical study', *Journal of Finance*, March; and R.A. Taggart (1977) 'A model of corporate financing decisions', *Journal of Finance*, December.

[19] The pecking-order theory is generally attributed to S.C. Myers (1984) 'The capital structure puzzle', *Journal of Finance*, **39**, July.

The pecking-order theory has at least two other implications. First, firms will hoard cash during good times to avoid the need to finance externally during bad times. Economists refer to the cash build-up as *financial slack.* Second, the pecking-order theory does not imply a well-defined target debt–equity ratio. Rather, the ratio varies as capital expenditures and retained earnings change.

One final note is in order. Because no formula supports them, the above four points may seem too nebulous to assist financial decision-making. Their industry's debt–equity ratio is an important factor for the capital-structure decisions of many real-world firms. While this may strike some as a cowardly approach, it at least keeps firms from deviating far from accepted practice. After all, the existing firms in any industry are the survivors. Therefore, one should pay at least some attention to their decisions.

Concept Question

• What are the factors to consider in establishing a debt-equity ratio?

17.8   Financial Distress, Bankruptcy and Reorganization

This chapter began with a discussion of financial distress, it ends with it, too. This is not coincidental. The possibility of financial distress puts limits on the use of debt. But **financial distress** is surprisingly hard to define precisely. This is true partly because of the variety of events befalling firms under financial distress. The list of events is almost endless but here are some examples:

Dividend reductions
Plant closures
Losses
Layoffs
Chief executive resignations
Plummeting share price

Financial distress is a situation where a firm's operating cash flows are not sufficient to satisfy current obligations (such as trade debts or interest expenses), and the firm is forced to take corrective action. Financial distress may lead a firm to default on a contract, and it may involve financial restructuring between the firm, its creditors and its equity investors. Usually, the firm is forced to take actions that it would not have taken if it had sufficient cash flow.

Our definition of financial distress can be expanded somewhat by linking it to insolvency. Insolvency can be defined as the inability to pay one's debts; lack of means of paying one's debts; or such a condition of a person's assets and liabilities that the former, made immediately available, would be insufficient to discharge the latter.

Firms deal with financial distress in several ways such as

1. Selling major assets
2. Merging with another firm
3. Reducing capital spending, dividends, research and development, training, etc.
4. Issuing new securities
5. Negotiating with banks and other creditors
6. Exchanging equity for debt
7. Filing for bankruptcy

Items (1), (2) and (3) concern the firm's assets. Items (4), (5), (6) and (7) involve the liabilities side of the firm's balance sheet and are examples of financial restructuring. Financial distress may involve both asset restructuring and financial restructuring (i.e. changes on both sides of the balance sheet).

Some firms may actually benefit from financial distress by restructuring their assets. Financial distress can serve as a firm's 'early warning' system for trouble. Firms with more debt experience financial distress earlier than firms with less debt. However, firms that experience financial distress earlier have more time for restructuring. Firms with low financial leverage experience financial distress later and, in many instances, be forced to liquidate.

Firms in most European countries that cannot or choose not to make contractually required payments to creditors have two basic options: liquidation or reorganization. **Liquidation** means termination of the firm as a going concern; it involves selling the assets of the firm for salvage value. The proceeds, net of transactions costs, are distributed to creditors in order of established priority. **Reorganization** is the option of keeping the firm as a going concern; it sometimes involves issuing new securities to replace old securities.

Liquidation and formal reorganization may be done by bankruptcy. *Bankruptcy* is a legal proceeding and can be done voluntarily with the company filing the petition or it can be done involuntarily with the creditors filing the petition.

The rules for corporate bankruptcy and liquidation vary substantially from one European country to another. Hence we present here a general view—for detail relating to individual countries, the interested reader is referred to local legislation. Corporate bankruptcy liquidation typically involves the following sequence of events:

1. A petition is filed in a court. Companies may file a voluntary petition, or involuntary petitions may be filed against the company by its unpaid and overdue creditors.
2. A trustee-in-bankruptcy is elected by the creditors to take over the assets of the debtor company. The trustees will attempt to liquidate the assets.
3. When the assets are liquidated, after payment of the costs of administration, assets are distributed among the creditors.
4. If any assets remain, after expenses and payments to creditors, they are distributed to the shareholders.

Once a company is determined to be bankrupt, liquidation may take place. The distribution of the proceeds of the liquidation occurs according to the following typical priority list—but beware because it does vary from country to country:

1. Administration expenses associated with liquidating the bankrupt's assets.
2. Unsecured claims arising after the filing of a non-voluntary bankruptcy petition.
3. Wages, salaries, commission and the like up to a specified amount per claimant.
4. Contributions to employee benefit plans.
5. Tax claims, including local taxes.
6. Secured and unsecured creditor's claims, including short- and long-term debt.
7. Preferred shareholders' claims.
8. Equity shareholders' claims.

The priority rule in liquidation is often referred to as the **absolute priority rule**.

One caveat to this list concerns secured creditors. Liens (or other charges) on property are outside absolute priority rule ordering. However, if the secured property is liquidated and provides cash insufficient to cover the amount owed them, the secured creditors join with unsecured creditors in dividing the remaining liquidating value. In contrast, if the secured property is liquidated for proceeds greater than the secured claim, the net proceeds are used to pay unsecured creditors and others.

An alternative to liquidation in most countries is **bankruptcy reorganization**. The general objective is to plan to restructure the company—perhaps selling off some divisions, parts or assets—with the intent of making better some provision for repayment of creditors. The exact details of bankruptcy reorganization vary substantially across frontiers, but essentially the company is restructured and reorganized with a view to paying off the unpaid creditors.

There is an inherent conflict of interest between equity investors and creditors, and the conflict is accentuated when both have incomplete information about the circumstances of financial distress. When a firm initially experiences a cash flow shortfall, it may not know whether the shortfall is permanent or temporary. If the shortfall is permanent, creditors will push for a formal reorganization or liquidation. However, if the cash flow shortfall is temporary, formal reorganization or liquidation may not be necessary. Equity investors will push for this latter stance. This conflict of interest cannot easily be resolved.

These last two points are especially important. They suggest that financial distress will be more expensive (cheaper) if complexity is high (low) and information is incomplete (complete).

Concept Questions

- How would you describe financial distress?
- Why doesn't financial distress always cause firms to die?
- What is a benefit of financial distress?

17.9   Summary and Conclusions

1. We mentioned in the last chapter that, according to theory, firms should create all-debt capital structures under corporate taxation. Because firms generally assume moderate amounts of debt in the real world, the theory must be missing something at this point. We point out in this chapter that costs of financial distress cause firms to restrain their issuance of debt. These costs are of two types: direct and indirect. Lawyers' and accountants' fees during the bankruptcy process are examples of direct costs. We mentioned four examples of indirect costs:
   a. Impaired ability to conduct business
   b. Incentive to take on risky projects
   c. Incentive toward underinvestment
   d. Distribution of funds to shareholders prior to bankruptcy
2. Because the above costs are substantial and the stockholders ultimately bear them, firms have an incentive for cost reduction. We suggest three cost-reduction techniques:
   a. Protective covenants
   b. Repurchase of debt prior to bankruptcy
   c. Consolidation of debt
3. Because costs of financial distress can be reduced but not eliminated, firms will not finance entirely with debt. Figure 17.1 illustrates the relationship between firm value and debt. In the figure, firms select the debt-to-equity ratio at which firm value is maximized.
4. While the trade-off between the tax shield and the cost of financial distress is the 'standard model' of capital structure, it is not the only model. A recent paper by Berens and Cuny

argues that significant equity financing can be explained by real growth and inflation, even in a world of low bankruptcy costs.

5. Debt-to-equity ratios vary across industries and countries. From a theoretical perspective and from empirical research, we present four factors determining the target debt-to-equity ratio:

   a. *Taxes*   Firms with high taxable income should rely more on debt than firms with little taxable income.

   b. *Types of Assets*   Firms with a high percentage of intangible assets such as research and development should have low debt. Firms with primarily tangible assets should have higher debt.

   c. *Uncertainty of Operating Income*   Firms with high uncertainty of operating income should rely mostly on equity.

   d. *Pecking Order*   The most profitable firms will use less debt because they have sufficient internal equity for all positive NPV projects.

   Some firms will accumulate financial slack to avoid using external equity.

6. Financial distress is a situation where a firm's operating cash flow is not sufficient to cover contractual obligations. Financially distressed firms are often forced to take corrective action and undergo financial restructuring. Financial restructuring involves exchanging new financial claims for old ones. Sometimes financially distressed firms are forced into liquidation.

KEY TERMS

Agency costs 392	Financial distress 404
Protective covenants 395	Liquidation 405
Negative covenant 395	Reorganization 405
Positive covenant 395	Absolute priority rule 405
Marketed claims 398	Bankruptcy reorganization 406
Non-marketed claims 398	

QUESTIONS AND PROBLEMS

Description of Costs of Financial Distress

17.1 What are the direct and indirect costs of bankruptcy? Briefly explain each.

17.2 Do you agree or disagree with the following statement? Explain your answer.

   A firm's stockholders would never want the firm to invest in projects with negative NPVs.

Can Costs of Debt Be Reduced?

17.3 What measures do shareholders undertake to minimize the costs of debt?

Integration of Tax Effect and Financial Distress Costs

17.4 How would the consideration of financial distress costs and agency costs affect the MM proposition in a world where corporations pay taxes?

CHAPTER 18 Valuation and Capital Budgeting for the Levered Firm

Instructors often structure the basic course in corporate finance around the two sides of the balance sheet. The lefthand side of the balance sheet contains assets. Chapters 5, 6, 7, 8 and 9 of this textbook treat the capital-budgeting decision, which is a decision concerning the assets of the firm. Chapters 10, 11, 12 and 13 treat the discount rate for a project, so those chapters also concern the lefthand side of the balance sheet. The righthand side of the balance sheet contains liabilities and owner's equity. Chapters 14, 15, 16 and 17 examine the debt-versus-equity decision, which is a decision about the righthand side of the balance sheet.

While the preceding chapters of this textbook have, for the most part, treated the capital-budgeting decision separately from the capital-structure decision, the two decisions are actually related. As we will see, a project of an all-equity firm might be rejected, while the same project might be accepted for a levered, but otherwise identical, firm. This occurs because the cost of capital frequently decreases with leverage, thereby turning some negative NPV projects into positive NPV projects.

Chapters 5 through 9 implicitly assumed that the firm is financed with only equity. The goal of this chapter is to value a project, or the firm itself, when leverage is employed. We point out that there are three standard approaches to valuation under leverage: the adjusted-present-value (APV) method, the flow-to-equity (FTE) method and the weighted-average-cost-of-capital (WACC) method. These three approaches may seem, at first glance, to be quite different. However, we aim in this chapter to stress their similarities. For certain situations, the different approaches provide exactly the same answer. For other situations, the three approaches may provide somewhat different answers, and we discuss which method is preferred.

The three methods discussed below can be used to value either the firm as a whole or a project. The example below discusses project value, though everything we say applies to an entire firm as well.

18.1 Adjusted-Present-Value Approach

The **adjusted-present-value (APV)** method is best described by the following formula:

$$APV = NPV + NPVF$$

In words, the value of a project to a levered firm (APV) is equal to the value of the project to an unlevered firm (NPV) plus the net present value of the financing side-effects (NPVF). One can generally think of four side-effects:

1. *The Tax Subsidy to Debt*   This was discussed in Chapter 16, where we pointed out that, for perpetual debt, the value of the tax subsidy is $T_C B$. (T_C is the corporate tax rate, and B is the value of the debt.) The material on valuation under corporate taxes in Chapter 16 is actually an application of the APV approach.
2. *The Costs of Issuing New Securities*   Investment bankers participate in the public issuance of corporate debt. These bankers must be compensated for their time and effort, a cost that lowers the value of the project.
3. *The Costs of Financial Distress*   The possibility of financial distress, and bankruptcy in particular, arises with debt financing. As stated in the previous chapter, financial distress imposes costs, thereby lowering value.
4. *Subsidies to Debt Financing*   Sometimes companies are able to raise debt where the interest cost is substantially below the market rate. This may occur because a project is undertaken in a poor region of a country or the EU or it may be because of some other socially desirable reason. However, the point is that, as with any subsidy, this subsidy adds value and its present value must be taken into account in determining the potential value.

While each of these four above side-effects is important, the tax deduction to debt almost certainly has the highest value in practice. For this reason, the following example considers the tax subsidy, but not the other three side-effects.

Consider the project of Bergkamp NV with the following characteristics:

Sales: NLG500,000 per year for the indefinite future
Cash costs: 72% of sales
Initial investment: NLG475,000
$T_C = 34\%$
$r_0 = 20\%$, where r_0 is the cost of capital for a project of an all-equity firm.

If both the project and the firm are financed with only equity, the project's cash flow is

Sales	NLG500,000
Cash costs	$-360,000$
Operating income	140,000
Corporate tax (0.34 tax rate)	$-47,600$
Unlevered cash flow (UCF)	NLG92,400

The distinction in Chapter 5 between present value and net present value is quite important for this example. As pointed out in Chapter 5, the *present value* of a project is determined before the initial investment at date 0 is subtracted. The initial investment is subtracted for the calculation of *net* present value.

Given a discount rate of 20 per cent, the present value of the project is

$$\frac{\text{NLG92,400}}{0.20} = \text{NLG462,000}$$

The net present value (NPV) of the project, that is, the value of the project to an all-equity firm, is

$$\text{NLG462,000} - \text{NLG475,000} = -\text{NLG13,000}$$

Since the NPV is negative, the project would be rejected by an all-equity firm.

Now imagine that the firm finances the project with exactly NLG126,229.50 in debt, so that the remaining investment of NLG348,770.5 (NLG475,000 − NLG126,229.50) is financed with equity. The *net* present value of the project under leverage, which we call APV, is

$$APV = NPV + T_C \times B$$
$$NLG29,918 = -NLG13,000 + 0.34 \times NLG126,229.50$$

That is, the value of the project when financed with some leverage is equal to the value of the project when financed with all equity plus the tax shield from the debt. Since this number is positive, the project should be accepted.

You may be wondering why we chose such a precise amount of debt. Actually, we chose it so that the ratio of debt to the present value of the project under leverage is 0.25.[1]

In this example, debt is a fixed proportion of the present value of the project, not a fixed proportion of the initial investment of NLG475,000. This is consistent with the goal of a target debt-*to-market*-value ratio, which we find in the real world. For example, commercial banks typically lend to real estate developers a fixed percentage of the market value of a project, not a fixed percentage of the initial investment.

Concept Questions

- How is the APV method applied?
- What additional information beyond NPV does one need to calculate APV?

18.2   Flow-to-Equity Approach

The **flow-to-equity (FTE)** approach is an alternative capital-budgeting approach. The formula simply calls for discounting the cash flow from the project to the equityholders of the levered firm at the cost of equity capital, r_S. For a perpetuity, this becomes

$$\frac{\text{Cash flow from project to equityholders of the levered firm}}{r_S}$$

There are three steps to the FTE approach.

---

[1] That is, the present value of the project after the initial investment has been made is NLG504,918 (NLG29,918 + NLG475,000). Thus, the debt-to-value ratio of the project is 0.25 (NLG126,229.5/NLG504,918).

This level of debt can be calculated directly. Note that

Present value of levered project = Present value of unlevered project + $T_C \times B$
$$V_{\text{With debt}} = NLG462,000 + 0.34 \times 0.25 \times V_{\text{With debt}}$$

Rearranging the last line, we have
$$V_{\text{With debt}} (1 - 0.34 \times 0.25) = NLG462,000$$
$$V_{\text{With debt}} = NLG504,918$$

Since debt is 0.25 of value, debt is NLG126,229.50 (0.25 × NLG504,918).

Step 1: Calculating Levered Cash Flow (LCF)[2]

Assuming an interest rate of 10 per cent, the perpetual cash flow to equityholders in our example is

Sales	NLG500,000.00
Cash costs	−360,000.00
Interest (10% × NLG126,229.50)	−12,622.95
Income after interest	127,377.05
Corporate tax (0.34 tax rate)	−43,308.20
Levered cash flow (LCF)	NLG84,068.85

Alternatively, one can calculate levered cash flow (LCF) directly from unlevered cash flow (UCF). The key here is that the difference between the cash flow that equityholders receive in an unlevered firm and the cash flow that equityholders receive in a levered firm is the after-tax interest payment. (Repayment of principal does not appear in this example, since the debt is perpetual.) One writes this algebraically as

$$UCF - LCF = (1 - T_C)r_B B$$

The term on the righthand side of this expression is the after-tax interest payment. Thus, since cash flow to the unlevered equityholders (UCF) is NLG92,400 and the after-tax interest payment is NLG8,331.15 [(0.66) × 0.10 × NLG126,229.50], cash flow to the levered equityholders (LCF) is

$$NLG92,400 - NLG8,331.15 = NLG84,068.85$$

which is exactly the number we calculated earlier.

Step 2: Calculating r_S

The next step is to calculate the discount rate, r_S. Note that we assumed that the discount rate on unlevered equity, r_0, is 0.20. As we saw in Chapter 16, the formula for r_S is

$$r_S = r_0 + \frac{B}{S}(1 - T_C)(r_0 - r_B)$$

Note that our target debt-to-value ratio of $\frac{1}{4}$ implies a target debt-to-equity ratio of $\frac{1}{3}$. Applying the above formula to this example, we have

$$r_S = 0.222 = 0.20 + \frac{1}{3}(0.66)(0.20 - 0.10)$$

Step 3: Valuation

The present value of the project's LCF is

$$\frac{LCF}{r_S} = \frac{NLG84,068.85}{0.222} = NLG378,688.50$$

---

[2] We use the term *levered cash flow* (LCF) for simplicity. A more complete term would be *cash flow from the project to the equityholders of a levered firm*. Similarly, a more complete term for *unlevered cash flow* (UCF) would be *cash flow from the project to the equityholders of an unlevered firm*.

Since the initial investment is NLG475,000 and NLG126,229.50 is borrowed, the firm must advance the project NLG348,770.50 (NLG475,000 − NLG126,229.50) out of its own cash reserves. The *net* present value of the project is simply the difference between the present value of the project's LCF and the investment not borrowed. Thus, the NPV is

$$NLG378,688.50 - NLG348,770.50 = NLG29,918$$

which is identical to the result found with the APV approach.

Concept Questions

• How is the FTE method applied?
• What information is needed to calculate FTE?

18.3   Weighted-Average-Cost-of-Capital Method

Finally, one can value a project using the **weighted-average-cost-of-capital** (WACC) method. While this method was discussed in Chapters 13 and 16, it is worth while to review it here. The WACC approach begins with the insight that projects of levered firms are simultaneously financed with both debt and equity. The cost of capital is a weighted average of the cost of debt and the cost of equity. As seen in Chapters 13 and 16, the cost of equity is r_S. Ignoring taxes, the cost of debt is simply the borrowing rate, r_B. However, with corporate taxes, the appropriate cost of debt is $(1 - T_C)r_B$, the after-tax cost of debt.

The formula for determining the weighted average cost of capital, r_{WACC}, is

$$r_{WACC} = \frac{S}{S + B} r_S + \frac{B}{S + B} r_B(1 - T_C)$$

The weight for equity, $S/S + B$, and the weight for debt, $B/S + B$, are target ratios. Target ratios are generally expressed in terms of market values, not accounting values. (Another phrase for accounting value is *book value*.)

The formula calls for discounting the *unlevered* cash flow of the project (UCF) at the weighted average cost of capital, r_{WACC}. The net present value of the project can be written algebraically as

$$\sum_{t=1}^{\infty} \frac{UCF_t}{(1 + r_{WACC})^t} - \begin{array}{c} \text{Initial} \\ \text{investment} \end{array}$$

If the project is a perpetuity, the net present value is

$$\frac{UCF}{r_{WACC}} - \text{Initial investment}$$

We previously stated that the target debt-to-value ratio of our project is $\frac{1}{4}$ and the corporate tax rate is 0.34, implying that the weighted average cost of capital is

$$r_{WACC} = \frac{3}{4} \times 0.222 + \frac{1}{4} \times 0.10(0.66) = 0.183$$

Note that r_{WACC}, 0.183, is lower than the cost of equity capital for an all-equity firm, 0.20. This must always be the case, since debt financing provides a tax subsidy that lowers the average cost of capital.

We previously determined the UCF of the project to be NLG92,400, implying that the present value of the project is

$$\frac{\text{NLG92,400}}{0.183} = \text{NLG504,918}$$

Since this initial investment is NLG475,000, the NPV of the project is

$$\text{NLG504,918} - \text{NLG475,000} = \text{NLG29,918}$$

In this example, all three approaches yield the same value.

Concept Question

- How is the WACC method applied?

18.4   A Comparison of the APV, FTE and WACC Approaches

Capital-budgeting techniques in the early chapters of this text applied to all-equity firms. Capital budgeting for the levered firm could not be handled early in the book because the effects of debt on firm value were deferred until the previous two chapters. We learned there that debt increases firm value through tax benefits but decreases value through bankruptcy and related costs.

In the present chapter, we provide three approaches to capital budgeting for the levered firm. The adjusted-present-value (APV) approach first values the project on an all-equity basis. That is, the project's after-tax cash flows under all-equity financing (UCF) are placed in the numerator of the capital-budgeting equation. The discount rate, assuming all-equity financing, appears in the denominator. At this point, the calculation is identical to that performed in the early chapters of this book. We then add the net present value of the debt. We point out that the net present value of the debt is likely to be the sum of four parameters: tax effects, flotation costs, bankruptcy costs and interest subsidies.

The flow-to-equity (FTE) approach discounts the after-tax cash flow from a project going to the equityholders of a levered firm (LCF). LCF is the residual to equityholders after interest has been deducted. The discount rate is r_S, the cost of capital to the equityholders of a levered firm. For a firm with leverage, r_S must be greater than r_0, the cost of capital for an unlevered firm. This follows from our material in Chapter 16 showing that leverage raises the risk to the equityholders.

The last approach is the weighted-average-cost-of-capital (WACC) method. This technique calculates the project's after-tax cash flows assuming all-equity financing (UCF). The UCF is placed in the numerator of the capital-budgeting equation. The denominator, r_{WACC}, is a weighted average of the cost of equity capital and the cost of debt capital. The tax advantage of debt is reflected in the denominator because the cost of debt capital is determined net of corporate tax. The numerator does not reflect debt at all.

All three approaches attempt the same task: valuation in the presence of debt financing. However, as we saw above, the approaches are markedly different in technique. Because of this, it is worth while to stress two points.

1. *APV versus WACC* As stated above, both the APV and the WACC approaches use unlevered cash flow (UCF). The APV discounts these flows at r_0, yielding the value of the unlevered project. Adding the present value of the

tax shield gives the value of the project under leverage. The WACC approach discounts UCF at r_{WACC}, which is lower than r_0. Thus, the APV and WACC approaches are different ways to determine the same value. While the APV approach adds a tax shield, the WACC approach lowers the denominator below r_0. Both approaches yield a value above that of the unlevered project.

2. *Entity Being Valued*   For both the APV and the WACC approaches, the initial investment is subtracted out in the final step (NLG475,000 in our example). However, for the FTE approach, only the firm's contribution to the initial investment (NLG348,770.50 = NLG475,000 − NLG126,229.50) is subtracted out. This occurs because, under the FTE approach, only the future cash flows to the levered equityholders (LCF) are included. Thus, since these future cash flows are reduced by interest payments, the initial investment is correspondingly reduced by debt financing.

A Suggested Guideline

The net present value of our project is exactly the same under each of the three methods. In theory, this should always be the case.[3] However, one method usually provides an easier computation than another, and, in many cases, one or more of the methods is virtually impossible computationally.

We first consider when it is best to use the WACC and FTE approaches. If the risk of a project stays constant throughout its life, it is plausible to assume that r_0 remains constant throughout the project's life. This assumption of constant risk appears to be reasonable for most real-world projects. In addition, if the debt-to-value ratio remains constant over the life of the project, both r_S and r_{WACC} will remain constant as well. Under this latter assumption, either the FTE or the WACC approach is easy to apply. However, if the debt-to-value ratio varies from year to year, both r_S and r_{WACC} vary from year to year as well. Using the FTE or the WACC approach when the denominator changes every year is computationally quite complex, and when computations become complex, the error rate rises. Thus, both the FTE and WACC approaches present difficulties when the debt-to-value *ratio* changes over time.

The APV approach is based on the *level* of debt in each future period. Consequently, when the debt level can be specified precisely for future periods, the APV approach is quite easy to use. However, when the debt level is uncertain, the APV approach becomes more problematic. For example, when the debt-to-value ratio is a constant, the debt level varies with the value of the project. Since the value of the project in a future year cannot be easily forecast, the level of debt cannot be easily forecast either.

Thus, the following guideline is suggested:

> Use WACC or FTE if a target debt-to-value *ratio* seems applicable to the project over its life.
> Use APV if the project's precise *level* of debt is known in advance over the life of the project.

---

[3] See I. Inselbag and H. Kaufold (1990) 'A Comparison of Alternative Discounted Cash Flow Approaches to Firm Valuation', The Wharton School, University of Pennsylvania, June, unpublished paper.

The Three Methods of Capital Budgeting with Leverage

1. Adjusted-Present-Value (APV) Method

$$\sum_{t=1}^{\infty} \frac{\text{UCF}_t}{(1 + r_0)^t} + \begin{array}{c}\text{Additional} \\ \text{effects of debt}\end{array} - \begin{array}{c}\text{Initial} \\ \text{investment}\end{array}$$

UCF_t = The project's cash flow at date t to the equityholders of an unlevered firm
r_0 = Cost of capital for project in an unlevered firm

2. Flow-to-Equity (FTE) Method

$$\sum_{t=1}^{\infty} \frac{\text{LCF}_t}{(1 + r_S)^t} - \left(\begin{array}{c}\text{Initial} \\ \text{investment}\end{array} - \begin{array}{c}\text{Amount} \\ \text{borrowed}\end{array} \right)$$

LCF_t = The project's cash flow at date t to the equityholders of a levered firm
r_S = Cost of equity capital with leverage

3. Weighted-Average-Cost-of-Capital (WACC) Method

$$\sum_{t=1}^{\infty} \frac{\text{UCF}_t}{(1 + r_{\text{WACC}})^t} - \begin{array}{c}\text{Initial} \\ \text{investment}\end{array}$$

r_{WACC} = Weighted average cost of capital

Notes:

1. The middle term in the APV formula implies that the value of a project with leverage is greater than the value of the project without leverage. Since $r_{\text{WACC}} < r_0$, the WACC formula implies that the value of a project with leverage is greater than the value of the project without leverage.

2. In the FTE method, cash flow *after interest* (LCF) is used. Initial investment is reduced by *amount borrowed* as well.

Guidelines:

1. Use WACC or FTE if a target debt-to-value *ratio* seems applicable to the project over its life.

2. Use APV if the project's precise *level* of debt is known in advance over the life of the project.

There are a number of situations where the APV approach is preferred. For example, in a leveraged buyout (LBO) the firm begins with a large amount of debt, but rapidly pays down the debt over a number of years. Since the schedule of debt reduction in the future is known when the LBO is arranged, tax shields in every future year can be easily forecast. Thus, the APV approach is easy to use here. (An illustration of the APV approach applied to LBOs is provided in Appendix 18A.) By contrast, the WACC and FTE approaches are virtually impossible to apply here, since the debt-to-equity ratio cannot be expected to be constant over time. In addition, situations involving interest subsidies and flotation costs are much easier to handle with the APV approach. (The Bicksler NV example in Section 18.6 applies the APV approach to subsidies and flotation costs.) Finally, the APV approach handles the lease-versus-buy decision much more easily than does either the FTE or the WACC approach. (A treatment of the lease-versus-buy decision appears in Chapter 24.)

The above examples are special situations. In order to see which approach is more appropriate for a typical capital-budgeting situation, we must answer the following question: When managers pursue debt policy, do they think of keeping the level of debt fairly constant through time, or do they think of keeping the debt–equity ratio fairly constant through time? This is ultimately an empirical question, and one that has not been rigorously investigated. However, we believe that managers should think in terms of an optimal debt–equity ratio. If a project does much better than expected, both its value and its debt capacity will be likely to rise. A shrewd financial manager will take advantage of this by increasing debt. Conversely, the firm should reduce debt if the value of a project were to decline unexpectedly. Because financing is a time-consuming task, the level of debt cannot be adjusted on a day-to-day or month-to-month basis. However, the adjustment should occur over time.

Because of this, we recommend that the WACC and the FTE approaches, rather than the APV approach, be used in most real-world situations. In addition, frequent discussions with business executives have convinced us that the WACC is the most widely used method in the real world, by far. Thus, practitioners seem to agree with us that, outside of the special situations mentioned above, the APV approach is a less important method of capital budgeting.

Concept Questions

- What is the main difference between APV and WACC?
- What is the main difference between the FTE approach and the other two approaches?
- When should the APV method be used?
- When should the FTE and WACC approaches be used?

18.5   Capital Budgeting for Projects that Are Not Scale-Enhancing

In Chapter 13, we covered scale-enhancing and non-scale-enhancing projects. A scale-enhancing project is one where the project is similar to the existing firm. For example, a project at Daimler-Benz to produce automobiles would be considered scale-enhancing. The analyses in Sections 18.1–18.3 can be used to value scale-enhancing projects. A somewhat different analysis is needed when a project is not scale-enhancing. This is best illustrated by an example.

● Example

European Enterprises NV (EE) is a large conglomerate headquartered in Amsterdam thinking of entering the widget (an entirely fictitious product found only in finance and economics books) business, where it plans to finance projects with a debt-to-value ratio of 25 per cent (or, alternatively, a debt-to-equity ratio of $\frac{1}{3}$). There is currently one firm in the widget industry, Euro Widgets (EW). This firm is financed with 40 per cent debt and 60 per cent equity. The beta of EW's equity is 1.5. EW has a borrowing rate of 12 per cent, and EE expects to borrow for its widget venture at 10 per cent. The corporate tax rate for both firms is 0.40, the market-risk premium is 8.5 per cent, and the riskless interest rate is 8 per cent. What is the appropriate discount rate for EE to use for its widget venture?

As mentioned in Sections 18.1–18.3, a company may use one of three capital-budgeting approaches: APV, FTE or WACC. The appropriate discount rates for these three approaches are r_0, r_S, and r_{WACC}, respectively. Since EW is EE's only competitor in widgets, we look at EW's cost of capital to calculate r_0, r_S, and r_{WACC} for EE's widget venture. The four-step procedure below will allow us to calculate all three discount rates.

1. *Determining EW's Cost of Equity Capital* First, we determine EW's cost of equity capital, using the security market line (SML) of Chapter 11.

EW's Cost of Equity Capital:

$$r_S = R_F + \beta \times (\bar{R}_M - R_F)$$
$$20.75\% = 8\% + 1.5 \times \quad 8.5\%$$

where $\bar{R}_M$ is the expected return on the market portfolio and R_F is the risk-free rate.

2. *Determining EW's Hypothetical All-Equity Cost of Capital* However, we must standardize the above number in some way, since EW and EE's widget ventures have different target debt-to-value ratios. The easiest approach is to calculate the hypothetical cost of equity capital for EW, assuming all-equity financing. This can be determined from MM's Proposition II under taxes (see Chapter 16).

EW's Cost of Capital If All-Equity:

$$r_S = r_0 + \frac{B}{S}(1 - T_C)(r_0 - r_B)$$

$$20.75\% = r_0 + \frac{0.4}{0.6}(0.60)(r_0 - 12\%)$$

In the examples in Chapter 16, the unknown in this equation was r_S.[4] However, for this example, the unknown is r_0. By solving the equation, one finds that $r_0 = 0.1825$. Of course, r_0 is less than r_S because the cost of equity capital would be less when the firm employs no leverage.

At this point, firms in the real world generally make the assumption that the business risk of their venture is about equal to the business risk of the firms already in the business. Applying this assumption to our problem, we assert that the hypothetical discount rate of EE's widget venture if all-equity financed is also 0.1825.[5] This discount rate would be employed if EE uses the APV approach, since the APV approach calls for r_0, the project's cost of capital in a firm with no leverage.

3. *Determining r_S for EE's Widget Venture.* Alternatively, EE might use the FTE approach, where the discount rate for levered equity is determined from

Cost of Equity Capital for EE's Widget Venture:

$$r_S = r_0 + \frac{B}{S} + (1 - T_C)(r_0 - r_B)$$

$$19.9\% = 18.25\% + \frac{1}{3}(0.60)(18.25\% - 10\%)$$

Note that the cost of equity capital for EE's widget venture, 0.199, is less than the cost of equity capital for EW, 0.2075. This occurs because EW has a higher debt-to-equity ratio. (As mentioned above, both firms are assumed to have the same business risk.)

---

[4] In this example we are implicitly assuming that the debt betas for EW and EE are not zero. This point is discussed in more detail in Section 18.7.

[5] Alternatively, a firm might assume that its venture would be somewhat riskier since it is a new entrant. Thus, the firm might select a discount rate slightly higher than 0.1825. Of course, no exact formula exists for adjusting the discount rate upwards.

4. *Determining* r_{WACC} *for EE's Widget Venture*   Finally, EE might use the WACC approach. The appropriate calculation here is

r_{WACC} **for EE's Widget Venture:**

$$r_{WACC} = \frac{B}{S + B} r_B (1 - T_C) + \frac{S}{S + B} r_S$$

$$16.425\% = \frac{1}{4} 10\%(0.60) + \frac{3}{4} 19.9\% \quad \bullet$$

18.6   APV Example

As mentioned above, the APV approach is effective in situations where flotation costs and subsidized financing arise. The FTE and the WACC approaches are less effective in these situations. The following is an example where the APV approach works well.

● **Example**
Bicksler NV is considering a NLG10 million project that will last five years, implying straight-line depreciation per year of NLG2 million. The cash revenues less cash expenses per year are NLG3,500,000. The corporate tax bracket is 34 per cent. The risk-free rate is 10 per cent, and the cost of unlevered equity is 20 per cent.
    The cash flow projections each year are

	C_0	C_1	C_2	C_3	C_4	C_5
Initial outlay	−NLG10,000,000					
Depreciation tax shield		0.34 × NLG2,000,000 = NLG680,000	NLG680,000	NLG680,000	NLG680,000	NLG680,000
Revenue less expenses		(1 − 0.34) × NLG3,500,000 = NLG2,310,000	NLG2,310,000	NLG2,310,000	NLG2,310,000	NLG2,310,000

We stated above that the APV of a project is the sum of its all-equity value plus the additional effects of debt. We examine each in turn.

All-Equity Value

Assuming the project is financed with all equity, the value of the project is

$$-NLG10,000,000 + \frac{NLG680,000}{0.10} \times \left[1 - \left(\frac{1}{1.10} \right)^5 \right] +$$

Initial cost   Depreciation tax shield

$$\frac{NLG2,310,000}{0.20} \times \left[1 - \left(\frac{1}{1.20} \right)^5 \right] = -NLG513,951$$

Present value of (Cash revenues − Cash expenses)

This calculation uses the techniques of the early chapters of this book. Notice that the depreciation tax shield is discounted at the riskless rate of 10 per cent. The revenues and expenses are discounted at the higher rate of 20 per cent.
    An all-equity firm would clearly reject this project, because the NPV is −NLG513,951. And equity-flotation costs (not mentioned in the example) would only make the NPV more negative. However, debt financing may add enough value to the project to justify acceptance. We consider the effects of debt below.

Additional Effects of Debt

Bicksler NV can obtain a five-year, non-amortizing loan for NLG7,500,000 after flotation costs at the risk-free rate of 10 per cent. Flotation costs are fees paid when stock or debt is issued. These fees may go to printers, lawyers and investment bankers, among others. Bicksler NV is informed that flotation costs will be 1 per cent of the gross proceeds of its loan. The previous chapter indicates that debt financing alters the NPV of a typical project. We look at the effects of debt below.

Flotation Costs

We represent the gross proceeds to be raised as *gross proceeds*. Given that flotation costs are 1 per cent of the gross proceeds, we have

$$\text{NLG7,500,000} = (1 - 0.01) \times \text{Gross proceeds} = 0.99 \times \text{Gross proceeds}$$

Thus, the gross proceeds are

$$\frac{\text{NLG7,500,000}}{1 - 0.01} = \frac{\text{NLG7,500,000}}{0.99} = \text{NLG7,575,758}$$

This implies flotation costs of NLG75,758 (1% $\times$ NLG7,575,758). To check the calculation, note that net proceeds are NLG7,500,000 (NLG7,575,758 − NLG75,758).

Flotation costs are paid immediately,[6] but are deducted from taxes by amortizing on a straight-line basis over the life of the loan. The cash flows from flotation costs are

	Date 0	Date 1	Date 2	Date 3	Date 4	Date 5
Floation costs Deduction	**−NLG75,758**	$\text{NLG15,152} = \dfrac{\text{NLG75,758}}{5}$	NLG15,152	NLG15,152	NLG15,152	NLG15,152
Tax shield from floatation costs		$0.34 \times \text{NLG15,152}$ = **NLG5,152**	**NLG5,152**	**NLG5,152**	**NLG5,152**	**NLG5,152**

The relevant cash flows from flotation costs are in boldface. When discounting at 10 per cent, the tax shield has a net present value of

$$\text{NLG5,152} \times A^5_{0.10} = \text{NLG19,530}$$

This implies a net cost of flotation of

$$-\text{NLG75,758} + \text{NLG19,530} = -\text{NLG56,228}$$

The net present value of the project after the flotation costs of debt, but before the benefits of debt, is

$$-\text{NLG513,951} - \text{NLG56,228} = -\text{NLG570,179}$$

Tax Subsidy

Interest must be paid on the gross proceeds of the loan, even though intermediaries receive the flotation costs. Since the gross proceeds of the loan are NLG7,575,578,

---

[6] In other words, Bicksler NV receives only NLG7,500,000. The flotation costs of NLG75,758 are received by intermediaries, for example, investment bankers.

annual interest is NLG757,576 (NLG7,575,758 × 0.10). The interest cost after taxes is NLG500,000 [NLG757,756 × (1 − 0.34)]. Because the loan is non-amortizing, the entire debt of NLG7,575,758 is repaid at date 5. These terms are indicated below:

	Date 0	Date 1	Date 2	Date 3	Date 4	Date 5
Loan (gross proceeds	**NLG7,575,758**					
Interest paid		10% × NLG7,575,758 = NLG757,576	NLG757,576	NLG757,576	NLG757,576	NLG757,576
Interest cost after taxes		(1 − 0.34) × NLG757,576 = **NLG500,000**	**NLG500,000**	**NLG500,000**	**NLG500,000**	**NLG500,000**
Repayment of debt						**NLG7,575,758**

The relevant cash flows are listed in boldface in the above table. They are (1) loan received, (2) annual interest cost after taxes and (3) repayment of debt. Note that we include the gross proceeds of the loan as an inflow, since the flotation costs have previously been subtracted.

In Chapter 16, we mentioned that the financing decision can be evaluated in terms of net present value. The net present value of the loan is simply the net present value of each of the three cash flows. This can be represented as

$$\text{NPV(Loan)} = + \begin{array}{c}\text{Amount} \\ \text{borrowed}\end{array} - \begin{array}{c}\text{Present value} \\ \text{of after-tax} \\ \text{interest payments}\end{array} - \begin{array}{c}\text{Present value} \\ \text{of loan} \\ \text{repayments}\end{array} \quad (18.1)$$

The calculations for this example are

$$\text{NLG976,415} = +\text{NLG7,575,758} - \frac{\text{NLG500,000}}{0.10} \times \left[1 - \left(\frac{1}{1.10}\right)^5 \right]$$

$$- \frac{\text{NLG7,575,758}}{(1.10)^5} \quad (18.1')$$

The NPV(Loan) is positive, reflecting the interest tax shield.[7]

The adjusted present value of the project with this financing is

$$\text{APV} = \text{All-equity value} - \text{Flotation costs of debt} + \text{NPV(Loan)} \quad (18.2)$$

$$\text{NLG406,236} = -\text{NLG513,951} - \text{NLG56,228} + \text{NLG976,415} \quad (18.2')$$

Though we previously saw that an all-equity firm would reject the project, a firm would *accept* the project if a NLG7,500,000 (net) loan could be obtained.

Because the loan discussed above was at the market rate of 10 per cent, we have considered only two of the three additional effects of debt (flotation costs and tax subsidy) so far. We now examine another loan where the third effect arises.

Non-Market-Rate Financing

A number of companies are fortunate enough to obtain subsidized debt financing from their governments. Suppose that the project of Bicksler NV is deemed socially

---

[7] The NPV(loan) must be zero in a no-tax world, because interest provides no tax shield there. To check this intuition, we calculate

$$\text{No-tax case: } 0 = +\text{NLG7,575,758} - \frac{\text{NLG757,576}}{0.10} \times \left[1 - \left(\frac{1}{1.10}\right)^5 \right] - \frac{\text{NLG7,575,758}}{(1.10)^5}$$

beneficial in the Netherlands and in the EU, and there are grants available in terms of a NLG7,500,000 loan at 8 per cent interest. In addition, all flotation costs are absorbed by the government. Clearly, the company will choose this loan over the one we previously assumed. The cash flows from the subsidized loan are

	Date 0	Date 1	Date 2	Date 3	Date 4	Date 5
Loan received	NLG7,500,000					
Interest paid		8% × NLG7,500,000 = NLG600,000	NLG600,000	NLG600,000	NLG600,000	NLG600,000
After-tax interest		(1 − 0.34) × NLG600,000 = NLG396,000	NLG396,000	NLG396,000	NLG396,000	NLG396,000
Repayment of debt						NLG7,500,000

Using (18.1), the NPV loan is

$$\text{NLG1,341,939} = + \text{NLG7,500,000} - \frac{\text{NLG396,000}}{0.10} \times \left[1 - \left(\frac{1}{1.10}\right)^5 \right]$$

$$- \frac{\text{NLG7,500,000}}{(1.10)^5} \tag{18.1''}$$

Why do we discount the cash flows in (18.1") at 10 per cent when the firm is borrowing at 8 per cent? We discount at 10 per cent because that is the fair or marketwide rate. That is, 10 per cent is the rate at which one could borrow without benefit of subsidization. The net present value of the subsidized loan is larger than the net present value of the earlier loan because the firm is now borrowing at the below-market rate of 8 per cent. Note that the NPV(loan) calculation in equation (18.1") captures both the tax effect and the non-market-rate effect.

The net present value of the project with subsidized debt financing is

$$\text{APV} = \text{All-equity value} - \text{Flotation costs of debt} + \text{NPV(Loan)} \tag{18.2}$$

$$+\text{NLG827,988} = -\text{NLG513,951} - 0 + \text{NLG1,341,939} \tag{18.2''}$$

The above example illustrates the adjusted-present-value (APV) approach. The approach begins with the present value of a project for the all-equity firm. Next, the effects of debt are added in. The approach has much to recommend it. It is intuitively appealing because individual components are calculated separately and added together in a simple way. And, if the debt from the project can be specified precisely, the present value of the debt can be calculated precisely. ●

18.7   Beta and Leverage

Chapter 13 provides the formula for the relationship between the beta of the common stock and the leverage of the firm in a world without taxes. We reproduce this formula here:

The no-tax case:

$$\beta_{\text{Equity}} = \beta_{\text{Asset}}\left(1 + \frac{\text{Debt}}{\text{Equity}}\right) \tag{18.3}$$

As pointed out in Chapter 13, this relationship holds under the assumption that the beta of debt is zero.

Since firms must pay corporate taxes in practice, it is worthwhile to provide the relationship in a world with corporate taxes. It can be shown that the relationship between the beta of the unlevered firm and the beta of the levered equity is[8]

The corporate-tax case:

$$\beta_{\text{Equity}} = \left(1 + \frac{(1 - T_C)\,\text{Debt}}{\text{Equity}}\right)\beta_{\text{Unlevered firm}} \tag{18.4}$$

when (1) the corporation is taxed at the rate of T_C and (2) the debt has a zero beta.

Because $[1 + (1 - T_C)\text{Debt/Equity}]$ must be more than 1 for a levered firm, it follows that $\beta_{\text{Unlevered firm}} < \beta_{\text{Equity}}$. The corporate-tax case of (18.4) is quite similar to the no-tax case of (18.3), because the beta of levered equity must be greater than the beta of the unlevered firm in either case. The intuition that leverage increases the risk of equity applies in both cases.

---

[8] This result holds only if the beta of debt equals zero. To see this, note that

$$V_U + T_C B = V_L = B + S \tag{a}$$

where

$$
\begin{aligned}
V_U &= \text{Value of unlevered firm}\\
V_L &= \text{Value of levered firm}\\
B &= \text{Value of debt in a levered firm}\\
S &= \text{Value of equity in a levered firm}
\end{aligned}
$$

As we stated in the text, the beta of the levered firm is a weighted average of the debt beta and the equity beta:

$$\frac{B}{B + S} \times \beta_B + \frac{S}{B + S} \times \beta_S$$

where β_B and β_S are the betas of the debt and the equity of the levered firm, respectively. Because $V_L = B + S$, we have

$$\frac{B}{V_L} \times \beta_B + \frac{S}{V_L} \times \beta_S \tag{b}$$

The beta of the levered firm can also be expressed as a weighted average of the beta of the unlevered firm and the beta of the tax shield:

$$\frac{V_U}{V_U + T_C B} \times \beta_U + \frac{T_C B}{V_U + T_C B} \times \beta_B$$

where β_U is the beta of the unlevered firm. This follows from equation (a). Because $V_L = V_U + T_C B$, we have

$$\frac{V_U}{V_L} \times \beta_U + \frac{T_C B}{V_L} \times \beta_B \tag{c}$$

We can equate (b) and (c) because both represent the beta of a levered firm. Equation (a) tells us that $V_U = S + (1 - T_C) \times B$. Under the assumption that $\beta_B = 0$, equating (b) and (c) and using equation (a) yields equation (18.4).

The generalized formula for the levered beta (where β_B is not zero) is:

$$\beta_S = \beta_U + (1 - T_C)(\beta_U - \beta_B)\frac{B}{S}$$

and

$$\beta_U = \frac{S}{B(1 - T_C) + S}\beta_S + \frac{B(1 - T_C)}{B(1 - T_C) + S}\beta_B$$

However, notice that the two equations are not equal. It can be shown that leverage increases the equity beta less rapidly under corporate taxes. This occurs because, under taxes, leverage creates a riskless tax shield, thereby lowering the risk of the entire firm.

● **Example**

Bogarde NV is considering a scale-enhancing project. The market value of the firm's debt is NLG100 million, and the market value of the firm's equity is NLG200 million. The debt is considered riskless. The corporate tax rate is 34 per cent. Regression analysis indicates that the beta of the firm's equity is 2. The risk-free rate is 10 per cent, and the expected market premium is 8.5 per cent. What would the project's discount rate be in the hypothetical case that Bogarde NV, is all-equity? ●

We can answer this question in two steps.

1. *Determining Beta of Hypothetical All-Equity Firm* Rearranging equation (18.4), we have

Unlevered beta:

$$\frac{\text{Equity}}{\text{Equity} + (1 - T_C) \times \text{Debt}} \times \beta_{\text{Equity}} = \beta_{\text{Unlevered firm}} \qquad (18.5)$$

$$\frac{\text{NLG200 million}}{\text{NLG200 million} + (1 - 0.34) \times \text{NLG100 million}} \times 2 = 1.50$$

2. *Determining Discount Rate* We calculate the discount rate from the security market line (SML) as

Discount Rate:

$$
\begin{array}{ccccccc}
r_S & = & R_F & + & \beta & \times & [\bar{R}_M - R_F] \\
22.75\% & = & 10\% & + & 1.50 & \times & 8.5\%
\end{array}
$$

The Project Is Not Scale-Enhancing

Because the above example assumed that the project is scale-enhancing, we began with the beta of the firm's equity. If the project is not scale-enhancing, one could begin with the equity betas of firms in the industry of the project. For each firm, the hypothetical beta of the unlevered equity could be calculated by equation (18.5). The SML could then be used to determine the project's discount rate from the average of these betas.

18.8 Summary and Conclusions

In earlier chapters, we have shown how to calculate net present value for projects of all-equity firms. In the last two chapters, we pointed out that the introduction of taxes and bankruptcy costs changes a firm's financing decisions. Rational corporations should employ some debt in a world of this type. Because of the benefits and costs associated with debt, the capital-budgeting decision is different for levered firms than for unlevered firms. The present chapter has discussed three methods for capital budgeting by levered firms: the adjusted-present-value (APV), flows-to-equity (FTE), and weighted-average-cost-of-capital (WACC) approaches.

1. The APV formula can be written as

$$\sum_{t=1}^{\infty} \frac{\text{UCF}_t}{(1 + r_0)^t} + \begin{matrix}\text{Additional}\\\text{effects of debt}\end{matrix} - \begin{matrix}\text{Initial}\\\text{investment}\end{matrix}$$

There are four additional effects of debt:
- Tax shield from debt financing
- Flotation costs
- Bankruptcy costs
- Benefit of non-market-rate financing.

2. The FTE formula can be written as

$$\sum_{t=1}^{\infty} \frac{\text{LCF}_t}{(1 + r_S)^t} - \left(\begin{matrix}\text{Initial}\\\text{investment}\end{matrix} - \begin{matrix}\text{Amount}\\\text{borrowed}\end{matrix}\right)$$

3. The WACC formula can be written as

$$\sum_{t=1}^{\infty} \frac{\text{UCF}_t}{(1 + r_{\text{WACC}})^t} - \begin{matrix}\text{Initial}\\\text{investment}\end{matrix}$$

4. Corporations frequently follow the guideline:

   Use WACC or FTE if the firm's target debt-to-value *ratio* applies to the project over its life.
   Use APV if the project's *level* of debt is known over the life of the project.

5. The APV method is frequently used for special situations like interest subsidies, LBOs and leases. The WACC and FTE methods are commonly used for more typical capital-budgeting situations. The APV approach is a rather unimportant method for typical capital-budgeting situations.

6. The beta of the equity of the firm is positively related to the leverage of the firm.

KEY TERMS

Adjusted present value (APV)   408   Weighted Average Cost of Capital   412
Flow to equity (FTE)   410

QUESTIONS AND PROBLEMS

Adjusted Present-Value Approach

18.1 Honda and GM are competing to sell a fleet of cars to Hertz. Hertz's policies on its rental cars include use of straight-line depreciation and disposing of the cars after five years. Hertz expects that the autos will have no salvage value. Hertz expects a fleet of 25 cars to generate USD100,000 per year in pretax income. Hertz is in the 34-percent tax bracket, and the firm's overall required return is 10 per cent. The addition of the new fleet will not add to the risk of the firm. Treasury bills are priced to yield 6 per cent.
   a. What is the maximum price that Hertz should be willing to pay for the fleet of cars?
   b. Suppose the price of the fleet (in US dollars) is USD325,000; both suppliers are charging this price. Hertz is able to issue USD200,000 in debt to finance the project. The bonds can be issued at par and will carry an 8 per cent interest rate. Hertz will incur no costs to issue the debt and no costs of financial distress. What is the APV of this project if Hertz uses debt to finance the auto purchase?
   c. To entice Hertz to buy the cars from Honda, the Japanese government is willing to lend Hertz USD200,000 at 5 per cent. Now what is the maximum price that Hertz is willing to pay Honda for the fleet of cars?

18.2 MEO Voedselen NV has made cat food for over 20 years. The company currently has a debt–equity ratio of 25 per cent, borrows at a 10 per cent interest rate, and is in the 40 per cent tax bracket. Its shareholders require an 18 per cent return.

MEO is planning to expand cat food production capacity. The equipment to be purchased would last three years and generate the following unlevered cash flows (UCF):

Unlevered cash flows by year (in NLG millions)

0	1	2	3	4+
−15	5	8	10	0

MEO has also arranged a NLG6 million debt issue to partially finance the expansion. Under the loan, the company would pay 10 per cent annually on the outstanding balance. The firm would also make year-end principal payments of NLG2 million per year, completely retiring the issue at the end of the third year.

Ignoring the costs of financial distress and issue costs, should MEO proceed with the expansion plan?

18.3 Smith, Jones and Brown plc have established a joint venture with Malaysia Road Construction Company to build a toll road in Malaysia. The initial investment in paving equipment is MYR20 million. MYR refers to the Malaysian ringgit, the local currency. Do all your calculations in MYR. Straight-line depreciation will be used, and the equipment has an economic life of five years with no salvage value. The annual construction costs are estimated to be MYR10 million. The project will be finished in two years. Net toll revenue collected from the usage of the road is projected to be MYR6 million per annum for 20 years starting from the end of the first year of usage. The local preferential corporate tax rate for joint ventures is 25 per cent. There are no other taxes. The required rate of return for the project under all-equity financing is 12 per cent. the prevailing market interest rate is 9 per cent a year. To encourage foreign capital participation in the infrastructure sector, the Malaysian government will subsidize the project with MYR10 million of 15-year, long-term loan, at an interest rate of 5 per cent a year. What is the NPV of this project in Malaysian ringgits?

Flow-to-Equity Approach

18.4 Milano Pizza in Nederland BV owns a chain of three identical restaurants popular for their Milan style pizza. Each store has an equity value of NLG900,000 and debt–equity ratio of 30 per cent. The prevailing market interest rate is 9.5 per cent. An equivalent all-equity-financed store would have a discount rate of 15 per cent. For each store, the estimated annual sales is NLG1,000,000, costs of goods sold is NLG400,000, general and administrative costs is NLG300,000. (Every cash flow stream is assumed to be a perpetuity.) The marginal tax rate is 40 per cent. What is the value of Milano Pizza in Nederland BV?

Weighted-Average-Cost-of-Capital Approach

18.5 The overall firm beta for Wild Widget Industries (WWI) is 0.9. WWI has a target debt–equity ratio of $\frac{1}{2}$. The expected return on the market is 16 per cent, and Treasury bills are currently selling to yield 8 per cent. WWI one-year bonds that carry a 7 per cent coupon are selling for GBP97.272. The corporate tax rate is 34 per cent.
a. What is WWI's cost of equity?
b. What is WWI's cost of debt?
c. What is WWI's weighted average cost of capital?

18.6 Baber plc's stock returns have a covariance with the market of 0.031. The standard deviation of the market returns is 0.16, and the historical market premium is 8.5 per cent. Baber bonds carry a 13 per cent coupon rate and are priced to yield 11 per cent. The market value of the bonds is GBP24 million. Baber shares, of which 4 million are outstanding, sell for GBP15 per share. Baber's finance director considers the firm's current debt–equity ratio optimal. The tax rate is 34 per cent and the Treasury bill rate is 7 per cent.

Baber must decide whether or not to purchase additional capital equipment. The cost of the equipment is GBP27.5 million. The expected cash flows from the new equipment are GBP9 million a year for five years. Purchasing the equipment will not change the risk level of Baber. Should Baber purchase the equipment?

A Comparison of the APV, FTE, and WACC Approaches

18.7 Kinedyne NV has decided to divest one of its divisions. The assets of the group have the same operating risk characteristics as those of the parent firm. The capital structure for the parent has been stable at 40 per cent debt/60 per cent equity (in market-value terms), the level determined to be optimal given the firm's assets. The required return on Kinedyne's assets is 16 per cent, and the firm (and the division) borrows at a rate of 10 per cent.

Sales revenue for the division is expected to remain stable indefinitely at last year's level of NLG19,740,000. Variable costs amount to 60 per cent of sales. Annual depreciation of NLG1.8 million is exactly matched each year by new investment in the division's equipment. The division would be taxed at the parent's current rate of 40 per cent.

a. How much is the division worth in unleveraged form?

b. If the division had the same capital structure as the parent firm, how much would it be worth?

c. At this optimal capital structure, what return will the equityholders of the division require?

d. Show that the market value of the equity of the division would be justified by the earnings to shareholders and the required return on equity.

APPENDIX 18A

THE ADJUSTED-PRESENT-VALUE APPROACH TO VALUING LEVERAGED BUYOUTS[9]

Introduction

A leveraged buyout (LBO) is the acquisition by a small group of equity investors of a public or private company financed primarily with debt. The equityholders service the heavy interest and principal payments with cash from operations and/or asset sales. The shareholders generally hope to reverse the LBO within three to seven years by way of a public offering or sale of the company to another firm. A buyout is therefore likely to be successful only if the firm generates enough cash to serve the debt in the early years, and if the company is attractive to other buyers as the buyout matures.

In a leveraged buyout, the equity investors are expected to pay off the outstanding principal according to a specific timetable. The owners know that the firm's debt–equity ratio will fall and can forecast the dollar amount of debt needed to finance future operations. Under these circumstances, the adjusted-present-value (APV) approach is more practical than the weighted-average-cost-of-capital (WACC) approach because the capital structure is changing. In this appendix, we illustrate the use of this procedure in valuing the RJR Nabisco transaction, the largest LBO in history.

The RJR Nabisco Buyout

In the summer of 1988, the price of RJR stock was hovering around USD55 a share. The firm had USD5 billion of debt. The firm's CEO, acting in concert with some other senior managers of the firm, announced a bid of USD75 per share to take the firm private in a management buyout. Within days of the management's offer, Kohlberg Kravis and Roberts (KKR) entered the fray with a USD90 bid of their own. By the end of November, KKR emerged from the ensuing bidding process with an offer of USD109 a share, or USD25 billion total. We now use the APV technique to analyse KKR's winning strategy.

The APV method as described in this chapter can be used to value companies as well as projects. Applied in this way, the maximum value of a levered firm (V_L) is its value as an all-equity entity (V_U) plus the discounted value of the interest tax shields from the debt its assets will support

---

[9] This appendix has been adapted by Isik Inselbag and Howard Kaufold, The Wharton School, University of Pennsylvania, from their unpublished manuscript entitled 'Analysing the RJR Nabisco Buyout: An Adjusted Present Value Approach'.

(PVTS).[10] This relation can be stated as

$$V_L = V_U + \text{PVTS}$$

$$= \sum_{t=1}^{\infty} \frac{\text{UCF}_t}{(1 + r_0)^t} + \sum_{t=1}^{\infty} \frac{T_C r_B B_{t-1}}{(1 + r_B)^t}$$

In the second part of this equation, UCF_t is the unlevered cash flow from operations for year t. Discounting these cash flows by the required return on assets, r_0, yields the all-equity value of the company. B_{t-1} represents the debt balance remaining at the end of year $(t - 1)$. Because interest in a given year is based on the debt balance remaining at the end of the previous year, the interest paid in year t is $r_B B_t - 1$. The numerator of the second term, $T_C r_B B_{t-1}$, is therefore the tax shield for year t. We discount this series of annual tax shields using the rate at which the firm borrows, r_B.[11]

KKR planned to sell several of RJR's food divisions and operate the remaining parts of the firm more efficiently. Table 18A.1 presents KKR's projected unlevered cash flows for RJR under the buyout, adjusting for planned asset sales and operational efficiencies.

With respect to financial strategy, KKR planned a significant increase in leverage with accompanying tax benefits. Specifically, KKR issued almost USD24 billion of new debt to complete the buyout, raising annual interest costs to more than USD3 billion.[12] Table 18A.2 presents the projected interest expense and tax shields for the transaction.

We now use the data from Tables 18A.1 and 18A.2 to calculate the APV of the RJR buyout. This valuation process is presented in Table 18A.3.

The valuation presented in Table 18A.3 involves four steps.

Step 1: Calculating the present value of unlevered cash flows for 1989–93   The unlevered cash flows for 1989–93 are shown in the last line of Table 18A.1 and the first line of Table 18A.3. These flows are discounted by the required asset return, r_0, which at the time of the buyout was approximately 14 per cent. The value as of the end of 1988 of the unlevered cash flows expected

---

TABLE 18A.1   RJR Operating Cash Flows (in USD millions)

	1989	*1990*	*1991*	*1992*	*1993*
Operating income	USD2,620	USD3,410	USD3,645	USD3,950	USD4,310
Tax on operating income	891	1,142	1,222	1,326	1,448
After-tax operating income	1,729	2,268	2,423	2,624	2,862
Add back depreciation	449	475	475	475	475
Less capital expenditures	522	512	525	538	551
Less change in working capital	(203)	(275)	200	225	250
Add proceeds from asset sales	3,545	1,805			
Unlevered cash flow (UCF)	USD5,404	USD4,311	USD2,173	USD2,336	USD2,536

---

[10] One should also deduct from this value any costs of financial distress. However, we would expect these costs to be small in the case of RJR for two reasons. As a firm in the tobacco and food industries, its cash flows are relatively stable and recession resistant. Furthermore, the firm's assets are divisible and attractive to a number of potential buyers, allowing the firm to receive full value if disposition is required.

[11] The pretax borrowing rate, r_B, represents the appropriate discount rate for the interest tax shields when there is a precommitment to a specific debt repayment schedule under the terms of the LBO. If debt covenants require that the entire free cash flow be dedicated to debt service, the amount of debt outstanding and, therefore, the interest tax shield at any point in time are a direct function of the operating cash flows of the firm. Since the debt balance is then as risky as the cash flows, the required return on assets should be used to discount the interest tax shields.

[12] A significant portion of this debt was of the payment in kind variety, which offers lenders additional bonds instead of cash interest. This payment in kind debt financing provided KKR with significant tax shields, while allowing it to postpone the cash burden of debt service to future years. For simplicity of presentation, Table 18A.2 does not separately show cash versus non-cash interest charges.

TABLE 18A.2   Projected Interest Expenses and Tax Shields (in USD millions)

	1989	1990	1991	1992	1993
Interest expenses	USD3,384	USD3,004	USD3,111	USD3,294	USD3,483
Interest tax shields ($T_C = 34\%$)	1,151	1,021	1,058	1,120	1,184

TABLE 18A.3   RJR LBO Valuation (in USD millions except share data)

	1989	1990	1991	1992	1993
Unlevered cash flow (UCF)	USD5,404	USD4,311	USD2,173	USD2,336	USD2,536
Terminal value: (3% growth after 1993)					
Unlevered terminal value (UTV)					23,746
Terminal value at target debt					26,654
Tax shield in terminal value					2,908
Interest tax shields	1,151	1,021	1,058	1,120	1,184
PV of UCF 1989–93 at 14%	12,224				
PV of UTV at 14%	12,333				
Total unlevered value	24,557				
PV of tax shields 1989–93 at 13.5%	3,877				
PV of tax shield in TV at 13.5%	1,544				
Total value of tax shields	5,421				
Total value	29,978				
Less value of assumed debt	5,000				
Value of equity	USD24,978				
Number of shares	229 million				
Value per share	USD109.07				

from 1989 through 1993 is

$$\frac{5.404}{1.14} + \frac{4.311}{1.14^2} + \frac{2.173}{1.14^3} + \frac{2.336}{1.14^4} + \frac{2.536}{1.14^5} = \text{USD}12.224 \text{ billion}$$

Step 2: Calculating the present value of the unlevered cash flows beyond 1993 (unlevered terminal value)   We assume the unlevered cash flows grow at the modest annual rate of 3 per cent after 1993. The value, as of the end of 1993, of these cash flows is equal to the following discounted value of a growing perpetuity:

$$\frac{2.536(1.03)}{0.14 - 0.03} = \text{USD}23.746 \text{ billion}$$

This translates to a 1988 value of

$$\frac{23.746}{1.14^5} = \text{USD}12.333 \text{ billion}$$

As in Step 1, the discount rate is the required asset rate of 14 per cent.

The total unlevered value of the firm is therefore (USD12.224 + USD12.333) = USD24.557 billion.

To calculate the total buyout value, we must add the interest tax shields expected to be realized by debt financing.

Step 3: Calculating the present value of interest tax shields for 1989–93.   Under the prevailing US tax laws in 1989, every dollar of interest reduces taxes by 34 cents. The present value of the interest tax shields for the period from 1989–93 can be calculated by discounting the annual tax savings at the pretax average cost of debt, which was approximately 13.5 per cent. Using the tax shields from Table 18A.2, the discounted value of these tax shields is calculated as

$$\frac{1.151}{1.135} + \frac{1.021}{1.135^2} + \frac{1.058}{1.135^3} + \frac{1.120}{1.135^4} + \frac{1.184}{1.135^5} = \text{USD3.877 billion}$$

Step 4: Calculating the present value of interest tax shields beyond 1993   Finally, we must calculate the value of tax shields associated with debt used to finance the operations of the company after 1993. We assume that debt will be reduced and maintained at 25 per cent of the value of the firm from that date forward.[13] Under this assumption it is appropriate to use the WACC method to calculate a terminal value for the firm at the target capital structure. This, in turn, can be decomposed into an all-equity value and a value from tax shields.

If, after 1993, RJR uses 25 per cent debt in its capital structure, its WACC at this target capital structure would be approximately 12.8 per cent.[14] Then the levered terminal value as of the end of 1993 can be estimated as

$$\frac{2.536(1.03)}{0.128 - 0.03} = \text{USD26,654 billion}$$

Since the levered value of the company is the sum of the unlevered value plus the value of interest tax shields, it is the case that

$$
\begin{aligned}
\text{Value of tax shields (end 1993)} &= V_L \text{ (end 1993)} - V_U \text{ (end 1993)} \\
&= \text{USD26.654 billion} - \text{USD23.746 billion} \\
&= \text{USD2.908 billion}
\end{aligned}
$$

To calculate the value, as of the end of 1988, of these future tax shields, we again discount by the borrowing rate of 13.5 per cent to get[15]

$$\frac{2.908}{1.135^5} = \text{USD1.544 billion}$$

The total value of interest tax shields therefore equals (USD3.877 + USD1.544) USD5.421 billion.

---

[13] This 24 per cent figure is consistent with the debt utilization in industries in which RJR Nabisco is involved. In fact, that was the debt-to-total-market-value ratio for RJR immediately before management's initial buyout proposal. The firm can achieve this target by 1993 if a significant portion of the convertible debt used to finance the buyout is exchanged for equity by that time. Alternatively, KKR could issue new equity (as would occur, for example, if the firm were taken public) and use the proceeds to retire some of the outstanding debt.

[14] To calculate this rate, use the weighted average cost of capital from this chapter:

$$r_{\text{WACC}} = \frac{S}{S + B} r_S + \frac{B}{S + B} r_B (1 - T_C)$$

and substitute the appropriate values for the proportions of debt and equity used, as well as their respective costs. Specifically, at the target debt-value ratio, $B/S + B = 25\%$, and $S/S + B = (1 - B/S + B) = 75\%$. Given this blend,

$$r_S = r_0 + \frac{B}{S} (1 - T_C) (r_0 - r_B)$$

$$= 0.14 + \frac{0.25}{0.75} (1 - 0.34) (0.14 - 0.135) = 0.141$$

Using these findings plus the borrowing rate of 13.5 per cent in r_{WACC}, we find

$$r_{\text{WACC}} = 0.75(0.141) + 0.25(0.135) (1 - 0.34) = 0.128$$

In fact, this value is an approximation to the weighted average cost of capital when the market debt-value blend is constant, or when the cash flows are growing. For a detailed discussion of this issue, see Isik Inselbag and Howard Kaufold (1990) 'A Comparison of Alternative Discounted Cash Flow Approaches for Firm Valuation', The Wharton School, University of Pennsylvania, June, unpublished paper.

[15] A good argument can be made that since post-1993 debt levels are proportional to firm value, the tax shields are as risky as the firm and should be discounted at the rate *e*.

Adding all of these components together, the total value of RJR under the buyout proposal is USD29.978 billion. Deducting the USD5 billion market value of assumed debt yields a value for equity of USD24.978 billion, or USD109.07 per share.

Concluding Comments on LBO Valuation Methods

As mentioned earlier in this chapter, the WACC method is by far the most widely applied approach to capital budgeting. One could analyse an LBO and generate the results of the second section of this appendix using this technique, but it would be a much more difficult process. We have tried to show that the APV approach is the preferred way to analyse a transaction in which the capital structure is not stable over time.

Consider the WACC approach to valuing the KKR bid for RJR. One could discount the operating cash flows of RJR by a set of weighted average costs of capital and arrive at the same USD30 billion total value for the company. To do this, one would need to calculate the appropriate rate for each year since the WACC rises as the buyout proceeds. This occurs because the value of the tax subsidy declines as debt principal is repaid. In other words, there is no single return that represents the cost of capital when the firm's capital structure is changing.

There is also a theoretical problem with the WACC approach to valuing a buyout. To calculate the changing WACC, one must know the market value of a firm's debt and equity. But if the debt and equity values are already known, the total market value of the company is also known. That is, one must know the value of the company to calculate the WACC. One must therefore resort to using book-value measures for debt and equity, or make assumptions about the evolution of their market values, in order to implement the WACC method.

Dividend Policy: Why Does It Matter?

Some companies pay out about 50 per cent of their net income as cash dividends. However, some no cash dividends and others pay more dividends than their net income.

Companies view the dividend decision as quite important because it determines what funds flow to investors and what funds are retained by the firm for reinvestment. Dividend policy can also provide information to the stockholder concerning the firm's performance. The bulk of this chapter considers the rationale both for a policy of high dividend payout and for a policy of low dividend payout.

All discussions of dividends are plagued by the 'two-handed economist' problem. What do we mean? Richard Nixon, while President of the USA, was reportedly discussing the economic implications of a decision and asked his staff to set up a meeting with an economic adviser. Supposedly Mr Nixon said, 'But I don't want one of those two-handed economists'. When asked what a two-handed economist was, he replied. 'You know, an economist who says, 'On the one hand I recommend you do so-and-so because of the following reasons, but on the other hand I recommend that you don't do it because of these other reasons'. 'Unfortunately, any sensible treatment of dividend policy will appear to be written by a two-handed economist. On the one hand, there are many good reasons for companies to pay high dividends, but, on the other hand, there are many good reasons to pay low dividends.

We begin this chapter with a discussion of some practical aspects of dividend payments. Next we treat dividend policy. Before delineating the pros and cons of different dividend levels, we examine a benchmark case in which the choice of the level of dividends is not important. Surprisingly, we will see that this conceptual setup is not merely an academic curiosity but, instead, quite applicable to the real world. Next we consider personal taxes, an imperfection, generally inducing a low level of dividends. This is followed by reasons justifying a high dividend level. Finally, we look at the empirical work on dividends.

19.1   Different Types of Dividends

The term *dividend* usually refers to cash distributions of earnings. If a distribution is made from sources other than current or accumulated retained earnings, the term *distribution* rather than dividend is used. However, it is acceptable to refer to a distribution from earnings as a *dividend* and a distribution from capital as a capital or *liquidating dividend*. More generally, any direct payment by the company to the shareholders may be considered part of dividend policy.

The most common type of dividend is in the form of cash. European companies tend to pay **regular cash dividends** twice a year. Sometimes firms will pay regular cash dividends and a *special dividend* which occurs irregularly. Paying a cash dividend reduces corporate cash and retained earnings shown in the balance sheet—except in the case of a liquidating dividend (where paid-in capital may be reduced).

Another type of dividend is paid out in shares. This dividend is referred to as a **stock dividend** or a **scrip dividend**. In this case, no cash leaves the firm. Rather, a stock dividend increases the number of shares outstanding. We frequently find that firms actually give shareholders the choice between a cash dividend or a stock dividend—although this alternative is, usually, impelled by corporate tax reasons.

When a firm declares a **share split**, it increases the number of shares outstanding. Because each share is now entitled to a smaller percentage of the firm's cash flow, the share price should fall. For example, if the managers of a firm whose shares are selling at GBP9 declare a 3 : 1 share split, the price of a share should fall to about GBP3. A share split strongly resembles a share dividend except it is usually much larger.

19.2   Standard Method of Cash Dividend Payment

The decision whether or not to pay a dividend rests in the hands of the board of directors of the corporation. A dividend is distributable to shareholders of record on a specific date. When a dividend has been declared, it becomes a liability of the firm and cannot be easily rescinded. The amount of the dividend is expressed as some money, pence, pfennigs, cents or whatever per share (*dividend per share*), as a percentage of the market price (*dividend yield*), or as a percentage of earnings per share (*dividend payout ratio*).

Somewhere between the date upon which the company declares the dividend and the date of payment, there is the **ex-dividend date**. Purchases of shares after this date involve the vendors in being entitled to keep the forthcoming dividend. In other words, the purchaser does not get the dividend. Obviously, the ex-dividend date is important, because an individual purchasing the security before the ex-dividend date will receive the current dividend, whereas another individual purchasing the security on or after this date will not receive the dividend. The share price should fall on the ex-dividend date.[1] It is worth while to note that this drop is an indication of market efficiency, not inefficiency, because the market rationally attaches value to a cash dividend. In a world with neither taxes nor transaction costs, the share price is expected to fall by the amount of the dividend:

Before ex-dividend date	Price = NLG(P + 1)
On or after ex-dividend date	Price = NLGP

This is illustrated in Figure 19.1.

Concept Question

• Why should the price of a share change when it goes ex-dividend?

---

[1] Empirically, the share price appears to fall within the first few minutes of the ex-dividend day.

FIGURE 19.1   Price Behaviour around the Ex-dividend Date for a NLG1 Cash Dividend

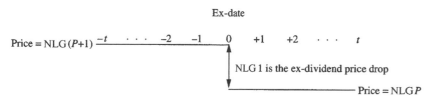

The share price will fall by the amount of the dividend on the ex-date (time 0). If the dividend is NLG1 per share, the price will be equal to P on the ex-date.

Before ex-date (-1)	Price $= \text{NLG}(P + 1)$
Ex-date (0)	Price $= \text{NLG}\,P$

19.3   The Benchmark Case: An Illustration of the Irrelevance of Dividend Policy

A powerful argument can be made that dividend policy does not matter. This will be illustrated with the Wharton Company. Wharton is an all-equity firm that has existed for 10 years. The current financial managers know at the present time (date 0) that the firm will dissolve in one year (date 1). At date 0 the managers are able to forecast cash flows with perfect certainty. The managers know that the firm will receive a cash flow of GBP10,000 immediately and another GBP10,000 next year. They believe that Wharton has no additional positive NPV projects it can use to its advantage.[2]

Current Policy: Dividends Set Equal to Cash Flow

At the present time, dividends (Div) at each date are set equal to the cash flow of GBP10,000. The NPV of the firm can be calculated by discounting these dividends. The firm's value can be expressed as

$$V_0 = \text{Div}_0 + \frac{\text{Div}_1}{1 + r_S}$$

where Div_0 and Div_1 are the cash flows paid out in dividends, and r_S is the discount rate. The first dividend is not discounted because it will be paid immediately.

Assuming $r_S = 10\%$, the value of the firm can be calculated by

$$\text{GBP19,090.91} = \text{GBP10,000} + \frac{\text{GBP10,000}}{1.1}$$

If 1,000 shares are outstanding, the value of each share is

$$\text{GBP19.09} = \text{GBP10} + \frac{\text{GBP10}}{1.1} \tag{19.1}$$

To simplify the example, we assume that the ex-dividend date is the same as the date of payment. After the imminent dividend is paid, the stock price will immediately fall

---

[2] Wharton's investment in physical assets is fixed.

to GBP9.09 (GBP19.09 − GBP10). Several members of the board of Wharton have expressed dissatisfaction with the current dividend policy and have asked you to analyse an alternative policy.

Alternative Policy: Initial Dividend Is Greater than Cash Flow

Another policy is for the firm to pay a dividend of GBP11 per share immediately, which is, of course, a total dividend of GBP11,000. Because the cash position is only GBP10,000, the extra GBP1,000 must be raised in one of a few ways. Perhaps the simplest would be to issue GBP1,000 of bonds or shares now (at date 0). Assume that shares are issued and the new shareholders will desire enough cash flow at date 1 to let them earn the required 10 per cent return on their date 0 investment.[3] The new shareholders will demand GBP1,100 of the date 1 cash flow,[4] leaving only GBP8,900 to the old shareholders. The dividends to the old shareholders will be

	Date 0	Date 1
Aggregate dividends to old shareholders	GBP11,000	GBP8,900
Dividends per share	GBP11.00	GBP8.90

The present value of the dividends per share is therefore

$$\text{GBP19.09} = \text{GBP11} + \frac{\text{GBP8.90}}{1.1} \tag{19.2}$$

Students often find it instructive to determine the price at which the new shares are issued. Because the new shareholders are not entitled to the immediate dividend, they would pay GBP8.09 (GBP8.90/1.1) per share. Thus, 123.61 (GBP1,000/GBP8.09) new shares are issued.

The Indifference Proposition

Note that the NPVs of equations (19.1) and (19.2) are equal. This leads to the initially surprising conclusion that the change in dividend policy did not affect the value of a share. However, upon reflection, the result seems quite sensible. The new shareholders are parting with their money at date 0 and receiving it back with the appropriate return at date 1. In other words, they are taking on a zero NPV investment. As illustrated in Figure 19.2, old shareholders are receiving additional funds at date 0, but must pay the new shareholders their money with the appropriate return at date 1. Because the old shareholders must pay back the principal plus the appropriate return, the act of issuing new shares at date 0 will not increase or decrease the value of the old shareholders' holdings. That is, they are giving up a zero NPV investment to the new shareholders. An increase in dividends at date 0 leads to the necessary reduction of dividends at date 1, so the value of the old shareholders' holdings remains unchanged.

This illustration is based on the pioneering work of Modigliani and Miller (MM).[5] Although our presentation is in the form of a numerical example, the MM paper proves

---

[3] The same results would occur after an issue of bonds, though the argument would be less easily resolved.

[4] Because the new shareholders buy at date 0, their first (and only) dividend is at date 1.

[5] M. H. Miller and F. Modigliani (1961) 'Dividend policy, growth and the valuation of shares', *Journal of Business*, October. Yes, this is the same MM who gave us a capital-structure theory.

FIGURE 19.2   Current and Alternative Dividend Policies

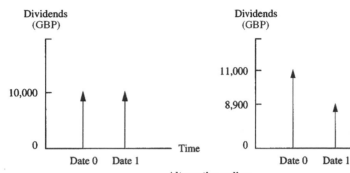

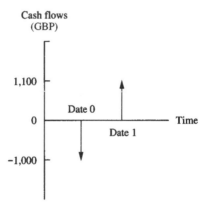

that investors are indifferent to dividend policy in the general algebraic case. MM make the following assumptions:

1. There are neither taxes nor brokerage fees, and no single participant can affect the market price of the security through his or her trades. Economists say that perfect markets exist when these conditions are met.
2. All individuals have the same beliefs concerning future investments, profits, and dividends. As mentioned in Chapter 11, these individuals are said to have *homogeneous expectations.*
3. The investment policy of the firm is set ahead of time, and is not altered by changes in dividend policy.

Homemade Dividends

To illustrate the indifference investors have toward dividend policy in our example, we used net-present-value equations. An alternative and perhaps more intuitively appealing explanation avoids the mathematics of discounted cash flows.

Suppose individual investor X prefers dividends per share of GBP10 at both dates 0 and 1. Would she be disappointed when informed that the firm's management is adopting the alternative dividend policy (dividends of GBP11 and GBP8.90 on the two dates, respectively)? Not necessarily, because she could easily reinvest the GBP1 of unneeded funds received on date 0, yielding an incremental return of GBP1.10 at date 1. Thus, she would receive her desired net cash flow of GBP11 − GBP1 = GBP10 at date 0 and GBP8.90 + GBP1.10 = GBP10 at date 1.

Conversely, imagine investor Z preferring GBP11 of cash flow at date 0 and GBP8.90 of cash flow at date 1, who finds that management will pay dividends of GBP10 at both dates 0 and 1. Here he can sell off shares of stock at date 0 to receive the desired amount of cash flow. That is, if he sells off shares (or fractions of shares) at date 0 totalling GBP1, his cash flow at date 0 becomes GBP10 + GBP1 = GBP11. Because a sale of GBP1 shares at date 0 will reduce his dividends by GBP1.10 at date 1, his net cash flow at date 1 would be GBP10 − GBP1.10 = GBP8.90.

The example illustrates how investors can make **homemade dividends**. In this instance, corporate dividend policy is being undone by a potentially dissatisfied shareholder. This homemade dividend is illustrated by Figure 19.3. Here the firm's cash flows of GBP10 at both dates 0 and 1 are represented by point A. This point also represents the initial dividend payout. However, as we just saw, the firm could alternatively pay out GBP11 at date 0 and GBP8.90 at date 1, a strategy represented by point B. Similarly, by either issuing new shares or buying back old shares, the firm could achieve a dividend payout represented by any point on the diagonal line.

FIGURE 19.3   Homemade Dividends: a Trade-off between Dividends at Date 0 and Dividends at Date 1

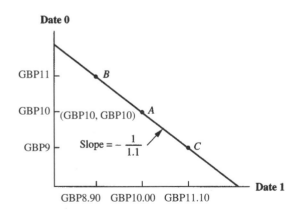

This graph illustrates both (1) how managers can vary policy and (2) how individuals can undo the firm's dividend policy.

Managers varying dividend policy. A firm paying out all cash flows immediately is at point A on the graph. The firm could achieve point B by issuing stock to pay extra dividends or achieve point C by buying back old shares with some of its cash.

Individuals undoing the firm's dividend policy. Suppose the firm adopts the dividend policy represented by point B: dividends of GBP11 at date 0 and GBP8.90 at date 1. An investor can reinvest GBP1 of the dividends at 10 per cent, which will place her at point A. Suppose, alternatively, the firm adopts the dividend policy represented at point A. An individual can sell off GBP1 of stock at date 0, placing him at point B. No matter what dividend policy the firm establishes, a shareholder can undo it.

The previous paragraph describes the choices available to the managers of the firm. The same diagonal line also represents the choices available to the shareholder. For example, if the shareholder receives a dividend distribution of (GBP11, GBP8.90), he or she can either reinvest some of the dividends to move down and to the right on the graph or sell off shares and move up and to the left.

The implications of the graph can be summarized in two sentences:

1. By varying dividend policy, the managers can achieve any payout along the diagonal line in Figure 19.3.
2. Either by reinvesting excess dividends at date 0 or by selling off shares of stock at this date, any individual investor can achieve any net cash payout along the diagonal line.

Thus, because both the corporation and the individual investor can move only along the diagonal line, dividend policy in this model is irrelevant. The changes the managers make in dividend policy can be undone by an individual who, by either reinvesting dividends or selling off shares, can move to a desired point on the diagonal line.

A Test

You can test your knowledge of this material by examining these true statements:

1. Dividends are relevant.
2. Dividend policy is irrelevant.

The first statement follows from common sense. Clearly, investors prefer higher dividends to lower dividends at any single date if the dividend level is held constant at every other date. In other words, if the dividend per share at a given date is raised while the dividend per share for each other date is held constant, the share price will rise. This act can be accomplished by management decisions that improve productivity, increase tax savings or strengthen product marketing.

The second statement is understandable once we realize that dividend policy cannot raise the dividend per share at one date while holding the dividend level per share constant at all other dates. Rather, dividend policy merely establishes the trade-off between dividends at one date and dividends at another date. As we saw in Figure 19.3, an increase in date 0 dividends can be accomplished only by a decrease in date 1 dividends. The extent of the decrease is such that the present value of all dividends is not affected.

Thus, in this simple world, dividend policy does not matter. That is, managers choosing either to raise or to lower the current dividend do not affect the current value of their firm. The above theory is a powerful one, and the work of MM is generally considered a classic in modern finance. With relatively few assumptions, a rather surprising result is shown to be perfectly true.[6] Because we want to examine many real-world factors ignored by MM, their work is only a starting point in this chapter's discussion of dividends. The next part of the chapter investigates these real-world considerations.

---

[6] One of the real contributions of MM has been to shift the burden of proof. Before MM, firm value was believed to be influenced by its dividend policy. After MM, it became clear that establishing a correct dividend policy was not obvious at all.

Dividends and Investment Policy

The above argument shows that an increase in dividends through issuance of new shares neither helps nor hurts the shareholders. Similarly, a reduction in dividends through share repurchase neither helps nor hurts shareholders.[7]

What about reducing capital expenditures to increase dividends? Earlier chapters show that a firm should accept all positive net-present-value projects. To do otherwise would reduce the value of the firm. Thus, we have an important point:

> Firms should never give up a positive NPV project to increase a dividend (or to pay a dividend for the first time).

This idea was implicitly considered by Miller and Modigliani. As we pointed out, one of the assumptions underlying their dividend-irrelevance proposition was: 'The investment policy of the firm is set ahead of time and is not altered by changes in dividend policy'.

Concept Questions

- How can an investor make homemade dividends?
- Are dividends irrelevant?
- What assumptions are needed to show that dividend policy is irrelevant?

19.4   Taxes, Issuance Costs and Dividends

The model we used to determine the level of dividends assumed that there were no taxes, no transactions costs and no uncertainty. It concluded that dividend policy is irrelevant. Although this model helps us to grasp some fundamentals of dividend policy, it ignores many factors that exist in reality. It is now time to investigate these real-world considerations. We first examine the effect of taxes on the level of a firm's dividends.

Cash dividends received are taxed as ordinary income. In some countries, but not all, capital gains may be taxed at somewhat lower rates. However, dividends are taxable when distributed, whereas taxes on capital gains are deferred until the shares are sold. Thus, for individual shareholders, the *effective* tax rate on dividend income is usually higher than the tax rate on capital gains. A discussion of dividend policy in the presence of personal taxes is facilitated by classifying firms into two types, those without sufficient cash to pay a dividend and those with sufficient cash to do so.

Firms without Sufficient Cash to Pay a Dividend

It is simplest to begin with a Dutch firm without cash and owned by a single entrepreneur. If this firm should decide to pay a dividend of NLG100, it must raise

---

[7] However, if we can make a share buyback at below fundamental value per share based upon present value calculations for the company, then shareholders who remain with the company should be pleased because, by so doing, we should create shareholder value. By a reverse process we can destroy shareholder value by managing a buyback at above fundamental value. The exception to both of these caveats is when the share buyback is via a tender offer pro-rata to all shareholders.

capital.[8] The firm might choose among a number of different stock and bond issues in order to pay the dividend. However, for simplicity, we assume that the entrepreneur contributes cash to the firm by issuing stock to himself. This transaction, diagrammed in the lefthand side of Figure 19.4, would clearly be a *wash* in a world of no taxes. NLG100 cash goes into the firm when stock is issued and is immediately paid out as a dividend. Thus, the entrepreneur neither benefits nor loses when the dividend is paid, a result consistent with Miller–Modigliani.

Now assume that dividends are taxed at the owner's personal tax rate of 30 per cent. The firm still receives NLG100 upon issuance of stock. However, the NLG100 dividend is not fully credited to the entrepreneur. Instead, the dividend payment is taxed, implying that the owner receives only NLG70 net after tax. Thus, the entrepreneur loses NLG30.

Though the above example is clearly contrived and unrealistic, similar results can be reached for more plausible situations. Thus, financial economists generally agree that, in a world of personal taxes, one should not issue stock to pay a dividend.

The direct costs of issuance will add to this effect. Investment bankers must be paid when new capital is raised. Thus, the net receipts due to the firm from a new issue are less than 100 per cent of total capital raised. Because the size of new issues can be lowered by a reduction in dividends, we have another argument in favour of a low-dividend policy.

An increase in dividends may lead to a decline in stock price for still another reason. The market price of a stock is determined by the interaction of the demand for and the supply of stock. New issues increase the outstanding supply of the stock, putting downward pressure on the market price of existing shares. Therefore, to the extent that dividends are financed by new issues, an increase in dividends may well contribute to a stock-price reduction.[9] However, in an efficient stock market, changes in the supply of stock should have a negligible effect on stock price.

FIGURE 19.4   Firm Issues Shares in Order to Pay a Dividend

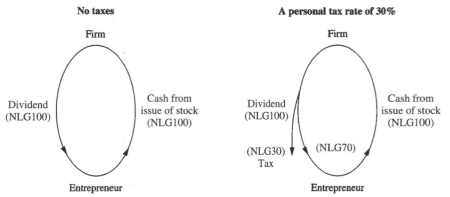

In the no-tax case, the entrepreneur receives the NLG100 in dividends that he gave to the firm when purchasing stock. The entire operation is called a *wash,* in other words, it has no economic effect. With taxes, the entrepreneur still receives NLG100 in dividends. However, he must pay NLG30 in taxes to the tax authority. The entrepreneur loses and the tax authority wins when a firm issues stock to pay a dividend.

---

[8] We do some examples in dollars because a non-European currency, tax regime or environment may be more appropriate given that there is such a colossal disparity on the point being illustrated from one European country to another.

[9] The empirical evidence on price pressure effects in Chapter 14 suggests that this is an unimportant effect.

Of course, our advice not to finance dividends through new stock issues might need to be modified somewhat in the real world. A company with a large and steady cash flow for many years in the past might be paying a regular dividend. If the cash flow unexpectedly dried up for a single year, should new stock be issued so that dividends could be continued? While our above discussion would imply that new stock should not be issued, many managers might issue the stock anyway for practical reasons. In particular, stockholders appear to prefer dividend stability. Thus, managers might be forced to issue stock to achieve this stability, knowing full well the adverse tax consequences.

An interesting empirical paper by Kalay and Shimrat sheds light on the above discussion.[10] They present evidence that very few companies issue stock to pay a dividend. Thus, in spite of possible practical problems, our recommendation seems to apply in the real world.

Firms with Sufficient Cash to Pay a Dividend

The previous discussion argues that, in a world with personal taxes, one should not issue stock to pay a dividend. Does the tax disadvantage of dividends imply the stronger policy, 'Never pay dividends in a world with personal taxes'?

We argue below that this prescription does not necessarily apply to firms with excess cash. To see this, imagine a firm with NLG1 million in extra cash after selecting all positive NPV projects and determining the level of prudent cash balances. The firm might consider the following alternatives to a dividend:

1. *Select Additional Capital-Budgeting Projects*   Because the firm has taken all the available positive NPV projects already, it must invest its excess cash in negative NPV projects. This is clearly a policy at variance with principles of corporate finance. In spite of our distaste for this strategy, Professor Michael Jensen of Harvard University has suggested that many managers choose to take on negative NPV projects in lieu of dividends, doing their stockholders a disservice in the process.[11] A host of British privatized utility companies appear to be particularly guilty of this policy. It is frequently argued that managers who adopt negative NPV projects are ripe for takeover.

2. *Acquire Other Companies*   To avoid the payment of dividends, a firm might use excess cash to acquire another company. This strategy has the advantage of acquiring profitable assets. However, a firm often incurs heavy costs when it embarks on an acquisition programme. In addition, acquisitions are invariably made above the market price. Premiums of 20 to 50 per cent are not uncommon. Because of this, a number of researchers have argued that mergers are not generally profitable to the acquiring company, even when firms are merged for a valid business purpose.[12] Therefore, a company making an acquisition merely to avoid a dividend is unlikely to succeed.

3. *Purchase Financial Assets*   The strategy of purchasing financial assets in lieu of a dividend payment can be illustrated with the following example.

[10] Avner Kalay and Adam Shimrat (1988) 'On the payment of equity financed dividends', University of Utah working paper.

[11] M. C. Jensen (1986) 'Agency costs of free cash flows, corporate finance and takeovers', *American Economic Review*, May.

[12] Richard Roll (1986) 'The hubris hypothesis of corporate takeovers', *Journal of Business*, pp. 197–216, explores this idea in depth.

● **Example**

The Regional Electric Company has Euro1,000 of extra cash. It can retain the cash and invest it in Treasury bills yielding 10 per cent, or it can pay the cash to shareholders as a dividend. Shareholders can also invest in Treasury bills with the same yield. Suppose the corporate tax rate is 34 per cent, and the individual tax rate is 28 per cent. How much cash will investors have after five years under each policy? ●

If dividends are paid now, shareholders will receive

$$\text{Euro}1{,}000 \times (1 - 0.28) = \text{Euro}720$$

today after personal tax. Because their return after personal tax is 7.2 per cent, they will have

$$\text{Euro}720 \times (1.072)^5 = \text{Euro}1{,}019.31 \qquad (19.3)$$

in five years. If Regional Electric Company retains the cash to invest in Treasury bills and pays out the proceeds five years from now, the firm will have

$$\text{Euro}1{,}000 \times (1.066)^5 = \text{Euro}1{,}376.53$$

in five years.

If this is paid as a dividend, the shareholders will receive

$$\text{Euro}1{,}376.53 \times (1 - 0.28) = \text{Euro}991.10 \qquad (19.4)$$

after personal taxes at date 5. The resulting formula (19.3) is greater than that in (19.4), implying that cash to shareholders will be greater if the firm pays the dividend now.

This example shows that, for a firm with extra cash, the dividend–payout decision will depend on personal and corporate tax rates. If personal tax rates are higher than corporate tax rates, a firm will have an incentive to reduce dividend payouts. However, if personal tax rates are lower than corporate tax rates, a firm will have an incentive to pay out any excess cash as dividends.

Summary on Taxes

Miller and Modigliani argue that dividend policy is irrelevant in a perfect capital market. However, because dividends are taxed as ordinary income, the MM irrelevance principle does not hold in the presence of personal taxes.

We make a couple of points for a regime of personal taxes:

1. A firm should not issue shares to pay a dividend.
2. Managers have an incentive to seek alternative uses for funds to reduce dividends especially where the firm can earn higher returns than shareholders.

19.5   Expected Return, Dividends and Personal Taxes

The material presented so far in this chapter can properly be called a discussion of *dividend policy*. That is, it is concerned with the level of dividends chosen by a firm. A related, but distinctly different, question is: 'What is the relationship between the expected return on a security and its dividend yield?' To answer this question, we consider an extreme situation where dividends are taxed as ordinary income and capital gains are not taxed. Corporate taxes are ignored.

Suppose every shareholder is in a 25 per cent tax bracket and is considering the stocks of firm g and firm d. Firm g pays no dividend; firm d does. Suppose the current price of the shares of firm g is Euro100 and next year's price is expected to be Euro120. The shareholder in firm g expects a Euro20 capital gain, implying a 20 per cent return. If capital gains are not taxed, the pretax and after-tax returns must be the same.

Suppose firm d will pay a Euro20 dividend per share next year. The price of firm d's shares are expected to be Euro100 after the dividend payment. If the stocks of firm g and firm d are equally risky, the market prices must be set so that their after-tax expected returns are equal, in this case, to 20 per cent. What will the current price of stock in firm d equal?

The current market price of a share in firm d can be calculated as follows:

$$P_0 = \frac{\text{Euro100} + \text{Euro20}\,(1 - T_d)}{1.20}$$

The first term in the numerator is Euro100, the expected price of the share at date 1. The second term represents the dividend after personal tax, where T_d is the personal tax rate on dividends. (The tax on capital gains is ignored under our assumption of no capital gains tax.) By discounting at 20 per cent, we are ensuring that the after-tax rate on stock d is 20 per cent, the same as the rate of return (both pre- and post-tax) for firm g.[13] Setting $T_d = 0.25$, $P_0 =$ Euro95.83.

Because the investor receives Euro120 from firm d at date 1 (Euro100 in value of shares plus Euro20 in dividends) before personal taxes, the expected pretax return on the security equals

$$\frac{\text{Euro120}}{\text{Euro95.83}} - 1 = 25.22\%$$

The above calculations are presented in Table 19.1.

This example shows that the expected *pretax* return on a security with a high dividend yield is greater than the expected *pretax* return on an otherwise identical security with a low dividend yield.[14] The result is graphed in Figure 19.5. Our conclusion is consistent with efficient capital markets because much of the pretax return for a security with a high dividend yield is taxed away.

Does the above example suggest that corporate managers should avoid paying dividends? One might think so at first glance, because firm g sells at a higher price at date 0 than does firm d. However, by deferring a potential Euro20 dividend, firm d might increase its share price at date 0 by far less than Euro20. For example, this is likely to be the case if firm d's best use for its cash is to pay Euro20 for a company whose market price is far below Euro20. Moreover, our previous discussion showed that deferment of dividends to purchase either bonds or shares is justified only when personal taxes go down by more than corporate taxes rise. Thus, this example does not imply that dividends should be avoided.

---

[13] More formally, the after-tax rate of return is

$$\frac{\text{Euro100}}{\text{Euro95.83}} + \frac{\text{Euro20} \times (1 - 0.25)}{\text{Euro95.83}} - 1 = 20\%$$

[14] Dividend yield is defined as Annual dividends per share/Current price per share

TABLE 19.1   Effect of Dividend Yield on Pretax Expected Returns

	Firm g *(no dividend)*	*Firm d* *(all dividend)*
Assumptions:		
Expected price at date 1	Euro120	Euro100
Dividend at date 1 (before tax)	0	Euro20
Dividend at date 1 (after tax)	0	Euro15
Price at date 0	Euro100	(to be solved)
Analysis:		
We solve that the price of firm *d* at date 0 is Euro95.83,* allowing us to calculate		
Capital gain	Euro20	Euro100 − Euro95.83 = Euro4.17
Total gain before tax (both dividend and capital gain)	Euro20	Euro20 + Euro4.17 = Euro24.17
Total percentage return (before tax)	$\dfrac{Euro20}{Euro100} = 0.20$	$\dfrac{Euro24.17}{Euro95.83} = 0.252$
Total gain after tax	Euro20	Euro15 + Euro4.17 = Euro19.17
Total percentage return (before tax)	$\dfrac{Euro20}{Euro100} = 0.20$	$\dfrac{Euro19.17}{Euro95.83} = 0.20$

Stocks with high dividend yields will have higher pretax expected returns than stocks with low-dividend yields. This is referred to as the *grossing up effect.*

* We solve for the price of firm *d* date 0 as

$$P_0 = \frac{Euro100 + Euro20 \times (1 - 0.25)}{1.20} = Euro95.83$$

FIGURE 19.5   Relationship between Expected Return and Dividend Yield

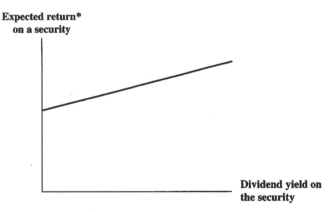

Because the tax rate on dividends at the personal level is higher than the *effective* rate on capital gains, stockholders demand higher expected returns on high-dividend stocks than on low-dividend stocks.
* Expected return includes both expected capital gain and dividend.

Empirical Evidence

As explained above, financial theory indicates that the expected return on a security should be related to its dividend yield. Although this issue has been researched thoroughly, the empirical results are not generally consistent with each other. On the one hand, Brennan as well as Litzenberger and Ramaswamy (LR) find a positive association between expected pretax returns and dividend yields.[15–17] In particular, LR find that a 1 per cent increase in dividend yield requires an extra 23 per cent in expected return. On the other hand, both Black and Scholes and Miller and Scholes find no relationship between expected pretax returns and dividend yields.[18,19]

It is surprising that the results of such uniformly high-quality research can be so contradictory. One can only hope that the ambiguities will be cleared up in the future. Unfortunately, optimal investment strategies for individuals cannot be easily formulated under the current confusion.

19.6   Real-World Factors Favouring a High-Dividend Policy

In a previous section, we pointed out that dividends are taxed at the personal level. This implies that financial managers seek out ways to reduce dividends, though a complete elimination of dividends would be unlikely for firms with a strong cash flow. In this section, we consider reasons why a firm might pay its shareholders high dividends, even in the presence of high personal taxes on dividends.

In a classic textbook, Graham, Dodd and Cottle[20] have argued that firms should generally have high dividend payouts because

1. 'The discounted value of near dividends is higher than the present worth of distant dividends.'
2. Between 'two companies with the same general earning power and same general position in an industry, the one paying the larger dividend will almost always sell at a higher price.'

Two factors favouring a high dividend payout have been mentioned frequently by proponents of this view: the desire for current income and the resolution of uncertainty.

Desire for Current Income

It has been argued that many individuals desire current income. The classic example is the group of retired people and others living on a fixed income, proverbially known as 'widows and orphans'. The argument further states that these individuals would bid up the share price should dividends rise and bid down the share price should dividends fall.

Miller and Modigliani point out that this argument is not relevant to their theoretical model. An individual preferring high current cash flow but holding low-dividend securities could easily sell off shares to provide the necessary funds. Thus, in

---

[15] M. Brennan (1970) 'Taxes: Market valuation and corporate financial policy', *National Tax Journal*, December.

[16] R. Litzenberger and K. Ramaswamy (1979) 'The effect of personal taxes and dividends on capital asset prices: Theory and Empirical Evidence', *Journal of Financial Economics*, June.

[17] R. Litzenberger and K. Ramaswamy (1982) 'The effects of dividends on common stock prices: Tax effects or information effect?', *Journal of Finance,* May.

[18] F. Black and M. Scholes (1974) 'The effects of dividend yield and dividend policy on common stock prices and returns', *Journal of Financial Economics*, May.

[19] M. Miller and M. Scholes (1982) 'Dividends and taxes: Some empirical evidence', J*ournal of Political Economics*, December.

[20] B. Graham, D. Dodd and S. Cottle (1961) *Security Analysis*, Homewood, Ill.: Irwin.

a world of no transactions costs, a high-current-dividend policy would be of no value to the shareholder. However, the current income argument does have relevance in the real world. Here the sale of low-dividend shares would involve brokerage fees and other transactions costs, direct cash expenses that could be avoided by an investment in high-dividend securities. In addition, the expenditure of the shareholder's own time when selling securities and the natural (but not necessarily rational) fear of consuming out of principal might further lead many investors to buy high-dividend securities.

However, to put this argument in perspective, it should be remembered that financial intermediaries such as mutual funds can perform these repackaging transactions for individuals at very low cost. Such intermediaries could buy low-dividend shares, and by a controlled policy of realizing gains they could pay their investors at a higher rate.

Uncertainty Resolution

We have just pointed out that investors with substantial needs for current consumption will prefer high current dividends. Gordon originally argued that a high-dividend policy also benefits stockholders because it resolves uncertainty.[21] He states that investors price a security by forecasting and discounting future dividends. According to Gordon, forecasts of dividends to be received in the distant future have greater uncertainty than do forecasts of near-term dividends. Because the discount rate is positively related to the degree of uncertainty surrounding dividends, the stock price should be low for those companies that pay small dividends now in order to remit higher dividends at later dates.

Dividends are easier to predict than capital gains; however, it would be false to conclude that increased dividends can make the firm less risky. A firm's overall cash flows are not necessarily affected by dividend policy, as long as capital spending and borrowing are not changed. It is hard to see how the risks of the overall cash flows can be changed with a change in dividend policy.

Agency Costs

When a firm has diffuse ownership, we have previously described how conflicts of interest can arise between stockholders and managers. Because of this, managers may be tempted to pursue selfish goals at the expense of shareholders. There are various mechanisms to help shareholders control management behaviour, thus reducing the conflict between shareholders and managers. Several scholars have suggested that dividends can serve as a way to reduce agency costs.[22] By paying dividends equal to the amount of 'surplus' cash flow, a firm can reduce management's ability to squander the firm's resources. Since dispersion of ownership among shareholders is a basic measure of agency costs, it would be expected that firms with high dispersed ownership would have high dividends.

Concept Question

- What are the real-world factors favouring a high-dividend policy?

---

[21] M. Gordon (1961) *The Investment, Financing, and Valuation of the Corporation*, Homewood, Ill.: Irwin.

[22] Michael Rozeff (1986) 'How companies set their dividend payout ratios', in *The Revolution in Corporate Finance* edited by Joel M. Stern and Donald H. Chew, New York: Blackwell. See also Robert S. Hansen, Raman Kumar and Dilip K. Shome (1994) 'Dividend policy and corporate monitoring: Evidence from the regulated electric utility industry', *Financial Management*, Spring.

19.7   A Resolution of Real-World Factors?

In the previous sections, we pointed out that, in all probability, the existence of personal taxes favours a low-dividend policy after all positive NPV projects are taken, whereas some other factors favour high dividends. The finance profession had hoped that it would be easy to determine which of these sets of factors dominates. Unfortunately, after years of research, no one has been able to conclude which of the two is more important. Thus, the dividend-policy question is not resolved.

A discussion of two important concepts—the information content of dividends and the clientele effect—will give the reader an appreciation of some of the relevant issues. The first topic illustrates the difficulty in interpreting empirical results on dividends and provides another reason for dividends. The second topic suggests that the dividend–payout ratio may not be as important as we originally imagined.

Information Content of Dividends: A Brainteaser with Practical Applications

Much of the material in corporate finance may not be inherently very interesting. However, the present topic is fascinating, because it is a brainteaser.

To begin with, let us quickly review some of our earlier discussion. Previously, we examined three different positions on dividends:

1. From the homemade-dividend argument of MM, dividend policy is irrelevant, given that future earnings are held constant.
2. Because of tax effects, a firm's share price may be negatively related to the current dividend when future earnings are held constant.
3. Because of the desire for current income and related factors, a firm's share price may be positively related to its current dividend, even when future earnings are held constant.

It has been empirically established that the price of a firm's stock will generally rise when its current dividend is increased. There is some convincing documentation of the information content of dividends. For example, Asquith and Mullins looked at a sample of firms that either paid the first dividend in their corporate history or initiated dividends after a 10-year period.[23] They found significant increases in stock price on the day the initial dividend was announced. The Asquith and Mullins results confirm the previous work of Pettit, Charest, and Ahroney and Swary.[24] What does this observation imply about any of the three positions just stated?

At first glance, the observation may seem consistent with position (3) and inconsistent with positions (1) and (2). In fact, many writers have argued this. However, other authors have countered that the observation itself is consistent with all three positions. They point out that companies do not like to cut a dividend. Thus, firms will raise the dividend only when future earnings, cash flow, and so on, are expected to rise enough so that the dividend is not likely to be reduced later to its

---

[23] P. Asquith and D. Mullins, Jr. (1983) 'The impact of initiating dividend payments on shareholder wealth', *Journal of Business*, January.

[24] R. Pettit (1972) 'Dividend announcements, security performance, and capital market efficiency', *Journal of Finance*; G. Charest (1978) 'Dividend information, stock returns and market efficiency', *Journal of Financial Economics*, **6**; J. Ahroney and I. Swary (1980) 'Quarterly dividend and earnings announcements and stockholders' returns: An empirical analysis', *Journal of Finance*, March.

original level. A dividend increase is management's signal to the market that the firm is expected to do well.

It is the expectation of good times, and not only the shareholder's affinity for current income, that raises stock price. The rise in the share price following the dividend signal is called the **information-content effect** of the dividend. To recapitulate, imagine that the share price is unaffected or negatively affected by the level of dividends, given that future earnings are held constant. Nevertheless, the information-content effect implies that share price may rise when dividends are raised—if dividends simultaneously cause stockholders to upwardly adjust their expectations of future earnings.

Several theoretical models of dividend policy incorporate managerial incentives to communicate information via dividends.[25] Here, dividends serve to signal to shareholders the firm's current and future performance.

The Clientele Effect

In the first part of this chapter, we established the MM proposition that dividend policy is irrelevant when certain conditions hold. The next section dealt with those imperfections likely to make dividend policy relevant. Because many imperfections were presented there, the reader might be sceptical that the imperfections could cancel each other out so perfectly that dividend policy would become irrelevant. However, the argument presented below suggests the irrelevancy of dividend policy in the real world.

Those individuals in high tax brackets are likely to prefer either no or low dividends. But there are also individual investors in low brackets. They are likely to prefer some dividends if they desire current income or favour resolution of uncertainty. Also, pension funds pay no taxes on either dividends or capital gains. Because they face no tax consequences, pension funds will also prefer dividends if they have a preference for current income. However it has to be stated that pension funds ultimate beneficiaries will be tax payers. This adds further to the complexities of the dividend problem.

Suppose that 40 per cent of all investors prefer high dividends and 60 per cent prefer low dividends, yet only 20 per cent of firms pay high dividends while 80 per cent pay low dividends. Here, the high-dividend firms will be in short supply, thus their shares should be bid up, while the shares of low-dividend firms should be bid down.

However, the dividend policies of all firms need not be fixed in the long run. In this example, we would expect enough low-dividend firms to increase their payout so that 40 per cent of the firms pay high dividends and 60 per cent of the firms pay low dividends. After this has occurred, no type of firm will be better off. Once payouts of corporations conform to the desires of shareholders, no single firm can affect its market value by switching from one dividend strategy to another.

Clienteles are likely to form in the following way:

Group	Shares
Individuals in high tax brackets	Zero-to-low-payout shares
Individuals in low tax brackets	Low-to-medium-payout shares
Tax-free institutions	Medium-payout shares

To see if you understand the clientele effect, consider the following statement: 'In

[25] S. Bhattacharya (1979) 'Imperfect information, dividend policy, and "the bird in the hand" Fallacy', *Bell Journal of Economics*, **10**; S. Bhattacharya (1980) 'Nondissipative signalling structure and dividend policy', *Quarterly Journal of Economics*, **95**; S. Ross (1977) 'The determination of financial structure: The incentive signalling approach', *Bell Journal of Economics*, **8**; M. Miller and K. Rock (1985) 'Dividend policy under asymmetric information', *Journal of Finance*.

spite of the theoretical argument that dividend policy is irrelevant or that firms should not pay dividends, many investors like high dividends. Because of this fact, a firm can boost its share price by having a higher dividend payout ratio.' True or false?

The statement is false. The very existence of clienteles makes this doubtful. As long as enough high-dividend firms satisfy dividend-loving investors, a firm will not be able to boost its share price by paying high dividends. A firm can boost its share price only if an unsatisfied clientele exists. There is no evidence that this is the case.

Our discussion on clienteles followed from the fact that tax brackets vary across investors. If shareholders care about taxes, shares should attract tax clienteles based on dividend yield. This appears to be true. Surveys by Blume, Crockett and Friend, and by Lewellen, Stanley, Lease and Schlarbaum, show that stocks with the highest dividend yields tend to be held by individual investors in low tax brackets.[26]

Concept Questions

- Do dividends have information content?
- What are tax clienteles?

19.8   What We Know and Do Not Know about Dividend Policy

Corporations Smooth Dividends

In 1956, John Lintner suggested that managers estimate what portion of the firm's earnings is likely to be permanent and what portion of the earnings is likely to be temporary. He looked at the dividend-payout patterns of firms and concluded that dividends are more likely to be raised following a permanent, rather than a temporary, increase in earnings and that firms have a long-run target for their dividend-to-earnings ratio. However, because managers need time to assess the permanence of any earnings rise, dividend changes appear to lag earnings changes by a number of periods. It follows from Lintner's analysis that the dividend-to-earnings ratio rises when a company begins a period of bad times, and the ratio falls when a company reaches a period of good times.[27]

John Lintner's work and the later work of Fama and Babiak[28] suggest that what is meant by dividend policy is related not only to the level of dividends but also to the change in dividends.

1. *Level of Dividends*   Managers tend to think of dividend payments in terms of a proportion of income and also think investors are entitled to a 'fair' share of corporate income. Companies appear to think in terms of a long-run *target payout ratio*.
2. *Change in Dividends*   Managers avoid making a change in the level of dividend payments if it will have to be reversed later. Thus, the level of dividends is more *stable* than the level of earnings. Firms smooth out changes in their dividends relative to changes in their earnings.

---

[26] M. Blume, J. Crockett and I. Friend (1974) 'Stockownership in the United States: Characteristics and trends', *Survey of Current Business*, **54**, 11; W. Lewellen, K.L. Stanley, R.C. Lease and G. G. Schlarbaum (1978) 'Some direct evidence on the dividend clientele phenomenon', *Journal of Finance*, 33, 5.

[27] J. Lintner (1968) 'Distribution and incomes of corporations among dividends, retained earnings and taxes', *American Economic Review*, **63**, (4).

[28] E. Fama and H. Babiak (1968) 'Dividend policy: An empirical analysis,' *Journal of the American Statistical Association*, **63**, (4).

Taken together, Lintner's observations suggest that two parameters describe dividend policy: the target payout ratio (t) and the speed of adjustment of current dividends to the target (s). Dividend changes will tend to conform to the following type of model:

$$\text{Div}_1 - \text{Div}_0 = s \cdot (t\text{EPS}_1 - \text{Div}_0)$$

where Div_1 and Div_0 are dividends in the next year and dividends in the current year, respectively. EPS_1 is earnings per share in the next year.

A conservative company will have a low adjustment rate and a less conservative company a high adjustment rate. As can be seen, if $s = 0$, $\text{Div}_1 = \text{Div}_0$, and if $s = 1$, the actual change in dividends will be equal to the target change in dividends. The level of dividends will be set by t. A firm will have a low t if it has many positive NPV projects and a high t if it has few positive NPV projects relative to available cash flow.

Dividends Provide Information to the Market

We previously observed that the price of a firm's shares will frequently rise when its current dividend is increased. This seems to suggest that there is information content in dividend changes. The price of a firm's shares can fall significantly when its dividend is cut. One reason may be that investors are looking at current dividends for clues concerning the level of future earnings and dividends.

A Sensible Dividend Policy

The knowledge of the finance profession varies across topic areas. For example, capital-budgeting techniques are both powerful and precise. A single net-present-value equation can accurately determine whether a multi-million dollar project should be accepted or rejected. The capital-asset-pricing model and the arbitrage-pricing model provide empirically validated relationships between expected return and risk.

Conversely, the field has less knowledge of capital-structure policy. Though a number of elegant theories relate firm value to the level of debt, no formula can be used to calculate the firm's optimum debt–equity ratio. Our profession is forced too frequently to employ rules of thumb, such as treating the industry's average ratio as the optimal one for the firm. The field's knowledge of dividend policy is, perhaps, similar to its knowledge of capital-structure policy. We do know that:

1. Firms should avoid having to cut back on positive NPV projects to pay a dividend, with or without personal taxes.
2. Firms should avoid issuing shares to pay a dividend in a world with personal taxes.
3. Repurchases should be considered when there are few positive new investment opportunities and there is a surplus of unneeded cash. But they are only likely to create shareholder value (at least in theory) if the shares bought back are undervalued on fundamental present value criteria or due to the consequent increase in gearing.

The above recommendations suggest that firms with many positive NPV projects relative to available cash flow should have low payout ratios. Firms with few positive NPV projects relative to available cash flow should have high payouts. In addition, we know that personal taxes can encourage a policy of low dividends, and other factors can encourage a high-dividend policy. However, there is no formula for calculating the optimal dividend-to-earnings ratio. There is some benefit to dividend stability, and unnecessary changes in dividend payout are avoided by most firms.

19.9 Summary and Conclusions

1. The dividend decision is important because it determines the payout received by shareholders and the funds retained by the firm for investment. Dividend policy is usually reflected by the current dividend-to-earnings ratio. This is referred to as the payout *ratio*. Unfortunately, the optimal payout ratio cannot be determined quantitatively. Rather, one can only indicate qualitatively what factors lead to low- or high-dividend policies.

2. We argue that the dividend policy of the firm is irrelevant in a perfect capital market because the shareholder can effectively undo the firm's dividend strategy. If a shareholder receives a greater dividend than desired, he or she can reinvest the excess. Conversely, if the shareholder receives a smaller dividend than desired, he or she can sell off extra shares of stock. This argument is due to MM and is similar to their homemade-leverage concept, discussed in Chapter 16.

3. Even in a perfect capital market, a firm should not reject positive NPV projects to increase dividend payments.

4. Although the MM argument is useful in introducing the topic of dividends, it ignores many factors in practice. We show that personal taxes and new-issue costs are real-world considerations that favour low-dividend payout. With personal taxes and new-issue costs, the firm should not issue stock to pay a dividend. However, our discussion does not imply that all firms should avoid dividends. Rather, those with high cash flow relative to positive NPV opportunities might pay dividends due to legal constraints and/or a dearth of investment opportunities.

5. The expected return on a security is positively related to its dividend yield in a world with personal taxes. This result suggests that individuals in low or zero tax brackets should consider investing in high-yielding shares. However, the result does not imply that firms should avoid all dividends.

6. The general consensus among financial analysts is that the tax effect is the strongest argument in favour of low dividends and the preference for current income is the strongest argument in favour of high dividends. Unfortunately, no empirical work has determined which of these two factors dominates, perhaps because the clientele effect argues that dividend policy is quite responsive to the needs of shareholders. For example, if 40 per cent of the shareholders prefer low dividends and 60 per cent prefer high dividends, approximately 40 per cent of companies will have a low dividend payout, and 60 per cent will have a high payout. This sharply reduces the impact of an individual firm's dividend policy on its market price.

7. Research has shown that many firms appear to have a long-run target dividend-payout policy. Firms that have few (many) positive NPV projects relative to available cash flow will have high (low) payouts. In addition, firms try to reduce the fluctuations in the level of dividends. There appears to be some value in dividend stability and smoothing.

8. The stock market reacts positively to increases in dividends (or an initial dividend payment) and negatively to decreases in dividends. This suggests that there is information content in dividend payments.

KEY TERMS

Regular cash dividends   432
Stock dividend   432
Scrip dividend   432
Share split   432

Ex-dividend date   432
Homemade dividends   436
Information-content effect   447
Clienteles   447

QUESTIONS AND PROBLEMS

The Benchmark Case: An Illustration of the Irrelevance of Dividend Policy

19.1   The growing-perpetuity model expresses the value of a share of stock as the present value of the expected dividends from that stock. How can you conclude that dividend policy is irrelevant when this model is valid?

19.2   Gibson Co. has a current period cash flow of $1.2 million and pays no dividends, and the present value of forecasted future cash flows are $15 million. It is an all-equity-financed company with 1 million shares outstanding. Assume the effective personal tax rate is zero.
   a. What is the share price of Gibson?
   b. Suppose the board of directors of Gibson Co. announces its plan to pay out 50 per cent of its current cash flow as cash dividends to their shareholders. How can Jeff Miller, who owns 1,000 shares of Gibson stock, achieve a zero payout policy on his own?

Taxes, Issuances Costs and Dividends

19.3   Cranfield University pays no taxes on capital gains, dividend income, or interest payments. Would you expect to find low-dividend, high-growth shares in the university's portfolio? Would you expect to find tax-free government bonds in the portfolio?

19.4   In their 1970 paper on dividends and taxes, Elton and Gruber reported that the ex-dividend-date drop in a share's price as a percentage of the dividend should equal the ratio of one minus the ordinary income tax rate to one minus the capital gains rate; that is,

$$\frac{P_e - P_b}{D} = \frac{1 - T_o}{1 - T_c}$$

where

P_e = The ex-dividend share price
P_b = The share price before it trades ex-dividend
D = The amount of the dividend
T_o = The tax rate on ordinary income
T_c = The effective tax rate on capital gains

Note: As we pointed out in the text, the effective tax rate of capital gains is usually less than the actual tax rate, because their realization may be postponed. Indeed, because investors could postpone their realizations indefinitely, the effective rate could be zero.

   a. If $T_o = T_c = 0$, how much will the share price fall?
   b. If $T_o \neq 0$ and $T_c = 0$, how much will it fall?
   c. Explain the results you found in *a* and *b*.
   d. Do the results of Elton and Gruber's study imply that firms will maximize shareholder wealth by not paying dividends?

Expected Return, Dividends, and Personal Taxes

19.5   Some time ago, a political advisory committee recommended wage and price controls to prevent the spiralling inflation that was experienced in the 1970s. Members of the investment community and several labour unions sent the committee reports that discuss whether or not dividends should be under the controls.

   The reports from the investment community demonstrated that the value of a share is equal to the discounted value of its expected dividend stream. Thus, they argued that any legislation that caps dividends will also hold down share prices, thereby increasing companies' costs of capital.

   The unions' reports conceded that dividend policy is important to firms that are trying to control costs. They also felt that dividends are important to shareholders, but only because the dividend is the shareholders' wage. In order to be fair, the unions argued, if the government controls labour's wage, it should also control dividends.

   Discuss these arguments and explain the fallacy in them.

19.6   Deaton Co. and Grebe Inc., are in the same risk class. Shareholders expect Deaton to pay a USD4 dividend next year when the share will sell for USD20. Grebe has a no-dividend policy. Currently, Grebe shares are selling for USD20 per share. Grebe shareholders expect a

USD4 capital gain over the next year. Capital gains are not taxed, but dividends are taxed at 25 per cent.

a. What is the current price of Deaton Co. shares?

b. If capital gains are also taxed at 25 per cent, what should be the price of Deaton Co. shares?

c. Explain the result you found in part *b.*

Real-World Factors Favouring a High-Dividend Policy

19.7 The bird-in-the-hand argument, which states that a dividend today is safer than the uncertain prospect of a capital gain tomorrow, is often used to justify high dividend-payout ratios. Explain the fallacy behind the argument.

19.8 The desire for current income is not a valid explanation for preference for high-current-dividend policy, as investors can always create homemade dividends by selling a portion of their stocks. Comment.

A Resolution of Real-World Factors?

19.9 In the May 4, 1981, issue of *Fortune*, an article entitled 'Fresh evidence that dividends don't matter' stated: 'All told, 115 companies of the 500 [largest industrial corporations] raised their payout every year during the period [1970–80]. Investors in this . . . group would have fared somewhat better than investors in the 500 as a whole: the median total [annual compound] return of the 115 was 10.7% during the decade vs. 9.4% for the 500.'

Is this evidence that investors prefer dividends to capital gains? Why or why not?

19.10 If the market places the same value on USD1 of dividends as on USD1 of capital gains, then firms with different payout ratios will appeal to different clienteles of investors. One clientele is as good as another; therefore, a firm cannot increase its value by changing its dividend policy. Yet empirical investigations reveal a strong correlation between dividend-payout ratios and other firm characteristics. For example, small, rapidly growing firms that have recently gone public almost always have payout ratios that are zero; all earnings are reinvested in the business. Explain this phenomenon if dividend policy is irrelevant.

19.11 In spite of the theoretical argument that dividend policy should be irrelevant, the fact remains that many investors like high dividends. If this preference exists, a firm can boost its share price by increasing its dividend-payout ratio. Explain the fallacy in this argument.

What We Know and Do Not Know about Dividend Policy

19.12 Empirical research found that there have been significant increases in share price on the day an initial dividend (i.e. the first time a firm pays a cash dividend) is announced. What does this finding imply about the information content of initial dividends?

PART V

Long-Term Financing

20 Issuing Equity Securities to the Public   455
21 Long-Term Debt   468
22 Options and Corporate Finance   487
23 Warrants and Convertibles   524
24 Leasing   542

Part IV discussed capital structure; we determined the relationship between the firm's debt–equity ratio and the firm's value. The debt we used in Part IV was stylized. In fact, there are many different types of debt. In Part V we discuss how financial managers choose the type of debt that makes the most sense, including straight debt, debt with options, and leasing.

In Chapter 20, we describe the range of ways employed by European firms to sell securities to the public. We describe the features of these methods and point out some counter-initiative implications.

In Chapter 21, we describe some basic features of long-term debt. One of the special features of most long-term bonds is that they can be called by the firm before the maturity date. We try to explain why call provisions exist. There are many types of long-term debt, including floating-rate bonds, income bonds and original-issue discount bonds. We discuss why they exist.

In Chapter 22, we describe options. First we describe the options that trade on organized exchanges. Options are contingent claims on the value of an underlying asset. Every issue of corporate security has option features. Later in the chapter we present a formal model that can be used to value options. The model bears no resemblance to net present value (NPV). Our goal is to present the underlying logic of option valuation. This is important because NPV does not work well for contingent claims.

In Chapter 23, we look at bonds with special option features. These bonds are sold as bonds with warrants and as bonds convertible into ordinary shares. A warrant gives the holder a right to buy ordinary shares for cash, and a convertible bond gives the holder the right to exchange it for ordinary shares. In Chapter 23, we discuss warrants and convertibles and explain why firms issue them.

Chapter 24 describes a special form of long-term debt called leasing. In general, a rental agreement that lasts for more than one year is a lease. Leases are a source of financing and displace debt in the balance sheet. Many silly reasons are given for leasing, and we present some of them. The major reason for long-term leasing is to lower taxes.

CHAPTER
20

Issuing Equity Securities to the Public

This chapter looks at how companies issue equity securities to the investing public. The general procedures for debt, which are quite similar, are presented in the next chapter.

Before securities can be traded on a securities market, they must be issued to the public. A firm making an issue to the public must satisfy requirements set out in local legislation and statutes. In general, investors must be given all material information in the form of a registration statement and prospectus. In the first part of this chapter, we discuss what this typically entails.

A public issue of equity can be sold directly to the public with the help of underwriters. Alternatively, a public equity issue can be sold to the firm's existing shareholders by what is called a *rights offer*. This chapter examines the differences between these offers.

Shares of companies going public for the first time are often underpriced. We describe this unusual phenomenon and provide a possible explanation.

20.1 How Shares are Issued to the Public

There are two kinds of public issues: the *general cash offer* and the *rights offer*. Cash offers are sold to interested investors, and rights offers are sold to existing shareholders. Equity is sold both by the cash offer and the rights offer, though almost all debt is sold by cash offer.

The procedures detailed below present a general picture of how shares are issued to the public under the general cash offer—obviously there are substantial variations on a theme and these are apparent as one moves from one country to another. Once a company has permission from the particular market's authority to come to the stockmarket it can go about it in a variety of ways. Different rules apply to shares in a company coming to the market for the first time and for extra new shares issued by companies which are already quoted and have a market price. Completely new shares may be issued in a variety of ways, the most common of which are listed below:

1. An **offer for sale**, underwritten by an issuing house, is one of the most common means by which new companies come to the market. Underwriting means that the issuing house (a financial intermediary specializing in share and debt issues, and in bringing together the business firm requiring cash and the investing community), commercial banks, investment banks (financial intermediaries who perform a wide variety of services for sale of securities, advising in mergers and takeovers, corporate reconstructions and trading on their own account) and

brokers, both domestic and foreign, will have already bought the shares at a marginally lower price than the one at which they are offered to the general investing public. If all the shares are sold, the underwriters make a profit. If the public does not like the issue, the underwriters cannot sell the shares back to the original sellers. They have to keep them or sell them, probably at a loss, when the shares are quoted. This is called leaving the shares with the underwriters. Naturally, the company offering the shares gets its money regardless of the success or failure of the issue.

Investors are invited by the issuing house, with the help of a detailed financial record and indication of business strategy contained in a **prospectus**, to subscribe for the shares. Where demand for an issue exceeds supply, the issue is said to be oversubscribed. In such cases, following what amounts to a raffle, some investors may not get any allotment of shares or the amount they have asked for may be severely scaled down. When such heavily oversubscribed issues are eventually quoted, they often do not start off dealing at the price at which they were issued, but at a higher one. This is called a premium, and may be substantial.

Of course, should an issue be undersubscribed with shares being left with the underwriter, when dealing commences it usually does so below the offer for sale price—in other words, the issue goes to a discount.

The shares marketed may be new shares which the company itself is selling or it may be the case that the shares in the offer for sale, come from substantial shareholders' existing holdings.

2. A **public issue** is similar to an offer for sale, but the issuing house acts as an adviser to the company selling shares to the public rather than as a principal in buying shares for the company and selling them to the public.

3. A **placing** is where the company sells shares, through an issuing house, to private clients of the issuing house at a specified price. This route is used for small **flotations** and is cheaper than an offer for sale and is not usually underwritten.

4. An **introduction** is where the company already has a fairly wide spectrum of shareholders, at least sufficient to make a market, but has not had a stockmarket quote before. The introduction mechanism is similar to a placing, but it is existing shareholders who are selling their shares to the public through the stock exchange with an issuing house advising.

5. A **tender** is like an offer for sale, but instead of the issuing company's setting a fixed price in advance the public bids for the shares as in an auction. Usually, the company sets a minimum level below which it is not prepared to sell; the bids are then made in writing. The bids are counted from the highest price bid down to the lowest, and an allocation plan devised so that all of the shares are taken up. Usually, everyone who eventually gets the shares pays the lowest price that is accepted. Tenders are becoming more accepted today; they have a fairly long history in France. The effect of selecting a market-clearing price is that the underpricing that may occur in an offer for sale is limited.

An increasingly popular means of issuing new shares to the public, particularly in the Netherlands and in Britain, is via **bookbuilding**. In a bookbuilding exercise, investment banks and their clients, stockbrokers and their clients, and other financial intermediaries and their clientele irrevocably indicate (and pay by a certain date) how many shares they will take of a particular issue at the specified price. Sometimes, a percentage of the issue is also available for general public subscription. Of course, in the case of an oversubscription, potential investors may receive less than they committed to in the bookbuilding exercise.

The first public equity issue that is made by a company is referred to as an **initial public offering (IPO)** or an **unseasoned new issue**. All initial public offerings are cash offers. A **seasoned new issue** refers to a new issue where the company's securities have been previously issued. A seasoned new issue of ordinary shares may be made by using a cash offer or a rights offer.

Investment Bankers

Investment bankers, also called merchant bankers in some countries, are at the heart of new security issues. They provide advice, market the securities (after investigating the market's potential receptiveness to the issue), and underwrite the amount an issue will raise. For corporate issuers, investment bankers perform services such as the following:

> Formulating and advising on the method used to issue the securities
> Pricing the new securities
> Selling the new securities

In addition, investment bankers have the responsibility of pricing fairly. When a firm goes public, particularly for the first time, the buyers know relatively little about the firm's operations. After all, it is not rational for a buyer of, say, only 1,000 shares to study the company at length. Instead, the buyer must rely on the judgement of the investment banker, who has presumably examined the firm in detail. Given this asymmetry of information, what prevents the investment banker from pricing the issued securities too high? While the underwriter may be argued to have a short-run incentive to price high, it has a long-run incentive to make sure that its customers do not pay too much; they might desert the underwriter in future deals if they lose money on this one. Thus, as long as an investment banker plans to stay in business over time, it is in their self-interest to price fairly. Some might even argue that they might have a self-interest in slight underpricing.

Financial economists argue that each investment bank has a reservoir of reputation capital. Mispricing of new issues, as well as unethical dealings, is likely to reduce this reputation capital.

The Offering Price

Determining the correct offering price is the most difficult thing an investment banker must do for an initial public offering. The issuing firm faces a potential cost if the offering price is set too high or too low. If the issue is priced too high, it may be unsuccessful and be withdrawn. If the issue is priced below the true market price, the issuer's existing shareholders will experience an opportunity loss.

Ibbotson has found that unseasoned new equity issues in the USA have been typically offered at 11 per cent below their true market price.[1] Underpricing helps new shareholders earn a higher return on the shares they buy. However, the existing shareholders of the issuing firm are not helped by underpricing. To them it is an indirect cost of issuing new securities. Several studies—but not all—have confirmed the early research of Ibbotson.

---

[1] R. Ibbotson (1975) 'Price performance of common stock new issues', *Journal of Financial Economics*, **2**.

Underpricing: A Possible Explanation

When the price of a new issue is too low, the issue is often *oversubscribed*. This means investors will not be able to buy all of the shares they want and the underwriters will have to allocate the shares among investors. The average investor will find it difficult to get shares in an oversubscribed offering because there will not be enough shares to go round. While initial public offerings have positive initial returns on average, a significant fraction of them have price drops. An investor submitting an order for all new issues may well find that he or she will be allocated more shares in issues that go down in price.

IN THEIR OWN WORDS . . . Jay R. Ritter on IPO Underpricing around the World

The United States is not the only country in which initial public offerings of common stock (IPOs) are underpriced. The phenomenon exists in every country with a stock market, although the amount of underpricing varies from country to country

Many countries have government regulators who force issuing companies to sell shares at a lower price than they otherwise would. Sometimes the purpose is to protect unsophisticated investors. However, in some denationalizations or privatizations, there has been another motive for underpricing.

For example, in 1979, when Margaret Thatcher became Prime Minister of Britain amid a wave of strikes and a declining economy, there were more union members than stockholders in Britain. To give British voters a positive experience with capitalism, as the government denationalized several government-owned businesses, it intentionally sought both to underprice the shares and allow as many voters as possible to buy them. As a result of this strategy, by the mid-1980s there were more shareholders than union members. As a by-product of the denationalizations, the British government ran a budget surplus, because of the cash raised as the asset sales continued.

The table below gives a summary of the average initial returns on IPOs in a number of countries collected from a number of studies by various authors.

Country	Sample size	Time period	Average initial return
Australia	266	1976–89	11.9%
Belgium	28	1984–90	10.1
Brazil	62	1979–90	78.5
Canada	258	1971–92	5.4
Chile	19	1982–90	16.3
Finland	85	1984–92	9.6
France	187	1983–92	4.2
Germany	170	1978–92	10.9
Hong Kong	80	1980–90	17.6
Italy	75	1985–91	27.1
Japan	472	1970–91	32.5
Korea	347	1980–90	78.1
Malaysia	132	1980–91	80.3
Mexico	37	1987–90	33.0
Netherlands	72	1982–91	7.2
New Zealand	149	1979–91	28.8
Portugal	62	1986–87	54.4
Singapore	66	1973–87	27.0
Spain	71	1985–90	35.0
Sweden	213	1970–91	39.0
Switzerland	42	1983–89	35.8
Taiwan	168	1971–90	45.0
Thailand	32	1988–89	58.1
United Kingdom	2,133	1959–90	12.0
United States	10,626	1960–92	15.3

Jay R. Ritter is Professor of Finance at the University of Illinois. An outstanding scholar, he is well respected for his insightful analyses of new issues and going public.

Consider this tale of two investors. Ms Smart knows precisely what companies are worth when their shares are offered. Mr Average knows only that prices usually rise one month after the IPO. Armed with this information, Mr Average decides to buy 1,000 shares of every IPO. Does Mr Average actually earn an abnormally high average return across all initial offerings?

The answer is no, and at least one reason is the strategy of Ms Smart and operators like her. Because Ms Smart knows that company *XYZ* is underpriced, she invests all her money in its IPO. When the issue is oversubscribed, the underwriters must allocate the shares between Ms Smart and Mr Average. If they do it on a pro rata basis and if Ms Smart has bid for twice as many shares as Mr Average, she will get two shares for each one Mr Average receives. The net result is that when an issue is underpriced, Mr. Average cannot buy as much of it as he wants.

Ms Smart also knows that company *ABC* is overpriced. In this case she avoids its IPO altogether, and Mr Average ends up with a full 1,000 shares. To summarize, Mr Average receives fewer shares when more knowledgeable investors swarm to buy an underpriced issue, but he gets all he wants when the smart money avoids the issue.

This is called the *winner's curse*, and it explains much of the reason why IPOs have such a large average return. When the average investor wins and gets his or her allocation, it is because those who knew better avoided the issue. To counteract the winner's curse and attract the average investor, underwriters underprice issues.[2]

Concept Questions

- Describe an offer for sale and a placing.
- Suppose that a stockbroker calls you up out of the blue and offers to sell you some shares of a new issue. Do you think the issue will do better or worse than average?

20.2   The Cost of New Issues

Issuing securities to the public is not free and the costs of different issuing methods are important determinants of which is used. The costs fall into five categories.

1. Spread or underwriting discount	The spread is the difference between the price the issuing form receives and the price offered to the public.
2. Other direct expenses	These are costs incurred by the issuer that are not part of the compensation to underwriters. They include filing fees, legal fees, and taxes.
3. Indirect expenses	These costs are not reported in the prospectus and include management time on the new issue.
4. Abnormal returns	In a seasoned issue of stock, the price drops by 1 per cent to 2 per cent upon the announcement of the issue.
5. Underpricing	For initial public offerings, the stock typically rises substantially after the issue date. This is a cost to the firm because the shares are sold for less than its efficient price in the aftermarket.

---

[2] This explanation was first suggested in K. Rock (1986) 'Why new issues are underpriced', *Journal of Financial Economics*, **15**.

Concept Question

• Describe the costs of a new issue of ordinary shares.

20.3   Rights

When new ordinary shares are offered to the general public, the proportionate ownership of existing shareholders is likely to be reduced. However, in many countries local company law dictates that companies must first offer any new issue of ordinary shares (perhaps with a very small number of limited exceptions) to existing shareholders. In most countries, it is possible for existing shareholders to waive this right by passing resolutions (approved by existing shareholders) to this effect. And in a few countries there are rules which do allow the company to issue shares to third parties without reference to existing shareholders. Obviously shareholders should resist this latter incursion into their rights.

An issue of ordinary shares for cash to existing stockholders is called a *rights offering*. Here, each shareholder is issued an *option* to buy a specified number of new shares from the firm at a specified price within a specified time, after which the rights expire. For example, a firm whose stock is selling at GBP3 may let current shareholders buy a fixed number of shares at GBP2 per share within two months. Such rights are often traded on the Stock Exchange even before the GBP2 has been paid by the shareholder.

The Mechanics of a Rights Offering

The various considerations confronting a financial manager in a rights offering are illustrated by the situation of the Regional Power Company, whose initial financial statements are given in Table 20.1.

Regional Power earns GBP2 million after taxes and has 1 million shares outstanding. Earnings per share are GBP2, and the shares sell at 10 times earnings

TABLE 20.1   Financial Statement before Rights Offering

REGIONAL POWER COMPANY		
Balance Sheet and Income Statement		
Balance Sheet		
Assets GBP20,000,000	Shareholder Funds	
	Ordinary shares	GBP10,000,000
	Retained earnings	10,000,000
Total GBP20,000,000	Total	GBP20,000,000
Income Statement		
Earnings before taxes	GBP 3,030,303	
Taxes (34%)	1,030,303	
Net income	GPB 2,000,000	
Earnings per share	GPB 2	
Shares outstanding	1,000,000	
Market price per share	GBP 20	
Total market value	GBP 20,000,000	

(that is, its price-earnings ratio is 10). The market price of each share is therefore GBP20. The company plans to raise GBP5 million of new equity funds by a rights issue.

The process of issuing rights follows this typical routine. Existing shareholders are notified that they have been given one right for each share they own. Exercise occurs when a shareholder sends payment to the firm's subscription agent (usually a bank). Shareholders of Regional Power will have several choices: (1) subscribe for the full number of entitled shares, (2) sell all of the rights or (3) do nothing and let the rights expire.

The financial management of Regional Power must answer the following questions:

1. What price should the existing shareholders be asked to pay for a new share?
2. How many rights will be required to purchase one share?
3. What effect will the rights offering have on the existing price of the share?

Subscription Price

In a rights offering, the **subscription price** is the price that existing shareholders are asked to pay for a new share. A rational shareholder will only subscribe to the rights offering if the subscription price is below the market price of the share on the offer's expiration date. For example, if the share price is GBP13 and the subscription price is GBP15, no rational shareholder will subscribe. Why pay GBP15 for something worth GBP13? Regional Power chooses a price of GBP10, which is well below the current market price of GBP20. As long as the market price does not fall by half before expiration of the rights offer, the rights issue should succeed.

Number of Rights Needed to Purchase a Share

Regional Power wants to raise GBP5 million in new equity. With a subscription price of GBP10, it must issue 500,000 new shares. This can be determined by dividing the total amount to be raised by the subscription price:

$$\text{Number of new shares} = \frac{\text{Funds to be raised}}{\text{Subscription price}} = \frac{\text{GBP5,000,000}}{\text{GBP10}} = 500,000 \text{ shares}$$

Because shareholders in this case get one right for each share they own, 1 million rights will be issued by Regional Power. To determine how many rights must be exercised to get one new share, we can divide the number of existing outstanding shares by the number of new shares:

$$\text{Number of rights needed to buy a new share} = \frac{\text{'Old' shares}}{\text{'New' shares}} = \frac{1,000,000}{500,000} = 2 \text{ rights}$$

Thus, a shareholder must give up two rights plus GBP10 to receive a share of new stock. If all the shareholders do this, Regional Power will raise the required GBP5 million.

It should be clear that the subscription price, the number of new shares and the number of new shares per old share are interrelated. If Regional Power lowers the subscription price, it must issue more new shares to raise GBP5 million in new equity.

Several possibilities appear here:

Subscription price	Number of new shares	Rights structure (new shares per old share held)
GBP20	250,000	1 for 4
10	500,000	1 for 2
5	1,000,000	1 for 1

Effect of Rights Offering on Price of a Share

Rights clearly have value. In the case of Regional Power, the right to be able to buy a share worth GBP20 for GBP10 is valuable.

Suppose a shareholder of Regional Power owns two shares just before the rights offering. This situation is depicted in Table 20.2. Initially, the price of Regional Power is GBP20 per share, so the shareholder's total holding is worth 2 × GBP20 = GBP40. The shareholder who has two shares will receive two rights. The Regional Power rights offer gives shareholders with two rights the opportunity to purchase one additional share for GBP10. The holding of the shareholder who exercises these rights and buys the new share would increase to three shares. The value of the new holding would be GBP40 + GBP10 = GBP50 (the GBP40 initial value plus the GBP10 paid to the company). Because the shareholder now holds three shares, the price per share would drop to GBP50/3 = GBP16.67 (rounded to two decimal places).

The difference between the old share price of GBP20 and the new share price of GBP16.67 reflects the fact that the old shares carried rights to subscribe to the new issue. The difference must be equal to the value of one right, that is, GBP20 − GBP16.67 = GBP3.33.

As there is an ex-dividend date with dividends, so there is an **ex-rights** date here. An individual buying the shares prior to the ex-rights date will receive the rights when distributed. An individual buying the shares on or after the ex-rights date will not receive the rights. In our example, the price of the shares prior to the

TABLE 20.2   The Value to the Individual Shareholder of Regional Power's Rights

	The shareholder
Initial position	
Number of shares	2
Share price	GBP20
Value of holding	GBP40
Terms of offer	
Subscription price	GBP10
Number of rights issued	2
Number of rights for a share	2
After offer	
Number of shares	3
Value of holdings	GBP50
Share price	GBP16.67
Value of right	
Old price − New price	GBP20 − GBP16.67 = GBP3.33
$\dfrac{\text{New price} - \text{Subscription price}}{\text{Number of rights for a share}}$	(GBP16.67 − GBP10)/2 = GBP3.33

ex-rights date is GBP20. An individual buying on or after the ex-rights date is not entitled to the rights. The price on or after the ex-rights date is GBP16.67. This is the ex-rights price.

Table 20.3 shows what happens to Regional Power. If all shareholders exercise their rights, the number of shares will increase to 1.5 million and the value of the firm will increase to GBP25 million. After the rights offering the value of each share will drop to GBP16.67 (= GBP25 million/1.5 million).

An investor holding no shares of Regional Power who wants to subscribe to the new issue can do so by buying rights. An outside investor buying two rights will pay GBP3.33 $\times$ 2 = GBP6.67 (to account for previous rounding). If the investor exercises the rights at a subscription cost of GBP10, the total cost would be GBP10 + GBP6.67 = GBP16.67. In return for this expenditure, the investor will receive a new share, which is worth GBP16.67.

TABLE 20.3   Regional Power Company Rights Offering

Initial position	
Number of shares	1 million
Share price	GBP20
Value of firm	GBP20 million
Terms of offer	
Subscription price	GBP10
Number of rights issued	1 million
Number of rights for a share	2
After offer	
Number of shares	1.5 million
Share price	GBP16.67
Value of firm	GBP25 million
Value of one right	GBP20 − GBP16.67 = GBP3.33
	or (GBP16.67 − GBP10)/2 = GBP3.33

In many countries, the parlance is slightly different. One would need two rights to subscribe for a new share. As we learned above, one right is worth GBP3.33. Two rights, in this case, enable one to purchase one new share. The stock market might talk in terms of one new share 'nil paid' being priced at GBP6.67. Indeed, this is the more usual phraseology in Britain.

Of course, referring back to our example, outside investors can also buy Regional Power shares directly at GBP16.67 per share. In an efficient stock market, it will make no difference whether new shares are obtained via rights or via direct purchase.

Effects on Shareholders

Shareholders can exercise their rights or sell them. In either case, the shareholder will neither win nor lose by the rights offering. The hypothetical holder of two shares of Regional Power has a portfolio worth GBP40. If the shareholder exercises the rights, he or she ends up with three shares worth a total of GBP50. In other words, by spending GBP10, the investor increases the value of the holding by GBP10, which means that he or she is neither better nor worse off.

On the other hand, a shareholder who sells the two rights for GBP3.33 each (or sells one Regional Power share 'nil paid') obtains GBP3.33 $\times$ 2 = GBP6.67 in cash.

Because the two shares held previously are each worth GBP16.67, the holdings are valued at

$$
\begin{array}{lll}
\text{Shares} & = 2 \times \text{GBP16.67} = & \text{GBP33.33} \\
\text{Sold rights} & = 2 \times \text{GBP3.33} \ \ = & \text{GBP6.67} \\
\text{Total} & = & \text{GBP40.00}
\end{array}
$$

The new GBP33.33 market value plus GBP6.67 in cash is exactly the same as the original holding of GBP40. Thus, shareholders can neither lose nor gain from exercising or selling rights.

It is obvious that the new market price of the firm's shares will be lower after the rights offering than it was before the rights offering. The lower the subscription price, the greater the price decline of a rights offering. However, our analysis shows that the shareholders have suffered no loss because of the rights offering.

If a shareholder ignores the offer, he or she may lose money. However, in many countries there are rules to cover this eventuality. Companies will sell the rights not taken up on behalf of the non-subscribing shareholders and remit the proceeds to them (less any dealing cost).

The Underwriting Arrangements

Undersubscription can occur if investors throw away rights or if bad news causes the market price of the shares to fall below the subscription price. To ensure against these possibilities, rights offerings are often arranged with **standby underwriting**. Here, the underwriter makes a firm commitment to purchase the unsubscribed portion of the issue at the subscription price less a small take-up fee. The underwriter usually receives a **standby fee** as compensation for his or her risk-bearing function.

In practice, the subscription price is usually set well below the current market price, making the probability of a rights failure quite small. Though a relatively small percentage (often well below 10 per cent) of shareholders fail to exercise valuable rights, shareholders may be allowed to purchase unsubscribed shares at the subscription price. This **oversubscription privilege** reduces the likelihood that the corporate issuer would need to turn to its underwriter for help. This practice is not necessarily typical of all—or even most—European countries.

Concept Questions

• Describe the details of a rights offering.
• What are the questions that financial management must answer in a rights offering?
• How is the value of a right determined?

20.4   The Announcement of New Equity and the Value of the Firm

It seems reasonable to believe that new long-term financing is arranged by firms after positive net-present-value projects are put together. As a consequence, when the announcement of external financing is made, the firm's market value should go up. This is precisely the opposite of what actually happens in the case of new equity financing. Asquith and Mullins, Masulis and Korwar, and Mikkelson and Partch have all found that the market value of existing equity drops on the announcement of a new issue of ordinary shares.[3] Plausible reasons for this strange result include:

1. *Managerial Information* If managers have superior information about the market value of the firm, they may know when the firm is overvalued. If they do, they might attempt to issue new shares to third parties when the market value exceeds the correct value. This will benefit existing shareholders. However, the potential new shareholders are not stupid. They will infer overvaluation from the new issue, thereby bidding down the share price on the announcement date of the issue.

2. *Debt Capacity* The stereotypical firm chooses a debt-to-equity ratio that balances the tax shield from debt with the cost of financial distress. When the managers of a firm have special information that the probability of financial distress has risen, the firm is more likely to raise capital through shares than through debt. If the market infers this chain of events, the share price should fall on the announcement date of an equity issue.

3. *Cash Planning* A new, unexpected issue alters the cash plan of the shareholder if he or she is to take up his or her rights. At the margin, this might mean, for a significant number of shareholders, sticking with their original cash plan and letting the rights lapse with the result that such rights are sold in the market by the company on behalf of the non-subscribing shareholder. This must create some downward pressure on the share price.

Concept Question

• What are some of the reasons for the price of shares to drop on the announcement of a new equity issue?

20.5 Venture Capital

The previous sections of this chapter assume that a company is big enough and old enough to raise capital in the public equity markets, but there are many firms that have not reached that stage. These small and young firms often find it more convenient to raise funds first of all by borrowing from banks, and then raising new equity from that part of the private financial marketplace known as the market for venture capital. Venture capital can be viewed as early-stage financing of new and young firms seeking to grow rapidly.

Suppliers of Venture Capital

A number of companies, private partnerships and even wealthy individuals provide investment funds for venture-capital investment. The organizers behind these partnerships might raise capital from institutional investors, such as insurance companies and pension funds. Alternatively, a group of individuals might provide the funds to be invested ultimately with budding entrepreneurs.

---

[3] P. Asquith and D. Mullins (1986) 'Equity issues and offering dilution', *Journal of Financial Economics*, **15**; R. Masulis and A. N. Korwar (1986) 'Seasoned equity offerings: An empirical investigation', *Journal of Financial Economics*, **15**; and W. H. Mikkelson and M. M. Partch (1986) 'The valuation effects of security offerings and the issuance process', *Journal of Financial Economics*, **15**.

20.6   Bonus Issues or Scrip Issues

The other type of share issue by a company which already has a share quotation is the bonus issue or scrip or capitalization issue. These terms all mean the same thing. Often described as 'free', they are nothing of the kind. A company may decide to make a scrip issue in the ratio of one new share for each one already held. Anyone who had 1,000 shares before the issue will have 2,000 afterwards. But nothing has happened to the total value of the holding. If the shares were quoted at GBP20 before the issue and were therefore worth GBP20,000, they will be quoted at GBP10 after it and still be worth GBP20,000.

So why do companies do it? Usually it is to capitalize the company's reserves. In the past, the company may have built up various reserve items on its balance sheet, such as retained profits or share premium account. Perhaps its issued share capital on the balance sheet looks small in relation to the reserves the company has built up. So it brings accumulated reserves and issued capital back into line by issuing more shares. It is simply a bookkeeping transaction.

Companies tend not to make bonus issues when they are doing badly; the issue may be inferred as an expression of confidence in the future and the directors may well not adjust the dividend down entirely to adjust for the new shares issued. Whether this means that there is an effective rise in the price of the shares following a scrip issue is a moot point. If there is, it is because investors are reading something about directors' confidence into the decision. Thus, the theoretical movement in share price in the example above, from GBP20 to GBP10, may be to something slightly above GBP10 (bringing investors an immediate profit). Of course, had the directors merely said that they were confident about good future performance, the same result may have resulted.

20.7   Summary and Conclusions

This chapter looks closely at how equity is issued. The main points follow.

1. Shares are frequently issued to the public by a range of methods from offers for sale, public issues, placings, introductions and tenders.
2. Initial public offerings generally involve an element of underpinning.
3. Large issues have proportionately much lower costs of issuing equity than small ones.
4. Rights offerings are cheaper than general cash offers as they eliminate the problem of underpricing.
5. Venture capitalists are an increasingly important influence in start-up firms and management buyout financing.

KEY TERMS

Offer for sale 455	Initial public offering (IPO) 457
Prospectus 456	Unseasoned new issue 457
Public issue 456	Seasoned new issue 457
Placing 456	Subscription price 461
Flotation 456	Ex-rights 462
Introduction 456	Standby underwriting 464
Tender 456	Standby fee 464
Bookbuilding 456	Oversubscription privilege 464

QUESTIONS AND PROBLEMS

The Cash Offer

20.1 Suppose the Newton Company has 10,000 shares. Each share is worth CHF40, and the company's market value of equity is CHF400,000. Suppose the firm issues 5,000 new shares at the following prices: CHF40, CHF20 and CHF10. What will be the effect of each of the alternative offering prices on the existing price per share?

20.2   In 1980, a certain assistant professor of finance in the USA bought 12 initial public offerings of common stock. He held each of these for approximately one month and then sold them. The investment rule he followed was to submit a purchase order for every firm-commitment initial public offering of oil- and gas-exploration companies. There were 22 such offerings, and he submitted a purchase order for approximately USD1,000 of stock for each one. With 10 of these, no shares were allocated to this assistant professor. With five of the 12 offerings that were purchased, fewer than the requested number of shares were allocated.

The year 1980 was very good for oil- and gas-exploration company owners: for the 22 stocks that went public, the stock was selling on average for 80 per cent above the offering price within a month. Yet, this assistant professor looked at his performance record and found the USD8,400 invested in the 12 companies had grown to only USD10,100, a return of only about 20 per cent. (Commissions were negligible.) Did he have bad luck, or should he have expected to do worse than the average initial-public-offering investor? Explain.

The Announcement of New Equity and the Value of the Firm

20.3   What are the possible reasons why the share price typically drops on the announcement of a seasoned new equity issue?

The Cost of New Issues

20.4   What are the costs of new issues?

Rights

20.5   A Danish company, Bountiful Butter Processors AS (abbreviated to BBP) wants to raise equity through a rights offering. BBP has 2,400,000 ordinary shares outstanding, and must raise DKK12,000,000. The subscription price of the rights will be DKK15.
   a. How many new shares must BBP issue?
   b. How many rights will be necessary to purchase one share?
   c. What must a shareholder remit to receive one new share?

20.6   Jelly Beans NV is proposing a rights offering. There are 100,000 outstanding shares at NLG25 each. There will be 10,000 new shares issued at a NLG20 subscription price.
   a. What is the value of a right?
   b. What is the ex-rights price?
   c. What is the new market value of the company?

20.7   Superior GmbH is a manufacturer of beta-blockers. Management has concluded that additional equity financing is required to increase production capacity, and that these funds are best attained through a rights offering. It has correctly concluded that, as a result of the rights offering, share price will fall from DEM50 to DEM45 (DEM50 is the rights-on price; DEM45 is the ex-rights price, also known as the when-issued price). The company is seeking DEM5 million in additional funds with a per-share subscription price equal to DEM25. How many shares were there before the offering?

20.8   A company's shares currently sell for FRF45 per share. Last week the firm issued rights to raise new equity. To purchase a new share, a shareholder must remit FRF10 on the basis of 1 for 3.
   a. What is the ex-rights share price?
   b. What is the price of one right?
   c. When will the price drop occur? Why will it occur then?

20.9   Shares of Summit SA are currently selling at FRF13 per share. There are 1 million shares outstanding. The firm is planning to raise FRF2 million to finance a new project. What is the ex-right share price, the value of a right and the appropriate subscription prices, if
   a. two shares of outstanding shares are entitled to purchase one additional share of the new issue;
   b. four shares of outstanding shares are entitled to purchase one additional share of the new issue.
   c. How does the shareholders' wealth change from *a* to *b*?

CHAPTER 21

Long-Term Debt

The previous chapter introduced the mechanics of new long-term financing, with an emphasis on equity. This chapter takes a closer look at long-term debt instruments.

The chapter begins with a review of the basic features of long-term debt, and a description of some important aspects of publicly issued long-term bonds. We also discuss forms of long-term financing that are not publicly issued: term loans and private-placement bonds. These are directly placed with lending institutions, such as a commercial bank or a life insurance company.

All bond agreements have protective covenants. These are restrictions on the firm that protect the bondholder. We present several types of protective covenants in this chapter.

Almost all publicly issued industrial bonds have call provisions, which enable a company to buy back its bonds at a predetermined call price. This chapter attempts to answer two questions about call provisions:

1. Should firms issue callable bonds?
2. When should such bonds be called?

There are many different kinds of long-term bonds. We discuss three: floating-rate bonds, income bonds and deep-discount bonds—and analyse what types of bonds are best in different circumstances.

21.1 Long-Term Debt: A Review

Long-term debt securities are promises by the issuing firm to pay interest and principal on the unpaid balance. The *maturity* of a long-term debt instrument refers to the length of time the debt remains outstanding with some unpaid balance. Debt securities can be *short-term* (maturities of one year or less) or *long-term* (maturities of more than one year).[1] Short-term debt is sometimes referred to as *unfunded debt* and long-term debt as *funded debt*.[2] The most frequently encountered form of short- term debt is the overdraft. This is a loan from a bank which is repayable on demand. Those last two words are very important. The bank can recall its loan whenever it wishes. Because of this feature of flexibility for the bank, overdraft finance is cheaper than other forms of borrowing—all other things being equal. Clearly, it is less risky to the bank lending the money. We discuss this kind of finance further in Chapter 26, Short-Term Finance and Planning.

---

[1] In addition, people often refer to intermediate-term debt, which has a maturity of more than one year and less than three to five years.

[2] The word *funding* generally implies long-term. Thus, a firm planning to fund its debt requirements may be replacing short-term debt with long-term debt.

Features of a Hypothetical Bond

	Terms	Explanations
Amount of issue	DEM100 million	The company will issue DEM100 million of bonds
Date of issue	21/10/95	The bonds will be sold on 21/10/95
Maturity	31/12/24	The principal will be paid in 30 years
Denomination	DEM1,000	Each individual bond will pay DEM1,000 at maturity
Annual coupon	5.50	Because the denomination of each bond is DEM1,000, each bondholder will receive DEM55 per bond per year
Offer price	100	The offer price will be 100 per cent of the denomination or DEM1,000 per bond
Yield to maturity	5.50%	If the bond is held to maturity, bondholders will receive a stated annual rate of return equal to 5.5 per cent
Dates of coupon payments	31/12, 30/6	Coupons of DEM27.50 will be paid on these dates
Security	None	No security
Sinking funds	Annual; begins In 2005	The sinking funds will be sufficient to pay 80 per cent of principal, the balance to be paid at maturity
Call provision	Not callable before 31/12/05 Call price: DEM1,100	The bonds have a deferred call feature. After 31/12/05 the company can buy back the bonds for DEM1,100 per bond
Rating	Moody's Aaa	This is Moody's highest rating. The bonds have the lowest probability of default

The two major forms of long-term debt are public issue and privately placed debt. We discuss public-issue bonds first; most of what we say about them holds true for privately placed long-term debt as well. The main difference between publicly issued and privately placed debt is that private debt is directly placed with a lending institution.

There are many other attributes to long-term debt, including security, call features, sinking funds, ratings and protective covenants. The boxed material illustrates these attributes. We will learn what these features mean as we progress through this chapter.

21.2   The Public Issue of Bonds

The general procedures followed for a **public issue** of bonds are the same as those for shares, as described in the previous chapter. The offering must be approved by the board of directors. Sometimes, a vote of the shareholders is also required. Usually, a registration statement is prepared for review by the financial supervisory authorities. If accepted, the registration becomes effective and the securities are sold.

A public issue of bonds usually includes an indenture, a document not found in the case of an issue of ordinary shares. An **indenture** is a written agreement between the corporation (the borrower) and a trust company. It is sometimes referred to as the *trust deed*.[3] The trust company is appointed by the borrowing corporation to represent the bondholders. The trust company must (1) be sure the terms of the indenture are obeyed, (2) manage the sinking fund and (3) represent bondholders if the company defaults on its payments.

The typical bond indenture can be a document of several hundred pages, and it generally includes the following provisions:

1. The basic terms of the bonds
2. A description of property used as security
3. Details of the protective covenants
4. The sinking-fund arrangements
5. The call provision

Each of these is discussed below

The Basic Terms

Bonds usually have a round number *face value* which varies from one country to another. This is also called the *principal value* or the *denomination* and it is stated on the bond certificate. The *par value* (i.e. initial accounting value) of a bond is almost always the same as the face value.

Transactions between bond buyers and bond sellers determine the market value of the bond. Actual bond-market values depend on the general level of interest rates, among other factors, and need not equal the face value. The bond price is quoted as a percentage of the denomination. Though interest is paid only twice a year, interest accrues continually over the year, and the quoted prices of a bond usually include accrued interest. This is illustrated in the example below.

● **Example**

Suppose the Black and White plc has issued 1000 bonds. The amount stated on each bond certificate is GBP100. The total face value or principal value of the bonds is GBP100,000. Further suppose the bonds are currently *priced* at 100, which means 100 per cent of GBP100. This means that buyers and sellers are holding bonds at a price per bond of GBP100. If interest rates rise, the price of the bond might fall to, say, 97, which means 97 per cent of GBP100, or GBP97. ●

Suppose the bonds have a stated interest rate of 12 per cent due on January 1, 2050. The bond indenture might read as follows:

> The bond will mature on January 1, 2050, and will be limited in aggregate principal amount to GBP100,000. Each bond will bear interest at the rate of 12.0 per cent per annum from January 1, 1990, or from the most recent Interest Payment Date to which interest has been paid or provided for. Interest is payable semiannually on July 1 and January 1 of each year.

Suppose an investor buys the bonds on April 1. Since the last interest payment, on January 1, three months of interest at 12 per cent per year would have accrued.

---

[3] The terms *loan agreement* or *loan contract* are usually used for privately placed debt and term loans.

Because interest of 12 per cent a year works out to 1 per cent per month, interest over the three months is 3 per cent. Therefore, the buyer of the bond must pay a price of 100 per cent plus the 3 per cent of accrued interest (GBP3). On July 1, the buyer will receive an interest payment of GBP6. This can be viewed as the sum of the GBP3 he or she paid the seller plus the 3 months of interest, GBP3, for holding the bond from April 1 to July 1.

As is typical of industrial bonds, the Black and White bonds are registered. The indenture might read as follows:

> Interest is payable semiannually on July 1 and January 1 of each year to the person in whose name the bond is registered at the close of business on June 15 or December 15, respectively.

This means that the company has a registrar who will record the ownership of each bond. The company will pay the interest and principal by cheque mailed directly to the address of the owner of record.

When a bond is registered and with attached coupons, the bondholder must separate a coupon from the bond certificate and send it to the company registrar (paying agent). Some bonds are in **bearer** form. This means that ownership is not recorded in the company books. As with a registered bond with attached coupons, the holder of the bond certificate separates the coupon and sends it in to the company to receive payment.

There are two drawbacks to bearer bonds. First, they can be easily lost or stolen. Second, because the company does not know who owns its bonds, it cannot notify bondholders of important events. However, bearer bonds have the advantage of secrecy, because even the issuing company does not know who the bond's owners are. This secrecy is particularly vexing to taxing authorities, because tax collection on interest is difficult if the holder is unknown.

Security

Debt securities are also classified according to the *collateral* protecting the bondholder. Collateral is a general term for the assets that are pledged as security for payment of debt. For example, *collateral trust bonds* involve a pledge of identified assets held by the company.

Some bonds represent unsecured obligations of the company, where no specific pledge of property is made. Holders have a claim on property not otherwise pledged—the property that remains after mortgages and collateral trusts are taken into account.

Protective Covenants

A **protective covenant** is that part of the indenture or loan agreement that limits certain actions of the borrowing company. Protective covenants can be classified into two types: negative covenants and positive covenants. A **negative covenant** limits or prohibits actions that the company may take. Here are some typical examples:

1. Limitations are placed on the amount of dividends a company may pay.
2. The firm cannot pledge any of its assets to other lenders.
3. The firm cannot merge with another firm.

4. The firm may not sell or lease its major assets without approval by the lender.
5. The firm cannot issue additional long-term debt.

A **positive covenant** specifies an action that the company agrees to take or a condition the company must abide by. Here are some examples:

1. The company agrees to maintain its working capital at a minimum level.
2. The company must furnish periodic financial statements to the lender.

The financial implications of protective covenants were treated in detail in the chapters on capital structure. In that discussion, we argued that protective covenants can benefit shareholders because, if bondholders are assured that they will be protected in times of financial stress, they will accept a lower interest rate.

The Sinking Fund

Bonds can be entirely repaid at maturity, at which time the bondholder will receive the stated value of the bond, or they can be repaid before maturity. Early repayment is typical.

In a direct, private placement of debt, the repayment schedule is specified in the loan contract. For public issues, the repayment usually takes place through the use of a sinking fund and a call provision.

A *sinking fund* is an account managed by the bond trustee for the purpose of repaying the bonds. Typically, the company makes yearly payments to the trustee. The trustee can purchase bonds in the market or can select the company's bonds concerned randomly and purchase them, generally at face value. There are many different kinds of sinking-fund arrangements:

- Frequently, sinking funds start between 5 and 10 years after the initial issuance.
- Some sinking funds establish equal payments over the life of the bond.
- Most high-quality bond issues establish payments to the sinking fund that are not sufficient to redeem the entire issue. As a consequence, there is the possibility of a large *balloon* payment at maturity.

Sinking funds have two opposing effects on bondholders:

1. *Sinking Funds Provide Extra Protection to Bondholders*   A firm experiencing financial difficulties would have trouble making sinking-fund payments. Thus, sinking-fund payments provide an early warning system to bondholders.
2. *Sinking Funds Give the Firm an Attractive Option*   If bond prices fall below the face value, the firm will satisfy the sinking fund by buying bonds at the lower market prices. If bond prices rise above the face value, the firm will buy the bonds back at the lower face value.

The Call Provision

A *call provision* lets the company repurchase or call the entire bond issue at a predetermined price over a specified period.

Generally, the call price is above the bond's face value. The difference between the call price and the face value is the **call premium**. For example, if the call price is 105, that is, 105 per cent of say, GBP100, the call premium is 5. The amount of the call premium usually becomes smaller over time. One typical arrangement is to set the call premium initially equal to the annual coupon payment and then make it decline to zero over the life of the bond.

Call provisions are not usually operative during the first few years of a bond's life. For example, a company may be prohibited from calling its bonds for the first 10 years. This is referred to as a **deferred call**. During this period the bond is said to be **call-protected**.

Concept Questions

* Do bearer bonds have any advantage? Why might Mr 'I Like to Keep My Affairs Private' prefer to hold bearer bonds?
* What advantages and what disadvantages do bondholders derive from the provisions of sinking funds?
* What is a call provision? What is the different between the call price and the stated price?

21.3 Bond Refunding

Replacing all or part of an issue of outstanding bonds is called bond **refunding**. Usually, the first step in a typical bond refunding is to call the entire issue of bonds at the call price. Bond refunding raises two questions:

1. Should firms issue callable bonds?
2. Given that callable bonds have been issued, when should the bonds be called?

We attempt to answer these questions in this section.

Should Firms Issue Callable Bonds?

Common sense tells us that call provisions have value. First, many publicly issued bonds have call provisions. Second, it is obvious that a call works to the advantage of the issuer. If interest rates fall and bond prices go up, the option to buy back the bonds at the call price is valuable. In bond refunding, firms will typically replace the called bonds with a new bond issue. The new bonds will have a lower coupon rate than the called bonds.

However, bondholders will take the call provision into account when they buy the bond. For this reason, we can expect that bondholders will demand higher interest rates on callable bonds than on non-callable bonds. In fact, financial economists view call provisions as being zero-sum in efficient capital markets.[4] Any expected gains to the issuer from being allowed to refund the bond at lower rates will be offset by higher initial interest rates. We illustrate the zero-sum aspect to callable bonds in the following example.

● Example

Suppose Kraus Intercable GmbH intends to issue perpetual bonds of DEM1,000 face value at a 10 per cent interest rate.[5] Annual coupons have been set at DEM100. There is

---

[4] See A. Kraus (1983) 'An analysis of call provisions and the corporate refunding decision', *Midland Corporate Finance Journal*, **1**, Spring, p. 1.

[5] Perpetual bonds have no maturity date.

an equal chance that by the end of the year interest rates will do one of the following:

1. Fall to $6\frac{2}{3}$ per cent. If so, the bond price will increase to DEM1,500.
2. Increase to 20 per cent. If so, the bond price will fall to DEM500. ●

Non-callable Bond

Suppose the market price of the non-callable bond is the expected price it will have next year plus the coupon, all discounted at the current 10 per cent interest rate.[6] The value of the non-callable bond is

Value of Non-callable Bond:

$$\frac{\text{First year coupon} + \text{Expected price at end of year}}{1 + r}$$

$$= \frac{\text{DEM100} + (0.5 \times \text{DEM1,500}) + (0.5 \times \text{DEM500})}{1.10}$$

$$= \text{DEM1,000}$$

Callable Bond

Now suppose the Kraus Intercable GmbH decides to issue callable bonds. The call premium is set at DEM100 over par value and the bonds can be called *only* at the end of the first year.[7] In this case, the call provision will allow the company to buy back its bonds at DEM1,100 (DEM1,000 par value plus the DEM100 call premium). Should interest rates fall, the company will buy for DEM1,100 a bond that would be worth DEM1,500 in the absence of a call provision. Of course, if interest rates rise, Kraus would not want to call the bonds for DEM1,100, because they are worth only DEM500 on the market.

Suppose rates fall and Kraus calls the bonds by paying DEM1,100. If the firm simultaneously issues new bonds with a coupon of DEM100, it will bring in DEM1,500 (DEM100/0.0667) at the $6\frac{2}{3}$ per cent interest rate. This will allow Kraus to pay an extra dividend to shareholders of DEM400 (DEM1,500 − DEM1,100). In other words, if rates fall from 10 per cent to $6\frac{2}{3}$ per cent, exercise of the call will transfer DEM400 of potential bondholder gains to the shareholders.

When investors purchase callable bonds, they realize that they will forfeit their anticipated gains to shareholders if the bonds are called. As a consequence, they will not pay DEM1,000 for a callable bond with a coupon of DEM100.

How high must the coupon on the callable bond be so that it can be issued at the par value of DEM1,000? We can answer this in three steps.

Step 1: Determining end-of-year value if interest rates drop   If the interest rate drops to $6\frac{2}{3}$ per cent by the end of the year, the bond will be called for DEM1,100. The bondholder will receive both this and the annual coupon payment. If we let C represent the coupon on the callable bond, the bondholder gets the following at the end of the year:

$$\text{DEM1,100} + C$$

---

[6] We are assuming that the current price of the non-callable bonds is the expected value discounted at the risk-free rate of 10 per cent. This is equivalent to assuming that the risk is unsystematic and carries no risk premium.

[7] Normally, bonds can be called over a period of many years. Our assumption that the bond can only be called at the end of the first year was introduced for simplicity.

Step 2: Determining end-of-year value if interest rates rise   If interest rates rise to 20 per cent, the value of the bondholder's position at the end of the year is:

$$\frac{C}{0.20} + C$$

That is, the perpetuity formula tells us that the bond will sell at $C/0.20$. In addition, the bondholder receives the coupon payment at the end of the year.

Step 3: Solving for C   Because interest rates are equally likely to rise or to fall, the expected value of the bondholder's end-of-year position is

$$(\text{DEM}1,100 + C) \times 0.5 + \left(\frac{C}{0.20} + C\right) \times 0.5$$

Using the current interest rate of 10 per cent, we set the present value of these payments equal to par:

$$\text{DEM}1,000 = \frac{(\text{DEM}1,100 + C) \times 0.5 + \left(\dfrac{C}{0.20} + C\right) \times 0.5}{1.10}$$

C is the unknown in the equation. The equation holds if $C = \text{DEM}157.14$. In other words, callable bonds can sell at par only if their coupon rate is 15.714 per cent.

The Paradox Restated

If Kraus issues a non-callable bond, it will only need to pay a 10 per cent interest rate. By contrast, Kraus must pay an interest rate of 15.7 per cent on a callable bond. The interest-rate differential makes an investor indifferent whether he or she buys one of the two bonds in our example or the other. Because the return to the investor is the same with either bond, the cost of debt capital is the same to Kraus with either bond. Thus, our example suggests that there is neither an advantage nor a disadvantage from issuing callable bonds.

Why, therefore, are callable bonds issued in the real world? This question has vexed financial economists for a long time. We now consider four specific reasons why a company might use a call provision:

1. Superior interest-rate predictions
2. Taxes
3. Financial flexibility for future investment opportunities
4. Less interest-rate risk

Superior Interest-Rate Forecasting

Company insiders may know more about interest-rate changes on its bonds than does the investing public. For example, managers may be better informed about potential changes in the firm's credit rating. Thus, a company may prefer the call provision at a particular time because it believes that the expected fall in interest rates (the probability of a fall multiplied by the amount of the fall) is greater than the bondholders believe.

Although this is possible, there is reason to doubt that inside information is the rationale for call provisions. Suppose firms really had superior ability to predict changes that would affect them. Bondholders would infer that a company expected an improvement in its credit rating whenever it issued callable bonds. Bondholders would require an increase in the coupon rate to protect them against a call if this occurred. As a result, we would expect that there would be no financial advantage to the firm from callable bonds over non-callable bonds.

Of course, there are many non-company-specific reasons why interest rates can fall. For example, the interest-rate level is connected to the anticipated inflation rate. But it is difficult to see how companies could have more information about the general level of interest rates than other participants in the bond markets.

Taxes

Call provisions may have tax advantages if the bondholder is taxed at a lower rate than the company. We have seen that callable bonds have higher coupon rates than non-callable bonds. Because the coupons provide a deductible interest expense to the corporation and are taxable income to the bondholder, the corporation will gain more than a bondholder in a low tax bracket will lose. Presumably, some of the tax saving can be passed on to the bondholders in the form of a high coupon.

Future Investment Opportunities

As we have explained, bond indentures contain protective covenants that restrict a company's investment opportunities. For example, protective covenants may limit the company's ability to acquire another firm or to sell certain assets (for example, a division of the company). If the covenants are sufficiently restrictive, the cost of the shareholders in lost net present value can be large. However, if bonds are callable, the company can buy back the bonds at the call price and take advantage of a superior investment opportunity.[8]

Less Interest-Rate Risk

The call provision will reduce the sensitivity of a bond's value to changes in the level of interest rates. As interest rates increase, the value of a non-callable bond will fall. Because the callable bond has a higher coupon rate, the value of a callable bond will fall less than the value of a non-callable bond. Kraus has argued that, by reducing the sensitivity of a bond's value to changes in interest rates, the call provision may reduce the risk of shareholders as well as bondholders.[9] He argues that, because the bond is a liability of the corporation, the equityholders bear risk as the bond changes value over time. Thus, it can be shown that, under certain conditions, reducing the risk of bonds through a call provision will also reduce the risk of equity.

Calling Bonds: When Does It Make Sense?

The value of the company is the value of the stock plus the value of the bonds. From

---

[8] This argument is from Z. Bodie and R. A. Taggart (1978) 'Future investment opportunities and the value of the call provision on a bond', *Journal of Finance*, **33**, p. 4.

[9] A. Kraus (1983) 'An analysis of call provisions and the corporate refunding decision', *Midland Corporate Finance Journal*, **1**, Spring. Kraus points out that the call provision will not always reduce the equity's interest-rate risk. If the firm as a whole bears interest-rate risk, more of this risk may be shifted from equity-holders to bondholders with non-callable debt. In this case, equityholders may actually bear more risk with callable debt.

the Modigliani–Miller theory and the pie model in earlier chapters, we know that firm value is unchanged by how it is divided between these two instruments. Therefore, maximizing shareholder wealth means minimizing the value of the callable bond. In a world with no transactions costs, it can be shown that the company should call its bonds whenever the callable-bond value exceeds the call price. This policy minimizes the value of the callable bonds.

The preceding analysis is modified slightly by including the costs from issuing new bonds. These extra costs change the refunding rule to allow bonds to trade at prices above the call price. The objective of the company is to minimize the sum of the value of the callable bonds plus new issue costs. It has been observed that many real-world firms do not call their bonds when the market value of the bonds reaches the call price. Perhaps these issue costs are the explanation.

Concept Questions

- What are the advantages to a firm of having a call provision?
- What are the disadvantages to bondholders of having a call provision?

21.4 Bond Ratings

Firms frequently pay to have their debt rated. The two leading bond-rating firms are Moody's Investor Service and Standard & Poor's. The debt ratings depend upon (1) the likelihood that the firm will default and (2) the protection afforded by the loan contract in the event of default. The ratings are constructed from information supplied by the corporation, primarily the financial statements of the firm. The rating classes are shown in the tabulation in the box.

The highest rating debt can have is AAA or Aaa. Debt rated AAA or Aaa is judged to be the best quality and to have the lowest degree of risk. The lowest rating is D, which indicates that the firm is in default. In the 1980s, a growing part of corporate borrowing has taken the form of *low-grade bonds*. These bonds are also known as either *high-yield bonds* or *junk bonds*. Low-grade bonds are corporate bonds that are rated below *investment grade* by the major rating agencies (that is, below BBB for Standard & Poor's or Baa for Moody's).

Bond ratings are important, because bonds with lower ratings tend to have higher interest costs. However, the most recent evidence is that bond ratings merely reflect bond risk. There is no conclusive evidence that bond ratings affect risk.[10] It is not surprising that the share prices and bond prices of firms do not show any unusual behaviour on the days around a rating change. Because the ratings are based on publicly available information, they probably do not, in themselves, supply new information to the market.[11]

---

[10] M. Weinstein (1981) 'The systematic risk of corporate bonds', *Journal of Financial and Quantitative Analysis*, September; J. P. Ogden (1987) 'Determinants of relative interest rate sensitivity of corporate bonds', *Financial Management*, Spring; and F. Reilly and M. Joehnk (1976) 'The association between market based risk measures for bonds and bond ratings', *Journal of Finance*, December.

[11] M. Weinstein (1977) 'The effect of a ratings change announcement on bond price', *Journal of Financial Economics*, **5**. However, R. W. Holthausen and R. W. Leftwich (1986) 'The effect of bond rating changes on common stock prices', *Journal of Financial Economics*, **17**, September, find that bond rating downgrades are associated with abnormal negative returns of the stock of the issuing firm.

Bond Ratings

	Very high quality	High quality	Specu-lative	Very poor
Standard & Poor's	AAA AA	A BBB	BB B	CCC CC C D
Moody's	Aaa Aa	A Baa	Ba B	Caa Ca C D

At times both Moody's and Standard & Poor's adjust these ratings. S&P uses plus and minus signs: A+ is the strongest A rating and A− the weakest. Moody's uses a 1, 2 or 3 designation, with 1 indicating the strongest.

Moody's	S&P	
Aaa	AAA	Debt rated Aaa and AAA has the highest rating. Capacity to pay interest and principal is extremely strong.
Aa	AA	Debt rated Aa and AA has a very strong capacity to pay interest and repay principal. Together with the highest rating, this group comprises the high-grade bond class.
A	A	Debt rated A has a strong capicity to pay interest and repay principal. However, it is somewhat more susceptible to adverse changes in circumstances and economic conditions.
Baa	BBB	Debt rated Baa and BBB is regarded as having adequate capacity to pay interest and repay principal. Whereas it normally exhibits adequate protection parameters, adverse economic conditions or changing circumstances are more likely to lead to a weakened capacity to pay interest and repay principal for debt in this category than in higher-rated categories. These bonds are medium grade obligations.
Ba B Caa Ca	BB B CCC CC	Debt rated in these categories is regarded, on balance, as predominantly speculative. Ba and BB indicate the lowest degree of speculation, and Ca and CC the highest. Although such debt is likely to have some quality and protective characterisitcs, these are outweighed by large uncertainties or major risk exposures to adverse conditions.
C	C	This rating is reserved for income bonds on which no interest is being paid.
D	D	Debt rated D is in default, and payment of interest and/or repayment is in arrears.

Data from various editions of *Standard & Poor's Bond Guide* and *Moody's Bond Guide*.

Junk Bonds

The investment community has labelled bonds with a Standard and Poor's rating of BB and below or a Moody's rating of Ba and below as **junk bonds**. These bonds are also called *high-yield* or *low-grade* and we shall use all three terms interchangeably. Issuance of junk bonds has grown greatly in recent years, leading to increased public interest in this form of financing.

Table 21.1 presents data on junk-bond financing in the USA in the recent past. Column (1) shows the great growth in junk-bond issuance over a six-year period. Column (3) shows the default rate on junk bonds increased from 1.71 per cent in 1985 to 10.27 per cent in 1994. The losses experienced are shown in Column (5). These losses have averaged about 2.88 per cent (of par) over this 10-year time period.

In our opinion, the growth in junk-bond financing can better be explained by the activities of one man than by a number of economic factors. While a graduate student at the Wharton School in the 1970s, Michael Milkin observed a large difference between the return on high-yield bonds and the return on safer bonds. Believing that this difference was greater than what the extra default risk would justify, he concluded that institutional investors would benefit from purchases of junk bonds.

TABLE 21.1   **Junk Bonds: 1985–1994**

	(1) Par value outstanding (in USD millions)	(2) Par value of default (in USD millions)	(3) Default rate (%)	(4) Weighed price after default	(5) Default loss (%)
1994	235,000	3,418	1.45%	39.9	0.96%
1993	206,907	2,287	1.11	56.6	0.52
1992	163,000	5,545	3.40	50.1	1.91
1991	183,600	18,862	10.27	36.0	7.16
1990	181,000	18,354	10.14	23.4	8.42
1989	189,258	8,110	4.29	38.3	2.93
1988	148,187	3,944	2.66	43.6	1.66
1987	129,557	7,486	5.78	75.9	1.74
1986	90,243	3,156	3.50	34.5	2.48
1985	58,088	999	1.71	45.9	1.04
Weighted average 1985–1994			4.55		2.88

Source: E. I. Altman (1995) 'Defaults and returns on high yields bonds: Analysis through 1994', New York University Saloman Center.

His later employment at Drexel Burnham Lambert allowed him to develop the junk-bond market. Milkin's salesmanship simultaneously increased the demand for junk bonds among institutional investors and the supply of junk bonds among corporations. Corporations were particularly impressed with Drexel's vast network of institutional clients, allowing capital to be raised quickly. However, with the demise of the junk-bond market, and with Michael Milkin's conviction for securities fraud, Drexel found it necessary to declare bankruptcy.

The junk-bond market took on increased importance when these bonds were used to finance mergers and other corporate restructurings. Whereas a firm can only issue a small amount of high-grade debt, the same firm can issue much more debt if low-grade financing is allowed as well. Therefore, the use of junk bonds lets acquirers effect takeovers that they could not do with only traditional bond-financing techniques. Drexel was particularly successful with this technique, primarily because their huge base of institutional clients allowed them to raise large sums of money quickly.

At present, it is not clear how the great growth in junk-bond financing has altered the returns on these instruments. On the one hand, financial theory indicates that the expected return on an asset should be negatively related to its marketability.[12] Because trading volume in junk bonds has greatly increased in recent years, the marketability has risen as well. This should lower the expected return on junk bonds, thereby benefiting corporate issuers. On the other hand, the increased interest in junk-bond financing by corporations (the increase in the supply schedule of junk bonds) is likely to raise the expected returns on these assets. The net effect of these two forces is unclear.[13]

---

[12] For example, see Y. Amihud and H. Mendelson (1986) 'Asset pricing and the bid-ask spread', *Journal of Financial Economics*, December.

[13] The actual risk of junk bonds is not known with certainty because it is not easy to measure default rate. P. Asquity, D. W. Mullins, Jr. and E. D. Wolff (1989) 'Original issue high yields bonds: Aging analysis and defaults, exchanges and calls, *Journal of Finance*, September, show that the default rate on junk bonds can be greater than 30 per cent over the life of the bond. They look at cumulative default rates and find that of all junk bonds issued in 1977 and 1978, 34 per cent had defaulted by December 31, 1988. Table 21.1 shows yearly default rates. E. I. Altman (1990) 'Setting the record straight on junk bonds: A review of the research on default rates and returns', *Journal of Applied Corporate Finance*, Summer, shows that yearly default rates of 5 per cent are consistent with cumulative default rates of over 30 per cent.

IN THEIR OWN WORDS . . . Edward I. Altman on Junk Bonds

One of the most important developments in corporate finance over the last 15 years has been the reemergence of publicly owned and traded low-rated corporate debt. Originally offered to the public in the early 1900s to help finance some of our emerging growth industries, these high-yield/high-risk bonds virtually disappeared after the rash of bond defaults during the Depression. Recently, however, the junk bond market has been catapulted from an insignificant element in the corporate fixed income market to one of the fastest growing and most controversial types of financing mechanisms.

The term *junk* emanates from the dominant type of low-rated bond issues outstanding prior to 1977 when the 'market' consisted almost exclusively of original-issue investment-grade bonds that fell from their lofty status to a higher default risk, speculative-grade level. These so-called 'fallen angels' amounted to about $8.5 billion in 1977. At the beginning of 1994, fallen angels comprised about 17 per cent of the $240 billion publicly owned junk bond market.

Beginning in 1977, issuers began to go directly to the public to raise capital for growth purposes. Early users of junk bonds were energy-related firms, cable TV companies, airlines, and assorted other industrial companies. This type of financing is a form of securitization of what heretofore was the sole province of private placements financed by banks and insurance companies. The emerging growth company rationale coupled with relatively high returns to early investors helped legitimize this sector. Most investment banks ignored junk bonds until 1983–1984, when their merits and profit potential became more evident.

Synonymous with the market's growth was the emergence of the investment banking firm Drexel Burnham Lambert and its junk bond wizard, Michael Milken. Drexel established a potent network of issuers and investors and rode the wave of new financing and the consequent surge in secondary trading to become one of the powerful investment banks in the late 1980s. The incredible rise in power of this firm was followed by an equally incredible fall resulting first in government civil and criminal convictions and huge fines for various misdealings and finally the firm's total collapse and bankruptcy in February 1990.

By far the most important and controversial aspect of junk bond financing was its role in the corporate restructuring movement from 1985-1989. High-leverage transactions and acquisitions, such as leveraged buyouts (LBOs), which occur when a firm is taken private, and leveraged recapitalizations (debt for equity swaps), transformed the face of corporate America, leading to a heated debate as to the economic and social consequences of firms being transformed from public to private enterprises with debt/equity ratios of at least 6:1.

These transactions involved increasingly large companies, and the multibillion dollar takeover became fairly common, finally capped by the huge $25+ billion RJR Nabisco LBO in 1989. LBOs were typically financed with about 60 per cent senior bank and insurance company debt, about 25–30 per cent subordinated public debt (junk bonds), and 10–15 per cent equity. The junk bond segment is sometimes referred to as 'mezzanine' financing because it lies between the 'balcony' senior debt and the 'basement' equity.

. These restructurings resulted in huge fees to advisors and underwriters and huge premiums to the old shareholders who were bought out, and they continued as long as the market was willing to buy these new debt offerings at what appeared to be a favorable risk/return trade-off. The bottom fell out of the market in the last six months of 1989 due to a number of factors including a marked increase in defaults, government regulation against S&Ls holding junk bonds, fears of higher interest rates and a recession, and, finally, the growing realization of the leverage excesses of certain ill-conceived restructurings.

The default rate rose dramatically to 4 per cent in 1989 and then skyrocketed in 1990 and 1991 to 10.1 per cent and 10.3 per cent respectively, with about $19 billion of defaults in 1991. By the end of 1990, the pendulum of growth in new junk bond issues and returns to investors swung dramatically downward as prices plummeted and the new issue market all but dried up. The year 1991 was a pivotal year in that despite record defaults, bond prices and new issues rebounded strongly as the prospects for the future brightened.

In the early 1990s, the financial market was questioning the very survival of the junk bond market. The answer was a resounding 'yes', as the amount of new issues soared to record annual levels of $38 billion in 1992 and an incredible almost $50 billion in 1993. Coupled with plummeting default rates (under 1.5 per cent in 1993) and returns in these years between 15–20 per cent, the risk-return characteristics have been extremely favorable. The junk-bond market in the mid-1990s is a quieter one compared to the 1980s, but, in terms of growth and returns, it is healthier than ever before.

Edward I Altman is Max L. Heine Professor of Finance and Vice-Director of the Saloman Center at the Stern School of Business of New York University. He is widely recognized as one of the world's experts on bankruptcy and credit analysis as well as the high-yield or 'junk' bond market.

Blume and Keim find that, from 1977 to 1986, the average rate of return on low-grade bonds was higher than the average rate of return on high-grade corporate bonds, while the standard deviation of return on junk bonds was *lower*.[14] This suggests that junk bonds have attractive investment characteristics. However, because the data prior to 1977 are so sketchy, one cannot easily determine what effect the recent growth in the junk-bond market had on the rates of return on these bonds.

Junk-bond financing has recently created much controversy. First, because the use of junk bonds increases the firm's interest deduction, US tax authorities have registered strong disapproval. Several legislators have suggested denying interest deductibility on junk bonds, particularly when the bonds are used to finance mergers in the USA. Second, the media has focused on the effect of junk-bond financing on corporate solvency. Clearly, this form of financing permits the possibility of higher debt–equity ratios. Whether or not this increased leverage will lead to wholesale defaults in an economic downturn, as some commentators have suggested, remains to be seen. Third, US mergers have often resulted in dislocations and loss of jobs. Because junk-bond financing has played a role in mergers, it has come under much criticism. The social policy implications of mergers are quite complex, and any final judgement on them is likely to be reserved for the distant future. At any rate, junk-bond financing should not be implicated too strongly in either the social benefits or the social costs of the recent wave of mergers. Perry and Taggart point out that, contrary to popular belief, this form of financing accounts for only a few per cent of all US mergers.[15]

Concept Questions

- List and describe the different bond-rating classes.
- Why don't bond prices change when bond ratings change?

21.5   Some Different Types of Bonds

Until now we have considered plain vanilla bonds.[16] In this section, we look at some more unusual types: floating-rate bonds, deep-discount bonds and income bonds.

Floating-Rate Bonds

The conventional bonds we have discussed in this chapter have *fixed-value obligations*. That is, the coupon rate is set as a fixed percentage of the par value.

With **floating-rate bonds**, the coupon payments are adjustable. The adjustments are tied to an *interest-rate index* such as the Treasury-bill interest rate or the 30-year Treasury-bond rate. For example, in 1974 Citibank, the large US and international bank, issued USD850 million of floating-rate notes maturing in 1989. The coupon rate was set at 1 per cent above the 90-day Treasury-bill rate and adjusted semiannually.

In most cases, the coupon adjusts with a lag to some base rate. For example, suppose a coupon-rate adjustment is made on June 1. The adjustment may be from a simple average of yields on six-month Treasury bills issued during March, April and

---

[14] M. Blume and D. Keim (1987) 'Lower grade bonds: Their risk and returns', *Financial Analysts Journal,* July/August.

[15] K. Perry and R. Taggart (1988) 'The growing role of junk bonds in corporate finance', *Journal of Applied Corporate Finance*, Spring.

[16] Plain vanilla bonds, like plain vanilla ice cream, means the basic type of bond—or ice cream.

May. In addition, the majority of these *floaters* have put provisions and floor-and-ceiling provisions:

1. With a *put provision* the holder has the right to redeem his or her note at par on the coupon payment date. Frequently, the investor is prohibited from redeeming at par during the first few years of the bond's life.
2. With floor-and-ceiling provisions the coupon rate is subject to a minimum and a maximum. For example, the minimum coupon rate might be 8 per cent and the maximum rate might be 14 per cent.

The popularity of floating-rate bonds is connected to inflation risk. When inflation is higher than expected, issuers of fixed-rate bonds tend to make gains at the expense of lenders, and when inflation is less than expected, lenders make gains at the expense of borrowers. Because the inflation risk of long-term bonds is borne by both issuers and bondholders, it is in their interests to devise loan agreements that minimize inflation risk.[17]

Floaters reduce inflation risk because the coupon rate is tied to the current interest rate, which, in turn, is influenced by the rate of inflation. This can most clearly be seen by considering the formula for the present value of a bond. As inflation increases the interest rate (the denominator of the formula), inflation increases a floater's coupon rate (the numerator of the formula). Hence, bond value is hardly affected by inflation. Conversely, the coupon rate of fixed-rate bonds cannot change, implying that the prices of these bonds are at the mercy of inflation.

As an alternative, an individual who is concerned with inflation risk can invest in short-term notes, such as Treasury bills, and *roll them over*.[18] The investor can accomplish essentially the same objective by buying a floater that is adjusted to the Treasury-bill rate. However, the purchaser of a floater can reduce transactions costs relative to rolling over short-term Treasury bills, because floaters are long-term bonds. The same type of reduction in transactions costs makes floaters attractive to some corporations.[19] They benefit from issuing a floater instead of issuing a series of short-term notes.

In an earlier section, we discussed callable bonds. Because the coupon on floaters varies with marketwide interest rates, floaters always sell at or near par. Therefore, it is not surprising that floaters do not generally have call features.

Deep-Discount Bonds (also called Zero-Coupon Bonds)

A bond that pays no coupon must be offered at a price that is much lower than its face value. Such bonds are known as **original-issue discount bonds**, **deep-discount bonds**, **pure-discount bonds** or **zero-coupon bonds**. They are frequently called *zeros* for short.

Suppose DDB GmbH issues DEM1,000 of five-year deep-discount bonds when the marketwide interest rate is 10 per cent. These bonds do not pay any coupons. The initial price is set at DEM621 because DEM621 = DEM1,000$/(1.10)^5$

---

[17] See B. Cornell (1986) 'The future of floating rate bonds', in *The Revolution in Corporate Finance*, I.M. Stern and D.H. Chew, Jr. (eds), New York: Blackwell.

[18] That is, he could buy a bill, receive the face value at maturity, use these proceeds to buy a second bill, receive the face value from the second bill at maturity, and so on.

[19] Cox, Ingersoll and Ross developed a framework for pricing floating-rate notes; see J. Cox, J. Ingersoll and S.A. Ross (1980) 'An analysis of variable rate loan contracts', *Journal of Finance*, **35**, May.

Because these bonds have no intermediate coupon payments, they are quite attractive to certain investors and quite unattractive to others. For example, consider an insurance company forecasting death-benefit payments of DEM1,000,000 five years from today. The company would like to be sure that it will have the funds to pay off the liability in five years' time. The company could buy five-year zero-coupon bonds with a face value of DEM1,000.000. The company is matching assets with liabilities here, a procedure that eliminates interest-rate risk. That is, regardless of the movement of interest rates, the firm's set of zeros will always be able to pay off the DEM1,000,000 liability.

Conversely, the firm would be at risk if it bought coupon bonds instead. For example, if it bought five-year coupon bonds, it would need to reinvest the coupon payments through to the fifth year. Because interest rates in the future are not known with certainty today, one cannot be sure if these bonds will be worth more or less than DEM1,000,000 by the fifth year.

Now, consider a couple saving for their child's university education in 15 years' time. They *expect* that, with inflation, six years of college should cost DEM150,000 in 15 years. Thus, they buy 15-year zero-coupon bonds with a face value of DEM150,000.[20] If they have forecasted inflation perfectly (and if university costs keep pace with inflation), their child's tuition will be fully funded. However, if inflation rises more than expected, the tuition will cost more than DEM150,000. As an alternative, the parents might have considered rolling over government 3-month bills. Because the yields on government bills rise and fall with the inflation rate, this simple strategy is likely to cause less risk than the strategy with zeros.

The key to these examples concerns the distinction between nominal and real quantities. The insurance company's liability is DEM1,000,000 in nominal dollars. Because the face value of a zero-coupon bond is a nominal quantity, the purchase of zeros eliminates risk. However, it is easier to forecast university costs in real terms than in nominal terms. Thus, a zero-coupon bond is a poor choice to reduce the financial risk of a child's university education.

Income Bonds

Income bonds are similar to conventional bonds, except that coupon payments are dependent on company income. Specifically, coupons are paid to bondholders only if the firm's income is sufficient.

Income bonds (where they are legal) are a financial puzzle because, from the firm's standpoint, they appear to be a cheaper form of debt than conventional bonds. Income bonds provide the same tax advantage to corporations from interest deductions that conventional bonds do. However, a company that issues income bonds is less likely to experience financial distress. When a coupon payment is omitted because of insufficient corporate income, an income bond is not in default.

Why don't firms issue more income bonds? Two explanations have been offered:

1. The '*Smell of Death*' *Explanation*   Firms that issue income bonds signal to the capital markets their increased prospect of financial distress.
2. The '*Dead-Weight Costs*' *Explanation*   The calculation of corporate income is crucial to determining the status of bondholders' income, and shareholders and bondholders will not necessarily agree on how to calculate the income. This creates agency costs associated with the firm's accounting methods.

---

[20] A more precise strategy would be to buy zeros maturing in years 15, 16, 17 and 18, respectively. In this way, the bonds might mature just in time to meet tuition payments.

Although these are possibilities, the work of McConnell and Schlarbaum suggests that no truly satisfactory reason exists for the lack of more investor interest in income bonds.[21]

Concept Question

- Create an idea of an unusual bond and analyse its features.

21.6   Direct Placement Compared to Public Issues

Earlier in this chapter, we described the mechanics of issuing debt to the public. However, over one half of all long-term debt is privately placed. There are two basic forms of direct private long-term financing: term loans and private placement.

Term loans are direct business loans with maturities of between 1 year and 15 years. The typical term loan is amortized over the life of the loan. That is, the loan is repaid by equal annual payments of interest and principal. The lenders are commercial banks and insurance companies. A **private placement**, which also involves the sale of a bond or loan directly to a limited number of investors, is very similar to a term loan except that the maturity is usually longer.

Some important differences between direct long-term financing and public issues are as follows:

1. A direct long-term loan avoids costs of registration in some countries.
2. Direct placement is likely to have more restrictive covenants.
3. It is easier to renegotiate a term loan and a private placement in the event of a default. It is harder to renegotiate a public issue because hundreds of holders are usually involved.
4. Life insurance companies and pension funds dominate the private-placement segment of the bond market. Commercial banks are significant participants in the term-loan market.
5. The costs of distributing bonds are lower in the private market.

The interest rates on term loans and private placements are usually higher than those on an equivalent public issue. Hays, Joehnk and Melicher found that the yield to maturity on private placements was 0.46 per cent higher than on similar public issues.[22] This finding reflects the trade-off between a higher interest rate and more flexible arrangements in the event of financial distress, as well as the lower transaction costs associated with private placements.

Concept Questions

- What are the differences between private and public bond issues?
- A private placement is more likely to have restrictive covenants than is a public issue. Why?

---

[21] J. McConnell and G. Schlarbaum (1986) 'The income bond puzzle', in *The Revolution in Corporate Finance*, J.M. Stern and D.H. Chew, Jr. (eds), New York: Blackwell.

[22] P.A. Hayes, M.D. Joehnk and R.W. Melicher (1979) 'Determinants of risk premiums in the public and private bond market', *Journal of Financial Research*, Fall.

21.7   Summary and Conclusions

This chapter describes some important aspects of long-term debt financing.

1. The written agreement describing the details of the long-term debt contract is called an *indenture*. Some of the main provisions are security, repayment, protective covenants and call provisions.
2. There are many ways that shareholders can take advantage of bondholders. Protective covenants are designed to protect bondholders from management decisions that favour stockholders at bondholders' expense.
3. Unsecured bonds are frequently called *debentures* or *notes*. They are general claims on the company's value. If the company defaults on secured bonds, the trustee can repossess the assets. This makes secured bonds more valuable than unsecured ones.
4. Long-term bonds usually provide for repayment of principal before maturity. This is accomplished by a sinking fund. With a sinking fund, the company retires a certain number of bonds each year. A sinking fund protects bondholders because it reduces the average maturity of the bond, and its payment signals the financial condition of the company.
5. Most publicly issued bonds are callable. A callable bond is less attractive to bondholders than a non-callable bond. A callable bond can be bought back by the company at a call price that is less than the true value of the bond. As a consequence, callable bonds are priced to obtain higher stated interest rates for bondholders than noncallable bonds.

   Generally, companies should exercise the call provision whenever the bond's value is greater than the call price.

   There is no single reason for call provisions. Some sensible reasons include taxes, greater flexibility, management's ability to predict interest rates, and the fact that callable bonds are less sensitive to interest-rate changes.
6. There are many different types of bonds, including floating-rate bonds, deep-discount bonds and income bonds. This chapter also compares private placement with public issuance.

KEY TERMS

Public issue 469	Refunding 473
Indenture 470	Junk bonds 478
Bearer 471	Floating-rate bonds 481
Protective covenant 471	Original-issue discount bonds 482
Negative covenant 471	Deep-discount bonds 482
Positive covenant 472	Pure-discount bonds 482
Call premium 472	Zero-coupon bonds 482
Deferred call 473	Income bonds 483
Call-protected 473	Private placement 484

QUESTIONS AND PROBLEMS

The Public Issue of Bonds

21.1 Define the following terms:
  a. Protective covenant
  b. Negative covenant
  c. Positive covenant
  d. Sinking fund

21.2 Sinking funds have both positive and negative characteristics to the bondholders. Why?

21.3 What is a call premium? During what period of time is a bond said to be call-protected?

Bond Refunding

21.4 KIC plc plans to issue GBP5 million of perpetual bonds. The face value of each bond is GBP100. The annual coupon on the bonds is 12 per cent. Market interest rates on one-year bonds are 11 per cent. With equal probability, the long-term market interest rate will be either 14 per cent or 7 per cent next year. Assume investors are risk-neutral.

a. If the KIC bonds are non-callable, what is the theoretical price of the bonds?

b. If the bonds are callable one year from today at GBP145, will their price be greater than or less than the price you computed in part *a*? Why?

21.5 Bowdeen Manufacturing plc intends to issue callable, perpetual bonds. The bonds are callable at GBP125. One-year interest rates are 12 per cent. There is a 60 per cent probability that long-term interest rates one year from today will be 15 per cent and a 40 per cent probability that long-term interest rates will be 8 per cent. To simplify the firm's accounting, Bowdeen would like to issue the bonds at par (GBP100). What must the coupon on the bonds be for Bowdeen to be able to sell them at par?

21.6 An outstanding issue of Public Express Airlines plc bonds has a call provision attached. The total principal value of the bonds is GBP250 million and the bonds pay an annual coupon of 8 per cent of face value. The total cost of refunding would be 12 per cent of the principal amount raised. The appropriate tax rate for the company is 35 per cent. How low does the borrowing cost of Public Express need to drop to justify refunding with a new bond issue?

21.7 Margret Kimberly, CFO of Purple Star Inc., a US company, is considering whether or not to refinance the two currently outstanding corporate bonds of the firm. The first one is an 8 per cent perpetual bond with a USD1000 face value with USD75 million outstanding. The second one is a 9 per cent perpetual bond with the same face value with USD87.5 million outstanding. The call premiums for the two bonds are 8.5 per cent and 9.5 per cent of the face value, respectively. The transaction costs of the refundings are USD10 million and USD12 million respectively. The current interest rates for the two bonds are 7 per cent and 7.25 per cent, respectively. Which bond should Ms Kimberly recommend be refinanced? What is the NPV of the refunding?

Some Different Types of Bonds

21.8 What is a junk bond? What are some of the controversies created by junk-bond financing?

21.9 Describe the following types of bonds:

a. Floating rate

b. Deep discount

c. Income

CHAPTER 22 Options and Corporate Finance

Options are special contractual arrangements giving the owner the right to buy or sell an asset at a fixed price at any time on or before a given date. Share options, the most familiar type, are options to buy and sell shares. Share options are frequently referred to as stock options. Both terms have the same meaning. Stock options are traded on numerous organized stock exchanges.

Corporate securities are very similar to the stock options that are traded on organized exchanges. Almost every issue of corporate bonds and stocks has option features. In addition, capital-structure decisions and capital-budgeting decisions can be viewed in terms of options.

We start this chapter with a description of different types of publicly traded options. We identify and discuss the factors that determine their values. Next, we show how common stocks and bonds can be thought of as options on the underlying value of the firm. This leads to several new insights concerning corporate finance. For example, we show how certain corporate decisions can be viewed as options.

22.1 Options

An **option** is a contract giving its owner the right to buy or sell an asset at a fixed price on or before a given date. For example, an option on a building might give the buyer the right to buy the building for DEM1 million on or at any time before the Saturday prior to the third Wednesday in January 2010. Options are a unique type of financial contract because they give the buyer the right, but not the obligation, to do something. The buyer uses the option only if it is a smart thing to do so; otherwise the option can be thrown away.

There is a special vocabulary associated with options. Here are some important definitions:

1. **Exercising the Option**   The act of buying or selling the underlying asset via the option contract is referred to as *exercising the option*.
2. **Strike or Exercise Price**   The fixed price in the option contract at which the holder can buy or sell the underlying asset is called the *strike price or exercise price*.
3. **Expiration Date**   The maturity date of the option is referred to as the *expiration date*. After this date, the option is dead.
4. **American and European Options**   An American option may be exercised anytime up to the expiration date. A European option differs from an American option in that it can be exercised only on the expiration date.

22.2   Call Options

The most common type of option is a **call option**. A call option gives the owner the right to buy an asset at a fixed price during a particular time period. There is no restriction on the kind of asset, but the most common ones traded on exchanges are options on shares and bonds. Usually, the assets involved are ordinary shares.

For example, call options on XYZ GmbH shares can be purchased on the Frankfurt Stock Exchange. XYZ does not issue (that is, sell) call options on its ordinary shares. Instead, individual investors are the original buyers and sellers of call options on XYZ ordinary shares. A representative call option on XYZ enables an investor to buy 100 shares of XYZ on or before July 15, 19XX, at an exercise price of DEM150. This is a valuable option if there is some probability that the price of XYZ ordinary shares will exceed DEM150 on or before July 15, 19XX.

Virtually all stock-option contracts specify that the exercise price and number of shares be adjusted for stock splits and stock dividends. Suppose that XYZ shares were selling for DEM180 on the day the option was purchased. Further suppose that the next day it split 6 for 1. Each share would drop in price to DEM30, and the probability that the stock would rise over DEM150 per share in the near future becomes very remote. To protect the option holder from such an occurrence, call options are typically adjusted for stock splits and stock dividends. In the case of a 6-for-1 split, the exercise price would become DEM25 (DEM150/6). Furthermore, the option contract would now include 600 shares, instead of the original 100 shares.[1]

The Value of a Call Option at Expiration

What is the value of a call-option contract on ordinary shares at expiration? The answer depends on the value of the underlying shares at expiration.

We shall define S_T as the market price of the underlying shares on the expiration date, T. Of course, this price is not known prior to expiration. Suppose that a particular call option can be exercised one year from now at the exercise price of DEM50. If the value of the ordinary shares at expiration, S_T, is greater than the exercise price of DEM50, the option will be worth the difference, S_T − DEM50. When S_T > DEM50, the call is said to be *in the money*.

For example, suppose the share price on expiration day is DEM60. The option holder has the right to buy the share from the option seller for DEM50.[2] Because the share is selling in the market for DEM60, the option holder will exercise the option, that is, buy the share for DEM50. If he wants to, he can then sell the share for DEM60 and pocket the difference of DEM10 (DEM60 − DEM50).[3]

Of course, it is also possible that the value of the share will turn out to be less than the exercise price. If S_T < DEM50, the call is *out of the money*. The holder will not exercise in this case. For example, if the share price at expiration date is DEM40, no rational investor would exercise. Why pay DEM50 for a share worth only DEM40? Because the option holder has no obligation to exercise the call, he can *walk away*

---

[1] No adjustment is made for the payment by XYZ of cash dividends to shareholders. This failure to adjust hurts holders of call options, though, of course, they should know the terms of option contracts before buying.

[2] We use *buyer, owner* and *holder* interchangeably.

[3] This example assumes that the call lets the holder purchase one share at DEM50. In reality, a call lets the holder purchase 100 shares @ DEM50 per share. The profit would then equal DEM1,000 [(DEM60 − DEM50) × 100].

from the option. As a consequence, if $S_T >$ DEM50 on the expiration date, the value of the call option will be 0. In this case, the value of the call option is not $S_T -$ DEM50, as it would be if the holder of the call option had the *obligation* to exercise the call. The payoff of a call option at expiration is

	Payoff on the Expiration Date	
	If $S_T \le$ DEM50	If $S_T >$ DEM50
Call-option value:	0	$S_T -$ DEM50

Figure 22.1 plots the value of the call at expiration against the value of the share. It is referred to as the *hockey-stick diagram* of call-option values. If $S_T <$ DEM50, the call is out of the money and worthless. If $S_T >$ DEM50, the call is in the money and rises one-for-one with increases in the share price. Notice that the call can never have a negative value. It is a *limited-liability* instrument, which means that all the holder can lose is the initial amount he paid for it.

● **Example**

Suppose Herr Optimist holds a one-year call option for 100 shares of XYZ GmbH. It is a European call option and can be exercised at DEM150 per share. Assume that the expiration date has arrived. What is the value of the XYZ call option on the expiration date? If XYZ is selling for DEM200 per share, Herr Optimist can exercise the option—purchase 100 shares of XYZ at DEM150 per share—and then immediately sell the shares at DEM200. Herr Optimist will have made DEM5,000 (100 shares × DEM50).

Instead, assume that XYZ is selling for DEM100 per share on the expiration date. If Herr Optimist still holds the call option, he will throw it away. The value of the XYZ call on the expiration date will be zero in this case. ●

Concept Questions

• What is a call option?
• How is a call option's price related to the underlying stock price at the expiration date?

FIGURE 22.1   The Value of a Call Option on the Expiration Date

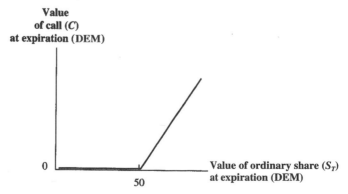

If $S_T >$ DEM50, then call-option value $= S_T -$ DEM50. If $S_T \le$ DEM50, then call-option value $= 0$.

 A call option gives the owner the right to *buy* an asset at a fixed price during a particular time period.

22.3   Put Options

A **put option** can be viewed as the opposite of a call option. Just as a call gives the holder the right to buy shares at a fixed price, a put gives the holder the right to *sell* shares for a fixed exercise price.

The Value of a Put Option at Expiration

The circumstances that determine the value of a put option are the opposite of those for a call option, because a put option gives the holder the right to sell shares. Let us assume that the exercise price of the put is DEM50. If the price, S_T, of the underlying ordinary shares at expiration is greater than the exercise price, it would be foolish to exercise the option and sell shares at DEM50. In other words, the put option is worthless if $S_T >$ DEM50. The put is out of the money in this case. However, if $S_T <$ DEM50, the put is in the money. It will pay to buy shares at S_T and use the option to sell shares at the exercise price of DEM50. For example, if the share price at expiration is DEM40, the holder should buy the shares in the open market at DEM40. By immediately exercising, he receives DEM50 for the sale. His profit is DEM10 (DEM50 − DEM40).

The payoff of a put option at expiration is

	Payoff on the Expiration Date	
	If $S_T <$ DEM50	If $S_T \geq$ DEM50
Put-option value:	DEM50 − S_T	0

Figure 22.2 plots the values of a put option for all possible values of the underlying stock. It is instructive to compare Figure 22.2 with Figure 22.1 which shows the call option. The call option is valuable whenever the stock is above the exercise price, and the put is valuable when the stock price is below the exercise price.

FIGURE 22.2   The Value of a Put Option on the Expiration Date

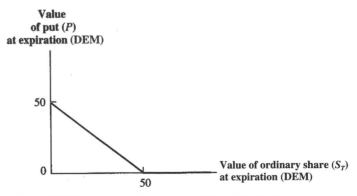

If $S_T \geq$ DEM50, then put-option value = 0. If $S_T <$ DEM50, then. put-option value = DEM50 − S_T.
   A put option gives the owner the right to *sell* an asset at a fixed price during a particular time period.

● **Example**
Frau Pessimist feels quite certain that ABC GmbH will fall from its current DEM160-per-share price. She buys a put. Her put-option contract gives her the right to sell 100 shares of ABC at DEM150 per share one year from now. If the price of ABC is DEM200 on the expiration date, she will tear up the put option contract because it is worthless. That is, she will not want to sell shares worth DEM200 for the exercise price of DEM150.

On the other hand, if ABC is selling for DEM100 on the expiration date, she will exercise the option. Frau Pessimist has the right to sell 100 shares of ABC for DEM150 per share. In this case, she can buy 100 shares of ABC in the market for DEM100 per share and turn around and sell the shares at the exercise price of DEM150 per share. Her profit will be DEM5,000 (100 shares × DEM50). The value of the put option on the expiration date therefore will be DEM5,000. ●

Concept Questions

• What is a put option?
• How is a put option related to the underlying share price at expiration date?

22.4   Writing Options

An investor who *writes* (or sells) a call on ordinary shares promises to deliver shares of it if required to do so by the call-option holder. Notice that the seller is *obligated* to do so. The seller of a call option obtains a cash payment from the holder (or buyer) at the time the option is bought. If, at the expiration date, the price of the ordinary share is below the exercise price, the call option will not be exercised and the seller's liability is zero.

If, at the expiration date, the price of the ordinary share is greater than the exercise price, the holder will exercise the call and the seller must give the holder shares in exchange for the exercise price. The seller loses the difference between the share price and the exercise price. For example, assume that the share price is DEM60 and the exercise price is DEM50. Knowing that exercise is imminent, the option seller buys shares in the open market at DEM60. Because he is obligated to sell at DEM50, he loses DEM10 (DEM50 − DEM60).

Conversely, an investor who sells a put on ordinary shares agrees to purchase shares if the put holder should so request. The seller loses on this deal if the share price falls below the exercise price and the holder puts the shares to the seller. For example, assume that the share price is DEM40 and the exercise price is DEM50. The holder of the put will exercise in this case. In other words, he will sell the underlying shares at the exercise price of DEM50. This means that the seller of the put must buy the underlying shares at the exercise price of DEM50. Because the share is only worth DEM40, the loss here is DEM10 (DEM40 − DEM50).

The values of the 'sell-a-call' and 'sell-a-put' positions are depicted in Figure 22.3. The graph on the lefthand side of the figure shows that the seller of a call loses nothing when the share price at expiration date is below DEM50. However, the seller loses a mark for every mark that the share price rises above DEM50. The graph in the centre of the figure shows that the seller of a put loses nothing when the share price at expiration date is above DEM50. However, the seller loses a mark for every mark that the share falls below DEM50.

FIGURE 22.3   **The Payoffs to Sellers of Calls and Puts, and to Buyers of Ordinary Shares**

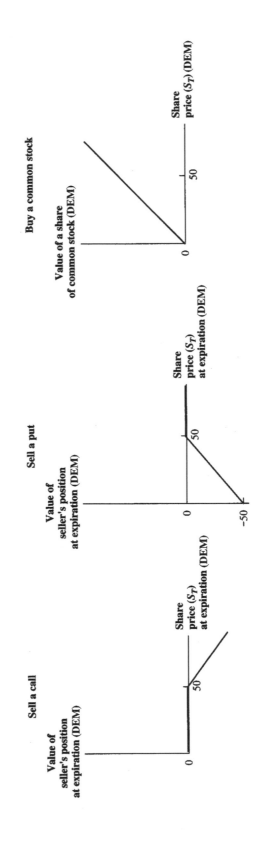

The graph also shows the value at expiration of simply buying ordinary shares. Notice that buying the shares is the same as buying a call option on the shares with an exercise price of zero. This is not surprising. If the exercise price is zero, the call holder can buy the shares for nothing, which is really the same as owning it.

22.5   Reading the *Financial Times*

Now that we understand the definitions for calls and puts, let's see how these options are quoted. Table 22.1 presents information on the options of British Airways from the Friday, November 22, 1996 issue of the *Financial Times* (FT). The options are traded on the London International Financial Futures Exchange (LIFFE), one of a number of options exchanges. The first column tells us that the shares of British Airways closed at $559\frac{1}{2}$ pence per share on the previous day (Thursday, November 21, 1996). Now consider the second and third columns. Thursday's closing price for an option maturing at the end of January 1997 with a strike price of 550 pence was $57\frac{1}{2}$ pence. Because the option is sold as a 1000-share contract, the cost of the contract is GBP575 ($1000 \times 57\frac{1}{2}$p) before commissions. The call maturing in January 1997 with an exercise price of 600p closed at $24\frac{1}{2}$p.

The last three columns display quotes on puts. For example, a put maturing in January 1997 with an exercise price of 550p sells at $3\frac{1}{2}$p.

TABLE 22.1   Information on the Options of British Airways

		LIFFE					
		Calls			**Puts**		
Option & *London close*	*Strike* *price*	*Jan.*	*Apr.*	*Jul.*	*Jan.*	*Apr.*	*Jul.*
British Airways							
$559\frac{1}{2}$	550	$57\frac{1}{2}$	$71\frac{1}{2}$	$79\frac{1}{2}$	$3\frac{1}{2}$	9	16
$559\frac{1}{2}$	600	$24\frac{1}{2}$	$40\frac{1}{2}$	$48\frac{1}{2}$	19	27	$35\frac{1}{2}$

Data from *Financial Times*, November 22, 1996

22.6   Combinations of Options

Puts and calls can serve as building blocks for more complex option contracts. For example, Figure 22.4 illustrates the payoff from buying a put option on a share and simultaneously buying the share.

If the share price is greater than the exercise price, the put option is worthless, and the value of the combined position is equal to the value of the ordinary share. If instead the exercise price is greater than the share price, the decline in the value of the shares will be exactly offset by the rise in value of the put.

Note that the combination of buying a put and buying the underlying share has the same *shape* in Figure 22.4 as the call purchase in Figure 22.1. Furthermore, the shape of the combination strategy in Figure 22.4 is the *mirror image* of the shape of the call sale in the upper lefthand corner of Figure 22.3. This suggests the following possibility:

> One strategy in the options market may offset another strategy, resulting in a riskless return.

FIGURE 22.4   **Payoffs to the Combination of Buying Puts and Buying Stock**

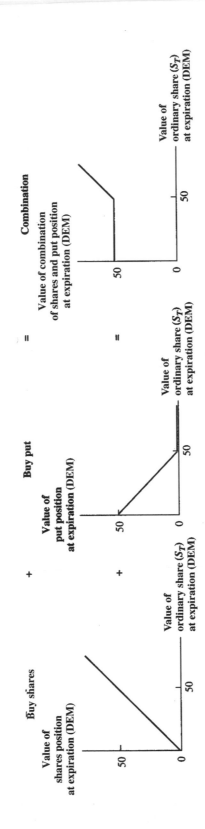

This possibility is in fact true, as evidenced by the following example.

● **Example**
Both the exercise price of the call and the exercise price of the put of Breitner GmbH are DEM55. Both options are European, so they cannot be exercised prior to expiration. The expiration date is one year from today. The share price is currently DEM44. At the expiration date, the stock will be at either DEM58 or DEM34. ●

The Offsetting Strategy   Suppose you pursue the following strategy:

> Buy the stock
> Buy the put
> Sell the call

The payoffs at expiration are

Payoffs on the Expiration Date

Initial transaction	Share price rises to DEM58	Share price falls to DEM34
Buy an ordinary share	DEM58	DEM34
Buy a put	0 (You let put expire.)	DEM21 = DEM55 − DEM34
Sell a call	−DEM3 = −(DEM58 − DEM55)	0 (Holder lets call expire)
Total	DEM55	DEM55

Note that, when the share price falls, the put is in the money and the call expires without being exercised. When the share price rises, the call is in the money and you let the put expire. The major point is that you end up with DEM55 in either case.

There is no risk to this strategy. While this result may bother students—or even shock some—it is actually quite intuitive. We pointed out earlier that the graph of the strategy of buying both a put and the underlying shares is the mirror image of the graph from the strategy of selling the call. Thus, combining both strategies, as we did in the example, should eliminate all risk.

The above payoff diagram separately valued each asset at the expiration date. Actually, a discussion of the actual exercise process may simplify things, because here the share is always linked with an option. Consider the following strategy tabulation:

Strategies on the Expiration Date

Share price rises to DEM58		Share price falls to DEM34	
You let put expire	0	Call expires	0
Call is exercised against you, obligating you to sell the share you own and receive the exercise price of	DEM55	You choose to exercise put, that is, you sell the share you own at the exercise price of	DEM55
Total	DEM55	Total	DEM55

Again, we show the riskless nature of the strategy. Regardless of the price movement of the share, exercise entails surrendering the share for DEM55.

Though we have specified the payoffs at expiration, we have ignored the earlier investment that you made. To remedy this, suppose that you originally pay DEM44 for the share and DEM7 for the put and receive DEM1 for selling the call.[4] In addition, the riskless interest rate is 10 per cent.

You have paid

$$-\text{DEM50} = \quad\quad -\text{DEM44} \quad\quad\quad -\text{DEM7} \quad\quad\quad +\text{DEM1}$$

| | Share purchase | Purchase of put | Sale of call |

Because you pay DEM50 today and are guaranteed DEM55 in one year, you are just earning the interest rate of 10 per cent. Thus, the prices in this example allow no possibility of arbitrage or easy money. Conversely, if the put sold for only DEM6, your initial investment would be DEM49. You would then have a non-equilibrium return of 12.2 per cent (DEM55/DEM49 − 1) over the year.

It can be proved that, in order to prevent arbitrage, the prices at the time you take on your original position must conform to the following fundamental relationship:

Put-call :	Value of	+	Value of	−	Value of	=	Present value of
parity	share		put		call		exercise price
	DEM44	+	DEM7	−	DEM1	=	DEM50 = DEM55/1.10

This result is called **put-call parity**. It shows that the values of a put and a call with the same exercise price and same expiration date are precisely related to each other. It holds generally, not just in the specific example we have chosen.[5]

Concept Question

- What is put-call parity?

22.7   Valuing Options

In the last section, we determined what options are worth on the expiration date. Now we wish to determine the value of options when you buy them well before expiration.[6] We begin by considering the upper and lower bounds on the value of a call.

Bounding the Value of a Call

Consider an American call that is in the money prior to expiration. For example, assume that the share price is DEM60 and the exercise price is DEM50. In this case, the option cannot sell below DEM10. To see this, note the simple strategy if the option sells at, say, DEM9.

---

[4] Note that the options are both European. An American put must sell for more than DEM11 (DEM55 − DEM44). That is, if the price of an American put is only DEM7, one would buy the put, buy the share and exercise immediately, generating an immediate arbitrage profit of DEM4 (−DEM7 − DEM44 + DEM55).

[5] However, the formula is applicable only when both the put and the call have the same expiration date and the same exercise price.

[6] Our discussion in this section is of American options, because they are traded in the real world. As necessary, we will indicate differences for European calls.

Date		Transaction	
Today	(1)	Buy call	−DEM9
Today	(2)	Exercise call, that is, buy underlying share at exercise price	−DEM50
Today	(3)	Sell stock at current market price	+DEM60
Arbitrage profit			+DEM1

The type of profit that is described in this transaction is an *arbitrage* profit. Arbitrage profits come from transactions that have no risk or cost and cannot occur regularly in normal, well-functioning financial markets. The excess demand for these options would quickly force the option price up to at least DEM10 (DEM60 − DEM50).[7]

Of course, the price of the option is likely to sell above DEM10. Investors will rationally pay more than DEM10 because of the possibility that the share price will rise above DEM60 before expiration. Is there an upper boundary for the option price as well? It turns out that the upper boundary is the price of the underlying share. That is, an option to buy ordinary shares cannot have a greater value than the ordinary share itself. A call option can be used to buy ordinary shares with a payment of an exercise price. It would be foolish to buy shares this way if the shares could be purchased directly at a lower price. The upper and lower bounds are represented in Figure 22.5.

FIGURE 22.5   The Upper and Lower Boundaries of Call-Option Values

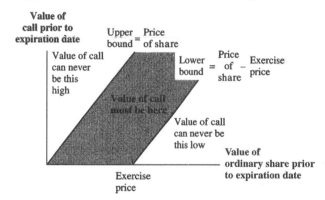

The precise option value will depend on five factors:
1. Exercise price
2. Expiration date
3. Share price
4. Risk-free interest rate
5. Variance of the share

The Factors Determining Call-Option Values

The previous discussion indicated that the price of a call option must fall somewhere in the shaded region of Figure 22.5. We will now determine more precisely where in the shaded region it should be. The factors that determine a call's value can be broken into two sets. The first set contains the features of the option contract. The two basic contractual features are the expiration price and the exercise date. The second set of factors affecting the call price concerns characteristics of the share and the market.

---

[7] It should be noted that this lower bound is strictly true for an American option, but not for a European option.

Exercise Price

It should be obvious that if all other things are held constant, the higher the exercise price, the lower the value of a call option. However, the value of a call option cannot be negative, no matter how high we set the exercise price. Furthermore, as long as there is some possibility that the price of the underlying asset will exceed the exercise price before the expiration date, the option will have value.

Expiration Date

The value of an American call option must be at least as great as the value of an otherwise identical option with a shorter term to expiration. Consider two American calls: One has a maturity of nine months and the other expires in six months. Obviously, the nine-month call has the same rights as the six-month call, and also has an additional three months within which these rights can be exercised. It cannot be worth less and will generally be more valuable.[8]

Share Price

Other things being equal, the higher the share price, the more valuable the call option will be. This is obvious, and is illustrated in any of our figures that plot the call price against the share price at expiration.

Now consider Figure 22.6, which shows the relationship between the call price and the share price prior to expiration. The curve indicates that the call price increases as the share price increases. Furthermore, it can be shown that the relationship is represented, not by a straight line, but by a *convex* curve. That is, the increase in the call price for a given change in the share price is greater when the share price is high than when the share price is low.

FIGURE 22.6   Value of a Call as a Function of Share Price

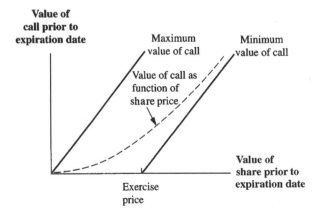

The call price is positively related to the share price. In addition, the change in the call price for a given change in the share price is greater when the share price is high than when it is low.

---

[8] This relationship need not hold for a European call option. Consider a firm with two otherwise identical European call options, one expiring at the end of May and the other expiring a few months later. Further assume that a *huge* dividend is paid in early June. If the first call is exercised at the end of May, its holder will receive the underlying share. If he does not sell the share, he will receive the large dividend shortly thereafter. However, the holder of the second call will receive the share through exercise after the dividend is paid. Because the market knows that the holder of this option will miss the dividend, the value of the second call option could be less than the value of the first.

The Key Factor: The Variability of the Underlying Asset

The greater the variability of the underlying asset, the more valuable the call option will be. Consider the following example. Suppose that just before the call expires, the share price will be either DEM100 with probability 0.5 or DEM80 with probability 0.5. What will be the value of a call with an exercise price of DEM110? Clearly, it will be worthless, because no matter what happens to the share, its price will always be below the exercise price.

Now let us see what happens if the share is more variable. Suppose that we add DEM20 to the best case and take DEM20 away from the worst case. Now the share has a one-half chance of being worth DEM60 and a one-half chance of being worth DEM120. We have spread the share returns, but, of course, the expected value of the share has stayed the same:

$$(\tfrac{1}{2} \times \text{DEM80}) + (\tfrac{1}{2} \times \text{DEM100}) = \text{DEM90} = (\tfrac{1}{2} \times \text{DEM60}) + (\tfrac{1}{2} \times \text{DEM120})$$

Notice that the call option now has value, because there is a one-half chance that the share price will be DEM120, or DEM10 above the exercise price of DEM110. This illustrates a very important point. There is a fundamental distinction between holding an option on an underlying asset and holding the underlying asset. If investors in the marketplace are risk-averse, a rise in the variability of the share will decrease its market value. However, the holder of a call receives payoffs from the positive tail of the probability distribution. As a consequence, a rise in the variability in the underlying share increases the market value of the call.

This result can also be seen from Figure 22.7. Consider two shares, *A* and *B*, each of which is normally distributed. For each security, the figure illustrates the probability of different share prices on the expiration date.[9] As can be seen from the figures, share *B* has more volatility than does share *A*. This means that share *B* has higher probability

---

FIGURE 22.7   Distribution of Ordinary Share Price at Expiration for Both Security *A* and Security *B*. Options on the Two Securities have the Same Exercise Price

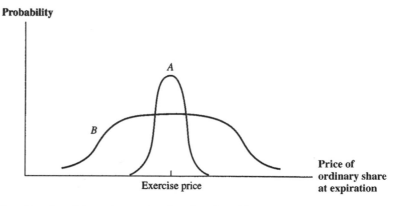

The call on share *B* is worth more than the call on share *A* because share *B* is more volatile. At expiration, a call that is way in the money is more valuable than a call that is way out of the money. However, at expiration, a call way out of the money is worth zero, just as is a call slightly out of the money.

---

[9] This graph assumes that, for each security, the exercise price is equal to the expected share price. This assumption is employed merely to facilitate the discussion. It is not needed to show the relationship between a call's value and the volatility of the underlying share.

of both abnormally high returns and abnormally low returns. Let us assume that options on each of the two securities have the same exercise price. To option holders, a return much below average on stock B is no worse than a return only moderately below average on share A. In either situation, the option expires out of the money. However, to option holders, a return much above average on share B is better than a return only moderately above average on share A. Because a call's price at the expiration date is the difference between the share price and the exercise price, the value of the call on B at expiration will be higher in this case.

The Interest Rate
Call prices are also a function of the level of interest rates. Buyers of calls do not pay the exercise price until they exercise the option, if they do so at all. The delayed payment is more valuable when interest rates are high and less valuable when interest rates are low. Thus, the value of a call is positively related to interest rates.

A Quick Discussion of Factors Determining Put-Option Values

Given our extended discussion of the factors influencing a call's value, we can examine the effect of these factors on puts very easily. Table 22.2 summarizes the five factors influencing the prices of both American calls and American puts. The effect of three factors on puts are the opposite of the effect of these three factors on calls:

1. The put's market price *decreases* as the share price increases because puts are in the money when the share sells below the exercise price.
2. The market value of a put with a high exercise price is *greater* than the value of an otherwise-identical put with a low exercise price for the reason given in (1) above.
3. A high interest rate *adversely* affects the value of a put. The ability to sell a share at a fixed exercise price sometime in the future is worth less if the present value of the exercise price is diminished by a high interest rate.

The effect of the other two factors on puts is the same as the effect of these factors on calls:

4. The value of an American put with a distant expiration date is greater than an otherwise identical put with an earlier expiration.[10] The longer time to maturity gives the put holder more flexibility, just as it did in the case of a call.

TABLE 22.2   Factors Affecting American Option Values

	Call option•	Put option*
Value of underlying asset (share price)	+	−
Exercise price	−	+
Share volatility	+	+
Interest rate	+	−
Time to exercise date	+	+

The signs (+, −) indicate the effect of the variables on the value of the option. For example, the two +s for share volatility indicate that an increase in volatility will increase both the value of a call and the value of a put.

[10] Though this result must hold in the case of an American put, it need not hold for a European put.

5. Volatility of the underlying share increases the value of the put. The reasoning is analogous to that for a call. At expiration, a put that is way in the money is more valuable than a put only slightly in the money. However, at expiration, a put way out of the money is worth zero, just as is a put only slightly out of the money.

Concept Questions

- List the factors that determine the value of options.
- Why does a share's variability affect the value of options written on it?

22.8   An Option-Pricing Formula

We have explained *qualitatively* that the value of a call option is a function of five variables:

1. The current price of the underlying asset, which for share options is the price of the ordinary shares
2. The exercise price
3. The time to expiration date
4. The variance of the underlying asset
5. The risk-free interest rate

It is time to replace the qualitative model with a precise option-valuation model. The model we choose is the famous Black–Scholes option-pricing model. You can put numbers into the Black–Scholes model and get values back.

The Black–Scholes model is represented by a rather imposing formula. A derivation of the formula is simply not possible in this textbook, as students will be happy to learn. However, some appreciation for the achievement as well as some intuitive understanding is in order.

In the early chapters of this book, we showed how to discount capital-budgeting projects using the net-present-value formula. We also used this approach to value stocks and bonds. 'Why', students sometimes ask, 'can't the same NPV formula be used to value puts and calls?' It is a good question because the earliest attempts at valuing options used NPV. Unfortunately, the attempts were simply not successful because no one could determine the appropriate discount rate. An option is generally riskier than the underlying share, but no one knew exactly how much riskier.

Black and Scholes attacked the problem by pointing out that a strategy of borrowing to finance a share purchase duplicates the risk of a call. Then, knowing the price of a share already, one can determine the price of a call such that its return is identical to that of the share-with-borrowing alternative.

We illustrate the intuition behind the Black–Scholes approach by considering a simple example where a combination of a call and a share eliminates all risk. This example works because we let the future share price be one of only two values. Hence, the example is called a *two-state option model*. By eliminating the possibility that the share price can take on other values, we are able to duplicate the call exactly.

A Two-State Option Model

To find the option price, we assume a market where there can never be an arbitrage possibility. To see how it works, consider the following example. Suppose the market price of a share is DEM50 and it will be either DEM60 or DEM40 at the end of the year. Further, suppose that there exists a call option for 100 shares with a one-year expiration date and a DEM50 exercise price. Investors can borrow at 10 per cent.

There are two possible trading strategies that we shall examine. The first is to buy a call on the share, and the second is to buy 50 shares and borrow a *duplicating* amount. The duplicating amount is the amount of borrowing necessary to make the future payoffs from buying stock and borrowing the same as the future payoffs from buying a call on the stock. In our example, the duplicating amount of borrowing is DEM1,818. With a 10 per cent interest rate, principal and interest at the end of the year total DEM2,000 (DEM1,818 × 1.10). At the end of one year, the future payoffs are set out as follows:

	Future Payoffs	
Initial transactions	*If share price is DEM60*	*If share price is DEM40*
1. Buy a call (100-share contract)	100 × (DEM60 − DEM50)= DEM1,000	0
2. Buy 50 shares	50 × DEM60 = DEM3,000	50 × DEM40 = DEM2,000
Borrow DEM1,818	−(DEM1,818 × 1.10) = −DEM2,000	−DEM2,000
Total from strategy 2	DEM1,000	0

Note that the future payoff structure of 'buy a call' is duplicated by the strategy of 'buy shares' and 'borrow'. These two trading strategies are equivalent as far as market traders are concerned. As a consequence, the two strategies must have the same cost. The cost of purchasing 50 shares while borrowing DEM1,818 is

Buy 50 shares	50 × DEM50 =	DEM2,500
Borrow DEM1,818 at 10%		−DEM1,818
		DEM682

Because the call option gives the same return, the call must be priced at DEM682. This is the value of the call option in a market where arbitrage profits do not exist.

Before leaving this simple example, we should comment on a remarkable feature. We found the exact value of the option without even knowing the probability that the share would go up or down! If an optimist thought the probability of an up move was very high and a pessimist thought it was very low, they would still agree on the option value. How could that be? The answer is that the current DEM50 share price already balances the views of the optimists and the pessimists. The option reflects that balance because its value depends on the share price.

The Black–Scholes Model

The above example illustrates the duplicating strategy. Unfortunately, a strategy such as this will not work in the real world over, say, a one-year time frame, because there are many more than two possibilities for next year's share price. However, the number of possibilities is reduced as the time period is shortened. In fact, the assumption that there are only two possibilities for the share price over the next infinitesimal instant is quite plausible.[11]

---

[11] A full treatment of this assumption can be found in J. Cox and M. Rubinstein (1985) *Option Markets*, Englewood Cliffs, N.J.: Prentice Hall, Ch. 5.

In our opinion, the fundamental insight of Black and Scholes is to shorten the time period. They show that a specific combination of shares and borrowing can indeed duplicate a call over an infinitesimal time horizon. Because the price of the share will change over the first instant, another combination of shares and borrowing is needed to duplicate the call over the second instant, and so on. By adjusting the combination from moment to moment, they can continually duplicate the call. It may boggle the mind that a formula can (1) determine the duplicating combination at any moment and (2) value the option based on this duplicating strategy. Suffice it to say that their dynamic strategy allows them to value a call in the real world, just as we showed how to value the call in the two-state model.

This is the basic intuition behind the Black–Scholes (BS) model. Because the actual derivation of their formula is, alas, far beyond the scope of this text, we simply present the formula itself. The formula is

Black–Scholes Model:

$$C = SN(d_1) - Ee^{-rt} N(d_2)$$

where

$$d_1 = [\ln(S/E) + (r + \tfrac{1}{2}\sigma^2)t]/\sqrt{\sigma^2 t}$$

$$d_2 = d_1 - \sqrt{\sigma^2 t}$$

This formula for the value of a call, C, is one of the most complex in finance. However, it involves only five parameters:

1. S = Current share price
2. E = Exercise price of call (some instructors and some textbooks use the notation X, not E)
3. r = Continuous risk-free rate of return (annualized)
4. σ^2 = Variance (per year) of the continuous return on the stock
5. t = Time (in years) to expiration date

In addition, there is the statistical concept:

$N(d)$ = Probability that a standardized, normally distributed, random
variable will be less than or equal to d

Rather than discuss the formula in its algebraic state, we illustrate the formula with an example.

● Example

Consider the German Company PEC GmbH. On October 4, 19X0, the PEC April 49 call option had a closing value of DEM4. The share itself is selling at DEM50. On October 4, the option had 199 days to expiration (maturity date = April 21, 19X1). The annual risk-free interest rate is 7 per cent.

The above information determines three variables directly:

1. The share price, S, is DEM50
2. The exercise price, E, is DEM49
3. The risk-free rate, r, is 0.07

In addition, the time to maturity, t, can be calculated quickly: The formula calls for t to be expressed in years.

4. We express the 199-day interval in years as $t = 199/365$

In the real world, an option trader would know S and E exactly. Traders generally view government bills as riskless, so a current quote from the *Financial Times* or a similar newspaper would be obtained for the interest rate. The trader would also know (or could count) the number of days to expiration exactly. Thus, the fraction of a year to expiration, t, could be calculated quickly. The problem comes in determining the variance of the share's return. The formula calls for the variance in operation between the purchase date of October 4 and the expiration date. Unfortunately, this represents the future, so the correct value for variance is simply not available. Instead, traders frequently estimate variance from past data, just as we calculated variance in an earlier chapter. In addition, some traders may use intuition to adjust their estimate. For example, if anticipation of an upcoming event is currently increasing the volatility of the share, the trader might adjust his estimate of variance upward to reflect this. (This problem was most severe right after the October 19, 1987, crash. The stock market was quite risky in the aftermath, so estimates using precrash data were too low.)

The above discussion was intended merely to mention the difficulties in variance estimation, not to present a solution.[12] For our purposes, we assume that a trader has come up with an estimate of variance:

5. The variance of PEC has been estimated to be 0.09 per year

Using the above five parameters, we calculate the Black–Scholes value of the PEC option in three steps:

Step 1: Calculate d_1 and d_2. These values can be determined by a straightforward, albeit tedious, insertion of our parameters into the basic formula. We have

$$d_1 = \left[\ln\!\left(\frac{S}{E}\right) + (r + \tfrac{1}{2}\sigma^2)t \right] \Big/ \sqrt{\sigma^2 t}$$

$$= \left[\ln\!\left(\frac{50}{49}\right) + (0.07 + \tfrac{1}{2} \times 0.09) \times \frac{199}{365} \right] \Big/ \sqrt{0.09 \times \frac{199}{365}}$$

$$= [0.0202 + 0.0627]/0.2215 = 0.3743$$

$$d_2 = d_1 - \sqrt{\sigma^2 t}$$

$$= 0.1528$$

Step 2: Calculate $N(d_1)$ *and* $N(d_2)$ The values $N(d_1)$ and $N(d_2)$ can best be understood by examining Figure 22.8. The figure shows the normal distribution with an expected value of 0 and a standard deviation of 1. This is frequently called the **standardized normal distribution**. We mentioned in an earlier chapter that the probability that a drawing from this distribution will be between s1 and r1 (within one standard deviation of its mean, in other words) is 68.26 per cent.

Now, let us ask a different question. What is the probability that a drawing from

---

[12] A more in-depth attempt to estimate variance can be found in Cox and Rubinstein (see ref. 11).

FIGURE 22.8   Graph of Cumulative Probability

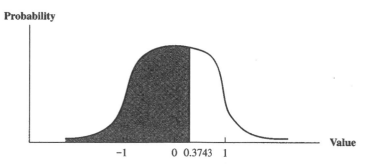

Shaded area represents cumulative probability. Because the probability is 0.6459 that a drawing from the standard normal distribution will be below 0.3743, we say that N(0.3743) = 0.6459. That is, the cumulative probability of 0.3743 is 0.6459.

the standardized normal distribution will be *below* a particular value? For example, the probability that a drawing will be below 0 is clearly 50 per cent because the normal distribution is symmetric. Using statistical terminology, we say that the **cumulative probability** of 0 is 50 per cent. Statisticians say N(0) = 50%. It turns out that

$$N(d_1) = N(0.3743) = 0.6459$$
$$N(d_2) = N(0.1528) = 0.5607$$

The first value means that there is a 64.59 per cent probability that a drawing from the standardized normal distribution will be below 0.3743. The second value means that there is a 56.07 per cent probability that a drawing from the standardized normal distribution will be below 0.1528. More generally, N(d) is the notation that a drawing from the standardized normal distribution will be below d. In other words, N(d) is the cumulative probability of d. Note that d_1 and d_2 in our example are slightly positive, so $N(d_1)$ and $N(d_2)$ are slightly greater than 0.50.

We can determine the cumulative probability from Table 22.3. For example, consider d = 0.37. This can be found in the table as 0.3 on the vertical and 0.07 on the horizontal. The value in the table for d = 0.37 is 0.1443. This value is not the cumulative probability of 0.37. One must first make an adjustment to determine cumulative probability. That is,

$$N(0.37) = 0.50 + 0.1443 = 0.6443$$
$$N(-0.37) = 0.50 - 0.1443 = 0.3557$$

Unfortunately, our table only handles two significant digits, whereas our value of 0.3743 has four significant digits. Hence, we must interpolate to find N(0.3743). Because N(0.37) = 0.6443 and N(0.38) = 0.6480, the difference between the two values is 0.0037 (0.6480 – 0.6443). Because 0.3743 is 43 per cent of the way between 0.37 and 0.38, we interpolate as[13]

$$N(0.3743) = 0.6443 + 0.43 \times 0.0037 = 0.6459$$

---

[13] This method is called *linear interpolation*. It is only one of a number of possible methods of interpolation.

TABLE 22.3   **Cumulative Probabilities of the Standard Normal Distribution Function**

d	00.00	0.01	0.02	0.03	0.04	0.05	0.06	0.07	0.08	0.09
0.0	0.0000	0.0040	0.0080	0.0120	0.0160	0.0199	0.0239	0.0279	0.0319	0.0359
0.1	0.0398	0.0438	0.0478	0.0517	0.0557	0.0596	0.0636	0.0675	0.0714	0.0753
0.2	0.0793	0.0832	0.0871	0.0910	0.0948	0.0987	0.1026	0.1064	0.1103	0.1141
0.3	0.1179	0.1217	0.1255	0.1293	0.1331	0.1368	0.1406	0.1443	0.1480	0.1517
0.4	0.1554	0.1591	0.1628	0.1664	0.1700	0.1736	0.1772	0.1808	0.1844	0.1879
0.5	0.1915	0.1950	0.1985	0.2019	0.2054	0.2088	0.2123	0.2157	0.2190	0.2224
0.6	0.2257	0.2291	0.2324	0.2357	0.2389	0.2422	0.2454	0.2486	0.2517	0.2549
0.7	0.2580	0.2611	0.2642	0.2673	0.2704	0.2734	0.2764	0.2794	0.2823	0.2852
0.8	0.2881	0.2910	0.2939	0.2967	0.2995	0.3023	0.3051	0.3078	0.3106	0.3133
0.9	0.3159	0.3186	0.3212	0.3238	0.3264	0.3289	0.3315	0.3240	0.3365	0.3389
1.0	0.3413	0.3438	0.3461	0.3485	0.3508	0.3531	0.3554	0.3577	0.3599	0.3621
1.1	0.3643	0.3665	0.3686	0.3708	0.3729	0.3749	0.3770	0.3790	0.3810	0.3830
1.2	0.3849	0.3869	0.3888	0.3907	0.3925	0.3944	0.3962	0.3980	0.3997	0.4015
1.3	0.4032	0.4049	0.4066	0.4082	0.4099	0.4115	0.4131	0.4147	0.4162	0.4177
1.4	0.4192	0.4207	0.4222	0.4236	0.4251	0.4265	0.4279	0.4292	0.4306	0.4319
1.5	0.4332	0.4345	0.4357	0.4370	0.4382	0.4394	0.4406	0.4418	0.4429	0.4441
1.6	0.4452	0.4463	0.4474	0.4484	0.4495	0.4505	0.4515	0.4525	0.4535	0.4545
1.7	0.4554	0.4564	0.4573	0.4582	0.4591	0.4599	0.4608	0.4616	0.4625	0.4633
1.8	0.4641	0.4649	0.4656	0.4664	0.4671	0.4678	0.4686	0.4693	0.4699	0.4706
1.9	0.4713	0.4719	0.4726	0.4732	0.4738	0.4744	0.4750	0.4756	0.4761	0.4767
2.0	0.4773	0.4778	0.4783	0.4788	0.4793	0.4798	0.4803	0.4808	0.4812	0.4817
2.1	0.4821	0.4826	0.4830	0.4834	0.4838	0.4842	0.4846	0.4850	0.4854	0.4857
2.2	0.4861	0.4866	0.4830	0.4871	0.4875	0.4878	0.4881	0.4884	0.4887	0.4890
2.3	0.4893	0.4896	0.4898	0.4901	0.4904	0.4906	0.4909	0.4911	0.4913	0.4916
2.4	0.4918	0.4920	0.4922	0.4925	0.4927	0.4929	0.4931	0.4932	0.4934	0.4936
2.5	0.4938	0.4940	0.4941	0.4943	0.4945	0.4946	0.4948	0.4949	0.4951	0.4952
2.6	0.4953	0.4955	0.4956	0.4957	0.4959	0.4960	0.4961	0.4962	0.4963	0.4964
2.7	0.4965	0.4966	0.4967	0.4968	0.4969	0.4970	0.4971	0.4972	0.4973	0.4974
2.8	0.4974	0.4975	0.4976	0.4977	0.4977	0.4978	0.4979	0.4979	0.4980	0.4981
2.9	0.4981	0.4982	0.4982	0.4982	0.4984	0.4984	0.4985	0.4985	0.4986	0.4986
3.0	0.4987	0.4987	0.4987	0.4988	0.4988	0.4989	0.4989	0.4989	0.4990	0.4990

$N(d)$ represents areas under the standard normal distribution function. Suppose that $d_1 = 0.24$. This table implies a cumulative probability of $0.5000 + 0.0948 = 0.5948$. If d_1 is equal to 0.2452, we must estimate the probability by interpolating between $N(0.25)$ and $N(0.24)$.

Step 3: *Calculate C*   We have

$$C = S \times [N(d_1)] - Ee^{-rt} \times [N(d_2)]$$
$$= DEM50 \times [N(d_1)] - DEM49 \times [e^{-0.07 \times (199/365)}] \times N(d_2)$$
$$= (DEM50 \times 0.6459) - (DEM49 \times 0.9626 \times 0.5607)$$
$$= DEM32.295 - DEM26.447$$
$$= DEM5.85$$

The estimated price of DEM5.85 is greater than the DEM4 actual price, implying that the call option is underpriced. A trader believing in the Black–Scholes model would buy a call. Of course, the Black–Scholes model is fallible. Perhaps the disparity between the model's estimate and the market price reflects error in the model's estimate of variance. ●

It is no exaggeration to say that the Black–Scholes formula is among the most important contributions in finance. It allows anyone to calculate the value of an option given a few parameters. The attraction of the formula is that four of the parameters are observable: the current price of the stock, S, the exercise price, E, the interest rate, r, and the time to expiration date, t. Only one of the parameters must be estimated: the variance of return, σ^2.

To see how truly attractive this formula is, note what parameters are not needed. First, the investor's risk aversion does not affect value. The formula can be used by anyone, regardless of willingness to bear risk. Second, it does not depend on the expected return on the share! Investors with different assessments of the share's expected return will nevertheless agree on the call price. As in the two-state example, this is because the call depends on the stock price and that price already balances investors' divergent views.

The assumptions for the Black–Scholes model appear to be severe:

1. There are no penalties for or restrictions on short selling.
2. Transaction costs and taxes are zero.
3. The option is European.
4. The share pays no dividends.
5. The share price is continuous, that is, there are no jumps.
6. The market operates continuously.
7. The short-term interest rate is known and constant.
8. The share price is 'lognormally' distributed.

These assumptions are the sufficient conditions for the Black–Scholes model to be correct.

We now refer to certain pieces of option market jargon. Where a call option on a share has an exercise price below the underlying share price, the holder of such a call is obviously in a profitable position. The fact that the exercise price of the call is below the share price is referred to in terms of the option being **in-the-money**. The same would be the case where the exercise price of a put option is above the underlying share price. When an option is in-the-money, it is said to have **intrinsic value**. In such circumstances, intrinsic value refers to the amount given, either, by the exercise price less the share price (if positive) for a put option, or, the share price less the exercise price (if positive) for a call option. Options that have intrinsic value are said to be in-the-money. It's easy to remember. Each begins with in.

By contrast, when a call option has an exercise price above the underlying share price, it is said to be **out-of-the-money**. Similarly, a put option on a share with an exercise price below the underlying share price would be out-of-the-money. Options which are out-of-the-money have no intrinsic value. Note, of course, that such options cannot have negative intrinsic value because were a European option to be out-of-the-money at maturity it would simply not be exercised. The option holder would not incur a loss in the sense that he or she would simply not exercise the option but let it lapse (of course, allowing for the option premium already paid, a loss could be said to have been incurred—but the option premium is clearly a sunk cost).

Where an option has time to run to maturity, the value of the option (assuming it is a call and the exercise price is below the underlying share price) will be more than $(S - E)$. The amount by which the option value exceeds $(S - E)$ is what the Black–Scholes model is all about. In all such circumstances, the amount by which the option premium exceeds intrinsic value is termed **time value**. Captured within the general expression, time value, will be the effects of time to run to maturity, volatility and the risk-free interest rate—that is, t, σ and r, respectively. An option with zero intrinsic value, but with time to run to maturity, will have time value only.

Where the exercise price of an option is equal to the underlying share price, whether it is a call option or a put, it is said to be **at-the-money**. Such options will have zero intrinsic value, but will have time value. Time value plus intrinsic value will always give the value of an option.

In circumstances where some of the eight assumptions, referred to earlier in this section, of the Black–Scholes model do not hold, a variation of the model often works. For example, the formula can be fine-tuned to account for dividends—see last paragraph of this section. Empirical studies suggest that the model, particularly when fine-tuned, does a good job in computing call-option value.

Note that the Black–Scholes option-pricing model applies to European options. It is worth mentioning that, where a share pays no dividends, an American call should be equal in terms of option premium to a European call with all other characteristics similar. The rationale for this is as follows. The value of a call option increases as the time to maturity increases. Thus, if exercised early, an American call option would lose its time value—if exercised early it would have intrinsic value only. Early exercise of an American call would seem pointless. Because an American call option should not be exercised early, its value should be the same as a European call option and the Black–Scholes model would be applicable to each.

As regards American puts, equality of price with a European put is not the case. On occasions, it can pay to exercise an American put before maturity. For example, imagine that, immediately after purchase of an American put, the share price falls to zero. In this case, there is no advantage to continuing to hold the option. It has reached its maximum value. It is better to exercise the option and invest the proceeds. This kind of situation applies, too, where the underlying share moves towards zero—it becomes 'bombed out'. This feature means that an American put will always be worth more than a European put with characteristics otherwise the same. Depending upon the situation, the difference may be significant, as in our extreme example. In other cases than this extreme, the difference is less marked. However, it remains the case that an American put might be exercised early where interest rates have moved sufficiently high to justify early exercise with reinvestment of the proceeds. This occurs where the interest-rate effect exceeds the volatility effect. Since the Black–Scholes formula does not allow for early exercise, it cannot be used to value an American put option. Note, of course, that put-call parity would not, therefore, apply to American options.

It is worth mentioning, too, that there are cases where an otherwise identical European put option, with a short time to maturity, is worth more than one with a long time to maturity. This occurs where a European put is deep in-the-money (the exercise price is a long way above the share price), maybe again the share has become 'bombed out'. The long time to expiry may have a negative influence on the premium value compared with the shorter maturity put because the longer maturity provides greater opportunity for the share to revive from being bombed out.

In the case of European options on dividend paying shares, the existing share price includes the present value of dividends during the period to maturity, to which the option holder is not entitled. Thus, to value a European option on a dividend-paying stock, one must disaggregate from the share price (S), the present value of dividends accruing before the maturity of the option.

Concept Questions

- How does the two-state option model work?
- What is the formula for the Black–Scholes option-pricing model?

22.9   An Option-Pricing Table

Earlier sections of this chapter have indicated that, for a share which pays no dividend, the five factors affecting an option's value are the exercise price, the underlying share price, the time to expiration of the option, the variance (σ^2)—or the standard deviation (σ), sometimes termed volatility—of returns on the share, and the risk-free rate of return. It is possible to bring all of these factors together to produce a table for pricing European call options (and hence put option value via put-call parity). The variability, per unit of time, of returns on a share is measured by the variance of returns, σ^2. Multiplying the variance per unit of time by the amount of time remaining gives **cumulative variance**, $\sigma^2 t$. Cumulative variance is a measure of how much things could change before time runs out and a decision must be made in relation to the option. $\sigma\sqrt{t}$ is simply the square root of cumulative variance. Of course, options for which either σ or t is zero have no cumulative variance. Were we to plot the share price dividend by the present value of the exercise price—that is the exercise price discounted at the risk-free rate of interest—against the square root of cumulative variance, given by $\sigma\sqrt{t}$, we would capture all five critical factors.

Table A.7 in Appendix A plots S/PV(E) on one axis against $\sigma\sqrt{t}$ on the other. The figure found in the appropriate part of the matrix represents a percentage of the underlying share price. This percentage multiplied by the share price gives the call option value.

● Example

Digital Couplets plc is quoted on the London stock market at a current price of GBP9.00. The problem is to value a twelve month European call option with an exercise price of GBP9.20. The estimated volatility (σ) is estimated at 12 per cent per annum and the risk-free rate is 5 per cent per annum on a continuously compounded basis.

The value of S/PV(E) can be calculated as:

$$9.00/9.20(0.9512) = 1.02845$$

Note that Table A.6 in Appendix A has been used to calculate the one year continuous discount factor at the risk-free rate of 5 per cent. The value of $\sigma\sqrt{t}$ is simply equal to:

$$0.12\sqrt{1} = 0.12$$

Since the exact value of S/PV(E) at 1.02845 does not appear in Table A.7, we have to use interpolation to value the option. The same goes for the value of $\sigma\sqrt{t}$ at 0.12. The relevant parts of the matrix, taken from Table A.7, for the purpose of interpolation, are:

S/PV(E)

		1.02	1.04
	0.10	5.0	6.1
$\sigma\sqrt{t}$			
	0.15	7.0	8.0

Interpolating downwards would give figures of 5.80 and 6.86 for a value of $\sigma\sqrt{t}$ of 0.12 against values of S/PV(E) of 1.02 and 1.04, respectively. Further interpolation between 1.02 and 1.04 to 1.02845 as a value for S/PV(E) gives a figure of 6.25 as the appropriate figure in the matrix. This figure is a percentage of the underlying share price. Thus, the value of the call option is simply:

$$GBP9.00\ (6.25\%) = GBP0.56$$

Were one to wish to value a twelve month European put option with a strike price at GBP 9.20, with all other factors identical, the put-call parity formula would enable us to do so. This is shown below:

$$Put = Call + PV(E) - S$$
$$= 0.56 + 9.20(0.9512) - 9.00$$
$$= 0.56 + 8.75 - 9.00$$
$$= GBP0.31$$

Note that it is also possible to determine the market's implied volatility (and implied variance) from Table A.7. Implied volatility relates to what the market is building into the Black–Scholes valuation for an option as a volatility factor. If the values of S, E, r, t and the amount of the option premium are known, as would typically be the case for an exchange-quoted option, the volatility that option traders are building into the option premium can be determined. In such a situation, the value of S/PV(E) can be calculated. The percentage which is given by the option premium divided by S can be calculated. Now, it is easy to read down Table A.7 for the value of S/PV(E) which has already been determined until one arrives at the figure calculated for the option premium divided by S. Reading across the matrix, this will enable a figure for $\sigma\sqrt{t}$ to be read off. Since t, the time the option has to run to maturity, is known, the value of σ, implied volatility, can be calculated.

Of course, if the data one has relate to a European put option, and if Table A.7 is to be used to determine implied volatility, then it is necessary to convert the put premium into a call price via the put-call parity formula.

Concept Questions

- What is cumulative variance?
- What is implied volatility?

22.10   Stocks and Bonds as Options

The previous material in this chapter described, explained, and valued publicly traded options. This is important material to any finance student because much trading occurs in these listed options. The study of options has another purpose for the student of corporate finance.

You may have heard the one-liner about the elderly gentleman who was surprised to learn that he had been speaking prose all of his life. The same can be said about the corporate finance student and options. Although options were formally defined for the first time in this chapter, many corporate policies discussed earlier in the text were actually options in disguise. Though it is beyond the scope of this chapter to recast all of corporate finance in terms of options, the rest of the chapter considers the implicit options in three topics:

1. Stocks and bonds as options
2. Capital-structure decisions as options
3. Capital-budgeting decisions as options

We begin by illustrating the implicit options in stocks and bonds through a simple example.

● **Example**

The Popov Company has been awarded the concessions at next year's Olympic Games in Antarctica. Because the firm's principals live in Antarctica, and because there is no other concession business in that continent, their enterprise will disband after the games. The firm has issued debt to help finance this venture. Interest and principal due on the debt next year will be USD800, at which time the debt will be paid off in full. The firm's cash flows next year are forecast as

	Popov's cash-flow schedule			
	Very successful games	*Moderately successful games*	*Moderately unsuccessful games*	*Outright failure*
Cash flow before interest and principal	USD1,000	USD850	USD700	USD550
Interest and principal	800	800	700	550
Cash flow to shareholders	USD200	USD50	0	0

As can be seen, the principals have forecast four equally likely scenarios. If either of the first two scenarios occurs, the bondholders will be paid in full. The extra cash flow goes to the shareholders. However, if either of the last two scenarios occurs, the bondholders will not be paid in full. Instead, they will receive the firm's entire cash flow, leaving the shareholders with nothing. ●

This example is similar to the bankruptcy examples presented in our chapters on capital structure. Our new insight is that the relationship between the ordinary shares and the firm can be expressed in terms of options. We consider call options first because the intuition is easier. The put-option scenario is treated next.

The Firm Expressed in Terms of Call Options

The Shareholders

We now show that shares can be viewed as a call option on the firm. To illustrate this, Figure 22.9 graphs the cash flow to the shareholders as a function of the cash flow to the firm. The shareholders receive nothing if the firm's cash flows are less than USD800; here, all of the cash flows go to the bondholders. However, the shareholders earn a dollar for every dollar that the firm receives above USD800. The graph looks exactly like the call-option graphs that we considered earlier in this chapter.

But what is the underlying asset upon which the stock is a call option? The underlying asset is the firm itself. That is, we can view the *bondholders* as owning the firm. However, the shareholders have a call option on the firm with an exercise price of USD800.

FIGURE 22.9   Cash Flow to Stockholders of Popov Corporation as a Function of Cash Flow of Firm

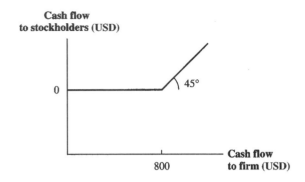

If the firm's cash flow is above USD800, the shareholders would choose to exercise this option. In other words, they would buy the firm from the bondholders for USD800. Their net cash flow is the difference between the firm's cash flow and their USD800 payment. This would be USD200 (USD1,000 − USD800) if the games are very successful and USD50 (USD850 − USD800) if the games are moderately successful.

Should the value of the firm's cash flows be less than USD800, the shareholders would not choose to exercise their option. Instead, they walk away from the firm, as any call-option holder would do. The bondholders then receive the firm's entire cash flow.

Bondholders

What about the bondholders? Our earlier cash flow schedule showed that they get the entire cash flow of the firm if the firm generates less cash than USD800. Should the firm earn more than USD800, the bondholders receive only USD800, that is, they are entitled only to interest and principal. This schedule is graphed in Figure 22.10.

In keeping with our view that the shareholders have a call option on the firm, what does the bondholders' position consist of? The bondholders' position can be described by two claims:

1. They own the firm.
2. They have written a call against the firm with an exercise price of USD800.

FIGURE 22.10   Cash Flow to Bondholders as a Function of Cash Flow of Firm

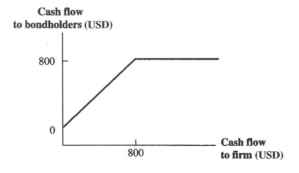

As we mentioned above, the shareholders walk away from the firm if cash flows are less than USD800. Thus, the bondholders retain ownership in this case. However, if the cash flows are greater than USD800, the shareholders exercise their option. They call the shares away from the bondholders for USD800.

The Firm Expressed in Terms of Put Options

The above analysis expresses the positions of the shareholders and the bondholders in terms of call options. We can now express the situation in terms of put options.

The Shareholders

The shareholders' position can be expressed by three claims:

1. They own the firm.
2. They owe USD800 in interest and principal to the bondholders.

If the debt were risk-free, these two claims would fully describe the shareholders' situation. However, because of the possibility of default, we have a third claim as well.

3. The shareholders own a put option on the firm with an exercise price of USD800. The group of bondholders is the seller of the put.

Now consider two possibilities:

Cash Flow Is Less than USD800   Because the put has an exercise price of USD800, the put is in the money. The shareholders 'put', that is, sell, the firm to the bondholders. Normally, the holder of a put receives the exercise price when the asset is sold. However, the shareholders already owe USD800 to the bondholders. Thus, the debt of USD800 is simply cancelled—and no money changes hands—when the stock is delivered to the bondholders. Because the shareholders give up the stock in exchange for extinguishing the debt, the stockholders end up with nothing if the cash flow is below USD800.

Cash Flow Is Greater than USD800   Because the put is out of the money here, the shareholders do not exercise. Thus, the shareholders retain ownership of the firm, but pay USD800 to the bondholders as interest and principal.

The Bondholders

The bondholders' position can be described by two claims:

1. The bondholders are owed USD800.
2. They have sold a put option on the firm to the shareholders with an exercise price of USD800.

Cash Flow Is Less than USD800   As mentioned above, the shareholders will exercise the put in this case. This means that the bondholders are obligated to pay USD800 for the firm. Because they are owed USD800, the two obligations offset each other. Thus, the bondholders simply end up with the firm in this case.

Cash Flow Is Greater than USD800   Here, the shareholders do not exercise the put. Thus, the bondholders merely receive the USD800 that is due them.

Expressing the bondholders' position in this way is illuminating. With a riskless default-free bond, the bondholders are owed USD800. Thus, we can express the risky bond in terms of a riskless bond and a put:

$$\text{Value of risky bond} = \text{Value of default-free bond} - \text{Value of put option}$$

That is, the value of the risky bond is the value of the default-free bond less the value of the shareholders' option to sell the company for USD800.

A Resolution of the Two Views

We have argued above that the positions of the shareholders and the bondholders can be viewed either in terms of calls or in terms of puts. These two viewpoints are summarized in Table 22.4. The two viewpoints can be related in terms of the put-call-parity relationship discussed earlier in this chapter:

$$\text{Value of ordinary shares} + \text{Value of put on ordinary shares} - \text{Value of call on ordinary shares} = \text{Present value of exercise price} \quad (22.1)$$

Using the results of this section, equation (22.1) can be rewritten as:

$$\underbrace{\text{Value of call on firm}}_{\substack{\text{Shareholders'} \\ \text{position in terms} \\ \text{of call options}}} = \underbrace{\text{Value of firm} + \text{Value of put on firm} - \text{Value of default-free bond}}_{\substack{\text{Shareholders' position} \\ \text{in terms of put options}}} \quad (22.2)$$

TABLE 22.4   Positions of Shareholders and Bondholders in Popov Company in Terms of Calls and Puts

Shareholders	*Bondholders*
Positions viewed in terms of call options 1. Shareholders own a call on the firm with exercise price of USD800.	1. Bondholders own the firm 2. Bondholders have sold a call on the firm to the shareholders.

Positions viewed in terms of put options
  1. Shareholders own the firm.
  2. Shareholders owe USD800 in interest and principal to bondholders.
  3. Shareholders own a put option on the firm with exercise price of USD800.
	1. Bondholders are owed USD800 in interest and principal.
	2. Bondholders have sold a put on the firm to the shareholders.

Going from equation (22.1) to equation (22.2) involves a few steps. First, we treat the firm, not the share, as the underlying asset in this section. Second, the exercise price is now USD800, the principal and interest on the firm's debt. Taking the present value of this amount at the riskless rate yields the value of a default-free bond. Third, the order of the terms in equation (22.1) is rearranged in equation (22.2).

Note that the lefthand side of equation (22.2) is the shareholders' position in terms of call options, as shown in Table 22.4. The righthand side of equation (22.2) is the shareholders' position in terms of put options, as shown in the table. Thus, put-call parity shows that viewing the shareholders' position in terms of call options is equivalent to viewing the shareholders' position in terms of put options. Now, let's rearrange terms in equation (22.2) to yield

$$\underset{\substack{\text{Bondholders' position in} \\ \text{terms of call options}}}{\underbrace{\begin{array}{c} \text{Value of} \\ \text{firm} \end{array} - \begin{array}{c} \text{Value of call} \\ \text{on firm} \end{array}}} = \underset{\substack{\text{Bondholders' position in} \\ \text{terms of put options}}}{\underbrace{\begin{array}{c} \text{Value of} \\ \text{default-free bond} \end{array} - \begin{array}{c} \text{Value of put} \\ \text{on firm} \end{array}}} \qquad (22.3)$$

The lefthand side of equation (22.3) is the bondholders' position in terms of call options, as shown in Table 22.4. The righthand side of the equation is the bondholders' position in terms of put options, as shown in Table 22.4. Thus, put-call parity shows that viewing the bondholders' position in terms of call options is equivalent to viewing the bondholders' position in terms of put options.

A Note on Loan Guarantees

In the Popov example above, the bondholders bore the risk of default. Of course, bondholders generally ask for an interest rate that is high enough to compensate them for bearing risk. When firms experience financial distress, they can no longer attract new debt at moderate interest rates. Thus, firms experiencing distress have frequently sought loan guarantees from the government. Our framework can be used to understand these guarantees.

If the firm defaults on a guaranteed loan, the government must make up the difference. In other words, a government guarantee converts a risky bond into a riskless bond. What is the value of this guarantee?

Recall that, with option pricing,

$$\begin{array}{c} \text{Value of} \\ \text{default-free bond} \end{array} = \begin{array}{c} \text{Value of} \\ \text{risky bond} \end{array} + \begin{array}{c} \text{Value of} \\ \text{put option} \end{array}$$

This equation shows that the government is assuming an obligation that has a cost equal to the value of a put option.

Our analysis differs from that of either politicians or company spokespeople. They generally say that the guarantee will cost the taxpayer nothing because the guarantee enables the firm to attract debt, thereby staying solvent. However, it should be pointed out that though solvency may be a strong possibility, it is never a certainty. Thus, at the time the guarantee is made, the government's obligation has a cost in terms of present value. To say that a government guarantee costs the government nothing is like saying a put on the shares of British Airways has no value because the share price is *likely* to rise in price.

Who benefits from a typical loan guarantee?

1. If existing risky bonds are guaranteed, all gains accrue to the existing bondholders. The shareholders gain nothing because the limited liability of companies absolves the shareholders of any obligation in bankruptcy.
2. If new debt is being issued and guaranteed, the new debtholders do not gain. Rather, in a competitive market, they must accept a low interest rate because of the debt's low risk. The shareholders gain here because they are able to issue debt at a low interest rate. In addition, some of the gains accrue to the old bondholders because the firm's value is greater than would otherwise be true. Therefore, if shareholders want all the gains from loan guarantees, they should renegotiate or retire existing bonds before the guarantee is in place.

Concept Questions

Concept Questions

- How can the firm be expressed in terms of call options?
- How can the firm be expressed in terms of put options?
- How does put-call parity relate these two expressions?

22.11   Capital-Structure Policy and Options

Recall our chapters on capital structure where we showed how managers, acting on behalf of the shareholders, can take advantage of bondholders. A number of these strategies can be explained in terms of options. To conserve space, we discuss only two of them. The first, selecting a high-risk project instead of a low-risk project, can be most easily explained in terms of a call option. The second, milking the firm, can be most easily understood in terms of a put option.[14]

Selecting High-Risk Projects

Imagine a levered firm considering two mutually exclusive projects, a low-risk one and a high-risk one. There are two equally likely outcomes, recession and boom. The firm is in such dire straits that should a recession hit, it will come near to bankruptcy if the low-risk project is selected and actually fall into bankruptcy if the high-risk project is selected. The cash flows for the firm if the low-risk project is taken can be described as

Low-Risk Project

	Probability	Value of firm	=	Shares	+	Bonds
Recession	0.5	GBP400	=	0	+	GBP400
Boom	0.5	GBP800	=	GBP400	+	GBP400

If recession occurs, the value of the firm will be GBP400, and if boom obtains, the value of the firm will be GBP800. The expected value of the firm is GBP600 (0.5 × GBP400 + 0.5 × GBP800). The firm has promised to pay the bondholders GBP400. Shareholders will obtain the difference between the total payoff and the amount paid to the bondholders. The bondholders have the prior claim on the payoffs, and the shareholders have the residual claim.

Now suppose that another, riskier, project can be substituted for the low-risk project. The payoffs and probabilities are as follows:

High-Risk Project

	Probability	Value of firm	=	Shares	+	Bonds
Recession	0.5	GBP200	=	0	+	GBP200
Boom	0.5	GBP1,000	=	GBP600	+	GBP400

---

[14] The put-call-parity relationship implies that a call option can be described as a put and vice versa. Thus, both selecting one project over another and choosing to milk the firm can be described by either a call or a put. In each case, out analysis uses the simplest approach, as the student will be happy to learn.

The expected value of the firm is GBP600 (0.5 × GBP200 + 0.5 × GBP1,000), which is identical to the value of the firm with the low-risk project. However, note that the expected value of the shares is GBP300 (0.5 × 0 + 0.5 × GBP600) with the high-risk project, but only GBP200 (0.5 × 0 + 0.5 × GBP400) with the low-risk project. Given the firm's present levered state, shareholders will select the high-risk project.

The shareholders benefit at the expense of the bondholders when the high-risk project is accepted. The explanation is quite clear. The bondholders suffer pound for pound when the firm's value falls short of the GBP400 bond obligation. However, the bondholders' payments are capped at GBP400 when the firm does well.

This can be explained in terms of call options. We argued earlier in this chapter that the value of a call rises with an increase in the volatility of the underlying asset. Because the share is a call option on the firm, a rise in the volatility of the firm increases the value of the share. In our example, the value of the share is higher if the high-risk project is accepted.

Table 22.4 showed that the value of a risky bond can be viewed as the difference between the value of the share and the value of a call on the firm. Because a call's value rises with the risk of the underlying asset, the value of the bond should decline if the firm increases its risk. In our example, the bondholders are hurt when the high-risk project is accepted.

Milking the Firm

The above considers the situation where the firm can choose between a high-risk and a low-risk project. The chapters on capital structure also examined the case where extra dividends and other distributions are paid out to shareholders in anticipation of financial distress. This strategy, which was previously referred to as milking the firm, hurts the bondholders. We can explain the option aspect of this strategy most easily by thinking in terms of puts, not calls. We stated earlier that

$$\text{Value of risky bond} = \text{Value of riskless bonds} - \text{Value of put option}$$

The put option represents the ability of the shareholders to sell the firm to the bondholders in exchange for the bondholders' promised payment. Earlier in this chapter, we learned that the value of the put increases as the value of the underlying asset falls. Because the value of the firm falls when a dividend is paid, a put on the firm must rise in value when the dividend payment is announced. By the above equation, the value of the risky bonds must decrease when the put option increases in value.

The above discussion is in terms of risky bonds. Of course, a loss to the bondholders implies a benefit to the stockholders. Hence, shareholders must gain when dividends are paid during periods of financial distress.

22.12   Investment in Real Projects and Options

Let us quickly review the material on capital budgeting presented earlier in the text. We first considered projects where forecasts for future cash flows were made at date 0. The expected cash flow in each future period was discounted at an appropriate risky rate, yielding an NPV calculation. For independent projects, a positive NPV meant acceptance and a negative NPV meant rejection.

This approach treated risk through the discount rate. We later considered decision-tree analysis, an approach that handles risk in a more sophisticated way. We pointed out that the firm will make investment and operating decisions on a project over its entire life. We value a project today, assuming that future decisions will be optimal. However, we do not yet know what these decisions will be, because much information remains to be discovered. The firm's ability to delay its investment and operating decisions until the release of information is an option. We now illustrate this option through an example.

● **Example**

Exoff Oil Corporation is considering the purchase of an oil field in a remote part of Russia. The seller has listed the property in US dollars as USD10,000 and is eager to sell immediately. Initial drilling costs are USD500,000. The firm anticipates that 10,000 barrels of oil can be extracted each year for many decades. Because the termination date is so far in the future and so hard to estimate, the firm views the cash flow stream from the oil as a perpetuity. With oil prices at USD20 per barrel and extraction costs at USD16 a barrel, the firm anticipates a net margin of USD4 per barrel. Because the firm budgets capital in real terms, it assumes that its cash flow per barrel will always be USD4. The appropriate real discount rate is 10 per cent. The firm has enough tax credits from bad years in the past so that it will not need to pay taxes on any profits from the oil field. Should Exoff buy the property?

The NPV of the oil field to Exoff is

$$-USD110,000 = -USD10,000 - USD500,000 + \frac{USD4 \times 10,000}{0.10} \quad (22.4)$$

According to this analysis, Exoff should not purchase the land.

Though this approach uses the standard capital-budgeting techniques of this and other textbooks, it is actually inappropriate for this situation. To see this, consider the analysis of Kirtley Thornton, a consultant to Exoff. He agrees that the price of oil is expected to rise at the rate of inflation. However, he points out that the next year is quite perilous for oil prices. On the one hand, OPEC is considering a long-term agreement that would raise oil prices to USD35 per barrel in real terms for many years in the future. On the other hand, National Motors recently indicated that cars using a mixture of sand and water for fuel are currently being tested. Thornton argues that oil will be priced at USD5 in real terms for many years, should this development prove successful. Full information on both these developments will be released in exactly one year.

Should oil prices rise to USD35 a barrel, the NPV of the project would be

$$USD1,390,000 = -USD10,000 - USD500,000 + \frac{(USD35 - USD16) \times 10,000}{0.10}$$

However, should oil prices fall to USD5 a barrel, the NPV of the oil field will be even more negative than it is today.

Thornton makes two recommendations to Exoff's board. He argues that

1. The land should be purchased.
2. The drilling decision should be delayed until information on both OPEC's new agreement and National Motor's new automobile are developed.

Thornton explains his recommendations to the board by first assuming that the land has already been purchased. He argues that, under this assumption, the drilling decision should be delayed. Second, he investigates his assumption that the land should have been purchased in the first place. This approach of examining the second decision (whether to drill) after assuming that the first decision (to buy the land) has been made was also used in our earlier presentation on decision trees.

Let us now work through Thornton's analysis.

Assume the land has already been purchased   If the land has already been purchased, should drilling begin immediately? If drilling begins immediately, the NPV is −USD110,000. If the drilling decision is delayed until new information is released in a year, the optimal choice can be made at that time. If oil prices drop to USD5 a barrel, Exoff should not drill. Instead, the firm walks away from the project, losing nothing beyond its USD10,000 purchase price for the land. If oil prices rise to USD35, drilling should begin.

Thornton points out that, by delaying, the firm will only invest the USD500,000 of drilling costs if oil prices rise. Thus, by delaying the firm saves USD500,000 in the case where oil prices drop. Kirtley concludes that, once the land is purchased, the drilling decision should be delayed.[15]

Should the land have been purchased in the first place?   We now know that, if the land had been purchased, it is optimal to defer the drilling decision until the release of information. Given that we know this optimal decision concerning drilling, should the land be purchased in the first place? Without knowing the exact probability that oil prices will rise, Thornton is nevertheless confident that the land should be purchased. The NPV of the project at USD35 oil prices is USD1,390,000 whereas the cost of the land is only USD10,000. He believes that an oil-price rise is possible, though by no means probable. Even so, he argues that the high potential return is clearly worth risk. ●

This example presents an approach that is similar to our decision-tree analysis of the Solar Equipment Company in a previous chapter. Our purpose in the present chapter is to discuss this type of decision in an option framework. When Exoff purchases the land, it is actually purchasing a call option. That is, once the land has been purchased, the firm has an option to buy an active oil field at an exercise price of USD500,000. As it turns out, one should generally not exercise a call option immediately.[16] In this case, the firm delays exercise until relevant information concerning future oil prices is released.

This section points out a serious deficiency in classical capital budgeting; net-present-value calculations typically ignore the flexibility that real-world firms have. In our example, the standard techniques generated a negative NPV for the land purchase.

---

[15] Actually, there are three separate effects here. First, the firm avoids drilling costs in the case of low oil prices by delaying the decision. This is the effect discussed by Kirtley Thornton. Second, the present value of the $500,000 payment is less when the decision is delayed, even if drilling eventually takes place. Third, the firm loses on year of cash inflows through delay.

The first two arguments support delaying the decision. The third argument supports immediate drilling. In this example, the first argument greatly outweighs the other two arguments. Thus, Thornton avoided the second and third arguments in his presentation.

[16] Actually, it can be shown that a call option that pays no dividend should *never* be exercised before expiration. However, for a dividend-paying share, it may be optimal to exercise prior to the ex-dividend date. The analogy applies to our example of an option in real assets.

The firm would receive cash flows from oil earlier if drilling begins immediately. This is equivalent to the benefit from exercising a call on a stock prematurely in order to capture the dividend. However, in our example, this dividend effect is far outweighed by the benefits from waiting.

Yet, by allowing the firm the option to change its investment policy according to new information, the land purchase can easily be justified.

We entreat our students to look for hidden options in projects. Because options are beneficial, managers are shortchanging their firm's projects if capital-budgeting calculations ignore flexibility.

Concept Question

• Why are the hidden options in projects valuable?

22.13   Summary and Conclusions

This chapter serves as an introduction to options.

1. The most familiar options are puts and calls. These options give the holder the right to sell or buy ordinary shares at a given exercise price. American options can be exercised any time up to and including the expiration date. European options can be exercised only on the expiration date.

2. Options can either be held in isolation or in combination. We focused on the strategy of
   • Buying the put
   • Buying the stock
   • Selling the call
   where the put and call have both the same exercise price and the same expiration date. This strategy yields a riskless return because the gain or loss on the call precisely offsets the gain or loss on the stock-and-put combination. In equilibrium, the return on this strategy must be exactly equal to the riskless rate. From this, the put-call-parity relationship was established:

$$\begin{array}{c} \text{Value of} \\ \text{stock} \end{array} + \begin{array}{c} \text{Value of} \\ \text{put} \end{array} - \begin{array}{c} \text{Value of} \\ \text{call} \end{array} = \begin{array}{c} \text{Present value of} \\ \text{exercise price} \end{array}$$

3. The value of an option depends on five factors:
   • The price of the underlying asset
   • The exercise price
   • The expiration date
   • The variability of the underlying asset
   • The interest rate on risk-free bonds
   The Black–Scholes model can determine the intrinsic price of an option from these five factors. An option pricing table is available to ease calculation.

4. Much of corporate financial theory can be presented in terms of options. In this chapter we pointed out that
   a. Ordinary shares can be represented as a call option on the firm.
   b. Shareholders enhance the value of their call by increasing the risk of their firm.
   c. Milking the firm can be expressed in options.
   d. Real projects have hidden options that enhance value.

KEY TERMS

Option   487
Exercising the option   487
Strike or exercise price   487
Expiration date   487
American options   487
European options   487
Call option   488
Put option   490
Put-call parity   496

Standardized normal distribution   504
Cumulative probability   505
In-the-money   507
Intrinsic value   507
Out-of-the money   507
Time value   507
At-the-money   508
Cumulative variance   509

QUESTIONS AND PROBLEMS

Options: General

22.1 Define the following terms associated with options:
 a. Option
 b. Exercise
 c. Strike price
 d. Expiration date
 e. Call option
 f. Put option

22.2 What is the difference between American options and European options?

22.3 Mr Goodie holds American put options on Delta Triangle stock. The exercise price of the put is GBP40 and Delta shares are selling for GBP35 per share. If the put sells for GBP$4\frac{1}{2}$, what is the best strategy for Mr Goodie?

22.4 A call option on Futura GmbH shares currently trades for DEM4. The expiration date is February 18 of next year. The exercise price of the option is DEM45.
 a. If this is an American option, on what dates can the option be exercised?
 b. If this is a European option, on what dates can the option be exercised?
 c. Suppose the current price of Futura corporation stock is DEM35. Is this option worthless?

22.5 The strike price of a call option on Simpsons NV ordinary shares is NLG50.
 a. What is the payoff at expiration on this call if, on the expiration date, Simpsons shares sell for NLG55?
 b. What is the payoff at expiration of this call if, on the expiration date, Simpsons shares sell for NLG45?
 c. Draw the payoff diagram for this option.

22.6 A put is trading on Simpsons NV stock. It has a strike price of NLG50.
 a. What is the payoff at expiration of this put if, on the expiration date, Simpsons shares sell for NLG55?
 b. What is the payoff at expiration of this put if, on the expiration date, Simpsons shares sell for NLG45?
 c. Draw the payoff diagram for this option.

22.7 Piersol Paper Mill's common stock (that is, ordinary shares) currently sells for USD145. Both puts and calls on Piersol Paper are being traded. These options all expire eight months from today, and they have a strike price of USD160. Eight months from today, Piersol Paper common stock will sell for USD172 with a probability of 0.5. It will sell for USD138 with a probability of 0.5. You own a put on Piersol Paper. Now, you are becoming nervous about the risk to which you are exposed.
 a. What other transactions should you make to eliminate this risk?
 b. What is the expected payoff at expiration of the strategy you developed in *a*?

22.8 Suppose you observe the following market prices:

| American Call (Strike = USD50) | USD8 |
| Stock | USD60 |

 a. What should you do?
 b. What is your profit or loss?
 c. What do opportunities such as this imply about the lower bound on the price of American calls?
 d. What is the upper bound on the price of American calls? Explain.

22.9 List the factors that determine the value of an American call option. State how a change in each factor alters the option's value.

22.10 List the factors that determine the value of an American put option. State how a change in each factor alters the option's value.

22.11 *a.* If the risk of a share increases, what is likely to happen to the price of call options on the share? Why?
 b. If the risk of a share increases, what is likely to happen to the price of put options on the share? Why?

The Two-State Option Model

22.12   You bought a 100-share call contract three weeks ago. The expiration date of the calls is five weeks from today. On that date, the price of the underlying share will be either FRF120 or FRF95. The two states are equally likely to occur. Currently, the share sells for FRF96; its strike price is FRF112. You are able to purchase 32 shares. You are able to borrow money at 10 per cent per annum.
What is the value of your call contract?

22.13   Assume only two states will exist one year from today when a call on the Danish company Delta AS shares expires. The price of Delta will be either DKK60 or DKK40 on that date. Today, Delta shares trade for DKK55. The strike price of the call is DKK50. The rate at which you can borrow is 9 per cent. How much are you willing to pay for a contract of this call?

The Black-Scholes Option Model

22.14   *a.* Use the Black-Scholes model to price a call with the following characteristics:
Share price = DKK62
Strike price = DKK70
Time to expiration = 4 weeks
Share-price variance = 0.35
Risk-free interest rate = 0.05
   b. Use the option pricing table to check your calculations.

22.15   *a.* Use the Black–Scholes model to price a call with the following characteristics:
Share price = DKK52
Strike price = DKK48
Time to expiration = 120 days
Share-price variance = 0.04
Risk-free interest rate = 0.05
   b. Use the option pricing table to check your calculations.

22.16   *a.* Use the Black–Scholes model to price a call with the following characteristics.
Share price = DKK45
Strike price = DKK52
Time to expiration = 6 months
Share-price variance = 0.40
Risk-free interest rate = 0.065
   b. Use the option pricing table to check your calculations.
   c. What does put-call parity imply the price of the corresponding put will be?

22.17   *a.* Use the Black-Scholes model to price a call with the following characteristics:
Share price = NLG70
Strike price = NLG90
Time to expiration = 6 months
Share-price variance = 0.25
Risk-free interest rate = 0.06
   b. Use the option pricing table to check your calculations.
   c. What does put-call parity imply the price of the corresponding put will be?

22.18   You have been asked by a client to determine the maximum price he should be willing to pay to purchase a Rocketeer NV call. The options have an exercise price of NLG25, and they expire in 120 days. The current price of Rocketeer shares is NLG27, the annual risk-free rate is 7 per cent, and the estimated variance of the share is 0.0576. No dividends are expected to be declared over the next six months. What is the maximum price your client should pay?

Application of Options to Corporate Finance

22.19   It is said that the equity in a levered firm is like a call option on the underlying assets. Explain what is meant by this statement.

22.20   London Real Estate & Investment plc is undertaking a new project. If the project is successful, the value of the firm in a year will be GBP650 million, but if it turns out to be a failure, the firm will be worth only GBP250 million. The current value of the firm is GBP400 million. The firm has outstanding bonds due in a year with a face value of GBP300 million. The three-month government bill rate is 7 per cent. What is the value of the equity? What is the value of the debt?

22.21   Suppose London Real Estate & Investment plc, in the above problem decided to undertake a riskier project. The value of the firm in a year will be either GBP800 million or GBP100 million, depending on the success of the project. What is the value of the equity? What is the value of the debt? Which project is preferred by bondholders?

CHAPTER 23

Warrants and Convertibles

We study two financing instruments in this chapter, warrants and convertibles. A warrant gives the holder the right to buy ordinary shares for cash. In this sense, it is very much like a call option. Warrants may be issued with bonds, though they are also combined with new issues of ordinary shares and preferred stock. In the case of new issues of shares, warrants may sometimes be given to investment bankers as compensation for underwriting services.

A convertible bond gives the holder the right to exchange the bond for ordinary shares. Therefore, it is a mixed security blurring the traditional line between equity and bonds. There is also convertible preferred stock.

The chapter describes the basic features of warrants and convertibles. Here are some of the most important questions concerning warrants and convertibles:

1. How can warrants and convertibles be valued?
2. What impact do warrants and convertibles have on the value of the firm?
3. What are the differences between warrants, convertibles, and call options?
4. Why do some companies issue bonds with warrants and convertible bonds?
5. Under what circumstances are warrants and convertibles converted into ordinary shares?

23.1 Warrants

Warrants are securities that give holders the right, but not the obligation, to buy shares directly from a company at a fixed price for a given period of time. Each warrant specifies the number of shares that the holder can buy, the exercise price, and the expiration date.

From the preceding description of warrants, it is clear that they are similar to call options. The differences in contractual features between warrants and the call options that trade on stock exchanges are small. For example, warrants have longer maturity periods.[1] In some countries, there are warrants that are actually perpetual, meaning that they never expire at all.

Warrants are sometimes referred to as *equity kickers* because they are usually issued in combination with bonds. In most cases, warrants are attached to the bonds when issued. The loan agreement will state whether the warrants are detachable from the bond, that is, whether they can be sold separately. Usually, the warrant can be detached immediately.

---

[1] Warrants are usually protected against share splits and dividends in the same way that call options are.

● **Example**

XYZ plc is a large supermarket chain in the UK. It has issued warrants, which trade separately from the bond to which they were originally attached. Each warrant gives the holder the right to purchase 0.279 shares of XYZ for GBP1.052 per warrant. To purchase one share, a holder must give up 3.584 warrants and pay an amount of GBP3.7691 per warrant. This makes the exercise price of the XYZ warrants equal to GBP13.5085 (3.584 × GBP3.7691 = GBP13.5085). The warrants expire on November 24, 2001.

XYZ plc has issued 10 million ordinary shares which are listed on the London Stock Exchange. The price of XYZ ordinary shares is GBP12.125. ●

The relationship between the value of XYZ's warrants and its share price can be viewed like the relationship between a call option and the share price, described in a previous chapter. Figure 23.1 depicts the relationship for XYZ warrants. The lower limit on the value of the warrants is zero if XYZ's share price is below GBP13.5085 per share. If the price of XYZ's shares rise above GBP13.5085 per share, the lower limit is the share price minus GBP13.5085 divided by 3.584.[2] The upper limit is the price of XYZ's ordinary shares divided by 3.584. A warrant to buy one share cannot sell at a price above the price of the underlying ordinary share.

FIGURE 23.1   XYZ Warrants on April 26, 1997

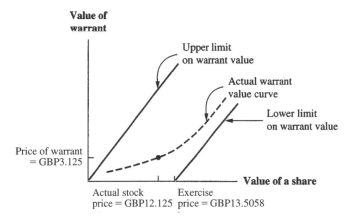

The price of XYZ warrants on April 26, 1997 was higher than the lower limit. The height of the warrant price above the lower limit will depend on the following:

1. The variance of XYZ's share returns.
2. The time to expiration date.
3. The risk-free rate of interest.
4. The share price of XYZ.
5. The exercise price.

These are the same factors that determine the value of a call option.

---

[2] We need to divide by 3.584 because it takes 3.584 warrants to purchase one share.

23.2   The Difference between Warrants and Call Options

From the holder's point of view, warrants are similar to call options on ordinary shares. A warrant, like a call option, gives its holder the right to buy ordinary shares at a specified price. Warrants usually have an expiration date, though in most cases they are issued with longer lives than call options. From the firm's point of view, however, a warrant is very different from a call option on the company's ordinary shares.

The most important difference between call options and warrants is that call options are issued by individuals and warrants are issued by firms. When a warrant is exercised, a firm must issue new shares. Each time a warrant is exercised, the number of shares outstanding increases.

To illustrate, suppose Eilts GmbH issues a warrant giving holders the right to buy one ordinary share at DEM25. Further, suppose the warrant is exercised. Eilts must issue one new share. In exchange for the share, it receives DEM25 from the holder.

In contrast, when a call option is exercised there is no change in the number of shares outstanding. Suppose Herr Reuter holds a call option on the ordinary shares of Eilts GmbH. The call option gives Herr Reuter the right to buy one share in Eilts GmbH for DEM25. If Herr Reuter chooses to exercise the call option, a seller, say Frau Berger, is obligated to give her one share of Eilts GmbH in exchange for DEM25. If Frau Berger does not already own a share, she must enter the stock market and buy one. The call option is a side bet between buyers and sellers on Eilts GmbH ordinary shares. When a call option is exercised, one investor gains and the other loses. The total number of shares outstanding of Eilts GmbH remains constant, and no new funds are made available to the company.

• Example

To see how warrants affect the value of the firm, imagine that Mr Gould and Ms Rockefeller are two investors who have together purchased six ounces of platinum. At the time they bought the platinum, Mr Gould and Ms Rockefeller each contributed one half of the cost, which we will assume was USD3,000 for six ounces,[3] or USD500 an ounce (they each contributed USD1,500). They incorporated, printed two stock certificates, and named the firm the GR Company. Each certificate represents a one-half claim to the platinum. Mr Gould and Ms Rockefeller each own one certificate. They have formed a company with platinum as its only asset.

A Call Is Issued   Suppose Mr Gould later decides to sell to Ms Fiske a call option issued on Mr Gould's share. The call option gives Ms Fiske the right to buy Mr Gould's share for USD1,800 within the next year. If the price of platinum rises above USD600 per ounce, the firm will be worth more than USD3,600, and each share will be worth more than USD1,800. If Ms Fiske decides to exercise her option, Mr Gould must turn over his stock certificate and receive USD1,800.

How would the firm be affected by the exercise? The number of shares will remain the same. There will still be two shares, now owned by Ms Rockefeller and Ms Fiske. If the price of platinum rises to USD700 an ounce, each share will be worth USD2,100 (USD4,200/2). If Ms Fiske exercises her option at this price, she will profit by USD300.

A Warrant Is Issued Instead   This story changes if a warrant is issued. Suppose that Mr Gould does not sell a call option to Ms Fiske. Instead, Mr Gould and Ms Rockefeller have a stockholders' meeting. They vote that GR Company will issue a warrant and sell it to Ms Fiske. The warrant will give Ms Fiske the right to receive a

---

[3] We use dollars in this example because platinum prices, like oil prices, are quoted in US dollars.

share of the company at an exercise price of USD1,800.[4] If Ms Fiske decides to exercise the warrant, the firm will issue another stock certificate and give it to Ms Fiske in exchange for USD1,800.

From Ms Fiske's perspective, the call option and the warrant seem to be the same. The exercise prices of the warrant and the call are the same: USD1,800. It is still advantageous for Ms Fiske to exercise the option when the price of platinum exceeds USD600 per ounce. However, we will show that Ms Fiske actually makes less in the warrant situation due to dilution.

The GR Company must also consider dilution. Suppose the price of platinum increases to USD700 an ounce and Ms Fiske exercises her warrant. Two things will occur:

1. Ms Fiske will pay USD1,800 to the firm.
2. The firm will print one stock certificate and give it to Ms Fiske. The stock certificate will represent a one-third claim on the platinum of the firm.

Because Ms Fiske contributes USD1,800 to the firm, the value of the firm increases. It is now worth

$$
\begin{aligned}
\text{New value of firm} &= \text{Value of platinum} + \text{Contribution to the firm by Ms Fiske} \\
&= \text{USD4,200} \qquad\quad + \text{USD1,800} \\
&= \text{USD6,000}
\end{aligned}
$$

Because Ms Fiske has a one-third claim on the firm's value, her share is worth USD2,000 (USD6,000/3). By exercising the warrant, Ms Fiske gains USD2,000 − USD1,800 = USD200. This is illustrated in Table 23.1.

TABLE 23.1   Effect of Call Option and Warrant on the GR Company*

	Price of platinum per share	
Value of firm if:	*USD700*	*USD600*
No warrant		
Mr Gould's share	USD2,100	USD1,800
Ms Rockefeller's share	2,100	1,800
Firm	USD4,200	USD3,600
Call option		
Mr Gould's claim	USD 0	USD1,800
Ms Rockefeller's claim	2,100	1,800
Ms Fiske's claim	2,100	0
Firm	USD4,200	USD3,600
Warrant		
Mr Gould's share	USD2,000	USD1,800
Ms Rockefeller's share	2,000	1,800
Ms Fiske's share	2,000	0
Firm	USD6,000	USD3,600

*If the price of platinum is USD700, the value of the firm is equal to the value of six ounces of platinum plus the excess dollars paid into the firm by Ms Fiske. This amount is USD4,200 + USD1,800 = USD6,000.

---

[4] The sale of the warrant brings cash into the firm. We assume that the sale proceeds immediately leave the firm through a cash dividend to Mr Gould and Ms Rockefeller. This simplifies the analysis, because the firm with warrants then has the same total value as the firm without warrants.

Dilution   Why does Ms Fiske only gain USD200 in the warrant case, while gaining USD300 in the call option case? The key is dilution, that is, the creation of another share. In the call option case, she contributes USD1,800 and receives one of the two outstanding shares. That is, she receives a share worth USD2,100($\frac{1}{2}$ × USD4,200). Her gain is USD300 (USD2,100 − USD1,800). We rewrite this gain as

Gain on Exercise of Call:

$$\frac{USD4,200}{2} - USD1,800 = USD300 \tag{23.1}$$

In the warrant case, she contributes USD1,800 and receives a newly created share. She now owns one of the three outstanding shares. Because the USD1,800 remains in the firm, her share is worth USD2,000 (USD4,200 + USD1,800)/3. Her gain is USD200 (USD2,000 − USD1,800). We rewrite this gain as

Gain on Exercise of Warrant:

$$\frac{USD4,200 + USD1,800}{2 + 1} - USD1,800 = USD200 \tag{23.2}$$

Warrants also affect accounting numbers. Warrants and (as we shall see) convertible bonds cause the number of shares to increase. This causes the firm's net income to be spread over a larger number of shares, thereby decreasing earnings per share. Firms with significant amounts of warrants and convertible issues report earnings per share in a *base case* format and a *fully diluted* basis. ●

How the Firm Can Hurt Warrant Holders

The platinum firm owned by Mr Gould and Ms Rockefeller has issued a warrant to Ms Fiske that is *in the money* and about to expire. One way that Mr Gould and Ms Rockefeller can hurt Ms Fiske is to pay themselves a large dividend. This could be funded by selling a substantial amount of platinum. The value of the firm would fall, and the warrant would be worth much less.

Concept Questions

- What is the key difference between a warrant and a traded call option?
- Why does dilution occur when warrants are exercised?
- How can the firm hurt warrant holders?

23.3   Warrant Pricing and the Black–Scholes Model (Advanced)

We now wish to express the gains from exercising a call and a warrant in more general terms. The gain on a call can be written as

Gain from Exercising a Single Call:

$$\underset{\text{(Value of a share)}}{\underbrace{\frac{\text{Firm's value net of debt}}{\#}}} - \text{Exercise price} \tag{23.3}$$

Equation (23.3) generalizes equation (23.1). We define the firm's *value net of debt* to be the total firm value less the value of the debt. The total firm value is USD4,200 in our example and there is no debt. The # stands for the number of shares outstanding, which is 2 in our example. The ratio on the left is the value of a share of stock. The gain on a warrant can be written as

Gain from Exercising a Single Warrant:

$$\frac{\text{Firm's value net of debt} + \text{Exercise price} \times \#_w}{\# + \#_w} - \text{Exercise price} \qquad (23.4)$$
(Value of a share after warrant is exercised)

Equation (23.4) generalizes (23.2). The numerator on the left-hand term is the firm's value net of debt *after* the warrant is exercised. It is the sum of the firm's value net of debt *prior* to the warrant's exercise plus the proceeds the firm receives from the exercise. The proceeds equal the product of the exercise price multiplied by the number of warrants. The number of warrants appears as $\#_w$. (Our analysis uses the plausible assumption that all warrants in the money will be exercised.) Note that $\#_w = 1$ in our numerical example. The denominator, $\# + \#_w$, is the number of shares outstanding after the exercise of the warrants. The ratio on the left is the value of a share of stock after exercise. By rearranging terms, (23.4) can be rewritten as[5]

Gain from Exercising a Single Warrant:

$$\frac{\#}{\# + \#_w} \times \left(\frac{\text{Firm's value net of debt}}{\#} - \text{Exercise price} \right) \qquad (23.5)$$
(Gain from a call on a firm with no warrants)

Formula (23.5) relates the gain on a warrant to the gain on a call. Note that the term within parentheses is (23.3). Thus, the gain from exercising a warrant is a proportion of the gain from exercising a call in a firm without warrants. The proportion $\#/(\# + \#_w)$ is the ratio of the number of shares in the firm without warrants to the number of shares after all the warrants have been exercised. This ratio must always be less than 1. Thus, the gain on a warrant must be less than the gain on an identical call in a firm without warrants. Note that $\#/(\# + \#_w) = 200/300 = \frac{2}{3}$ in our example, which explains why Ms Fiske gains USD300 on her call yet gains only USD200 on her warrant.

The above implies that the Black–Scholes model must be adjusted for warrants. When a call option is issued to Ms Fiske, we know that the exercise price is USD1,800 and the time to expiration is one year. Though we have posited neither the price of the stock, the variance of the stock, nor the interest rate, we could easily provide these data for a real-world situation. Thus, we could use the Black–Scholes model to value Ms Fiske's call.

Suppose that the warrant is to be issued tomorrow to Ms Fiske. We know the number of warrants to be issued, the warrant's expiration date and the exercise price. Using our assumption that the warrant proceeds are immediately paid out as a dividend, we could use the Black–Scholes model to value the warrant. We would first calculate the value of an identical call. The warrant price is the call price multiplied by the ratio $\#/(\# + \#_w)$. As mentioned earlier, this ratio is $\frac{2}{3}$ in our example.

---

[5] To derive (23.5), one should separate 'Exercise price' in (23.4). This yields

$$\frac{\text{Firm's value net of debt}}{\# + \#_w} - \frac{\#}{\# + \#_w} \times \text{Exercise price}$$

By rearranging terms, one can obtain (23.5).

23.4   Convertible Bonds

A **convertible bond** is similar to a bond with warrants. The most important difference is that a bond with warrants can be separated into distinct securities and a convertible bond cannot. A convertible bond gives the holder the right to exchange it for a given number of shares anytime up to and including the maturity date of the bond.

Preferred shares can frequently be converted into ordinary shares. A convertible preferred share is the same as a convertible bond except that it has an infinite maturity date.

● Example

LMN GmbH is a German retailer listed on the Frankfurt Stock Exchange.

In June 1996, LMN raised DEM72 million by issuing 6 per cent convertible subordinated debentures due in 2021. It planned to use the proceeds to add new stores to its chain. Like many debentures, they had a sinking fund and were callable after two years. LMN bonds differed from other debentures in their convertible feature. Each bond was convertible into 21.62 shares of ordinary shares of LMN any time before maturity. The number of shares received for each bond (21.62 in this example) is called the **conversion ratio**.

Bond traders also speak of the **conversion price** of the bond. This is calculated as the ratio of the face value of the bond to the conversion ratio. Because the face value of each LMN bond was DEM1,000, the conversion ratio was DEM46.25 (DEM1,000/21.62). The bondholders of LMN could give up bonds with a face value of DEM1,000 and receive 21.62 shares of LMN. This was equivalent to paying DEM46.25 (DEM1,000/21.62) for each LMN share.

When LMN issued its convertible bonds, its ordinary shares were trading at DEM38 per share. The conversion price of DEM46.25 was 22 per cent higher than the actual share price. This 22 per cent is referred to as the **conversion premium**. It reflects the fact that the conversion option in LMN convertible bonds was *out of the money*. This conversion premium is typical.

Convertibles are almost always protected against stock splits and stock dividends. If LMN's shares had been split two for one, the conversion ratio would have been increased from 21.62 to 43.24. ●

Conversion ratio, conversion price and conversion premium are well-known terms in the real world. For that reason alone, the student should master the concepts. However, conversion price and conversion premium implicitly assume that the bond is selling at par. If the bond is selling at another price, the terms have little meaning. By contrast, conversion ratio can have a meaningful interpretation regardless of the price of the bond.

Concept Question

• What are the conversion ratio, the conversion price, and the conversion premium?

23.5   The Value of Convertible Bonds

The value of a convertible bond can be described in terms of three components: straight bond value, conversion value and option value. We examine these three components below.

Straight Bond Value

The straight bond value is what the convertible bonds would sell for if they could not be converted into ordinary shares. It will depend on the general level of interest rates and on the default risk. Suppose that straight debentures issued by LMN had been rated A, and A-rated bonds were priced to yield 10 per cent in June 1996. The straight bond value of LMN convertible bonds can be determined by discounting the coupon payment and principal amount at 10 per cent:[6]

$$
\begin{aligned}
\text{Straight bond} &= \sum_{t=1}^{25} \frac{\text{DEM60}}{(1.1)^t} + \frac{\text{DEM1,000}}{(1.1)^{25}} \\
&= \text{DEM60} \times A_{0.10}^{25} + \frac{\text{DEM1,000}}{(1.1)^{25}} \\
&= \text{DEM544.6} + \text{DEM92.3} \\
&= \text{DEM636.9}
\end{aligned}
$$

The straight bond value of a convertible bond is a minimum value. The price of LMN's convertible could not have gone lower than the straight bond value. The straight-bond-value portion of a convertible will depend on the market's assessment of default risk.

When LMN experienced poor economic results, its bond value declined. We know from previous discussions that the value of straight bonds is related to the value of the firm. The upper lefthand corner of Figure 23.2 illustrates the relationship between straight bond value and firm value. If the value of LMN's retail stores became zero, the value of LMN's bonds would be zero. Conversely, LMN's straight debt could be worth, at most, only the value of an equivalent risk-free bond.

Conversion Value

The value of convertible bonds depends on conversion value. **Conversion value** is what the bonds would be worth if they were immediately converted into the ordinary shares at current prices. Typically, conversion value is computed by multiplying the number of shares that will be received when the bond is converted by the current price of the ordinary shares.

In June 1996, each LMN convertible bond could have been converted into 21.62 shares of LMN. Shares in LMN were selling for DEM38. Thus, the conversion value was 21.62 × DEM38 = DEM821.56. A convertible cannot sell for less than its conversion value. Arbitrage prevents this from happening. If LMN's convertible sold for less than DEM821.56, investors would have bought the bonds and converted them into ordinary shares and sold the shares. The profit would have been the difference between the value of the shares sold and the bond's conversion value.

Thus, convertible bonds have two minimum values: the straight bond value and the conversion value. The conversion value is determined by the value of the firm's underlying shares. This is illustrated in the upper righthand corner of Figure 23.2. As the value of ordinary shares rises and falls, the conversion price rises and falls with it. When the value of LMN's shares increases by DEM1, the conversion value of its convertible bonds would increase by DEM21.62.

---

[6] This formula assumes that coupons are paid annually.

FIGURE 23.2   **The Market Value of Convertible Bonds**

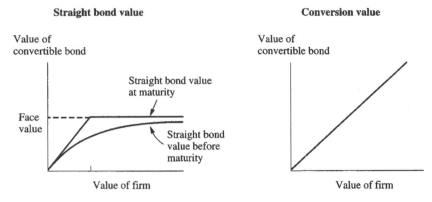

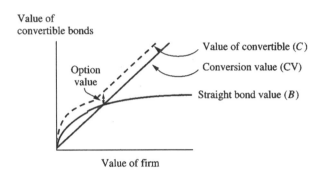

The actual value of a convertible is always higher than either its straight bond value or its conversion value.

Option Value

The value of a convertible bond will generally exceed both the straight bond value and the conversion value.[7] This occurs because holders of convertibles need not convert immediately. Instead, by waiting they can take advantage of whichever is greater in the future, the straight bond value or the conversion value. This option to wait has value, and it raises the value over both the straight bond value and the conversion value.

When the value of the firm is low, the value of convertible bonds is most significantly influenced by their underlying value as straight debt. However, when the value of the firm is very high, the value of convertible bonds is mostly determined by their underlying conversion value. This is illustrated in the bottom portion of Figure 23.2.

The bottom portion of the figure implies that the value of a convertible bond is the maximum of its straight bond value and its conversion value, plus its option value:

$$\text{Value of convertible bond} = \frac{\text{The greater of (Straight bond value, Conversion value)}}{+ \text{ Option Value}}$$

---

[7] The most plausible exception is when conversion would provide the investor with a dividend much greater than the interest available prior to conversion. The optimal strategy here could very well be to convert immediately, implying that the market value of the bond would exactly equal the conversion value. Other exceptions occur when the firm is in default or the bondholders are forced to convert.

- **Example**

Suppose that Windmolen NV has outstanding 1,000 ordinary shares and 100 bonds. Each bond has a face value of NLG1,000 at maturity. They are zero coupon bonds and pay no interest. At maturity, each bond can be converted into 10 shares of newly issued ordinary shares.

What are the circumstances that will make it advantageous for the holders of Windmolen convertible bonds to convert to ordinary shares at maturity?

If the holders of the convertible bonds convert, they will receive $100 \times 10 = 1,000$ shares. Because there were already 1,000 shares, the total number of shares outstanding becomes 2,000 upon conversion. Thus, converting bondholders own 50 per cent of the value of the firm, V. If they do not convert, they will receive NLG100,000 or V, whichever is less. The choice for the holders of the Windmolen bonds is obvious. They should convert if 50 per cent of V is greater than NLG100,000. This will be true whenever V is greater than NLG200,000. This is illustrated as follows:

Payoff to Convertible Bondholders and Shareholders of the Windmolen NV

	(1) $V \leqslant NLG100,000$	*(2)* $NLG100,000 < V \leqslant NLG200,000$	*(3)* $V > NLG200,000$
Decision: Convertible	Bondholder Will Not Convert	Bondholders Will Not Convert	Bondholders Will Convert
bondholders	V	NLG100,000	0.5V
Shareholders	0	V − NLG100,000	0.5V ●

Concept Questions

- What three elements make up the value of a convertible bond?
- Describe the payoff structure of convertible bonds.

23.6   Reasons for Issuing Warrants and Convertibles

Probably there is no other area of corporate finance where real-world practitioners get as confused as they do about the reasons for issuing convertible debt. In order to separate fact from fantasy, we present a structured argument. We first compare convertible debt with straight debt. Then we compare convertible debt with equity. For each comparison, we ask in what situations is the firm better off with convertible debt and in what situations is it worse off.

Convertible Debt versus Straight Debt

Convertible debt pays a lower interest rate than does otherwise-identical straight debt. For example, if the interest rate is 10 per cent on straight debt, the interest rate on convertible debt might be 9 per cent. Investors will accept a lower interest rate on a convertible because of the potential gain from conversion.

Imagine a firm that seriously considers both convertible debt and straight debt finally deciding to issue convertibles. When would this decision have benefited the firm and when would it have hurt the firm? We consider two situations.

The Share Price Later Rises so that Conversion Is Indicated

The firm clearly likes to see the share price rise. However, it would have benefited even more had it previously issued straight debt instead of a convertible. While the firm paid out a lower interest rate than it would have with straight debt, it was obligated to sell the convertible holders a chunk of the equity at a below-market price.

The Share Price Later Falls or Does Not Rise Enough to Justify Conversion
The firm hates to see the share price fall. However, as long as the share price does fall, it is glad that it had previously issued convertible debt instead of straight debt. This is because the interest rate on convertible debt is lower. Because conversion does not take place, our comparison of interest rates is all that is needed.

Summary
Compared to straight debt, the firm is worse off having issued convertible debt if the underlying share subsequently does well. The firm is better off having issued convertible debt if the underlying share subsequently does poorly. In an efficient market, one cannot predict future share prices. Thus, we cannot argue that convertibles either dominate or are dominated by straight debt.

Convertible Debt versus Ordinary Shares

Next, imagine a firm that seriously considers both convertible debt and ordinary shares, finally deciding to issue convertibles. When would this decision have benefited the firm and when would it have hurt the firm? We consider our two situations.

The Share Price Later Rises so that Conversion Is Indicated
The firm is better off having previously issued a convertible instead of equity. To see this, consider the LMN case. The firm could have issued stock for DEM38. Instead, by issuing a convertible, the firm effectively received DEM46.25 for a share upon conversion.

The Share Price Later Falls or Does Not Rise Enough to Justify Conversion
No firm wants to see the share price fall. However, given that the price did fall, the firm would have been better off if it had previously issued shares instead of a convertible. The firm would have benefited by issuing shares above its later market price. That is, the firm would have received more than the subsequent worth of the shares. However, the drop in share price did not affect the value of the convertible much because the straight bond value serves as a floor.

Summary
Compared with equity, the firm is better off having issued convertible debt if the underlying share subsequently does well. The firm is worse off having issued convertible debt if the underlying share subsequently does poorly. One cannot predict future share prices in an efficient market. Thus, we cannot argue that issuing convertibles is better or worse than issuing equity. The above analysis is summarized in Table 23.2.

Modigliani–Miller (MM) pointed out that, abstracting from taxes and bankruptcy costs, the firm is indifferent to whether it issues shares or issues debt. The MM relationship is a quite general one. Their pedagogy could be adjusted to show that the firm is indifferent to whether it issues convertibles or issues other instruments. To save space (and the patience of students), we have omitted a full-blown proof of MM in a world with convertibles. However, the above results are perfectly consistent with MM. Now we turn to the real-world view of convertibles.

TABLE 23.2   The Case For and Against Convertible Bonds (CBs)

	If firm subsequently does poorly	*If firm subsequently prospers*
Convertible bonds (CBs) Compared to:	No conversion because of low share price	Conversion because of high share price
Straight bonds	CBs provide cheap financing because coupon rate is lower.	CBs provide expensive financing because bonds are converted, which dilutes existing equity.
Ordinary shares	CBs provide expensive financing because firm could have issued ordinary share finance at high prices.	CBs provide cheap financing because firm issues shares at high prices when bonds are converted.

The 'Free Lunch' Story

The above discussion suggests that issuing a convertible bond is no better and no worse than issuing other instruments. Unfortunately, many corporate executives fall into the trap of arguing that issuing convertible debt is actually better than issuing alternative instruments. This is a free lunch type of explanation, of which we are quite critical.

● **Example**

The stock price of GmbH is DEM20. Suppose this company can issue subordinated debentures at 10 per cent. It can also issue convertible bonds at 6 per cent with a conversion value of DEM800. The conversion value means that the holders can convert a convertible bond into 40 (DEM800/DEM20) ordinary shares.

A company treasurer who believes in free lunches might argue that convertible bonds should be issued because they represent a cheaper source of financing than either subordinated bonds or ordinary shares. The treasurer will point out that if the company does poorly and the price does not rise above DEM20, the convertible bondholders will not convert the bonds into ordinary shares. In this case, the company will have obtained debt financing at below market rates by attaching worthless equity kickers. On the other hand, if the firm does well and the price of its ordinary shares rises to DEM25 or above, convertible holders will convert. The company will issue 40 shares. The company will receive a bond with face value of DEM1,000 in exchange for issuing 40 shares of ordinary shares, implying a conversion price of DEM25. The company will have issued shares *de facto* at DEM25 per share, or 20 per cent above the DEM20 share price prevailing when the convertible bonds were issued. This enables it to lower its cost of equity capital. Thus, the treasurer happily points out, regardless of whether the company does well or poorly, convertible bonds are the cheapest form of financing.

Although this argument may sound quite plausible at first glance, there is a flaw. The treasurer is comparing convertible financing *with straight debt* when the share subsequently falls. However, the treasurer compares convertible financing with ordinary shares when the shares subsequently rise. This is an unfair mixing of comparisons. By contrast, our analysis of Table 23.2 was fair, because we examined both share price increases and decreases when comparing a convertible with each alternative instrument. We found that no single alternative dominated convertible bonds in both up and down markets. ●

The 'Expensive Lunch' Story

Suppose we stand the treasurer's argument on its head by comparing (1) convertible financing with straight debt when the stock rises and (2) convertible financing with equity when the share falls.

From Table 23.2, we see that convertible debt is more expensive than straight debt when the share subsequently rises. The firm's obligation to sell convertible holders a chunk of the equity at a below-market price more than offsets the lower interest rate on a convertible.

Also from Table 23.2, we see that convertible debt is more expensive than equity when the share subsequently falls. Had the firm issued shares, it would have received a price higher than its subsequent worth. Therefore, the expensive lunch story implies that convertible debt is an inferior form of financing. Of course, we dismiss both the free lunch and the expensive lunch arguments.

A Reconciliation

In an efficient financial market there is neither a free lunch nor an expensive lunch. Convertible bonds can be neither cheaper nor more expensive than other instruments. A convertible bond is a package of straight debt and an option to buy ordinary shares. The difference between the market value of a convertible bond and the value of a straight bond is the price investors pay for the call-option feature. In an efficient market this is a fair price.

In general, if a company prospers, issuing convertible bonds will turn out to be worse than issuing straight bonds and better than issuing ordinary shares. In contrast, if a company does poorly, convertible bonds will turn out to be better than issuing straight bonds and worse than issuing ordinary shares.

Concept Questions

- What is wrong with the simple view that it is cheaper to issue a bond with a warrant or a convertible feature because the required coupon is lower?
- What is wrong with the free lunch story?
- What is wrong with the expensive lunch story?

23.7   Why Are Warrants and Convertibles Issued?

From studies in the USA, it is known that firms that issue convertible bonds are different from other firms. Here are some of the differences:

1. The bond ratings of firms using convertibles are lower than those of other firms.[8]
2. Convertibles tend to be used by smaller firms with high growth rates and more financial leverage.[9]
3. Convertibles are usually subordinated and unsecured.

The kind of company that uses convertibles provides clues to why they are issued. Here are some explanations that make sense.

---

[8] E. F. Brigham (1966) 'An analysis of convertible debentures', *Journal of Finance*, 21.
[9] W. H. Mikkelson (1981) 'Convertible calls and security returns', *Journal of Financial Economics*, **9**, September.

Matching Cash Flows

If financing is costly, it makes sense to issue securities whose cash flows match those of the firm. A young, risky, and, it hopes, growing firm might prefer to issue convertibles or bonds with warrants because these will have lower initial interest costs. When the firm is successful, the convertibles (or warrants) will be converted. This causes expensive dilution, but it occurs when the firm can most afford it.

Risk Synergy

Another argument for convertible bonds and bonds with warrants is that they are useful when it is very costly to assess the risk of the issuing company. Suppose you are evaluating a new product by a start-up company. The new product is a biogenetic virus that may increase the yields of corn crops in northern climates. It may also cause cancer. This type of product is difficult to value properly. Thus, the risk of the company is very hard to determine. It may be high, or it may be low. If you could be sure the risk of the company was high, you would price the bonds for a high yield, say 15 per cent. If it was low, you would price them at a lower yield, say 10 per cent.

Convertible bonds and bonds with warrants can protect somewhat against mistakes of risk evaluation. Convertible bonds and bonds with warrants have two components: straight bonds and call options on the company's underlying shares. If the company turns out to be a low-risk company, the straight bond component will have high value and the call option will have low value. However, if the company turns out to be a high-risk company, the straight bond component will have low value and the call option will have high value. This is illustrated in Table 23.3.

TABLE 23.3   **A Hypothetical Case of the Yields on Convertible Bonds***

	Firm risk	
	Low (%)	*High (%)*
Straight bond yield	10	15
Convertible bond yield	6	7

*The yields on straight bonds reflect the risk of default. The yields on convertibles are not sensitive to default risk.

However, although risk has effects on value that cancel each other out in convertibles and bonds with warrants, the market and the buyer nevertheless must make an assessment of the firm's potential to value securities, and it is not clear that the effort involved is that much less than is required for a straight bond.

Agency Costs

Convertible bonds can resolve agency problems associated with raising money. In a previous chapter we showed that straight bonds are like risk-free bonds minus a put option on the assets of the firm. This creates an incentive for creditors to force the firm into low-risk activities. In contrast, holders of ordinary shares have incentives to adopt high-risk projects. High-risk projects with negative NPV transfer wealth from bondholders to shareholders. If these conflicts cannot be resolved, the firm may be forced to pass up profitable investment opportunities. However, because convertible bonds have an equity component, less expropriation of wealth can occur when convertible debt is issued instead of straight debt.[10] In other words, convertible bonds mitigate agency costs. One implication is that convertible bonds have less-restrictive debt covenants than do straight bonds in the real world. Casual empirical evidence seems to bear this out.

Concept Question

- Why do firms issue convertible bonds and bonds with warrants?

23.8   Conversion Policy

There is one aspect of convertible bonds that we have omitted so far. Firms are frequently granted a call option on the bond. The typical arrangements for calling a convertible bond are simple. When the bond is called, the holder has about 30 days to choose between the following:

1. Converting the bond to ordinary shares at the conversion ratio.
2. Surrendering the bond and receiving the call price in cash.

What should bondholders do? It should be obvious that if the conversion value of the bond is greater than the call price, conversion is better than surrender; and if the conversion value is less than the call price, surrender is better than conversion. If the conversion value is greater than the call price, the call is said to **force conversion.**

What should financial managers do? Calling the bonds does not change the value of the firm as a whole. However, an optimal call policy can benefit the shareholders at the expense of the bondholders. Because we are speaking of dividing a pie of fixed size, the optimal call policy is very simple: Do whatever the bondholders do not want you to do.

Bondholders would love the shareholders to call the bonds when the bond's market value is below the call price. Shareholders would be giving bondholders extra value. Alternatively, should the value of the bonds rise above the call price, the bondholders would love the shareholders not to call the bonds, because bondholders would be allowed to hold on to a valuable asset.

There is only one policy left. This is the policy that maximizes shareholder value and minimizes bondholder value. This policy is

> Call the bond when its value is equal to the call price.

It is a puzzle that firms do not always call convertible bonds when the conversion value reaches the call price. Ingersoll examined the call policies of 124 firms in the USA between 1968 and 1975.[11] In most cases, he found that the company waited to call the bonds until the conversion value was much higher than the call price. The

---

[10] A. Barnea, R. A. Haugen and L. Senbet (1985) *Agency Problems and Financial Contracting*, Prentice Hall Foundations of Science Series, New York: Prentice Hall, Ch. VI.

[11] J. Ingersoll (1977) 'An examination of corporate call policies on convertible bonds', *Journal of Finance*, May. See also M. Harris and A. Raviv (1985) 'A sequential signalling model of convertible debt policy,' *Journal of Finance*, December. Harris and Raviv describe a signal equilibrium that is consistent with Ingersoll's result. They show that managers with favourable information will delay calls to avoid depressing share prices.

median company waited until the conversion value of its bonds was 44 per cent higher than the call price. This is not even close to the optimal strategy.

Concept Questions

- Why will convertible bonds not be voluntarily converted to stock before expiration?
- When should firms force conversion of convertibles? Why?

23.9 Summary and Conclusions

1. A warrant gives the holder the right to buy shares at an exercise price for a given period of time. Typically, warrants are issued in a package with bonds. Afterwards they become detached and trade separately.
2. A convertible bond is a combination of a straight bond and a call option. The holder can give up the bond in exchange for shares.
3. Convertible bonds and warrants are like call options. However, there are some important differences:
   a. Warrants and convertible securities are issued by corporations. Call options are traded between individual investors.
      i. Warrants are usually issued privately and are combined with a bond. In most cases, the warrants can be detached immediately after the issue. In some cases, warrants are issued with preferred stock, with ordinary shares or in executive compensation programmes.
      ii. Convertibles are usually bonds that can be converted into ordinary shares.
      iii. Call options are sold separately by individual investors (called *writers* of call options).
   b. Warrants and call options are exercised for cash. The holder of a warrant gives the company cash and receives new shares of the company. The holder of a call option gives another individual cash in exchange for shares. When someone converts a bond, it is exchanged for ordinary shares. As a consequence, bonds with warrants and convertible bonds have different effects on corporate cash flow and capital structure.
   c. Warrants and convertibles cause dilution to the existing shareholders. When warrants are exercised and convertible bonds converted, the company must issue new ordinary shares. The percentage ownership of the existing shareholders will decline. New shares are not issued when call options are exercised.
4. Many arguments, both plausible and implausible, are given for issuing convertible bonds and bonds with warrants. One plausible rationale for such bonds has to do with risk. Convertibles and bonds with warrants are associated with risky companies. Lenders can do several things to protect themselves from high-risk companies:
   a. They can require high yields.
   b. They can lend less or not at all to firms whose risk is difficult to assess.
   c. They can impose severe restrictions on such debt.
   Another useful way to protect against risk is to issue bonds with equity kickers. This gives the lenders the chance to benefit from risks and reduces the conflicts between bondholders and shareholders concerning risk.
5. A puzzle particularly vexes financial researchers. Convertible bonds usually have call provisions. Companies appear to delay calling convertibles until the conversion value greatly exceeds the call price. From the shareholders' standpoint, the optimal call policy would be to call the convertibles when the conversion value equals the call price.

KEY TERMS

Warrants	524	Conversion premium	530
Convertible bond	530	Conversion value	531
Conversion ratio	530	Force conversion	538
Conversion price	530		

QUESTIONS AND PROBLEMS

23.1 Define:
   a. Warrants
   b. Convertibles

Warrants

23.2 Explain why the following limits on warrant prices exist.
   a. The lower limit is zero if the share price is below the exercise price.
   b. The lower limit is share price less exercise price if the share price is above the exercise price.
   c. The upper limit is the price of the share.

23.3 *a.* What is the primary difference between warrants and calls?
   b. What is the implication of that difference?

23.4 Suppose the GR Company, which was discussed in the text, sells Ms Fiske a warrant. Prior to the sale, the company had two shares outstanding. Mr Gould owns one share and Ms Rockefeller owns the other share. The assets of the firm are seven ounces of platinum, which was purchased at USD500 per ounce. The exercise price of the warrant is USD1,800. All funds that enter the firm are used to purchase more platinum. Ms Fiske is sold the warrant moments after incorporation for USD500.
   a. What is the price of GR stock before the warrant is sold?
   b. At what price for platinum will Ms Fiske exercise her warrant?
   c. Suppose the price of platinum suddenly rises to USD520 per ounce.
       i.   What is the value of GR?
       ii. What will Ms Fiske do?
       iii. What is the new price per GR share?
       iv. What was Ms Fiske's gain from exercise?
   d. What would Ms Fiske's gain have been if Mr Gould had sold her a call?
   e. Why are Ms Fiske's gains different?

23.5 General Autos has its warrants traded in the market and will expire five years from today. Each warrant is entitled to purchase 0.25 shares of General Autos shares at DEM10 per share.
   a. Suppose General Autos shares are currently selling for DEM8, what is the lower limit on the warrant value? What is the upper limit?
   b. Suppose General Autos shares are currently selling for DEM12, what is the lower limit on the warrant value? What is the upper limit?

23.6 Babbel GmbH, has outstanding 10 million ordinary shares and 200,000 warrants. Each warrant can purchase five ordinary shares at DEM15 per share. Warrant holders exercised all of their warrants today. The share price of Babbel GmbH before the exercise was DEM17. What should the new share price be after the exercise? Assume there is no information content on the exercise of the warrants.

23.7 A warrant entitles the holder to buy 10 ordinary shares at NLG21 per share. When the market price of the shares are NLG15, will the market price of the warrant equal zero? Why or why not?

23.8 Grand Mills plc has 4 million ordinary shares outstanding. The company has 500,000 warrants being traded in the market. Each warrant has the right to buy one ordinary share at GBP20 per share. The warrant will expire one year from today. Grand Mills shares are selling for GBP22 per share and the variance of the return on the shares is 0.005. The risk-free rate is 5 per cent. Use the Black–Scholes model to price the warrant.

23.9 Consider the following warrants.
   Warrant X: For each warrant held, three ordinary shares can be purchased at an exercise price of CHF20 per share.
   Warrant Y: For each warrant held, two ordinary shares can be purchased at an exercise price of CHF30 per share.
   The current market price of share X is CHF30 per share. The current market price of share Y is CHF40 per share.
   a. What is the minimum value of warrant X?
   b. What is the minimum value of warrant Y?

Convertibles

23.10 At issuance of Bierhoff GmbH convertible bonds, one of the two following sets of characteristics were true.

	A	B
Offering price of bond	DEM900	DEM1,000
Bond value (straight debt)	DEM900	DEM950
Share price	DEM20	DEM30
Conversion ratio	50	30

Which of the relationships do you believe was more likely to have prevailed? Why?

23.11 The following facts apply to a convertible security:

Conversion price	CHF25/share
Coupon rate	6%
Par value	CHF1,000
Yield on non-convertible debenture of same quality	10%
Market value of straight bond of same quality with coupon rate of 10%	CHF950
Share price	CHF24/share

a. What is the minimum price at which the convertible should sell?
b. What accounts for any premium in the market price of the convertible over the value of the ordinary shares into which it can be converted?

23.12 Strunz GmbH issued DEM430,000 of 8 per cent convertible debentures. Each bond is convertible into 28 ordinary shares any time before maturity.
a. Suppose the current price of the bonds is DEM1,000 and the current price of a Strunz share is DEM31.25.
  i. What is the conversion ratio?
  ii. What is the conversion price?
  iii. What is the conversion premium?
b. Suppose the current price of the bonds is DEM1,180 and the current price of a Strunz share is DEM31.25.
  i. What is the conversion ratio?
  ii. What is the conversion price?
  iii. What is the conversion premium?
c. What is the conversion value of the debentures?
d. If the value of Strunz shares increases by DEM2, what will the conversion value be?

23.13 Basler GmbH issued a zero coupon convertible bond due 10 years from today. The bond has a face value of DEM1,000 at maturity. Each bond can be converted into 25 Basler ordinary shares. The appropriate interest rate is 10 per cent. The company's shares are selling for DEM12 per share. Each convertible bond is traded at DEM400 in the market.
a. What is the straight bond value?
b. What is the conversion value?
c. What is the option value of the bond?

23.14 A DEM1,000 par convertible debenture has a conversion price per ordinary share of DEM180. With the ordinary shares selling at DEM60, what is the conversion value of the bond?

CHAPTER 24 Leasing

Almost any asset that can be purchased can be leased, from aircraft to computers. When we take vacations or business trips, renting a car for a few days frequently seems a convenient thing to do. This is an example of a short-term lease. After all, buying a car and selling it a few days later would be a great nuisance.

Companies lease both short-term and long-term, but this chapter is primarily concerned with long-term leasing over a term of more than two or three years. Long-term leasing is a method of financing property, plant and equipment. More equipment is financed today by long-term leases than by any other method of equipment financing.

Every lease contract has two parties: the lessee and the lessor. The **lessee** is the user of the equipment, and the **lessor** is the owner. Typically, the lessee first decides on the asset needed and then negotiates a lease contract with a lessor. From the lessee's standpoint, long-term leasing is similar to buying the equipment with a secured loan. The terms of the lease contract are compared to what a banker might arrange with a secured loan. Thus, long-term leasing is a form of financing.

Many questionable advantages are claimed for long-term leasing, such as 'leasing provides 100 per cent financing', or 'leasing conserves capital'. However, in most countries, the principal benefit of long-term leasing is tax reduction. Leasing allows the transfer of tax benefits from those who need equipment but cannot take full advantage of the tax benefits associated with ownership to a party who can. If corporate tax laws were completely repealed, long-term leasing would virtually disappear.

24.1 Leasing —The Basics

A *lease* is a contractual agreement between a lessee and a lessor. The agreement establishes that the lessee has the right to use an asset and in return must make periodic payments to the lessor, the owner of the asset. The lessor is either the asset's manufacturer or an independent leasing company. If the lessor is an independent leasing company, it must buy the asset from a manufacturer. Then the lessor delivers the asset to the lessee, and the lease goes into effect.

As far as the lessee is concerned, it is the use of the asset that is most important, not who owns the asset. The use of an asset can be obtained by a lease contract. Because the user can also buy the asset, leasing and buying involve alternative financing arrangements for the use of an asset. This is illustrated in Figure 24.1.

The specific example in Figure 24.1 often happens in the computer industry. Firm *U*, the lessee, might be a hospital, a law firm or any other firm that uses computers. The lessor is an independent leasing company who purchased the equipment from a manufacturer such as IBM or Apple. Leases of this type are called **direct leases**. In the figure, the lessor issued both debt and equity to finance the purchase.

FIGURE 24.1   **Buying versus Leasing**

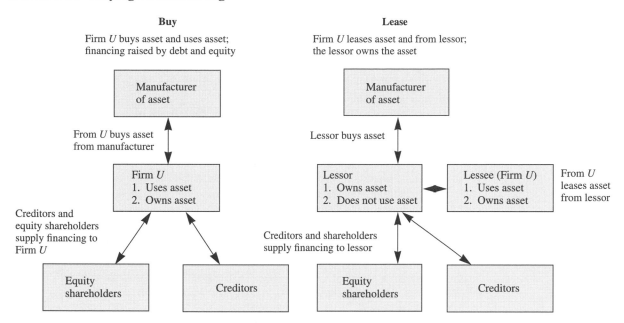

Of course, a manufacturer like IBM could lease its own computers, though we do not show this situation in the example. In such a case, IBM would compete with the independent computer-leasing company.

One of the biggest problems in the area of leasing is that taxation and accounting rules with respect to leases vary from one European country to another. Having said this, it is worth while beginning with definitions that emanate from the USA.[1] There a lease meeting one or more of the following criteria is to be classified as a capital lease by the lessee and the requirement is that such leases (called financial leases) are capitalized in the accounts of the lessee. The asset involved in the lease appears as a fixed asset in the accounts, with the amount remaining due in future years appearing as a liability. The requirements are:

1. The lease transfers ownership of the property to the lessee by the end of the lease term.
2. The lease contains a bargain purchase option.
3. The lease term is equal to 75 per cent or more of the estimated economic life of the leased property.
4. The present value at the beginning of the lease term of the minimum lease payments (excluding that portion of the payments representing executory costs such as insurance, maintenance and taxes to be paid by the lessor, including any profit thereon) equals or exceeds 90 per cent of the excess of the fair value of the leased property to the lessor at the inception of the lease over any related investment tax credit retained by the lessor and expected to be realized by him (the so-called 90 per cent recovery test).

---

[1] Your authors are fully aware that Europe does not include the USA, neither does the USA include Europe. But since US accounting classifications of leases are well developed, this seems a very good place to start.

The latter two criteria are not applicable when the beginning of the lease term falls within the last 25 per cent period of the total estimated economic life of the leased property.

A lease which does not meet the above criteria is to be classified as an operating lease from the lessee's perspective. This means that the lessee need not capitalize the lease. But for operating leases having (remaining) non-cancellable lease terms in excess of one year, information of the future obligations must be disclosed in the lessee's financial statements.

So US regulations mean that **financial leases** (sometimes also called capital leases or finance leases) are the exact opposite of **operating leases**, as is seen from their important characteristics:

1. Financial leases do not provide for maintenance or service by the lessor.
2. Financial leases are fully depreciated or amortized.
3. The lessee usually has a right to renew the lease on expiration.
4. Generally, financial leases cannot be cancelled. In other words, the lessee must make all payments or face the risk of bankruptcy.

Because of the above characteristics, particularly (2), the financial lease provides an alternative method of financing to purchase. Hence, its name is a good one.

Two special types of financial leases are the sale and lease-back arrangement and the leveraged lease.

Sale and Lease-Back
A sale and lease-back occurs when a company sells an asset it owns to another firm and immediately leases it back. In a sale and lease-back, two things happen:

1. The lessee receives cash from the sale of the asset.
2. The lessee makes periodic lease payments, thereby retaining use of the asset.

Leveraged Leases
A **leveraged lease** is a three-sided arrangement among the lessee, the lessor and the lenders:

1. As in other leases, the lessee uses the assets and makes periodic lease payments.
2. As in other leases, the lessor purchases the assets, delivers them to the lessee, and collects the lease payments. However, the lessor puts up no more than 40 to 50 per cent of the purchase price.
3. The lenders supply the remaining financing and receive interest payments from the lessor. Thus, the arrangement on the righthand side of Figure 24.1 would be a leveraged lease if the bulk of the financing was supplied by creditors.

The lenders in a leveraged lease typically use a non-recourse loan. This means that the lessor is not obligated to the lender in case of a default. However, the lender is protected in two ways:

1. The lender has a first lien on the asset.
2. In the event of loan default, the lease payments are made directly to the lender.

The lessor puts up only part of the funds but gets the lease payments and all the tax benefits of ownership. These lease payments are used to pay the debt service of the non-recourse loan. The lessee benefits because, in a competitive market, the lease payment is lowered when the lessor saves taxes.

Concept Questions

- What are some reasons that assets like automobiles would be leased with operating leases, whereas machines or real estate would be leased with financial leases?
- What are the differences between an operating lease and a financial lease?

In the USA, before November 1976, a firm could arrange to use an asset through a lease and not disclose the asset or the lease contract on the balance sheet. Lessees needed only to report information on leasing activity in the footnotes of their financial statements. Thus, leasing led to **off-balance-sheet financing**. Since November 1976, in the USA certain leases have been classified as capital or financial leases. For a capital lease, the present value of the lease payments appears on the liabilities side of the balance sheet. The identical value appears on the lefthand side of the balance sheet as an asset. The US accounting regulators classify all other leases as operating leases. No mention of the lease appears on the balance sheet for operating leases.

24.2   European Lease Accounting

Different rules apply in different European countries as regards accounting for leases. In this brief overview, we focus upon only four countries: Britain, Germany, France and the Netherlands. For a fuller picture, readers are referred to the detailed accounting rules in individual countries.

Britain

In the UK, a finance lease is one that transfers all the risks and rewards of ownership (but not legal title) of an asset to the lessee. It is presumed that a lease is a finance lease if, at the inception of the lease, the present value of the minimum lease payments (including any initial payment) amounts to substantially all (90 per cent+) of the leased asset's fair value to the lessor at the inception of the lease. All other leases are operating leases.

The definition of a finance lease is only slightly different to that applicable in the USA. Defining leases in this manner ensures that all leases are either finance leases or operating leases. As in the USA, similar rules of accounting for leases apply.

For the lessor, the appropriate UK accounting standard requires that assets that are held for leasing under operating leases are capitalized as fixed assets and depreciated over their useful economic life. Rental income is recognized on an accruals basis irrespective of when such rentals are due for payment.

In the books of the lessor, items that are classified as finance leases are not shown as assets. The lessor records, as a debtor in current assets, the amount due from the lessee, and that amount should be equal to the net investment in the lease after making provisions for bad and doubtful rentals receivable. Income is recognized in the profit and loss account, using an actuarial method based on present value arithmetic, such that a constant return on the net investment is reported.

For the lessee, rentals due on operating leases are usually charged to the profit and loss account on a straight-line basis unless an alternative systematic and rational basis is more applicable.

The lessee records both a fixed asset and an obligation (in creditors) when entering into finance leases. The fixed asset is depreciated over the term of the lease or the asset's useful life, whichever is the shorter. The obligation is reduced as rentals are paid, and the finance charge that is built into this rental is charged on a systematic basis so as to give a constant charge on the outstanding obligation.

Germany

The only regulation contained within the German Commercial Code is the disclosure requirement requiring the lessee to include within a note on financial commitments the future obligations under lease contracts, but these obligations do not have to be separately identified.

The rules relating to accounting for leases are contained within the tax regulations where there are identification criteria for recognizing finance leases that should be capitalized by the lessee. German businesses, however, tend to formulate their lease contracts in such a way that the lessor shows the asset on its balance sheet.

France

The capitalization of finance lease commitments and their disclosure as a fixed asset and related liability appears only in French consolidated accounts, and even then only rarely.

The legislation relating to individual companies does not allow the capitalization of finance leases and therefore all leases are effectively accounted for as operating leases with no effort being made to reflect the economic substance of the transaction in the books of either the lessee or the lessor. The only time a leased asset will appear on the balance sheet of the lessee is when the asset is purchased under an option in the lease in which case it is treated as an acquisition at the actual option exercise price.

The notes to the accounts must include details of the fair value of the asset at the start of the lease, the depreciation charge for the period and the accumulated depreciation provision as if the leased asset had been purchased at the inception of the lease. This would enable a reader to adjust the financial statements to reflect the position based on the substance over form concept whereby capitalization of finance leases occurs.

Netherlands

The usual distinction between finance leases, where the economic risks lie with the lessee, but legal ownership remains with the lessor, and operating leases, exists with the accounting requirements reflecting the two forms of contract.

For finance leases, the lessee capitalizes the asset and shows the relevant lease rental obligations in liabilities. The accounts must clearly show that the lessee is the economic, but not the legal owner. The lessor shows the outstanding rentals under accounts receivable. Most finance leases involve the use of a finance company and either entitle the lessee to acquire the asset at well below market value at the end of the lease term or gain use of the asset for approximately all of its useful economic life. For operating leases, the item is carried as an asset in the accounts of the lessor but the lessee, while not recording the obligations in its balance sheet, must disclose details of any long-term commitments to pay rentals involving substantial amounts.

Other European Countries

As mentioned earlier, rules differ. However it is fair to say that most other European countries tend to adopt the French method of accounting for leases rather than the British one.

24.3   The Cash Flows of Leasing

In this section we identify the basic cash flows used in evaluating a lease. In all countries, leasing is a tax-driven financing arrangement. Given a lack of homogeneity between European countries on corporate tax, in the example here we assume a country with a 34 per cent corporation tax rate which allows straight-line depreciation of assets for tax purposes and allows interest charges to be set off as an expense against tax payable.

Consider the decision confronting the Xomox Corporation, which manufactures pipe. Business has been expanding and Xomox currently has a five-year backlog of pipe orders for the Trans-European Pipeline.

The International Boring Machine Corporation (IBMC) makes a pipe-boring machine that can be purchased for Euro10,000. The Euro is the designation of the common European currency should Economic and Monetary Union (EMU) become a reality in parts of Europe. Xomox has determined that it needs a new machine, and the IBMC model will save Xomox Euro6,000 per year in reduced electricity bills for the next five years. These savings are known with certainty because Xomox has a long-term electricity purchase agreement with various electricity utilities.

Xomox has a corporate tax rate of 34 per cent. We assume that five-year straight-line depreciation is used for the pipe-boring machine, and the machine will be worthless after five years.

However, Friendly Leasing Corporation has offered to lease the same pipe-boring machine to Xomox for Euro2,500 per year for five years. With the lease, Xomox would remain responsible for maintenance, insurance, and operating expenses.[2]

Simon Smart, a recently hired MBA, has been asked to calculate the incremental cash flows from leasing the IBMC machine in lieu of buying it. He has prepared Table 24.1, which shows the direct cash flow consequences of buying the pipe-boring machine and also signing the lease agreement with Friendly Leasing.

To simplify matters, Simon Smart has prepared Table 24.2, which subtracts the direct cash flows of buying the pipe-boring machine from those of leasing it. Noting that only the net advantage of leasing is relevant to Xomox, he concludes the following from his analysis:

1. Operating costs are not directly affected by leasing. Xomox will save Euro3,960 (after taxes) from use of the IBMC boring machine regardless of whether the machine is owned or leased. Thus, this cash flow stream does not appear in Table 24.2.
2. If the machine is leased, Xomox will save the Euro10,000 it would have used to purchase the machine. This saving shows up as an initial cash *inflow* of Euro10,000 in year 0.
3. If Xomox leases the pipe-boring machine, it will no longer own this machine

---

[2] For simplicity, we have assumed that lease payments are made at the end of each year. Actually, most leases require lease payments to be made at the beginning of the year.

TABLE 24.1   **Cash Flows to Xomox from Using the IBMC Pipe-Boring Machine: Buy versus Lease**

	Year 0	Year 1	Year 2	Year 3	Year 4	Year 5
Buy						
Cost of machine	−Euro10,000					
After-tax operating savings [Euro3,960 = Euro6,000 × (1 − 0.34)]		Euro3,960	Euro3,960	Euro3,960	Euro3,960	Euro3,960
Depreciation tax benefit		680	680	680	680	680
	−Euro10,000	Euro4,640	Euro4,640	Euro4,640	Euro4,640	Euro4,640
Lease						
Lease payments		−Euro2,500	−Euro2,500	−Euro2,500	−Euro2,500	−Euro2,500
Tax benefits of lease payments Euro860 = Euro2,500 × 0.34)		850	850	850	850	850
After-tax operating savings		3,960	3,960	3,960	3,960	3,960
Total		Euro2,310	Euro2,310	Euro2,310	Euro2,310	Euro2,310

Depreciation is straight line. Because the depreciable base is Euro10,000, depreciation expense per year is Euro10,000/5 = Euro2,000.
The depreciation tax benefit per year is equal to

$$\text{Tax rate} \times \text{Depreciation expense per year} = \text{Depreciation tax benefit}$$
$$0.34 \quad \times \quad \text{Euro2,000} \quad = \quad \text{Euro680}$$

TABLE 24.2   **Incremental Cash Flow Consequences for Xomox from Leasing instead of Purchasing**

	Year 0	Year 1	Year 2	Year 3	Year 4	Year 5
Lease						
Lease payment		−Euro2,500	−Euro2,500	−Euro2,500	−Euro2,500	−Euro2,500
Tax benefit of lease payment		850	850	850	850	850
Buy (minus)						
Cost of machine	−(−Euro10,000)					
Lost depreciation tax benefit		−680	−680	−680	−680	−680
Total	Euro10,000	−Euro2,330	−Euro2,330	−Euro2,330	−Euro2,330	−Euro2,330

The bottom line presents the cash flows from leasing relative to the cash flows from purchase. The cash flows would be exactly the *opposite* if we considered the purchase relative to the lease.

and must give up the depreciation tax benefits. These tax benefits show up as an *outflow*.

4. If Xomox chooses to lease the machine, it must pay Euro2,500 per year for five years. The first payment is due at the end of the first year. (This is a break, because sometimes the first payment is due immediately.) The lease payments are tax deductible and, as a consequence, generate tax benefits of Euro850 (0.34 × Euro2,500).

The net cash flows have been placed in the bottom line of Table 24.2. These numbers represent the cash flows from *leasing* relative to the cash flows from the purchase. It is arbitrary that we express the flows in this way. We could have expressed the cash flows from the *purchase* relative to the cash flows from leasing. These cash flows would be

	Year 0	Year 1	Year 2	Year 3	Year 4	Year 5
Net cash flows from purchase alternative relative to lease alternative	−Euro10,000	Euro2,330	Euro2,330	Euro2,330	Euro2,330	Euro2,330

Of course, the cash flows here are the opposite of those in the bottom line of Table 24.2. Depending on our purpose, we may look at either the purchase relative to the lease or vice versa. Thus, the student should become comfortable with either viewpoint.

Now that we have the cash flows, we can make our decision by discounting the flows properly. However, because the discount rate is tricky, we take a detour in the next section before moving back to the Xomox case. In this next section, we show that cash flows in the lease-versus-buy decision should be discounted at the *after-tax* interest rate (i.e. the after-tax cost of debt capital).

24.4   A Detour on Discounting and Debt Capacity with Corporate Taxes

The analysis of leases is difficult, and both financial practitioners and academics have made conceptual errors. These errors revolve around taxes. We hope to avoid their mistakes by beginning with the simplest type of example, a loan for one year. Though this example is unrelated to our lease-versus-buy situation, principles developed here will apply directly to lease-buy analysis.

Present Value of Riskless Cash Flows

Consider a corporation that lends Euro100 for a year. If the interest rate is 10 per cent, the firm will receive Euro110 at the end of the year. Of this amount, Euro10 is interest and the remaining Euro100 is the original principal. A corporate tax rate of 34 per cent implies taxes on the interest of Euro3.40 ($0.34 \times$ Euro10). Thus, the firm ends up with Euro106.60 (Euro110 − Euro3.40) after taxes on a Euro100 investment.

Now, consider a company that borrows Euro100 for a year. With a 10 per cent interest rate, the firm must pay Euro110 to the bank at the end of the year. However, the borrowing firm can take the Euro10 of interest as a tax deduction. The corporation pays Euro3.40 ($0.34 \times$ Euro10) less in taxes than it would have paid had it not borrowed the money at all. Thus, considering this reduction in taxes, the firm must pay Euro106.60 (Euro110 − Euro3.40) on a Euro100 loan. The cash flows from both lending and borrowing are displayed in Table 24.3.

The above two paragraphs show a very important result: The firm could not care less whether it received Euro100 today or Euro106.60 next year.[3] If it received Euro100 today, it could lend it out, thereby receiving Euro106.60 after corporate taxes at the end of the year. Conversely, if it knows today that it will receive Euro106.60 at the end of the year, it could borrow Euro100 today. The after-tax interest and principal

---

[3] For simplicity, assume that the firm received Euro100 or Euro106.60 after corporate taxes. Since $0.66 = 1 - 0.34$, the pretax inflows would be Euro151.52 (Euro100/0.66) and Euro161.52 (Euro106.60/0.66), respectively.

TABLE 24.3   Lending and Borrowing in a World with Corporate Taxes (Interest rate is 10 per cent and corporate tax rate is 34 per cent)

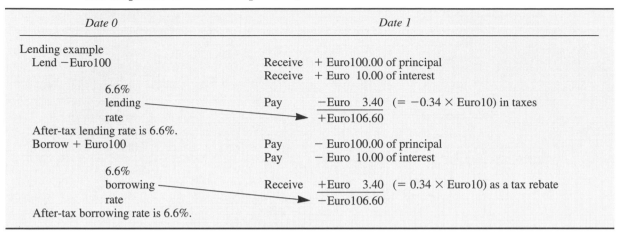

	Date 0	Date 1
Lending example		
Lend −Euro100		Receive + Euro100.00 of principal
		Receive + Euro 10.00 of interest
	6.6% lending rate	Pay −Euro 3.40 (= −0.34 × Euro10) in taxes
		+Euro106.60
After-tax lending rate is 6.6%.		
Borrow + Euro100		Pay − Euro100.00 of principal
		Pay − Euro 10.00 of interest
	6.6% borrowing rate	Receive +Euro 3.40 (= 0.34 × Euro10) as a tax rebate
		−Euro106.60
After-tax borrowing rate is 6.6%.		

General principle: In a world with corporate taxes, riskless cash flows should be discounted at the after-tax interest rate.

payments on the loan would be paid with the Euro106.60 that the firm will receive at the end of the year. Because of the interchangeability illustrated above, we say that a payment of Euro106.60 next year has a present value of Euro100. Because Euro100 = Euro106.60/1.066, a riskless cash flow should be discounted at the after-tax interest rate of 0.066 [0.10 × (1 − 0.34)].

Of course, the above discussion considered a specific example. The general principle is

> In a world with corporate taxes, the firm should discount riskless cash flows at the after-tax rate of interest.

Optimal Debt Level and Riskless Cash Flows (Advanced)

In addition, our simple example can illustrate a related point concerning optimal debt level. Consider a firm that has just determined that the current level of debt in its capital structure is optimal. Immediately following that determination, it is surprised to learn that it will receive a guaranteed payment of Euro106.60 in one year from, say, a tax-exempt government lottery. This future windfall is an asset that, like any asset, should raise the firm's optimal debt level. How much does this payment raise the firm's optimal level?

Our above analysis implies that the firm's optimal debt level must be Euro100 more than it previously was. That is, the firm could borrow Euro100 today, perhaps paying the entire amount out as a dividend. It would owe the bank Euro110 at the end of the year. However, because it receives a tax rebate of Euro3.40 (0.34 × Euro10), its net repayment will be Euro106.60. Thus, its borrowing of Euro100 today is fully offset by next year's government lottery proceeds of Euro106.60. In other words, the lottery proceeds act as an irrevocable trust that can service the increased debt. Note that we need not know the optimal debt level before the lottery was announced. We are merely saying that, whatever this prelottery optimal level was, the optimal debt level is Euro100 more after the lottery announcement.

Of course, this is just one example. The general principle is[4]

> In a world with corporate taxes, one determines the increase in the firm's optimal debt level by discounting a future guaranteed after-tax inflow at the after-tax riskless interest rate.

Conversely, suppose that a second and unrelated firm is surprised to learn that it must pay Euro106.60 next year to the government for back taxes. Clearly, this additional liability impinges on the second firm's debt capacity. By the above reasoning, it follows that the second firm's optimal debt level must be lowered by exactly Euro100.

Concept Question

• How should one discount a riskless cash flow?

24.5   NPV Analysis of the Lease-versus-Buy Decision

The detour leads to a simple method for evaluating leases: discount all cash flows at the after-tax interest rate. From the bottom line of Table 24.2, Xomox's incremental cash flows from leasing versus purchasing are

	Year 0	*Year 1*	*Year 2*	*Year 3*	*Year 4*	*Year 5*
Net cash flows from lease alternative relative to purchase alternative	Euro10,000	−Euro2,330	−Euro2,330	−Euro2,330	−Euro2,330	−Euro2,330

Let us assume that Xomox can either borrow or lend at the interest rate of 7.57575 per cent. If the corporate tax rate is 34 per cent, the correct discount rate is the after-tax rate of 5 per cent [7.57575% × (1 − 0.34)]. When 5 per cent is used to compute the NPV of the lease, we have

$$\text{NPV} = \text{Euro}10{,}000 - \text{Euro}2{,}330 \times A_{0.05}^{5} = -\text{Euro}87.68 \qquad (24.1)$$

Because the net present value of the incremental cash flows from leasing relative to purchasing is negative, Xomox prefers to purchase.

Equation (24.1) is the correct approach to lease-versus-buy analysis. However, students are often bothered by two things. First, they question whether the cash flows in Table 24.2 are truly riskless. We examine this issue below. Second, they feel that this approach lacks intuition. We address this concern a little later.

The Discount Rate

Because we discounted at the after-tax riskless rate of interest, we have implicitly assumed that the cash flows in the Xomox example are riskless. Is this appropriate?

A lease payment is like the debt service on a secured bond issued by the lessee, and the discount rate should be approximately the same as the interest rate on such

---

[4] This principle holds for riskless or guaranteed cash flows only. Unfortunately, there is no easy formula for determining the increase in optimal debt level from a *risky* cash flow.

debt. In general, this rate will be slightly higher than the riskless rate considered in the previous section. The various tax shields could be somewhat riskier than the lease payments for two reasons. First, the value of the depreciation tax benefits depends on the ability of Xomox to generate enough taxable income to use them. Second, the corporate tax rate may change in the future. For these two reasons, a firm might be justified in discounting the depreciation tax benefits at a rate higher than that used for the lease payments. However, our experience is that real-world companies discount both the depreciation tax shield and lease payments at the same rate. This implies that financial practitioners view the above two risks as minor. We adopt the real-world convention of discounting the two flows at the same rate. This rate is the after-tax interest rate on secured debt issued by the lessee.

At this point some students still ask the question: Why not use r_{WACC} as the discount rate in lease-versus-buy analysis? Of course, r_{WACC} should not be used for lease analysis because the cash flows are more like debt-service cash flows than operating cash flows and, as such, the risk is much less. The discount rate should reflect the risk of the incremental cash flows.

24.6   Debt Displacement and Lease Valuation

The Basic Concept of Debt Displacement (Advanced)

The previous analysis allows one to calculate the right answer in a simple manner. This clearly must be viewed as an important benefit. However, the analysis has little intuitive appeal. To remedy this, we hope to make lease–buy analysis more intuitive by considering the issue of debt displacement.

A firm that purchases equipment will generally issue debt to finance the purchase. The debt becomes a liability of the firm. A lessee incurs a liability equal to the present value of all future lease payments. Because of this, we argue that leases displace debt. The balance sheets in Table 24.4 illustrate how leasing might affect debt.

TABLE 24.4   Debt Displacement Elsewhere in the Firm When a Lease is Instituted

Assets		*Liabilities*	
Initial situation			
Current	Euro 50,000	Debt	Euro 60,000
Fixed	50,000	Equity	60,000
Total	Euro100,000	Total	Euro100,000
Buy with secured loan			
Current	Euro 50,000	Debt	Euro 66,000
Fixed	50,000	Equity	44,000
Machine	10,000		
Total	Euro110,000	Total	Euro110,000
Lease			
Current	Euro 50,000	Lease	Euro 10,000
Fixed	50,000	Debt	56,000
Machine	10,000	Equity	44,000
Total	Euro110,000	Total	Euro110,000

This example shows that leases reduce the level of debt elsewhere in the firm. Though the example illustrates a point, it is not meant to show a *precise* method for calculating debt displacement.

Suppose a firm initially has Euro100,000 of assets and a 150 per cent optimal debt–equity ratio. The firm's debt is Euro60,000, and its equity is Euro40,000. As in the Xomox case, suppose the firm must use a new Euro10,000 machine. The firm has two alternatives:

1. *The Firm Can Purchase the Machine*   If it does, it will finance the purchase with a secured loan and with equity. The debt capacity of the machine is assumed to be the same as for the firm as a whole.
2. *The Firm Can Lease the Asset and Get 100 per cent Financing*   That is, the present value of the future lease payments will be Euro10,000.

If the firm finances the machines with both secured debt and new equity, its debt will increase by Euro6,000 and its equity by Euro4,000. Its optimal debt–equity ratio of 150 per cent will be maintained.

Conversely, consider the lease alternative. Because the lessee views the lease payment as a liability, the lessee thinks in terms of a *liability-to-equity* ratio, not just a debt-to-equity ratio. As mentioned above, the present value of the lease liability is Euro10,000. If the leasing firm is to maintain a liability-to-equity ratio of 150 per cent, debt elsewhere in the firm must fall by Euro4,000 when the lease is instituted. Because debt must be repurchased, net liabilities only rise by Euro6,000 (Euro10,000 − Euro4,000) when Euro10,000 of assets are placed under lease.[5]

Debt displacement is a hidden cost of leasing. If a firm leases, it will not use as much regular debt as it would otherwise. The benefits of debt capacity will be lost, particularly the lower taxes associated with interest expense.

Optimal Debt Level in the Xomox Example (Advanced)

The previous section showed that leasing displaces debt. Though the section illustrated a point, it was not meant to show the precise method for calculating debt displacement. Below, we describe the precise method for calculating the difference in optimal debt levels between purchase and lease in the Xomox example.

From the last line of Table 24.2, we know that the cash flows from the purchase alternative relative to the cash flows from the lease alternative are[6]

	Year 0	Year 1	Year 2	Year 3	Year 4	Year 5
Net cash flows from purchase alternative relative to lease alternative	−Euro10,000	Euro 2,330	Euro2,330	Euro2,330	Euro2,330	Euro2,330

An increase in the optimal debt level at year 0 occurs because the firm learns at that time of guaranteed cash flows beginning at year 1. Our detour on discounting and debt capacity told us to calculate this increased debt level by discounting the future riskless cash inflows at the after-tax interest rate.[7] Thus, additional debt level of the

---

[5] Growing firms in the real world will not generally repurchase debt when instituting a lease. Rather, they will issue less debt in the future than they would have without the lease.

[6] The last line of Table 24.2 presents the cash flows from the lease alternative relative to the purchase alternative. As pointed out earlier, our cash flows are now reversed because we are now presenting the cash flows from the purchase alternative relative to the lease alternative.

[7] Though our detour considered only riskless cash flows, the cash flows in a leasing example are not necessarily riskless. As we explained earlier, we therefore adopt the real-world convention of discounting at the after-tax interest rate on secured debt issued by the lessee.

purchase alternative relative to the lease alternative is

Increase in optimal debt level from purchase alternative relative to lease alternative:

$$Euro10{,}087.68 = \frac{Euro2{,}330}{1.05} + \frac{Euro2{,}330}{(1.05)^2}$$

$$+ \frac{Euro2{,}330}{(1.05)^3} + \frac{Euro2{,}330}{(1.05)^4} + \frac{Euro2{,}330}{(1.05)^5}$$

That is, whatever the optimal amount of debt would be under the lease alternative, the optimal amount of debt would be Euro10,087.68 more under the purchase alternative.

This result can be stated in another way. Imagine there are two identical firms except that one firm purchases the boring machine and the other leases it. From Table 24.2, we know that the purchasing firm generates Euro2,330 more cash flow after taxes in each of the five years than does the leasing firm. Further, imagine that the same bank lends money to both firms The bank should lend the purchasing firm more money because it has a greater cash flow each period. How much extra money should the bank loan the purchasing firm so that the incremental loan can be paid off by the extra cash flows of Euro2,330 per year? The answer is exactly Euro10,087.68, the increase in the optimal debt level we calculated earlier.

To see this, let us work through the example on a year-by-year basis. Because the purchasing firm borrows Euro10,087.68 more at year 0 than does the leasing firm, the purchasing firm will pay interest of Euro764.22 (Euro10,087.68 × 0.0757575) at year 1 on the additional debt. The interest allows the firm to reduce its taxes by Euro259.83 (Euro764.22 × 0.34), leaving an after-tax outflow of Euro504.39 (Euro764.22 − Euro259.83) at year 1.

We know from Table 24.2 that the purchasing firm generates Euro2,330 more cash at year 1 than does the leasing firm. Because the purchasing firm has the extra Euro2,330 coming in at year 1 but must pay interest on its loan, how much of the loan can the firm repay at year 1 and still have the same cash flow as the leasing firm has? The purchasing firm can repay Euro1,825.61 (Euro2,330 − Euro504.39) of the loan at year 1 and still have the same net cash flow that the leasing firm has. After the repayment, the purchasing firm will have a remaining balance of Euro8,262.07 (Euro10,087.68 − Euro1,825.61) at year 1. For each of the five years, this sequence of cash flows is displayed in Table 24.5. The outstanding balance goes to zero over the five years. Thus, the annual cash flow of Euro2,330, which represents the extra cash from purchasing instead of not leasing, fully amortizes the loan of Euro10,087.68.

Our analysis on debt capacity has two purposes. First, we want to show the additional debt capacity from purchasing. We just completed this task. Second, we want to determine whether or not the lease is preferred to the purchase. This decision rule follows easily from the above discussion. By leasing the equipment and having Euro10,087.68 less debt than under the purchase alternative, the firm has exactly the same cash flow in years 1 to 5 that it would have through a levered purchase. Thus, we can ignore cash flows beginning in year 1 when comparing the lease alternative with the purchase with debt alternative. However, the cash flows differ between the alternatives at year 0. These differences are

1. *The Purchase Cost at Year 0 of Euro10,000 Is Avoided by Leasing* This should be viewed as a cash inflow under the leasing alternative.
2. *The Firm Borrows Euro10,087.68 Less at Year 0 under the Lease Alternative*

TABLE 24.5 Calculation of Increase in Optimal Debt Level if Xomox Purchases instead of Leases

	Year 0	*Year 1*	*Year 2*	*Year 3*	*Year 4*	*Year 5*
Outstanding balance of loan	Euro10,087.68	Euro8,262.07*	Euro6,345.17	Euro4,332.42	Euro2,219.05	Euro 0
Interest		764.22	625.91	480.69	328.22	168.11
Tax deduction on interest		259.83	212.81	163.44	111.59	57.16
After-tax interest expense		Euro 504.39	Euro 413.10	Euro 317.25	Euro 216.63	Euro 110.95
Extra cash that purchasing firm generates over leasing firm (from Table 24.2)		Euro2,330.00	Euro2,330.00	Euro2,330.00	Euro2,330.00	Euro2,330.00
Repayment of loan		Euro1,825.61†	Euro1,916.90	Euro2,012.75	Euro2,113.37	Euro2,219.05

Assume that there are two otherwise-identical firms where one leases and the other purchases. The purchasing firm can borrow Euro10,087.68 more than the leasing firm. The extra cash flow each year of Euro2,330 from purchasing instead of leasing can be used to pay off the loan in five years.
*Euro8,262.07 = Euro10,087.68 − Euro1,825.61.
†Euro1,825.61 = Euro2,330 − Euro504.39.

than It Can under the Purchase Alternative   This should be viewed as a cash outflow under the leasing alternative.

Because the firm borrows Euro10,087.68 less by leasing, but saves only Euro10,000 on the equipment, the lease alternative requires an extra cash outflow at year 0 relative to the purchase alternative of −Euro87.68 (Euro10,000 − Euro10,087.68). Because cash flows in later years from leasing are identical to those from purchasing with debt, the firm should purchase.

This is exactly the same answer we got when, earlier in this chapter, we discounted all cash flows at the after-tax interest rate. Of course, this is no coincidence because the increase in the optimal debt level is also determined by discounting all flows at the after-tax interest rate. The accompanying box presents both methods. (The numbers in the box are in terms of the NPV of the lease relative to the purchase. Thus, a negative NPV indicates that the purchase alternative should be taken.)

Two Methods for Calculating Net Present Value of Lease Relative to Purchase*

Method 1: Discount all cash flows at the after-tax interest rate

$$-\text{Euro}87.68 = \text{Euro}10,000 - \text{Euro}2,330 \times A^5_{0.05}$$

Method 2: Compare pruchase price with reduction in optimal debt level under leasing alternative

$$-\text{Euro}87.68 = \underset{\substack{\text{Purchase} \\ \text{price}}}{\text{Euro}10,000} - \underset{\substack{\text{Reduction in} \\ \text{optimal debt} \\ \text{level if leasing}}}{\text{Euro}10,087.68}$$

---

*Because we are calculating the NPV of the lease relative to the purchase, a negative value indicates that the purchase alternative is preferred

24.7   Does Leasing Ever Pay: The Base Case

We previously looked at the lease–buy decision from the point of view of the potential lessee, Xomox. Let's now look at the decision from the point of view of the lessor, Friendly Leasing. This firm faces three cash flows, all of which are displayed in Table 24.6. First, Friendly purchases the machine for Euro10,000 at year 0. Second, because the asset is depreciated straight-line over five years, the depreciation expense at the end of each of the five years is Euro2,000 (Euro10,000/5). The yearly depreciation tax shield is Euro680 (Euro2,000 × 0.34). Third, because the yearly lease payment is Euro2,500, the after-tax lease payment is Euro1,650 [Euro2,500 × (1 − 0.34)].

TABLE 24.6   **Cash Flows to Friendly Leasing as Lessor of IBMC Pipe-Boring Machine**

	Year 0	Year 1	Year 2	Year 3	Year 4	Year 5
Cash for machine	−Euro10,000					
Depreciation tax benefit (Euro680 = Euro2,000 × 0.34)		Euro 680	Euro 680	Euro 680	Euro 680	Euro 680
After-tax lease payment [Euro1,650 = Euro 2,500 × (1 − 0.34)]		Euro1,650	Euro1,650	Euro1,650	Euro1,650	Euro1,650
Total	−Euro10,000	Euro2,330	Euro2,330	Euro2,330	Euro2,330	Euro2,330

These cash flows are the opposite of the cash flows to Xomox, the lessee (see the bottom line of Table 24.2).

Now examine the total cash flows to Friendly Leasing, as displayed in the bottom line of Table 24.6. Those of you with a healthy memory will notice something very interesting. These cash flows are exactly the *opposite* of those of Xomox, as displayed in the bottom line of Table 24.2. Those of you with a healthy sense of scepticism may be thinking something very interesting: 'If the cash flows of the lessor are exactly the opposite of those of the lessee, the combined cash flow of the two parties must be zero each year. Thus, there does not seem to be any joint benefit to this lease. Because the net present value to the lessee was −Euro87.68, the NPV to the lessor must be Euro87.68. The joint NPV is Euro0 (−Euro87.68 + Euro87.68). There does not appear to be any way for the NPV of both the lessor and the lessee to be positive at the same time. Because one party would inevitably lose money, the leasing deal could never fly.'

This is one of the most important results of leasing. Though Table 24.6 concerns one particular leasing deal, the principle can be generalized. As long as (1) both parties are subject to the same interest and tax rates and (2) transaction costs are ignored, there can be no leasing deal that benefits both parties. However, there is a lease payment for which both parties would calculate an NPV of zero. Given that fee, Xomox would be indifferent to whether it leased or bought, and Friendly Leasing would be indifferent to whether it leased or not.[8]

A student with an even healthier sense of scepticism might be thinking, 'This textbook appears to be arguing that leasing is not beneficial. Yet, we know that leasing occurs frequently in the real world. Maybe, just maybe, the textbook is wrong.' Although we will not admit to being wrong (what textbook would?), we freely admit to being incomplete at this point. The next section considers factors that give benefits to leasing.

---

[8] The break-even lease payment is Euro2,469.32 in our example. Both the lessor and lessee can solve for this as

$$\text{Euro}10,000 = \text{Euro}680 \times A_{0.05}^{5} + L \times (1 - 0.34) \times A_{0.05}^{5}$$

In this case, $L = \text{Euro}2,469.32$.

24.8   Reasons for Leasing

Proponents of leasing make many claims about why firms should lease assets rather than buy them. Some of the reasons given to support leasing are good, and some are not. We discuss here the reasons for leasing we think are good and some of the ones we think aren't.

Good Reasons for Leasing

If leasing is a good choice, it will be because one or more of the following will be true:

1. Taxes may be reduced by leasing.
2. The lease contract may reduce certain types of uncertainty.
3. Transactions costs can be higher for buying an asset and financing it with debt or equity than for leasing the asset.

Tax Advantages

The most important reason for long-term leasing is tax reduction. If the corporate income tax were repealed, long-term leasing would probably disappear. The tax advantages of leasing exist because firms are in different tax brackets.

Should a user in a low tax bracket purchase, he will receive little tax benefit from depreciation and interest deductions. Should the user lease, the lessor will receive the depreciation shield and the interest deductions. In a competitive market, the lessor must charge a low lease payment to reflect these tax shields. Thus, the user is likely to lease rather than purchase.

In our example with Xomox and Friendly Leasing, the value of the lease to Friendly was Euro87.68. That is,

$$\text{Euro87.68} = -\text{Euro10,000} + \text{Euro2,330} \times A^5_{0.05}$$

However, the value of the lease to Xomox was exactly the opposite (-Euro87.68). Because the lessor's gains came at the expense of the lessee, no deal could be arranged.

However, if Xomox pays no taxes and the lease payments are reduced to Euro2,475 from Euro2,500, both Friendly and Xomox will find there is positive NPV in leasing. Xomox can rework Table 24.2 with $T_c = 0$, finding that its cash flows from leasing are

	Year 0	*Year 1*	*Year 2*	*Year 3*	*Year 4*	*Year 5*
Cost of machine	Euro10,000					
Lease payment		−Euro2,475	−Euro2,475	−Euro2,475	−Euro2,475	−Euro2,475

The value of the lease to Xomox is

$$\text{Value of lease} = \text{Euro10,000} - \text{Euro2,475} \times A^5_{0.0757575}$$
$$= \text{Euro6.55}$$

Notice that the discount rate is the interest rate of 7.57575 per cent because tax rates are zero. In addition, the full lease payment of Euro2,475—and not some lower, after-tax number—is used since there are no taxes. Finally, note that depreciation is ignored, also because no taxes apply.

Given a lease payment of Euro2,475, the cash flows to Friendly Leasing are

	Year 0	Year 1	Year 2	Year 3	Year 4	Year 5
Cost of machine	−Euro10,000					
Depreciation tax shield (Euro680 = Euro2,000 × 0.34)		Euro680	Euro680	Euro680	Euro680	Euro680
After-tax lease payment [Euro1,633.50 = Euro2,475 × (1 − 0.34)]		Euro1,633.50	Euro1,633.50	Euro1,633.50	Euro1,633.50	Euro1,633.50
Total		Euro2,313.50	Euro2,313.50	Euro2,313.50	Euro2,313.50	Euro2,313.50

The value of the lease to Friendly is

$$
\begin{aligned}
\text{Value of lease} &= -\text{Euro}10{,}000 + \text{Euro}2{,}313.50 \times A_{0.05}^5 \\
&= -\text{Euro}10{,}000 + \text{Euro}10{,}016.24 \\
&= \text{Euro}16.24
\end{aligned}
$$

As a consequence of different tax rates, the lessee (Xomox) gains Euro6.55 and the lessor (Friendly) gains Euro16.24. Both the lessor and the lessee can gain if their tax rates are different, because the lessor uses the depreciation and interest tax shields that cannot be used by the lessee. The tax authority loses tax revenue, and some of the tax gains to the lessor are passed on to the lessee in the form of lower lease payments.

Because both parties can gain when tax rates differ, the lease payment is agreed upon through negotiation. Before negotiation begins, each party needs to know the *reservation* payment of both parties. This is the payment such that one party will be indifferent to whether it entered the lease deal or not. In other words, this is the payment such that the value of the lease is zero. These payments are calculated below.

Reservation Payment of Lessee. We now solve for L_{MAX}, the payment such that the value of the lease to the lessee is zero. When the lessee is in a zero tax bracket, his cash flows, in terms of L_{MAX}, are

	Year 0	Year 1	Year 2	Year 3	Year 4	Year 5
Cost of machine	Euro10,000					
Lease payment		$-L_{\text{MAX}}$	$-L_{\text{MAX}}$	$-L_{\text{MAX}}$	$-L_{\text{MAX}}$	$-L_{\text{MAX}}$

This chart implies that

$$
\text{Value of lease} = \text{Euro}10{,}000 - L_{\text{MAX}} \times A_{0.0757575}^5
$$

The value of the lease equals zero when

$$
L_{\text{MAX}} \times \frac{\text{Euro}10{,}000}{A_{0.0757575}^5} = \text{Euro}2{,}476.62
$$

After performing this calculation, the lessor knows that he will never be able to charge a payment above Euro2,476.62.

Reservation Payment of Lessor We now solve for L_{MIN}, the payment such that the value of the lease to the lessor is zero. The cash flows to the lessor, in terms of L_{MIN}, are

	Year 0	Year 1	Year 2	Year 3	Year 4	Year 5
Cost of machine	−Euro10,000					
Depreciation tax shield (Euro680 = Euro2,000 × 0.34)		Euro680	Euro680	Euro680	Euro680	Euro680
After-tax lease payment ($T_C = 0.34$)		$L_{MIN} \times (0.66)$	$L_{MIN} \times (0.66)$	$L_{MIN} \times (0.66)$	$L_{MIN} \times (0.66)$	$L_{MIN} \times (0.66)$

This chart implies that

$$\text{Value of lease} = -\text{Euro}10{,}000 + \text{Euro}680 \times A_{0.05}^{5} + L_{MIN} \times (0.66) \times A_{0.05}^{5}$$

The value of the lease equals zero when

$$L_{MIN} = \frac{\text{Euro}10{,}000}{0.66 \times A_{0.05}^{5}} - \frac{\text{Euro}680}{0.66}$$

$$= \text{Euro}3{,}499.62 - \text{Euro}1{,}030.30$$

$$= \text{Euro}2{,}469.32$$

After performing this calculation, the lessee knows that the lessor will never agree to a lease payment below Euro2,469.32.

A Reduction of Uncertainty

We have noted that the lessee does not own the property when the lease expires. The value of the property at this time is called the *residual value*, and the lessor has a firm claim to it. When the lease contract is signed, there may be substantial uncertainty as to what the residual value of the asset will be. Thus, under a lease contract, this residual risk is borne by the lessor. Conversely, the user bears this risk when purchasing.

It is common sense that the party best able to bear a particular risk should do so. If the user has little risk aversion, he will not suffer by purchasing. However, if the user is highly averse to risk, he should find a third-party lessor more capable of assuming this burden.

This latter situation frequently arises when the user is a small and/or newly formed firm. Because the risk of the entire firm is likely to be quite high, and because the principal stockholders are likely to be undiversified, the firm desires to maximize risk wherever possible. A potential lessor, such as a large and publicly held financial institution, is far more capable of bearing the risk. Conversely, this situation is not expected to happen when the user is a blue chip corporation. That potential lessor is more able to bear risk.

Transactions Costs

The costs of changing an asset's ownership are generally greater than the costs of writing a lease agreement. Consider the choice that confronts a person who lives in Munich but must do business in Manchester for two days. It will clearly be cheaper to rent a hotel room for two nights than it would be to buy an apartment for two days and then to sell it.

Unfortunately, leases generate agency costs as well. For example, the lessee might misuse or overuse the asset, since she has no interest in the asset's residual value. This cost will be implicitly paid by the lessee through a high lease payment. Although the lessor can reduce these agency costs through monitoring, monitoring itself is costly.

Thus, leasing is most beneficial when the transaction costs of purchase and resale outweigh the agency costs and monitoring costs of a lease.

Bad Reasons for Leasing

Leasing and Accounting Income
In our discussion on accounting and leasing, we implied that a firm's balance sheet may show fewer liabilities with an operating lease than with either a capitalized lease or a purchase financed with debt. We indicated that a firm desiring to project a strong balance sheet might select an operating lease. In addition, the firm's return on assets (ROA) is generally higher with an operating lease than with either a capitalized lease or a purchase.

Of course, in an efficient capital market, accounting information cannot be used to fool investors. It is unlikely, then, that leasing's impact on accounting numbers should create value for the firm. Clever investors should be able to see through attempts by management to improve the firm's financial statements. Whether capital markets are efficient in every country in Europe is, of course, a moot point worthy of much further research. We rather doubt it—at least we doubt whether semistrong efficiency would be exhibited in all European stock markets.

One Hundred per cent Financing
It is often claimed that leasing provides 100 per cent financing, whereas secured equipment loans require an initial down payment. However, we argued earlier that leases tend to displace debt elsewhere in the firm. Our earlier analysis suggests that leases do not permit a greater level of total liabilities than do purchases with borrowing.

Other Reasons
There are, of course, many special reasons for some companies to find advantages in leasing. In a case from the other side of the Atlantic, the US Navy leased a fleet of tankers instead of asking government departments for appropriations. The US Navy was using leasing to circumvent capital-expenditure systems set up to control them.

Concept Question
• Summarize the good and bad arguments for leasing.

24.9   Some Unanswered Questions

Our analysis suggests that the primary advantage of long-term leasing results from the differential tax rates of the lessor and the lessee. Other valid reasons for leasing are lower contracting costs and risk reduction. There are several questions our analysis has not specifically answered.

Are the Uses of Leases and of Debt Complementary?

In the USA, Ang and Peterson find that firms with high debt tend to lease frequently as well.[9] This result should not be puzzling. The corporate attributes that provide high-

---
[9] J. Ang and P. P. Peterson (1984) 'The leasing puzzle', *Journal of Finance*, **39**, September.

debt capacity may also make leasing advantageous. Thus, even though leasing displaces debt (that is, leasing and borrowing are substitutes) for an individual firm, high debt and high leasing can be positively associated when one looks at a number of firms.

Why Are Leases Offered by Both Manufacturers and Third-Party Lessors?

The offsetting effects of taxes can explain why both manufacturers (for example, computer firms) and third-party lessors offer leases.

1. For manufacturer lessors, the basis for determining depreciation is the manufacturer's cost. For third-party lessors, the basis is the sales price that the lessor paid to the manufacturer. Because the sales price is generally greater than the manufacturer's cost, this is an advantage to third-party lessors.
2. However, the manufacturer must recognize a profit for tax purposes when selling the asset to the third-party lessor. The manufacturer's profit for some equipment can be deferred if the manufacturer becomes the lessor. This provides an incentive for manufacturers to lease.

Why Are Some Assets Leased More than Others?

Certain assets appear to be leased more frequently than others. Smith and Wakeman have looked at non-tax incentives affecting leasing in the USA.[10] Their analysis suggests many asset and firm characteristics that are important in the lease-or-buy decision. The following are among the things they mention:

1. The more sensitive the value of an asset is to use and maintenance decisions, the more likely it is that the asset will be purchased instead of leased. They argue that ownership provides a better incentive to minimize maintenance costs than does leasing.
2. Price-discrimination opportunities may be important. Leasing may be a way of circumventing laws against charging too *low* a price.

24.10   Summary and Conclusions

A large fraction of European equipment is leased rather than purchased. This chapter both describes the institutional arrangements surrounding leases and shows how to evaluate leases financially.

1. Leases can be separated into two types. Operating leases allow the lessee to use the equipment, ownership remains with the lessor. Although the lessor in a financial lease legally owns the equipment, the lessee maintains effective ownership.
2. Accounting rules on lease capitalization vary from one European country to another.
3. Firms' leasing decisions are generally tax-driven. To protect its interests, the tax authorities allow financial arrangements to be classified as leases only if a number of criteria are met.
4. Risk-free cash flows should be discounted at the after-tax risk-free rate. Because both lease payments and depreciation tax shields are nearly riskless, all relevant cash flows in the lease–buy decision should be discounted at a rate near this after-tax rate. We use the real-world convention of discounting at the after-tax interest rate on the lessee's secured debt.

[10] C. W. Smith, Jr. and L. M. Wakeman (1985) 'Determinants of corporate leasing policy', *Journal of Finance*, July.

5. Though this method is simple, it lacks certain intuitive appeal. In an optional section, we presented an alternative method in the hopes of increasing the reader's intuition. Relative to a lease, a purchase generates debt capacity. This increase in debt capacity can be calculated by discounting the difference between the cash flows of the purchase and the cash flows of the lease by the after-tax interest rate. The increase in debt capacity from a purchase is compared to the extra outflow at year 0 from a purchase.

6. If the lessor is in the same tax bracket as the lessee, the cash flows to the lessor are exactly the opposite of the cash flows to the lessee. Thus, the sum of the value of the lease to the lessee plus the value of the lease to the lessor must be zero. While this suggests that leases can never fly, there are actually at least three good reasons for leasing:
   a. Differences in tax brackets between lessor and lessee.
   b. Shift of risk-bearing to the lessor.
   c. Minimization of transaction costs.
   We also document a number of bad reasons for leasing.

KEY TERMS

Lessee 542	Operating leases 544
Lessor 542	Leveraged lease 544
Direct leases 542	Off-balance-sheet financing 545
Financial leases 544	Debt displacement 553

QUESTIONS AND PROBLEMS

24.1 Discuss the validity of each of the following statements.
   a. Leasing reduces risk and can reduce a firm's cost of capital.
   b. Leasing provides 100 per cent financing.
   c. Firms that do a large amount of leasing will not do much borrowing.
   d. If the tax advantages of leasing were eliminated, leasing would disappear.

24.2 Super Sonics Entertainment is considering to borrow money at 11 per cent and to purchase a facility that costs Euro350,000. The machine will be tax depreciated over five years by straight-line method and will be worthless in five years. Super Sonics can lease the machine with the year-end payments of Euro94,200. The corporate tax rate is 35 per cent. Should Super Sonics buy or lease?

24.3 High electricity costs have made Farmer Corporation's chicken-plucking machine economically worthless. There are only two machines available to replace it.
   The International Plucking Machine (IPM) model is available only on a lease basis. The annual, end-of-year payments are Euro2,100 for five years. This machine will save Farmer Euro6,000 per year through reductions in electricity costs in each of the five years.
   As an alternative, Farmer can purchase a more energy-efficient machine from Basic Machine Corporation (BMC) for Euro15,000. This machine will save Euro9,000 per year in electricity costs. A local bank has offered to finance the machine with a Euro15,000 loan. The interest rate on the loan will be 10 per cent on the remaining balance and five annual principal payments of Euro3,000.
   Farmer has a target debt-to-asset ratio of 67 per cent. Farmer is in the 34 per cent tax bracket. After five years, both machines are worthless. Only straight-line tax depreciation is allowed for chicken-plucking machines. The savings that Farmer will enjoy are known with certainty, because Farmer has a long-term chicken purchase agreement with State Food Products, and a four-year backlog of orders.
   a. Should Farmer lease the IPM machine or purchase the more efficient BMC machine?
   b. Does your answer depend on the form of financing for direct purchase?
   c. How much debt is displaced by this lease?

24.4 Wolfson has decided to purchase a new machine that costs Euro3 million. The machine will be worthless after three years. Only the straight-line method over three years is allowed by the tax authorities for this type of machine. Wolfson is in the 35 per cent tax bracket.

The Sur Bank has offered Wolfson a three-year loan for Euro3 million. The repayment schedule is three yearly principal repayments of Euro1 million and an interest charge of 12 per cent on the outstanding balance of the loan at the beginning of each year. Twelve per cent is the marketwide rate of interest. Both principal repayments and interest are due at the end of each year.

Cal Leasing offers to lease the same machine to Wolfson. Lease payments of Euro1.2 million per year are due at the end of each of the three years of the lease.

a. Should Wolfson lease the machine or buy it with bank financing?

b. What is the annual lease payment that will make Wolfson indifferent to whether it leases the machine or purchases it?

APPENDIX 24A

APV APPROACH TO LEASING

The box that appeared earlier in this chapter showed two methods for calculating the NPV of the lease relative to the purchase:

1. Discount all cash flows at the after-tax interest rate.
2. Compare the purchase price with reduction in optimal debt level under the leasing alternative.

Surprisingly (and perhaps unfortunately) there is still another method. We feel compelled to present this third method, because it has important links with the adjusted present value (APV) approach discussed earlier in this text. We illustrate this approach using the Xomox example developed in Table 24.2.

In a previous chapter, we learned that the APV of any project can be expressed as

$$APV = \text{All-equity value} + \text{Additional effects of debt}$$

In other words, the adjusted present value of a project is the sum of the net present value of the project when financed by all-equity plus the additional effects from debt financing. In the context of the lease-versus-buy decision, the APV method can be expressed as

Adjusted present value of the lease relative to the purchase	=	Net present value of the lease relative to the purchase when purchase is financed by all-equity	−	Additional effects when purchase is financed with some debt

All-Equity Value

From an earlier chapter, we know that the all-equity value is simply the NPV of the cash flows discounted at the pretax interest rate. For the Xomox example, we know from Table 24.2 that this value is

$$Euro592.03 = Euro10,000 - Euro2,330 \times A^5_{0.0757575}$$

This calculation is identical to method 1 in the earlier box except that we are now discounting at the pretax interest rate. The calculation states that the lease is preferred over the purchase by Euro592.03 if the purchase is financed by all-equity. Because debt financing generates a tax subsidy, it is not surprising that the lease alternative would be preferred by almost Euro600 over the purchase alternative if debt were not allowed.

Additional Effects of Debt

We learned earlier in the text that the interest tax shield in any year is the interest multiplied by the corporate tax rate. Taking the interest in each of the five years from Table 24.5, the present value of the interest tax shield is

$$Euro679.71 = 0.34 \left[\frac{Euro764.22}{1.0757575} + \frac{Euro625.91}{(1.0757575)^2} \right.$$

$$\left. + \frac{Euro480.69}{(1.0757575)^3} + \frac{Euro328.21}{(1.0757575)^4} + \frac{Euro168.11}{(1.0757575)^5} \right]$$

This tax shield must be subtracted from the NPV of the lease because it represents interest deductions not available under the lease alternative. The adjusted present value of the lease relative to the purchase is

$$-Euro87.68 = Euro592.03 - Euro679.71$$

A Third Method for Calculating Net Present Value of Lease Relative to Purchase*†

Method 3: Calculate APV

All-equity value: $Euro592.03 = Euro10,000 - Euro2,330 \times A^5_{0.0757575}$

Additional effects of debt‡

$$-Euro679.7 = -0.34 \left[\frac{Euro764.22}{1.0757575} + \frac{Euro625.91}{(1.0757575)^2} + \frac{Euro480.69}{(1.0757575)^3} + \right.$$

$$\left. \frac{Euro328.21}{(1.0757575)^4} + \frac{Euro168.11}{(1.0757575)^5} \right]$$

APV = $-Euro87.68 = Euro592.03 - Euro679.71$

*Because we are calculating the NPV of the lease relative to the purchase, a neghative value indicates that the purchase alternative is preferred.
†The first two methods are shown in the earlier box appearing in this chapter.
‡The firm misses the interest deductions if it leases. Because we are calculating the NPV of the lease relative to the purchase, the additional effect of debt is a negative number.

This value is the same as our calculations from the previous two approaches, implying that all three approaches are equivalent. The accompanying box presents the APV approach.

Which approach is easiest to calculate? The first approach is easiest because one need only discount the cash flows at the after-tax interest rate. Though the second and third approaches (in the two boxes) look easy, the extra step of calculating the increased debt capacity is needed for both of them.

Which approach is more intuitive? Our experience is that students generally find the third method the most intuitive. This is probably because they have already learned the APV method from a previous chapter. The second method is generally straightforward to those students who have taken the time to understand the increased-debt-level concept. However, the first method seems to have the least intuitive appeal because it is merely a mechanical approach.

Which approach should the practitioner use? The practitioner should use the simplest approach, which is the first. We included the others only for the sake of completeness.

PART VI

Financial Planning, Short-Term Finance and Working Capital Management

25 Corporate Financial Models and Long-Term Planning 567
26 Short-Term Finance and Planning 578
27 Credit Management 600

Financial planning establishes the blueprint for change in a firm. It is necessary because (1) it includes putting forward the firm's goals to motivate the organization and provide benchmarks for performance measurement, (2) the firm's financing and investment decisions are not independent and their interaction must be identified and (3) the firm must anticipate changing conditions and surprises.

Most of Chapter 25 is devoted to long-term financial planning. Long-term financial planning incorporates decisions such as capital budgeting, capital structure and dividend policy. An important part of Chapter 25 is the discussion of building corporate financial models. Here we introduce the concept of sustainable growth and show that a firm's growth rate depends on its spending characteristics (profit margin and asset turnover) and financial policies (dividend policy and capital structure).

In Chapter 26, we introduce short-term financial planning, which involves short-lived assets and liabilities. We discuss various aspects of short-term financial planning. The primary tool for short-term financial planning, the cash budget, is described. It incorporates the short-term financial goals of the firm and tells the financial manager the amount of necessary short-term financing.

Chapter 27 describes what is involved when a firm makes the decision to grant credit to its customers. This decision involves three types of analysis:

1. A firm must decide on the conditions under which it sells its goods and services for credit. These conditions are the terms of the sale.
2. Before granting credit, the firm must analyse the risk that the customer will not pay; this is called credit analysis.
3. After credit is extended, the firm must determine how to collect its cash.

CHAPTER
25

Corporate Financial Models and Long-Term Planning

Financial planning establishes guidelines for change in the firm. They should include (1) an identification of the firm's financial goals, (2) an analysis of the differences between these goals and the current financial status of the firm and (3) a statement of the actions needed for the firm to achieve its financial goals.

The basic policy elements of financial planning have been discussed in various chapters in this book. They comprise (1) the investment opportunities the firm elects to take advantage of, (2) the degree of financial leverage the firm chooses to employ and (3) the amount of cash the firm thinks is necessary and appropriate to pay shareholders. These are the financial policies that the firm must decide upon for its growth and profitability.

Almost all firms use an explicit, companywide growth rate as a major component of their long-term financial planning. There are direct connections between the growth that a company can achieve and its financial policy. One purpose of this chapter is to look at the financial aspects of strategic decisions.

The chapter first describes what is usually meant by corporate financial planning. Mostly we talk about long-term financial planning. Short-term financial planning is discussed in the next chapter. We examine what the firm can accomplish by developing a long-term financial plan. This enables us to make an important point: investment and financing decisions frequently interact. The different interactions of investment and financing decisions can be analysed in the planning model.

Finally, financial planning forces the corporation to think about goals. The goal most frequently espoused by corporations is growth. Indeed, one of the consequences of accepting positive NPV projects is growth. We show how financial-planning models can be used to better understand how growth is achieved.

25.1 What Is Corporate Financial Planning?

Financial planning formulates the method by which financial goals are to be achieved. It has two dimensions: a time frame and a level of aggregation.

A financial plan is a statement of what is to be done in a future time. Most decisions have long lead-times, which means they take a long time to implement. In an uncertain world, this requires that decisions be made far in advance of their implementation. If a firm wants to build a factory in 2000, it may need to line up contractors in 1998. It is sometimes useful to think of the future as having a short run and a long term. The short term, in practice, is usually the coming 12 months. Initially, we focus our attention on financial planning over the long term, which is usually taken to be a two-year to five-year period of time.

Financial plans are compiled from the capital-budgeting analyses of each of a firm's projects. In effect, the smaller investment proposals of each operational unit are added up and treated as a big project. This process is called **aggregation**.

Financial plans always entail alternative sets of assumptions. For example, suppose a company has two separate divisions: one for consumer products and one for gas turbine engines. The financial-planning process might require each division to prepare three alternative business plans for the next three years:

1. *A Worst Case*   This plan would require making the worst possible assumptions about the company's products and the state of the economy. It could mean divestiture and liquidation.
2. *A Normal Case*   This plan would require making most likely assumptions about the company and the economy.
3. *A Best Case*   Each division would be required to work out a case based on the most optimistic assumptions. It could involve new products and expansion.

Because the company is likely to spend a lot of time preparing proposals on different scenarios that will become the basis for the company's financial plan, it seems reasonable to ask what the planning process will accomplish:

1. *Interactions*   The financial plan must make explicit the linkages between investment proposals for the different operating activities of the firm and the financing choices available to the firm. For example, a firm setting itself a 15 per cent growth in earnings per share target must set this aspiration in such a way that it articulates with its financing programme.
2. *Options*   The financial plan provides the opportunity for the firm to work through various investment and financing options. The firm addresses questions of what financing arrangements are optimal, and evaluates options of closing plants or marketing new products.
3. *Feasibility*   The different plans must fit into the overall corporate objective of maximizing shareholder wealth.
4. *Avoiding Surprises*   Financial planning should identify what may happen in the future if certain events take place. Thus, one of the purposes of financial planning is to avoid surprises.

Concept Questions

- What are the two dimensions of the financial-planning process?
- Why should firms draw up financial plans?

25.2   A Financial-Planning Model: The Ingredients

Just as companies differ in size and products, financial plans are not the same for all companies. However, there are some common elements:

1. **Sales Forecast**   All financial plans require a sales forecast. Perfectly accurate sales forecasts are not possible, because sales depend on the uncertain future state of the economy. Firms can get help from businesses specializing in macroeconomic and industry projections.
2. **Pro Forma Statements**   The financial plan will have a forecast balance sheet, an income statement, and a sources-and-uses statement. These are called *pro forma statements*, or *pro formas*.

3. **Asset Requirements**   The plan will describe projected capital spending. In addition, it will discuss the proposed uses of net working capital.

4. **Financial Requirements**   The plan will include a section on financing arrangements. This part of the plan should discuss dividend policy and debt policy. Sometimes firms will expect to raise equity by selling new shares. In this case the plan must consider what kinds of securities must be sold and what methods of issuance are most appropriate.

5. **Plug**   Suppose a financial planner assumes that sales, costs, and net income will rise at a particular rate, g_1. Further suppose that the planner desires assets and liabilities to grow at a different rate, g_2. These two different growth rates may be incompatible unless a third variable is also adjusted. For example, compatibility may only be reached if outstanding shares grow at a different rate, g_3. In this example, we treat the growth in outstanding shares as the *plug* variable. That is, the growth rate in outstanding shares is chosen to make the growth rate in income-statement items consistent with the growth rate in balance-sheet items. Surprisingly, even if the income-statement items grow at the *same* rate as the balance-sheet items, consistency might be achieved only if outstanding shares grow at a different rate.

   Of course, the growth rate in outstanding shares need not be the plug variable. One could have income-statement items grow at g_1, and assets, long-term debt and outstanding shares grow at g_2. In this case, compatibility between g_1 and g_2 might be achieved by letting short-term debt grow at a rate of g_2.

6. **Economic assumptions**   The plan must explicitly state the economic environment in which the firm expects to reside over the life of the plan. Among the economic assumptions that must be made is the level of interest rates.

● Example

The Computerfield Company's 19X1 financial statements are as follows:

Profit and Loss Account 19X1		**Balance Sheet Year-End, 19X1**			
Sales	GBP1,000	Assets	GBP500	Debt	GBP250
Costs	800			Equity	250
Net income	GBP200	Total	GBP500	Total	GBP500

In 19X1, Computerfield's profit margin is 20 per cent, and it has never paid a dividend. Its debt–equity ratio is 1. This is also the firm's *target* debt–equity ratio. Unless otherwise stated, the financial planners at Computerfield assume that all variables are tied directly to sales and that current relationships are optimal.

Suppose that sales increase by 20 per cent from 19X1 to 19X2. Because the planners would then also forecast a 20 per cent increase in costs, the pro forma income statement would be

Profit and Loss Account 19X2	
Sales	GBP1,200
Costs	960
Net income	GBP240

The assumption that all variables will grow by 20 per cent will enable us to construct the pro forma balance sheet as well:

Balance Sheet
Year-End, 19X2

Assets	GBP600	Debt	GBP300
		Equity	300
Total	GBP600	Total	GBP600

Now we must reconcile these two pro formas. How, for example, can net income be equal to GBP240 and equity increase by only GBP50? The answer is that Computerfield must have paid a dividend or repurchased stock equal to GBP190. In this case, dividends are the plug variable.

Suppose Computerfield does not pay a dividend and does not repurchase its own stock. With these assumptions, Computerfield's equity will grow to GBP490, and debt must be retired to keep total assets equal to GBP600. In this case, the debt–equity ratio is the plug variable. This example shows the interaction of sales growth and financial policy. The next example focuses on the need for external funds. It identifies a six-step procedure for constructing the pro forma balance sheet. Of course, all of the financial planning procedures explained in this chapter and the one following are easily simulated by spreadsheet analysis on a computer, however it is best if the finance student fully understands the long-hand ramifications set out here. ●

● **Example**

Rosenhof NV is thinking of acquiring a new machine. With this new machine the company expects sales to increase from NLG20 million to NLG22 million—10 per cent growth. The corporation believes that its assets and liabilities vary directly with its level of sales. Its profit margin on sales is 10 per cent, and its dividend-payout ratio is 50 per cent.

The company's current balance sheet (reflecting the purchase of the new machine) is as follows:

Current Balance Sheet		**Pro Forma Balance Sheet**	
			Explanation
Current assets	NLG6,000,000	NLG6,600,000	30% of sales
Fixed assets	24,000,000	26,400,000	120% of sales
Total assets	NLG30,000,000	NLG33,000,000	150% of sales
Short-term debt	NLG10,000,000	NLG11,000,000	50% of sales
Long-term debt	6,000,000	6,600,000	30% of sales
Common stock	4,000,000	4,000,000	Constant
Retained earnings	10,000,000	11,100,000	Net income
Total financing	NLG30,000,000	NLG32,700,000	
		NLG300,000	Funds needed (the difference between total assets and total financing)

From this information we can determine the pro forma balance sheet, which is on the righthand side. The change in retained earnings will be

$$\text{Net income} \quad - \quad \text{Dividends} \quad = \quad \text{Change in}$$
$$\text{retained earnings}$$
$$(0.10 \times \text{NLG22 million}) - (0.5 \times 0.10 \times \text{NLG22 million}) = \text{NLG1.1 million}$$

In this example the plug variable is new shares. The company must issue NLG300,000 of new shares. The equation that can be used to determine if external funds are needed is

External Funds Needed (EFN):

$$\left(\frac{\text{Assets}}{\text{Sales}}\right) \times \Delta\text{Sales} - \frac{\text{Debt}}{\text{Sales}} \times \Delta\text{Sales} - (p \times \text{Project sales}) \times (1 - d)$$

$$= (1.5 \times \text{NLG2 million}) - (0.80 \times \text{NLG2 million}) - (0.10 \times \text{NLG22 million} \times 0.5)$$

$$= \text{NLG1.4 million} - \text{NLG1.1 million}$$

$$= \text{NLG0.3 million}$$

where

$$\frac{\text{Assets}}{\text{Sales}} = 1.5$$

$$\frac{\text{Debt}}{\text{Sales}} = 0.8$$

$$p = \text{Net profit margin} = 0.10$$

$$d = \text{Dividend payout ratio} = 0.5$$

$$\Delta\text{Sales} = \text{Projected change in sales}$$

The steps in the estimation of the pro forma sheet for Rosenhof NV and the external funds needed (EFN) are as follows:

1. Express balance-sheet items that vary with sales as a percentage of sales.
2. Multiply the percentages determined in step (1) by projected sales to obtain the amounts for the future period.
3. Where no percentage applies, simply insert the previous balance-sheet figure in the future period.
4. Compute projected retained earnings as follows:

Projected retained earnings = Present retained earnings
+ Projected net income – Cash dividends

5. Add the asset accounts to determine projected assets. Next, add the liabilities and equity accounts to determine the total financing; any difference is the *shortfall*. This equals external funds needed (EFN).
6. Use the plug to fill EFN. ●

25.3   What Determines Growth?

Firms frequently make growth forecasts an explicit part of financial planning. For instance, a firm might state a financial objective as achieving a 15 per cent growth rate in sales per year to 1999. Donaldson reports on the pervasiveness of stating corporate goals in terms of growth rates.[1] This may seem puzzling in the light of our previous emphasis on maximizing the firm's value as the central goal of management. One way to reconcile the difference is to think of growth as an intermediate goal that leads to higher value. Rappaport correctly points out that, in applying the NPV approach, growth should not be a goal but must be a consequence of decisions that maximize NPV.[2] In fact, if the firm is willing to accept negative NPV projects just to grow in size, growth will probably make the shareholders (but perhaps not the managers) worse off.

Donaldson also concludes that most major US industrial companies are very reluctant to use external equity as a regular part of their financial planning. To illustrate the linkages between the ability of a firm to grow and its financial policy when the firm does not issue equity, we can make some planning assumptions that are consistent with the financial policy of Hoffman plc.

1. The firm's assets will grow in proportion to its sales.
2. Net income is a constant proportion of its sales.
3. The firm has a given dividend-payout policy and a given debt–equity ratio.
4. The firm will not change the number of outstanding shares.

There is only one growth rate that is consistent with the preceding assumptions. In effect, with these assumptions, growth has been made a plug variable. To see this, recall that a change in assets must always be equal to a change in debt plus a change in equity:

$$\boxed{\begin{array}{c}\text{Change}\\\text{in}\\\text{assets}\end{array}} = \boxed{\begin{array}{c}\text{Change}\\\text{in}\\\text{debt}\\\hline\text{Change}\\\text{in}\\\text{equity}\end{array}}$$

Now we can write the conditions that ensure this equality and solve for the growth rate that will give it to us.

The variables used in this demonstration are the following:

T = The ratio of total assets to sales
p = The net profit margin on sales
d = The dividend-payout ratio
L = The debt–equity ratio
S_0 = Sales this year
ΔS = The change in sales ($S_1 - S_0 = \Delta S$)
RE = Retained earnings = Net income × Retention ratio = $S_1 \times p \times (1 - d)$
NI = Net income = $S_1 \times p$

If the firm is to increase sales by ΔS during the year, it must increase assets by $T\Delta S$. The firm is assumed not to be able to change the number of shares outstanding, so the equity financing must come from retained earnings. Retained earnings will depend on next year's sales, the payout ratio, and the profit margin. The amount of

[1] G. Donaldson (1984) *Managing Corporation Wealth: The Operations of a Comprehensive Financial Goals System*, New York: Praeger.
[2] A. Rappaport (1986) *Creating Shareholder Value: The New Standard for Business Performance*, New York: Free Press.

borrowing will depend on the amount of retained earnings and the debt–equity ratio.

New equity: $S_1 \times p \times (1 - d)$

plus

Borrowing: $[S_1 \times p \times (1 - d)] \times L$

equals

Capital spending: $T\Delta S$

Moving things around a little gives the following:

$$T\Delta S = [S_1 \times p \times (1 - d)] + [S_1 \times p \times (1 - d) \times L]$$

and

$$\frac{\Delta S}{S_0} = \frac{p \times (1 - d) \times (1 + L)}{T - p \times (1 - d) \times (1 + L)} = \text{Growth rate in sales} \qquad (25.1)$$

This is the growth-rate equation. Given the profit margin (p), the payout ratio (d), the debt–equity ratio (L), and the asset-requirement ratio (T), the growth rate can be determined.[3] It is the only growth possible with the preset values for the four variables. Higgins has referred to this growth rate as the firm's **sustainable growth rate**.[4]

● Example

Table 25.1 shows the current income statement, the sources-and-uses-of-funds statement, and the balance sheet for Hoffman plc. Net income for the company was 16.5 per cent (GBP1,650/GBP10,000) of sales revenue. The company paid out 72.4 per cent (GBP1,195/GBP1,650) of its net income in dividends. The interest rate on debt was 10 per cent, and the long-term debt was 50 per cent (GBP5,000/GBP10,000) of assets. (Notice that, for simplicity, we use the single term *net working capital*, in Table 25.1, instead of separating current assets from current liabilities.) Hoffman's assets grew at the rate of 10 per cent (GBP910/GBP9,090). In addition, sales grew at 10 per cent, though this increase is not shown in Table 25.1.

The cash flow generated by Hoffman was enough not only to pay a dividend but also to increase net working capital and fixed assets by GBP455 each. The company did not issue any shares during the year. Its debt–equity ratio and dividend-payout ratio remained constant throughout the year.

The sustainable growth rate for Hoffman plc is 10 per cent, or

$$\frac{0.165 \times 0.276 \times 2}{1 - (0.165 \times 0.276 \times 2)} = 0.1$$

However, suppose its desired growth rate was to be 20 per cent. It is possible for Hoffman's desired growth to exceed its sustainable growth because Hoffman is able to issue new shares. A firm can do several things to increase its sustainable growth rate as

---

[3] This is approximately equal to the rate of return on equity (ROE) multiplied by the retention rate (RR): ROE × RR. This expression is only precisely equal to equation (25.1) above in continuous time; otherwise it is an approximation. More precisely:

$$\text{Growth rates in sales} = \frac{\text{ROE} \times \text{RR}}{1 - (\text{ROE} \times \text{RR})}$$

[4] R.C. Higgins (1981) 'Sustainable growth under inflation', *Financial Management*, Autumn. The definition of sustainable growth was popularized by the Boston Consulting Group and others.

TABLE 25.1   Current Financial Statements: Hoffman plc (in thousands)

HOFFMAN plc
Profit and Loss Account

	This Year
Net sales (S)	GBP10,000
Cost of sales	7,000
Earnings before taxes and interest	3,000
Interest expense	500
Earnings before taxes	2,500
Taxes	850
Net income (NI)	GBP1,650

Sources and Uses of Cash

	This Year
Sources:	
Net income (NI)	GBP1,650
Depreciation	500
Operating cash flow	2,150
Borrowing	455
New stock issue	0
Total sources	2,605
Uses:	
Increase in net working capital	455
Capital spending	955
Dividends	1,195
Total uses	2,605

Balance Sheet

	This Year	Last Year	Change
Assets			
Net working capital	GBP5,000	GBP4,545	GBP455
Fixed assets	5,000	4,545	455
Total assets	GBP10,000	GBP9,090	GBP910
Liabilities and Stockholders' Equity			
Debt	GBP5,000	GBP4,545	GBP455
Equity	5,000	4,545	455
Total liabilities and stockholders' equity	GBP10,000	GBP9,090	GBP910

seen from the Hoffman example:

1. Sell new shares.
2. Increase its reliance on debt.
3. Reduce its dividend-payout ratio.
4. Increase profit margins.
5. Decrease its asset-requirement ratio.

Now we can see the use of a financial-planning model to test the feasibility of the planned growth rate. If sales are to grow at a rate higher than the sustainable growth rate, the firm must improve operating performance, increase financial leverage, decrease dividends or sell new shares. Of course, the planned rates of growth should be the result of a complete NPV-based planning process. ●

IN THEIR OWN WORDS . . .
Robert C. Higgins on Sustainable Growth

Most financial officers know intuitively that it takes money to make money. Rapid sales growth requires increased assets in the form of accounts receivable, inventory, and fixed plant, which, in turn, require money to pay for assets. They also know that if their company does not have the money when needed, it can literally 'grow broke.' The sustainable growth equation states these intuitive truths explicitly.

Sustainable growth is often used by bankers and other external analysts to assess a company's credit wothiness. They are aided in this exercise by several sophisticated computer software packages that provide detailed analyses of the company's past financial performance, including its annual sustainable growth rate,.

Bankers use this information in several ways. Quick comparison of a company's actual growth rate to its sustainable rate tells the banker what issues will be at the top of management's financial agenda. If actual growth consistently exceeds sustainable growth, management's problem will be where to get the cash to finance growth. The banker thus can anticipate interest in loan products. Conversely, if sustainable growth consistently exceeds actual, the banker had best be prepared to talk about investment products, because management's problem will be what to do with all the cash that keeps piling up in the till.

Bankers also find the sustainable growth equation useful for explaining to financially inexperienced small business owners and overly optimistic entrepreneurs that, for the long-run viability of their business, it is necessary to keep growth and profitability in proper balance.

Finally, comparison of actual to sustainable growth rates helps a banker understand why a loan applicant needs money and for how long the need might continue. In one instance, a loan applicant requested $100,000 to pay off insistent suppliers and promised to repay in a few months when he collected some accounts receivable that were coming due. A sustainable growth analysis revealed that the firm had been growing at four to six times its sustainable growth rate and that this pattern was likely to continue in the forseeable future. This alerted the banker that impatient suppliers were only a symptom of the much more fundamental disease of overly rapid growth, and that $100,000 loan would likely prove to be only the down payment on a much larger, multiyear committment.

Robert C. Higgins is Professor of Finance at the University of Washington. He pioneered the use of sustainable growth as a tool for financial analysis.

Concept Questions

- When might the goals of growth and value maximization be in conflict, and when would they be aligned?
- What are the determinants of growth?

25.4   Some Caveats of Financial-Planning Models

Financial-planning models suffer from a great deal of criticism. We present two commonly voiced attacks below.

First, financial-planning models do not indicate which financial policies are the best. For example, our model could not tell us whether Hoffman's decision to issue new equity to achieve a higher growth rate raises the NPV of the firm.

Second, financial-planning models are too simple. In reality, costs are not always proportional to sales, assets need not be a fixed percentage of sales, and capital budgeting involves a sequence of decisions over time. These assumptions are generally not incorporated into financial plans.

Financial-planning models are necessary to assist in planning the future investment and financial decisions of the firm. Without some sort of long-term financial plan, the firm may find itself adrift in a sea of change without a rudder for guidance. But, because of the assumptions and the abstractions from reality necessary in the construction of the financial plan, we also think that they should carry the label: Let the user beware!

25.5   Summary and Conclusions

Financial planning forces the firm to think about and forecast the future. It involves the following:

1. Building a corporate financial model.
2. Describing different scenarios of future development from worst to best cases.
3. Using the models to construct pro forma financial statements.
4. Running the model under different scenarios (conduct sensitivity analysis).
5. Examining the financial implications of ultimate strategic plans.

Corporate financial planning should not become a purely mechanical activity. If it does, it will probably focus on the wrong things. In particular, plans are formulated all too often in terms of a growth target with an explicit linkage to creation of value. Nevertheless, the alternative to financial planning is stumbling into the future.

KEY TERMS

Aggregation 568	Financial requirements 569
Sales forecast 568	Plug 569
Pro forma statements 568	Economic assumptions 569
Asset requirements 569	Sustainable growth rate 573

QUESTIONS AND PROBLEMS

Financial-Planning Models: The Ingredients

25.1 Cheryl Colby, the finance director of Charming Flowers plc, has created the firm's pro forma balance sheet for the next financial year. Sales are projected to grow at 10 per cent to the level of GBP330 million. Current assets, fixed assets, short-term debt and long-term debt are 25 per cent, 150 per cent, 40 per cent, and 45 per cent of the total sales, respectively. Charming Flowers pays out 40 per cent of the net income. The value of ordinary shares is constant at GBP50 million. The post-tax profit margin on sales is 12 percent.

    a. Based on Ms Colby's forecast, how much external fund does Charming Flowers need?

    b. Reconstruct the current balance sheet based on the projected figures.

    c. Lay out the firm's pro forma balance sheet for the next financial year.

What Determines Growth?

25.2 The Stieben Company has determined that the following will be true next year:

$$T = \text{Ratio of total assets to sales} = 1$$
$$P = \text{Net profit margin on sales (net of tax)} = 5\%$$
$$d = \text{Dividend-payout ratio} = 50\%$$
$$L = \text{Debt-equity ratio} = 1$$

    a. What is Stieben's sustainable growth rate in sales?

    b. Can Stieben's actual growth rate in sales be different from its sustainable growth rate? Why or why not?

    c. How can Stieben change its sustainable growth?

25.3 The Optimal Scam Company would like to see its sales grow at 20 per cent for the foreseeable future. Its financial statements for the current year are presented below.

Profit and Loss Account *(GBP millions)*		*Balance Sheet* *(GBP millions)*	
Sales	32.00	Current assets	16
Costs	28.97	Fixed assets	16
Gross profit	3.03	Total assets	32
Taxes	1.03		
Net income	2.00	Current debt	10
		Long-term debt	4
Dividends	1.40	Total debt	14
Retained earnings	0.60	Common stock	14
		Ret. earnings	4
		Total liabilities and equity	32

The current financial policy of the Optimal Scam Company includes

Dividend-payout ratio $(d) = 70\%$
Debt-to-equity ratio $(L) = 77.78\%$
Net profit margin $(P) = 6.25\%$ (margin is net of tax)
Assets-sales ratio $(T) = 1$

a. Determine Optimal Scam's need for external funds next year.
b. Construct a pro forma balance sheet for Optimal Scam.
c. Calculate the sustainable growth rate for the Optimal Scam Company.
d. How can Optimal Scam change its financial policy to achieve its growth objective?

25.4 MBI Company does not want to grow. The company's financial management believes it has no positive NPV projects. The company's operating financial characteristics are

Profit margin $= 10\%$ (net of tax)
Assets-sales ratio $= 150\%$
Debt-equity ratio $= 100\%$
Dividend-payout ratio $= 50\%$

a. Calculate the sustainable growth rate for the MBI Company.
b. How can MBI Company achieve its stated growth goal?

25.5 Throughout this text, you have learned that financial managers should select positive net-present-value projects. How does this project-selection criterion relate to financial-planning models?

25.6 Your firm recently hired a new MBA. She insists that your firm is incorrectly computing its sustainable growth rate. Your firm computes the sustainable growth rate using the following formula:

$$\frac{P \times (1-d) \times (1+L)}{T - P \times (1-d) \times (1+L)}$$

P = Net of tax profit margin on sales
d = Dividend-payout ratio
L = Debt-equity ratio
T = Ratio of total assets to sales

Your new employee claims that the correct formula is ROE $\times (1 - d)$ where ROE is net profit divided by net worth and d is dividends divided by net profit. Is your new employee correct?

25.7 Atlantic Transportation has a payout ratio of 60 per cent, debt-equity ratio of 50 per cent, return on equity of 16 per cent, and an assets–sales ratio of 175 per cent.
a. What is its sustainable growth rate?
b. What must its profit margin be in order to achieve its sustainable growth rate?

Some Caveats of Financial-Planning Models
25.8 What are the shortcomings of financial-planning models that we should be aware of?

<table>
<tr><td>CHAPTER
26</td><td># Short-Term Finance and Planning</td></tr>
</table>

Up to now we have described many of the decisions of long-term finance: capital budgeting, dividend policy and capital structure. This chapter introduces short-term finance. Short-term finance is an analysis of decisions that affect current assets and current liabilities, and will frequently have an impact on the firm within a year.

The term *net working capital* is often associated with short-term financial decision-making. Net working capital is the difference between current assets and current liabilities. The focus of short-term finance on net working capital seems to suggest that it is an accounting subject. However, making net-working-capital decisions still relies on cash flow and net present value.

There is no universally accepted definition of short-term finance. The most important difference between short-term and long-term finance is the timing of cash flows. Short-term financial decisions involve cash inflows and outflows within a year or less. For example, a short-term financial decision is involved when a firm orders raw materials, pays in cash, and anticipates selling finished goods in one year for cash, as illustrated in Figure 26.1. A long-term financial decision is involved when a firm purchases a special machine that will reduce operating costs over the next five years, as illustrated in Figure 26.2.

FIGURE 26.1 Short-Term Financial Decision

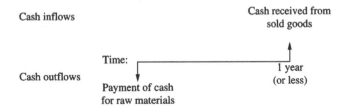

FIGURE 26.2 Long-Term Financial Decision

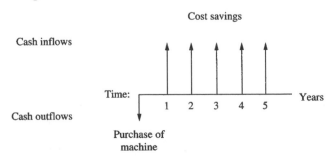

Here are some questions of short-term finance:

1. What is a reasonable level of cash to keep on hand (in a bank) to pay bills?
2. How much raw material should be ordered?
3. How much credit should be extended to customers?

This chapter introduces the basic elements of short-term financial decisions. First, we describe the short-term operating activities of the firm, and then we identify alternative short-term financial policies. Finally, we outline the basic elements in a short-term financial plan and describe short-term financing instruments.

26.1   Tracing Cash and Net Working Capital

In this section we trace the components of cash and net working capital as they change from one year to the next. Our goal is to describe the short-term operating activities of the firm and their impact on cash and working capital.

Current assets are cash and other assets that are expected to be converted to cash within the year. Current assets are presented in the balance sheet in order of their accounting **liquidity**—the ease with which they can be converted to cash at a fair price and the time it takes to do so. Table 26.1 gives the balance sheet and profit and loss

TABLE 26.1   **Financial Statements**

TRADEWINDS MANUFACTURING
December 31, 19X2, and December 31, 19X1
Balance Sheet

	19X2	19X1
Assets		
Current assets:		
Cash	Euro 500,000	Euro 500,000
Marketable securities (at cost)	500,000	450,000
Accounts receivable less allowance for bad debts	2,000,000	1,600,000
Inventories	3,000,000	2,000,000
Total current assets	6,000,000	4,550,000
Fixed assets (property, plant and equipment):		
Land	450,000	450,000
Building	4,000,000	4,000,000
Machinery	1,500,000	800,000
Office equipment	50,000	50,000
Less: Accumulated depreciation	2,000,000	1,700,000
Net fixed assets	4,000,000	3,600,000
Prepayments and deferred charges	400,000	300,000
Intangibles	100,000	100,000
Total assets	Euro10,500,000	Euro 8,550,000
Liabilities		
Current liabilities:		
Accounts payable	Euro 1,000,000	Euro 750,000
Notes payable	1,500,000	500,000
Accrued expenses payable	250,000	225,000
Taxes payable	250,000	225,000
Total current liabilitiess	3,000,000	1,700,000
Long-term liabilities:		
First mortgage bonds, 5% interest, due 2025	3,000,000	3,000,000
Deferred taxes	600,000	600,000
Total liabilities	Euro 6,600,000	Euro 5,300,000

TABLE 26.1   (Concluded)

TRADEWINDS MANUFACTURING
December 31, 19X2, and December 31, 19X1
Shareholders' Equity

Ordinary Shares, Euro5 nominal value each; authorized, issued, and outstanding 300,000 shares	1,500,000	1,500,000
Reserve	500,000	500,000
Accumulated retained earnings	1,900,000	1,250,000
Total shareholders' equity	3,900,000	3,250,000
Total liabilities and shareholders' equity	Euro10,500,000	Euro 8,550,000

Profit and Loss Account

	19X2	*19X1*
Net sales	Euro11,500,000	Euro10,700,000
Cost of sales and operating expenses:		
Cost of goods sold	8,200,000	7,684,000
Depreciation	300,000	275,000
Selling and administration expenses	1,400,000	1,325,000
Operating profit	1,600,000	1,416,000
Other income:		
Dividends and interest...................................	50,000	50,000
Total income from operations	1,650,000	1,466,000
Less: Interest on bonds and other liabilities	300,000	150,000
Income before provision for income tax	1,350,000	1,316,000
Provision for income tax	610,000	600,000
Net profit	Euro 740,000	Euro 716,000
Dividends paid out	Euro 90,000	Euro 132,000
Retained earnings	Euro 650,000	Euro 584,000

account of the Tradewinds Manufacturing for 19X2 and 19X1. The four major items found in the current asset section of the Tradewinds balance sheet are cash, marketable securities, accounts receivable and inventories.

Analogous to their investment in current assets, firms use several kinds of short-term debt, called current liabilities. Current liabilities are obligations that are expected to require cash payment within one year or within the operating cycle, whichever is shorter.[1] The three major items found as *current liabilities* are accounts payable; accrued wages, taxes and other expenses payable; and notes payable.

26.2   Defining Cash in Terms of Other Elements

Now we will define cash in terms of the other elements of the balance sheet. The balance sheet equation is

$$\text{Net working capital} + \text{Fixed assets} = \text{Long-term debt} + \text{Equity} \qquad (26.1)$$

---

[1] As we will learn in this chapter, the operating cycle begins when inventory is received and ends when cash is collected from the sale of the inventory.

Net working capital is cash plus the other elements of net working capital; that is,

$$\text{Net working capital} = \text{Cash} + \text{Other current assets} - \text{Current liabilities} \quad (26.2)$$

Substituting equation (26.2) into (26.1) yields

$$\text{Cash} + \begin{matrix}\text{Other}\\\text{current}\\\text{assets}\end{matrix} - \begin{matrix}\text{Current}\\\text{liabilities}\end{matrix} = \begin{matrix}\text{Long term}\\\text{debt}\end{matrix} + \text{Equity} - \begin{matrix}\text{Fixed}\\\text{assets}\end{matrix} \quad (26.3)$$

and rearranging we find that

$$\text{Cash} = \begin{matrix}\text{Long term}\\\text{debt}\end{matrix} + \text{Equity} - \begin{matrix}\text{Net working capital}\\\text{(excluding cash)}\end{matrix} - \begin{matrix}\text{Fixed}\\\text{assets}\end{matrix} \quad (26.4)$$

The natural interpretation of equation (26.4) is that increasing long-term debt and equity and decreasing fixed assets and net working capital (excluding cash) will increase cash to the firm.

The Sources-and-Uses-of-Cash Statement

From the righthand side of equation (26.4), we can see that an increase in long-term debt and/or equity leads to an increase in cash. Moreover, a decrease in net working capital and/or fixed assets leads to an increase in cash. In addition, the sum of net income and depreciation increases cash, whereas dividend payments decrease cash. This reasoning allows an accountant to create a sources-and-uses-of-cash statement, which shows all the transactions that affect a firm's cash position.

Let us trace the changes in cash for Tradewinds during the year. Notice that Tradewinds' cash balance remained constant during 19X2, even though cash flow from operations was Euro1.04 million (net income plus depreciation). Why did cash remain the same? The answer is simply that the sources of cash were equal to the uses of cash. From the firm's sources-and-uses-of-cash statement (Table 26.2), we find that Tradewinds generated cash as shown below:

1. It generated cash flow from operations of Euro1.04 million.
2. It increased its accounts payable by Euro250,000. This is the same as increasing borrowing from suppliers.
3. It increased its borrowing from banks by Euro1 million. This shows up as an increase in notes payable.
4. It increased accrued expenses by Euro25,000.
5. It increased taxes payable by Euro25,000, in effect borrowing from the tax authorities.

Tradewinds used cash for the following reasons:

1. It invested Euro700,000 in fixed assets.
2. It increased prepayments by Euro100,000.
3. It paid a Euro90,000 dividend.
4. It invested in inventory worth Euro1 million.
5. It lent its customers additional money. Hence, accounts receivable increased by Euro400,000.
6. It purchased Euro50,000 worth of marketable securities.

TABLE 26.2   Sources and Use of Cash

TRADEWINDS MANUFACTURING
Sources and Use of Cash
(in thousands)

Sources of cash:	
Cash flow from operations:	
Net income	Euro 740
Depreciation	300
Total cash flow from operations:	1,040
Decrease in net working capital:	
Increase in accounts payable	250
Increase in notes payable	1,000
Increase in accrued expenses	25
Increase in taxes payable	25
Total sources of cash	2,340
Uses of cash:	
Increase in fixed assets	700
Increase in prepayments	100
Dividends	90
Increase in net working capital:	
Investment in inventory	1,000
Increase in accounts receivable	400
Increase in marketable securities	50
Total uses of cash	2,340
Change in cash balance	0

This example illustrates the difference between a firm's cash position on the balance sheet and cash flows from operations.

Concept Questions

- What is the difference between net working capital and cash?
- Will net working capital always increase when cash increases?
- List the potential uses of cash.
- List the potential sources of cash.

26.3   The Operating Cycle and the Cash Cycle

Short-term finance is concerned with the firm's **short-run operating activities**. A typical manufacturing firm's short-run operating activities consist of a sequence of events and decisions:

Events	*Decisions*
1. Buying raw materials	1. How much inventory to order?
2. Paying cash for purchases	2. To borrow, or draw down cash balance?
3. Manufacturing the product	3. What choice of production technology?
4. Selling the product	4. To offer cash terms or credit terms to customers?
5. Collecting cash	5. How to collect cash?

These activities create patterns of cash inflows and cash outflows that are both unsynchronized and uncertain. They are unsynchronized because the payment of cash for raw materials does not happen at the same time as the receipt of cash from selling the product. They are uncertain because future sales and costs are not known with certainty.

Figure 26.3 depicts the short-term operating activities and cash flows for a typical manufacturing firm along the **cash flow time line**. The **operating cycle** is the time interval between the arrival of inventory stock and the date when cash is collected from receivables. The **cash cycle** begins when cash is paid for materials and ends when cash is collected from receivables. The cash flow time line consists of an operating cycle and a cash cycle. The need for short-term financial decision-making is suggested by the gap between the cash inflows and cash outflows. This is related to the lengths of the operating cycle and the accounts payable period. This gap can be filled either by borrowing or by holding a liquidity reserve for marketable securities. The gap can be shortened by changing the inventory, receivable, and payable periods. Now we take a closer look at the operating cycle.

FIGURE 26.3   Cash Flow Time Line and the Short-Term Operating Activities of a Typical Manufacturing Firm

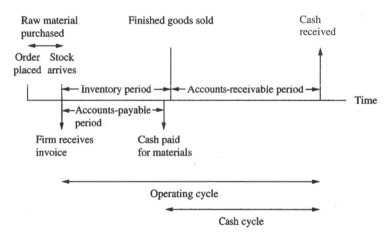

The *operating cycle* is the time period from the arrival of stock until the receipt of cash. (Sometimes the operating cycle is defined to include the time from placement of the order until arrival of the stock.) The *cash cycle* begins when cash is paid for materials and ends when cash is collected from receivables.

The length of the operating cycle is equal to the sum of the lengths of the inventory and accounts receivable periods. The inventory period is the length of time required to order, produce and sell a product. The accounts receivable period is the length of time required to collect cash receipts

The cash cycle is the time between cash disbursement and cash collection. It can be thought of as the operating cycle less the accounts-payable period, that is,

$$\text{Cash cycle} = \text{Operating cycle} - \text{Accounts payable period}$$

The accounts payable period is the length of time the firm is able to delay payment on the purchase of various resources, such as wages and raw materials.

In practice, the inventory period, the accounts receivable period, and the accounts payable period are measured by days in inventory, days in receivables and days in payables, respectively. We illustrate how the operating cycle and the cash cycle can be measured in the following example.

● **Example**

Tradewinds Manufacturing is a diversified manufacturing firm with the balance sheet and income statement shown in Table 26.1 for 19X1 and 19X2. The operating cycle and the cash cycle can be determined for Tradewinds after calculating the appropriate ratios for inventory, receivables and payables. Consider inventory first. The average inventory is

$$\text{Average inventory} = \frac{\text{Euro3 million} + \text{Euro2 million}}{2} = \text{Euro2.5 million}$$

The terms in the numerator are the ending inventory in the second and first years, respectively.

We next calculate the inventory-turnover ratio:

$$\text{Inventory–turnover ratio} = \frac{\text{Cost of goods sold}}{\text{Average inventory}} = \frac{\text{Euro8.2 million}}{\text{Euro2.5 million}} = 3.3$$

This implies that the inventory cycle occurs 3.3 times a year. Finally, we calculate days in inventory:

$$\text{Days in inventory} = \frac{365 \text{ days}}{3.3} = 110.6 \text{ days}$$

Our calculation implies that the inventory cycle is slightly more than 110 days.

We perform analogous calculations for receivables and payables.[2]

$$\frac{\text{Average}}{\text{accounts receivable}} = \frac{\text{Euro1.8 million} + \text{Euro1.6 million}}{2} = \text{Euro1.8 million}$$

$$\frac{\text{Average}}{\text{receivable turnover}} = \frac{\text{Credit sales}}{\text{Average accounts receivable}} = \frac{\text{Euro11.5 million}}{\text{Euro1.8 million}} = 6.4$$

$$\text{Days in receivables} = \frac{365}{6.4} = 57 \text{ days}$$

$$\text{Average payables} = \frac{\text{Euro1.0 million} + \text{Euro0.75 million}}{2} = \text{Euro0.875 million}$$

$$\text{Accounts payable deferral period} = \frac{\text{Cost of goods sold}}{\text{Average payables}} = \frac{\text{Euro8.2 million}}{\text{Euro0.875 million}} = 9.4$$

$$\text{Days in payables} = \frac{365}{9.4} = 38.8 \text{ days}$$

The above calculations allow us to determine both the operating cycle and the cash cycle.

------

[2] We assume that the Tradewinds Manufacturing makes no cash sales.

$$\text{Operating cycle} = \text{Days in Inventory} + \text{Days in receivables}$$
$$= 110.6 \text{ days} + 57 \text{ days} = 167.6 \text{ days}$$

$$\text{Cash cycle} = \text{Operating cycle} - \text{Days in payables}$$
$$= 167.6 \text{ days} - 38.8 \text{ days} = 128.8 \text{ days} \bullet$$

The need for short-term financial decision-making is suggested by the gap between the cash inflows and cash outflows. This is related to the lengths of the operating cycles and accounts payable period. This gap can be filled either by borrowing or by holding a liquidity reserve for marketable securities. The gap can be shortened by changing the inventory, receivable and payable periods. Now we take a closer look at this aspect of short-term financial policy.

Concept Questions

- What does it mean to say that a firm has an inventory–turnover ratio of four?
- Describe the operating cycle and cash cycle. What are the differences between them?

26.4   Some Aspects of Short-Term Financial Policy

The policy that a firm adopts for short-term finance will be composed of at least two elements:

1. *The Size of the Firm's Investment in Current Assets*   This is usually measured relative to the firm's level of total operating revenues. A flexible or accommodative short-term financial policy would maintain a high ratio of current assets to sales. A restrictive short-term financial policy would entail a low ratio of current assets to sales.
2. *The Financing of Current Assets*   This is measured as the proportion of short-term debt to long-term debt. A restrictive short-term financial policy means a high proportion of short-term debt relative to long-term financing, and a flexible policy means less short-term debt and more long-term debt.

The Size of the Firm's Investment in Current Assets

Flexible short-term financial policies include

1. Keeping large balances of cash and marketable securities.
2. Making large investments in inventory.
3. Granting liberal credit terms, which result in a high level of accounts receivable.

Restrictive short-term financial policies are

1. Keeping low cash balances and no investment in marketable securities.
2. Making small investments in inventory.
3. Allowing no credit sales and no accounts receivable.

Determining the optimal investment level in short-term assets requires an identification of the different costs of alternative short-term financing policies. The objective is to trade off the cost of restrictive policies against those of the flexible ones to arrive at the best compromise.

Current asset holdings are highest with a flexible short-term financial policy and lowest with a restrictive policy. Thus, flexible short-term financial policies are costly in that they require higher cash outflows to finance cash and marketable securities, inventory and accounts receivable. However, future cash inflows are highest with a flexible policy. Sales are stimulated by the use of a credit policy that provides liberal financing to customers. A large amount of inventory on hand ('on the shelf') provides a quick delivery service to customers and increases sales.[3] In addition, the firm can probably charge higher prices for the quick delivery service and the liberal credit terms of flexible policies. A flexible policy also may result in fewer production stoppages because of inventory shortages.[4]

Managing current assets can be thought of as involving a trade-off between costs that rise with the level of investment and costs that fall with the level of investment. Costs that rise with the level of investment in current assets are called **carrying costs**. Costs that fall with increases in the level of investment in current assets are called **shortage costs**.

Carrying costs are generally of two types. First, because the rate of return on current assets is low compared with that of other assets, there is an opportunity cost. Second, there is the cost of maintaining the economic value of the item. For example, the cost of warehousing inventory belongs here.

Shortage costs are incurred when the investment in current assets is low. If a firm runs out of cash, it will be forced to sell marketable securities. If a firm runs out of cash and cannot readily sell marketable securities, it may need to borrow or default on an obligation. (This general situation is called a *cash-out*.) If a firm has no inventory (a *stock-out*) or if it cannot extend credit to its customers, it will lose customers.

There are two kinds of shortage costs:

1. *Trading or Order Costs*   Order costs are the costs of placing an order for more cash (brokerage costs) or more inventory (production set-up costs).
2. *Costs Related to Safety Reserves*   These are the costs of lost sales, lost customer goodwill, and disruption of the production schedule.

Figure 26.4 illustrates the basic nature of carrying costs. The total costs of investing in current assets are determined by adding the carrying costs and the shortage costs. The minimum point on the total cost curve (CA*) reflects the optimal balance of current assets. The curve is generally quite flat at the optimum, and it is difficult, if not impossible, to find the precise optimal balance of shortage and carrying costs. Usually we are content with a choice near the optimum.

If carrying costs are low and/or shortage costs are high, the optimal policy calls for substantial current assets. In other words, the optimal policy is a flexible one. This is illustrated in the middle graph of Figure 26.4.

If carrying costs are high and/or shortage costs are low, the optimal policy is a restrictive one. That is, the optimal policy calls for modest current assets. This is illustrated in the bottom graph of the figure.

One of the most significant impacts on inventory levels over recent years has been the emphasis on just-in-time systems. This technique has probably halved inventory levels in companies where it has been adopted. Just-in-time (JIT) inventory management works on the assumption that raw materials and work in progress should

---

[3] This is true of some types of finished goods.

[4] This is true of inventory of raw material, but not of finished goods.

FIGURE 26.4   **Carrying Costs and Shortage Costs**

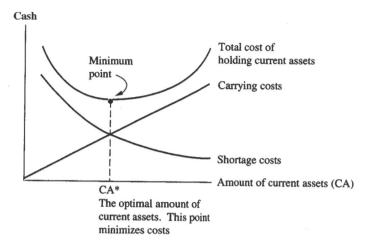

The optimal amount of
current assets. This point
minimizes costs

Flexible policy

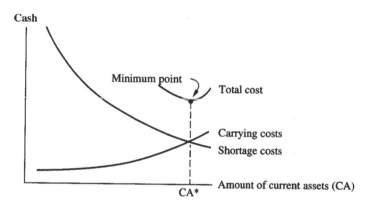

Restrictive policy

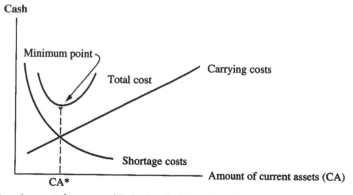

Carrying costs increase with the level of investment in current assets. They
include both opportunity costs and the costs of maintaining the asset's
economic value. *Shortage costs* decrease with increases in the level of
investment in current assets. They include trading costs and the costs of
running out of the current asset (for example, being short of cash).

flow from start to finish without stopping. They arrive where needed just in time, rather than becoming part of a substantial inventory. On its introduction, planning requires top to bottom reform of manufacturing and procurement operations.

By having suppliers deliver parts and materials to a factory only as they are needed, inventories are held down. At first sight, it might be thought that JIT would lead to higher prices being charged by the supplier. The just-in-time technique works because it leads to a reduction in the level of inventory required by both customers and suppliers.

Lower inventories reduce warehousing and financing costs. Just-in-time must ensure fast identification of poor-quality parts and permit manufacturers to change to new products without being stuck with surplus components. Very successful JIT factories have reduced their inventories to levels for only two or three days' (or even hours) production.

Just-in-time does more than just reduce carrying costs. With minimal inventory at each stage of production, inefficiencies, bottlenecks and quality problems are revealed and must be corrected. To be successful, JIT requires big investments in plant redesign, and significant effort in retraining managers and workers.

Alternative Financing Policies for Current Assets

In the previous section, we examined the level of investment in current assets. Now we turn to the level of current liabilities, assuming the investment in current assets is optimal.

An Ideal Model
In an ideal economy, short-term assets can always be financed with short-term debt, and long-term assets can be financed with long-term debt and equity. In this economy, net working capital is always zero.

Imagine the simple case of a grain-elevator operator. Grain-elevator operators buy crops after harvest, store them and sell them during the year. They have high inventories of grain after the harvest, and end with low inventories just before the next harvest.

Bank loans with maturities of less than one year are used to finance the purchase of grain. These loans are paid with the proceeds from the sale of grain.

The situation is shown in Figure 26.5. Long-term assets are assumed to grow over time, whereas current assets increase at the end of the harvest and then decline during the year. Short-term assets end at zero just before the next harvest. These assets are

---

FIGURE 26.5   Financing Policy for an Idealized Economy

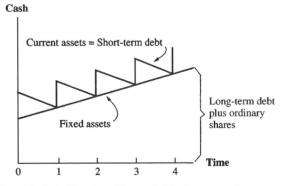

In an ideal world, net working capital is always zero because short-term assets are financed by short-term debt.

financed by short-term debt, and long-term assets are financed with long-term debt and equity. Net working capital—current assets minus current liabilities—is always zero.

Different Strategies in Financing Current Assets

Current assets cannot be expected to drop to zero in the real world, because a long-term rising level of sales will result in some permanent investment in current assets. A growing firm can be thought of as having both a permanent requirement for current assets and one for long-term assets. This total asset requirement will exhibit balances over time reflecting (1) a secular growth trend, (2) a seasonal variation around the trend and (3) unpredictable day-to-day and month-to-month fluctuations. This is depicted in Figure 26.6. (We have not tried to show the unpredictable day-to-day and month-to-month variations in the total asset requirement.)

FIGURE 26.6   The Total Asset Requirement over Time

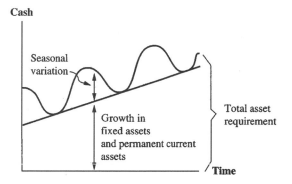

Now, let us look at how this asset requirement is financed. First, consider the strategy (strategy *F* in Figure 26.7) where long-term financing covers more than the total asset requirement, even at seasonal peaks. The firm will have excess cash available for investment in marketable securities when the total asset requirement falls from peaks. Because this approach implies chronic short-term cash surpluses and a large investment in net working·capital, it is considered a flexible strategy.

When long-term financing does not cover the total asset requirement, the firm must borrow short-term to make up the deficit. This restrictive strategy is labelled strategy *R* in Figure 26.7.

Which Is Best?

What is the most appropriate amount of short-term borrowing? There is no definitive answer. Several considerations must be included in a proper analysis:

1. *Cash Reserves*   The flexible financing strategy implies surplus cash and little short-term borrowing. This strategy reduces the probability that a firm will experience financial distress. Firms may not need to worry as much about meeting recurring, short-run obligations. However, investments in cash and marketable securities are zero net-present-value investments at best.
2. *Maturity Hedging*   Most firms finance inventories with short-term bank loans and fixed assets with long-term financing. Firms tend to avoid financing long-lived assets with short-term borrowing. This type of maturity mismatching

FIGURE 26.7   **Alternative Asset-Financing Policies**

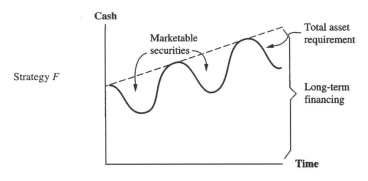

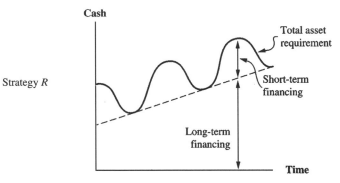

Strategy *F* always implies a short-term cash surplus and a
large investment in cash and marketable securities.
Strategy *R* uses long-term financing for on-going asset
requirements only, and short-term borrowing for seasonal
variations.

would necessitate frequent financing and is inherently risky, because short-term
interest rates are more volatile than longer rates.

3. *Term Structure*   Short-term interest rates are normally lower than long-term
interest rates. This implies that, on average, it is more costly to rely on long-
term borrowing than on short-term borrowing.

Concept Questions

- What keeps the real world from being an ideal one where net working capital could
always be zero?
- What considerations determine the optimal compromise between flexible and
restrictive net-working-capital policies?

26.5   Cash Budgeting

The **cash budget** is a primary tool of short-run financial planning. It allows the
financial manager to identify short-term financial needs (and opportunities). It will tell
the manager the required borrowing in the short term. It is the way of identifying the
cash-flow gap on the cash-flow time line. The idea of the cash budget is simple: It

records estimates of cash receipts and disbursements. We illustrate cash budgeting with the following example of Fun Toys.

● **Example**

All of Fun Toys' cash inflows come from the sale of toys. Cash budgeting for Fun Toys starts with a sales forecast for the next year, by quarter:

	First Quarter	*Second Quarter*	*Third Quarter*	*Fourth Quarter*
Sales (Euro millions)	Euro100	Euro200	Euro150	Euro100

Fun Toys' fiscal year starts on July 1. Fun Toys' sales are seasonal and are usually very high in the second quarter, due to Christmas sales. But Fun Toys sells to department stores on credit, and sales do not generate cash immediately. Instead, cash comes later from collections on accounts receivable. Fun Toys has a 90-day collection period, and 100 per cent of sales are collected the following quarter. In other words,

$$\text{Collections} = \text{Last quarter's sales}$$

This relationship implies that

$$\frac{\text{Accounts receivable}}{\text{at end of last quarter}} = \text{Last quarter's sales} \qquad (26.5)$$

We assume that sales in the fourth quarter of the previous fiscal year were Euro100 million. From equation (26.5), we know that accounts receivable at the end of the fourth quarter of the previous fiscal year were Euro100 million and collections in the first quarter of the current fiscal year are Euro100 million.

The first quarter sales of the current fiscal year of Euro100 million are added to the accounts receivable, but Euro100 million of collections are subtracted. Therefore, Fun Toys ended the first quarter with accounts receivable of Euro100 million. The basic relation is

$$\frac{\text{Ending accounts}}{\text{receivable}} = \frac{\text{Starting accounts}}{\text{receivable}} + \text{Sales} - \text{Collections}$$

Table 26.3 shows cash collections for Fun Toys for the next four quarters. Though collections are the only source of cash here, this need not always be the case. Other sources of cash could include sales of assets, investment income and long-term financing. ●

TABLE 26.3   Sources of Cash (in millions)

	First quarter	*Second quarter*	*Third quarter*	*Fourth quarter*
Sales	Euro100	Euro200	Euro150	Euro100
Cash collections	100	100	200	150
Starting receivables	100	100	200	150
Ending receivables	100	200	150	100

Cash Outflow

Next, we consider the cash disbursements. They can be put into four basic categories, as shown in Table 26.4.

1. *Payments of Accounts Payable*   These are payments for goods or services, such as raw materials. These payments will generally be made after purchases. Purchases will depend on the sales forecast. In the case of Fun Toys, assume that

   Payments = Last quarter's purchases
   Purchases = $\frac{1}{2}$ next quarter's sales forecast

2. *Wages, Taxes and Other Expenses*   This category includes all other normal costs of doing business that require actual expenditures. Depreciation, for example, is often thought of as a normal cost of business, but it requires no cash outflow.
3. *Capital Expenditures*   These are payments of cash for long-lived assets. Fun Toys plans a major capital expenditure in the fourth quarter.
4. *Long-Term Financing*   This category includes interest and principal payments on long-term outstanding debt and dividend payments to shareholders.

The total forecasted outflow appears in the last line of Table 26.4.

TABLE 26.4   Disbursement of Cash (in millions)

	First quarter	Second quarter	Third quarter	Fourth quarter
Sales	Euro100	Euro200	Euro150	Euro100
Purchases	100	75	50	50
Uses of cash				
Payments of accounts payable	50	100	75	50
Wages, taxes, and other expenses	20	40	30	20
Capital expenditures	0	0	0	100
Long-term financing expenses: interest and dividends	10	10	10	10
Total uses of cash	Euro 80	Euro150	Euro115	Euro180

The Cash Balance

The net cash balance appears in Table 26.5, and a large net cash outflow is forecast in the second quarter. This large outflow is not caused by an inability to earn a profit. Rather, it results from delayed collections on sales. This results in a cumulative cash shortfall of Euro30 million in the second quarter.

Fun Toys had established a minimum operating cash balance equal to Euro5 million to facilitate transactions, protect against unexpected contingencies and maintain compensating balances at its commercial banks. This means that it has a cash shortfall in the second quarter equal to Euro35 million.

TABLE 26.5   **The Cash Balance (in millions)**

	First quarter	Second quarter	Third quarter	Fourth quarter
Total cash receipts	Euro100	Euro100	Euro200	Euro150
Total cash disbursements	80	150	115	180
Net cash flow	20	(50)	85	(30)
Cumulative excess cash balance	20	(30)	55	25
Minimum cash balance	5	5	5	5
Cumulative finance surplus (deficit) requirement	15	(35)	50	20

Concept Questions

- How would you conduct a sensitivity analysis for Fun Toys' net cash balance?
- What could you learn from such an analysis?

26.6   The Short-Term Financial Plan

Fun Toys has a short-term financing problem. It cannot meet the forecasted cash outflows in the second quarter from internal sources. Its financing options include (1) overdraft borrowing (2) other unsecured bank borrowing, (3) other secured borrowing and (4) other sources.

Overdraft Borrowing

Overdraft finance is available in most European countries although, when looked at from a global perspective, it is not available in some of the most important countries in the world, for example the USA. **Overdrafts** are relatively easy to negotiate and are flexible, allowing the borrower to borrow up to a specified ceiling, run down the loan and then to increase borrowing again as required. The operation of an overdraft facility is usually linked to a current account. Interest rates fluctuate, linked to some marker rate, such as bank base rate. Interest is determined on the daily amount outstanding. Overdrafts were developed originally to cope with firms' needs to finance seasonal working capital, and banks traditionally liked to see their customers' overdrafts run down to zero during the year when seasonal working capital requirement declined. To some extent, at least for good creditworthy firms, this requirement has been relaxed in some European countries so that the overdraft has become a source of core finance. However, the great drawback with this source of finance, which is typically cheaper than longer term money, is that it is repayable on demand. This latter feature makes it a highly risky source of ongoing finance and, when used in this way, banks may request that customers refinance on some more appropriate and more permanent basis. Of course, it has to be said that although technically repayable on demand, most banks do not make a habit of enforcing this option and usually give reasonable notice of their intentions.

In the UK, the very best customers pay an interest rate of 1 per cent over base rate, while small or weaker customers may pay nearer 4 or 5 per cent over base rate.

Unsecured Loans

Another way to finance a temporary cash deficit is to arrange a short-term unsecured bank loan. Firms that use short-term bank loans usually ask their bank for either a non committed or a committed *line of credit*. A *non committed* line is an informal arrangement that allows firms to borrow up to a previously specified limit without going through the normal paperwork. The interest rate on the line of credit is usually set equal to the bank's base lending rate plus an additional percentage. In some European countries (and many South American countries), banks may also require that compensating balances be kept at the bank by the firm. For example, a firm might be required to keep an amount equal to 5 per cent on the line of credit.

Committed lines of credit are formal legal arrangements and usually involve a commitment fee paid by the firm to the bank (the fee may be around 0.25 per cent of the total committed funds per year). For larger firms the interest rate is often tied to the London Interbank Offered Rate (LIBOR) or Paris Interbank Offered Rate (PIBOR) or Amsterdam Interbank Offered Rate (AIBOR), and so on, or merely to the bank's cost of funds. In some parts of Europe, medium-sized and smaller firms are often required to keep compensating balances in the bank. Compensating balances are deposits the firm keeps with the bank in low-interest or non-interest-bearing accounts.

Compensating balances are commonly of the order of 2 to 5 per cent of the amount used. By leaving these funds with the bank without receiving interest, the firm increases the effective interest earned by the bank on the line of credit. For example, if a firm borrowing Euro100,000 must keep Euro5,000 as a compensating balance, the firm effectively receives only Euro95,000. A stated interest rate of 10 per cent implies yearly interest payments of Euro10,000 (Euro100,000 × 0.10). The effective interest rate is 10.53 per cent (Euro10,000/Euro95,000).

Secured Loans

Banks and other finance companies often require *security* for a loan. Security for short-term loans usually consists of accounts receivable or inventories.

Under **accounts receivable financing**, receivables are either *assigned* or *factored*. Under assignment, the lender not only has a lien on the receivables but also has recourse to the borrower. Factoring involves the sale of accounts receivable. The purchaser, who is called a *factor*, must then collect on the receivables. The factor assumes the full risk of default on bad accounts.

As the name implies, an **inventory loan** uses inventory as collateral.

Other Sources

There are a variety of other sources of short-term funds employed by corporations. The most important of these are the issuance of **commercial paper** and financing through **banker's acceptances**. Commercial paper consists of short-term notes issued by large and highly rated firms. Typically these notes are of short maturity, ranging up to 270 days. Because the firm issues these directly, and because it usually backs the issue with a special bank line of credit, the rate the firm obtains is often below the usual rate the bank would charge it for a direct loan.

A banker's acceptance is an agreement by a bank to pay a sum of money. These agreements typically arise when a seller sends a bill or draft to a customer. The customer's bank *accepts* this bill and notes the acceptance on it, which makes it an obligation of the bank. In this way a firm that is buying something from a supplier can effectively arrange for the bank to pay the outstanding bill. Of course, the bank charges the customer a fee for this service.

The Banker's View

In advancing loans, bankers like to see detailed cash forecasts together with income statement and balance sheet projections into the future plus a business plan. The essential point is that the banker wants to be sure that the customer can generate sufficient cash to repay the borrowing plus interest in accordance with the terms of the loan. The banker frequently runs 'what if' scenarios with different sets of assumptions than those that the customer has built into the projections. Bankers often assess debt proposals using simple checklists. Table 26.6 shows two that are widely used. Some banks introduce more complex checklists that are closer to credit scoring systems. They assess the management, market, strategy and general competitive environment, using a statistically determined weighted scoring system. Opinions vary as to the value of these. Many bankers place great weight on their judgment of how the entrepreneur will cope in a business crisis. The banker may suggest changes in the potential borrowers proposal in order to reduce the bank's exposure to acceptable levels.

TABLE 26.6 Two Common Banker's Checklists

The Five Cs	Campari
Character of borrower	Character of borrower
Capacity to repay	Ability to borrow and repay
Capital provided (debt–equity ratio)	Margin to profit
Collateral, or security	Purpose of the loan
Conditions (product, industry, economy)	Amount of the loan
	Repayment terms
	Insurance against non-payment (security)

Concept Questions

- What are the two basic forms of short-term financing?
- Describe two types of secured loans.

26.7 Managing the Collection and Disbursement of Cash

A firm's cash balance as reported in its financial statements *(book cash or ledger cash)* is not the same thing as the balance shown in its bank account *(bank cash or collected bank cash)*. The difference between bank cash and book cash is called **float** and represents the net effect of checks in the process of collection.

● Example

Imagine that General Mechanics Industries (GMI), currently has Euro100,000 on deposit with its bank. It purchases some raw materials, paying its vendors with a cheque written on July 8 for Euro100,000. The company's books (that is, ledger balances) are changed to show the Euro100,000 reduction in the cash balance. But the firm's bank will not find out about this cheque until it has been deposited at the vendor's bank and has been presented to the firm's bank for payment on, say, July 15. Until the cheque's presentation, the firm's bank cash is greater than its book cash, and it has *positive float*.

Position Prior to July 8:

$$\text{Float} = \text{Firm's bank cash} - \text{Firm's book cash}$$
$$= \text{Euro}100{,}000 - \text{Euro}100{,}000$$
$$= 0$$

Position from July 8 through July 14:

$$\text{Disbursement float} = \text{Firm's bank cash} - \text{Firm's book cash}$$
$$= \text{Euro}100{,}000 \quad - 0$$
$$= \text{Euro}100{,}000$$

During the period of time that the cheque is *clearing*, GMI has a balance with the bank of Euro100,000. It can obtain the benefit of this cash while the cheque is clearing. For example, the bank cash could be invested in financial securities. Cheques written by the firm generate *disbursement float*, causing an immediate decrease in book cash but no immediate change in bank cash. ●

● Example

Imagine that GMI receives a cheque from a customer for Euro100,000. Assume, as before, that the company has Euro100,000 deposited at its bank and has neutral float position. It deposits the cheque and increases its book cash by Euro100,000 on November 8. However, the cash is not available to GMI until its bank has presented the check to the customer's bank and received Euro100,000 on, say, November 15. In the meantime, the cash position at GMI will reflect a collection float of Euro100,000.

Position Prior to November 8:

$$\text{Float} = \text{Firm's bank cash} - \text{Firm's book cash}$$
$$= \text{Euro}100{,}000 - \text{Euro}100{,}000$$
$$= 0$$

Position from November 8 through November 14:

$$\text{Collection float} = \text{Firm's bank cash} - \text{Firm's book cash}$$
$$= \text{Euro}100{,}000 \quad - \text{Euro}200{,}000$$
$$= -\text{Euro}100{,}000 ●$$

Cheques received by the firm represent *collection float*, which increases book cash immediately, but does not immediately change bank cash. The firm is helped by disbursement float and is hurt by collection float. The sum of disbursement float and collection float is *net float*.

A firm should be more concerned with net float and bank cash than with book cash. If a financial manager knows that a cheque will not clear for several days, he or she will be able to keep a lower cash balance at the bank than might be true otherwise. Good float management can generate a great deal of money. For example, the average daily sales of the US oil giant Exxon are about USD248 million. If Exxon speeds up the collection process or slows down the disbursement process by one day, it frees up USD248 million, which can be invested in marketable securities. With an interest rate of 10 per cent, this represents overnight interest of approximately USD68,000 [(USD248 million/365) $\times$ 0.10].

Float management involves controlling the collection and disbursement of cash. The objective in cash collection is to reduce the lag between the time customers pay their bills and the time the cheques are collected. The objective in cash disbursement is to slow down payments, thereby increasing the time between when cheques are written and when cheques are presented. In other words, collect early and pay late. Of course, to the extent that the firm succeeds in doing this, the customers and suppliers lose money, and the trade-off is the effect on the firm's relationship with them. But late payment must not be pushed too far lest your reputation becomes so bad that no one deals with you, or if they do they put their prices up. Often, before a supplier grants credit, references are obtained from independent agencies set up to monitor trade payment practices (among other things). Poor payment practices could mean that suppliers are cautious about granting credit. In such circumstances, slowing payment creates an obvious problem. Suppliers may be reluctant to grant credit or they might increase prices. The moral is fairly obvious. Don't push the practice of slow payment too far—it will rebound.

Collection float can be broken down into three parts: mail float, in-house processing float and availability float:

1. *Mail Float* is the part of the collection and disbursement process where cheques are trapped in the postal system.
2. *In-House Processing Float* is the time it takes the receiver of a cheque to process the payment and deposit it in a bank for collection.
3. *Availability Float* refers to the time required to clear a cheque through the banking system.

In some European countries, banks can take so long to credit your account for float purposes when cheques have been paid into the bank that it may pay to arrange special clearance terms. Banks may demand payment for this, but it can be beneficial to pay in respect of large cheques. Clearly, a calculation based on interest versus the special clearance payment must be made. Various techniques are available, and reported in specialist texts, to companies to negotiate adverse and significant float machinations of local banks, and these vary from European country to country. Suffice to say that the problem is a very real one, particularly in southern and eastern Europe.

26.8   Summary and Conclusions

1. This chapter introduces the management of short-term finance. Short- term finance involves short-lived assets and liabilities. We trace and examine the short-term sources and uses of cash as they appear on the firm's financial statements. We see how current assets and current liabilities arise in the short-term operating activities and the cash cycle of the firm. From an accounting perspective, short-term finance involves net working capital.
2. Managing short-term cash flows involves the minimization of costs. The two major costs are carrying costs—the interest and related costs incurred by overinvesting in short-term assets such as cash—and shortage costs, the cost of running out of short-term assets. The objective of managing short-term finance and short-term financial planning is to find the optimal trade-off between these two costs.
3. In an ideal economy, the firm could perfectly predict its short-term uses and sources of cash, and net working capital could be kept at zero. In the real world, net working capital provides a buffer that lets the firm meet its ongoing obligations. The financial manager seeks the optimal level of each of the current assets.
4. The financial manager can use the cash budget to identify short-term financial needs. The cash budget tells the manager what borrowing is required or what lending will be possible in the short run. The firm has available to it a number of ways of acquiring funds to meet short-term shortfalls, including unsecured and secured loans.

KEY TERMS

Liquidity   579
Short-run operating activities   582
Cash flow time line   583
Operating cycle   583
Cash cycle   583
Carrying costs   586
Shortage costs   586
Cash budget   590

Overdrafts   593
Compensating balance   594
Accounts receivable financing   594
Inventory loan   594
Commercial paper   594
Banker's acceptances   594
Float   595

QUESTIONS AND PROBLEMS

Tracing Cash and Net Working Capital

26.1 Derive the cash equation from the basic balance sheet equation: assets = liabilities + equity.

26.2 Indicate whether the following corporate actions increase, decrease, or cause no change to cash.
  a. Cash is paid for raw materials purchased for inventory.
  b. A dividend is paid.
  c. Merchandise is sold on credit.
  d. Ordinary shares are issued.
  e. Raw material is purchased for inventory on credit.
  f. A piece of machinery is purchased and paid for with long-term debt.
  g. Payments for previous sales are collected.
  h. Accumulated depreciation is increased.
  i. Merchandise is sold for cash.
  j. Payment is made for a previous purchase.
  k. A short-term bank loan is received.
  l. A dividend is paid with funds received from a sale of ordinary shares.
  m. Allowance for bad debts is decreased.
  n. A piece of office equipment is purchased and paid for with a short-term borrowing.
  o. Marketable securities are purchased with retained earnings.
  p. Last year's taxes are paid.
  q. This year's tax liability is increased.
  r. Interest on long-term debt is paid.

Defining Cash in Terms of Other Elements

26.3 Below are the 19X6 balance sheet and profit and loss account of Country Kettles. Use this information to construct a sources-and-uses-of-cash statement.

COUNTRY KETTLES
Balance Sheet
December 31, 19X6

	19X6	19X5
Assets		
Cash	Euro42,000	Euro35,000
Accounts receivable	94,250	84,500
Inventory	78,750	75,000
Property, plant, equipment	181,475	168,750
Less: Accumulated depreciation	61,475	56,250
Total assets	Euro335,000	Euro307,000
Liabilities and Equity		
Accounts payable	Euro60,500	Euro55,000
Accrued expenses	5,150	8,450
Long-term debt	15,000	30,000
Ordinary shares	28,000	25,000
Retained earnings	226,350	188,550
Total liabilities and equity	Euro335,000	Euro307,000

COUNTRY KETTLES
Profit and Loss Account
December 31, 19X6

Net sales	Euro765,000
Cost of goods sold	459,000
Sales, general and administrative costs	91,800
Advertising	26,775
Rent	45,000
Depreciation	5,225
Profit before taxes	137,200
Taxes	68,600
Net profit	Euro68,600
Dividends	Euro30,800
Retained earnings	Euro37,800

The Operating Cycle and Cost Cycle

26.4 On Eastern Printing Machine Co.'s profit and loss account for 1996, the cost of goods sold and the credit sales are Euro200 million and Euro240 million, respectively. The following data are from its balance sheets.

	(Euro million)	
	Dec. 31, 1996	*Dec. 31, 1997*
Inventory	40	60
Accounts receivable	30	50
Accounts payable	10	30

　　a. How many days is Eastern Printing Machine's operating cycle?
　　b. How many days is Eastern Printing Machine's cash cycle?

26.5 Define:
　　a. Operating cycle
　　b. Cash cycle
　　c. Accounts payable period

26.6 Indicate whether the following company actions increase, decrease, or cause no change to the cash cycle and the operating cycle.
　　a. The use of discounts offered by suppliers is decreased.
　　b. More finished goods are being produced for order instead of for inventory.
　　c. A greater percentage of raw materials purchases is paid for with cash.
　　d The terms of discounts offered to customers are made more favourable for the customers.
　　e. A larger than usual amount of raw materials is purchased as a result of a price decline.
　　f. An increased number of customers pays with cash instead of credit.

Cash Budgeting

26.7 The sales budget for your company in the coming year is based on a 20 per cent quarterly growth rate with the first quarter projection at Euro100 million. In addition to this basic trend, the seasonal adjustments for the four quarters are 0, -10, -5 and 15 million Euros, respectively. Generally, 30 per cent of the sales can be collected within the month and 50 per cent in the following month; the rest of the sales are bad debts. All sales are credit sales. Compute the cash collections from sales for each quarter from the second to the fourth quarter.

Credit Management

When a firm sells goods and services it can (1) be paid in cash immediately or (2) wait for a time to be paid, that is, extend credit to customers. Granting credit is investing in a customer, an investment tied to the sale of a product or service. This chapter examines the firm's decision to grant credit.

An account receivable is created when credit is granted. These receivables include credit granted to other firms, called *trade credit*, and credit granted consumers, called *consumer credit*. About one-sixth of all the assets of industrial firms are in the form of accounts receivable.

The investment in accounts receivable for any firm depends on both the amount of credit sales and the average collection period. For example, if a firm's credit sales per day equal DEM1,000 and its average collection period is 30 days, its accounts receivable will be equal to DEM30,000. Thus, a firm's investment in accounts receivable depends on factors influencing credit sales and collection. A firm's credit policy affects these factors.

The following are the components of credit policy:

1. **Terms of the Sale** A firm must decide on certain conditions when selling its goods and services for credit. For example, the terms of sale may specify the credit period, the cash discount and the type of credit instrument.
2. **Credit Analysis** When granting credit, a firm tries to distinguish between customers that will pay and customers that will not pay. Firms use a number of devices and procedures to determine the probability that customers will pay.
3. **Collection Policy** Firms that grant credit must establish a policy for collecting the cash when it becomes due.

This chapter discusses each of the components of credit policy that make up the decision to grant credit.

In some ways, the decision to grant credit is connected to the cash collection process described in the previous chapter. This is illustrated in Figure 27.1 with a cash flow diagram.

FIGURE 27.1   **The Cash Flows of Granting Credit**

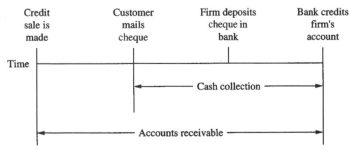

The typical sequence of events when a firm grants credit is (1) the credit sale is made, (2) the customer sends a cheque to the firm, (3) the firm deposits the cheque and (4) the firm's account is credited for the amount of the cheque.

27.1   Terms of the Sale

The terms of sale refer to the period for which credit is granted, the cash discount and the type of credit instrument. For example, suppose a customer is granted credit with terms of 2/10, net 30. This means that the customer has 30 days from the **invoice** date within which to pay.[1] In addition, a cash discount of 2 per cent from the stated sales price is to be given if payment is made in 10 days. If the stated terms are net 60, the customer has 60 days from the invoice date to pay and no discount is offered for early payment.

Credit Period

Credit periods vary among different industries and within different European countries. Generally a firm must consider three factors in setting a credit period:

1. *The Probability that the Customer Will Not Pay*   A firm whose customers are in high-risk businesses may find itself offering restrictive credit terms.
2. *The Size of the Account*   If the account is small, the credit period will be shorter. Small accounts are more costly to manage, and customers are less important.
3. *The Extent to which the Goods Are Perishable*   If the collateral values of the goods are low and cannot be sustained for a long period, less credit will be granted.

Lengthening the credit period effectively reduces the price paid by the customer. Generally this increases sales.

Cash Discounts

Cash discounts are often part of the terms of sale. One reason they are offered is to speed up the collection of receivables. The firm must trade this off against the cost of the discount.

● Example
Carl Manalt, the chief financial officer of the Swedish firm, Ruptbank Company, is considering the request of the company's largest customer, who wants to take a 3 per cent discount for payment within 20 days on a SEK100,000 purchase. In other words, he intends to pay SEK97,000 [SEK100,000 × (1 − 0.03)]. Normally, this customer pays in 30 days with no discount. The cost of debt capital for Ruptbank is 10 per cent. Carl has worked out the cash flow implications illustrated in Figure 27.2. He assumes that the time required to cash the cheque when the customer

---

[1] An invoice is a bill written by a seller of goods or services and submitted to the buyer. The invoice date is sensibly the same as the shipping date. But slippage behind that tight schedule often occurs.

FIGURE 27.2   **Cash Flows for Different Credit Terms**

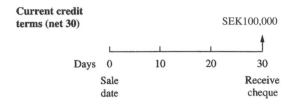

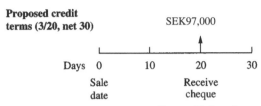

Current situation: customers usually pay 30 days from the sale date and receive no discount.

Proposed situation: customer will pay 20 days from the sale date at a 3 per cent discount from the SEK100,000 purchase price.

receives it is the same under both credit arrangements. He has calculated the present value of the two proposals as:

Current Policy:

$$PV = \frac{SEK100,000}{1 + (0.1 \times 30/365)} = SEK99,184.8$$

Proposed Policy:

$$PV = \frac{SEK97,000}{1 + (0.1 \times 20/365)} = SEK96,471.4$$

His calculation shows that granting the discount would cost Ruptbank SEK2713.4 (SEK99,184.8 − SEK96,471.4) in present value. Consequently, Ruptbank is better off with the current credit arrangement. ●

In the previous example, we implicitly assumed that granting credit had no side effects. However, the decision to grant credit may generate higher sales and involve a different cost structure. The next example illustrates the impact of changes in the level of sales and costs in the credit decision.

● Example

Suppose that Ruptbank has variable costs of SEK0.50 per SEK1 of sales. If offered a discount of 3 per cent, customers will increase the order size by 10 per cent. This new information is shown in Figure 27.3. That is, the customer will increase the order size to SEK110,000 and, with the 3 per cent discount, will remit SEK106,700 [SEK110,000 × (1 − 0.03)] to Ruptbank in 20 days. It will cost more to fill the larger order because

FIGURE 27.3   **Cash Flows for Different Credit Terms: The Impact of New Sales and Costs**

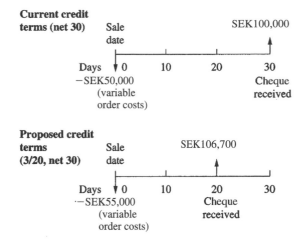

variable costs are SEK55,000. The net present values are worked out here:

Current Policy:

$$\text{NPV} = -\text{SEK}50{,}000 + \frac{\text{SEK}100{,}000}{1 + (0.1 \times 30/365)} = \text{SEK}49{,}184.8$$

Proposed Policy:

$$\text{NPV} = -\text{SEK}55{,}000 + \frac{\text{SEK}106{,}700}{1 + (0.1 \times 20/365)} = \text{SEK}51{,}118.5$$

Now it is clear that the firm is better off with the proposed credit policy. This increase is the net effect of several different factors including the larger initial costs, the earlier receipt of the cash inflows, the increased sales level and the discount. ●

Credit Instruments

Most credit is offered on *open account*. This means that the only formal **credit instrument** is the invoice, which is sent with the shipment of goods, and which the customer signs as evidence that the goods have been received. Afterwards, the firm and its customers record the exchange on their accounting books.

At times, the firm may require that the customer sign a *promissory note* or IOU. This is used when the order is large and when the firm anticipates a problem in collections. Promissory notes can eliminate controversies later about the existence of a credit agreement.

One problem with promissory notes is that they are signed after delivery of the goods. One way to obtain a credit commitment from a customer before the goods are delivered is through the use of a *commercial draft*. The selling firm typically writes a commercial draft calling for the customer to pay a specific amount by a specified date. The draft is then sent to the customer's bank with the shipping invoices. The bank requires the buyer to sign the draft before turning over the invoices. The goods can then be shipped to the buyer. If immediate payment is required, it is called a *sight draft*. Here, funds must be turned over to the bank before the goods are shipped.

Frequently, even the signed draft is not enough for the seller. In this case, he might demand that the banker pay for the goods and collect the money from the customer. When the banker agrees to do so in writing, the document is called a *banker's acceptance* or *bill of exchange*. Here the banker *accepts* responsibility for payment. Because banks generally are well-known and well-respected institutions, the banker's acceptance becomes a liquid instrument. In other words, the seller can then sell (*discount*) the banker's acceptance in the secondary market.

A firm can also use a *conditional sales* contract as a credit instrument. This is an arrangement where the firm retains legal ownership of the goods until the customer has completed payment. Conditional sales contracts usually are paid off in instalments and have interest costs built into them.

Credit Periods

Within Europe, business culture and practice varies by country and even by region within countries. This is most strikingly reflected in the credit norms of different parts of the continent. Quite remarkably, the policies on credit from Scandinavian to southern Europe show a tremendous contrast. In fact, as can be seen from Table 27.1, Sweden, Norway, Finland and Denmark, with national average payment times of around $1\frac{1}{2}$ months, compare very favourably indeed with the relatively lax credit control found in Greece, Spain and Italy, where average payment times average from $3\frac{1}{2}$ months to over 5 months—despite Italy, Spain and Greece having legislation to force payment of interest on late settlement.

Concept Question

• What considerations enter into the determination of the terms of sale?

TABLE 27.1   Credit Norms and Averages in 1995

	Normal payment terms (days)	Average national payment times (days)
Sweden	30	40
Norway	15–30	46
Finland	30	46
Denmark	30–45	55
Netherlands	30	61
Belgium	30–60	63
Germany	30–60	65
Britain	30–60	75
Austria	30–60	87
France	90	90
Portugal	60	95
Cyprus	75	99
Italy	60–90	104
Spain	90	130
Greece	65–120	158

Source: Association of British Factors and Discounters Survey of Small to Medium Enterprises

27.2   The Decision to Grant Credit: Risk and Information

Locust Industries BV, a Netherlands-based business headquartered in Utrecht, has been in existence for two years. It is one of several successful firms that develop computer programs. The present financial managers have set out two alternative credit strategies. The firm can offer credit or the firm can refuse credit.

Suppose Locust has determined that, if it offers no credit to its customers, it can sell its existing computer software for NLG50 per program. It estimates that the costs to produce a typical computer program are equal to NLG20 per program.

The alternative is to offer credit. In this case, customers of Locust will pay one period later. Locust has determined that if it offers credit, it can charge higher prices and expect higher sales.

Strategy 1: Refuse Credit   If Locust refuses to grant credit, cash flows will not be delayed, and period 0 net cash flows, NCF, will be

$$P_0 Q_0 - C_0 Q_0 = \text{NCF}$$

The subscripts denote the time when the cash flows are incurred, where

P_0 = Price per unit received at time 0
C_0 = Cost per unit received at time 0
Q_0 = Quantity sold at time 0

The net cash flows at period 1 are zero, and the net present value to Locust of refusing credit will simply be the period 0 net cash flow:

$$\text{NPV} = \text{NCF}$$

For example, if credit is not granted and $Q_0 = 100$, the NPV can be calculated as

$$\text{NLG}50 \times 100 - \text{NLG}20 \times 100 = \text{NLG}3{,}000$$

Strategy 2: Offer Credit   Alternatively, let us assume that Locust grants credit to all customers for one period. The factors that influence the decision are listed below.

	Strategy 1 Refuse Credit	Strategy 2 Offer Credit
Price per unit	P_0 = NLG50	P_0' = NLG50
Quantity sold	Q_0 = 100	Q_0' = 200
Cost per unit	C_0 = NLG20	C_0' = NLG25
Probability of payment	h = 1	h = 0.90
Credit period	0	1 period
Discount rate	0	r_B = 0.01

The prime ($'$) denotes the variables under the second strategy. If the firm offers credit and the new customers pay, the firm will receive revenues of $P_0' Q_0'$ one period hence, but its costs, $C_0' Q_0'$, are incurred in period 0. If new customers do not pay, the firm incurs costs $C_0' Q_0'$ and receives no revenues. The probability that customers will pay, h, is 0.90 in the example. Quantity sold is higher with credit, because new customers are attracted. The cost per unit is also higher with credit because of the costs of operating a credit policy.

The expected cash flows for each policy are set out as follows:

	Expected Cash Flows	
	Time 0	*Time 1*
Refuse credit	$P_0Q_0 - C_0Q_0$	0
Offer credit	$-C_0'Q_0'$	$h \times P_0'Q_0'$

Note that granting credit produces delayed expected cash inflows equal to $h \times P_0'Q_0'$. The costs are incurred immediately and require no discounting. The net present value if credit is offered is

$$\text{NPV(offer)} = \frac{h \times P_0'Q_0'}{1 + r_B} - C_0'Q_0'$$

$$= \frac{0.9 \times \text{NLG50} \times 200}{1.01} - \text{NLG5,000} = \text{NLG3,910.89}$$

Locust Industries' decision should be to adopt the proposed credit policy. The NPV of granting credit is higher than that of refusing credit. This decision is very sensitive to the probability of payment. If it turns out that the probability of payment is 81 per cent, Locust Industries is indifferent to whether it grants credit or not. In this case, the NPV of granting credit is NLG3,000, which we previously found to be the NPV of not granting credit:

$$\text{NLG3,000} = h \times \frac{\text{NLG50} \times 200}{1.01} - \text{NLG5,000}$$

$$\text{NLG8,000} = h \times \frac{\text{NLG50} \times 200}{1.01}$$

$$h = 80.8\%$$

The decision to grant credit depends on four factors:

1. The delayed revenues from granting credit, $P_0'Q_0'$.
2. The immediate costs of granting credit, $C_0'Q_0'$.
3. The probability of payment, h.
4. The appropriate required rate of return for delayed cash flows, r_B.

The Value of New Information about Credit Risk

Obtaining a better estimate of the probability that a customer will default can lead to a better decision. How can a firm determine when to acquire new information about the creditworthiness of its customers?

It may be sensible for Locust Industries to determine which of its customers are most likely not to pay. The overall probability of non-payment is 10 per cent. But credit checks by an independent firm show that 90 per cent of Locust's customers (computer stores) have been profitable over the last five years and that these customers have never defaulted on payments. The less profitable customers are much more likely to default. In fact, 100 per cent of the less profitable customers have defaulted on previous obligations.

Locust would like to avoid offering credit to the deadbeats. Consider its projected number of customers per year of $Q'_0 = 200$ if credit is granted. Of these customers, 180 have been profitable over the last five years and have never defaulted on past obligations. The remaining 20 have not been profitable. Locust expects that all of these less profitable customers will default. This information is set out in a table:

Type of Customer	Number	Probability of Non-payment	Expected Number of Defaults
Profitable	180	0	0
Less profitable	20	100%	20
Total customers	200	10%	20

The NPV of granting credit to the customers who default is:

$$\frac{hP'_0Q'_0}{1 + r_B} - C'_0Q'_0 = \frac{0 \times \text{NLG50} \times 20}{1.01} - \text{NLG25} \times 20 = -\text{NLG500}$$

the cost of providing them with the software. If Locust can identify these customers without cost, it would certainly deny them credit.

In fact, it actually costs Locust NLG3 per customer to figure out whether a customer has been profitable over the last five years. The expected payoff of the credit cheque on its 200 customers is then given by:

$$\begin{array}{l} \text{Gain from not} \\ \text{extending credit} \\ \text{NLG500} \end{array} - \begin{array}{l} \text{Cost of} \\ \text{credit checks} \\ - \text{NLG3} \times 200 = -\text{NLG100} \end{array}$$

For Locust, credit is not worth checking. It would need to pay NLG600 to avoid a NLG500 loss.

Future Sales

Up to this point, Locust has not considered the possibility that offering credit will permanently increase the level of sales in future periods (beyond next month). In addition, payment and non-payment patterns in the current period will provide credit information that is useful for the next period. These two factors should be analysed.

In the case of Locust, there is a 90 per cent probability that the customer will pay in period 1. But, if payment is made, there will be another sale in period 2. The probability that the customer will pay in period 2, if the customer has paid in period 1, is 100 per cent. Locust can refuse to offer credit in period 2 to customers that have refused to pay in period 1. This is shown in Figure 27.4.

Concept Question

• List the factors that influence the decision to grant credit.

FIGURE 27.4   Future Sales and the Credit Decision

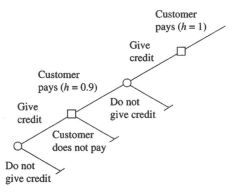

There is a 90-per cent probability that a customer will pay in period 1. However, if payment is made, there will be another sale in period 2. The probability that the customer will pay in period 2 is 100 per cent—if the customer has paid in period 1.

27.3   Optimal Credit Policy

So far we have discussed how to compute net present value for two alternative credit policies. However, we have not discussed the optimal amount of credit. At the optimal amount of credit, the incremental cash flows from increased sales are exactly equal to the carrying costs from the increase in accounts receivable.

Consider a firm that does not currently grant credit. This firm has no bad debts, no credit department and relatively few customers. Now consider another firm that grants credit. This firm has lots of customers, a credit department and a bad-debt expense.

It is useful to think of the decision to grant credit in terms of carrying costs and opportunity costs:

1. *Carrying costs* are the costs associated with granting credit and making an investment in receivables. Carrying costs include the delay in receiving cash, the losses from bad debts and the costs of managing credit.
2. *Opportunity costs* are the lost sales from refusing to offer credit. These costs drop as credit is granted.

We represent these costs in Figure 27.5.

The sum of the carrying costs and the opportunity costs of a particular credit policy is called the *total-credit-cost curve*. A point is identified as the minimum of the total-credit-cost curve. If the firm extends more credit than the minimum, the additional net cash flow from new customers will not cover the carrying costs of this investment in receivables.

The concept of optimal credit policy in the context of modern principles of finance should be somewhat analogous to the concept of the optimal inventory level discussed earlier in the text. In perfect financial markets, there should be no optimal credit policy. Alternative amounts of credit for a firm should not affect the value of the firm. Thus, the decision to grant credit would be a matter of indifference to financial managers.

FIGURE 27.5   The Costs of Granting Credit

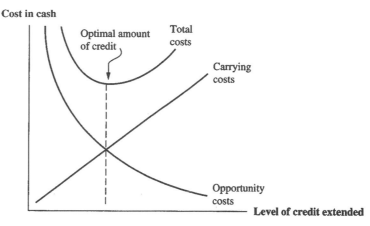

Carrying costs are the cash flows that must be incurred when credit is granted. They are positively related to the amount of credit extended.

Opportunity costs are the lost sales from refusing credit. These costs drop when credit is granted.

We could expect taxes, monopoly power, bankruptcy costs and agency costs to be important in determining an optimal credit policy in a world of imperfect financial markets. For example, customers in high tax brackets would be better off borrowing and taking advantage of cash discounts offered by firms than would customers in low tax brackets. Companies in low tax brackets would be less able to offer credit, because borrowing would be relatively more expensive than for firms in high tax brackets.

In general, a firm extends trade credit if it has a comparative advantage in doing so. Trade credit is likely to be advantageous if the selling firm has a cost advantage over other potential lenders, if the selling firm has monopoly power it can exploit, and if the selling firm can reduce taxes by extending credit. Firm size may be important if there are size economies in managing credit.

The optimal credit policy depends on characteristics of particular firms. Assuming that the firm has more flexibility in its credit policy than in the prices it charges, firms with excess capacity, low variable operating costs, high tax brackets and repeat customers should extend credit more liberally than others.

27.4   Credit Analysis

When granting credit, a firm tries to distinguish between customers that will pay and customers that will not pay. There are a number of sources of information for determining creditworthiness.

Credit Information

Information commonly used to assess creditworthiness includes the following:

1. *Financial Statements* A firm can ask a customer to supply financial statements. Rules of thumb based on financial ratios can be calculated.

2. *Credit Reports on Customer's Payment History with Other Firms*   Many organizations sell information on the credit strength of business firms. The best known and largest firm of this type worldwide is Dun & Bradstreet, which provides subscribers with a credit-reference book and credit reports on individual firms. The reference book has credit ratings on many thousands of businesses.
3. *Banks*   Banks will generally provide some assistance to their business customers in acquiring information on the creditworthiness of other firms.
4. *The Customer's Payment History with the Firm*   The most obvious way to obtain an estimate of a customer's probability of non-payment is whether he or she has paid previous bills.

Credit Scoring

Once information has been gathered, the firm faces the hard choice of either granting or refusing credit. Many firms use the traditional and subjective guidelines referred to as the 'five Cs of credit' which were referred to in Table 26.6 in the previous chapter. These are:

1. *Character*   The customer's reputation, self-presentation and willingness to meet credit obligations.
2. *Capacity*   The customer's ability to meet credit obligations out of operating cash flows.
3. *Capital*   The customer's financial strength.
4. *Collateral*   A pledged asset in the case of default.
5. *Conditions*   General economic conditions.

Firms such as credit-card issuers have developed elaborate statistical models (called **credit-scoring** models) for determining the probability of default. Usually all of the relevant and observable characteristics of a large pool of customers are studied to find their historic relation to default. Because these models determine who is and who is not creditworthy, not surprisingly they have been the subject of government regulation in some parts of the world. For example, if a model were to find that women default more than men, it might be used to deny women credit. This regulation may remove such models from the domain of the statistician and make them a subject for politicians.

Concept Questions

- What is credit analysis?
- What are the five Cs of credit?

27.5   Collection Policy

Collection refers to obtaining payment of past-due accounts. The credit manager keeps a record of payment experiences with each customer.

Average Collection Period

Acme Compact Disc Players sells 100,000 compact disc players a year at Euro300 each. All sales are for credit with terms of 2/20, net 60.

Suppose that 80 per cent of Acme customers take the discounts and pay on day 20; the rest pay on day 60. The **average collection period (ACP)** measures the average amount of time required to collect an account receivable. The ACP for Acme is 28 days:

$$0.8 \times 20 \text{ days} + 0.2 \times 60 \text{ days} = 28 \text{ days}$$

(The average collection period is frequently referred to as *days' sales outstanding* or *days in receivables.*)

Of course, this is an idealized example where customers pay on either one of two dates. In reality, payments arrive in a random fashion, so that the average collection period must be calculated differently.

To determine the ACP in the real world, firms first calculate average daily sales. The **average daily sales (ADS)** equal annual sales divided by 365. The ADS of Acme are

$$\text{Average daily sales} = \frac{\text{Euro}300 \times 100,000}{365 \text{ days}} = \text{Euro}82,192$$

If receivables today are Euro2,301,376, the average collection period is

$$\text{Average collection period} = \frac{\text{Accounts receivable}}{\text{Average daily sales}}$$

$$= \frac{\text{Euro}2,301,376}{\text{Euro}82,192}$$

$$= 28 \text{ days}$$

In practice, firms observe sales and receivables on a daily basis. Consequently, an average collection period can be computed and compared to the stated credit terms. For example, suppose Acme had computed its ACP at 40 days for several weeks, versus its credit terms of 2/20, net 60. With a 40-day ACP, some customers are paying later than usual. It may be that some accounts are overdue.

However, firms with seasonal sales will often find the *calculated* ACP changing during the year, making the ACP a somewhat flawed tool. This occurs because receivables are low before the selling season and high after the season. Thus, firms may keep track of seasonal movement in the ACP over past years. In this way, they can compare the ACP for today's date with the average ACP for that date in previous years. To supplement the information in the ACP, the credit manager may make up a schedule of ageing of receivables.

Ageing Schedule

The **ageing schedule** tabulates receivables by age of account. In the following schedule, 75 per cent of the accounts are on time, but a significant number are more than 60 days past due. This signifies that some customers are in arrears.

Ageing Schedule

Age of Account	Percentage of Total Value of Accounts Receivable
0–20 days	50
21–60 days	25
61–80 days	20
Over 80 days	5
	100

The ageing schedule changes during the year. Comparatively, the ACP is a somewhat flawed tool because it only gives the yearly average. Some firms have refined it so that they can examine how it changes with peaks and valleys in their sales. Similarly, the ageing schedule is often augmented by the payments pattern. The payments pattern describes the lagged collection pattern of receivables. Like a mortality table that describes the probability that a 23-year-old will live to be 24, the payments pattern describes the probability that a 67-day-old account will still be unpaid when it is 68 days old.

Collection Effort

The firm usually employs the following procedures for customers that are overdue:

1. Sends a delinquency letter informing the customer of the past-due status of the account.
2. Makes a telephone call to the customer.
3. Employs a collection agency.
4. Takes legal action against the customer.

At times, a firm may refuse to grant additional credit to customers until arrears are paid. This may antagonize a normally good customer, and points to a potential conflict of interest between the collections department and the sales department. Of course, the firm can manage its credit management better by simply getting bills out earlier and mailing them more speedily.

Factoring and Discounting

Factoring refers to the sale of a firm's accounts receivable to a financial institution known as a *factor*. The firm and the factor agree on the basic credit terms for each customer. The customer sends payment directly to the factor, and the factor bears the risk of non-paying customers. The factor buys the receivables at a discount, which may range from 0.5 per cent to around 6 or 7 per cent of the value of the invoice amount, and may even be higher than this in some parts of Europe.

One point should be stressed. We have presented the elements of credit policy as though they were almost independent of each other. In fact, they are closely interrelated. For example, the optimal credit policy is not independent of collection and monitoring policies. A tighter collection policy can reduce the probability of default, and this, in turn, can raise the NPV of a more liberal credit policy.

Concept Question

- What tools can a manager use to analyse a collection policy?

27.6   How to Finance Trade Credit

There are other, more sophisticated, ways of financing accounting receivables found in some parts of Europe. These are secured debt, a captive finance company and securitization.

The use of secured debt is usually referred to as asset-based receivables financing. This is the predominant form of receivables financing. Many lenders will not lend without security to firms with substantive uncertainty or little equity. With secured debt, if the borrower gets into financial difficulty, the lender can repossess the asset and sell it for its fair market value.

Many large firms with good credit ratings use captive finance companies. The captive finance companies are subsidiaries of the parent firm. This is similar to the use of secured debt, because the creditors of the captive finance company have a claim on its assets and, as a consequence, the accounts receivable of the parent firm. A captive finance company is attractive if economies of scale are important and if an independent subsidiary with limited liability is warranted.

Securitization occurs when the selling firm sells its accounts receivables to a financial institution. The financial institution pools the receivables with other receivables and issues securities to finance items.

27.7   Summary and Conclusions

1. The components of a firm's credit policy are the terms of sale, the credit analysis and the collection policy.
2. The terms of sale describe the amount and period of time for which credit is granted and the type of credit instrument.
3. The decision to grant credit is a straightforward NPV decision, and can be improved by additional information about the payment characteristics of the customers. Additional information about the customers' probability of defaulting is valuable, but this value must be traded off against the expense of acquiring the information.
4. The optimal amount of credit the firm offers is a function of the competitive conditions in which it finds itself. These conditions will determine the carrying costs associated with granting credit and the opportunity costs of the lost sales from refusing to offer credit. The optimal credit policy minimizes the sum of these two costs.
5. We have seen that knowledge of the probability that customers will default is valuable. To enhance its ability to assess customers' default probability, a firm can score credit. This relates the default probability to observable characteristics of customers.
6. The collection policy is the method of dealing with past-due accounts. The first step is to analyse the average collection period and to prepare an ageing schedule that relates the age of accounts to the proportion of the accounts receivable they represent. The next step is to decide on the collection method and to evaluate the possibility of factoring, that is, selling the overdue accounts.

KEY TERMS

Terms of the sale 600	Credit instrument 603
Credit analysis 600	Credit scoring 610
Collection policy 600	Average collection period (ACP) 610
Invoice 601	Average daily sales (ADS) 611
Credit periods 601	Ageing schedule 611
Cash discounts 601	Factoring 612

QUESTIONS AND PROBLEMS

Terms of the Sale

27.1 North Country Publishing Ltd has provided the following data:

> Annual credit sales = GBP10 million
> Average collection period = 60 days
> Terms: Net 30
> Interest rate = 10%

North Country Publishing proposes to offer a discount policy of 2/10, net 30. It anticipates that 50 per cent of its customers will take advantage of this new policy. As a result, the collection period will be reduced to 30 days. Should the North Country Publishing offer the new credit terms?

27.2   Webster's GmbH sells on credit terms of net 45. Its accounts are on average 45 days past due. If annual credit sales are DEM5 million, what is the company's balance in accounts receivable?

The Decision to Grant Credit: Risk and Information

27.3   De Goeij Sport BV operates a sports shoe business by mail order. Management is considering dropping its policy of no credit. The credit policy under consideration by de Goeij follows:

	No Credit	Credit
Price per unit	NLG35	NLG40
Cost per unit	NLG25	NLG32
Quantity sold	2,000	3,000
Probability of payment	100%	85%
Credit period	0	1
Discount rate	0	3%

  a.   Should de Groeij offer credit to its customers?

  b.   What must the probability of payment be before de Groeij would adopt the policy?

27.4   Silver Spokes Bicycle Company (SSBC) has decided to offer credit to its customers during the spring selling season. Sales are expected to be 300 cycles. The average cost to SSBC of a cycle is GBP240. The owner of SSBC knows that only 95 per cent of the customers will be able to make their payments. To identify the remaining 5 per cent, he is considering subscribing to the services of a credit rating agency. The initial charge for this service is GBP500, with an additional charge of GBP4 per individual report. Should he subscribe to the agency?

Optimal Credit Policy

27.5   In principle, how should we decide the optimal credit policy?

Credit Analysis

27.6   What is the information commonly used to assess creditworthiness of a client?

Collection Policy

27.7   Major Electronics sells 85,000 personal stereos each year at a price per unit of CHF55. All sales are on credit. The terms are 3/15, net 40. The discount is taken by 40 per cent of the customers. What is the investment in accounts receivable?

   In reaction to a competitor, Major Electronics is considering changing its credit terms to 5/15, net 40 in order to preserve its sales level. Describe how this policy change will affect the investment in accounts receivable.

27.8   The Allen Company Ltd has monthly credit sales of GBP600,000. The average collection period is 90 days. The cost of production is 70 per cent of the selling price. What is the Allen Company's average investment in accounts receivable?

27.9   The factoring department of Inter Dansk Bank (IDB) is processing 100,000 invoices per year with average invoice value of DKK1,500. IDB buys the accounts receivables at 4 per cent off the invoice value. The average collection period is 30 days. Currently 2 per cent of the accounts receivable turn out to be bad debts. The annual interest rate is 10 per cent. The annual operating expense of this department is DKK400,000. What is the gross profit before interest and tax for the factoring department of IDB?

PART VII

Special Topics

28 Mergers and Acquisitions   617
29 International Corporate Finance and Derivative Securities   644
30 The Road to Economic and Monetary Union   677

In Part VII we discuss three special topics: mergers and acquisitions, international corporate finance and derivative securities and European monetary union.

Chapter 28 describes the corporate finance of mergers and acquisitions. The acquisition of one firm by another is a capital-budgeting decision and the basic principles of NPV apply; that is, a firm should be acquired if it generates positive NPV to the shareholders of the acquiring firm. The purpose of Chapter 28 is to discuss how to value an acquisition candidate. However, the NPV of an acquisition candidate is more difficult to determine than that of a typical investment project because of complex accounting, tax and legal effects.

Chapter 29 concerns international corporate finance. Many firms have significant foreign operations and must consider special financial factors that do not directly affect purely domestic firms. These factors include foreign exchange rates and interest rates in foreign currencies. The problems created may be managed by a range of derivative securities.

Finally, our last chapter relates to European monetary union, and embraces such topics as the European Monetary System (EMS) and Economic and Monetary Union (EMU). The purpose, structure, functioning, special features and tensions in the EMS are described. The EMS is paving the way towards monetary union in Europe. There is a timetable in place and agreed criteria for qualification for a single European currency. Undoubtedly, entry into EMU will be staged with a small number of EU countries adopting EMU to start with and subsequent entry by some other countries and currencies at later dates.

CHAPTER 28
Mergers and Acquisitions

There is no more dramatic or controversial activity in corporate finance than the acquisition of one firm by another or the merger of two firms. It is the stuff of which reporters' dreams are made, and it can also be a source of scandal and rumour.

The acquisition of one firm by another is, of course, an investment made under uncertainty. The basic principle of valuation applies. A firm should be acquired if it generates a positive net present value to the shareholders of the acquiring firm. However, because the NPV of an acquisition candidate is very difficult to determine, mergers and acquisitions are interesting topics in their own right. Here are some of the special features of this area of finance:

1. The benefits from acquisitions are called *synergies*. It is hard to estimate synergies using discounted cash flow techniques.
2. There are complex accounting, tax and legal effects when one firm is acquired by another.
3. Acquisitions are an important control device of shareholders. It appears that some acquisitions are a consequence of an underlying conflict between the interests of existing managers and of shareholders. Acquisition by another firm is one way that shareholders can remove managers with whom they are unhappy.
4. Acquisition analysis frequently focuses on the total value of the firms involved. But usually an acquisition will affect the relative values of shares and bonds, as well as their total value.
5. Mergers and acquisitions sometimes involve unfriendly transactions. Thus, when one firm attempts to acquire another, it does not always involve quiet, gentlemanly negotiations. The sought-after firm may use defensive tactics to fight an unwanted approach.

This chapter starts by introducing the basic legal, accounting, and value aspects of acquisitions. These will be explained throughout the chapter. The chapter discusses how to determine the NPV of an acquisition candidate. The NPV of an acquisition candidate is the difference between the synergy from the merger and the premium to be paid. We consider the following types of synergy: (1) revenue enhancement, (2) cost reduction, (3) lower taxes and (4) lower cost of capital. The premium paid for an acquisition is the price paid minus the market value of the acquisition prior to the merger. The premium may depend on whether cash or securities are used to finance the offer price.

28.1   The Basic Forms of Acquisition

Exact mechanisms and possibilities of takeovers vary from one European country to another (as we mentioned in Chapter 1), but there are some common themes and we attempt to focus upon these. There are three basic legal procedures that one firm can use to acquire another firm: (1) merger or consolidation, (2) acquisition of shares and (3) acquisition of assets.

Merger or Consolidation

A **merger** refers to the absorption of one firm by another. The acquiring firm retains its name and its identity, and it acquires all of the assets and liabilities of the acquired firm. After a merger, the acquired firm ceases to exist as a separate business entity.

A **consolidation** is the same as a merger except that an entirely new firm is created. In a consolidation, both the acquiring firm and the acquired firm terminate their previous legal existence and become part of the new firm. In a consolidation, the distinction between the acquiring and the acquired firm is not important. However, the rules for mergers and consolidations are basically the same. Acquisitions by merger and consolidation result in combinations of the assets and liabilities of acquired and acquiring firms.

- **Example**

Suppose firm *A* acquires firm *B* in a merger. Further, suppose firm *B* shareholders are given one share of firm *A* in exchange for two shares of firm *B*. From a legal standpoint, firm *A*'s shareholders are not directly affected by the merger. However, firm *B*'s shares cease to exist. In a consolidation, the shareholders of firm *A* and firm *B* would exchange their shares for the share of a new firm (e.g. firm *C*). Because the differences between mergers and consolidations are not all that important for our purposes, we shall refer to both types of reorganizations as mergers. ●

There are some advantages and some disadvantages to using a merger to acquire a firm:

1. A merger is legally straightforward and does not cost as much as other forms of acquisition. It avoids the necessity of transferring title of each individual asset of the acquired firm to the acquiring firm.
2. A merger must, in most European countries, be approved by a vote of the shareholders of each firm.

Acquisition of Shares

A second way to acquire another firm is to purchase the firm's voting shares in exchange for cash, shares of the acquisition or other securities. This usually begins with an offer from the management of one firm to another. Alternatively it may be accomplished by what is technically a tender offer. A **tender offer** is a public offer to buy shares of a target firm. It is made by one firm directly to the shareholders of another firm. The offer is communicated to the target firm's shareholders by a general mailing. In some countries, a general mailing is very difficult because it requires the names and addresses of the shareholders in the target company, which may not be available—especially where bearer shares are used in common practice. In such cases, the purchaser has to resort to public announcement in newspapers.

Acquisition of Assets

One firm can acquire another firm by buying all of its assets. A formal vote of the shareholders of the selling firm is usually required. This approach to acquisition will avoid the potential problem of having minority shareholders, which can occur in an acquisition of shares. Acquisition of assets involves transferring title to assets. The legal process of transferring assets can be costly.

A Classification Scheme

Financial analysts have typically classified acquisitions into three types:

1. *Horizontal Acquisition*   This is an acquisition of a firm in the same industry as the acquiring firm. The firms compete with each other in their product market.
2. *Vertical Acquisition*   A vertical acquisition involves firms at different steps of the production process. The acquisition by an airline company of a travel agency would be a vertical acquisition.
3. *Conglomerate Acquisition*   The acquiring firm and the acquired firm are not related to each other. The acquisition of a food-products firm by a computer firm would be considered a conglomerate acquisition.

A Note on Takeovers

Takeover is a general and imprecise term referring to the transfer of control of a firm from one group of shareholders to another.[1] A firm that has decided to take over another firm is usually referred to as the **bidder**. The bidder offers to pay cash or securities to obtain the shares or assets of another company. If the offer is accepted, the target firm will give up control over its shares or assets to the bidder in exchange for the consideration (i.e. its shares, its debt or cash).

For example, when a bidding firm acquires a target firm, the right to control the operating activities of the target firm is transferred to a newly elected board of directors of the acquiring firm. This is a takeover by acquisition.

Takeovers can occur by acquisition, proxy contests and going-private transactions. Thus, takeovers encompass a broader set of activities than acquisitions. Figure 28.1 depicts this.

If a takeover is achieved by acquisition, it will be by merger, tender offer for shares or purchase of assets. In mergers and tender offers, the acquiring firm buys the voting shares of the acquired firm.

FIGURE 28.1   Varieties of Takeovers

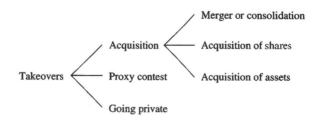

---

[1] *Control* may be defined as having a majority vote on the board of directors.

Takeovers can occur with *proxy contests*. Proxy contests occur when a group of shareholders attempts to gain controlling seats on the board of directors by voting in new directors. A *proxy* authorizes the proxy holder to vote on all matters in a shareholders' meeting. In a proxy contest, proxies from the rest of the shareholders are solicited by an insurgent group of shareholders. This mechanism is very rare in Europe.

In *going-private transactions*, all the equity shares of a public firm are purchased by a small group of investors. The group usually includes members of incumbent management and some outside investors. The shares of the firm are delisted from stock exchanges and can no longer be purchased in the open market.

Concept Questions

- What is a merger? How does a merger differ from other forms of acquisition?
- What is a takeover?

28.2   Accounting for Acquisitions

When one firm acquires another firm, the acquisition will be treated as either a purchase or a pooling of interests on the books of account.

The Purchase Method

The **purchase method** of reporting acquisitions requires that the assets of the acquired firm be reported at their fair market value on the books of the acquiring firm. This allows the acquiring firm to establish a new cost basis for the acquired assets.

In a purchase, an accounting term called *goodwill* is created. **Goodwill** is the excess of the purchase price over the sum of the fair market values of the individual assets acquired.

● Example

Suppose firm *A* acquires firm *B*, creating a new firm, *AB*. Firm *A*'s and firm *B*'s financial positions at the date of the acquisition are shown in Table 28.1. The book

---

TABLE 28.1   **Accounting for Acquisitions: Purchase (in Euro millions)**

Firm A				Firm B			
Cash	Euro 4	Equity	Euro20	Cash	Euro 2	Equity	Euro10
Land	16			Land	0		
Buildings	0			Buildings	8		
Total	Euro20		Euro20	Total	Euro10		Euro10

Firm AB			
Cash	Euro 6	Debt	Euro19
Land	16	Equity	20
Buildings	14		
Goodwill	3		
Total	Euro39		Euro39

When the purchase method is used, the assets of the acquired firm (firm *B*) appears in the combined firm's books at their fair market value.

value of firm *B* on the date of the acquisition is Euro10 million. This is the sum of Euro8 million in buildings and Euro2 million in cash. However, an appraiser states that the sum of the fair market values of the individual buildings is Euro14 million. With Euro2 million in cash, the sum of the market values of the individual assets in firm *B* is Euro16 million. This represents the value to be received if the firm is liquidated by selling off the individual assets separately. However, the whole is often worth more than the sum of the parts in business. Firm *A* pays Euro19 million in cash for firm *B*. This difference of Euro3 million (Euro19 million − Euro16 million) is goodwill. It represents the increase in value by keeping the firm intact as an ongoing business. Firm *A* issued Euro19 million in new debt to finance the acquisition. The last balance sheet in Table 28.1 shows what happens under purchase accounting.

1. The total assets of firm *AB* increase to Euro39 million. The buildings of firm *B* appear in the new balance sheet at their current market value. That is, the market value of the assets of the acquired firm become part of the book value of the new firm. However, the assets of the acquiring firm (firm *A*) remain at their old book value. They are not revalued upwards when the new firm is created.
2. The excess of the purchase price over the sum of the fair market values of the individual assets acquired is Euro3 million. This amount is reported as goodwill. In some countries, the practice is to write off goodwill against capital reserves in the acquirer's books, in others goodwill is amortized over a period of years in the books of account. In most European countries, goodwill amortization expenses are not tax deductible. ●

Pooling of Interests

Under a **pooling of interests**, the assets of the new firm are valued at the same level at which they were carried on the books of the acquired and acquiring firms. Using the previous example, assume that firm *A* issues ordinary shares with a market value of Euro19 million to acquire firm *B*. Table 28.2 illustrates this merger.

The new firm is owned jointly by all the shareholders of the previously separate firms. The total assets and the total equity are unchanged by the acquisition. No goodwill is created. Furthermore, the Euro19 million used to acquire firm *B* does not appear in Table 28.2.

TABLE 28.2   Accounting for Acquisitions: Pooling of Interests (in Euro millions)

Firm A				**Firm B**			
Cash	Euro 4	Equity	Euro20	Cash	Euro 2	Equity	Euro10
Land	16			Land	0		
Buildings	0			Buildings	8		
Total	Euro20		Euro20	Total	Euro10		Euro10

Firm AB			
Cash	Euro 6	Equity	Euro30
Land	16		
Buildings	8		
Total	Euro30		Euro30

In a pooling of interests, the assets appear in the combined firm's books at the same value they had in each separate firm's books prior to the merger.

Purchase or Pooling of Interests: A Comparison

Rules on accounting for acquisitions varies from one European country to another. Pooling of interests is often used when the acquiring firm issues voting stock in exchange for at least 90 per cent of the outstanding voting stock of the acquired firm, purchase accounting is being used under other financing arrangements.

In purchase accounting, goodwill is usually amortized over a period of years in the books of account. Therefore, just like depreciation, the amortization expense reduces reported income. In addition, the assets of the acquired firm are written up in the books in purchase accounting. This creates a higher depreciation expense for the combined firm than would be the case for a pooling. Due to both goodwill and asset write-ups, purchase accounting will usually result in lower reported income than will pooling.

The above paragraph concerns effects in the books of account, not the tax position. Because the amount of tax-deductible expenses (usually) is not affected by the method of acquisition accounting, cash flows are not (usually) affected. Hence, the net present value of the acquisition should be the same whether pooling or purchase accounting is used in most European countries; however, where goodwill amortization is tax deductible, this conclusion would not hold.

Concept Question

• What is the difference between purchase accounting and pooling-of-interests accounting?

28.3   Determining the Synergy from an Acquisition

Suppose firm A is contemplating acquiring firm B. The value of firm A is V_A and the value of firm B is V_B. (It is reasonable to assume that, for public companies, V_A and V_B can be determined by observing the market price of the outstanding securities.) The difference between the value of the combined firm (V_{AB}) and the sum of the values of the firms as separate entities is the synergy from the acquisition:

$$\text{Synergy} = V_{AB} - (V_A + V_B)$$

The acquiring firm must generally pay a premium for the acquired firm. For example, if shares of the target are selling for Euro50, the acquirer might need to pay Euro60 a share, implying a premium of Euro10 or 20 per cent. Firm A will want to determine the synergy before entering into negotiations with firm B on the premium.

The synergy of an acquisition can be determined from the usual discounted cash flow model:

$$\text{Synergy} = \sum_{t=1}^{T} \frac{\Delta \text{CF}_t}{(1 + r)^t}$$

where ΔCF_t is the difference between the cash flows at date t of the combined firm and the sum of the cash flows of the two separate firms. In other words, ΔCF_t is the incremental cash flow at date t from the merger. The term, r, is the risk-adjusted discount rate appropriate for the incremental cash flows. This is generally considered to be the required rate of return on the equity of the target.

From the chapters on capital budgeting, we know that the incremental cash flows can be separated into four parts:

$$\Delta CF_t = \Delta Rev_t - \Delta Costs_t - \Delta Taxes_t - \Delta Capital\ requirements_t$$

where ΔRev_t is the incremental revenue of the acquisition, $\Delta Costs_t$ is the incremental costs of the acquisition, $\Delta Taxes_t$ is the incremental acquisition taxes and $\Delta Capital\ requirements_t$ is the incremental new investment required in working capital and fixed assets.

28.4 Source of Synergy from Acquisitions

It follows from our classification of incremental cash flows that the possible sources of synergy fall into four basic categories: revenue enhancement, cost reduction, lower taxes, and lower cost of capital.

Revenue Enhancement

One important reason for acquisitions is that a combined firm may generate greater revenues than two separate firms. Increased revenues may come from marketing gains, strategic benefits, and market power.

Marketing Gains

It is frequently claimed that mergers and acquisitions can produce greater operating revenues from improved marketing. Improvements can be made in the following:

1. Previously ineffective media programming and advertising efforts
2. A weak existing distribution network
3. An unbalanced product mix

Strategic Option Benefits

Some acquisitions promise *strategic* or real option advantages. This is an opportunity to take advantage of the competitive environment if certain situations materialize. In this regard, a strategic benefit is more like an option than it is a standard investment opportunity. For example, imagine that a sewing machine company acquired a computer company. The firm will be well positioned if technological advances allow computer-driven sewing machines in the future. Michael Porter has used the word *beachhead* in his description of the process of entering a new industry to exploit perceived opportunities.[2] The beachhead is used to spawn new opportunities based on *intangible* relationships. He uses the example of Procter & Gamble's initial acquisition of the Charmin Paper Company as a beachhead that allowed Procter & Gamble to develop a highly interrelated cluster of paper products: disposable nappies, paper towels, feminine hygiene products and bathroom tissue.

Market or Monopoly Power

One firm may acquire another to reduce competition. If so, prices can be increased and monopoly profits obtained. Mergers that reduce competition do not benefit society and may be challenged by government and EU regulatory authorities.

---

[2] M. Porter (1985) *Competitive Advantage*, New York: Free Press.

Cost Reduction

One of the most basic reasons to merge is that a combined firm may operate more efficiently than two separate firms. A firm can obtain greater operating efficiency in several different ways through a merger or an acquisition.

Economies of Scale

If the average cost of production falls while the level of production increases, there is said to be an economy of scale. Figure 28.2 illustrates that economies of scale result while the firm grows to its optimal size. After this point, diseconomies of scale occur. In other words, average cost increases with further firm growth.

Though the precise nature of economy of scale is not known, it is one obvious benefit of horizontal mergers. The phrase *spreading overhead* is frequently used in connection with economies of scale. This refers to the sharing of central facilities, such as corporate headquarters, top management and a large mainframe computer.

FIGURE 28.2   Economies of Scale and the Optimal Size of the Firm

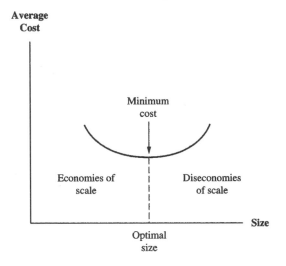

Economies of Vertical Integration

Operating economies can be gained from vertical combinations as well as from horizontal combinations. The main purpose of vertical acquisitions is to make coordination of closely related operating activities easier. This is probably the reason why most forest product firms that cut timber also own sawmills and haulage equipment. Economies from vertical integration probably explain why most airline companies own airplanes; it also may explain why some airline companies have purchased hotels and car-rental companies.

Technology transfers are another reason for vertical integration. An automobile manufacturer might well acquire an advanced electronics firm if the special technology of the electronics firm can improve the quality of the automobile.

Complementary Resources

Some firms acquire others to make better use of existing resources or to provide the missing ingredient for success. Think of a ski-equipment store that could merge with a tennis-equipment store to produce more even sales over both the winter and summer seasons—and make better use of store capacity.

Elimination of Inefficient Management

There are firms whose value could be increased with a change in management. For example, Jensen and Ruback argue that acquisitions can occur because of changing technology or market conditions that require a restructuring of the corporation.[3] Incumbent managers in some cases do not understand changing conditions. They have trouble abandoning strategies and styles they have spent years formulating.

The oil industry is an example of managerial inefficiency cited by Jensen. In the late 1970s, changes in the oil industry included reduced expectations of the future price of oil, increased exploration and development costs, and increased real interest rates. As a result of these changes, substantial reductions in exploration and development were called for. However, many oil company managers were unable to 'downsize' their firms. Acquiring companies sought out oil firms in order to reduce the investment levels of these oil companies. For example, T. Boone Pickens of Mesa Petroleum perceived the changes taking place in the oil industry and attempted to buy several oil companies: Unocal, Phillips and Getty. The results of these attempted acquisitions have been reduced expenditures on exploration and development and huge gains to the shareholders of the affected firms.

Mergers and acquisitions may be viewed as part of the labour market for top management. Jensen and Ruback have used the phrase *market for corporate control*, in which alternative management teams compete for the rights to manage corporate activities.

Tax Gains

Tax gains may be a powerful incentive for some acquisitions. The possible tax gains that can come from an acquisition are the following:

1. The use of tax losses from net operating losses
2. The use of unused debt capacity
3. The use of surplus funds

Net Operating Losses

Sometimes firms have tax losses they cannot take advantage of. These tax losses are referred to as NOL (an acronym for net operating losses). Consider the situation of firm *A* and firm *B*.

Table 28.3 shows the pretax income, taxes, and after-tax income for firms *A* and *B*. Firm *A* will earn Euro200 under state 1, but will lose money under state 2. The firm will pay taxes under state 1, but is not entitled to a tax rebate under state 2. Conversely, firm *B* will pay tax of Euro68 under state 2. Thus, if firms *A* and *B* are separate, the tax authorities will obtain Euro68 in taxes, regardless of which state occurs. However, if *A* and *B* merge, the combined firm will pay Euro34 in taxes under both state 1 and state 2.

It is obvious that if firms *A* and *B* merge, they will pay lower taxes than if they remain separate. Without merger, they do not take advantage of potential tax losses.

The message of the preceding example is that firms need taxable profits to take advantage of potential tax losses. Mergers can sometimes accomplish this.

---

[3] M. C. Jensen and R. S. Ruback (1983) 'The market for corporate control: The scientific evidence', *Journal of Financial Economics*, **11**, April; and M. C. Jensen (1986) 'Agency costs of free cash flow, corporate finance, and takeovers', *American Economic Review*, May.

TABLE 28.3   Tax Effect of Merger of Firms *A* and *B*

	Before merger				After merger	
	Firm *A*		**Firm *B***		**Firm *AB***	
	If state 1	*If state* 2	*If state* 1	*If state* 2	*If state* 1	*If state* 2
Taxable income	Euro200	−Euro100	−Euro100	Euro200	Euro100	Euro100
Taxes	68	0	0	68	34	34
Net income	Euro132	−Euro100	−Euro100	Euro132	Euro 66	Euro 66

Neither firm will be able to deduct its losses prior to the merger. The merger allows the losses from *A* to offset the taxable profits from *B*—and vice versa.

Unused Debt Capacity

It can be argued that the optimal debt–equity ratio is the one where the marginal tax benefit from additional debt is equal to the marginal increase in the financial distress costs from additional debt. All other things being equal, because some diversification occurs when firms merge, the cost of financial distress is likely to be less for the combined firm than is the sum of these present values for the two separate firms. Thus, the acquiring firm might be able to increase its debt–equity ratio after a merger, creating additional tax benefits—and additional value.[4]

Surplus Funds

Consider a firm that has *free cash flow*. That is, it has cash flow available after payment of all taxes and after all positive net-present-value projects have been provided for. In this situation, aside from purchasing fixed-income securities, the firm has several ways to spend the free cash flow, including

1. Pay dividends
2. Buy back its own shares
3. Acquire shares in another firm

An extra dividend will increase the tax paid by some investors. Investors may pay lower taxes in a share repurchase. However, this may not be so where the marginal personal tax rate of a shareholder equals his or her capital gains tax rate band.

The firm can buy the shares of another firm. Thus, the firm's shareholders avoid taxes from dividends that would have been paid.

The Cost of Capital

The cost of capital can often be reduced when two firms merge because the costs of issuing securities are subject to economies of scale. The costs of issuing both debt and equity are much lower for larger issues than for smaller issues.

---

[4] Michael C. Jensen ('Agency costs of free cash flow, corporate finance, and takeovers', *American Economic Review*, May 1986) offers another reason why debt is frequently used in mergers and acquisitions. He argues that using more debt provides incentives for the new management to create efficiencies so that debt can be repaid.

28.5 Calculating the Value of the Firm after an Acquisition

Now that we have listed the possible sources of synergy from a merger, let us see how one would value these sources. Consider two firms. Smooth plc, manufactures and markets soaps and cosmetics. The firm has a reputation for its ability to attract, develop and keep talented people. The firm has successfully introduced several major products in the past two years. It would like to enter the over-the-counter pharmacy market to round out its product line. Nosneeze plc, is a well-known maker of cold remedies. Alan Squires, the great-grandson of the founder of Nosneeze plc, became chairman of the firm last year. Unfortunately, Alan knows nothing about cold remedies, and as a potential consequence Nosneeze plc has had lacklustre financial performance. For the most recent year, pretax profits and cash flow fell by 15 per cent. The firm's share price is at an all-time low.

The financial management of Smooth finds Nosneeze an attractive acquisition candidate. It believes that the cash flows from the combined firms would be far greater than what each firm would have alone. The cash flows and present values from the acquisition are shown in Table 28.4. The increased cash flows (CF_t) come from three benefits:

1. *Tax Gains* If Smooth acquires Nosneeze, Smooth will be able to use some tax-loss carryforwards to reduce its tax liability. The additional cash flows from tax gains might be discounted at the cost of debt capital because they can be determined and unlocked with relatively little uncertainty. It is contended that a margin above the risk-free rate must be used because such tax shelter could be disallowed by the tax authorities. In some countries, this disallow might look more certain and in such circumstances tax losses might be discounted at a higher rate—for example, the weighted average cost of capital. The financial management of Smooth estimates that the acquisition will reduce taxes by GBP1 million per year in perpetuity. The relevant discount rate is 5 per cent, and the present value of the tax reduction is GBP20 million.

2. *Operating Efficiencies* The financial management of Smooth has determined that Smooth can take advantage of some of the unused production capacity of Nosneeze. At times, Smooth has been operating at full capacity with a large backlog of orders. Nosneeze's manufacturing facilities, with a little reconfiguration, can be used to produce Smooth's soaps. Thus, more soaps and cold remedies can be produced without adding to the combined firm's capacity and cost. These operating efficiencies will increase after-tax cash flows by GBP1.5 million per year. Using Nosneeze's discount rate and assuming perpetual gains, the PV of the unused capacity is determined to be GBP10 million.

TABLE 28.4 Acquisition of Nosneeze plc by Smooth plc

	Net cash flow per year (perpetual)	Discount rate	Value
Smooth plc	GBP10.0 million	0.10	GBP100 million
Nosneeze plc	4.5 million	0.15	30 million*
Benefits from acquisition	5.5 million	0.122	45 million
Strategic option benefits	3.0 million	0.20	15 million
Tax shelters	1.0 million	0.05	20 million
Operating efficiences	1.5 million	0.15	10 million
Smooth–Nosneeze	20.0 million	0.114	175 million

*The market value of Nosneeze's outstanding ordinary shares is GBP30 million; 1 million shares are outstanding.

3. *Strategic Option Benefits* The financial management of Smooth has determined that the acquisition of Nosneeze will give Smooth strategic option benefits. The management of Smooth believes that the addition of the Nosneeze Bac-Rub ointment for sore backs to its existing product mix will give it a better chance to launch successful new skincare cosmetics if these markets develop in the future. Management of Smooth estimates that there is a 50 per cent probability that GBP6 million in after-tax cash flow can be generated with the new skincare products. These opportunities are contingent on factors that cannot be easily quantified. Because of the lack of precision here, the managers decided to use a high discount rate. Smooth chooses a 20 per cent rate, and it estimates that the present value of the strategic factors is GBP15 million (0.50 × GBP6 million/0.20).

Avoiding Mistakes

The Smooth–Nosneeze illustration is very straightforward. It is deceptive because the incremental cash flows have already been determined. In practice, an analyst must estimate these cash flows and determine the proper discount rate. Valuing the benefits of a potential acquisition is harder than valuing benefits for standard capital-budgeting projects. Many mistakes can be made. Some of the general rules follows:

1. *Do Not Ignore Market Values* In many cases it is very difficult to estimate values using discounted cash flows. Because of this, an expert at valuation should know the market prices of comparable opportunities. In an efficient market, prices should reflect value. Because the market value of Nosneeze is GBP30 million, we use this to estimate Smooth's existing value.
2. *Estimate Only Incremental Cash Flows* Only incremental cash flows from an acquisition will add value to the acquiring firm. Thus, it is important to estimate the cash flows that are incremental to the acquisition.
3. *Use the Correct Discount Rate* The discount rate should be the required rate of return for the incremental cash flows associated with the acquisition.[5] It should reflect the risk associated with the *use* of funds, not their *source*. It would be a mistake for Smooth to use its own cost of capital to value the cash flows from Nosneeze. If this is not intuitively obvious, consider an airline acquiring an electricity utility. The airline is reckoned to be risky with a beta of 1.5 while the utility has a beta of 0.5. Clearly, the utility's relatively low risk cash flow should be evaluated at a relating low discount rate—presumably one based on a beta of 0.5 rather than 1.5.
4. *If Smooth and Nosneeze Combine, There Will Be Transaction Costs* These will include fees to investment bankers, legal fees and other requirements.

28.6   A Cost to Shareholders from Reduction in Risk

The previous section discussed gains to the firm from a merger. In a firm with debt, these gains are likely to be shared by both bondholders and shareholders. We now consider a benefit to the bondholders from a merger, which occurs at the expense of the shareholders.

---

[5] Recall that the required rate of return is sometimes referred to as the *cost of capital*, or the *opportunity cost of capital*.

When two firms merge, the variability of their combined values is usually less than would be true if the firms remained separate entities. A reduction of the variability of firm values can occur if the values of the two firms are less than perfectly correlated. The reduction in variability can reduce the cost of borrowing and make the creditors better off than before. This will occur if the probability of financial distress is reduced by the merger.

Unfortunately, the shareholders are likely to be worse off. The gains to creditors are at the expense of the shareholders if the total value of the firm does not change. The relationship among the value of the merged firm, debt capacity and risk is very complicated. We now consider two examples.

The Base Case

Consider a base case where two all-equity firms merge. Table 28.5 gives the net present values of firm *A* and firm *B* in three possible states of the economy: prosperity, average and depression. The market value of firm *A* is Euro60, and the market value of firm *B* is Euro40. The market value of each firm is the weighted average of the values in each of the three states. For example, the value of firm *A* is

$$\text{Euro60} = \text{Euro80} \times 0.5 + \text{Euro50} \times 0.3 + \text{Euro25} \times 0.2$$

The values in each of the three states for firm *A* are Euro80, Euro50 and Euro25, respectively. The probabilities of each of the three states occurring are 0.5, 0.3 and 0.2, respectively.

TABLE 28.5   **Share-Swap Mergers**

	NPV			Market Value
	State 1	*State 2*	*State 3*	
Base case: two all-equity firms before merger				
Firm *A*	Euro 80	Euro50	Euro25	Euro 60
Firm *B*	Euro 50	Euro40	Euro15	Euro 40
Probability	0.5	0.3	0.2	
After merger*				
Firm *AB*	Euro130	Euro90	Euro40	Euro100
Firm *A*, equity and risky debt before merger				
Firm *B*, all-equity before merger				
Firm *A*	Euro 80	Euro50	Euro25	Euro 60
Debt	Euro 40	Euro40	Euro25	Euro 37
Equity	Euro 40	Euro10	Euro 0	Euro 23
Firm *B*	Euro 50	Euro40	Euro15	Euro 40
After merger†				
Firm *AB*	Euro130	Euro90	Euro40	Euro100
Debt	Euro 40	Euro40	Euro40	Euro 40
Equity	Euro 90	Euro50	Euro 0	Euro 60

Value of debt rises after merger. Value of original stock in acquiring firm falls correspondingly.

* Stockholders in *B* receive shares value of Euro40. Therefore, shareholders of *A* have a value of Euro100 − Euro40 = Euro60 and are *indifferent to merger.*

† Because firm *B*'s shareholders receive stock in firm *A* worth Euro40, original shareholders in firm *A* have shares worth Euro20 (Euro60 − Euro40). Gains and losses from merger are

Euro20 − Euro23 = −Euro3:   Therefore, shareholders of *A* lose Euro3.

Euro40 − Euro37 = Euro3:   Therefore, bondholders of *A* gain Euro3.

When firm *A* merges with firm *B*, the combined firm *AB* will have a market value of Euro100. There is no synergy from this merger, and consequently the value of firm *AB* is the sum of the values of firm *A* and firm *B*. Shareholders of *B* receive shares with a value of Euro40, and therefore shareholders of *A* have a value of Euro100 − Euro40 = Euro60. Thus, shareholders of *A* and *B* are indifferent to the proposed merger.

One Firm Has Debt

Alternatively, imagine firm *A* has some debt and some equity outstanding before the merger.[6] Firm *B* is an all-equity firm. Firm *A* will default on its debt in state 3 because the net present value of firm *A* in this state is Euro25, and the value of the debt claim is Euro40. As a consequence, the full value of the debt claim cannot be paid by firm *A*. The creditors take this into account, and the value of the debt is Euro37 (Euro40 × 0.5 + Euro40 × 0.3 + Euro25 × 0.2).

Though default occurs without a merger, no default occurs with a merger. To see this, notice that, when the two firms are separate, firm *B* does not guarantee firm *A*'s debt. That is, if firm *A* defaults on its debt, firm *B* does not help the bondholders of firm *A*. However, after the merger the bondholders can draw on the cash flows from both *A* and *B*. When one of the divisions of the combined firm fails, creditors can be paid from the profits of the other division. This mutual guarantee, which is called the *coinsurance effect*, makes the debt less risky and more valuable than before.

The bonds are worth Euro40 after the merger. Thus, the bondholders of *AB* gain Euro3 (Euro40 − Euro37) from the merger.

The shareholders of firm *A* lose Euro3 (Euro20 − Euro23) from the merger. That is, firm *A*'s shares are worth Euro23 prior to the merger. The shares are worth Euro60 after the merger. However, shareholders in firm *B* receive Euro40 of shares in firm *A*. Hence, those individuals who were shareholders in firm *A* prior to the merger have stock worth only Euro20 (Euro60 − Euro40) after the merger.

There is no net benefit to the firm as a whole. The bondholders gain the coinsurance effect, and the stockholders lose the coinsurance effect. Some general conclusions emerge from the preceding analysis.

1. Bondholders in the aggregate will usually be helped by mergers and acquisitions. The size of the gain to bondholders depends on the reduction of bankruptcy states after the combination. That is, the less risky the combined firm is, the greater are the gains to bondholders.
2. Shareholders of the acquiring firm will be hurt by the amount that bondholders gain.
3. The conclusions apply to mergers and acquisitions where no synergy is present. In the case of synergistic combinations, much depends on the size of the synergy.

How Can Shareholders Reduce Their Losses from the Coinsurance Effect?

The coinsurance effect allows some mergers to increase bondholder values by reducing shareholder values. However, there are at least two ways that shareholders can reduce or eliminate the coinsurance effect. First, the shareholders in firm *A* could retire its debt *before* the merger announcement date and reissue an equal amount of debt after the merger. Because debt is retired at the low, premerger price, this type of refinancing transaction can neutralize the coinsurance effect to the bondholders.

---

[6] This example was provided by David Babbel.

Also, note that the debt capacity of the combined firm is likely to increase, because the acquisition reduces the probability of financial distress. Thus, the shareholders' second alternative is simply to issue more debt after the merger. An increase in debt following the merger will have two effects, even without the prior action of debt retirement. The interest deduction from new corporate debt raises firm value. In addition, an increase in debt after merger raises the probability of financial distress, thereby reducing or eliminating the bondholders' gain from the coinsurance effect.

28.7   Two 'Bad' Reasons for Mergers

Earnings Growth

An acquisition can create the appearance of earnings growth, which may fool investors into thinking that the firm is worth more than it really is. Suppose Global Resources plc acquires Regional Enterprises plc. The financial positions of Global and Regional before the acquisition are shown in Table 28.6. Regional has had very poor earnings growth and sells at a price–earnings ratio much lower than that of Global. The merger creates no additional value. If the market is smart, it will realize that the combined firm is worth the sum of the values of the separate firms. In this case, the market value of the combined firm will be GBP3,500, which is equal to the sum of the values of the separate firms before the merger.

At these values, Global will acquire Regional by exchanging 40 of its shares for 100 Regional shares,[7] so that Global will have 140 shares outstanding after the merger. Because the share price of Global after the merger is the same as before the merger, the price–earnings ratio must fall. This is true because the market is smart and recognizes that the total market has not been altered by the merger. This scenario is represented by the third column of Table 28.6.

Let us now consider the possibility that the market is fooled. One can see from Table 28.6 that the acquisition enables Global to increase its earnings per share from GBP1 to GBP1.43. If the market is fooled, it might mistake the 43 per cent increase in earnings per share for true growth. In this case, the price–earnings ratio of Global may not fall after the merger. Suppose the price-earnings ratio of Global remains

TABLE 28.6   Financial Positions of Global Resources plc and Regional Enterprises plc

	Global Resources before merger	*Regional Enterprises before merger*	Global Resources after merger	
			The market is 'smart'	*The market is 'fooled'*
Earnings per share	GBP 1.00	GBP 1.00	GBP 1.43	GBP 1.43
Price per share	GBP25.00	GBP10.00	GBP25.00	GBP35.71
Price–earnings ratio	25	10	17.5	25
Number of shares	100	100	140	140
Total earnings	GBP 100	GBP 100	GBP 200	GBP 200
Total value	GBP2,500	GBP1,000	GBP3,500	GBP5,000

Exchange ratio: 1 share in Global for 2.5 shares in Regional.

[7] This ratio implies a fair exchange because a share of Regional is selling for 40 per cent (GBP10/GBP25) of the price of a share of Global.

equal to 25. The total value of the combined firm will increase to GBP5,000 (25 × GBP200), and the share price per share of Global will increase to GBP35.71 (GBP5,000/140). This is reflected in the last column of Table 28.6.

This is earnings-growth magic. Like all good magic, it is an illusion and the shareholders of Global and Regional will receive something for nothing. This may work for a while, but in the long run the efficient market will work its wonders and the value will decline.

Diversification

Diversification is often mentioned as a benefit of one firm acquiring another. Earlier in this chapter, we noted that it is not uncommon to see firms with surplus cash articulating a need for diversification.

However, we argue that diversification, by itself, cannot produce increases in value. To see this, recall that a business's variability of return can be separated into two parts: (1) what is specific to the business and called *unsystematic* and (2) what is *systematic* because it is common to all businesses.

Systematic variability cannot be eliminated by diversification, so mergers will not eliminate this risk at all. By contrast, unsystematic risk can be diversified away through mergers. However, the investor does not need widely diversified companies to eliminate unsystematic risk. Shareholders can diversify more easily than companies simply purchasing ordinary shares in different companies. Thus, diversification through conglomerate merger may not benefit shareholders.[8]

Diversification can produce gains to the acquiring firm only if two things are true:

1. Diversification decreases the unsystematic variability at lower costs than by investors via adjustments to personal portfolios. This seems very unlikely.
2. Diversification reduces risk and thereby increases debt capacity. This possibility was mentioned earlier in the chapter.

Concept Question

- Why can a merger create the appearance of earnings growth?

28.8   The NPV of a Merger

Since the acquisition of one company by another basically involves parting with value now by the bidder (the consideration) to acquire a stream of cash flows in the future, then it follows in financial theory that firms should use NPV analysis when making acquisitions. The analysis is relatively straightforward when the consideration is cash. The analysis becomes more complex when the consideration is in shares.

Cash

Suppose firm A and firm B have values as separate entities of GBP500 and GBP100, respectively. They are both all-equity firms. If firm A acquires firm B, the merged firm AB will have a combined value of GBP700 due to synergies of GBP100. The board of firm B has indicated that it will sell firm B if it is offered GBP150 in cash.

---

[8] Recent evidence suggests that diversification can actually hurt shareholders. R. Mork, A. Shleifer and R. W. Vishney ('Do managerial objectives drive bad acquisitions', *Journal of Finance*, **45**, 1990, pp. 31–48) show that shareholders did poorly in firms that diversified by acquisition in the 1980s.

Should firm A acquire firm B? Assuming that firm A finances the acquisition out of its own retained earnings, its value after the acquisition is[9]

$$
\begin{aligned}
\begin{array}{l}\text{Value of} \\ \text{firm } A \text{ after} \\ \text{the acquisition}\end{array}
&= \begin{array}{l}\text{Value of} \\ \text{combined firm}\end{array} - \begin{array}{l}\text{Cash} \\ \text{paid}\end{array} \\
&= \text{GBP700} \quad\; - \quad \text{GBP150} \\
&= \text{GBP550}
\end{aligned}
$$

Because firm A was worth GBP500 prior to the acquisition, the NPV to firm A's shareholders is

$$\text{GBP50} = \text{GBP550} - \text{GBP500} \tag{28.1}$$

Assuming that there are 25 shares in firm A, each share of the firm is worth GBP20 (GBP500/25) prior to the merger and GBP22 (GBP550/25) after the merger. These calculations are displayed in the first and third columns of Table 28.7. Looking at the rise in share price, we conclude that firm A should make the acquisition.

TABLE 28.7   Cost of Acquisition: Cash versus Ordinary Shares

	Before acquisition		After acquisition: Firm A		
	(1)	*(2)*	*(3)*	*(4)* Ordinary shares:† Exchange ratio *(0.75:1)*	*(5)* Ordinary shares:† Exchange ratio *(0.6819:1)*
	Firm A	*Firm B*	*Cash**		
Market value (V_A, V_B)	GBP500	GBP100	GBP550	GBP 700	GBP700
Number of shares	25	10	25	32.5	31.819
Price per share	GBP 20	GBP 10	GBP22	GBP21.54	GBP 22

* Value of firm A after acquisition: cash
$\quad V_A = V_{AB} - \text{Cash}$
$\quad \text{GBP550} = \text{GBP700} - \text{GBP150}$
† Value of firm A after acquisition: ordinary shares
$\quad V_A = V_{AB}$
$\quad \text{GBP700} = \text{GBP700}$

We spoke earlier of both the synergy and the premium of a merger. We can also value the NPV of a merger to the acquirer as

$$\text{NPV of a merger to acquirer} = \text{Synergy} - \text{Premium}$$

Because the value of the combined firm is GBP700 and the premerger values of A and B were GBP500 and GBP100, respectively, the synergy is GBP100 [GBP700 − (GBP500 + GBP100)]. The premium is GBP50 (GBP150 − GBP100). Thus, the NPV of the merger to the acquirer is

$$\text{NPV of a merger to firm } A = \text{GBP100} - \text{GBP50} = \text{GBP50}$$

---

[9] The analysis will be essentially the same if new stock is issued. However, the analysis will differ if new debt is issued to fund.

One caveat is in order. In this book, we have consistently argued that the market value of a firm is the best estimate of its true value. However, we must adjust our analysis when discussing mergers. If the true price of firm *A without the merger* is GBP500, the market value of firm *A* may actually be above GBP500 when merger negotiations take place. This occurs because the market price reflects the possibility that the merger will occur. For example, if the probability is 60 per cent that the merger will take place, the market price of firm *A* will be

Market value of firm *A* with merger	×	Probability of merger	+	Market value of firm *A* without merger	×	Probability of no merger
GBP530 = GBP550	×	0.60	+	GBP500	×	0.40

The managers would underestimate the NPV from merger in equation (28.1) if the market price of firm *A* is used. Thus, managers are faced with the difficult task of valuing their own firm without the acquisition.

Ordinary Shares

Of course, firm *A* could purchase firm *B* with ordinary shares instead of cash. Unfortunately, the analysis is not as straightforward here. In order to handle this scenario, we need to know how many shares are outstanding in firm *B*. We assume that there are 10 shares outstanding, as indicated in column 2 of Table 28.7.

Suppose firm *A* exchanges 7.5 of its shares for the entire 10 shares of firm *B*. We call this an exchange ratio of 0.75:1. The value of each share of firm *A* before the acquisition is GBP20. Because $7.5 \times GBP20 = GBP150$, this exchange *appears* to be the equivalent of purchasing firm *B* in cash for GBP150.

This is incorrect: the true cost is greater than GBP150. To see this, note that firm *A* has 32.5 (25 + 7.5) shares outstanding after the merger. Firm *B* shareholders own 23 per cent (7.5/32.5) of the combined firm. Their holdings are valued at GBP161 (23% × GBP700). Because these shareholders receive shares in firm *A* worth GBP161, the cost of the merger to firm *A*'s shareholders must be GBP161, not GBP150.

This result is shown in column 4 of Table 28.7. The value of each share of firm *A* after a share-for-share transaction is only GBP21.54 (GBP700/32.5). We found out earlier that the value of each share is GBP22 after a cash-for-share transaction. The difference is that the cost of the share-for-share transaction to firm *A* is higher.

This non-intuitive result occurs because the exchange ratio of 7.5 shares of firm *A* for 10 shares of firm *B* was based on the *premerger* prices of the two firms. However, since the share of firm *A* rises after the merger, firm *B* shareholders receive more than GBP150 in firm *A* shares. They participate in the NPV of the merger to the acquirer given by (synergy − premium).

What should the exchange ratio be so that firm *B* shareholders receive only GBP150 of firm *A*'s shares? We begin by defining α, the proportion of the shares in the combined firm that firm *B*'s shareholders own. Because the combined firm's value is GBP700, the value of firm *B* shareholders after the merger is

Value of Firm *B* Shareholders after Merger:

$$\alpha \times GBP700$$

Setting $\alpha \times GBP700 = GBP150$, we find that $\alpha = 21.43\%$. In other words, firm *B*'s shareholders will receive shares worth GBP150 if they receive 21.43 per cent of the firm after merger. Now we determine the number of shares issued to firm B's shareholders. The proportion, α, that firm B's shareholders have in the combined firm can be expressed as

$$\alpha = \frac{\text{New shares issued}}{\text{Old shares} + \text{New shares issued}} = \frac{\text{New shares issued}}{25 + \text{New shares issued}}$$

Plugging our value of α into the equation yields

$$0.2143 = \frac{\text{New shares issued}}{25 + \text{New shares issued}}$$

Solving for the unknown, we have

$$\text{New shares} = 6.819 \text{ shares}$$

Total shares outstanding after the merger is 31.819 (25 + 6.819). Because 6.819 shares of firm A are exchanged for 10 shares of firm B, the exchange ratio is 0.6819:1.

Results at the exchange ratio of 0.6819:1 are displayed in column 5 of Table 28.7. Each ordinary share is worth GBP22, exactly what it is worth in the share-for-cash transaction. Thus, given that the board of firm B will sell its firm for GBP150, this is the fair exchange ratio, not the ratio of 0.75:1 mentioned earlier.

Cash versus Ordinary Shares

Whether to finance an acquisition by cash or by shares is an important decision. The choice depends on several factors, as follows:

1. *Overvaluation*   If in the opinion of management the acquiring firm's shares are overvalued, using shares can be less costly than using cash.
2. *Undervaluation*   If in the opinion of management the acquiring firms shares are undervalued, using shares can prove more costly than using cash.
3. *Taxes*   Acquisition by cash usually results in a taxable transaction. Acquisition by exchanging shares is tax free in most European countries.
4. *Sharing Gains*   If cash is used to finance an acquisition, the selling firm's shareholders receive a fixed price. In the event of a hugely successful merger, they will not participate in any additional gains. Of course, if the acquisition is not a success, the losses will not be shared and shareholders of the acquiring firm will be worse off than if shares were used.

Note that under the first two numbers immediately above we refer to share overvaluation and undervaluation for the bidder company. Even in an efficient market, this is possible. Remember that US and British markets among others, where significant research has been undertaken, have been found to be semi-strong efficient. Of course, managers within a company have insider information and can therefore calculate a strong form efficient value of the firm based upon future cash generative capabilities. Such an analysis of fundamental value might well produce a situation where this value differed from the market value hence the overvaluation or undervaluation. This difference would be based upon strong-form valuation versus semistrong valuation.

Concept Question

• In an efficient market with no tax effects, should an acquiring firm use cash or stock?

28.9   Defensive Tactics

Target-firm managers frequently resist takeover attempts. Resistance usually starts with press releases and mailings to shareholders that present management's viewpoint. It may eventually lead to legal action and solicitation of competing bids. Managerial action to defeat a takeover attempt may make target shareholders better off if it elicits a higher offer premium from the bidding firm or another firm. Of course, management resistance may simply reflect pursuit of self-interest at the expense of shareholders. That is, the target managers may resist a takeover in order to preserve their jobs. In this section, we describe various defensive tactics that have been used by target-firm managements to resist unfriendly takeover attempts.

Profit Forecast

The management may pursue various accounting alternatives or release profit provisions for warranties or on long-term contract such that in the near future profit will be enhanced. The idea is that the release of such new information might be used as evidence for the inadequacy of the bidder's approach. Of course, the tactical timing of this release of information can be critical. Timed after the bidder has made his initial sighting offer, it may have less impact than if timed after the bidder's 'final offer'. There are various accounting ruses underpinning this defence.

Revalue Assets

The demonstration that accounting values of assets per share fall far short of market value of assets per share is an often-used defence. Again, the ploy is to show the inadequacy of an existing takeover bid.

Profit, Dividend and Share Price Record

Pointing to shortcomings in profit, dividend and share price record against peer companies of the bidder is a tactic designed to indicate that the bidder's management track record leaves something to be desired. Of course, this generally produces an aggressive tactic from the bidder in which the target company is shown to be far less competent than the bidder, and the rhetorical question is left dangling in front of the shareholder: we perform better than them, so who do you prefer?

This defence essentially involves finding the bidder's strategic, operational or financial Achilles heel and attacking it for all that one's worth.

Dividend Increase

Defending companies often increase dividend as a defensive ploy. According to the financial theory to which we have already been exposed, such a tactic without any underlying profit increment, merely results in the ordinary share finance falling by the amount of the dividend following its ex-dividend date. On its own it is really a rather weak defence. Because of this it invariably features as part of a package of other defensive moves.

Monopolies Reference

Lobbying at national or EU level to the effect that the proposed bid will cre..
monopoly within the legislation rules can buy time or even stop a potential bidder.

White Knight

Another ploy that is often used is to seek out a friendly bidder with whom the
management of the target company would rather merge than with the company
mounting the unfriendly attack. Closely related to this defence, although not legal in
all countries, is that of placing shares in friendly hands.

Golden Parachutes

Some target firms provide compensation contracts for high severance payments to top-
level management if a takeover occurs. This can be viewed as a payment to
management to make it less concerned for its own welfare and more interested in
shareholders when considering a takeover bid. Alternatively, the payment can be seen
as an attempt to enrich management at the shareholders' expense.

Crown Jewels

Firms often sell major assets—crown jewels—when faced with a takeover threat. This
is sometimes referred to as the *scorched earth strategy*.

Poison Pill

Poison pill is a term taken from the world of espionage. Agents are supposed to
bite a pill of cyanide rather than permit capture. Presumably this prevents enemy
interrogators from learning important secrets. In finance, poison pills are used to make
a stock repellent to others. A poison pill is generally a right to buy shares in the
merged firm at a bargain price. The right is granted to the target firm's shareholders,
contingent on another firm acquiring control. The right dilutes the shares so much that
the bidding firm loses money on its shares. Thus, wealth is transferred from the bidder
to the target. This tactic is not legal in many countries.

Repurchase Standstill Agreements

Managers may arrange a *targeted share repurchase* to forestall a takeover attempt. In a
targeted repurchase, a firm buys back its own shares from a potential bidder, usually at
a substantial premium. These premiums can be thought of as payments to potential
bidders to delay or stop unfriendly takeover attempts. Such payments are labelled as
greenmail and are not legal in all countries.

Going Private and Leveraged Buyouts

Going private refers to what happens when the publicly owned stock in a firm is
purchased by a private group, usually composed of existing management. As a
consequence, the firm's stock is taken off the market (if it is an exchange-traded stock,
it is delisted) and is no longer traded. Thus, in going-private transactions, shareholders
of publicly held firms are forced to accept cash for their shares.

637

Going-private transactions are frequently *leveraged buyouts* (LBOs). In a leveraged buyout, the cash-offer price is financed with large amounts of debt. LBOs have recently become quite popular because the arrangement calls for little equity capital. This equity capital is generally supplied by a small group of investors, some of whom are likely to be managers of the firm being purchased.

The selling shareholders are invariably paid a premium above market price in an LBO, just as they are in a merger. As with a merger, the acquirer profits only if the synergy created is greater than the premium. Synergy is quite plausible in a merger of two firms, and we delineated a number of types of synergy earlier in the chapter. However, it is much more difficult to explain synergy in an LBO, because only one firm is involved.

There are generally two reasons given for the ability of an LBO to create value. First, the extra debt provides a tax deduction, which, as earlier chapters suggested, leads to an increase in firm value. Most LBOs are on firms with stable earnings and with low to moderate debt. The LBO may simply increase the firm's debt to its optimum level.

Second, the LBO usually turns the previous managers into owners, thereby increasing their incentive to work hard. The increase in debt is a further incentive because the managers must earn more than the debt service to obtain any profit for themselves.

Concept Question

• What can a firm do to make a takeover less likely?

28.10 Some Evidence on Acquisitions

One of the most controversial issues surrounding our subject is whether mergers and acquisitions benefit shareholders.

Do Acquisitions Benefit Shareholders?

Much research—especially in the USA—has attempted to estimate the effect of mergers and takeovers on share prices of the bidding and target firms. These studies are called *event studies* because they estimate abnormal stock-price changes on and around the offer-announcement date—the event. Abnormal returns are usually defined as the difference between actual stock returns and a market index, to take account of the influence of marketwide effects on the returns of individual securities.

An overview of the US evidence is reported in Jensen and Ruback. Tables 28.8 and 28.9 summarize the results of numerous studies that look at the effects of mergers and tender offers on stock prices. Table 28.8 shows that the shareholders of target companies in successful takeovers achieve large abnormal returns. When the takeover is done by merger the gains are 20 per cent, and when the takeover is done by tender offer the gains are 30 percent.

The shareholders of bidding firms do not fare nearly as well. According to the studies summarized in Table 28.8, bidders experience abnormal returns of 4 per cent in tender offers, and in mergers the percentage is zero. These numbers are sufficiently small to leave doubt about the effect on bidders. Table 28.9 shows that the shareholders of firms involved in unsuccessful takeover attempts experience small negative returns in both mergers and tender offers. What conclusions can be drawn from Tables 28.8 and 28.9?

TABLE 28.8   **Abnormal Stock-Price Changes Associated with Successful Corporate Takeover Bids**

Takeover technique	Target	Bidders
Tender offer	30%	4%
Merger	20%	0
Proxy contest	8%	n.a.

n.a. = Not applicable.
Modified from Michael C. Jensen and Richard S. Ruback (1983) 'The market for corporate control: The scientific evidence', *Journal of Financial Econimics*, **11**, April, pp. 7, 8. © Elsevier Science Publishers B. V. (North-Holland).

TABLE 28.9   **Abnormal Stock-Price Changes Associated with Unsuccessful Corporate Takeover Bids**

Takeover technique	Target	Bidders
Tender offer	−3%	−1%
Merger	−3%	−5%
Proxy contest	8%	n.a.

n.a. = Not applicable.
Modified from Michael C. Jensen and Richard S. Ruback (1983) 'The market for corporate control: The scientific evidence', *Journal of Financial Economics*, **11**, April, pp. 7, 8. © Elsevier Science Publishers B. V. (North-Holland).

1. The results of all event studies suggest that the shareholders of target firms achieve substantial gains as a result of successful takeovers. The gains appear to be larger in tender offers than in mergers. This may reflect the fact that takeovers sometimes start with a friendly merger proposal from the bidder to the management of the target firm. If management rejects the offer, the bidding firm may take the offer directly to the shareholders with an unfriendly tender offer. The target management may actively oppose the offer with defensive tactics. This often has the result of raising the tender offer from the bidding firm, and thus, on the average, friendly mergers are arranged at a lower premium than unfriendly tender offers.

2. The shareholders of bidding firms earn comparatively little from takeovers. They earn an average of only 4 per cent from tender offers and do not appear to earn anything from mergers. In fact, in a study by Asquith, the shareholders of acquiring firms in successful mergers experienced significantly abnormal losses after the announcement of the merger.[10] These findings are a puzzle.

    a. One possible explanation is that anticipated merger gains were not completely achieved, and thus shareholders experienced losses. Managers of bidding firms may tend to overestimate the gains from acquisition.

---

[10] P. Asquith (1983) 'Merger bids, uncertainty and stockholder returns', *Journal of Financial Economics*, **11**, April.

b. The bidding firms are usually much larger than the target firms. Thus, the money gains to the bidder may be approximately the same as the money gains to the shareholders of the target firm at the same time that the percentage returns are much lower for the bidding firms.

c. Management may not be acting in the interests of shareholders when it attempts to acquire other firms. Perhaps it is attempting to increase the size of its firm, even if this reduces its value.

d. Several studies indicate that the returns of bidding firms cannot be measured very easily. Many of the gains to the shareholders of bidding firms come when acquisition programmes commence. The incremental effect of each acquisition on share price may be very small, because the share price at commencement reflects the anticipated gains from future acquisitions.

3. The return to the shareholders of targets of unsuccessful merger, measured from the offer date to the cancellation date, is negative. Thus, all the initial gains are lost over the time period during which the merger failure becomes known. The overall average return to shareholders of unsuccessful tender offers is about the same as for unsuccessful merger attempts. However, the story is more complicated. Bradley, Desai and Kim report that how well shareholders of target firms do in unsuccessful tender offers depends on whether or not future takeover offers are forthcoming. They find that target-firm shareholders realize additional positive gains when a new offer is made but lose everything previously gained if no other offer occurs.[11]

Concept Question

• What does the evidence say about the benefits of mergers and acquisitions?

28.11   Summary and Conclusions

1. One firm can acquire another in several different ways. The three usual forms of acquisition are merger and consolidation, acquisition of shares and acquisition of assets.

2. Mergers and acquisitions require an understanding of tax and accounting rules. Tax rules vary from country to country and are too complicated to evaluate here.

   Accounting for mergers and acquisitions involves a choice of the purchase method or the pooling-of-interests method. The choice between these two methods does not, in most countries, affect after-tax cash flows of the combined firm. However, most financial managers prefer the pooling-of-interests method, because net income of the combined firm under this method is usually higher than it is under the purchase method.

3. The synergy from an acquisition is defined as the value of the combined firm (V_{AB}) less the value of the two firms as separate entities (V_A and V_B), or

$$\text{Synergy} = V_{AB} - (V_A + V_B)$$

   The shareholders of the acquiring firm will gain if the synergy from the merger is greater than the premium.

4. The possible benefits of an acquisition come from the following:
   a. Revenue enhancement
   b. Cost reduction
   c. Lower taxes
   d. Lower cost of capital
   In addition, the reduction in risk from a merger may actually help bondholders and hurt shareholders.

---

[11] M. Bradley, A. Desai and E.H. Kim (1983) 'The rationale behind interfirm tender offers: Information or synergy', *Journal of Financial Economics*, **11**, April.

5. Some of the most colourful language of finance stems from defensive tactics in acquisition battles. *Poison pills, golden parachutes, crown jewels*, and *greenmail* are terms that describe various antitakeover tactics. These tactics are discussed in this chapter.
6. The empirical research on mergers and acquisitions is extensive. Its basic conclusions are that, on average, the shareholders of acquired firms fare very well, while the shareholders of acquiring firms do not gain much.

KEY TERMS

Merger   618
Consolidation   618
Tender offer   618
Bidder   619
Purchase method   620
Goodwill   620

Pooling of interests   621
White knight   637
Golden parachutes   637
Crown jewels   637
Poison pill   637

QUESTIONS AND PROBLEMS

The Basic Forms of Acquisitions

28.1 Lager Brewing has acquired the Canned Brewing in a vertical merger. Lager Brewing has issued Euro300,000 in new long-term debt to pay for its purchase. (Euro300,000 is the purchase price.) Construct the balance sheet for the new company if the merger is treated as a purchase for accounting purposes. The balance sheets shown here represent the assets of both firms at their true market values. Assume these market values are also the book values.

LAGER BREWING
Balance Sheet
(in thousands)

Current assets	Euro400	Current liabilities	Euro200
Other assets	100	Long-term debt	100
Net fixed assets	500	Equity	700
Total	Euro1,000	Total	Euro1,000

CANNED BREWING
Balance Sheet
(in thousands)

Current assets	Euro80	Current liabilities	Euro80
Other assets	40	Equity	120
Net fixed assets	80		
Total	Euro200	Total	Euro200

28.2 Suppose the balance sheet for Canned Brewing in problem 28.1 shows the assets at their book value and not their market value of Euro240,000. Construct the balance sheet for the new corporation. Again, treat the transaction as a purchase.

28.3 Keep the assumptions of 28.2. Construct the balance sheet for the new corporation. Use pooling interest method to treat the transaction.

Source of Synergy from Acquisitions

28.4 Indicate whether you think the following claims regarding takeovers are true or false. In each case provide a brief explanation for your answer.
   a. By merging competitors, takeovers have created monopolies that will raise product prices, reduce production, and harm consumers.
   b. Managers act in their own interest at times and, in reality, may not be answerable to shareholders. Takeovers may reflect runaway management.

c. In an efficient market, takeovers would not occur because market price would reflect the true value of corporations. Thus, bidding firms would not be justified in paying premiums above market prices for target firms.

d. Traders and institutional investors, having extremely short time horizons, are influenced by their perceptions of what other market traders will be thinking of share prospects and do not value takeovers based on fundamental factors. Thus, they will sell shares in target firms despite the true value of the firms.

e. Acquisitions analysis frequently focuses on the total value of the firms involved. An acquisition, however, will usually affect relative values of shares and bonds, as well as their total value.

Calculating the Value of the Firm after an Acquisition

28.5 The following table shows the projected cash flows and their respective discount rates after the acquisition of Small Fry Co. by Whale Co. Fill in the blanks and calculate the share price of the new firm if it has Euro100 million of debt and 5 million shares outstanding.

	Net Cash Flow Per Year (Perpetual) (in Euro million)	Discount Rate (%)	Value (in Euro million)
Small Fry Co.	8	16%	?
Whale Co.	20	10	?
Benefits from Acquisition	5	?	42.5
Revenue enhancement	2.5	?	12.5
Cost reduction	2	10	?
Tax shelters	0.5	5	?
Whale Co.	33	?	?

A Cost to Shareholders from Reduction in Risk

28.6 The Chocolate Ice Cream Company and the Vanilla Ice Cream Company have agreed to merge and form Fudge Swirl Consolidated. Both companies are exactly alike except that they are located in different towns. The end-of-period value of each firm is determined by the weather, as shown.

State	Probability	Value
Rainy	0.1	GBP100,000
Warm	0.4	200,000
Hot	0.5	400,000

The weather conditions in each town are independent of those in the other. Furthermore, each company has an outstanding debt claim of GBP200,000. Assume that no premium is paid in the merger.

a. What is the distribution of joint values?

b. What is the distribution of end-of-period debt values and share values after the merger?

c. Show that the value of the combined firm is the sum of the individual values.

d. Show that the bondholders are better off and the shareholders are worse off in the combined firm than they would have been if the firms remained separate.

Two 'Bad' Reasons for Mergers

28.7 Refer to the Global Resources example in Section 28.7 of the text. Suppose that instead of 40 shares, Global exchanges 100 of its shares for the 100 shares of Regional. The new Global Resources will now have 200 shares outstanding and earnings of GBP200. Assume the market is smart.

a. Calculate Global's value after the merger.

b. Calculate Global's earnings per share.

c. Calculate Global's price per share.

d. Redo your answers to (a), (b) and (c) if the market is fooled.

28.8 Coldran Aviation has voted in favour of being bought out by Arcadia Financial Corporation. Information about each company is presented below.

	Arcadia Financial	Coldran Aviation
Price–earnings ratio	16	10.8
Number of shares	100,000	50,000
Earnings	CHF225,000	CHF100,000

Shareholders in Coldran Aviation will receive six-tenths of a share of Arcadia for each share they hold.

a. How will the earnings per share (EPS) for these shareholders be changed?

b. What will be the effect on the original Arcadia shareholders of changes in the EPS?

The NPV of a Merger

28.9 Fly-By-Night Couriers NV is analysing the possible acquisition of Flash-in-the-Pan Restaurants NV. Neither firm has debt. The forecasts of Fly-By-Night show that the purchase would increase its annual after-tax cash flow by NLG600,000 indefinitely. The current market value of Flash-in-the-Pan is NLG20 million. The current market value of Fly-By-Night is NLG35 million. The appropriate discount rate for the incremental cash flows is 8 per cent.

a. What is the synergy from the merger?

b. What is the value of Flash-in-the-Pan to Fly-By-Night?

Fly-By-Night is trying to decide whether it should offer 25 per cent of its shares or GBP15 million in cash to Flash-in-the-Pan.

c. What is the cost to Fly-by-Night of each alternative?

d. What is the NPV to Fly-by-Night of each alternative?

e. Which alternative should Fly-By-Night use?

28.10 Freeport Manufacturing is considering making an offer to purchase Portland Industries. The treasurer of Freeport has collected the following information:

	Freeport	*Portland*
Price-earnings ratio	15	12
Number of shares	1,000,000	250,000
Earnings	NLG1,000,000	NLG750,000

The treasurer also knows that securities analysts expect the earnings and dividends (currently NLG1.80 per share) of Portland to grow at a constant rate of 5 per cent each year. Her research indicates, however, that the acquisition would provide Portland with some economies of scale that would improve this growth rate to 7 per cent per year.

a. What is the value of Portland to Freeport?

b. If Freeport offers NLG40 in cash for each outstanding Portland share, what would the NPV of the acquisition be?

c. If instead Freeport were to offer 600,000 of its shares in exchange for the outstanding shares of Portland, what would the NPV of the acquisition be?

d. Should the acquisition be attempted, and if so, should it be a cash or share offer?

e. Freeport's management thinks that 7 per cent growth is too optimistic and that 6 per cent is more realistic. How does this change your previous answers?

CHAPTER 29 International Corporate Finance and Derivative Securities

So far, all of our examples have used only one currency within that particular example. We may have used different European currencies in individual instances but, thus far, we have not mixed them in any of our questions and problems at the back of chapters nor in our examples within chapters. That is about to change now.

Companies that have significant foreign operations are often referred to as *international corporations* or *multinationals*. International corporations must consider many financial factors that do not directly affect purely domestic firms. These include foreign exchange rates, different interest rates from country to country, complex accounting methods for foreign operations, foreign tax rates and foreign government intervention.

The basic principles of corporate finance still apply to international corporations; like domestic companies, they seek to invest in projects that create more value for the shareholders than they cost and to arrange financing that raises cash at the lowest possible cost. That is, the net-present-value principle holds for both foreign and domestic operations. However, it is usually more complicated to apply the NPV principle to foreign operations.

Perhaps the most important complication of international finance is foreign exchange. The foreign exchange markets provide information and opportunities for an international corporation when it undertakes capital-budgeting and financing decisions. The relationship among foreign exchange, interest rates and inflation is defined by the basic theories of exchange rates: purchasing-power parity, interest-rate parity and the expectations theory.

Typically, international financing decisions involve a choice of three basic approaches:

1. Export domestic cash to the foreign operations.
2. Borrow in the country where the investment is located.
3. Borrow in a third country.

We discuss the merits of each approach.

Finally, we briefly consider the topic of derivative securities. We look at what they are and how they may be used to hedge risk exposures.

29.1   The Foreign Exchange Markets

For the majority of **foreign exchange markets**, there are no individual, physical marketplaces. The market is made up of banks and dealers carrying out transactions via telephone, computer, telex and other similar devices.

The total foreign exchange market is the largest of all markets in the world. It has been estimated that foreign exchange deals, worldwide, averaged USD1,300 billion per day in 1995. This market size is two hundred times that of the New York Stock Exchange. The market is a 24 hour market which moves from one centre to another—from Tokyo to Hong Kong to Singapore to Kuwait to London to New York to San Francisco to Sydney and then back to Tokyo—as the sun appears to move round the world.

About 95 per cent of all foreign exchange transactions involve banks on both sides of the deal. This high percentage is reflected by banks taking and unravelling positions in currencies in order to trade for profit and to offset imbalances by their purchase and sales with customers. Some 96 per cent of all trades involve the US dollar. If a French importer wishes to pay a British exporter, the bank will quote a sterling/franc rate based upon the franc/dollar rate and the dollar/sterling rate.

Nowadays, trade accounts for only a small proportion of all foreign exchange deals, maybe only 1 to 2 per cent of total transactions. The lion's share is made up of capital movements from one centre to another and the taking of positions by bankers in different currencies.

There is a **spot market** in which deals are arranged for immediate delivery (technically, a spot deal has delivery two working days after the spot transaction) and there is a forward market in which purchase or sale is arranged today at an agreed rate, but with delivery some time in the future. Forward markets do not exist for all currencies, for example there is no forward market for the Argentine peso. But, for the currencies of major Western economies, forward markets can go out to ten years; for others it is only in existence for up to six months or a year. The term deep market is used to refer to those currencies which are widely dealt, for example dollars, sterling, deutschemarks, etc. At the opposite end of the spectrum, the terms shallow or thin market are applied synonymously to currencies which are traded only occasionally.

London is the largest foreign exchange centre, followed by New York and then Tokyo. London's average daily turnover is around USD464 billion; the next two centres' averages amount to USD244 billion and USD161 billion, respectively. Half of London's turnover is accounted for by spot transactions and almost 40 per cent involves forward deals maturing within one month.

The foreign exchange market is the cheapest market in the world in which to deal. If one were to start with USD1 million and switch this into deutschemarks and then immediately reverse the transaction so that one returned to US dollars, the proceeds would be less than USD1 million by approximately twice the bid/offer spread (the rate for selling and the rate for buying) for deutschemarks against US dollars (after all, two deals have been done). But assuming exchange rates had not moved, the total amount by which one would be out of pocket would be only USD300 or so. For major currencies, the large banks act as market makers. This means that they hold stocks of foreign currencies and are prepared to deal in large amounts at stated prices. In other currencies, banks may operate as brokers thereby avoiding the risk of price movements.

Foreign exchange dealers can make or lose a lot of money for the banks that employ them. They can make a million dollars a day for the bank, but they can also lose that sum. Their salaries and bonuses are high; some make USD500,000 per annum. But their business life is strenuous. Watching currency movements for 10 hours a day in the bank (and taking a Reuters foreign exchange rate screen home) and dealing on the finest margins all take their toll. Dealers on banks' foreign exchange desks seem to be aged between 20 and just over 30. Perhaps beyond 30, reflexes are slower. Perhaps the adrenalin flows more slowly. Or maybe dealers have made so much money already that motivation is not quite what it used to be and dealers move on to a less frenetic life style.

29.2   Eurocurrency Markets

With a few minor exceptions, the definition of a **Eurodollar** is a dollar deposited in a bank outside the USA. A Eurodeutschemark is a deutschemark deposited in a bank outside Germany. A Eurosterling deposit is created by depositing British pounds in a bank account outside the UK. The term Eurocurrency is used to embrace all forms of Euro-deposits. But beware! When people talk about the Eurodollar market a certain amount of caution is called for. This is because the term Eurodollar is sometimes used as a generic term for all Eurocurrency deposits.

Eurocurrency markets exist outside the borders of the country of the underlying currency concerned. As such, they escape controls which may be imposed on domestic currency markets. Indeed, they escape controls altogether. Markets for lending and borrowing in Eurocurrencies operate in the world of classical economies—a world without a regulating authority, a world without controls. In this respect, a contrast must be drawn with domestic currency and domestic money markets.

The domestic central bank is usually the institution through which the home government intervenes in domestic interest rate markets and currency markets. In Eurocurrency and Euro-interest rate markets, there is no intervention by a central bank for Euromarkets because there is no central bank for Euromarkets.

In domestic interest rate markets, governments have, at various points in the past, fixed maximum interest rates payable by commercial banks to depositors. In domestic banking markets, governments frequently specify that banks must deposit some proportion of their own lendings to clients or deposits received from customers with the local central bank at rates substantially below market rates—so-called reserve asset requirements.

The effect of the former control was that it forced depositors to seek market rates by placing their monies in non-regulated markets, such as **Euromarkets**. Via this kind of mechanism, investors have been able to access higher deposits in Euromarkets than they have in domestic markets.

The impact of the latter control, exercised through reserve asset requirements, has a similar distorting effect. With reserve requirements, a commercial bank aiming for a return of, say 15 per cent per annum on its total loan portfolio would have to charge borrowers above this rate at a submarket rate. By contrast, in the Euromarkets, the commercial bank would lend at 15 per cent per annum to earn an overall return of 15 per cent since no requirements for below market rate depositing exist. All other things being equal, borrowers are able to access Euromarkets more cheaply than their domestic counterpart.

It is interesting to note that the effect of the domestic regulations referred to in the foregoing paragraph means that both lenders and borrowers may get a better deal in the Euromarkets than in the domestic markets. Hardly surprising, then, that Euromarkets offer a vast reservoir of lending and borrowing potential for companies, governments, quasi-government organizations, high net-worth individuals and so on. It is also of interest to note that, in the absence of exchange controls, Euromarkets and domestic markets should not get much out of line, because it is always possible for an operator (whether an individual, or a company or a bank) to borrow in the Euromarket and invest in the domestic market. The possibility of arbitrage of this kind should keep rates fairly close.

The advantages referred to above are based upon regulation of domestic financial markets as opposed to non-regulation of Euromarkets. To some extent, deregulation of domestic markets is putting these two marketplaces on to the same footing. The Euromarkets have, none the less, developed a momentum of their own, and they have experienced no problem in terms of maintaining their attractiveness to investors and borrowers alike, even though domestic markets are frequently quite competitive.

The key significance of Euromarkets in much of our analysis of international finance is that they represent unregulated (or free) markets in which to place or borrow money. In other words, these markets demonstrate the unfettered interaction of demand and supply in arriving at the price of money.

The genesis of the Eurocurrency markets in the 1950s occurred because Soviet government agencies wanted to maintain currency deposits in dollars. This was because the dollar was the most acceptable currency for financing their international transactions. They were reluctant to hold their dollars in deposits in New York, because the threat existed that the US authorities might freeze these deposits. So the dollars held by the USSR moved to London, as the Soviets believed that the political risk of London dollar deposits was lower than in New York. And the banks in which these offshore dollars were deposited on-lent thus gave birth to the Eurocurrency market.

While the Soviets may have been the cause of the rapid growth of offshore deposits during the 1950s, the really big take-off in the 1960s reflected other factors. The foremost of these was the increasing differential between Eurodollar and domestic interest rates, which made it increasingly profitable to escape national regulations in the USA. On top of this, growth was fuelled by the increasing size of the multinational firm and the great competitive expansion of banks. The Eurocurrency markets were on the move, and they have not stopped advancing.

29.3   Currency Calculations

Multinational financing management involves manipulation with more than one currency. Understanding it necessarily involves confronting such questions as how foreign exchange markets work, what makes exchange rates move and how protection can be bought to avoid currency risk. Making sense of the complexities of international finance has no magic answer, but this section presents the single most important theorem of foreign exchange. Unless it is understood, the serious student will always flounder in the dark when confronted with exchange rates and interest rates. However, the key to understanding the mysteries of this fascinating facet of finance is at hand. That key concerns the relationship between interest rates, inflation rates, spot and forward exchange rates.

Foreign Exchange Markets

An American company importing goods from Germany with their price denominated in deutschemarks may buy marks in order to pay for the goods. An American company exporting goods to Germany, again with the price denominated in marks, receives deutschemarks which it may then sell in exchange for dollars. The currency aspects of these transactions involve use of the foreign exchange markets.

In most centres, the foreign exchange market has no central, physical marketplace. Business is conducted by telephone or telex. The main dealers are commercial banks and central banks. Most companies wishing to buy or sell currency usually do so through a commercial bank.

In the UK, exchange rates are quoted in terms of the number of units of foreign currency bought for one unit of home currency, that is GBP1. This method of quotation is termed the indirect quote. By contrast, exchange rates throughout continental Europe are quoted in terms of the number of units of home currency, that is the number of deutschemarks, French francs or whatever, necessary to buy one unit of foreign currency. This is the direct quotation method. In the USA, the convention is to use the direct quote when dealing internally with residents of the USA and the indirect quote with foreigners. The exception to this latter rule is that the direct quote is used when dealing with British-based banks or UK businesses. This practice means that New York uses the same figure when talking to foreign dealers as such foreign dealers use for their own transactions and quotations. A quote of USD0.7271 per DEM in New York means that each deutschemark costs USD0.7271. In other words, to put it in indirect terms, there are DEM1.3753 to the dollar given by:

$$\frac{1}{0.7271}$$

On the face of it, buying or selling a currency at the spot rate of exchange implies immediate delivery and payment. The practice of the foreign exchange market is for delivery to be at two working days after the deal, but this applies only to spot transactions.

There is also the forward market where deals for future delivery—usually in one, three, six or 12 months' time, although other durations can be dealt. The forward market enables companies and others to insure themselves against foreign exchange losses (or, of course, to speculate on future movements to exchange rates). If you are going to need DEM100,000 in six months' time, you can enter into a six-month forward contract. The forward rate on this contract is the price agreed now to be paid in six months when the DEM100,000 are delivered.

If the six-month forward rate for the deutschemark against the dollar is quoted at USD0.7331 per DEM as opposed to a spot price of USD0.7271, the implication is that you pay more dollars if you buy forward than if you buy deutschemarks spot. In this case the dollar is said to trade at a forward discount on the deutschemark. Put another way, the deutschemark trades at a forward premium on the dollar. Expressed as an annual rate, the forward premium is:

$$\frac{0.7331 - 0.7271}{0.7271} \times \frac{12 \text{ months}}{6 \text{ months}} \times 100 = 1.65\% \text{ p.a.}$$

Assuming the forward markets and interest rates are in equilibrium, the currency of the country with the higher interest rate is said to be at a discount on the other currency. At the same time, looking at things from the opposite side of the fence, the currency of the country with lower interest rates will be at a premium on the other currency.

Inflation, Interest and Exchange Rates

In the absence of barriers to international capital mobility, there is a relationship between spot exchange rates, forward rates, interest rates and inflation rates. Many national governments attempt to restrict the mobility of their citizens' money; they erect exchange controls and they seek to regulate domestic interest rate markets. But money is internationally mobile in the Eurocurrency markets which are unfettered by government controls. Before considering the relationship between the four variables referred to, it will be helpful to set out the notation to be used. This appears in Table 29.1.

TABLE 29.1   Foreign Exchange Notation to be used

£/$ exchange rates	s_0 = spot rate now
	f_0 = forward rate now
	$^*s_t$ = expected spot rate at time t
Interest rates per annum	$i_\$$ = Eurodollar unterest rate
	$i_£$ = Eurosterling interest rate
	$p_\$$ = US general price level now
Inflation rates per annum	$p_£$ = UK general price level now
	$^*p_\$$ = expected US inflation rate
	$^*p_£$ = expected UK inflation rate

It can be shown by deductive reasoning or by a mathematical approach that, if equilibrium holds, differences between forward and spot rates, differences in interest rates, expected differences in inflation rates and expected changes in spot rates are equal to one another. Figure 29.1 summarizes the relationship. A form of proof of the relationship is available in the appendix to this chapter, but this can be omitted without affecting basic understanding of the ideas developed here.

It must be stressed that the model in Figure 29.1 is an equilibrium model. In the real world, markets move towards equilibrium, but rarely demonstrate total equilibrium at any particular point in time. So it should not be surprising if some of the arms of the four-way equivalence model do not hold in the real world of financial markets in the short-term.

According to Figure 29.1, the relationship between the spot and the forward exchange rate is underpinned by interest rate differentials. Note, and this is most important, that we should be looking at free market interest rates, that is those quoted in the unfettered Eurocurrency markets; it is these that underpin the difference between spot and forward foreign exchange rates. This relationship is technically referred to as **interest rate parity**, although it clearly involves exchange rates as well as interest rates. In Eurocurrency markets, interest rate parity is found to hold good virtually all of the time. That is not to say that bankers and dealers do not have opportunities to make profits from temporary disequilibria in interest rates and exchange rates; indeed, they make substantial profits from such sources. However, except at the level of bankers, dealers and the most sophisticated of industrial corporate treasuries, these opportunities are rare. In taking advantage of them, dealers are undertaking what is referred to as a covered interest arbitrage. The term sounds complicated but the mechanism is easy. Take an example.

Assume that an investor has GBP1 million to invest for a period of twelve months. He has a whole spectrum of investment opportunities; he could put the money into sterling or dollar investments, or into yen or into deutschemarks, or whatever. But for

FIGURE 29.1   **Four-Way Equivalence in the Foreign Exchange Market**

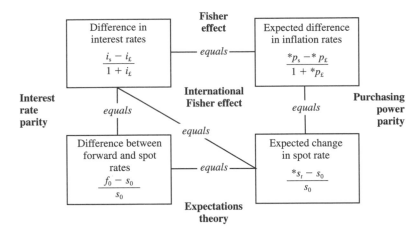

Note: Using the notation as here, f_0, s_0 and $*s_t$ must all be stated in terms of the number of dollars to one pound sterling. Great care must be taken on this point whenever using the equations in the model. Should currencies other than dollars and sterling be under consideration, substitution in the model is a relatively simple process. To get approximate results, the number of months may be used. Thus a three-month forward premium or discount would have to be treated as:

$$\frac{f_0 - s_0}{s_0} \times \frac{12}{3}$$

In practice, the actual number of days, rather than months, has to be used in calculations. A further slight modification is necessary because US dollar interest rates are quoted on a 360-day year basis whereas sterling rates are quoted on a 365-day basis. All Eurocurrencies use a 360-day year.

Approximation
For quick, approximate calculations the four-way relationship may be written as:

$$i_\$ - i_£ = *p_\$ - *p_£ = \frac{f_0 - s_0}{s_0} = \frac{*s_t - s_0}{s_0}$$

This approximation becomes less accurate as higher inflation economies are dealt with.

simplicity, suppose we look at only two of these opportunities. The currency markets are quoting the dollar against sterling at USD1.6800 spot and USD1.6066 for 12 months forward. Euromarket fixed interest rates are 13 per cent per annum for 12 months sterling and 8⅟₁₆ per cent per annum for US dollars for a similar period. The investor may either.

1. Invest GBP1 million in Eurosterling at a 13 per cent per annum fixed interest rate for twelve months; or
2. Convert GBP1 million into US dollars at USD1.6800; invest the proceeds in the Eurodollar interest market at an $8\frac{1}{16}$ per cent per annum fixed interest rate for one year and sell the precalculated proceeds forward twelve months at a rate of USD1.6066.

What are the expected proceeds? Obviously the sterling investment yields GBP1,130,000 at the end of 12 months. The dollar investment yields, to all intents and purposes, the same amount. The proceeds from the spot transaction are USD1,680,000.

Investing at $8\frac{1}{16}$ per cent per annum, the proceeds in 12 months' time will total USD1,815,450 and selling this forward at USD1.6066 yields GBP1,129,995. This is, more or less, the same outturn as from the sterling investment opportunity. This is what one might expect: after all, each investment opportunity is of equal risk (the investor carries the credit risk associated with the bank with whom he invests, but if he invests with the same Eurobank then the credit risk associated with each opportunity is equal), and investments of equal risk should, according to financial theory, promise equal returns.

Were this not the case, arbitrageurs in the foreign exchange and interest rate markets would borrow currency in one centre, swap it to the other, invest there and sell the proceeds forward. Such proceeds would, if equilibrium did not hold, exceed the amount repayable in terms of the borrowing plus accrued interest and thereby yield a virtually riskless profit to the operator. This mechanism is the covered interest arbitrage referred to earlier. The actions of dealers ensure that profitable opportunities of this kind do not last for more than fleeting instants. Exploitation of these brief opportunities creates movements in spot and forward exchange rates and in interest rates, and such movements ensure that the tendency in the currency and interest rate markets is towards equilibrium.

Covered interest arbitrage involves borrowing in centre *A* for a specified period at a fixed interest rate and shipping the proceeds borrowed to centre *B*. The sum shipped is deposited there for the same period as the borrowing in centre *A*, again at a fixed interest rate. The total proceeds of investment in centre *B* that will accrue at the end of the investment period can be calculated, since the interest rate is fixed. Such proceeds are sold via the forward market for the period of the borrowing and lending, and the sum received in centre *A* from this forward transaction will more than repay the borrowing in centre *A* plus accrued interest. This profit is said to be covered interest arbitrage profit.

By contrast, **uncovered interest arbitrage** involves a borrowing in centre *A* for a specified period at a fixed interest rate and shipping the proceeds borrowed to centre *B* via the spot market. The sum is again placed on deposit for the same period as that for which the borrowing was arranged in centre *A* and again it is at a fixed rate. This time the investor speculates that the proceeds from lending in centre *B*, when shipped to centre *A* at the spot rate prevailing at the end of the investment period, will exceed the borrowing accrued interest in centre *A*. Note that, under uncovered interest arbitrage, the operator speculated on the future spot rate. Any profit earned is a risky profit. Under covered interest arbitrage, the operator is not speculating, but making a risk-free profit based on momentary disequilibria in interest differentials and forward and spot rates.

According to the **Fisher effect** (see Figure 29.1), a term coined because it was observed by US economist Irving Fisher, quoted interest rates in a country reflect anticipated real returns adjusted for local inflation expectations. In a world where investors are internationally mobile, expected real rates of return should tend towards equality reflecting the fact that, in search of higher real returns, investors' arbitraging actions will force these returns towards each other. At least this should hold with respect to the free market Eurocurrency interest rates. Constraints on international capital mobility prevent this relationship from holding in domestic interest rate markets, so quoted Eurocurrency interest rates may differ for different currencies, but, according to the Fisher effect, only by virtue of different inflation expectations; and these inflation differentials should underpin expected changes in the spot rates of exchange. In other words, we would expect US and UK free market interest investment to yield equal real returns. Difference in nominal returns would reflect expected inflation differentials.

We now move on to **purchasing power parity**. At its simplest, this theory suggests that exchange rates move to make good changes in inflation rates. Assume an example in which there are no costs of transporting goods. If the US dollar/sterling exchange rate is USD1.70 and British widgets sell at GBP10 each, the US-produced widget should be marketed at USD17 to be in line on price. If this were initially the case, and inflation in the UK and the USA amounted to 8 per cent and 4 per cent per annum, respectively, the widget prices (assuming they were to move in line with general inflation) would be GBP10.80 and USD17.68, respectively. However, an exchange rate movement which took account of these relative inflations would ensure continuing competitiveness, such that a rate would have to be USD1.6370 = GBP1.

There are a number of reservations about purchasing power parity. First, the prices of individual goods and services rarely move exactly in line with general inflation, whether it be measured by retail prices, wholesale prices or whatever. Furthermore, the index that would be most relevant would be one based upon export prices.

The diagonal in Figure 29.1, the **international Fisher effect**, suggest a relationship between interest differences and expected movements of the spot exchange rate. It will be recalled that interest rate parity is based upon covered interest arbitrage. The international Fisher effect is built upon uncovered interest arbitrage. The argument is that rational investors make estimates of future spot rates of exchange. If their judgments are such as to justify excess profits from uncovered interest arbitrage, their actions in purchasing one currency and selling another will move exchange rates until such excess profits are eliminated. The effect of this speculation would be to bring interest rate differentials into line with spot exchange rates and expectations of their movement.

The test of any theory is how well it stands up in the real world. We have seen that interest rate parity is extraordinarily well supported when tested against evidence from financial markets. In the real world, the Fisher effect and the international Fisher effect are found to hold in the long-term, but there are substantial short-run deviations from equilibrium. Of course, if the international Fisher effect were to hold immutably, then interest rates on borrowing in different countries would always be exactly offset by exchange rate movements. And if the Fisher effect were to hold immutably, then real interest returns (that is, quoted interest rates less expected inflation) from investment in different currencies would always be equated, too.

When tested against evidence from economic statistics, purchasing power parity is found to hold up moderately well in the long term. But in the short term there are substantial deviations; so much so that using purchasing power parity as a short-term predictor of exchange rates is utterly unjustifiable. Having said this, its use as a long-term forecasting device seems better merited by the evidence. As mentioned above, purchasing power parity predicts that exchange rates change to compensate for differences in inflation between two countries. If a country's nominal exchange rate falls, and that decline is an exact compensation for inflation differentials, then its real effective exchange rate is said to remain constant. Purchasing power parity predicts that real effective exchange rates will remain constant through time.

One of the major problems with using purchasing power parity as a long-term predictive device for exchange rate forecasting is the choice of base year. Exchange rate movements may be weighted according to international trade and corrected for inflation relativities to obtain real effective exchange rates. If real effective exchange rates are indexed to 100 for the base year, it follows that for currencies where the current figure is over 100, the exchange rate is overvalued on purchasing power criteria and vice versa. But there is a problem: the answer obtained about valuation may vary according to which year is chosen as a base date.

Referring to Figure 29.2, if 1992 is used as the base year with currencies trade

FIGURE 29.2   **Real Effective Exchange Rates (1992 = 100)**

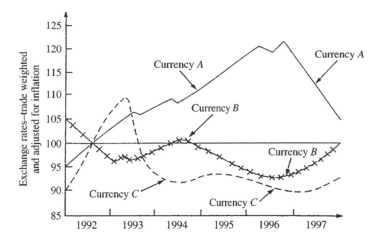

weighted and corrected for inflation, then by 1994, currency *A* appears overvalued, currency *B* appears correctly valued and currency *C* appears undervalued. But if 1995 is taken as the base year, currency *A* appears undervalued by 1997; at this time currency *B* looks overvalued and currency *C* looks correctly valued. So how does one get over this problem?

The answer is that one should start the analysis at a time when the exchange rate of the country being analysed is in equilibrium. And what is meant by an exchange rate being in equilibrium? One approach is to commence at a time when the exchange rate is such that the overall balance of trade plus invisibles is equal (or approximately equal) to zero. In this sense, exchange rate equilibrium may be defined as that level at which it results in the balance on trade and invisibles coming out at zero overall. However, the question of capital flows affecting exchange rate equilibrium has become so significant that a theory of fundamental equilibrium exchange rates (FEERs) has been developed. Here the notion is that the equilibrium exchange rate is that rate which is consistent with overall external balance, given underlying capital flows.

Lastly, turning to the **expectations theory** arm of the model outlined in Figure 29.1, the forward rate is generally (but not always) found to be an unbiased long-term predictor of the future spot rate. This means that if the forward rate is used to predict the future spot rate, the sum of gains will equal the sum of losses in the long-term. But, again, there may be substantial short-term deviations.

Do these deviations show any consistency? The answer is yes. Evidence suggests that, in the short-term, when a currency is substantially strengthening, the forward rate underestimates the future spot value of the strengthening currency. And, when a currency is on a significantly weakening trend, the forward rate tends to overestimate its future spot rate.

Practicalities

In practical treasury work, the interest rate parity side of Figure 29.1 is used in computer aids to identify whether opportunities for covered interest arbitrage exist. The international Fisher effect is resorted to in order to estimate future exchange rates implied by market interest rates in different currencies. Purchasing power parity is often used to forecast long-term foreign exchange rate movements.

In raising foreign-denominated long-term borrowings, identification of whether a currency is out of equilibrium can be a valuable exercise. All other things being equal, it is better to raise such borrowings denominated in an overvalued currency. If movements of exchange rates are towards equilibrium, there will be opportunities to repay such borrowings and make a gain in so doing.

Concept Questions

- What is the theoretical relationship between interest rates, exchange rates and inflation rates?
- How well do these relationships stand up in the real world?

29.4   Foreign Exchange Quotations

The foreign exchange market is the framework of individuals, firms, banks and brokers who buy and sell foreign currencies. The foreign exchange market for any one currency, for example the French franc, consists of all the locations such as Paris, London, New York, Zurich, Frankfurt, and so on, in which the French franc is bought and sold for other currencies. Foreign exchange markets tend to be located in national financial centres near the local financial markets. The most important foreign exchange markets are found in London, New York, Tokyo, Frankfurt, Amsterdam, Paris, Zurich, Toronto, Brussels, Milan, Singapore and Hong Kong.

There are four main types of transaction undertaken in these foreign exchange markets: spot transactions, forward deals, futures transactions and currency options.

In the spot market, currencies are bought and sold for immediate delivery. In practice, this means that settlement is made two working days after the spot date. The intervention of these two days allows for necessary paperwork to be completed. In the forward market, currencies are bought and sold at prices agreed now, but for future delivery at an agreed date. Not only is delivery made in the future, but payment is also made at the future date.

The Players

The main participants in the market are companies and individuals. Commercial banks, central banks and brokers. Companies and individuals need foreign currency for business or travel reasons. Commercial banks are the source from which companies and individuals obtain their foreign currency. Through their extensive network of dealing rooms, their arbitrage operations (buying in one centre and selling in another), banks ensure that quotations in different centres tend towards the same price. There are also foreign exchange brokers who bring buyers, sellers and banks together and receive commissions on deals arranged. The other main player operating in the market is the central bank, the main part of whose foreign exchange activities involves the buying and selling of the home currency or foreign currencies with a view to ensuring that the exchange rate moves in line with established targets set for it by the government.

Not only are there numerous foreign exchange market centres around the world, but dealers in different locations can communicate with one another via the telephone, telex and computers. The overlapping of time zones means that, apart from weekends, there is always one centre that is open.

Methods of Quotation

A foreign exchange rate is the price on one currency in terms of another. Foreign exchange dealers quote two prices, one for selling, one for buying. The first area of mystique in foreign exchange quotations arises from the fact that there are two ways of quoting rates: the direct quote and the indirect quote. The former gives the quotation in terms of the number of units of home currency necessary to buy one unit of foreign currency. The latter gives the quotation in terms of the number of units of foreign currency bought with one unit of home currency.

Continental Europe dealers normally quote via the direct method. In London dealers use the indirect method. In the USA, both quotation methods are used. When a bank is dealing with a customer within the USA a direct quotation is given, but when dealing with other banks in Europe (except the UK), the indirect quotation is used.

Foreign exchange dealers quote two prices: the rate at which they are prepared to sell a currency and that at which they are prepared to buy. The difference between the bid rate and the offer is the dealer's spread which is one of the potential sources of profit for dealers. Whether using the direct quotation method or the indirect quote, the smaller rate is always termed the bid rate and the higher is called the offer, or ask, rate.

If we assume that the middle quote (that is, halfway between the sell and buy price) for deutschemarks to the US dollar is DEM1.3753 = USD1, then the New York internal quote for this rate would be USD0.7271 and the Frankfurt quote would be DEM1.3753. Where both centres use the same method of quotation (that is, they both use the direct quote or they both use the indirect quote method), and when they are both in effect quoting the same price (in other words there are no arbitrage opportunities), the quote in one centre is the reciprocal of the other. Thus, the two quotes multiplied together will equal 1.0. To the extent that this condition fails to hold, possibilities for profitable arbitrage (selling in one centre and buying in the other) exist. Of course, operators need to look at the buy rate in one centre and the sell rate in the other in terms of assessing arbitrage opportunities. In carrying out a profitable arbitrage, dealers force the prices in various centres towards equality.

If, in terms of the middle quote, the sterling/US dollar rate is USD1.6015 equal GBP1, then the New York quote (using the local direct method) will be USD1.6015 and the London quote (using the indirect method) will also be USD1.6015. Where one centre uses the direct quotation method and the other uses the indirect method, the two quotations will, assuming no profitable arbitrage opportunities exist, be exactly the same.

The size of the bid/offer spread varies according to the depth of the market and its ability at any particular time. Depth of a market refers to the volume of transactions in a particular currency. Deep markets have many deals; shallow markets have few. High percentage spreads are associated with high uncertainty (perhaps due to impending devaluation) and low volumes of transactions in a currency. Lower spreads are associated with stable, high-volume markets. Deep markets usually have narrower spreads than shallow ones.

If US dollars are quoted in terms of sterling as USD1.6050/USD1.6060, it means that the dealer is prepared to sell dollars at USD1.6050 to the pound, or buy dollars at USD1.6060. Conversely, the dealer is prepared to buy pounds at the rate of USD1.6050 or sell pounds at USD1.6060. In the above example, the spread is equal to USD0.0010, at 10 points. A point (or pip, as it is widely called) is a unit of a decimal, usually the fourth place to the right of the decimal point.

Next, it is necessary to consider the meaning of cross rates. A cross rate may be defined as an exchange rate which is calculated from two (or more) other rates. Thus the rate for the deutschemark to the Swedish krona will be derived as the cross rate from the US dollar to the deutschemark and the US dollar to the krona.

The practice in world foreign exchange markets is that currencies are quoted against the US dollar. If one bank asks another for its deutschemark rate, that rate will be quoted against the US dollar unless otherwise specified. Most dealings are done against the US dollar, hence it follows that the market rate for a currency at any moment is most accurately reflected in its exchange rate against the US dollar. A bank that was asked to quote sterling against the Swiss franc would normally do so by calculating this rate from the GBP/USD rate and the USD/CHF rate. It would therefore be using cross rates to arrive at its quotation.

Let us suppose that we require a quote for Swiss francs against the deutschemark. The quotation which we would receive would be derived through the quote of both currencies against the US dollar. If these rates against the dollar were USD1 − CHF1.1326/1.1336 and USD1 = DEM1.3750/1.3755, it would be possible to derive the cross rate for the Swiss franc against the deutschemark. Our goal is to derive the selling and buying rates for Swiss francs in terms of deutschemarks. If we are selling Swiss francs we will be buying deutschemarks. So we begin with the rate for selling Swiss francs and buying dollars; we then move to selling dollars and buying deutschemarks. The amalgamation of these two rates gives us the rate for selling Swiss francs and buying deutschemarks. The rate for selling Swiss francs to the dealer and buying dollars is CHF1.1336; the rate for selling dollars and buying deutschemarks is DEM1.3750. So selling CHF1 gives USD0.8822. Selling USD0.8822 gives DEM1.2130. Thus the rate for selling Swiss francs and buying deutschemarks is CHF1 = DEM1.2130, or DEM1 = CHF0.8244.

Similarly, in our example, if we are buying Swiss francs we will be selling deutschemarks. This time we begin with the rate for buying Swiss francs from the dealer and selling dollars to him, and then we move to buying dollars and selling deutschemarks. Amalgamating these two rates gives us the rate for buying Swiss francs and selling deutschemarks. The rate for buying Swiss francs and selling dollars is CHF1.1326; the rate for buying dollars and selling deutschemarks is DEM1.3755. Selling DEM1 give USD0.7270. Selling USD0.7270 gives CHF0.8234. Thus the rate for buying Swiss francs and selling deutschemarks is DEM1 = CHF0.8234, or CHF1 = DEM1.2145. Thus the cross rate quotation using direct Zurich figures would be CHF0.8234/0.8244 = DEM1 and the direct Frankfurt quote would be DEM1.2130/1.2145.

Forward Contracts and Quotations

It is necessary to consider next how **forward rates** are quoted by foreign exchange dealers. A forward foreign exchange contract is an agreement between two parties to exchange one currency for another at some future date. The rate at which the exchange is to be made, the delivery date and the amounts involved are fixed at the time of the agreement.

One of the major problems that newcomers to foreign exchange markets have is understanding how the **forward premium** and **forward discount** works and how foreign exchange dealers quote for forward delivery. Assume that a quoted currency is more expensive in the future than it is now in terms of the base currency. The quoted currency is then said to stand at a premium in the forward market relative to the base currency. Conversely, the base currency is said to stand at a discount relative to the quoted currency.

Consider an example in which the US dollar is the base currency and the Deutschemark is the quoted currency. Assume that the spot rate is USD1 = DEM1.3753. The rate quoted by a bank today for delivery in three months' time (today's three-month forward rate) is USD1 = DEM1.3748. In this example, the dollar buys fewer deutschemarks in three months' time than it does today. So the deutschemark is more expensive in the forward market. Thus the dollar stands at a discount relative to the deutschemark; conversely, the deutschemark stands at a premium relative to the dollar. The size of the dollar discount or deutschemark premium is the difference between 1.3753 and 1.3748, that is, 0.05 pfennigs. The convention in the foreign exchange market is frequently to quote in terms of points, or hundredths of a unit. Hence 0.05 pfennigs is frequently quoted as 5 points.

In order to arrive at the forward prices, the deutschemark premium or dollar discount must be subtracted from the spot rate. Were there a deutschemark discount or dollar premium, this would be added to the spot rate. But care has to be taken: in our example we used a New York indirect quote. Had we used a New York direct quote, the reverse would apply: in other words, the deutschemark premium or dollar discount would have to be added to the spot quotation. An easier way to deal with this little problem is always to remember (and this has never, in practice, been found to be otherwise) that the bid/offer spread on the forward quote is always wider than the spread on the spot figure. If this is remembered, it is an easy process to compare the two spreads and, if the forward spread is narrower than the spot spread, the sums have been done incorrectly and recomputation is necessary.

Just as in the spot market, dealers quote selling and buying rates in the forward market, too. As in the spot market the convention, whether using direct of indirect quotation methods, it is the smaller rate that is quoted first. In the above example, the spot rate for deutschemark to US dollar might be quoted as DEM1.3748/1.3758 and the three-month deutschemark premium (or dollar discount) might be 6/3. Thus, if the foreign exchange dealer is buying dollars forward, there will be a deutschemark premium of 6 points, or 0.6 pfennigs. But if he is buying the deutschemark, the premium will only be 3 points of 0.03 pfennigs. Using the convention that the forward quotation comes out at DEM1.3742/1.3755.

	Bid rate	Offer rate	Spread in Points
Spot quotation	1.3748	1.3758	10
Forward spread	6	3	3
Subtract to make forward spread 13 points	1.3742	1.3755	13

Sometimes forward quotes are given as −10/ +10 or 10P10. In this situation the forward market is said to be 'round par'. Thus, to get the forward rate, 10 points have to be added to either the bid or offer and 10 points have to be subtracted so that the forward spread widens on the spot spread. For example, take the quotation of:

$$1.3748/1.3758 \qquad -10/ +10$$

The forward rate could be construed as 1.3738/1.3768, i.e. it may be quoted in full rather than as points distance from spot. This is called the outright forward price. It would be computed as:

	Bid rate	Offer rate	Spread in Points
Spot quotation	1.3748	1.3758	10
Forward spread	(10)	10	20
	1.3738	1.3768	30

Sometimes this kind of situation is quoted in terms of the spread from the spot rate as 10 pfennigs discount, 10 pfennigs premium.

It is important to bear in mind that the currency quoted at a discount in the forward market relative to another currency will have higher Eurocurrency interest rates than the currency which is at the premium. The rationale for this was discussed in the previous chapter.

As an adjunct to the above methods of quoting forward foreign exchange rates, we sometimes see the percentage per annum cost of forward cover. What does this mean and how is it calculated? The annualized forward premium may be expressed as a percentage by reference to the formula:

$$\frac{\text{Forward rate} - \text{Spot rate}}{\text{Spot rate}} \times \frac{12}{n} \times 100$$

where n is the number of months in the forward contract. It should be noted that small differences in the annual percentage cost for forward cover arise when using the direct quotation method as opposed to using the indirect quote. Slightly different results also arise from using the buying rate as opposed to the selling rate or the middle price. The problem of differing costs of forward cover for buying and selling is easily resolved. While different figures are achieved using mathematics, the relevant figure for a company executive using the forward market is the percentage cost of doing the transaction that he or she wishes to undertake.

Let us look at an example. Suppose again that we have a spot rate of USD1 = DEM1.3748/1.3758 and that the three-month forward quote is 6/3. The forward rate came out (see above) as DEM1.3742/1.3755. If we were a buyer of deutschemarks forward, the forward premium would be obtained by comparing the rates for buying deutschemarks (that is DEM1.3748 spot and DEM1.3742 three months forward). The annualized forward premium for buying deutschemarks would therefore amount to:

$$\frac{1.3742 - 1.3748}{1.3748} \times \frac{12}{3} \times 100 = -0.17\% \text{ p.a.}$$

The deutschemark is said to be at an annualized premium of 0.17 per cent in the three-month forward market based on rates for buying marks.

Concept Question

- Why should the bid/offer spread on the forward rate always be wider than the spot bid/offer spread? (Hint: Think about how the forward rate is derived from the spot rate.)

29.5   International Investment Decisions

Analysing capital investment decisions involves comparing inflows with cash outflows from a project. Investment appraisal systems are frequently collectively termed capital budgeting, and this focuses upon expected incremental cash flows associated with a project. The specification of these flows for the overseas project creates the usual difficulties found in a domestic capital project, but international project analysis is much more complex. Although the basic pattern follows the same model as that suggested by corporate financial theory, the multinational firm must consider factors peculiar to international operations.

A project may be estimated to produce considerable cash flows in a foreign territory but, because of exchange control restrictions, the bulk of these foreign cash flows may not be distributable to the parent company. In these circumstances, looking at the project purely in terms of cash flows accruing in the foreign territory may indicate that it is worth investing. Is this good enough? Surely the present value to the parent company is a function of future cash flows accruing to it which are distributable to the parent company's investors. But we stated that for the project concerned, the bulk of foreign cash flows were blocked by exchange controls. Surely it is only incremental cash flows which are remittable back to the parent company which add value for its shareholders? This means that our capital project might be looked at from at least two standpoints: incremental project cash flows and incremental parent cash flows. To the international company, though, it is only incremental parent cash flows that matter.

The International Complications

There are six key categories of complexity in international capital budgeting about which analysts are advised to beware. These embrace situations where:

1. Full remittance of cash flows arising from a project are restricted in terms of payment to the parent.
2. Part of the parent input is via equipment.
3. Exchange rates are not expected to be constant throughout the project's life.
4. Different rates of tax apply in the country of the project and in the parent's country.
5. Royalties and management fees are involved.
6. There are knock-on effects impinging upon operations in the group elsewhere in the world.

We now consider each of these complexities in turn.

Remittance Constraints on Cash Flows

In international capital budgeting, a significant difference may exist between the cash generation of a project and the amount that is remittable to the parent. The main reason for this is the existence of exchange controls in the host nation. Management in an overseas subsidiary can be excused for focusing only upon project cash flows accruing locally. Overseas managers often ignore the consequences of an investment upon the rest of the corporation and, in particular, the impact of the project at the level of distributable cash flows of the parent company. For the project, the appropriate incremental cash inflows are those additional cash outturns resulting from new operations after adjustment for local corporate taxes. From the parent's view, the critical incremental cash flow figures are the additional remittable funds to the parent treasury in London, New York, or wherever. From the central treasury's point of view, the important cash flows relating to a new investment are incremental cash flows that are distributable to the multinational's shareholders. This means that management fees (net of the costs of providing supervision), royalties, interest, dividend remittances, loan inputs and repayments and equity inputs are all key cash flows.

According to corporate financial theory, the value of a project is determined by the net present value of future cash flows available for the investor. The parent multinational corporation should therefore value only those cash flows that are available for repatriation. This should be done net of any transfer costs, since it is only these remaining funds that can be used to pay corporate interest and dividends; it is only these funds that represent free cash flow. The estimation of parent cash flows involves focusing upon incremental remittable cash flows; whether they are actually remitted or not is immaterial, what is important is that they *may* be remitted.

In those countries without exchange controls, project cash flows may readily translate into parent cash flows. In other countries, international project evaluation should involve two key stages of analysis. First, project cash flows should be computed from the overseas subsidiary's standpoint, as if it were a separate free-standing entity. Focus, in the second stage of analysis, moves to the parent. Here analysis requires forecasts of the amounts and timing of distributable cash flows. It also requires information about taxes payable. In summary, then, it is distributable parent cash flows which matter.

For an overseas investment in a country where there are no restrictions on remittance, incremental cash flows accruing to the multinational corporation need to be forecast in local currency and then converted into the multinational corporation's home currency in accordance with expected exchange rates prevailing when such cash flows accrue. If when subjected to home territory tax rules, which is the harshest tax treatment, the project still looks attractive, then a clear green light is indicated.

Where a project is in a country from which cash flow repatriation is restricted, the relevant focus should be upon remittable incremental parent cash flows. Analysis might embrace the cash flows set out in Table 29.2.

Table 29.2   Parent Cash Flows

- Equity put into overseas project
- Dividends back from overseas project
- Equity capital remitted back to parent
- Loans put into overseas project
- Loan interest back from overseas
- Management fees, etc. received from overseas project net of supervision costs
- Royalties
- Equipment or inventory contributions to overseas project (here the opportunity cost is the relevant figures)
- Contribution accruing to the parent or to a subsidiary in a country where repatriation of funds is not restricted (or to other subsidiaries when repatriation is possible) on incremental sales to the project
- Appropriate tax effect on remittance
- The value of growth options

There are various means at the disposal of the group treasurer in order to unlock blocked overseas cash flows; such techniques as countertrade and barter are the most obvious. In overseas project evaluation, it is perfectly permissible to take credit as a parent cash flow for blocked cash generation to the extent that it can be unlocked by such means as to countertrade and barter, subject to the costs of unblocking.

Equipment Input to a Project

The second major complication in international capital budgeting arises in situations in which the home-based company puts up part of its equity or loan capital in an overseas subsidiary by way of equipment or inventory. Clearly, the project should be debited with its input for the purpose of calculating project returns but, since it is parent returns that are of paramount importance, how should we treat this factor at the level of parent incremental cash flows?

The home territory company has surrendered value (in the form of equipment or inventory) in the expectation of obtaining greater value later on in terms of remittable, incremental parent cash flows. The problem that the financial analyst has is to put a value on the equipment or inventory surrendered. There is an ideally suited technique for valuing the property put in by the home territory company and this involves the use of the concept of deprival value. This has been defined by Bonbright, the originator of the concept, in his book *The Valuation of Property*, as the 'adverse value of the entire loss, direct or indirect, that the owner might expect to suffer if he were to be deprived of the property'. In effect, in subscribing equipment or inventory, the home-territory company is voluntarily being deprived of assets in favour of the foreign business.

Bonbright advances three meaningful bases for valuation of an asset. These are:

1. The current purchase price of an asset in a comparable state of wear and tear: this is replacement cost (*RC*).
2. The net realizable value (*NRV*) of the asset: this is the current net disposable value.
3. The present value of the expected future earnings stream flowing from the asset (*PV*).

The Bonbright approach seems the relevant and logical way to assess the value forgone by the home-territory company in surrendering assets to an overseas venture. The correct basis of valuation is summarized in Table 29.3.

TABLE 29.3   Basis of Asset Valuation

Circumstances	*Correct basis*
$NRV > PV > RC$	*RC*
$NRV > RC > PV$	*RC*
$PV > RC > NRV$	*RC*
$PV > NRV > RC$	*RC*
$RC > PV > NRV$	*PV*
$RC > NRV > PV$	*NRV*

Obviously when an asset subscribed to an overseas venture is completely unnecessary to the home operations, then the relevant valuation basis would be *NRV*. After all, the home company had forgone the opportunity to sell the asset for its realizable value.

Having identified the appropriate valuation method in respect of the asset subscribed to an overseas project, this becomes the initial minus item in the parent cash flow projections against which subsequent estimated inflows are set.

It is worth noting that, whether in a domestic or international situation, were one company to subscribe equipment and inventory to another company in return for a share of its equity, deprival value would provide the correct basis for valuing the input as part of the process of investment appraisal.

Exchange Rates

We now turn to the third area of complication: exchange rates. If exchange rates are in equilibrium at the time the project commences, and if future exchange rates move in line with purchasing power parity, and furthermore, if more project cash inflows and outflows move in line with general inflation in the overseas territory, then assuming that there are no exchange control restrictions and assuming that host territory and home country taxes are at similar rates, project cash flow analysis will give exactly the same indication about investment viability as parent cash flow analysis. Rarely, if ever, will all of these conditions hold.

Consequently, it is recommended that estimated future project cash flows (net of local tax) be shown in money terms (that is, gross of expected host country inflation) and the project net present value should be calculated following the application of a money terms host country discount rate. Parent cash flows should be estimated by applying the expected future exchange rate to host country net cash flows if there are no exchange controls, or remittable net cash flows if exchange controls are in place or where they are expected to be introduced. Due allowance must be made for host and home country taxation impacts and a parent net present value would be estimated following the application of a risk-adjusted parent discount rate.

Estimation of future exchange rates might follow from projections of inflation rates with corrections arising through purchasing power parity. Of course, it must be remembered that while purchasing power parity is found empirically to hold in the long-term, movements in exchange rates often follow discontinuous paths with governments supporting currencies for long periods before giving in and letting the economics of inflation rate differentials have their full effect. Given that exchange rate movements are discontinuous, wise analysts may wish to reflect this in their forecasts, although the timing of when purchasing power parity is likely to reassert itself is incredibly difficult to predict. Perhaps this problem is best handled via sensitivity analysis with various sets of figures being prepared for different timings of purchasing power parity asserting itself.

Taxation

The fourth area of complication concerns taxation. Clearly, project cash flows should be estimated net of local taxation and parent cash flows should be calculated net of parent taxation.

Royalties and Management Fees

If royalties and management fees are charged by a home-based company to an overseas operating subsidiary, then these should be shown as a debit to the project cash flow and as a credit in the parent cash flow analysis. Strictly speaking, of course, income to be forgone and/or incremental costs to be incurred in deploying management in pursuit of the project should be set against parent cash inflows.

Impact Elsewhere in the Group

The final problem area in overseas capital budgeting involves investment projects where there are substantial knock-on effects on operations elsewhere within the group. For example, a motor manufacturer contemplating the establishment of a plant in Spain may find that the proposed investment will affect the operations of other units within the multinational group. This may arise, in part, through the new project's effect on sales of other parts of the multinational in Europe (for example, sales deriving from French and German plants). But it may also arise through vertical integration by, for example, affecting the output of a mining operation in South America which is owned by the multinational corporation. It could be the case that the new plant is expected to absorb output from the mine. Where such knock-on effects exist, the firm needs to evaluate the project by aggregating all incremental cash flows accruing. Thus, while cash flows in Spain are clearly relevant, so are reduced cash flows accruing to the French and German operations, and so are increased flows accruing to the South American mine.

Furthermore, international investment is one of the most fertile sources of growth option. Such impacts should be allowed for in the appraisal of international investment opportunities.

Concept Questions

• How do exchange control regulations create problems in analysing international capital investment decisions?
• What are the main sources of difference between international capital budgeting and domestic capital budgeting?

29.6   International Financing Decisions

Companies, whether they operate within national boundaries or beyond them, may borrow in their own domestic capital markets or they may move further afield and tap international markets to finance their operations. The Eurocurrency market is the largest international source of funds and its growth has been astounding. The Eurocurrency market is that market in which banks, often termed Eurobanks, accept deposits and make loans denominated in currencies other than that of the country in which the banks are located. Eurodollars are dollars held in the form of time deposits in banks outside the United States. Eurodeutschemarks are marks deposited in banks outside Germany,. The prefix 'Euro' really means external and refers to funds that are intermediated outside the country of the currency in which the funds are denominated.

The Eurocredit market is defined as the market for loans in currencies which are not native to the country in which the bank officer making the loans is located. The Eurocredit market is concerned with medium- and long-term loans. Multinational companies and governments are the main borrowers.

A **Eurobond** is an international bond underwritten by an international syndicate and sold in countries other than the country of the currency in which the issue is denominated. This market, too, has seen phenomenal growth over the last two decades.

The Eurobond Market

The Eurobond markets possess a number of advantages for borrowers. These include the following.

1. The size and depth of the market are such that it has the capacity to absorb large and frequent issues.
2. The Eurobond market has a freedom and flexibility not found in domestic markets. The issuing techniques make it possible to bypass restrictions, such as requirements for official authorization, queueing arrangements, formal disclosure, exchange listing obligations and so forth, which govern the issue of securities by domestic as well as foreign borrowers in the individual national

markets. All the financial institutions involved in Eurobond issues are subject to at least one national jurisdiction. National authorities can, and sometimes do, make their influence felt, especially when their own currency is used to denominate the issue.

3. The costs of issue of Eurobonds, up to $2\frac{1}{2}$ per cent of the face value of the issue, are relatively low.

4. Interest costs on dollar Eurobonds are competitive with domestic bonds in New York. It is usual that multinationals are able to raise funds at a slightly lower cost in the Eurobond market than in their corresponding domestic market.

5. Maturities in the Eurobond market are suited to long-term funding requirements. Maturities may reach 30 years, but 15-year Eurobonds are more common. In the medium-term range, 5- to 10-year Eurobonds run into competition with medium-term Eurocurrency loans.

6. A key feature of the Eurobond market is the development of a reliable and extensive institutional framework for underwriting, distribution and placing of securities.

On the other side of the equation, there are a number of special characteristics of the Eurobond market which make it particular attractive to investors. These include the following features:

1. Eurobonds are issued in such a way that interest can be paid free of income tax or withholding taxes. Besides this, the bonds are issued in bearer form and held outside the country of the investor, enabling the less than scrupulous to evade domestic income tax and maintain anonymity. Some countries' exchange control regulations limit an investor's ability to purchase Eurobonds.

2. Issuers of Eurobonds have, on the whole, an excellent reputation for creditworthiness. Most of the borrowers, whether governments, international organizations or large multinational companies, have first-class reputations. The market is very much oriented to companies with well-known names.

3. A special advantage to borrowers, as well as lenders, is provided by convertible Eurobonds. Holders of convertibles are given an option to exchange their bonds at a fixed price and within a specified period for the stock of the parent company of the financing subsidiary. A bond with a warrant gives the bondholder an option to buy a certain number of ordinary shares at a stated price. The more the price of the underlying share rises, the more valuable the warrant becomes. Because warrants are usually detachable, the bondholder may retain the bond but sell the warrants.

4. The Eurobond market is active both as a primary and as a secondary market. This secondary market expanded in the late 1960s and early 1970s. Eurobonds are traded over the counter both locally and internationally by financial institutions that are ready to buy or sell Eurobonds for their own accounts or on behalf of clients. Just as telephone and telex linkages have integrated foreign exchange markets, so have they integrated the secondary market in Eurobonds. International trading in Eurobonds is greatly facilitated by a clearing house arrangement in Brussels called Euroclear. Participants in Euroclear can complete transactions by means of book entries rather than physical movements of the securities. This has removed the main barrier to secondary market trading, which had been the inability to deliver bonds on time. There are now various other clearing arrangements in the market.

Borrowing Internationally

Tapping foreign capital markets may be done by the parent company or a subsidiary borrowing in local markets. There are a number of special advantages associated with such a financial strategy.

Many companies carry on their main operations in countries whose domestic capital markets are comparatively small and possibly subject to drying up. Should the parent company be located in such a country, and should that company have fairly substantial needs for cash to invest in order to compete in world markets, then its growth and competitive ability may be constrained by the existence of shallow domestic financial markets, unless it taps international financing sources. This was one of the major problems confronting Novo Industri A/S, the pharmaceutical group based in Denmark, when in 1978 it launched its first dollar convertible Eurobond issue. The economics of the pharmaceutical industry, with its high added value, research and development levels, high capital intensity and its need for constant innovation, makes access to deep capital markets a necessary precondition to successful competition on a world scale. Novo was aware that the scale of its corporate strategy pivoted about the availability of substantial cash resources on an ongoing basis. It saw its domestic capital market as being small and subject to periods of illiquidity which meant that, if it wanted to pursue its strategic plan, it was necessary to look outside domestic capital markets.

These kinds of consideration are not too critical for companies based in the UK or the USA, but they can be very relevant in many other countries. Indeed, the lack of depth coupled with the illiquidity of some countries' capital markets may be the historical reasons for most large multinational businesses being based in countries with sophisticated financing sources. We believe that the lack of ready access to substantial domestic capital markets has constrained the growth of businesses in many smaller European countries and elsewhere in the world.

Besides the benefit of access to deeper financial markets, tapping capital markets outside its home country should enable the international company to take advantage of market imperfections that prevent the Fisher effect from holding in the short-term. It will be recalled that, according to the four-way equivalence model developed earlier in this chapter, real interest rates (that is, nominal rates adjusted for anticipated inflation) should tend towards equality. But, given that out model is rarely, if ever, totally in equilibrium, the company which has access to world financial markets, rather than just its domestic one, should be able to lower its costs of borrowing. Schematically, we would suggest a relationship like that shown in Figure 29.3. It is worth mentioning, however, that when a company taps international financial sources for the first time, it generally finds itself paying slightly more than an established borrower in terms of interest rates plus underwriting fees.

The Risks of Borrowing Internationally

International financing can be broadly categorized as falling into three classes embracing the following situations:

1. Financing in the currency in which cash inflows are expected.
2. Financing in a currency other than that in which cash inflows are expected, but with cover in the forward or swap market.
3. Financing in a currency other than that in which cash inflows are expected, but without forward cover or an appropriate swap.

Financing by way of the first two methods avoids foreign exchange risk. With funds

FIGURE 29.3   The International Cost of Borrowing

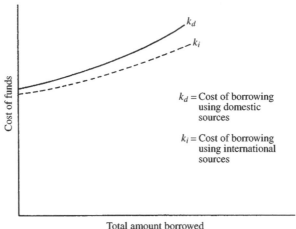

raised via the third method, though, foreign exchange risk is taken on. If the international Fisher effect were always to hold as an immutable iron law, and if foreign exchange markets were always in equilibrium, then the benefit accruing to the company through lower nominal interest rates on financing in a hard currency would be offset exactly by the amount by which the harder currency appreciated relative to other currencies. In other words, if the international Fisher effect holds the true cost of funds, at the pretax level, would be equal to the nominal interest rates in the home currency and this rate would apply irrespective of whence the international company were to draw its funds. As we know from the earlier discussion, the international Fisher effect does not hold in the short-term in the real world, and there is some doubt whether it holds in the long-term. If it is the case that we cannot feel confident about the international Fisher effect asserting itself in the long-run, and if it is also the case that exchange rate markets and interest rates are not always in equilibrium, then the international treasurer may seek either to avoid financing risk by hedging using such techniques as forward markets or to profit in this area by personal insights. Thus the international treasurer may seek to raise money denominated in overvalued currencies for relatively long maturities; and by the same token will avoid raising funds in undervalued currencies.

Just as disequilibrium in the international Fisher effect can give rise to financing opportunities for the astute corporate treasurer who is prepared to take on foreign exchange risk, so can market imperfections which flow from different tax regimes create opportunities. However, it must be borne in mind that financing in a currency other than that in which cash inflows are expected, but without forward cover, is a risky course of action.

This whole area of foreign currency financing without forward cover is full of pitfalls. Short-cuts are ill-advised. There is no substitute for careful analysis of the interaction between past movements of exchange rates, interest rates and inflation rates.

29.7 Derivatives and Hedging of Risk

The name *derivative* is fairly self-explanatory. A **derivative security** is a financial instrument whose payoffs and values are derived from, or depend on, something else. Often we speak of the thing that the derivative depends on as *underlying*. For example, in Chapter 22 we studied how options work. An option is a derivative. The value of a call option depends on the value of the underlying stock on which it is written. Actually, call options are quite complicated examples of derivatives. The vast majority of derivatives are simpler than call options. Most derivatives are forwards or futures contracts or what are called swaps and we will study each of these very briefly in this section. However, a complete picture of this area of finance is outside the scope of this book and interested readers should seek detailed coverage elsewhere in the specialist literature.[1]

Why do firms use derivatives? The answer is that derivatives are tools for changing the firm's risk exposure. Derivatives are to finance what scalpels are to surgery. By using derivatives, the firm can cut away unwanted portions of risk exposure and even transform the exposures into quite different forms. A central point in finance is that risk is undesirable. In our chapters on risk and return, we pointed out that individuals would choose risky securities only if the expected return compensated for the risk. Similarly, a firm will accept a project with high risk only if the return on the project compensates for this risk. Not surprisingly, then, firms are usually looking for ways to reduce their risk. When the firm reduces its risk exposure, it is said to be **hedging**. Hedging offsets the firm's risk, such as the risk in a project, by one or more transactions in the financial markets. Generally, hedging involves a risk position created by trading and an opposite position created in financial markets. Assume a US company has a DEM10 million receivable, due for receipt in three months' time, created by exporting (the US company has a DEM asset). It might enter into a three-month forward contract under which it undertakes to pay the bank DEM10 million in return for an agreed sum now of US dollars in three months' time. Thus, it takes on a DEM liability with the bank. By doing this, it has taken on a financial position which reverses the trading position as to currency, amount and timing of payment. It, therefore, converts a DEM asset into a USD asset.

Derivatives can also be used merely to change or even increase the firm's risk exposure. When this occurs, the firm is **speculating** on the movement of some economic variables—those that underlie the derivative. For example, if a derivative is purchased that will rise in value if interest rates rise and if the firm has no offsetting exposure to interest rate changes, then the firm is speculating that interest rates will rise and give it a profit on its derivatives position. Using derivatives to translate an opinion about whether interest rates or some other economic variable will rise or fall is the opposite of hedging—it is risk enhancing. Speculating on your views on the economy, and using derivatives to profit if that view turns out to be correct, is not necessarily wrong, but the speculator should always remember that sharp tools cut deep, and if the opinions on which the derivatives position is based turn out to be incorrect, the consequences can prove costly. Efficient market theory teaches how difficult it is to predict what markets will do. Most of the sad experiences with derivatives occurred not from their use as instruments for hedging and offsetting risk, but, rather, from speculation.

We have already looked at **forward contracts** in the context of foreign exchange. Remember, though, that a forward contract is not an option. Both the buyer and the seller are obligated to perform under the terms of the contract. Conversely, the buyer of an option *chooses* whether or not to exercise the option.

A forward contract should be contrasted with a **cash transaction**, that is, a transaction where exchange is immediate. No cash changes hands under a forward

---

[1] See, for example, the excellent text of John C. Hull (1997) *Options, Futures and Other Derivatives*, 3rd edn, 1997, Prentice Hall.

contract until the maturity date. A variant of the forward contract takes place on financial exchanges. Contracts on exchanges are usually called **futures contracts**. A futures contract differs somewhat from a forward contract. First, futures contracts are traded on an exchange whereas forward contracts are not generally traded on an exchange. Because of this, there is generally a liquid market in futures contracts. A buyer can net out her futures position with a sale. A seller can net out his futures position with a purchase. This procedure is analogous to the *netting-out* process in the options markets. However, the buyer of an options contract can also walk away from the contract by not exercising it. If a buyer of a futures contract does not subsequently sell her contract, she must take delivery.

Second, and most important, the prices of futures contracts are **marked to market** on a daily basis. This means that they are revalued, day by day, and accrued profits or losses are settled day by day. The consequence of this is that there are clearly many cash flows in futures contracts. However, after all the dust settles, the *net price* to the buyer is the price at which the contract was bought originally. Futures contracts entered into by a buyer and a seller are, technically, each with the futures exchange clearing house.

The mark-to-market provision on futures contracts has two related effects. The first concerns differences in net present value. For example, a large price drop immediately following purchase means an immediate outpayment for the buyer of a futures contract. Of course, the present value of the cash outflows is less to the buyer of a futures contract if a price rise followed purchase. Though this effect could be substantial in certain theoretical circumstances, it appears to be of quite limited importance in the real world.

Second, the firm must have extra liquidity to handle a sudden outflow prior to expiration. This added risk may make the futures contract less attractive than the forward contract.

The mark-to-market provisions minimize the chance of default on a futures contract. Because of this default issue, futures contracts generally involve individuals and institutions who know and can trust each other. Textbooks on futures contracts from one or two decades ago frequently included a statement such as, 'No major default has ever occurred on the commodity exchanges'. No textbook published after the Hunt Brothers defaulted on silver contracts in the 1970s can make that claim. Nevertheless, the extremely low default rate in futures contracts is truly amazing.

Futures contracts are traded in three main areas: agricultural commodities, metals and oil, and financial assets. This enables firms to hedge (and speculate) on prices of agricultural commodities, metals and oil, and financial assets, such as exchange rates, interest rates and levels of stock markets.

Swaps are close cousins to forwards and futures contracts. Swaps are arrangements between two counterparties to exchange cash flows over time. There is enormous flexibility in the forms that swaps can take, but the two basic types are **interest-rate swaps** and **currency swaps**. Often these are combined when interest received in one currency is swapped for interest in another currency. So, swaps are agreements to exchange flows over time. The fist major type is an interest-rate swap in which one pattern of coupon payments, say fixed payments, are exchanged for another, say, coupons that float with LIBOR. LIBOR stands for the London Interbank Offered Rate and it is the rate that most international banks charge one another for loans in the London market. LIBOR is commonly used as the marker reference for a floating-rate commitment, and, depending on the creditworthiness of the borrower, the rate can vary from LIBOR to LIBOR plus one percentage point or more over LIBOR. The second major type is a currency swap in which an agreement is struck to swap payments denominated in one currency for payments in another currency over time.

Swaps, like forwards and futures, are essentially zero-sum transactions, which is to say that in both cases the market sets prices at a fair level, and neither party has any substantial bargain or loss at the moment the deal is struck. For example, in the currency swap, the swap rate is some average of the market expectation of what the exchange rate will be over the life of the swap. In the interest-rate swap, the rates are set as the fair floating and fixed rates for the creditor, taking account of the creditworthiness of the counterparties.

29.8   Summary and Conclusions

1. Figure 29.1 sets out a model relating spot and forward exchange rates, interest differentials, inflation differentials and expected movements in spot. The model is most important. Indeed, in the study of foreign exchange it is perhaps the single most important set of theoretical ideas.

    The model itself is an equilibrium model. In the real world, markets are rarely, if ever, in equilibrium. Therefore, it should not be surprising if, for lengthy periods, parts of the model do not hold in the real world. Markets move towards equilibrium and the same is true of foreign exchange markets.

2. Evidence suggests that interest rate parity holds virtually all the time at the level of quotations to companies, but the remaining parts of the model are found to be long-run phenomena. Short-term deviations are the order of the day with the Fisher effect, purchasing power parity, the international Fisher effect and expectations theory. While this imposes threats to companies, it also creates the opportunities that were referred to in the subsection headed 'Practicalities' in Section 29.3.

3. Foreign exchange markets comprise the framework of individuals, firms, banks and brokers who buy and sell foreign currencies. Market participants include companies, individuals, commercial banks, central banks and brokers. Between 90 and 95 per cent of all foreign exchange transactions involve banks on both sides of the deal. Trade accounts for only 1 or 2 per cent of all transactions nowadays.

4. Time zones around the world overlap, hence the foreign exchange markets are in effect open all the time in one centre or another, except at weekends.

5. International capital budgeting, like its domestic counterpart, focuses upon expected incremental cash flows associated with a project. But international capital budgeting is more complex because of certain factors peculiar to international operations.

6. There are six main categories of complexity. These embrace situations where exchange controls prevent full remittance of overseas incremental cash generation created via the new project, where part of the parent input is by way of equipment, where exchange rates are not expected to be constant throughout a project's life (and this probably applies to all overseas projects) where different tax rates apply in the host and home country, where royalties and fees are to be paid out of income of the new investment to a group company in the home country and where there are substantial knock-on effects and growth options. These distinctive characteristics are extremely important. They are rarely fully appreciated, even within the most sophisticated of companies, and the astute treasurer can play a big part in helping his or her company grapple with the difficulties surrounding international investment appraisal. Many poor international investment decisions have been made because of the failure of the multinational company fully to comprehend that it is distributable parent cash flows that matter rather than mere project cash flows.

7. International borrowing enables companies to lower their average cost of finance, and it may be an important part of the funding equation for companies whose base is within countries with shallow capital markets, as well as for major multinational companies.

8. International financing can be categorized into three classes. First, a company may borrow

internationally in currencies in which it expects cash inflows to accrue. Second, it may borrow in a currency other than that in which cash inflows are expected, but it may cover foreign exchange exposure. Third, the company may finance itself in a currency other than that in which cash inflows are expected, but not take forward cover. The last of these funding options is the most risky. While the interest rate and capital repayments are fixed in foreign currency terms the problem is that, because exchange rates may change, the home currency cost of borrowing is uncertain. It is possible to estimate the true cost of an uncovered foreign borrowing by taking into account expected exchange rate movements and timing of cash inflows. This is done using the discounted cash flow technique with cash flows expressed in home currency terms after allowing for expected foreign exchange rate movements. With flows expressed in home currency, the calculation of the true cost of the loan (in home currency terms) is the discounted cash flow rate which equates expected inflows and outflows under the financing.

9. Firms hedge to reduce risk.

10. A forward contract is an agreement by two parties to sell an item for cash at a later date. The price is set at the time the agreement is signed. However, cash changes hands on the date of delivery. Forward contracts are generally not traded on organized exchanges.

11. Futures contracts are also agreements for future delivery. They have certain advantages, such as liquidity, that forward contracts do not. An unusual feature of futures contracts is the mark-to-market convention. If the price of a futures contract falls on a particular day, every buyer of the contract must pay money to the clearing house. Every seller of the contract receives money from the clearing house. Everything is reversed if the price rises. The mark-to-market convention is designed to prevent defaults on futures contracts.

KEY TERMS

Foreign exchange markets   645
Spot market   645
Eurodollar   646
Eurocurrency   646
Euromarkets   646
Interest rate parity   649
Covered interest arbitrage   651
Uncovered interest arbitrage   651
Fisher effect   651
Purchasing power parity   652
International Fisher effect   652
Expectations theory   653
Forward rates   656

Forward premium   656
Forward discount   656
Eurobond   663
Derivative security   666
Hedging   667
Speculating   667
Forward contract   667
Cash transaction   667
Futures contract   668
Marked to market   668
Swaps   668
Interest-rate swaps   668
Currency swaps   668

QUESTIONS AND PROBLEMS

Foreign Exchange Rates

In the problems to this chapter, assume that all interest rates quoted are per annum rates. Calculate 90 day rates by taking one-quarter of the annual rate. Also assume that: only one rate is quoted, rather than a bid/offer rate, deals may be done at this rate whether they are purchase or sale deals, lend or borrow deals. This is, of course, a simplifying assumption. Also disregard any transaction costs; for substantial deals these are generally taken care of in the bid/offer spread. Take one month as one-twelfth of a year, two months as one-sixth, and so on.

29.1 The spot rate for the deutschemark in New York is USD0.55
    a. What should the spot price for the US dollar be in Frankfurt?
    b. Should the dollar be quoted at DEM1.85 in Frankfurt, how would the market react?

29.2 When the deutschmark spot rate was quoted at USD0.55 in New York, the US market was quoting sterling at GBP1.60

      a. What should the price of the pound be in Frankfurt?

      b. If sterling were quoted at DEM2.80/GBP in Frankfurt, what profit opportunities would exist?

29.3 Your company has to make a USD1 million payment in three months' time. The dollars are available now. You decide to invest them for three months and you are given the following information

    ● the US dollar deposit rate is 8 per cent p.a.

    ● the sterling deposit rate is 10 per cent p.a.

    ● the spot exchange rate is USD1.80/GBP

    ● the three-month forward rate is USD1.78/GBP

      a. Where should your company invest for the better return?

      b. Assuming that interest rates and the spot exchange rate remain as above, what forward rate would yield an equilibrium situation?

      c. Assuming that the US dollar interest rate and the spot and forward rates remain as in the original question, where would you invest if the sterling rate were 14 per cent per annum?

      d. With the originally stated spot and forward rates and the same dollar deposit rate, what is the equilibrium sterling deposit rate?

29.4 The spot rate for the French franc is USD0.1500 and the three-month forward rate is USD0.1505. Your company is prepared to speculate that the French franc will move to USD0.1650 by the end of three months.

      a. Are the quotations given direct or indirect Paris quotations?

      b. How would the speculation be undertaken using the spot market only?

      c. How would the speculation be arranged using forward markets?

      d. If your company were prepared to put USD1 million at risk on the deal, what would the profit outturns be if expectations were met ignore all interest rate implications.

      e. How would your answer to (*d*) above differ were you to take into account interest rate implications.

29.5 A foreign exchange trader gives the following quotes for the Belgian franc spot, one-month, three-month and six-month to a US-based treasurer.

      USD0.02478/80   4/6   9/8   14/11

      a. Calculate the outright quotes for one, three and six months forward.

      b. If the treasurer wished to buy Belgian francs three months forward, how much would he or she pay in dollars?

      c. If he or she wished to purchase US dollars one month forward, how much would the treasurer have to pay in Belgian francs?

      d. Assuming that Belgian francs are being bought, what is the premium or discount, for the one-, three-, and six-month forward rates in annual percentage terms?

      e. What do the above quotations imply in respect of the term structure of interest rates in the USA and Belgium?

29.6 You are given the following spot quotations in London:

      USD1 = CHF1.5485/95

      USD1 = DEM1.7935/45

      GBP1 = USD1.6325/35

    Calculate the following bid/offer quotations, also in London:

      a. CHF against DEM

      b. GBP against DEM

International Investment and Financing Decisions

29.7 The Inter-Continental Hotel Company is considering investing in a new chalet hotel at Verbier in Switzerland. The initial investment required is for USD2 million, or CHF4 million at the current exchange rate of USD1 = CHF2. Profits for the first ten years will be reinvested, at which time Inter-Continental expects to sell out. Inter-Continental estimates that its interest in the hotel will realise CHF6.5 million in six years' time

      a. Indicate what factors you would regard as relevant in evaluating this investment

      b. How will changes in the value of the Swiss franc affect the investment?

      c. Indicate possible ways of forecasting the USD:CHF exchange rate ten years ahead

29.8 Compare and contrast international investment and financing decisions with their domestic counterparts.

APPENDIX 29A

A DEDUCTIVE PROOF OF THE FOUR-WAY EQUIVALENCE MODEL

Interest Rate Parity

Assume that an investor has GBP1 million to invest for a period of one year. The exchange rate quotation for the US dollar is USD1.610000 spot, and USD1.530949 for twelve months forward.[2] Twelve-month interest rates are $8\frac{15}{16}$ per cent for Eurodollar deposits, and $14\frac{9}{16}$ per cent for Eurosterling deposits. The investor has at least two options which avoid foreign exchange risk:

1. Invest GBP1 million in a Eurosterling deposit at $14\frac{9}{16}$ per cent.
2. *a.* Convert GBP1 million into US dollars at USD1.610000.
   b. Invest the proceeds in a Eurodollar deposit (the point being that the deposit is a dollar deposit attracting an interest rate appropriate to dollar placements; for one year the rate is $8\frac{15}{16}$ per cent).
   c. Sell the calculated proceeds forward one year at GBP1.530949.

Investing in Eurosterling, the proceeds after one year will be GBP1.145,625. Investing in Eurodollars the proceeds after one year may be calculated as follows:

1. The amount invested will be the spot proceeds of USD1,610,000.
2. These will accumulate at $8\frac{15}{16}$ per cent to USD1,753,894 after one year.
3. The sterling proceeds from selling this forward will be:

$$1,753,894 \div 1.530949 = \text{GBP}1,145,625$$

Thus the two opportunities offer the same return. Were this not so, operators in the foreign exchange markets could buy in on centre, convert the money into another currency, and invest at a profit in another centre.

The actions of arbitrageurs ensure that profitable opportunities based on the above kind of operation do not last for more than very short periods. Where profitable opportunities do exist, the market would say that there are opportunities for profitable covered interest arbitrage. But exploitation of these opportunities themselves creates movements in exchange and interest rates, ensuring that the tendency in the foreign exchange market is towards equilibrium between differences in interest rates and differences between forward and spot rates.

The interest rate differential, called the *interest agio*, is calculated as:

$$\frac{i_\$ - i_£}{1 + i_£} = 8\tfrac{15}{16}\% - \frac{14\tfrac{9}{16}\%}{1.14\tfrac{9}{16}\%}$$
$$= -0.0491$$
$$= -4.91\%$$

Notice that calculating the interest differential precisely in this way, which is the correct method, differs from making a straight deduction:

$$i_\$ - i_£ = 8\tfrac{15}{16} - 14\tfrac{9}{16} = -5\tfrac{5}{8}\%$$

The annual forward premium is the *exchange agio* and is given by:

$$\frac{f_0 - s_0}{s_0} = \frac{1.530949 - 1.610000}{1.610000}$$
$$= -0.0491$$
$$= -4.91\%$$

If there are no opportunities for profitable covered interest arbitrage then the interest agio will exactly equal the exchange agio. This is the interest rate parity theorem and it is summarized in Table 29A.1. An algebraic proof of the theory is given in Table 29A.2.

---

[2] The foreign exchange market quotes the US dollar sterling to four decimal places. In this appendix, the quotation is to six places to explain more clearly the principles involved.

TABLE 29A.1   **Interest Rate Parity**

Difference in interest rates		Difference between forward and spot rate
$\dfrac{i_\$ - i_\pounds}{1 + i_\pounds}$	$=$	$\dfrac{f_0 - s_0}{s_0}$

TABLE 29A.2   **Interest Rate Parity Proved**

A US exporter due to receive GBP*A* in one year (at time t where $t = 12$ months) might avoid foreign exchange risk in one of two ways.

Using the forward market his US dollar proceeds at time t would be \$$f_0 A$. Alternatively, he could borrow GBP$A/(1 + i_\pounds)$ and convert it into US dollars, giving \$$[A/(1 + i_\pounds)]s_0$. Investing this now would yield at time t the sum of:

$$\$ \frac{A}{(1 + i_\pounds)} s_0 (1 + i_\$)$$

Assuming equilibrium between money markets and foreign exchange markets, this must equal \$$f_0 A$. Written mathematically:

$$\frac{A}{(1 + i_\pounds)} s_0 (1 + i_\$) = f_0 A$$

Dividing by A and rearranging:

$$f_0 = s_0 \frac{(1 + i_\$)}{(1 + i_\pounds)}$$

Dividing by s_0 and deducting 1:

$$\frac{f_0}{s_0} - 1 = \frac{(1 + i_\$)}{(1 + i_\pounds)} - 1$$

That is:

$$\frac{f_0 - s_0}{s_0} = \frac{(1 + i_\$)}{(1 + i_\pounds)} - 1$$

$$= \frac{(i_\$ - i_\pounds)}{(1 + i_\pounds)}$$

Purchasing Power Parity

If a commodity sells in the US at USD300 per kilo and in the UK at GBP220, with the spot exchange rate at USD1.50/GBP, a profitable opportunity exists to buy in the USA, ship to the UK and sell there. Arbitrageurs buying in New York and selling in London would tend to increase the US price and reduce the UK price until no profit potential existed. Within the range of costs such as shipping and insurance, the prices of an otherwise identical commodity in two centres should not differ. Thus:

$$\text{GBP price of commodity} \times \text{USD price of GBP} = \text{USD price of commodity}$$

that is

$$\text{USD price of GBP} = \frac{\text{USD price of commodity}}{\text{GBP price of commodity}}$$

This kind of relationship should tend to hold for all internationally traded goods, that is

$$\text{Price of GBP} = \frac{\text{USD price of an internationally traded commodity}}{\text{GBP price of the internationally traded commodity}}$$

Changes in the ratio of domestic prices of internationally traded goods in two centres should be reflected in changes in the price of currencies—the exchange rates.

In order to take the argument to the next stage, we should strictly speaking, limit our attention to relative prices of internationally traded goods. But we approximate. Purchasing power parity (PPP) theory uses relative general price changes as a proxy for prices of internationally traded goods. Applying it to the previous equation, we should obtain:

$$\text{Change in USD price of GBP} = \frac{\text{Change in USD price level}}{\text{Change in GBP price level}}$$

Thus, if inflation in the USA is 8 per cent p.a. and it is 12 per cent p.a. in the UK, then applying purchasing power parity theory we would expect the pound sterling to fall against the dollar by $(0.08 - 0.12)/1.12$, that is 3.6 per cent. Again, this calculation is precise. A quick approximation based merely on straight inflation differentials would suggest a devaluation of 4 per cent p.a. (The justification for using the precise formulation, rather than the approximate one, is considered in the algebraic formulation in Table 29A.4.

Purchasing power parity theory, itself an approximation since it uses the general price level as a proxy for the price level for internationally traded goods, suggests that changes in the spot rate of exchange may be estimated by reference to expected inflation differentials. Table 29A.3 summarizes the purchasing power parity theorem and Table 29A.4 gives an algebraic proof.

TABLE 29A.3   Purchasing Power Parity

Expected difference in inflation rates		Expected change in spot rates
$\dfrac{{}^{*}p_\$ - {}^{*}p_\pounds}{1 + {}^{*}p_\pounds}$	$=$	$\dfrac{{}^{*}s_t - s_0}{s_0}$

TABLE 29A.4   Purchasing Power Parity Proved

Given that relative price levels underpin the spot rate of exchange at any date, the values of the spot rate now and the expected spot rate at time t are given respectively by:

$$s_0 = \frac{p_\$}{p_\pounds} \quad \text{and} \quad {}^{*}s_t = \frac{p_\$(1 + {}^{*}p_\$)}{p_\pounds(1 + {}^{*}p_\pounds)}$$

Subtracting these two equations:

$$ {}^{*}s_k - s_0 = \frac{p_\$}{p_\pounds}\left[\frac{(1 + {}^{*}p_\$)}{(1 + {}^{*}p_\pounds)} - 1\right]$$

Dividing by s_0 (which is the equivalent of multiplying by $p_\pounds/p_\$$)

$$\frac{{}^{*}s_t - s_0}{s_0} = \frac{{}^{*}p_\$ - {}^{*}p_\pounds}{1 + {}^{*}p_\pounds}$$

Although simplest, then, purchasing power parity predicts that the exchange rate changes to compensate for differences in inflation between two countries. Thus, if country A has a higher inflation rate than its trading partners, the exchange rate of the former should weaken to compensate for this relativity. If country A's nominal exchange rate falls, and if that fall is an exact compensation for inflation differentials, its real effective exchange rate is said to remain constant. Purchasing power parity predicts that real effective exchange rates will remain constant through time.

The Fisher Effect

According to the Fisher effect (sometimes referred to as Fisher's closed hypothesis) nominal interest rates in a country reflect anticipated real returns adjusted for local inflation expectations. In a world where investors are internationally mobile, expected real rates of return should tend towards equality, reflecting the fact that in search of higher real returns, investors' arbitraging actions will force these returns towards each other. At least, this should hold with respect to the free market Eurocurrency interest rates. Constraints on international capital mobility create imperfections which, among other things, prevent this relationship from holding in domestic interest rate markets. So nominal Eurocurrency interest rates may differ for different currencies but, according to the Fisher effect, only by virtue of different inflation expectations. And these inflation differentials should underpin expected changes in the spot rates of exchange. In other words, we would expect US and UK free market interest investment to yield equal real returns. Differences in nominal returns would reflect expected inflation differentials. This would give us the Fisher effect theorem summarized in Table 29A.5 and proved using elementary mathematics in Table 29A.6.

TABLE 29A.5   The Fisher Effect

Difference in interest rates		Difference between forward and spot rates
$\dfrac{i_\$ - i_£}{1 + i_£}$	$=$	$\dfrac{{}^*p_\$ - {}^*p_£}{1 + {}^*p_£}$

Table 29A.6   The Fisher Effect Proved

Local interest rates will equal the international real return (r) adjusted for expected local inflation. Thus:

$$1 + i_\$ = (1 + r)(1 + {}^*p_\$) \quad \text{and} \quad 1 + i_£ = (1 + r)(1 + {}^*p_£)$$

Subtracting these two equations:

$$i_\$ - i_£ = (1 + r)({}^*p_\$ - {}^*p_£)$$

Dividing by $(1 + r)$:

$$\frac{i_\$ - i_£}{1 + r} = {}^*p_\$ - {}^*p_£$$

Dividing by $(1 + {}^*p_£)$:

$$\frac{i_\$ - i_£}{1 + i_£} = \frac{{}^*p_\$ - {}^*p_£}{1 + {}^*p_£}$$

Expectations Theory

We have already demonstrated the following equivalues:

Differences between forward and spot rates	$=$	Differences in interest rates
Differences in interest rates	$=$	Differences in expected inflation rates
Differences in expected inflation rates	$=$	Expected change in spot rate

By logic it follows that the difference between the forward and spot rates equals the expected change in the spot rate. This is the expectations theory of exchange rates.

If users of the foreign exchange market were not interested in risk, then the forward rate of exchange would depend solely on what people expected the future spot rate to be. A 12-month forward rate of USD1.530949 to the pound would exist only because traders expected the spot rate in 12 months to be USD1.530949 to the pound. If they anticipated that it would be higher than this, nobody would sell sterling at the forward rate. By the same token, if they expected it to be lower, nobody would buy at the forward rate.

If traders do care about risk, the forward rate might be higher or lower than the expected spot rate. Suppose that a US exporter is certain to receive GBP1 million in six months' time, he might wait until six months have elapsed then convert to dollars or he might sell the pound forward. The first action involves exchange risk; the latter does not. To avoid foreign exchange risk, the trader may be willing to pay something slightly different from the expected spot price.

On the other side of the equation, there may be traders who wish to buy sterling six months away. To avoid the risk associated with movements in foreign exchange rates, they may be prepared to pay a forward price a little higher than the expected spot price.

Some traders find it safer to sell sterling forward; some traders find it safer to buy sterling forward. If the former group predominates, the forward price of sterling is likely to be less than the expected spot price. If the latter group predominates, the forward price is likely to be greater than the expected spot price. The actions of the predominant group are likely to adjust rates until they arrive at the hypothesized position in Table 29A.7.

TABLE 29A.7 Expectations Theory

Difference between forward and spot rates		Expected change in spot rate
$\dfrac{f_0 - s_0}{s_0}$	$=$	$\dfrac{{}^{*}s_t - s_0}{s_0}$

The International Fisher Effect

The hypothesis that differences in interest rate should underpin the expected movement in the spot rate of exchange is termed the international Fisher effect; it is sometimes also called Fishers' open hypothesis. Again, it follows by logic from the equivalences already proved, and it is shown as the diagonal in Table 29.1

We can now combine the separate relationships we have been discussing to show the four-way equivalence in the foreign exchange market. This relationship is summarized in Table 29A.1.

The Road to Economic and Monetary Union

No overview of foreign exchange markets would be complete without reference, however brief, to the **European Monetary System (EMS)** and **Economic and Monetary Union (EMU)**. The purpose, structure, functioning, special features and tensions of the EMS are summarized in this chapter. It is worth beginning this section by being clear that the EMS is neither a pure fixed exchange rate system nor a pure floating rate mechanism.

The EMS was created in 1979 by the European Union (EU) countries with the dual objectives of establishing a zone of exchange rate stability to encourage trade and growth and of accelerating the convergence and integration of economic policies within the EU.

30.1   Principal Features of the EMS

The main characteristic of the EMS is the operation of its exchange rate system. The **European Currency Unit (ECU)** is the nucleus of the EMS. The ECU comprises a basket of fixed amounts of EU currencies. The ECU will become the Euro, the common European currency, should EMU proceed to its planned goal under the **Maastricht Treaty**—see section 30.2.

The ECU is used both as the numeraire of the **Exchange Rate Mechanism (ERM)** and as a means of settlement between central banks within the EU. Additionally, it exists as a unit of account for official EU business. The ECU is frequently used as a currency of denomination in the international credit and bond markets. Around 3 per cent of international bond issues are denominated in ECUs and some EU country's governments also issue domestic treasury bills in ECUs. However, only around 5 per cent of European trade is invoiced in ECUs. ECU interest rates are equal to a weighted average of the component domestic rates of the EU currencies. In practice, synthetic ECU yields and forward exchange rates are often calculated from a hypothetical basket containing only those currencies with liquid domestic money markets. Note that sterling is a component of the ECU. At the time of writing, however, the British pound was not a member of the exchange rate mechanism (ERM) of the EMS.

The Exchange Rate Mechanism

The central idea underpinning the European Monetary System was to achieve currency stability through co-ordinated exchange rate management. This would facilitate trade within the EU and set the stage for moves towards a single currency around the end of the twentieth century.

The exchange rate mechanism, a system of flexible exchange rates, was the central plank of the EMS. Originally, countries participating in the ERM would keep the value of their currencies within margins of $2\frac{1}{4}$ per cent either side of central rates against the other currencies in the mechanism. Sterling, the peseta and the escudo, which joined the ERM several years after its start-up, were allowed to move within margins of 6 per cent upwards and downwards. But all this has subsequently changed—see 'The Wake of Black Wednesday' in Section 30.2.

The ERM worked by requiring members to intervene in the foreign exchange markets to prevent currencies breaching their ceilings or floors against the other currencies. Thus, if the peseta fell to its floor within the system, the Bank of Spain would be required to buy pesetas and/or sell other ERM currencies to bolster the peseta against its fellow European exchange rates. Other members would be required to help by intervening on behalf of the weak currency. In our example, this would prop up the peseta before it fell through its floor.

As a second resort, the country whose currency was under pressure could raise its short-term interest rates to make its currency more attractive to investors. If intervention on the foreign exchanges and adjustment of interest rates failed to stop a currency from moving outside its ERM limits, a last resort would be a realignment of the central rates to relieve the tensions in the system.

In the early years of the ERM, there were several realignments. But from 1987 until the massive tensions of the autumn of 1992 there were none. Many would argue that it was the failure of the mechanism to realign in response to the strength of the deutschemark that led to these very tensions. So let us look at these problems further. But before we do, there are a couple of highly pertinent aspects that require discussion—these relate to the EMU and German Reunification.

Concept Question

- What are the differences between the EMS and the ERM?

30.2   Economic and Monetary Union

Countries may link their currencies together in various ways. At one end of the spectrum would be a relatively light linkage with little sacrifice of independence of monetary policy; at the other, there might be a convergence of policy such that independence is given up all together. In 1989, a committee headed by Jacques Delors, who was then president of the European Commission, recommended a three-stage transition to a goal of monetary union at the strongly convergent end of the above financial spectrum. The ultimate goal was for Economic and Monetary Union (EMU), a European Union in which national currencies are replaced by a single EU currency managed by a sole central bank operating on behalf of all EU members.

The Delors vision involved three stages. In the first, all EU members would join the ERM. In stage 2, exchange rate margins would be narrowed and certain macroeconomic policy decisions placed under more centralized EU control. In essence, stage 3 of the plan involves the replacement of national currencies by a European currency and the vesting of monetary policy decisions in a European System of Central Banks, similar to the US Federal Reserve System and headed by a European Central Bank.

On December 10, 1991, the leaders of the EU countries met at Maastricht in the province of Limburg at the most southerly tip of the Netherlands. They proposed far reaching amendments to the Treaty of Rome. These amendments would put the EU squarely on course to EMU. Included in the 250-page Maastricht Treaty were provisions calling for a start to stage 2 of the Delors plan on January 1, 1994 and a start to stage 3 no later than January 1, 1999. In addition to its monetary policy provisions, the Maastricht Treaty proposed steps towards harmonizing social policy within the EU (with rules on workplace safety, consumer protection and immigration) and towards centralizing foreign and defence policy decisions that EU members currently make on their own.

In terms of moving to stage 3, **convergence criteria** are set for individual countries as follows:

- The inflation rate must be within 1.5 percentage points of the average rate of the three EU states with the lowest inflation.
- The long-term interest rates must be within 2 percentage points of the average rate of the three EU states with the lowest interest rates.
- The national budget deficit must be below 3 per cent of GNP.
- The national debt must not exceed 60 per cent of GNP.
- The national currency must not have been devalued for two years and must have remained within the 2.25 per cent fluctuation margin provided for by the EMS.

Despite the optimism of Maastricht, the treaty was soon being viewed with scepticism. Many Europeans began to question whether their countries would be wise to sacrifice control over their national economic policies. The Maastricht Treaty could not come into force until all EU countries had ratified it through national referendum or parliamentary vote. In June 1992, the treaty, in its very first electoral test, was narrowly rejected by Danish voters. Prospects for EMU worsened later that year. In September 1992, ERM parities were hit by speculative attacks that led to the British pound and the Italian lira making their exits from the ERM on September 16, 1992—called 'Black Wednesday'. Investors and speculators shifted vast funds out of sterling and the lira into the deutschemark. Both sank well below their ERM floors as the authorities gave up the struggle to keep them within their old bands. On that day, the UK government tried to save the pound by intervening heavily and by announcing an increase in interest rates from 10 per cent to 15 per cent. But this was not enough to stem the flow against sterling, and after a steady drain on reserves the British government pulled out and lowered interest rates back to 10 per cent—and all on the same day.

For the next eleven months or so, relative calm returned to the ERM currencies. But, in August 1993 tensions rose again—this time centred on the French franc. France was in a recession with high unemployment yet was unable to cut its very high interest rates much below Germany's because both were within the same currency zone.

One solution might have been for Germany to lower its lending rates, but the Bundesbank, the German central bank, did not contemplate such a move for fear of encouraging inflation at home. The prime duty of the Bundesbank, an independent central bank, as set out in its constitution, is to monitor domestic monetary policy. The Bundesbank is required, by law, to put the need for low German inflation before the troubles of the ERM.

Pressure mounted. Finance ministers of the EU countries met to find a solution. Their answer was to widen the currency bands for all except the deutschemark and the Dutch guilder to 15 per cent. The mark/guilder band remained at $2\frac{1}{4}$ per cent. For the rest, the bands were so wide that although the ERM survives, at the time of writing, in name, the currencies are effectively floating. With the new bands, a currency could move by 30 per cent—from its ceiling to its floor—against another member without falling out of the system.

One of the key sources of tension for the ERM in its recent years of turmoil flowed from German Reunification. Its effects on European currency rates are now considered.

German Reunification

The reunification of East and West Germany in 1990 created an economic disturbance that deeply affected the EMS. East German wages, initially far below those in the West, moved upwards as East German workers demanded parity with workers elsewhere in the country. But many East German workers lacked the skills, training and modern equipment of those in the West. Expected flows of private investment to modernize eastern Germany failed to materialize. Coupled with high European recession, the result was high unemployment in the East and a steep fall in East German output. The western side of Germany soon found itself making payments to the east—to support and retrain unemployed workers, to renovate antiquated capital stock and to clean up the East's polluted environment. By 1991, western Germans were transferring an amount well over 5 per cent of their income to the east. The German government borrowed much of the necessary sums rather than raise taxes. Hence the public fiscal deficit widened sharply.

Further inflationary pressures came from the liberal spending of the eastern Germans, who had received a liberal trade of their ostmarks into deutschemarks, to purchase the high-quality consumer durables they had been denied under Communism. To halt rising prices, Germany's Bundesbank tightened monetary controls in 1992 and also pushed interest rates to historically high levels. By then, the European economies, other than Germany, had been weakening for more than a year. One factor partially underpinning this weakness may have been the German aggregate demand expansion itself, which had already raised interest rates in Germany and throughout the EMS. A second factor behind Europe's recession was continuing slow economic activity in the USA and the resulting real depreciation of the dollar—this moved world demand away from European goods and toward American goods.

Germany's decision to tighten monetary policy passed a problem on to France and Germany's other ERM partners. Should they tighten their own monetary policies in unison with Germany's to maintain ERM exchange rates? Or should they devalue their currencies against the mark as a way of stimulating international demand for their products? While criticizing Germany's tight monetary policy, the ERM partners allowed their own interest rates to rise in line with Germany and thereby resisted devaluation. With EMU seemingly in reach, governments wanted to avoid being forced into a new alignment. The defence of EMS exchange rate levels deepened the European recession outside of Germany. Germany denied any responsibility for the rest of Europe's economic problems and refused to make substantial policy changes, although it could be argued that a temporary withdrawal of the German mark from the ERM might better have kept the ERM on course and avoided the turmoil that subsequently affected exchange rate markets in Europe. The Germans themselves worried that a European central bank, following EMU, would be less zealous than their own Bundesbank in fighting inflation. With unemployment on the rise throughout Europe, job losses were blamed on the European Union's liberal trade and migration policies and the ERM.

Black Wednesday

In June 1992, Denmark, the first country to vote on the Maastricht accord, rejected the treaty by a small margin. Danish rejection raised serious legal problems because amendments to the Treaty of Rome required unanimous approval of all EU members.

A similar referendum was scheduled for September in France. The prospect of a French refusal to ratify Maastricht encouraged foreign exchange market participants to gamble that weak currencies would devalue. The first currencies to be hit by speculative attacks were the Finnish markka and the Swedish krona. Neither belonged to the ERM, but both wished for EU membership and had pegged their currencies to the ECU. Finland capitulated on September 8, 1992 letting the markka depreciate steeply against the ECU. Sweden was successful temporarily in defending the krona. Speculation only died down after the Swedish central bank, the Riksbank, allowed interest rates on overnight loans to reach 500 per cent per annum, about 1.35 per cent per day. At the same time, the UK and Italian governments were struggling to keep their currencies above the floors of their ERM bands.

Speculation against the pound and lira continued. By the evening of Friday September 11, the Bundesbank had spent USD16 billion in EMS intervention supporting the lira. The Bundesbank was reluctant to spend any more. Over the weekend, the EMS agreed to let Italy devalue its currency by 7 per cent against the ECU. The lira's parity change was the first ERM realignment since January 1987. It signified to players in the foreign exchange market that attacks on other ERM currencies might succeed.

On Tuesday, September 15, Bundesbank President Helmut Schlesinger was reported in a German newspaper as saying that a broad currency realignment would be needed to ease existing tensions in the ERM. His remark set off a massive speculative attack against the pound and the lira in particular. On September 16, a day now known as Black Wednesday because of the damage done to the ERM, the pound was allowed to float after the Bank of England lost billions of dollars defending it. This action followed numerous repeated pledges by the UK government not to realign. Despite having devalued only two days before, Italy took the lira out of the ERM rather than lose more reserves. Spain devalued the peseta and reimposed exchange controls.

Then the French franc came under attack, despite an inflation rate lower than Germany's. Heavy and prolonged intervention by the Bank of France and the Bundesbank, plus a sharp rise in French interest rates, eventually extricated the franc from the bottom of its ERM band. After the most turbulent week in ERM history, French voters narrowly approved the Maastricht Treaty on September 20 and thereby gave the EMU another chance, albeit a relatively slim and faltering one.

The Wake of Black Wednesday

Currency upheavals continued through 1992 and into the spring of 1993. Later in 1992 the Portuguese escudo was devalued, the Spanish peseta devalued again and the Swedish krona and Norwegian krone, although not in the EMS but linked to it, were set afloat. Early in 1993, the Irish punt was devalued, the escudo devalued a second time, and the Spanish peseta devalued a third time. The French franc and Danish krone continued to be under periodic speculative attack. These events took place against deepening recession in the ERM economies, not helped by the Bundesbank's insistence on making only gradual cuts in German interest rates.

In the spring of 1993, Denmark held a second referendum on the Maastricht Treaty after the EU had given Denmark the right to refuse participation in the common monetary and defence policies which the treaty would create. Second time round, Denmark agreed and the British government followed suit by a narrow parliamentary majority for ratification. By 1993, all EU members but Germany had approved the Maastricht Treaty.

During July 1993, speculators attacked the French franc and other ERM currencies again after a new disagreement over interest rates between Germany and other ERM members. On Friday, July 30, alone, the Bundesbank sold nearly USD30 billion worth of deutschemarks to help prop up the French franc. The Bank of France itself used up all of its foreign reserves in pursuit of this goal. The following Monday, August 2, ERM rates, with the exception of the mark/Dutch guilder rate, would float within widened bands of plus or minus 15 per cent around the existing central parities. This change in ERM rules was extended to avoid a formal devaluation of the French franc, a step the French government had pledged to avoid at all costs, while leaving the Bundesbank free to lower German interest rates slowly.

EU leaders insisted that these problems would not alter the Maastricht Treaty's timetable for EMU. Despite such sentiments even the most enthusiastic of European monetary supporters might be excused for being somewhat sceptical about the timing of EMU.

Where does EMU go from here? With the 1995 entry of Sweden, Finland and Austria into the EU it is very possible to think of a two-speed, or three-speed move to a common currency. Germany, Austria and the Netherlands plus one or two others (including, probably, France and Belgium) look to be in the vanguard of currency integration, with the Bundesbank making obvious claims for central bank status within the new system.

On May 31, 1995 the European Commission launched a blueprint for achieving a shift to a single currency by the end of the century. Their Green Paper adopts a gradual approach, but the Commission remains confident that an unspecified number of countries in the 15-strong European Union will move to a single currency by the beginning of 1999, with the introduction of Euro-banknotes and coins following within a maximum of three years. The Green Paper proposes three stages in transition towards the adoption of the ECU as the new currency of legal tender. These stages are:

1. *Phase A*   There is a gap of one year between commitment by participating countries and locking of exchange rates.
2. *Phase B*   The European Central Bank fixes parities and begins operating a single monetary policy.
3. *Phase C*   The final changeover to the single currency would follow three years later with participating countries' national notes and coins phased out and the ECU becoming their sole legal tender. For participating countries all cheques, transfers and credit cards would be converted into ECU.

The 74-page Green Paper lists the benefits of a single currency as a more efficient single market, stimulation of trade, growth and employment, elimination of transaction costs and an increase in international monetary stability.

The United Kingdom's position outside of the first wave towards a common currency is almost certain. In the longer term, the UK parliamentary system and culture create problems. Most Western European countries effectively have coalitions in government with the result that the attempt of the ruling party to engineer an economic boom in the run-up to a general election does not occur—unlike the political environment in the UK. There are many who would argue that Britain's two party system is well past its sell-by date. When contrasted with its European counterparts, claims that it achieves superior performance are ludicrous. A coalition would avoid all the pointless economically engineered booms before elections, and it would mean that economic policies could be aligned with the UK's European neighbours.

As of early 1997, plans are well afoot with the new currency being called the Euro and its value set equal to an ECU and bank notes have already been designed and are scheduled to be in circulation in 2002.

Although there is a lot of water to flow under the bridge yet, the path to EMU seems highly possible. Governments seem determined not to fudge the previously agreed convergence criteria, and although some are failing to meet them currently a couple of major privatizations could well put that right.

Concept Questions

- What are the key aspects of Economic and Monetary Union?
- What are the three stages of EMU
- What are the convergence criteria for moving to stage 3 of EMU?

30.3   Summary and Conclusions

1. The exchange rate mechanism of the EMS, as originally conceived, constrained the fluctuations of participating member countries' currencies relative to one another. Cross rates were defined in terms of units of currency to the ECU and intervention was called for such that there was only modest deviation in exchange rates between ERM currencies, although such currencies would fluctuate substantially against non-ERM countries' exchange rates.

2. The ERM is now operating such wide bands of currency movement for participating countries (mainly plus or minus 15 per cent) as to render its original objectives of a cleavage of exchange rates of ERM members' currencies virtually non-existent. That the German and the Dutch exchange rates remain in a band of plus or minus $2\frac{1}{4}$ per cent of each others' ECU parities probably puts them in pole position as the race to a common European currency gets firmly under way. The entry of Austria into the EU adds an obvious other state to the front line. Maybe these three countries will move to a common European currency in the twentieth century. The circulation of this currency elsewhere in Europe might well quickly lead to its more widespread adoption. This scenario, or one very like it, is a strong certainty in the early twenty-first century.

KEY TERMS

European Monetary System (EMS) 677	Maastricht Treaty 677
Economic and Monetary Union (EMU) 677	Exchange Rate Mechanism (ERM) 677
European Currency Unit (ECU) 677	Convergence criteria 677

Mathematical Tables

TABLE A.1   **Present value of USD1 to be received after T periods $= 1/(1 + r)^T$**

					Interest rate				
Period	1%	2%	3%	4%	5%	6%	7%	8%	9%
1	0.9901	0.9804	0.9709	0.9615	0.9524	0.9434	0.9346	0.9259	0.9174
2	0.9803	0.9612	0.9426	0.9246	0.9070	0.8900	0.8734	0.8573	0.8417
3	0.9706	0.9423	0.9151	0.8890	0.8638	0.8396	0.8163	0.7938	0.7722
4	0.9610	0.9238	0.8885	0.8548	0.8227	0.7921	0.7629	0.7350	0.7084
5	0.9515	0.9057	0.8626	0.8219	0.7835	0.7473	0.7130	0.6806	0.6499
6	0.9420	0.8880	0.8375	0.7903	0.7462	0.7050	0.6663	0.6302	0.5963
7	0.9327	0.8706	0.8131	0.7599	0.7107	0.6651	0.6227	0.5835	0.5470
8	0.9235	0.8535	0.7894	0.7307	0.6768	0.6274	0.5820	0.5403	0.5019
9	0.9143	0.8368	0.7664	0.7026	0.6446	0.5919	0.5439	0.5002	0.4604
10	0.9053	0.8203	0.7441	0.6756	0.6139	0.5584	0.5083	0.4632	0.4224
11	0.8963	0.8043	0.7224	0.6496	0.5847	0.5268	0.4751	0.4289	0.3875
12	0.8874	0.7885	0.7014	0.6246	0.5568	0.4970	0.4440	0.3971	0.3555
13	0.8787	0.7730	0.6810	0.6006	0.5303	0.4688	0.4150	0.3677	0.3262
14	0.8700	0.7579	0.6611	0.5775	0.5051	0.4423	0.3878	0.3405	0.2992
15	0.8613	0.7430	0.6419	0.5553	0.4810	0.4173	0.3624	0.3152	0.2745
16	0.8528	0.7284	0.6232	0.5339	0.4581	0.3936	0.3387	0.2919	0.2519
17	0.8444	0.7142	0.6050	0.5134	0.4363	0.3714	0.3166	0.2703	0.2311
18	0.8360	0.7002	0.5874	0.4936	0.4155	0.3503	0.2959	0.2502	0.2120
19	0.8277	0.6864	0.5703	0.4746	0.3957	0.3305	0.2765	0.2317	0.1945
20	0.8195	0.6730	0.5537	0.4564	0.3769	0.3118	0.2584	0.2145	0.1784
21	0.8114	0.6598	0.5375	0.4388	0.3589	0.2942	0.2415	0.1987	0.1637
22	0.8034	0.6468	0.5219	0.4220	0.3418	0.2775	0.2257	0.1839	0.1502
23	0.7954	0.6342	0.5067	0.4057	0.3256	0.2618	0.2109	0.1703	0.1378
24	0.7876	0.6217	0.4919	0.3901	0.3101	0.2470	0.1971	0.1577	0.1264
25	0.7798	0.6095	0.4776	0.3751	0.2953	0.2330	0.1842	0.1460	0.1160
30	0.7419	0.5521	0.4120	0.3083	0.2314	0.1741	0.1314	0.0994	0.0754
40	0.6717	0.4529	0.3066	0.2083	0.1420	0.0972	0.0668	0.0460	0.0318
50	0.6080	0.3715	0.2281	0.1407	0.0872	0.0543	0.0339	0.0213	0.0134

*The factor is zero to four decimal places.

TABLE A.1 (*Concluded*)

					Interest rate					
10%	*12%*	*14%*	*15%*	*16%*	*18%*	*20%*	*24%*	*28%*	*32%*	*36%*
0.9091	0.8929	0.8772	0.8696	0.8621	0.8475	0.8333	0.8065	0.7813	0.7576	0.7353
0.8264	0.7972	0.7695	0.7561	0.7432	0.7182	0.6944	0.6504	0.6104	0.5739	0.5407
0.7513	0.7118	0.6750	0.6575	0.6407	0.6086	0.5787	0.5245	0.4768	0.4348	0.3975
0.6830	0.6355	0.5921	0.5718	0.5523	0.5158	0.4823	0.4230	0.3725	0.3294	0.2923
0.6209	0.5674	0.5194	0.4972	0.4761	0.4371	0.4019	0.3411	0.2910	0.2495	0.2149
0.5645	0.5066	0.4556	0.4323	0.4104	0.3704	0.3349	0.2751	0.2274	0.1890	0.1580
0.5132	0.4523	0.3996	0.3759	0.3538	0.3139	0.2791	0.2218	0.1776	0.1432	0.1162
0.4665	0.4039	0.3506	0.3269	0.3050	0.2660	0.2326	0.1789	0.1388	0.1085	0.0854
0.4241	0.3606	0.3075	0.2843	0.2630	0.2255	0.1938	0.1443	0.1084	0.0822	0.0628
0.3855	0.3220	0.2697	0.2472	0.2267	0.1911	0.1615	0.1164	0.0847	0.0623	0.0462
0.3505	0.2875	0.2366	0.2149	0.1954	0.1619	0.1346	0.0938	0.0662	0.0472	0.0340
0.3186	0.2567	0.2076	0.1869	0.1685	0.1372	0.1122	0.0757	0.0517	0.0357	0.0250
0.2897	0.2292	0.1821	0.1625	0.1452	0.1163	0.0935	0.0610	0.0404	0.0271	0.0184
0.2633	0.2046	0.1597	0.1413	0.1252	0.0985	0.0779	0.0492	0.0316	0.0205	0.0135
0.2394	0.1827	0.1401	0.1229	0.1079	0.0835	0.0649	0.0397	0.0247	0.0155	0.0099
0.2176	0.1631	0.1229	0.1069	0.0930	0.0708	0.0541	0.0320	0.0193	0.0118	0.0073
0.1978	0.1456	0.1078	0.0929	0.0802	0.0600	0.0451	0.0258	0.0150	0.0089	0.0054
0.1799	0.1300	0.0946	0.0808	0.0691	0.0508	0.0376	0.0208	0.0118	0.0068	0.0039
0.1635	0.1161	0.0829	0.0703	0.0596	0.0431	0.0313	0.0168	0.0092	0.0051	0.0029
0.1486	0.1037	0.0728	0.0611	0.0514	0.0365	0.0261	0.0135	0.0072	0.0039	0.0021
0.1351	0.0926	0.0638	0.0531	0.0443	0.0309	0.0217	0.0109	0.0056	0.0029	0.0016
0.1228	0.0826	0.0560	0.0462	0.0382	0.0262	0.0181	0.0088	0.0044	0.0022	0.0012
0.1117	0.0738	0.0491	0.0402	0.0329	0.0222	0.0151	0.0071	0.0034	0.0017	0.0008
0.1015	0.0659	0.0431	0.0349	0.0284	0.0188	0.0126	0.0057	0.0027	0.0013	0.0006
0.0923	0.0588	0.0378	0.0304	0.0245	0.0160	0.0105	0.0046	0.0021	0.0010	0.0005
0.0573	0.0334	0.0196	0.0151	0.0116	0.0070	0.0042	0.0016	0.0006	0.0002	0.0001
0.0221	0.0107	0.0053	0.0037	0.0026	0.0013	0.0007	0.0002	0.0001	*	*
0.0085	0.0035	0.0014	0.0009	0.0006	0.0003	0.0001	*	*	*	*

TABLE A.2 **Present value of an annuity of USD1 per period for T periods $= [1 - 1/(1 + r)^T]/r$**

Number of periods	Interest rate								
	1%	*2%*	*3%*	*4%*	*5%*	*6%*	*7%*	*8%*	*9%*
1	0.9901	0.9804	0.9709	0.9615	0.9524	0.9434	0.9346	0.9259	0.9174
2	1.9704	1.9416	1.9135	1.8861	1.8594	1.8334	1.8080	1.7833	1.7591
3	2.9410	2.8839	2.8286	2.7751	2.7232	2.6730	2.6243	2.5771	2.5313
4	3.9020	3.8077	3.7171	3.6299	3.5460	3.4651	3.3872	3.3121	3.2397
5	4.8534	4.7135	4.5797	4.4518	4.3295	4.2124	4.1002	3.9927	3.8897
6	5.7955	5.6014	5.4172	5.2421	5.0757	4.9173	4.7665	4.6229	4.4859
7	6.7282	6.4720	6.2303	6.0021	5.7864	5.5824	5.3893	5.2064	5.0330
8	7.6517	7.3255	7.0197	6.7327	6.4632	6.2098	5.9713	5.7466	5.5348
9	8.5660	8.1622	7.7861	7.4353	7.1078	6.8017	6.5152	6.2469	5.9952
10	9.4713	8.9826	8.5302	8.1109	7.7217	7.3601	7.0236	6.7101	6.4177
11	10.3676	9.7868	9.2526	8.7605	8.3064	7.8869	7.4987	7.1390	6.8052
12	11.2551	10.5753	9.9540	9.3851	8.8633	8.3838	7.9427	7.5361	7.1607
13	12.1337	11.3484	10.6350	9.9856	9.3936	8.8527	8.3577	7.9038	7.4869
14	13.0037	12.1062	11.2961	10.5631	9.8986	9.2950	8.7455	8.2442	7.7862
15	13.8651	12.8493	11.9379	11.1184	10.3797	9.7122	9.1079	8.5595	8.0607
16	14.7179	13.5777	12.5611	11.6523	10.8378	10.1059	9.4466	8.8514	8.3126
17	15.5623	14.2919	13.1661	12.1657	11.2741	10.4773	9.7632	9.1216	8.5436
18	16.3983	14.9920	13.7535	12.6593	11.6896	10.8276	10.0591	9.3719	8.7556
19	17.2260	15.6785	14.3238	13.1339	12.0853	11.1581	10.3356	9.6036	8.9501
20	18.0456	16.3514	14.8775	13.5903	12.4622	11.4699	10.5940	9.8181	9.1285
21	18.8570	17.0112	15.4150	14.0292	12.8212	11.7641	10.8355	10.0168	9.2922
22	19.6604	17.6580	15.9369	14.4511	13.1630	12.0416	11.0612	10.2007	9.4424
23	20.4558	18.2922	16.4436	14.8568	13.4886	12.3034	11.2722	10.3741	9.5802
24	21.2434	18.9139	16.9355	15.2470	13.7986	12.5504	11.4693	10.5288	9.7066
25	22.0232	19.5235	17.4131	15.6221	14.0939	12.7834	11.6536	10.6748	9.8226
30	25.8077	22.3965	19.6004	17.2920	15.3725	13.7648	12.4090	11.2578	10.2737
40	32.8347	27.3555	23.1148	19.7928	17.1591	15.0463	13.3317	11.9246	10.7574
50	39.1961	31.4236	25.7298	21.4822	18.2559	15.7619	13.8007	12.2335	10.9617

TABLE A.2   (*Concluded*)

					Interest rate				
10%	*12%*	*14%*	*15%*	*16%*	*18%*	*20%*	*24%*	*28%*	*32%*
0.9091	0.8929	0.8772	0.8696	0.8621	0.8475	0.8333	0.8065	0.7813	0.7576
1.7355	1.6901	1.6467	1.6257	1.6052	1.5656	1.5278	1.4568	1.3916	1.3315
2.4869	2.4018	2.3216	2.2832	2.2459	2.1743	2.1065	1.9813	1.8684	1.7663
3.1699	3.0373	2.9137	2.8550	2.7982	2.6901	2.5887	2.4043	2.2410	2.0957
3.7908	3.6048	3.4331	3.3522	3.2743	3.1272	2.9906	2.7454	2.5320	2.3452
4.3553	4.1114	3.8887	3.7845	3.6847	3.4976	3.3255	3.0205	2.7594	2.5342
4.8684	4.5638	4.2883	4.1604	4.0386	3.8115	3.6046	3.2423	2.9370	2.6775
5.3349	4.9676	4.6389	4.4873	4.3436	4.0776	3.8372	3.4212	3.0758	2.7860
5.7590	5.3282	4.9464	4.7716	4.6065	4.3030	4.0310	3.5655	3.1842	2.8681
6.1446	5.6502	5.2161	5.0188	4.8332	4.4941	4.1925	3.6819	3.2689	2.9304
6.4951	5.9377	5.4527	5.2337	5.0286	4.6560	4.3271	3.7757	3.3351	2.9776
6.8137	6.1944	5.6603	5.4206	5.1971	4.7932	4.4392	3.8514	3.3868	3.0133
7.1034	6.4235	5.8424	5.5831	5.3423	4.9095	4.5327	3.9124	3.4272	3.0404
7.3667	6.6282	6.0021	5.7245	5.4675	5.0081	4.6106	3.9616	3.4587	3.0609
7.6061	6.8109	6.1422	5.8474	5.5755	5.0916	4.6755	4.0013	3.4834	3.0764
7.8237	6.9740	6.2651	5.9542	5.6685	5.1624	4.7296	4.0333	3.5026	3.0882
8.0216	7.1196	6.3729	6.0472	5.7487	5.2223	4.7746	4.0591	3.5177	3.0971
8.2014	7.2497	6.4674	6.1280	5.8178	5.2732	4.8122	4.0799	3.5294	3.1039
8.3649	7.3658	6.5504	6.1982	5.8775	5.3162	4.8435	4.0967	3.5386	3.1090
8.5136	7.4694	6.6231	6.2593	5.9288	5.3527	4.8696	4.1103	3.5458	3.1129
8.6487	7.5620	6.6870	6.3125	5.9731	5.3837	4.8913	4.1212	3.5514	3.1158
8.7715	7.6446	6.7429	6.3587	6.0113	5.4099	4.9094	4.1300	3.5558	3.1180
8.8832	7.7184	6.7921	6.3988	6.0442	5.4321	4.9245	4.1371	3.5592	3.1197
8.9847	7.7843	6.8351	6.4338	6.0726	5.4509	4.9371	4.1428	3.5619	3.1210
9.0770	7.8431	6.8729	6.4641	6.0971	5.4669	4.9476	4.1474	3.5640	3.1220
9.4269	8.0552	7.0027	6.5660	6.1772	5.5168	4.9789	4.1601	3.5693	3.1242
9.7791	8.2438	7.1050	6.6418	6.2335	5.5482	4.9966	4.1659	3.5712	3.1250
9.9148	8.3045	7.1327	6.6605	6.2463	5.5541	4.9995	4.1666	3.5714	3.1250

TABLE A.3   Future value of USD1 at the end of T periods $= (1 + r)^T$

	Interest rate								
Period	1%	2%	3%	4%	5%	6%	7%	8%	9%
1	1.0100	1.0200	1.0300	1.0400	1.0500	1.0600	1.0700	1.0800	1.0900
2	1.0201	1.0404	1.0609	1.0816	1.1025	1.1236	1.1449	1.1664	1.1881
3	1.0303	1.0612	1.0927	1.1249	1.1576	1.1910	1.2250	1.2597	1.2950
4	1.0406	1.0824	1.1255	1.1699	1.2155	1.2625	1.3108	1.3605	1.4116
5	1.0510	1.1041	1.1593	1.2167	1.2763	1.3382	1.4026	1.4693	1.5386
6	1.0615	1.1262	1.1941	1.2653	1.3401	1.4185	1.5007	1.5869	1.6771
7	1.0721	1.1487	1.2299	1.3159	1.4071	1.5036	1.6058	1.7138	1.8280
8	1.0829	1.1717	1.2668	1.3686	1.4775	1.5938	1.7182	1.8509	1.9926
9	1.0937	1.1951	1.3048	1.4233	1.5513	1.6895	1.8385	1.9990	2.1719
10	1.1046	1.2190	1.3439	1.4802	1.6289	1.7908	1.9672	2.1589	2.3674
11	1.1157	1.2434	1.3842	1.5395	1.7103	1.8983	2.1049	2.3316	2.5804
12	1.1268	1.2682	1.4258	1.6010	1.7959	2.0122	2.2522	2.5182	2.8127
13	1.1381	1.2936	1.4685	1.6651	1.8856	2.1329	2.4098	2.7196	3.0658
14	1.1495	1.3195	1.5126	1.7317	1.9799	2.2609	2.5785	2.9372	3.3417
15	1.1610	1.3459	1.5580	1.8009	2.0789	2.3966	2.7590	3.1722	3.6425
16	1.1726	1.3728	1.6047	1.8730	2.1829	2.5404	2.9522	3.4259	3.9703
17	1.1843	1.4002	1.6528	1.9479	2.2920	2.6928	3.1588	3.7000	4.3276
18	1.1961	1.4282	1.7024	2.0258	2.4066	2.8543	3.3799	3.9960	4.7171
19	1.2081	1.4568	1.7535	2.1068	2.5270	3.0256	3.6165	4.3157	5.1417
20	1.2202	1.4859	1.8061	2.1911	2.6533	3.2071	3.8697	4.6610	5.6044
21	1.2324	1.5157	1.8603	2.2788	2.7860	3.3996	4.1406	5.0338	6.1088
22	1.2447	1.5460	1.9161	2.3699	2.9253	3.6035	4.4304	5.4365	6.6586
23	1.2572	1.5769	1.9736	2.4647	3.0715	3.8197	4.7405	5.8715	7.2579
24	1.2697	1.6084	2.0328	2.5633	3.2251	4.0489	5.0724	6.3412	7.9111
25	1.2824	1.6406	2.0938	2.6658	3.3864	4.2919	5.4274	6.8485	8.6231
30	1.3478	1.8114	2.4273	3.2434	4.3219	5.7435	7.6123	10.063	13.268
40	1.4889	2.2080	3.2620	4.8010	7.0400	10.286	14.974	21.725	31.409
50	1.6446	2.6916	4.3839	7.1067	11.467	18.420	29.457	46.902	74.358
60	1.8167	3.2810	5.8916	10.520	18.679	32.988	57.946	101.26	176.03

*FVIV > 99,999.

TABLE A.3 (*Concluded*)

					Interest rate					
10%	*12%*	*14%*	*15%*	*16%*	*18%*	*20%*	*24%*	*28%*	*32%*	*36%*
1.1000	1.1200	1.1400	1.1500	1.1600	1.1800	1.2000	1.2400	1.2800	1.3200	1.3600
1.2100	1.2544	1.2996	1.3225	1.3456	1.3924	1.4400	1.5376	1.6384	1.7424	1.8496
1.3310	1.4049	1.4815	1.5209	1.5609	1.6430	1.7280	1.9066	2.0972	2.3000	2.5155
1.4641	1.5735	1.6890	1.7490	1.8106	1.9388	2.0736	2.3642	2.6844	3.0360	3.4210
1.6105	1.7623	1.9254	2.0114	2.1003	2.2878	2.4883	2.9316	3.4360	4.0075	4.6526
1.7716	1.9738	2.1950	2.3131	2.4364	2.6996	2.9860	3.6352	4.3980	5.2899	6.3275
1.9487	2.2107	2.5023	2.6600	2.8262	3.1855	3.5832	4.5077	5.6295	6.9826	8.6054
2.1436	2.4760	2.8526	3.0590	3.2784	3.7589	4.2998	5.5895	7.2058	9.2170	11.703
2.3579	2.7731	3.2519	3.5179	3.8030	4.4355	5.1598	6.9310	9.2234	12.166	15.917
2.5937	3.1058	3.7072	4.0456	4.4114	5.2338	6.1917	8.5944	11.806	16.060	21.647
2.8531	3.4785	4.2262	4.6524	5.1173	6.1759	7.4301	10.657	15.112	21.199	29.439
3.1384	3.8960	4.8179	5.3503	5.9360	7.2876	8.9161	13.215	19.343	27.983	40.037
3.4523	4.3635	5.4924	6.1528	6.8858	8.5994	10.699	16.386	24.759	36.937	54.451
3.7975	4.8871	6.2613	7.0757	7.9875	10.147	12.839	20.319	31.691	48.757	74.053
4.1772	5.4736	7.1379	8.1371	9.2655	11.974	15.407	25.196	40.565	64.359	100.71
4.5950	6.1304	8.1372	9.3576	10.748	14.129	18.488	31.243	51.923	84.954	136.97
5.0545	6.8660	9.2765	10.761	12.468	16.672	22.186	38.741	66.461	112.14	186.28
5.5599	7.6900	10.575	12.375	14.463	19.673	26.623	48.039	86.071	148.02	253.34
6.1159	8.6128	12.056	14.232	16.777	23.214	31.948	59.568	108.89	195.39	344.54
6.7275	9.6463	13.743	16.367	19.461	27.393	38.338	73.864	139.38	257.92	468.57
7.4002	10.804	15.668	18.822	22.574	32.324	46.005	91.592	178.41	340.45	637.26
8.1403	12.100	17.861	21.645	26.186	38.142	55.206	113.57	228.36	449.39	866.67
8.9543	13.552	20.362	24.891	30.376	45.008	66.247	140.83	292.30	593.20	1178.7
9.8497	15.179	23.212	28.625	35.236	53.109	79.497	174.63	374.14	783.02	1603.0
10.835	17.000	26.462	32.919	40.874	62.669	95.396	216.54	478.90	1033.6	2180.1
17.449	29.960	50.950	66.212	85.850	143.37	237.38	634.82	1645.5	4142.1	10143.
45.259	93.051	188.88	267.86	378.72	750.38	1469.8	5455.9	19427.	66521.	*
117.39	289.00	700.23	1083.7	1670.7	3927.4	9100.4	46890.	*	*	*
304.48	897.60	2595.9	4384.0	7370.2	20555.	56348.	*	*	*	*

TABLE A.4　Sum of annuity of USD1 per period for T periods $= [(1 + r)^T - 1]/r$

Number of periods	Interest rate								
	1%	2%	3%	4%	5%	6%	7%	8%	9%
1	1.0000	1.0000	1.0000	1.0000	1.0000	1.0000	1.0000	1.0000	1.0000
2	2.0100	2.0200	2.0300	2.0400	2.0500	2.0600	2.0700	2.0800	2.0900
3	3.0301	3.0604	3.0909	3.1216	3.1525	3.1836	3.2149	3.2464	3.2781
4	4.0604	4.1216	4.1836	4.2465	4.3101	4.3746	4.4399	4.5061	4.5731
5	5.1010	5.2040	5.3091	5.4163	5.5256	5.6371	5.7507	5.8666	5.9847
6	6.1520	6.3081	6.4684	6.6330	6.8019	6.9753	7.1533	7.3359	7.5233
7	7.2135	7.4343	7.6625	7.8983	8.1420	8.3938	8.6540	8.9228	9.2004
8	8.2857	8.5830	8.8932	9.2142	9.5491	9.8975	10.260	10.637	11.028
9	9.3685	9.7546	10.159	10.583	11.027	11.491	11.978	12.488	13.021
10	10.462	10.950	11.464	12.006	12.578	13.181	13.816	14.487	15.193
11	11.567	12.169	12.808	13.486	14.207	14.972	15.784	16.645	17.560
12	12.683	13.412	14.192	15.026	15.917	16.870	17.888	18.977	20.141
13	13.809	14.680	15.618	16.627	17.713	18.882	20.141	21.495	22.953
14	14.947	15.974	17.086	18.292	19.599	21.015	22.550	24.215	26.019
15	16.097	17.293	18.599	20.024	21.579	23.276	25.129	27.152	29.361
16	17.258	18.639	20.157	21.825	23.657	25.673	27.888	30.324	33.003
17	18.430	20.012	21.762	23.698	25.840	28.213	30.840	33.750	36.974
18	19.615	21.412	23.414	25.645	28.132	30.906	33.999	37.450	41.301
19	20.811	22.841	25.117	27.671	30.539	33.760	37.379	41.446	46.018
20	22.019	24.297	26.870	29.778	33.066	36.786	40.995	45.762	51.160
21	23.239	25.783	28.676	31.969	35.719	39.993	44.865	50.423	56.765
22	24.472	27.299	30.537	34.248	38.505	43.392	49.006	55.457	62.873
23	25.716	28.845	32.453	36.618	41.430	46.996	53.436	60.893	69.532
24	26.973	30.422	34.426	39.083	44.502	50.816	58.177	66.765	76.790
25	28.243	32.030	36.459	41.646	47.727	54.865	63.249	73.106	84.701
30	34.785	40.568	47.575	56.085	66.439	79.058	94.461	113.28	136.31
40	48.886	60.402	75.401	95.026	120.80	154.76	199.64	259.06	337.88
50	64.463	84.579	112.80	152.67	209.35	290.34	406.53	573.77	815.08
60	81.670	114.05	163.05	237.99	353.58	533.13	813.52	1253.2	1944.8

*FVIFA > 99,999.

TABLE A.4 (*Concluded*)

					Interest rate					
10%	*12%*	*14%*	*15%*	*16%*	*18%*	*20%*	*24%*	*28%*	*32%*	*36%*
1.0000	1.0000	1.0000	1.0000	1.0000	1.0000	1.0000	1.0000	1.0000	1.0000	1.0000
2.1000	2.1200	2.1400	2.1500	2.1600	2.1800	2.2000	2.2400	2.2800	2.3200	2.3600
3.3100	3.3744	3.4396	3.4725	3.5056	3.5724	3.6400	3.7776	3.9184	4.0624	4.2096
3.6410	4.7793	4.9211	4.9934	5.0665	5.2154	5.3680	5.6842	6.0156	6.3624	6.7251
6.1051	6.3528	6.6101	6.7424	6.8771	7.1542	7.4416	8.0484	8.6999	9.3983	10.146
7.7156	8.1152	8.5355	8.7537	8.9775	9.4420	9.9299	10.980	12.136	13.406	14.799
9.4872	10.089	10.730	11.067	11.414	12.142	12.916	14.615	16.534	18.696	21.126
11.436	12.300	13.233	13.727	14.240	15.327	16.499	19.123	22.163	25.678	29.732
13.579	14.776	16.085	16.786	17.519	19.086	20.799	24.712	29.369	34.895	41.435
15.937	17.549	19.337	20.304	21.321	23.521	25.959	31.643	38.593	47.062	57.352
18.531	20.655	23.045	24.349	25.733	28.755	32.150	40.238	50.398	63.122	78.998
21.384	24.133	27.271	29.002	30.850	34.931	39.581	50.895	65.510	84.320	108.44
24.523	28.029	32.089	34.352	36.786	42.219	48.497	64.110	84.853	112.30	148.47
27.975	32.393	37.581	40.505	43.672	50.818	59.196	80.496	109.61	149.24	202.93
31.772	37.280	43.842	47.580	51.660	60.965	72.035	100.82	141.30	198.00	276.98
35.950	42.753	50.980	55.717	60.925	72.939	87.442	126.01	181.87	262.36	377.69
40.545	48.884	59.118	65.075	71.673	87.068	105.93	157.25	233.79	347.31	514.66
45.599	55.750	68.394	75.836	84.141	103.74	128.12	195.99	300.25	459.45	700.94
51.159	64.440	78.969	88.212	98.603	123.41	154.74	244.03	385.32	607.47	954.28
57.275	72.052	91.025	102.44	115.38	146.63	186.69	303.60	494.21	802.86	1298.8
64.002	81.699	104.77	118.81	134.84	174.02	225.03	377.46	633.59	1060.8	1767.4
71.403	92.503	120.44	137.63	157.41	206.34	271.03	469.06	812.00	1401.2	2404.7
79.543	104.60	138.30	159.28	183.60	244.49	326.24	582.63	1040.4	1850.6	3271.3
88.497	118.16	158.66	184.17	213.98	289.49	392.48	723.46	1332.7	2443.8	4450.0
98.347	133.33	181.87	212.79	249.21	342.60	471.98	898.09	1706.8	3226.8	6053.0
164.49	241.33	356.79	434.75	530.31	790.95	1181.9	2640.9	5873.2	12941.	28172.3
442.59	767.09	1342.0	1779.1	2360.8	4163.2	7343.9	22729.	69377.	*	*
1163.9	2400.0	4994.5	7217.7	10436.	21813.	45497.	*	*	*	*
3034.8	7471.6	18535.	29220.	46058.	*	*	*	*	*	*

TABLE A.5   Future value of USD1 with a continuously compounded rate *r* for *T* periods: Values of e^{rT}

Period (T)	Continuously compounded rate (r)									
	1%	*2%*	*3%*	*4%*	*5%*	*6%*	*7%*	*8%*	*9%*	*10%*
1	1.0101	1.0202	1.0305	1.0408	1.0513	1.0618	1.0725	1.0833	1.0942	1.1052
2	1.0202	1.0408	1.0618	1.0833	1.1052	1.1275	1.1503	1.1735	1.1972	1.2214
3	1.0305	1.0618	1.0942	1.1275	1.1618	1.1972	1.2337	1.2712	1.3100	1.3499
4	1.0408	1.0833	1.1275	1.1735	1.2214	1.2712	1.3231	1.3771	1.4333	1.4918
5	1.0513	1.1052	1.1618	1.2214	1.2840	1.3499	1.4191	1.4918	1.5683	1.6487
6	1.0618	1.1275	1.1972	1.2712	1.3499	1.4333	1.5220	1.6161	1.7160	1.8221
7	1.0725	1.1503	1.2337	1.3231	1.4191	1.5220	1.6323	1.7507	1.8776	2.0138
8	1.0833	1.1735	1.2712	1.3771	1.4918	1.6161	1.7507	1.8965	2.0544	2.2255
9	1.0942	1.1972	1.3100	1.4333	1.5683	1.7160	1.8776	2.0544	2.2479	2.4596
10	1.1052	1.2214	1.3499	1.4918	1.6487	1.8221	2.0138	2.2255	2.4596	2.7183
11	1.1163	1.2461	1.3910	1.5527	1.7333	1.9348	2.1598	2.4109	2.6912	3.0042
12	1.1275	1.2712	1.4333	1.6161	1.8221	2.0544	2.3164	2.6117	2.9447	3.3201
13	1.1388	1.2969	1.4770	1.6820	1.9155	2.1815	2.4843	2.8292	3.2220	3.6693
14	1.1503	1.3231	1.5220	1.7507	2.0138	2.3164	2.6645	3.0649	3.5254	4.0552
15	1.1618	1.3499	1.5683	1.8221	2.1170	2.4596	2.8577	3.3201	3.8574	4.4817
16	1.1735	1.3771	1.6161	1.8965	2.2255	2.6117	3.0649	3.5966	4.2207	4.9530
17	1.1853	1.4049	1.6653	1.9739	2.3396	2.7732	3.2871	3.8962	4.6182	5.4739
18	1.1972	1.4333	1.7160	2.0544	2.4596	2.9447	3.5254	4.2207	5.0531	6.0496
19	1.2092	1.4623	1.7683	2.1383	2.5857	3.1268	3.7810	4.5722	5.5290	6.6859
20	1.2214	1.4918	1.8221	2.2255	2.7183	3.3201	4.0552	4.9530	6.0496	7.3891
21	1.2337	1.5220	1.8776	2.3164	2.8577	3.5254	4.3492	5.3656	6.6194	8.1662
22	1.2461	1.5527	1.9348	2.4109	3.0042	3.7434	4.6646	5.8124	7.2427	9.0250
23	1.2586	1.5841	1.9937	2.5093	3.1582	3.9749	5.0028	6.2965	7.9248	9.9742
24	1.2712	1.6161	2.0544	2.6117	3.3201	4.2207	5.3656	6.8210	8.6711	11.0232
25	1.2840	1.6487	2.1170	2.7183	3.4903	4.4817	5.7546	7.3891	9.4877	12.1825
30	1.3499	1.8221	2.4596	3.3204	4.4817	6.0496	8.1662	11.0232	14.8797	20.0855
35	1.4191	2.0138	2.8577	4.0552	5.7546	8.1662	11.5883	16.4446	23.3361	33.1155
40	1.4918	2.2255	3.3201	4.9530	7.3891	11.0232	16.4446	24.5235	36.5982	54.5982
45	1.5683	2.4596	3.8574	6.0496	9.4877	14.8797	23.3361	36.5982	57.3975	90.0171
50	1.6487	2.7183	4.4817	7.3891	12.1825	20.0855	33.1155	54.5982	90.0171	148.4132
55	1.7333	3.0042	5.2070	9.0250	15.6426	27.1126	46.9931	81.4509	141.1750	244.6919
60	1.8221	3.3201	6.0496	11.0232	20.0855	36.5982	66.6863	121.5104	221.4064	403.4288

TABLE A.5 (*Continued*)

					Continuously compounded rate (*r*)					
11%	*12%*	*13%*	*14%*	*15%*	*16%*	*17%*	*18%*	*19%*	*20%*	*21%*
1.1163	1.1275	1.1388	1.1503	1.1618	1.1735	1.1853	1.1972	1.2092	1.2214	1.2337
1.2461	1.2712	1.2969	1.3231	1.3499	1.3771	1.4049	1.4333	1.4623	1.4918	1.5220
1.3910	1.4333	1.4770	1.5220	1.5683	1.6161	1.6653	1.7160	1.7683	1.8221	1.8776
1.5527	1.6161	1.6820	1.7507	1.8221	1.8965	1.9739	2.0544	2.1383	2.2255	2.3164
1.7333	1.8221	1.9155	2.0138	2.1170	2.2255	2.3396	2.4596	2.5857	2.7183	2.8577
1.9348	2.0544	2.1815	2.3164	2.4596	2.6117	2.7732	2.9447	3.1268	3.3201	3.5254
2.1598	2.3164	2.4843	2.6645	2.8577	3.0649	3.2871	3.5254	3.7810	4.0552	4.3492
2.4109	2.6117	2.8292	3.0649	3.3201	3.5966	3.8962	4.2207	4.5722	4.9530	5.3656
2.6912	2.9447	3.2220	3.5254	3.8574	4.2207	4.6182	5.0531	5.5290	6.0496	6.6194
3.0042	3.3201	3.6693	4.0552	4.4817	4.9530	5.4739	6.0496	6.6859	7.3891	8.1662
3.3535	3.7434	4.1787	4.6646	5.2070	5.8124	6.4883	7.2427	8.0849	9.0250	10.0744
3.7434	4.2207	4.7588	5.3656	6.0496	6.8210	7.6906	8.6711	9.7767	11.0232	12.4286
4.1787	4.7588	5.4195	6.1719	7.0287	8.0045	9.1157	10.3812	11.8224	13.4637	15.3329
4.6646	5.3656	6.1719	7.0993	8.1662	9.3933	10.8049	12.4286	14.2963	16.4446	18.9158
5.2070	6.0496	7.0287	8.1662	9.4877	11.0232	12.8071	14.8797	17.2878	20.0855	23.3361
5.8124	6.8210	8.0045	9.3933	11.0232	12.9358	15.1803	17.8143	20.9052	24.5325	28.7892
6.4883	7.6906	9.1157	10.8049	12.8071	15.1803	17.9933	21.3276	25.2797	29.9641	35.5166
7.2427	8.6711	10.3812	12.4286	14.8797	17.8143	21.3276	25.5337	30.5694	36.5982	43.8160
8.0849	9.7767	11.8224	14.2963	17.2878	20.9052	25.2797	30.5694	36.9661	44.7012	54.0549
9.0250	11.0232	13.4637	16.4446	20.0855	24.5325	29.9641	36.5982	44.7012	54.5982	66.6863
10.0744	12.4286	15.3329	18.9158	23.3361	28.7892	35.5166	43.8160	54.0549	66.6863	82.2695
11.2459	14.0132	17.4615	21.7584	27.1126	33.7844	42.0980	52.4573	65.3659	81.4509	101.4940
12.5535	15.7998	19.8857	25.0281	31.5004	39.6464	49.8990	62.8028	79.0436	99.4843	125.2110
14.0132	17.8143	22.6464	28.7892	36.5982	46.5255	59.1455	75.1886	95.5835	121.5104	154.4700
15.6426	20.0855	25.7903	33.1155	42.5211	54.5982	70.1054	90.0171	115.5843	148.4132	190.5663
27.1126	36.5982	49.4024	66.6863	90.0171	121.5104	164.0219	221.4064	298.8674	403.4288	544.5719
46.9931	66.6863	94.6324	134.2898	190.5663	270.4264	383.7533	544.5719	772.7843	1096.633	1556.197
81.4509	121.5104	181.2722	270.4264	403.4288	601.8450	897.8473	1339.431	1998.196	2980.958	4447.067
141.1750	221.4064	347.2344	544.5719	854.0588	1339.431	2100.646	3294.468	5166.754	8103.084	12708.17
244.6919	403.4288	665.1416	1096.633	1808.042	2980.958	4914.769	8103.084	13359.73	22026.47	36315.50
424.1130	735.0952	1274.106	2208.348	3827.626	6634.244	11498.82	19930.37	34544.37	59874.14	103777.0
735.0952	1339.431	2440.602	4447.067	8103.084	14764.78	26903.19	49020.80	89321.72	162754.8	296558.6

TABLE A.5 (*Concluded*)

Period (T)	Continuously compounded rate (r)						
	22%	23%	24%	25%	26%	27%	28%
1	1.2461	1.2586	1.2712	1.2840	1.2969	1.3100	1.3231
2	1.5527	1.5841	1.6161	1.6487	1.6820	1.7160	1.7507
3	1.9348	1.9937	2.0544	2.1170	2.1815	2.2479	2.3164
4	2.4109	2.5093	2.6117	2.7183	2.8292	2.9447	3.0649
5	3.0042	3.1582	3.3201	3.4903	3.6693	3.8574	4.0552
6	3.7434	3.9749	4.2207	4.4817	4.7588	5.0531	5.3656
7	4.6646	5.0028	5.3656	5.7546	6.1719	6.6194	7.0993
8	5.8124	6.2965	6.8210	7.3891	8.0045	8.6711	9.3933
9	7.2427	7.9248	8.6711	9.4877	10.3812	11.3589	12.4286
10	9.0250	9.9742	11.0232	12.1825	13.4637	14.8797	16.4446
11	11.2459	12.5535	14.0132	15.6426	17.4615	19.4919	21.7584
12	14.0132	15.7998	17.8143	20.0855	22.6464	25.5337	28.7892
13	17.4615	19.8857	22.6464	25.7903	29.3708	33.4483	38.0918
14	21.7584	25.0281	28.7892	33.1155	38.0918	43.8160	50.4004
15	27.1126	31.5004	36.5982	42.5211	49.4024	57.3975	66.6863
16	33.7844	39.6464	46.5255	54.5982	64.0715	75.1886	88.2347
17	42.0980	49.8990	59.1455	70.1054	83.0963	98.4944	116.7459
18	52.4573	62.8028	75.1886	90.0171	107.7701	129.0242	154.4700
19	65.3659	79.0436	95.5835	115.5843	139.7702	169.0171	204.3839
20	81.4509	99.4843	121.5104	148.4132	181.2722	221.4064	270.4264
21	101.4940	125.2110	154.4700	190.5663	235.0974	290.0345	357.8092
22	126.4694	157.5905	196.3699	244.6919	304.9049	379.9349	473.4281
23	157.5905	198.3434	249.6350	314.1907	395.4404	497.7013	626.4068
24	196.3699	249.6350	317.3483	403.4288	512.8585	651.9709	828.8175
25	244.6919	314.1907	403.4288	518.0128	665.1416	854.0588	1096.633
30	735.0952	992.2747	1339.431	1808.042	2440.602	3294.468	4447.067
35	2208.348	3133.795	4447.067	6310.688	8955.293	12708.17	18033.74
40	6634.244	9897.129	14764.78	22026.47	32859.63	49020.80	73130.44
45	19930.37	31257.04	49020.80	76879.92	120571.7	189094.1	296558.6
50	59874.14	98715.77	162754.8	268337.3	442413.4	729416.4	1202604
55	179871.9	311763.4	540364.9	936589.2	1623346	2813669	4876801
60	540364.9	984609.1	1794075	3269017	5956538	10853520	19776403

TABLE A.6   **Present value of USD1 with a continuous discount rate *r* for *T* periods: Values of e^{-rT}**

Period (T)	Continuous discount rate (r)						
	1%	*2%*	*3%*	*4%*	*5%*	*6%*	*7%*
1	0.9900	0.9802	0.9704	0.9608	0.9512	0.9418	0.9324
2	0.9802	0.9608	0.9418	0.9231	0.9048	0.8869	0.8694
3	0.9704	0.9418	0.9139	0.8869	0.8607	0.8353	0.8106
4	0.9608	0.9231	0.8869	0.8521	0.8187	0.7866	0.7558
5	0.9512	0.9048	0.8607	0.8187	0.7788	0.7408	0.7047
6	0.9418	0.8869	0.8353	0.7866	0.7408	0.6977	0.6570
7	0.9324	0.8694	0.8106	0.7558	0.7047	0.6570	0.6126
8	0.9231	0.8521	0.7866	0.7261	0.6703	0.6188	0.5712
9	0.9139	0.8353	0.7634	0.6977	0.6376	0.5827	0.5326
10	0.9048	0.8187	0.7408	0.6703	0.6065	0.5488	0.4966
11	0.8958	0.8025	0.7189	0.6440	0.5769	0.5169	0.4630
12	0.8869	0.7866	0.6977	0.6188	0.5488	0.4868	0.4317
13	0.8781	0.7711	0.6771	0.5945	0.5220	0.4584	0.4025
14	0.8694	0.7558	0.6570	0.5712	0.4966	0.4317	0.3753
15	0.8607	0.7408	0.6376	0.5488	0.4724	0.4066	0.3499
16	0.8521	0.7261	0.6188	0.5273	0.4493	0.3829	0.3263
17	0.8437	0.7118	0.6005	0.5066	0.4274	0.3606	0.3042
18	0.8353	0.6977	0.5827	0.4868	0.4066	0.3396	0.2837
19	0.8270	0.6839	0.5655	0.4677	0.3867	0.3198	0.2645
20	0.8187	0.6703	0.5488	0.4493	0.3679	0.3012	0.2466
21	0.8106	0.6570	0.5326	0.4317	0.3499	0.2837	0.2299
22	0.8025	0.6440	0.5169	0.4148	0.3329	0.2671	0.2144
23	0.7945	0.6313	0.5016	0.3985	0.3166	0.2516	0.1999
24	0.7866	0.6188	0.4868	0.3829	0.3012	0.2369	0.1864
25	0.7788	0.6065	0.4724	0.3679	0.2865	0.2231	0.1738
30	0.7408	0.5488	0.4066	0.3012	0.2231	0.1653	0.1225
35	0.7047	0.4966	0.3499	0.2466	0.1738	0.1225	0.0863
40	0.6703	0.4493	0.3012	0.2019	0.1353	0.0907	0.0608
45	0.6376	0.4066	0.2592	0.1653	0.1054	0.0672	0.0429
50	0.6065	0.3679	0.2231	0.1353	0.0821	0.0498	0.0302
55	0.5769	0.3329	0.1920	0.1108	0.0639	0.0369	0.0213
60	0.5488	0.3012	0.1653	0.0907	0.0498	0.0273	0.0150

TABLE A.6   (*Continued*)

Period (T)	Continuous discount rate (r)									
	8%	*9%*	*10%*	*11%`*	*12%*	*13%*	*14%*	*15%*	*16%*	*17%*
1	0.9231	0.9139	0.9048	0.8958	0.8869	0.8781	0.8694	0.8607	0.8521	0.8437
2	0.8521	0.8353	0.8187	0.8025	0.7866	0.7711	0.7558	0.7408	0.7261	0.7118
3	0.7866	0.7634	0.7408	0.7189	0.6977	0.6771	0.6570	0.6376	0.6188	0.6005
4	0.7261	0.6977	0.6703	0.6440	0.6188	0.5945	0.5712	0.5488	0.5273	0.5066
5	0.6703	0.6376	0.6065	0.5769	0.5488	0.5220	0.4966	0.4724	0.4493	0.4274
6	0.6188	0.5827	0.5488	0.5169	0.4868	0.4584	0.4317	0.4066	0.3829	0.3606
7	0.5712	0.5326	0.4966	0.4630	0.4317	0.4025	0.3753	0.3499	0.3263	0.3042
8	0.5273	0.4868	0.4493	0.4148	0.3829	0.3535	0.3263	0.3012	0.2780	0.2576
9	0.4868	0.4449	0.4066	0.3716	0.3396	0.3104	0.2837	0.2592	0.2369	0.2165
10	0.4493	0.4066	0.3679	0.3329	0.3012	0.2725	0.2466	0.2231	0.2019	0.1827
11	0.4148	0.3716	0.3329	0.2982	0.2671	0.2393	0.2144	0.1920	0.1720	0.1541
12	0.3829	0.3396	0.3012	0.2671	0.2369	0.2101	0.1864	0.1653	0.1466	0.1300
13	0.3535	0.3104	0.2725	0.2393	0.2101	0.1845	0.1620	0.1423	0.1249	0.1097
14	0.3263	0.2837	0.2466	0.2144	0.1864	0.1620	0.1409	0.1225	0.1065	0.0926
15	0.3012	0.2592	0.2231	0.1920	0.1653	0.1423	0.1225	0.1054	0.0907	0.0781
16	0.2780	0.2369	0.2019	0.1720	0.1466	0.1249	0.1065	0.0907	0.0773	0.0659
17	0.2567	0.2165	0.1827	0.1541	0.1300	0.1097	0.0926	0.0781	0.0659	0.0556
18	0.2369	0.1979	0.1653	0.1381	0.1153	0.0963	0.0805	0.0672	0.0561	0.0469
19	0.2187	0.1809	0.1496	0.1237	0.1023	0.0846	0.0699	0.0578	0.0478	0.0396
20	0.2019	0.1653	0.1353	0.1108	0.0907	0.0743	0.0608	0.0498	0.0408	0.0334
21	0.1864	0.1511	0.1225	0.0993	0.0805	0.0652	0.0529	0.0429	0.0347	0.0282
22	0.1720	0.1381	0.1108	0.0889	0.0714	0.0573	0.0460	0.0369	0.0296	0.0238
23	0.1588	0.1262	0.1003	0.0797	0.0633	0.0503	0.0400	0.0317	0.0252	0.0200
24	0.1466	0.1153	0.0907	0.0714	0.0561	0.0442	0.0347	0.0273	0.0215	0.0169
25	0.1353	0.1054	0.0821	0.0639	0.0498	0.0388	0.0302	0.0235	0.0183	0.0143
30	0.0907	0.0672	0.0498	0.0369	0.0273	0.0202	0.0150	0.0111	0.0082	0.0061
35	0.0608	0.0429	0.0302	0.0213	0.0150	0.0106	0.0074	0.0052	0.0037	0.0026
40	0.0408	0.0273	0.0183	0.0123	0.0082	0.0055	0.0037	0.0025	0.0017	0.0011
45	0.0273	0.0174	0.0111	0.0071	0.0045	0.0029	0.0018	0.0012	0.0007	0.0005
50	0.0183	0.0111	0.0067	0.0041	0.0025	0.0015	0.0009	0.0006	0.0003	0.0002
55	0.0123	0.0071	0.0041	0.0024	0.0014	0.0008	0.0005	0.0003	0.0002	0.0001
60	0.0082	0.0045	0.0025	0.0014	0.0007	0.0004	0.0002	0.0001	0.0001	0.0000

TABLE A.6 (*Continued*)

				Continuous discount rate (*r*)						
18%	*19%*	*20%*	*21%*	*22%*	*23%*	*24%*	*25%*	*26%*	*27%*	*28%*
0.8353	0.8270	0.8187	0.8106	0.8025	0.7945	0.7866	0.7788	0.7711	0.7634	0.7558
0.6977	0.6839	0.6703	0.6570	0.6440	0.6313	0.6188	0.6065	0.5945	0.5827	0.5712
0.5827	0.5655	0.5488	0.5326	0.5169	0.5016	0.4868	0.4724	0.4584	0.4449	0.4317
0.4868	0.4677	0.4493	0.4317	0.4148	0.3985	0.3829	0.3679	0.3535	0.3396	0.3263
0.4066	0.3867	0.3679	0.3499	0.3329	0.3166	0.3012	0.2865	0.2725	0.2592	0.2466
0.3396	0.3198	0.3012	0.2837	0.2671	0.2516	0.2369	0.2231	0.2101	0.1979	0.1864
0.2837	0.2645	0.2466	0.2299	0.2144	0.1999	0.1864	0.1738	0.1620	0.1511	0.1409
0.2369	0.2187	0.2019	0.1864	0.1720	0.1588	0.1466	0.1353	0.1249	0.1153	0.1065
0.1979	0.1809	0.1653	0.1511	0.1381	0.1262	0.1153	0.1054	0.0963	0.0880	0.0805
0.1653	0.1496	0.1353	0.1225	0.1108	0.1003	0.0907	0.0821	0.0743	0.0672	0.0608
0.1381	0.1237	0.1108	0.0993	0.0889	0.0797	0.0714	0.0639	0.0573	0.0513	0.0460
0.1154	0.1023	0.0907	0.0805	0.0714	0.0633	0.0561	0.0498	0.0442	0.0392	0.0347
0.0963	0.0846	0.0743	0.0652	0.0573	0.0503	0.0442	0.0388	0.0340	0.0299	0.0263
0.0805	0.0699	0.0608	0.0529	0.0460	0.0400	0.0347	0.0302	0.0263	0.0228	0.0198
0.0672	0.0578	0.0498	0.0429	0.0369	0.0317	0.0273	0.0235	0.0202	0.0174	0.0150
0.0561	0.0478	0.0408	0.0347	0.0296	0.0252	0.0215	0.0183	0.0156	0.0133	0.0113
0.0469	0.0396	0.0334	0.0282	0.0238	0.0200	0.0169	0.0143	0.0120	0.0102	0.0086
0.0392	0.0327	0.0273	0.0228	0.0191	0.0159	0.0133	0.0111	0.0093	0.0078	0.0065
0.0327	0.0271	0.0224	0.0185	0.0153	0.0127	0.0105	0.0087	0.0072	0.0059	0.0049
0.0273	0.0224	0.0183	0.0150	0.0123	0.0101	0.0082	0.0067	0.0055	0.0045	0.0037
0.0228	0.0185	0.0150	0.0122	0.0099	0.0080	0.0065	0.0052	0.0043	0.0034	0.0028
0.0191	0.0153	0.0123	0.0099	0.0079	0.0063	0.0051	0.0041	0.0033	0.0026	0.0021
0.0159	0.0127	0.0101	0.0080	0.0063	0.0050	0.0040	0.0032	0.0025	0.0020	0.0016
0.0133	0.0105	0.0082	0.0065	0.0051	0.0040	0.0032	0.0025	0.0019	0.0015	0.0012
0.0111	0.0087	0.0067	0.0052	0.0041	0.0032	0.0025	0.0019	0.0015	0.0012	0.0009
0.0045	0.0033	0.0025	0.0018	0.0014	0.0010	0.0007	0.0006	0.0004	0.0003	0.0002
0.0018	0.0013	0.0009	0.0006	0.0005	0.0003	0.0002	0.0002	0.0001	0.0001	0.0001
0.0007	0.0005	0.0003	0.0002	0.0002	0.0001	0.0001	0.0000	0.0000	0.0000	0.0000
0.0003	0.0002	0.0001	0.0001	0.0001	0.0000	0.0000	0.0000	0.0000	0.0000	0.0000
0.0001	0.0001	0.0000	0.0000	0.0000	0.0000	0.0000	0.0000	0.0000	0.0000	0.0000
0.0001	0.0000	0.0000	0.0000	0.0000	0.0000	0.0000	0.0000	0.0000	0.0000	0.0000
0.0000	0.0000	0.0000	0.0000	0.0000	0.0000	0.0000	0.0000	0.0000	0.0000	0.0000

TABLE A.6   (*Concluded*)

Period (T)	Continuous discount rate (r)						
	29%	30%	31%	32%`	33%	34%	35%
1	0.7483	0.7408	0.7334	0.7261	0.7189	0.7188	0.7047
2	0.5599	0.5488	0.5379	0.5273	0.5169	0.5066	0.4966
3	0.4190	0.4066	0.3946	0.3829	0.3716	0.3606	0.3499
4	0.3135	0.3012	0.2894	0.2780	0.2671	0.2567	0.2466
5	0.2346	0.2231	0.2122	0.2019	0.1920	0.1827	0.1738
6	0.1755	0.1653	0.1557	0.1466	0.1381	0.1300	0.1225
7	0.1313	0.1225	0.1142	0.1065	0.0993	0.0926	0.0863
8	0.0983	0.0907	0.0837	0.0773	0.0714	0.0659	0.0608
9	0.0735	0.0672	0.0614	0.0561	0.0513	0.0469	0.0429
10	0.0550	0.0498	0.0450	0.0408	0.0369	0.0334	0.0302
11	0.0412	0.0369	0.0330	0.0296	0.0265	0.0238	0.0213
12	0.0308	0.0273	0.0242	0.0215	0.0191	0.0169	0.0150
13	0.0231	0.0202	0.0178	0.0156	0.0137	0.0120	0.0106
14	0.0172	0.0150	0.0130	0.0113	0.0099	0.0086	0.0074
15	0.0129	0.0111	0.0096	0.0082	0.0071	0.0061	0.0052
16	0.0097	0.0082	0.0070	0.0060	0.0051	0.0043	0.0037
17	0.0072	0.0061	0.0051	0.0043	0.0037	0.0031	0.0026
18	0.0054	0.0045	0.0038	0.0032	0.0026	0.0022	0.0018
19	0.0040	0.0033	0.0028	0.0023	0.0019	0.0016	0.0013
20	0.0030	0.0025	0.0020	0.0017	0.0014	0.0011	0.0009
21	0.0023	0.0018	0.0015	0.0012	0.0010	0.0008	0.0006
22	0.0017	0.0014	0.0011	0.0009	0.0007	0.0006	0.0005
23	0.0013	0.0010	0.0008	0.0006	0.0005	0.0004	0.0003
24	0.0009	0.0007	0.0006	0.0005	0.0004	0.0003	0.0002
25	0.0007	0.0006	0.0004	0.0003	0.0003	0.0002	0.0002
30	0.0002	0.0001	0.0001	0.0001	0.0001	0.0000	0.0000
35	0.0000	0.0000	0.0000	0.0000	0.0000	0.0000	0.0000
40	0.0000	0.0000	0.0000	0.0000	0.0000	0.0000	0.0000
45	0.0000	0.0000	0.0000	0.0000	0.0000	0.0000	0.0000
50	0.0000	0.0000	0.0000	0.0000	0.0000	0.0000	0.0000
55	0.0000	0.0000	0.0000	0.0000	0.0000	0.0000	0.0000
60	0.0000	0.0000	0.0000	0.0000	0.0000	0.0000	0.0000

TABLE A.7 Black–Scholes value of call option expressed as a percentage of the share price

Share price divided by present value of exercise price, that is S/PV(*E*)

Square root of cumulative variance, that is $\sigma\sqrt{t}$

	0.30	0.35	0.40	0.45	0.50	0.55	0.60	0.65	0.70	0.75	0.80	0.82	0.84	0.86	0.88	0.90	0.92	0.94	0.96	0.98	1.00	1.02	1.04	1.06	1.08	1.10	1.12	1.14	1.16	1.18	1.20	1.25	1.30	1.35	1.40	1.45	1.50	1.75	2.00	2.50	
0.05	0.0	0.0	0.0	0.0	0.0	0.0	0.0	0.0	0.0	0.0	0.0	0.0	0.0	0.0	0.0	0.0	0.1	0.3	0.6	1.2	2.0	3.1	4.5	6.0	7.5	9.1	10.7	12.3	13.8	15.3	16.7	20.0	23.1	25.9	28.6	31.0	33.3	42.9	50.0	60.0	0.05
0.10	0.0	0.0	0.0	0.0	0.0	0.0	0.0	0.0	0.0	0.0	0.0	0.1	0.2	0.3	0.5	0.8	1.2	1.7	2.3	3.1	4.0	5.0	6.1	7.3	8.6	10.0	11.3	12.7	14.1	15.4	16.8	20.0	23.1	25.9	28.6	31.0	33.3	42.9	50.0	60.0	0.10
0.15	0.0	0.0	0.0	0.0	0.0	0.0	0.0	0.0	0.1	0.2	0.5	0.7	1.0	1.3	1.7	2.2	2.8	3.5	4.2	5.1	6.0	7.0	8.0	9.1	10.2	11.4	12.6	13.8	15.0	16.2	17.4	20.4	23.3	26.0	28.6	31.0	33.3	42.9	50.0	60.0	0.15
0.20	0.0	0.0	0.0	0.0	0.0	0.0	0.0	0.1	0.4	0.8	1.5	1.9	2.3	2.8	3.4	4.0	4.7	5.4	6.2	7.1	8.0	8.9	9.9	10.9	11.9	13.0	14.1	15.2	16.3	17.4	18.5	21.2	23.9	26.4	28.9	31.2	33.5	42.9	50.0	60.0	0.20
0.25	0.0	0.0	0.0	0.0	0.0	0.1	0.2	0.5	1.0	0.8	2.8	3.3	3.9	4.5	5.2	5.9	6.6	7.4	8.2	9.1	9.9	10.9	11.8	12.8	13.7	14.7	15.7	16.7	17.7	18.7	19.8	22.3	24.7	27.1	29.4	31.7	33.8	42.9	50.0	60.0	0.25
0.30	0.0	0.0	0.0	0.1	0.1	0.3	0.7	1.2	2.0	3.1	4.4	5.0	5.7	6.3	7.0	7.8	8.6	9.4	10.2	11.1	11.9	12.8	13.7	14.6	15.6	16.5	17.4	18.4	19.3	20.3	21.2	23.5	25.8	28.1	30.2	32.3	34.3	43.1	50.1	60.0	0.30
0.35	0.0	0.0	0.1	0.2	0.4	0.8	1.4	2.3	3.3	4.6	6.2	6.8	7.5	8.2	9.0	9.8	10.6	11.4	12.2	13.0	13.9	14.8	15.6	16.5	17.4	18.3	19.2	20.1	21.0	21.9	22.7	24.9	27.1	29.2	31.2	33.2	35.1	43.5	50.2	60.0	0.35
0.40	0.0	0.1	0.2	0.5	0.9	1.6	2.4	3.5	4.8	6.3	8.0	8.7	9.4	10.2	11.0	11.7	12.5	13.4	14.2	15.0	15.9	16.7	17.5	18.4	19.2	20.1	20.9	21.8	22.6	23.5	24.3	26.4	28.4	30.4	32.3	34.2	36.0	44.0	50.5	60.1	0.40
0.45	0.1	0.2	0.5	1.0	1.7	2.6	3.7	5.0	6.5	8.1	9.9	10.6	11.4	12.2	12.9	13.7	14.5	15.3	16.2	17.0	17.8	18.6	19.4	20.3	21.1	21.9	22.7	23.5	24.3	25.1	25.9	27.9	29.8	31.7	33.5	35.3	37.0	44.6	50.8	60.2	0.45
0.50	0.2	0.5	1.0	1.7	2.6	3.7	5.1	6.6	8.2	10.0	11.8	12.6	13.4	14.2	14.9	15.7	16.5	17.3	18.1	18.9	19.7	20.5	21.3	22.1	22.9	23.7	24.5	25.3	26.1	26.8	27.6	29.5	31.3	33.1	34.8	36.4	38.1	45.3	51.3	50.4	0.50
0.55	0.5	1.0	1.7	2.6	3.8	5.1	6.6	8.3	10.0	11.9	13.8	14.6	15.4	16.1	16.9	17.7	18.5	19.3	20.1	20.9	21.7	22.4	23.2	24.0	24.8	25.5	26.3	27.0	27.8	28.5	29.2	31.0	32.8	34.5	36.1	37.7	39.2	46.1	51.9	60.7	0.55
0.60	0.9	1.6	2.5	3.7	5.1	6.6	8.3	10.1	11.9	13.8	15.8	16.6	17.4	18.1	18.9	19.7	20.5	213.	22.0	22.8	23.6	24.3	25.1	25.8	26.6	27.3	28.1	28.8	29.5	30.2	30.9	32.6	34.3	35.9	37.5	39.0	40.4	47.0	52.5	61.0	0.60
0.65	1.4	2.4	3.6	4.9	6.5	8.2	10.0	11.9	13.8	15.8	17.8	18.6	19.3	20.1	20.9	21.7	22.5	23.2	24.0	24.7	25.5	26.2	27.0	27.7	28.4	29.1	29.8	30.5	31.2	31.9	32.6	34.2	35.8	37.4	38.9	40.3	41.7	48.0	53.3	61.4	0.65
0.70	2.1	3.3	4.7	6.3	8.1	9.9	11.9	13.8	15.8	17.8	19.8	20.6	21.3	22.1	22.9	23.6	24.4	25.2	25.9	26.6	27.4	28.1	28.8	29.5	30.2	30.9	31.6	32.3	32.9	33.6	34.2	35.8	37.3	38.8	40.3	41.6	43.0	49.0	54.0	61.9	0.70
0.75	3.0	4.4	6.1	7.9	9.8	11.7	13.7	15.8	17.8	19.8	21.8	22.5	23.3	24.1	24.8	25.6	26.3	27.1	27.8	28.5	29.2	29.9	30.6	31.3	32.0	32.7	33.3	34.0	34.6	35.3	35.9	37.4	38.9	40.3	41.7	43.0	44.3	50.0	54.9	62.4	0.75
0.80	4.0	5.7	7.5	9.5	11.5	13.6	15.7	17.7	19.8	21.8	23.7	24.5	25.3	26.0	26.8	27.5	28.3	29.0	29.7	30.4	31.1	31.8	32.4	33.1	33.8	34.4	35.1	35.7	36.3	36.9	37.5	39.0	40.4	41.8	43.1	44.4	45.6	51.1	55.8	63.0	0.80
0.85	5.1	7.1	9.1	11.2	13.3	15.5	17.6	19.7	21.8	23.8	25.7	26.5	27.2	28.0	28.7	29.4	30.2	30.9	31.6	32.2	32.9	33.6	34.2	34.9	35.5	36.2	36.8	37.4	38.0	38.6	39.2	40.6	41.9	43.3	44.5	45.8	46.9	52.2	56.7	63.6	0.85
0.90	6.4	8.5	10.7	13.0	15.2	17.4	19.6	21.7	23.8	25.8	27.2	28.4	29.2	29.9	30.6	31.3	32.0	32.7	33.4	34.1	34.7	35.4	36.0	36.6	37.3	37.9	38.5	39.1	39.6	40.2	40.8	42.1	43.5	44.7	46.0	47.1	48.3	53.3	57.6	64.3	0.90
0.95	7.8	10.1	12.5	14.8	17.1	19.4	21.6	23.7	25.7	27.7	29.6	30.4	31.1	31.8	32.5	33.2	33.9	34.6	35.2	35.9	36.5	37.2	37.8	38.4	39.0	39.6	40.1	40.7	41.3	41.8	42.4	43.7	43.5	44.7	46.0	48.5	49.6	54.5	58.6	65.0	0.95
1.00	9.3	11.8	14.3	16.7	19.1	21.4	23.6	25.7	27.7	29.7	31.6	32.3	33.0	33.7	34.4	35.1	35.7	36.4	37.0	37.7	38.3	38.9	39.5	40.1	40.7	41.2	41.8	42.4	42.9	43.4	44.0	45.2	46.5	47.6	48.8	49.9	50.9	55.6	59.5	65.7	1.00
1.05	10.9	13.6	16.1	18.6	21.0	23.3	25.6	27.7	29.7	31.6	33.5	34.2	34.9	35.6	36.2	36.9	37.6	38.2	38.8	39.4	40.0	40.6	41.2	41.8	42.4	42.9	43.5	44.0	44.5	45.0	45.5	46.8	48.0	49.1	50.2	51.2	52.2	56.7	60.5	66.5	1.05
1.10	12.6	15.4	18.0	20.6	23.0	25.3	27.5	29.6	31.6	33.5	35.4	36.1	36.7	37.4	38.1	38.7	39.3	40.0	40.6	41.2	41.8	42.3	42.9	43.5	44.0	44.5	45.1	45.6	46.1	46.6	47.1	48.3	49.4	50.5	51.6	52.6	53.5	57.9	61.5	67.2	1.10
1.15	14.4	17.2	20.0	22.5	25.0	27.3	29.5	31.6	33.6	35.4	37.2	37.9	38.6	39.2	39.9	40.5	41.1	41.7	42.3	42.9	43.5	44.0	44.6	45.1	45.6	46.2	46.7	47.2	47.7	48.2	48.6	49.8	50.9	51.9	52.9	53.9	54.9	59.0	62.5	68.0	1.15
1.20	16.2	19.1	21.9	24.5	27.0	29.3	31.5	33.6	35.5	37.3	39.1	39.7	40.4	41.0	41.7	42.3	42.9	43.5	44.0	44.6	45.1	45.7	46.2	46.7	47.3	47.8	48.3	48.7	49.2	49.7	50.1	51.3	52.3	53.4	54.3	55.2	56.1	60.2	63.5	68.8	1.20
1.25	18.1	21.1	23.9	26.5	29.0	31.3	33.5	35.5	37.4	39.2	40.9	41.5	42.2	42.8	43.4	44.0	44.6	45.2	45.7	46.3	46.8	47.3	47.8	48.4	48.8	49.3	49.8	50.3	50.7	51.2	51.6	52.7	53.7	54.7	55.7	56.6	57.4	61.3	64.5	69.6	1.25
1.30	20.0	23.0	25.9	28.5	31.0	33.3	35.4	37.4	39.3	41.0	42.7	43.3	43.9	44.5	45.1	45.7	46.3	46.8	47.4	47.9	48.4	48.9	49.4	49.9	50.4	50.9	51.3	51.8	52.2	52.7	53.1	54.1	55.1	56.1	57.0	57.9	58.7	62.4	65.5	70.4	1.30
1.35	21.9	25.0	27.9	30.5	33.0	35.2	37.3	39.3	41.1	42.8	44.4	45.1	45.7	46.3	46.8	47.4	47.9	48.5	49.0	49.5	50.0	50.5	51.0	51.5	52.0	52.4	52.9	53.3	53.7	54.1	54.6	55.6	56.5	57.4	58.3	59.1	59.9	63.5	66.5	71.1	1.35
1.40	23.9	27.0	29.9	32.5	34.9	37.1	39.2	41.1	42.9	44.6	46.2	46.8	47.4	47.9	48.5	49.0	49.6	50.1	50.6	51.1	51.6	52.1	52.6	53.0	53.5	53.9	54.3	54.8	55.2	55.6	56.0	56.9	57.9	58.7	59.6	60.4	61.2	64.6	67.5	71.9	1.40
1.45	25.8	29.0	31.9	34.5	36.9	39.1	41.1	43.0	44.7	46.4	47.9	48.5	49.0	49.6	50.1	50.7	51.2	51.7	52.2	52.7	53.2	53.6	54.1	54.5	55.0	55.4	55.8	56.2	56.6	57.0	57.4	58.3	59.2	60.0	60.9	61.6	62.4	65.7	68.4	72.7	1.45
1.50	27.8	31.0	33.8	36.4	38.8	40.9	42.9	44.8	46.5	48.1	49.6	50.1	50.7	51.2	51.8	52.3	52.8	53.3	53.7	54.2	54.7	55.1	55.6	56.0	56.4	56.8	57.2	57.6	58.0	58.4	58.8	59.7	60.5	61.3	62.1	62.9	63.6	66.8	69.4	73.5	1.50
1.55	29.8	33.0	35.8	38.4	40.7	42.8	44.8	46.6	48.2	49.8	51.2	51.8	52.3	52.8	53.3	53.8	54.3	54.8	55.3	55.7	56.2	56.6	57.0	57.4	57.8	58.2	58.6	59.0	59.4	59.7	60.1	61.0	61.8	62.6	63.3	64.1	64.7	67.8	70.3	74.3	1.55
1.60	31.8	35.0	37.8	40.3	42.6	44.6	46.5	48.3	49.9	51.4	52.8	53.4	53.9	54.4	54.9	55.4	55.9	56.3	56.8	57.2	57.6	58.0	58.5	58.9	59.2	59.6	60.0	60.4	60.7	61.1	61.4	62.3	63.1	63.8	64.5	65.2	65.9	68.8	71.3	75.1	1.60
1.65	33.8	36.9	39.7	42.2	44.4	46.4	48.3	50.0	51.6	53.1	54.4	54.9	55.4	55.9	56.4	56.9	57.3	57.8	58.2	58.6	59.1	59.5	59.9	60.2	60.6	61.0	61.4	61.7	62.1	62.4	62.7	63.5	64.3	65.0	65.7	66.4	67.0	69.9	72.2	75.9	1.65
1.70	35.8	38.9	41.6	44.0	46.2	48.2	50.0	51.7	53.2	54.7	56.0	56.5	57.0	57.5	57.9	58.4	58.8	59.2	59.7	60.1	60.5	60.9	61.2	61.6	62.0	62.3	62.7	63.0	63.4	63.7	64.0	64.8	65.5	66.2	66.9	67.5	68.2	70.9	73.1	76.6	1.70
1.75	37.7	40.8	43.5	45.9	48.0	50.0	51.7	53.4	54.8	56.2	57.5	58.0	58.5	58.9	59.4	59.8	60.7	60.7	61.1	61.5	61.8	62.2	62.6	62.9	63.3	63.6	64.0	64.3	64.6	64.9	65.3	66.0	66.7	67.4	68.0	68.7	69.2	71.9	74.0	77.4	1.75
2.00	47.3	50.1	52.5	54.6	56.5	58.2	59.7	61.1	62.4	63.6	64.6	65.0	65.4	65.8	66.2	66.6	66.9	67.3	67.6	67.9	68.3	68.6	68.9	69.2	69.5	69.8	70.0	70.3	70.6	70.8	71.1	71.7	72.3	72.9	73.4	73.9	74.4	76.5	78.3	81.0	2.00
2.25	56.1	58.6	60.7	62.5	64.1	65.6	66.8	68.0	69.1	70.0	70.9	71.5	71.6	71.9	72.2	72.5	72.8	73.1	73.4	73.7	73.9	74.2	74.4	74.7	74.9	75.2	75.4	75.6	75.8	76.0	76.3	76.8	77.2	77.7	78.1	78.5	78.9	80.6	82.1	84.3	2.35
2.50	64.0	66.1	67.9	69.4	70.8	72.0	73.1	74.0	74.9	75.7	76.4	76.7	77.0	77.2	77.5	77.7	78.0	78.2	78.4	78.7	78.9	79.1	79.3	79.5	79.7	79.9	80.0	80.2	80.4	80.6	80.7	81.1	81.5	81.9	82.2	82.6	82.9	84.3	85.4	87.2	2.50
2.75	70.9	72.7	74.2	75.4	76.6	77.5	78.4	79.2	79.9	80.5	81.1	81.4	81.6	81.8	82.0	82.2	82.4	82.6	82.7	82.9	83.1	83.3	83.4	83.6	83.7	83.9	84.0	84.2	84.3	84.4	84.6	84.9	85.2	85.5	85.8	86.0	86.3	87.4	88.3	89.7	2.75
3.00	76.9	78.3	79.5	80.5	81.4	82.2	82.9	83.5	84.1	84.6	85.1	85.3	85.4	85.6	85.8	85.9	86.1	86.2	86.4	86.5	86.6	86.8	86.9	87.0	87.1	87.3	87.4	87.5	87.6	87.7	87.8	88.1	88.3	88.5	88.8	89.0	89.2	90.0	90.7	91.8	3.00
3.50	86.0	86.9	87.6	88.3	88.8	89.3	89.7	90.1	90.5	90.8	91.1	91.2	91.3	91.4	91.5	91.6	91.6	91.7	91.8	9.19	92.0	92.1	92.1	92.2	92.3	92.4	92.4	92.5	92.6	92.6	92.7	92.8	93.0	93.1	93.3	93.4	93.5	94.0	94.4	95.1	3.50
4.00	92.0	92.5	92.9	93.3	93.6	93.9	94.2	94.4	94.6	94.8	94.9	95.0	95.0	05.1	95.2	95.2	95.3	95.3	95.4	95.4	95.4	95.5	95.5	95.6	95.6	95.7	95.7	95.7	95.8	95.8	95.8	95.9	96.0	96.1	96.2	96.2	96.3	96.6	96.8	97.2	4.00
4.50	95.7	96.0	96.2	96.4	96.6	96.7	96.9	97.0	97.1	97.2	97.3	97.3	97.3	97.4	97.4	97.4	97.5	97.5	97.5	97.5	97.6	97.6	97.6	97.6	97.6	97.7	97.7	97.7	97.7	97.8	97.8	97.8	97.9	97.9	97.9	98.0	98.0	98.2	98.3	98.5	4.50
5.00	97.8	97.9	98.1	98.2	98.3	98.3	98.4	98.5	98.5	98.6	98.6	98.6	98.6	98.7	98.7	98.7	98.7	09.7	98.7	98.7	98.8	98.8	98.8	98.8	98.8	98.8	98.8	98.8	98.8	98.9	98.9	98.9	98.9	98.9	98.0	99.0	99.0	99.1	99.1	99.2	5.00
6.00	99.5	99.5	99.6	99.6	99.6	99.6	99.7	99.7	99.7	99.7	99.7	99.7	99.7	99.7	99.7	99.7	99.7	99.7	99.7	99.7	99.7	99.7	99.7	99.7	99.7	99.7	99.7	99.7	99.7	99.8	99.8	99.8	99.8	99.8	99.8	99.8	99.8	99.8	99.8	99.8	6.00

Note: Values in the table represent percentages of the underlying share price: for example, 40.4 denotes a call option worth 40.4 per cent of the underlying share price.
Values in the table were computed from the Black–Scholes option pricing model

Solutions to Selected End-of-Chapter Problems

Chapter 3

3.1   Total assets $=$ DEM128,000
       Ordinary shares $=$ DEM88,000
3.2   Ordinary shares $=$ NLG110,000,000
                RE $=$ NLG22,000,000
3.7   *a.* FRF25 million
       b. $-$FRF25 million

Chapter 5

5.1   *a.* GBP1,628.89
       b. GBP1,967.15
       c. GBP2,653.30
5.4   GBP92.30
5.5   CHF187,780.23
5.6   *a.* $PV_1 =$ GBP10,000 $PV_2 =$ GBP20,000
       b. $PV_1 =$ GBP9,090.91 $PV_2 =$ GBP12,418.43
       c. $PV_1 =$ GBP 8,333.33 $PV_2 =$ GBP8,037.55
       d. $r = 18.921\%$
5.9   NLG6,714.61
5.10   CHF1,609,866.18
5.15   *a.* DEM1,259.71
       b. DEM1,265.32
       c. DEM1,270.24
       d. DEM1,271.25
5.19 $P =$ GBP800
5.22   *a.* ESB10,000
       b. ESB 4,545.45
       c. ESB20,000
5.28   NPV $=$ FRF201.88
5.29   NLG16,834.88
5.31   9.0648%
5.32   *a.* CHF4,347.26
       b. CHF17,824.65
5.37   GBP440,011.07
5.38   NPV $=$ NLG282.87, purchase the machine

Chapter 6

6.2   *a.* NLG1,000.00
       b. NLG828.41
       c. NLG1,231.15
6.6   *a.* 12.36%
       b. DEM748.48

c. DEM906.15
6.10 $P =$ GBP7.50
6.13 $r = 14\%$
6.18   NLG26.95
6.20 $P =$ CHF23.75

Chapter 7

7.1   *a.* Project *A*
       b. Project *B*
7.3   *a.* 56.25%
7.5   12.87%
7.7   For Project *A*: $IRR_1 = 0\%$
                        $IRR_2 = 100\%$
       For Project *B*: $IRR = 36.1944\%$
7.8   *a.* IRR (Project *A*) $= 25.69\%$
           IRR (Project *B*) $= 19.43\%$
       e. 19.09%
       g. $NPV_A =$ GBP689.98
           $NPV_B =$ GBP5,671.08
       Choose Project *B*
7.15   *a.* Project *A*
       b. AAR (Sunday) $= 22.22\%$
           AAR (Saturday) $= 19.05\%$

Chapter 8

8.3   EPS $=$ GBP4
       NPVGO $=$ GBP3
         Price $=$ GBP36.33
8.4 $NPV_A =$ CHF1,446.76
       $NPV_B =$ CHF119.17
       Choose Project *A*
8.6   DEM705,882.35
8.8   DEM150,100

Chapter 9

9.5   *a.* 265,625 abalones
       b. GBP28,600

Chapter 10

10.1   *a.* USD1 per share

b. USD1,500

c. 8.11%

10.4 $E(R) = 14.7\%$

10.7   *b.* 8.49%

Chapter 11

11.1   *a.* $\bar{R} = 10.57\%$

b. $\sigma = 5.73\%$

11.4   Weight of Atlas stock $= \frac{2}{3}$

Weight of Beta stock $= \frac{1}{3}$

11.5 $\bar{R}_p = 16.2\%$

$\sigma_p = 18.23\%$

11.16 $E(R_M) - R_f = 15\%$

$E(R_p) - R_f = 20\%$

$\beta_p = 1.33$

$\sigma(R_m) = 3\%$

$E(R_S) = 10\%$

Chapter 12

12.3   *a.* $R_A = 10.5 + 1.2 \times (R_M - 14.2) + \epsilon_A$

$R_B = 13.0 + 0.98 \times (R_M - 14.2) + \epsilon_B$

$R_C = 15.7 + 1.37 \times (R_M - 14.2) + \epsilon_C$

b. $R_p = 12.925 + 1.1435 \times (R_M - 14.2) + 0.30\epsilon_A + 0.45\epsilon_B + 0.25\epsilon_C$

c. $R_p = 13.8398\%$

12.5   *a.* $\text{Var}(R_{1p}) = 0.0225$

$\text{Var}(R_{2p}) = 0.00225$

A risk averse investor will prefer to invest in the second market.

b. $\text{Var}(R_{1p}) = 0.0585$

$\text{Var}(R_{2p}) = 0.0025$

A risk averse investor will prefer to invest in the second market.

c. $\text{Var}(R_{1p}) = 0.0225$

$\text{Var}(R_{2p}) = 0.0225$

Indifferent between investing in the two markets.

d. Indifference implies that the variances of the portfolios in the two markets are equal.

$\text{Corr}(\epsilon_{2i}, \epsilon_{2j}) = \text{Corr}(\epsilon_{1i}, \epsilon_{1j}) + 0.5$

Chapter 13

13.3   *a.* $\bar{R}_T = 0.01633; \beta_T = 1.14036$

13.4   *b.*   *i.* $\bar{R}_m = 0.18$

iii. $\sigma_M = 0.01265$

d.   *i.* $\bar{R}_j = 0.2$

ii. $\sigma^2_j = 0.00048$

e. $\text{Corr}(R_m, R_i) = 0.635$

f. $\beta_j = 1.1$

Chapter 15

15.1   *a.* 67,715 shares

b. Average price = GBP5 per share

c. Book value = GBP40 per share

15.2   *a.* Ordinary shares = GBP500

Total = GBP150,500

Chapter 16

16.3   12.5%

16.6   *a.* 18%

b. $r_S = 20\%$

16.8   *a.* Value = FRF300 million

b. Value = FRF300 million

c. $r_S = 10.14\%$

16.11   *a.* $V_U = $ NLG1,530,000

b. NLG273,000

16.12   GBP2,800,000

Chapter 18

18.1   *a.* $I = $ USD350,625.29

b. B/C NPV = USD18,285.17

APV = USD40,005.51

c. $I = $ USD403,222.85

18.5   *a.* $r_S = 17.576\%$

b. $r_B = 10\%$, pre-tax

After-tax cost of debt = 6.6%

c. 13.917%

18.6 $\beta_S = 1.21; r_S = 17.293\%$

$V = $ GBP84,000,000; WACC = 14.426%

NPV = GBP3.084 million

Chapter 19

19.6   *a.* $P_0 = $ USD19.17

b. $P_0 = $ USD20.00

Chapter 20

20.1   At CHF40, $P = $ CHF40.00

At CHF20, $P = $ CHF33.33

At CHF10, $P = $ CHF30.00

20.5   *a.* 800,000 shares

b. 3

c. DKK15 and three rights

20.6   *a.* Ex-rights price = NLG24.55

b. Value of a right = NLG0.45

c. Value = NLG2,700,500

20.8   *a.* FRF36.25

b. FRF 8.75

Chapter 21

21.4   *a.* $P = $ GBP126.64

21.5   Coupon rate = 12.4%

Chapter 22

22.5   *a.* NLG5

b. NLG0

22.6   *a.* NLG0

b. NLG5

22.12   FRF0.5974

22.14 $C = $ DKK1.61

22.16   *a.* $C = $ DKK5.89

b. $P = $ DKK11.28

Chapter 23

23.4 *a.* USD1,750
   b. USD514.29
   c. i. USD3,640
      iii. USD5,440/3 = USD1,813.33
      iv. Gain = USD13.33
   d. USD20
23.5 *a.* Lower limit = DEM0
      Upper limit = DEM2
   b. Lower limit = DEM0.5
      Upper limit = DEM3
23.12 *a. i.* 28
      ii. DEM35.71
      iii. 14.27%
   b. i. 28
      ii. The conversion price is only meaningful if the bond is selling at par.
   c. DEM875
   d. Method One = DEM931
      Method Two = DEM931
23.14 DEM333.33

Chapter 24

24.3 *a.* Lease vs. buy NPV = −Euro3,177.78
   c. Euro18,177.78

Chapter 25

25.2 *a.* 5.26%
25.4 *a.* 7.14%
   b. Increase dividend payout ratio to $d = 1$.

Chapter 26

26.3 Total sources = Euro82,325

Chapter 27

27.1 PV(Old) = GBP26,948.12
   $T = 50$ days (for customers not taking the discount)
27.2 DEM1,232,876.71
27.3 *a.* NPV(Credit) = NLG3,029.13
   b. 99.57%
27.7 Accounts receivable = CHF384,247

Chapter 28

28.6 *b.* Prob (Joint value = GBP200,000) = 0.01
      Prob (Joint value = GBP600,000) = 0.40
      Prob (Debt value = GBP300,000) = 0.08
      Prob (Debt value = GBP400,000) = 0.91
      Prob (Stock value = GBP0) = 0.25
   c. Value of each company = GBP290,000
   d. Total debt value before merger = GBP380,000
      Total debt value after merger = GBP390,000
28.9 *a.* NLG7,500,000
   b. V = NLG27,500,000
   c. Cash: NLG15,000,000
      Shares: NLG15,625,000
28.10 *a.* NLG14,815,385

Chapter 29

29.1 *a.* USD0.55 or DEM1.8181
   b. Buy DEM sell USD in Frankfurt
      Sell DEM buy USD in New York
29.2 *a.* GBP1 = DEM2.9091
   b. Buy DEM sell GBP in New York
      Sell DEM buy GBP in Frankfurt
29.3 *a.* Invest in USD
   b. USD1.7912
   c. Invest in GBP
   d. 12.56%
29.6 *a.* CHF1 = DEM1.157470 − 1.158863 or
      DEM1 = CHF0.8629 − 0.8640
   b. GBP1 = DEM2.9279 − 2.9313 or
      DEM1 = GBP0.3411 − 0.3415

Glossary

AAR   Average accounting return.

APT   Arbitrage pricing theory.

Accounting insolvency   Total liabilities exceed total assets. A firm with negative net worth is insolvent on the books.

Accounting liquidity   The ease and quickness with which assets can be converted to cash.

Accounts payable   Money the firm owes to suppliers.

Accounts receivable   Money owed to the firm by customers.

Accounts receivable financing   A secured short-term loan that involves either the assigning of receivables or the factoring of receivables. Under assignment, the lender has a lien on the receivables and recourse to the borrower. Factoring involves the sale of accounts receivable. Then the purchaser, called the factor, collects the receivables.

Accounts receivable turnover   Credit sales divided by average accounts receivable.

Additions to net working capital   Component of cash flow of firm, along with operating cash flow and capital spending.

Agency costs   Costs of conflicts of interest among shareholders, bondholders and managers. Agency costs are the costs of resolving these conflicts. They include the costs of providing managers with an incentive to maximize shareholder wealth and then monitoring their behaviour and the cost of protecting bondholders from shareholders. Agency costs are borne by shareholders.

Agency theory   The theory of the relationship between principals and agents. It involves the nature of the costs of resolving conflicts of interest between principals and agents.

Aggregation   Process in corporate financial planning whereby the smaller investment proposals of each of the firm's operational units are added up and in effect treated as a big picture.

Ageing schedule   A compilation of accounts receivable by the age of account.

American Depository Receipt (ADR)   A security issued in the United States to represent shares of a foreign company, enabling those shares to be traded in the United States.

American option   An option contract that may be exercised anytime up to the expiration date. A European option may be exercised only on the expiration date.

Amortization   Repayment of a loan in instalments. Also refers to depreciation of leasehold property.

Annualized holding-period return   The annual rate of return that, when compounded T times, would have given the same T-period holding return as actually occurred from period 1 to period T.

Annuity   A level stream of equal cash payments that lasts for a fixed time. An example of an annuity is the coupon part of a bond with level annual payments.

Annuity factor   The term used to calculate the present value of the stream of level payments for a fixed period.

Annuity in advance   An annuity with an immediate initial payment.

Annuity in arrears   An annuity with a first payment one full period hence, rather than immediately. The first payment occurs on date 1 rather than on date 0.

Arbitrage   Buying an asset in one market at a lower price and simultaneously selling an identical asset in another market at a higher price. This is done with no risk.

Arbitrage pricing theory (APT)   An equilibrium asset pricing theory that is derived from a factor model by using diversification and arbitrage. It shows that the expected return on any risky asset is a linear combination of various factors.

Arithmetic average   The sum of the values observed divided by the total number of observations—sometimes referred to as the mean.

Assets   Anything that the firm owns.

At the money   An option when the value of its underlying security is equal to the option strike price.

Auction market   A market where all traders in a certain good meet at one place to buy or sell an asset. A stock exchange is an example.

Autocorrelation   The correlation of a variable with itself over successive time intervals.

Availability float   Refers to the time required to clear a cheque through the banking system.

Average accounting return (AAR) The average project earnings before taxes but after depreciation divided by the average book value of the investment during its life.

Average collection period Average amount of time required to collect an account receivable. Also referred to as days sales outstanding.

Average cost of capital A firm's required return to the bondholders and the shareholders expressed as a percentage of capital contributed to the firm. Average cost of capital is computed by dividing the total required cost of capital by the total amount of contributed capital.

Average daily sales Annual sales divided by 365 days.

Balance sheet A statement showing a firm's accounting value on a particular date. It reflects the equation, Assets = Liabilities + Shareholders' equity.

Balloon The principal amount repaid on maturity of a loan that is significantly larger than the annual repayments. For example an issue could have six payments of 10 per cent, followed by a balloon of 40 per cent at maturity.

Balloon payment See **Balloon**.

Banker's acceptance Agreement by a bank to pay a given sum of money at a future date.

Bankruptcy State of being unable to pay debts. Thus the ownership of the firm's assets is transferred from the shareholders to the bondholders.

Bankruptcy costs See **Financial distress costs.**

Bargain-purchase-price option Gives lessee the option to purchase the asset at a price below fair market value when the lease expires.

Basic IRR rule Accept the project if IRR is greater than the hurdle rate; reject the project if IRR is less than the hurdle rate.

Basket An artificial currency, based on a mixture of actual currencies. For example, the ECU is an artificial currency based upon a basket of EU currencies.

Bearer bond A bond issued without record of the owner's name. Whoever holds the bond (the bearer) is the owner.

Bells and whistles The additional features of a security intended to attract investors or reduce issue costs or both.

Best-efforts underwriting An offering in which an underwriter agrees to distribute as much of the offering as possible and to return any unsold shares to the issuer.

Beta coefficient A measure of the sensitivity of a security's return to movements in an underlying factor. It is a measured systematic risk.

Bidder A firm or person that has made an offer to take over another firm.

Bill of exchange A negotiable instrument, used mainly in international trade, instructing one person, the drawee, to pay a certain sum of money to another named person, the drawer, on demand or at a certain future time. If the drawee, or acceptor, of the bill is a bank, the bill is a bank bill (known as a banker's acceptance); if it is a trader, the bill is a trade bill; if it is the UK or US government, it is a Treasury bill. Such bills are normally issued with 90-day lives, and their marketability depends on the standing of the drawee or acceptor, the nature of the underlying transaction and whether the bill is eligible for rediscounting with the central bank. Such latter bills of exchange are called eligible bills.

Black–Scholes call pricing equation An exact formula for the price of a call option. The formula requires five variables: the risk-free interest rate, the variance of the underlying share the exercise price, the price of the underlying share, and the time to expiration.

Blanket inventory lien A secured loan that gives the lender a lien against all the borrower's inventories.

Bond A long-term debt of a firm. In common usage, the term *bond* often refers to both secured and unsecured debt.

Book cash A firm's cash balance as reported in its financial statements.

Book value per share Per-share accounting equity value of a firm. Total accounting equity divided by the number of outstanding shares.

Bookbuilding A mechanism of new issue of shares in which investment banks, brokers and other financial intermediaries and their respective clienteles indicate to the issuing house the number of shares which they are prepared to apply for at the specified price.

Borrow To obtain or receive money on loan with the promise or understanding of returning it or its equivalent.

Break-even analysis Analysis of the level of sales at which a project would make exactly zero profit.

Bubble theory (of speculative markets) Security prices sometimes move wildly above their true values.

Bullet A straight debt issue with repayment in one go at maturity.

Business angels Individuals providing venture capital.

Business failure A business that has terminated with a loss to creditors.

Business risk The risk that the firm's shareholders bear if the firm is financed only with equity.

Buying the index Purchasing the shares in an index, for example the Financial Times - Stock Exchange 100, in the same proportion as the index to achieve the same return.

CAPM Capital asset pricing model.

CAR Cumulative abnormal return.

Call option The right, but not the obligation, to buy a fixed number of shares at a stated price within a specified time.

Call premium The price of a call option on ordinary shares.

Call price of a bond Amount at which a firm has the right to repurchase its bonds or debentures before the stated maturity date.

Call protected Describes a bond that is not allowed to be called, usually for a certain early period in the life of the bond.

Call provision A written agreement between an issuing company and its bondholders that gives the company the option to redeem the bond at a specified price before the maturity date.

Callable Refers to a bond that may be repurchased at a stated call price before maturity.

Cannibalization Cash flow amount transferred to a new product line from customers and sales of other products of the firm. Also called erosion.

Capital asset pricing model (CAPM) An equilibrium asset pricing theory that shows that equilibrium rates of expected return on all risky assets are a function of their covariance with the market portfolio.

Capital budgeting Planning and managing expenditures for long-lived assets.

Capital gains The positive change in the value of an asset. A negative capital gain is a capital loss.

Capital market line The efficient set of all assets, both risky and riskless, which provides the investor with the best possible opportunities.

Capital markets Financial markets for long-term debt and for equity shares.

Capital rationing The case where funds are limited to a fixed cash amount and must be allocated among competing projects.

Capital structure The mix of the various debt and equity capital maintained by a firm. Also called financial structure. The composition of a company's securities used to finance its investment activities; the relative proportions of short-term debt, long-term debt, and owners' equity.

Carrying costs Costs that increase with increases in the level of investment in current assets.

Cash budget A forecast of cash receipts and disbursements expected by a firm in the coming year. It is a short-term financial planning tool.

Cash cow A business that generates substantial cash after allowing for reinvestment and taxation.

Cash cycle In general, the time between cash disbursement and cash collection. In net working capital management, it can be thought of as the operating cycle less the accounts payable payment period.

Cash discount A discount given for a cash purchase. One reason a cash discount may be offered is to speed up the collection of receivables.

Cash flow Cash generated by the firm and paid to creditors and shareholders. It can be classified as (1) cash flow from operations, (2) cash flow from changes in fixed assets, and (3) cash flow from changes in net working capital.

Cash flow after interest and taxes Net income plus depreciation.

Cash flow time line Line depicting the operating activities and cash flows for a firm over a particular period.

Cash offer A public equity issue that is sold to interested investors.

Cash transaction A transaction where exchange is immediate, as contrasted to a forward contract, which calls for future delivery of an asset at an agreed-upon price.

Cashout Refers to situation where a firm runs out of cash and cannot readily sell marketable securities.

Certificates of deposit Short-term loans to commercial banks.

Change in net working capital Difference between net working capital from one period to another.

Changes in fixed assets Component of cash flow that equals sales of fixed assets minus the acquisition of fixed assets.

Characteristic line The line relating the expected return on a security to different returns on the market.

Chartism See **Technical analysis**

Clearing The exchange of cheques and balancing of accounts between banks.

Clientele effect Argument that shares attract clienteles based on dividend yield or taxes. For example, a tax clientele effect is induced by the difference in tax treatment of dividend income and capital gains income; high tax-bracket individuals tend to prefer low-dividend yields.

Coinsurance effect Refers to the fact that the merger of two firms decreases the probability of default on either's debt.

Collateral Assets that are pledged as security for payment of debt.

Collection float An increase in book cash with no immediate change in bank cash, generated by cheques deposited by the firm that have not cleared.

Collection policy Procedures followed by a firm in attempting to collect accounts receivable.

Commercial draft Demand for payment.

Commercial paper Short-term, unsecured promissory notes issued by companies with a high credit standing.

Common stock See **Ordinary shares**

Compensating balance Deposit that the firm keeps with the bank in a low-interest or non-interest-bearing account to compensate banks for loans or services.

Competitive offer Method of selecting an investment banker for a new issue by offering the securities to the underwriter bidding highest.

Compound interest Interest that is earned both on the initial principal and on interest earned on the initial principal in previous periods. The interest earned in one period becomes in effect part of the principal in a following period.

Compound value Value of a sum after investing it over one or more periods. Also called future value.

Compounding Process of reinvesting each interest payment to earn more interest. Compounding is based on the idea that interest itself becomes principal and therefore also earns interest in subsequent periods.

Concentration banking The use of geographically dispersed collection centres to speed up the collection of accounts receivable.

Conditional sales contract An arrangement whereby the firm retains legal ownership of the goods until the customer has completed payment.

Conflict between bondholders and shareholders These two groups may have interests in the company that conflict. Sources of conflict include dividends, dilution, distortion of investment and underinvestment. Protective covenants work to resolve these conflicts.

Conglomerate acquisition Acquisition in which the

acquired firm and the acquiring firm are not related, unlike a horizontal or a vertical acquisition.

Consol A bond that carries a promise to pay a coupon forever. It has no final maturity date and therefore never matures.

Consumer credit Credit granted to consumers. Trade credit is credit granted to other firms.

Contingent claim Claim whose value is directly dependent on, or is contingent on, the value of its underlying assets. For example, the debt and equity securities issued by a firm derive their value from the total value of the firm.

Continuous compounding Interest compounded continuously, every instant, rather than at fixed intervals.

Contribution margin Amount that each additional product contributes to profit, that is (Sales price − Variable cost).

Conversion premium Difference between the conversion price and the current share price divided by the current share price.

Conversion price The amount of value exchangeable for one ordinary share. This term really refers to the share price and means the cash amount of the bond's face value that is exchangeable for one share.

Conversion ratio The number of shares per GBP100 (or mark or franc or whatever) bond (or debenture) that a bondholder would receive if the bond were converted into shares.

Conversion value What a convertible bond would be worth if it were immediately converted into the ordinary shares at the current price.

Convertible bond A bond that may be converted into another form of security, typically ordinary shares, at the option of the holder at a specified price for a specified period of time.

Corporation Form of business organization that is created as a distinct 'legal person' composed of one or more actual individuals or legal entities. Primary advantages of a corporation include limited liability, ease of ownership transfer and perpetual succession.

Correlation A standardized statistical measure of the dependence of two random variables. It is defined as the covariance divided by the standard deviations of two variables.

Cost of equity capital The required return on the company's ordinary shares in capital markets. It is also called the equity holders' required rate of return because it is what equity holders can expect to obtain in the capital market. It is a cost from the firm's perspective.

Coupon The stated interest on a debt instrument.

Covariance A statistical measure of the degree to which random variables move together.

Credit analysis The process of determining whether a credit applicant meets the firm's standards and what amount of credit the applicant should receive.

Credit instrument Device by which a firm offers credit, such as an invoice, a promissory note, or a conditional sales contract.

Credit period Time allowed a credit purchaser to remit the full payment for credit purchases.

Credit scoring Determining the probability of default when granting customers credit.

Creditor Person or institution that holds the debt issued by a firm or individual.

Cross rate The exchange rate between two foreign currencies, neither of which is the US dollar.

Crown jewels An antitakeover tactic in which major assets—the crown jewels—are sold by a firm when faced with a takeover threat.

Cum dividend With dividend.

Cumulative abnormal return (CAR) Sum of differences between the expected return on a share and the actual return that comes from the release of news to the market.

Cumulative preference dividend Dividend on preferred shares that takes priority over dividend payments on ordinary shares. Dividends may not be paid on the ordinary shares until all past dividends on the preferred shares have been paid.

Cumulative probability The probability that a drawing from the standardized normal distribution will be below a particular value.

Cumulative variance Multiplying variance per unit of time by the time an option has to run to maturity gives cumulative variance.

Cumulative voting A procedure whereby a shareholder may cast all of his or her votes for one member of the board of directors.

Current asset Asset that is in the form of cash or that is expected to be converted into cash in the next 12 months, such as inventory.

Current liabilities Obligations that are expected to require cash payment within one year or the operating period.

Current ratio Total current assets divided by total current liabilities. Used to measure short-term solvency of a firm.

Date of dividend payment Date that dividend cheques are mailed.

Date of record Date on which holders of record in a firm's share register are designated as the recipients of either dividends or share rights.

Dates convention Treating cash flows as being received on exact dates—date 0, date 1, and so forth—as opposed to the end-of-year convention.

Days in receivables Average collection period.

Days sales outstanding Average collection period.

De facto Existing in actual fact although not by official legal recognition.

Dealer market A market where traders specializing in particular commodities buy and sell assets for their own account.

Debenture A loosely used term generally meaning an unsecured medium-term bond. A debt obligation backed by the general credit of the issuing company.

Debt Loan agreement that is a liability of the firm. An obligation to repay a specified amount at a particular time.

Debt capacity Ability to borrow. The amount a firm can borrow up to the point where the firm value no longer increases.

Debt displacement The amount of borrowing that leasing displaces. Firms that do a lot of leasing will be forced to cut back on borrowing.

Debt ratio Total debt divided by total assets.

Debt service Interest payments plus repayments of principal to creditors, that is, retirement of debt.

Decision trees A graphical representation of possible sequential decisions and the possible outcomes of those decisions.

Declaration date Date on which the board of directors passes a resolution to pay a dividend of a specified amount to all qualified holders of record on a specified date.

Deep-discount bond A bond issued with a very low coupon or no coupon and selling at a price far below par value. When the bond has no coupon, it is also called a zero coupon bond or pure-discount or original-issue-discount bond.

Default risk The chance that interest or principal will not be paid on the due date and in the promised amount.

Deficit The amount by which a sum of money is less than the required amount. An excess of liabilities over assets, of losses over profits or of expenditure over income.

Deliverable instrument The asset in a forward contract that will be delivered in the future at an agreed-upon price.

Denomination Face value or principal of a bond.

Depreciation A non-cash expense, such as the cost of plant or equipment, charged against earnings to write off the cost of an asset during its estimated useful life.

Depreciation tax shield Portion of an investment that can be deducted from taxable income.

Dilution Loss in existing shareholders' value. There are several kinds of dilution, for example (1) dilution of ownership, (2) dilution of market value and (3) dilution of book value and earnings, as with warrants and convertible issues. Firms with significant amounts of warrants or convertible issues outstanding are required to report earnings on a 'fully diluted' basis.

Direct lease A lease under which a lessor buys equipment from a manufacturer and leases it to a lessee.

Disbursement float A decrease in book cash, but no immediate change in bank cash, generated by cheques written by the firm.

Discount If a bond is selling below its face value, it is said to sell at a discount.

Discount rate Rate used to calculate the present value of future cash flows.

Discounted payback period rule An investment decision rule in which the cash flows are discounted at an interest rate and the payback rule is applied on these discounted cash flows.

Discounting Calculating the present value of a future amount. The process is the opposite of compounding.

Diversifiable risk A risk that specifically affects a single asset or a small group of assets. Also called unique or unsystematic risk.

Dividend Payment made by a firm to its owners, either in cash or in shares.

Dividend growth model A model wherein dividends are assumed to be at a constant rate in perpetuity.

Dividend payout Amount of cash paid to shareholders expressed as a percentage of earnings per share.

Dividend yield Dividends per ordinary share divided by market price per share.

Dividends per share Amount of cash paid to shareholders expressed as pence, dollars, pfennig (or whatever) per share.

Duration The weighted average time of an asset's cash flows. The weights are determined by present value factors.

EAC Equivalent annual cost.

EBIT Earnings before interest and taxes.

ECU See **European Currency Unit.**

EMH Efficient market hypothesis.

EMS See **European Monetary System**.

EMU See **Economic and Monetary Union.**

ERM See **Exchange Rate Mechanism.**

Economic and Monetary Union (EMU) The ultimate goal of Economic and Monetary Union (sometimes loosely referred to as European Monetary Union) is a European Union in which national currencies are replaced by a single European currency managed by a sole central bank operating on behalf of EMU members. It is planned to be phased in.

Economic assumptions Economic environment in which the firm is expected to reside over the life of the financial plan.

Effective annual interest rate The interest rate as if it were compounded once per time period rather than several times per period.

Efficient market hypothesis (EMH) The prices of securities fully reflect available information. Investors buying bonds and shares in an efficient market should expect to obtain an equilibrium rate of return. Firms should expect to receive the "fair" value (present value) for the securities they sell.

Efficient set Graph representing a set of portfolios that maximize expected return at each level of portfolio risk.

End-of-year convention Treating cash flows as if they occur at the end of a year (or, alternatively, at the end of a period), as opposed to the date convention. Under the end-of-year convention, the end of year 0 is the present, the end of year 1 occurs one period hence, and so on.

Equilibrium rate of interest The interest rate that clears the market. Also called market-clearing interest rate.

Equity Ownership interest of ordinary shareholders in a company. Given by total assets minus total liabilities (total liabilities to include preference shares).

Equity kicker Used to refer to warrants issued in combination with bonds.

Equity share An ownership interest which bears most risk in a company and participates in any residual return.

Erosion Cash-flow amount transferred to a new project from customers and sales of other products of the firm. Also called cannibalization.

Eurobanks Banks that make loans and accept deposits in foreign currencies.

Eurobond An international bond sold primarily in countries other than the country in whose currency the issue is denominated.

Eurocurrency Money deposited in a financial centre outside of the country whose currency is involved.

Eurodollar A dollar deposited in a bank outside the United States.

Eurodollar CD Deposit of dollars with foreign banks.

European Currency Unit (ECU) A basket currency of European foreign exchange originally devised in 1979. It is the forerunner of the Euro, the planned European common currency.

European option An option contract that may be exercised only on the expiration date. An American option may be exercised any time up to the expiration date.

European monetary system (EMS) A structure of agreements governing the exchange market activities of participating members of the European Union. Agreements require members to manage closely the exchange values of their currencies relative to those of other members.

Event study A statistical study that examines how the release of information affects prices at a particular time.

Ex rights or ex dividend Phrases used to indicate that a share is selling without a recently declared right or dividend.

Exchange controls Restrictions imposed by the central bank or other government authorities on the convertibility of a currency, or on the movement of funds in that currency.

Exchange rate Price of one country's currency in terms of another.

Exchange rate mechanism (ERM) A system of intervention in the foreign exchange markets designed to keep participating EU countries within a narrow range versus the ECU.

Exercise price Price at which the holder of an option can buy (in the case of a call option) or sell (in the case of a put option) the underlying share. Also called the strike price.

Exercising the option The act of buying or selling the underlying asset via the option contract.

Expectations theory (of foreign exchange rates) Theory that forward exchange rates are unbiased estimates of expected future exchange rates.

Expectations hypothesis (of interest rates) Theory that forward interest rates are unbiased estimates of expected future interest rates.

Expected return Average of possible returns weighted by their probability.

Expiration date Maturity date of an option.

Extinguish Retire or pay off debt.

Face value The value of a bond that appears on its face. Also referred to as par value or principal.

FTSE 100 Financial Times-Stock Exchange composite index of 100 British ordinary shares.

Factor A financial institution that buys a firm's accounts receivables and collects the debt.

Factoring Sale of a firm's accounts receivable to a financial institution known as a factor.

Fair market value Amount at which a financial instrument would change hands between a willing buyer and a willing seller, both having knowledge of the relevant facts. Also called market price.

Feasible set Opportunity set.

Financial distress Events preceding and including bankruptcy, such as violation of loan contracts.

Financial distress costs Legal and administrative costs of liquidation or reorganization (direct costs) plus an impaired ability to do business and an incentive towards selfish strategies such as taking large risks, underinvesting and milking the property (indirect costs).

Financial intermediaries Institutions that provide the market function of matching borrowers and lenders or traders.

Financial lease A long-term non cancellable lease generally requiring the lessee to pay all maintenance costs. Also called finance lease or capital lease.

Financial leverage Extent to which a firm relies on debt. Also called gearing.

Financial markets Markets that deal with cash flows over time, where the savings of lenders are allocated to the financing needs of borrowers.

Financial requirements In the financial plan, financing arrangements that are necessary to meet the overall corporate objective.

Financial risk The additional risk that the firm's shareholders bear when the firm is financed with debt as well as equity.

Firm commitment underwriting An underwriting in which an investment banking firm commits to buy the entire issue and assumes all financial responsibility for any unsold shares.

Fixed asset Long-lived property owned by a firm that is used by a firm in the production of its income. Tangible fixed assets include real property, plant and equipment. Intangible fixed assets include patents, trademarks and brands.

Fixed cost A cost that is fixed in total. It is not dependent on the amount of goods or services produced during the period.

Float The difference between bank cash and book cash. Float represents the net effect of cheques in the process of collection, or clearing.

Floater Floating-rate bond.

Floating-rate bond A debt obligation with an adjustable coupon payment.

Forced conversion If the conversion value of a convertible is greater than the call price, the call can be used to force conversion.

Foreign bonds   An international bond issued by foreign borrowers in another nation's capital market and traditionally denominated in that nation's currency.

Foreign exchange market   Market in which arrangements are made today for future exchange of major currencies; used to hedge against major swings in foreign exchange rates.

Forward contract   An arrangement calling for future delivery of an asset at an agreed-upon price.

Forward exchange rate   Averaged future day's exchange rate between two major currencies. It is agreed as of now.

Forward trade   An agreement to buy or sell based on exchange rates established today for settlement in the future.

Frequency distribution   The organization of data to show how often certain values or ranges of values occur.

Fully diluted   See **Dilution**.

Funded debt   Long-term debt.

Future value   Value of a sum after investing it over one or more periods. Also called compound value.

Futures contract   Obliges traders to purchase or sell an asset at an agreed-upon price on a specified future date. The long position is held by the trader who commits to purchase. The short position is held by the trader who commits to sell. Futures differ from forward contracts in their standardization, exchange trading, margin requirements, and daily settling (marking to market).

GAAP   Generally Accepted Accounting Principles.

Gearing   Extent to which a firm relies on debt. Also called financial leverage.

General partnership   Form of business organization in which all partners agree to provide some portion of the work and cash and to share profits and losses. Each partner is liable for the debts of the partnership.

Generally Accepted Accounting Principles (GAAP)   A common set of accounting concepts, standards and procedures by which financial statements are prepared.

Geometric mean   Annualized holding-period return.

Gilts   UK and Irish government securities.

Going-private transactions   Publicly owned shares in a firm are replaced with complete equity ownership by a private group. The shares are delisted from stock exchanges and can no longer be purchased in the open market.

Golden parachute   Compensation paid to top-level management by a target firm if a takeover occurs.

Goodwill   The excess of the purchase price over the sum of the book (or fair market) values of the individual assets acquired.

Greenmail   Payments to potential bidders to cease unfriendly takeover attempts. Its legality varies from country to country.

Green-shoe provision   A contract provision that gives the underwriter the option to purchase additional shares at the offering price to cover overallotments.

Growing perpetuity   A constant stream of cash flows without end that is expected to rise indefinitely. For example, cash flows to the landlord of a block of flats might be expected to rise by a certain percentage each year.

Growth opportunity   Opportunity to invest in profitable projects.

Hedging   Taking a position in two or more securities that are negatively correlated (taking opposite trading positions) to reduce risk.

High-yield bond   Junk bond.

Holding period   Length of time that an individual holds a security.

Holding-period return   The rate of return over a given period.

Homemade dividends   An individual investor can undo corporate dividend policy by reinvesting excess dividends or selling off shares to receive a desired cash flow.

Homemade leverage   Idea that as long as individuals borrow (and lend) on the same terms as the firm, they can duplicate the effects of corporate leverage on their own. Thus, if levered firms are priced too high, rational investors will simply borrow on personal accounts to buy shares in unlevered firms.

Homogeneous expectations   Idea that all individuals have the same beliefs concerning future investments, profits, and dividends.

Horizontal acquisition   Merger or takeover between two companies producing similar goods or services.

IPO   Initial public offering.

IRR   Internal rate of return.

Immunized   Immune to interest-rate risk.

In the money   Describes an option whose exercise would produce profits. Out of the money describes an option whose exercise would not be profitable.

Income bond   A bond on which the payment of income is contingent on sufficient earnings. Income bonds are commonly used during the reorganization of a failed or failing business.

Income statement   Financial report that summarizes a firm's performance over a specified time period. Also called profit and loss account.

Incremental cash flows   Difference between the firm's cash flows with and without a project.

Incremental IRR   IRR on the incremental investment from choosing one project rather than another, for example from choosing a larger project instead of a smaller project.

Indenture   Written agreement between the corporate debt issuer and the lender, setting forth maturity date, interest rate and other terms.

Independent project   A project whose acceptance or rejection is independent of the acceptance or rejection of other projects.

Inflation   An increase in the amount of money in circulation, resulting in a fall in its value and rise in prices.

Inflation-escalator clause   A clause in a contract providing for increases or decreases in price based on fluctuations in inflation which may be measured by the cost of living, production costs, and so forth.

Information-content effect   The rise in the share price following the dividend signal.

Initial public offering (IPO)   The original sale of a

company's securities to the public. Also called an unseasoned new issue.

Inside information Non-public knowledge about a company possessed by people in special positions inside a firm.

Instruments Financial securities, such as money market instruments or capital market instruments.

Interest coverage ratio Earnings before interest and taxes divided by interest expense. Used to measure a firm's ability to pay interest.

Interest on interest Interest earned on reinvestment of each interest payment on money invested.

Interest rate The price paid for borrowing money. It is the rate of exchange of present consumption for future consumption, or the price of current cash in terms of future cash.

Interest rate on debt The firm's cost of debt capital. Also called return on the debt.

Interest-rate-parity theorem The interest rate differential between two countries will be equal to the difference between the forward-exchange rate and the spot-exchange rate.

Interest-rate risk The chance that a change in the interest rate will result in a change in the value of a security.

Interest subsidy A firm's deduction of the interest payments on its debt from its earnings before it calculates its tax bill.

Internal financing Net income (after interest and taxes) plus depreciation minus dividends. Internal financing comes from internally generated cash flow.

Internal rate of return (IRR) A discount rate at which the net present value of an investment is zero. The IRR is a method of evaluating capital expenditure proposals.

Inventory A current asset composed of raw materials to be used in production, work in process and finished goods.

Inventory loan A secured short-term loan to purchase inventory.

Inventory turnover ratio Ratio of annual sales to average inventory that measures how quickly inventory is produced and sold.

Investment bankers Financial intermediaries who perform a variety of services, including aiding in the sale of securities, facilitating mergers and other corporate reorganizations, acting as brokers to both individual and institutional clients, and trading for their own accounts. Also called merchant bankers.

Investment grade bond Debt that is rated BBB and above by Standard & Poor's or Baa and above by Moody's.

Invoice Bill written by a seller of goods or services and submitted to the purchaser.

Junk bond A speculative grade bond, rated Ba or lower by Moody's, or BB or lower by Standard & Poor's, or an unrated bond. Because they are speculative, they carry high interest rates. Also called a high-yield or low-grade bond.

LBO Leveraged buyout.

LIBOR London interbank offered rate.

LIFFE See **London International Financial Futures Exchange**.

Law of one price (LOP) A commodity will cost the same regardless of what currency is used to purchase it.

Lease A contractual arrangement to grant the use of specific fixed assets for a specified time in exchange for payment, usually in the form of rent. An operating lease is generally a short-term cancellable arrangement, whereas a financial, or capital, lease is a long-term non-cancellable agreement.

Lend To provide money temporarily on the condition that it or its equivalent will be returned, often with an interest fee.

Lessee One that receives the use of assets under a lease.

Lessor One that conveys the use of assets under a lease.

Level-coupon bond Bond with a stream of coupon payments that are the same throughout the life of the bond.

Leveraged buyout Takeover of a company by using borrowed funds, usually by a group including some member of existing management.

Leveraged equity Shares in a firm that relies on financial leverage. Holders of leveraged equity face the benefits and costs of using debt.

Leveraged lease Tax-oriented leasing arrangement that involves one or more third-party lenders.

Liabilities Debts of the firm in the form of financial claims on a firm's assets.

Limited partnership Form of business organization that permits the liability of some partners to be limited by the amount of cash contributed by them to the partnership.

Line of credit A *non-committed* line of credit is an informal agreement that allows firms to borrow up to a previously specified limit without going through the normal paperwork. A *committed* line of credit is a formal legal arrangement and usually involves a commitment fee paid by the firm to the bank.

Lintner's observations John Lintner's work (1956) suggested that dividend policy is related to a target level of dividends and the speed of adjustment of change in dividends.

Liquidation Termination of the firm as a going concern. Liquidation involves selling the assets of the firm for salvage value. The proceeds, net of transaction costs, are distributed to creditors in order of established priority.

Liquidity Refers to the ease and quickness of converting assets to cash. Also called marketability.

Lockbox Post office box set up to intercept accounts receivable payments. Lockboxes are a widely used device to speed up collection of cash.

Lombard rate A German term for the rate of interest charged for a loan against the security of a pledged promissory note. Particularly used by the Bundesbank, which normally maintains its Lombard rate at about 0.5 per cent above its discount rate.

London interbank bid rate (LIBID) The London rate at which the major banks will bid to take deposits from each other for a given maturity, normally between overnight and five years.

London interbank mean rate (LIMEAN) The average of LIBID and LIBOR.

London interbank offered rate (LIBOR) Rate that the most creditworthy banks charge one another for large loans in the London market.

London International Forward Futures Exchange (LIFFE) A centralized market in London where standardized currency contracts, currency options and financial futures are traded.

Long run A period of time in which all costs are variable.

Long-term debt An obligation having a maturity of more than one year from the date it was issued.

Low-grade bond Junk bond.

MM Proposition I A proposition of Modigliani and Miller (MM) which states that a firm cannot change the total value of its outstanding securities by changing its capital structure proportions.

MM Proposition II A proposition of Modigliani and Miller (MM) which states that the cost of equity is a linear function of the firm's debt–equity ratio.

Mail float Refers to the part of the collection and disbursement process where cheques are trapped in the postal system.

Make a market The obligation of a specialist to offer to buy and sell shares. It is assumed that this makes the market liquid, because the specialist assumes the role of a buyer for investors if they wish to sell and a seller if they wish to buy.

Making delivery Refers to the seller's actually turning over to the buyer the asset agreed upon in a forward contract.

Marked to market Describes the daily settlement of obligations on futures positions.

Market capitalization Price per share multiplied by the number of shares outstanding.

Market clearing Total demand for loans by borrowers equals total supply of loans from lenders. The market clears at the equilibrium rate of interest.

Market model A one-factor model for returns where the index that is used for the factor is an index of the returns on the whole market.

Market portfolio In concept, a value-weighted index of all securities. In practice, it is an index, such as the FTSE 100 or S&P 500, that describes the stock market. The return on the index approximates the return of the entire stock market. A market portfolio represents the average investor's investment.

Market price The current price at which a security is trading in a market.

Market risk Systematic risk. This term emphasizes the fact that systematic risk influences to some extent all assets in the market.

Market value The price at which willing buyers and sellers trade a firm's assets.

Marketability Refers to the ease and quickness of converting an asset to cash. Also called liquidity.

Market-to-book (M/B) ratio Market price per share of an ordinary share divided by book value per share.

Material adverse clause The clause in a loan agreement or similar contract under which the loan will become repayable in the event that there should be a serious (or material) deterioration in the borrower's credit standing. The clause is used by banks as a substitute where they are not able to negotiate a stronger covenant such as a borrowings limitation clause or a ratio covenant. The difficulty with such clauses lies in the definition of materiality. The normal wording in the loan agreement gives no indication of how to interpret the clause. Attempts to define materiality are almost certain to have the effect of changing the clause into a ratio covenant.

Maturity date The date on which the final repayment on a bond is due.

Merchant bankers See **Investment bankers**.

Merger Combination of two or more companies.

Minimum variance portfolio The portfolio of risky assets with the lowest possible variance. By definition, this portfolio must also have the lowest possible standard deviation.

Money markets Financial markets for debt securities that pay off in the short term (usually less than one year).

Mortgage securities A debt obligation secured by a mortgage on the real property of the borrower.

Multiple rates of return More than one rate of return from the same project that make the net present value of the project equal to zero. This situation arises when the IRR method is used for a project in which negative cash flows follow positive ones.

Multiples Another name for price/earnings ratios.

Mutually exclusive investment decisions Investment decisions in which the acceptance of one project precludes the acceptance of other projects.

NPV Net present value.

NPVGO model A model valuing the firm in which net present value of new investment opportunities is explicitly examined. NPVGO stands for net present value of growth opportunities.

Negative covenant Part of the indenture or loan agreement that limits or prohibits actions that the company may take.

Net-present-value (NPV) The present value of future cash returns, discounted at the appropriate market interest rate, minus the present value of the cost of the investment.

Net-present-value rule An investment is worth making if it has a positive NPV. If an investment's NPV is negative, it should be rejected.

Net working capital Current assets minus current liabilities.

Net worth See **Shareholders' interest**.

Nominal cash flow A cash flow expressed in nominal terms if the actual cash amounts to be received (or paid out) are given.

Nominal interest rate Interest rate unadjusted for inflation.

Non-cash item Expense against revenue that does not directly affect cash flow, such as depreciation and deferred taxes.

Normal distribution   Symmetric bell-shaped frequency distribution that can be defined by its mean and standard deviation.

Note   Unsecured debt, usually with a medium-term maturity.

Odd lot   Share trading unit of less than 100 shares.

Off balance sheet financing   Financing that is not shown as a liability on a company's balance sheet.

One-factor APT   A special case of the arbitrage pricing theory that is derived from the one-factor model by using diversification and arbitrage. It shows the expected return on any risky asset is a linear function of a single factor. The CAPM can be expressed as one-factor APT in which a single factor is the market portfolio.

Open account   A credit account for which the only formal instrument of credit is the invoice.

Operating activities   Sequence of events and decisions that create the firm's cash inflows and cash outflows before financing. These activities include buying and paying for raw materials, manufacturing and selling a product, and collecting cash.

Operating cash flow   Earnings before interest and depreciation minus taxes. It measures the cash generated from operations, not counting capital spending or working capital requirements.

Operating cycle   The time interval between the arrival of inventory and the date when cash is collected from receivables.

Operating lease   Type of lease in which the period of contract is less than the life of the equipment and the lessor pays all maintenance and servicing costs.

Operating leverage   The degree to which a company's costs of operation are fixed as opposed to variable. A firm with high operating costs compared to a firm with a low operating leverage implies larger percentage changes in EBIT with respect to a change in the sales revenue.

Opportunity cost   Most valuable alternative that is given up. The rate of return used in NPV computation is an opportunity interest rate.

Opportunity set   The possible expected return-standard deviation pairs of all portfolios that can be constructed from a given set of assets. Also called a feasible set.

Option   A right—but not an obligation—to buy or sell underlying assets at a fixed price during a specified time period.

Ordinary shares   Equity claims held by the 'residual owners' of the firm, who are the last to receive any distribution of earnings or assets. Also called common stock.

Original-issue-discount bond   A bond issued with a discount from par value.

Out of the money   Describes an option whose exercise would not be profitable. In the money describes an option whose exercise would produce profits.

Oversubscribed issue   Investors are not able to buy all the shares they want, so underwriters must allocate the shares among investors. This occurs when a new issue is underpriced.

Oversubscription privilege   Allows shareholders to purchase unsubscribed shares in a rights offering at the subscription price.

Over-the-counter (OTC) market   An informal network of brokers and dealers who negotiate sales of securities.

Par value   The nominal or face value of shares or bonds. For shares, it is a relatively unimportant value except for bookkeeping purposes. Also called nominal value.

Partnership   Form of business organization in which two or more co-owners form a business. Usually, in a general partnership each partner has unlimited liability for the debts of the partnership. Limited partnership permits some partners to have limited liability.

Payback period rule   An investment decision rule which states that all investment projects that have payback periods equal to or less than a particular cutoff period are accepted, and all of those that pay off in more than the particular cutoff period are rejected. The payback period is the number of years required for a firm to recover its initial investment required by a project from the cash flow it generates.

Payout ratio   Proportion of net income paid out in cash dividends.

Pecking order in long-term financing   Hierarchy of long-term financing strategies, in which using internally generated cash is at the top and issuing new equity is at the bottom.

Perfect markets   Perfectly competitive financial markets.

Perfectly competitive financial markets   Markets in which no trader has power to change the price of goods or services. Perfect markets are characterized by the following conditions: (1) Trading is costless, and access to the financial markets is free. (2) Information about borrowing and lending opportunities is freely available. (3) There are many traders, and no single trader can have a significant impact on market prices. (4) Goods and services offered are homogeneous.

Performance shares   Shares given to managers on the basis of performance as measured by earnings per share and similar criteria—a control device used by shareholders to tie management to the self-interest of shareholders.

Perpetuity   A constant stream of cash flows without end.

Perquisites   Management amenities such as a big office, a company car or expense-account meals. 'Perks' are agency costs of equity because managers of the firm are agents of the shareholders.

Pie model of capital structure   A model of the debt–equity ratio of the firms, graphically depicted in slices of a pie that represents the value of the firm in the capital markets.

Plug   A variable that handles financial slack in the financial plan.

Poison pill   Strategy by a takeover target company to make the target company less appealing to an acquiring company that wishes to purchase it.

Pooling of interests   Accounting method of reporting acquisitions under which the balance sheets of the two companies are simply added together item by item.

Portfolio   Combined holding of assets of an investor, for example more than one share, bond, real estate asset, or other asset.

Portfolio variance   Weighted sum of the covariances and variances of the assets in a portfolio.

Positive covenant   Part of the indenture or loan agreement that specifies an action that the company must abide by.

Preemptive right   The right to share proportionally in any new shares sold.

Preference share   See **Preferred share**.

Preferred share   A type of share whose holders are given certain priority over ordinary shareholders in the payment of dividends. Usually the dividend rate is fixed at the time of issue. Preferred shareholders normally do not receive voting rights. Also called preference shares.

Premium   If a bond is selling above its face value, it is said to sell at a premium.

Present value   The value of a future cash steam discounted at the appropriate market interest rate.

Present value factor   Factor used to calculate an estimate of the present value of an amount to be received in a future period.

Price takers   Individuals who respond to rates and prices by acting as though they have no influence on them.

Price-to-earnings (P/E) ratio   Current market price of ordinary share divided by current annual earnings per share.

Primary market   Where new issues of securities are offered to the public.

Principal   The value of a bond that must be repaid at maturity. Also called the face value or par value.

Principle of diversification   Highly diversified portfolios will have negligible unsystematic risk. In other words, unsystematic risks disappear in portfolios and only systematic risks survive.

Private placement   The sale of a bond or other security directly to a limited number of investors.

Pro forma statements   Projected income statements, balance sheets and sources and uses statements for future years.

Profit and loss account   Financial report that summarizes a firm's performance over a specified time period. Also called income statement.

Profit margin   Profits divided by total operating revenue (or turnover).

Profitability index   A method used to evaluate projects. It is the ratio of the present value of the future expected cash flows after initial investment divided by the amount of the initial investment.

Promissory note   Written promise to pay.

Prospectus   A legal document that is given to would-be investors contemplating purchasing securities in an offering. It describes the details of the company and the particular offering.

Protective covenant   A part of the indenture or loan agreement that limits certain actions a company takes during the term of the loan to protect the lender's interest.

Proxy   A grant of authority by the shareholder to transfer his or her voting rights to someone else.

Public issue   Sale of securities to the public.

Purchase accounting   Method of reporting acquisitions requiring that the assets of the acquired firm be reported at their fair market value on the books of the acquiring firm.

Purchasing power parity (PPP)   Idea that the exchange rate adjusts to keep purchasing power constant among currencies.

Pure discount bond   Bonds that pay no coupons and only pay back face value at maturity having been initially issued at a price less than face value.. Also referred to as zero coupon bonds or ZCBs.

Put option   The right, but not the obligation, to sell a specified number of units of a particular security at a stated price on or before a specified time.

Put provision   Gives holder of a bond the right to redeem his or her note at par on the coupon payment date.

Put-call parity   The value of a call equals the value of buying the share plus buying the put plus borrowing at the risk-free rate.

Q ratio or Tobin's Q ratio   Market value of firm's assets divided by replacement value of firm's assets.

Quick assets   Current assets minus inventories.

Quick ratio   Quick assets (current assets minus inventories) divided by total current liabilities. Used to measure short-term solvency of a firm.

R squared (R^2)   Square of the correlation coefficient proportion of the variability explained by the linear model.

Random walk   Theory that share prices change from day to day are at random. The changes are independent of each other and have the same probability distribution.

Real cash flow   A cash flow is expressed in real terms if the current, or date 0, purchasing power of the cash flow is given.

Real interest rate   Interest rate expressed in terms of real goods; that is, the nominal interest rate minus the expected inflation rate.

Receivables turnover ratio   Total operating revenues divided by average receivables. Used to measure how effectively a firm is managing its accounts receivable.

Refunding   The process of replacing outstanding bonds, typically to issue new securities at a lower interest rate than those replaced.

Registration statement   The registration that discloses all the pertinent information concerning the corporation that wants to make a security offering. The statement is filed with regulatory authorities.

Relative purchasing power parity (RPPP)   Idea that the rate of change in the price level of commodities in one country relative to the price level in another determines the rate of change of the exchange rate between the two countries' currencies.

Reorganization   Financial restructuring of a failed firm. Both the firm's asset structure and its financial structure are changed to reflect their true value, and claims are settled or renegotiated.

Replacement value   Current cost of replacing the firm's assets.

Repurchase agreement (repos)   Short-term, often overnight, sales of government securities with an agreement to repurchase the securities at a slightly higher price.

Residual dividend approach   An approach that suggests that a firm pay dividends if and only if acceptable investment opportunities for those funds are currently unavailable.

Restrictive covenants   Provisions that place constraints on the operations of borrowers, such as restrictions on working capital, fixed assets, future borrowing, and payment of dividend.

Retained earnings   Earnings not paid out as dividends.

Retention ratio   Retained earnings for a period divided by net income for that period.

Return   Profit on capital investment or securities.

Return on assets (ROA)   Income divided by average total assets.

Return on equity (ROE)   Net income after interest and taxes divided by average ordinary shareholders' equity.

Reverse split   The procedure whereby the number of outstanding shares is reduced; for example, two outstanding shares are combined to create only one.

Rights offer   An offering of shares for cash to existing shareholders that gives a current shareholder the opportunity to maintain the same proportionate interest in the company.

Risk-averse   A risk-averse investor will consider risky portfolios only if they provide ample compensation for risk via a risk premium.

Risk class   A partition of the universal set of risk measure so that projects that are in the same risk class can be comparable.

Risk premium   The excess return on the risky asset that is the difference between expected return on risky assets and the return on risk-free assets.

Round lot   Ordinary shares trading unit of 100 shares or multiples of 100 shares.

S&P 500   Standard & Poor's Composite Index of 500 US ordinary shares.

SML   Security market line.

SMP   Security market plane.

Sale and lease-back   An arrangement whereby a firm sells its existing assets to a financial company which then leases them back to the firm. This is often done to generate cash for the firm.

Sales forecast   A key input to the firm's financial planning process. External sales forecasts are based on historical experience, statistical analysis and consideration of various macroeconomic factors.

Scenario analysis   Analysis of the effect on a project of different scenarios, each scenario involving a confluence of factors.

Seasoned new issue   A new issue of shares after the company's securities have previously been issued.

Secondary markets   Already-existing securities bought and sold on the exchanges as opposed to an IPO.

Security market line (SML)   A straight line that shows the equilibrium relationship between systematic risk and expected rates of return for individual securities. According to the SML, the excess return on a risky asset is equal to the excess return on the market portfolio multiplied by the beta coefficient.

Semistrong-form efficiency   Theory that the market is efficient with respect to all publicly available information.

Seniority   The order of repayment. In the event of bankruptcy, senior debt must be repaid before subordinated debt receives any payment.

Sensitivity analysis   Analysis of the effect on the project when there is some change in critical variables such as sales and costs.

Separation principle   The principle that portfolio choice can be separated into two independent tasks: (1) determination of the optimal risky portfolio, which is a purely technical problem, and (2) the personal choice of the best mix of the risky portfolio and the risk-free asset.

Separation theorem   The value of an investment to an individual is not dependent on consumption preferences. All investors will want to accept or reject the same investment projects by using the NPV rule, regardless of personal preference.

Serial covariance   The covariance between a variable and the lagged value of the variable. The same as autocovariance.

Set of contracts perspective   View of company as a set of contracting relationships among individuals who have conflicting objectives, such as shareholders or managers.

Shareholder   Holder of equity shares. The terms *shareholders* and *stockholders* usually refer to owners of ordinary shares (sometimes called common stock) in a company.

Shareholders' interest   The residual claims that shareholders have against a firm's assets, calculated by subtracting total liabilities from total assets. It includes the claims of ordinary shareholders and preference shareholders too. Also called net worth.

Shelf life   Number of days it takes to get goods purchased and sold, or days in inventory.

Shirking   The tendency to do less work when the return is smaller. Owners may have more incentive to shirk if they issue equity as opposed to debt, because they retain less ownership interest in the company and therefore may receive a smaller return. Thus, shirking is considered an agency cost of equity.

Short run   That period of time in which certain equipment, resources and commitments of them are fixed.

Short sale   Sale of a security that an investor doesn't own, but has instead borrowed or plans to buy in subsequently.

Short-run operating activities   Events and decisions concerning the short-term finance of a firm, such as how much inventory to order and whether to offer cash terms or credit terms to customers.

Short-term debt   An obligation having a maturity of one year or less from the date it was issued.

Side-effects   Effects of a proposed project on other parts of the firm.

Sight draft   A commercial draft demanding immediate payment.

Signalling approach   Approach to the determination of optimal capital structure asserting that insiders in a firm have information that the market does not; therefore the choice of capital structure by insiders can signal information to outsiders and change the value of the firm. This theory is also called the asymmetric information approach.

Simple interest   Interest calculated by considering only the original principal amount.

Sinking fund   An account managed by the bond trustee for the purpose of repaying the bonds.

Sole proprietorship   A business owned by a single individual. The sole proprietorship pays no corporate income tax, but has unlimited liability for business debts and obligations; personal income tax is assessed on the owner who is a sole proprietor.

Spot exchange rate   Exchange rate between two currencies for immediate delivery.

Spot interest rate   Interest rate fixed today on a loan that is made today.

Spreadsheet   A computer program that organizes numerical data into rows and columns on a terminal screen for calculating and making adjustments based on new data.

Standard deviation   The positive square root of the variance. This is the standard statistical measure of the spread of a sample.

Standardized normal distribution   A normal distribution with an expected value of 0 and a standard deviation of 1.

Standby fee   Usually an amount paid to an underwriter who agrees to purchase any shares that are not subscribed by the public investor in a rights offering.

Standby underwriting   An agreement whereby an underwriter agrees to purchase any shares that are not purchased by the public investor.

Stated annual interest rate   The interest rate expressed as a percentage per annum, by which interest payment is determined.

Stock dividend   Payment of a dividend in the form of shares rather than cash.

Stock split   The increase in the number of outstanding shares while making no change in shareholders' equity.

Stockholder   Holder of equity shares in a firm. The terms *stockholder* and *shareholders* usually refer to owners of ordinary shares.

Stockout   Running out of inventory.

Straight-line depreciation   A method of depreciation whereby each year the firm depreciates a constant proportion of the initial investment less salvage value.

Strike price   Price at which the put option or call option can be exercised. Also called the exercise price.

Strong-form efficiency   Theory that the market is efficient with respect to all available information, public or private.

Subordinated debt   Debt whose holders have a claim on the firm's assets only after senior debtholder's claims have been satisfied.

Subscription price   Price that existing shareholders are allowed to pay for a share in a rights offering.

Sum-of-the-year's-digits depreciation   Method of accelerated depreciation.

Sunk cost   A cost that has already occurred and cannot be removed. Because sunk costs are in the past, such costs should be ignored when deciding whether to accept or reject a project.

Sustainable growth rate   The only growth rate possible with preset values for four variables: profit margin, payout ratio, debt–equity ratio and asset utilization ratio if the firm issues no new equity.

Swap   Exchange between two securities or currencies. One type of swap involves the sale (or purchase) of a foreign currency with a simultaneous agreement to repurchase (or sell) it.

Swap rate   The difference between the sale (purchase) price and the price to repurchase (resell) it in a swap.

Sweep account   Account in which the bank takes all excess available funds at the close of each business day and invests them for the firm.

Syndicate   A group of investment banking companies that agrees to co-operate in a joint venture to underwrite an offering of securities for resale to the public.

Systematic   Common to all businesses.

Systematic risk   Any risk that affects a wide range of assets, each to a greater or lesser degree. Also called market risk.

Systematic risk principle   Only the systematic portion of risk matters in large, well-diversified portfolios. Thus, the expected returns must be related only to systematic risks.

T-bill   Treasury bill.

Takeover   General term referring to transfer of control of a firm from one group of shareholders to another.

Taking delivery   Refers to the buyer's actually assuming possession from the seller of the asset agreed upon in a forward contract.

Target firm   A firm that is the object of a takeover by another firm.

Target payout ratio   A firm's long-run dividend-to-earnings ratio. The firm's policy is to attempt to pay out a certain percentage of earnings, but it pays a stated dividend and adjusts it to the target as increases in earnings occur.

Targeted repurchase   The firm buys back its own shares from a potential bidder, usually at a substantial premium, to forestall a takeover attempt. Not legal in all countries.

Taxable income   Gross income less a set of deductions.

Technical analysis   Research to identify mispriced securities that focuses on recurrent and predictable share price patterns. Also called chartism.

Technical insolvency   Default on a legal obligation of the firm. For example, technical insolvency occurs when a firm doesn't pay a bill.

Tender offer   Public offer to buy shares of a takeover target firm.

Term structure   Relationship between interest rates for various maturities.

Terms of sale   Conditions on which firm proposes to sell its goods and services for cash or credit.

Time value of money   Price or value put on time. Time value of money reflects the opportunity cost of investing at a risk-free rate. The certainty of having a given sum of money today is worth more than the certainty of having an equal sum at a later date because money can be put to profitable use during the intervening time.

Tobin's Q   Market value of assets divided by replacement value of assets. A Tobin's Q ratio greater than 1 indicates the firm has done well with its investment decisions.

Tombstone   An advertisement that announces an offering of securities. It identifies the issuer, the type of security, the underwriters and where additional information is available.

Total asset-turnover ratio   Turnover divided by average total assets. Used to measure how effectively a firm is managing its assets.

Total cash flow of the firm   Total cash inflow minus total cash outflow.

Trade acceptance   Written demand that has been accepted by a firm to pay a given sum of money at a future date.

Trade credit   Credit granted to other firms.

Trading range   Price range between highest and lowest prices at which a security is traded.

Transactions motive   A reason for holding cash that arises from normal disbursement and collection activities of the firm.

Treasury bill   Short-term discount government debt maturing in less than one year. T-bills are issued periodically by the government and are virtually risk free.

Treasury bond or note   Debt obligations of the government that make coupon payments and are sold at or near par value. They have original maturities of more than one year.

Triangular arbitrage   Striking offsetting deals among three markets simultaneously to obtain an arbitrage profit.

Underpricing   Issuing of securities below the fair market value.

Underwriter   An investment firm that buys an issue of security from the firm and resells it to the investors.

Unfunded debt   Short-term debt.

Unseasoned new issue   Initial public offering (IPO).

Unsystematic   What is specific to a firm.

Unsystematic risk   See **Diversifiable risk.**

VA principle   Value additivity principle.

Value additivity (VA) principle   In an efficient market the value of the sum of two cash flows is the sum of the values of the individual cash flows.

Variable cost   A cost that varies directly with volume and is zero when production is zero.

Variance of the probability distribution   The expected value of squared deviation from the expected return.

Venture capital   Early-stage financing for young companies seeking to grow.

Vertical acquisition   Acquisition in which the acquired firm and the acquiring firm are at different steps in the production process.

WACC   Weighted average cost of capital.

Warrant   A security that gives the holder the right—but not the obligation—to buy shares directly from a company at a fixed price for a given time period.

Weak-form efficiency   Theory that the market is efficient with respect to historical price information.

Weighted average cost of capital (WACC)   The average cost of capital on the firm's existing projects and activities. The weighted average cost of capital for the firm is calculated by weighting the cost of each source of funds by its proportion of the total market value of the firm.

Weighted average maturity   A measure of the level of interest-rate risk calculated by weighting cash flows by the time to receipt and multiplying by the fraction of total present value represented by the cash flow at that time.

Winner's curse   The average investor wins; that is, gets the desired allocation of a new issue because those who knew better avoided the issue.

Wire transfer   An electronic transfer of funds from one bank to another that eliminates the mailing and cheque-clearing times associated with other cash-transfer methods.

Yankee bonds   Foreign bonds issued in the United States by foreign banks and corporations.

Yield to maturity   The discount rate that equates the present value of interest payments and redemption value with the present price of the bond.

Zero-balance account (ZBA)   A bank account in which a zero balance is maintained by transfers of funds from a master account in an amount only large enough to cover cheques presented.

Zero coupon bond   Bonds that pay no interest, but only pay back face value at maturity having initially been issued at a price less than face value. Also called pure discount bonds.

Index

Abandon, option to, 204
Accounting
  efficient markets and, 338
  leasing and, 545–547
  for mergers and acquisitions,
    620–622
Accounting statements, 33–34
  analysis of, 56–64
  balance sheet, 30–31, 45–48
  income statement, 48–50
  statement of cash flows, 51–53,
    62–64
Acquisitions, See Mergers and
  acquisitions
Adjusted-present-value approach
  (APV), 408–410
  example of, 418–421
  leasing, 563–564
  leveraged buyouts and, 426–430,
    475–480
Agency cost of equity, 399–400
Agency costs, 40
  convertible bonds and, 537–538
  high-dividend policy and, 445
Aging schedule, 611–612
Alternatives to net present value
  average accounting return, 150–153
  discounted payback period rule, 150
  internal rate of return, 153–165
  payback period rule, 147–150
  profitability index, 165–167
American options, 487
Amortization, 351
Annuity, 98–104
Arbitrage pricing model, capital-asset-
  pricing model and, 291–292
Arbitrage pricing theory, 277–295
Asset beta, 307–308
Assets
  on balance sheet, 45
  current, 30–31, 50–51
  fixed, 30–31
Average accounting return, 150–153

Average collection period, 610–611
Average daily sales, 611
Average stock returns, 222–223

Balance sheet, 3–4, 22–23, 30–31,
  45–48
Bankruptcy, 388
Basic principle of investment
  decision making, 72
Bearer bond, 471
Beta(s), 228–229
  asset beta, 307–308
  cyclicity of revenues, 305
  determinants of, 305–308
  equity beta, 307–308
  expected returns and, 288–290
  financial leverage and, 307–308
  formula for, 302
  leveraged and, 421–423
  measurement of, 304
  as measure of responsiveness,
    265–266
  as measure of risk, 265
  operating leverage, 305–307
  risk and, 228–229
  systematic risk and, 280–284
  unlevered, 423
Beta coefficient, 281
Beta risk, 301
Black–Scholes model, 502–510
  warrants and, 528–529
Black Wednesday, 680–682
Bondholders
  call options and, 512–513
  put options and, 513–514
Bond ratings, 477–481
Bonds, 29
  basic terms, 470–471
  in bearer form, 471
  call provision, 472–473, 554–555
  consols, 114–115
  convertible bonds. See Convertible

bonds
  coupons, 112–114
  deep-discount, 482–483
  defined, 111
  example of, 111
  face value, 470, 551
  floating-rate, 481–482
  income, 483–484
  interest rates related to bond prices,
    115–116
  junk bonds, 477–481
  level-coupon bonds, 112–114
  as options, 510–516
  present value formulas for, 116
  protective covenants, 471–472
  pure discount bonds, 111–112
  sinking fund, 472
  types of, 481–484
  yield to maturity, 116
Bond valuation, 111–116
Bookbuilding, 456–457
Book value, 47–48, 347
Borrowing, riskless, 260–264
Break-even analysis, 201–204
Bubble theory, 336–337
Business organization, 36–40
  corporation, 38–40
  partnership, 37–38
  sole proprietorship, 37

Callable bond, 473–474
Callable debt, 351
Call options, 488–489
  firm expressed in terms of,
    511–513
  valuation of, 496–501
Call premium, 472–473
Capital-asset pricing model (CAPM),
  238–276
  arbitrage pricing model and,
    291–292
  arbitrage pricing theory and, 277

expected return on individual
    security, 268–271
expected return on market, 268
formula for, 269
Capital budgeting, 4, 31, 159–160,
    168
    adjusted-present-value approach
        408–410
    (APV), 418, 421
    all-equity value, 418, 465–466
    comparison of approaches, 413–416
    debt, effects of, 419–421
    flow-to equity approach (FTE),
        410–412
    incremental cash flows, 174–176
    inflation and, 182–184
    investments of unequal lives,
        184–189
    net present value and, 174–190
    time-value-of-money concept, 78
    weighted-average-cost-capital
        (WACC) method, 412–413
Capital expenditure, 31
Capital market line, 263
Capital markets, 42–43
    Capital market theory, 211–212
    average stock returns, 222–223
    returns, 212–216
    holding-period returns, 216–220
    percentage returns, 216–220
    risk-free returns, 222–223, 231–233
    risk statistics, 223–225, 233
    statistics for returns, 221–222,
        229–233
Capital rationing, 167
Capital structure, 4–5, 31–32, 357–384
    agency cost of equity, 399–400
    bankruptcy, 388
    capital structure question, 457–458
    costs of financial distress, 388–391
    debt, limits to use of, 388–407
    establishment of, 402–404
    financial leverage and firm value,
        example of, 362–366
    growth and debt-equity ratio,
        400–402
    maximizing firm value, 358–360
    maximizing shareholder interests,
        358–360
    Modigliani and Miller (MM)
        Proposition I, 362
    Modigliani and Miller (MM)
        Proposition II, 366–374
    optimal, determination of, 360–362
    pie model, 357–358, 397–398
    taxes, 374–383
Capital-structure policy, options and,
    516–517
Cash
    collection and disbursement of,
        595–597

defined in terms of other elements of
    balance sheet, 580–582
    generation of, 30
    management of, 595–597
Cash budgeting, 590–593
Cash discounts, 601–603
Cash flow(s), 32–35, 51–53, 180
    inflation and, 183–184
Change in net working capital, 50–51
Characteristic line, 267
Commercial paper, 594
Compensating balances, 594
Compounding
    compounding periods, 90–94
    continuous, 92–94
    defined, 82
    future value and, 82–86
    over many years, 92
    power of, 86
Compound interest, 82–83
Conglomerate acquisition, 619
Consols, 94–97, 114–115
Contingent claims, 36
Continuous compounding, 92–94
Contribution margin, 202
Convergence criteria, 679
Conversion price, 530
Conversion ratio, 530
Conversion value, 531–532
Convertible bonds and debt, 530–533
    conversion policy, 538–539
    conversion value, 531–532
    defined, 530
    option value, 532–533
    reasons for issuing, 533–536
    value of, 530–533
Corporate discount rate, 308–311, 323
Corporate financial models, long-term
    planning and, 567
Corporate financial planning. See also
    Financial planning model defined,
    567–568
    growth forecasts and, 571–575
Corporate governance, 10–20
    and corporate finance, 18–20
    Britain, 10–12
    France, 14–16
    Germany, 12–14
    Netherlands, 16–17
Corporate strategy
    positive NPV and, 193–195
    stock market and, 194–195
Corporate strategy analysis, 193–195
Corporation, 38–39
    compared with partnership, 39
    control of, 41–42
    goals of, 40–42
    investment decision making in, 75–76
Correlation coefficients, 331
Cost of capital, 308
    with debt, 309–311

equity capital, 300–304
    mergers and acquisitions and, 626
    relationship to security market line,
        308–309
    weighted average cost of capital,
        310
Cost of equity, 300
    agency cost of equity, 399–400
Cost of equity capital, 300–304, 417
Coupons, 112
Covariance
    defined, 239
    individual securities, 241–244
    portfolio, 255–256
Covered interest arbitrage, 651
Credit
    collection policy, 610–612
    generally, 600–601
    information and, 605–608
    offer of, 605–606
    optimal policy, 608–609
    refusal of, 605–608
Credit analysis, 600, 605–610,
Creditor, 350
Credit periods, 601, 604
Credit scoring, 610
Crown jewels, 637
Cumulative abnormal return, 333
Cumulative dividends, 353
Cumulative voting, 347–348
Currency calculations, 647–658
Current assets, 31, 50–51
    alternative financing policies for,
        588–590
    defined, 578–579
    short-term financial policy and,
        585–590
Current liabilities, 50–51
Cutoff rate, 308
Cyclicity of revenues, 305

Debt, 31–32
    cost of, 309
    differentiated from equity, 35–36,
        47, 350
    limits to use of, 388–406
    optimal debt level, 553–555
    preferred stock as, 353–354
    reduction of costs of, 395–396
    straight debt compared with
        convertible debt, 533–536
    taxes related to, 374–383
Debt-equity financing, agency cost of
    equity and, 400
Debt-equity ratio
    evaluation of optimal, 402–404
    growth and, 400–402
    no-growth and, 401
Decision trees in NPV analysis,
    195–197

Deep-discount bonds, 482–483
Defensive tactics, mergers and
    acquisitions, 636–638
Deferred call, 470
Depreciation, 49–50
Deprival value, 661
Derivatives
    defined, 666–667
    generally, 666–669
Derivative securities, 666–669
Dilution, 526–527
Discount in foreign exchange, 657
Discounted cash flow method of
    capital budgeting, 168
Discounted payback period rule, 150
Discounting and present value, 86–90
Discount rate, 551–552
    calculation of, 410–412
    project versus firm, 308–309
    risk-adjusted, 301–303
    for risky projects, 225–228
Diversifiable risk, 259
Diversification, 228–229
Dividend-growth model, 128
Dividend policy
    dividends set equal to cash flow,
        433–434
    indifference proposition, 434–435
    initial dividend greater than cash
        flow, 434
    irrelevance of, 433–438
    real-world factors favouring high-
        dividend policy, 444–445
Dividends
    information content of, 446–447
    information to market provided by,
        449
    investment policy and, 438
    policy, 433–438, 444–450
    types of, 431–432
Dollar returns, 216–223

Economic and Monetary Union
    (EMU), 677–683
Economies of scale, 624
Economies of vertical integration, 624
Effective annual interest rate, 91
Efficient capital markets, 322–324
    accounting and, 338
    defined, 319
    price-pressure effects, 340–341
Efficient-market hypothesis (EMH),
    322
    evidence regarding, 330–337
    misconceptions about, 328–329
    price fluctuations and, 329
    semistrong-form efficiency,
        327–328, 332–337
    strong-form efficiency, 327–328,
        337

types of efficiency, 325–330
    weak-form efficiency, 325–327,
        330–332
Empirical models of asset pricing,
    292–293
Equity, differentiated from debt,
    35–36, 47, 350
Equity beta, 302–304
Equity capital, cost of, 299–304
Equity shares, 30–31
Eurobonds, 663–665
Eurocurrency markets, 646–647
European corporate reporting, 20–24
European corporate taxation, 25–27
European Currency Unit (ECU),
    677–683
European equity markets, 3–10
    concentration, 7–8
    market capitalisation, 4–6
European Monetary System (EMS),
    677–683
European options, 487
Exchange Rate Mechanism (ERM),
    677–683
Exercise price of option, 487, 498
Exercising option, 487
Expand, option to, 204
Expectations theory of exchange rates,
    650–653, 675–676
Expected return
    betas and, 288–290
    defined, 238
    dividend yield and, 441–444
Expiration date, of option, 487, 498

Financial cash flow, 51–53
Financial distress, 404–406
Financial leases, 543–544
Financial leverage, beta and, 307–308
Financial plan, defined, 567–568
Financial planning, 567
Financing decisions, creation of value,
    319–322
Fisher effect, 650–653, 675
Fixed assets, 30–31
Fixed costs, 198
Floating-rate bonds, 481–482
Flow-to-equity approach (FTE),
    410–412
Foreign exchange markets, 645–658,
    661–662
Forward markets in foreign exchange,
    648–651, 656–658
Free cash flow, 626
Future cash flows
    algebraic formula for, 90
    present value of, 86–88
    value of firms and, 104–105
Future value (FV), 74, 78–79
    compounding and, 82–86

Golden parachutes, 637
Goodwill, 620–621
Growing annuity, 103–104
Growing perpetuity, 96–98
Growth forecasts, 571–575
Growth portfolio, 293–294

Historical market risk premium,
    236–237
Holding-period returns, 216–220
Homemade dividends, 435–437
Homemade leverage, 362
Horizontal acquisition, 619
Hurdle rate, 308

Income
    defined, 48–49
    determination of, 179–180
Incremental cash flows, 174–176
Inflation
    capital budgeting and, 182–184
    cash flow and, 183–184
Inflation and foreign exchange rates,
    649–653
Initial public offering (IPO), 339–340,
    457–459
Interest
    compound, 82–86
    effective annual interest rate, 91
    equilibrium rate of interest, 70
    simple, 82–83
    stated annual interest rate, 91
Interest and foreign exchange rates,
    649–653
Interest rate(s), 68,70
    bond prices, relation to, 115–116
    call prices, and, 500
    competitive market and, 70–71
    international, 649–654, 665–666
    term structure of, 137–144
Interest rate parity in foreign
    exchange, 649–653, 672–673
Internal financing, 354
Internal rate of return (IRR), 153–165
International financing decisions,
    663–666
International Fisher effect, 650–653,
    676
International investment decisions,
    658–663
Introduction, 456
Investment decisions, 67–68
    basic principle of investment
        decision making, 72
    corporate, 75–76
Investment policy, dividends and, 438

Junk bonds, 477–481

Leases
  defined, 542–545
  financial leases, 544
  generally, 542–545
  leveraged leases, 544
  operating lease, 544
  sale and lease-back, 544
  types of, 542–545
Leasing
  accounting and, 545–547
  APV approach to, 563–564
  cash flows, 547–549
  taxation and, 557–559
Level-coupon bonds, 112–114
Leverage. See also Valuation under
    leverage
  beta and, 421–423
  corporate taxes and, 374–383
  firm value and, 362–366
  homemade leverage, 362
  Modigliani and Miller (MM)
    Proposition I, 360–362
  Modigliani and Miller (MM)
    Proposition II, 366–374
  value of leveraged firm, 378–379
Leveraged buyouts, 426–430,
  637–638
Leveraged leases, 544
Levered cash flow (LCF), 411
Liabilities
  on balance sheet, 45
  current, 50–51
Liquidity, 579
Long-term debt, 31
  basic feature of, 351
  differentiating debt from equity,
    349–350
  different types of, 351, 372
  interest versus dividends, 350
  overview of, 468–469
  repayment, 351
  security, 352
  seniority, 352
Long-term financing
  convertible bonds, 530–539
  corporate long-term debt, 349–352
  warrants, 524–529, 533–538
Long-term planning, corporate
    financial models and, 567–576

Maastricht Treaty, 677–683
Managerial goals of corporation, 40–41
Marked to market, 668
Market efficiency. See Efficient capital
    markets
Market risk, 259
Market risk premium, 236–237
Market value, 347
Maturity date, of bond, 111
Mergers and acquisitions, 617–640

accounting for, 620–622
acquisition of assets, 619
acquisition of shares, 618
basic forms of, 617–620
benefit to shareholders, 638–640
consolidation, 618
defensive tactics, 636–638
diversification and, 632
example of, 803–807
merger, defined, 618
net present value (NPV) of,
  632–636
risk reduction and, 628–631
source of synergy from, 623–626
synergy and, 622–626
takeovers, 619–620
value of firm after, 627–628
Modigliani and Miller (MM)
    Proposition I, 360–366
  example of, 368–373
Modigliani and Miller (MM)
    Proposition II, 366–374
  example of, 368–373
Multiple rates of return, 158–160
Mutually exclusive projects, 160–165

Negative covenant, 395, 471–472
Net present value (NPV), 180,
  299–300
  annuity, 98–103
  capital budgeting and, 174–190
  compounding periods, 90–94
  corporate investment, 75–76
  formula for, 80
  of future cash flow, algebraic
    formula for, 90
  growing annuity, 103–104
  growing perpetuity, 96–98
  incremental cash flows, 174–176
  investments of unequal lives,
    184–189
  perpetuity, 94–96
Net present value (NPV) analysis
  break-even analysis, 197–204
  decision trees, 195–197
  options, 204–206
  positive NPV, 193–195
  sensitivity analysis, 197–204
Net working capital, 31,50–51, 177,
  180–181
  formula for, 579–580
No-dividend shares, 127–128
No-growth and debt-equity ratio, 401
Nominal interest rate, 182
Noncallable bond, 474
Noncash items, 49–50
NPVGO model, 128–130

Offer for sale, 455–456

Operating cash flow(s), 53, 184–186
Operating lease, 544
Operating leverage, 305–307
Opportunity costs, 175, 179
Optimal capital structure, 386–388
Optimal debt level, 550–551
Option-pricing formulas, 501–508
  Black-Scholes model, 502–508
  two-state option model, 501–502
Option-pricing table, 509–510, 701
Options
  call options, 488–489
  capital-structure policy and,
    516–517
  combinations of, 493–496
  defined, 487
  investment in real projects, and
    517–520
  put options, 490–491
  selling options, 491–493
  stocks and bonds as, 510–516
  valuation of, 496–501
Option value, 532–533
Ordinary shares
  authorized, 345
  classes of shares, 349
  convertible debt and, 534–535
  dividends, 348–349
  long-term financing, 344–355
  NPV of merger and, 634–635
  rate of return, 214–216
  retained earnings, 346–347
  share premium account, 345
  shareholders' rights, 347–348

Parent cash flows, 659–660
Partnership, 37–38
Payback period rule, 147–150
Payout ratio, 124
Pecking order, 354–355
Pension funds, 8–9
Perpetuity, 94–98
Pie model, 32, 357–358, 375–376,
  397–398
Placing, 456
Poison pill, 637
Pooling of interests, 621
  purchase compared with, 622
Portfolio(s)
  diversification and, 286–288
  efficient set for many securities,
    253–256
  efficient set for two assets, 249–253
  market-equilibrium portfolio,
    264–268
  optimal, 262–264
  return and risk for, 244–256
  standard deviation, 247, 255–256
  value portfolio, 293–294
  variance, 246–249, 255–256

Portfolio risk, 259
Positive covenant, 395–396, 424, 472, 553
Positive NPV, 193–195
Preferred shares
  as debt, 353–354
  defined, 352–353
  dividends, 353
  preference, defined, 352–353
Premium in foreign exchange, 657
Present value analysis, 79
Present value (PV) 79–80
  of annuity, 98–103
  of ordinary shares, 117–121
  discounting and, 86–90
  of firm, 104–105
  formulas for bonds, 116
  of growing annuity, 103–104
  of growing perpetuity, 96–98
  of perpetuity, 94–96
  riskless cash flows, 549–551
Price-earnings ratio, 130–133
Primary market, 18–19
Profitability index, 165–167
Project cash flows, 659–660
Prospectus, 456
Protective covenants, 395–396
  bonds, 471–472
Public issue of equity securities
  cash offer, 455–459
  general procedure for, 455–459
  initial public offering, 457–459
  investment bankers and, 457
  offering price, 457
  rights offering, 460–465
  underpricing, 457–459
  venture capital, 465
Purchase method of reporting
  acquisitions, 620–622
  pooling of interests compared with, 622
Purchasing Power Parity (PPP), 650, 652–654, 673–674
Put-call parity, 496, 510
Put options, 490–491
  combinations with, 493–496
  firm expressed in terms of, 513–514
  valuation of, 500–501, 510

Random walk, 325, 330
Real cash flow, 183
Real interest rate, 182–183
Retained earnings, 346–347
Retention ratio, 122
Return. See also Expected return
  arbitrage pricing theory and, 278–279
  average share returns, 9, 222–223, 229–233

capital-asset-pricing model (CAPM), 268–271
  for individual securities, 238–244
  for portfolios, 244–256
  risk, relationship with, 268–271
  risk-free returns, 222–223, 231
  risk statistics, 223–225, 231–233
  statistics for, 9, 222–233
Return on equity, 122
Returns
  generally, 212–216
  holding-period returns, 216–220
  percentage returns, 9, 219–223, 229–233
Returns on European equities and other assets, 9, 229–233
Rights share issues
Risk
  beta and, 228–229
  beta as measure of, 265–268
  capital-asset-pricing model (CAPM), 268–271
  of cash flows, 34–35
  discount rate for risky projects, 225–228
  diversifiable risk, 259
  for individual securities, 238–239
  investors holding market portfolio, 265–269
  market risk, 259
  portfolio risk, 257–259
  for portfolios, 244–249
  of project versus firm, 308–311
  return, relationship with, 268–271
  risk-free returns, 222–223, 229–233
  riskless borrowing and lending, 260–264
  systematic risk, 259, 279–280
  unique risk, 259
  unsystematic risk, 259, 279–280
Risk-adjusted discount rate, 301–302
Risk averse, 259
Risk-free returns, 222–223, 231
Riskless cash flows
  optimal debt level and, 550–551
  present value of, 549–550
Risk premium, 222–223, 229–233

Sales forecast, 568
Secondary market, 43
Secured loans, 594
Security market line, 269
  relationship to cost of capital, 309
Semistrong-form efficiency, 327–328
  contrary results, 335–337
  event studies, 332–334
  evidence regarding, 332–337
Sensitivity analysis, 197–201
Shareholders
  cumulative voting, 347–348

defined, 31, 344
  effects of rights offering on, 463–464
  mergers and acquisitions benefits, 638–640, 794–796
  rights of, 368–369
Shareholders and options
  call options and, 511–513
  put options and, 513–514
  shareholders' equity
  on balance sheet, 45
  defined, 47
Short-term debt, 31
Short-term finance
  cash budgeting, 590–593
  cash cycle, 582–585
  defined, 578–579
  operating cycle, 582–585
  overdrafts, 593
  short-run operating activities, 582–583
Short-term financial plan
  banker's acceptance, 594
  commercial paper, 594
  secured loans, 594
  unsecured loans, 594
Simple interest, 82–83
Sinking fund, 351, 372, 472, 554
Small-capitalization stocks, rate of return, 223
Sole proprietorship, 37
Sources and uses of cash statement, 581–582
Spot foreign exchange rate, 649–653, 655–658
Standard deviation, 223–225
  calculation of, 241–242
  defined, 241–242
  portfolio, 247
  portfolio of many assets, 255–256
Standard deviation, risk-free investment, 262
Striking price of option, 487
Strong-form efficiency, 327–328
  evidence regarding, 337
Subordinated debt, 352
Subscription price, in rights offering, 461
Sunk cost, 175
Sustainable growth rate, 573, 575
Swaps, 668–669
Synergy, 617
  acquisitions and, 622–626
  source of, 623–626
Systematic risk, 259–260, 279–284, 288
  betas and, 279–284

Takeovers, 617–640
Taxation

leases and, 557–559
Modigliani and Miller (MM)
    Proposition I. See Modigliani
    and Miller (MM) Proposition I
Modigliani and Miller (MM)
    Proposition II. See Modigliani
    and Miller (MM) Proposition II
    share price and leverage under,
      382–383
    weighted average cost of capital
      and, 382
Tax effects, firm value and, 396–399
Tax shield, 377–378
Technical analysis, 325–327
Term loans, 566–567
Term structure, 590
    of interest rates, 137–144
Timing, of cash flows, 34

Uncertainty
    high-dividend policy and, 445
Uncovered interest arbitrage, 651
Underwriting, rights offering, 464
Unique risk, 259
Unseasoned new issue, 457–459
Unsecured loans, 593–594
Unsystematic risk, 259, 279–280

Valuation
    bonds. See Bond valuation
    stocks. See Stock valuation
Valuation under leverage
    adjusted-present-value approach
      (APV), 408–410, 418–421
    comparison of approaches,
      413–416
    flow-to equity approach (FTE).
      410–412
    weighted-average-cost-capital
      (WACC) method, 412–413
Value
    versus cost, 47–48
    creation with financing decisions,
      319–322
Value creation, 30, 32
Value of firm, 104–105
    announcement of new equity and,
      464–465
    integration of tax effects and
      financial distress costs,
      396–399
    maximizing, 358–360
    after mergers and acquisitions,
      628–631
    pie model, 357–358, 397–398
Variable costs, 198

Variance, 223–224
    individual securities, 239–241
    portfolio, 246–249
    portfolio of many assets, 255–256
    risk-free investment, 261
Venture capital, 465
Vertical acquisition, 619

Warrants, 524–529
    attributes of firms that issue, 536–538
    Black-Scholes model and, 528–529
    call options compared with 526–528
    defined, 524
    pricing of, 528–529
    reasons for issuing, 533–536
Weak-form efficiency, 325–327
    evidence regarding, 330–332
Weighted-average-cost-capital
    (WACC)
    corporate taxes and, 382
    method, 310, 412–413
Working capital, 177

Yield to maturity, 116

Zero-coupon bonds, 112, 482–483